Lecture Notes in Computer Science 14442

The series Lecture Notes in Computer Science (LNCS), including its subseries Lecture Notes in Artificial Intelligence (LNAI) and Lecture Notes in Bioinformatics (LNBI), has established itself as a medium for the publication of new developments in computer science and information technology research, teaching, and education.

LNCS enjoys close cooperation with the computer science R & D community, the series counts many renowned academics among its volume editors and paper authors, and collaborates with prestigious societies. Its mission is to serve this international community by providing an invaluable service, mainly focused on the publication of conference and workshop proceedings and postproceedings. LNCS commenced publication in 1973.

Jian Guo · Ron Steinfeld
Editors

Advances in Cryptology – ASIACRYPT 2023

29th International Conference on the Theory
and Application of Cryptology and Information Security
Guangzhou, China, December 4–8, 2023
Proceedings, Part V

Springer

Editors
Jian Guo
Nanyang Technological University
Singapore, Singapore

Ron Steinfeld
Monash University
Melbourne, VIC, Australia

ISSN 0302-9743 ISSN 1611-3349 (electronic)
Lecture Notes in Computer Science
ISBN 978-981-99-8732-0 ISBN 978-981-99-8733-7 (eBook)
https://doi.org/10.1007/978-981-99-8733-7

This Springer imprint is published by the registered company Springer Nature Singapore Pte Ltd.
The registered company address is: 152 Beach Road, #21-01/04 Gateway East, Singapore 189721, Singapore

Preface

The 29th Annual International Conference on the Theory and Application of Cryptology and Information Security (Asiacrypt 2023) was held in Guangzhou, China, on December 4–8, 2023. The conference covered all technical aspects of cryptology, and was sponsored by the International Association for Cryptologic Research (IACR).

We received an Asiacrypt record of 376 paper submissions from all over the world, and the Program Committee (PC) selected 106 papers for publication in the proceedings of the conference. Due to this large number of papers, the Asiacrypt 2023 program had 3 tracks.

The two program chairs were supported by the great help and excellent advice of six area chairs, selected to cover the main topic areas of the conference. The area chairs were Kai-Min Chung for Information-Theoretic and Complexity-Theoretic Cryptography, Tanja Lange for Efficient and Secure Implementations, Shengli Liu for Public-Key Cryptography Algorithms and Protocols, Khoa Nguyen for Multi-Party Computation and Zero-Knowledge, Duong Hieu Phan for Public-Key Primitives with Advanced Functionalities, and Yu Sasaki for Symmetric-Key Cryptology. Each of the area chairs helped to lead discussions together with the PC members assigned as paper discussion lead. Area chairs also helped to decide on the submissions that should be accepted from their respective areas. We are very grateful for the invaluable contribution provided by the area chairs.

To review and evaluate the submissions, while keeping the load per PC member manageable, we selected a record size PC consisting of 105 leading experts from all over the world, in all six topic areas of cryptology. The two program chairs were not allowed to submit a paper, and PC members were limited to submit one single-author paper, or at most two co-authored papers, or at most three co-authored papers all with students. Each non-PC submission was reviewed by at least three reviewers consisting of either PC members or their external sub-reviewers, while each PC member submission received at least four reviews. The strong conflict of interest rules imposed by IACR ensure that papers are not handled by PC members with a close working relationship with the authors. There were approximately 420 external reviewers, whose input was critical to the selection of papers. Submissions were anonymous and their length was limited to 30 pages excluding the bibliography and supplementary materials.

The review process was conducted using double-blind peer review. The conference operated a two-round review system with a rebuttal phase. After the reviews and first round discussions the PC selected 244 submissions to proceed to the second round and the authors were then invited to participate in an interactive rebuttal phase with the reviewers to clarify questions and concerns. The remaining 131 papers were rejected, including one desk reject. The second round involved extensive discussions by the PC members. After several weeks of additional discussions, the committee selected the final 106 papers to appear in these proceedings.

The eight volumes of the conference proceedings contain the revised versions of the 106 papers that were selected. The final revised versions of papers were not reviewed again and the authors are responsible for their contents.

The PC nominated and voted for two papers to receive the Best Paper Awards, and one paper to receive the Best Early Career Paper Award. The Best Paper Awards went to Thomas Espitau, Alexandre Wallet and Yang Yu for their paper "On Gaussian Sampling, Smoothing Parameter and Application to Signatures", and to Kaijie Jiang, Anyu Wang, Hengyi Luo, Guoxiao Liu, Yang Yu, and Xiaoyun Wang for their paper "Exploiting the Symmetry of Z^n: Randomization and the Automorphism Problem". The Best Early Career Paper Award went to Maxime Plancon for the paper "Exploiting Algebraic Structure in Probing Security". The authors of those three papers were invited to submit extended versions of their papers to the Journal of Cryptology. In addition, the program of Asiacrypt 2023 also included two invited plenary talks, also nominated and voted by the PC: one talk was given by Mehdi Tibouchi and the other by Xiaoyun Wang. The conference also featured a rump session chaired by Kang Yang and Yu Yu which contained short presentations on the latest research results of the field.

Numerous people contributed to the success of Asiacrypt 2023. We would like to thank all the authors, including those whose submissions were not accepted, for submitting their research results to the conference. We are very grateful to the area chairs, PC members and external reviewers for contributing their knowledge and expertise, and for the tremendous amount of work that was done with reading papers and contributing to the discussions. We are greatly indebted to Jian Weng and Fangguo Zhang, the General Chairs, for their efforts in organizing the event and to Kevin McCurley and Kay McKelly for their help with the website and review system. We thank the Asiacrypt 2023 advisory committee members Bart Preneel, Huaxiong Wang, Kai-Min Chung, Yu Sasaki, Dongdai Lin, Shweta Agrawal and Michel Abdalla for their valuable suggestions. We are also grateful for the helpful advice and organization material provided to us by the Eurocrypt 2023 PC co-chairs Carmit Hazay and Martijn Stam and Crypto 2023 PC co-chairs Helena Handschuh and Anna Lysyanskaya. We also thank the team at Springer for handling the publication of these conference proceedings.

December 2023

Jian Guo
Ron Steinfeld

Organization

General Chairs

Jian Weng	Jinan University, China
Fangguo Zhang	Sun Yat-sen University, China

Program Committee Chairs

Jian Guo	Nanyang Technological University, Singapore
Ron Steinfeld	Monash University, Australia

Program Committee

Behzad Abdolmaleki	University of Sheffield, UK
Masayuki Abe	NTT Social Informatics Laboratories, Japan
Miguel Ambrona	Input Output Global (IOHK), Spain
Daniel Apon	MITRE Labs, USA
Shi Bai	Florida Atlantic University, USA
Gustavo Banegas	Qualcomm, France
Zhenzhen Bao	Tsinghua University, China
Andrea Basso	University of Bristol, UK
Ward Beullens	IBM Research Europe, Switzerland
Katharina Boudgoust	Aarhus University, Denmark
Matteo Campanelli	Protocol Labs, Denmark
Ignacio Cascudo	IMDEA Software Institute, Spain
Wouter Castryck	imec-COSIC, KU Leuven, Belgium
Jie Chen	East China Normal University, China
Yilei Chen	Tsinghua University, China
Jung Hee Cheon	Seoul National University and Cryptolab Inc, South Korea
Sherman S. M. Chow	Chinese University of Hong Kong, China
Kai-Min Chung	Academia Sinica, Taiwan
Michele Ciampi	University of Edinburgh, UK
Bernardo David	IT University of Copenhagen, Denmark
Yi Deng	Institute of Information Engineering, Chinese Academy of Sciences, China

Patrick Derbez	University of Rennes, France
Xiaoyang Dong	Tsinghua University, China
Rafael Dowsley	Monash University, Australia
Nico Döttling	Helmholtz Center for Information Security, Germany
Maria Eichlseder	Graz University of Technology, Austria
Muhammed F. Esgin	Monash University, Australia
Thomas Espitau	PQShield, France
Jun Furukawa	NEC Corporation, Japan
Aron Gohr	Independent Researcher, New Zealand
Junqing Gong	ECNU, China
Lorenzo Grassi	Ruhr University Bochum, Germany
Tim Güneysu	Ruhr University Bochum, Germany
Chun Guo	Shandong University, China
Siyao Guo	NYU Shanghai, China
Fuchun Guo	University of Wollongong, Australia
Mohammad Hajiabadi	University of Waterloo, Canada
Lucjan Hanzlik	CISPA Helmholtz Center for Information Security, Germany
Xiaolu Hou	Slovak University of Technology, Slovakia
Yuncong Hu	Shanghai Jiao Tong University, China
Xinyi Huang	Hong Kong University of Science and Technology (Guangzhou), China
Tibor Jager	University of Wuppertal, Germany
Elena Kirshanova	Technology Innovation Institute, UAE and I. Kant Baltic Federal University, Russia
Eyal Kushilevitz	Technion, Israel
Russell W. F. Lai	Aalto University, Finland
Tanja Lange	Eindhoven University of Technology, Netherlands
Hyung Tae Lee	Chung-Ang University, South Korea
Eik List	Nanyang Technological University, Singapore
Meicheng Liu	Institute of Information Engineering, Chinese Academy of Sciences, China
Guozhen Liu	Nanyang Technological University, Singapore
Fukang Liu	Tokyo Institute of Technology, Japan
Shengli Liu	Shanghai Jiao Tong University, China
Feng-Hao Liu	Florida Atlantic University, USA
Hemanta K. Maji	Purdue University, USA
Takahiro Matsuda	AIST, Japan
Christian Matt	Concordium, Switzerland
Tomoyuki Morimae	Kyoto University, Japan
Pierrick Méaux	University of Luxembourg, Luxembourg

Benjamin Wesolowski	CNRS and ENS Lyon, France
Shuang Wu	Huawei International, Singapore, Singapore
Keita Xagawa	Technology Innovation Institute, UAE
Chaoping Xing	Shanghai Jiao Tong University, China
Jun Xu	Institute of Information Engineering, Chinese Academy of Sciences, China
Takashi Yamakawa	NTT Social Informatics Laboratories, Japan
Kang Yang	State Key Laboratory of Cryptology, China
Yu Yu	Shanghai Jiao Tong University, China
Yang Yu	Tsinghua University, Beijing, China
Yupeng Zhang	University of Illinois Urbana-Champaign and Texas A&M University, USA
Liangfeng Zhang	ShanghaiTech University, China
Raymond K. Zhao	CSIRO's Data61, Australia
Hong-Sheng Zhou	Virginia Commonwealth University, USA

Additional Reviewers

Amit Agarwal
Jooyoung Lee
Léo Ackermann
Akshima
Bar Alon
Ravi Anand
Sarah Arpin
Thomas Attema
Nuttapong Attrapadung
Manuel Barbosa
Razvan Barbulescu
James Bartusek
Carsten Baum
Olivier Bernard
Tyler Besselman
Ritam Bhaumik
Jingguo Bi
Loic Bidoux
Maxime Bombar
Xavier Bonnetain
Joppe Bos
Mariana Botelho da Gama
Christina Boura
Clémence Bouvier
Ross Bowden
Pedro Branco
Lauren Brandt
Alessandro Budroni
Kevin Carrier
André Chailloux
Suvradip Chakraborty
Debasmita Chakraborty
Haokai Chang
Bhuvnesh Chaturvedi
Caicai Chen
Rongmao Chen
Mingjie Chen
Yi Chen
Megan Chen
Yu Long Chen
Xin Chen
Shiyao Chen
Long Chen
Wonhee Cho
Qiaohan Chu
Valerio Cini
James Clements
Ran Cohen
Alexandru Cojocaru
Sandro Coretti-Drayton

Anamaria Costache
Alain Couvreur
Daniele Cozzo
Hongrui Cui
Giuseppe D'Alconzo
Zhaopeng Dai
Quang Dao
Nilanjan Datta
Koen de Boer
Luca De Feo
Paola de Perthuis
Thomas Decru
Rafael del Pino
Julien Devevey
Henri Devillez
Siemen Dhooghe
Yaoling Ding
Jack Doerner
Jelle Don
Mark Douglas Schultz
Benjamin Dowling
Minxin Du
Xiaoqi Duan
Jesko Dujmovic
Moumita Dutta
Avijit Dutta
Ehsan Ebrahimi
Felix Engelmann
Reo Eriguchi
Jonathan Komada Eriksen
Andre Esser
Pouria Fallahpour
Zhiyong Fang
Antonio Faonio
Pooya Farshim
Joël Felderhoff
Jakob Feldtkeller
Weiqi Feng
Xiutao Feng
Shuai Feng
Qi Feng
Hanwen Feng
Antonio Flórez-Gutiérrez
Apostolos Fournaris
Paul Frixons
Ximing Fu
Georg Fuchsbauer
Philippe Gaborit
Rachit Garg
Robin Geelen
Riddhi Ghosal
Koustabh Ghosh
Barbara Gigerl
Niv Gilboa
Valerie Gilchrist
Emanuele Giunta
Xinxin Gong
Huijing Gong
Zheng Gong
Robert Granger
Zichen Gui
Anna Guinet
Qian Guo
Xiaojie Guo
Hosein Hadipour
Mathias Hall-Andersen
Mike Hamburg
Shuai Han
Yonglin Hao
Keisuke Hara
Keitaro Hashimoto
Le He
Brett Hemenway Falk
Minki Hhan
Taiga Hiroka
Akinori Hosoyamada
Chengan Hou
Martha Norberg Hovd
Kai Hu
Tao Huang
Zhenyu Huang
Michael Hutter
Jihun Hwang
Akiko Inoue
Tetsu Iwata
Robin Jadoul
Hansraj Jangir
Dirmanto Jap
Stanislaw Jarecki
Santos Jha

Ashwin Jha
Dingding Jia
Yanxue Jia
Lin Jiao
Daniel Jost
Antoine Joux
Jiayi Kang
Gabriel Kaptchuk
Alexander Karenin
Shuichi Katsumata
Pengzhen Ke
Mustafa Khairallah
Shahram Khazaei
Hamidreza Amini Khorasgani
Hamidreza Khoshakhlagh
Ryo Kikuchi
Jiseung Kim
Minkyu Kim
Suhri Kim
Ravi Kishore
Fuyuki Kitagawa
Susumu Kiyoshima
Michael Klooß
Alexander Koch
Sreehari Kollath
Dimitris Kolonelos
Yashvanth Kondi
Anders Konring
Woong Kook
Dimitri Koshelev
Markus Krausz
Toomas Krips
Daniel Kuijsters
Anunay Kulshrestha
Qiqi Lai
Yi-Fu Lai
Georg Land
Nathalie Lang
Mario Larangeira
Joon-Woo Lee
Keewoo Lee
Hyeonbum Lee
Changmin Lee
Charlotte Lefevre
Julia Len
Antonin Leroux
Andrea Lesavourey
Jannis Leuther
Jie Li
Shuaishuai Li
Huina Li
Yu Li
Yanan Li
Jiangtao Li
Song Song Li
Wenjie Li
Shun Li
Zengpeng Li
Xiao Liang
Wei-Kai Lin
Chengjun Lin
Chao Lin
Cong Ling
Yunhao Ling
Hongqing Liu
Jing Liu
Jiahui Liu
Qipeng Liu
Yamin Liu
Weiran Liu
Tianyi Liu
Siqi Liu
Chen-Da Liu-Zhang
Jinyu Lu
Zhenghao Lu
Stefan Lucks
Yiyuan Luo
Lixia Luo
Jack P. K. Ma
Fermi Ma
Gilles Macario-Rat
Luciano Maino
Christian Majenz
Laurane Marco
Lorenzo Martinico
Loïc Masure
John McVey
Willi Meier
Kelsey Melissaris
Bart Mennink

Charles Meyer-Hilfiger
Victor Miller
Chohong Min
Marine Minier
Arash Mirzaei
Pratyush Mishra
Tarik Moataz
Johannes Mono
Fabrice Mouhartem
Alice Murphy
Erik Mårtensson
Anne Müller
Marcel Nageler
Yusuke Naito
Barak Nehoran
Patrick Neumann
Tran Ngo
Phuong Hoa Nguyen
Ngoc Khanh Nguyen
Thi Thu Quyen Nguyen
Hai H. Nguyen
Semyon Novoselov
Julian Nowakowski
Arne Tobias Malkenes Ødegaard
Kazuma Ohara
Miyako Ohkubo
Charles Olivier-Anclin
Eran Omri
Yi Ouyang
Tapas Pal
Ying-yu Pan
Jiaxin Pan
Eugenio Paracucchi
Roberto Parisella
Jeongeun Park
Guillermo Pascual-Perez
Alain Passelègue
Octavio Perez-Kempner
Thomas Peters
Phuong Pham
Cécile Pierrot
Erik Pohle
David Pointcheval
Giacomo Pope
Christopher Portmann
Romain Poussier
Lucas Prabel
Sihang Pu
Chen Qian
Luowen Qian
Tian Qiu
Anaïs Querol
Håvard Raddum
Shahram Rasoolzadeh
Divya Ravi
Prasanna Ravi
Marc Renard
Jan Richter-Brockmann
Lawrence Roy
Paul Rösler
Sayandeep Saha
Yusuke Sakai
Niels Samwel
Paolo Santini
Maria Corte-Real Santos
Sara Sarfaraz
Santanu Sarkar
Or Sattath
Markus Schofnegger
Peter Scholl
Dominique Schröder
André Schrottenloher
Jacob Schuldt
Binanda Sengupta
Srinath Setty
Yantian Shen
Yixin Shen
Ferdinand Sibleyras
Janno Siim
Mark Simkin
Scott Simon
Animesh Singh
Nitin Singh
Sayani Sinha
Daniel Slamanig
Fang Song
Ling Song
Yongsoo Song
Jana Sotakova
Gabriele Spini

Marianna Spyrakou
Lukas Stennes
Marc Stoettinger
Chuanjie Su
Xiangyu Su
Ling Sun
Akira Takahashi
Isobe Takanori
Atsushi Takayasu
Suprita Talnikar
Benjamin Hong Meng Tan
Ertem Nusret Tas
Tadanori Teruya
Masayuki Tezuka
Sri AravindaKrishnan Thyagarajan
Song Tian
Wenlong Tian
Raphael Toledo
Junichi Tomida
Daniel Tschudi
Hikaru Tsuchida
Aleksei Udovenko
Rei Ueno
Barry Van Leeuwen
Wessel van Woerden
Frederik Vercauteren
Sulani Vidhanalage
Benedikt Wagner
Roman Walch
Hendrik Waldner
Han Wang
Luping Wang
Peng Wang
Yuntao Wang
Geng Wang
Shichang Wang
Liping Wang
Jiafan Wang
Zhedong Wang
Kunpeng Wang
Jianfeng Wang
Guilin Wang
Weiqiang Wen
Chenkai Weng
Thom Wiggers
Stella Wohnig
Harry W. H. Wong
Ivy K. Y. Woo
Yu Xia
Zejun Xiang
Yuting Xiao
Zhiye Xie
Yanhong Xu
Jiayu Xu
Lei Xu
Shota Yamada
Kazuki Yamamura
Di Yan
Qianqian Yang
Shaojun Yang
Yanjiang Yang
Li Yao
Yizhou Yao
Kenji Yasunaga
Yuping Ye
Xiuyu Ye
Zeyuan Yin
Kazuki Yoneyama
Yusuke Yoshida
Albert Yu
Quan Yuan
Chen Yuan
Tsz Hon Yuen
Aaram Yun
Riccardo Zanotto
Arantxa Zapico
Shang Zehua
Mark Zhandry
Tianyu Zhang
Zhongyi Zhang
Fan Zhang
Liu Zhang
Yijian Zhang
Shaoxuan Zhang
Zhongliang Zhang
Kai Zhang
Cong Zhang
Jiaheng Zhang
Lulu Zhang
Zhiyu Zhang

Chang-An Zhao
Yongjun Zhao
Chunhuan Zhao
Xiaotong Zhou
Zhelei Zhou
Zijian Zhou
Timo Zijlstra
Jian Zou
Ferdinando Zullo
Cong Zuo

Sponsoring Institutions

- Gold Level Sponsor: Ant Research
- Silver Level Sponsors: Sansec Technology Co., Ltd., Topsec Technologies Group
- Bronze Level Sponsors: IBM, Meta, Sangfor Technologies Inc.

Contents – Part V

Functional Encryption, Commitments and Proofs

Improved Fully Adaptive Decentralized MA-ABE for NC1 from MDDH 3
Jie Chen, Qiaohan Chu, Ying Gao, Jianting Ning, and Luping Wang

Verifiable Decentralized Multi-client Functional Encryption for Inner Product 33
Dinh Duy Nguyen, Duong Hieu Phan, and David Pointcheval

Registered ABE via Predicate Encodings 66
Ziqi Zhu, Kai Zhang, Junqing Gong, and Haifeng Qian

Registered (Inner-Product) Functional Encryption 98
Danilo Francati, Daniele Friolo, Monosij Maitra, Giulio Malavolta, Ahmadreza Rahimi, and Daniele Venturi

Robust Decentralized Multi-client Functional Encryption: Motivation, Definition, and Inner-Product Constructions 134
Yamin Li, Jianghong Wei, Fuchun Guo, Willy Susilo, and Xiaofeng Chen

Cuckoo Commitments: Registration-Based Encryption and Key-Value Map Commitments for Large Spaces 166
Dario Fiore, Dimitris Kolonelos, and Paola de Perthuis

Lattice-Based Functional Commitments: Fast Verification and Cryptanalysis 201
Hoeteck Wee and David J. Wu

Non-interactive Zero-Knowledge Functional Proofs 236
Gongxian Zeng, Junzuo Lai, Zhengan Huang, Linru Zhang, Xiangning Wang, Kwok-Yan Lam, Huaxiong Wang, and Jian Weng

Zero-Knowledge Functional Elementary Databases 269
Xinxuan Zhang and Yi Deng

Secure Messaging and Broadcast

WhatsUpp with Sender Keys? Analysis, Improvements and Security Proofs 307
David Balbás, Daniel Collins, and Phillip Gajland

Efficient Updatable Public-Key Encryption from Lattices ... 342
Calvin Abou Haidar, Alain Passelègue, and Damien Stehlé

CCA-1 Secure Updatable Encryption with Adaptive Security ... 374
Huanhuan Chen, Yao Jiang Galteland, and Kaitai Liang

Distributed Broadcast Encryption from Bilinear Groups ... 407
Dimitris Kolonelos, Giulio Malavolta, and Hoeteck Wee

Author Index ... 443

Functional Encryption, Commitments and Proofs

Improved Fully Adaptive Decentralized MA-ABE for NC1 from MDDH

Jie Chen[1], Qiaohan Chu[1](✉), Ying Gao[2,3], Jianting Ning[4], and Luping Wang[5]

[1] Shanghai Key Laboratory of Trustworthy Computing, Software Engineering Institute, East China Normal University, Shanghai, China
52205902004@stu.ecnu.edu.cn

[2] School of Cyber Science and Technology, Beihang University, Beijing, China

[3] Zhongguancun Laboratory, Beijing, China

[4] College of Computer and Cyberspace Security, Fujian Normal University, Fuzhou, China

[5] School of Electronic and Information Engineering, Suzhou University of Science and Technology, Suzhou, China

Abstract. We improve the first and the only existing prime-order fully adaptively secure decentralized Multi-Authority Attribute-Based Encryption (MA-ABE) scheme for NC1 in Datta-Komargodski-Waters [Eurocrypt '23]. Compared with Datta-Komargodski-Waters, our decentralized MA-ABE scheme extra enjoys shorter parameters and meanwhile supports many-use of attribute. Shorter parameters is always the goal for Attribute-Based Encryption (ABE), and many-use of attribute is a native property of decentralized MA-ABE for NC1. Our scheme relies on the Matrix Decision Diffie-Hellman (MDDH) assumption and is in the random oracle model, as Datta-Komargodski-Waters.

Keywords: Attribute-Based Encryption · Decentralized · Fully Adaptive Security

1 Introduction

Attribute-Based Encryption (ABE) [22,36] is a public key encryption primitive that supports fine-grained access control for encrypted data. Concretely, ABE allows the encryptor to embed some attribute vector or policy into the ciphertext, and only the user who holds a secret key associated with a satisfied policy or satisfied attribute vector can decrypt the ciphertext successfully. Since the introduction of ABE, there have been plenty of works focusing on ABE, about security, efficiency, expressiveness and more [1,3,6,9,10,19–21,23,25–27,30,31,33,38,40,41].

Decentralized Multi-authority ABE. Traditional ABE requires a central authority that is in charge of generating and storing the master secret key. With

J. Guo and R. Steinfeld (Eds.): ASIACRYPT 2023, LNCS 14442, pp. 3–32, 2023.
https://doi.org/10.1007/978-981-99-8733-7_1

the master secret key, this central authority can generate any secret key and thus decrypt all the ciphertexts. Therefore, if this central authority is malicious, the security of the ABE system is destroyed. To mitigate such a trust reliance on the central authority, the notion of Multi-Authority Attribute-Based Encryption (MA-ABE) has been introduced and studied. There have been some earlier works about MA-ABE [7,8,29,32], however, these earlier works are limited in either functionality or security. Later, Lewko and Waters [28] proposed the first truly decentralized MA-ABE scheme for NC1 (it is well known that NC1 can be realized by (monotone) Linear Secret Sharing Scheme (LSSS) [4,28,33], below, we use the policy NC1 and LSSS interchangeably) in composite-order groups under the Subgroup Decision (SD) assumptions achieving adaptive security. In decentralized MA-ABE, anyone can become an authority, and each authority controls a set of attributes. Each authority generates the public keys and the master secret keys associated with the attributes he controls, and issues the corresponding secret keys to the users. Since the encryption algorithm takes as input the public keys, which are generated by different authorities, each authority cannot generate valid secret keys associated with the attributes that are not controlled by him, thus the central trust is distributed. The decryption of decentralized MA-ABE requires a user to collect the secret keys associated with the attributes that satisfy the policy embedded in the ciphertext, from a set of authorities. In decentralized MA-ABE, no global coordination is needed, except the creation of an initial set of common reference parameters, i.e., the global parameters.

Fully Adaptive Security. For the security of decentralized MA-ABE, it is required that for a challenge ciphertext, it is collusion-resistant against an arbitrary number of unauthorized secret keys, which corresponds to an arbitrary number of unauthoried secret key queries in the security game (below, we regard secret key queries as an arbitrary number of unauthorized secret key queries, by default), and is against corruptions of some authorities, which corresponds to some corruption queries in the security game. Before Datta, Komargodski, and Waters [15], the best security level of decentralized MA-ABE is against static corruption queries of some authorities (which means the corruption queries of some authorities should be made at the beginning, even before seeing any secret key), and adaptive ciphertext and secret key queries (which means the ciphertext and secret key queries can be made at any time). Recently, Datta, Komargodski, and Waters [15] proposed the first fully adaptively secure decentralized MA-ABE schemes, which are against not only adaptive ciphertext and secret key queries, but also adaptive corruption queries of some authorities (which means the corruption queries of some authorities can be made at any time).

A Sequence of Works. Subsequent to Lewko and Waters's work [28], a number of decentralized MA-ABE constructions have been proposed. Rouselakis and Waters [35] proposed a decentralized MA-ABE scheme for NC1 that improves the efficiency, but under the non-standard q-type assumption and achieving only static security. Okamoto and Takashima [34] proposed a decentralized MA-ABE scheme for NC1 in prime-order groups under the Decision Linear (DLin) assumption [5] and achieving adaptive security. Ambrona and Gay [2] proposed decentralized MA-ABE schemes for NC1 either achieving adaptive security in the generic group model (GGM), or achieving selective security under the Symmetric External Diffie-Hellman (SXDH) assumption. Datta, Komargodski, and Waters [12] proposed the first decentralized MA-ABE scheme under the Learning With Errors (LWE) assumption, but supporting a non-trivial DNF access policy and achieving only static security. Datta, Komargodski, and Waters [13] also proposed the first decentralized MA-ABE scheme for NC1 under the standard computational or decisional bilinear Diffie-Hellman (C/DBDH) assumptions, but achieving only static security. Waters, Wee, and Wu [39] proposed a decentralized MA-ABE scheme for DNF without random oracles, under the recently-introduced evasive LWE assumption [37,42], but achieving only static security. Recently, Datta, Komargodski, and Waters [15] proposed the first decentralized MA-ABE schemes for NC1 achieving fully adaptive security, under the SD assumptions and MDDH assumption.

Many-Use of Attribute. Traditionally, pairing-based ABE for LSSS usually confronts the one-use of attribute limitation, which means that the mapping ρ of LSSS is restricted to be injective. This is because in the security analysis, we usually need the property that the master secret key $\mathbf{W}_{\rho(x)}$ is random. However, it is expected that the attribute can be used for many times, since many-use of attribute is closer to the real world in the sense that attributes are usually reused. One rescue for one-use limitation is using a simple encoding technique [26,28], but this will incur the ciphertext size growing with the policy size. Rouselakis and Waters [35] proposed a decentralized MA-ABE scheme for LSSS allowing many-use of attribute without sacrificing the ciphertext size. In [35], they use the random oracle to overcome the one-use limitation. Later, Kowalczyk and Wee [24] proposed ABE schemes for LSSS that allow many-use of attribute without sacrficing the ciphertext size. In [24], they mainly rely on a single-queried adaptively secure ABE for LSSS (which is called Core 1-ABE in [24]) to achieve many-use of attribute. Ambrona and Gay [2] also constructed decentralized MA-ABE schemes for LSSS without the one-use limitation. In [2], the one-use limitation is overcome by the underlying Identity-Based Functional Encryption scheme for inner products.

1.1 Results

We improve the first and the only existing fully adaptively secure decentralized MA-ABE scheme in prime-order groups of [15]. Concretely, our construction is almost in the same style as the construction of [15], except that

- we prove that our construction allows many-use of attribute without sacrificing the ciphertext size;

- in our construction, the dimension of the ciphertext matrix is of $2k+1$ and the dimension of secret key matrix is of $3k$, while in the construction of [15], both the ciphertext matrix and the secret key matrix are of $3k$-dimension, where k is the parameter of the MDDH assumption.

Our construction relies on the MDDH assumption and is in the random oracle model, as [15].

We present detailed comparisons in Table 1 and Table 2.

Table 1. A comparison of current decentralized MA-ABE schemes for NC1

Scheme	Assumption	Security	Bounded Policy Size?	Many-Use?
AG21 [2]	GGM	Adaptive	No	Yes
AG21 [2]	SXDH	Selective	No	Yes
LW11 [28]	SD	Adaptive	No	No
OT20 [34]	DLin	Adaptive	No	No
RW15 [35]	q-type	Static	No	Yes
DKW21b [13]	C/DBDH	Static	Yes	No
DKW23 [15]	SD	Fully Adaptive	No	No
DKW23 [15]	MDDH	Fully Adaptive	No	No
Ours	MDDH	Fully Adaptive	No	Yes

- Adaptive security means the corruption queries are made at the beginning, but the ciphertext and secret key queries can be made adaptively; Selective security means the ciphertext and corruption queries are made before the secret key queries, while the secret key queries can be made adaptively; Static security means the ciphertext, secret key and corruption queries are made before the public key of any attribute authority is published; Fully adaptive security means the ciphertext, secret key and corruption queries can all be made adaptively.
- For "Bounded Policy Size?", "No" denotes that the corresponding scheme is not required to declare the maximal size of policy during the system setup, and "Yes" denotes that the corresponding scheme is required to declare the maximal size of policy during the system setup.
- For "Many-Use?", "No" denotes that the corresponding scheme does not allow many-use of attribute without parameter size expansion, and "Yes" denotes that the corresponding scheme allows many-use of attribute without parameter size expansion.
- All the schemes in the Table are in the random oracle model.

1.2 Technical Overview

Before we proceed to the details of our technical overview, we first provide a summary in Fig. 1 to make our approaches clear.

Table 2. A comparison of fully adaptively secure decentralized MA-ABE in prime-order groups

Scheme	$\lvert \mathsf{PK}_u \rvert$	$\lvert \mathsf{MSK}_u \rvert$	$\lvert \mathsf{CT} \rvert$	$\lvert \mathsf{sk}_{\mathsf{GID},u} \rvert$	Many-Use?
DKW23 [15]	$6k^2\lvert G_1\rvert$	$18k^2\lvert \mathbb{Z}_p\rvert$	$12k\ell\lvert G_1\rvert$	$6k\lvert G_2\rvert$	No
Ours	$6k^2\lvert G_1\rvert$	$(12k^2+6k)\lvert \mathbb{Z}_p\rvert$	$(10k\ell+2\ell)\lvert G_1\rvert$	$(4k+2)\lvert G_2\rvert$	Yes

- We omit C and the access policy $(\mathbf{M}, \rho)$ in CT.
- k denotes the parameter of the MDDH assumption, and ℓ denotes the number of the rows of $\mathbf{M}$ in access policy $(\mathbf{M}, \rho)$.
- We assume that each authority controls a single attribute, thus the subscripts of $\mathsf{PK}, \mathsf{MSK}$ and $\mathsf{sk}_{\mathsf{GID}}$ are all u.

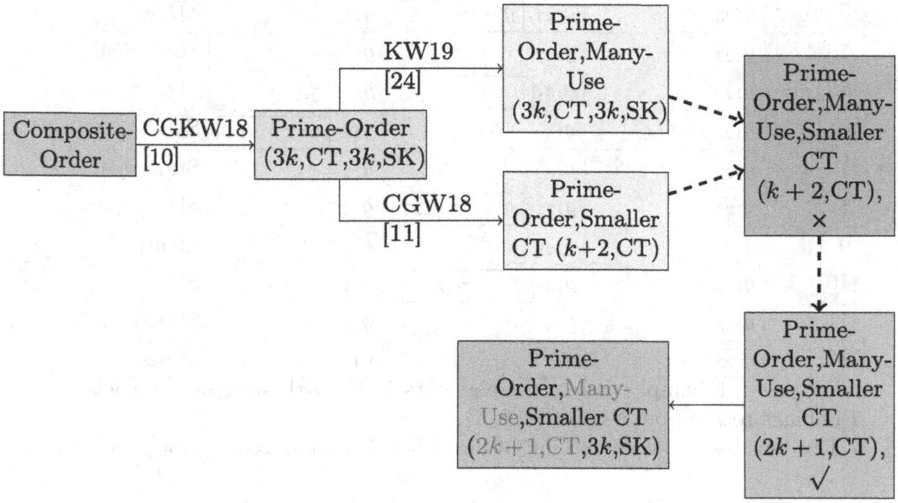

Fig. 1. Summary of our approaches. The dashed line shows an attempt, which is described in the pointed box. The cross shows that we failed in the attempt, and the check mark shows that we succeeded in the attempt. For the format like "(2k + 1, CT, 3k, SK)", $2k + 1$ describes the matrix size of the ciphertext and $3k$ describes the matrix size of the secret key. We highlight our contributions in green (Color figure online).

Recap of Datta-Komargodski-Waters Composite-Order Decentralized MA-ABE. We start with recapping the security proofs of the composite-order decentralized MA-ABE construction in [15], which is shown in Table 3.

Observe that throughout the hybrids, three subgroups are involved, thus, for the prime-order construction, it should involve three subspaces. For CT and h, it needs the SD assumptions of "g_1 to g_{13}", and "g_1 to g_{12}", which are both based on the first subgroup g_1. For $\mathsf{H}(\mathsf{GID})$, it needs the SD assumptions of "g_{123} to g_1", "g_1 to g_{12}", "g_{12} to g_1", which are based on the first subgroup g_1, and "g_{12} to g_{123}", which is implicitly based on the second subgroup g_2, and "g_{13} to g_{123}", "g_{123} to g_{13}", which are implicitly based on the third subgroup g_3. Note that

Table 3. Hybrid sequence for the composite-order decentralized MA-ABE in [15]

Hybrid	CT	H(GID)	h	Justification
0	g_1	g_{123}	g_1	–
1	g_1	g_1, $\boxed{g_{123} \mapsto g_1}$	g_1	SD
2	g_{13}, $\boxed{g_1 \mapsto g_{13}}$	g_1	g_1	SD
3	g_{13}	g_1	g_1	Statistical
4	g_{123}, $\boxed{g_1 \mapsto g_{12}}$	g_1	g_1	SD
5:j:1	g_{123}	g_{12}, $\boxed{g_1 \mapsto g_{12}}$	g_1	SD
5:j:2	g_{123}	g_{12}	g_1	Statistical
5:j:3	g_{123}	g_{123}, $\boxed{g_{12} \mapsto g_{123}}$	g_1	SD
5:j:4	g_{123}	g_{123}	g_1	Statistical
5:(j+1)	g_{123}	g_{13}, $\boxed{g_{12} \mapsto g_1}$	g_1	SD
6	g_{123}	g_{13}	g_{12}, $\boxed{g_1 \mapsto g_{12}}$	SD
7	g_{123}	g_{13}	g_{12}	Statistical
8	g_{123}	g_{123}, $\boxed{g_{13} \mapsto g_{123}}$	g_{12}	SD
9	g_{123}	g_{123}	g_{12}	Identical
10	g_{123}	g_{13}, $\boxed{g_{123} \mapsto g_{13}}$	g_{12}	SD
11	g_{123}	g_{13}	g_{12}	Statistical
12	g_{123}	g_{13}	g_{12}	Statistical

- We use g_i to simply denote the elements in the i-th subgroup, for which i belongs to the power set of $\{1, 2, 3\}$.
- The box describes which kind of Subgroup Decision assumption is used.

for CT, the "based on" subgroup consists of only g_1, and for H(GID) and h, the (implicitly) "based on" subgroups consist of g_1, g_2 and g_3. The analysis of the "based on" subgroups is prepared for the later "horter matrix" part. Roughly speaking, the subspace corresponding to the "based on" subgroup must be of k-dimension, where k is the parameter of the MDDH assumption.

Straight-Forward Transformation from Composite-Order to Prime-Order. We transform the above composite-order construction into prime-order construction by using the framework of [10] in a straight-forward way. Let's recall the framework of [10]. In the framework, there is a correspondence as follows:

$$\text{for CT}, \; g_i \mapsto [\mathbf{A}_i]_1, g_i^{s_i} \mapsto [\mathbf{s}_i \mathbf{A}_i^\top]_1,$$
$$\text{for H(GID) and } h, \; g_j \mapsto [\mathbf{B}_j]_2, g_j^{r_j} \mapsto [\mathbf{B}_j \mathbf{r}_j]_2,$$

where $i, j \in \{1, 2, 3\}$, $\mathbf{A}_i \in \mathbb{Z}_p^{\ell'_A \times \ell_i}$, $\mathbf{s}_i \leftarrow_R \mathbb{Z}_p^{1 \times \ell_i}$, $\mathbf{B}_j \in \mathbb{Z}_p^{\ell'_B \times \ell_j}$, $\mathbf{r}_j \leftarrow_R \mathbb{Z}_p^{\ell_j \times 1}$, and $\ell'_A = \sum_i \ell_i, \ell'_B = \sum_j \ell_j$.

Naturally, as in [17,18], we would like to set $\ell_i = \ell_j = k$, for all $i, j \in \{1, 2, 3\}$, where k is the parameter of the MDDH assumption, and below we default k to this meaning. Then, the ℓ'_A and ℓ'_B are equal to $3k$, which is the same as in the prime-order decentralized MA-ABE construction of [15].

Equipped with Many-Use of Attribute. To equip the above prime-order construction with many-use of attribute, we roughly leverage the technique in Kowalczyk and Wee's work [24]. Roughly speaking, their technique can be regarded as replacing statistical indistinguishability with computational indistinguishability. Recall that in [24], Kowalczyk and Wee first defined a single-queried ABE, called Core 1-ABE, which demonstrates the indistinguishability between the random secrets μ_0 and μ_1 of LSSS. Then they programmed the Core 1-ABE into a centralized ABE scheme, and changed the secret in the central ABE scheme into a random value. Note that in their work, the Core 1-ABE is applied into a centralized ABE, while we hope to apply it into a decentralized ABE. Fortunately, in a similar way, we can successfully program the Core 1-ABE to change the secrets in our construction. Following the technique in [24] directly, we need to set the ℓ'_A in our construction as $3k$. This is because the Core 1-ABE is based on a MDDH-based CPA-secure symmetric encryption, when changing a secret, we need a k-dimensional space to assist to program it. Since throughout the proofs, two kinds of secrets need to be changed, thus, intuitively, we need a $2k$-dimensional space. That is, the number of the columns of $\mathbf{A}_2$ and $\mathbf{A}_3$ (i.e., the ℓ_2 and ℓ_3 of "$\mathbf{A}$") should be set as k, thus, plus the number of the columns of $\mathbf{A}_1$ (i.e., the ℓ_1 of "$\mathbf{A}$"), which is k, we have $\ell'_A = 3k$. Note that this exactly matches the ℓ'_A we have set in the last section. That is, from the aspect of many-use of attribute, the ℓ'_A is $3k$, and from the aspect of straight-forward transformation in the last section, the ℓ'_A is also $3k$.

Smaller Ciphertext Matrix. Inspired by Chen, Gong, and Wee's work [11], we would like to explore whether we can improve $3k$ to a smaller dimension, like $k+2$. Recall that for ciphertext, the "based on" subgroup consists of only g_1, therefore, when transforming composite-order into prime-order, it is sufficient to set $\mathbf{A}_1 \in \mathbb{Z}_p^{(k+2)\times k}$ and $\mathbf{A}_2, \mathbf{A}_3 \in \mathbb{Z}_p^{(k+2)\times 1}$, rather than set $\mathbf{A}_1, \mathbf{A}_2, \mathbf{A}_3 \in \mathbb{Z}_p^{3k\times k}$, if we don't consider many-use of attribute.

Challenge: Many-Use of Attribute and Smaller Ciphertext Matrix Simultaneously. To program the Core 1-ABE, we require the ℓ_2, ℓ_3 of "$\mathbf{A}$" to be k. While, for smaller ciphertext matrix, we expect the ℓ_2, ℓ_3 of "$\mathbf{A}$" to be 1. This seems to tell us that many-use of attribute cannot coexist with smaller ciphertext matrix.

An Attempt. Our observation is that in fact, we only need one "k" matrix to help us to program the Core 1-ABE. That is, the "two kinds of secrets" can share one k-dimensional space. Then, can we use $\mathbf{A}_1$ to help us to program the Core 1-ABE and finally achieve $(k+2)$-dimensional ciphertext matrix? The answer is negative. The essential point is that the simulator can only query a proportion of the secret keys of the CPA-secure symmetric encryption, thus the simulator cannot simulate all the public keys of the decentralized MA-ABE construction.

Final Solution. The fact that gaining "k" from $\mathbf{A}_1$ cannot work suggests that we have to use another shared "k" matrix, so that we can preserve the public keys unchanged (by the orthogonality). However, to successfully program the Core 1-ABE, we need this another "k" matrix not to be orthogonal to the matrices that have existed in the ciphertext. Fortunately, when we set $\mathbf{A}_3$ as the another "k" matrix, we can successfully program the Core 1-ABE in all the related proofs (while, if we set $\mathbf{A}_2$ as the another "k" matrix, we cannot successfully program the Core 1-ABE in some proofs). Then by setting $\mathbf{A}_1, \mathbf{A}_3 \in \mathbb{Z}_p^{(2k+1)\times k}, \mathbf{A}_2 \in \mathbb{Z}_p^{(2k+1)\times 1}$, we finally achieve $(2k+1)$-dimensional ciphertext matrix and meanwhile achieve many-use of attribute.

To better demonstrate our construction, we provide a summary of the hybrid sequence of our construction in Table 4.

Table 4. Hybrid sequence for our prime-order decentralized MA-ABE

Hybrid	CT	H(GID)	h	Justification
0	$\mathbf{A}_1$	$\mathbf{B}_1, \mathbf{B}_2, \mathbf{B}_3$	$\mathbf{B}_1$	-
1	$\mathbf{A}_1$	$\mathbf{B}_1$, $\boxed{\mathbf{B}_1, \mathbf{B}_2, \mathbf{B}_3 \mapsto \mathbf{B}_1}$	$\mathbf{B}_1$	MDDH
2	$\mathbf{A}_1, \mathbf{A}_3$, $\boxed{\mathbf{A}_1 \mapsto \mathbf{A}_1, \mathbf{A}_3}$	$\mathbf{B}_1$	$\mathbf{B}_1$	MDDH
3	$\mathbf{A}_1, \mathbf{A}_3$	$\mathbf{B}_1$	$\mathbf{B}_1$	Core 1-ABE
4	$\mathbf{A}_1, \mathbf{A}_2, \mathbf{A}_3$, $\boxed{\mathbf{A}_1 \mapsto \mathbf{A}_1, \mathbf{A}_2}$	$\mathbf{B}_1$	$\mathbf{B}_1$	MDDH
5:j:1	$\mathbf{A}_1, \mathbf{A}_2, \mathbf{A}_3$	$\mathbf{B}_1, \mathbf{B}_2$, $\boxed{\mathbf{B}_1 \mapsto \mathbf{B}_1, \mathbf{B}_2}$	$\mathbf{B}_1$	MDDH
5:j:2	$\mathbf{A}_1, \mathbf{A}_2, \mathbf{A}_3$	$\mathbf{B}_1, \mathbf{B}_2$	$\mathbf{B}_1$	Core 1-ABE
5:j:3	$\mathbf{A}_1, \mathbf{A}_2, \mathbf{A}_3$	$\mathbf{B}_1, \mathbf{B}_2, \mathbf{B}_3$, $\boxed{\mathbf{B}_2 \mapsto \mathbf{B}_2, \mathbf{B}_3}$	$\mathbf{B}_1$	MDDH
5:j:4	$\mathbf{A}_1, \mathbf{A}_2, \mathbf{A}_3$	$\mathbf{B}_1, \mathbf{B}_2, \mathbf{B}_3$	$\mathbf{B}_1$	Core 1-ABE
5:(j+1)	$\mathbf{A}_1, \mathbf{A}_2, \mathbf{A}_3$	$\mathbf{B}_1, \mathbf{B}_3$, $\boxed{\mathbf{B}_1, \mathbf{B}_2 \mapsto \mathbf{B}_1}$	$\mathbf{B}_1$	MDDH
6	$\mathbf{A}_1, \mathbf{A}_2, \mathbf{A}_3$	$\mathbf{B}_1, \mathbf{B}_3$	$\mathbf{B}_1, \mathbf{B}_2$, $\boxed{\mathbf{B}_1 \mapsto \mathbf{B}_1, \mathbf{B}_2}$	MDDH
7	$\mathbf{A}_1, \mathbf{A}_2, \mathbf{A}_3$	$\mathbf{B}_1, \mathbf{B}_3$	$\mathbf{B}_1, \mathbf{B}_2$	Core 1-ABE
8	$\mathbf{A}_1, \mathbf{A}_2, \mathbf{A}_3$	$\mathbf{B}_1, \mathbf{B}_2, \mathbf{B}_3$, $\boxed{\mathbf{B}_3 \mapsto \mathbf{B}_2, \mathbf{B}_3}$	$\mathbf{B}_1, \mathbf{B}_2$	MDDH
9	$\mathbf{A}_1, \mathbf{A}_2, \mathbf{A}_3$	$\mathbf{B}_1, \mathbf{B}_2, \mathbf{B}_3$	$\mathbf{B}_1, \mathbf{B}_2$	Identical
10	$\mathbf{A}_1, \mathbf{A}_2, \mathbf{A}_3$	$\mathbf{B}_1, \mathbf{B}_3$, $\boxed{\mathbf{B}_2, \mathbf{B}_3 \mapsto \mathbf{B}_3}$	$\mathbf{B}_1, \mathbf{B}_2$	MDDH
11	$\mathbf{A}_1, \mathbf{A}_2, \mathbf{A}_3$	$\mathbf{B}_1, \mathbf{B}_3$	$\mathbf{B}_1, \mathbf{B}_2$	Core 1-ABE
12	$\mathbf{A}_1, \mathbf{A}_2, \mathbf{A}_3$	$\mathbf{B}_1, \mathbf{B}_3$	$\mathbf{B}_1, \mathbf{B}_2$	Statistical

- We use $\mathbf{A}_1 \in \mathbb{Z}_p^{(2k+1)\times k}, \mathbf{A}_2 \in \mathbb{Z}_p^{(2k+1)\times 1}, \mathbf{A}_3 \in \mathbb{Z}_p^{(2k+1)\times k}$ and $\mathbf{B}_1, \mathbf{B}_2, \mathbf{B}_3 \in \mathbb{Z}_p^{3k\times k}$ to denote the subspaces in CT and the subspaces in H(GID), h, respectively.
- The box describes the transition of the subspaces.

2 Preliminaries

2.1 Notations

We use $\leftarrow_R$ to denote random sampling, and use $\|$ to denote concatenation of matrices. For an integer N, we use $[N]$ to denote the set $\{1, ..., N\}$. We use $\equiv$ to denote two distributions being identically indistinguishable. For a matrix $\mathbf{A}$, we use $\mathsf{span}(\mathbf{A})$ to denote the column span of $\mathbf{A}$ and use $\mathsf{basis}(\mathbf{A})$ to denote a basis of $\mathsf{span}(\mathbf{A})$. We use $\mathbf{I}$ to denote an identity matrix of proper size, and use $\mathbf{0}$ to denote a zero matrix of proper size.

2.2 Prime-Order Bilinear Groups

A prime-order group generator $\mathcal{G}$ takes as input the security parameter λ in unary notation and outputs a description $\mathbb{G} = (p, G_1, G_2, G_T, e)$, where p is a prime, G_1, G_2, G_T are cyclic groups of order p, and $e : G_1 \times G_2 \to G_T$ is an asymmetric non-degenerated bilinear mapping. Let $[1]_1 = g_1 \in G_1, [1]_2 = g_2 \in G_2$ and $[1]_T = g_T = e(g_1, g_2) \in G_T$ be the respective generators. For any $a, b \in \mathbb{Z}_p$, we have $e(g_1^a, g_2^b) = e(g_1, g_2)^{ab} = g_T^{ab} = [ab]_T$. We define $[\mathbf{M}]_1 = g_1^{\mathbf{M}}, [\mathbf{M}]_2 = g_2^{\mathbf{M}}$ and $[\mathbf{M}]_T = g_T^{\mathbf{M}}$, where $\mathbf{M}$ is a matrix over $\mathbb{Z}_p$, and exponentiation is carried out component-wise. We also define $e([\mathbf{A}]_1, [\mathbf{B}]_2) = [\mathbf{AB}]_T$, where $\mathbf{A}, \mathbf{B}$ are matrices over $\mathbb{Z}_p$.

2.3 Basis Structure

Fix parameters $\ell_1, \ell_2, \ell_3 \geq 1$. Sample

$$\mathbf{A}_1 \leftarrow_R \mathbb{Z}_p^{\ell' \times \ell_1}, \mathbf{A}_2 \leftarrow_R \mathbb{Z}_p^{\ell' \times \ell_2}, \mathbf{A}_3 \leftarrow_R \mathbb{Z}_p^{\ell' \times \ell_3},$$

where $\ell' := \ell_1 + \ell_2 + \ell_3$. Let $(\mathbf{A}_1^{\|} \| \mathbf{A}_2^{\|} \| \mathbf{A}_3^{\|})^{\top}$ denote the inverse of $(\mathbf{A}_1 \| \mathbf{A}_2 \| \mathbf{A}_3)$, so that $\mathbf{A}_i^{\top} \mathbf{A}_i^{\|} = \mathbf{I}$ (known as non-degeneracy) and $\mathbf{A}_i^{\top} \mathbf{A}_j^{\|} = \mathbf{0}$ if $i \neq j$ (known as orthogonality), as depicted in Fig. 2.

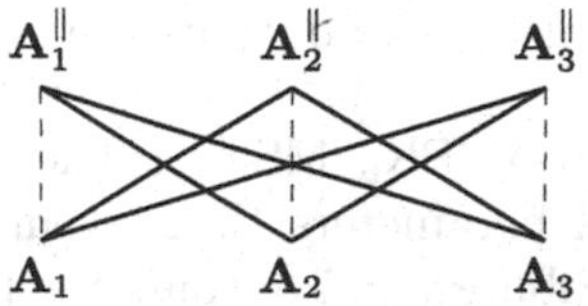

Fig. 2. Basis relations. Solid lines mean orthogonal, dashed lines mean non-degeneracy. Similar relations hold in composite-order groups.

By symmetry, we can permute the indexes for $\mathbf{A}_1, \mathbf{A}_2, \mathbf{A}_3$.

2.4 Assumptions

Matrix Decision Diffie-Hellman Assumption. Let $k, l, d \in \mathbb{N}$. The Matrix Decision Diffie-Hellman (MDDH) assumption [16] says that for all p.p.t adversaries $\mathcal{A}$, the following advantage function is negligible in λ:

$$\mathsf{Adv}_{\mathcal{A}}^{\mathrm{MDDH}_{k,l}^{d}}(\lambda) := |\Pr[\mathcal{A}(\mathbb{G}, [\mathbf{M}]_1, [\mathbf{MS}]_1) = 1] - \Pr[\mathcal{A}(\mathbb{G}, [\mathbf{M}]_1, [\mathbf{U}]_1) = 1]|,$$

where $\mathbb{G} = (p, G_1, G_2, G_T, e) \leftarrow \mathcal{G}(1^\lambda), \mathbf{M} \leftarrow_R \mathbb{Z}_p^{l\times k}, \mathbf{S} \leftarrow_R \mathbb{Z}_p^{k\times d}$, and $\mathbf{U} \leftarrow_R \mathbb{Z}_p^{l\times d}$.

MDDH assumption also holds similarly in G_2.

Lemma 1 ($\mathbf{MDDH}_{\ell_1\to\ell_1+\ell_2} \Longrightarrow SD^{G_1}_{\mathbf{A}_1\mapsto\mathbf{A}_1,\mathbf{A}_2}$). *Under the $MDDH_{\ell_1,\ell_1+\ell_2}$ assumption in G_1, there exists an efficient sampler outputting random ($[\mathbf{A}_1]_1$, $[\mathbf{A}_2]_1, [\mathbf{A}_3]_1$) (as described in Sect. 2.3) along with base $\mathsf{basis}(\mathbf{A}_1^{\|}), \mathsf{basis}(\mathbf{A}_3^{\|})$, $\mathsf{basis}(\mathbf{A}_1^{\|}, \mathbf{A}_2^{\|})$ (of arbitrary choice) such that the following advantage function is negligible in λ.*

$$\mathsf{Adv}_{\mathcal{A}}^{SD^{G_1}_{\mathbf{A}_1\mapsto\mathbf{A}_1,\mathbf{A}_2}}(\lambda) := |\Pr[\mathcal{A}(D, [T_0]_1) = 1] - \Pr[\mathcal{A}(D, [T_1]_1) = 1]|,$$

where

$$D := ([\mathbf{A}_1]_1, [\mathbf{A}_2]_1, [\mathbf{A}_3]_1, \mathsf{basis}(\mathbf{A}_1^{\|}), \mathsf{basis}(\mathbf{A}_3^{\|}), \mathsf{basis}(\mathbf{A}_1^{\|}, \mathbf{A}_2^{\|})),$$
$$T_0 \leftarrow_R \mathsf{span}(\mathbf{A}_1), T_1 \leftarrow_R \mathsf{span}(\mathbf{A}_1, \mathbf{A}_2).$$

Remark 1. Lemma 1 is similarly stated in [10,11,17,18], and similar lemma also holds in G_2.

2.5 Decentralized Multi-authority Attribute-Based Encryption for LSSS

Syntax. We assume that each authority controls a single attribute. A decentralized Multi-Authority Attribute-Based Encryption scheme for Linear Secret Sharing Scheme consists of five efficient algorithms:

- $\mathsf{GlobalSetup}(1^\lambda) \to \mathsf{GP}$: The global setup algorithm takes as input the security parameter λ in unary notation, and outputs the global parameters GP for the system.
- $\mathsf{AuthSetup}(\mathsf{GP}, u \in \mathcal{AU}) \to (\mathsf{PK}_u, \mathsf{MSK}_u)$: The authority setup algorithm takes as input the global parameters GP and an attribute $u \in \mathcal{AU}$, where $\mathcal{AU}$ is the universe of attributes, and outputs the public key PK_u of u as well as the master secret key MSK_u of u.
- $\mathsf{Enc}(\mathsf{GP}, msg, (\mathbf{M}, \rho), \{\mathsf{PK}_{u'}\}_{u'\in\rho([\ell])}) \to \mathsf{CT}$: The encryption algorithm takes as input the global parameters GP, a message $msg \in \mathbb{M}$, where $\mathbb{M}$ is the message space, an LSSS access policy $(\mathbf{M}, \rho)$ in which ρ maps each row of $\mathbf{M}$ to an attribute in $\mathcal{AU}$, and the public keys set $\{\mathsf{PK}_{u'}\}_{u'\in\rho([\ell])}$ for all the attributes in the range of ρ on the constraint of $[\ell]$. Then output a ciphertext CT.

- $\mathsf{KeyGen}(\mathsf{GP}, \mathsf{GID}, \mathsf{MSK}_u) \to \mathsf{sk}_{\mathsf{GID},u}$: The key generation algorithm takes as input the global parameters GP, a user's global identifier $\mathsf{GID} \in \mathcal{GID}$, where $\mathcal{GID}$ is the universe of global identifiers, and a master secret key of attribute $u \in \mathcal{AU}$. Then output a secret key of GID and u.
- $\mathsf{Dec}(\mathsf{GP}, \mathsf{CT}, \{\mathsf{sk}_{\mathsf{GID},u''}\}_{u'' \in \mathcal{U}}) \to msg' / \perp$: The decryption algorithm takes as input the global parameters GP, a ciphertext CT and a collection of secret keys $\{\mathsf{sk}_{\mathsf{GID},u''}\}_{u'' \in \mathcal{U}}$ of the user ID-attribute pairs $\{(\mathsf{GID}, u'')\}$ possessed by a user with global identifier GID, and $u'' \in \mathcal{U} \subseteq \mathcal{AU}$, where $\mathcal{U}$ is a subset of $\mathcal{AU}$. Then output a message msg', or $\perp$.

Correctness. A decentralized MA-ABE scheme for LSSS is correct, if for all $\lambda \in \mathbb{N}$, $msg \in \mathbb{M}$, $\mathsf{GID} \in \mathcal{GID}$, LSSS access policy $(\mathbf{M}, \rho)$, and $\mathcal{U} \subseteq \mathcal{AU}$ containing attributes that satisfy the LSSS access structure, we have

$$\Pr\left[msg' = msg \left| \begin{array}{l} \mathsf{GP} \leftarrow \mathsf{GlobalSetup}(1^\lambda); \\ \forall u \in \mathcal{AU}, \mathsf{PK}_u, \mathsf{MSK}_u \leftarrow \mathsf{AuthSetup}(\mathsf{GP}, u); \\ \mathsf{CT} \leftarrow \mathsf{Enc}(\mathsf{GP}, msg, (\mathbf{M}, \rho), \{\mathsf{PK}_{u'}\}_{u' \in \rho([\ell])}); \\ \forall u'' \in \mathcal{U}, \mathsf{sk}_{\mathsf{GID},u''} \leftarrow \mathsf{KeyGen}(\mathsf{GP}, \mathsf{GID}, \mathsf{MSK}_{u''}); \\ msg' = \mathsf{Dec}(\mathsf{GP}, \mathsf{CT}, \{\mathsf{sk}_{\mathsf{GID},u''}\}_{u'' \in \mathcal{U}}); \end{array} \right. \right] = 1.$$

Fully Adaptive Security. For a stateful adversary $\mathcal{A}$, define the advantage function $\mathsf{Adv}_{\mathcal{A}}^{\text{MA-ABE}}(\lambda) :=$

$$\Pr\left[b' = b \left| \begin{array}{l} \mathsf{GP} \leftarrow \mathsf{GlobalSetup}(1^\lambda); \\ \forall u \in \mathcal{AU}, \mathsf{PK}_u, \mathsf{MSK}_u \leftarrow \mathsf{AuthSetup}(\mathsf{GP}, u); \\ ((\mathbf{M}, \rho), msg_0, msg_1) \leftarrow \\ \mathcal{A}^{\mathsf{AuthSetup}(\mathsf{GP},\cdot),\mathsf{KeyGen}(\mathsf{GP},\cdot,\mathsf{MSK}_u)}(\mathsf{GP}, \{\mathsf{PK}_u\}_{u \in \mathcal{AU}}); \\ b \leftarrow_R \{0,1\}; \\ \mathsf{CT}_b \leftarrow \mathsf{Enc}(\mathsf{GP}, msg_b, (\mathbf{M}, \rho), \{\mathsf{PK}_{u'}\}_{u' \in \rho([\ell])}); \\ b' \leftarrow \mathcal{A}^{\mathsf{AuthSetup}(\mathsf{GP},\cdot),\mathsf{KeyGen}(\mathsf{GP},\cdot,\mathsf{MSK}_u)}(\mathsf{GP}, \{\mathsf{PK}_u\}_{u \in \mathcal{AU}}, \mathsf{CT}_b); \end{array} \right. \right] - \frac{1}{2},$$

where $\mathsf{AuthSetup}(\mathsf{GP}, \cdot)$ denotes that $\mathcal{A}$ can make authority setup queries and authority master key queries adaptively, and $\mathsf{KeyGen}(\mathsf{GP}, \cdot, \mathsf{MSK}_u)$ denotes that $\mathcal{A}$ can make secret key queries adaptively, with the restriction that all the information that $\mathcal{A}$ gets from the queries cannot make $\mathcal{A}$ decrypt the challenge ciphertext CT_b successfully by following a legitimate decryption process. A decentralized MA-ABE scheme is fully adaptively secure, if for all p.p.t adversaries $\mathcal{A}$, the advantage $\mathsf{Adv}_{\mathcal{A}}^{\text{MA-ABE}}(\lambda)$ is a negligible function in λ.

Many-Use of Attribute. If the mapping ρ in the LSSS access policy $(\mathbf{M}, \rho)$ is not restricted to be an injective mapping, then we say the attributes in $\mathcal{AU}$ can be used for many times, i.e., many-use of attribute.

Core 1-ABE. Core 1-ABE is defined in [24]. For a stateful adversary $\mathcal{A}$, define the advantage function $\mathsf{Adv}_{\mathcal{A}}^{\text{1-ABE}}(\lambda) :=$

$$\Pr\left[b' = b \left| \begin{array}{l} \mathbf{w}_i \leftarrow \mathsf{CPA.Setup}(1^\lambda); \\ (\mu_0, \mu_1) \leftarrow \mathcal{A}^{\mathcal{O}_X(\cdot), \mathcal{O}_E(\cdot,\cdot)}; \\ b \leftarrow_R \{0,1\}; \\ \mathsf{ct}_b \leftarrow \mathcal{O}_F((f, \mu_b)); \\ b' \leftarrow \mathcal{A}^{\mathcal{O}_X(\cdot), \mathcal{O}_E(\cdot,\cdot)}(\mathsf{ct}_b); \end{array} \right. \right] - \frac{1}{2},$$

where $\mathcal{O}_F((f, \mu_b)) = \mathsf{ct} := \{\mathsf{sk}'_f = \{\mu_j\}_{\rho'(j)=0} \cup \{\mathsf{CPA.Enc}(\mathbf{w}_{\rho'(j)}, \mu_j)\}_{\rho'(j) \neq 0}\}$, $(\{\mu_j\}, \rho') \leftarrow \mathsf{share}(f, \mu_b)$, and $\mathcal{O}_X(x) := (\mathsf{ct}'_x = \{\mathbf{w}_i\}_{x_i=1})$, and $\mathcal{O}_E(i, m) := \mathsf{CPA.Enc}(\mathbf{w}_i, m)$, with the restriction that (i) only one query is made to each $\mathcal{O}_F(\cdot)$ and $\mathcal{O}_X(\cdot)$, and (ii) the queries f and x to $\mathcal{O}_F(\cdot), \mathcal{O}_X(\cdot)$ respectively, satisfy $f(x) = 0$.

The CPA-secure symmetric encryption scheme in [24] is constructed as follows:

- $\mathsf{CPA.Setup}(1^\lambda)$: Run $\mathbb{G} \leftarrow \mathcal{G}(1^\lambda)$. Sample $\mathbf{w} \leftarrow_R \mathbb{Z}_p^{1\times k}$. Output $\mathsf{sk} = \mathbf{w}$.
- $\mathsf{CPA.Enc}(\mathsf{sk}, [M]_2)$: Sample $\mathbf{r} \leftarrow_R \mathbb{Z}_p^{k\times 1}$. Output $(ct_1, ct_2) = ([M + \mathbf{wr}]_2, [\mathbf{r}]_2)$.
- $\mathsf{CPA.Dec}(\mathsf{sk}, (ct_1, ct_2))$: Output $ct_1 \cdot (\mathsf{sk} \cdot ct_2)^{-1}$.

The correctness follows that $ct_1 \cdot (\mathsf{sk} \cdot ct_2)^{-1} = [M + \mathbf{wr} - \mathbf{wr}]_2 = [M]_2$.

In [24], $\mathsf{Adv}_{\mathcal{A}}^{\text{1-ABE}}(\lambda)$ is proved to be a negligible function in λ under the MDDH assumption.

3 Decentralized MA-ABE in Prime-Order Groups

We assume that each authority controls a single attribute. The hash function H is modeled as a random oracle in the security analysis.

3.1 Construction

- $\mathsf{GlobalSetup}(1^\lambda)$: Take as input the security parameter λ in unary notation. Run $\mathbb{G} = (p, G_1, G_2, G_T, e) \leftarrow \mathcal{G}(1^\lambda)$. We use a strong seeded randomness extractor $\mathsf{Ext} : G_T \times \mathsf{S} \to \mathbb{M}$, where $\mathbb{M} \subset \{0,1\}^*$ is the message space and $\mathsf{S} \subset \{0,1\}^*$ is the seed space. Sample $\mathsf{seed} \leftarrow_R \mathsf{S}$, $\mathbf{A}_1 \leftarrow_R \mathbb{Z}_p^{(2k+1)\times k}$, $\mathbf{B}_1 \leftarrow_R \mathbb{Z}_p^{3k\times k}$, $\mathbf{r} \leftarrow_R \mathbb{Z}_p^{k\times 1}$. We also use a hash function $\mathsf{H} : \{0,1\}^* \to G_2^{3k\times 1}$, which maps global identifier $\mathsf{GID} \in \mathcal{GID} \subset \{0,1\}^*$ to elements in $G_2^{3k\times 1}$, where $\mathcal{GID}$ is the universe of global identifiers. Concretely, for a $\mathsf{GID} \in \mathcal{GID}$, $\mathsf{H}(\mathsf{GID}) = [\mathbf{h}_{\mathsf{GID}}]_2$, where $\mathbf{h}_{\mathsf{GID}} \leftarrow_R \mathbb{Z}_p^{3k\times 1}$. Output $\mathsf{GP} = (\mathbb{G}, [\mathbf{A}_1]_1, h = [\mathbf{B}_1\mathbf{r}]_2, \mathsf{seed})$.
- $\mathsf{AuthSetup}(\mathsf{GP}, u \in \mathcal{AU})$: Take as input GP and an attribute $u \in \mathcal{AU}$, where $\mathcal{AU}$ is the universe of attributes. Sample $\mathbf{W}_{A,u}, \mathbf{W}_{B,u} \leftarrow_R \mathbb{Z}_p^{(2k+1)\times 3k}$. Output

$$\mathsf{PK}_u = ([P_{A,u}]_1 = [\mathbf{A}_1^\top \mathbf{W}_{A,u}]_1, [P_{B,u}]_1 = [\mathbf{A}_1^\top \mathbf{W}_{B,u}]_1),$$
$$\mathsf{MSK}_u = (\mathbf{W}_{A,u}, \mathbf{W}_{B,u}).$$

– $\mathsf{Enc}(\mathsf{GP}, msg, (\mathbf{M} \in \mathbb{Z}_p^{\ell\times d}, \rho : [\ell] \to \mathcal{AU}), \{\mathsf{PK}_{u'}\}_{u'\in\rho([\ell])})$: Take as input GP, the message msg, an LSSS access structure $(\mathbf{M} \in \mathbb{Z}_p^{\ell\times d}, \rho : [\ell] \to \mathcal{AU})$, and the public keys $\{\mathsf{PK}_{u'}\}_{u'\in\rho([\ell])}$ used for encryption. Sample

$$\mathbf{K} \leftarrow_R \mathbb{Z}_p^{1\times 3k}, \mathbf{K}'_A \leftarrow_R \mathbb{Z}_p^{(d-1)\times 3k}, \mathbf{K}'_B \leftarrow_R \mathbb{Z}_p^{(d-1)\times 3k},$$
$$\mathbf{s}_{A,x}, \mathbf{s}_{B,x} \leftarrow_R \mathbb{Z}_p^{1\times k}.$$

Output $\mathsf{CT} = ((\mathbf{M}, \rho), C, \{C_{1,A,x}, C_{1,B,x}, C_{2,A,x}, C_{2,B,x}\}_{x\in[\ell]})$, where

$$C = msg \oplus \mathsf{Ext}(e([\mathbf{K}]_1, h), \mathsf{seed}),$$
$$C_{1,A,x} = [\mathbf{s}_{A,x}\mathbf{A}_1^\top]_1,$$
$$C_{1,B,x} = [\mathbf{s}_{B,x}\mathbf{A}_1^\top]_1,$$
$$C_{2,A,x} = [\mathbf{s}_{A,x}\mathbf{A}_1^\top \mathbf{W}_{A,\rho(x)} + \mathbf{M}_x \begin{pmatrix}\mathbf{K}\\ \mathbf{K}'_A\end{pmatrix}]_1,$$
$$C_{2,B,x} = [\mathbf{s}_{B,x}\mathbf{A}_1^\top \mathbf{W}_{B,\rho(x)} + \mathbf{M}_x \begin{pmatrix}-\mathbf{K}\\ \mathbf{K}'_B\end{pmatrix}]_1,$$

and $\mathbf{M}_x$ denotes the x-th row of $\mathbf{M}$.

– $\mathsf{KeyGen}(\mathsf{GP}, \mathsf{H}, \mathsf{GID} \in \mathcal{GID}, \mathsf{MSK}_u)$: Take as input $\mathsf{GP}, \mathsf{H}, \mathsf{GID} \in \mathcal{GID}, \mathsf{MSK}_u$. Output $\mathsf{sk}_{\mathsf{GID},u} = (K_{\mathsf{GID},A,u}, K_{\mathsf{GID},B,u})$, where

$$K_{\mathsf{GID},A,u} = [\mathbf{W}_{A,u}\mathbf{h}_{\mathsf{GID}} + \mathbf{W}_{A,u}\mathbf{B}_1\mathbf{r}]_2,$$
$$K_{\mathsf{GID},B,u} = [\mathbf{W}_{B,u}\mathbf{h}_{\mathsf{GID}}]_2.$$

– $\mathsf{Dec}(\mathsf{GP}, \mathsf{H}, \mathsf{CT}, \mathsf{GID}, \{\mathsf{sk}_{\mathsf{GID},u''}\}_{u''\in\rho(\mathbf{I})})$: Compute $\{\omega_x \in \mathbb{Z}_p\}_{x\in\mathbf{I}}$, such that $\sum_{x\in\mathbf{I}} \omega_x \cdot \mathbf{M}_x = (1, 0, ..., 0)$. Then compute

$$D_{A,x} = e(C_{2,A,x}, \mathsf{H}(\mathsf{GID}) \cdot h) \cdot e(C_{1,A,x}, K_{\mathsf{GID},A,\rho(x)})^{-1},$$
$$D_{B,x} = e(C_{2,B,x}, \mathsf{H}(\mathsf{GID})) \cdot e(C_{1,B,x}, K_{\mathsf{GID},B,\rho(x)})^{-1}.$$

And compute

$$D = \prod_{x\in\mathbf{I}} (D_{A,x} \cdot D_{B,x})^{\omega_x}.$$

Output

$$C \oplus \mathsf{Ext}(D, \mathsf{seed}).$$

Correctness. We have

$$\begin{aligned}
D_{A,x} =& e(C_{2,A,x}, \mathsf{H}(\mathsf{GID}) \cdot h) \cdot e(C_{1,A,x}, K_{\mathsf{GID},A,\rho(x)})^{-1} \\
=& e([\mathbf{s}_{A,x}\mathbf{A}_1^\top \mathbf{W}_{A,\rho(x)} + \mathbf{M}_x \begin{pmatrix} \mathbf{K} \\ \mathbf{K}'_A \end{pmatrix}]_1, [\mathbf{h}_{\mathsf{GID}} + \mathbf{B}_1\mathbf{r}]_2) \cdot \\
& e([\mathbf{s}_{A,x}\mathbf{A}_1^\top]_1, [\mathbf{W}_{A,\rho(x)}\mathbf{h}_{\mathsf{GID}} + \mathbf{W}_{A,\rho(x)}\mathbf{B}_1\mathbf{r}]_2)^{-1} \\
=& [\mathbf{s}_{A,x}\mathbf{A}_1^\top \mathbf{W}_{A,\rho(x)}\mathbf{h}_{\mathsf{GID}} + \mathbf{s}_{A,x}\mathbf{A}_1^\top \mathbf{W}_{A,\rho(x)}\mathbf{B}_1\mathbf{r} + \mathbf{M}_x \begin{pmatrix} \mathbf{K} \\ \mathbf{K}'_A \end{pmatrix} \mathbf{h}_{\mathsf{GID}} + \\
& \mathbf{M}_x \begin{pmatrix} \mathbf{K} \\ \mathbf{K}'_A \end{pmatrix} \mathbf{B}_1\mathbf{r} - \mathbf{s}_{A,x}\mathbf{A}_1^\top \mathbf{W}_{A,\rho(x)}\mathbf{h}_{\mathsf{GID}} - \mathbf{s}_{A,x}\mathbf{A}_1^\top \mathbf{W}_{A,\rho(x)}\mathbf{B}_1\mathbf{r}]_T \\
=& [\mathbf{M}_x \begin{pmatrix} \mathbf{K} \\ \mathbf{K}'_A \end{pmatrix} \mathbf{h}_{\mathsf{GID}} + \mathbf{M}_x \begin{pmatrix} \mathbf{K} \\ \mathbf{K}'_A \end{pmatrix} \mathbf{B}_1\mathbf{r}]_T,
\end{aligned}$$

and

$$\begin{aligned}
D_{B,x} =& e(C_{2,B,x}, \mathsf{H}(\mathsf{GID})) \cdot e(C_{1,B,x}, K_{\mathsf{GID},B,\rho(x)})^{-1} \\
=& e([\mathbf{s}_{B,x}\mathbf{A}_1^\top \mathbf{W}_{B,\rho(x)} + \mathbf{M}_x \begin{pmatrix} -\mathbf{K} \\ \mathbf{K}'_B \end{pmatrix}]_1, [\mathbf{h}_{\mathsf{GID}}]_2) \cdot \\
& e([\mathbf{s}_{B,x}\mathbf{A}_1^\top]_1, [\mathbf{W}_{B,\rho(x)}\mathbf{h}_{\mathsf{GID}}]_2)^{-1} \\
=& [\mathbf{s}_{B,x}\mathbf{A}_1^\top \mathbf{W}_{B,\rho(x)}\mathbf{h}_{\mathsf{GID}} + \mathbf{M}_x \begin{pmatrix} -\mathbf{K} \\ \mathbf{K}'_B \end{pmatrix} \mathbf{h}_{\mathsf{GID}} - \mathbf{s}_{B,x}\mathbf{A}_1^\top \mathbf{W}_{B,\rho(x)}\mathbf{h}_{\mathsf{GID}}]_T \\
=& [\mathbf{M}_x \begin{pmatrix} -\mathbf{K} \\ \mathbf{K}'_B \end{pmatrix} \mathbf{h}_{\mathsf{GID}}]_T.
\end{aligned}$$

Then if $\sum_{x \in \mathbf{I}} \omega_x \cdot \mathbf{M}_x = (1, 0, ..., 0)$, we have

$$\begin{aligned}
D =& \prod_{x \in \mathbf{I}} (D_{A,x} \cdot D_{B,x})^{\omega_x} \\
=& \prod_{x \in \mathbf{I}} [\omega_x \mathbf{M}_x \begin{pmatrix} \mathbf{K} \\ \mathbf{K}'_A \end{pmatrix} \mathbf{h}_{\mathsf{GID}} + \omega_x \mathbf{M}_x \begin{pmatrix} \mathbf{K} \\ \mathbf{K}'_A \end{pmatrix} \mathbf{B}_1\mathbf{r} + \omega_x \mathbf{M}_x \begin{pmatrix} -\mathbf{K} \\ \mathbf{K}'_B \end{pmatrix} \mathbf{h}_{\mathsf{GID}}]_T \\
=& [\mathbf{K}\mathbf{B}_1\mathbf{r}]_T \\
=& e([\mathbf{K}]_1, [\mathbf{B}_1\mathbf{r}]_2) \\
=& e([\mathbf{K}]_1, h).
\end{aligned}$$

3.2 Security Analysis

Theorem 1. *The above decentralized MA-ABE scheme for NC1 is fully adaptively secure and allows many-use of attribute, under the MDDH assumption in the random oracle model. Moreover, we have*

$$\begin{aligned}\mathsf{Adv}_{\mathcal{A}}^{MA\text{-}ABE}(\lambda) \leq & \mathsf{Adv}_{\mathcal{B}^1}^{MDDH^q_{G_2,k,3k}}(\lambda) + \mathsf{Adv}_{\mathcal{B}^2}^{SD^{G_1}_{\mathbf{A}_1 \mapsto \mathbf{A}_1,\mathbf{A}_3}}(\lambda) + \mathsf{Adv}_{\mathcal{B}^3}^{SD^{G_1}_{\mathbf{A}_1 \mapsto \mathbf{A}_1,\mathbf{A}_2}}(\lambda) \\ & + (2q+1) \cdot \mathsf{Adv}_{\mathcal{B}^4}^{SD^{G_2}_{\mathbf{B}_1 \mapsto \mathbf{B}_1,\mathbf{B}_2}}(\lambda) + q \cdot \mathsf{Adv}_{\mathcal{B}^5}^{SD^{G_2}_{\mathbf{B}_2 \mapsto \mathbf{B}_2,\mathbf{B}_3}}(\lambda) \\ & + 2 \cdot \mathsf{Adv}_{\mathcal{B}^6}^{SD^{G_2}_{\mathbf{B}_3 \mapsto \mathbf{B}_2,\mathbf{B}_3}}(\lambda) + (4q+4) \cdot \mathsf{Adv}_{\mathcal{B}^7}^{1\text{-}ABE}(\lambda) + \mathsf{negl}(\lambda),\end{aligned}$$

where q is the total number of global identifiers GID *that the simulator generates the* H *oracle outputs for, $\mathcal{B}^1$ is a* p.p.t *adversary for the $MDDH^q_{k,3k}$ assumption in G_2, $\mathcal{B}^2$ is a* p.p.t *adversary for the $SD_{\mathbf{A}_1 \mapsto \mathbf{A}_1,\mathbf{A}_3}$ assumption in G_1, $\mathcal{B}^3$ is a* p.p.t *adversary for the $SD_{\mathbf{A}_1 \mapsto \mathbf{A}_1,\mathbf{A}_2}$ assumption in G_1, $\mathcal{B}^4$ is a* p.p.t *adversary for the $SD_{\mathbf{B}_1 \mapsto \mathbf{B}_1,\mathbf{B}_2}$ assumption in G_2, $\mathcal{B}^5$ is a* p.p.t *adversary for the $SD_{\mathbf{B}_2 \mapsto \mathbf{B}_2,\mathbf{B}_3}$ assumption in G_2, $\mathcal{B}^6$ is a* p.p.t *adversary for the $SD_{\mathbf{B}_3 \mapsto \mathbf{B}_2,\mathbf{B}_3}$ assumption in G_2, $\mathcal{B}^7$ is a* p.p.t *adversary for the Core 1-ABE, which is based on the MDDH assumption and with polynomial security loss, and* $\mathsf{negl}(\lambda)$ *is a negligible function in λ incurred by a statistical indistinguishability from* Ext.

Hybrids. Before we proceed to the details of security analysis, we clarify some notations and explain some complicated points.

Notations. In the security analysis, we set

$$\begin{aligned}&\mathbf{A}_1 \leftarrow_R \mathbb{Z}_p^{(2k+1)\times k}, \mathbf{A}_2 \leftarrow_R \mathbb{Z}_p^{(2k+1)\times 1}, \mathbf{A}_3 \leftarrow_R \mathbb{Z}_p^{(2k+1)\times k}, \\ &\mathbf{A}_1^{\|} \leftarrow_R \mathbb{Z}_p^{(2k+1)\times k}, \mathbf{A}_2^{\|} \leftarrow_R \mathbb{Z}_p^{(2k+1)\times 1}, \mathbf{A}_3^{\|} \leftarrow_R \mathbb{Z}_p^{(2k+1)\times k}, \\ &\mathbf{B}_1, \mathbf{B}_2, \mathbf{B}_3 \leftarrow_R \mathbb{Z}_p^{3k\times k}, \\ &\mathbf{B}_1^{\|}, \mathbf{B}_2^{\|}, \mathbf{B}_3^{\|} \leftarrow_R \mathbb{Z}_p^{3k\times k},\end{aligned}$$

which satisfy the basis structure in Sect. 2.3, respectively.

Let Y denote the subset of rows of the challenge access matrix $\mathbf{M}$ labeled by the authorities for which $\mathcal{A}$ supplies the authority public keys $\{\mathsf{PK}_{u'} = ([P_{A,u'}]_1, [P_{B,u'}]_1)\}$. Let $\bar{Y} = [\ell] \backslash Y$.

Below, we use $\mathsf{Reconstruct}(\{\mathsf{share}_i\})$ to denote the secret from the reconstruction of shares $\{\mathsf{share}_i\}$.

Sampling of Secrets. This statement is similarly stated in Lemma 4.3 of [14]. Recall that we require the information $\mathcal{A}$ gain from the corruption and secret key queries cannot help $\mathcal{A}$ decrypt the challenge ciphertext CT_b successfully following a legitimate decryption process. For the form of the secret $\mathbf{K}$, this means that there must exist a vector $\mathbf{u} \in \mathbb{Z}_p^d$ such that $\mathbf{u}$ is orthogonal to all the rows of $\mathbf{M}$ labeled by corrupted authorities, but is not orthogonal to $(1, 0, ..., 0)$, i.e., the first entry of $\mathbf{u}$ is non-zero, and the truly secret values of $\mathbf{K}$ are attached to $\mathbf{u}$. Concretely, consider a basis $\mathbb{U}$ of $\mathbb{Z}_p^d$ involving the vector $\mathbf{u}$, set

$$\mathbf{v}_A^{\prime(1)} = \widehat{\mathbf{v}_A}^{(1)} + a_1\mathbf{u},$$

$$\vdots$$

$$\mathbf{v}_A^{\prime(3k)} = \widehat{\mathbf{v}_A}^{(3k)} + a_{3k}\mathbf{u},$$

where for each $i \in [3k]$, $\widehat{\mathbf{v}_A}^{(i)}$ is in the span of $\mathbb{U}\backslash\{\mathbf{u}\}$, and $a_i \leftarrow_R \mathbb{Z}_p$ is the truly secret value of $\mathbf{K}$. Set

$$\begin{pmatrix} \mathbf{K} \\ \mathbf{K}'_A \end{pmatrix} = \begin{pmatrix} \mathbf{v}_A^{\prime(1)} \\ \vdots \\ \mathbf{v}_A^{\prime(3k)} \end{pmatrix}^\top .$$

Then we have $\mathbf{K} = (\widehat{\mathbf{v}_{A1}}^{(1)}, ..., \widehat{\mathbf{v}_{A1}}^{(3k)}) + (a_1u_1, ..., a_{3k}u_1) \in \mathbb{Z}_p^{1\times 3k}$.

Similarly, we can set

$$\mathbf{v}_B^{\prime(1)} = \widehat{\mathbf{v}_B}^{(1)} - a_1\mathbf{u},$$

$$\vdots$$

$$\mathbf{v}_B^{\prime(3k)} = \widehat{\mathbf{v}_B}^{(3k)} - a_{3k}\mathbf{u},$$

and set

$$\begin{pmatrix} -\mathbf{K} \\ \mathbf{K}'_B \end{pmatrix} = \begin{pmatrix} \mathbf{v}_B^{\prime(1)} \\ \vdots \\ \mathbf{v}_B^{\prime(3k)} \end{pmatrix}^\top ,$$

where

$$\widehat{\mathbf{v}_{B1}}^{(1)} = -\widehat{\mathbf{v}_{A1}}^{(1)},$$

$$\vdots$$

$$\widehat{\mathbf{v}_{B1}}^{(3k)} = -\widehat{\mathbf{v}_{A1}}^{(3k)},$$

and for each $i \in [3k]$, $\widehat{\mathbf{v}_B}^{(i)}$ is in the span of $\mathbb{U}\backslash\{\mathbf{u}\}$.

For simplicity, below, we just write $\mathbf{K} \leftarrow_R \mathbb{Z}_p^{1\times 3k}, \mathbf{K}'_A, \mathbf{K}'_B \leftarrow_R \mathbb{Z}_p^{(d-1)\times 3k}$ to implicitly mean that $\mathbf{K}, \mathbf{K}'_A, \mathbf{K}'_B$ satisfy the above conditions.

- Hybrid_0: This is as the real hybrid.
- Hybrid_1: This is the same as Hybrid_0, except that we replace $\mathsf{H}(\mathsf{GID}) = [\mathbf{h}_{\mathsf{GID}}]_2$ with $[\mathbf{B}_1\mathbf{r}_{\mathsf{GID}}]_2$, where $\mathbf{r}_{\mathsf{GID}} \leftarrow_R \mathbb{Z}_p^{k\times 1}$. Thus, $\mathsf{sk}_{\mathsf{GID},u}$ becomes

$$K_{\mathsf{GID},A,u} = [\mathbf{W}_{A,u}\boxed{\mathbf{B}_1\mathbf{r}_{\mathsf{GID}}} + \mathbf{W}_{A,u}\mathbf{B}_1\mathbf{r}]_2, K_{\mathsf{GID},B,u} = [\mathbf{W}_{B,u}\boxed{\mathbf{B}_1\mathbf{r}_{\mathsf{GID}}}]_2.$$

- Hybrid_2: This is the same as Hybrid_1, except that for $x \in \bar{Y}$, we replace the challenge CT generated by the simulator with

$$C_{1,A,x} = [\boxed{\mathbf{s}_{A,x}^{(13)}(\mathbf{A}_1\|\mathbf{A}_3)^\top}]_1, C_{1,B,x} = [\boxed{\mathbf{s}_{B,x}^{(13)}(\mathbf{A}_1\|\mathbf{A}_3)^\top}]_1,$$
$$C_{2,A,x} = [\boxed{\mathbf{s}_{A,x}^{(13)}(\mathbf{A}_1\|\mathbf{A}_3)^\top}\mathbf{W}_{A,\rho(x)} + \mathbf{M}_x\begin{pmatrix}\mathbf{K}\\ \mathbf{K}'_A\end{pmatrix}]_1,$$
$$C_{2,B,x} = [\boxed{\mathbf{s}_{B,x}^{(13)}(\mathbf{A}_1\|\mathbf{A}_3)^\top}\mathbf{W}_{B,\rho(x)} + \mathbf{M}_x\begin{pmatrix}-\mathbf{K}\\ \mathbf{K}'_B\end{pmatrix}]_1,$$

where $\mathbf{s}_{A,x}^{(13)}, \mathbf{s}_{B,x}^{(13)} \leftarrow_R \mathbb{Z}_p^{1\times 2k}$.
- Hybrid_3: This is the same as Hybrid_2, except that for $x \in \bar{Y}$, we replace the challenge CT generated by the simulator with

$$C_{1,A,x} = [\mathbf{s}_{A,x}^{(13)}(\mathbf{A}_1\|\mathbf{A}_3)^\top]_1, C_{1,B,x} = [\mathbf{s}_{B,x}^{(13)}(\mathbf{A}_1\|\mathbf{A}_3)^\top]_1,$$
$$C_{2,A,x} = [\mathbf{s}_{A,x}^{(13)}(\mathbf{A}_1\|\mathbf{A}_3)^\top\mathbf{W}_{A,\rho(x)} + \mathbf{M}_x\begin{pmatrix}\mathbf{K}\\ \mathbf{K}'_A\end{pmatrix} + \boxed{\sigma'_{A,x}\mathbf{N}'_A\mathbf{B}_3^{\|\top}}]_1,$$
$$C_{2,B,x} = [\mathbf{s}_{B,x}^{(13)}(\mathbf{A}_1\|\mathbf{A}_3)^\top\mathbf{W}_{B,\rho(x)} + \mathbf{M}_x\begin{pmatrix}-\mathbf{K}\\ \mathbf{K}'_B\end{pmatrix} + \boxed{\sigma'_{B,x}\mathbf{N}'_B\mathbf{B}_3^{\|\top}}]_1,$$

where

$$\mathbf{N}'_A, \mathbf{N}'_B \leftarrow_R \mathbb{Z}_p^{1\times k},$$
$$\sigma'_{A,x} = \mathbf{M}_x\begin{pmatrix}\sigma'_A\\ \mathbf{k}_A^{(3)}\end{pmatrix}, \sigma'_A \leftarrow_R \mathbb{Z}_p, \mathbf{k}_A^{(3)} \leftarrow_R \mathbb{Z}_p^{(d-1)\times 1},$$
$$\sigma'_{B,x} = \mathbf{M}_x\begin{pmatrix}\sigma'_B\\ \mathbf{k}_B^{(3)}\end{pmatrix}, \sigma'_B \leftarrow_R \mathbb{Z}_p, \mathbf{k}_B^{(3)} \leftarrow_R \mathbb{Z}_p^{(d-1)\times 1}.$$

- Hybrid_4: This is the same as Hybrid_3, except that for $x \in \bar{Y}$, we replace the challenge CT generated by the simulator with

$$C_{1,A,x} = [\boxed{\mathbf{s}_{A,x}^{(123)}(\mathbf{A}_1\|\mathbf{A}_2\|\mathbf{A}_3)^\top}]_1, C_{1,B,x} = [\boxed{\mathbf{s}_{B,x}^{(123)}(\mathbf{A}_1\|\mathbf{A}_2\|\mathbf{A}_3)^\top}]_1,$$
$$C_{2,A,x} = [\boxed{\mathbf{s}_{A,x}^{(123)}(\mathbf{A}_1\|\mathbf{A}_2\|\mathbf{A}_3)^\top}\mathbf{W}_{A,\rho(x)} + \mathbf{M}_x\begin{pmatrix}\mathbf{K}\\ \mathbf{K}'_A\end{pmatrix} + \sigma'_{A,x}\mathbf{N}'_A\mathbf{B}_3^{\|\top}]_1,$$
$$C_{2,B,x} = [\boxed{\mathbf{s}_{B,x}^{(123)}(\mathbf{A}_1\|\mathbf{A}_2\|\mathbf{A}_3)^\top}\mathbf{W}_{B,\rho(x)} + \mathbf{M}_x\begin{pmatrix}-\mathbf{K}\\ \mathbf{K}'_B\end{pmatrix} + \sigma'_{B,x}\mathbf{N}'_B\mathbf{B}_3^{\|\top}]_1,$$

where $\mathbf{s}_{A,x}^{(123)}, \mathbf{s}_{B,x}^{(123)} \leftarrow_R \mathbb{Z}_p^{1\times(2k+1)}$.
- $\mathsf{Hybrid}_{5:j}$ $(j \in [q])$: In this hybrid, for $t \le j$, $\mathsf{H}(\mathsf{GID}_t) = [(\mathbf{B}_1\|\mathbf{B}_3)\mathbf{r}_{\mathsf{GID}_t}^{(13)}]_2$, where $\mathbf{r}_{\mathsf{GID}_t}^{(13)} \leftarrow_R \mathbb{Z}_p^{2k\times 1}$; for $t > j$, $\mathsf{H}(\mathsf{GID}_t) = [\mathbf{B}_1\mathbf{r}_{\mathsf{GID}_t}]_2$, where $\mathbf{r}_{\mathsf{GID}_t} \leftarrow_R \mathbb{Z}_p^{k\times 1}$. And $\mathsf{Hybrid}_{5:0}$ is Hybrid_4.

- $\mathsf{Hybrid}_{5:j:1}(j \in [q])$: This is the same as $\mathsf{Hybrid}_{5:(j-1)}$, except that for the j-th global identifier GID_j, we replace $\mathsf{H}(\mathsf{GID}_j) = [\mathbf{B}_1\mathbf{r}_{\mathsf{GID}_j}]_2$ with $\mathsf{H}(\mathsf{GID}_j) = [(\mathbf{B}_1\|\mathbf{B}_2)\mathbf{r}^{(12)}_{\mathsf{GID}_j}]_2$, where $\mathbf{r}^{(12)}_{\mathsf{GID}_j} \leftarrow_R \mathbb{Z}_p^{2k\times 1}$. Thus, $\mathsf{sk}_{\mathsf{GID}_j,u}$ becomes

$$K_{\mathsf{GID}_j,A,u} = [\mathbf{W}_{A,u}\boxed{(\mathbf{B}_1\|\mathbf{B}_2)\mathbf{r}^{(12)}_{\mathsf{GID}_j}} + \mathbf{W}_{A,u}\mathbf{B}_1\mathbf{r}]_2,$$
$$K_{\mathsf{GID}_j,B,u} = [\mathbf{W}_{B,u}\boxed{(\mathbf{B}_1\|\mathbf{B}_2)\mathbf{r}^{(12)}_{\mathsf{GID}_j}}]_2.$$

- $\mathsf{Hybrid}_{5:j:2}(j \in [q])$: This is the same as $\mathsf{Hybrid}_{5:j:1}$, except that for $x \in \bar{Y}$, we replace the challenge CT generated by the simulator with

$$C_{1,A,x} = [\mathbf{s}^{(123)}_{A,x}(\mathbf{A}_1\|\mathbf{A}_2\|\mathbf{A}_3)^\top]_1, C_{1,B,x} = [\mathbf{s}^{(123)}_{B,x}(\mathbf{A}_1\|\mathbf{A}_2\|\mathbf{A}_3)^\top]_1,$$
$$C_{2,A,x} = [\mathbf{s}^{(123)}_{A,x}(\mathbf{A}_1\|\mathbf{A}_2\|\mathbf{A}_3)^\top\mathbf{W}_{A,\rho(x)} + \mathbf{M}_x\begin{pmatrix}\mathbf{K}\\ \mathbf{K}'_A\end{pmatrix} +$$
$$\boxed{\sigma''_{A,x}\mathbf{N}''_A\mathbf{B}_2^{\|\top}} + \sigma'_{A,x}\mathbf{N}'_A\mathbf{B}_3^{\|\top}]_1,$$
$$C_{2,B,x} = [\mathbf{s}^{(123)}_{B,x}(\mathbf{A}_1\|\mathbf{A}_2\|\mathbf{A}_3)^\top\mathbf{W}_{B,\rho(x)} + \mathbf{M}_x\begin{pmatrix}-\mathbf{K}\\ \mathbf{K}'_B\end{pmatrix} +$$
$$\boxed{\sigma''_{B,x}\mathbf{N}''_B\mathbf{B}_2^{\|\top}} + \sigma'_{B,x}\mathbf{N}'_B\mathbf{B}_3^{\|\top}]_1,$$

where

$$\mathbf{N}''_A, \mathbf{N}''_B \leftarrow_R \mathbb{Z}_p^{1\times k},$$
$$\sigma''_{A,x} = \mathbf{M}_x\begin{pmatrix}\sigma''_A\\ \mathbf{k}^{(2)}_A\end{pmatrix}, \sigma''_A \leftarrow_R \mathbb{Z}_p, \mathbf{k}^{(2)}_A \leftarrow_R \mathbb{Z}_p^{(d-1)\times 1},$$
$$\sigma''_{B,x} = \mathbf{M}_x\begin{pmatrix}\sigma''_B\\ \mathbf{k}^{(2)}_B\end{pmatrix}, \sigma''_B \leftarrow_R \mathbb{Z}_p, \mathbf{k}^{(2)}_B \leftarrow_R \mathbb{Z}_p^{(d-1)\times 1}.$$

- $\mathsf{Hybrid}_{5:j:3}(j \in [q])$: This is the same as $\mathsf{Hybrid}_{5:j:2}$, except that for the j-th global identifier GID_j, we replace $\mathsf{H}(\mathsf{GID}_j) = [(\mathbf{B}_1\|\mathbf{B}_2)\mathbf{r}^{(12)}_{\mathsf{GID}_j}]_2$ with $\mathsf{H}(\mathsf{GID}_j) = [(\mathbf{B}_1\|\mathbf{B}_2\|\mathbf{B}_3)\mathbf{r}^{(123)}_{\mathsf{GID}_j}]_2$, where $\mathbf{r}^{(123)}_{\mathsf{GID}_j} \leftarrow_R \mathbb{Z}_p^{3k\times 1}$. Thus, $\mathsf{sk}_{\mathsf{GID}_j,u}$ becomes

$$K_{\mathsf{GID}_j,A,u} = [\mathbf{W}_{A,u}\boxed{(\mathbf{B}_1\|\mathbf{B}_2\|\mathbf{B}_3)\mathbf{r}^{(123)}_{\mathsf{GID}_j}} + \mathbf{W}_{A,u}\mathbf{B}_1\mathbf{r}]_2,$$
$$K_{\mathsf{GID}_j,B,u} = [\mathbf{W}_{B,u}\boxed{(\mathbf{B}_1\|\mathbf{B}_2\|\mathbf{B}_3)\mathbf{r}^{(123)}_{\mathsf{GID}_j}}]_2.$$

– $\mathsf{Hybrid}_{5:j:4}(j \in [q])$: This is the same as $\mathsf{Hybrid}_{5:j:3}$, except that for $x \in \bar{Y}$, we replace the challenge CT generated by the simulator back with

$$C_{1,A,x} = [\mathbf{s}_{A,x}^{(123)}(\mathbf{A}_1\|\mathbf{A}_2\|\mathbf{A}_3)^\top]_1, C_{1,B,x} = [\mathbf{s}_{B,x}^{(123)}(\mathbf{A}_1\|\mathbf{A}_2\|\mathbf{A}_3)^\top]_1,$$
$$C_{2,A,x} = [\mathbf{s}_{A,x}^{(123)}(\mathbf{A}_1\|\mathbf{A}_2\|\mathbf{A}_3)^\top \mathbf{W}_{A,\rho(x)} + \mathbf{M}_x \begin{pmatrix} \mathbf{K} \\ \mathbf{K}'_A \end{pmatrix} +$$
$$\boxed{\cancel{\sigma''_{A,x}\mathbf{N}''_A\mathbf{B}_2^{\|\top}} + \sigma'_{A,x}\mathbf{N}'_A\mathbf{B}_3^{\|\top}}]_1,$$
$$C_{2,B,x} = [\mathbf{s}_{B,x}^{(123)}(\mathbf{A}_1\|\mathbf{A}_2\|\mathbf{A}_3)^\top \mathbf{W}_{B,\rho(x)} + \mathbf{M}_x \begin{pmatrix} -\mathbf{K} \\ \mathbf{K}'_B \end{pmatrix} +$$
$$\boxed{\cancel{\sigma''_{B,x}\mathbf{N}''_B\mathbf{B}_2^{\|\top}} + \sigma'_{B,x}\mathbf{N}'_B\mathbf{B}_3^{\|\top}}]_1.$$

– $\mathsf{Hybrid}_{5:(j+1)}(j \in [q])$: This is the same as $\mathsf{Hybrid}_{5:j:4}$, except that for the j-th global identifier GID_j, we replace $\mathsf{H}(\mathsf{GID}_j) = [(\mathbf{B}_1\|\mathbf{B}_2\|\mathbf{B}_3)\mathbf{r}_{\mathsf{GID}_j}^{(123)}]_2$ with $\mathsf{H}(\mathsf{GID}_j) = [(\mathbf{B}_1\|\mathbf{B}_3)\mathbf{r}_{\mathsf{GID}_j}^{(13)}]_2$, where $\mathbf{r}_{\mathsf{GID}_j}^{(13)} \leftarrow_R \mathbb{Z}_p^{2k\times 1}$. Thus, $\mathsf{sk}_{\mathsf{GID}_j,u}$ becomes

$$K_{\mathsf{GID}_j,A,u} = [\mathbf{W}_{A,u}\boxed{(\mathbf{B}_1\|\mathbf{B}_3)\mathbf{r}_{\mathsf{GID}_j}^{(13)}} + \mathbf{W}_{A,u}\mathbf{B}_1\mathbf{r}]_2,$$
$$K_{\mathsf{GID}_j,B,u} = [\mathbf{W}_{B,u}\boxed{(\mathbf{B}_1\|\mathbf{B}_3)\mathbf{r}_{\mathsf{GID}_j}^{(13)}}]_2.$$

– Hybrid_6: This is the same as $\mathsf{Hybrid}_{5:(q+1)}$, except that we replace $h = [\mathbf{B}_1\mathbf{r}]_2$ in GP with $h = [(\mathbf{B}_1\|\mathbf{B}_2)\mathbf{r}^{(12)}]_2$, where $\mathbf{r}^{(12)} \leftarrow_R \mathbb{Z}_p^{2k\times 1}$. Then C in the challenge CT generated by the simulator becomes

$$C = msg_b \oplus \mathsf{Ext}(e([\mathbf{K}]_1, [\boxed{(\mathbf{B}_1\|\mathbf{B}_2)\mathbf{r}^{(12)}}]_2), \mathsf{seed}).$$

And $\mathsf{sk}_{\mathsf{GID},u}$ becomes

$$K_{\mathsf{GID},A,u} = [\mathbf{W}_{A,u}(\mathbf{B}_1\|\mathbf{B}_3)\mathbf{r}_{\mathsf{GID}}^{(13)} + \mathbf{W}_{A,u}\boxed{(\mathbf{B}_1\|\mathbf{B}_2)\mathbf{r}^{(12)}}]_2,$$
$$K_{\mathsf{GID},B,u} = [\mathbf{W}_{B,u}(\mathbf{B}_1\|\mathbf{B}_3)\mathbf{r}_{\mathsf{GID}}^{(13)}]_2.$$

– Hybrid_7: This is the same as Hybrid_6, except that for $x \in \bar{Y}$, we replace the challenge CT generated by the simulator with

$$C_{1,A,x} = [\mathbf{s}_{A,x}^{(123)}(\mathbf{A}_1\|\mathbf{A}_2\|\mathbf{A}_3)^\top]_1, C_{1,B,x} = [\mathbf{s}_{B,x}^{(123)}(\mathbf{A}_1\|\mathbf{A}_2\|\mathbf{A}_3)^\top]_1,$$
$$C_{2,A,x} = [\mathbf{s}_{A,x}^{(123)}(\mathbf{A}_1\|\mathbf{A}_2\|\mathbf{A}_3)^\top \mathbf{W}_{A,\rho(x)} + \mathbf{M}_x \begin{pmatrix} \mathbf{K} \\ \mathbf{K}'_A \end{pmatrix} + \sigma'_{A,x}\mathbf{N}'_A\mathbf{B}_3^{\|\top}]_1,$$
$$C_{2,B,x} = [\mathbf{s}_{B,x}^{(123)}(\mathbf{A}_1\|\mathbf{A}_2\|\mathbf{A}_3)^\top \mathbf{W}_{B,\rho(x)} + \mathbf{M}_x \begin{pmatrix} -\mathbf{K} \\ \mathbf{K}'_B \end{pmatrix} + \boxed{\sigma''_{B,x}\mathbf{N}''_B\mathbf{B}_2^{\|\top}} +$$
$$\sigma'_{B,x}\mathbf{N}'_B\mathbf{B}_3^{\|\top}]_1,$$

where

$$\mathbf{N}''_B \leftarrow_R \mathbb{Z}_p^{1\times k}, \sigma''_{B,x} = \mathbf{M}_x \begin{pmatrix} \sigma''_B \\ \mathbf{k}_B^{(2)} \end{pmatrix}, \sigma''_B \leftarrow_R \mathbb{Z}_p, \mathbf{k}_B^{(2)} \leftarrow_R \mathbb{Z}_p^{(d-1)\times 1}.$$

- Hybrid_8: This is the same as Hybrid_7, except that we replace $\mathsf{H(GID)} = [(\mathbf{B}_1\|\mathbf{B}_3)\mathbf{r}_{\mathsf{GID}}^{(13)}]_2$ with $\mathsf{H(GID)} = [(\mathbf{B}_1\|\mathbf{B}_2\|\mathbf{B}_3)\mathbf{r}_{\mathsf{GID}}^{(123)}]_2$, where $\mathbf{r}_{\mathsf{GID}}^{(123)} \leftarrow_R \mathbb{Z}_p^{3k\times 1}$. Thus, $\mathsf{sk}_{\mathsf{GID},u}$ becomes

$$K_{\mathsf{GID},A,u} = [\mathbf{W}_{A,u}\boxed{(\mathbf{B}_1\|\mathbf{B}_2\|\mathbf{B}_3)\mathbf{r}_{\mathsf{GID}}^{(123)}} + \mathbf{W}_{A,u}(\mathbf{B}_1\|\mathbf{B}_2)\mathbf{r}^{(12)}]_2,$$
$$K_{\mathsf{GID},B,u} = [\mathbf{W}_{B,u}\boxed{(\mathbf{B}_1\|\mathbf{B}_2\|\mathbf{B}_3)\mathbf{r}_{\mathsf{GID}}^{(123)}}]_2.$$

- Hybrid_9: This is the same as Hybrid_8, except that we replace $\mathsf{H(GID)} = [(\mathbf{B}_1\|\mathbf{B}_2\|\mathbf{B}_3)\mathbf{r}_{\mathsf{GID}}^{(123)}]_2$ with $\mathsf{H(GID)} \equiv \mathsf{H(GID)}/h = [(\mathbf{B}_1\|\mathbf{B}_2\|\mathbf{B}_3)\mathbf{r}_{\mathsf{GID}}^{(123)} - (\mathbf{B}_1\|\mathbf{B}_2)\mathbf{r}^{(12)}]_2$, where $h = [(\mathbf{B}_1\|\mathbf{B}_2)\mathbf{r}^{(12)}]_2$. Thus, $\mathsf{sk}_{\mathsf{GID},u}$ becomes

$$K_{\mathsf{GID},A,u} = [\mathbf{W}_{A,u}\boxed{(\mathbf{B}_1\|\mathbf{B}_2\|\mathbf{B}_3)\mathbf{r}_{\mathsf{GID}}^{(123)}}]_2,$$
$$K_{\mathsf{GID},B,u} = [\mathbf{W}_{B,u}\boxed{(\mathbf{B}_1\|\mathbf{B}_2\|\mathbf{B}_3)\mathbf{r}_{\mathsf{GID}}^{(123)}} - \mathbf{W}_{B,u}\boxed{(\mathbf{B}_1\|\mathbf{B}_2)\mathbf{r}^{(12)}}]_2.$$

- Hybrid_{10}: This is the same as Hybrid_9, except that we replace $\mathsf{H(GID)} = [(\mathbf{B}_1\|\mathbf{B}_2\|\mathbf{B}_3)\mathbf{r}_{\mathsf{GID}}^{(123)} - (\mathbf{B}_1\|\mathbf{B}_2)\mathbf{r}^{(12)}]_2$ with $\mathsf{H(GID)} = [(\mathbf{B}_1\|\mathbf{B}_3)\mathbf{r}_{\mathsf{GID}}^{(13)} - (\mathbf{B}_1\|\mathbf{B}_2)\mathbf{r}^{(12)}]_2$, where $\mathbf{r}_{\mathsf{GID}}^{(13)} \leftarrow_R \mathbb{Z}^{2k\times 1}$. Thus, $\mathsf{sk}_{\mathsf{GID},u}$ becomes

$$K_{\mathsf{GID},A,u} = [\mathbf{W}_{A,u}\boxed{(\mathbf{B}_1\|\mathbf{B}_3)\mathbf{r}_{\mathsf{GID}}^{(13)}}]_2,$$
$$K_{\mathsf{GID},B,u} = [\mathbf{W}_{B,u}\boxed{(\mathbf{B}_1\|\mathbf{B}_3)\mathbf{r}_{\mathsf{GID}}^{(13)}} - \mathbf{W}_{B,u}(\mathbf{B}_1\|\mathbf{B}_2)\mathbf{r}^{(12)}]_2.$$

- Hybrid_{11}: This is the same as Hybrid_{10}, except that for $x \in \bar{Y}$, we replace the challenge CT generated by the simulator back with

$$C_{1,A,x} = [\mathbf{s}_{A,x}^{(123)}(\mathbf{A}_1\|\mathbf{A}_2\|\mathbf{A}_3)^\top]_1, C_{1,B,x} = [\mathbf{s}_{B,x}^{(123)}(\mathbf{A}_1\|\mathbf{A}_2\|\mathbf{A}_3)^\top]_1,$$
$$C_{2,A,x} = [\mathbf{s}_{A,x}^{(123)}(\mathbf{A}_1\|\mathbf{A}_2\|\mathbf{A}_3)^\top\mathbf{W}_{A,\rho(x)} + \mathbf{M}_x\begin{pmatrix}\mathbf{K}\\ \mathbf{K}'_A\end{pmatrix} + \boxed{\sigma''_{A,x}\mathbf{N}''_A\mathbf{B}_2^{\|\top}} +$$
$$\sigma'_{A,x}\mathbf{N}'_A\mathbf{B}_3^{\|\top}]_1,$$
$$C_{2,B,x} = [\mathbf{s}_{B,x}^{(123)}(\mathbf{A}_1\|\mathbf{A}_2\|\mathbf{A}_3)^\top\mathbf{W}_{B,\rho(x)} + \mathbf{M}_x\begin{pmatrix}-\mathbf{K}\\ \mathbf{K}'_B\end{pmatrix} + \sigma''_{B,x}\mathbf{N}''_B\mathbf{B}_2^{\|\top} +$$
$$\sigma'_{B,x}\mathbf{N}'_B\mathbf{B}_3^{\|\top}]_1,$$

where

$$\sigma''_{A,x} = \mathbf{M}_x\begin{pmatrix}\sigma''_A\\ \mathbf{k}_A^{(2)}\end{pmatrix}, \sigma''_A \leftarrow_R \mathbb{Z}_p, \mathbf{k}_A^{(2)} \leftarrow_R \mathbb{Z}_p^{(d-1)\times 1}.$$

- Hybrid_{12}: This is the same as Hybrid_{11}, except that we replace msg_b with $\boxed{msg_R} \leftarrow_R \mathbb{M}$.

Proofs.

Lemma 2. *We have* $|\mathsf{Adv}_{\mathcal{A}}^{\mathsf{Hybrid}_0}(\lambda) - \mathsf{Adv}_{\mathcal{A}}^{\mathsf{Hybrid}_1}(\lambda)| \leq \mathsf{Adv}_{\mathcal{B}_1}^{MDDH^q_{G_2,k,3k}}(\lambda)$, *where* $\mathcal{B}_1$ *is the adversary for the* $MDDH^q_{k,3k}$ *assumption in* G_2.

Proof. This proof is a conventional use of the MDDH assumption, we leave the proof in the full version.

Lemma 3. *We have* $|\mathsf{Adv}_{\mathcal{A}}^{\mathsf{Hybrid}_1}(\lambda) - \mathsf{Adv}_{\mathcal{A}}^{\mathsf{Hybrid}_2}(\lambda)| \leq \mathsf{Adv}_{\mathcal{B}_2}^{SD^{G_1}_{\mathbf{A}_1 \mapsto \mathbf{A}_1, \mathbf{A}_3}}(\lambda)$, *where* $\mathcal{B}_2$ *is the adversary for the* $SD_{\mathbf{A}_1 \mapsto \mathbf{A}_1, \mathbf{A}_3}$ *assumption in* G_1.

Proof. Since this proof is similar to the proof of Lemma 6, we leave this proof in the full version.

Lemma 4. *We have* $|\mathsf{Adv}_{\mathcal{A}}^{\mathsf{Hybrid}_2}(\lambda) - \mathsf{Adv}_{\mathcal{A}}^{\mathsf{Hybrid}_3}(\lambda)| \leq 2 \cdot \mathsf{Adv}_{\mathcal{B}_3}^{1\text{-}ABE}(\lambda)$, *where* $\mathcal{B}_3$ *is the adversary for the Core 1-ABE.*

Proof. Since this proof is similar to the proof of Lemma 7, and the proof of Lemma 7 is more illustrative for the use of Core 1-ABE, thus we leave this proof in the full version.

Lemma 5. *We have* $|\mathsf{Adv}_{\mathcal{A}}^{\mathsf{Hybrid}_3}(\lambda) - \mathsf{Adv}_{\mathcal{A}}^{\mathsf{Hybrid}_4}(\lambda)| \leq \mathsf{Adv}_{\mathcal{B}_4}^{SD^{G_1}_{\mathbf{A}_1 \mapsto \mathbf{A}_1, \mathbf{A}_2}}(\lambda)$, *where* $\mathcal{B}_4$ *is the adversary for the* $SD_{\mathbf{A}_1 \mapsto \mathbf{A}_1, \mathbf{A}_2}$ *assumption in* G_1.

Proof. Since this proof is similar to the proof of Lemma 6, we leave the proof in the full version.

Lemma 6. *We have* $|\mathsf{Adv}_{\mathcal{A}}^{\mathsf{Hybrid}_{5:(j-1)}}(\lambda) - \mathsf{Adv}_{\mathcal{A}}^{\mathsf{Hybrid}_{5:j:1}}(\lambda)| \leq \mathsf{Adv}_{\mathcal{B}_5}^{SD^{G_2}_{\mathbf{B}_1 \mapsto \mathbf{B}_1, \mathbf{B}_2}}(\lambda)$, *where* $\mathcal{B}_5$ *is the adversary for the* $SD_{\mathbf{B}_1 \mapsto \mathbf{B}_1, \mathbf{B}_2}$ *assumption in* G_2.

Proof. Suppose there exists a simulator $\mathcal{B}_5$. $\mathcal{B}_5$ receives

$$(\mathbb{G}, [\mathbf{B}_1]_2, [\mathbf{B}_2]_2, [\mathbf{B}_3]_2, \mathsf{basis}(\mathbf{B}_1^{\parallel}), \mathsf{basis}(\mathbf{B}_1^{\parallel}, \mathbf{B}_2^{\parallel}), \mathsf{basis}(\mathbf{B}_3^{\parallel})), \text{ and } [T]_2.$$

$\mathcal{B}_5$ uses a strong seeded randomness extractor $\mathsf{Ext} : G_T \times \mathsf{S} \to \mathbb{M}$, and a hash function $\mathsf{H} : \{0,1\}^* \to G_2^{3k \times 1}$, which is modeled as a random oracle. Then $\mathcal{B}_5$ proceeds as follows:

Generating the Global Public Parameters: Sample seed $\leftarrow_R \mathsf{S}, \mathbf{r} \leftarrow_R \mathbb{Z}_p^{k \times 1}$. Output

$$\mathsf{GP} = (\mathbb{G}, [\mathbf{A}_1]_1, h = [\mathbf{B}_1 \mathbf{r}]_2, \mathsf{seed}).$$

Generating Authority Public-Master Keys: For a valid Authority Setup query of $u \in \mathcal{AU}$, $\mathcal{B}_5$ samples $\mathbf{W}_{A,u}, \mathbf{W}_{B,u} \leftarrow_R \mathbb{Z}_p^{(2k+1) \times 3k}$. $\mathcal{B}_5$ sets

$$\mathsf{PK}_u = ([\mathbf{A}_1^\top \mathbf{W}_{A,u}]_1, [\mathbf{A}_1^\top \mathbf{W}_{B,u}]_1),$$
$$\mathsf{MSK}_u = (\mathbf{W}_{A,u}, \mathbf{W}_{B,u}).$$

$\mathcal{B}_5$ sends PK_u to $\mathcal{A}$, and stores $(\mathsf{PK}_u, \mathsf{MSK}_u)$. Whenever $\mathcal{A}$ requests MSK_u at a later time, $\mathcal{B}_5$ provides it to $\mathcal{A}$.

Generating the H Oracle Outputs: Whenever $\mathcal{A}$ queries the random oracle H for some $\mathsf{GID} \in \mathcal{GID}$, $\mathcal{B}_5$ proceeds as follows: For $t \leq j-1$, $\mathcal{B}_5$ sets $\mathsf{H}(\mathsf{GID}_t) = [(\mathbf{B}_1\|\mathbf{B}_3)\mathbf{r}^{(13)}_{\mathsf{GID}_t}]_2$, where $\mathbf{r}^{(13)}_{\mathsf{GID}_t} \leftarrow_R \mathbb{Z}_p^{2k\times 1}$; For $t = j$, $\mathcal{B}_5$ sets $\mathsf{H}(\mathsf{GID}_t) = [T]_2$; For $t \geq j+1$, $\mathcal{B}_5$ sets $\mathsf{H}(\mathsf{GID}_t) = [\mathbf{B}_1\mathbf{r}^{(1)}_{\mathsf{GID}_t}]_2$, where $\mathbf{r}^{(1)}_{\mathsf{GID}_t} \leftarrow_R \mathbb{Z}_p^{k\times 1}$. It stores $\mathsf{H}(\mathsf{GID}_t)$ so that it can respond consistently if $\mathsf{H}(\mathsf{GID}_t)$ is queried again.

Generating Secret Keys: For a valid Secret Key query of $(\mathsf{GID}_t, u) \in \mathcal{GID}\times\mathcal{AU}$, $\mathcal{B}_5$ runs the real KeyGen to generate $\mathsf{sk}_{\mathsf{GID}_t,u}$ with $\mathsf{H}(\mathsf{GID}_t)$, $h = [\mathbf{B}_1\mathbf{r}]_2$ and $\mathsf{MSK}_u = (\mathbf{W}_{A,u}, \mathbf{W}_{B,u})$. If $\mathsf{H}(\mathsf{GID}_t)$ has not been generated before, then generate it following the above procedure.

Generating the Challenge Ciphertext: At some point, $\mathcal{A}$ queries the challenge $(msg_0, msg_1, \mathbf{M}, \rho)$, and also submits the public keys $\{\mathsf{PK}_{u'} = ([P_{A,u'}]_1, [P_{B,u'}]_1)\}$ for a subset U_A of attribute authorities appearing in the LSSS access structure $(\mathbf{M}, \rho)$. If U_A passes the validation test, $\mathcal{B}_5$ flips a random coin $b \leftarrow_R \{0,1\}$ and generates CT as follows:

Let Y denote the subset of rows of the challenge access matrix $\mathbf{M}$ labeled by the authorities for which $\mathcal{A}$ supplies the authority public keys $\{\mathsf{PK}_{u'} = ([P_{A,u'}]_1, [P_{B,u'}]_1)\}$. Let $\bar{Y} = [\ell]\backslash Y$. $\mathcal{B}_5$ samples $\mathbf{K} \leftarrow_R \mathbb{Z}_p^{1\times 3k}, \mathbf{K}'_A \leftarrow_R \mathbb{Z}_p^{(d-1)\times 3k}, \mathbf{K}'_B \leftarrow_R \mathbb{Z}_p^{(d-1)\times 3k}, \mathbf{s}^{(1)}_{A,x}, \mathbf{s}^{(1)}_{B,x} \leftarrow_R \mathbb{Z}_p^{1\times k}, \mathbf{s}^{(23)}_{A,x}, \mathbf{s}^{(23)}_{B,x} \leftarrow_R \mathbb{Z}_p^{1\times(k+1)}$, and $\mathbf{N}'_A, \mathbf{N}'_B \leftarrow_R \mathbb{Z}_p^{1\times k}, \sigma'_A \leftarrow_R \mathbb{Z}_p, \mathbf{k}^{(3)}_A \leftarrow_R \mathbb{Z}_p^{(d-1)\times 1}, \sigma'_B \leftarrow_R \mathbb{Z}_p, \mathbf{k}^{(3)}_B \leftarrow_R \mathbb{Z}_p^{(d-1)\times 1}$. Set

$$\mathbf{s}^{(123)}_{A,x} = (\mathbf{s}^{(1)}_{A,x}\|\mathbf{s}^{(23)}_{A,x}), \mathbf{s}^{(123)}_{B,x} = (\mathbf{s}^{(1)}_{B,x}\|\mathbf{s}^{(23)}_{B,x}),$$
$$\sigma'_{A,x} = \mathbf{M}_x \begin{pmatrix} \sigma'_A \\ \mathbf{k}^{(3)}_A \end{pmatrix}, \sigma'_{B,x} = \mathbf{M}_x \begin{pmatrix} \sigma'_B \\ \mathbf{k}^{(3)}_B \end{pmatrix}.$$

$\mathcal{B}_5$ sets $C = msg_b \oplus \mathsf{Ext}(e([\mathbf{K}]_1, h), \mathsf{seed})$.

For each $x \in Y$, $\mathcal{B}_5$ forms $C_{1,A,x}, C_{1,B,x}, C_{2,A,x}, C_{2,B,x}$ as:

$$C_{1,A,x} = [\mathbf{s}^{(1)}_{A,x}\mathbf{A}_1^\top]_1, C_{1,B,x} = [\mathbf{s}^{(1)}_{B,x}\mathbf{A}_1^\top]_1,$$
$$C_{2,A,x} = [\mathbf{s}^{(1)}_{A,x}P_{A,\rho(x)} + \mathbf{M}_x \begin{pmatrix} \mathbf{K} \\ \mathbf{K}'_A \end{pmatrix}]_1, C_{2,B,x} = [\mathbf{s}^{(1)}_{B,x}P_{B,\rho(x)} + \mathbf{M}_x \begin{pmatrix} -\mathbf{K} \\ \mathbf{K}'_B \end{pmatrix}]_1.$$

For each $x \in \bar{Y}$, $\mathcal{B}_5$ forms $C_{1,A,x}, C_{1,B,x}, C_{2,A,x}, C_{2,B,x}$ as:

$$C_{1,A,x} = [\mathbf{s}^{(123)}_{A,x}(\mathbf{A}_1\|\mathbf{A}_2\|\mathbf{A}_3)^\top]_1, C_{1,B,x} = [\mathbf{s}^{(123)}_{B,x}(\mathbf{A}_1\|\mathbf{A}_2\|\mathbf{A}_3)^\top]_1,$$
$$C_{2,A,x} = [\mathbf{s}^{(123)}_{A,x}(\mathbf{A}_1\|\mathbf{A}_2\|\mathbf{A}_3)^\top\mathbf{W}_{A,\rho(x)} + \mathbf{M}_x \begin{pmatrix} \mathbf{K} \\ \mathbf{K}'_A \end{pmatrix} + \sigma'_{A,x}\mathbf{N}'_A\mathsf{basis}(\mathbf{B}_3^\|)^\top]_1,$$
$$C_{2,B,x} = [\mathbf{s}^{(123)}_{B,x}(\mathbf{A}_1\|\mathbf{A}_2\|\mathbf{A}_3)^\top\mathbf{W}_{B,\rho(x)} + \mathbf{M}_x \begin{pmatrix} -\mathbf{K} \\ \mathbf{K}'_B \end{pmatrix} + \sigma'_{B,x}\mathbf{N}'_B\mathsf{basis}(\mathbf{B}_3^\|)^\top]_1.$$

$\mathcal{B}_5$ sends $\mathsf{CT} = (C, \{C_{1,A,x}, C_{1,B,x}, C_{2,A,x}, C_{2,B,x}\}_{x\in[\ell]})$ to $\mathcal{A}$.

Guess: $\mathcal{A}$ eventually outputs a guess bit $b' \in \{0,1\}$. $\mathcal{B}_5$ outputs 1 if $b = b'$ and 0 otherwise.

Observe that if $T = \mathbf{B}_1\mathbf{r}^{(1)}_{\mathsf{GID}_j}$, where $\mathbf{r}^{(1)}_{\mathsf{GID}_j} \leftarrow_R \mathbb{Z}_p^{k\times 1}$, the distributions are exactly as in $\mathsf{Hybrid}_{5:(j-1)}$; if $T = (\mathbf{B}_1\|\mathbf{B}_2)\mathbf{r}^{(12)}_{\mathsf{GID}_j}$, where $\mathbf{r}^{(12)\top}_{\mathsf{GID}_j} = (\mathbf{r}^{(1)\top}_{\mathsf{GID}_j}\|\mathbf{r}^{(2)\top}_{\mathsf{GID}_j}), \mathbf{r}^{(2)}_{\mathsf{GID}_j} \leftarrow_R \mathbb{Z}_p^{k\times 1}$, the distributions are exactly as in $\mathsf{Hybrid}_{5:j:1}$. Then if $\mathcal{A}$ can distinguish $\mathsf{Hybrid}_{5:(j-1)}$ and $\mathsf{Hybrid}_{5:j:1}$, $\mathcal{B}_5$ can use $\mathcal{A}$ to break the $\mathrm{SD}_{\mathbf{B}_1\mapsto\mathbf{B}_1,\mathbf{B}_2}$ assumption in G_2. Thus, we obtain a contradiction.

Lemma 7. *We have* $|\mathsf{Adv}_{\mathcal{A}}^{\mathsf{Hybrid}_{5:j:1}}(\lambda) - \mathsf{Adv}_{\mathcal{A}}^{\mathsf{Hybrid}_{5:j:2}}(\lambda)| \le 2\cdot\mathsf{Adv}_{\mathcal{B}_6}^{1\text{-}ABE}(\lambda)$, *where* $\mathcal{B}_6$ *is the adversary for the Core 1-ABE.*

Proof. Suppose there exists a simulator $\mathcal{B}_6$. $\mathcal{B}_6$ challenges

$$(\mu_{0,A} = \mu_0, \mu_{1,A}) \text{ and } (-\mu_{0,B} = -\mu_0, -\mu_{1,B}),$$

respectively, to the underlying Core 1-ABE, where $\mu_0, \mu_{1,A}, \mu_{1,B} \leftarrow_R \mathbb{Z}_p$, and queries $\mathcal{O}_F(((\mathbf{M},\rho),\mu_{\beta,A})), \mathcal{O}_{X,A}(\{u\}), \mathcal{O}_F(((\mathbf{M},\rho),-\mu_{\beta,B})), \mathcal{O}_{X,B}(\{u\})$, which are defined in Sect. 2.5. Then $\mathcal{B}_6$ receives

$$\{[\mu_{\beta,A,x} + \eta_{A,\rho(x)}\mathbf{s}^{(3)}_{A,x}]_1, [\mathbf{s}^{(3)}_{A,x}]_1\}, \{\eta_{A,u}\},$$

and

$$\{[-\mu_{\beta,B,x} + \eta_{B,\rho(x)}\mathbf{s}^{(3)}_{B,x}]_1, [\mathbf{s}^{(3)}_{B,x}]_1\}, \{\eta_{B,u}\},$$

respectively.

$\mathcal{B}_6$ samples $\mathbf{N}''_A, \mathbf{N}''_B \leftarrow_R \mathbb{Z}_p^{1\times k}$, and for $\mathbf{M}_x\begin{pmatrix}\mathbf{K}\\ \mathbf{K}'_A\end{pmatrix}$, sets

$$\mathbf{K} = \widetilde{\mathbf{K}} + \mu_{\beta,A}\mathbf{N}''_A\mathbf{B}_2^{\|\top},$$

for $\mathbf{M}_x\begin{pmatrix}-\mathbf{K}\\ \mathbf{K}'_B\end{pmatrix}$, sets

$$\mathbf{K} = \widetilde{\mathbf{K}} + \mu_{\beta,B}\mathbf{N}''_B\mathbf{B}_2^{\|\top},$$

where $\widetilde{\mathbf{K}} \leftarrow_R \mathbb{Z}_p^{1\times 3k}$. Then set

$$\mathbf{W}_{A,u} = \widetilde{\mathbf{W}_{A,u}} + \mathbf{A}_3^{\|}\eta_{A,u}\mathbf{N}''_A\mathbf{B}_2^{\|\top}, \mathbf{W}_{B,u} = \widetilde{\mathbf{W}_{B,u}} + \mathbf{A}_3^{\|}\eta_{B,u}\mathbf{N}''_B\mathbf{B}_2^{\|\top},$$

where $\widetilde{\mathbf{W}_{A,u}}, \widetilde{\mathbf{W}_{B,u}} \leftarrow_R \mathbb{Z}_p^{(2k+1)\times 3k}$, and $\eta_{A,u}, \eta_{B,u} \in \mathbb{Z}_p^{k\times 1}$ are from the answers of $\mathcal{O}_{X,A}(\{u\}), \mathcal{O}_{X,B}(\{u\})$, respectively.

Observe that, when we change $\mathbf{W}_{A,u}, \mathbf{W}_{B,u}$ and $\mathbf{K}$, only $\mathsf{PK}_u, \mathsf{sk}_{\mathsf{GID}_t,u}$ and CT are changed.

For PK_u, we have

$$\mathbf{A}_1^\top \mathbf{W}_{A,u} \equiv \mathbf{A}_1^\top (\widetilde{\mathbf{W}_{A,u}} + \mathbf{A}_3^{\|} \eta_{A,u} \mathbf{N}_A'' \mathbf{B}_2^{\|\top}) = \mathbf{A}_1^\top \widetilde{\mathbf{W}_{A,u}},$$

and

$$\mathbf{A}_1^\top \mathbf{W}_{B,u} \equiv \mathbf{A}_1^\top (\widetilde{\mathbf{W}_{B,u}} + \mathbf{A}_3^{\|} \eta_{B,u} \mathbf{N}_B'' \mathbf{B}_2^{\|\top}) = \mathbf{A}_1^\top \widetilde{\mathbf{W}_{B,u}}.$$

Thus, PK_u remains unchanged.

For $\mathsf{sk}_{\mathsf{GID}_t,u}$, we have

when $t \le j-1$,

$$\begin{aligned}\mathbf{W}_{A,u}((\mathbf{B}_1\|\mathbf{B}_3)\mathbf{r}^{(13)}_{\mathsf{GID}_t} + \mathbf{B}_1\mathbf{r}) \equiv& (\widetilde{\mathbf{W}_{A,u}} + \mathbf{A}_3^{\|}\eta_{A,u}\mathbf{N}_A''\mathbf{B}_2^{\|\top})((\mathbf{B}_1\|\mathbf{B}_3)\mathbf{r}^{(13)}_{\mathsf{GID}_t} + \mathbf{B}_1\mathbf{r})\\ =&\widetilde{\mathbf{W}_{A,u}}((\mathbf{B}_1\|\mathbf{B}_3)\mathbf{r}^{(13)}_{\mathsf{GID}_t} + \mathbf{B}_1\mathbf{r}),\end{aligned}$$

and

$$\begin{aligned}\mathbf{W}_{B,u}(\mathbf{B}_1\|\mathbf{B}_3)\mathbf{r}^{(13)}_{\mathsf{GID}_t} \equiv& (\widetilde{\mathbf{W}_{B,u}} + \mathbf{A}_3^{\|}\eta_{B,u}\mathbf{N}_B''\mathbf{B}_2^{\|\top})(\mathbf{B}_1\|\mathbf{B}_3)\mathbf{r}^{(13)}_{\mathsf{GID}_t}\\ =&\widetilde{\mathbf{W}_{B,u}}(\mathbf{B}_1\|\mathbf{B}_3)\mathbf{r}^{(13)}_{\mathsf{GID}_t},\end{aligned}$$

where $\mathbf{r}^{(13)}_{\mathsf{GID}_t} \leftarrow_R \mathbb{Z}_p^{2k\times 1}$;

when $t = j$,

$$\begin{aligned}\mathbf{W}_{A,u}((\mathbf{B}_1\|\mathbf{B}_2)\mathbf{r}^{(12)}_{\mathsf{GID}_t} + \mathbf{B}_1\mathbf{r}) \equiv& (\widetilde{\mathbf{W}_{A,u}} + \mathbf{A}_3^{\|}\eta_{A,u}\mathbf{N}_A''\mathbf{B}_2^{\|\top})((\mathbf{B}_1\|\mathbf{B}_2)\mathbf{r}^{(12)}_{\mathsf{GID}_t} + \mathbf{B}_1\mathbf{r})\\ =&\widetilde{\mathbf{W}_{A,u}}((\mathbf{B}_1\|\mathbf{B}_2)\mathbf{r}^{(12)}_{\mathsf{GID}_t} + \mathbf{B}_1\mathbf{r}) + \mathbf{A}_3^{\|}\eta_{A,u}\mathbf{N}_A''\mathbf{r}^{(2)}_{\mathsf{GID}_t},\end{aligned}$$

and

$$\begin{aligned}\mathbf{W}_{B,u}(\mathbf{B}_1\|\mathbf{B}_2)\mathbf{r}^{(12)}_{\mathsf{GID}_t} \equiv& (\widetilde{\mathbf{W}_{B,u}} + \mathbf{A}_3^{\|}\eta_{B,u}\mathbf{N}_B''\mathbf{B}_2^{\|\top})(\mathbf{B}_1\|\mathbf{B}_2)\mathbf{r}^{(12)}_{\mathsf{GID}_t}\\ =&\widetilde{\mathbf{W}_{B,u}}(\mathbf{B}_1\|\mathbf{B}_2)\mathbf{r}^{(12)}_{\mathsf{GID}_t} + \mathbf{A}_3^{\|}\eta_{B,u}\mathbf{N}_B''\mathbf{r}^{(2)}_{\mathsf{GID}_t},\end{aligned}$$

where $\mathbf{r}^{(1)}_{\mathsf{GID}_t}, \mathbf{r}^{(2)}_{\mathsf{GID}_t} \leftarrow_R \mathbb{Z}_p^{k\times 1}, \mathbf{r}^{(12)\top}_{\mathsf{GID}_t} = (\mathbf{r}^{(1)\top}_{\mathsf{GID}_t}\|\mathbf{r}^{(2)\top}_{\mathsf{GID}_t})$, and $\eta_{A,u}$, $\eta_{B,u}$ are from the answers of $\mathcal{O}_{X,A}(\{u\}), \mathcal{O}_{X,B}(\{u\})$;

when $t \ge j+1$,

$$\begin{aligned}\mathbf{W}_{A,u}(\mathbf{B}_1\mathbf{r}^{(1)}_{\mathsf{GID}_t} + \mathbf{B}_1\mathbf{r}) \equiv& (\widetilde{\mathbf{W}_{A,u}} + \mathbf{A}_3^{\|}\eta_{A,u}\mathbf{A}_2^\top\mathbf{N}_A''\mathbf{B}_2^{\|\top})(\mathbf{B}_1\mathbf{r}^{(1)}_{\mathsf{GID}_t} + \mathbf{B}_1\mathbf{r})\\ =&\widetilde{\mathbf{W}_{A,u}}(\mathbf{B}_1\mathbf{r}^{(1)}_{\mathsf{GID}_t} + \mathbf{B}_1\mathbf{r}),\end{aligned}$$

and

$$\begin{aligned}\mathbf{W}_{B,u}\mathbf{B}_1\mathbf{r}^{(1)}_{\mathsf{GID}_t} \equiv& (\widetilde{\mathbf{W}_{B,u}} + \mathbf{A}_3^{\|}\eta_{B,u}\mathbf{N}_B''\mathbf{B}_2^{\|\top})\mathbf{B}_1\mathbf{r}^{(1)}_{\mathsf{GID}_t}\\ =&\widetilde{\mathbf{W}_{B,u}}\mathbf{B}_1\mathbf{r}^{(1)}_{\mathsf{GID}_t},\end{aligned}$$

where $\mathbf{r}^{(1)}_{\mathsf{GID}_t} \leftarrow_R \mathbb{Z}_p^{k\times 1}$.

For the challenge CT, observe that only the components of $x \in \bar{Y}$ are changed. Then for each $x \in \bar{Y}$, $C_{1,A,x}, C_{1,B,x}, C_{2,A,x}, C_{2,B,x}$ are formed as

$$
\begin{aligned}
C_{1,A,x} =& [\mathbf{s}^{(123)}_{A,x}(\mathbf{A}_1\|\mathbf{A}_2\|\mathbf{A}_3)^\top]_1, C_{1,B,x} = [\mathbf{s}^{(123)}_{B,x}(\mathbf{A}_1\|\mathbf{A}_2\|\mathbf{A}_3)^\top]_1,\\
C_{2,A,x} =& [\mathbf{s}^{(123)}_{A,x}(\mathbf{A}_1\|\mathbf{A}_2\|\mathbf{A}_3)^\top \mathbf{W}_{A,\rho(x)} + \sigma'_{A,x}\mathbf{N}'_A\mathbf{B}_3^{\|\top} + \mathbf{M}_x \begin{pmatrix}\mathbf{K}\\ \mathbf{K}'_A\end{pmatrix}]_1\\
\equiv& [\mathbf{s}^{(123)}_{A,x}(\mathbf{A}_1\|\mathbf{A}_2\|\mathbf{A}_3)^\top \widetilde{\mathbf{W}_{A,\rho(x)}} + \mathbf{s}^{(123)}_{A,x}(\mathbf{A}_1\|\mathbf{A}_2\|\mathbf{A}_3)^\top \mathbf{A}_3^{\|}\eta_{A,\rho(x)}\mathbf{N}''_A\mathbf{B}_2^{\|\top} +\\
& \sigma'_{A,x}\mathbf{N}'_A\mathbf{B}_3^{\|\top} + \mathbf{M}_x \begin{pmatrix}\mathbf{K}\\ \mathbf{K}'_A\end{pmatrix}]_1\\
=& [\mathbf{s}^{(123)}_{A,x}(\mathbf{A}_1\|\mathbf{A}_2\|\mathbf{A}_3)^\top \widetilde{\mathbf{W}_{A,\rho(x)}} + \mathbf{s}^{(3)}_{A,x}\mathbf{A}_3^\top \mathbf{A}_3^{\|}\eta_{A,\rho(x)}\mathbf{N}''_A\mathbf{B}_2^{\|\top} + \sigma'_{A,x}\mathbf{N}'_A\mathbf{B}_3^{\|\top} +\\
& \mathbf{M}_x \begin{pmatrix}\mathbf{K}\\ \mathbf{K}'_A\end{pmatrix}]_1\\
=& [\mathbf{s}^{(123)}_{A,x}(\mathbf{A}_1\|\mathbf{A}_2\|\mathbf{A}_3)^\top \widetilde{\mathbf{W}_{A,\rho(x)}} + \mathbf{s}^{(3)}_{A,x}\eta_{A,\rho(x)}\mathbf{N}''_A\mathbf{B}_2^{\|\top} +\\
& \sigma'_{A,x}\mathbf{N}'_A\mathbf{B}_3^{\|\top} + \mathbf{M}_x \begin{pmatrix}\mathbf{K}\\ \mathbf{K}'_A\end{pmatrix}]_1\\
\equiv& [\mathbf{s}^{(12)}_{A,x}(\mathbf{A}_1\|\mathbf{A}_2)^\top \widetilde{\mathbf{W}_{A,\rho(x)}} + \sigma'_{A,x}\mathbf{N}'_A\mathbf{B}_3^{\|\top} +\\
& \underbrace{\mathbf{M}_x \begin{pmatrix}\widetilde{\mathbf{K}}\\ \mathbf{K}'_A\end{pmatrix} + \mathbf{s}^{(3)}_{A,x}\mathbf{A}_3^\top \widetilde{\mathbf{W}_{A,\rho(x)}} + (\mu_{\beta,A,x} + \mathbf{s}^{(3)}_{A,x}\eta_{A,\rho(x)})\mathbf{N}''_A\mathbf{B}_2^{\|\top}}_{\mathbf{M}_x \begin{pmatrix}\mathbf{K}\\ \mathbf{K}'_A\end{pmatrix} + \mathbf{s}^{(3)}_{A,x}\mathbf{A}_3^\top \mathbf{W}_{A,\rho(x)}}]_1,\\
C_{2,B,x} =& [\mathbf{s}^{(123)}_{B,x}(\mathbf{A}_1\|\mathbf{A}_2\|\mathbf{A}_3)^\top \mathbf{W}_{B,\rho(x)} + \sigma'_{B,x}\mathbf{N}'_B\mathbf{B}_3^{\|\top} + \mathbf{M}_x \begin{pmatrix}-\mathbf{K}\\ \mathbf{K}'_B\end{pmatrix}]_1\\
\equiv& [\mathbf{s}^{(123)}_{B,x}(\mathbf{A}_1\|\mathbf{A}_2\|\mathbf{A}_3)^\top \widetilde{\mathbf{W}_{B,\rho(x)}} + \mathbf{s}^{(123)}_{B,x}(\mathbf{A}_1\|\mathbf{A}_2\|\mathbf{A}_3)^\top \mathbf{A}_3^{\|}\eta_{B,\rho(x)}\mathbf{N}''_B\mathbf{B}_2^{\|\top} +\\
& \sigma'_{B,x}\mathbf{N}'_B\mathbf{B}_3^{\|\top} + \mathbf{M}_x \begin{pmatrix}-\mathbf{K}\\ \mathbf{K}'_B\end{pmatrix}]_1\\
=& [\mathbf{s}^{(123)}_{B,x}(\mathbf{A}_1\|\mathbf{A}_2\|\mathbf{A}_3)^\top \widetilde{\mathbf{W}_{B,\rho(x)}} + \mathbf{s}^{(3)}_{B,x}\mathbf{A}_3^\top \mathbf{A}_3^{\|}\eta_{B,\rho(x)}\mathbf{N}''_B\mathbf{B}_2^{\|\top} +\\
& \sigma'_{B,x}\mathbf{N}'_B\mathbf{B}_3^{\|\top} + \mathbf{M}_x \begin{pmatrix}-\mathbf{K}\\ \mathbf{K}'_B\end{pmatrix}]_1\\
=& [\mathbf{s}^{(123)}_{B,x}(\mathbf{A}_1\|\mathbf{A}_2\|\mathbf{A}_3)^\top \widetilde{\mathbf{W}_{B,\rho(x)}} + \mathbf{s}^{(3)}_{B,x}\eta_{B,\rho(x)}\mathbf{N}''_B\mathbf{B}_2^{\|\top} + \sigma'_{B,x}\mathbf{N}'_B\mathbf{B}_3^{\|\top} +\\
& \mathbf{M}_x \begin{pmatrix}-\mathbf{K}\\ \mathbf{K}'_B\end{pmatrix}]_1\\
\equiv& [\mathbf{s}^{(12)}_{B,x}(\mathbf{A}_1\|\mathbf{A}_2)^\top \widetilde{\mathbf{W}_{B,\rho(x)}} + \sigma'_{B,x}\mathbf{N}'_B\mathbf{B}_3^{\|\top} +\\
& \underbrace{\mathbf{M}_x \begin{pmatrix}-\widetilde{\mathbf{K}}\\ \mathbf{K}'_B\end{pmatrix} + \mathbf{s}^{(3)}_{B,x}\mathbf{A}_3^\top \widetilde{\mathbf{W}_{B,\rho(x)}} + (-\mu_{\beta,B,x} + \mathbf{s}^{(3)}_{B,x}\eta_{B,\rho(x)})\mathbf{N}''_B\mathbf{B}_2^{\|\top}}_{\mathbf{M}_x \begin{pmatrix}-\mathbf{K}\\ \mathbf{K}'_B\end{pmatrix} + \mathbf{s}^{(3)}_{B,x}\mathbf{A}_3^\top \mathbf{W}_{B,\rho(x)}}]_1
\end{aligned}
$$

where $\mathbf{N}'_A, \mathbf{N}'_B \leftarrow_R \mathbb{Z}_p^{1\times k}$, $\mathbf{s}^{(1)}_{A,x}, \mathbf{s}^{(1)}_{B,x} \leftarrow_R \mathbb{Z}_p^{1\times k}$, $\mathbf{s}^{(2)}_{A,x}, \mathbf{s}^{(2)}_{B,x} \leftarrow_R \mathbb{Z}_p$, and $\mathbf{s}^{(123)}_{A,x} = (\mathbf{s}^{(1)}_{A,x} \| \mathbf{s}^{(2)}_{A,x} \| \mathbf{s}^{(3)}_{A,x}), \mathbf{s}^{(123)}_{B,x} = (\mathbf{s}^{(1)}_{B,x} \| \mathbf{s}^{(2)}_{B,x} \| \mathbf{s}^{(3)}_{B,x})$, $\mathbf{s}^{(12)}_{A,x} = (\mathbf{s}^{(1)}_{A,x} \| \mathbf{s}^{(2)}_{A,x}), \mathbf{s}^{(12)}_{B,x} = (\mathbf{s}^{(1)}_{B,x} \| \mathbf{s}^{(2)}_{B,x})$, and $([\mu_{\beta,A,x} + \mathbf{s}^{(3)}_{A,x}\eta_{A,\rho(x)}]_1, [\mathbf{s}^{(3)}_{A,x}]_1)$, $([-\mu_{\beta,B,x} + \mathbf{s}^{(3)}_{B,x}\eta_{B,\rho(x)}]_1, [\mathbf{s}^{(3)}_{B,x}]_1)$ are from the answers of $\mathcal{O}_F(((\mathbf{M},\rho),\mu_{\beta,A})), \mathcal{O}_F(((\mathbf{M},\rho),-\mu_{\beta,B}))$, respectively.

Observe that if $\mu_{\beta,A} = \mu_{0,A}$ and $\mu_{\beta,B} = \mu_{0,B}$, the distributions are as in $\mathsf{Hybrid}_{5:j:1}$; if $\mu_{\beta,A} = \mu_{1,A}$ and $\mu_{\beta,B} = \mu_{1,B}$, the distributions are as in $\mathsf{Hybrid}_{5:j:2}$, which implicitly sets $\sigma''_A = \mathsf{Reconstruct}(\{\sigma''_{A,x}\}) = \mu_{1,A} - \mu_{0,A}$, and $\sigma''_B = \mathsf{Reconstruct}(\{\sigma''_{B,x}\}) = \mu_{1,B} - \mu_{0,B}$.

We can conclude that $\mathsf{Hybrid}_{5:j:1}$ and $\mathsf{Hybrid}_{5:j:2}$ are indistinguishable under the Core 1-ABE.

Lemma 8. *We have* $|\mathsf{Adv}_{\mathcal{A}}^{\mathsf{Hybrid}_{5:j:2}}(\lambda) - \mathsf{Adv}_{\mathcal{A}}^{\mathsf{Hybrid}_{5:j:3}}(\lambda)| \leq \mathsf{Adv}_{\mathcal{B}_7}^{SD^{G_2}_{\mathbf{B}_2 \mapsto \mathbf{B}_2,\mathbf{B}_3}}(\lambda)$, *where* $\mathcal{B}_7$ *is the adversary for the* $SD_{\mathbf{B}_2 \mapsto \mathbf{B}_2,\mathbf{B}_3}$ *assumption in* G_2.

Proof. Since this proof is similar to the proof of Lemma 6, we leave the proof in the full version.

Lemma 9. *We have* $|\mathsf{Adv}_{\mathcal{A}}^{\mathsf{Hybrid}_{5:j:3}}(\lambda) - \mathsf{Adv}_{\mathcal{A}}^{\mathsf{Hybrid}_{5:j:4}}(\lambda)| \leq 2\cdot\mathsf{Adv}_{\mathcal{B}_8}^{1\text{-}ABE}(\lambda)$, *where* $\mathcal{B}_8$ *is the adversary for the Core 1-ABE.*

Proof. Since this proof is similar to the proof of Lemma 7, we leave the proof in the full version.

Lemma 10.
We have $|\mathsf{Adv}_{\mathcal{A}}^{\mathsf{Hybrid}_{5:j:4}}(\lambda) - \mathsf{Adv}_{\mathcal{A}}^{\mathsf{Hybrid}_{5:(j+1)}}(\lambda)| \leq \mathsf{Adv}_{\mathcal{B}_9}^{SD^{G_2}_{\mathbf{B}_1 \mapsto \mathbf{B}_1,\mathbf{B}_2}}(\lambda)$, *where* $\mathcal{B}_9$ *is the adversary for the* $SD_{\mathbf{B}_1 \mapsto \mathbf{B}_1,\mathbf{B}_2}$ *assumption in* G_2.

Proof. Since this proof is similar to the proof of Lemma 6, we leave the proof in the full version.

Lemma 11. *We have* $|\mathsf{Adv}_{\mathcal{A}}^{\mathsf{Hybrid}_{5:(q+1)}}(\lambda) - \mathsf{Adv}_{\mathcal{A}}^{\mathsf{Hybrid}_{6}}(\lambda)| \leq \mathsf{Adv}_{\mathcal{B}_{10}}^{SD^{G_2}_{\mathbf{B}_1 \mapsto \mathbf{B}_1,\mathbf{B}_2}}(\lambda)$, *where* $\mathcal{B}_{10}$ *is the adversary for the* $SD_{\mathbf{B}_1 \mapsto \mathbf{B}_1,\mathbf{B}_2}$ *assumption in* G_2.

Proof. Since this proof is similar to the proof of Lemma 6, we leave the proof in the full version.

Lemma 12. *We have* $|\mathsf{Adv}_{\mathcal{A}}^{\mathsf{Hybrid}_{6}}(\lambda) - \mathsf{Adv}_{\mathcal{A}}^{\mathsf{Hybrid}_{7}}(\lambda)| \leq \mathsf{Adv}_{\mathcal{B}_{11}}^{1\text{-}ABE}(\lambda)$, *where* $\mathcal{B}_{11}$ *is the adversary for the Core 1-ABE.*

Proof. Since this proof is similar to the proof of Lemma 7, we leave the proof in the full version.

Lemma 13. *We have* $|\mathsf{Adv}_{\mathcal{A}}^{\mathsf{Hybrid}_{7}}(\lambda) - \mathsf{Adv}_{\mathcal{A}}^{\mathsf{Hybrid}_{8}}(\lambda)| \leq \mathsf{Adv}_{\mathcal{B}_{12}}^{SD^{G_2}_{\mathbf{B}_3 \mapsto \mathbf{B}_2,\mathbf{B}_3}}(\lambda)$, *where* $\mathcal{B}_{12}$ *is the adversary for the* $SD_{\mathbf{B}_3 \mapsto \mathbf{B}_2,\mathbf{B}_3}$ *assumption in* G_2.

Proof. Since this proof is similar to the proof of Lemma 6, we leave the proof in the full version.

Lemma 14. *We have* $|\mathsf{Adv}_{\mathcal{A}}^{\mathsf{Hybrid}_8}(\lambda) - \mathsf{Adv}_{\mathcal{A}}^{\mathsf{Hybrid}_9}(\lambda)| = 0$.

Proof. By simply setting $\mathsf{H}(\mathsf{GID}) \equiv \mathsf{H}(\mathsf{GID})/h$ for the queried $\mathsf{GID} \in \mathcal{GID}$ of H, where h is the component in GP, we can easily conclude that Hybrid_8 and Hybrid_9 are identically distributed.

Lemma 15. *We have* $|\mathsf{Adv}_{\mathcal{A}}^{\mathsf{Hybrid}_9}(\lambda) - \mathsf{Adv}_{\mathcal{A}}^{\mathsf{Hybrid}_{10}}(\lambda)| \leq \mathsf{Adv}_{\mathcal{B}_{13}}^{SD^{G_2}_{\mathbf{B}_3 \mapsto \mathbf{B}_2, \mathbf{B}_3}}(\lambda)$, *where* $\mathcal{B}_{13}$ *is the adversary for the* $SD_{\mathbf{B}_3 \mapsto \mathbf{B}_2, \mathbf{B}_3}$ *assumption in* G_2.

Proof. Since this proof is similar to the proof of Lemma 6, we leave the proof in the full version.

Lemma 16. *We have* $|\mathsf{Adv}_{\mathcal{A}}^{\mathsf{Hybrid}_{10}}(\lambda) - \mathsf{Adv}_{\mathcal{A}}^{\mathsf{Hybrid}_{11}}(\lambda)| \leq \mathsf{Adv}_{\mathcal{B}_{14}}^{1\text{-}ABE}(\lambda)$, *where* $\mathcal{B}_{14}$ *is the adversary for the Core 1-ABE.*

Proof. Since this proof is similar to the proof of Lemma 7, we leave the proof in the full version.

Lemma 17. *We have* $|\mathsf{Adv}_{\mathcal{A}}^{\mathsf{Hybrid}_{11}}(\lambda) - \mathsf{Adv}_{\mathcal{A}}^{\mathsf{Hybrid}_{12}}(\lambda)| \leq \mathsf{negl}(\lambda)$.

Proof. Since the symmetric key $e([\mathbf{K}]_1, [(\mathbf{B}_1 \| \mathbf{B}_2)\mathbf{r}^{(12)}]_2)$ is masked by the randomness from the second subspace, we can replace msg_b with $msg_R \leftarrow_R \mathbb{M}$ with a negligible difference by the statistical indistinguishability from Ext, if Ext is parameterized correctly.

Acknowledgements. We thank all the anonymous reviewers for helpful feedback on the write-up. This work is supported by the National Key Research and Development Program of China (2022YFB2701600, 2018YFA0704701), National Natural Science Foundation of China (61972156, 62372180, 61972094, 62032005), NSFC-ISF Joint Scientific Research Program (61961146004), "Digital Silk Road" Shanghai International Joint Lab of Trustworthy Intelligent Software (22510750100) and Innovation Program of Shanghai Municipal Education Commission (2021-01-07-00-08-E00101).

References

1. Agrawal, S., Yamada, S.: Optimal broadcast encryption from pairings and LWE. In: Canteaut, A., Ishai, Y. (eds.) EUROCRYPT 2020, Paqrt I. LNCS, vol. 12105, pp. 13–43. Springer, Cham (2020). https://doi.org/10.1007/978-3-030-45721-1_2
2. Ambrona, M., Gay, R.: Multi-authority abe, revisited. IACR Cryptol. ePrint Arch. p. 1381 (2021)
3. Attrapadung, N.: Dual system encryption framework in prime-order groups via computational pair encodings. In: Cheon, J.H., Takagi, T. (eds.) ASIACRYPT 2016, Part II. LNCS, vol. 10032, pp. 591–623. Springer, Heidelberg (2016). https://doi.org/10.1007/978-3-662-53890-6_20
4. Benaloh, J., Leichter, J.: Generalized secret sharing and monotone functions. In: Goldwasser, S. (ed.) CRYPTO 1988. LNCS, vol. 403, pp. 27–35. Springer, New York (1990). https://doi.org/10.1007/0-387-34799-2_3

5. Boneh, D., Boyen, X., Shacham, H.: Short group signatures. In: Franklin, M. (ed.) CRYPTO 2004. LNCS, vol. 3152, pp. 41–55. Springer, Heidelberg (2004). https://doi.org/10.1007/978-3-540-28628-8_3
6. Boneh, D., et al.: Fully key-homomorphic encryption, arithmetic circuit ABE and compact garbled circuits. In: Nguyen, P.Q., Oswald, E. (eds.) EUROCRYPT 2014. LNCS, vol. 8441, pp. 533–556. Springer, Heidelberg (2014). https://doi.org/10.1007/978-3-642-55220-5_30
7. Chase, M.: Multi-authority Attribute Based Encryption. In: Vadhan, S.P. (ed.) TCC 2007. LNCS, vol. 4392, pp. 515–534. Springer, Heidelberg (2007). https://doi.org/10.1007/978-3-540-70936-7_28
8. Chase, M., Chow, S.S.M.: Improving privacy and security in multi-authority attribute-based encryption. In: Al-Shaer, E., Jha, S., Keromytis, A.D. (eds.) CCS 2009, pp. 121–130. ACM (2009)
9. Chen, J., Gay, R., Wee, H.: Improved dual system ABE in prime-order groups via predicate encodings. In: Oswald, E., Fischlin, M. (eds.) EUROCRYPT 2015, Part II. LNCS, vol. 9057, pp. 595–624. Springer, Heidelberg (2015). https://doi.org/10.1007/978-3-662-46803-6_20
10. Chen, J., Gong, J., Kowalczyk, L., Wee, H.: Unbounded ABE via bilinear entropy expansion, revisited. In: Nielsen, J.B., Rijmen, V. (eds.) EUROCRYPT 2018, Part I. LNCS, vol. 10820, pp. 503–534. Springer, Cham (2018). https://doi.org/10.1007/978-3-319-78381-9_19
11. Chen, J., Gong, J., Wee, H.: Improved inner-product encryption with adaptive security and full attribute-hiding. In: Peyrin, T., Galbraith, S. (eds.) ASIACRYPT 2018, Part II. LNCS, vol. 11273, pp. 673–702. Springer, Cham (2018). https://doi.org/10.1007/978-3-030-03329-3_23
12. Datta, P., Komargodski, I., Waters, B.: Decentralized multi-authority ABE for DNFs from LWE. In: Canteaut, A., Standaert, F.-X. (eds.) EUROCRYPT 2021, Part I. LNCS, vol. 12696, pp. 177–209. Springer, Cham (2021). https://doi.org/10.1007/978-3-030-77870-5_7
13. Datta, P., Komargodski, I., Waters, B.: Decentralized multi-authority ABE for nc^1 from computational-bdh. IACR Cryptol. ePrint Arch. p. 1325 (2021)
14. Datta, P., Komargodski, I., Waters, B.: Fully adaptive decentralized multi-authority ABE. IACR Cryptol. ePrint Arch. p. 1311 (2022). https://eprint.iacr.org/2022/1311
15. Datta, P., Komargodski, I., Waters, B.: Fully adaptive decentralized multi-authority ABE. In: Hazay, C., Stam, M. (eds.) EUROCRYPT 2023, Part III. LNCS, vol. 14006, pp. 447–478. Springer, Cham (2023). https://doi.org/10.1007/978-3-031-30620-4_15
16. Escala, A., Herold, G., Kiltz, E., Ràfols, C., Villar, J.: An algebraic framework for Diffie-Hellman assumptions. In: Canetti, R., Garay, J.A. (eds.) CRYPTO 2013, Part II. LNCS, vol. 8043, pp. 129–147. Springer, Heidelberg (2013). https://doi.org/10.1007/978-3-642-40084-1_8
17. Gay, R., Hofheinz, D., Kiltz, E., Wee, H.: Tightly CCA-secure encryption without pairings. In: Fischlin, M., Coron, J.-S. (eds.) EUROCRYPT 2016, Part I. LNCS, vol. 9665, pp. 1–27. Springer, Heidelberg (2016). https://doi.org/10.1007/978-3-662-49890-3_1
18. Gong, J., Dong, X., Chen, J., Cao, Z.: Efficient IBE with tight reduction to standard assumption in the multi-challenge setting. In: Cheon, J.H., Takagi, T. (eds.) ASIACRYPT 2016. LNCS, vol. 10032, pp. 624–654. Springer, Heidelberg (2016). https://doi.org/10.1007/978-3-662-53890-6_21

19. Gong, J., Waters, B., Wee, H.: ABE for DFA from k-Lin. In: Boldyreva, A., Micciancio, D. (eds.) CRYPTO 2019. LNCS, vol. 11693, pp. 732–764. Springer, Cham (2019). https://doi.org/10.1007/978-3-030-26951-7_25
20. Gong, J., Wee, H.: Adaptively secure ABE for DFA from k-Lin and more. In: Canteaut, A., Ishai, Y. (eds.) EUROCRYPT 2020. LNCS, vol. 12107, pp. 278–308. Springer, Cham (2020). https://doi.org/10.1007/978-3-030-45727-3_10
21. Gorbunov, S., Vaikuntanathan, V., Wee, H.: Attribute-based encryption for circuits. In: Boneh, D., Roughgarden, T., Feigenbaum, J. (eds.) STOC'13, 2013, pp. 545–554. ACM (2013)
22. Goyal, V., Pandey, O., Sahai, A., Waters, B.: Attribute-based encryption for fine-grained access control of encrypted data. In: Juels, A., Wright, R.N., di Vimercati, S.D.C. (eds.) CCS 2006, pp. 89–98. ACM (2006)
23. Jain, A., Lin, H., Luo, J.: On the optimal succinctness and efficiency of functional encryption and attribute-based encryption. In: Hazay, C., Stam, M. (eds.) EUROCRYPT 2023, Part III. LNCS, vol. 14006, pp. 479–510. Springer, Cham (2023). https://doi.org/10.1007/978-3-031-30620-4_16
24. Kowalczyk, L., Wee, H.: Compact adaptively secure ABE for NC^1 from k-lin. In: Ishai, Y., Rijmen, V. (eds.) EUROCRYPT 2019, Part I. LNCS, vol. 11476, pp. 3–33. Springer, Cham (2019). https://doi.org/10.1007/978-3-030-17653-2_1
25. Lewko, A.: Tools for simulating features of composite order bilinear groups in the prime order setting. In: Pointcheval, D., Johansson, T. (eds.) EUROCRYPT 2012. LNCS, vol. 7237, pp. 318–335. Springer, Heidelberg (2012). https://doi.org/10.1007/978-3-642-29011-4_20
26. Lewko, A., Okamoto, T., Sahai, A., Takashima, K., Waters, B.: Fully secure functional encryption: attribute-based encryption and (hierarchical) inner product encryption. In: Gilbert, H. (ed.) EUROCRYPT 2010. LNCS, vol. 6110, pp. 62–91. Springer, Heidelberg (2010). https://doi.org/10.1007/978-3-642-13190-5_4
27. Lewko, A., Waters, B.: New techniques for dual system encryption and fully secure hibe with short ciphertexts. In: Micciancio, D. (ed.) TCC 2010. LNCS, vol. 5978, pp. 455–479. Springer, Heidelberg (2010). https://doi.org/10.1007/978-3-642-11799-2_27
28. Lewko, A., Waters, B.: Decentralizing attribute-based encryption. In: Paterson, K.G. (ed.) EUROCRYPT 2011. LNCS, vol. 6632, pp. 568–588. Springer, Heidelberg (2011). https://doi.org/10.1007/978-3-642-20465-4_31
29. Lin, H., Cao, Z., Liang, X., Shao, J.: Secure threshold multi authority attribute based encryption without a central authority. In: Chowdhury, D.R., Rijmen, V., Das, A. (eds.) INDOCRYPT 2008. LNCS, vol. 5365, pp. 426–436. Springer, Heidelberg (2008). https://doi.org/10.1007/978-3-540-89754-5_33
30. Lin, H., Luo, J.: Compact adaptively secure ABE from k-lin: Beyond NC^1 and towards NL. In: Canteaut, A., Ishai, Y. (eds.) EUROCRYPT 2020, Part III. LNCS, vol. 12107, pp. 247–277. Springer, Cham (2020). https://doi.org/10.1007/978-3-030-45727-3_9
31. Liu, T., Vaikuntanathan, V., Wee, H.: Conditional disclosure of secrets via non-linear reconstruction. In: Katz, J., Shacham, H. (eds.) CRYPTO 2017. LNCS, vol. 10401, pp. 758–790. Springer, Cham (2017). https://doi.org/10.1007/978-3-319-63688-7_25
32. Müller, S., Katzenbeisser, S., Eckert, C.: Distributed attribute-based encryption. In: Lee, P.J., Cheon, J.H. (eds.) ICISC 2008. LNCS, vol. 5461, pp. 20–36. Springer, Heidelberg (2009). https://doi.org/10.1007/978-3-642-00730-9_2

33. Okamoto, T., Takashima, K.: Fully secure functional encryption with general relations from the decisional linear assumption. In: Rabin, T. (ed.) CRYPTO 2010. LNCS, vol. 6223, pp. 191–208. Springer, Heidelberg (2010). https://doi.org/10.1007/978-3-642-14623-7_11
34. Okamoto, T., Takashima, K.: Decentralized attribute-based encryption and signatures. IEICE **103–A**(1), 41–73 (2020)
35. Rouselakis, Y., Waters, B.: Efficient statically-secure large-universe multi-authority attribute-based encryption. In: Böhme, R., Okamoto, T. (eds.) FC 2015. LNCS, vol. 8975, pp. 315–332. Springer, Heidelberg (2015). https://doi.org/10.1007/978-3-662-47854-7_19
36. Sahai, A., Waters, B.: Fuzzy identity-based encryption. In: Cramer, R. (ed.) EUROCRYPT 2005. LNCS, vol. 3494, pp. 457–473. Springer, Heidelberg (2005). https://doi.org/10.1007/11426639_27
37. Tsabary, R.: Candidate witness encryption from lattice techniques. In: Dodis, Y., Shrimpton, T. (eds.) CRYPTO 2022, Part I. LNCS, vol. 13507, pp. 535–559. Springer, Cham (2022). https://doi.org/10.1007/978-3-031-15802-5_19
38. Waters, B.: Dual system encryption: realizing fully secure IBE and HIBE under simple assumptions. In: Halevi, S. (ed.) CRYPTO 2009. LNCS, vol. 5677, pp. 619–636. Springer, Heidelberg (2009). https://doi.org/10.1007/978-3-642-03356-8_36
39. Waters, B., Wee, H., Wu, D.J.: Multi-authority ABE from lattices without random oracles. In: Kiltz, E., Vaikuntanathan, V. (eds.) TCC 2022, Part I. LNCS, vol. 13747, pp. 651–679. Springer, Cham (2022). https://doi.org/10.1007/978-3-031-22318-1_23
40. Wee, H.: Dual system encryption via predicate encodings. In: Lindell, Y. (ed.) TCC 2014. LNCS, vol. 8349, pp. 616–637. Springer, Heidelberg (2014). https://doi.org/10.1007/978-3-642-54242-8_26
41. Wee, H.: Broadcast encryption with size $N^{1/3}$ and more from k-lin. In: Malkin, T., Peikert, C. (eds.) CRYPTO 2021, Part IV. LNCS, vol. 12828, pp. 155–178. Springer, Cham (2021). https://doi.org/10.1007/978-3-030-84259-8_6
42. Wee, H.: Optimal broadcast encryption and CP-ABE from evasive lattice assumptions. In: Dunkelman, O., Dziembowski, S. (eds.) EUROCRYPT 2022, Part II. LNCS, vol. 13276, pp. 217–241. Springer, Cham (2022). https://doi.org/10.1007/978-3-031-07085-3_8

Verifiable Decentralized Multi-client Functional Encryption for Inner Product

Dinh Duy Nguyen[1(✉)], Duong Hieu Phan[1], and David Pointcheval[2]

[1] LTCI, Telecom Paris, Institut Polytechnique de Paris, Palaiseau, France
dinh.nguyen@telecom-paris.fr, hieu.phan@telecom-paris.fr

[2] DIENS, École normale supérieure, CNRS, Inria, PSL University, Paris, France
david.pointcheval@ens.fr

Abstract. Joint computation on encrypted data is becoming increasingly crucial with the rise of cloud computing. In recent years, the development of multi-client functional encryption (MCFE) has made it possible to perform joint computation on private inputs, without any interaction. Well-settled solutions for linear functions have become efficient and secure, but there is still a shortcoming: if one user inputs incorrect data, the output of the function might become meaningless for all other users (while still useful for the malicious user). To address this issue, the concept of verifiable functional encryption was introduced by Badrinarayanan *et al.* at Asiacrypt '16 (BGJS). However, their solution was impractical because of strong statistical requirements. More recently, Bell *et al.* introduced a related concept for secure aggregation, with their ACORN solution, but it requires multiple rounds of interactions between users. In this paper,

- we first propose a computational definition of verifiability for MCFE. Our notion covers the computational version of BGJS and extends it to handle any valid inputs defined by predicates. The BGJS notion corresponds to the particular case of a fixed predicate in our setting;
- we then introduce a new technique called *Combine-then-Descend*, which relies on the class group. It allows us to construct One-time Decentralized Sum (ODSUM) on verifiable private inputs. ODSUM is the building block for our final protocol of a verifiable decentralized MCFE for inner-product, where the inputs are within a range. Our approach notably enables the efficient identification of malicious users, thereby addressing an unsolved problem in ACORN.

Keywords: Verifiability · Decentralized · Functional Encryption · Inner Product

1 Introduction

Multi-client Functional Encryption. Functional Encryption (FE) [8] is a paradigm designed to overcome the *all-or-nothing* limitation of traditional encryption, allowing the sender to control access to their encrypted data in a

J. Guo and R. Steinfeld (Eds.): ASIACRYPT 2023, LNCS 14442, pp. 33–65, 2023.
https://doi.org/10.1007/978-981-99-8733-7_2

more fine-grained manner through *functional decryption keys*. This paradigm enables the preservation of user's privacy in cloud computing services, where clouds can learn nothing beyond the delegated function evaluated on user's private data. FE with a single user appears to be quite restrictive in practice, as the number of useful functions may be small. In this case, the Public Key Encryption (PKE) can be transformed into FE by encrypting the evaluations of various functions using specific keys. However, this approach is not feasible for multi-user settings, even if a fixed function only is considered. To address this, Multi-Input Functional Encryption (MIFE) and Multi-Client Functional Encryption (MCFE) were thus introduced [20,21], allowing multiple clients to encrypt their individual data independently and contribute encrypted inputs to a joint function, with the help of possibly a trusted authority who runs the setup procedure and generates functional decryption keys. Among the classes of functions for MIFE/MCFE, the inner product is an expressive class that allows computing weighted averages and sums over encrypted data, making it especially useful for statistical analysis.

Chotard *et al.* [14] first introduced the notion of decentralized MCFE (DMCFE) in which there is no requirement for a trusted authority, and each client can have a complete control over their encrypted individual data and over the generation of functional decryption keys. The authors also provided a DMCFE scheme for inner product that is secure in random oracle model and in which all clients only need to run an MPC protocol once during the setup. As follow-up works, new constructions of DMCFE for inner product that improve the security model such as by allowing incomplete ciphertext queries [2], by removing the random oracle [1,22], or by allowing dynamic join of new users [15] have been introduced. In particular, the MPC protocol in [14] was removed by a decentralized sum protocol in [15], making the DMCFE for inner product completely non-interactive and eliminating the need for pairings in the groups. In this paper, we focus on the decentralized MCFE.

Importance of Verifiability in MCFE. Historically, the security of an encryption scheme has focused on the confidentiality of the message being encrypted. The (multi-client) functional encryption is not an exception, with its indistinguishability security ensuring that given two encrypted values and decryption keys for functions that evaluate the same at these two values, then it is computationally hard to distinguish between the ciphertexts of these two values. However, Badrinarayanan et al. [5] showed that the security of computation for an honest-but-curious receiver is necessary: a malicious sender could provide a false ciphertext and false functional decryption keys, so that the value encrypted within the ciphertext can vary when computed with these different functions through an honest decryption process. An analogous notion for the receiver in the multi-input setting is also provided.

In this work, we address a practical concern when using (decentralized) multi-client FE for inner product in real-world applications. The DMCFE for inner-product protocol can be run by thousands of senders, but they may not be all honest. If we assume that a small percentage of them are malicious, trying to bias the function evaluations by sending random data, or even fake data, and contributing dishonest functional key shares. To minimize the impact of these malicious clients, we propose a verification scheme for ciphertexts and one for functional decryption key shares, so that once all are valid, the decryption result is guaranteed to not be significantly biased. Furthermore, our concrete DMCFE scheme allows practically-efficient identification of malicious senders. Beyond the inner products, we define a verifiable DMCFE, which consequently provides input validation for the receiver as in [6]. Compared to their scheme, our verifiable MCFE scheme works on a larger class of functions than the sum, and does not require interaction between senders and receiver during the verification process.

Verifiable DMCFE for Inner Product. Verifiability for DMCFE in the general case is very difficult, because a small modification of the input can cause a significant difference in the output (e.g. inverse functions). We can formalize the validity condition as a predicate, depending on each application. However, for linear functions with small coefficients and small inputs (which are the most useful in practice, like average functions for example), a change in the input does not result in a major change in the output, unless there is a significant modification to an input. When the number of users is large enough, the inputs are bounded (which are often considered in Inner-Product Functional Encryption) then if an input is changed but still remains within a reasonable range, the output function will be quite close to the exact value. Additionally, most of the IP-DMCFE schemes need a final discrete logarithm computation to get the result, which requires it to be small enough, and so the inputs should also be in a reasonable range. For these reasons, we target DMCFE for inner product, and verifiability checks that the inputs stay within a specific range. Such a range verification will be our predicate in the general framework (for both the encrypted inputs and the functions in the keys).

A Real-Life Example. We consider *Aggregating Household Energy Consumption* as a practical motivation. For optimization purpose, an energy supplier may want to aggregate the units of energy (kilowatt-hours or kWh) consumed by its customers during some specific periods of the day. However, the energy consumption of each customer is a private information, as it may include, for example, the time they get up in the morning, leave their house, return home and which electronic devices they use. Still, they may be willing to help the supplier with their data to improve its service. To protect user's privacy, the customers are recommended to use a decentralized multi-client functional encryption to send their data in an encrypted form. However, nothing guarantees that the electricity supplier receives a correct aggregate of the metered energy consumption or at least an approximation of this value. In fact, some customers may provide malformed ciphertexts and malformed functional key shares to bias the joint-input function. Therefore, if we can enforce each client to correctly encrypt a value in some valid range and to generate a correct functional key share, the noise from the input made by a small number of malicious clients can be mitigated when the aggregate value is computed among a large number of clients.

The fact that this scenario has not been captured in prior work of (decentralized) MCFE is historically reasonable: in single-input FE, there is only one encryptor. When this encryptor wants to bias the result computed by the functional decryptor, he can encrypt an invalid input, such as values out of the use domain or singular points of the function. Since this FE is single-input, a receiver can trivially identify the invalidity of the input by looking at the result of the function. Therefore, the standard security notion of single-input FE only considers the confidentiality of the individual input, which is later inherited by DMCFE. On the other hand, a receiver in DMCFE, can only learn the joint function evaluated on the joint inputs, then it seems not trivial to efficiently identify invalid individual inputs of the malicious clients out of the valid ones. We stress that using functional encryption schemes for modular inner product over $\mathbb{Z}_p$ where p can be any prime [4] to reduce the inner-product value space would not solve this problem. An adversary can always inject an arbitrary value to make the computation over $\mathbb{Z}_p$ become uniformly random over the space. Therefore, guaranteeing that each encrypted input is within a specified range will cause overhead costs but plays an important step in tackling this issue.

Our Contributions for verifiable DMCFE can be listed as:

- **Concept**: We introduce the definition of verifiable DMCFE with the ability to identify malicious senders. The verifiability guarantees that the decryption process, given as input a vector of ciphertexts and functional key shares that passed public verification schemes, always outputs the delegated functions evaluated on a vector of inputs satisfying specific predicates. If any verification fails, verifiability guarantees that malicious senders will be identified.
- **Technique**: We develop a technique called *Combine-then-Descend*. This technique enables senders to combine their verifiable private inputs in exponents in a decentralized manner. Subsequently, the final result is descended to obtain the sum in scalars, which can be used within a pairing-based protocol. Private inputs are put in exponent to facilitate efficient verification using Σ-protocols. We exploit the particular setting of class group in which the final result falls in a subgroup where the discrete logarithm problem is easy. Then, we construct the One-time Decentralized Sum (ODSUM) scheme in class groups, which serves as the building block for subsequent constructions.
- **Construction**: We present a concrete construction of range-verifiable DMCFE for inner product. We show a technique of extending from one-time security to multiple-time security for the ODSUM scheme that preserves the efficiency of the proof of correct encoding. The resulting DMCFE scheme then has verifiability with overhead costs depending only on the range proof for the ciphertext. Notably, our approach efficiently addresses the problem of identifying an unbounded number of malicious senders, which remained unsolved in secure aggregation protocols like ACORN.

1.1 Technical Overview

Combine-then-Descend Technique. We construct a new decentralized sum scheme (DSUM) in a DDH group that has an easy DL subgroup (class group, [12]). Our DSUM scheme will not compute the pair-wise shared masks for private input by using a pseudo-random function (PRF) as in [15]. The reason is that using a general non-interactive zero-knowledge argument (NIZK) to prove the correct computation of a PRF on input an exchanged key can be very expensive. Instead, each private input will be encoded as a power of the generator f of the easy DL subgroup and masked directly by pair-wise exchanged keys in the bigger group as follows

$$C_i = f^{x_i} \cdot \left(\prod_{i<j} T_j \cdot \prod_{i>j} T_j^{-1} \right)^{t_i}.$$

Here, C_i is the ciphertext of a sender $\mathcal{S}_i$ that encrypts x_i under a secret key t_i and each $(T_j)^{t_i}$ is a Diffie-Hellman exchanged key with a public key T_j of another sender $\mathcal{S}_j$. Given public parameters $(f, (T_j)_{j \neq i})$, then proving that C_i is encrypted correctly with the witness (x_i, t_i) can be done efficiently by using a Σ-protocol in an unknown-order group [11,19]. After verifying that all ciphertexts are valid, a receiver can combine them into $f^{\sum_i x_i} = \prod_i C_i$, then efficiently descend the sum $\sum_i x_i$ from the power of f. Unlike in the standard DDH group, there is no restriction on the size of the sum to be descended when this DSUM scheme is instantiated in a class group. Therefore, with only a constant overhead for proving time and proof size, this DSUM scheme allows senders to jointly compute the sum of private random shares of other cryptographic protocols and to efficiently identify the senders who gave malformed ciphertexts. However, to decentralize an MCFE scheme for inner product as in [14], this DSUM scheme is not yet enough since for each setup of pair-wise key exchanges, the scheme only supports one-time encryption (ODSUM). We then show an extension from one-time secure DSUM to multiple-time secure DSUM by leveraging the encryption with labels of inner-product MCFE scheme in [14] itself so that the correct encryption of the resulting DSUM scheme can still be efficicntly proved and verified by a Σ-protocol.

Range-Verifiable DMCFE *for Inner Product.* To mitigate the effect of malicious inputs on the inner-product evaluation, each sender is restricted to encrypt values within a data range, which is relatively small compared to the possible range of the plaintexts. We design a decentralized MCFE scheme where anybody can verify the correctness of each encryption and each functional key share. Our work will not focus on the proof schemes, but on the design of encryption scheme such that the relations for proofs of correct generation are simplified.

We use the following building blocks: the MCFE scheme for inner product from [14], a Σ-protocol, a range proof on Pedersen commitments, and the ODSUM scheme that we presented above.

To recall, a ciphertext in the MCFE scheme [14] is computed in the form of a Pedersen commitment with message x_i and an opening $\boldsymbol{s}_{\mathsf{MCFE},i}$, namely $[c_i] = [\boldsymbol{u}_\ell^\top] \cdot \boldsymbol{s}_{\mathsf{MCFE},i} + [x_i]$ where $[\boldsymbol{u}_\ell] \in \mathbb{G}^2$ is the output of a random oracle taking a label ℓ as input, and $s_{\mathsf{MCFE},i}$ is a private encryption key that is chosen uniformly from $\mathbb{Z}_p^2$, and $x_i \in \mathbb{Z}_p$ is the value to encrypt. For an inner-product function $\boldsymbol{y}$, the functional decryption key is computed as $\mathsf{dk}_{\boldsymbol{y}} = (\mathsf{dk} := \sum_i s_{\mathsf{MCFE},i} \cdot y_i, \boldsymbol{y})$. This scheme can be transformed into a decentralized MCFE by letting each sender use DSUM to encrypt his share of functional key $s_{\mathsf{MCFE},i} \cdot y_i$, so that $\mathsf{dk}_{\boldsymbol{y}}$ will be revealed as the sum of all senders' shares.

For the ciphertext verification (and also for the key share verification), a commitment of private key $s_{\mathsf{MCFE},i}$ needs to be produced as $([\boldsymbol{u}_{\ell_{\mathsf{MCFE},b}}^{\top}] \cdot s_{\mathsf{MCFE},i})_{b \in [2]}$ where $[\boldsymbol{u}_{\ell_{\mathsf{MCFE},b}}] \in \mathbb{G}^2$ is the output of a random oracle taking an initialization label $\ell_{\mathsf{MCFE},b}$ as input, and published since the key generation process. The relation for a proof of correct encryption now states that a ciphertext is correct if it encrypts a value within a data range under the committed private key. A proof scheme for this relation is a combination of a Pedersen-commitment range proof and a Σ-protocol in the standard DDH group.

For the key share verification, on one hand we want a DSUM scheme that supports multi-label encryption as in [15], that is, only ciphertexts generated under the same label can be combined to decrypt the sum of encrypted inputs. If an adversary mixes and matches ciphertexts of different labels, he receives nothing. On the other hand, the relation for a proof of correct encryption has to be simple so that it can be proved by a Σ-protocol. An MCFE for inner product (so for the sum) has the former property, while an ODSUM has the latter. Therefore, we leverage both these schemes to achieve a label-supporting LDSUM with efficient proofs of correctness: in the key generation process, each sender publishes an ODSUM encryption of his private MCFE key $s_{\mathsf{LDSUM},i} \in \mathbb{Z}_p$ as his public key, then each input x_i is encrypted by the MCFE scheme under a label ℓ and a private key $s_{\mathsf{LDSUM},i}$. To decrypt the sum $\sum_i x_i$, a receiver first collects all senders' public keys to reveal $\mathsf{dk}_{\mathbf{1}} = \sum_i s_{\mathsf{LDSUM},i} \in \mathbb{Z}_p$, which is exactly the MCFE functional decryption key for vector $\mathbf{1} = (1, ..., 1)$ (the sum). Using $\mathsf{dk}_{\mathbf{1}}$, he can continue to decrypt the sum of x_i that is encrypted by the MCFE scheme. An important point is that the order of the easy-DL subgroup in the class group can be instantiated to be equal to the prime order p of the standard DDH group. Therefore, both the encryption-key space of LDSUM and the plaintext space of ODSUM are $\mathbb{Z}_p$.

A final point to note is that when using the LDSUM scheme to encrypt MCFE key shares $s_{\mathsf{MCFE},i} \cdot y_i$, the functional key dk in $\mathsf{dk}_{\boldsymbol{y}} = (\mathsf{dk} := \sum_i s_{\mathsf{MCFE},i} \cdot y_i, \boldsymbol{y})$ may not be revealed as a scalar. The reason is that LDSUM is technically a particular instantiation of the MCFE scheme for inner product in [14], which can only decrypt when the inner product is small enough by computing a discrete logarithm. Therefore, we will use a pairing group to solve this issue.

1.2 Related Work and Comparisons

Formalization. Our definition of verifiable decentralized MCFE is a generalized computational version of the verifiability for MIFE in [5]. The first additional point is that the verifiability in our definition implies the validation of encrypted inputs with respect to a class of predicates. Moreover, the decentralized multi-client setting is a more general context: there is no central functional key authority, and each sender generates ciphertexts and functional key shares independently. While this setting is not considered in [5], our verifiability guarantees that any malicious sender, who gave malformed ciphertexts and functional key shares to make a global public verification with those of other honest senders fail, will be identified. On the other hand, if we restrict the functionality to be the sum of encrypted inputs, then we can obtain an analogous input validation for secure aggregation (ACORN protocols) as in [6]. Our protocol and ACORN protocols [6] have been independently developed using completely different approaches, which we consider below.

Solutions for Efficient Malicious Sender Identification. For all protocols that allow multiple senders to compute a joint function on their private inputs, Malicious Sender Identification is a desirable feature, but it is not obvious to obtain within a practical efficiency. An example is that both our DMCFE scheme and the ACORN protocols in [6] need a decentralized sum to allow senders to generate ciphertexts that encrypt the decryption key shares of the bigger protocol in a decentralized manner. We both had the same problem in achieving the input validation: it could be very costly to use a general NIZK to prove and verify the correct encryption of the initial underlying decentralized sum.

To overcome this issue, the authors in [6] proposed two protocols: ACORN-detect and ACORN-robust. The first allows validating the aggregated (decryption) key, which is combined from all key shares of senders. Each key share is committed by a Pedersen commitment, and the combined key is compared with the aggregation of committed key shares thanks to the homomorphic property of the commitment. Besides requiring an interactive Σ-protocol between the server and each sender, a major drawback is that now a sender can send a malicious key share to make the combined key broken without being identified. The second protocol ACORN-robust can identify malicious senders and remove their inputs based on the help of neighbour honest senders, but allows at most $\frac{1}{3}$ number of senders to be malicious and at least 6 rounds of interaction between each sender and the server (more rounds of interaction may happen with a decreasing probability). In our verifiable inner-product DMCFE scheme, we gain the efficiency by constructing and then adapting a new decentralized sum that is efficient to verify. The result covers all and even better advantages of the two previous ACORN protocols: our DMCFE scheme has malicious sender identification, requires no round of interaction between each sender and a receiver, allows an unbounded number of malicious senders, and eventually allows a larger class of functionality (inner product over sum). Notably, in our verifiable DMCFE scheme, the constant time (group exponentiations) and the constant size (group elements) for proving each key share can even be more efficient than those for each ciphertext, which are dominated by a range proof as in ACORN.

2 Preliminaries

2.1 Groups and Assumptions

Prime Order Group. Let GGen be a prime-order group generator, a probabilistic polynomial time (PPT) algorithm that on input the security parameter 1^λ returns a description $\mathcal{G} = (\mathbb{G}, p, P)$ of an additive cyclic group $\mathbb{G}$ of order p for a 2λ-bit prime p, whose generator is P. For $a \in \mathbb{Z}_p$, define $[a] = aP \in \mathbb{G}$ as the *implicit representation* of a in $\mathbb{G}$.

From a random element $[a] \in \mathbb{G}$, it is computationally hard to compute the value a (the discrete logarithm problem). Given $[a], [b] \in \mathbb{G}$ and a scalar $x \in \mathbb{Z}_p$, one can efficiently compute $[ax] \in \mathbb{G}$ and $[a+b] = [a] + [b] \in G$.

Definition 1 (Decisional Diffie-Hellman Assumption). *The Decisional Diffie-Hellman Assumption states that, in a prime-order group $\mathcal{G} \xleftarrow{\$} \mathsf{GGen}(1^\lambda)$, no PPT adversary can distinguish between the two following distributions with non-negligible advantage:*

$$\{([a],[r],[ar]) | a, r \xleftarrow{\$} \mathbb{Z}_p\} \text{ and } \{([a],[r],[s]) | a, r, s \xleftarrow{\$} \mathbb{Z}_p\}.$$

Equivalently, this assumption states it is hard to distinguish, knowing $[a]$, a random element from the span of $[\boldsymbol{a}]$ for $\boldsymbol{a} = (1, a)$, from a random element in $\mathbb{G}^2$: $[\boldsymbol{a}] \cdot r = [\boldsymbol{a}r] = ([r],[ar]) \approx ([r],[s])$.

Pairing Group. Let PGGen be a pairing group generator, a PPT algorithm that on input the security parameter 1^λ returns a description $\mathcal{PG} = (\mathbb{G}_1, \mathbb{G}_2, \mathbb{G}_T, p, P_1, P_2, e)$ of asymmetric pairing groups where $\mathbb{G}_1$, $\mathbb{G}_2$, $\mathbb{G}_T$ are additive cyclic groups of order p for a 2λ-bit prime p, P_1 and P_2 are generators of $\mathbb{G}_1$ and $\mathbb{G}_2$, respectively, and $e : \mathbb{G}_1 \times \mathbb{G}_2 \to \mathbb{G}_T$ is an efficiently computable (non-degenerate) bilinear group elements. For $s \in \{1, 2, T\}$ and $a \in \mathbb{Z}_p$, define $[a]_s = aP_s \in \mathbb{G}_s$ as the implicit representation of a in $\mathbb{G}_s$. Given $[a]_1$, $[b]_2$, one can efficiently compute $[ab]_T$ using the pairing e.

Definition 2 (Symmetric eXternal Diffie-Hellman Assumption). *The Symmetric eXternal Diffie-Hellman (SXDH) Assumption states that, in a pairing group $\mathcal{PG} \xleftarrow{\$} \mathsf{PGen}(1^\lambda)$, the DDH assumption holds in both $\mathbb{G}_1$ and $\mathbb{G}_2$.*

Class Group. We recall the notion of a DDH group with an easy DL subgroup (first introduced in [12]), which can be instantiated from class groups of imaginary quadratic fields and also recall the corresponding computational assumptions.

Definition 3 (Generator for a DDH group with an easy DL subgroup [10,11]). *Let GenClassGroup be a pair of algorithms* $(\mathsf{Gen}, \mathsf{Solve})$. *The* Gen *algorithm is a group generator which takes as inputs a security parameter λ and* *a prime p and outputs a tuple* $(p, \tilde{s}, \hat{g}, f, \hat{g}_p, \hat{G}, F, \hat{G}^p)$. *The set* $(\hat{G}, \cdot)$ *is a cyclic group of odd order ps where s is an integer, p is a* μ*-bit prime, and* $\gcd(p, s) = 1$. *The algorithm* Gen *only outputs an upper bound* $\tilde{s}$ *of s. The set* $\hat{G}^p = \{x^p, x \in \hat{G}\}$ *is the subgroup of order s of* $\hat{G}$*, and F is the subgroup of order p of* $\hat{G}$*, so that* $\hat{G} = F \times \hat{G}^p$. *The algorithm* Gen *outputs* f, $\hat{g}_p$ *and* $\hat{g} = f.\hat{g}_p$ *which are respective generators of* $F, \hat{G}^p$ *and* $\hat{G}$. *Moreover, the DL problem is easy in F, which means that the* Solve *algorithm is a deterministic polynomial time algorithm that solves the discrete logarithm problem in F.*

An important feature of the GenClassGroup is that we can choose the same prime order as in the standard DDH (including pairing groups) for the easy DL subgroup. A concrete instantiation of such a group can be found in [10].

Let g_p be a random power of $\hat{g}_p$, G^p be a subgroup generated by g_p, and G be a subgroup generated by $g := g_p f$. The following assumption is called *Hard subgroup membership* assumption, which states that it is hard to distinguish random elements of G^p in G.

Definition 4 (HSM assumption [11]**).** *Let GenClassGroup* = (Gen, Solve) *be a generator for DDH groups with an easy DL subgroup. Let* $(\tilde{s}, f, \hat{g}_p, \hat{G}, F)$ *be an output of* Gen, g_p *be a random power of* $\hat{g}_p$, *and* $g := g_p f$. *We denote by* $\mathcal{D}$ *(resp.* $\mathcal{D}_p$*) a distribution over the integers s.t. the distribution* $\{g^x, x \hookleftarrow \mathcal{D}\}$ *(resp.* $\{\hat{g}_p^x, x \hookleftarrow \mathcal{D}_p\}$*) is at distance less than* $2^{-\lambda}$ *from the uniform distribution in* $\langle g \rangle$ *(resp. in* $\langle \hat{g}_p \rangle$*). Let* $\mathcal{A}$ *be an adversary for the HSM problem, its advantage is defined as:*

$$\mathsf{Adv}_{\mathcal{A}}^{\mathit{HSM}}(\lambda) := \left| \Pr\left[\begin{array}{l} (\tilde{s}, f, \hat{g}_p, F, \hat{G}^p) \leftarrow \mathsf{Gen}(1^\lambda, p), t \leftarrow \mathcal{D}_p, g_p = \hat{g}_p^t, \\ x \hookleftarrow \mathcal{D}, x' \hookleftarrow \mathcal{D}_p, b \xleftarrow{\$} \{0,1\}, \\ Z_0 \leftarrow g^x, Z_1 \leftarrow g_p^{x'}, \\ b' \leftarrow \mathcal{A}(p, \tilde{s}, f, \hat{g}_p, g_p, F, \hat{G}^p, Z_b, \mathsf{Solve}(\cdot)) \end{array} : b = b' \right] - \frac{1}{2} \right|$$

The HSM problem is said to be hard in G if for all probabilistic polynomial time attacker $\mathcal{A}$, $\mathsf{Adv}_{\mathcal{A}}^{\mathit{HSM}}(\lambda)$ *is negligible.*

From [10,13], one can set $S := 2^{\lambda-2} \cdot \tilde{s}$, and instantiate $\mathcal{D}_p$ as the uniform distribution on $\{0, ..., S\}$ and $\mathcal{D}$ as the uniform distribution on $\{0, ..., pS\}$. We also put the *Low order assumption* and the *Strong root assumption* in the full version [23], which is used to prove the soundness of our Σ-protocol over the class group.

2.2 Non-interactive Zero-Knowledge Proofs

Zero-Knowledge Proofs. Let $\mathcal{R}$ be a polynomial-time decidable relation. We call w a witness for a statement u if $\mathcal{R}(u; w) = 1$. A language L associated with $\mathcal{R}$ is defined as $L = \{u | \exists w : \mathcal{R}(u; w) = 1\}$. A zero-knowledge proof for

L consists of a pair of algorithms $(\mathcal{P}, \mathcal{V})$ where $\mathcal{P}$ convinces $\mathcal{V}$ that a common input $u \in L$ without revealing information about a witness w. If $u \notin L$, $\mathcal{P}$ has a negligible chance of convincing $\mathcal{V}$ to accept that $u \in L$. In a zero-knowledge proof of knowledge, $\mathcal{P}$ additionally proves that it owns a witness w as input such that $\mathcal{R}(u; w) = 1$. In this work, we focus on the non-interactive proofs where $\mathcal{P}$ sends only one message π to $\mathcal{V}$. On the input π, some public parameters and its own inputs, $\mathcal{V}$ decides to accept or not. A formal definition, from [3,7,18], is given below.

Definition 5 (Non-interactive Zero-knowledge Argument). *A NIZK argument for a language L defined by an NP relation $\mathcal{R}$ consists of a triple of PPT algorithms* (SetUp, Prove, Verify)*:*

- $\mathsf{SetUp}(\lambda)$*: Takes as input a security parameter λ, and outputs a common reference string (CRS) σ. The CRS is implicit input to other algorithms;*
- $\mathsf{Prove}(u, w)$*: Takes as input a statement u and a witness w, and outputs an argument π.*
- $\mathsf{Verify}(u, \pi)$*: Takes as input a statement u and an argument π, outputs either 1 accepting the argument or 0 rejecting it.*

Sometimes in this paper we will call π a proof. The algorithms satisfy the following properties.

1. *Completeness. For all u, w such that $\mathcal{R}(u; w) = 1$,*

$$\Pr\left[\begin{array}{l}\sigma \leftarrow \mathsf{SetUp}(\lambda),\\ \pi \leftarrow \mathsf{Prove}(u, w)\end{array} : \mathsf{Verify}(u, \pi) = 1\right] = 1.$$

2. *Computational Soundness. For all PPT adversaries $\mathcal{A}$, there is a negligible function $\mu(\lambda)$ such that*

$$\Pr\left[\begin{array}{l}\sigma \leftarrow \mathsf{SetUp}(\lambda),\\ (u, \pi) \leftarrow \mathcal{A}(\sigma)\end{array} : \mathsf{Verify}(u, \pi) = 1 \wedge u \notin L\right] \leq \mu(\lambda).$$

3. *Zero-Knowledge. There exists a PPT simulator $(\mathcal{S}_1, \mathcal{S}_2)$ such that for all PPT adversaries $(\mathcal{A}_1, \mathcal{A}_2)$, there is a negligible function $\mu(\lambda)$ such that*

$$\left|\begin{array}{l}\Pr\left[\begin{array}{l}\sigma \leftarrow \mathsf{SetUp}(\lambda),\\ (u, w, \mathsf{st}) \leftarrow \mathcal{A}_1(\sigma) :\\ \pi \leftarrow \mathsf{Prove}(u, w)\end{array} \begin{array}{r}\mathcal{A}_2(\sigma, \pi, \mathsf{st}) = 1\\ \wedge\, \mathcal{R}(u; w) = 1\end{array}\right]\\ -\Pr\left[\begin{array}{l}(\sigma, \tau) \leftarrow \mathcal{S}_1(\lambda),\\ (u, w, \mathsf{st}) \leftarrow \mathcal{A}_1(\sigma) :\\ \pi \leftarrow \mathcal{S}_2(\sigma, u, \tau)\end{array} \begin{array}{r}\mathcal{A}_2(\sigma, \pi, \mathsf{st}) = 1\\ \wedge\, \mathcal{R}(u; w) = 1\end{array}\right]\end{array}\right| \leq \mu(\lambda).$$

where τ is a trapdoor for σ and st *is an internal state.*

We defer the definitions and notations for non-interactive zero-knowledge arguments of knowledge and range proof in the full version [23].

2.3 Decentralized Sum

The decentralized sum (DSUM) [15] is a primitive that allows several parties of a group to commit to values, so that only the sum of their values can be revealed when all parties of the group have sent the shares. Another important feature of DSUM is that there is no trusted party: each party totally controls the generation of its secret key. The definition of this primitive was first introduced as a particular case of the general Dynamic Decentralized Functional Encryption in [15]. For the use in this work, we focus on a more relaxed security: given all senders' shares, a receiver cannot learn any information about individual inputs beyond their sum.

Definition 6 (Decentralized Sum). *A decentralized sum over an Abelian group $\mathcal{M}$ and a set of n senders consists of four algorithms:*

- $\mathsf{SetUp}(\lambda)$: *Takes as input the security parameter λ, and outputs the public parameters* pp. *The public parameters are implicit arguments to all the other algorithms;*
- $\mathsf{KeyGen}()$: *This is a protocol between the senders $(\mathcal{S}_i)_{i\in[n]}$ that eventually each generates its own secret key* sk_i. *The protocol also outputs a public key* pk, *which can be an implicit argument;*
- $\mathsf{Encrypt}(\mathsf{sk}_i, m_i)$: *Takes as input a secret key* sk_i *and a message m_i. Parses $m_i = (x_i, \ell)$ where $x_i \in \mathcal{M}$ and ℓ can be considered as an encryption label. Outputs the ciphertext* $\mathsf{ct}_{\ell,i}$;
- $\mathsf{Decrypt}(\epsilon, (\mathsf{ct}_{\ell,i})_{i\in[n]})$: *Takes as input an empty key ϵ (no private decryption key is required) and an n-vector ciphertext $(\mathsf{ct}_{\ell,i})_{i\in[n]}$ under the same label ℓ. Returns $\sum_{i\in[n]} x_i \in \mathcal{M}$ or $\perp$.*

Correctness. Given $\mathsf{pp} \leftarrow \mathsf{SetUp}(\lambda)$, $((\mathsf{sk}_i)_{i\in[n]}, \mathsf{pk}) \leftarrow \mathsf{KeyGen}()$, and $\mathsf{ct}_{i,\ell} \leftarrow \mathsf{Encrypt}(\mathsf{sk}_i, m_i)$ where $m_i = (x_i, \ell)$ for all $i \in [n]$, then the probability that $\mathsf{Decrypt}(\epsilon, (\mathsf{ct}_{\ell,i})_{i\in[n]}) = \sum_{i\in[n]} x_i$ is equal to 1.

Definition 7 (IND-Security Game for *DSUM*). *Let us consider a* DSUM *scheme over a message space $\mathcal{M}$ and a set of n senders. No adversary $\mathcal{A}$ should be able to win the following security game with a non-negligible probability against a challenger $\mathcal{C}$:*

- *Initialization: the challenger $\mathcal{C}$ runs the setup algorithm* $\mathsf{pp} \leftarrow \mathsf{SetUp}(\lambda)$ *and the key generation* $((\mathsf{sk}_i)_{i\in[n]}, \mathsf{pk}) \leftarrow \mathsf{KeyGen}()$ *and chooses a random bit $b \xleftarrow{\$} \{0,1\}$. It sends* $(\mathsf{pp}, \mathsf{pk})$ *to the adversary $\mathcal{A}$.*
- *Encryption queries* $\mathsf{QEncrypt}(i, x^0, x^1, \ell)$: *$\mathcal{A}$ has unlimited and adaptive access to a Left-or-Right encryption oracle, and receives the ciphertext* $\mathsf{ct}_{\ell,i}$ *generated by* $\mathsf{Encrypt}(\mathsf{sk}_i, (x_i, \ell))$. *Any further query for the same pair (ℓ, i) will later be ignored.*
- *Corruption queries* $\mathsf{QCorrupt}(i)$: *$\mathcal{A}$ can make an unlimited number of adaptive corruption queries on input index i, to get the secret key* sk_i *of any sender i of its choice.*

- *Finalize: $\mathcal{A}$ provides its guess b' on the bit b, and this procedure outputs the result β of the security game, according to the analysis given below.*

The output β of the game depends on some conditions, where $\mathcal{CS}$ is the set of corrupted senders (the set of indexes i input to QCorrupt *during the whole game), and $\mathcal{HS}$ is the set of honest (non-corrupted) senders. We set the output to $\beta \leftarrow b'$, unless one of the three cases below is true, in which case we set $\beta \xleftarrow{\$} \{0,1\}$:*

1. *some* $\mathsf{QEncrypt}(i, x_i^0, x_i^1, \ell)$*-query has been asked for an index $i \in \mathcal{CS}$ with $x_i^0 \neq x_i^1$;*
2. *for some label ℓ, an encryption-query* $\mathsf{QEncrypt}(i, x_i^0, x_i^1, \ell)$ *has been asked for some $i \in \mathcal{HS}$, but encryption-queries* $\mathsf{QEncrypt}(j, x_j^0, x_j^1, \ell)$ *have not all been asked for all $j \in \mathcal{HS}$;*
3. *for some label ℓ, there exists a pair of vectors $(\boldsymbol{x}^0 = (x_i^0)_i, \boldsymbol{x}^1 = (x_i^1)_i)$ such that $\sum_i x_i^0 \neq \sum_i x_i^1$, when*
   - *$x_i^0 = x_i^1$, for all $i \in \mathcal{CS}$;*
   - $\mathsf{QEncrypt}(i, x_i^0, x_i^1, \ell)$*-queries have been asked for all $i \in \mathcal{HS}$.*

We say this DSUM *is* IND*-secure if for any adversary $\mathcal{A}$,*

$$\mathsf{Adv}^{\mathsf{ind}}_{\mathsf{DSUM}}(\mathcal{A}) = |P[\beta = 1 | b = 1] - P[\beta = 1 | b = 0]|$$

is negligible.

Weaker Notions. For some weaker variants of indistinguishability, some queries can only be sent before the initialization phase:

- Selective Security (sel – IND): the encryption queries (QEncrypt) are sent before the initialization;
- Static Security (sta – IND): the corruption queries (QCorrupt) are sent before the initialization.

3 ODSUM from Combine-then-Descend Technique

3.1 Motivation

In a high level overview, we want to develop a concrete DSUM scheme such that no adversary playing on behalf of some senders can make the decryption with other honest senders' encryptions fail, for example by behaving maliciously in the KeyGen process or sending maliciously generated encryptions.

A straight approach is letting each sender use a general NIZK to prove the correctness of his encryptions and send the proofs with them. However, this approach may bring a heavy computational overhead for the encryption time. For example, given a simplified instantiation (without the All-or-Nothing Encapsulation layer) of DSUM scheme from the construction in [15], to encrypt a message $x_i \in \mathbb{Z}_p$ under a label $\ell \in \{0,1\}^*$, a sender $\mathcal{S}_i$ computes a ciphertext

$$c_{\ell,i} = x_i + \sum_{i<j} \mathsf{PRF}((T_j)^{t_i}, \ell) - \sum_{i>j} \mathsf{PRF}((T_j)^{t_i}, \ell) \in \mathbb{Z}_p.$$

where PRF is a pseudorandom function, and each $(T_j)^{t_i}$ is a pair-wise exchanged key in a DDH group $\mathbb{G}$ with a public key T_j and a secret key t_i. The complex part to be implemented for NIZK is the computation of the pseudorandom function on input a pair-wise exchanged key and an encryption label.

Our expected DSUM scheme will remove the use of PRF in the above manner. Instead, the input is encoded as a power of a (sub)-group generator f and is directly masked by group multiplications with the pair-wise exchanged keys. This helps greatly simplify the relation of correct encryption so that each ciphertext can be proved and verified by using a Σ-protocol only. As the computational cost and communication cost of such a Σ-protocol arc constant, then the overhead is asymptotically optimal. After *combining* all valid encryptions by multiplying them together, the pair-wise masks vanish, and we want the receiver to efficiently *descend* the sum from the exponent of f. We refer to this technique as the *combine-then-descend* technique. The DDH groups with an easy DL subgroup [12], which are instantiated in class groups of imaginary quadratic fields, is an extremely suitable environment to construct our DSUM scheme with those desired properties. Moreover, unlike the composite modulus for plaintext in Paillier encryption, we can choose a prime for the order of f before creating a class group, which makes the sum computed by the DSUM scheme automatically compatible with other applications in pairing groups.

3.2 Class Group-Based One-Time Decentralized Sum (ODSUM)

We construct a DSUM scheme from the combine-then-descend technique:

- SetUp(λ): It generates a DDH group with an easy DL subgroup $(\tilde{s}, f, \hat{g}_p, \hat{G}, F) \leftarrow \mathsf{GenClassGroup}(1^\lambda, p)$. It samples a $t \hookleftarrow \mathcal{D}_p$ and sets $g_p = \hat{g}_p^{t}$[1]. The public parameters are $\mathsf{pp} = (\tilde{s}, f, \hat{g}_p, g_p, \hat{G}, F, p)$, which is an implicit input to other algorithms.
- KeyGen(): Each sender generates a secret key $\mathsf{sk}_i = t_i \hookleftarrow \mathcal{D}_p$ and publishes $T_i = g_p^{t_i}$. The public key is defined as $\mathsf{pk} = (T_i)_{i \in [n]}$.
- Encrypt($x_i, \mathsf{pk}, \mathsf{sk}_i$): The encryption is supposed to be done one time for one message in the protocol, so there is no label. It generates a ciphertext

$$C_i = f^{x_i} \cdot \left(\prod_{i<j} T_j \cdot \prod_{i>j} T_j^{-1} \right)^{t_i}.$$

- Decrypt($\epsilon, (C_i)_{i \in [n]}$) : No decryption key is required (empty key ϵ). It computes $M = \prod_{i \in [n]} C_i$ and outputs $\alpha \leftarrow \mathsf{Solve}(M) \in \mathbb{Z}_p$ or $\perp$.

[1] This step can be done in a decentralized manner, with up to $n_{\mathsf{SetUp}} - 1$ malicious parties out of n_{SetUp} as in the interactive setup for the CL scheme in [11].

Correctness. Given $\mathsf{pp} \leftarrow \mathsf{SetUp}(\lambda)$, $((\mathsf{sk}_i)_i, \mathsf{pk}) \leftarrow \mathsf{KeyGen}()$, and the ciphertexts $C_i \leftarrow \mathsf{Encrypt}(x_i, \mathsf{pk}, \mathsf{sk}_i)$ for $i \in [n]$, we have

$$\begin{aligned} M = \prod_{i\in[n]} C_i &= \prod_{i\in[n]} \left(f^{x_i} \cdot \left(\prod_{i<j} T_j \cdot \prod_{i>j} T_j^{-1} \right)^{t_i} \right) \\ &= f^{\sum_{i\in[n]} x_i} \cdot \prod_{i\in[n]} g_p^{\sum_{i<j} t_j t_i - \sum_{i>j} t_j t_i} = f^{\sum_{i\in[n]} x_i}, \end{aligned}$$

and $\mathsf{Solve}(M) = \sum_{i\in[n]} x_i$.

An important advantage of this scheme is that a proof of correct encryption can be generated by using a Σ-protocol in an unknown-order group [19], which has a soundness based on the Strong Root Assumption and the γ-Low Order Assumption in class groups [11]. Moreover, thanks to the easy DL subgroup generated by f, there is no restriction on the size of the sum to be aggregated. If the above scheme is in a standard DDH group, a range proof for each encrypted input is required and thus the computational overhead and the proof size can not be constant anymore.

On the other hand, we call the above scheme as one-time decentralized sum (ODSUM), as it only supports one-time secure encryption. Therefore, each sender is supposed to encrypt a message once only. Without this restriction, an adversary can mix and match between (possibly) multiple ciphertexts of the same sender with other senders' ciphertexts in decryption to extract information related to the mixed-and-matched encrypted inputs. Later, we will provide a technique to extend from one-time security to multiple-time security and show that the extended DSUM scheme is applicable to be used in verifiable decentralized MCFE for inner product.

One-time Security Model. The DSUM scheme described in Sect. 3.2 is one-time secure, therefore the security model is as defined in Definition 7, except for the encryption oracle:

- Encryption queries $\mathsf{QEncrypt}(i, x^0, x^1)$: $\mathcal{A}$ has unlimited and adaptive access to a Left-or-Right encryption oracle, and receives the ciphertext ct_i generated by $\mathsf{Encrypt}(\mathsf{sk}_i, x_i)$ (no label ℓ). Any further query for the same sender i will later be ignored.

Theorem 1. *The One-time Decentralized Sum scheme described in Sect. 3.2 is* IND*-secure under the HSM assumption, as in the one-time security model above. More precisely, we have*

$$\mathsf{Adv}^{\mathsf{ind}}_{\mathsf{ODSUM}}(t, q_E) \leq 2n(n-1)^2 \cdot (\mathsf{Adv}_{\mathsf{HSM}}(t) + 2^{-2\lambda})$$

where

- $\mathsf{Adv}^{\mathsf{ind}}_{\mathsf{ODSUM}}(t, q_E)$ *is the best advantage of any PPT adversary running in time t with q_E encryption queries against the* IND*-security game of the* ODSUM *scheme;*

- $\mathsf{Adv}_{\mathsf{HSM}}(t)$ *is best advantage of any PPT adversary running in time t to distinguish a HSM instance.*
- $q_E \leq n$ *according to the security model of* ODSUM.

Proof. We may note that to have a non-negligible advantage of winning the game, the adversary has to let at least two clients be non-corrupted (honest) such that each of them has two different messages (x^0, x^1) for encryption queries. We call such clients as explicitly honest clients. Indeed,

- if there is no explicitly honest client: unless the game output β is randomized by the finalizing condition 1 in Definition 7, the adversary has only access to the QEncrypt for any client index i of the same message $x_i^b = x_i^0 = x_i^1$, which implies that the adversary has no information about b;
- if there is only one explicitly honest client: we denote by (i, x_i^0, x_i^1) with $x_i^0 \neq x_i^1$ be the only query of two different messages to QEncrypt, then the game output β is randomized by the finalizing condition 3 in Definition 7.

From above, we consider all PPT adversaries that let at least two clients be explicitly honest. We proceed by using a hybrid argument. Let $\mathcal{A}$ be a PPT adversary running in time t. For any game $\mathbf{G}$, we write $\mathsf{Adv}_{\mathbf{G}}$ the advantage of $\mathcal{A}$ in the game $\mathbf{G}$. Note that $\mathbf{G}_0$ is the security game defined in the one-time security model, whereas $\mathsf{Adv}_{\mathbf{G}_1} = 0$, since the adversary's view in $\mathbf{G}_1$ does not depend on the random bit $b \xleftarrow{\$} \{0, 1\}$.

Game $\mathbf{G}_0^*$: this game is as $\mathbf{G}_0$, except the challenger guesses the number of explicitly honest clients. The challenger samples $\kappa \xleftarrow{\$} [2, n]$. If eventually the number of explicitly honest clients is not κ, the game output is $\beta \xleftarrow{\$} \{0, 1\}$. We have that $\mathsf{Adv}_{\mathbf{G}_0^*} = \frac{\mathsf{Adv}_{\mathbf{G}_0}}{n-1}$. For all $t \in [2, \kappa]$, we define the following games.

Game $\mathbf{G}_{0,t}^*$: this game is as $\mathbf{G}_0^*$, except that for the first explicitly honest client $\mathsf{id}_1 \in [n]$, $\mathsf{QEncrypt}(\mathsf{id}_1, x_{\mathsf{id}_1}^0, x_{\mathsf{id}_1}^1)$ uses

$$C_{\mathsf{id}_1} = f^{x_{\mathsf{id}_1}^b \boxed{- \sum_{j \in \{2,t\}} u_j}} \cdot \prod_{\mathsf{id}_1 < j} (T_j)^{t_{\mathsf{id}_1}} \cdot \prod_{\mathsf{id}_1 > j} (T_j)^{-t_{\mathsf{id}_1}},$$

where $u_j \xleftarrow{\$} \mathbb{Z}_p$ for all $j \in [t]$. For the ρ'th explicitly honest client id_ρ with $1 < \rho \leq t$, $\mathsf{QEncrypt}(\mathsf{id}_\rho, x_{\mathsf{id}_\rho}^0, x_{\mathsf{id}_\rho}^1)$ uses

$$C_{\mathsf{id}_\rho} = f^{x_{\mathsf{id}_\rho}^b \boxed{+ u_\rho}} \cdot \prod_{\mathsf{id}_\rho < j} (T_j)^{t_{\mathsf{id}_\rho}} \cdot \prod_{\mathsf{id}_\rho > j} (T_j)^{-t_{\mathsf{id}_\rho}}$$

The changes from $\mathbf{G}_0^*$ are highlighted in gray. From $\mathbf{G}_0^*$ to $\mathbf{G}_{0,2}^*$, we construct a sub-transition with a similar strategy as in the IND-security proof for the CL encryption scheme [13]:

- **Game $\mathbf{G}_{sub}^0$:** this game is as $\mathbf{G}_0^*$, except that the challenger guesses the second explicitly honest client, denoted by id_2. If the guess is incorrect, the challenger aborts and returns a random bit. This incurs a security loss of n.

- **Game $\mathbf{G}^1_{sub}$**: this game is as $\mathbf{G}^0_{sub}$ except that the challenger creates secret keys $(t_i)_{i\in[n]}$ from a distribution $\mathcal{D}$ instead of $\mathcal{D}_p$, so that $(t_i)_{i\in[n]}$ are close to be uniform over the order of G (the subgroup generated by g_pf). For the pairwise-shared mask $K_{\mathsf{id}_2,i} := (T_{\mathsf{id}_2})^{t_i} = (T_i)^{t_{\mathsf{id}_2}}$ with $i \neq \mathsf{id}_2$ that appears in the encryption queries for id_2 and i respectively, the challenger will now compute $K_{\mathsf{id}_2,i} = (T_{\mathsf{id}_2})^{t_i}$. These two modifications does not change the adversary's view, so the simulation remains perfect.
- **Game $\mathbf{G}^2_{sub}$**: by guessing as in $\mathbf{G}^0_{sub}$, the challenger creates $T_{\mathsf{id}_2} = f^u g_p^{t_{\mathsf{id}_2}}$ with $u \xleftarrow{\$} \mathbb{Z}_p$ and $t_{\mathsf{id}_2} \hookleftarrow \mathcal{D}_p$. In other words, T_{id_2} is close to be uniform over G. It computes $K_{\mathsf{id}_2,i}$ with $i \neq \mathsf{id}_2$ as in the previous game, so we have
$$K_{\mathsf{id}_2,\mathsf{id}_1} = (T_{\mathsf{id}_2})^{t_{\mathsf{id}_1}} = f^{ut_{\mathsf{id}_1}} g_p^{t_{\mathsf{id}_2}t_{\mathsf{id}_1}}.$$
The gap between $\mathbf{G}^0_{sub}$ and $\mathbf{G}^2_{sub}$ is
$$\left|\mathsf{Adv}_{\mathbf{G}^0_{sub}} - \mathsf{Adv}_{\mathbf{G}^2_{sub}}\right| \leq \mathsf{Adv}_{\mathsf{HSM}}(t).$$
As p is a 2λ-bit prime, the probability that $u = 0 \mod p$ is a negligible $2^{-2\lambda}$. On the other hand, t_{id_1} is close to be uniform over the order $n_G = ps_p$ of G with $\gcd(p, s_p) = 1$. Therefore the value $(t_{\mathsf{id}_1} \mod p)$ appearing in the exponent of f and the value $(t_{\mathsf{id}_1} \mod s_p)$ appearing in the exponent of g_p are independent (more details in Lemma 1, [10]). Unless $u = 0 \mod p$, the value $(ut_{\mathsf{id}_1} \mod p)$ is then uniformly random over modulus p, even when an unbounded adversary can extract $(t_{\mathsf{id}_1} \mod s_p)$ from T_{id_1} and $(K_{i,\mathsf{id}_1})_{i\neq\mathsf{id}_1}$.
- **Game $\mathbf{G}^3_{sub}$**: this game is as $\mathbf{G}^2_{sub}$, except that $K_{\mathsf{id}_2,\mathsf{id}_1}$ is computed as
$$K_{\mathsf{id}_2,\mathsf{id}_1} = f^{\mu_2+ut_{\mathsf{id}_1}} g_p^{t_{\mathsf{id}_2}t_{\mathsf{id}_1}} = f^{\mu_2}(T_{\mathsf{id}_2})^{t_{\mathsf{id}_1}}$$
where $\mu_2 \xleftarrow{\$} \mathbb{Z}_p$. Unless $u = 0 \mod p$, the distributions $\{ut_{\mathsf{id}_1} \mod p : t_{\mathsf{id}_1} \xleftarrow{\$} \mathbb{Z}_p\}$ in $\mathbf{G}^2_{sub}$ and $\{\mu_2 + ut_{\mathsf{id}_1} : \mu_2 \xleftarrow{\$} \mathbb{Z}_p, t_{\mathsf{id}_1} \xleftarrow{\$} \mathbb{Z}_p\}$ in $\mathbf{G}^3_{sub}$ are the same, so we have
$$\left|\mathsf{Adv}_{\mathbf{G}^2_{sub}} - \mathsf{Adv}_{\mathbf{G}^3_{sub}}\right| \leq 2^{-2\lambda}.$$

By switching $T_{\mathsf{id}_2} = f^u g_p^{t_{\mathsf{id}_2}}$ back to $T_{\mathsf{id}_2} = g_p^{t_{\mathsf{id}_2}}$ and lifting the requirement that the challenger has to guess id_2, we obtain the game $\mathbf{G}^*_{0,2}$. Formally, we have
$$\left|\mathsf{Adv}_{\mathbf{G}^*_0} - \mathsf{Adv}_{\mathbf{G}^*_{0,2}}\right| \leq 2n \cdot (\mathsf{Adv}_{\mathsf{HSM}}(t) + 2^{-2\lambda}).$$
The transition from $\mathbf{G}^*_{0,t-1}$ to $\mathbf{G}^*_{0,t}$ for $t \in [3, \kappa]$ is similar: the challenger has to guesses the t-th explicitly honest client. If the guess is unsuccessful, the challenger aborts and returns a random bit. As before, this incurs a security loss of n. We then use a similar game-based sub-transition as above. Eventually, we obtain
$$\left|\mathsf{Adv}_{\mathbf{G}^*_0} - \mathsf{Adv}_{\mathbf{G}^*_{0,\kappa}}\right| \leq 2(n-1)n \cdot (\mathsf{Adv}_{\mathsf{HSM}}(t) + 2^{-2\lambda}).$$

Game $\mathbf{G}^*_{1,\kappa}$: For all $i \in [n]$, we put $\Delta_i = x_i^0 - x_i^b$. This game is as $\mathbf{G}^*_{0,\kappa}$ except that u_t is replaced by $u_t + \Delta_{\mathsf{id}_t}$ for all $t \in [2, \kappa]$. As u_t is sampled uniformly, then the transition from $\mathbf{G}^*_{0,t}$ to $\mathbf{G}^*_{1,t}$ remains perfect.
On the other hand, by the condition (b) in the security game, we know that $\sum_{t\in[\kappa]} x^0_{\mathsf{id}_t} = \sum_{t\in[\kappa]} x^1_{\mathsf{id}_t}$, this implies that $x^0_{\mathsf{id}_1} = x^b_{\mathsf{id}_1} - \sum_{j\in\{2,t\}} \Delta_{\mathsf{id}_t}$. Therefore, we have

$$f^{x^b_{\mathsf{id}_1} - \sum_{j\in[2,\kappa]}(u_j + \Delta_{\mathsf{id}_t})} = f^{x^0_{\mathsf{id}_1} - \sum_{j\in[2,\kappa]} u_j}$$

and

$$f^{x^b_{\mathsf{id}_\rho} + (u_\rho + \Delta_{\mathsf{id}_\rho})} = f^{x^0_{\mathsf{id}_\rho} + u_\rho}$$

for $1 < \rho \leq \kappa$. In other words, this game is as $\mathbf{G}^*_{0,\kappa}$ except that $x^b_{\mathsf{id}_\rho}$ is replaced by $x^0_{\mathsf{id}_\rho}$ for all $\rho \in [\kappa]$. We transition gradually from $\mathbf{G}^*_{1,\kappa}$ to $\mathbf{G}^*_1$ as a switch back from $\mathbf{G}^*_{0,\kappa}$ to $\mathbf{G}^*_0$ when $x^b_{\mathsf{id}_\rho}$ is replaced by $x^0_{\mathsf{id}_\rho}$ for all $\rho \in [\kappa]$. Hence, all the answers to encryption queries in $\mathbf{G}^*_1$ are encryptions of x^0, which is independent of b. In the game $\mathbf{G}_1$, we finally lift the requirement that the challenger has to guess the number of explicitly honest clients κ.
In conclusion, we have

$$\mathsf{Adv}_{\mathbf{G}_0} \leq 2n(n-1)^2 \cdot (\mathsf{Adv}_{\mathsf{HSM}}(t) + 2^{-2\lambda}).$$

4 Verifiable Decentralized MCFE

We denote by $\mathcal{F}$ a class of n-ary functions from $\mathcal{M}^n$ to $\mathcal{X}$. We also denote by $\mathcal{P}^{\mathtt{m}} \subset \{0,1\}^*$ a class of polynomially-time-decidable predicates for message to encrypt and by $\mathcal{P}^{\mathtt{f}} \subset \{0,1\}^*$ a class of polynomially-time-decidable predicates for function in a functional decryption key.

Definition 8 (Verifiable Decentralized Multi-client Functional Encryption). *A verifiable decentralized multi-client functional encryption on $\mathcal{M}$ over $(\mathcal{F}, \mathcal{P}^{\mathtt{m}}, \mathcal{P}^{\mathtt{f}})$, and a set of n senders $(\mathcal{S}_i)_i$ consists of eight algorithms :*

- $\mathsf{SetUp}(\lambda)$: *Takes as input the security parameter λ. Outputs the public parameters pp. Those parameters are implicit arguments to all the other algorithms.*
- $\mathsf{KeyGen}()$: *This is a protocol between the senders $(\mathcal{S}_i)_i$ that eventually each generates its own secret key sk_i, its private encryption key ek_i. The protocol also outputs a verification key for ciphertexts $\mathsf{vk}_{\mathsf{CT}}$, a verification key for functional keys $\mathsf{vk}_{\mathsf{DK}}$, a public key pk. Similar to pp, pk can be an implicit argument.*
- $\mathsf{Encrypt}(\mathsf{ek}_i, x_i, \ell, \mathsf{P}^{\mathtt{m}}_i)$: *Takes as input an encryption key ek_i, a value x_i to encrypt, a label ℓ and a predicate $\mathsf{P}^{\mathtt{m}}_i \in \mathcal{P}^{\mathtt{m}}$. Outputs the ciphertext $C_{\ell,i}$.*
- $\mathsf{DKeyGenShare}(\mathsf{sk}_i, \ell_f, \mathsf{P}^{\mathtt{f}})$: *Takes as input a user secret key sk_i, a function label ℓ_f for $f \in \mathcal{F}$, and a predicate $\mathsf{P}^{\mathtt{f}} \in \mathcal{P}^{\mathtt{f}}$. Outputs a functional decryption key share $\mathsf{dk}_{f,i}$.*
- $\mathsf{VerifyDK}((\mathsf{dk}_{f,i})_{i\in[n]}, \mathsf{vk}_{\mathsf{DK}}, \mathsf{P}^{\mathtt{f}})$: *Takes as input functional decryption key shares $(\mathsf{dk}_{f,i})_{i\in[n]}$, a verification key $\mathsf{vk}_{\mathsf{DK}}$ and a predicate $\mathsf{P}^{\mathtt{f}} \in \mathcal{P}^{\mathtt{f}}$. Outputs 1 for accepting or 0 with a set of malicious senders $\mathcal{MS}_{\mathsf{dk}} \neq \emptyset$ for rejecting.*

- $\mathsf{VerifyCT}(\boldsymbol{C}_\ell, \mathsf{vk}_{\mathsf{CT}}, (\mathsf{P}_i^{\mathtt{m}})_{i\in[n]})$: *Takes as input an n-vector ciphertext* $\boldsymbol{C}_\ell = (C_{\ell,i})_{i\in[n]}$, *a verification key* $\mathsf{vk}_{\mathsf{CT}}$, *and message predicates* $(\mathsf{P}_i^{\mathtt{m}})_{i\in[n]} \in (\mathcal{P}^{\mathtt{m}})^n$. *Outputs* 1 *for accepting or* 0 *with a set of malicious senders* $\mathcal{MS}_{\mathsf{ct}} \neq \emptyset$ *for rejecting.*
- $\mathsf{DKeyComb}((\mathsf{dk}_{f,i})_{i\in[n]}, \ell_f)$: *Takes as input the functional decryption key shares* $(\mathsf{dk}_{f,i})_{i\in[n]}$, *a function label* ℓ_f, *and outputs the functional decryption key* dk_f.
- $\mathsf{Decrypt}(\mathsf{dk}_f, \boldsymbol{C}_\ell)$: *Takes as input a functional decryption key* dk_f, *an n-vector ciphertext* $\boldsymbol{C}_\ell := (C_{\ell,i})_{i\in[n]}$. *Outputs* $f(\boldsymbol{x})$ *or* $\perp$.

Correctness. Given any set of message predicates $(\mathsf{P}_i^{\mathtt{m}})_{i\in[n]} \in (\mathcal{P}^{\mathtt{m}})^n$ *and any function predicate* $\mathsf{P}^{\mathtt{f}} \in \mathcal{P}^{\mathtt{f}}$: *for all functions* $f \in \mathcal{F}$ *such that* $\mathsf{P}^{\mathtt{f}}(f) = 1$, *and all sets of values* $(x_1, ..., x_n) \in \mathcal{M}^n$ *such that* $\mathsf{P}_i^{\mathtt{m}}(x_i) = 1$ *for all* $i \in [n]$, *and*

$$\begin{cases} \mathsf{pp} \leftarrow \mathsf{SetUp}(\lambda) \\ ((\mathsf{sk}_i, \mathsf{ek}_i)_{i\in[n]}, \mathsf{vk}_{\mathsf{CT}}, \mathsf{vk}_{\mathsf{DK}}, \mathsf{pk}) \leftarrow \mathsf{KeyGen}() \\ C_{\ell,i} \leftarrow \mathsf{Encrypt}(\mathsf{ek}_i, x_i, \ell, \mathsf{P}_i^{\mathtt{m}}) \forall i \in [n] \\ \mathsf{dk}_{f,i} \leftarrow \mathsf{DKeyGenShare}(\mathsf{sk}_i, \ell_f, \mathsf{P}^{\mathtt{f}}) \forall i \in [n] \end{cases}$$

then

$$\begin{cases} \mathsf{VerifyDK}((\mathsf{dk}_{f,i})_{i\in[n]}, \mathsf{vk}_{\mathsf{DK}}, \mathsf{P}^{\mathtt{f}}) = 1 \\ \mathsf{VerifyCT}(\boldsymbol{C}_\ell, \mathsf{vk}_{\mathsf{CT}}, (\mathsf{P}_i^{\mathtt{m}})_{i\in[n]}) = 1 \\ \mathsf{Decrypt}(\mathsf{dk}_f, \boldsymbol{C}_\ell) = f(x_1, ..., x_n) \end{cases}$$

with probability 1.

Verifiability with Malicious Sender Identification. For all PPT adversaries $\mathcal{A}$, *the advantage* $\mathsf{Adv}_{\mathsf{VDMCFE}}^{\mathsf{verif}}(\mathcal{A})$ *in the following game is negligible in* λ.

- *Initialization: Challenger initializes by choosing classes of predicates* $\mathcal{P}^{\mathtt{m}}, \mathcal{P}^{\mathtt{f}}$ *and running* $\mathsf{pp} \leftarrow \mathsf{SetUp}(\lambda)$. *It sends* $(\mathsf{pp}, \mathcal{P}^{\mathtt{m}}, \mathcal{P}^{\mathtt{f}})$ *to* $\mathcal{A}$.
- *Key generation queries* $\mathsf{QKeyGen}()$: *For only one time in the game,* $\mathcal{A}$ *can play on behalf of corrupted senders and call other non-corrupted senders to join a key generation protocol and together compute* $(\mathsf{vk}_{\mathsf{CT}}, \mathsf{vk}_{\mathsf{DK}}, \mathsf{pk})$.
- *Corruption queries* $\mathsf{QCorrupt}(i)$: $\mathcal{A}$ *can make an unlimited number of adaptive corruption queries on input an index* i, *to play on behalf of sender* $\mathcal{S}_i$ *in the protocol. If* i *was queried after* $\mathsf{QKeyGen}$, *then* $\mathcal{A}$ *additionally receives* $(\mathsf{sk}_i, \mathsf{ek}_i, \mathsf{vk}_{\mathsf{CT}}, \mathsf{vk}_{\mathsf{DK}})$ *and cannot play on behalf of* $\mathcal{S}_i$ *in the key generation process anymore.*
- *Encryption queries* $\mathsf{QEncrypt}(i, \ell, \mathsf{P}_i^{\mathtt{m}})$: $\mathcal{A}$ *has unlimited and adaptive access to call an honest (non-corrupted) sender* $\mathcal{S}_i$ *to provide a correct encryption* $C_{\ell,i} = \mathsf{Encrypt}(\mathsf{ek}_i, x_i, \ell, \mathsf{P}_i^{\mathtt{m}})$ *for some* x_i *such that* $\mathsf{P}_i^{\mathtt{m}}(x_i) = 1$. $\mathcal{A}$ *can only choose any message predicate* $\mathsf{P}_i^{\mathtt{m}} \in \mathcal{P}^{\mathtt{m}}$, *otherwise the query is ignored.*

- *Functional key share queries* $\mathsf{QDKeyGen}(i, f, \mathsf{P}^{\mathtt{f}})$*: $\mathcal{A}$ has unlimited and adaptive access to call an honest (non-corrupted) sender $\mathcal{S}_i$ to provide a correct functional key share* $\mathsf{dk}_{f,i} = \mathsf{DKeyGenShare}(\mathsf{sk}_i, f, \mathsf{P}^{\mathtt{f}})$*. $\mathcal{A}$ can only choose any message predicate $\mathsf{P}^{\mathtt{f}} \in \mathcal{P}^{\mathtt{f}}$ and then a function f such that $\mathsf{P}^{\mathtt{f}}(f) = 1$, otherwise the query is ignored.*
- *Finalize: let $\mathcal{MS}_{\mathcal{A}}$ be the set of corrupted senders, then $\mathcal{A}$ has to output verification keys* $(\mathsf{vk}_{\mathsf{CT}}, \mathsf{vk}_{\mathsf{DK}})$ *and public key* pk *from* $\mathsf{QKeyGen}()$*, message predicates $(\mathsf{P}^{\mathtt{m}}_i)_{i\in[n]} \in (\mathcal{P}^{\mathtt{m}})^n$, a function predicate $\mathsf{P}^{\mathtt{f}} \in \mathcal{P}^{\mathtt{f}}$, a label ℓ, malicious ciphertexts $(C_{\ell,i})_{i\in\mathcal{MS}_{\mathcal{A}}}$, and malicious functional key shares $(\mathsf{dk}_{f_j,i})_{j,i\in\mathcal{MS}_{\mathcal{A}}}$ for a polynomially number of functions f_j such that $\mathsf{P}^{\mathtt{f}}(f_j) = 1$. The ciphertexts of honest senders $(C_{\ell,i})_{i\notin\mathcal{MS}_{\mathcal{A}}}$ and their functional key shares $(\mathsf{dk}_{f_j,i})_{j,i\notin\mathcal{MS}_{\mathcal{A}}}$ are automatically completed by using the oracles* $\mathsf{QEncrypt}$ *and* $\mathsf{QDKeyGen}$.
- *$\mathcal{A}$ wins the game if one of the following cases happens:*
  - *If* $\mathsf{VerifyCT}(\boldsymbol{C}_\ell, \mathsf{vk}_{\mathsf{CT}}, (\mathsf{P}^{\mathtt{m}}_i)_{i\in[n]}) = 1$ *and, for all function queries f_j,* $\mathsf{VerifyDK}((\mathsf{dk}_{f_j,i})_{i\in[n]}, \mathsf{vk}_{\mathsf{DK}}, \mathsf{P}^{\mathtt{f}}) = 1$*: there does not exist a tuple of messages $(x_i)_{i\in[n]}$ such that, for all $i \in [n]$, $\mathsf{P}^{\mathtt{m}}_i(x_i) = 1$, and*
  $$\mathsf{Decrypt}(\mathsf{dk}_{f_j}, \boldsymbol{C}_\ell) = f_j(x_1, ..., x_n)$$
  with $\mathsf{dk}_{f_j} = \mathsf{DKeyComb}((\mathsf{dk}_{f_j,i})_{i\in[n]}, f_j)$ *for all functions f_j.*
  - *If* $\mathsf{VerifyCT}(\boldsymbol{C}_\ell, \mathsf{vk}_{\mathsf{CT}}, (\mathsf{P}^{\mathtt{m}}_i)_{i\in[n]}) = 0$ *or* $\mathsf{VerifyDK}((\mathsf{dk}_{f_j,i})_{i\in[n]}, \mathsf{vk}_{\mathsf{DK}}, \mathsf{P}^{\mathtt{f}}) = 0$ *for some f_j: the union $\mathcal{MS} = \mathcal{MS}_{\mathsf{ct}} \cup \mathcal{MS}_{\mathsf{dk}}$ contains an honest sender $\mathcal{S}_i$, in other words $i \in \mathcal{MS}$ but $i \notin \mathcal{MS}_{\mathcal{A}}$.*

In our definition of verifiable decentralized MCFE, each functional key share $\mathsf{dk}_{f,i}$ is assumed to contain the description of its corresponding function f, and then a receiver can easily detect if $\mathsf{P}^{\mathtt{f}}(f) \neq 1$ in VerifyDK and reject the key share. Therefore, the condition that $\mathsf{P}^{\mathtt{f}}(f_j) = 1$ in the finalization phase of the verifiability game makes sense. The first winning condition is determined statistically: the validity of ciphertext verification and functional key verification guarantees that an adversary could not produce (maliciously generated) ciphertexts $(C_{\ell,i})_{i\in[n],i\in\mathcal{MS}_{\mathcal{A}}}$ and functional key shares $(\mathsf{dk}_{f_j,i})_{i\in\mathcal{MS}_{\mathcal{A}}}$, such that there exists no tuple of inputs $(x_1, .., x_n)$ that satisfy all message predicates and are consistent in the decryption to $f_j(x_1, ..., x_n)$ for all f_j. The second winning case guarantees that if any verification fails, then there is a negligible chance that an honest sender is accused.

Our definition of verifiability for decentralized MCFE, in particular the first winning condition, is partially inspired by the definition of verifiability for MIFE in [5]. The intuition of verifiability in [5] guarantees that no matter how the setup is done, for (possibly maliciously generated) every n-vector ciphertext $\boldsymbol{C}$ that is valid to a publicly known verification, there must exist an n-vector plaintext $\boldsymbol{x}$ such that for (possibly maliciously generated) every functional decryption key $\mathsf{dk}_f = (\mathsf{dk}, f)$ that is valid to another publicly known verification, the decryption algorithm on input $(\boldsymbol{C}, \mathsf{dk}_f)$ must output $f(\boldsymbol{x})$. By introducing predicates for messages to encrypt and a predicate for function to generate a functional decryption key, our definition additionally validates the content of messages within ciphertexts and the content of functions within functional decryption keys. Furthermore, we formalize the property of malicious sender identification in a general context where multiple independent clients join the protocol.

To be more detailed, using our syntax for the verifiability game, the definition of verifiable MIFE in [5] differs in the following points:

- **Functional encryption.** Multi-input setting is considered instead of multi-client setting, i.e. in MIFE, there is no restriction that only ciphertexts under the same label ℓ can decrypt.
- **Message and function predicates.** In verifiable MIFE, it is fixed from the initialization that $\mathsf{P}^{\mathtt{m}}_i(x) = 1$ iff $x \in \mathcal{M}$ for all $i \in [n]$ and $\mathsf{P}^{\mathtt{f}}(f) = 1$ iff $f \in \mathcal{F}$.
- **Malicious Sender Identification**: In verifiable MIFE, each ciphertext is verified separately, and the functional decryption keys dk_f to be verified are given by a central key authority.
- **Adversary assumption.** In verifiable MIFE, the verifiability game is defined for any adversary that has unlimited computing power and this adversary is allowed to choose pp. The advantage of such adversary in the game is 0 (verifiability with no trusted party and perfect soundness).

Our verifiability requires computational soundness and the adversary is not allowed to create all the setup parameters (pp must be chosen by the challenger). This relaxation might help us to obtain verifiable MCFE schemes with practical efficiency and it might be reasonable in practice to have minimal public parameters that only consist of computational assumptions and random oracle.

If we restrict the functionality of verifiable decentralized MCFE to be the sum of encrypted inputs, then we can obtain a protocol with the same feature as the validation for secure aggregation with input validation in [6]. In their ACORN protocols, each encrypted input is guaranteed to satisfy pre-defined predicates.

Indistinguishability Security. In addition to verifiability, privacy is still an essential security goal: it is derived from the indistinguishability security notion of decentralized MCFE [14] as follows.

Definition 9 (IND-Security Game for Verifiable DMCFE). *Let us consider a Verifiable DMCFE scheme over a set of n senders, a class function predicates $\mathcal{P}^{\mathtt{f}}$, and a class of message predicates $\mathcal{P}^{\mathtt{m}}$. No adversary $\mathcal{A}$ should be able to win the following security game with a non-negligible probability against a challenger $\mathcal{C}$:*

- *Initialization: the challenger $\mathcal{C}$ runs the setup algorithm $\mathsf{pp} \leftarrow \mathsf{SetUp}(\lambda)$ and the key generation $\big((\mathsf{sk}_i, \mathsf{ek}_i)_{i\in[n]}, \mathsf{vk}_{\mathsf{CT}}, \mathsf{vk}_{\mathsf{DK}}, \mathsf{pk}\big) \leftarrow \mathsf{KeyGen}()$ and chooses a random bit $b \xleftarrow{\$} \{0,1\}$. It sends $(\mathsf{vk}_{\mathsf{CT}}, \mathsf{vk}_{\mathsf{DK}}, \mathsf{pk})$ to the adversary $\mathcal{A}$.*
- *Encryption queries $\mathsf{QEncrypt}(i, x^0, x^1, \ell, \mathsf{P}^{\mathtt{m}}_i)$: $\mathcal{A}$ has unlimited and adaptive access to a Left-or-Right encryption oracle. If $\mathsf{P}^{\mathtt{m}}_i \in \mathcal{P}^{\mathtt{m}}$ and $\mathsf{P}^{\mathtt{m}}_i(x^0_i) = \mathsf{P}^{\mathtt{m}}_i(x^1_i) = 1$, then $\mathcal{A}$ receives the ciphertext $C_{\ell,i}$ generated by $\mathsf{Encrypt}(\mathsf{ek}_i, x^b_i, \ell, \mathsf{P}^{\mathtt{m}}_i)$. Otherwise, the query is ignored. We note that any further query for the same pair (ℓ, i) will later be ignored.*

- *Functional decryption key queries* $\mathsf{QDKeyGen}(i, f, \mathcal{P}^{\mathtt{f}})$*:* $\mathcal{A}$ *has unlimited and adaptive access to the senders running* $\mathsf{DKeyGenShare}(\mathsf{sk}_i, \ell_f, \mathsf{P}^{\mathtt{f}})$ *algorithm for any input function* f *of its choice. If* $\mathsf{P}^{\mathtt{f}} \in \mathcal{P}^{\mathtt{f}}$ *and* $\mathsf{P}^{\mathtt{f}}(f) = 1$*, it is given back the functional decryption key share* $\mathsf{dk}_{f,i}$*. Otherwise, the query is ignored.*
- *Corruption queries* $\mathsf{QCorrupt}(i)$*:* $\mathcal{A}$ *can make an unlimited number of adaptive corruption queries on input index* i*, to get the secret and encryption keys* $(\mathsf{sk}_i, \mathsf{ek}_i)$ *of any sender* i *of its choice.*
- *Finalize:* $\mathcal{A}$ *provides its guess* b' *on the bit* b*, and this procedure outputs the result* β *of the security game, according to the analysis given below.*

The output β *of the game depends on some conditions, where* $\mathcal{CS}$ *is the set of corrupted senders (the set of indexes* i *input to* $\mathsf{QCorrupt}$ *during the whole game), and* $\mathcal{HS}$ *is the set of honest (non-corrupted) senders. We set the output to* $\beta \leftarrow b'$*, unless one of the three cases below is true, in which case we set* $\beta \stackrel{\$}{\leftarrow} \{0,1\}$*:*

1. *some* $\mathsf{QEncrypt}(i, x_i^0, x_i^1, \ell)$*-query has been asked for an index* $i \in \mathcal{CS}$ *with* $x_i^0 \neq x_i^1$*;*
2. *for some label* ℓ*, an encryption-query* $\mathsf{QEncrypt}(i, x_i^0, x_i^1, \ell)$ *has been asked for some* $i \in \mathcal{HS}$*, but encryption-queries* $\mathsf{QEncrypt}(j, x_j^0, x_j^1, \ell)$ *have not all been asked for all* $j \in \mathcal{HS}$*;*
3. *for some label* ℓ *and for some function* f *asked to* $\mathsf{QDKeyGen}$*, there exists a pair of vectors* $(\boldsymbol{x}^0 = (x_i^0)_i, \boldsymbol{x}^1 = (x_i^1)_i)$ *such that* $f(\boldsymbol{x}^0) \neq f(\boldsymbol{x}^1)$*, when*
   - $x_i^0 = x_i^1$*, for all* $i \in \mathcal{CS}$*;*
   - $\mathsf{QEncrypt}(i, x_i^0, x_i^1, \ell)$*-queries have been asked for all* $i \in \mathcal{HS}$*.*

We say this verifiable DMCFE *is* IND*-secure with respect to* $\mathcal{P}^{\mathtt{f}}$ *and* $\mathcal{P}^{\mathtt{m}}$ *if for any adversary* $\mathcal{A}$*,*

$$\mathsf{Adv}^{\mathsf{ind}}_{\mathsf{VDMCFE}}(\mathcal{A}) = |P[\beta = 1|b = 1] - P[\beta = 1|b = 0]|$$

is negligible.

In this work, we also use the following weaker notion:

- Static Security ($\mathtt{sta-IND}$): the corruption queries ($\mathsf{QCorrupt}$) are sent before the initialization, while encryption queries can be sent adaptively during the game.

5 A Range-Verifiable **DMCFE** for Inner Product

5.1 Ciphertext Verification

For each encryption label ℓ, the ciphertext of the MCFE scheme in [14] is $[c_i] = [\boldsymbol{u}_\ell^\top] \cdot \boldsymbol{s}_i + [x_i]$ where $[\boldsymbol{u}_\ell] \in \mathbb{G}^2$ is the output of a random oracle taking label ℓ as input, and $\boldsymbol{s}_i$ is a private encryption key that is chosen uniformly from $\mathbb{Z}_p^2$, and $x_i \in \mathbb{Z}_p$ is the value to encrypt. The ciphertext is in the form of a Pedersen commitment, where x_i is the committed value and $\boldsymbol{s}_i$ is a two-dimensional opening. There is a number of efficient range proof schemes [9,16,17] for the committed value in the Pedersen commitment:

$$\mathcal{R}_{\mathsf{range}}([c], l, r; \boldsymbol{s}, x) = 1 \leftrightarrow [c] = [\boldsymbol{u}^\top] \cdot \boldsymbol{s} + [x] \wedge x \in [l, r]$$

The functional key for an inner product with $\boldsymbol{y}$ in the MCFE scheme is $\mathsf{dk}_{\boldsymbol{y}} = (\mathsf{dk} := \sum_{i=1}^{n} y_i \cdot \boldsymbol{s}_i \in \mathbb{Z}_p^2, \boldsymbol{y})$. To avoid encryption under a false encryption key that is not consistent with the share $\boldsymbol{s}_i y_i$ (and vice versa), our scheme will require each sender to publish a commitment of his private encryption key as $\mathsf{com}_{\mathsf{ek}} = ([\boldsymbol{u}_{\ell_{\mathsf{MCFE},b}}^\top] \cdot \boldsymbol{s}_i)_{b \in [2]} \in \mathbb{G}^2$ during the key generation process, where $([\boldsymbol{u}_{\ell_{\mathsf{MCFE},b}}^\top])_{b \in [2]}$ are generated by a random oracle taking initialization labels $(\ell_{\mathsf{MCFE},b})_{b \in [2]}$ as input. This commitment is perfectly binding, which later makes proofs for ciphertexts and functional keys become proofs of membership. By using the soundness of these proofs, we can avoid a large security loss from multiple rewinding-based extractions [24,25] when proving the verifiability of our inner-product decentralized MCFE scheme.

Now each sender is required to provide a proof for the relation $\mathcal{R}_{\mathsf{Encrypt}}$:

$$\mathcal{R}_{\mathsf{Encrypt}}([c], \mathsf{com}_{\mathsf{ek}}, l, r; \boldsymbol{s}, x) = 1 \leftrightarrow \begin{cases} [c] = [\boldsymbol{u}^\top] \cdot \boldsymbol{s} + [x] \\ \wedge\ x \in [l, r] \\ \wedge\ \mathsf{com}_{\mathsf{ek}} = ([\boldsymbol{u}_{\ell_{\mathsf{MCFE},b}}^\top] \cdot \boldsymbol{s})_{b \in [2]} \end{cases}$$

The above relation defines a non-trivial language $L_{\mathsf{Encrypt}} \subsetneq \mathbb{G}^3$ for $([c], \mathsf{com}_{\mathsf{ek}})$. On the other hand, a Σ-protocol, denoted by $\mathsf{NIZK}_{\mathsf{key}}$, can be used to prove the relation $\mathcal{R}_{\mathsf{key}}$:

$$\mathcal{R}_{\mathsf{key}}([c], \mathsf{com}_{\mathsf{ek}}; \boldsymbol{s}, x) = 1 \leftrightarrow \begin{cases} [c] = [\boldsymbol{u}^\top] \cdot \boldsymbol{s} + [x] \\ \wedge\ \mathsf{com}_{\mathsf{ek}} = ([\boldsymbol{u}_{\ell_{\mathsf{MCFE},b}}^\top] \cdot \boldsymbol{s})_{b \in [2]} \end{cases}$$

One can combine a Σ-protocol and a range proof scheme to obtain a NIZK for the relation $\mathcal{R}_{\mathsf{Encrypt}}$. The details are provided by Lemma 1 in the full version [23].

5.2 Functional Key Share Verification

The MCFE scheme in [14] can be transformed into a decentralized MCFE by allowing each sender to use a DSUM scheme [15] to encrypt his share of functional key $\boldsymbol{s}_{\mathsf{MCFE},i} \cdot y_i$, so that $\mathsf{dk}_{\boldsymbol{y}}$ will be revealed as the sum of all senders' shares. A requirement is that the DSUM scheme must support multi-label encryption, that is, only ciphertexts under the same label can be combined to decrypt the sum of encrypted inputs. For the context of decentralized MCFE, by controlling the (inner-product function) label in the decryption, an adversary cannot mixes shares of different functional keys of a sender and matches them with other senders' in the DSUM decryption to obtain valid functional keys of non-agreed functions. As shown in Sect. 3.2, the ODSUM scheme does not have this property, since we removed the pseudo-random function in the encryption to obtain efficiency for the proof of correct encryption.

From ODSUM *to Label-Supporting* DSUM. To solve the problem that ODSUM does not support multi-label encryption, we leverage again the inner-product MCFE scheme in [14] that has this property. We first give an intuitive construction for a DSUM scheme that both supports multi-label encryption and preserves the efficiency for the proof of correct encryption. We call this scheme LDSUM to differentiate with ODSUM and other DSUM schemes.

- **Key Generation**: Each client i generates its own secret key $\mathsf{sk}_{\mathsf{MCFE},i}$ for the MCFE scheme. He joins the key generation of ODSUM with other senders to obtain a secret key $\mathsf{sk}_{\mathsf{ODSUM},i}$ and public key ODSUM.pk in a decentralized manner. His secret key is now $(\mathsf{sk}_{\mathsf{MCFE},i}, \mathsf{sk}_{\mathsf{ODSUM},i})$. He uses ODSUM to encrypt $\mathsf{sk}_{\mathsf{MCFE},i}$ under the keys $(\mathsf{sk}_{\mathsf{ODSUM},i}, \mathsf{ODSUM.pk})$. The resulting ciphertext, denoted by pk_i, is public.
- **Encryption**: Each sender $\mathcal{S}_i$ uses the MCFE scheme to encrypt his message x_i under the key $\mathsf{sk}_{\mathsf{MCFE},i}$ and a label ℓ. The resulting ciphertext is denoted by $c_{i,\ell}$.
- **Decryption**: The receiver first collects all pk_i and uses ODSUM to decrypt dk. Then he collects all MCFE ciphertexts $c_{i,\ell}$ under the same label and uses the MCFE scheme to decrypt $\sum_i x_i$ with the key dk.

The correctness of the above scheme comes from the fact that an MCFE functional key for sum, which is presented by vector $\mathbf{1} = (1, ..., 1)$, is the sum of all senders' MCFE secret keys. We have $\mathsf{dk} = \mathsf{ODSUM.Decrypt}((\mathsf{pk}_i)_i) = \sum_i \mathsf{sk}_{\mathsf{MCFE},i}$. Therefore, the correctness is implied by the correctness of ODSUM and MCFE.

A formal description of the LDSUM scheme is given as follows.

- $\mathsf{SetUp}(\lambda)$:
  1. It generates a prime-order group $\mathcal{G} := (\mathbb{G}, p, P) \xleftarrow{\$} \mathsf{GGen}(1^\lambda)$, and $\mathcal{H}$ a full-domain hash function onto $\mathbb{G}^2$.
  2. It generates the setup of One-time Decentralized Sum $\mathsf{ODSUM.SetUp}(\lambda) = (\tilde{s}, f, \hat{g}_p, g_p, \hat{G}, F, p)$ (a class group).
  3. The public parameters pp consist of $((\mathcal{G}, \mathcal{H}), (\tilde{s}, f, \hat{g}_p, g_p, \hat{G}, F, p))$ and are implicit arguments to all other algorithms.
- $\mathsf{KeyGen}()$:
  1. Each sender generates $\boldsymbol{s}_i \xleftarrow{\$} \mathbb{Z}_p^2$ for all $i \in [n]$.
  2. Each sender joins ODSUM.KeyGen() and obtains two instances $(t_{i,b}, T_{i,b}, \mathsf{ODSUM.pk}_b)_{b\in[2]}$.
  3. Each sender computes and publishes a global key share for the sum:

$$\mathsf{dk}_i = (\mathsf{ODSUM.Encrypt}(s_{i,b}, \mathsf{ODSUM.pk}_b, t_{i,b}))_{b\in[2]} \in G^2$$

  4. For each sender, the secret key is $\mathsf{sk}_i = (\boldsymbol{s}_i, \boldsymbol{t}_i := (t_{i,1}, t_{i,2}))$. The public key is $\mathsf{pk} = ((\mathsf{ODSUM.pk}_b)_{b\in[2]}, (\mathsf{dk}_i)_{i\in[n]})$.
- $\mathsf{Encrypt}(\mathsf{sk}_i, x_i, \ell)$:
  1. It parses $\mathsf{sk}_i = (\boldsymbol{s}_i, \boldsymbol{t}_i)$.

2. It computes $[\boldsymbol{u}_\ell] = \mathcal{H}(\ell)$, and computes $[c_{\ell,i}] = [\boldsymbol{u}_\ell^\top \boldsymbol{s}_i + x_i] \in \mathbb{G}$.
3. The ciphertext is $C_{\ell,i} := (\ell, [c_{\ell,i}])$.

– $\mathsf{Decrypt}(\boldsymbol{C}_\ell, \mathsf{pk})$:
1. It parses $\boldsymbol{C}_\ell := (C_{\ell,i})_{i\in[n]}$ and $\mathsf{pk} = ((\mathsf{ODSUM.pk}_b)_{b\in[2]}, (\mathsf{dk}_i)_{i\in[n]})$.
2. It recovers the (public) decryption key for the sum:

$$\mathsf{dk}_1 \leftarrow (\mathsf{ODSUM.Decrypt}((\mathsf{dk}_{i,b})_{i\in[n]}))_{b\in[2]} \in \mathbb{Z}_p^2.$$

3. Decryption for the sum: from $C_{\ell,i} = (\ell, [c_{\ell,i}])$, it computes

$$[\alpha] = \sum_i [c_i] - [\boldsymbol{u}_\ell^\top] \cdot \mathsf{dk}_1,$$

and eventually solves the discrete logarithm to extract and return α. For efficient decryption, we require α to be small enough.

A formal proof of correctness and a security analysis of the above scheme are provided in the full version [23]. It is also more convenient to leave the relation for proof of correct generation and the corresponding Σ-protocol in the description of the verifiable inner-product DMCFE scheme.

5.3 Description of Range-Verifiable Inner-Product DMCFE Scheme

Let n be the number of senders. The message predicate $\mathsf{P}^{\mathsf{m}}(x) = 1 \leftrightarrow x \in [0, 2^m - 1]$ and the function predicate $\mathsf{P}^{\mathsf{f}}(\boldsymbol{y}) = 1 \leftrightarrow y_i \in [0, 2^m - 1]$ for all $i \in [n]$ are parameterized by a polynomially bounded m.

– $\mathsf{SetUp}(\lambda)$:
1. It generates a pairing group $\mathcal{PG} := (\mathbb{G}_1, \mathbb{G}_2, \mathbb{G}_T, p) \xleftarrow{\$} \mathsf{PGGen}(1^\lambda)$, and $\mathcal{H}_b$ a full-domain hash function onto $\mathbb{G}_b^2$ for $b \in [2]$.
2. It generates initialization labels $(\ell_{\mathsf{DMCFE},b})_{b\in[2]} := (\{0,1\}^*)^2$.
3. It generates the setup of LDSUM in $\mathbb{G}_2$: $\mathsf{LDSUM.pp} = \mathsf{LDSUM.SetUp}(\lambda, \mathbb{G}_2)$.
4. The public parameters pp consist of $(\mathcal{PG}, (\mathcal{H}_b)_{b\in[2]}, \mathsf{LDSUM.pp}, \ell_{\mathsf{DMCFE}})$ and are implicit arguments to all other algorithms.

– $\mathsf{KeyGen}()$:
1. Each sender joins $\mathsf{LDSUM.KeyGen}()$ to obtain $(\mathsf{LDSUM.sk}_i, \mathsf{LDSUM.pk})$.
2. Each sender generates $\boldsymbol{s}_{\mathsf{DMCFE},i} \xleftarrow{\$} \mathbb{Z}_p^2$ and commits $\boldsymbol{s}_{\mathsf{DMCFE},i}$ as

$$\mathsf{com}_{\mathsf{DMCFE},i} = ([\boldsymbol{v}_{\mathsf{DMCFE},b}^\top \cdot \boldsymbol{s}_{\mathsf{DMCFE},i}]_1)_{b\in[2]};$$

where $[\boldsymbol{v}_{\mathsf{DMCFE},b}]_1 = \mathcal{H}_1(\ell_{\mathsf{DMCFE},b})$ for $b \in [2]$.
3. For each sender, the encryption key is $\mathsf{ek}_i = \boldsymbol{s}_{\mathsf{DMCFE},i}$ and the secret key is $\mathsf{sk}_i = (\boldsymbol{s}_{\mathsf{DMCFE},i}, \mathsf{LDSUM.sk}_i)$.
4. The verification key for ciphertexts is $\mathsf{vk}_{\mathsf{CT}} = (\mathsf{com}_{\mathsf{DMCFE},i})_{i\in[n]}$, while for functional keys it is $\mathsf{vk}_{\mathsf{DK}} = (\mathsf{LDSUM.pk}, (\mathsf{com}_{\mathsf{DMCFE},i})_{i\in[n]})$.
5. The public key is $\mathsf{pk} = \mathsf{LDSUM.pk}$.

- $\mathsf{Encrypt}(\mathsf{ek}_i, x_i, \ell, m)$:
  1. It parses $\mathsf{ek}_i = \boldsymbol{s}_{\mathsf{DMCFE},i}$ and computes $[c_{\ell,i}]_1 = [\boldsymbol{u}_\ell^\top \boldsymbol{s}_{\mathsf{DMCFE},i} + x_i]_1$ where $[\boldsymbol{u}_\ell]_1 = \mathcal{H}_1(\ell)$.
  2. It re-computes $\mathsf{com}_{\mathsf{DMCFE},i}$ and a proof $\pi_{\mathsf{Encrypt},i}$ for the relation $\mathcal{R}_{\mathsf{Encrypt}}$ on input $(\ell, [c_{\ell,i}]_1, \mathsf{com}_{\mathsf{DMCFE},i}, m; x_i, \mathsf{ek}_i)$.
  3. It outputs the ciphertext $C_{\ell,i} = (\ell, [c_{\ell,i}]_1, \pi_{\mathsf{Encrypt},i})$.
- $\mathsf{DKeyGenShare}(\mathsf{sk}_i, \ell_{\boldsymbol{y}}, m, \mathsf{pk})$:
  1. It parses $\mathsf{sk}_i = (\boldsymbol{s}_{\mathsf{DMCFE},i}, \mathsf{LDSUM.sk}_i)$, $\ell_{\boldsymbol{y}} = (\ell_{\boldsymbol{y},b})_{b\in[2]}$ and $\mathsf{pk} = \mathsf{LDSUM.pk}$.
  2. It computes $\mathsf{dk}_i = (\mathsf{LDSUM.Encrypt}(\mathsf{LDSUM.sk}_i, s_{\mathsf{DMCFE},i,b} \cdot y_i, \ell_{\boldsymbol{y},b}))_{b\in[2]}$.
  3. It re-computes $\mathsf{com}_{\mathsf{DMCFE},i}$ and a proof $\pi_{\mathsf{DKeyGenShare},i}$ for the relation $\mathcal{R}_{\mathsf{DKeyGenShare}}$ on input $(\mathsf{LDSUM.pk}, \mathsf{com}_{\mathsf{DMCFE},i}, \mathsf{dk}_i, \ell_{\boldsymbol{y}}; \mathsf{sk}_i)$.
  4. It outputs the functional key share $\mathsf{dk}_{i,\boldsymbol{y}} = (\mathsf{dk}_i, \ell_{\boldsymbol{y}}, \pi_{\mathsf{DKeyGenShare},i})$.
- $\mathsf{VerifyCT}((C_{\ell,i})_{i\in[n]}, \mathsf{vk}_{\mathsf{CT}}, m)$:
  1. It parses $C_{\ell,i} = (\ell, [c_{\ell,i}]_1, \pi_{\mathsf{Encrypt},i})$ for $i \in [n]$, and $\mathsf{vk}_{\mathsf{CT}} = (\mathsf{com}_{\mathsf{DMCFE},i})_{i\in[n]}$.
  2. For $i \in [n]$: it verifies the proof $\pi_{\mathsf{Encrypt},i}$ for the relation $\mathcal{R}_{\mathsf{Encrypt}}$ on input $(\ell, [c_{\ell,i}]_1, \mathsf{com}_{\mathsf{DMCFE},i}, m)$.
  3. It outputs 1 for accepting if $\pi_{\mathsf{Encrypt},i}$ is valid for all $i \in [n]$, otherwise outputs 0 with the set $\mathcal{MS} = \{i : \pi_{\mathsf{Encrypt},i} \text{ is not valid}\}$ for rejecting.
- $\mathsf{VerifyDK}((\mathsf{dk}_{i,\boldsymbol{y}})_{i\in[n]}, \mathsf{vk}_{\mathsf{DK}})$:
  1. It parses the keys $\mathsf{dk}_{i,\boldsymbol{y}} = (\mathsf{dk}_i, \ell_{\boldsymbol{y}}, \pi_{\mathsf{DKeyGenShare},i})$ and $\mathsf{vk}_{\mathsf{DK}} = (\mathsf{LDSUM.pk}, (\mathsf{com}_{\mathsf{DMCFE},i})_{i\in[n]})$.
  2. From the function label $\ell_{\boldsymbol{y}}$, it verifies that $y_i \in [0, 2^m - 1]$ for $i \in [n]$. It stops and outputs 0 if $\boldsymbol{y}$ is not valid.
  3. For $i \in [n]$: it verifies $\pi_{\mathsf{DKeyGenShare},i}$ for the relation $\mathcal{R}_{\mathsf{DKeyGenShare}}$ on input $(\mathsf{LDSUM.pk}, \mathsf{com}_{\mathsf{DMCFE},i}, \mathsf{dk}_i, \ell_{\boldsymbol{y}})$.
  4. It outputs 1 for accepting if $\pi_{\mathsf{DKeyGenShare},i}$ is valid for all $i \in [n]$, otherwise outputs 0 with the set $\mathcal{MS} = \{i : \pi_{\mathsf{DKeyGenShare},i} \text{ is not valid}\}$ for rejecting.
- $\mathsf{DKeyComb}((\mathsf{dk}_{i,\boldsymbol{y}})_{i\in[n]}, \ell_{\boldsymbol{y}}, \mathsf{pk})$:
  1. It parses the keys $\mathsf{dk}_{i,\boldsymbol{y}} = (\mathsf{dk}_i, \ell_{\boldsymbol{y}}, \pi_{\mathsf{DKeyGenShare},i})$ and $\mathsf{pk} = \mathsf{LDSUM.pk}$.
  2. It outputs $[\mathsf{dk}_{\boldsymbol{y}}]_2 = (\mathsf{LDSUM.Decrypt}((\mathsf{dk}_{i,b})_{i\in[n]}, \ell_{\boldsymbol{y},b}, \mathsf{LDSUM.pk}))_{b\in[2]} \in \mathbb{G}_2^2$. In the LDSUM decryption, it is hard to obtain $\mathsf{dk}_{\boldsymbol{y}} \in \mathbb{Z}_p^2$ from $[\mathsf{dk}_{\boldsymbol{y}}]_2$, since $\mathsf{dk}_{\boldsymbol{y}}$ is random over $\mathbb{Z}_p^2$. Therefore, we stop the LDSUM decryption once obtaining $[\mathsf{dk}_{\boldsymbol{y}}]_2$.
- $\mathsf{Decrypt}(\boldsymbol{C}_\ell, [\mathsf{dk}_{\boldsymbol{y}}]_2)$: It gets $[\alpha]_T = \sum_{i\in[n]} e([c_{\ell,i}]_1, [y_i]_2) - e([\boldsymbol{u}_\ell]_1^\top, [\mathsf{dk}_{\boldsymbol{y}}]_2)$, and eventually solves the discrete logarithm in basis $[1]_T$ to return α.

The relation $\mathcal{R}_{\mathsf{Encrypt}}$ that guarantees a correct encryption of a valid input x_i under a committed encryption key $\boldsymbol{s}_{\mathsf{DMCFE},i}$ is defined as in Sect. 5.1. We can use $\mathsf{NIZK}_{\mathsf{Encrypt}}$ that is constructed as in Sect. 5.1 to prove this relation. Since the LDSUM scheme uses the ODSUM as a sub-protocol (see Sect. 5.2) in its key generation, we express all the terms LDSUM.pk, $\mathsf{LDSUM.sk}_i$ explicitly as follows

- $\mathsf{LDSUM.pk} = ((T_{\mathsf{ODSUM},i})_{i\in[n]}, (\mathsf{dk}_{\mathsf{LDSUM},i})_{i\in[n]}) \in G^{2\times n} \times G^n$;
- $\mathsf{LDSUM.sk}_i = (\boldsymbol{s}_{\mathsf{LDSUM},i}, \boldsymbol{t}_{\mathsf{ODSUM},i}) \in \mathbb{Z}_p^2 \times \mathbb{Z}^2$.

The relation $\mathcal{R}_{\mathsf{DKeyGenShare}}$ is defined in Fig. 1 and proved by $\mathsf{NIZK}_{\mathsf{DKeyGenShare}}$ in Fig. 2. A remark is that the key $s_{\mathsf{LDSUM},i}$ is verified to be consistent in between $\mathsf{dk}_{\mathsf{LDSUM},i}$ (in class group) and dk_i (in pairing group), so we need a Σ-protocol that proves the DL equality between these two groups.

$\mathcal{R}_{\mathsf{DKeyGenShare}}$

Parameters: $i, \ell_{\boldsymbol{y}}, \ell_{\mathsf{DMCFE}}$
Statement: $(T_{\mathsf{ODSUM},j})_{j\in[n]}, \mathsf{dk}_{\mathsf{LDSUM},i}, \mathsf{com}_{\mathsf{DMCFE},i}, \mathsf{dk}_i$
Witness: $\boldsymbol{s}_{\mathsf{DMCFE},i}, \boldsymbol{s}_{\mathsf{LDSUM},i}, \boldsymbol{t}_{\mathsf{ODSUM},i}$
Relation:

1. $T_{\mathsf{ODSUM},i} = (g^{t_{\mathsf{ODSUM},i,1}}, g^{t_{\mathsf{ODSUM},i,2}})$
2. $\mathsf{dk}_{\mathsf{LDSUM},i} = (f^{s_{\mathsf{LDSUM},i,b}}(\prod_{i<j} T_{\mathsf{ODSUM},j,b} \cdot \prod_{i>j} T^{-1}_{\mathsf{ODSUM},j,b})^{t_{\mathsf{ODSUM},i,b}})_{b\in[2]}$
3. $\mathsf{com}_{\mathsf{DMCFE},i} = ([\boldsymbol{v}^\top_{\mathsf{DMCFE},b} \cdot \boldsymbol{s}_{\mathsf{DMCFE},i}]_1)_{b\in[2]}$ with $[\boldsymbol{v}_{\mathsf{DMCFE},b}]_1 = \mathcal{H}_1(\ell_{\mathsf{DMCFE},b})$
4. $\mathsf{dk}_i = ([\boldsymbol{u}^\top_{\ell_{\boldsymbol{y}},b} \boldsymbol{s}_{\mathsf{LDSUM},i} + s_{\mathsf{DMCFE},i,b} \cdot y_i]_2)_{b\in[2]}$ with $[\boldsymbol{u}_{\ell_{\boldsymbol{y}},b}]_2 = \mathcal{H}_2(\ell_{\boldsymbol{y},b})$

Fig. 1. The relation defines the correct generation of each functional key share

The above scheme is compatible with the definition of verifiable DMCFE in Sect. 4 by the following theorem.

Theorem 2. *The decentralized MCFE for inner product scheme described in Sect. 5.3 has correctness and verifiability for range predicates in the random oracle, as in Definition 8. More precisely,*

$$\mathsf{Adv}^{\mathsf{verif}}_{\mathsf{DMCFE}}(t, q_C, q_F) \le q_C \cdot \max\{\mathsf{Adv}^{\mathsf{snd}}_{\mathsf{NIZK}_{\mathsf{Encrypt}}}(t), q_F \cdot \mathsf{Adv}^{\mathsf{snd}}_{\mathsf{NIZK}_{\mathsf{DKeyGenShare}}}(t)\}$$

where

- $\mathsf{Adv}^{\mathsf{verif}}_{\mathsf{DMCFE}}(t, q_c, q_F)$ *is the best advantage of any PPT adversary running in time t against the verifiability game in Definition 8 with q_C corruption queries and q_F functions for the finalization phase;*
- $\mathsf{Adv}^{\mathsf{snd}}_{\mathsf{NIZK}_{\mathsf{Encrypt}}}(t)$ *is the best advantage of any PPT adversary running in time t against the soundness of $\mathsf{NIZK}_{\mathsf{Encrypt}}$.*
- $\mathsf{Adv}^{\mathsf{snd}}_{\mathsf{NIZK}_{\mathsf{DKeyGenShare}}}(t)$ *is the best advantage of any PPT adversary running in time t against the soundness of $\mathsf{NIZK}_{\mathsf{DKeyGenShare}}$.*

Proof. We start with the correctness and then with the range-verifiability.

Correctness. Given a range predicate for input and for inner product function $[0, 2^m - 1]$, a vector $\boldsymbol{y}$ such that $y_i \in [0, 2^m - 1]$, an n-vector plaintext $\boldsymbol{x}$ such that $x_i \in [0, 2^m - 1]$. We consider the following case

$$\begin{cases} \mathsf{pp} \leftarrow \mathsf{SetUp}(\lambda) \\ ((\mathsf{sk}_i, \mathsf{ek}_i)_{i\in[n]}, \mathsf{vk}_{\mathsf{CT}}, \mathsf{vk}_{\mathsf{DK}}, \mathsf{pk}) \leftarrow \mathsf{KeyGen}() \\ C_{\ell,i} \leftarrow \mathsf{Encrypt}(\mathsf{ek}_i, x_i, \ell, m) \forall i \in [n] \\ \mathsf{dk}_{i,\boldsymbol{y}} \leftarrow \mathsf{DKeyGenShare}(\mathsf{sk}_i, \ell_{\boldsymbol{y}}, m) \forall i \in [n] \end{cases}$$

Σ-protocol for the relation $\mathcal{R}_{\mathsf{DKeyGenShare}}$:

Parameters: $(\mathcal{PG}, \mathcal{H}_1, \mathcal{H}_2)$, $(\hat{G}, F, g_p, f, S, p)$, $(i, \ell_{\boldsymbol{y}}, \ell_{\mathsf{DMCFE}})$

Statement: $(T_{\mathsf{ODSUM},j})_{j\in[n]}, \mathsf{dk}_{\mathsf{LDSUM},i}, \mathsf{com}_{\mathsf{DMCFE},i}, \mathsf{dk}_i$

Witness: $\boldsymbol{s}_{\mathsf{DMCFE},i}, \boldsymbol{s}_{\mathsf{LDSUM},i}, \boldsymbol{t}_{\mathsf{ODSUM},i}$

Output: 1 if $\mathcal{V}$ accepts, and 0 otherwise.

Protocol:

- $\mathcal{V}$ verifies that $\mathsf{dk}_{\mathsf{LDSUM},i}, T_{\mathsf{ODSUM},j} \in \hat{G}^2$ for $j \in [n]$.
- $\mathcal{P}$ commits the randomness:
  1. $\boldsymbol{\rho}_{\mathsf{LDSUM},i}, \boldsymbol{\rho}_{\mathsf{DMCFE},i} \xleftarrow{\$} \mathbb{Z}_p^2$, $\boldsymbol{\rho}_{\mathsf{ODSUM},i} \xleftarrow{\$} [0, 2^\lambda pS]^2$
  2. $R_{\mathsf{ODSUM},i} = (g_p^{\rho_{\mathsf{ODSUM},i,b}})_{b\in[2]}$
  3. $R_{\mathsf{dk}_i} = ([\boldsymbol{u}_{\ell_{\boldsymbol{y}},b}^\top \boldsymbol{\rho}_{\mathsf{LDSUM},i} + \rho_{\mathsf{DMCFE},i,b} \cdot y_i]_2)_{b\in[2]}$
  4. $R_{\mathsf{DMCFE},i} = ([\boldsymbol{v}_{\mathsf{DMCFE},b}^\top \cdot \boldsymbol{\rho}_{\mathsf{DMCFE},i}]_1)_{b\in[2]}$
  5. Let $K_{\Sigma,i} := \prod_{i<j} T_{\mathsf{ODSUM},j,b} \cdot (\prod_{i>j} T_{\mathsf{ODSUM},j,b})^{-1} \in G$, then $R_{\mathsf{dk}_{\mathsf{LDSUM},i}} = (f^{\rho_{\mathsf{LDSUM},i,b}} K_{\Sigma,i}^{\rho_{\mathsf{ODSUM},i,b}})_{b\in[2]}$
- $\mathcal{P}$ sends $(R_{\mathsf{ODSUM},i}, R_{\mathsf{dk}_i}, R_{\mathsf{DMCFE},i}, R_{\mathsf{dk}_{\mathsf{LDSUM},i}})$ to $\mathcal{V}$
- $\mathcal{V}$ chooses a random challenge $\alpha \xleftarrow{\$} [0, p-1]$ and sends it to $\mathcal{P}$.
- $\mathcal{P}$ computes the response:
  1. $\boldsymbol{z}_{\mathsf{ODSUM},i} = \alpha \cdot \boldsymbol{t}_{\mathsf{ODSUM},i} + \boldsymbol{\rho}_{\mathsf{ODSUM},i} \in \mathbb{Z}$
  2. $\boldsymbol{z}_{\mathsf{LDSUM},i} = \alpha \cdot \boldsymbol{s}_{\mathsf{LDSUM},i} + \boldsymbol{\rho}_{\mathsf{LDSUM},i} \in \mathbb{Z}_p$
  3. $\boldsymbol{z}_{\mathsf{DMCFE},i} = \alpha \cdot \boldsymbol{s}_{\mathsf{DMCFE},i} + \boldsymbol{\rho}_{\mathsf{DMCFE},i} \in \mathbb{Z}_p$
- $\mathcal{P}$ sends $(\boldsymbol{z}_{\mathsf{ODSUM},i}, \boldsymbol{z}_{\mathsf{LDSUM},i}, \boldsymbol{z}_{\mathsf{DMCFE},i})$ to $\mathcal{V}$.
- $\mathcal{V}$ verifies that:
  1. $\boldsymbol{z}_{\mathsf{ODSUM},i} \in [0, (2^\lambda+1)pS]^2$ and $\boldsymbol{z}_{\mathsf{LDSUM},i}, \boldsymbol{z}_{\mathsf{DMCFE},i} \in \mathbb{Z}_p^2$
  2. $T_{\mathsf{ODSUM},i}^\alpha \cdot R_{\mathsf{ODSUM},i} = (g_p^{z_{\mathsf{ODSUM},i,b}})_{b\in[2]}$
  3. $\alpha \cdot \mathsf{dk}_i + R_{\mathsf{dk}_i} = ([\boldsymbol{u}_{\ell_{\boldsymbol{y}},b}^\top \boldsymbol{z}_{\mathsf{LDSUM},i} + z_{\mathsf{DMCFE},i,b} \cdot y_i]_2)_{b\in[2]}$
  4. $\alpha \cdot \mathsf{com}_{\mathsf{DMCFE},i} + R_{\mathsf{DMCFE},i} = ([\boldsymbol{v}_{\mathsf{DMCFE},b}^\top \cdot \boldsymbol{z}_{\mathsf{DMCFE},i}]_1)_{b\in[2]}$
  5. Let $K_{\Sigma,i} := \prod_{i<j} T_{\mathsf{ODSUM},j,b} \cdot (\prod_{i>j} T_{\mathsf{ODSUM},j,b})^{-1} \in G$, then $\mathsf{dk}_{\mathsf{LDSUM},i}^\alpha \cdot R_{\mathsf{dk}_{\mathsf{LDSUM},i}} = (f^{z_{\mathsf{LDSUM},i,b}} K_{\Sigma,i}^{z_{\mathsf{ODSUM},i,b}})_{b\in[2]}$
- $\mathcal{V}$ rejects and stops the protocol if any check is invalid, and accepts otherwise.

Fig. 2. Note that $S = 2^{\lambda-2} \cdot \tilde{s}$ and $\mathcal{D}_p$ is a uniform distribution over $\{0, ..., S\}$. We let $\rho_{\mathsf{ODSUM},i}$ be uniform in $[0, 2^\lambda pS]$ to obtain statistical zero-knowledge as in [19].

Parse $C_{\ell,i} = (\ell, [c_{\ell,i}]_1, \pi_{\mathsf{Encrypt},i})$ and $\mathsf{dk}_{i,\boldsymbol{y}} = (\mathsf{dk}_i, \ell_{\boldsymbol{y}}, \pi_{\mathsf{DKeyGenShare},i})$, by the completeness of $\mathsf{NIZK}_{\mathsf{Encrypt}}$ and $\mathsf{NIZK}_{\mathsf{DKeyGenShare}}$ respectively, we have that all $\pi_{\mathsf{Encrypt},i}$ and $\pi_{\mathsf{DKeyGenShare},i}$ are respectively valid. Therefore,

$$\mathsf{VerifyCT}((C_{\ell,i})_{i\in[n]}, \mathsf{vk}_{\mathsf{CT}}, m) = \mathsf{VerifyDK}((\mathsf{dk}_{i,\boldsymbol{y}})_{i\in[n]}, \mathsf{vk}_{\mathsf{DK}}) = 1.$$

For the decryption, we parse $\mathsf{dk}_{i,\boldsymbol{y}} = (\mathsf{dk}_i, \ell_{\boldsymbol{y}}, \pi_{\mathsf{DKeyGenShare},i})$ and $\mathsf{pk} = \mathsf{LDSUM.pk}$. By the correctness of LDSUM (Sect. 5.2) and the fact that LDSUM stops and outputs $[\mathsf{dk}_{\boldsymbol{y},b}]_2$ before computing the discrete logarithm, we have

$$\begin{aligned}[\mathsf{dk}_{\boldsymbol{y}}]_2 &= (\mathsf{LDSUM.Decrypt}((\mathsf{dk}_{i,b})_{i\in[n]}, \ell_{\boldsymbol{y},b}, \mathsf{LDSUM.pk}))_{b\in[2]} \\ &= ([\sum_{i\in[n]} s_{\mathsf{DMCFE},i,b} \cdot y_i]_2)_{b\in[2]}.\end{aligned}$$

Then we have $[\alpha]_T$ equal to

$$\sum_{i\in[n]} e([c_{\ell,i}]_1, [y_i]_2) - e([\boldsymbol{u}_\ell]_1^\top, [\mathsf{dk}_{\boldsymbol{y}}]_2)$$

$$= \sum_{i\in[n]} \left[(\boldsymbol{u}_\ell^\top \boldsymbol{s}_{\mathsf{DMCFE},i} + x_i)\cdot y_i\right]_T - \left[\boldsymbol{u}_\ell^\top \cdot (\sum_{i\in[n]} \boldsymbol{s}_{\mathsf{DMCFE},i}\cdot y_i)\right]_T = \left[\sum_{i\in[n]} x_i \cdot y_i\right]_T$$

As the inner product $\sum_{i\in[n]} x_i \cdot y_i$ is small, computing α can be done efficiently.

Verifiability. We suppose that there exists a PPT adversary $\mathcal{A}$ that can win the verifiability game in Definition 8 with a non-negligible probability. Without loss of generality, the range predicate for input and inner product function can be fixed to be $[0, 2^m - 1]$.

Except using a trivial attack, $\mathcal{A}$ cannot win the game by making other honest senders accused of sending invalid ciphertexts or invalid functional key shares (the second winning condition). Indeed, to accuse an honest sender $\mathcal{S}_i$, $\mathcal{A}$ has to broadcast some malicious share that makes the proof of correct generation for $\mathcal{S}_i$'s ciphertext or for $\mathcal{S}_i$'s functional key share invalid. By the design of the scheme, the only broadcast elements among senders and the receiver are the ODSUM public keys $(T_{\mathsf{ODSUM},j})_{j\in[n]}$ (included in $\mathsf{LDSUM.pk}$), which are not used in the relation $\mathcal{R}_{\mathsf{Encrypt}}$. For the relation $\mathcal{R}_{\mathsf{DKeyGenShare}}$, the condition involving $(T_{\mathsf{ODSUM},j})_{j\in[n],j\neq i}$ is the generation of $\mathsf{dk}_{\mathsf{LDSUM},i}$, which only requires $(T_{\mathsf{ODSUM},j})_{j\in[n],j\neq i}$ to be group elements in class group $\hat{G}$. Therefore, sending an incorrect group-encoding $T_{\mathsf{ODSUM},j}$ can make the generation and then the proof fail. However, this is a trivial attack and can be excluded, as each $T_{\mathsf{ODSUM},j}$ can be efficiently verified to be in group by the public (and by the verifier in Fig. 2 also) and the public will already know it is the corrupted sender $\mathcal{S}_j$ who broadcast a malicious share.

We now consider $\mathcal{A}$ that wins the game by winning the first condition. We let $(\mathsf{vk}_{\mathsf{CT}}, \mathsf{vk}_{\mathsf{DK}}, \mathsf{pk}, \ell, (C_{\ell,i})_{i\in\mathcal{MS}_\mathcal{A}}, (\mathsf{dk}_{\boldsymbol{y}_j,i})_{j,i\in\mathcal{MS}_\mathcal{A}})$ be the transcript that makes $\mathcal{A}$ win the game. In this case we have

$$\mathsf{VerifyCT}((C_{\ell,i})_{i\in[n]}, \mathsf{vk}_{\mathsf{CT}}, m) = \mathsf{VerifyDK}((\mathsf{dk}_{i,\boldsymbol{y}})_{i\in[n]}, \mathsf{vk}_{\mathsf{DK}}) = 1.$$

Suppose that the transcript output by $\mathcal{A}$ satisfies the relations $\mathcal{R}_{\mathsf{DKeyGenShare}}$ and $\mathcal{R}_{\mathsf{Encrypt}}$.

- From $\mathcal{R}_{\mathsf{DKeyGenShare}}$, $(\mathsf{vk_{CT}}, \mathsf{vk_{DK}}, \mathsf{pk})$ is generated from KeyGen with secret keys $\mathsf{sk}_i = (\boldsymbol{s}_{\mathsf{DMCFE},i}, (\boldsymbol{s}_{\mathsf{LDSUM},i}, \boldsymbol{t}_{\mathsf{ODSUM},i}))$ and encryption keys $\mathsf{ek}_i = \boldsymbol{s}_{\mathsf{DMCFE},i}$. For each $i \in [n]$ and each inner product function $\boldsymbol{y}_j$, $\mathsf{dk}_{\boldsymbol{y}_j,i}$ is generated from $\mathsf{DKeyGenShare}$ on input $(\mathsf{sk}_i, \ell_{\boldsymbol{y}}, \mathsf{pk})$.
- From $\mathcal{R}_{\mathsf{Encrypt}}$, $C_{\ell,i}$ is generated from $\mathsf{Encrypt}$ on input a message $x_i \in [0, 2^m - 1]$ and an encryption key $\boldsymbol{s'}_{\mathsf{DMCFE},i}$ for each $i \in [n]$.

We model the hash function $\mathcal{H}_1$ as a random oracle onto $\mathbb{G}^2$. Then $\mathsf{com}_{\mathsf{DMCFE},i}$ is perfectly binding. From above, we have $\boldsymbol{s}_{\mathsf{DMCFE},i} = \boldsymbol{s'}_{\mathsf{DMCFE},i}$. By the proved correctness of the scheme, the decryption process with input $\boldsymbol{C}_\ell = (C_{\ell,i})_{i\in[n]}$ and $[\mathsf{dk}_{\boldsymbol{y}}]_2 = \mathsf{DKeyComb}((\mathsf{dk}_{\boldsymbol{y}_j,i})_{i\in[n]}, \ell_{\boldsymbol{y}}, \mathsf{pk})$ will output the inner product $\langle \boldsymbol{x}, \boldsymbol{y}_j \rangle$ for all vectors $\boldsymbol{y}_j$. This contradicts the first winning condition, so $\mathcal{A}$ must break either the soundness of $\mathsf{NIZK}_{\mathsf{Encrypt}}$ or the soundness of $\mathsf{NIZK}_{\mathsf{DKeyGenShare}}$ with the same probability of winning the game.

If $\mathcal{A}$ wins the game by breaking the soundness $\mathsf{NIZK}_{\mathsf{Encrypt}}$ with a non-negligible probability, an adversary $\mathcal{B}$ against the soundness of $\mathsf{NIZK}_{\mathsf{Encrypt}}$ can be constructed as follows: $\mathcal{B}$ plays as a challenger in the game with $\mathcal{A}$, after $\mathcal{A}$ finalized the game, $\mathcal{B}$ guesses an index i from the corrupted set $\mathcal{MS}_{\mathcal{A}}$ and outputs the instance $(\ell, [c_{\ell,i}]_1, \mathsf{com}_{\mathsf{DMCFE},i}, \pi^i_{\mathsf{Encrypt}}, m)$ from $\mathcal{A}$'s transcript. Given q_C corrupted senders, in the case $\mathcal{A}$ wins the game, the probability that $\mathcal{B}$ breaks the soundness of $\mathsf{NIZK}_{\mathsf{Encrypt}}$ is $\frac{1}{q_C}$. Similarly for $\mathsf{NIZK}_{\mathsf{DKeyGenShare}}$, given q_F inner-product functions $\boldsymbol{y}_j$ to be finalized, $\mathcal{B}$ outputs one in $n \cdot q_F$ instances of $((T_{\mathsf{ODSUM},i})_{i\in[n]}, \mathsf{dk}_{\mathsf{LDSUM},i}, \mathsf{com}_{\mathsf{DMCFE},i}, \mathsf{dk}_i, \boldsymbol{y}_j)$ from $\mathcal{A}$, which incurs a security loss of $q_C \cdot q_F$. To finalize, we have

$$\mathsf{Adv}^{\mathsf{verif}}_{\mathsf{DMCFE}}(\mathcal{A}, t, q_C, q_F) \le q_C \cdot \max\{\mathsf{Adv}^{\mathsf{snd}}_{\mathsf{NIZK}_{\mathsf{Encrypt}}}(t), q_F \cdot \mathsf{Adv}^{\mathsf{snd}}_{\mathsf{NIZK}_{\mathsf{DKeyGenShare}}}(t)\}.$$

As $\mathsf{Adv}^{\mathsf{snd}}_{\mathsf{NIZK}_{\mathsf{Encrypt}}}(t)$ and $\mathsf{Adv}^{\mathsf{snd}}_{\mathsf{NIZK}_{\mathsf{DKeyGenShare}}}(t)$ are negligible, and q_C and q_F are polynomially bounded, the proof is complete.

5.4 Indistinguishability Security

Theorem 3. *The Range-Verifiable DMCFE for Inner Product scheme described in Sect. 5.3 is* $\mathtt{sta} - \mathtt{IND}$*-secure under the SXDH and HSM assumptions, as in Definition 9.*

The proof is provided in the full version [23].

5.5 Efficiency Analysis

We assume that $\mathsf{NIZK}_{\mathsf{Encrypt}}$ is instantiated with the Σ-protocol $\mathsf{NIZK}_{\mathsf{key}}$ and the Bulletproof for range [9] (for the relation $\mathcal{R}_{\mathsf{range}}$ in Sect. 5.1). As far as we know, Bulletproof offers better efficiency for batch verification than other transparent-setup non-interactive range proof schemes. Since the scalar operation in $\mathbb{Z}_p$ is cheap compared to the group exponentiation, we do not detail them here. Let n be the number of senders and m be a binary upper bound of a input range $[0, 2^m - 1]$.

- **Proving time**: $\mathsf{NIZK}_{\mathsf{Encrypt}}$ costs about $12m+17$ exponentiations with $O(m)$ scalar operations, while $\mathsf{NIZK}_{\mathsf{DKeyGenShare}}$ costs 16 exponentiations with $O(1)$ scalar operations.
- **Proof size**: each $\pi_{\mathsf{Encrypt},i}$ has the size of $2\log_2\lceil m \rceil + 7$ group elements and 10 scalars, while each $\pi_{\mathsf{DKeyGenShare}}$ has the size of 8 group elements and 6 scalars.
- **Verifying time**: $\mathsf{NIZK}_{\mathsf{Encrypt}}$ costs about a single multi-exponentiation of size $2m + 2\log_2\lceil m \rceil + 19$ with $O(m)$ scalar operations for each ciphertext, while $\mathsf{NIZK}_{\mathsf{DKeyGenShare}}$ costs 24 exponentiations for each key share.

For a practical parameter, one can have $n = 2^{10}$ and $m \leq 16$. Then the costs for functional key share are even more efficient than those for ciphertext. Compared to the DMCFE in [14], the overhead costs from verifiability for each sender and each receiver asymptotically depend only on m (range proof costs). Therefore, the approach of verifying each functional key share, which has the advantage of identifying up to all n malicious senders in a non-interactive manner, is no more prohibitively expensive in our scheme.

On the other hand, this approach is avoided in [6] for the ACORN-robust protocol since each key share for sum can not be verified efficiently. Their alternative approach requires the help of checking from $\log(n)$ neighboring senders, which incurs more interaction during verification and overhead costs additionally depending on $\log(n)$ (besides range proof costs) for each sender. Their approach also assumes that at most 1/3 number of senders misbehave.

6 Discussions

6.1 Batch Verification

In our inner-product DMCFE scheme in Sect. 5.3, if a receiver wants to verify that the combined functional decryption key $\mathsf{dk}_{\boldsymbol{y}}$ is generated correctly with respect to a vector $\boldsymbol{y}$, there is a more efficient way than verifying each sender's functional key share. The receiver can directly check the following equalities

$$e\left(\sum_{i=1}^{n} \mathsf{com}_{\mathsf{DMCFE},i,b} \cdot y_i, [1]_2\right) = e([\boldsymbol{v}_{\mathsf{DMCFE},b}^{\top}]_1, [\mathsf{dk}_b]_2)$$

for $b \in [2]$. When $\mathsf{dk}_{\boldsymbol{y}}$ is correct, the above equalities are equivalent to

$$\left[\sum_{i\in[n]} (\boldsymbol{v}_{\mathsf{DMCFE},b}^{\top} \cdot \boldsymbol{s}_{\mathsf{DMCFE},i}) \cdot y_i\right]_T = \left[\boldsymbol{v}_{\mathsf{DMCFE},b}^{\top} \cdot \left(\sum_{i\in[n]} \boldsymbol{s}_{\mathsf{DMCFE},i} \cdot y_i\right)\right]_T$$

for $b \in [2]$. If any equality does not hold, then dk_y is maliciously generated. This verification has perfect soundness under the condition that $(v_{\mathsf{DMCFE},b})_{b\in[2]} \in \mathbb{Z}_p^{2\times 2}$ are linearly independent. The verification time is $2n$ exponentiations and 6 pairings compared to $24n$ exponentiations for verifying each of n key shares. In a hybrid use, a receiver can first use this quick verification to see if dk_y is correct. If it is not the case, he can continue to verify each key share to identify malicious senders.

Similarly, for batch verification of n independent ciphertexts under the same label for a range $[0, 2^m - 1]$, $\mathsf{NIZK}_{\mathsf{Encrypt}}$ when instantiated with Bulletproof costs about 3 multi-exponentiations of size $3+2n$, a multi-exponentiation of size $2m + 3 + n(2\log_2\lceil m\rceil + 5)$, and $\mathcal{O}(n \cdot m)$ scalar operations.

6.2 Privacy Improvement with AoNE

The All-or-Nothing Encapsulation AoNE in [15] is an encryption which guarantees that a receiver can reveal either *all* encrypted messages under the same label of senders by collecting all their ciphertexts, or *nothing*. By adding a AoNE encryption layer on DSUM or DMCFE ciphertexts, the leakage from incomplete ciphertexts can be ruled out. Due to space constraints, we put an heuristic of applying AoNE to the verifiable DMCFE scheme while still preserving the efficiency of malicious sender identification in the full version [23].

6.3 Perspectives

Natural questions from our work include improving the static security of the verifiable DMCFE scheme for inner product and allowing dynamic join of new users as in [15]. Furthermore, obtaining practical overhead costs from verifiability for function-hiding DMCFE schemes is an interesting direction.

Acknowledgements. This work was supported in part by the France 2030 ANR Project ANR-22-PECY-003 SecureCompute and by Beyond5G, a project funded by the French government as part of the plan "France Relance".

References

1. Abdalla, M., Benhamouda, F., Gay, R.: From single-input to multi-client inner-product functional encryption. In: Galbraith, S.D., Moriai, S. (eds.) ASIACRYPT 2019. LNCS, vol. 11923, pp. 552–582. Springer, Cham (2019). https://doi.org/10.1007/978-3-030-34618-8_19
2. Abdalla, M., Benhamouda, F., Kohlweiss, M., Waldner, H.: Decentralizing inner-product functional encryption. In: Lin, D., Sako, K. (eds.) PKC 2019. LNCS, vol. 11443, pp. 128–157. Springer, Cham (2019). https://doi.org/10.1007/978-3-030-17259-6_5
3. Agrawal, S., Ganesh, C., Mohassel, P.: Non-interactive zero-knowledge proofs for composite statements. In: Shacham, H., Boldyreva, A. (eds.) CRYPTO 2018. LNCS, vol. 10993, pp. 643–673. Springer, Cham (2018). https://doi.org/10.1007/978-3-319-96878-0_22

4. Agrawal, S., Libert, B., Stehlé, D.: Fully secure functional encryption for inner products, from standard assumptions. In: Robshaw, M., Katz, J. (eds.) CRYPTO 2016. LNCS, vol. 9816, pp. 333–362. Springer, Heidelberg (2016). https://doi.org/10.1007/978-3-662-53015-3_12
5. Badrinarayanan, S., Goyal, V., Jain, A., Sahai, A.: Verifiable functional encryption. In: Cheon, J.H., Takagi, T. (eds.) ASIACRYPT 2016. LNCS, vol. 10032, pp. 557–587. Springer, Heidelberg (2016). https://doi.org/10.1007/978-3-662-53890-6_19
6. Bell, J., Gascón, A., Lepoint, T., Li, B., Meiklejohn, S., Raykova, M., Yun, C.: ACORN: input validation for secure aggregation. Cryptology ePrint Archive, Report 2022/1461 (2022). https://eprint.iacr.org/2022/1461
7. Blum, M., Feldman, P., Micali, S.: Non-interactive zero-knowledge and its applications (extended abstract). In: 20th ACM STOC, pp. 103–112. ACM Press, May 1988. https://doi.org/10.1145/62212.62222
8. Boneh, D., Sahai, A., Waters, B.: Functional encryption: definitions and challenges. In: Ishai, Y. (ed.) TCC 2011. LNCS, vol. 6597, pp. 253–273. Springer, Heidelberg (2011). https://doi.org/10.1007/978-3-642-19571-6_16
9. Bünz, B., Bootle, J., Boneh, D., Poelstra, A., Wuille, P., Maxwell, G.: Bulletproofs: short proofs for confidential transactions and more. In: 2018 IEEE Symposium on Security and Privacy, pp. 315–334. IEEE Computer Society Press, May 2018. https://doi.org/10.1109/SP.2018.00020
10. Castagnos, G., Catalano, D., Laguillaumie, F., Savasta, F., Tucker, I.: Two-party ECDSA from hash proof systems and efficient instantiations. In: Boldyreva, A., Micciancio, D. (eds.) CRYPTO 2019. LNCS, vol. 11694, pp. 191–221. Springer, Cham (2019). https://doi.org/10.1007/978-3-030-26954-8_7
11. Castagnos, G., Catalano, D., Laguillaumie, F., Savasta, F., Tucker, I.: Bandwidth-efficient threshold EC-DSA. In: Kiayias, A., Kohlweiss, M., Wallden, P., Zikas, V. (eds.) PKC 2020. LNCS, vol. 12111, pp. 266–296. Springer, Cham (2020). https://doi.org/10.1007/978-3-030-45388-6_10
12. Castagnos, G., Laguillaumie, F.: Linearly homomorphic encryption from DDH. In: Nyberg, K. (ed.) CT-RSA 2015. LNCS, vol. 9048, pp. 487–505. Springer, Cham (2015). https://doi.org/10.1007/978-3-319-16715-2_26
13. Castagnos, G., Laguillaumie, F., Tucker, I.: Practical fully secure unrestricted inner product functional encryption modulo p. In: Peyrin, T., Galbraith, S. (eds.) ASIACRYPT 2018. LNCS, vol. 11273, pp. 733–764. Springer, Cham (2018). https://doi.org/10.1007/978-3-030-03329-3_25
14. Chotard, J., Dufour Sans, E., Gay, R., Phan, D.H., Pointcheval, D.: Decentralized multi-client functional encryption for inner product. In: Peyrin, T., Galbraith, S. (eds.) ASIACRYPT 2018. LNCS, vol. 11273, pp. 703–732. Springer, Cham (2018). https://doi.org/10.1007/978-3-030-03329-3_24
15. Chotard, J., Dufour-Sans, E., Gay, R., Phan, D.H., Pointcheval, D.: Dynamic decentralized functional encryption. In: Micciancio, D., Ristenpart, T. (eds.) CRYPTO 2020. LNCS, vol. 12170, pp. 747–775. Springer, Cham (2020). https://doi.org/10.1007/978-3-030-56784-2_25
16. Couteau, G., Goudarzi, D., Klooß, M., Reichle, M.: Sharp: Short relaxed range proofs. In: Yin, H., Stavrou, A., Cremers, C., Shi, E. (eds.) ACM CCS 2022, pp. 609–622. ACM Press, November 2022. https://doi.org/10.1145/3548606.3560628
17. Couteau, G., Klooß, M., Lin, H., Reichle, M.: Efficient range proofs with transparent setup from bounded integer commitments. In: Canteaut, A., Standaert, F.-X. (eds.) EUROCRYPT 2021. LNCS, vol. 12698, pp. 247–277. Springer, Cham (2021). https://doi.org/10.1007/978-3-030-77883-5_9

18. Feige, U., Lapidot, D., Shamir, A.: Multiple non-interactive zero knowledge proofs based on a single random string (extended abstract). In: 31st FOCS. pp. 308–317. IEEE Computer Society Press, October 1990. https://doi.org/10.1109/FSCS.1990.89549
19. Girault, M., Poupard, G., Stern, J.: On the fly authentication and signature schemes based on groups of unknown order. J. Cryptol. **19**(4), 463–487 (2006). https://doi.org/10.1007/s00145-006-0224-0
20. Goldwasser, S., Gordon, S.D., Goyal, V., Jain, A., Katz, J., Liu, F.-H., Sahai, A., Shi, E., Zhou, H.-S.: Multi-input functional encryption. In: Nguyen, P.Q., Oswald, E. (eds.) EUROCRYPT 2014. LNCS, vol. 8441, pp. 578–602. Springer, Heidelberg (2014). https://doi.org/10.1007/978-3-642-55220-5_32
21. Gordon, S.D., Katz, J., Liu, F.H., Shi, E., Zhou, H.S.: Multi-input functional encryption. Cryptology ePrint Archive, Report 2013/774 (2013). https://eprint.iacr.org/2013/774
22. Libert, B., Ţiţiu, R.: Multi-client functional encryption for linear functions in the standard model from LWE. In: Galbraith, S.D., Moriai, S. (eds.) ASIACRYPT 2019. LNCS, vol. 11923, pp. 520–551. Springer, Cham (2019). https://doi.org/10.1007/978-3-030-34618-8_18
23. Nguyen, D.D., Phan, D.H., Pointcheval, D.: Verifiable decentralized multi-client functional encryption for inner product. Cryptology ePrint Archive, Paper 2023/268 (2023). https://eprint.iacr.org/2023/268, https://eprint.iacr.org/2023/268
24. Pointcheval, D., Stern, J.: Security proofs for signature schemes. In: Maurer, U. (ed.) EUROCRYPT 1996. LNCS, vol. 1070, pp. 387–398. Springer, Heidelberg (1996). https://doi.org/10.1007/3-540-68339-9_33
25. Shoup, V., Gennaro, R.: Securing threshold cryptosystems against chosen ciphertext attack. In: Nyberg, K. (ed.) EUROCRYPT 1998. LNCS, vol. 1403, pp. 1–16. Springer, Heidelberg (1998). https://doi.org/10.1007/BFb0054113

Registered ABE via Predicate Encodings

Ziqi Zhu[1], Kai Zhang[2], Junqing Gong[1,3](✉), and Haifeng Qian[1]

[1] East China Normal University, Shanghai, China
jqgong@sei.ecnu.edu.cn
[2] Shanghai University of Electric Power, Shanghai, China
[3] Shanghai Qi Zhi Institute, Shanghai, China

Abstract. This paper presents the first generic black-box construction of registered attribute-based encryption (Reg-ABE) via predicate encoding [TCC'14]. The generic scheme is based on k-Lin assumption in the prime-order bilinear group and implies the following concrete schemes that improve existing results:

- the first Reg-ABE scheme for span program in the *prime-order group*; prior work uses *composite-order group*;
- the first Reg-ABE scheme for zero inner-product predicate from *k-Lin assumption*; prior work relies on *generic group model (GGM)*;
- the first Reg-ABE scheme for *arithmetic branching program (ABP)* which has not been achieved previously.

Technically, we follow the blueprint of Hohenberger *et al.* [EUROCRYPT'23] but start from the prime-order dual-system ABE by Chen et al. [EUROCRYPT'15], which transforms a predicate encoding into an ABE. The proof follows the dual-system method in the context of Reg-ABE: we conceptually consider helper keys as secret keys; furthermore, malicious public keys are handled via pairing-based quasi-adaptive non-interactive zero-knowledge argument by Kiltz and Wee [EUROCRYPT'15].

Keywords: Attribute-based encryption · Black-box construction · Dual-system method · Key escrow problem · Prime-order bilinear group

1 Introduction

Registered attribute-based encryption (Reg-ABE) [23] is an emerging primitive that extends attribute-based encryption (ABE) [21,33] to avoid key escrow issue. Conceptually, this is an extension of registration-based encryption (RBE) [13]. A Reg-ABE for predicate $P : X \times Y \to \{0,1\}$ is established by publishing a common reference string crs. A user can generate his/her own key pair $(\mathsf{pk}, \mathsf{sk})$ locally and register (pk, y) for some $y \in Y$ into the system. The registration is carried out by the curator in a public and deterministic manner, and will produce a master public key mpk for encryption as traditional ABE. The user can decrypt a ciphertext for $x \in X$ using his/her sk when $P(x, y) = 1$ along with so-called

J. Guo and R. Steinfeld (Eds.): ASIACRYPT 2023, LNCS 14442, pp. 66–97, 2023.
https://doi.org/10.1007/978-981-99-8733-7_3

helper key hsk obtained from the curator during registration phase. Furthermore, each registration might trigger an update to all users' helper keys.

Existing Reg-ABE can be classified into two classes: (1) Early work [6,13, 14,20] uses non-black-box technique based on garbling scheme [4,37] or indistinguishable obfuscation (iO) [11,25]; while (2) recent work [7,9,16,23] uses black-box technique based on concrete assumptions in bilinear group or integral lattice.

This work explores a *systematic* way to build pairing-based Reg-ABE in a black-box fashion: we want to cover a large set of functionalities in a *unified* framework. All prior work [9,16,23] focused on a single *specific* predicate. See Fig. 1 for more details.

1.1 Results

In this work, we propose a generic Reg-ABE scheme via predicate encoding [5,36]. It works with prime-order bilinear group and the security is based on the well-known k-Lin assumption for $k \geq 1$. Given our knowledge of existing predicate encoding [5,36], this implies:

- the first Reg-ABE scheme for span program in the *prime-order* group; this improves the result of [23] which supports the same predicate in *composite-order* groups;
- the first Reg-ABE scheme for zero inner-product predicate from *standard assumption* (k-Lin); this *partially* resolved the open problem posted in [9]: the RIPE in [9] relies on generic group model (GGM) but achieves attribute-hiding; note that, even without attribute-hiding, the RIPE [9] does not seem to get rid of GGM;
- the first Reg-ABE scheme for arithmetic branching program (ABP) that goes *beyond span program.*

See Fig. 1 for more details. We also highlight more implications thanks to the result in [2] and more subsequent work on predicate encodings: we are able to come up with different variants of all Reg-ABE schemes mentioned above, such as dual of policy (i.e., "key-policy vs ciphertext-policy" transformation) and composition of policies (i.e., disjunction, conjunction and negation of predicates).

Strategy. We follow the blueprint by [23] and focus on a weaker primitive called *slotted Reg-ABE.* A slotted Reg-ABE scheme for $L \in \mathbb{N}$ slots (L-slot Reg-ABE for short) is similar to the standard Reg-ABE except that the curator is replaced by an *aggregator* who simply collects all L public keys and generate mpk and hsk's *once for all.* Here, the aggregator is stateless while the curator is stateful which allows us to register the L public keys in a one-by-one fashion. By this, we do not worry about update operations for now which can be handled by so-called "powers-of-two" approach by [23]. In particular, [23] shows that one can use the approach to generically transform any slotted Reg-ABE to a (full-fledged) Reg-ABE while preserving basic features such as predicates, assumptions, etc. In this work, we give a pairing-based slotted Reg-ABE via predicate encodings

reference	functionality	assumption
[16]	Equality Check (IBE)	prime, q-type/DBDH
[23]	Span Program	composite, static
[9]	Inner-Product Predicate †	prime, GGM
full paper	Span Program	prime ✓, k-Lin ✓
full paper	Inner-Product Predicate	prime, k-Lin ✓
§ 4	Arithmetic Branching Program ✓	prime ✓, k-Lin ✓

Fig. 1. Summary of black-box construction of pairing-based Reg-ABE. In the column **assumption**, "composite" and "prime" indicate composite- and prime-order bilinear groups respectively; "static" means a specific set of static assumptions, "GGM" stands for generic group model; for k-Lin assumption, we allow $k \geq 1$. We use ✓ to highlight the advantage of our scheme over prior ones supporting the same predicate.
† [9] also achieves attribute-hiding while ours in the full paper does not; we note that, without considering attribute-hiding, their scheme does not seem to be provably secure under standard assumption.

from k-Lin assumption. We provide a detailed technical overview of our slotted Reg-ABE scheme in the next two subsections.

Remarks. Before we proceed, we remark that our Reg-ABE inherits several restrictions from [23], compared with prior RBE [6,7,13,14,20]. We highlight two of them:

- Our Reg-ABE only accommodates *bounded number of users*, the size of crs depends on the number of users. Note that, almost all known RBE schemes supporting unbounded number of users [6,13,14,20] require non-black-box techniques; the only exception is the recent LWE-based scheme by Döttling *et al.* [7].
- Our Reg-ABE requires an explicit verification of public key before registration, only those "valid" public keys can be registered to the system, see Sect. 2.2. This is introduced by [23] to handle malicious public keys, see Sect. 1.3, paragraph **Handle Malicious pk**; however, this is not needed in prior RBE schemes.

It is an interesting open problem to explore whether these restrictions or relaxations are necessary to support expressive predicates. See Sect. 1.4 for more discussions and open problems.

1.2 Overview of Slotted ABE

In this overview, we explain our construction of slotted Reg-ABE from predicate encodings. A L-slotted Reg-ABE for $P : X \times Y \to \{0,1\}$ is governed by a crs; given $(\mathsf{pk}_1, y_1), \ldots, (\mathsf{pk}_L, y_L)$ and crs, an aggregator can generate a master public key mpk for encryption. For correctness, we require that one can use sk_i, the corresponding secret key of pk_i, to decrypt when $P(x, y_i) = 1$ where x is associated with the ciphertext. For security, when sk_i is leaked, we require that $P(x, y_i) = 0$; when sk_i is secret, it is allowed to have $P(x, y_i) = 1$; here we neglect the case where pk_i is malicious for now and handle this case later on.

Starting Point: Predicate Encoding and Dual-System ABE. Let lower-case boldface denote *row* vectors and upper-case boldface denote matrices. We first review the notion of predicate encoding and dual-system ABE [5,36] with the notation in [1,2]. A predicate $P : X \times Y \to \{0,1\}$ has an (n, n_c, n_k)-predicate encoding (PE) if: For all $x \in X$, $y \in Y$, one can efficiently and deterministically find

$$\mathbf{C}_x \in \mathbb{Z}_p^{n \times n_c},\ \mathbf{K}_y \in \mathbb{Z}_p^{n \times n_k},\ \mathbf{a}_y \in \mathbb{Z}_p^{1 \times n_k},\ \mathbf{d}_{x,y} \in \mathbb{Z}_p^{n_c + n_k}$$

that forms $\mathbf{M}_{x,y} = \begin{pmatrix} \mathbf{a}_y & \mathbf{0}_{n_c} \\ \mathbf{K}_y & \mathbf{C}_x \end{pmatrix}$ such that

- when $P(x, y) = 1$, we have $\mathbf{M}_{x,y}\mathbf{d}_{x,y}^\top = \mathbf{e}_1^\top$;
- when $P(x, y) = 0$, we have $\{x, y, \alpha, (\alpha \| \mathbf{w})\mathbf{M}_{x,y}\} \approx_s \{x, y, \alpha, (0 \| \mathbf{w})\mathbf{M}_{x,y}\}$ where $\mathbf{w} \leftarrow \mathbb{Z}_p^n$.

In the literature, they are called α-reconstruction and α-privacy which are used to ensure correctness and security of ABE, respectively. (For the reader who is familiar with the notations in [5], $\mathbf{C}_x, \mathbf{K}_y, \mathbf{a}_y$ correspond to $\mathsf{sE}, \mathsf{rE}, \mathsf{kE}$, and $\mathbf{d}_{x,y}$ corresponds to sD, rD.) Let $\mathbb{G}$ be a finite cyclic group with generator g and denote $[x] = g^x$, we will start from the following one-key ABE scheme:

$$\begin{aligned} \mathsf{mpk} &: [\mathbf{w}, \alpha]; \\ \mathsf{ct}_x &: [s, s\mathbf{w}\mathbf{C}_x], [s\alpha] \cdot \mathsf{m}; \\ \mathsf{sk}_y &: \alpha\mathbf{a}_y + \mathbf{w}\mathbf{K}_y. \end{aligned} \tag{1}$$

Decryption relies on the following equation:

$$(s \cdot (\alpha\mathbf{a}_y + \mathbf{w}\mathbf{K}_y) \| s\mathbf{w}\mathbf{C}_x)\mathbf{d}_{x,y}^\top = (s\alpha \| s\mathbf{w})\mathbf{M}_{x,y}\mathbf{d}_{x,y}^\top = (s\alpha \| s\mathbf{w})\mathbf{e}_1^\top = s\alpha \tag{2}$$

where the second equation uses the α-reconstruction of PE; security follows from the α-privacy of PE. The actual proof needs a composite-order group with subgroup decision assumption; we omit the details.

Zero-Slot Scheme. The left-hand side of Eq. (2) immediately inspires the following (oversimplified) Reg-ABE scheme where we can embed y to mpk so that an encryption under x reveals m if and only $P(x, y) = 1$. We call this *zero-slot* scheme since there is no user to register at all.

$$\begin{aligned} \mathsf{crs} &: [\mathbf{w}, \alpha]; \\ \mathsf{mpk}_y &: [\alpha\mathbf{a}_y + \mathbf{w}\mathbf{K}_y, \mathbf{w}, \alpha]; \\ \mathsf{ct}_x &: [s\alpha\mathbf{a}_y + s\mathbf{w}\mathbf{K}_y, s\mathbf{w}\mathbf{C}_x], [s\alpha] \cdot \mathsf{m}. \end{aligned} \tag{3}$$

Observe that the structure of ct_x is quite similar to the left-hand side of (2); conceptually, we embed the *decryption procedure* (not just the functional key sk_y in scheme (1)) into mpk. Decryption uses the same equation as in scheme (1), i.e., Eq. (2). The security follows from the α-privacy as well as DDH assumption. In particular, the proof works in two steps: DDH assumption allows us to change the ciphertext ct_x to

$$[\tilde{\alpha}\mathbf{a}_y + \tilde{\mathbf{w}}\mathbf{K}_y, \tilde{\mathbf{w}}\mathbf{C}_x], [\tilde{\alpha}] \cdot \mathsf{m}$$

where $\tilde{\alpha}, \tilde{\mathbf{w}}$ are uniform and independent of $\alpha, \mathbf{w}$; then privacy applies w.r.t. $\tilde{\alpha}$ and $\tilde{\mathbf{w}}$. The proof is quite simple due to the fact that we actually work in the one-key setting.

From Zero to One. We proceed to modify the zero-slot scheme to allow user registration. As [23], the user will generate an ElGamal key pair: $\mathsf{pk} = [u]$ and $\mathsf{sk} = u$ where u is uniformly sampled by the user himself/herself. To register this user, we simply replace α with $\alpha + u$ in mpk_y and ct_x. This means that, in ct_x, we actually encrypt $[s\alpha]$ by ElGamal encryption under pk; the user who holds $\mathsf{sk} = u$ can recover the ciphertext in zero-slot scheme (3). In more details, the one-slot scheme is

$$\begin{aligned} \mathsf{crs} &: [\mathbf{w}, \alpha]; \\ \mathsf{pk}, \mathsf{sk} &: [u], u; \\ \mathsf{mpk}_{\mathsf{pk},y} &: [(\alpha + u)\mathbf{a}_y + \mathbf{w}\mathbf{K}_y, \mathbf{w}, \alpha]; \\ \mathsf{ct}_x &: [s, s(\alpha + u)\mathbf{a}_y + s\mathbf{w}\mathbf{K}_y, s\mathbf{w}\mathbf{C}_x], [s\alpha] \cdot \mathsf{m}. \end{aligned} \tag{4}$$

Here we add $[s]$ for correctness. Clearly, one can publicly and deterministically compute $\mathsf{mpk}_{\mathsf{pk},y}$ from $\mathsf{crs}, \mathsf{pk}$ and y; this is an important feature for Reg-ABE. For security, we consider two cases:

- when u is leaked, we require that $P(x, y) = 0$, the security reduced to that for zero-slot scheme (3);
- when u is secret, we allow that $P(x, y) = 1$, the security relies on the fact that $[s\alpha]$ is hidden by $[su]$ which is basically the security of ElGamal encryption.

A caveat is that we should also allow pk to be maliciously generated by the adversary; this is a stronger attack than the first case and *cannot* be captured by the current scheme; we will defer the solution to the end of this overview. Before we proceed, we mention that an alternative way to implement our strategy is to embed $[u]$ as follows:

$$\begin{aligned} \mathsf{mpk}_{\mathsf{pk},y} &: [\alpha\mathbf{a}_y + \mathbf{w}\mathbf{K}_y, \mathbf{w}, \alpha + u]; \\ \mathsf{ct}_x &: [s, s\alpha\mathbf{a}_y + s\mathbf{w}\mathbf{K}_y, s\mathbf{w}\mathbf{C}_x], [s(\alpha + u)] \cdot \mathsf{m}. \end{aligned}$$

They are basically equivalent. We will work with (4) that makes the follow-up discussion simpler.

From One to Many: Observation. We follow the strategy of [9,23] to build L-slot scheme based on one-slot scheme that allows us to register $(\mathsf{pk}_1, y_1), \ldots, (\mathsf{pk}_L, y_L)$ for a priori known $L \in \mathbb{N}$: we generate L parallel one-slot schemes, register (pk_j, y_j) to j-th instance of one-slot scheme (or slot j for short) and "add" the corresponding $\mathsf{mpk}_{\mathsf{pk}_j, y_j}$ and ciphertext in a "component-wise" way. In particular, the scheme is as follows:

$$\begin{aligned}
\mathsf{crs} &: [\mathbf{w}_j, \alpha_j], \forall j; \qquad (5)\\
\mathsf{pk}_i &: [u_i];\\
\mathsf{sk}_i &: u_i;\\
\mathsf{mpk} &: [\textstyle\sum_j ((\alpha_j + u_j)\mathbf{a}_{y_j} + \mathbf{w}_j \mathbf{K}_{y_j}), \sum_j \mathbf{w}_j, \sum_j \alpha_j];\\
\mathsf{ct}_x &: [s, s\textstyle\sum_j ((\alpha_j + u_j)\mathbf{a}_{y_j} + \mathbf{w}_j \mathbf{K}_{y_j}), s\sum_j \mathbf{w}_j \mathbf{C}_x], [s\sum_j \alpha_j] \cdot \mathsf{m};
\end{aligned}$$

where j ranges over $1, \ldots, L$ and those terms with subscript j correspond to slot j. We encounter the same issue as in [23]: even with $\mathsf{sk}_i = u_i$ and $P(x, y_i) = 1$ for some i, we still cannot decrypt successfully as before due to the "add" operation and the solution is to issue an extra helper key hsk_i for each slot $i \in [L]$. Omitting the term with message m and fixing $i \in [L]$, the ciphertext is the "sum" of two parts:

$$\begin{aligned}
&[s, s((\alpha_i + u_i)\mathbf{a}_{y_i} + \mathbf{w}_i \mathbf{K}_{y_i}), s\mathbf{w}_i \mathbf{C}_x], && \text{// local part;}\\
&[s, s\textstyle\sum_{j \neq i} ((\alpha_j + u_j)\mathbf{a}_{y_j} + \mathbf{w}_j \mathbf{K}_{y_j}), s\sum_{j \neq i} \mathbf{w}_j \mathbf{C}_x], && \text{// mixed part.}
\end{aligned}$$

The local part corresponds to one-slot scheme for slot i and can be handled via sk_i as before, i.e., scheme (4); the mixed part involves terms from all other slots. The helper key hsk_i is designed to remove the mixed part.

From One to Many: Helper Keys via Pairing. A naive solution is to set

$$\mathsf{hsk}_i : \textstyle\sum_{j \neq i} ((\alpha_j + u_j)\mathbf{a}_{y_j} + \mathbf{w}_j \mathbf{K}_{y_j}), \sum_{j \neq i} \mathbf{w}_j.$$

This definitely works but may suffer from "mix-and-match" attack. As an example, for $L = 3$, we have:

$$\mathsf{hsk}_2 - \mathsf{hsk}_1 + \mathsf{hsk}_3 = 2((\alpha_1 + u_1)\mathbf{a}_{y_1} + \mathbf{w}_1 \mathbf{K}_{y_1}, \mathbf{w}_1)$$

this allows user in slot 1 to recover α_1 since u_1 is known to this user and $\mathsf{hsk}_1, \mathsf{hsk}_2, \mathsf{hsk}_3$ should be public. Therefore, the scheme is entirely broken. We fix the issue using the idea of achieving collusion resistance in ABE: we introduce different random coins into different hsk_i which avoids the above attack; this requires bilinear group. Let $\mathbb{G}_1 = \langle g_1 \rangle, \mathbb{G}_2 = \langle g_2 \rangle$ be finite cyclic source groups of bilinear maps e and $\mathbb{G}_T$ be the target group. Write $[x]_1 = g_1^x, [x]_2 = g_2^x$. We embed mpk,ct_x in $\mathbb{G}_1$ and set hsk_i over $\mathbb{G}_2$ with random coin r_i:

$$\mathsf{hsk}_i : [r_i, r_i \textstyle\sum_{j \neq i} ((\alpha_j + u_j)\mathbf{a}_{y_j} + \mathbf{w}_j \mathbf{K}_{y_j}), r_i \sum_{j \neq i} \mathbf{w}_j]_2.$$

This is analogous to the secret key in ABE and helps to recover the local part of ct_x in the same form as before but over $\mathbb{G}_T$ with random coin sr_i instead of s:

$$[sr_i((\alpha_i + u_i)\mathbf{a}_{y_i} + \mathbf{w}_i\mathbf{K}_{y_i}), sr_i\mathbf{w}_i\mathbf{C}_x]_T$$

Then, decryption of one-slot scheme gives $[sr_i\alpha_i]_T$ when $P(x, y_i) = 1$. However, one cannot use this to carry message m: since α_i and r_i are fresh for each $i \in [L]$, we have to include terms $[sr_1\alpha_1]_T \cdot \mathsf{m}, \ldots, [sr_L\alpha_L]_T \cdot \mathsf{m}$ in ct_x for correctness, this further requires us to publish $[r_1\alpha_1]_T, \ldots, [r_L\alpha_L]_T$ in mpk, i.e., we have $|\mathsf{mpk}| = O(L)$, which is disallowed in Reg-ABE. A common trick in the context of ABE is sufficient to fix this: we will include term $[s\alpha]_T \cdot \mathsf{m}$ in ct_x as usual and connect α_i and α via term $[r_i\alpha_i + \alpha]_2$ in hsk_i. By this, we do not make any change to ct and user in slot i can compute

$$e([s]_1, [r_i\alpha_i + \alpha]_2) = [sr_i\alpha_i]_T \cdot [s\alpha]_T$$

which recovers m given $[sr_i\alpha_i]_T$ we computed before and $[s\alpha]_T \cdot \mathsf{m}$ in ct_x.

Summary. Putting all these together and writing α_j as v_j, we have the following scheme:

$$\begin{aligned} \mathsf{crs} &= [\alpha]_T, [v_j, \mathbf{w}_j]_1, \quad \forall j; \\ &\quad\; [r_i, r_iv_j, r_i\mathbf{w}_j, r_iv_i + \alpha]_2, \quad \forall i \neq j; \\ \mathsf{pk}_i &= [u_i]_1, [u_ir_j]_2, \quad \forall j \neq i; \\ \mathsf{sk}_i &= u_i; \\ \mathsf{mpk} &= [\textstyle\sum_j((v_j + u_j)\mathbf{a}_{y_j} + \mathbf{w}_j\mathbf{K}_{y_j}), \sum_j \mathbf{w}_j]_1, [\alpha]_T; \\ \mathsf{hsk}_i &= [r_i, r_i\textstyle\sum_{j\neq i}((v_j + u_j)\mathbf{a}_{y_j} + \mathbf{w}_j\mathbf{K}_{y_j}), r_i\sum_{j\neq i}\mathbf{w}_j, r_iv_i + \alpha]_2; \\ \mathsf{ct}_x &= [s, s\textstyle\sum_j((v_j + u_j)\mathbf{a}_{y_j} + \mathbf{w}_j\mathbf{K}_{y_j}), s\sum_j \mathbf{w}_j\mathbf{C}_x]_1, [s\alpha]_T \cdot \mathsf{m}. \end{aligned} \tag{6}$$

Here crs is constructed so that one can use it to generate mpk and $\mathsf{hsk}_1, \ldots, \mathsf{hsk}_L$ in a public way. To prove the security, we will need to embed (6) into composite-order group. We decide not to dive into details in the composite-order group and focus on prime-order scheme where we will handle malicious public key. Before that, we quickly mention the connect to broadcast encryption (BE) by Gentry and Waters [15]: neglecting all terms involving $\mathbf{w}_1, u_1, \ldots, \mathbf{w}_L, u_L$, the first row of crs is the master public key of BE, the second row of crs gives the secret keys for users $1, \ldots, L$ and ct_x is the BE ciphertext for set $[L]$. In another words, by introducing term $[r_i\alpha_i + \alpha]_2$ in hsk_i and crs in the previous paragraph, we actually employ Gentry-Waters BE [15] to reduce the size of ct_x and mpk from $O(L)$ to $O(1)$. Two recent results formally clarify the connection, see Sect. 1.4, paragraph **Concurrent Work**.

1.3 Final Slotted Reg-ABE in Prime-Order Group

Our final scheme is based on the prime-order version of scheme (6). We first explain how to get this prime-order scheme and then reach the final slotted Reg-ABE scheme with an additional concern on malicious public keys.

Prime-Order Scheme. Applying the "composite-order-to-prime-order" transformation in [5], we can get our scheme in the prime-order group. In more details, discarding all subscripts i and j, we do the following substitution with $\mathbf{A} \in \mathbb{Z}_p^{k\times(k+1)}$ and $\mathbf{B} \in \mathbb{Z}_p^{(k+1)\times k}$:

$$\alpha \in \mathbb{Z}_N,\ v \in \mathbb{Z}_N,\ \mathbf{w} \in \mathbb{Z}_N^n \mapsto \mathbf{k} \in \mathbb{Z}_p^{k+1},\ \mathbf{V} \in \mathbb{Z}_p^{(k+1)\times(k+1)},\ \mathbf{W} \in \mathbb{Z}_p^{(k+1)\times(k+1)n};$$

and

$$\begin{aligned}
[s]_1 \in \mathbb{G}_1, [r]_2 \in \mathbb{G}_2, [\alpha]_2 \in \mathbb{G}_2 &\mapsto [\mathbf{sA}]_1 \in \mathbb{G}_1^{1\times(k+1)}, [\mathbf{Br}^\top]_2 \in \mathbb{G}_2^{k+1}, [\mathbf{k}]_2 \in \mathbb{G}_2^{k+1}\\
[\alpha]_T \in \mathbb{G}_T, [s\alpha]_T \in \mathbb{G}_T &\mapsto [\mathbf{Ak}^\top]_T \in \mathbb{G}_T^k, [\mathbf{sAk}^\top]_T \in \mathbb{G}_T\\
[v]_1 \in \mathbb{G}_1, [\mathbf{w}]_1 \in \mathbb{G}_1^n &\mapsto [\mathbf{AV}]_1 \in \mathbb{G}_1^{k\times(k+1)}, [\mathbf{AW}]_1 \in \mathbb{G}_1^{k\times(k+1)n}\\
[sv]_1 \in \mathbb{G}_1, [s\mathbf{w}]_1 \in \mathbb{G}_1^n &\mapsto [\mathbf{sAV}]_1 \in \mathbb{G}_1^{1\times(k+1)}, [\mathbf{sAW}]_1 \in \mathbb{G}_1^{1\times(k+1)n}\\
[rv]_2 \in \mathbb{G}_2, [r\mathbf{w}]_2 \in \mathbb{G}_2^n &\mapsto [\mathbf{VBr}^\top]_2 \in \mathbb{G}_2^{k+1}, [\mathbf{W}(\mathbf{I}_n \otimes \mathbf{Br}^\top)]_2 \in \mathbb{G}_2^{(k+1)\times n}
\end{aligned}$$

Note that $u \in \mathbb{Z}_N$ is translated to $\mathbf{U} \in \mathbb{Z}_p^{(k+1)\times(k+1)}$ as $v \in \mathbb{Z}_N$ and each entry in $\mathbf{w}$ is actually treated as v too[1]. The proof is analogous to the dual-system proof for ABE [5,35,36]:

1. we switch $[\mathbf{sA}]_1$ to a random vector $[\mathbf{c}]_1$ over $\mathbb{G}_1$;
2. for $j = 1, \ldots, L$, we switch $[\mathbf{Br}_j^\top]_2$ to a random vector $[\mathbf{d}_j^\top]_2$ over $\mathbb{G}_2$ and make use of the entropy in $\mathbf{U}_j, \mathbf{V}_j, \mathbf{W}_j$ to argue the "partial" secrecy of $\mathbf{k}$ in term $\mathbf{V}_j\mathbf{Br}_j^\top + \mathbf{k}^\top$.

Recall that we use the idea of collusion resistance to build $\mathsf{hsk}_1, \ldots, \mathsf{hsk}_L$. Therefore, in the proof, we conceptually view $\mathsf{hsk}_1, \ldots, \mathsf{hsk}_L$ as secret keys in ABE and exactly follow the dual-system method. Of course, the actual proof makes changes in crs instead of $\mathsf{hsk}_1, \ldots, \mathsf{hsk}_L$ since aggregation is public and the adversary with crs along with a series of public keys can compute them by itself, see Sect. 2 for formal definition.

Handle Malicious pk. We finally mention a subtlety in the proof. Recall that, in Sect. 1.2, we neglect the case where pk is malicious. In this case, the first step mentioned in the proof overview can not go through since the simulator does not know $\mathsf{sk} = \mathbf{U}$. In particular, the simulator takes $[\mathbf{A}, \mathbf{t}]_1$ as input where $\mathbf{t} = \mathbf{sA}$ or $\mathbf{t} = \mathbf{c}$ and need to simulate the term $[\mathbf{sAU}]_1$ (or $[\mathbf{cU}]_1$) appeared in the challenge ciphertext where $[\mathbf{AU}]_1$ is the public key registered by the adversary;

[1] Let $\mathbf{w} = (w_1, \ldots, w_n)$. With the same substitution $w_i \in \mathbb{Z}_N \mapsto \mathbf{W}_i \in \mathbb{Z}_p^{(k+1)\times(k+1)}$ and

$$[sw_i]_1 \mapsto [\mathbf{sAW}_i]_1, \quad [rw_i]_2 \mapsto [\mathbf{W}_i\mathbf{Br}^\top]_2,$$

we have

$$\begin{aligned}
[s\mathbf{w}]_1 &= [sw_1\|\ldots\|sw_n]_1 = [\mathbf{sAW}_1\|\cdots\|\mathbf{sAW}_n]_1 = [\mathbf{sA}(\mathbf{W}_1\|\cdots\|\mathbf{W}_n)]_1\\
[r\mathbf{w}]_2 &= [rw_1\|\ldots\|rw_n]_2 = [\mathbf{W}_1\mathbf{Br}^\top\|\cdots\|\mathbf{W}_n\mathbf{Br}^\top]_2 = [(\mathbf{W}_1\|\cdots\|\mathbf{W}_n)(\mathbf{I}_n \otimes \mathbf{Br}^\top)]_2
\end{aligned}$$

where we obtain $\mathbf{W} = (\mathbf{W}_1\|\cdots\|\mathbf{W}_n) \in \mathbb{Z}_p^{(k+1)\times(k+1)n}$.

clearly, this is infeasible without $\mathbf{U}$. Our solution is to allow the simulator to "program" $[\mathbf{sA}]_1$ (or $[\mathbf{c}]_1$) into crs so that the user is forced to compute $[\mathbf{sAU}]_1$ (or $[\mathbf{cU}]_1$) for us when the user submitted pk. In particular, we make two changes to the prime-order scheme.

1. We introduce an extra term $[\mathbf{R}]_1$ where $\mathbf{R} \leftarrow \mathbb{Z}_p^{(k+2)\times(k+1)}$ to crs; user's public key also includes an extra term $[\mathbf{RU}]_1$. In the reduction, we program

$$\mathbf{R} = \widetilde{\mathbf{R}} \begin{pmatrix} \mathbf{t} \\ \mathbf{I}_{k+1} \end{pmatrix}, \quad \widetilde{\mathbf{R}} \leftarrow \mathbb{Z}_p^{(k+2)\times(k+2)}$$

   In both cases, $\widetilde{\mathbf{R}}$ ensures that $\mathbf{R}$ is random. Receiving $\mathsf{pk} = [\mathbf{T} = \mathbf{AU}, \mathbf{Q} = \mathbf{RU}]_1$, we use $[\mathbf{e}_1\widetilde{\mathbf{R}}^{-1}\mathbf{Q}]_1 = [\mathbf{tU}]_1$ to simulate the ciphertext, which is either $[\mathbf{sAU}]_1$ or $[\mathbf{cU}]_1$ as required.
2. Since the adversary can give an inconsistent pk where $\mathbf{T} = \mathbf{AU}$ and $\mathbf{Q} = \mathbf{RU}'$ with $\mathbf{U} \neq \mathbf{U}'$. We additionally ask for a proof π showing

$$\begin{pmatrix} \mathbf{T} \\ \mathbf{Q} \end{pmatrix} \in \mathsf{span} \begin{pmatrix} \mathbf{A} \\ \mathbf{R} \end{pmatrix}$$

   This ensures $\mathbf{U} = \mathbf{U}'$. One can generate the proof via any non-interactive zero-knowledge proof/argument (NIZK) for sufficiently large language such as Groth-Sahai Proof [22]. In this work, we choose to employ quasi-adaptive NIZK (QA-NIZK) for linear space from pairing [26] due to the fact that $[\mathbf{A}]_1$ and $[\mathbf{R}]_1$ (i.e., the language) are determined at a quite early stage. We mention that we need a stronger unbounded simulation soundness [19,31] where the adversary is given $\mathbf{A}$ and $\mathbf{R}$ "in the clear"; we leave more details to Sect. 2.4.

However, the additional term $[\mathbf{Q}]_1$ leaks almost all information of $\mathbf{U}$, which is crucial for the security when the user is honest. To fix the issue, we employ a wider $\mathbf{A}$ and $\mathbf{R}$ along with a higher $\mathbf{U}$ so that given $\mathbf{AU}, \mathbf{RU}$, we still have left-over entropy in $\mathbf{cU}$ for the security; see Sect. 3.4 for more details. We finally note that our method is indeed inspired by the idea of [23] in the composite-order group, however, this is not derived from theirs via a composite-order-to-prime-order transformation.

1.4 Discussions

On Hohenberger et al.'s Reg-ABE [23]. The recent work [23] showed a registered CP-ABE for span program and mentioned that "... if we ignore the slot-specific ciphertext component, then the structure of the ciphertexts in our scheme coincides with those in the ciphertext policy ABE scheme of Lewko et al. [30]." But the connection with predicate encoding is not as straightforward as stated. For $S \subseteq [n]$, let us define $\mathbf{x} = (x_1, \ldots, x_n) \in \{0,1\}^n$ where $x_i = 1$ for $i \in S$ and $x_i = 0$ for $i \notin S$. [23] uses the following unusual structure to encode

S in mpk and ct (Note that we are not showing mpk and ct *accurately*, there are some minor differences.):

$$\mathsf{mpk} : \{(1 - x_i)w_i\}_{i\in[n]} \quad \text{and} \quad \mathsf{ct} : \{\alpha_i + (1 - x_i)w_i s_i, s_i\}_{i\in[n]}$$

where $\mathbf{w} = (w_1, \ldots, w_n)$ is the public parameter and α_i are secret sharings of a secret value according to the policy that associated with ct. The key point is the fact that term $\alpha_i + (1 - x_i)w_i s_i$ in ct encodes both the policy (via α_i's) and set (i.e., x_i); this is not the case in predicate encodings where we encode them separately (due to the syntax of standard ABE). However, a simple calculation shows that

$$\alpha_i + (1 - x_i)w_i s_i = (\alpha_i + w_i s_i) - (x_i w_i s_i), \quad \forall i \in [n] \tag{7}$$

namely we can easily "unpack" ct as

$$\mathsf{ct}' : s_i, \{\alpha_i + w_i s_i\}_{i\in[n]}, \{x_i w_i s_i\}_{i\in[n]}$$

where the two terms encode policy (via α_i) and set separately; in fact, they are exactly the encoding for CP-ABE presented in [5, Appendix A.5] and equation (7) is actually the first step of *decryption*. This clarifies the connection between ours and [23]; this also suggests a possibility of optimizing the efficiency. Roughly, this requires some kind of pre-processing property for predicate encoding and we leave this as a future work.

Towards (Weak) Attribute-Hiding. As we have mentioned in Sect. 1.1, the RIPE proposed in [9] achieves attribute-hiding which roughly means that x associated with the ciphertext is also hidden from the adversary. Given the notion of attribute-hiding predicate encoding formulated in [5], it is expected that our scheme can also support *weak* attribute-hiding (as the dual-system ABE via predicate encoding in [5]). However, we argue that this is not straight-forward as expected: in order to remove the mixed part from the ciphertext using helper key, the decryption procedure needs to know x to get $\mathbf{C}_x$, see scheme (6) and Sect. 3.1; therefore, even with attribute-hiding predicate encoding, our Reg-ABE does not achieve (weak) attribute-hiding. It is still open to get (weak) attribute-hiding *under standard assumption* such as k-Lin; note that the Reg-IPE by [9] indeed achieves attribute-hiding but in the *generic group model*.

More Expressive Reg-ABE from Pair Encoding. Pair Encoding proposed by Attrapadung [3] is a more powerful tool to build ABE; for instance, this allows us to support multi-use of attribute and uniform computation such as DFA. However, our scheme can not work with pair encoding in a straight-forward way. We provide a quick discussion: Compared with the predicate encoding whose security is information-theoretical, the security of pair encoding (especially, for those predicates we just mentioned) is defined computationally when encodings w.r.t. ciphertext and key (analogous to $\mathbf{C}_x$ and $\mathbf{K}_y$) are encoded over $\mathbb{G}_1$ and $\mathbb{G}_2$, respectively. However, in the context of our Reg-ABE scheme, we encode both of them over $\mathbb{G}_1$ and thus all existing pair encodings with computational security should be revised. We leave this as a future work to adapt the notion of pair encoding and build Reg-ABE from this. Furthermore, we point out that the use of pair encoding may introduce strong assumptions such as q-type assumption. To obtain those functionalities and properties we mentioned at the beginning under standard assumptions, more work will be needed to adapt specialized solutions for ABE such as [17,18,29,32] to the context of Reg-ABE.

Concurrent Work. As an independent work, Freitag *et al.* [10] proposed a Reg-ABE scheme for arbitrary circuit families from witness encryption (WE) [12] and newly proposed function-binding hash function. Given the WE in [34], the scheme can be based on (evasive) LWE. In contract to our work and the pairing-based construction in [23], this construction is more like iO-based Reg-ABE in [23]: it enjoys transparent setup, supports unbounded number of users. However, it only achieves a weaker notion of selective-policy security without corruption in the standard model; the restriction on corruption can be removed in the random oracle model. Furthermore, this work also pointed out that Reg-ABE implies flexible/distributed broadcast encryption. Applying this observation, we mention that our Reg-ABE scheme implies the recent distributed broadcast encryption based on k-Lin assumption [28]; their another construction based on DBHE assumption [28] does not seem to be relevant to our Reg-ABE scheme.

Organization. Our paper is organized as follows: We review some background knowledge in Sect. 2. Section 3 presents our slotted Reg-ABE via predicate encoding, this readily implies full-fledged Reg-ABE. We show the first slotted Reg-ABE for ABP in Sect. 4 and more concrete instantiations in the full paper.

2 Preliminaries

Notations. For a finite set S, we use $s \leftarrow S$ to denote the procedure of sampling s from S uniformly. For an ordered list or array $\mathcal{L}$, we use $|\mathcal{L}|$ to denote its size (i.e., the number of entries in the list) and use $\mathcal{L}[i]$ to refer to its i-th entry. When $i > |\mathcal{L}|$ or $i < 1$, we define $\mathcal{L}[i] = \perp$; when we append x to $\mathcal{L}$, we set $\mathcal{L}[|\mathcal{L}|+1] = x$. We use $\star$ as wildcard. Let $\approx_s$ (resp. $\approx_c$) stand for two distributions being statistically (resp. computationally) indistinguishable. We use lower-case boldface to denote *row* vectors (e.g., $\mathbf{a}$) and upper-case boldface to denote matrices (e.g. $\mathbf{M}$). We let $\mathbf{e}_1 = (1, 0, \ldots, 0)$ of proper dimension (which is clear from the context) and use "$\|$" to denote vector or matrix concatenation (e.g. $(\mathbf{A}\|\mathbf{B})$).

Kronecker Product. Let $\mathbb{F}$ be a field. The *Kronecker Product* for matrices $\mathbf{A} = (a_{i,j}) \in \mathbb{F}^{\ell \times m}$ and $\mathbf{B} \in \mathbb{F}^{n \times p}$ is

$$\mathbf{A} \otimes \mathbf{B} = (a_{i,j}\mathbf{B}) = \begin{pmatrix} a_{1,1}\mathbf{B} \cdots a_{1,m}\mathbf{B} \\ \vdots \qquad \vdots \\ a_{\ell,1}\mathbf{B} \ldots a_{\ell,m}\mathbf{B} \end{pmatrix} \in \mathbb{F}^{\ell n \times mp}. \tag{8}$$

For matrices $\mathbf{A}, \mathbf{B}, \mathbf{C}, \mathbf{D}$ of proper sizes, we have $(\mathbf{A} \otimes \mathbf{B})(\mathbf{C} \otimes \mathbf{D}) = \mathbf{AC} \otimes \mathbf{BD}$.

2.1 Prime-Order Bilinear Groups

Assume an efficient algorithm $\mathcal{G}$ that takes as input a security parameter 1^λ and outputs $\mathbb{G} := (p, \mathbb{G}_1, \mathbb{G}_2, \mathbb{G}_T, e)$. Here $\mathbb{G}_1$, $\mathbb{G}_2$ and $\mathbb{G}_T$ are cyclic groups of prime order p, $e : \mathbb{G}_1 \times \mathbb{G}_2 \to \mathbb{G}_T$ is a non-degenerate bilinear map, and all group operations and bilinear map are efficient. Let $\mathbb{G}_1 = \langle g_1 \rangle$, $\mathbb{G}_2 = \langle g_2 \rangle$ and $g_T = e(g_1, g_2)$, we employ *implicit representation* of group elements: for a matrix $\mathbf{M} = (m_{ij})$ over $\mathbb{Z}_p$, define $[\mathbf{M}]_s = g_s^{\mathbf{M}} = (g_s^{m_{ij}})$ for all $s \in \{1, 2, T\}$; given $[\mathbf{A}]_1, [\mathbf{B}]_2$, we write $e([\mathbf{A}]_1, [\mathbf{B}]_2) = [\mathbf{AB}]_T$. We review *matrix Diffie-Hellman (MDDH) assumption* [8]; it is shown that it is implied by k-Lin [8].

Assumption 1 (**(k, ℓ, d)-MDDH over $\mathbb{G}_s$, $s \in \{1, 2\}$**). *Let $k, \ell, d \in \mathbb{N}$ with $k < \ell$. We say that the (k, ℓ, d)-MDDH assumption holds in $\mathbb{G}_s$ if for all PPT adversaries $\mathcal{A}$, the following advantage function is negligible in λ.*

$$\mathsf{Adv}^{\mathrm{MDDH}}_{\mathcal{A},s,k,\ell,d}(\lambda) = \big| \Pr[\mathcal{A}(\mathbb{G}, [\mathbf{M}]_s, [\mathbf{SM}]_s) = 1] - \Pr[\mathcal{A}(\mathbb{G}, [\mathbf{M}]_s, [\mathbf{U}]_s) = 1] \big|$$

where $\mathbb{G} := (p, \mathbb{G}_1, \mathbb{G}_2, \mathbb{G}_T, e) \leftarrow \mathcal{G}(1^\lambda)$, $\mathbf{M} \leftarrow \mathbb{Z}_p^{k \times \ell}$, $\mathbf{S} \leftarrow \mathbb{Z}_p^{d \times k}$ *and* $\mathbf{U} \leftarrow \mathbb{Z}_p^{d \times \ell}$.

2.2 Slotted Registered Attribute-Based Encryption

We review the notion of *slotted* registered attribute-based encryption (Reg-ABE) adapted from [23]. The formal definition of Reg-ABE can be found in the full paper along with a brief overview of "slotted Reg-ABE $\Longrightarrow$ Reg-ABE".

Algorithms. A slotted registered attribute-based encryption (Reg-ABE) for predicate $P : X \times Y \to \{0, 1\}$ consists of six efficient algorithms:

- $\mathsf{Setup}(1^\lambda, P, 1^L) \to \mathsf{crs}$: It takes as input the security parameter 1^λ, description of predicate P and the upper bound 1^L of the number of slots, outputs a common reference string crs.
- $\mathsf{Gen}(\mathsf{crs}, i) \to (\mathsf{pk}_i, \mathsf{sk}_i)$: It takes as input crs and slot number $i \in [L]$, outputs key pair $(\mathsf{pk}_i, \mathsf{sk}_i)$.
- $\mathsf{Ver}(\mathsf{crs}, i, \mathsf{pk}_i) \to 0/1$: It takes as input $\mathsf{crs}, i, \mathsf{pk}_i$ and outputs a bit indicating whether pk_i is valid.
- $\mathsf{Agg}(\mathsf{crs}, (\mathsf{pk}_i, y_i)_{i \in [L]}) \to (\mathsf{mpk}, (\mathsf{hsk}_j)_{j \in [L]})$: It takes as input crs and a series of pk_i with $y_i \in Y$ for all $i \in [L]$, outputs master public key mpk and a series of helper keys hsk_j for all $j \in [L]$. This algorithm is deterministic.

- $\mathsf{Enc}(\mathsf{mpk}, x, \mathsf{m}) \to \mathsf{ct}$: It takes as input mpk, $x \in X$ and message m, outputs a ciphertext ct.
- $\mathsf{Dec}(\mathsf{sk}, \mathsf{hsk}, \mathsf{ct}) \to \mathsf{m}/\bot$: It takes as input $\mathsf{sk}, \mathsf{hsk}, \mathsf{ct}$ and outputs m or a special symbol $\bot$.

For Setup, input P has different meanings for different predicates: for span program, it indicates the number of attributes, see Sect. 4 and the full paper; for inner-product predicates, it indicates the dimension of vectors, see the full paper. We also note that we use two different indices i and j for pk_i and hsk_j, respectively; both of them range from 1 to L but this convention will simplify the exposition.

Completeness. For all $\lambda, L \in \mathbb{N}$, all P, and all $i \in [L]$, we have

$$\Pr\left[\mathsf{Ver}(\mathsf{crs}, i, \mathsf{pk}_i) = 1 \,\middle|\, \mathsf{crs} \leftarrow \mathsf{Setup}(1^\lambda, P, 1^L);\ (\mathsf{pk}_i, \mathsf{sk}_i) \leftarrow \mathsf{Gen}(\mathsf{crs}, i)\right] = 1.$$

Correctness. For all $\lambda, L \in \mathbb{N}$, all P, all $i^* \in [L]$, all $\mathsf{crs} \leftarrow \mathsf{Setup}(1^\lambda, P, 1^L)$, all $(\mathsf{pk}_{i^*}, \mathsf{sk}_{i^*}) \leftarrow \mathsf{Gen}(\mathsf{crs}, i^*)$, all $\{\mathsf{pk}_i\}_{i \in [L] \setminus \{i^*\}}$ such that $\mathsf{Ver}(\mathsf{crs}, i, \mathsf{pk}_i) = 1$, all $x \in X$ and $y_1, \ldots, y_L \in Y$ such that $P(x, y_{i^*}) = 1$, and all m, we have

$$\Pr\left[\mathsf{Dec}(\mathsf{sk}_{i^*}, \mathsf{hsk}_{i^*}, \mathsf{ct}) = \mathsf{m} \,\middle|\, \begin{array}{r} (\mathsf{mpk}, (\mathsf{hsk}_j)_{j \in [L]}) \leftarrow \mathsf{Agg}(\mathsf{crs}, (\mathsf{pk}_i, y_i)_{i \in [L]}); \\ \mathsf{ct} \leftarrow \mathsf{Enc}(\mathsf{mpk}, x, \mathsf{m}) \end{array}\right] = 1.$$

Compactness. For all $\lambda, L \in \mathbb{N}$, all P, and all $i \in [L]$, we have

$$|\mathsf{mpk}| = \mathsf{poly}(\lambda, P, \log L) \quad \text{and} \quad |\mathsf{hsk}_i| = \mathsf{poly}(\lambda, P, \log L).$$

Security. For all stateful adversary $\mathcal{A}$, the advantage

$$\Pr\left[b = b' \,\middle|\, \begin{array}{l} L \leftarrow \mathcal{A}(1^\lambda);\ \mathsf{crs} \leftarrow \mathsf{Setup}(1^\lambda, P, 1^L) \\ (\mathsf{pk}_i^*, y_i^*)_{i \in [L]}, x^*, \mathsf{m}_0^*, \mathsf{m}_1^* \leftarrow \mathcal{A}^{\mathsf{OGen}(\cdot), \mathsf{OCor}(\cdot)}(\mathsf{crs}) \\ (\mathsf{mpk}, (\mathsf{hsk}_j)_{j \in [L]}) \leftarrow \mathsf{Agg}(\mathsf{crs}, (\mathsf{pk}_i^*, y_i^*)_{i \in [L]}) \\ b \leftarrow \{0,1\}, \mathsf{ct}^* \leftarrow \mathsf{Enc}(\mathsf{mpk}, x^*, \mathsf{m}_b^*);\ b' \leftarrow \mathcal{A}(\mathsf{ct}^*) \end{array}\right] - \frac{1}{2}$$

is negligible in λ, where the oracles work as follows with initial setting $\mathcal{C} = \emptyset$ and $\mathcal{D}_i = \emptyset$ for all $i \in [L]$:

- $\mathsf{OGen}(i)$: run $(\mathsf{pk}, \mathsf{sk}) \leftarrow \mathsf{Gen}(\mathsf{crs}, i)$, set $\mathcal{D}_i[\mathsf{pk}] = \mathsf{sk}$ and return pk.
- $\mathsf{OCor}(i, \mathsf{pk})$: return $\mathcal{D}_i[\mathsf{pk}]$ and update $\mathcal{C} = \mathcal{C} \cup \{(i, \mathsf{pk})\}$.

and, for all $i \in [L]$, we require that

$$\begin{aligned} \mathcal{D}_i[\mathsf{pk}_i^*] = \bot &\implies \mathsf{Ver}(\mathsf{crs}, i, \mathsf{pk}_i^*) = 1, \\ (i, \mathsf{pk}_i^*) \in \mathcal{C} \vee \mathcal{D}_i[\mathsf{pk}_i^*] = \bot &\implies P(x^*, y_i^*) = 0. \end{aligned}$$

We use $\mathsf{Adv}_{\mathcal{A}}^{\text{sReg-ABE}}(\lambda)$ to denote the advantage function. Note that [23] showed that there is no need to give mpk and $\mathsf{hsk}_1, \ldots, \mathsf{hsk}_L$ to $\mathcal{A}$ explicitly and to consider post-challenge queries.

2.3 Predicate Encodings

We review the notion of predicate encoding [5,36]; for simplicity, we use the formulation in [1,2]. A predicate $P : X \times Y \rightarrow \{0,1\}$ has a (n, n_c, n_k)-predicate encoding if: For all $x \in X$, $y \in Y$, there exist

$$\mathbf{C}_x \in \mathbb{Z}_p^{n \times n_c},\ \mathbf{K}_y \in \mathbb{Z}_p^{n \times n_k},\ \mathbf{a}_y \in \mathbb{Z}_p^{1 \times n_k},\ \mathbf{d}_{x,y} \in \mathbb{Z}_p^{1 \times (n_k + n_c)}$$

such that, letting

$$\mathbf{M}_{x,y} = \begin{pmatrix} \mathbf{a}_y & \mathbf{0}_{n_c} \\ \mathbf{K}_y & \mathbf{C}_x \end{pmatrix} \in \mathbb{Z}_p^{(1+n) \times (n_k + n_c)}$$

we have

- **correctness:** for $x \in X$ and $y \in Y$ such that $P(x, y) = 1$:
$$\mathbf{M}_{x,y} \mathbf{d}_{x,y}^{\top} = \mathbf{e}_1^{\top};$$
- **security:** for $x \in X$ and $y \in Y$ such that $P(x, y) = 0$ and for all $\alpha \in \mathbb{Z}_p$:
$$\{x, y, \alpha, (\alpha \| \mathbf{w}) \mathbf{M}_{x,y}\} \approx_s \{x, y, \alpha, (0 \| \mathbf{w}) \mathbf{M}_{x,y}\}, \quad \mathbf{w} \leftarrow \mathbb{Z}_p^n.$$

Also, we require that (1) given P, one can efficiently determine n, n_c, n_k; (2) given x, one can efficiently compute $\mathbf{C}_x$; (3) given y, one can efficiently compute $\mathbf{K}_y$ and $\mathbf{a}_y$; (4) given both x and y, one can efficiently compute $\mathbf{d}_{x,y}$.

2.4 Quasi-Adaptive Non-interactive Zero-Knowledge Argument

We review the notion of quasi-adaptive non-interactive zero-knowledge argument (QA-NIZK) tailored for linear space over group [26,27]. In this paper, we require a stronger unbounded simulation soundness in [19,31].

Algorithms. A Quasi-adaptive Non-interactive Zero-knowledge Argument (QA-NIZK) for linear space over bilinear group $\mathbb{G}$ [26,27] consists of four efficient algorithms:

- $\mathsf{LGen}(1^\lambda, 1^n, 1^m, 1^\ell, [\mathbf{M}]_1) \rightarrow (\mathsf{crs}, \mathsf{td})$: It takes as input the security parameter 1^λ, language parameter $1^n, 1^m, 1^\ell$, and a matrix $[\mathbf{M}]_1 \leftarrow \mathbb{G}_1^{n \times m}$ defining a linear space, outputs common reference string crs and trapdoor td.
- $\mathsf{LPrv}(\mathsf{crs}, [\mathbf{Y}]_1, \mathbf{X}) \rightarrow \pi$: It takes as input crs, a matrix $[\mathbf{Y}]_1 \in \mathbb{G}_1^{n \times \ell}$ with witness $\mathbf{X} \in \mathbb{Z}_p^{m \times \ell}$, outputs a proof π.
- $\mathsf{LVer}(\mathsf{crs}, [\mathbf{Y}]_1, \pi) \rightarrow 0/1$: It takes as input crs, $[\mathbf{Y}]_1$ and π, outputs a bit indicating the validity of π.
- $\mathsf{LSim}(\mathsf{crs}, \mathsf{td}, [\mathbf{Y}]_1) \rightarrow \widetilde{\pi}$: It takes as input crs, td, $[\mathbf{Y}]_1$, outputs a simulated proof $\widetilde{\pi}$.

Perfect Completeness. For all λ, $\mathbf{M}$, and all $\mathbf{X}, \mathbf{Y}$ such that $\mathbf{Y} = \mathbf{MX}$:

$$\Pr\left[\mathsf{LVer}(\mathsf{crs}, [\mathbf{Y}]_1, \pi) = 1 \;\middle|\; \begin{array}{c}(\mathsf{crs}, \mathsf{td}) \leftarrow \mathsf{LGen}(1^\lambda, 1^n, 1^m, 1^\ell, [\mathbf{M}]_1);\\ \pi \leftarrow \mathsf{LPrv}(\mathsf{crs}, [\mathbf{Y}]_1, \mathbf{X})\end{array}\right] = 1.$$

Perfect Zero-Knowledge. For all λ, $\mathbf{M}$, $(\mathsf{crs}, \mathsf{td}) \leftarrow \mathsf{LGen}(1^\lambda, 1^n, 1^m, 1^\ell, [\mathbf{M}]_1)$, and all $\mathbf{X}, \mathbf{Y}$ such that $\mathbf{Y} = \mathbf{MX}$:

$$\mathsf{LPrv}(\mathsf{crs}, [\mathbf{Y}]_1, \mathbf{X}) \equiv \mathsf{LSim}(\mathsf{crs}, \mathsf{td}, [\mathbf{Y}]_1).$$

Stronger Unbounded Simulation Soundness. For all adversary $\mathcal{A}$, the advantage

$$\Pr\left[\begin{array}{l}([\mathbf{Y}^*]_1, \mathsf{pk}^*) \notin \mathcal{Q} \quad \wedge\\ \mathbf{Y}^* \notin \mathsf{span}(\mathbf{M}) \quad \wedge\\ \mathsf{LVer}(\mathsf{crs}, [\mathbf{Y}^*]_1, \pi^*) = 1\end{array} \;\middle|\; \begin{array}{l}\mathbf{M} \leftarrow \mathbb{Z}_p^{n\times m}\\ (\mathsf{crs}, \mathsf{td}) \leftarrow \mathsf{LGen}(1^\lambda, 1^n, 1^m, 1^\ell, [\mathbf{M}]_1)\\ ([\mathbf{Y}^*]_1, \pi^*) \leftarrow \mathcal{A}^{\mathsf{LSim}(\mathsf{crs},\mathsf{td},\cdot)}(1^\lambda, \mathsf{crs}, \mathbf{M})\end{array}\right]$$

is negligible in λ, where $\mathcal{Q}$ records all queries to $\mathsf{LSim}(\mathsf{crs}, \mathsf{td}, \cdot)$ along with responses. We use $\mathsf{Adv}^{\mathrm{USS}}_{\mathcal{A},n,m,\ell}(\lambda)$ to denote the advantage function. Note that our definition is stronger in the sense that the adversary is given $\mathbf{M}$ instead of $[\mathbf{M}]_1$, this allows us to manipulate $\mathbf{M}$ in reduction (see the proof in full paper and [19,31] for more discussions).

Scheme from Pairings. Due to the simplicity and efficiency, we choose to use QA-NIZK in [27] for the case $\ell = 1$. It is direct to verify that this scheme achieves stronger unbounded simulation soundness (defined above) under MDDH assumption; see the full paper. For general $\ell > 1$, we simply employ ℓ parallel fresh instances.

3 Our Slotted Registered ABE

This section presents our slotted Reg-ABE via predicate encoding from k-Lin assumption. By the generic transformation in [23], this yields a Reg-ABE scheme via predicate encoding under the k-Lin assumption, see more details in the full paper. We provide a concrete slotted Reg-ABE for arithmetic branching program in Sect. 4, and more concrete instances in the full paper.

3.1 Scheme

Assuming a QA-NIZK $\Pi = (\mathsf{LGen}, \mathsf{LPrv}, \mathsf{LVer}, \mathsf{LSim})$ for linear space over bilinear groups, our slotted Reg-ABE scheme for predicates that have predicate encoding works as follows in the prime-order bilinear group:

– $\mathsf{Setup}(1^\lambda, P, 1^L)$: Run $\mathbb{G} := (p, \mathbb{G}_1, \mathbb{G}_2, \mathbb{G}_T, e) \leftarrow \mathcal{G}(1^\lambda)$. Sample

$$\mathbf{A} \leftarrow \mathbb{Z}_p^{k\times(2k+1)},\ \mathbf{B} \leftarrow \mathbb{Z}_p^{(k+1)\times k},\ \mathbf{k} \leftarrow \mathbb{Z}_p^{1\times(2k+1)}.$$

Compute parameter (n, n_c, n_k) from P, see Sect. 2.3. For all $i \in [L]$, sample

$$\mathbf{V}_i \leftarrow \mathbb{Z}_p^{(2k+1)\times(k+1)},\ \mathbf{W}_i \leftarrow \mathbb{Z}_p^{(2k+1)\times(k+1)n},\ \mathbf{R}_i \leftarrow \mathbb{Z}_p^{(2k+2)\times(2k+1)},\ \mathbf{r}_i \leftarrow \mathbb{Z}_p^{1\times k}.$$

For all $i \in [L]$, write $\mathbf{A}_i = \begin{pmatrix}\mathbf{A}\\ \mathbf{R}_i\end{pmatrix} \in \mathbb{Z}_p^{(3k+2)\times(2k+1)}$ and run

$$(\mathsf{crs}_i, \mathsf{td}_i) \leftarrow \mathsf{LGen}(1^\lambda, \mathbb{G}_1, [\mathbf{A}_i]_1).$$

Output

$$\mathsf{crs} = \begin{pmatrix} [\mathbf{A}]_1,\ [\mathbf{A}\mathbf{k}^\top]_T,\ \{\mathsf{crs}_i, [\mathbf{R}_i, \mathbf{A}\mathbf{V}_i, \mathbf{A}\mathbf{W}_i]_1\}_{i\in[L]} \\ \{[\mathbf{B}\mathbf{r}_j^\top, \mathbf{V}_j\mathbf{B}\mathbf{r}_j^\top + \mathbf{k}^\top]_2\}_{j\in[L]} \\ \{[\mathbf{V}_i\mathbf{B}\mathbf{r}_j^\top, \mathbf{W}_i(\mathbf{I}_n \otimes \mathbf{B}\mathbf{r}_j^\top)]_2\}_{j\in[L], i\in[L]\setminus\{j\}} \end{pmatrix}.$$

We note that we employ i as the index for $\mathbf{V}$'s and $\mathbf{W}$'s while j is the index for $\mathbf{r}$'s; both of them range from 1 to L. One exception is the terms with $\mathbf{k}$, which is conceptually $\mathbf{V}_i\mathbf{B}\mathbf{r}_j^\top$ with $i = j$. This is different from our notation in Sect. 1.2. Note that we do not use $\mathsf{td}_1, \ldots, \mathsf{td}_L$ in the actual scheme.

– $\mathsf{Gen}(\mathsf{crs}, i)$: Sample $\mathbf{U}_i \leftarrow \mathbb{Z}_p^{(2k+1)\times(k+1)}$. Define $\mathbf{M}_i = \begin{pmatrix}\mathbf{T}_i\\ \mathbf{Q}_i\end{pmatrix} = \begin{pmatrix}\mathbf{A}\mathbf{U}_i\\ \mathbf{R}_i\mathbf{U}_i\end{pmatrix} = \mathbf{A}_i\mathbf{U}_i \in \mathbb{Z}_p^{(3k+2)\times(k+1)}$ and run

$$\pi_i \leftarrow \mathsf{LPrv}(\mathsf{crs}_i, [\mathbf{M}_i]_1, \mathbf{U}_i).$$

Fetch $[\mathbf{R}_i]_1$ and $\{[\mathbf{B}\mathbf{r}_j^\top]_2\}_{j\in[L]\setminus\{i\}}$ from crs and output

$$\mathsf{pk}_i = \big([\underbrace{\mathbf{A}\mathbf{U}_i}_{\mathbf{T}_i}, \underbrace{\mathbf{R}_i\mathbf{U}_i}_{\mathbf{Q}_i}]_1, \{[\underbrace{\mathbf{U}_i\mathbf{B}\mathbf{r}_j^\top}_{\mathbf{h}_{i,j}^\top}]_2\}_{j\in[L]\setminus\{i\}}, \pi_i\big) \quad \text{and} \quad \mathsf{sk}_i = \mathbf{U}_i.$$

– $\mathsf{Ver}(\mathsf{crs}, i, \mathsf{pk}_i)$: Parse $\mathsf{pk}_i = \big([\mathbf{T}_i, \mathbf{Q}_i]_1, \{[\mathbf{h}_{i,j}^\top]_2\}_{j\in[L]\setminus\{i\}}, \pi_i\big)$. Write $\mathbf{M}_i = \begin{pmatrix}\mathbf{T}_i\\ \mathbf{Q}_i\end{pmatrix}$ and check

$$\mathsf{LVer}(\mathsf{crs}_i, [\mathbf{M}_i]_1, \pi_i) \stackrel{?}{=} 1.$$

For each $j \in [L] \setminus \{i\}$, check

$$e([\mathbf{A}]_1, [\mathbf{h}_{i,j}^\top]_2) \stackrel{?}{=} e([\mathbf{T}_i]_1, [\mathbf{B}\mathbf{r}_j^\top]_2).$$

If all these checks pass, output 1; otherwise, output 0.

– $\mathsf{Agg}(\mathsf{crs}, (\mathsf{pk}_i, y_i)_{i\in[L]})$: For all $i \in [L]$, compute $\mathbf{K}_{y_i}$ from y_i, and parse $\mathsf{pk}_i = ([\mathbf{T}_i, \mathbf{Q}_i]_1, \{[\mathbf{h}_{i,j}^\top]_2\}_{j\in[L]\setminus\{i\}}, \pi_i)$. Output:

$$\mathsf{mpk} = \left([\mathbf{A}]_1, \left[\sum_{i\in[L]}((\mathbf{AV}_i + \mathbf{T}_i)(\mathbf{a}_{y_i} \otimes \mathbf{I}_{k+1}) + \mathbf{AW}_i(\mathbf{K}_{y_i} \otimes \mathbf{I}_{k+1}))\right]_1, \left[\sum_{i\in[L]} \mathbf{AW}_i\right]_1, [\mathbf{Ak}^\top]_T\right)$$

and for all $j \in [L]$

$$\mathsf{hsk}_j = \Bigg(\underbrace{[\mathbf{Br}_j^\top]_2}_{\mathbf{k}_0^\top}, \underbrace{[\mathbf{V}_j\mathbf{Br}_j^\top + \mathbf{k}^\top]_2}_{\mathbf{k}_1^\top}, \underbrace{\left[\sum_{i\in[L]\setminus\{j\}} ((\mathbf{V}_i\mathbf{Br}_j^\top + \mathbf{h}_{i,j}^\top)\mathbf{a}_{y_i} + \mathbf{W}_i(\mathbf{I}_n \otimes \mathbf{Br}_j^\top)\mathbf{K}_{y_i})\right]_2}_{\mathbf{K}_2}, \underbrace{\left[\sum_{i\in[L]\setminus\{j\}} \mathbf{W}_i(\mathbf{I}_n \otimes \mathbf{Br}_j^\top)\right]_2}_{\mathbf{K}_3}\Bigg).$$

– $\mathsf{Enc}(\mathsf{mpk}, x, \mathsf{m})$: Sample $\mathbf{s} \leftarrow \mathbb{Z}_p^{1\times k}$ and compute $\mathbf{C}_x$. Output:

$$\mathsf{ct}_x = \Bigg(\underbrace{[\mathbf{sA}]_1}_{\mathbf{c}_0}, \underbrace{\left[\sum_{i\in[L]}((\mathbf{sAV}_i + \mathbf{sT}_i)(\mathbf{a}_{y_i} \otimes \mathbf{I}_{k+1}) + \mathbf{sAW}_i(\mathbf{K}_{y_i} \otimes \mathbf{I}_{k+1}))\right]_1}_{\mathbf{c}_1}, \underbrace{\left[\sum_{i\in[L]} \mathbf{sAW}_i(\mathbf{C}_x \otimes \mathbf{I}_{k+1})\right]_1}_{\mathbf{c}_2}, \underbrace{[\mathbf{sAk}^\top]_T \cdot \mathsf{m}}_{C}\Bigg).$$

– $\mathsf{Dec}(\mathsf{sk}_{i^*}, \mathsf{hsk}_{i^*}, \mathsf{ct}_x)$: Parse

$$\mathsf{sk}_{i^*} = \mathbf{U}_{i^*}, \quad \mathsf{hsk}_{i^*} = [\mathbf{k}_0^\top, \mathbf{k}_1^\top, \mathbf{K}_2, \mathbf{K}_3]_2, \quad \mathsf{ct}_x = ([\mathbf{c}_0, \mathbf{c}_1, \mathbf{c}_2]_1, C).$$

Compute $\mathbf{C}_x$ from x and recover

$$[\mathbf{z}_1]_T = e([\mathbf{c}_1\|\mathbf{c}_2]_1, [\mathbf{I}_{n_k+n_c} \otimes \mathbf{k}_0^\top]_2), \qquad [\mathbf{z}_2]_T = e([\mathbf{c}_0]_1, [\mathbf{K}_2\|\mathbf{K}_3\mathbf{C}_x]_2),$$
$$[z_3]_T = e([\mathbf{c}_0\mathbf{U}_{i^*}]_1, [\mathbf{k}_0^\top]_2), \qquad [z_4]_T = e([\mathbf{c}_0]_1, [\mathbf{k}_1^\top]_2).$$

Compute $\mathbf{d}_{x,y_{i^*}}$ from x and y_{i^*} and output

$$z = [(\mathbf{z}_1 - \mathbf{z}_2)\mathbf{d}_{x,y_{i^*}}^\top - z_3 - z_4]_T \cdot C.$$

Completeness. For all $\lambda, L \in \mathbb{N}$, all P, all $i \in [L]$, all $\mathsf{crs} \leftarrow \mathsf{Setup}(1^\lambda, P, 1^L)$ and $(\mathsf{pk}_i, \mathsf{sk}_i) \leftarrow \mathsf{Gen}(\mathsf{crs}, i)$, we have

$$\mathsf{pk}_i = ([\mathbf{T}_i, \mathbf{Q}_i]_1, \{[\mathbf{H}_{i,j}]_2\}_{j\in[L]\setminus\{i\}}, \pi_i) = ([\mathbf{AU}_i, \mathbf{R}_i\mathbf{U}_i]_1, \{[\mathbf{U}_i\mathbf{Br}_j^\top]_2\}_{j\in[L]\setminus\{i\}}, \pi_i)$$

for some $\mathbf{U}_i \leftarrow \mathbb{Z}_p^{(2k+1)\times(k+1)}$ and $\pi_i \leftarrow \mathsf{LPrv}(\mathsf{crs}_i, [\mathbf{A}_i\mathbf{U}_i]_1, \mathbf{U}_i)$, where $(\mathsf{crs}_i, \mathsf{td}_i) \leftarrow \mathsf{LGen}(1^\lambda, \mathbb{G}_1, [\mathbf{A}_i]_1)$ and $\mathbf{A}_i = \begin{pmatrix}\mathbf{A}\\ \mathbf{R}_i\end{pmatrix}$ with $\mathbf{A} \leftarrow \mathbb{Z}_p^{k\times(2k+1)}$, $\mathbf{R}_i \leftarrow \mathbb{Z}_p^{(2k+2)\times(2k+1)}$. Then

- Write $\mathbf{M}_i = \begin{pmatrix}\mathbf{T}_i\\ \mathbf{Q}_i\end{pmatrix} = \begin{pmatrix}\mathbf{AU}_i\\ \mathbf{R}_i\mathbf{U}_i\end{pmatrix}$, we have $\mathsf{LVer}(\mathsf{crs}_i, [\mathbf{M}_i]_1, \pi_i) = 1$ by the perfect completeness of Π (see Sect. 2.4) and the fact that $\mathbf{M}_i = \mathbf{A}_i\mathbf{U}_i$;
- For each $j \in [L] \setminus \{i\}$, we have $e([\mathbf{A}]_1, [\mathbf{U}_i\mathbf{Br}_j^\top]_2) = e([\mathbf{AU}_i]_1, [\mathbf{Br}_j^\top]_2)$ by the definition of bilinear map e (see Sect. 2.1) and the fact that $\mathbf{A} \cdot \mathbf{U}_i\mathbf{Br}_j^\top = \mathbf{AU}_i \cdot \mathbf{Br}_j^\top$.

This ensures that $\mathsf{Ver}(\mathsf{crs}, i, \mathsf{pk}_i) = 1$ by the specification of Ver and readily proves the completeness.

Correctness. For all $\lambda, L \in \mathbb{N}$, all P, all $i^* \in [L]$, all $\mathsf{crs} \leftarrow \mathsf{Setup}(1^\lambda, P, 1^L)$, all $(\mathsf{pk}_{i^*}, \mathsf{sk}_{i^*}) \leftarrow \mathsf{Gen}(\mathsf{crs}, i^*)$, all $\{\mathsf{pk}_i\}_{i\in[L]\setminus\{i^*\}}$ such that $\mathsf{Ver}(\mathsf{crs}, i, \mathsf{pk}_i) = 1$, for all $y_1, \ldots, y_L \in Y$ and $x \in X$ with $P(x, y_{i^*}) = 1$ and all m, we have:

$$\begin{aligned}
\mathsf{sk}_{i^*} &= \mathbf{U}_{i^*},\\
\mathsf{ct}_x &= \Bigg(\underbrace{[\mathbf{sA}]_1}_{\mathbf{c}_0}, \underbrace{\Big[\sum_{i\in[L]}((\mathbf{sAV}_i + \mathbf{sT}_i)(\mathbf{a}_{y_i}\otimes\mathbf{I}_{k+1}) + \mathbf{sAW}_i(\mathbf{K}_{y_i}\otimes\mathbf{I}_{k+1}))\Big]_1}_{\mathbf{c}_1},\\
&\qquad \underbrace{\Big[\sum_{i\in[L]}\mathbf{sAW}_i(\mathbf{C}_x\otimes\mathbf{I}_{k+1})\Big]_1}_{\mathbf{c}_2}, \underbrace{[\mathbf{sAk}^\top]_T\cdot\mathsf{m}}_{C}\Bigg)\\
\mathsf{hsk}_{i^*} &= \Bigg(\underbrace{[\mathbf{Br}_{i^*}^\top]_2}_{\mathbf{k}_0^\top}, \underbrace{[\mathbf{V}_{i^*}\mathbf{Br}_{i^*}^\top + \mathbf{k}^\top]_2}_{\mathbf{k}_1^\top},\\
&\qquad \underbrace{\Big[\sum_{i\in[L]\setminus\{i^*\}}((\mathbf{V}_i\mathbf{Br}_{i^*}^\top + \mathbf{h}_{i,i^*}^\top)\mathbf{a}_{y_i} + \mathbf{W}_i(\mathbf{I}_n\otimes\mathbf{Br}_{i^*}^\top)\mathbf{K}_{y_i})\Big]_2}_{\mathbf{K}_2},\\
&\qquad \underbrace{\Big[\sum_{i\in[L]\setminus\{i^*\}}\mathbf{W}_i(\mathbf{I}_n\otimes\mathbf{Br}_{i^*}^\top)\Big]_2}_{\mathbf{K}_3}\Bigg)
\end{aligned}$$

where

$$\mathbf{A}\mathbf{h}_{i,i^*}^{\top} = \mathbf{T}_i\mathbf{B}\mathbf{r}_{i^*}^{\top} \quad \forall i \in [L] \setminus \{i^*\} \quad \text{and} \quad \mathbf{A}\mathbf{U}_{i^*} = \mathbf{T}_{i^*}. \tag{9}$$

Note that here we actually consider hsk_j for $j = i^*$ and sk_i for $i = i^*$ and all above equalities are ensured by Ver and Gen. Then, as in Sect. 2.3, let

$$\mathbf{M}_{x,y_i} = \begin{pmatrix} \mathbf{a}_{y_i} & \mathbf{0}_{n_c} \\ \mathbf{K}_{y_i} & \mathbf{C}_x \end{pmatrix}, \quad \forall i \in [L],$$

we have

$$\begin{aligned}
\mathbf{z}_1 &= \sum_{i\in[L]} (\mathbf{sAV}_i + \mathbf{sT}_i \| \mathbf{sAW}_i)(\mathbf{M}_{x,y_i} \otimes \mathbf{I}_{k+1})(\mathbf{I}_{n_k+n_c} \otimes \mathbf{Br}_{i^*}^{\top}) \\
&= \sum_{i\in[L]} (\mathbf{sAV}_i + \mathbf{sT}_i \| \mathbf{sAW}_i)(\mathbf{I}_{1+n} \otimes \mathbf{Br}_{i^*}^{\top})\mathbf{M}_{x,y_i} \qquad (10) \\
&= \sum_{i\in[L]} (\mathbf{sAV}_i\mathbf{Br}_{i^*}^{\top} + \mathbf{sT}_i\mathbf{Br}_{i^*}^{\top} \| \mathbf{sAW}_i(\mathbf{I}_n \otimes \mathbf{Br}_{i^*}^{\top}))\mathbf{M}_{x,y_i} \\
\mathbf{z}_2 &= \sum_{i\in[L]\setminus\{i^*\}} (\mathbf{sAV}_i\mathbf{Br}_{i^*}^{\top} + \mathbf{sAh}_{i,i^*}^{\top} \| \mathbf{sAW}_i(\mathbf{I}_n \otimes \mathbf{Br}_{i^*}^{\top}))\mathbf{M}_{x,y_i} \\
z_3 &= \mathbf{sAU}_{i^*}\mathbf{Br}_{i^*}^{\top} \\
z_4 &= \mathbf{sAV}_{i^*}\mathbf{Br}_{i^*}^{\top} + \mathbf{sAk}^{\top}
\end{aligned}$$

and then

$$\begin{aligned}
z &= [(\mathbf{z}_1 - \mathbf{z}_2)\mathbf{d}_{x,y_{i^*}}^{\top} - z_3 - z_4]_T \cdot [\mathbf{sAk}^{\top}]_T \cdot \mathsf{m} \\
&= [(\mathbf{sAV}_{i^*}\mathbf{Br}_{i^*}^{\top} + \mathbf{sT}_{i^*}\mathbf{Br}_{i^*}^{\top} \| \mathbf{sAW}_{i^*}(\mathbf{I}_n \otimes \mathbf{Br}_{i^*}^{\top}))\mathbf{M}_{x,y_{i^*}}\mathbf{d}_{x,y_{i^*}}^{\top} \\
&\quad -\mathbf{sAU}_{i^*}\mathbf{Br}_{i^*}^{\top} - (\mathbf{sAV}_{i^*}\mathbf{Br}_{i^*}^{\top} + \mathbf{sAk}^{\top})]_T \cdot [\mathbf{sAk}^{\top}]_T \cdot \mathsf{m} \qquad (11) \\
&= [(\mathbf{sAV}_{i^*}\mathbf{Br}_{i^*}^{\top} + \mathbf{sT}_{i^*}\mathbf{Br}_{i^*}^{\top}) \\
&\quad -\mathbf{sAU}_{i^*}\mathbf{Br}_{i^*}^{\top} + \mathbf{sAk}^{\top} - (\mathbf{sAV}_{i^*}\mathbf{Br}_{i^*}^{\top} + \mathbf{sAk}^{\top})]_T \cdot \mathsf{m} \qquad (12) \\
&= \mathsf{m} \qquad (13)
\end{aligned}$$

Here, equality (10) follows from the property of tensor product: $(\mathbf{M}\otimes\mathbf{I})(\mathbf{I}\otimes\mathbf{a}^{\top}) = \mathbf{M}\otimes\mathbf{a}^{\top} = (\mathbf{I}\otimes\mathbf{a}^{\top})\mathbf{M}$ for matrices of proper size; equality (11) follows from the fact that $\mathbf{Ah}_{i,i^*}^{\top} = \mathbf{T}_i\mathbf{Br}_{i^*}^{\top}$ for all $i \in [L] \setminus \{i^*\}$ (see equality (9)); equality (12) follows from the correctness of predicate encoding; equality (13) follows from the fact that $\mathbf{T}_{i^*} = \mathbf{AU}_{i^*}$ (see equality (9)). This proves the correctness.

Compactness. Assume P has (n, n_c, n_k)-predicate encoding, our slotted Reg-ABE has the following properties:

$$|\mathsf{mpk}| = (n_k + n) \cdot \mathsf{poly}(\lambda) \quad \text{and} \quad |\mathsf{hsk}_j| = (n_k + n) \cdot \mathsf{poly}(\lambda)$$

We also have

$$|\mathsf{crs}| = L^2 \cdot n \cdot \mathsf{poly}(\lambda) \quad \text{and} \quad |\mathsf{ct}| = (n_k + n_c) \cdot \mathsf{poly}(\lambda).$$

Here $\mathsf{crs}_1, \ldots, \mathsf{crs}_L$ contribute $L \cdot \mathsf{poly}(\lambda)$ according to the efficiency of the pairing-based QA-NIZK scheme by Kiltz and Wee [27] and the fact that the size of language description is $\mathsf{poly}(\lambda)$.

Security. We have the following theorem. Given pairing-based QA-NIZK in [27], our slotted Reg-ABE scheme uses prime-order bilinear group and the security can be reduced to MDDH assumption.

Theorem 1. *Assume* $\Pi = (\mathsf{LGen}, \mathsf{LPrv}, \mathsf{LVer}, \mathsf{LSim})$ *is a QA-NIZK with perfect completeness, perfect zero-knowledge and stronger unbounded simulation soundness for linear space defined in Sect. 2.4, our slotted Reg-ABE scheme achieves the security defined in Sect. 2.2 under* MDDH *assumption.*

3.2 Proof

We prove the following technical lemma; this immediately proves Theorem 1.

Lemma 1. *For all adversaries* $\mathcal{A}$*, there exist adversaries* $\mathcal{B}_1$ *and* $\mathcal{B}_2$ *such that:*

$$\mathsf{Adv}_{\mathcal{A}}^{\mathrm{sReg\text{-}ABE}}(\lambda) \leq L \cdot \mathsf{Adv}_{\mathcal{B}_1}^{\mathrm{USS}}(\lambda) + (2L + 2L \cdot Q + 1) \cdot \mathsf{Adv}_{\mathcal{B}_2}^{\mathrm{MDDH}} + \mathsf{negl}(\lambda)$$

where L *is the number of slots,* Q *is the maximum number of queries on a slot made by* $\mathcal{A}$ *and* $\mathsf{Time}(\mathcal{B}_1), \mathsf{Time}(\mathcal{B}_2) \approx \mathsf{Time}(\mathcal{A})$.

Game Sequence. Let L be the number slots chosen by the adversary, crs be the common reference string, x^* be the challenge "attribute", $(\mathsf{m}_0^*, \mathsf{m}_1^*)$ be challenge message pair, $(\mathsf{pk}_i^*, y_i^*)_{i \in [L]}$ be challenge public keys and challenge "policy" to be registered and ct^* be the challenge ciphertext. For all $i \in [L]$, define $D_i = \{\mathsf{pk}_i : \mathcal{D}_i[\mathsf{pk}_i] = \mathsf{sk}_i \neq \perp\}$ which records responses to $\mathsf{OGen}(i)$ and $C_i = \{\mathsf{pk}_i : (i, \mathsf{pk}_i) \in \mathcal{C}\}$ which records public keys in D_i that have been sent to $\mathsf{OCor}(i, \cdot)$. Recall that, we require that, for each $i \in [L]$,

$$\mathsf{pk}_i^* \notin D_i \implies \mathsf{Ver}(\mathsf{crs}, i, \mathsf{pk}_i^*) = 1,$$
$$\mathsf{pk}_i^* \in C_i \vee \mathsf{pk}_i^* \notin D_i \implies P(x^*, y_i^*) = 0.$$

Note that pk_i serves as a *general* entry in D_i while pk_i^* is the *specific* challenge public for slot i; there can be more than one assignment for pk_i since the adversary can invoke $\mathsf{OGen}(i)$ for many times. We prove the Lemma 1 via dual-system method using the following game sequence.

- G_0: Real game. Recall that we have
  - crs is in the form:

$$\mathsf{crs} = \begin{pmatrix} [\mathbf{A}]_1,\ [\mathbf{A}\mathbf{k}^\top]_T,\ \{\mathsf{crs}_i, [\mathbf{R}_i, \mathbf{A}\mathbf{V}_i, \mathbf{A}\mathbf{W}_i]_1\}_{i \in [L]} \\ \{[\mathbf{B}\mathbf{r}_j^\top, \mathbf{V}_j\mathbf{B}\mathbf{r}_j^\top + \mathbf{k}^\top]_2\}_{j \in [L]} \\ \{[\mathbf{V}_i\mathbf{B}\mathbf{r}_j^\top, \mathbf{W}_i(\mathbf{I}_n \otimes \mathbf{B}\mathbf{r}_j^\top)]_2\}_{j \in [L], i \in [L] \setminus \{j\}} \end{pmatrix}$$

where $\mathsf{crs}_i \in \mathsf{LGen}(1^\lambda, \mathbb{G}_1, [\mathbf{A}_i]_1)$ and $\mathbf{A}_i = \begin{pmatrix} \mathbf{A} \\ \mathbf{R}_i \end{pmatrix}$.

- For each $i \in [L]$, each $\mathsf{pk}_i \in D_i$ is in the form:

$$\mathsf{pk}_i = ([\mathbf{AU}_i, \mathbf{R}_i\mathbf{U}_i]_1, \{[\mathbf{U}_i\mathbf{B}\mathbf{r}_j^\top]_2\}_{j\in[L]\setminus\{i\}}, \pi_i)$$

where $\pi_i \leftarrow \mathsf{LPrv}(\mathsf{crs}_i, [\mathbf{M}_i]_1, \mathbf{U}_i)$ and $\mathbf{M}_i = \begin{pmatrix} \mathbf{AU}_i \\ \mathbf{R}_i\mathbf{U}_i \end{pmatrix}$; note that $\mathbf{U}_i$ is the corresponding secret key sk_i.

- For all $i \in [L]$, pk_i^* is in the form:

$$\mathsf{pk}_i^* = ([\mathbf{T}_i^*, \mathbf{Q}_i^*]_1, \{[{\mathbf{h}_{i,j}^*}^\top]_2\}_{j\in[L]\setminus\{i\}}, \pi_i^*)$$

such that $\mathsf{Ver}(\mathsf{crs}, i, \mathsf{pk}_i^*) = 1$ which means $\mathsf{LVer}\left(\mathsf{crs}_i, \begin{bmatrix} \mathbf{T}_i^* \\ \mathbf{Q}_i^* \end{bmatrix}_1, \pi_i^*\right) = 1$ and $\mathbf{A}{\mathbf{h}_{i,j}^*}^\top = \mathbf{T}_i^*\mathbf{B}\mathbf{r}_j^\top$ for each $j \in [L] \setminus \{i\}$.

- ct^* for x^* and $(\mathsf{m}_0^*, \mathsf{m}_1^*)$ is in the form:

$$\mathsf{ct}^* = \Bigg(\underbrace{[\mathbf{sA}]_1}_{\mathbf{c}_0^*}, \underbrace{\left[\sum_{i\in[L]} ((\mathbf{sAV}_i + \mathbf{sT}_i^*)(\mathbf{a}_{y_i^*} \otimes \mathbf{I}_{k+1}) + \mathbf{sAW}_i(\mathbf{K}_{y_i^*} \otimes \mathbf{I}_{k+1}))\right]_1}_{\mathbf{c}_1^*},$$
$$\underbrace{\left[\sum_{i\in[L]} \mathbf{sAW}_i(\mathbf{C}_{x^*} \otimes \mathbf{I}_{k+1})\right]_1}_{\mathbf{c}_2^*}, \underbrace{[\mathbf{sAk}^\top]_T \cdot \mathsf{m}_b^*}_{C^*} \Bigg)$$

where $b \leftarrow \{0, 1\}$ is the secret bit.

- G_1: Identical to G_0 except that, for all $i \in [L]$ and all $\mathsf{pk}_i \in D_i$, we replace π_i in pk_i with

$$\widetilde{\pi}_i \leftarrow \boxed{\mathsf{LSim}}(\mathsf{crs}_i, \mathsf{td}_i, [\mathbf{M}_i]_1) \quad \text{where} \quad \mathbf{M}_i = \begin{pmatrix} \mathbf{AU}_i \\ \mathbf{R}_i\mathbf{U}_i \end{pmatrix}.$$

We have $\mathsf{G}_1 \equiv \mathsf{G}_0$. This follows from the perfect zero-knowledge of Π. See the full paper for more details.

- G_2: Identical to G_1 except that we sample $\mathbf{s} \leftarrow \mathbb{Z}_p^{1\times k}$ along with $\mathbf{A}$ and replace all $\mathbf{R}_i$ in crs with

$$\widehat{\mathbf{R}}_i = \widetilde{\mathbf{R}}_i \begin{pmatrix} \mathbf{sA} \\ \mathbf{I}_{2k+1} \end{pmatrix}, \quad \widetilde{\mathbf{R}}_i \leftarrow \mathbb{Z}_p^{(2k+2)\times(2k+2)}$$

We have $\mathsf{G}_2 \approx_s \mathsf{G}_1$. This follows from the fact that both $\mathbf{R}_i$ (in G_1) and $\widehat{\mathbf{R}}_i$ (in G_2) are truly random since matrix $\begin{pmatrix} \mathbf{sA} \\ \mathbf{I}_{2k+1} \end{pmatrix}$ is full rank. See the full paper for more details.

- G_3: Identical to G_2 except that we replace $\mathbf{sT}_i^*$ with $\mathbf{e}_1\widetilde{\mathbf{R}}_i^{-1}\mathbf{Q}_i^*$ in $\mathbf{c}_1^*$; namely, we have

$$\mathbf{c}_1^* = \sum_{i\in[L]} ((\mathbf{sAV}_i + \boxed{\mathbf{e}_1\widetilde{\mathbf{R}}_i^{-1}\mathbf{Q}_i^*})(\mathbf{a}_{y_i^*} \otimes \mathbf{I}_{k+1}) + \mathbf{sAW}_i(\mathbf{K}_{y_i^*} \otimes \mathbf{I}_{k+1})).$$

We have $\mathsf{G}_3 \approx_c \mathsf{G}_2$. This follows from stronger unbounded simulation soundness of Π along with the fact that $\mathsf{LVer}(\mathsf{crs}_i, [\mathbf{M}_i^*], \pi_i^*) = 1$ for all $i \in [L]$ where $\mathbf{M}_i^* = \begin{pmatrix} \mathbf{T}_i^* \\ \mathbf{Q}_i^* \end{pmatrix}$. Assume $\mathsf{pk}_{i^*}^* \notin D_{i^*}$, i.e., $\mathsf{pk}_{i^*}^*$ is malicious. In the reduction, we guess $i^* \leftarrow [L]$ and obtain $\mathbf{A}, \widehat{\mathbf{R}}_{i^*}, \mathsf{crs}_{i^*}$ as input; we simulate honestly as in G_3 except that for all $\mathsf{pk}_{i^*} \in D_{i^*}$, we make an oracle query $[\mathbf{M}_{i^*}]_1$ and get $\widetilde{\pi}_{i^*}$ in it; we finally output $([\mathbf{M}_{i^*}^*]_1, \pi_{i^*}^*)$ in $\mathsf{pk}_{i^*}^* \notin D_{i^*}$. Observe that once it happens that $\mathbf{e}_1\widetilde{\mathbf{R}}_{i^*}^{-1}\mathbf{Q}_{i^*}^* \neq \mathbf{s}\mathbf{T}_{i^*}^*$, we must have $\mathbf{M}_{i^*}^* \notin \mathsf{span}(\mathbf{A}_{i^*})$. When $\mathsf{pk}_{i^*}^* \in D_{i^*}$, we always have $\mathsf{G}_3 \equiv \mathsf{G}_2$. See the full paper for more details.

- G_4: Identical to G_3 except that we replace all $\mathbf{sA}$ with $\mathbf{c} \leftarrow \mathbb{Z}_p^{1\times(2k+1)}$; in particular, we generate all $\widehat{\mathbf{R}}_i$ as follows:

$$\widehat{\mathbf{R}}_i = \widetilde{\mathbf{R}}_i \begin{pmatrix} \boxed{\mathbf{c}} \\ \mathbf{I}_{2k+1} \end{pmatrix}, \quad \widetilde{\mathbf{R}}_i \leftarrow \mathbb{Z}_p^{(2k+2)\times(2k+2)}$$

and generate the challenge ciphertext as follows:

$$\mathsf{ct}^* = \Bigg(\underbrace{[\boxed{\mathbf{c}}]_1}_{\mathbf{c}_0^*}, \underbrace{\Big[\sum_{i\in[L]} ((\boxed{\mathbf{c}}\mathbf{V}_i + \mathbf{e}_1\widetilde{\mathbf{R}}_i^{-1}\mathbf{Q}_i^*)(\mathbf{a}_{y_i^*} \otimes \mathbf{I}_{k+1}) + \boxed{\mathbf{c}}\mathbf{W}_i(\mathbf{K}_{y_i^*} \otimes \mathbf{I}_{k+1})) \Big]_1}_{\mathbf{c}_1^*},$$
$$\underbrace{\Big[\sum_{i\in[L]} \boxed{\mathbf{c}}\mathbf{W}_i(\mathbf{C}_{x^*} \otimes \mathbf{I}_{k+1}) \Big]_1}_{\mathbf{c}_2^*}, \underbrace{[\boxed{\mathbf{c}}\mathbf{k}^\top]_T \cdot \mathsf{m}_b^*}_{C^*} \Bigg).$$

We have $\mathsf{G}_4 \approx_c \mathsf{G}_3$. This follows from MDDH assumption which ensures that $([\mathbf{A}]_1, [\mathbf{sA}]_1) \approx_c ([\mathbf{A}]_1, [\mathbf{c}]_1)$ when $\mathbf{A} \leftarrow \mathbb{Z}_p^{k\times(2k+1)}$, $\mathbf{s} \leftarrow \mathbb{Z}_p^{1\times k}$ and $\mathbf{c} \leftarrow \mathbb{Z}_p^{1\times(2k+1)}$. This is analogous to the transition from normal ciphertext to semi-functional ciphertext in the dual-system method [35]. See the full paper for more details.

- $\mathsf{G}_{5,\ell}$, $(\ell \in [0, L])$: Identical to G_4 except we change $[\mathbf{V}_j\mathbf{B}\mathbf{r}_j^\top + \mathbf{k}^\top]_2$ for all $j \in [\ell]$ as follows:

$$[\mathbf{V}_j\mathbf{B}\mathbf{r}_j^\top + \mathbf{k}^\top + \boxed{\mathbf{c}^\perp\alpha}]_2$$

where $\mathbf{c}^\perp \in \mathbb{Z}_p^{2k+1}$ such that $\mathbf{c}\mathbf{c}^\perp = 1$ and $\mathbf{A}\mathbf{c}^\perp = \mathbf{0}$ and $\alpha \leftarrow \mathbb{Z}_p$. We have that
  - $\mathsf{G}_{5,0} = \mathsf{G}_4$; the two games are exactly identical, since $[0] = \emptyset$;
  - $\mathsf{G}_{5,\ell} \approx_c \mathsf{G}_{5,\ell-1}$ for all $\ell \in [L]$; this is analogous to the transition from normal keys to semi-functional keys one-by-one in the dual-system method. However, the situation is much more complicated in the context of Reg-ABE, we will describe the sub-sequence of games for this step later in Sect. 3.3.

- G_6: Identical to $\mathsf{G}_{5,L}$ except that we replace term C^* in ct^* as $\boxed{C^* \leftarrow \mathbb{G}_T}$. We have $\mathsf{G}_6 \equiv \mathsf{G}_{5,L}$. This follows from the following statistical argument:

$$(\overbrace{\mathbf{A}\mathbf{k}^\top, \mathbf{k}^\top + \mathbf{c}^\perp\alpha}^{\mathsf{crs}}, \overbrace{\mathbf{c}\mathbf{k}^\top}^{C^* \text{ in } \mathsf{ct}^*}) \equiv (\mathbf{A}\mathbf{k}^\top, \mathbf{k}^\top, \mathbf{c}\mathbf{k}^\top - \alpha)$$

when $\mathbf{k} \leftarrow \mathbb{Z}_p^{1\times(2k+1)}$ and the fact that $[\alpha]_T$ only appears in C^*. We can prove the statement via change of variable $\mathbf{k}^\top \mapsto \mathbf{k}^\top - \mathbf{c}^\perp\alpha$. See the full paper for more details.

Observe that, in G_6, the challenge ciphertext ct^* is independent of b and the adversary's advantage is exactly 0.

3.3 From $\mathsf{G}_{5,\ell-1}$ to $\mathsf{G}_{5,\ell}$

We prove $\mathsf{G}_{5,\ell-1} \approx_c \mathsf{G}_{5,\ell}$ which completes our proof of Lemma 1. For this, we need the following sub-sequence of games for each $\ell \in [L]$:

- $\mathsf{G}_{5,\ell-1,0}$: Identical to $\mathsf{G}_{5,\ell-1}$. We recall crs and $\mathsf{pk}_i \in D_i$ in the following form, where we highlight $\mathbf{r}_\ell$-related terms using dashed boxes which will be changed in this sub-sequence.

$$\mathsf{crs} = \begin{pmatrix} [\mathbf{A}]_1, [\mathbf{A}\mathbf{k}^\top]_T, \{\mathsf{crs}_i, [\widehat{\mathbf{R}}_i, \mathbf{A}\mathbf{V}_i, \mathbf{A}\mathbf{W}_i]_1\}_{i\in[L]} \\ \{[\mathbf{B}\mathbf{r}_j^\top, \mathbf{V}_j\mathbf{B}\mathbf{r}_j^\top + \mathbf{k}^\top + \mathbf{c}^\perp\alpha]_2\}_{j\in[\ell-1]}, \\ \boxed{[\mathbf{B}\mathbf{r}_\ell^\top, \mathbf{V}_\ell\mathbf{B}\mathbf{r}_\ell^\top + \mathbf{k}^\top]_2}, \\ \{[\mathbf{B}\mathbf{r}_j^\top, \mathbf{V}_j\mathbf{B}\mathbf{r}_j^\top + \mathbf{k}^\top]_2\}_{j\in[L]\setminus[\ell]} \\ \{[\mathbf{V}_i\mathbf{B}\mathbf{r}_j^\top, \mathbf{W}_i(\mathbf{I}_n \otimes \mathbf{B}\mathbf{r}_j^\top)]_2\}_{j\in[L]\setminus\{\ell\}, i\in[L]\setminus\{j\}}, \\ \boxed{\{[\mathbf{V}_i\mathbf{B}\mathbf{r}_\ell^\top, \mathbf{W}_i(\mathbf{I}_n \otimes \mathbf{B}\mathbf{r}_\ell^\top)]_2\}_{i\in[L]\setminus\{\ell\}}} \end{pmatrix},$$

$$\mathsf{pk}_i = \begin{cases} ([\mathbf{A}\mathbf{U}_i, \widehat{\mathbf{R}}_i\mathbf{U}_i]_1, \{[\mathbf{U}_i\mathbf{B}\mathbf{r}_j^\top]_2\}_{j\in[L]\setminus\{i,\ell\}}, \boxed{[\mathbf{U}_i\mathbf{B}\mathbf{r}_\ell^\top]_2}, \widetilde{\pi}_i) & \text{if } i \neq \ell \\ ([\mathbf{A}\mathbf{U}_\ell, \widehat{\mathbf{R}}_\ell\mathbf{U}_\ell]_1, \{[\mathbf{U}_\ell\mathbf{B}\mathbf{r}_j^\top]_2\}_{j\in[L]\setminus\{\ell\}}, \widetilde{\pi}_\ell) & \text{if } i = \ell \end{cases}$$

  Clearly, we have $\mathsf{G}_{5,\ell-1,0} = \mathsf{G}_{5,\ell-1}$; all changes are conceptual.
- $\mathsf{G}_{5,\ell-1,1}$: Identical to $\mathsf{G}_{5,\ell-1,0}$ except that we replace all $\mathbf{B}\mathbf{r}_\ell^\top$ with $\mathbf{d}_\ell^\top \leftarrow \mathbb{Z}_p^{k+1}$ in crs; in particular, we change the dashed boxed term as follows:

$$[\boxed{\mathbf{d}_\ell^\top}, \mathbf{V}_\ell\boxed{\mathbf{d}_\ell^\top} + \mathbf{k}^\top]_2, \{[\mathbf{V}_i\boxed{\mathbf{d}_\ell^\top}, \mathbf{W}_i(\mathbf{I}_n \otimes \boxed{\mathbf{d}_\ell^\top})]_2, [\mathbf{U}_i\boxed{\mathbf{d}_\ell^\top}]_2\}_{i\in[L]\setminus\{\ell\}}$$

  We have $\mathsf{G}_{5,\ell-1,1} \approx_c \mathsf{G}_{5,\ell-1,0}$. This follows from MDDH assumption w.r.t. $[\mathbf{B}]_2$ which ensures that $([\mathbf{B}]_2, [\mathbf{B}\mathbf{r}_\ell^\top]_2) \approx_c ([\mathbf{B}]_2, [\mathbf{d}_\ell^\top]_2)$ when $\mathbf{B} \leftarrow \mathbb{Z}_p^{(k+1)\times k}$, $\mathbf{r}_\ell \leftarrow \mathbb{Z}_p^{1\times k}$, $\mathbf{d}_\ell \leftarrow \mathbb{Z}_p^{1\times(k+1)}$. See the full paper for more details.
- $\mathsf{G}_{5,\ell-1,2}$: Identical to $\mathsf{G}_{5,\ell-1,1}$ except that we change the dashed boxed terms as follows:

$$[\mathbf{d}_\ell^\top, \mathbf{V}_\ell\mathbf{d}_\ell^\top + \mathbf{k}^\top + \boxed{\mathbf{c}^\perp\alpha}]_2, \{[\mathbf{V}_i\mathbf{d}_\ell^\top, \mathbf{W}_i(\mathbf{I}_n \otimes \mathbf{d}_\ell^\top)]_2, [\mathbf{U}_i\mathbf{d}_\ell^\top]_2\}_{i\in[L]\setminus\{\ell\}}$$

  We have $\mathsf{G}_{5,\ell-1,2} \approx_c \mathsf{G}_{5,\ell-1,1}$. We provide an overview of the proof in Sect. 3.4.
- $\mathsf{G}_{5,\ell-1,3}$: Identical to $\mathsf{G}_{5,\ell-1,2}$ except that we replace all $\mathbf{d}_\ell^\top$ with $\mathbf{B}\mathbf{r}_\ell^\top$ where $\mathbf{r}_\ell^\top \leftarrow \mathbb{Z}_p^k$ in crs; in particular, we generate crs as follow:

$$[\boxed{\mathbf{B}\mathbf{r}_\ell^\top}, \mathbf{V}_\ell\boxed{\mathbf{B}\mathbf{r}_\ell^\top} + \mathbf{k}^\top + \mathbf{c}^\perp\alpha]_2, \{[\mathbf{V}_i\boxed{\mathbf{B}\mathbf{r}_\ell^\top}, \mathbf{W}_i(\mathbf{I}_n \otimes \boxed{\mathbf{B}\mathbf{r}_\ell^\top})]_2, [\mathbf{U}_i\boxed{\mathbf{B}\mathbf{r}_\ell^\top}]_2\}_{i\in[L]\setminus\{\ell\}}$$

We have $\mathsf{G}_{5,\ell-1,3} \approx_c \mathsf{G}_{5,\ell-1,2}$. Analogous to $\mathsf{G}_{5,\ell-1,1} \approx_c \mathsf{G}_{5,\ell-1,0}$, it follows from MDDH assumption w.r.t. $[\mathbf{B}]_2$ which ensures that $([\mathbf{B}]_2, [\mathbf{Br}_\ell^\top]_2) \approx_c ([\mathbf{B}]_2, [\mathbf{d}_\ell^\top]_2)$ when $\mathbf{B} \leftarrow \mathbb{Z}_p^{(k+1)\times k}$, $\mathbf{r}_\ell \leftarrow \mathbb{Z}_p^{1\times k}$, $\mathbf{d}_\ell \leftarrow \mathbb{Z}_p^{1\times(k+1)}$. See the full paper for more details.

Observe that, we have $\mathsf{G}_{5,\ell-1,3} = \mathsf{G}_{5,\ell}$ and this proves $\mathsf{G}_{5,\ell-1} \approx_c \mathsf{G}_{5,\ell}$.

3.4 From $\mathsf{G}_{5,\ell-1,1}$ to $\mathsf{G}_{5,\ell-1,2}$

We review $\mathsf{G}_{5,\ell-1,1}$ and $\mathsf{G}_{5,\ell-1,2}$ in the following form. Here we use solid boxes to indicate the difference between two games and use dashed boxes to highlight those terms that are relevant to our proof.

$$\mathsf{crs} = \begin{pmatrix} [\mathbf{A}]_1, [\mathbf{Ak}^\top]_T, \{\mathsf{crs}_i, [\widehat{\mathbf{R}}_i, \mathbf{AV}_i, \mathbf{AW}_i]_1\}_{i\in[L]} \\ \{[\mathbf{Br}_j^\top, \mathbf{V}_j\mathbf{Br}_j^\top + \mathbf{k}^\top + \mathbf{c}^\perp\alpha]_2\}_{j\in[\ell-1]}, \\ [\mathbf{d}_\ell^\top, \mathbf{V}_\ell\mathbf{d}_\ell^\top + \mathbf{k}^\top + \boxed{\mathbf{c}^\perp\alpha}]_2, \\ \{[\mathbf{Br}_j^\top, \mathbf{V}_j\mathbf{Br}_j^\top + \mathbf{k}^\top]_2\}_{j\in[L]\setminus[\ell]}; \\ \{[\mathbf{V}_i\mathbf{Br}_j^\top, \mathbf{W}_i(\mathbf{I}_n \otimes \mathbf{Br}_j^\top)]_2\}_{j\in[L]\setminus\{\ell\}, i\in[L]\setminus\{j\}}, \\ \{[\mathbf{V}_i\mathbf{d}_\ell^\top, \mathbf{W}_i(\mathbf{I}_n \otimes \mathbf{d}_\ell^\top)]_2\}_{i\in[L]\setminus\{\ell\}} \end{pmatrix},$$

$$\mathsf{pk}_i = \begin{cases} ([\mathbf{AU}_i, \widehat{\mathbf{R}}_i\mathbf{U}_i]_1, \{[\mathbf{U}_i\mathbf{Br}_j^\top]_2\}_{j\in[L]\setminus\{i,\ell\}}, [\mathbf{U}_i\mathbf{d}_\ell^\top]_2, \widetilde{\pi}_i) & \text{if } i \neq \ell \\ ([\mathbf{AU}_\ell, \widehat{\mathbf{R}}_\ell\mathbf{U}_\ell]_1, \{[\mathbf{U}_\ell\mathbf{Br}_j^\top]_2\}_{j\in[L]\setminus\{\ell\}}, \widetilde{\pi}_\ell) & \text{if } i = \ell \end{cases}$$

$$\mathbf{c}_1^* = (\mathbf{cV}_\ell + \mathbf{e}_1\widetilde{\mathbf{R}}_\ell^{-1}\mathbf{Q}_\ell^*)(\mathbf{a}_{y_\ell^*} \otimes \mathbf{I}_{k+1}) + \mathbf{cW}_\ell(\mathbf{K}_{y_\ell^*} \otimes \mathbf{I}_{k+1}) + \sum_{i\in[L]\setminus\{\ell\}} ((\mathbf{cV}_i + \mathbf{e}_1\widetilde{\mathbf{R}}_i^{-1}\mathbf{Q}_i^*)(\mathbf{a}_{y_i^*} \otimes \mathbf{I}_{k+1}) + \mathbf{cW}_i(\mathbf{K}_{y_i^*} \otimes \mathbf{I}_{k+1}))$$

$$\mathbf{c}_2^* = \mathbf{cW}_\ell(\mathbf{C}_{x^*} \otimes \mathbf{I}_{k+1}) + \sum_{i\in[L]\setminus\{\ell\}} \mathbf{cW}_i(\mathbf{C}_{x^*} \otimes \mathbf{I}_{k+1})$$

we define $\mathbf{c}^\perp \in \mathbb{Z}_p^{2k+1}$ and $\mathbf{d}^\perp \in \mathbb{Z}_p^{1\times(k+1)}$ such that $\mathbf{Ac}^\perp = \mathbf{0}$, $\mathbf{cc}^\perp = 1$, $\mathbf{d}^\perp\mathbf{B} = \mathbf{0}$ and $\mathbf{d}^\perp\mathbf{d}_\ell = 1$. We will proof $\mathsf{G}_{5,\ell-1,2} \approx_c \mathsf{G}_{5,\ell-1,1}$ by considering two cases: (1) pk_ℓ^* is honest; (2) pk_ℓ^* is corrupted or maliciously generated by the adversary.

Useful Lemma. Before we proceed, we prepare the following lemma.

Lemma 2. *For all* $\mathbf{B} \leftarrow \mathbb{Z}_p^{(k+1)\times k}$ *and* $\mathbf{d}^\perp \leftarrow \mathbb{Z}_p^{1\times(k+1)}$ *such that* $\mathbf{d}^\perp\mathbf{B} = 0$. *For any adversary* $\mathcal{A}$, *there exist an adversary* $\mathcal{B}_2$ *such that*

$$\begin{aligned} &\big|\Pr[\mathcal{A}(\mathbf{M}, [\mathbf{R}]_1, \mathbf{B}, \mathbf{d}^\perp, \mathbf{MU}, [\mathbf{RU}]_1, \mathbf{UB}) = 1] - \\ &\Pr[\mathcal{A}(\mathbf{M}, [\mathbf{R}]_1, \mathbf{B}, \mathbf{d}^\perp, \mathbf{MU}, [\mathbf{RU} + \boxed{\mathbf{u}^\top\mathbf{d}^\perp}]_1, \mathbf{UB}) = 1]\big| \\ \le\ & 2 \cdot \mathsf{Adv}_{\mathcal{B}_2}^{\mathrm{MDDH}} + \mathsf{negl}(\lambda) \end{aligned}$$

where $\mathbf{M} \leftarrow \mathbb{Z}_p^{(k+1)\times(2k+1)}$, $\mathbf{R} \leftarrow \mathbb{Z}_p^{(2k+2)\times(2k+1)}$, $\mathbf{U} \leftarrow \mathbb{Z}_p^{(2k+1)\times(k+1)}$ *and* $\mathbf{u} \leftarrow \mathbb{Z}_p^{1\times(2k+2)}$.

Before proving the lemma, we give some intuition by investigating a simplified version without $\mathbf{B}$ and $\mathbf{d}$:

$$\mathbf{M}, [\mathbf{R}]_1, \mathbf{MU}, [\mathbf{RU}]_1 \approx_c \mathbf{M}, [\mathbf{R}]_1, \mathbf{MU}, [\widehat{\mathbf{U}}]_1$$

where $\mathbf{M}, \mathbf{R}, \mathbf{U}$ are defined as before and $\widehat{\mathbf{U}} \leftarrow \mathbb{Z}_p^{(2k+2)\times(k+1)}$. If we encode $\mathbf{M}$ and $\mathbf{MU}$ over $\mathbb{G}_1$, this is simply MDDH assumption and there is nothing special. The main point here is that we give out $\mathbf{M}$ directly to the adversary. This allows it to get the kernel space of $\mathbf{M}$ which is crucial for its future application. Looking ahead, we will set $\mathbf{M} = \binom{\mathbf{A}}{\mathbf{c}}$ and want to know/simulate $\mathbf{c}^\perp$. However, this hurts the indistinguishability; the adversary can recover $\mathbf{U}$ and check whether the last term is truly random. At this point the shape of $\mathbf{M}$ saves us. Note that $\mathbf{M}$ is a wide matrix rather than a square one. The main idea behind the proof is that given $\mathbf{M}, \mathbf{MU}$, there is still some entropy left inside $[\mathbf{RU}]_1$ so that we can argue its pseudorandomness even given $[\mathbf{R}]_1$ as MDDH. A detailed proof of the lemma is as follows.

Proof. We prove the lemma with the following argument:

$$\begin{aligned}
&\mathbf{M}, [\mathbf{R}]_1, \quad \mathbf{B}, \mathbf{d}^\perp, \mathbf{MU}, [\mathbf{RU}]_1, && \mathbf{UB} \\
\approx_c\ &\mathbf{M}, [\boxed{\widetilde{\mathbf{R}}\mathbf{D}}]_1, \mathbf{B}, \mathbf{d}^\perp, \mathbf{MU}, [\boxed{\widetilde{\mathbf{R}}\mathbf{D}}\mathbf{U}]_1, && \mathbf{UB} \quad // \text{ MDDH} \\
\approx_s\ &\mathbf{M}, [\widetilde{\mathbf{R}}\mathbf{D}]_1, \mathbf{B}, \mathbf{d}^\perp, \mathbf{MU}, [\widetilde{\mathbf{R}}\mathbf{DU} + \boxed{\widetilde{\mathbf{R}}\widetilde{\mathbf{u}}^\top\mathbf{d}^\perp}]_1, && \mathbf{UB} \quad // \text{ change of variable} \\
\approx_c\ &\mathbf{M}, [\boxed{\mathbf{R}}]_1, \mathbf{B}, \mathbf{d}^\perp, \mathbf{MU}, [\boxed{\mathbf{R}}\mathbf{U} + \boxed{\mathbf{u}^\top}\mathbf{d}^\perp]_1, && \mathbf{UB} \quad // \text{ MDDH}
\end{aligned}$$

where $\widetilde{\mathbf{R}} \leftarrow \mathbb{Z}_p^{(2k+2)\times k}$, $\mathbf{D} \leftarrow \mathbb{Z}_p^{k\times(2k+1)}$ and $\widetilde{\mathbf{u}} \leftarrow \mathbb{Z}_p^{1\times k}$. We justify each step as follows: The first $\approx_c$ follows from MDDH assumption w.r.t. $[\widetilde{\mathbf{R}}]_1$ which ensures that $[\mathbf{R}]_1 \approx_c [\widetilde{\mathbf{R}}\mathbf{D}]_1$. The second $\approx_s$ follows from change of variable

$$\mathbf{U} \mapsto \mathbf{U} + \mathbf{D}^\perp\widetilde{\mathbf{u}}^\top\mathbf{d}^\perp$$

where $\widetilde{\mathbf{u}} \leftarrow \mathbb{Z}_p^{1\times k}$ and $\mathbf{D}^\perp \in \mathbb{Z}_p^{(2k+1)\times k}$ such that $\mathbf{DD}^\perp = \mathbf{I}$ and $\mathbf{MD}^\perp = \mathbf{0}$; this uses the fact that $\begin{pmatrix}\mathbf{M}\\ \mathbf{D}\end{pmatrix}$ has full rank w.h.p. The third $\approx_c$ follows from MDDH assumption w.r.t. $[\widetilde{\mathbf{R}}]_1$ which ensures that $[\widetilde{\mathbf{R}}, \widetilde{\mathbf{R}}(\mathbf{D}\|\widetilde{\mathbf{u}}^\top)]_1 \approx_c [\widetilde{\mathbf{R}}, (\mathbf{R}\|\mathbf{u}^\top)]_1$. This readily proves the lemma. □

Honest Case. In this case, we have $\mathsf{pk}_\ell^* = ([\mathbf{T}_\ell^*, \mathbf{Q}_\ell^*]_1, \{[\mathbf{h}_{\ell,j}^{*\,\top}]_2\}_{j\in[L]\setminus\{\ell\}}, \pi_\ell^*) \in D_\ell \setminus C_\ell$. Namely, we know $\mathbf{U}_\ell^*$ (such that $\mathbf{T}_\ell^* = \mathbf{AU}_\ell^*$ and $\mathbf{Q}_\ell^* = \widehat{\mathbf{R}}_\ell\mathbf{U}_\ell^*$) and $\mathbf{U}_\ell^*$ is hidden from the adversary. We can write the dashboxed terms in $\mathbf{c}_1^*$ as follows:

$$(\mathbf{cV}_\ell + \boxed{\mathbf{cU}_\ell^*})(\mathbf{a}_{y_\ell^*} \otimes \mathbf{I}_{k+1}) + \mathbf{cW}_\ell(\mathbf{K}_{y_\ell^*} \otimes \mathbf{I}_{k+1})$$

and replace $\widehat{\mathbf{R}}_\ell$ in crs with a random $\mathbf{R}_\ell$ as in G_1. We prove $\mathsf{G}_{5,\ell-1,2} \approx_c \mathsf{G}_{5,\ell-1,1}$ in this case using the following argument for all $b \in \{0,1\}$:

$$\begin{aligned}
&\mathbf{A}, \mathbf{c}^\perp, \mathbf{B}, [\mathbf{R}_\ell]_1, \mathbf{d}_\ell^\top, \mathbf{A}\mathbf{V}_\ell, \mathbf{V}_\ell\mathbf{B}, \mathbf{V}_\ell\mathbf{d}_\ell^\top + b\mathbf{c}^\perp\alpha && //\mathsf{crs}, \mathsf{pk}_\ell\\
&\mathbf{c}, \mathbf{c}\mathbf{V}_\ell + \mathbf{c}\mathbf{U}_\ell^*;\ \mathbf{A}\mathbf{U}_\ell^*, [\mathbf{R}_\ell\mathbf{U}_\ell^*]_1, \mathbf{U}_\ell^*\mathbf{B} && //\mathsf{ct}^*, \mathsf{pk}_\ell^*\\
\approx_c\ &\mathbf{A}, \mathbf{c}^\perp, \mathbf{B}, [\mathbf{R}_\ell]_1, \mathbf{d}_\ell^\top, \mathbf{A}\mathbf{V}_\ell, \mathbf{V}_\ell\mathbf{B}, \mathbf{V}_\ell\mathbf{d}_\ell^\top + b\mathbf{c}^\perp\alpha\\
&\mathbf{c}, \mathbf{c}\mathbf{V}_\ell + \mathbf{c}\mathbf{U}_\ell^*;\ \mathbf{A}\mathbf{U}_\ell^*, [\mathbf{R}_\ell\mathbf{U}_\ell^* + \boxed{\widehat{\mathbf{u}}^\top\mathbf{d}^\perp}]_1, \mathbf{U}_\ell^*\mathbf{B}\\
\approx_s\ &\mathbf{A}, \mathbf{c}^\perp, \mathbf{B}, [\mathbf{R}_\ell]_1, \mathbf{d}_\ell^\top, \mathbf{A}\mathbf{V}_\ell, \mathbf{V}_\ell\mathbf{B}, \mathbf{V}_\ell\mathbf{d}_\ell^\top + \boxed{\mathbf{c}^\perp v_\ell} + b\mathbf{c}^\perp\alpha\\
&\mathbf{c}, \mathbf{c}\mathbf{V}_\ell + \mathbf{c}\mathbf{U}_\ell^* + \boxed{v_\ell\mathbf{d}^\perp + u_\ell\mathbf{d}^\perp};\ \mathbf{A}\mathbf{U}_\ell^*, [\mathbf{R}_\ell\mathbf{U}_\ell^* + \boxed{\mathbf{R}_\ell\mathbf{c}^\perp u_\ell\mathbf{d}^\perp} + \widehat{\mathbf{u}}^\top\mathbf{d}^\perp]_1, \mathbf{U}_\ell^*\mathbf{B}\\
\approx_s\ &\mathbf{A}, \mathbf{c}^\perp, \mathbf{B}, [\mathbf{R}_\ell]_1, \mathbf{d}_\ell^\top, \mathbf{A}\mathbf{V}_\ell, \mathbf{V}_\ell\mathbf{B}, \mathbf{V}_\ell\mathbf{d}_\ell^\top + \mathbf{c}^\perp v_\ell + \cancel{b\mathbf{c}^\perp\alpha}\\
&\mathbf{c}, \mathbf{c}\mathbf{V}_\ell + \mathbf{c}\mathbf{U}_\ell^* + v_\ell\mathbf{d}^\perp + u_\ell\mathbf{d}^\perp;\ \mathbf{A}\mathbf{U}_\ell^*, [\mathbf{R}_\ell\mathbf{U}_\ell^* + \mathbf{R}_\ell\mathbf{c}^\perp u_\ell\mathbf{d}^\perp + \widehat{\mathbf{u}}^\top\mathbf{d}^\perp]_1, \mathbf{U}_\ell^*\mathbf{B}
\end{aligned}$$

where $\widehat{\mathbf{u}} \leftarrow \mathbb{Z}_p^{1\times(2k+2)}$ and $v_\ell, u_\ell \leftarrow \mathbb{Z}_p$. We justify each step as below: The first $\approx_c$ uses Lemma 2 with $\mathbf{M} = \begin{pmatrix}\mathbf{A}\\ \mathbf{c}\end{pmatrix}$, $\mathbf{R} = \mathbf{R}_\ell$, $\mathbf{U} = \mathbf{U}_\ell^*$ and $\mathbf{u} = \widehat{\mathbf{u}}$; in the reduction, we sample $\mathbf{V}_\ell$, α and $\mathbf{c}^\perp$. The second $\approx_s$ uses change of variables

$$\mathbf{V}_\ell \mapsto \mathbf{V}_\ell + \mathbf{c}^\perp v_\ell\mathbf{d}^\perp \quad \text{and} \quad \mathbf{U}_\ell^* \mapsto \mathbf{U}_\ell^* + \mathbf{c}^\perp u_\ell\mathbf{d}^\perp.$$

The last $\approx_s$ is straight-forward with the observation that $\widehat{\mathbf{u}}^\top$ hides $\mathbf{R}_\ell\mathbf{c}^\perp u_\ell$. See the full paper for more details.

Corrupted and Malicious Case. In this case, we have $\mathsf{pk}_\ell^* = ([\mathbf{T}_\ell^*, \mathbf{Q}_\ell^*]_1, \{[\mathbf{h}_{\ell,j}^{*\top}]_2\}_{j\in[L]\setminus\{\ell\}}, \pi_\ell^*) \in C_\ell \cup \overline{D}_\ell$. It is required that $P(x^*, y_\ell^*) = 0$. We prove $\mathsf{G}_{5,\ell-1,2} \approx_s \mathsf{G}_{5,\ell-1,1}$ in this case using the following argument for all $b \in \{0,1\}$:

$$\begin{aligned}
&\mathbf{A}, \mathbf{c}^\perp, \mathbf{B}, \mathbf{d}_\ell^\top, \mathbf{A}\mathbf{V}_\ell, \mathbf{V}_\ell\mathbf{B}, \mathbf{A}\mathbf{W}_\ell, \mathbf{W}_\ell(\mathbf{I}_n \otimes \mathbf{B}), \mathbf{V}_\ell\mathbf{d}_\ell^\top + b\mathbf{c}^\perp\alpha && //\mathsf{crs}\\
&\mathbf{c}, \mathbf{c}\mathbf{V}_\ell(\mathbf{a}_{y_\ell^*} \otimes \mathbf{I}_{k+1}) + \mathbf{c}\mathbf{W}_\ell(\mathbf{K}_{y_\ell^*} \otimes \mathbf{I}_{k+1}), && //\mathsf{ct}_0^*, \mathsf{ct}_1^*\\
&\mathbf{c}\mathbf{W}_\ell(\mathbf{C}_{x^*} \otimes \mathbf{I}_{k+1}) && //\mathsf{ct}_2^*\\
\approx_s\ &\mathbf{A}, \mathbf{c}^\perp, \mathbf{B}, \mathbf{d}_\ell^\top, \mathbf{A}\mathbf{V}_\ell, \mathbf{V}_\ell\mathbf{B}, \mathbf{A}\mathbf{W}_\ell, \mathbf{W}_\ell(\mathbf{I}_n \otimes \mathbf{B}), \mathbf{V}_\ell\mathbf{d}_\ell^\top + \boxed{\mathbf{c}^\perp v_\ell} + b\mathbf{c}^\perp\alpha\\
&\mathbf{c}, \mathbf{c}\mathbf{V}_\ell(\mathbf{a}_{y_\ell^*} \otimes \mathbf{I}_{k+1}) + \mathbf{c}\mathbf{W}_\ell(\mathbf{K}_{y_\ell^*} \otimes \mathbf{I}_{k+1}) + \boxed{v_\ell\mathbf{a}_{y_\ell^*} \otimes \mathbf{d}^\perp + \mathbf{w}_\ell\mathbf{K}_{y_\ell^*} \otimes \mathbf{d}^\perp},\\
&\mathbf{c}\mathbf{W}_\ell(\mathbf{C}_{x^*} \otimes \mathbf{I}_{k+1}) + \boxed{\mathbf{w}_\ell\mathbf{C}_{x^*} \otimes \mathbf{d}^\perp}\\
\approx_s\ &\mathbf{A}, \mathbf{c}^\perp, \mathbf{B}, \mathbf{d}_\ell^\top, \mathbf{A}\mathbf{V}_\ell, \mathbf{V}_\ell\mathbf{B}, \mathbf{A}\mathbf{W}_\ell, \mathbf{W}_\ell(\mathbf{I}_n \otimes \mathbf{B}), \mathbf{V}_\ell\mathbf{d}_\ell^\top + \mathbf{c}^\perp v_\ell + b\mathbf{c}^\perp\alpha\\
&\mathbf{c}, \mathbf{c}\mathbf{V}_\ell(\mathbf{a}_{y_\ell^*} \otimes \mathbf{I}_{k+1}) + \mathbf{c}\mathbf{W}_\ell(\mathbf{K}_{y_\ell^*} \otimes \mathbf{I}_{k+1}) + \cancel{v_\ell\mathbf{a}_{y_\ell^*} \otimes \mathbf{d}^\perp} + \mathbf{w}_\ell\mathbf{K}_{y_\ell^*} \otimes \mathbf{d}^\perp,\\
&\mathbf{c}\mathbf{W}_\ell(\mathbf{C}_{x^*} \otimes \mathbf{I}_{k+1}) + \mathbf{w}_\ell\mathbf{C}_{x^*} \otimes \mathbf{d}^\perp\\
\approx_s\ &\mathbf{A}, \mathbf{c}^\perp, \mathbf{B}, \mathbf{d}_\ell^\top, \mathbf{A}\mathbf{V}_\ell, \mathbf{V}_\ell\mathbf{B}, \mathbf{A}\mathbf{W}_\ell, \mathbf{W}_\ell(\mathbf{I}_n \otimes \mathbf{B}), \mathbf{V}_\ell\mathbf{d}_\ell^\top + \mathbf{c}^\perp v_\ell + \cancel{b\mathbf{c}^\perp\alpha}\\
&\mathbf{c}, \mathbf{c}\mathbf{V}_\ell(\mathbf{a}_{y_\ell^*} \otimes \mathbf{I}_{k+1}) + \mathbf{c}\mathbf{W}_\ell(\mathbf{K}_{y_\ell^*} \otimes \mathbf{I}_{k+1}) + \mathbf{w}_\ell\mathbf{K}_{y_\ell^*} \otimes \mathbf{d}^\perp,\\
&\mathbf{c}\mathbf{W}_\ell(\mathbf{C}_{x^*} \otimes \mathbf{I}_{k+1}) + \mathbf{w}_\ell\mathbf{C}_{x^*} \otimes \mathbf{d}^\perp
\end{aligned}$$

where $v_\ell \leftarrow \mathbb{Z}_p$ and $\mathbf{w}_\ell \leftarrow \mathbb{Z}_p^n$. We justify each step as follows: The first $\approx_s$ uses the change of variables:

$$\mathbf{V}_\ell \mapsto \mathbf{V}_\ell + \mathbf{c}^\perp v_\ell\mathbf{d}^\perp \quad \text{and} \quad \mathbf{W}_\ell \mapsto \mathbf{W}_\ell + \mathbf{c}^\perp(\mathbf{w}_\ell \otimes \mathbf{d}^\perp)$$

The second $\approx_s$ uses the fact that $P(x^*, y^*_\ell) = 0$ and the security of predicate encoding defined in Sect. 2.3. The last $\approx_s$ is straight-forward. See the full paper for more details.

4 Concrete Slotted Reg-ABE

This section presents our concrete slotted Reg-ABE for arithmetic branching programs (ABP), derived from the generic scheme in Sect. 3. We use the predicate encoding of arithmetic span programs (ASP) [5, Appendix A] which captures ABP [24]. As mentioned before, we employ the pairing-based QA-NIZK scheme by Kiltz and Wee, see the full paper. Our concrete slotted Reg-ABE for span program and zero inner-product predicate and slotted RBE are deferred to the full paper.

Preliminaries. An Arithmetic Span Program [24], denoted by V, is defined by $(\mathbf{Y}, \mathbf{Z}) \in \mathbb{Z}_p^{m\times\ell} \times \mathbb{Z}_p^{m\times\ell}$ where

$$V(\mathbf{x}) = 1 \iff \mathbf{x} \in \mathbb{Z}_p^{1\times m} \text{ satisfies } V \iff \exists \boldsymbol{\omega} \in \mathbb{Z}_p^{1\times m} \text{ s.t. } \mathbf{e}_1 = \boldsymbol{\omega}(\mathsf{diag}(\mathbf{x}) \cdot \mathbf{Y} + \mathbf{Z}).$$

Here we use notation: $\mathsf{diag}(\mathbf{x}) := \begin{pmatrix} x_1 & & \\ & \ddots & \\ & & x_m \end{pmatrix} \in \mathbb{Z}_p^{m\times m}$ for $\mathbf{x} = (x_1, \ldots, x_m)$

and note that $\mathsf{diag}(\mathbf{x}) = \mathsf{diag}(\mathbf{x})^\top$. We review the predicate encoding for ASP predicate (ciphertext-policy variant):

$$P(V, \mathbf{x}) = 1 \iff V(\mathbf{x}) = 1$$

as follows [5, Appendix A.6]: let $n = 2m + \ell$, $n_c = 2m$ and $n_k = m + 1$, define

$$\mathbf{C}_{\mathbf{Y},\mathbf{Z}} = \begin{pmatrix} \mathbf{I}_m & \mathbf{0}_{m\times m} \\ \mathbf{0}_{m\times m} & \mathbf{I}_m \\ \mathbf{Y}^\top & \mathbf{Z}^\top \end{pmatrix}, \qquad \mathbf{K}_{\mathbf{x}} = \begin{pmatrix} \mathbf{0}_m^\top & \mathsf{diag}(\mathbf{x}) \\ \mathbf{0}_m^\top & \mathbf{I}_m \\ \mathbf{e}_1^\top & \mathbf{0}_{\ell\times m} \end{pmatrix},$$

$$\mathbf{a}_{\mathbf{x}} = (1 \| \mathbf{0}_m), \qquad \mathbf{d}_{\mathbf{x},\mathbf{Y},\mathbf{Z}} = (1 \| \boldsymbol{\omega} \| - \boldsymbol{\omega} \cdot \mathsf{diag}(\mathbf{x}) \| - \boldsymbol{\omega})$$

where $\mathbf{0}_m$ is a *row* zero vector of size m. Note that we work with *read-once* ASP as in [5].

Scheme. Our concrete slotted Registered CP-ABE for read-once ASP from SXDH (1-Lin) assumption works as follows:

- $\mathsf{Setup}(1^\lambda, P, 1^L)$: Run $\mathbb{G} := (p, \mathbb{G}_1, \mathbb{G}_2, \mathbb{G}_T, e) \leftarrow \mathcal{G}(1^\lambda)$. Sample

  $$\mathbf{a} \leftarrow \mathbb{Z}_p^{1\times 3},\ \mathbf{b}^\top \leftarrow \mathbb{Z}_p^2,\ \mathbf{k} \leftarrow \mathbb{Z}_p^{1\times 3}.$$

  For all $i \in [L]$, sample

  $$\mathbf{V}_i \leftarrow \mathbb{Z}_p^{3\times 2},\ \mathbf{W}_i \leftarrow \mathbb{Z}_p^{3\times 2(2m+\ell)},\ \mathbf{R}_i \leftarrow \mathbb{Z}_p^{4\times 3},\ r_i \leftarrow \mathbb{Z}_p.$$

For all $i \in [L]$, write $\mathbf{A}_i = \binom{\mathbf{a}}{\mathbf{R}_i}$ and sample

$$\mathbf{a}_i' \leftarrow \mathbb{Z}_p^{1\times 2},\ \mathbf{b}_i'^\top \leftarrow \mathbb{Z}_p^2,\ \mathbf{K}_i' \leftarrow \mathbb{Z}_p^{5\times 2},\ \mathbf{K}_{i,0}', \mathbf{K}_{i,1}' \leftarrow \mathbb{Z}_p^{2\times 2}$$

and compute

$$\mathbf{P}_i = \mathbf{A}_i^\top \mathbf{K}_i', \quad \mathbf{p}_{i,0} = \mathbf{a}_i'\mathbf{K}_{i,0}', \quad \mathbf{p}_{i,1} = \mathbf{a}_i'\mathbf{K}_{i,1}';$$

$$\mathbf{c}_i'^\top = \mathbf{K}_i'\mathbf{b}_i'^\top, \quad \mathbf{c}_{i,0}'^\top = \mathbf{K}_{i,0}'\mathbf{b}_i'^\top, \quad \mathbf{c}_{i,1}'^\top = \mathbf{K}_{i,1}'\mathbf{b}_i'^\top.$$

For all $i \in [L]$, set

$$\mathsf{crs}_i = ([\mathbf{a}_i', \mathbf{P}_i, \mathbf{p}_{i,0}, \mathbf{p}_{i,1}]_1, [\mathbf{b}_i'^\top, \mathbf{c}_i'^\top, \mathbf{c}_{i,0}'^\top, \mathbf{c}_{i,1}'^\top]_2) \quad \mathsf{td}_i = \mathbf{K}_i'.$$

Output

$$\mathsf{crs} = \begin{pmatrix} [\mathbf{a}]_1, [\mathbf{a}\mathbf{k}^\top]_T, \{\mathsf{crs}_i, [\mathbf{R}_i, \mathbf{a}\mathbf{V}_i, \mathbf{a}\mathbf{W}_i]_1\}_{i\in[L]} \\ \{[\mathbf{b}^\top r_j, \mathbf{V}_j\mathbf{b}^\top r_j + \mathbf{k}^\top]_2\}_{j\in[L]} \\ \{[\mathbf{V}_i\mathbf{b}^\top r_j, \mathbf{W}_i(\mathbf{I}_{2m+\ell} \otimes \mathbf{b}^\top r_j)]_2\}_{j\in[L], i\in[L]\setminus\{j\}} \end{pmatrix}.$$

– $\mathsf{Gen}(\mathsf{crs}, i)$: Sample $\mathbf{U}_i \leftarrow \mathbb{Z}_p^{3\times 2}$. Define $\mathbf{M}_i = \binom{\mathbf{t}_i}{\mathbf{Q}_i} = \binom{\mathbf{a}\mathbf{U}_i}{\mathbf{R}_i\mathbf{U}_i}$, sample $\mathbf{s}_i^\top \leftarrow \mathbb{Z}_p^2$, and compute

$$\pi_i = [\underbrace{\mathbf{U}_i^\top \mathbf{P}_i + \mathbf{s}_i^\top(\mathbf{p}_{i,0} + \mathbf{p}_{i,1})}_{\pi_{i,0}}, \underbrace{\mathbf{s}_i^\top \mathbf{a}_i'}_{\pi_{i,1}}]_1$$

Fetch $[\mathbf{R}_i]_1$ and $\{[\mathbf{b}^\top r_j]_2\}_{j\in[L]\setminus\{i\}}$ from crs and output

$$\mathsf{pk}_i = ([\underbrace{\mathbf{a}\mathbf{U}_i}_{\mathbf{t}_i}, \underbrace{\mathbf{R}_i\mathbf{U}_i}_{\mathbf{Q}_i}]_1, \{[\underbrace{\mathbf{U}_i\mathbf{b}^\top r_j}_{\mathbf{h}_{i,j}^\top}]_2\}_{j\in[L]\setminus\{i\}}, \pi_i) \quad \text{and} \quad \mathsf{sk}_i = \mathbf{U}_i.$$

– $\mathsf{Ver}(\mathsf{crs}, i, \mathsf{pk}_i)$: Parse $\mathsf{pk}_i = ([\mathbf{t}_i, \mathbf{Q}_i]_1, \{[\mathbf{h}_{i,j}^\top]_2\}_{j\in[L]\setminus\{i\}}, \pi_i)$ and fetch $[\mathbf{b}_i'^\top, \mathbf{c}_i'^\top, \mathbf{c}_{i,0}'^\top, \mathbf{c}_{i,1}'^\top]_2$ from crs_i in crs. Write $\mathbf{M}_i = \binom{\mathbf{t}_i}{\mathbf{Q}_i}$ and parse $\pi_i = [\pi_{i,0}, \pi_{i,1}]_1$, check

$$e([\pi_{i,0}]_1, [\mathbf{b}_i'^\top]_2) \stackrel{?}{=} e([\mathbf{M}_i^\top]_1, [\mathbf{c}_i'^\top]_2) \cdot e([\pi_{i,1}]_1, [\mathbf{c}_{i,0}'^\top + \mathbf{c}_{i,1}'^\top]_2)$$

For each $j \in [L] \setminus \{i\}$, check

$$e([\mathbf{a}]_1, [\mathbf{h}_{i,j}^\top]_2) \stackrel{?}{=} e([\mathbf{t}_i]_1, [\mathbf{b}^\top r_j]_2).$$

If all these checks pass, output 1; otherwise, output 0.

– $\mathsf{Agg}(\mathsf{crs}, (\mathsf{pk}_i, \mathbf{x}_i)_{i\in[L]})$: For all $i \in [L]$, parse

$$\mathsf{pk}_i = ([\mathbf{t}_i, \mathbf{Q}_i]_1, \{[\mathbf{h}_{i,j}^\top]_2\}_{j\in[L]\setminus\{i\}}, \pi_i).$$

Output:

$$\mathsf{mpk} = \left([\mathbf{a}]_1, \left[\sum_{i \in [L]} \left((\mathbf{aV}_i + \mathbf{t}_i)((1\|\mathbf{0}_m) \otimes \mathbf{I}_2) + \mathbf{aW}_i \left(\begin{pmatrix} \mathbf{0}_m & \mathsf{diag}(\mathbf{x}_i) \\ \mathbf{0}_m & \mathbf{I}_m \\ \mathbf{e}_1^\top & \mathbf{0}_{\ell \times m} \end{pmatrix} \otimes \mathbf{I}_2 \right) \right) \right]_1, \left[\sum_{i \in [L]} \mathbf{aW}_i \right]_1, [\mathbf{ak}^\top]_T \right)$$

and for all $j \in [L]$

$$\mathsf{hsk}_j = \Bigg(\underbrace{[\mathbf{b}^\top r_j]_2}_{\mathbf{k}_0^\top}, \underbrace{[\mathbf{V}_j \mathbf{b}^\top r_j + \mathbf{k}^\top]_2}_{\mathbf{k}_1^\top}, \underbrace{\left[\sum_{i \in [L] \setminus \{j\}} \left((\mathbf{V}_i \mathbf{b}^\top r_j + \mathbf{h}_{i,j}^\top)(1\|\mathbf{0}_m) + \mathbf{W}_i (\mathbf{I}_{2m+\ell} \otimes \mathbf{b}^\top r_j) \begin{pmatrix} \mathbf{0}_m & \mathsf{diag}(\mathbf{x}_i) \\ \mathbf{0}_m & \mathbf{I}_m \\ \mathbf{e}_1^\top & \mathbf{0}_{\ell \times m} \end{pmatrix} \right) \right]_2}_{\mathbf{K}_2}, \underbrace{\left[\sum_{i \in [L] \setminus \{j\}} \mathbf{W}_i (\mathbf{I}_{2m+\ell} \otimes \mathbf{b}^\top r_j) \right]_2}_{\mathbf{K}_3} \Bigg).$$

- $\mathsf{Enc}(\mathsf{mpk}, (\mathbf{Y}, \mathbf{Z}), \mathsf{m})$: Sample $s \leftarrow \mathbb{Z}_p$. Output:

$$\mathsf{ct}_{\mathbf{Y},\mathbf{Z}} = \Bigg([\underbrace{s\mathbf{a}}_{\mathbf{c}_0}]_1, \underbrace{\left[\sum_{i \in [L]} \left((s\mathbf{aV}_i + s\mathbf{t}_i)((1\|\mathbf{0}_m) \otimes \mathbf{I}_2) + s\mathbf{aW}_i \left(\begin{pmatrix} \mathbf{0}_m & \mathsf{diag}(\mathbf{x}_i) \\ \mathbf{0}_m & \mathbf{I}_m \\ \mathbf{e}_1^\top & \mathbf{0}_{\ell \times m} \end{pmatrix} \otimes \mathbf{I}_2 \right) \right) \right]_1}_{\mathbf{c}_1}, \underbrace{\left[\sum_{i \in [L]} s\mathbf{aW}_i \left(\begin{pmatrix} \mathbf{I}_m & \mathbf{0}_{m \times m} \\ \mathbf{0}_{m \times m} & \mathbf{I}_m \\ \mathbf{Y}^\top & \mathbf{Z}^\top \end{pmatrix} \otimes \mathbf{I}_2 \right) \right]_1}_{\mathbf{c}_2}, \underbrace{[s\mathbf{ak}^\top]_T \cdot \mathsf{m}}_{C} \Bigg).$$

- $\mathsf{Dec}(\mathsf{sk}_{i^*}, \mathsf{hsk}_{i^*}, \mathsf{ct}_{\mathbf{Y},\mathbf{Z}})$: Parse

$$\mathsf{sk}_{i^*} = \mathbf{U}_{i^*}, \quad \mathsf{hsk}_{i^*} = [\mathbf{k}_0^\top, \mathbf{k}_1^\top, \mathbf{K}_2, \mathbf{K}_3]_2, \quad \mathsf{ct}_x = ([\mathbf{c}_0, \mathbf{c}_1, \mathbf{c}_2]_1, C).$$

recover

$$\begin{aligned} [\mathbf{z}_1]_T &= e([\mathbf{c}_1 \| \mathbf{c}_2]_1, [\mathbf{I}_{3m+1} \otimes \mathbf{k}_0^\top]_2), \\ [\mathbf{z}_2]_T &= e\left([\mathbf{c}_0]_1, \left[\mathbf{K}_2 \| \mathbf{K}_3 \begin{pmatrix} \mathbf{I}_m & \mathbf{0}_{m \times m} \\ \mathbf{0}_{m \times m} & \mathbf{I}_m \\ \mathbf{Y}^\top & \mathbf{Z}^\top \end{pmatrix} \right]_2 \right), \\ [z_3]_T &= e([\mathbf{c}_0 \mathbf{U}_{i^*}]_1, [\mathbf{k}_0^\top]_2), \\ [z_4]_T &= e([\mathbf{c}_0]_1, [\mathbf{k}_1^\top]_2). \end{aligned}$$

Compute $\boldsymbol{\omega}$ such that $\mathbf{e}_1 = \boldsymbol{\omega}(\mathsf{diag}(\mathbf{x}_{i^*}) \cdot \mathbf{Y} + \mathbf{Z})$, output

$$\mathsf{m}' = [(\mathbf{z}_1 - \mathbf{z}_2) \cdot (1 \| \boldsymbol{\omega} \| - \boldsymbol{\omega} \cdot \mathsf{diag}(\mathbf{x}_{i^*}) \| - \boldsymbol{\omega})^\top - z_3 - z_4]_T \cdot C.$$

Acknowledgement. We want to thank anonymous reviewers from Asiacrypt 2023 for their insightful comments and Hoeteck Wee for his encouragement! This work is partially supported by National Natural Science Foundation of China (62002120), Shanghai Rising-Star Program (22QA1403800), Innovation Program of Shanghai Municipal Education Commission (2021-01-07-00-08-E00101) and the "Digital Silk Road" Shanghai International Joint Lab of Trustworthy Intelligent Software (22510750100).

References

1. Abdalla, M., Catalano, D., Gay, R., Ursu, B.: Inner-product functional encryption with fine-grained access control. In: Moriai, S., Wang, H. (eds.) ASIACRYPT 2020. LNCS, vol. 12493, pp. 467–497. Springer, Cham (2020). https://doi.org/10.1007/978-3-030-64840-4_16
2. Ambrona, M., Barthe, G., Schmidt, B.: Generic transformations of predicate encodings: constructions and applications. In: Katz, J., Shacham, H. (eds.) CRYPTO 2017. LNCS, vol. 10401, pp. 36–66. Springer, Cham (2017). https://doi.org/10.1007/978-3-319-63688-7_2
3. Attrapadung, N.: Dual system encryption via doubly selective security: framework, fully secure functional encryption for regular languages, and more. In: Nguyen, P.Q., Oswald, E. (eds.) EUROCRYPT 2014. LNCS, vol. 8441, pp. 557–577. Springer, Heidelberg (2014). https://doi.org/10.1007/978-3-642-55220-5_31
4. Bellare, M., Hoang, V.T., Rogaway, P.: Foundations of garbled circuits. In: Yu, T., Danezis, G., Gligor, V.D. (eds.) ACM CCS 2012, pp. 784–796. ACM Press (2012)
5. Chen, J., Gay, R., Wee, H.: Improved dual system ABE in prime-order groups via predicate encodings. In: Oswald, E., Fischlin, M. (eds.) EUROCRYPT 2015. LNCS, vol. 9057, pp. 595–624. Springer, Heidelberg (2015). https://doi.org/10.1007/978-3-662-46803-6_20
6. Cong, K., Eldefrawy, K., Smart, N.P.: Optimizing registration based encryption. IACR Cryptol. ePrint Arch., p. 499 (2021)
7. Döttling, N., Kolonelos, D., Lai, R.W.F., Lin, C., Malavolta, G., Rahimi, A.: Efficient laconic cryptography from learning with errors. In: Hazay, C., Stam, M. (eds.) EUROCRYPT 2023. Part III, vol. 14006 of LNCS, pp. 417–446. Springer, Heidelberg (2023). https://doi.org/10.1007/978-3-031-30620-4_14
8. Escala, A., Herold, G., Kiltz, E., Ràfols, C., Villar, J.: An algebraic framework for Diffie-Hellman assumptions. In: Canetti, R., Garay, J.A. (eds.) CRYPTO 2013. LNCS, vol. 8043, pp. 129–147. Springer, Heidelberg (2013). https://doi.org/10.1007/978-3-642-40084-1_8
9. Francati, D., Friolo, D., Maitra, M., Malavolta, G., Rahimi, A., Venturi, D.: Registered (inner-product) functional encryption. Cryptology ePrint Archive, Paper 2023/395 (2023). https://eprint.iacr.org/2023/395
10. Freitag, C., Waters, B., Wu, D.J.: How to use (plain) witness encryption: registered ABE, flexible broadcast, and more. Cryptology ePrint Archive, Paper 2023/812 (2023). https://eprint.iacr.org/2023/812
11. Garg, S., Gentry, C., Halevi, S., Raykova, M., Sahai, A., Waters, B.: Candidate indistinguishability obfuscation and functional encryption for all circuits. In: 54th FOCS, pp. 40–49. IEEE Computer Society Press (2013)
12. Garg, S., Gentry, G., Sahai, A., Waters, B.: Witness encryption and its applications. In: Boneh, D., Roughgarden, T., Feigenbaum, J. (eds.) 45th ACM STOC, pp. 467–476. ACM Press (2013)

13. Garg, S., Hajiabadi, M., Mahmoody, M., Rahimi, A.: Registration-based encryption: removing private-key generator from IBE. In: Beimel, A., Dziembowski, S. (eds.) TCC 2018. LNCS, vol. 11239, pp. 689–718. Springer, Cham (2018). https://doi.org/10.1007/978-3-030-03807-6_25
14. Garg, S., Hajiabadi, M., Mahmoody, M., Rahimi, A., Sekar, S.: Registration-based encryption from standard assumptions. In: Lin, D., Sako, K. (eds.) PKC 2019. LNCS, vol. 11443, pp. 63–93. Springer, Cham (2019). https://doi.org/10.1007/978-3-030-17259-6_3
15. Gentry, C., Waters, B.: Adaptive security in broadcast encryption systems (with short ciphertexts). In: Joux, A. (ed.) EUROCRYPT 2009. LNCS, vol. 5479, pp. 171–188. Springer, Heidelberg (2009). https://doi.org/10.1007/978-3-642-01001-9_10
16. Glaeser, N., Kolonelos, D., Malavolta, G., Rahimi, A.: Efficient registration-based encryption. Cryptology ePrint Archive, Report 2022/1505 (2022).https://eprint.iacr.org/2022/1505
17. Gong, J., Waters, B., Wee, H.: ABE for DFA from k-Lin. In: Boldyreva, A., Micciancio, D. (eds.) CRYPTO 2019. LNCS, vol. 11693, pp. 732–764. Springer, Cham (2019). https://doi.org/10.1007/978-3-030-26951-7_25
18. Gong, J., Wee, H.: Adaptively secure ABE for DFA from k-Lin and more. In: Canteaut, A., Ishai, Y. (eds.) EUROCRYPT 2020. LNCS, vol. 12107, pp. 278–308. Springer, Cham (2020). https://doi.org/10.1007/978-3-030-45727-3_10
19. González, A., Hevia, A., Ràfols, C.: QA-NIZK arguments in asymmetric groups: new tools and new constructions. In: Iwata, T., Cheon, J.H. (eds.) ASIACRYPT 2015. LNCS, vol. 9452, pp. 605–629. Springer, Heidelberg (2015). https://doi.org/10.1007/978-3-662-48797-6_25
20. Goyal, R., Vusirikala, S.: Verifiable registration-based encryption. In: Micciancio, D., Ristenpart, T. (eds.) CRYPTO 2020. LNCS, vol. 12170, pp. 621–651. Springer, Cham (2020). https://doi.org/10.1007/978-3-030-56784-2_21
21. Goyal, V., Pandey, O., Sahai, A., Waters, B.: Attribute-based encryption for fine-grained access control of encrypted data. In: Juels, A., Wright, R.N., De Capitani di Vimercati, S. (eds.) ACM CCS 2006, pp. 89–98. ACM Press (2006). Available as Cryptology ePrint Archive Report 2006/309
22. Groth, J., Sahai, A.: Efficient non-interactive proof systems for bilinear groups. In: Smart, N. (ed.) EUROCRYPT 2008. LNCS, vol. 4965, pp. 415–432. Springer, Heidelberg (2008). https://doi.org/10.1007/978-3-540-78967-3_24
23. Hohenberger, S., George, L., Waters, B., David, J.W.: Registered attribute-based encryption. In: Hazay, C., Stam, M. (eds.) EUROCRYPT 2023. LNCS, vol. 14006, pp. 511–542. Springer, Heidelberg (2023). https://doi.org/10.1007/978-3-031-30620-4_17
24. Ishai, Y., Wee, H.: Partial garbling schemes and their applications. Cryptology ePrint Archive, Paper 2014/995 (2014). https://eprint.iacr.org/2014/995
25. Jain, A., Lin, H., Sahai, A.: Indistinguishability obfuscation from LPN over $\mathbb{F}_p$, DLIN, and PRGs in NC^0. In: Dunkelman, O., Dziembowski, S. (eds.) EUROCRYPT 2022, Part I, vol. 13275, pp. 670–699. Springer, Heidelberg (2022). https://doi.org/10.1007/978-3-031-06944-4_23
26. Jutla, C.S., Roy, A.: Shorter quasi-adaptive NIZK proofs for linear subspaces. In: Sako, K., Sarkar, P. (eds.) ASIACRYPT 2013. LNCS, vol. 8269, pp. 1–20. Springer, Heidelberg (2013). https://doi.org/10.1007/978-3-642-42033-7_1
27. Kiltz, E., Wee, H.: Quasi-adaptive NIZK for linear subspaces revisited. In: Oswald, E., Fischlin, M. (eds.) EUROCRYPT 2015. LNCS, vol. 9057, pp. 101–128. Springer, Heidelberg (2015). https://doi.org/10.1007/978-3-662-46803-6_4

28. Kolonelos, D., Malavolta, G., Wee, H.: Distributed broadcast encryption from bilinear groups. Cryptology ePrint Archive, Paper 2023/874 (2023).https://eprint.iacr.org/2023/874
29. Kowalczyk, L., Wee, H.: Compact adaptively secure ABE for NC^1 from k-Lin. In: Ishai, Y., Rijmen, V. (eds.) EUROCRYPT 2019. LNCS, vol. 11476, pp. 3–33. Springer, Cham (2019). https://doi.org/10.1007/978-3-030-17653-2_1
30. Lewko, A., Okamoto, T., Sahai, A., Takashima, K., Waters, B.: Fully secure functional encryption: attribute-based encryption and (hierarchical) inner product encryption. In: Gilbert, H. (ed.) EUROCRYPT 2010. LNCS, vol. 6110, pp. 62–91. Springer, Heidelberg (2010). https://doi.org/10.1007/978-3-642-13190-5_4
31. Libert, B., Peters, T., Joye, M., Yung, M.: Compactly hiding linear spans - tightly secure constant-size simulation-sound QA-NIZK proofs and applications. In: Iwata, T., Cheon, J.H. (eds.) ASIACRYPT 2015. LNCS, vol. 9452, pp. 681–707. Springer, Heidelberg (2015). https://doi.org/10.1007/978-3-662-48797-6_28
32. Lin, H., Luo, J.: Compact adaptively secure ABE from k-Lin: beyond NC^1 and towards NL. In: Canteaut, A., Ishai, Y. (eds.) EUROCRYPT 2020. LNCS, vol. 12107, pp. 247–277. Springer, Cham (2020). https://doi.org/10.1007/978-3-030-45727-3_9
33. Sahai, A., Waters, B.: Fuzzy identity-based encryption. In: Cramer, R. (ed.) EUROCRYPT 2005. LNCS, vol. 3494, pp. 457–473. Springer, Heidelberg (2005). https://doi.org/10.1007/11426639_27
34. Vaikuntanathan, V., Wee, H., Wichs, D.: Witness encryption and null-IO from evasive LWE. In: Agrawal, S., Lin, D. (eds.) ASIACRYPT 2022. LNCS, vol. 13791, pp. 195–221. Springer, Heidelberg (2022). https://doi.org/10.1007/978-3-031-22963-3_7
35. Waters, B.: Dual system encryption: realizing fully secure IBE and HIBE under simple assumptions. In: Halevi, S. (ed.) CRYPTO 2009. LNCS, vol. 5677, pp. 619–636. Springer, Heidelberg (2009). https://doi.org/10.1007/978-3-642-03356-8_36
36. Wee, H.: Dual system encryption via predicate encodings. In: Lindell, Y. (ed.) TCC 2014. LNCS, vol. 8349, pp. 616–637. Springer, Heidelberg (2014). https://doi.org/10.1007/978-3-642-54242-8_26
37. Yao, A.C.C.: Theory and applications of trapdoor functions (extended abstract). In: 23rd Annual Symposium on Foundations of Computer Science, Chicago, Illinois, USA, 3–5 November 1982, pp. 80–91. IEEE Computer Society (1982)

Registered (Inner-Product) Functional Encryption

Danilo Francati[1], Daniele Friolo[2], Monosij Maitra[3,5], Giulio Malavolta[4,5](✉), Ahmadreza Rahimi[5], and Daniele Venturi[2]

[1] Aarhus University, Aarhus, Denmark
dfrancati@cs.au.dk
[2] Sapienza University of Rome, Rome, Italy
{friolo,venturi}@di.uniroma1.it
[3] Ruhr-Universität Bochum, Bochum, Germany
monosij.maitra@rub.de
[4] Bocconi University, Milan, Italy
[5] Max-Planck Institute for Security and Privacy, Bochum, Germany
giulio.malavolta@unibocconi.it, ahmadrezar@pm.me

Abstract. Registered encryption (Garg *et al.*, TCC'18) is an emerging paradigm that tackles the key-escrow problem associated with identity-based encryption by replacing the private-key generator with a much weaker entity known as the key curator. The key curator holds no secret information, and is responsible to: (i) update the master public key whenever a new user registers its own public key to the system; (ii) provide helper decryption keys to the users already registered in the system, in order to still enable them to decrypt after new users join the system. For practical purposes, tasks (i) and (ii) need to be efficient, in the sense that the size of the public parameters, of the master public key, and of the helper decryption keys, as well as the running times for key generation and user registration, and the number of updates, must be small.

In this paper, we generalize the notion of registered encryption to the setting of functional encryption (FE).

As our main contribution, we show an efficient construction of registered FE for the special case of (*attribute hiding*) inner-product predicates, built over asymmetric bilinear groups of prime order. Our scheme supports a *large* attribute universe and is proven secure in the bilinear generic group model. We also implement our scheme and experimentally demonstrate the efficiency requirements of the registered settings. Our second contribution is a feasibility result where we build registered FE for P/poly based on indistinguishability obfuscation and somewhere statistically binding hash functions.

Keywords: Registered encryption · functional encryption · inner-product predicate encryption

J. Guo and R. Steinfeld (Eds.): ASIACRYPT 2023, LNCS 14442, pp. 98–133, 2023.
https://doi.org/10.1007/978-981-99-8733-7_4

1 Introduction

Functional encryption (FE) [18,51,53] enriches standard public-key encryption with fine-grained access control over encrypted data. This added feature is made possible by having a so-called master secret key msk that can be used (by an authority) to generate decryption keys sk_f associated with functions f, in such a way that decrypting any ciphertext c, corresponding to a plaintext m, reveals $f(m)$ and nothing more. Recent years have seen a flourish of works exploring FE constructions in various settings and from different assumptions [1–3,5,6,8,9,17,19,20,27,28,32–34,36,37,43–45,48,52,56], and its applications to building powerful cryptographic tools such as reusable garbled circuits [36], adaptive garbling [40], multi-party non-interactive key exchange [31], universal samplers [31], verifiable random functions [15,38], and indistinguishability obfuscation (iO) [7,16] (which, in turn, implies a plethora of other cryptographic primitives [52]).

An important limitation of FE is the well-known *key escrow* problem: the authority holding the master secret key (sometimes referred to as the private key generator – PKG) can generate secret keys for any function, allowing it to arbitrarily decrypt messages intended for specific recipients. This requires a fully trusted PKG which severely restricts the applicability of FE in many scenarios.

Registered Encryption. A recent line of research proposes to tackle the key-escrow problem in the much simpler case of identity-based encryption[1] (IBE) [54]. This led to the notion of *registered* IBE (RIBE) [29][2], where the main idea is to replace the PKG with a much weaker entity called the key curator (KC), whose role is to register the public keys of the users (without possessing any secret key). In particular, in a RIBE scheme there is an initial setup phase in which a common reference string (CRS) is sampled. The CRS is given to the KC which publishes an (initially empty) master public key. Each user now can also use the CRS and sample its own public and secret key, and can register its identity and the chosen public key to the KC; the KC is required to generate a new master public key, which includes the newly registered public keys, and which will permit encrypting messages to any of the registered users. Moreover, since the master public key is updated over time, the KC is responsible for providing any decrypting party with a so-called helper decryption key, i.e., auxiliary information connecting its public key with the updated master public key.

Recently, the notion of RIBE has been extended to the setting of attribute-based encryption (ABE) [41], where one can encrypt messages with respect to policies, and where decryptors can recover the message if their attributes satisfy the policy embedded in the ciphertext. However, their registered ABE (RABE)

[1] IBE can be seen as a special case of FE for equality predicates f_y such that $f_y(x, m) = m$ if and only if $y = x$ (and $\perp$ otherwise). Here, x and y have the role of the parties' identities (which do not need to be secret), and m is the encrypted message.

[2] The original paper define the primitive as registration based encryption. However, we choose to call it as registered IBE, in line with the more recent work in [41].

schemes [41] are required to hide only messages in the ciphertext. In particular, they do not hide the policies embedded in the ciphertexts, since they are required in the clear for decryption to work. This restricts using RABE in scenarios where hiding the policy is also important.

More generally, the current state of affairs leaves open the question of building registered FE (RFE), where any user can sample its own key pair $(\mathsf{pk}, \mathsf{sk})$ as before, along with fixing a function of its choice (say f, from a class of functions), and register (pk, f) with the KC. In such a setting, one can then encrypt messages m that the registered user can decrypt with sk and a helper secret key to learn only $f(m)$. Overall, this would achieve the analogous functionality to that of the celebrated notion of FE, without suffering from the key escrow issue. The focus of our work is to make progress on this problem.

1.1 Our Contributions

We initiate the study of RFE in this paper by providing two constructions – one for a special class of FE, and another for the general class of all functions.

In particular, as our first contribution, we provide the *first* RFE scheme for the class of inner-product predicates (a.k.a. (attribute hiding) inner-product predicate encryption), i.e., a registered IPE (RIPE) from asymmetric bilinear maps on prime-order groups. More concretely, our scheme supports the function class $\mathcal{F} = \{f_{\mathbf{x}}(\cdot, \cdot)\}_{\mathbf{x} \in \mathbb{Z}_q^{n^+}}$ defined as:

$$f_{\mathbf{x}}(m, \mathbf{y}) = \begin{cases} m & \text{if } \langle \mathbf{x}, \mathbf{y} \rangle = 0 \\ \perp & \text{otherwise} \end{cases} \tag{1}$$

where $\mathbf{x}$ and $\mathbf{y}$ are n-size vectors over $\mathbb{Z}_q^{n^+} = \mathbb{Z}_q^n \setminus \{\mathbf{0}^n\}$, and q is a prime. Below we summarize our result informally in Theorem 1 and also later in Table 1 (Sect. 3) when we discuss related works to compare it with existing registered encryption schemes.

Theorem 1 (Informal). *Let λ be a security parameter, n be the length of supported vectors, and L be a bound on the maximum number of users. There is a (black-box) construction of RIPE supporting a large universe and up to L users in the generic bilinear group model, satisfying the following properties:*

- *The CRS is of size $n \cdot L^2 \cdot \mathsf{poly}(\lambda, \log L)$.*
- *The master public key and each helper decryption key is of size $n \cdot \mathsf{poly}(\lambda, \log L)$.*
- *Key-generation and registration runs in time $L \cdot \mathsf{poly}(\lambda, \log L)$ and $n \cdot L^2 \cdot \mathsf{poly}(\lambda, \log L)$, respectively.*
- *Each registered user receives at most $O(\log L)$ updates from the KC over the entire lifetime of the system.*

Moreover, both encryption and decryption runs in time $n \cdot \mathsf{poly}(\lambda, \log L)$.

Our scheme is proven secure in the bilinear generic group model [12,14]. We emphasize that our scheme supports *attribute-hiding* and a *large universe* unlike [41]. In particular, our scheme satisfies the strong notion of *two-sided* security[3] [26,46], where no information on the attribute vector $\mathbf{y}$ is revealed (besides the orthogonality test) even if decryption succeeds, akin to what [46] achieved.[4]

Somewhat interestingly, our proof strategy and construction template are substantially different from the typical inner-product predicate encryption schemes in the literature (e.g., [46]). Roughly speaking, traditional proof strategies work by "programming" the function output (for the challenge ciphertext) in the key given by the adversary, and then arguing that this new key is indistinguishable from the original distribution. In the registered setting, the adversary can sample its own key, so the reduction has no control over it and cannot modify its distribution. Hence, we see RIPE as the main technical contribution of this work.

We also implemented our scheme and describe the results in Sect. 7. The benchmarks are achieved with a set of $L = 100$ to $L = 1000$ users with attribute vectors of length varying between $n = 10$ and $n = 100$. Our results demonstrate concrete, practical efficiency of our scheme beyond the realms of only feasibility. Further, following the *generic* and *non-cryptographic* transformations described in [46, Section 5], our RIPE scheme can also support constant-degree polynomial evaluations, disjunctions, conjunctions, and evaluating CNF and DNF formulas.

As our second contribution, we build RFE for all circuits from indistinguishability obfuscation (iO). This is a feasibility result extending the iO-based RABE schemes in [41] to the setting of RFE. In more detail, we achieve the following:

Theorem 2 (Informal). *Let λ be the security parameter. Assuming somewhere statistically binding hash functions [42, 50] and iO [13], there is a (non black-box) construction of RFE supporting arbitrary functions and an arbitrary number of users, satisfying the following properties:*

- *The CRS, master public key, and each helper decryption key is of size* $\mathsf{poly}(\lambda)$.
- *Key-generation and registration runs in time* $\mathsf{poly}(\lambda)$ *and* $L \cdot \mathsf{poly}(\lambda)$*, respectively, where L stands for the* current *number of registered users.*
- *Each registered user receives at most* $O(\log L)$ *updates from the KC over the entire lifetime of the system, where L is as defined in the previous item.*

Moreover, both encryption and decryption runs in time $\mathsf{poly}(\lambda)$*. Further, the above scheme achieves the same efficiency as that of iO-based RABE from [41].*

---

[3] Two-sided security in PE allows an adversary to obtain secret keys for predicates that *can* decrypt a challenge ciphertext, provided the challenge message pair consists of the same message.

[4] Generic compilers from any ABE for LSSS (or equivalently, monotone span programs) to (hierarchical) IPE are known (e.g., [11]). However, such compilers *do not ensure* attribute-privacy which we crucially require from our (registered) IPE scheme.

2 Technical Overview

In the following, we first describe the notion of registered FE and its properties of interest. Next, we provide a brief overview of the techniques behind our schemes.

RFE Definition. We discuss the notion of RFE at a high level. Fundamentally, RFE allows users to generate their own keys (associated to functions of their choice) without the need of a trusted authority, which is replaced with a KC that does not hold any secret. The KC is simply responsible of managing a data structure containing the public keys (plus the corresponding functions) of registered users. Roughly, the RFE syntax goes as follows: For some security parameter λ and a function class $\mathcal{F}$, the algorithm $\mathsf{Setup}(1^n, |\mathcal{F}|)$ initializes the system to output a common reference string crs.[5] Given crs, the KC initializes a state $\alpha = \perp$ (i.e., the data structure) and the master public key $\mathsf{mpk} = \perp$. A user can now register its own (pk, f) pair as follows: it samples $(\mathsf{pk}, \mathsf{sk}) \leftarrow\$ \mathsf{KGen}(\mathsf{crs}, \alpha)$ and submits a registration request (pk, f) to the KC, where $f \in \mathcal{F}$ is a function it wishes to associate with pk. The KC updates its state as $\alpha = \alpha'$ and $\mathsf{mpk} = \mathsf{mpk}'$ where (mpk', α') are output by the *deterministic* registration algorithm $\mathsf{RegPK}(\mathsf{crs}, \alpha, \mathsf{pk}, f)$. Intuitively, a ciphertext $c \leftarrow\$ \mathsf{Enc}(\mathsf{mpk}, m)$ computed with mpk can be later decrypted by the users registered before or during mpk was generated. The registered user uses sk to decrypt c. However, mpk is updated periodically (after each registration) – so the user issues an update request to the KC that, in turn, *deterministically* returns a helper secret key $\mathsf{hsk} = \mathsf{Update}(\mathsf{crs}, \alpha, \mathsf{pk})$. The hsk provides necessary information to make a (previously registered) user's secret key sk valid with respect to a new mpk. With hsk, the user can decrypt to learn $f(m) = \mathsf{Dec}(\mathsf{sk}, \mathsf{hsk}, c)$. For optimal efficiency, an RFE system with L registered users should satisfy the following properties:

(1) <u>*Compact parameters:*</u> The sizes of $\mathsf{crs}, \mathsf{mpk}, \mathsf{hsk}$ must be small, e.g., $\mathsf{poly}(\lambda, \log L)$.
(2) <u>*Efficiency:*</u> This measures key-generation and registration runtimes, and the number of updates as described below.
    (a) Each execution of KGen and RegPK should run in time $\mathsf{poly}(\lambda, \log L)$.
    (b) Each registered user receives at most $O(\log L)$ number of new updates (i.e., new hsks) over the lifetime of the system.

RFE can support an unbounded or a bounded number of users. In particular, for the unbounded case, the setup is independent of the number of users. (In this case, the parameter L in efficiency conditions refer to the *current* number of registered users.) For the bounded case, the setup depends on a bound L (fixed a-priori). Security of RFE is analogous to that of RIBE [29] and RABE [41]. In particular, an adversary A corrupting a subset of k registered users (i.e., A knows the

[5] Although the common reference string is generated by a trusted setup, the important difference is that there is no long-term secret that needs to be stored throughout the lifetime of the system. Furthermore, in some cases, the setup algorithm could be "transparent", and therefore computable using just a hash function.

set $\{(\mathsf{sk}_i, (\mathsf{pk}_i, f_i))\}_{i\in[k]}$) cannot distinguish $\mathsf{Enc}(\mathsf{mpk}, m_0)$ from $\mathsf{Enc}(\mathsf{mpk}, m_1)$, as long as $f_i(m_0) = f_i(m_1), \forall i \in [k]$. This should hold even if A registers *malformed* public keys. We refer to the full version [25] for more details.

Slotted RFE. Following Hohenberger *et al.* [41], we first define and use *slotted* RFE as a stepping stone towards building full-fledged RFE. Differently to RFE, there is only a single update (referred to as *aggregation*) in slotted RFE, where users are assigned to "slots" and the master public key is only computed once all slots are filled. In more detail, initialization and key generation work as before, except now that the Setup (resp. KGen) takes as an extra input the maximum number of slots/keys L that can be aggregated (resp. a user index $i \in [L]$). The KC takes all L pairs $\{(\mathsf{pk}_i, f_i)\}_{i\in[L]}$ *together*, aggregrates (i.e. updates) it to compute a short mpk and L helper secret keys $\{\mathsf{hsk}_i\}_{i\in[L]}$ for each user. Encryption and decryption again works as before.

Akin to RFE, slotted RFE security requires that, for an aggregated mpk w.r.t. to all L slots, $\mathsf{Enc}(\mathsf{mpk}, m_0)$ and $\mathsf{Enc}(\mathsf{mpk}, m_1)$ are computationally indistinguishable, so long as $f_j(m_0) = f_j(m_1)$ for all *corrupted* slots $j \in [L]$. We refer to the full version [25] for more details.

Hohenberger *et al.*[41] lifted slotted RABE to a standard RABE via a generic compiler, and the same holds for slotted RFE (with minor syntactic changes). Loosely speaking, they use a "powers-of-two" approach, where users are assigned to different slotted schemes with increasing capacities, and they are moved forward as new users join the system. The same idea yields a fully-fledged RFE that supports $O(\log L)$ number of updates and incurs a multiplicative $O(\log L)$ overhead on the size of $\mathsf{crs}, \mathsf{mpk}, \mathsf{hsk}$, and the key-generation and encryption runtimes compared to that of the underlying slotted RFE scheme. The registration runtime is dominated by $O(t_{\mathsf{Aggr}} + L \cdot t_{\mathsf{hsk}})$, where t_{Aggr} and t_{hsk} are the aggregation runtime and the helper decryption key size of the slotted RFE respectively. For completeness, we present the transformation in our full version [25].

2.1 (Bounded Users) Slotted RIPE from Pairings

We begin with an overview of our scheme for inner-product predicates. This is a special case of FE, where vectors $\mathbf{x} \in \mathbb{Z}_q^{n^+} (= \mathbb{Z}_q^n \setminus \{\mathbf{0}^n\})$ denote functions $f_{\mathbf{x}}$ (associated to keys), and messages consist of a tuple $(\mathbf{y}, m)$. The function $f_{\mathbf{x}}$ can be recast as:

$$f_{\mathbf{x}}(\mathbf{y}, m) = \begin{cases} m & \text{if } \langle \mathbf{x}, \mathbf{y} \rangle = 0 \\ \perp & \text{otherwise} \end{cases}$$

where we denote the length of vectors by $n = n(\lambda)$, and assume the attribute space to be $\mathcal{U} = \mathbb{Z}_q^{n^+}$ (i.e., domain of vectors). Our scheme follows the blueprint of [41]. However, unlike [41], that reveals the policy in clear, achieving attribute-hiding security in this setting of predicate encryption requires us to introduce crucial modifications, which we highlight after the overview of our scheme below. Furthermore, the security analysis is completely different.

Single-Slot Scheme. We begin by discussing a simplified scheme with $L = 1$ (i.e., there is a single slot). Below is a description of each algorithm in the scheme.

- **Generating the CRS:** We first describe the CRS generation. The CRS can be split into three different parts, a general part, a slot-specific part, and a key-specific part. We will describe how each part is generated individually.
  - *General part*: First, we generate an asymmetric pairing group of prime order q, denoted as $\mathcal{G} = (\mathbb{G}_1, \mathbb{G}_2, \mathbb{G}_T, q, g_1, g_2, e)$. Then, we sample $\alpha, \beta, \gamma \leftarrow_\$ \mathbb{Z}_q$ and set $h = g_1^\beta, Z = e(g_1, g_2)^\alpha$. (We will need γ for the multi-slot scheme, which we describe later.)
  - *Slot-specific part*: We associate each slot with a set of group elements, for this case we sample $t \leftarrow_\$ \mathbb{Z}_q$ and set $A = g_2^t$ and $B = g_2^\alpha A^\beta = g_2^{\alpha+\beta t}$.
  - *Key-specific part*: We also associate a group element to each component of the key vector, plus the secret key. To do this, for each $w \in [n+1]$, we sample $u_w \leftarrow \mathbb{Z}_q$ and set $U_w = g_1^{u_w}$.

  In the end, we set the CRS to be:

$$\mathsf{crs} = \left(\mathcal{G}, Z, h, A, B, \{U_w\}_{w\in[n+1]}\right).$$

- **Generating keys:** To compute a new pair of public/secret keys, we sample a non-zero secret key $\mathsf{sk} \leftarrow_\$ \mathbb{Z}_q$ and set $\mathsf{pk} = U_{n+1}^{-\mathsf{sk}}$. Note that we are conceptually treating the secret key as one more element of the predicate vector. This is an important structural difference with respect to [41].
- **Key Aggregation:** Since we only have one slot, given pk and crs, and a predicate vector (or key) $\mathbf{x} = (x_1, \ldots, x_n)$, we set the master public key as:

$$\mathsf{mpk} = \left(\mathcal{G}, h, Z, \{U_w\}_{w\in[n+1]}, \mathsf{pk} \cdot \prod_{w=1}^{n} U_w^{-x_w}\right).$$

- **Encryption:** To encrypt a message $m \in \mathbb{G}_T$ with respect to a non-zero attribute vector $\mathbf{y} = (y_1, \ldots, y_n) \in \mathbb{Z}_q^{n^+}$, and the master public key mpk, we create a ciphertext that has two components, a message-embedding component, and a key-slot-embedding component.
  - *Message embedding:* We sample $s \leftarrow_\$ \mathbb{Z}_q^*$, and set $C_1 = m \cdot Z^s, C_2 = g_1^s$.
  - *Key-slot embedding:* First, we sample $r, z \leftarrow_\$ \mathbb{Z}_q \setminus \{0\}$. Then, we set

$$C_{3,w} = h^{y_w \cdot r+s} \cdot U_w^{-z} \ (\forall w \in [n]), \quad C_{3,n+1} = h^s \cdot U_{n+1}^{-z}, \quad \text{and}$$

$$C_{3,n+2} = h^s \cdot \mathsf{pk}^{-z} \prod_{w=1}^{n} U_w^{z\cdot x_w}.$$

  The final ciphertext will be $(C_1, C_2, \{C_{3,w}\}_{w\in[n+1]})$.

- **Decryption:** Before describing the actual decryption, let us check the intuition behind each element of the ciphertext. The first component $C_1 = m \cdot Z^s$ is just a masking of the message with a random power of Z from the CRS. Consider B from crs, and the ciphertext components C_1 and C_2, and observe:

$$\frac{C_1}{e(C_2, B)} = \frac{m \cdot e(g_1, g_2)^{\alpha \cdot s}}{e(g_1, g_2)^{\alpha \cdot s} \cdot e(g_1, g_2)^{s\beta t}} = \frac{m}{e(h^s, A)}.$$

Thus, to recover the message, it suffices to recompute $e(h^s, A)$. Note that h^s is already present in some form in the $C_{3,*}$ components. We can partition $C_{3,*}$ terms into three different groups, and see how h^s appears in each one:

1. For all $w \in [n]$, we have $C_{3,w} = h^s \cdot h^{y_w \cdot r} \cdot U_w^{-z}$. In this case, there are extra terms $y_w \cdot r$ as well as U_w present in the ciphertext. However, since $\mathbf{x}$ and $\mathbf{y}$ are orthogonal (otherwise decryption fails), we can eliminate these extra terms by raising each $C_{3,w}$ to the power of x_w for $w \in [n]$ and compute their product. Thus, we will have:

$$\begin{aligned}\prod_{w=1}^{n} C_{3,w}^{x_w} &= \prod_{w=1}^{n} h^{x_w \cdot s} \cdot h^{x_w \cdot y_w \cdot r} \cdot \prod_{w=1}^{n} U_w^{-z \cdot x_w} \\ &= h^{s \cdot \sum_{w=1}^{n} x_w} \cdot \underbrace{h^{r \cdot \sum_{w=1}^{n} x_w \cdot y_w}}_{=1} \cdot \prod_{w=1}^{n} U_w^{-z \cdot x_w}.\end{aligned}$$

Therefore, we are left with two terms $h^{s \cdot \sum_{w=1}^{n} x_w}$ and $\prod_{w=1}^{n} U_w^{-z \cdot x_w}$.
2. For $w = n+1$, we have $C_{3,n+1} = h^s \cdot U_{n+1}^{-z}$, where the term h^s is masked with U_{n+1}^{-z}.
3. For $w = n+2$, we have $C_{3,n+2} = h^s \cdot \mathsf{pk}^{-z} \prod_{w=1}^{n} U_w^{z \cdot x_w} = h^s \cdot U_{n+1}^{z \cdot \mathsf{sk}} \cdot \prod_{w=1}^{n} U_w^{z \cdot x_w}$.

Multiplying together the remaining components we obtain:

$$C_{3,n+2} \cdot C_{3,n+1}^{\mathsf{sk}} \cdot \prod_{w=1}^{n} C_{3,w}^{x_w} = h^s \cdot h^{s \cdot \mathsf{sk}} \cdot h^{s \cdot \sum_{w=1}^{n} x_w} = h^{s \cdot (1 + \mathsf{sk} + \sum_{w=1}^{n} x_w)}.$$

The decryptor can now raise $h^{s \cdot (1 + \mathsf{sk} + \sum_{w=1}^{n} x_w)}$ to the power of $(1 + \mathsf{sk} + \sum_{w=1}^{n} x_w)^{-1}$ to get h^s. Once h^s is obtained, it can be paired with A, available from crs, to decrypt the message.

Multi-slot Scheme. To gain an intuition on how our scheme handles multiple slots, we describe a toy example where $L = 2$, i.e., we are in the two-slot setting. Notice that one trivial generalization is to individually generate public keys as before, and concatenate them into the master public key. However, this approach will not work, since we want the master public key size to be independent of the number of slots. Instead, we expand the slot-specific components in the CRS to A_1, B_1 (for slot 1) and A_2, B_2 (for slot 2), which are generated in the same way as A, B in the one-slot setting, but using independent random elements $t_1, t_2 \leftarrow_{\$} \mathbb{Z}_q$

in generating A_1, A_2. We will also need to link the slots to the keys, so that we can use the slot in the key-generation algorithm. For this, instead of generating only one set of $\{U_w\}_{w\in[n]}$, we generate them with respect to both slots

$$\{U_{w,1} = g_1^{u_{w,1}}\}_{w\in[n+1]} \qquad \text{and} \qquad \{U_{w,2} = g_1^{u_{w,2}}\}_{w\in[n+1]}$$

where the elements $\{u_{w,i}\}_{i\in\{1,2\}}$ are chosen independently and uniformly at random. Accordingly, in the key generation we can set

$$\mathsf{pk}_1 = U_{n+1,1}^{-\mathsf{sk}_1} \qquad \text{and} \qquad \mathsf{pk}_2 = U_{n+1,1}^{-\mathsf{sk}_2}$$

and we aggregate the keys as

$$\{\widehat{U}_w = U_{w,1} \cdot U_{w,2}\}_{w\in[n+1]} \quad \text{and} \quad \widehat{U}_{n+2} = \mathsf{pk}_1 \cdot \mathsf{pk}_2 \cdot \prod_{w=1}^{n} U_{w,1}^{-x_{w,1}} \prod_{w=1}^{n} U_{w,2}^{-x_{w,2}}$$

where $\mathbf{x}_1$ and $\mathbf{x}_2$ are the chosen keys. One can encrypt using the new $\widehat{U}$ values instead of U, however, once we try to decrypt and expand the corresponding equations, we realize that many terms will not cancel out as before. For example, if a message is encrypted for slot 1, during decryption we will have,

$$\begin{aligned}
\prod_{w\in[n]} C_{3,w}^{x_{w,1}} &= \prod_{w\in[n]} h^{(y_w \cdot r+s)\cdot x_{w,1}} \cdot \prod_{w=1}^{n} U_{w,1}^{-z\cdot x_{w,1}} \cdot \prod_{w=1}^{n} U_{w,2}^{-z\cdot x_{w,1}} \\
C_{3,n+1}^{\mathsf{sk}_1} &= h^{s\cdot \mathsf{sk}_1} \cdot U_{n+1,1}^{-z\cdot \mathsf{sk}_1} \cdot U_{n+1,2}^{-z\cdot \mathsf{sk}_1} \\
C_{3,n+2} &= h^{s} \cdot U_{n+1,1}^{z\cdot \mathsf{sk}_1} \cdot U_{n+1,2}^{z\cdot \mathsf{sk}_2} \cdot \prod_{w=1}^{n} U_{w,1}^{z\cdot x_{w,1}} \prod_{w=1}^{n} U_{w,2}^{z\cdot x_{w,2}}
\end{aligned}$$

where the terms in blue can be canceled out using a similar multiplication trick as before. However, the terms $U_{n+1,2}^{-z\cdot \mathsf{sk}_1}, U_{n+1,2}^{z\cdot \mathsf{sk}_2}, \prod_{w\in[n]} U_{w,2}^{-z\cdot x_{w,1}}$ and $\prod_{w=1}^{n} U_{w,2}^{z\cdot x_{w,2}}$ *cannot* be canceled as they do not appear anywhere else, and further we assume the decryptor only knows sk_1, but not sk_2. We can circumvent this issue by introducing some "cross-terms" into the CRS, and use them in the aggregation to compute helper secret keys that enables the decryptor (holding sk_1 and $\mathbf{x}_1$) to cancel such terms. We create these terms such that they include both slot-specific and key-specific parts. Intuitively, they bind each slot to other slots and keys together. For slots $i, j \in [2]$ where $i \neq j$ and key indices $w \in [n+1]$, we define these terms as:

$$W_{i,j,w} = A_i^{u_{j,w}}.$$

We add $\{W_{i,j,w}\}_{i\neq j\in[2],w\in[n+1]}$ to the CRS as:

$$\mathsf{crs} = \left(\mathcal{G}, Z, h, \{A_i, B_i\}_{i\in[2]}, \left\{\{U_{w,i}\}, \{W_{i,j,w}\}_{i\neq j}\right\}_{i,j\in[2],w\in[n+1]}\right).$$

In addition, we will let the user publish $\{W_{j,i,n+1}^{\mathsf{sk}_i}\}_{i\in\{1,2\},j\neq i}$ in their respective public keys, to enable the other users to cancel out the desired cross terms, and publish in the ciphertext an additional element $C_4 = g_1^z$, to be paired with the W's in order to compute the correct terms.

The above scheme is correct but unfortunately *insecure*. At a high level, the problem is that the adversary can pair C_4 with wrong elements and generate unintended relations between z and other components, in the exponent. To prevent this, instead of putting g_1^z directly in the ciphertext, we introduce an extra component $\Gamma = g_1^\gamma, \gamma \leftarrow\!\!\$\ \mathbb{Z}_q$ in the CRS, and set $C_4 = \Gamma^z$. The only other modification that we must apply is the generation of the CRS itself, where for slots $i, j \in \{1, 2\}$ with $i \neq j$, and key indices $w \in [n+1]$, we define:

$$W_{i,j,w} = A_i^{u_{j,w}/\gamma}.$$

This forces a (possibly malicious) decryptor to pair C_4 *only* with the elements $W_{i,j,w}$ and remove the additional cross-terms described above. The rest of the construction remains the same. See Sect. 6 for more details.

Proof Sketch. We prove the above slotted RIPE scheme secure in the generic bilinear group model (GGM). Recall that in the GGM, the adversary is supplied with handles to the corresponding group elements from the scheme. Further, it can also learn handles to arbitrary linear combinations of existing and new elements (in the same group $\mathbb{G}_t, t \in \{1, 2, T\}$) via the group oracles it is provided with. Additionally, since we are in the bilinear setting, the adversary also gets access to the pairing oracle that allows it to learn handles referring to the product of any two terms from the source groups $\mathbb{G}_1$ and $\mathbb{G}_2$. However, the only crucial information it can actually learn in this whole interaction is via the zero-tests that work again only in $\mathbb{G}_T$.

Our formal multi-slot RIPE scheme in Sect. 6 introduces several variables with different combinations of indices. To argue indistinguishability in a convenient way between subsequent hybrids in the proof, we first switch from the GGM to the symbolic group model (SGM) via the Schwarz-Zippel lemma. In particular, the SGM allows us to represent all the terms, that the adversary can learn in the security game, as multivariate polynomials (in respective groups) from a ring of variables. The heart of the proof relies on arguing properties of the *coefficients* of these polynomials that correspond to *successful* zero-tests, which aids in proving indistinguishability directly. In particular, these claims set in while proving attribute hiding by switching the challenge attribute from $\mathbf{y}_0$ to $\mathbf{y}_1$ in the ciphertext elements $C_{3,w}\ \forall w \in [n+2]$, and helps in arguing the following:

1. Coefficients of such polynomials formed by pairing terms $C_{3,w} \in \mathbb{G}_1$ with *any* element in $\mathbb{G}_2$, except $A_i, i \in [2]$, must be *all zero.*
2. Such a coefficient vector must be *orthogonal* to $\mathbf{y}_b$ for $b \in \{0, 1\}$, and in particular, either be a *constant multiple* of the vector $\widetilde{\mathbf{x}}_i = (\mathbf{x}_i, \mathsf{sk}_i), i \in [2]$ or be *all zero*.

The claim in Item 1 follows from observing that the monomials formed symbolically (in the exponent) when pairing $C_{3,w}$ with *anything* in $\mathbb{G}_2$ (except A_1

or A_2) are all linearly independent and do not cancel out. Item 2 follows from two observations. The first one is that the randomness r (appearing as an independent symbolic term, but only in the components $C_{3,w}$'s) can only cancel out in zero-tests when the coefficients are orthogonal to $\mathbf{y}_b$. The second one follows additionally from linear independence of some specific symbolic terms and observing further that the vector of first $n+1$ coefficients can be expressed as a constant multiple of $\widetilde{\mathbf{x}}_i$. Overall, these claims ensure that the only non-trivial adversarial queries can be for vectors lying in the span of both *registered and valid* predicates. The rest of the proof follows from the admissibility of the adversary, and by reusing these claims. We refer to Theorem 6 for more details.

Comparison with the Slotted RABE of [41]. Our slotted RIPE scheme from prime-order pairings (in Sect. 6) shares some similarities at a high level with the slotted RABE from composite-order pairings by Hohenberger *et al.*[41]. For instance, the message-embedding mechanism in both schemes are same, which is by masking the message with the randomness in the term $e(h^s, A_i)$. (This is also a standard technique in many other pairing-based schemes.) The use of "slot"-based framework to embed users' keys is also similar, but only at the level of a blueprint. In particular, that is where the similarity ends. More specifically, the way slots and attributes are "glued" together in our scheme is fundamentally different: in [41], the ciphertext has two specific components, an attribute-specific component and a slot-specific one, where one party can decrypt a message if it manages to succeed to decrypt the slot-specific component and the attribute-specific component simultaneously. But in our scheme, the slot and attribute elements are entwined in the same ciphertext component. In essence, we conceptually treat the secret key as "one more dimension" in the predicate vector, whereas the scheme in [41] uses a separate machinery that takes care of the key component. Further, unlike [41] which reveals the policy in the ciphertext, we carefully ensure attribute hiding by multiplying a randomizer $r \in \mathbb{Z}_q^+$ to the attribute $\mathbf{y}$. As a result, we achieve totally different functionalities and stronger security notions. Finally, our scheme supports vectors from $\mathbb{Z}_q^{n^+}$ where q is a λ-bit prime and n denotes supported the vector length. As stated in [41, Section 7.2], this enables our scheme to support a large attribute universe in contrast to the pairing-based RABE in [41], that only supports a small attribute universe.

2.2 (Unbounded Users) Slotted RFE from iO

As a feasibility result, we show (slotted) RFE for all circuits based on indistinguishability obfuscation (iO) [13] and (succinct) somewhere statistically binding hash functions (SSB) [42,50]. In particular, we generalize the techniques from Hohenberger *et al.* [41] to get a slotted RFE from iO (which can be lifted to RFE with the powers-of-two trick). Below is a brief overview of this slotted RFE.

The CRS is set as the SSB hash key hk, and users' keys are generated through a PRG PRG and a seed s (i.e., $(\mathsf{pk}, \mathsf{sk}) = (\mathsf{PRG}(s), s)$). To aggregate $((\mathsf{pk}_i, f_i))_{i\in[L]}$, the KC computes a Merkle tree hash $h = \mathsf{Hash}(\mathsf{hk}, ((\mathsf{pk}_i, f_i))_{i\in[L]})$ and sets $\mathsf{mpk} = (\mathsf{hk}, h)$. The helper secret key hsk_i (of the i-th slot) is essentially the SSB opening π_i for the i-th (hashed) block (pk_i, f_i). A ciphertext c (encrypting m) is simply the obfuscation $\widetilde{C}$ of a circuit $C_{h,m}$ that, on input $(i, \mathsf{pk}_i, f_i, \pi_i, \mathsf{sk}_i)$, returns $f_i(m)$ if the following two conditions are satisfied: π_i is a *valid opening* for the i-th block (pk_i, f_i) *and* $(\mathsf{pk}_i, \mathsf{sk}_i)$ is a *valid* key-pair. Decryption works using sk_i and $\mathsf{hsk}_i = \pi_i$ to evaluate $\widetilde{C}$ on input $(i, \mathsf{pk}_i, f_i, \pi_i, \mathsf{sk}_i)$. The scheme supports the function class $\mathsf{P/poly}$. Compactness of parameters is evident from SSB succinctness. Due to a poly-logarithmic overhead from the powers-of-two trick, the final RFE can support an arbitrary number of users by setting $L = 2^\lambda$. The registration runtime remains linear in the *current/effective* number of registered users at the time of registration. We provide more details in our full version [25].

2.3 On Function Privacy in (Slotted) RFE

By definition, RFE allows users to sample their own keys and functions. Thus, the notion of function-privacy, that is typically considered in the setting of (secret-key) FE [21,55], does not make much sense from this perspective. However, one can still define function-privacy w.r.t. any other registered or unregistered party. In more detail, in the case of RFE, a user choosing its own keys and functions may want to hide its function from any party including the KC. Capturing this requires a mild change in the RFE syntax, where the function can be input to the KGen algorithm instead of RegPK and also require that the generated user key-pair is tied to this function. The KC gets access of only the users' public

Table 1. Comparing known registered encryption schemes in terms of efficiency and assumptions. We only consider worst-case time complexity. For schemes supporting an unbounded (resp. bounded) number of users, L denotes the *current* number of registered (resp. the maximum number of supported) users. We omit λ to simplify the table, e.g. for $k \in \mathbb{N}$, $O(k)$ and $\mathsf{poly}(\log k)$ respectively denote $k \cdot \mathsf{poly}(\lambda)$ and $\mathsf{poly}(\lambda, \log k)$ etc. $\mathcal{U}$ (from [41]) denotes the attribute space supported by the corresponding scheme. $\mathcal{F}$ denotes the function space supported by our schemes (each function $f \in \mathcal{F}$ of our RIPE is an n-length vector from $\mathbb{Z}_q^{n^+}$). Above, **BB** is an abbreviation for "black-box".

Reference	Type	CRS size	Keygen runtime	Registration key runtime	Master public key size	Helper dec. key size	# Updates	Unbounded users	BB	Assumptions
[29]	IBE	$O(1)$	$O(1)$	$\mathsf{poly}(\log L)$	$\mathsf{poly}(\log L)$	$\mathsf{poly}(\log L)$	$O(\log L)$	✓	✗	iO + SSB
[29]	IBE	$O(1)$	$O(1)$	$O(L)$	$\mathsf{poly}(\log L)$	$\mathsf{poly}(\log L)$	$O(\log L)$	✓	✗	CDH/LWE
[30]	Anon. IBE	$O(1)$	$O(1)$	$\mathsf{poly}(\log L)$	$\mathsf{poly}(\log L)$	$\mathsf{poly}(\log L)$	$O(\log L)$	✓	✗	CDH/LWE
[39]	IBE	$O(1)$	$O(1)$	$\mathsf{poly}(\log L)$	$\mathsf{poly}(\log L)$	$\mathsf{poly}(\log L)$	$O(\log L)$	✓	✗	CDH/LWE
[23]	IBE	$O(1)$	$O(1)$	$\mathsf{poly}(\log L)$	$O(\sqrt{L})$	$\mathsf{poly}(\log L)$	$O(\log L)$	✓	✗	CDH/LWE
[35]	IBE $O(1)$-size ciphertexts	$O(\sqrt{L})$	$O(\sqrt{L})$	$O(\sqrt{L})$	$O(\sqrt{L})$	$O(\sqrt{L})$	$O(\sqrt{L})$	✗	✓	Pairings of Prime Order
[35]	IBE $O(\log L)$-size ciphertexts	$O(\sqrt{L})$	$O(\sqrt{L})$	$O(\sqrt{L}\log L)$	$O(\sqrt{L}\log L)$	$O(\log L)$	$O(\log L)$	✗	✓	Pairings of Prime Order
[24]	IBE	$\mathsf{poly}(\log L)$	$\mathsf{poly}(\log L)$	$O(L)$	$\mathsf{poly}(\log L)$	$\mathsf{poly}(\log L)$	$O(\log L)$	✓	✓	LWE
[41]	ABE small attribute space $\mathcal{U}$ LSSS policies	$L^2 \cdot \mathsf{poly}(\lvert\mathcal{U}\rvert, \log L)$	$L \cdot \mathsf{poly}(\lvert\mathcal{U}\rvert, \log L)$	$L \cdot \mathsf{poly}(\lvert\mathcal{U}\rvert, \log L)$	$\lvert\mathcal{U}\rvert \cdot \mathsf{poly}(\log L)$	$\lvert\mathcal{U}\rvert \cdot \mathsf{poly}(\log L)$	$O(\log L)$	✗	✓	Pairings of Composite Order
[41]	ABE large attribute space $\mathcal{U}$ arbitrary policies	$O(1)$	$O(1)$	$O(L)$	$O(1)$	$O(1)$	$O(\log L)$	✓	✗	iO + SSB
Ours §6	Inner-Product PE large function space $\mathcal{F}$ n-size vectors	$n \cdot L^2 \cdot \mathsf{poly}(\log L)$	$L \cdot \mathsf{poly}(\log L)$	$n \cdot L^2 \cdot \mathsf{poly}(\log L)$	$n \cdot \mathsf{poly}(\log L)$	$n \cdot \mathsf{poly}(\log L)$	$O(\log L)$	✗	✓	Pairings of Prime Order + GGM
Ours [25]	FE large function space $\mathcal{F}$ arbitrary functions	$O(1)$	$O(1)$	$O(L)$	$O(1)$	$O(1)$	$O(\log L)$	✓	✗	iO + SSB

keys to aggregate and generate $\mathsf{mpk}, \mathsf{hsk}$.[6] The security definition would need to change accordingly. In particular, it would now additionally require each public key to computationally hide the function tied to it.

All our schemes can be modified to satisfy this syntax. For example, our slotted RIPE from pairings can be easily adapted to this notion since the *extended* key $\widetilde{\mathbf{x}}_i = (\mathbf{x}_i, \mathsf{sk}_i, 1)$ is embedded in the public-key pk_i for slot $i \in [2]$ as $\mathsf{pk}_i = \prod_{w=1}^{n+1} U_{w,i}^{-\widetilde{x}_{w,i}}$. This holds similarly for the cross-terms as well. Using a NIZK, the users can prove that they always choose a non-zero vector as its predicate. It is also easy to verify the same for our slotted RFE from iO. However, for simplicity, we avoid formalizing this in our definitions and schemes. Both our formal constructions from Sect. 6 and the one based on iO are thus in the standard registered setting (i.e., without function-privacy). Building more efficient function-private RFE for specific functions is left as a future work.

3 Related Work

The first paper [29] defined and built RIBE from iO and SSB hashes; this was later improved by Garg *et al.* [30] building RIBE (with the same level of efficiency) from standard assumptions (e.g., from CDH/LWE) even for *anonymous* IBE. Subsequent work on RIBE focused on adding verifiability [39], proving lower bounds on the number of decryption updates [49], improving on practical efficiency of the garbled circuit construction [23], providing effcient black-box construction from pairings with $O(\sqrt{L})$ mpk [35]. More recently, Döttling *et al.* [24] obtain a lattice-based RIBE with the sizes of $\mathsf{crs}, \mathsf{mpk}, \mathsf{hsk}$ as well as key generation runtime growing as $\mathsf{poly}(\log L)$, with a $O(L)$ registration runtime and $O(\log L)$ number of updates. Very recently, [41] extended RIBE to the setting of ABE. They built a (black-box) registered ABE (RABE) scheme supporting a *bounded* number of users and linear secret sharing schemes as access policies from assumptions on composite-order pairing groups. However, their (pairing-based) scheme, the size of CRS and runtime of aggregate and keygen depend linearly on the size of attribute space $|\mathcal{U}|$. The dependence on $|\mathcal{U}|$ allows their scheme to only support a small attribute space (e.g., $|\mathcal{U}| \in \mathsf{poly}(n)$). Notably, our (paring-based) RIPE does not suffer from this limitation since our parameters depend only on the vector length $n = n(\lambda)$ (see Table 1); so we can support a exponential size function class $\mathcal{F}$.

In [39], the authors further introduced an RABE extension to more general access structures. Specifically, they proposed a universal definition of registration-based encryption in which the algorithms take as an additional input the description of an FE scheme (although no construction was presented). Such algorithms compile the standard algorithmic behavior of the FE scheme into

[6] In such a setting (rogue) users can try to register arbitrary functions of their choice which would allow them to learn arbitrary information about encrypted messages. To prevent this, one can restrict the function class at setup meaningfully (e.g., excluding trivial functions like identity). Any user wanting to register its public key would then need to prove the validity of its chosen function w.r.t. this class of functions.

a (verifiable) registration-based one. However, our tailored notion for the functional encryption setting is more natural and follows directly from the RABE definition.

Finally, we also mention a related work on dynamic decentralized FE [22] (DDFE), where there is no trusted authority and users sample their own keys. DDFE, as a notion, posits other general (and albeit unrelated) requirements like (conditional) aggregation of labelled data which comes from different users using seperate FE instances. However, a crucial difference from the registered setting, is that in DDFE there is no requirement on the master public key size, which can be as large as the number of registered users. This is a major challenge (and arguably the defining feature) of all registered settings. Chotard *et al.*[22] also built IP-DDFE, that outputs the inner-product value $\langle \mathbf{x}, \mathbf{y} \rangle$, while our scheme is for the more challenging orthogonality-test predicate (with two-sided security).

Open Problems. We view our work as an initial first step in the world of registered FE, however many open problems remain. For example, a natural question is if registered FE can be obtained generically from any compact, polynomially-hard FE. Another interesting direction is to design schemes for specialized function classes from weaker assumptions. Finally, a technical open problem is to prove our pairing-based RIPE scheme (or some modification thereof) secure in the standard model.

4 Organization

We organize the rest of the paper as follows. The formal definitions of both RFE and slotted RFE extend the same for the RABE setting from [41] in a straighforward way. Hence, we provide the RFE definitions in our full version [25]. Our main focus in this paper is on building (slotted) registered IPE. Thus, we first define slotted RIPE formally in Sect. 5.1 and extend it to slotted RFE for the case of general functions in our full version [25]. Our slotted RIPE scheme from bilinear pairings is provided in Sect. 6. We demonstrate our implementation results of the above slotted RIPE scheme in Sect. 7. Our slotted RFE for general functions and unbounded users, built on iO (plus an SSB hash and a PRG), generalizes a construction from [41] and is presented in [25]. Further, the transformation from slotted RFE to RFE extending the generic compiler from [41] is again provided in our full version [25].

5 Preliminaries

Notations. We write $[n] = \{1, 2, \ldots, n\}$ and $[0, n] = \{0\} \cup [n]$. Capital bold-face letters (such as $\mathbf{X}$) are used to denote random variables, small bold-face letters (such as $\mathbf{x}$) to denote vectors, small letters (such as x) to denote concrete values, calligraphic letters (such as $\mathcal{X}$) to denote sets, serif letters (such as A) to denote algorithms. All of our algorithms are modeled as (possibly interactive) Turing machines. For a string $x \in \{0,1\}^*$, we let $|x|$ be its length; if $\mathcal{X}$ is a set or a list, $|\mathcal{X}|$ represents the cardinality of $\mathcal{X}$. When x is chosen uniformly in $\mathcal{X}$, we write $x \leftarrow\!\!\$\ \mathcal{X}$. If A is an algorithm, we write $y \leftarrow\!\!\$\ \mathsf{A}(x)$ to denote a run of A on input x and output y; if A is randomized, y is a random variable and $\mathsf{A}(x;r)$ denotes a run of A on input x and (uniform) randomness r. An algorithm A is *probabilistic polynomial-time* (PPT) if A is randomized and for any input $x, r \in \{0,1\}^*$ the computation of $\mathsf{A}(x;r)$ terminates in a polynomial number of steps (in the input size). We write $C(x) = y$ to denote the evaluation of the circuit C on input x and output y. For any integer $k \in \mathbb{N}$, we denote $\mathbb{Z}_q^{k^+} = \mathbb{Z}_q^k \setminus \{\mathbf{0}^k\}$ as the set of all non-zero k-size vectors over $\mathbb{Z}_q$, and $\mathbb{Z}_q^+ = \mathbb{Z}_q \setminus \{0\}$.

Negligible Functions. Throughout the paper, we denote the security parameter by $\lambda \in \mathbb{N}$ and we implicitly assume that every algorithm takes λ as input. A function $\nu(\lambda)$ is called negligible in $\lambda \in \mathbb{N}$ if it vanishes faster than the inverse of any polynomial in λ, i.e. $\nu(\lambda) \in O(1/p(\lambda))$ for all positive polynomials $p(\lambda)$.

5.1 Slotted Registered Inner-Product Encryption

We now present the slotted RIPE definitions below. Let $n = n(\lambda)$ be a polynomial in λ and q be a prime. A slotted RIPE with message space $\mathcal{M}$ and attribute space $\mathcal{U}$ is composed of the following polynomial-time algorithms:

$\mathsf{Setup}(1^\lambda, 1^n, 1^L)$: On input the security parameter 1^n, the vector length n, and the number of slots L, the randomized setup algorithm outputs a common reference string crs.

$\mathsf{KGen}(\mathsf{crs}, i)$: On input the common reference string crs and a slot index $i \in [L]$, the randomized key-generation algorithm outputs a public key pk_i and a secret key sk_i.

$\mathsf{IsValid}(\mathsf{crs}, i, \mathsf{pk}_i)$: On input the common reference string crs, a slot index $i \in [L]$, and a public key pk_i, the deterministic key validation algorithm outputs a decision bit $b \in \{0,1\}$.

$\mathsf{Aggr}(\mathsf{crs}, ((\mathsf{pk}_i, \mathbf{x}_i))_{i \in [L]})$: On input the common reference string crs and a L pairs $(\mathsf{pk}_1, \mathbf{x}_1), \ldots, (\mathsf{pk}_L, \mathbf{x}_L)$ each composed of a public key pk_i and its corresponding (non-zero) vector $\mathbf{x}_i \in \mathcal{U}$, the deterministic aggregation algorithm outputs the master public key mpk and a L helper decryption keys $\mathsf{hsk}_1, \ldots, \mathsf{hsk}_L$.

$\mathsf{Enc}(\mathsf{mpk}, \mathbf{y}, m)$: On input the master public key mpk, a (non-zero) attribute vector $\mathbf{y} \in \mathcal{U}$, and a message $m \in \mathcal{M}$, the randomized encryption algorithm outputs a ciphertext c.

$\mathsf{Dec}(\mathsf{sk}, \mathsf{hsk}, c)$: On input a secret key sk, an helper decryption key hsk, and a ciphertext c, the deterministic decryption algorithm outputs a message $m \in \mathcal{M} \cup \{\perp\}$.

Completeness, Correctness, and Efficiency. Completeness of slotted RIPE says that honestly generated public keys for a slot index $i \in [L]$ are valid with respect to the same slot i, i.e., $\mathsf{IsValid}(\mathsf{crs}, i, \mathsf{pk}_i) = 1$. Similarly, correctness says that honest ciphertexts correctly decrypt (to functions of the plaintext) under honestly generated and aggregated keys. For compactness and efficiency, we extend the requirements of RFE to the slotted RIPE setting. The formal definitions are provided in our full version [25]. Below we define the security of slotted RIPE formally.

Definition 1 (Security of slotted RIPE). *Let* $\Pi_{\mathsf{sRIPE}} = (\mathsf{Setup}, \mathsf{KGen}, \mathsf{IsValid}, \mathsf{Aggr}, \mathsf{Enc}, \mathsf{Dec})$ *be a slotted RIPE scheme with message space* $\mathcal{M}$ *and attribute space* $\mathcal{U}$. *For any adversary* A, *define the following security game* $\mathbf{Game}^{\mathsf{sRIPE}}_{\Pi_{\mathsf{sRIPE}},\mathsf{A}}(\lambda, b)$ *with respect to a bit* $b \in \{0,1\}$ *between* A *and a challenger.*

- **Setup phase:** *Upon getting an attribute length* n *and a slot count* L *from the adversary* A, *the challenger samples* $\mathsf{crs} \leftarrow\$ \mathsf{Setup}(1^\lambda, 1^n, 1^L)$ *and gives* crs *to* A. *The challenger also initializes a counter* $\mathsf{ctr} = 0$, *a dictionary* D, *and a set of slot indices* $C_L = \emptyset$ *to account for corrupted slots.*
- **Pre-challenge query phase:** A *can issue the following queries.*
  - **Key-generation query:** A *specifies a slot index* $i \in [L]$. *As a response, the challenger increments* $\mathsf{ctr} = \mathsf{ctr} + 1$, *samples* $(\mathsf{pk}_{\mathsf{ctr}}, \mathsf{sk}_{\mathsf{ctr}}) \leftarrow\$ \mathsf{KGen}(\mathsf{crs}, i)$, *updates the dictionary as* $\mathsf{D}[\mathsf{ctr}] = (i, \mathsf{pk}_{\mathsf{ctr}}, \mathsf{sk}_{\mathsf{ctr}})$ *and replies with* $(\mathsf{ctr}, \mathsf{pk}_{\mathsf{ctr}})$ *to* A.
  - **Corruption query:** A *specifies an index* $c \in [\mathsf{ctr}]$. *In response, the challenger looks up the tuple* $\mathsf{D}[c] = (i', \mathsf{pk}', \mathsf{sk}')$ *and replies with* sk' *to* A.
- **Challenge phase:** *For each* $i \in [L]$, A *specifies a tuple* $(c_i, \mathbf{x}_i, \mathsf{pk}^*_i)$ *where:*
  - *either* $c_i \in [\mathsf{ctr}]$ *that refers to a challenger-generated key from before which it associates with a non-zero predicate* $\mathbf{x}_i \in \mathcal{U}$: *in this case, the challenger looks up* $\mathsf{D}[c_i] = (i', \mathsf{pk}', \mathsf{sk}')$ *and halts if* $i \neq i'$. *Else, the challenger sets* $\mathsf{pk}^*_i = \mathsf{pk}'$. *Further, if* A *issued a corrupt query before on* c_i, *the challenger adds* i *to* C_L.
  - *or* $c_i = \perp$ *that refers to a self-generated (and corrupt) secret key for an arbitrary non-zero predicate* $\mathbf{x}_i \in \mathcal{U}$: *in this case, the challenger aborts if* $\mathsf{IsValid}(\mathsf{crs}, i, \mathsf{pk}^*_i) = 0$. *Else if* pk^*_i *is valid, it adds the index* i *to* C_L.

  Additionally, A *sends a challenge pair* $(\mathbf{y}_0, m_0), (\mathbf{y}_1, m_1) \in \mathcal{U} \times \mathcal{M}$. *In response, the challenger computes* $(\mathsf{mpk}, (\mathsf{hsk}_i)_{i\in[L]}) = \mathsf{Aggr}(\mathsf{crs}, (\mathsf{pk}^*_i, \mathbf{x}_i)_{i\in[L]})$ *and* $c^* \leftarrow\$ \mathsf{Enc}(\mathsf{mpk}, \mathbf{y}_b, m_b)$, *and replies with* c^* *to* A.
- **Output phase:** A *returns a bit* $b' \in \{0,1\}$ *which is also the output of the experiment.*

A *is called admissible if the challenge pair* $(\mathbf{y}_0, m_0), (\mathbf{y}_1, m_1)$ *satisfy the following:*

- $\forall \mathbf{x}_i \in \mathcal{U}$ *with* $i \in C_L$, *it holds that:*

$$\text{either } \langle \mathbf{x}_i, \mathbf{y}_0 \rangle = \langle \mathbf{x}_i, \mathbf{y}_1 \rangle = 0 \quad \text{or} \quad \text{both} \langle \mathbf{x}_i, \mathbf{y}_0 \rangle, \langle \mathbf{x}_i, \mathbf{y}_1 \rangle \neq 0, \text{ and}$$

- *if* $\exists \mathbf{x}_i \in \mathcal{U}$ *with* $i \in C_L$ *such that* $\langle \mathbf{x}_i, \mathbf{y}_0 \rangle = \langle \mathbf{x}_i, \mathbf{y}_1 \rangle = 0$, *then* $m_0 = m_1$.

We say that Π_{sRIPE} *is secure if for all polynomials* $n = n(\lambda), L = L(\lambda)$ *and for all PPT and admissible* A *in the above security hybrid, there exists a negligible function* $\mathsf{negl}(\cdot)$ *such that for all* $\lambda \in \mathbb{N}$,

$$\left|\Pr[\mathbf{Game}^{\mathsf{sRIPE}}_{\Pi_{\mathsf{sRIPE}},\mathsf{A}}(\lambda, 0) = 1] - \Pr[\mathbf{Game}^{\mathsf{sRIPE}}_{\Pi_{\mathsf{sRIPE}},\mathsf{A}}(\lambda, 1) = 1]\right| = \mathsf{negl}(\lambda).$$

Remark 1. We argue in our full version [25] that for general RFE, security without post-challenge queries imply security with post-challenge queries in the slotted setting as well. This is because Aggr is deterministic and does not require any secret. Hence, an adversary can simulate the post-challenge queries itself.

6 Slotted Registered IPE from Prime-Order Pairings

Bilinear Groups. Our slotted RIPE is based on asymmetric bilinear groups. We use cyclic groups of prime order q with an asymmetric bilinear map endowed on them. We assume a PPT algorithm $\mathsf{GroupGen}$ that takes a security parameter λ as input and outputs $\mathcal{G} = (\mathbb{G}_1, \mathbb{G}_2, \mathbb{G}_\mathsf{T}, q, g_1, g_2, e)$, where $\mathbb{G}_1, \mathbb{G}_2, \mathbb{G}_\mathsf{T}$ are cyclic groups of prime order q, g_1 (resp. g_2) is random generator in $\mathbb{G}_1$ (resp. $\mathbb{G}_2$) and $e : \mathbb{G}_1 \times \mathbb{G}_2 \to \mathbb{G}_\mathsf{T}$ is a non-degenerate bilinear map.

We assume the message space $\mathcal{M} = \mathbb{G}_\mathsf{T}$ for our scheme. Our slotted RIPE supports an a-priori fixed number of slots $L = L(\lambda)$, i.e., the scheme supports a bounded number of slots. Below, we describe our formal scheme.

Construction 1. *The slotted RIPE scheme* $\Pi_{\mathsf{sRIPE}} = (\mathsf{Setup}, \mathsf{KGen}, \mathsf{IsValid}, \mathsf{Aggr}, \mathsf{Enc}, \mathsf{Dec})$ *with message space* $\mathcal{M} = \mathbb{G}_\mathsf{T}$ *and attribute space* $\mathcal{U} = \mathbb{Z}_q^{n^+}$ *is as follows:*

$\mathsf{Setup}(1^\lambda, 1^n, 1^L)$: *On input the security parameter* λ, *the attribute size* n *and the number of slots* L, *compute* $\mathcal{G} = (\mathbb{G}_1, \mathbb{G}_2, \mathbb{G}_\mathsf{T}, q, g_1, g_2, e) \leftarrow_{\$} \mathsf{GroupGen}(1^\lambda)$ *and generate the common reference string as follows.*

1. *Sample* $\alpha, \beta, \gamma \leftarrow_{\$} \mathbb{Z}_q^+$ *and set* $h = g_1^\beta, Z = e(g_1, g_2)^\alpha, \Gamma = g_1^\gamma, n' = n + 1$.
2. *For each index* $i \in [0, L]$, *do the following:*
   1. *for each* $w \in [n']$, *sample* $u_{w,i} \leftarrow_{\$} \mathbb{Z}_q$ *and set* $U_{w,i} = g_1^{u_{w,i}}$.
   2. *for a slot index* $i > 0$, *sample* $t_i \leftarrow_{\$} \mathbb{Z}_q$ *and set* $A_i = g_2^{t_i}, B_i = g_2^\alpha \cdot A_i^\beta$.
   3. *for a slot index* $i > 0$, $\forall w \in [n'], j \in [0, L] \setminus \{i\}$, *set* $W_{i,j,w} = A_i^{u_{w,j}/\gamma}$.
3. *Sample* $\widetilde{\mathbf{x}}_0 = (\widetilde{x}_{1,0}, \ldots, \widetilde{x}_{n,0}, \widetilde{r}_0) \leftarrow_{\$} \mathbb{Z}_q^{n'^+}$. *Set* $\mathsf{sk}_0 = \widetilde{\mathbf{x}}_0$ *and*

$$T_0 = \left(\prod_{w=1}^{n} U_{w,0}^{-\widetilde{x}_{w,0}}\right) \cdot U_{n',0}^{-\widetilde{r}_0} \quad , \quad \widetilde{W}_{i,0} = \left(\prod_{w=1}^{n} W_{i,0,w}^{\widetilde{x}_{w,0}}\right) \cdot W_{i,0,n'}^{\widetilde{r}_0}, \quad \forall i \in [L].$$

Also, set $\mathsf{pk}_0 = \left(T_0, \left\{\widetilde{W}_{i,0}\right\}_{i \in [L]}\right)$.

Finally, output the common reference string

$$\mathsf{crs} = (\mathcal{G}, Z, h, \Gamma, \{A_i, B_i\}_{i\in[L]}, \{\{U_{w,i}\}_{i\in[0,L]}, \{W_{i,j,w}\}_{i\in[L],j\in[0,L]\setminus\{i\}}\}_{w\in[n']}, \mathsf{pk}_0)$$

$\mathsf{KGen}(\mathsf{crs}, i)$: *On input the common reference string* crs *and a slot index* $i \in [L]$, *do the following.*

1. *Parse the common reference string*
$$\mathsf{crs} = \Big(\mathcal{G}, Z, h, \Gamma, \{A_i, B_i\}_{i\in[L]},$$
$$\Big\{\{U_{w,i}\}_{i\in[0,L]}, \{W_{i,j,w}\}_{i\in[L], j\in[0,L]\setminus\{i\}}\Big\}_{w\in[n']}, \mathsf{pk}_0\Big).$$
2. *Sample* $\widetilde{r}_i \leftarrow_\$ \mathbb{Z}_q^+$ *and pick elements* $U_{n',i}$ *and* $\{W_{j,i,n'}\}_{j\in[L]\setminus\{i\}}$ *from* crs.
3. *Compute* $T_i = U_{n',i}^{-\widetilde{r}_i}$ *and* $\widetilde{W}_{j,i} = W_{j,i,n'}^{\widetilde{r}_i}, \forall j \in [L] \setminus \{i\}$.
4. *Output* $\mathsf{pk}_i = \Big(T_i, \{\widetilde{W}_{j,i}\}_{j\in[L]\setminus\{i\}}\Big)$ *and* $\mathsf{sk}_i = \widetilde{r}_i$.

$\mathsf{IsValid}(\mathsf{crs}, i, \mathsf{pk}_i)$: *On input the common reference string* crs, *a slot index* $i \in [L]$ *and a purported public key* $\mathsf{pk}_i = \Big(T_i, \{\widetilde{W}_{j,i}\}_{j\in[L]\setminus\{i\}}\Big)$, *the key-validation algorithm first affirms that each of the components in* pk_i *is a valid group element, namely:* $\Big(T_i \overset{?}{\in} \mathbb{G}_1 \setminus \{1_{\mathbb{G}_1}\} \;\;\wedge\;\; \widetilde{W}_{j,i} \overset{?}{\in} G_2 \setminus \{1_{\mathbb{G}_2}\},\;\; \forall j \in [L] \setminus \{i\}\Big)$ *where* $1_{\mathbb{G}_t}$ *denotes the identity in* $\mathbb{G}_t$ *for* $\mathsf{t} \in [2]$. *If the checks pass, it picks the elements* $U_{n',i}$ *and* $\{W_{j,i,n'}\}_{j\in[L]\setminus\{i\}}$ *from* crs *and checks further that*
$$e\left(T_i^{-1}, W_{j,i,n'}\right) \overset{?}{=} e\left(U_{n',i}, \widetilde{W}_{j,i}\right), \forall j \in [L] \setminus \{i\}.$$
If all checks pass, it outputs 1. *Else, it outputs* 0.

$\mathsf{Aggr}(\mathsf{crs}, ((\mathsf{pk}_i, \mathbf{x}_i))_{i\in[L]})$: *On input the common reference string* crs *and a set of* L *public keys* $\mathsf{pk}_i = \Big(T_i, \{\widetilde{W}_{j,i}\}_{j\in[L]\setminus\{i\}}\Big)$ *together with vectors* $\mathbf{x}_i = (x_{1,i}, \ldots, x_{n,i}) \in \mathbb{Z}_q^{n^+}$ *(representing predicates* $f_{\mathbf{x}_i}$*), compute the following.*

1. *Parse the common reference string*
$$\mathsf{crs} = \Big(\mathcal{G}, Z, h, \Gamma, \{A_i, B_i\}_{i\in[L]},$$
$$\Big\{\{U_{w,i}\}_{i\in[0,L]}, \{W_{i,j,w}\}_{i\in[L], j\in[0,L]\setminus\{i\}}\Big\}_{w\in[n']}, \mathsf{pk}_0\Big).$$
2. *Fuse the predicate vector* $\mathbf{x}_i$ *into* pk_i *by updating each of its components as*
$$T_i = \left(\prod_{w=1}^{n} U_{w,i}^{-x_{w,i}}\right) \cdot T_i \quad , \quad \widetilde{W}_{j,i} = \left(\prod_{w=1}^{n} W_{j,i,w}^{x_{w,i}}\right) \cdot \widetilde{W}_{j,i}, \forall j \in [L] \setminus \{i\}$$
and set $\mathsf{pk}_i = \left(T_i, \left\{\widetilde{W}_{j,i}\right\}_{j\in[L]\setminus\{i\}}\right)$. *Further, parse* pk_0 *as follows:*
$$\mathsf{pk}_0 = \left(T_0, \left\{\widetilde{W}_{j,0}\right\}_{j\in[0,L]\setminus\{0\}}\right).$$
3. *For each* $w \in [n']$, *compute* $\widehat{U}_w = \prod_{i\in[0,L]} U_{w,i}$ *and* $\widehat{U}_{n'+1} = \prod_{i\in[0,L]} T_i$.

4. *Compute the cross-terms as follows. For each slot index* $i \in [L]$:
   (a) *for each* $w \in [n']$, *compute* $\widehat{W}_{w,i} = \prod_{j \in [0,L] \setminus \{i\}} W_{i,j,w}$.
   (b) *compute* $\widehat{W}_{n'+1,i} = \left(\prod_{j \in [0,L] \setminus \{i\}} \widetilde{W}_{i,j}\right)^{-1}$.
5. *Output the master public key and the slot-specific helper secret keys as* $\mathsf{mpk} = \left(\mathcal{G}, h, Z, \Gamma, \left\{\widehat{U}_w\right\}_{w \in [n'+1]}\right)$, *and*

$$\mathsf{hsk}_i = \left(\mathcal{G}, i, \mathbf{x}_i, A_i, B_i, \left\{\widehat{W}_{w,i}\right\}_{w \in [n'+1]}\right), \forall i \in [L].$$

$\mathsf{Enc}(\mathsf{mpk}, \mathbf{y}, m)$: *On input the master public key* mpk, *a vector* $\mathbf{y} = (y_1, \ldots, y_n) \in \mathbb{Z}_q^{n^+}$ *(as an attribute) and a message* $m \in \mathbb{G}_\mathsf{T}$, *the ciphertext is computed as:*
1. *Parse* $\mathsf{mpk} = \left(\mathcal{G}, h, Z, \Gamma, \left\{\widehat{U}_w\right\}_{w \in [n'+1]}\right)$.
2. *Set* $\widetilde{\mathbf{y}} = (\mathbf{y}, 0, 0) \in \mathbb{Z}_q^{n'+1}$ *and sample* $s, r, z \leftarrow\!\!\$\, \mathbb{Z}_q^+$. *Also, parse* $\widetilde{\mathbf{y}} = (\widetilde{y}_1, \ldots, \widetilde{y}_{n'+1})$.
3. *Message embedding: set* $C_1 = m \cdot Z^s$ *and* $C_2 = g_1^s$.
4. *Attribute and Slot embedding: for each* $w \in [n'+1]$, *set* $C_{3,w} = h^{\widetilde{y}_w \cdot r + s} \cdot \widehat{U}_w^{-z}$. *Set* $C_4 = \Gamma^z$.
5. *Output the ciphertext* $c = \left(C_1, C_2, \{C_{3,w}\}_{w \in [n'+1]}, C_4\right)$.

$\mathsf{Dec}(\mathsf{sk}, \mathsf{hsk}, c)$: *Parse the input secret key* sk, *helper secret key* hsk *and ciphertext* c *as* $\mathsf{sk} = \widetilde{r}_i$, *and*

$$\mathsf{hsk} = \left(\mathcal{G}, i, \mathbf{x}_i, A_i, B_i, \left\{\widehat{W}_{w,i}\right\}_{w \in [n'+1]}\right), c = \left(C_1, C_2, \{C_{3,w}\}_{w \in [n'+1]}, C_4\right),$$

for some $i \in [L]$. *Let* $\widetilde{\mathbf{x}}_i = (\widetilde{x}_{1,i}, \ldots, \widetilde{x}_{n'+1,i}) = (\mathbf{x}_i, \widetilde{r}_i, 1) \in \mathbb{Z}_q^{n'+1}, X_i = \sum_{w=1}^{n'+1} \widetilde{x}_{w,i} \in \mathbb{Z}_q$. *Compute and output the following:*

$$\frac{C_1}{e(C_2, B_i)} \cdot \left[\prod_{w=1}^{n'+1} \left\{e\left(C_{3,w}^{\widetilde{x}_{w,i}}, A_i\right) \cdot e\left(C_4, \widehat{W}_{w,i}^{\widetilde{x}_{w,i}}\right)\right\}\right]^{X_i^{-1}}.$$

Remark: In the setup algorithm in our scheme, we introduce a *dummy* slot "0" and pre-register an *honestly* generated dummy key pk_0. This slot does not impact the security definition in any way because the associated secret key sk_0 is thrown away once the one-time setup is executed. This modification is done only for a simpler analysis of the security proof in the GGM.

Theorem 3 (Completeness of Construction 1). *The slotted RIPE scheme* Π_{sRIPE} *with message space* $\mathcal{M} = \mathbb{G}_\mathsf{T}$ *and attribute space* $\mathcal{U} = \mathbb{Z}_q^{n^+}$ *from Construction 1 is complete.*

Theorem 4 (Compactness and Efficiency of Construction 1). *The slotted RIPE scheme* Π_{sRIPE} *with message space* $\mathcal{M} = \mathbb{G}_\mathsf{T}$ *and attribute space* $\mathcal{U} = \mathbb{Z}_q^{n^+}$ *from Construction 1 satisfies the following properties:*

- $|\mathsf{crs}| = n \cdot L^2 \cdot \mathsf{poly}(\lambda), |\mathsf{mpk}| = n \cdot \mathsf{poly}(\lambda), |\mathsf{hsk}| = (n \cdot \mathsf{poly}(\lambda) + O(\log L))$
- **Runtime**$(\mathsf{KGen}) = O(L) \cdot \mathsf{poly}(\lambda)$, **Runtime**$(\mathsf{IsValid}) = L \cdot \mathsf{poly}(\lambda)$
- **Runtime**$(\mathsf{Aggr}) = n \cdot L^2 \cdot \mathsf{poly}(\lambda)$

We refer to the full version [25] for the proofs of Theorems 4 and 3.

Theorem 5 (Perfect Correctness of Construction 1). *The slotted RIPE scheme* Π_{sRIPE} *with message space* $\mathcal{M} = \mathbb{G}_\mathsf{T}$ *and attribute space* $\mathcal{U} = \mathbb{Z}_q^{n^+}$ *from Construction 1 is perfectly correct.*

Proof. Fix some λ, attribute size $n = n(\lambda)$, a slot count $L = L(\lambda)$ and an index $i \in [L]$. Let $\mathsf{crs} \leftarrow\!\!\$\ \mathsf{Setup}(1^\lambda, 1^n, 1^L)$ and $(\mathsf{pk}_i, \mathsf{sk}_i) \leftarrow\!\!\$\ \mathsf{KGen}(\mathsf{crs}, i)$ be defined as in the scheme from Construction 1. Take any set of public keys $\{\mathsf{pk}_j\}_{j\in[L]\setminus\{i\}}$, where $\mathsf{IsValid}(\mathsf{crs}, j, \mathsf{pk}_j) = 1$. Therefore, we have

$$\mathsf{pk}_j = \left(T_j, \left\{\widetilde{W}_{\ell,j}\right\}_{\ell\in[L]\setminus\{j\}}\right), \forall j \in [L] \setminus \{i\} \quad , \quad \mathsf{sk}_j = \widetilde{r}_j \text{ for some } \widetilde{r}_j \in \mathbb{Z}_q^+.$$

For each $j \in [L]$, let $\mathbf{x}_j \in \mathbb{Z}_q^{n^+}$ be the predicate vector associated to pk_j and let $\widetilde{\mathbf{x}}_j = (\mathbf{x}_j, \widetilde{r}_j, 1)$. Further, let mpk and hsk_i be as computed by $\mathsf{Aggr}(\mathsf{crs}, ((\mathsf{pk}_j, \mathbf{x}_j))_{j\in[L]})$. Now, note that in the Dec algorithm, the computation associated to the message components yield

$$\frac{C_1}{e(C_2, B_i)} = \frac{m \cdot Z^s}{e\left(g_1^s, g_2^\alpha \cdot A_i^\beta\right)} = \frac{m \cdot e\left(g_1, g_2\right)^{\alpha\cdot s}}{e\left(g_1, g_2\right)^{\alpha\cdot s} \cdot e\left(g_1, g_2\right)^{s\beta t_i}} = \frac{m}{e\left(g_1, g_2\right)^{s\beta t_i}} \tag{2}$$

Now observe that for any vector $\mathbf{x}_i \in \mathbb{Z}_q^{n^+}$ for some $i \in [L]$ and an attribute $\mathbf{y} \in \mathbb{Z}_q^{n^+}$ with $\langle \mathbf{x}_i, \mathbf{y}\rangle = 0$, it also holds that $\langle \widetilde{\mathbf{x}}_i, \widetilde{\mathbf{y}}\rangle = \langle \mathbf{x}_i, \mathbf{y}\rangle + \langle \widetilde{r}_i, 0\rangle + 1 \cdot 0 = 0$. For brevity, we set up the notations $g_\mathsf{T} = e\left(g_1, g_2\right)$ and the discrete logarithm as $\mathsf{DL}(K) = k$, where $K = g_\mathsf{t}^k$ for any $k \in \mathbb{Z}_q$ (i.e., irrespective of any group type $\mathsf{t} \in \{1, 2, \mathsf{T}\}$) for the rest of the proof. To ensure correctness with the rest of decryption above, it is thus enough to show that

$$\prod_{w=1}^{n'+1} \left\{e\left(C_{3,w}^{\widetilde{x}_{w,i}}, A_i\right) \cdot e\left(C_4, \widehat{W}_{w,i}^{\widetilde{x}_{w,i}}\right)\right\} = g_\mathsf{T}^{s\beta t_i X_i} \tag{3}$$

so that Dec yields the message $m \in \mathbb{G}_\mathsf{T}$. We will analyze individual pairing products in the above form separately. Before that we note a few things about the public keys *after they are fused with the predicate vectors* during Aggr. For any $i \in [L], j \in [0, L]$, we have

$$T_j = \left(\prod_{w \in [n]} U_{w,j}^{-x_{w,j}} \right) \cdot U_{n',j}^{-\widetilde{r}_j} = \prod_{w \in [n']} g_1^{-u_{w,j} \widetilde{x}_{w,j}} = g_1^{-\sum_{w \in [n']} u_{w,j} \widetilde{x}_{w,j}}$$
$$\Longrightarrow \mathsf{DL}(T_j) = - \sum_{w \in [n']} u_{w,j} \widetilde{x}_{w,j},$$

$$\widetilde{W}_{i,j} = \left(\prod_{w \in [n]} W_{i,j,w}^{x_{w,j}} \right) \cdot W_{i,j,n'}^{\widetilde{r}_j} = \prod_{w \in [n']} \left(A_i^{u_{w,j}/\gamma} \right)^{\widetilde{x}_{w,j}}$$
$$= A_i^{\frac{1}{\gamma} \cdot \sum_{w \in [n']} u_{w,j} \widetilde{x}_{w,j}} = A_i^{-\mathsf{DL}(T_j)/\gamma},$$

where we redefined $\widetilde{x}_{n',0} = \widetilde{r}_0$. Further, for any $w \in [n']$ and $i \in [L]$, we have:

$$\widehat{W}_{w,i}^{\widetilde{x}_{w,i}} = \prod_{j \in [0,L] \setminus \{i\}} W_{i,j,w}^{\widetilde{x}_{w,i}} = \prod_{j \in [0,L] \setminus \{i\}} \left(A_i^{u_{w,j}/\gamma} \right)^{\widetilde{x}_{w,i}} = A_i^{\left(\widetilde{x}_{w,i} \cdot \sum_{j \in [0,L] \setminus \{i\}} u_{w,j} \right) / \gamma} \tag{4}$$

Defining the first pairing product as $\theta_1 = \prod_{w=1}^{n'+1} e\left(C_{3,w}^{\widetilde{x}_{w,i}}, A_i \right)$, we have:

$$\begin{aligned}
\theta_1 &= \prod_{w=1}^{n'+1} e\left(\left(h^{\widetilde{y}_w \cdot r + s} \cdot \widehat{U}_w^{-z} \right)^{\widetilde{x}_{w,i}}, A_i \right) \\
&= \prod_{w=1}^{n'+1} \left\{ e\left(h^{r \cdot \widetilde{x}_{w,i} \widetilde{y}_w}, A_i \right) \cdot e\left(h^{s \cdot \widetilde{x}_{w,i}}, A_i \right) \cdot e\left(\widehat{U}_w^{-z \widetilde{x}_{w,i}}, A_i \right) \right\} \\
&= e\left(h^{r \cdot \sum_{w=1}^{n'+1} \widetilde{x}_{w,i} \widetilde{y}_w}, A_i \right) \cdot e\left(g_1^{s\beta \sum_{w=1}^{n'+1} \widetilde{x}_{w,i}}, A_i \right) \cdot \prod_{w=1}^{n'+1} e\left(\widehat{U}_w^{-z \widetilde{x}_{w,i}}, A_i \right) \\
&= e\left(h^0, A_i \right) \cdot e\left(g_1^{s\beta X_i}, g_2^{t_i} \right) \cdot \prod_{w=1}^{n'+1} e\left(\widehat{U}_w^{-z \widetilde{x}_{w,i}}, A_i \right) \\
&= g_{\mathsf{T}}^{s\beta t_i X_i} \cdot \theta_{11} \cdot \theta_{12},
\end{aligned}$$

where $\theta_{11} = \prod_{w=1}^{n'} e\left(\widehat{U}_w^{-z \widetilde{x}_{w,i}}, A_i \right)$ and $\theta_{12} = e\left(\widehat{U}_{n'+1}^{-z}, A_i \right)$ (recall $\widetilde{x}_{n'+1,i} = 1$)

$$\theta_{11} = \prod_{w \in [n']} e\left(\prod_{j=0}^{L} U_{w,j}^{-z \widetilde{x}_{w,i}}, A_i \right) = \prod_{w \in [n']} e\left(\left(g_1^{\sum_{j=0}^{L} u_{w,j}} \right)^{-z \widetilde{x}_{w,i}}, g_2^{t_i} \right)$$
$$= \prod_{w \in [n']} g_{\mathsf{T}}^{-z t_i \widetilde{x}_{w,i} \sum_{j=0}^{L} u_{w,j}} = \prod_{w \in [n']} g_{\mathsf{T}}^{z t_i \left(-\widetilde{x}_{w,i} u_{w,i} \right)} \cdot \prod_{w \in [n']} g_{\mathsf{T}}^{-z t_i \widetilde{x}_{w,i} \sum_{j \in [0,L] \setminus \{i\}} u_{w,j}}$$

$$\Rightarrow \theta_{11} = g_{\mathsf{T}}^{zt_i \mathsf{DL}(T_i)} \cdot \zeta_1, \text{ where } \zeta_1 = \prod_{w\in[n']} g_{\mathsf{T}}^{-zt_i \widetilde{x}_{w,i} \sum_{j\in[0,L]\setminus\{i\}} u_{w,j}} \text{ and}$$

$$\begin{aligned}\theta_{12} &= e\left(\widehat{U}_{n'+1}^{-z}, A_i\right) = e\left(\prod_{j=0}^{L} T_j^{-1}, A_i^z\right) = \prod_{j=0}^{L} e\left(T_j^{-1}, A_i^z\right) = \prod_{j=0}^{L} e\left(\prod_{w=1}^{n'} U_{w,j}^{\widetilde{x}_{w,j}}, A_i^z\right)\\ &= \prod_{j=0}^{L} e\left(g_1^{\sum_{w\in[n']} u_{w,j}\widetilde{x}_{w,j}}, A_i^z\right) = \prod_{j=0}^{L} e\left(g_1^{-\mathsf{DL}(T_j)}, g_2^{zt_i}\right) = \prod_{j=0}^{L} g_{\mathsf{T}}^{-zt_i \mathsf{DL}(T_j)}\\ &= g_{\mathsf{T}}^{-zt_i \mathsf{DL}(T_i)} \cdot \zeta_2, \text{ where } \zeta_2 = g_{\mathsf{T}}^{-zt_i \sum_{j\in[0,L]\setminus\{i\}} \mathsf{DL}(T_j)}.\end{aligned}$$

We have $\theta_1 = g_{\mathsf{T}}^{s\beta t_i X_i} \cdot \left(\cancel{g_{\mathsf{T}}^{zt_i \mathsf{DL}(T_i)}} \cdot \zeta_1\right) \cdot \left(\cancel{g_{\mathsf{T}}^{-zt_i \mathsf{DL}(T_i)}} \cdot \zeta_2\right) \Rightarrow \theta_1 = g_{\mathsf{T}}^{s\beta t_i X_i} \cdot \zeta_1 \cdot \zeta_2$

Defining the second pairing product as $\theta_2 = \prod_{w=1}^{n'+1} e\left(C_4, \widehat{W}_{w,i}^{\widetilde{x}_{w,i}}\right)$, we have:

$$\begin{aligned}\theta_2 &= \left\{\prod_{w\in[n']} e\left(g_1^{z\gamma}, \widehat{W}_{w,i}^{\widetilde{x}_{w,i}}\right)\right\} \cdot e\left(g_1^{z\gamma}, \widehat{W}_{n'+1,i}\right) (\text{recall } \widetilde{x}_{n'+1,i} = 1 \text{ and } C_4 = \Gamma^z = g^{z\gamma})\\ &= \left\{\prod_{w\in[n']} e\left(g_1^{z\gamma}, A_i^{\left(\widetilde{x}_{w,i}\cdot\sum_{j\in[0,L]\setminus\{i\}} u_{w,j}\right)/\gamma}\right)\right\} \cdot e\left(g_1^{z\gamma}, \left(\prod_{j\in[0,L]\setminus\{i\}} \widetilde{W}_{i,j}\right)^{-1}\right)\\ &= \prod_{w\in[n']} e\left(g_1^{z\gamma}, g_2^{\left(t_i\widetilde{x}_{w,i}\cdot\sum_{j\in[0,L]\setminus\{i\}} u_{w,j}\right)/\gamma}\right)\Bigg\} \cdot \prod_{j\in[0,L]\setminus\{i\}} e\left(g_1^{z\gamma}, \left(A_i^{-\mathsf{DL}(T_j)/\gamma}\right)^{-1}\right)\\ &= \prod_{w\in[n']} g_{\mathsf{T}}^{zt_i\widetilde{x}_{w,i}\cdot\sum_{j\in[0,L]\setminus\{i\}} u_{w,j}} \cdot \prod_{j\in[0,L]\setminus\{i\}} e\left(g_1^{z\gamma}, g_2^{t_i \mathsf{DL}(T_j)/\gamma}\right)\\ &= \zeta_1^{-1} \cdot \prod_{j\in[0,L]\setminus\{i\}} g_{\mathsf{T}}^{zt_i \mathsf{DL}(T_j)} = \zeta_1^{-1} \cdot g_{\mathsf{T}}^{zt_i \sum_{j\in[0,L]\setminus\{i\}} \mathsf{DL}(T_j)} = \zeta_1^{-1} \cdot \zeta_2^{-1}\end{aligned}$$

This completes the proof since

$$\prod_{w=1}^{n'+1}\left\{e\left(C_{3,w}^{\widetilde{x}_{w,i}}, A_i\right)\cdot e\left(C_4, \widehat{W}_{w,i}^{\widetilde{x}_{w,i}}\right)\right\} = \theta_1 \cdot \theta_2 = g_{\mathsf{T}}^{s\beta t_i X_i} \cdot \zeta_1 \cdot \zeta_2 \cdot \zeta_1^{-1} \cdot \zeta_2^{-1} = g_{\mathsf{T}}^{s\beta t_i X_i}.$$

Theorem 6 (Security of Construction 1**).** *The slotted RIPE scheme* Π_{sRIPE} *with message space* $\mathcal{M} = \mathbb{G}_{\mathsf{T}}$ *and attribute space* $\mathcal{U} = \mathbb{Z}_q^{n^+}$ *from Construction 1 is secure in the* GGM.

Below, we show that our slotted RIPE scheme Π_{sRIPE} (Construction 1) is secure in the generic group model. We start with some notations and definitions for generic and symbolic group models.

Generic Bilinear Group Model. Our definitions for generic bilinear group model is adapted from [4,12]. Let $\mathcal{G} = (\mathbb{G}_1, \mathbb{G}_2, \mathbb{G}_T, q, g_1, g_2, e)$ be a bilinear group setting, $\mathcal{L}_1, \mathcal{L}_2, \mathcal{L}_T$ be lists of group elements in $\mathbb{G}_1, \mathbb{G}_2$, and $\mathbb{G}_T$ respectively. Let $\mathcal{D}$ be a distribution over $\mathcal{L}_1, \mathcal{L}_2, \mathcal{L}_T$. The generic group model for a bilinear group setting $\mathcal{G}$ and a distribution $\mathcal{D}$ is described in Fig. 1. In this model, the challenger first initializes the lists $\mathcal{L}_1, \mathcal{L}_2, \mathcal{L}_T$ by sampling the group elements according to $\mathcal{D}$, and the adversary receives handles for the elements in the lists. For $\mathsf{t} \in \{1, 2, \mathsf{T}\}$, $\mathcal{L}_\mathsf{t}[h]$ denotes the h-th element in the list $\mathcal{L}_\mathsf{t}$. The handle to this element is simply the pair (t, h). An adversary A running in the generic bilinear group model can apply group operations and the bilinear map e to the elements in the lists. To do this, A has to call the appropriate oracle specifying handles for the input elements. A also gets access to the internal state variables of the challenger via handles, and we assume that the equality queries are "free", in the sense that they do not count when measuring the computational complexity A. For $\mathsf{t} \in \{1, 2, \mathsf{T}\}$, the challenger computes the result of a query, say $\delta \in \mathbb{G}_\mathsf{t}$, and stores it in the corresponding list as $\mathcal{L}_\mathsf{t}[\mathsf{pos}] = \delta$ where pos is its next *empty* position in $\mathcal{L}_\mathsf{t}$, and returns to A its (newly created) handle $(\mathsf{t}, \mathsf{pos})$. Handles are not unique (i.e., the same group element may appear more than once in a list under different handles). As in [4], the equality test oracle in [12] is replaced with the zero-test oracle $\mathsf{Zt}_\mathsf{T}(\cdot)$ that, on input a handle (t, h), returns 1 if $\mathcal{L}_\mathsf{t}[h] = 0$ and 0 otherwise only for the case $\mathsf{t} = \mathsf{T}$.

State: Lists $\mathcal{L}_1, \mathcal{L}_2, \mathcal{L}_T$ over $\mathbb{G}_1, \mathbb{G}_2, \mathbb{G}_T$ respectively.

Initializations: Lists $\mathcal{L}_1, \mathcal{L}_2, \mathcal{L}_T$ sampled according to distribution $\mathcal{D}$.

Oracles: The oracles provide black-box access to the group operations, the bilinear map, and zero-tests.

- $\forall \mathsf{t} \in \{1, 2, \mathsf{T}\}$: $\mathsf{Add}_\mathsf{t}(h_1, h_2)$ appends $\mathcal{L}_\mathsf{t}[h_1] + \mathcal{L}_\mathsf{t}[h_2]$ to $\mathcal{L}_\mathsf{t}$ and returns its handle $(\mathsf{t}, |\mathcal{L}_\mathsf{t}|)$.
- $\forall \mathsf{t} \in \{1, 2, \mathsf{T}\}$: $\mathsf{Neg}_\mathsf{t}(h)$ appends $-\mathcal{L}_\mathsf{t}[h]$ and returns its handle $(\mathsf{t}, |\mathcal{L}_\mathsf{t}|)$.
- $\mathsf{Map}_e(h_1, h_2)$ appends $e(\mathcal{L}_1[h_1], \mathcal{L}_2[h_2])$ and returns its handle $(\mathsf{T}, |\mathcal{L}_\mathsf{T}|)$.
- $\mathsf{Zt}_\mathsf{T}(h)$ returns 1 if $\mathcal{L}_\mathsf{T}[h] = 0$ and 0 otherwise.

All oracles return $\perp$ when given invalid indices.

Fig. 1. GGM for bilinear group setting $\mathcal{G} = (\mathbb{G}_1, \mathbb{G}_2, \mathbb{G}_T, q, g_1, g_2, e)$ and distribution $\mathcal{D}$.

Symbolic Group Model. The symbolic group model (SGM) for a bilinear group setting $\mathcal{G}$ and a distribution $\mathcal{D}$ gives to the adversary the same interface as the corresponding generic group model (GGM), except that internally the challenger stores lists of elements from the ring $\mathbb{Z}_q[\mathtt{x}_1, \ldots, \mathtt{x}_k]$ instead of lists of group elements, where $\{\mathtt{x}_k\}_{k \in \mathbb{N}}$ are indeterminates. The

$\mathsf{Add_t}(\cdot,\cdot), \mathsf{Neg_t}(\cdot), \mathsf{Map}_e(\cdot,\cdot), \mathsf{Zt_T}(\cdot)$ oracles respectively compute addition, negation, multiplication, and zero tests in the ring. For our proof, we will work in the ring $\mathbb{Z}_q[\mathrm{x}_1, \ldots, \mathrm{x}_k, 1/\mathrm{x}_i]$ for some $i \in [k]$. Note that any element $f \in \mathbb{Z}_q[\mathrm{x}_1, \ldots, \mathrm{x}_k, 1/\mathrm{x}_i]$ can be represented as

$$f(\mathrm{x}_1, \ldots, \mathrm{x}_n) = \sum_{\mathbf{c} \in \mathbb{Z}^k} \eta_{\mathbf{c}} \prod_{i=1}^{k} \mathrm{x}_i^{c_i} \text{ with } \mathbf{c} = (c_1, \ldots, c_k) \in \mathbb{Z}^k$$

using $\{\eta_{\mathbf{c}} \in \mathbb{Z}_q\}_{\mathbf{c} \in \mathbb{Z}^k}$, where $\eta_{\mathbf{c}} = 0$ for all but finite $\mathbf{c} \in \mathbb{Z}^k$. Note that this expression is unique. We now begin our proof for Theorem 6 below.

Proof. At a high level, we show a sequence of hybrids each of which is a game between a challenger and a PPT adversary A. In the first (resp., last) hybrid, the challenger encrypts a pair $(\mathbf{y}_b, m_b)$ corresponding to bit $b = 0$ (resp., $b = 1$). The intermediate hybrids ensure that the distributions in any pair of subsequent hybrids from the first to the last one are statistically indistinguishable.

Since the proof is in the GGM, w.l.o.g. the challenger simulates all the generic bilinear group oracle queries for A. In particular, the challenger stores the actual computed elements in the list $\mathcal{L}_\mathsf{t}$ based on its group type $\mathsf{t} \in \{1, 2, \mathsf{T}\}$. The handle to an actual element stored in any of these lists are just a tuple $(\mathsf{t}, \mathsf{pos})$ specifying the group type t and its position in the table $\mathcal{L}_\mathsf{t}$. Since our scheme contains several variables, we will refrain from explicitly specifying the handles to the actual elements for convenience. Further, when we move to the SGM, we will denote any literal variable v as v and composite terms like $v_1 v_2$ (resp., $\frac{v_1}{v_2}$) as $\mathrm{v}_1\mathrm{v}_2$ (resp., $\frac{\mathrm{v}_1}{\mathrm{v}_2}$) to represent an individual monomial in a (possibly multivariate) polynomial. For variables denoted with Greek alphabets, say α, β, γ, we represent their corresponding formal variables as $\upalpha, \upbeta, \upgamma$. We also define $\mathbb{Z}_q\text{-}\mathsf{span}(\mathcal{S})$ as the set of $\mathbb{Z}_q$-linear combinations of all elements in any set $\mathcal{S}$. Assume A issues an arbitrary polynomial number $Q_{\mathsf{zt}}(\lambda)$ of queries to its $\mathsf{Zt_T}$ oracle in each hybrid.

$\mathbf{H}_1(\lambda)$: This is the real scheme corresponding to bit $b = 0$ in the GGM. In more detail, the hybrid goes as follows.

- **Setup phase:** A sends an attribute length $n = n(\lambda)$ and slot count $L = L(\lambda)$ to the challenger, upon which it first initializes $\mathsf{ctr} = 0$, a dictionary D, and the set $\mathcal{C}_L = \emptyset$ to account for corrupted slots. Next, it computes $\mathcal{G} = (\mathbb{G}_1, \mathbb{G}_2, \mathbb{G}_\mathsf{T}, q, g_1, g_2, e) \leftarrow_\$ \mathsf{GroupGen}(1^\lambda)$ and initializes three tables as $\mathcal{L}_\mathsf{t}[1] = g_\mathsf{t}, \forall \mathsf{t} \in \{1, 2, \mathsf{T}\}$. The challenger prepares a tuple $(\mathbb{G}_1, \mathbb{G}_2, \mathbb{G}_\mathsf{T}, q, \{(\mathsf{t}, 1)\}_{\mathsf{t} \in \{1,2,\mathsf{T}\}})$, where $(\mathsf{t}, 1)$ represents the handle to $g_\mathsf{t}, \forall \mathsf{t} \in \{1, 2, \mathsf{T}\}$. To allow A to compute the group operations including the bilinear map e, the challenger also simulates all the oracles $\mathsf{Add_t}, \mathsf{Neg_t}, \mathsf{Map}_e, \mathsf{Zt_T}$ with implicit access to the lists $\{\mathcal{L}_\mathsf{t}\}_{\mathsf{t} \in \{1,2,\mathsf{T}\}}$. It then computes the crs components as follows:

1. Set $n' = n + 1$. Compute $h = g_1^\beta, \Gamma = g_1^\gamma \in \mathbb{G}_1$ and $Z = e(g_1, g_2)^\alpha \in \mathbb{G}_\mathsf{T}$ as in the real Setup algorithm. Update $\mathcal{L}_1$ with the elements β, γ and $\mathcal{L}_\mathsf{T}$ with α respectively.

2. For each slot index $i \in [0, L]$, do the following:
   (a) $\forall w \in [n']$, compute $U_{w,i} = g_1^{u_{w,i}} \in \mathbb{G}_1$ as in the real scheme and update $\mathcal{L}_1$ with $u_{w,i}$.
   (b) $\forall i > 0$, compute $A_i = g_2^{t_i}, B_i = g_2^{\alpha+\beta \cdot t_i} \in \mathbb{G}_2$ as in the real scheme and update $\mathcal{L}_2$ with $t_i, (\alpha + \beta \cdot t_i)$ in order.
   (c) $\forall i > 0, w \in [n']$ and for each $j \in [0, L] \setminus \{i\}$, compute $W_{i,j,w} = g_2^{\frac{t_i \cdot u_{j,w}}{\gamma}} \in \mathbb{G}_2$ as in the real scheme and update $\mathcal{L}_2$ with $\frac{t_i \cdot u_{j,w}}{\gamma}$.
3. For $\widetilde{\mathbf{x}}_0 = (\widetilde{x}_{1,0}, \ldots, \widetilde{x}_{n',0}) \leftarrow_{\$} \mathbb{Z}_q^{n'^+}$, set $\mathsf{pk}_0 = \left(T_0, \left\{\widetilde{W}_{i,0}\right\}_{i \in [L]}\right)$ as in the real scheme. Define $u_0' = \sum_{w=1}^{n'} u_{w,0} \cdot \widetilde{x}_{w,0} = -\mathsf{DL}(T_0)$ so that

$$T_0 = g_1^{u_0'} \in \mathbb{G}_1 \quad , \quad \widetilde{W}_{i,0} = g_2^{\frac{t_i \cdot u_0'}{\gamma}} \in \mathbb{G}_2, \forall i \in [L].$$

   Update $\mathcal{L}_1$ with u_0' and $\mathcal{L}_2$ with $\left\{\frac{t_i \cdot u_0'}{\gamma}\right\}_{i \in [L]}$ in order.
4. Set

$$\mathsf{crs} = \Big(\mathcal{G}, Z, h, \Gamma, \{A_i, B_i\}_{i \in [L]},$$
$$\left\{\{U_{w,i}\}_{i \in [0,L]}, \{W_{i,j,w}\}_{i \in [L], j \in [0,L] \setminus \{i\}}\right\}_{w \in [n']}, \mathsf{pk}_0\Big).$$

5. Return to A a tuple crs' that includes $(\mathbb{G}_1, \mathbb{G}_2, \mathbb{G}_T, q, \{(\mathsf{t}, 1)\}_{\mathsf{t} \in \{1,2,\mathsf{T}\}})$ along with the handles to all elements in the same order as they are arranged in the crs above.

- **Pre-challenge query phase:** A can issue *key generation* queries or *corruption* queries in this phase.

1. Consider the key-generation queries first. Upon getting a slot index $i \in [L]$, the challenger updates $\mathsf{ctr} = \mathsf{ctr} + 1$, sets $\mathbf{x}_i^{\mathsf{ctr}} = \mathbf{x}_i$ and does the following:
   (a) Sample $\widetilde{r}_i^{\mathsf{ctr}} \leftarrow_{\$} \mathbb{Z}_q^+$ and compute $\mathsf{pk}_i^{\mathsf{ctr}} = \left(T_i^{\mathsf{ctr}}, \left\{\widetilde{W}_{j,i}^{\mathsf{ctr}}\right\}_{j \in [L] \setminus \{i\}}\right)$ as in KGen.
   (b) Note that the element $T_i^{\mathsf{ctr}} \in \mathbb{G}_1$ from $\mathsf{pk}_i^{\mathsf{ctr}}$ has the following structure:

$$T_i^{\mathsf{ctr}} = g_1^{-\widetilde{r}_i^{\mathsf{ctr}} u_{n',i}}, \text{ where } \mathsf{sk}_i^{\mathsf{ctr}} = \widetilde{r}_i^{\mathsf{ctr}} \text{ is the secret key.}$$

   Even given the handle to $u_{n',i}$, A cannot compute a handle for $\mathsf{DL}(T_i^{\mathsf{ctr}}) = -\widetilde{r}_i^{\mathsf{ctr}} u_{n',i}$ on its own. Hence, the challenger updates $\mathcal{L}_1$ with $\mathsf{DL}(T_i^{\mathsf{ctr}})$.
   (c) Further, each term in $\left\{\widetilde{W}_{j,i}^{\mathsf{ctr}} \in \mathbb{G}_2\right\}_{j \in [L] \setminus \{i\}}$ has the following structure:

$$\widetilde{W}_{j,i}^{\mathsf{ctr}} = W_{j,i,n'}^{\widetilde{r}_i^{\mathsf{ctr}}} = g_2^{\frac{t_j u_{n',i}}{\gamma} \cdot \widetilde{r}_i^{\mathsf{ctr}}}$$

   For reasons similar to Item (b) above, the challenger updates $\mathcal{L}_2$ with each element individually from the set $\left\{\widetilde{r}_i^{\mathsf{ctr}} \cdot \frac{t_j u_{n',i}}{\gamma}\right\}_{j \in [L] \setminus \{i\}}$.

(d) Define $\mathsf{pk}_{\mathsf{ctr}} = \mathsf{pk}_i^{\mathsf{ctr}}, \mathsf{sk}_{\mathsf{ctr}} = \mathsf{sk}_i^{\mathsf{ctr}}$ and $\mathsf{pk}'_{\mathsf{ctr}}$ as a sequence of handles to all elements in the same order as they are arranged in $\mathsf{pk}_{\mathsf{ctr}}$.

(e) Return the tuple $(\mathsf{ctr}, \mathsf{pk}'_{\mathsf{ctr}})$ to A and update $\mathsf{D}[\mathsf{ctr}] = (i, \mathsf{pk}_{\mathsf{ctr}}, \mathsf{sk}_{\mathsf{ctr}})$.

2. When A sends $c \in [\mathsf{ctr}]$ issuing a corruption query, the challenger returns sk' to A where $\mathsf{D}[c] = (i', \mathsf{pk}', \mathsf{sk}')$.

- **Challenge phase:** In this phase, A specifies the following challenge information:

$$\{(c_i, \mathbf{x}_i, \mathsf{pk}_i^*)\}_{i\in[L]} \quad \text{and} \quad ((\mathbf{y}_0, m_0), (\mathbf{y}_1, m_1)) \in (\mathbb{Z}_q^{n+} \times \mathbb{G}_\mathsf{T})^2.$$

Preproccssing the challenge information. For each $i \in [L]$, the challenger checks that $\mathbf{x}_i \neq \mathbf{0}^n$ and does the following:

1. If $c_i \in [\mathsf{ctr}]$, it checks $\mathsf{D}[c_i] = (i', \mathsf{pk}', \mathsf{sk}')$. If $i \neq i'$, it halts. Else, it sets $\mathsf{pk}_i^* = \mathsf{pk}'$. Further, if A issued a corruption query for c_i before, it updates $\mathcal{C}_L = \mathcal{C}_L \cup \{i\}$.
2. If $c_i = \perp$, pk_i^* represents a corrupt secret key generated by A itself. Hence, it parses pk_i^* and halts if $\mathsf{IsValid}(\mathsf{crs}, i, \mathsf{pk}_i^*) = 0$.[7] Else, it updates $\mathcal{C}_L = \mathcal{C}_L \cup \{i\}$.

Computing key aggregation. The challenger then computes

$$\left(\mathsf{mpk}, (\mathsf{hsk}_i)_{i\in[L]}\right) = \mathsf{Aggr}\left(\mathsf{crs}, ((\mathsf{pk}_i^*, \mathbf{x}_i))_{i\in[L]}\right), \text{ where}$$

$$\mathsf{mpk} = (\mathcal{G}, g, h, Z, \Gamma, \{\widehat{U}_w\}_{w'\in[n'+1]}), \text{ and } \{\mathsf{hsk}_i = (\mathcal{G}, i, A_i, B_i, \{\widehat{W}_{w,i}\}_{w\in[n'+1]})\}_{i\in[L]}.$$

Computing the challenge ciphertext. The challenger now uses mpk and the pair $(\mathbf{y}_0, m_0)$, and generates $c^* \leftarrow\!\!\$\ \mathsf{Enc}(\mathsf{mpk}, \mathbf{y}_0, m_0)$ where $c^* = \left(C_1, C_2, \{C_{3,w}\}_{w\in[n'+1]}, C_4\right)$.

1. Note that $C_1 = m_0 \cdot e(g_1, g_2)^{\alpha s} \in \mathbb{G}_\mathsf{T}$ and $C_2 = g_1^s \in \mathbb{G}_1$. Accordingly, the challenger updates $\mathcal{L}_\mathsf{T}$ with αs and $\mathcal{L}_1$ with s respectively.
2. With $\widetilde{\mathbf{y}}_0 = (\mathbf{y}_0, 0, 0) = (y_1^0, \ldots, y_n^0, 0, 0)$, note that the elements $\{C_{3,w} \in \mathbb{G}_1\}_{w\in[n'+1]}$ have the following structure:

$$\text{for all } w \in [n],\ C_{3,w} = h^{y_w^0 \cdot r + s} \cdot \widehat{U}_w^{-z} = g_1^{r\beta y_w^0 + s\beta - z\cdot u_w}$$

$$\text{for } w = n',\ C_{3,n'} = g_1^{r\beta\cdot 0 + s\beta - z\cdot u'_n} = g_1^{s\beta - z\cdot u_{n'}}$$

$$\text{for } w = n'+1, C_{3,n'+1} = g_1^{r\beta\cdot 0 + s\beta} \cdot \widehat{U}_{n'+1}^{-z} = g_1^{s\beta} \cdot \prod_{i=0}^{L} T_i^{-z}$$

$$= g_1^{s\beta} \cdot \prod_{i=0}^{L} g_1^{z\sum_{w=1}^{n'} \widetilde{x}_{w,i}\cdot u_{w,i}}$$

[7] By Definition 1, A is supposed to send well-formed keys that passes the $\mathsf{IsValid}(\mathsf{crs}, \cdot, \cdot)$ test. Hence, from now on we do not mention it any more, but assume the challenger checks it implicitly.

$$= g_1^{s\beta} \cdot \prod_{i=0}^{L} g_1^{z \cdot u'_i} = g_1^{s\beta + z \cdot u'_0 - z \sum_{i=1}^{L} \mathsf{DL}(T_i)}$$

$$where u_w = \sum_{i=0}^{L} u_{w,i} \text{ ,and } u_{n'} = \sum_{i=0}^{L} u_{n',i}.$$

Accordingly, the challenger updates $\mathcal{L}_1$ with the elements $\{r\beta y_w^0 + s\beta - z \cdot u_w\}_{w \in [n]}$, $(s\beta - z \cdot u_{n'})$, and $\left[s\beta + z \cdot u'_0 - z \cdot \sum_{i=1}^{L} \mathsf{DL}(T_i)\right]$ in order.
3. Since $C_4 = g_1^{\gamma z} \in \mathbb{G}_1$, it updates $\mathcal{L}_1$ with $z\gamma$.

Group oracle queries. Since Aggr is deterministic, A is able to compute $(\mathsf{mpk}, (\mathsf{hsk}_i)_{i \in [L]})$ on its own. In the GGM, A is able to compute handles for the elements in mpk and $\{\mathsf{hsk}_i\}_{i \in [L]}$. To this end, it queries the appropriate group oracles to generate such handles as follows:

1. A only needs to compute the handles for $\{\widehat{U}_w\}_{w \in [n'+1]}$ to complete its information about mpk. Note that $\forall w \in [n']$, $\widehat{U}_w = \prod_{i=0}^{L} U_{w,i} = g_1^{u_w}$, where $u_w = \sum_{i=0}^{L} u_{w,i}$. Hence, $\forall w \in [n']$, A invokes the Add_1 oracle L times *iteratively* on the handles in $\mathcal{L}_1$ for $\{u_{w,i}\}_{i \in [0,L]}$ and gets a handle for u_w. Further, to get a handle for $\widehat{U}_{n'+1} = \prod_{i=0}^{L} T_i$, it has to first a get a handle for each T_i that is fused with the predicate $\mathbf{x}_i$. Note the structure of each T_i after Step (2) in Aggr:

$$T_i = g_1^{\sum_{w=1}^{n'} -\widetilde{x}_{w,i} \cdot u_{w,i}} = g_1^{\sum_{w=1}^{n} (-x_{w,i} \cdot u_{w,i})} \times g_1^{\left(-\widetilde{r}_i \cdot u_{n',i}\right)} \in \mathbb{G}_1.$$

Given a handle for the second multiplicand, it is easy to note that the first one is publicly computable using Neg_1 and Add_1 oracles. Once A obtains the handles for $\{T_i\}_{i \in [L]}$, it can call Add_1 oracle on these handles to get the same for $\widehat{U}_{n'+1}$.
2. A only needs to compute the handles for $\{\widehat{W}_{w,i}\}_{w \in [n'+1]}$ to get complete information about hsk_i for each $i \in [L]$. Note that $\forall w \in [n']$, $\widehat{W}_{w,i} = \prod_{j \in [0,L] \setminus \{i\}} W_{i,j,w} = g_2^{t_i \cdot (u_w - u_{w,i})/\gamma}$, since $(u_w - u_{w,i}) = \sum_{j \in [0,L] \setminus \{i\}} u_{w,j}$. It is again easy to see that a handle for such an element can be computed by calling the Add_2 oracle $L - 1$ times *iteratively* on the handles in $\mathcal{L}_2$ for $\{\frac{t_i \cdot u_{w,j}}{\gamma}\}_{j \in [0,L] \setminus \{i\}}$. Further, note that to get a handle for $\widehat{W}_{n'+1,i} = \prod_{j \in [0,L] \setminus \{i\}} \widetilde{W}_{i,j}^{-1}$, it has to first a get a handle for each $\widetilde{W}_{j,i}$ that is fused with the predicate $\mathbf{x}_i$. Note the structure of each $\widetilde{W}_{j,i}$ after Step (2) in Aggr:

$$\widetilde{W}_{j,i} = \left(\prod_{w=1}^{n} W_{i,j,w}^{\widetilde{x}_{w,i}}\right) \cdot W_{i,j,n'}^{\widetilde{r}_i} = g_2^{\sum_{w=1}^{n} \frac{t_j u_{w,i}}{\gamma} \cdot x_{w,i}} \times g_2^{\left(\frac{t_j u_{n',i}}{\gamma} \cdot \widetilde{r}_i\right)} \in \mathbb{G}_2.$$

Again, given a handle for the second multiplicand, the same can be computed publicly for the entire product using handles for $\{W_{i,j,w}\}$. Once A obtains the handles to each element in $\{\widetilde{W}_{j,i}\}_{j \in [L] \setminus \{i\}}$, it can call Add_2 oracle on these handles to get the same for $\widehat{W}_{n+1,i}$.

3. Finally, it defines mpk' and each hsk'_i as sequences of handles to all elements (except $i, \mathbf{x}_i$) in the same order as arranged in mpk and each $\mathsf{hsk}_i, \forall i \in [L]$.

- **Output phase:** A outputs a bit $b' \in \{0, 1\}$.

For ease of presentation, in Table 2 we show all unit and composite terms generated in the scheme itself, and stored in the respective lists.

Table 2. The above table shows all terms from the scheme for which handles are stored in the respective lists $\mathcal{L}_t, \forall t \in \{1, 2, T\}$. Assume $\mathcal{A}$ issues some arbitrary polynomial number, Q_k, of key queries in the pre-challenge query phase (some of which may be corrupted). The table lists all the terms for each of these keys $\{\mathsf{pk}_c\}_{c\in[Q_k]}$ received by $\mathcal{A}$ in the second row. Hence, these terms are also indexed with superscripts for the key query count $c \in [Q_k]$ (along with the slot index, say $i \in [L]$, for which $\mathcal{A}$ asked the key). The terms corresponding to mpk and hsk_i are not shown in the table, since the handles for these are publicly computable by $\mathcal{A}$ using the group oracles. Note that such terms correspond to keys for all the registered L slots (possibly all of which may be corrupted or even adversarially generated). Hence, the individual variables in each of those terms in mpk and hsk_i are independent of the counter variable $c \in [Q_k]$ respectively. In c, observe that we also have $(\mathsf{DL}(m) + \alpha s)$ in $\mathcal{L}_T$, where $\mathsf{DL}(m) \in \mathbb{Z}_q$ is w.r.t. g_T.

	$\mathcal{L}_1$	$\mathcal{L}_2$	$\mathcal{L}_T$
crs	$\boxed{g_1}$, $\boxed{\beta}$, $\boxed{\gamma}$ $\boxed{u'_0} = \sum_{w=1}^{n'} u_{w,0}\widetilde{x}_{w,0}$, $\left\{\boxed{u_{w,i}}\right\}_{i\in[0,L], w\in[n']}$	$\boxed{g_2}$, $\left\{\boxed{t_i}, \boxed{\alpha + \beta t_i}\right\}_{i\in[L]}$ $\boxed{\dfrac{t_i u'_0}{\gamma}}$, $\left\{\boxed{\dfrac{t_i u_{w,j}}{\gamma}}\right\}_{i\in[L], j\in[0,L]\setminus\{i\}, w\in[n']}$	$\boxed{g_T}$ $\boxed{\alpha}$
$\{\mathsf{pk}_c\}_{c\in[Q_k]}$	$\left\{\boxed{-\widetilde{r}_i^c u_{n',i}}\right\}_{c\in[Q_k]}$ (for $\{T_i^c\}_{c\in[Q_k]}$)	$\left\{\boxed{\widetilde{r}_i^c \cdot \dfrac{t_j u_{n',i}}{\gamma}}\right\}_{j\in[L]\setminus\{i\}, c\in[Q_k]}$ (for $\left\{\widetilde{W}_{j,i}^c\right\}_{j\in[L]\setminus\{i\}, c\in[Q_k]}$)	–
c	$\boxed{s}$ (for C_2) , $\boxed{z\gamma}$ (for C_4) , $\boxed{r\beta y_w^0 + s\beta - z u_w}$ (for $C_{3,w}, \forall w \in [n]$), $\boxed{s\beta - z u_{n'}}$ (for $C_{3,n'}$) , where $u_{n'} = \sum_{i=0}^{L} u_{n',i}$ $\boxed{s\beta - z\mathsf{DL}(T)}$ (for $C_{3,n'+1}$) , where $\mathsf{DL}(T) = \sum_{i=0}^{L} \mathsf{DL}(T_i)$	–	$\boxed{\mathsf{DL}(m) + \alpha s}$

$\mathbf{H}_2(\lambda)$: In this hybrid, we switch to the SGM *partially*. Namely, the interaction between challenger and A remains exactly as it was in $\mathbf{H}_1(\lambda)$, but now the challenger stores formal variables for all the terms from Table 2 in the respective lists $\mathcal{L}_t, \forall t \in \{1, 2, T\}$. Thus, all the handles A receives refer to multivariate polynomials from the following ring:

$$\zeta = \mathbb{Z}_q \Big[\alpha, \beta, \gamma, u_0', \{u_{w,i}\}_{i\in[L],w\in[n']}, \{\tilde{r}_i^c\}_{i\in[L],c\in[Q_k]}, \{t_i\}_{i\in[L]}, \frac{1}{\gamma}, s, r, z, \{y_w\}_{w\in[n'+1]}\Big].$$

Concretely, A gets handles to formal polynomials from $\mathcal{L}_t$ for each $t \in \{1, 2, T\}$, where:

1. $\mathcal{L}_T = \{1, \alpha, \mathsf{DL}(m) + \alpha s\}$.
2. $\mathcal{L}_1 = \mathcal{L}_1^{\mathsf{crs}} \cup \mathcal{L}_1^{\mathsf{key}} \cup \mathcal{L}_1^c$, where
   (a) $\mathcal{L}_1^{\mathsf{crs}} = \left(1, \beta, \gamma, u_0', \{u_{w,i}\}_{i\in[0,L],w\in[n']}\right)$,
   (b) $\mathcal{L}_1^{\mathsf{key}} = \left(\{-\tilde{r}_i^c u_{n',i}\}_{c\in[Q_k]}\right)$ for some $i \in [L]$, and
   (c) $\mathcal{L}_1^c = \left(s, zg, \left\{rby_w + sb - z\sum_{i=0}^{L} u_{w,i}\right\}_{w\in[n]}, sb - zu_{n'}, sb - z\mathsf{DL}(T)\right)$.
3. $\mathcal{L}_2 = \mathcal{L}_2^{\mathsf{crs}} \cup \mathcal{L}_2^{\mathsf{key}}$, where
   (a) $\mathcal{L}_2^{\mathsf{crs}} = \left(1, \{t_i, a + bt_i\}_{i\in[L]}, \frac{t_i u_0'}{g}, \left\{\frac{t_i u_{w,j}}{g}\right\}_{i\in[L],j\in[0,L]\setminus\{i\},w\in[n']}\right)$, and
   (b) $\mathcal{L}_2^{\mathsf{key}} = \left(\left\{\frac{\tilde{r}_i^c t_j u_{n',i}}{g}\right\}_{j\in[L]\setminus\{i\},c\in[Q_k]}\right)$ for some $i \in [L]$.

However, when A issues any zero-test query via Zt_T oracle, the challenger replaces the formal variables with their corresponding elements from $\mathbb{Z}_q$. In this case, if the variable is not assigned a value in $\mathbb{Z}_q$, it samples the corresponding value from the same distribution as it did in $\mathbf{H}_1(\lambda)$. However, once a value is assigned to a variable, it is fixed throughout the rest of $\mathbf{H}_2(\lambda)$. We show in [25] that $\mathbf{H}_1(\lambda) \equiv \mathbf{H}_2(\lambda)$.

Given the tuple $\mathsf{P} = (\mathcal{L}_1, \mathcal{L}_2, \mathcal{L}_T)$, we define $\mathcal{C}(\mathcal{L}_T) = \mathcal{L}_T \cup \{V_1 \cdot V_2 \mid \forall V_1 \in \mathcal{L}_1, V_2 \in \mathcal{L}_2\}$. Basically, it is the set of all monomials from ζ with variables in $\mathbb{G}_T$ that $\mathcal{A}$ can compute querying Map_e on the handles it received for elements in $\mathcal{L}_1, \mathcal{L}_2$. We estimate the size of $\mathcal{C}(\mathcal{L}_T)$ as follows. Note that we have $|\mathcal{C}(\mathcal{L}_T)| = |\mathcal{L}_T| + |\mathcal{L}_1| \cdot |\mathcal{L}_2|$ where $|\mathcal{L}_T| = 3$,

$$\begin{aligned} |\mathcal{L}_1| &= |\mathcal{L}_1^{\mathsf{crs}}| + \left|\mathcal{L}_1^{\mathsf{key}}\right| + |\mathcal{L}_1^c| \\ &\leq \{(L+1)n' + 4\} + LQ_k + (n+4) = L(n + Q_k + 1) + 2n + 9, \text{ and} \\ |\mathcal{L}_2| &= |\mathcal{L}_2^{\mathsf{crs}}| + \left|\mathcal{L}_2^{\mathsf{key}}\right| \\ &\leq \{2 + 2L + n'L^2\} + \{L(L-1)Q_k\} = L^2(n + Q_k + 1) - L(Q_k - 2) + 2. \end{aligned}$$

There are several variables in ζ and several terms in $\mathcal{L}_1, \mathcal{L}_2$. Hence, for brevity, we do not state all the elements of $\mathcal{C}(\mathcal{L}_\mathsf{T})$ explicitly with all possible cross combinations of the monomials from $\mathcal{L}_1, \mathcal{L}_2$. However, it is easy to see by inspection that the maximal total degree of each term in $\mathcal{C}(\mathcal{L}_\mathsf{T})$ is $d = 7$ corresponding to the term $\left[\mathtt{rby_w} \cdot \frac{\widetilde{\mathtt{r}}_\mathtt{i}^\mathtt{c} \mathtt{t_j u_{n',i}}}{\mathtt{g}}\right]$ for any $w \in [n'], i \in [L], j \in [0, L] \setminus \{i\}, c \in [Q_\mathsf{k}]$. We also note that any handle submitted by $\mathcal{A}$ to the $\mathsf{Zt_T}$ oracle during its interaction refers to a polynomial $f \in \zeta$ as

$$f\Big(\alpha, \beta, \gamma, \mathtt{u}'_0, \{\mathtt{u_{w,i}}\}_{\mathtt{i}\in[\mathtt{L}],\mathtt{w}\in[\mathtt{n}']}, \{\widetilde{\mathtt{r}}_\mathtt{i}^\mathtt{c}\}_{\mathtt{i}\in[\mathtt{L}],\mathtt{c}\in[\mathtt{Q_k}]}, \{\mathtt{t_i}\}_{\mathtt{i}\in[\mathtt{L}]}, \frac{1}{\gamma}, \mathtt{s}, \mathtt{r}, \mathtt{z}, \{\mathtt{y_w}\}_{\mathtt{w}\in[\mathtt{n}'+1]}\Big) = \sum_{\theta \in \mathcal{C}(\mathcal{L}_\mathsf{T})} \eta_\Theta \Theta,$$

where the coefficients $\{\eta_\Theta \in \mathbb{Z}_q\}_{\Theta \in \mathcal{C}(\mathcal{L}_\mathsf{T})}$ can be computed efficiently. Further, since all the monomials in $\mathcal{C}(\mathcal{L}_\mathsf{T})$ are distinct, the coefficients η_Θ are unique.

$\mathbf{H}_3(\lambda)$: In this hybrid, *all* queries to $\mathsf{Zt_T}$ oracle are answered using formal variables. Namely, for any $\mathsf{Zt_T}$ query on a handle to a polynomial $f \in \zeta$, the challenger returns 1 if:

$$f\Big(\alpha, \beta, \gamma, \mathtt{u}'_0, \{\mathtt{u_{w,i}}\}_{\mathtt{i}\in[\mathtt{L}],\mathtt{w}\in[\mathtt{n}']}, \{\widetilde{\mathtt{r}}_\mathtt{i}^\mathtt{c}\}_{\mathtt{i}\in[\mathtt{L}],\mathtt{c}\in[\mathtt{Q_k}]}, \{\mathtt{t_i}\}_{\mathtt{i}\in[\mathtt{L}]}, \frac{1}{\gamma}, \mathtt{s}, \mathtt{r}, \mathtt{z}, \{\mathtt{y_w}\}_{\mathtt{w}\in[\mathtt{n}'+1]}\Big) = 0.$$

We show in [25] that $\mathbf{H}_2(\lambda) \approx \mathbf{H}_3(\lambda)$.

$\mathbf{H}_4(\lambda)$: In this hybrid, the challenge ciphertext computes an encryption of m_0 with respect to $\mathbf{y}_1$. That is, everything remains as it is in $\mathbf{H}_3(\lambda)$ except that the challenger generates

$$c^* = (C_1, C_2, \{C_{3,w}\}_{w\in[n'+1]}, C_4) \leftarrow_\$ \mathsf{Enc}(\mathsf{mpk}, \mathbf{y}_1, m_0).$$

Arguing indistinguishability between $\mathbf{H}_3(\lambda)$ and $\mathbf{H}_4(\lambda)$ is the crux of this proof. We provide this analysis in our full version [25]. From here on, the challenger moves to $\mathbf{H}_6(\lambda)$ directly if $m_0 = m_1$. Else if $m_0 \neq m_1$, it still moves to $\mathbf{H}_6(\lambda)$, but via the next hybrids.

$\mathbf{H}_{5,1}(\lambda)$: In this hybrid, $Z^s \in \mathbb{G}_\mathsf{T}$ is replaced with $\mathfrak{U} \leftarrow_\$ \mathbb{G}_\mathsf{T}$.
$\mathbf{H}_{5,2}(\lambda)$: In this hybrid, the challenge ciphertext encrypts m_1 instead of m_0.
$\mathbf{H}_{5,3}(\lambda)$: In this hybrid, $\mathfrak{U}$ is changed to the honestly computed Z^s again.
$\mathbf{H}_6(\lambda)$: In this hybrid, the challenger moves to GGM from the symbolic setting of SGM. This is the real scheme corresponding to bit $b = 1$ in the GGM.

Hybrid Indistinguishability. Due to space constraints, we defer all the formal proofs for the indistinguishability of hybrids in our full version [25].

Final pairing-based RIPE scheme. By combining the slotted RIPE scheme of Construction 1 and the ("powers-of-two") transformation provided in our full version [25] , we obtain a secure registered IPE with an extra $O(\log L)$ factor in all its compactness and efficiency measures.

7 Implementation and Benchmarks

We developed a Python prototype[8] of our sRIPE scheme from Sect. 6 with the BLS12-381 elliptic curve for pairings, which we implemented via the petrelic Python wrapper [47] around RELIC [10]. This configuration allows each element in $\mathbb{G}_1, \mathbb{G}_2, \mathbb{G}_T$ to be represented using 49, 97 and 384 bytes respectively. We obtained the benchmarks below on a personal computer with an Intel Core i7-10700 3.8GHz CPU and 128GB of RAM running Ubuntu 22.04.1 LTS with kernel 5.15.0-58-generic. Exponentiations in $\mathbb{G}_1$ (resp., $\mathbb{G}_2$) and each pairing took 0.13 (resp., 0.18) milliseconds and 0.68 milliseconds on average on our machine.

Benchmarks. We provide benchmarks in Fig. 2, showing the sizes of mpk and the |crs| as well as the execution times of setup, aggregate, encrypt and decrypt in relation to parameters L and n. For encryption and decryption, we executed

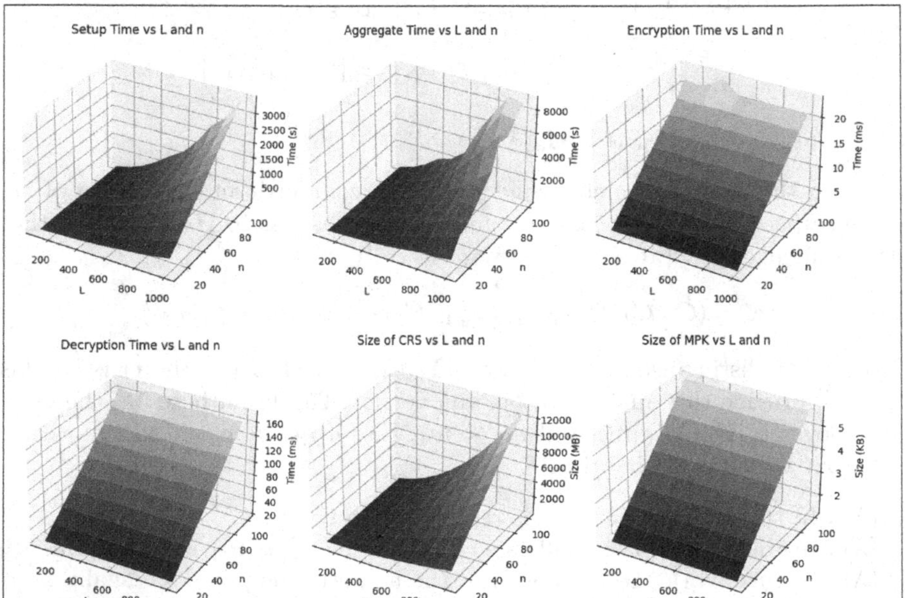

Fig. 2. Benchmarks for $L \in \{100, 200, \cdots, 1000\}$ and $n \in \{10, 20, \cdots, 100\}$

[8] https://anonymous.4open.science/r/slotted-ripe-DD12/.

the algorithms 100 times for each pair (L, n), and then computed the average runtime. The setup and aggregate were run once for each unique pair of (L, n). We did not plot the sizes of the ciphertexts, but these can be determined deterministically based on n as $|c| = 580 + 49n$ bytes. The size of the helper secret key for each user is $|\mathsf{hsk}| = 340 + 97n$ bytes. Note that the setup and aggregation time grows acutely with L and n. Improving the efficiency of our sRIPE scheme is left as a future work.

Acknowledgments. The authors thank the anonymous reviewers for their helpful comments. The first author was supported by the Carlsberg Foundation under the Semper Ardens Research Project CF18-112 (BCM). The second and the sixth author were partially supported by project SERICS (PE00000014) under the MUR National Recovery and Resilience Plan funded by the European Union - NextGenerationEU and by Sapienza University under the project SPECTRA. The third author was partially supported by the European Union (ERC AdG REWORC - 101054911), and by True Data 8 (Distributed Ledger & Multiparty Computation) under the Hessen State Ministry for Higher Education, Research and the Arts within their joint support of the National Research Center for Applied Cybersecurity ATHENE. The fourth author was partially funded by the German Federal Ministry of Education and Research (BMBF) in the course of the 6GEM research hub under grant number 16KISK038 and by the Deutsche Forschungsgemeinschaft (DFG, German Research Foundation) under Germany's Excellence Strategy - EXC 2092 CASA - 390781972.

References

1. Agrawal, S.: Indistinguishability obfuscation without multilinear maps: new methods for bootstrapping and instantiation. In: Ishai, Y., Rijmen, V. (eds.) EUROCRYPT 2019. LNCS, vol. 11476, pp. 191–225. Springer, Cham (2019). https://doi.org/10.1007/978-3-030-17653-2_7
2. Agrawal, S., Kitagawa, F., Modi, A., Nishimaki, R., Yamada, S., Yamakawa, T.: Bounded functional encryption for turing machines: adaptive security from general assumptions. In: Kiltz, E., Vaikuntanathan, V. (eds.) Theory of Cryptography: 20th International Conference, TCC 2022, Chicago, IL, USA, 7–10 November 2022, Proceedings, Part I, pp. 618–647. Springer, Heidelberg (2022). https://doi.org/10.1007/978-3-031-22318-1_22
3. Agrawal, S., Maitra, M., Vempati, N.S., Yamada, S.: Functional encryption for turing machines with dynamic bounded collusion from LWE. In: Malkin, T., Peikert, C. (eds.) CRYPTO 2021. LNCS, vol. 12828, pp. 239–269. Springer, Cham (2021). https://doi.org/10.1007/978-3-030-84259-8_9
4. Agrawal, S., Yamada, S.: Optimal broadcast encryption from pairings and LWE. In: Canteaut, A., Ishai, Y. (eds.) EUROCRYPT 2020. LNCS, vol. 12105, pp. 13–43. Springer, Cham (2020). https://doi.org/10.1007/978-3-030-45721-1_2
5. Ananth, P., Brakerski, Z., Segev, G., Vaikuntanathan, V.: From selective to adaptive security in functional encryption. In: Gennaro, R., Robshaw, M. (eds.) CRYPTO 2015. LNCS, vol. 9216, pp. 657–677. Springer, Heidelberg (2015). https://doi.org/10.1007/978-3-662-48000-7_32
6. Ananth, P., Jain, A., Lin, H., Matt, C., Sahai, A.: Indistinguishability obfuscation without multilinear maps: new paradigms via low degree weak pseudorandomness

and security amplification. In: Boldyreva, A., Micciancio, D. (eds.) CRYPTO 2019. LNCS, vol. 11694, pp. 284–332. Springer, Cham (2019). https://doi.org/10.1007/978-3-030-26954-8_10
7. Ananth, P., Jain, A.: Indistinguishability obfuscation from compact functional encryption. In: Gennaro, R., Robshaw, M. (eds.) CRYPTO 2015. LNCS, vol. 9215, pp. 308–326. Springer, Heidelberg (2015). https://doi.org/10.1007/978-3-662-47989-6_15
8. Ananth, P., Sahai, A.: Projective arithmetic functional encryption and indistinguishability obfuscation from degree-5 multilinear maps. In: Coron, J.-S., Nielsen, J.B. (eds.) EUROCRYPT 2017. LNCS, vol. 10210, pp. 152–181. Springer, Cham (2017). https://doi.org/10.1007/978-3-319-56620-7_6
9. Ananth, P., Vaikuntanathan, V.: Optimal bounded-collusion secure functional encryption. In: Hofheinz, D., Rosen, A. (eds.) TCC 2019. LNCS, vol. 11891, pp. 174–198. Springer, Cham (2019). https://doi.org/10.1007/978-3-030-36030-6_8
10. Aranha, D.F., Gouvêa, C.P.L., Markmann, T., Wahby, R.S., Liao, K.: RELIC is an Efficient LIbrary for Cryptography (2020). https://github.com/relic-toolkit/relic
11. Attrapadung, N., Hanaoka, G., Yamada, S.: Conversions among several classes of predicate encryption and applications to ABE with various compactness tradeoffs. In: Iwata, T., Cheon, J.H. (eds.) ASIACRYPT 2015. LNCS, vol. 9452, pp. 575–601. Springer, Heidelberg (2015). https://doi.org/10.1007/978-3-662-48797-6_24
12. Baltico, C.E.Z., Catalano, D., Fiore, D., Gay, R.: Practical functional encryption for quadratic functions with applications to predicate encryption. In: Katz, J., Shacham, H. (eds.) CRYPTO 2017. LNCS, vol. 10401, pp. 67–98. Springer, Cham (2017). https://doi.org/10.1007/978-3-319-63688-7_3
13. Barak, B., et al.: On the (im) possibility of obfuscating programs. J. ACM (JACM) **59**(2), 1–48 (2012)
14. Barthe, G., Fagerholm, E., Fiore, D., Mitchell, J.C., Scedrov, A., Schmidt, B.: Automated analysis of cryptographic assumptions in generic group models. J. Cryptol. **32**(2), 324–360 (2019)
15. Bitansky, N.: Verifiable random functions from non-interactive witness-indistinguishable proofs. J. Cryptol. **33**(2), 459–493 (2020)
16. Bitansky, N., Vaikuntanathan, V.: Indistinguishability obfuscation from functional encryption. In: Guruswami, V. (ed.) 56th FOCS, pp. 171–190. IEEE Computer Society Press (2015)
17. Boneh, D., et al.: Fully key-homomorphic encryption, arithmetic circuit ABE and compact garbled circuits. In: Nguyen, P.Q., Oswald, E. (eds.) EUROCRYPT 2014. LNCS, vol. 8441, pp. 533–556. Springer, Heidelberg (2014). https://doi.org/10.1007/978-3-642-55220-5_30
18. Boneh, D., Sahai, A., Waters, B.: Functional encryption: definitions and challenges. In: Ishai, Y. (ed.) TCC 2011. LNCS, vol. 6597, pp. 253–273. Springer, Heidelberg (2011). https://doi.org/10.1007/978-3-642-19571-6_16
19. Brakerski, Z., Döttling, N., Garg, S., Malavolta, G.: Candidate iO from homomorphic encryption schemes. In: Canteaut, A., Ishai, Y. (eds.) EUROCRYPT 2020, Part I. LNCS, vol. 12105, pp. 79–109. Springer, Heidelberg (May (2020). https://doi.org/10.1007/s00145-023-09471-5
20. Brakerski, Z., Döttling, N., Garg, S., Malavolta, G.: Factoring and pairings are not necessary for io: circular-secure lwe suffices. In: 49th International Colloquium on Automata, Languages, and Programming (ICALP 2022). Schloss Dagstuhl-Leibniz-Zentrum für Informatik (2022)

21. Brakerski, Z., Segev, G.: Function-private functional encryption in the private-key setting. In: Dodis, Y., Nielsen, J.B. (eds.) TCC 2015. LNCS, vol. 9015, pp. 306–324. Springer, Heidelberg (2015). https://doi.org/10.1007/978-3-662-46497-7_12
22. Chotard, J., Dufour-Sans, E., Gay, R., Phan, D.H., Pointcheval, D.: Dynamic decentralized functional encryption. In: Micciancio, D., Ristenpart, T. (eds.) CRYPTO 2020. LNCS, vol. 12170, pp. 747–775. Springer, Cham (2020). https://doi.org/10.1007/978-3-030-56784-2_25
23. Cong, K., Eldefrawy, K., Smart, N.P.: Optimizing registration based encryption. In: Paterson, M.B. (ed.) IMACC 2021. LNCS, vol. 13129, pp. 129–157. Springer, Cham (2021). https://doi.org/10.1007/978-3-030-92641-0_7
24. Döttling, N., Kolonelos, D., Lai, R.W.F., Lin, C., Malavolta, G., Rahimi, A.: Efficient laconic cryptography from learning with errors. In: Hazay, C., Stam, M. (eds.) EUROCRYPT 2023. LNCS, vol. 14006, pp. 417–446. Springer, Cham (2023). https://doi.org/10.1007/978-3-031-30620-4_14
25. Francati, D., Friolo, D., Maitra, M., Malavolta, G., Rahimi, A., Venturi, D.: Registered (inner-product) functional encryption. Cryptology ePrint Archive (2023)
26. Francati, D., Friolo, D., Malavolta, G., Venturi, D.: Multi-key and multi-input predicate encryption from learning with errors. In: Advances in Cryptology-EUROCRYPT 2023: 42nd Annual International Conference on the Theory and Applications of Cryptographic Techniques, Lyon, France, 23–27 April 2023, Proceedings, Part III, pp. 573–604. Springer, Heidelberg (2023). https://doi.org/10.1007/978-3-031-30620-4_19
27. Garg, S., Gentry, C., Halevi, S., Raykova, M., Sahai, A., Waters, B.: Candidate indistinguishability obfuscation and functional encryption for all circuits. In: 54th FOCS, pp. 40–49. IEEE Computer Society Press (2013)
28. Garg, S., Gentry, C., Halevi, S., Zhandry, M.: Functional encryption without obfuscation. In: Kushilevitz, E., Malkin, T. (eds.) TCC 2016. LNCS, vol. 9563, pp. 480–511. Springer, Heidelberg (2016). https://doi.org/10.1007/978-3-662-49099-0_18
29. Garg, S., Hajiabadi, M., Mahmoody, M., Rahimi, A.: Registration-based encryption: removing private-key generator from IBE. In: Beimel, A., Dziembowski, S. (eds.) TCC 2018. LNCS, vol. 11239, pp. 689–718. Springer, Cham (2018). https://doi.org/10.1007/978-3-030-03807-6_25
30. Garg, S., Hajiabadi, M., Mahmoody, M., Rahimi, A., Sekar, S.: Registration-based encryption from standard assumptions. In: Lin, D., Sako, K. (eds.) PKC 2019. LNCS, vol. 11443, pp. 63–93. Springer, Cham (2019). https://doi.org/10.1007/978-3-030-17259-6_3
31. Garg, S., Pandey, O., Srinivasan, A., Zhandry, M.: Breaking the sub-exponential barrier in obfustopia. In: Coron, J.-S., Nielsen, J.B. (eds.) EUROCRYPT 2017. LNCS, vol. 10212, pp. 156–181. Springer, Cham (2017). https://doi.org/10.1007/978-3-319-56617-7_6
32. Gay, R., Jain, A., Lin, H., Sahai, A.: Indistinguishability obfuscation from simple-to-state hard problems: new assumptions, new techniques, and simplification. In: Canteaut, A., Standaert, F.-X. (eds.) EUROCRYPT 2021. LNCS, vol. 12698, pp. 97–126. Springer, Cham (2021). https://doi.org/10.1007/978-3-030-77883-5_4
33. Gay, R., Pass, R.: Indistinguishability obfuscation from circular security. In: Proceedings of the 53rd Annual ACM SIGACT Symposium on Theory of Computing, pp. 736–749 (2021)
34. Gentry, C., Lewko, A.B., Sahai, A., Waters, B.: Indistinguishability obfuscation from the multilinear subgroup elimination assumption. In: Guruswami, V. (ed.) 56th FOCS, pp. 151–170. IEEE Computer Society Press (2015)

35. Glaeser, N., Kolonelos, D., Malavolta, G., Rahimi, A.: Efficient registration-based encryption. Cryptology ePrint Archive, Paper 2022/1505 (2022). https://eprint.iacr.org/2022/1505
36. Goldwasser, S., Kalai, Y.T., Popa, R.A., Vaikuntanathan, V., Zeldovich, N.: Reusable garbled circuits and succinct functional encryption. In: Boneh, D., Roughgarden, T., Feigenbaum, J. (eds.) 45th ACM STOC, pp. 555–564. ACM Press (2013)
37. Gorbunov, S., Vaikuntanathan, V., Wee, H.: Functional encryption with bounded collusions via multi-party computation. In: Safavi-Naini, R., Canetti, R. (eds.) CRYPTO 2012. LNCS, vol. 7417, pp. 162–179. Springer, Heidelberg (2012). https://doi.org/10.1007/978-3-642-32009-5_11
38. Goyal, R., Hohenberger, S., Koppula, V., Waters, B.: A generic approach to constructing and proving verifiable random functions. In: Kalai, Y., Reyzin, L. (eds.) TCC 2017. LNCS, vol. 10678, pp. 537–566. Springer, Cham (2017). https://doi.org/10.1007/978-3-319-70503-3_18
39. Goyal, R., Vusirikala, S.: Verifiable registration-based encryption. In: Micciancio, D., Ristenpart, T. (eds.) CRYPTO 2020. LNCS, vol. 12170, pp. 621–651. Springer, Cham (2020). https://doi.org/10.1007/978-3-030-56784-2_21
40. Hemenway, B., Jafargholi, Z., Ostrovsky, R., Scafuro, A., Wichs, D.: Adaptively secure garbled circuits from one-way functions. In: Robshaw, M., Katz, J. (eds.) CRYPTO 2016. LNCS, vol. 9816, pp. 149–178. Springer, Heidelberg (2016). https://doi.org/10.1007/978-3-662-53015-3_6
41. Hohenberger, S., Lu, G., Waters, B., Wu, D.J.: Registered attribute-based encryption. Cryptology ePrint Archive (2022)
42. Hubacek, P., Wichs, D.: On the communication complexity of secure function evaluation with long output. In: Roughgarden, T. (ed.) ITCS 2015, pp. 163–172. ACM (2015)
43. Jain, A., Lin, H., Matt, C., Sahai, A.: How to leverage hardness of constant-degree expanding polynomials overa $\mathbb{R}$ to build $i\mathcal{O}$. In: Ishai, Y., Rijmen, V. (eds.) EUROCRYPT 2019. LNCS, vol. 11476, pp. 251–281. Springer, Cham (2019). https://doi.org/10.1007/978-3-030-17653-2_9
44. Jain, A., Lin, H., Sahai, A.: Indistinguishability obfuscation from well-founded assumptions. In: Proceedings of the 53rd Annual ACM SIGACT Symposium on Theory of Computing, pp. 60–73 (2021)
45. Jain, A., Lin, H., Sahai, A.: Indistinguishability obfuscation from LPN over $\mathbb{F}_p$, DLIN, and PRGs in NC^0. In: Dunkelman, O., Dziembowski, S. (eds.) EUROCRYPT 2022, Part I. LNCS, vol. 13275, pp. 670–699. Springer, Heidelberg (2022). https://doi.org/10.1007/978-3-031-06944-4_23
46. Katz, J., Sahai, A., Waters, B.: Predicate encryption supporting disjunctions, polynomial equations, and inner products. In: Smart, N. (ed.) EUROCRYPT 2008. LNCS, vol. 4965, pp. 146–162. Springer, Heidelberg (2008). https://doi.org/10.1007/978-3-540-78967-3_9
47. Laurent Girod, W.L.: Petrelic is a python wrapper around relic (2022). https://github.com/spring-epfl/petrelic
48. Lin, H.: Indistinguishability obfuscation from constant-degree graded encoding schemes. In: Fischlin, M., Coron, J.-S. (eds.) EUROCRYPT 2016. LNCS, vol. 9665, pp. 28–57. Springer, Heidelberg (2016). https://doi.org/10.1007/978-3-662-49890-3_2
49. Mahmoody, M., Qi, W., Rahimi, A.: Lower bounds for the number of decryption updates in registration-based encryption. Cryptology ePrint Archive, Report 2022/1285 (2022). https://eprint.iacr.org/2022/1285

50. Okamoto, T., Pietrzak, K., Waters, B., Wichs, D.: New realizations of somewhere statistically binding hashing and positional accumulators. In: Iwata, T., Cheon, J.H. (eds.) ASIACRYPT 2015. LNCS, vol. 9452, pp. 121–145. Springer, Heidelberg (2015). https://doi.org/10.1007/978-3-662-48797-6_6
51. O'Neill, A.: Definitional issues in functional encryption. Cryptology ePrint Archive, Report 2010/556 (2010). https://eprint.iacr.org/2010/556
52. Sahai, A., Waters, B.: How to use indistinguishability obfuscation: deniable encryption, and more. In: Shmoys, D.B. (ed.) 46th ACM STOC, pp. 475–484. ACM Press (2014)
53. Sahai, A., Waters, B.: Fuzzy identity-based encryption. In: Cramer, R. (ed.) EUROCRYPT 2005. LNCS, vol. 3494, pp. 457–473. Springer, Heidelberg (2005). https://doi.org/10.1007/11426639_27
54. Shamir, A.: Identity-based cryptosystems and signature schemes. In: Blakley, G.R., Chaum, D. (eds.) CRYPTO 1984. LNCS, vol. 196, pp. 47–53. Springer, Heidelberg (1985). https://doi.org/10.1007/3-540-39568-7_5
55. Shen, E., Shi, E., Waters, B.: Predicate privacy in encryption systems. In: Reingold, O. (ed.) TCC 2009. LNCS, vol. 5444, pp. 457–473. Springer, Heidelberg (2009). https://doi.org/10.1007/978-3-642-00457-5_27
56. Wee, H., Wichs, D.: Candidate obfuscation via oblivious LWE sampling. In: Canteaut, A., Standaert, F.-X. (eds.) EUROCRYPT 2021. LNCS, vol. 12698, pp. 127–156. Springer, Cham (2021). https://doi.org/10.1007/978-3-030-77883-5_5

Robust Decentralized Multi-client Functional Encryption: Motivation, Definition, and Inner-Product Constructions

Yamin Li[1], Jianghong Wei[2], Fuchun Guo[3], Willy Susilo[3], and Xiaofeng Chen[1](✉)

[1] State Key Laboratory of Integrated Service Networks (ISN), Xidian University, Xi'an 710071, China
liyamin97@126.com, xfchen@xidian.edu.cn

[2] State Key Laboratory of Mathematical Engineering and Advanced Computing, Zhengzhou 450001, China
jianghong.wei.xxgc@gmail.com

[3] School of Computing and Information Technology, University of Wollongong, Wollongong, NSW 2522, Australia
{fuchun,wsusilo}@uow.edu.au

Abstract. Decentralized Multi-Client Functional Encryption (DMCFE) is a multi-user extension of Functional Encryption (FE) without relying on a trusted third party. However, a fundamental requirement for DMCFE is that the decryptor must collect the partial functional keys and the ciphertexts from all clients. If one client does not generate the partial functional key or the ciphertext, the decryptor cannot obtain any useful information. We found that this strong requirement limits the application of DMCFE in scenarios such as statistical analysis and machine learning.

In this paper, we first introduce a new primitive named *Robust Decentralized Multi-Client Functional Encryption* (RDMCFE), a notion generalized from DMCFE that aims to tolerate the problem of negative clients leading to nothing for the decryptor, where negative clients represent participants that are unable or unwilling to compute the partial functional key or the ciphertext. Conversely, a client is said to be a positive one if it is able and willing to compute both the partial functional key and the ciphertext. In RDMCFE scheme, the positive client set S is known by each positive client such that the generated partial functional keys help to eliminate the influence of negative clients, and the decryptor can learn the function value corresponding to the sensitive data of all positive clients when the cardinality of the set S is not less than a given threshold. We present such constructions for functionalities corresponding to the evaluation of inner products.

1. We provide a basic RDMCFE construction through the technique of double-masking structure, which is inspired by the work of Bonawitz et al. (CCS 2017). The storage and communication overheads of the construction are small and independent of the length of the vector.

J. Guo and R. Steinfeld (Eds.): ASIACRYPT 2023, LNCS 14442, pp. 134–165, 2023.
https://doi.org/10.1007/978-981-99-8733-7_5

However, in the basic construction, for the security guarantee, one set of secret keys can be used to generate partial functional keys for only one function.
2. We show how to design the enhanced construction so that partial functional keys for different functions can be generated with the same set of secret keys, at the cost of increasing storage and communication overheads. Specifically, in the enhanced RDMCFE construction, we protect the mask through a single-input FE scheme and a threshold secret sharing scheme having the additively homomorphic property.

Keywords: Functional Encryption · Decentralization · Inner Product · Robustness

1 Introduction

As an innovative paradigm of encryption, Functional Encryption (FE) [22], allows users to perform computations on data while ensuring data confidentiality. Specifically, when the FE scheme supports the function family $\mathcal{F}$, given a ciphertext $\mathsf{Enc}(x)$ and a functional key sk_f for a function $f \in \mathcal{F}$, the user can solely acquire the value $f(x)$ while nothing else about x. Nowadays, FE is no longer just a useful tool for plenty of theoretical applications [11,12]. The growing practicality of FE schemes has sparked a surge in demand for their application across diverse contexts, including but not limited to machine learning [35,38].

Multi-Client Functional Encryption (MCFE) [28] is the multi-user version of FE. Specifically, in the setting of MCFE, an authority generates $(\mathsf{msk}, \{\mathsf{ek}_i\}_{i\in[n]})$, where msk is the master secret key, which is used to compute the functional key sk_f. The authority distributes the encryption key ek_i to each client and sends sk_f to the decryptor. The client with the encryption key ek_i generates the ciphertext $\mathsf{Enc}(x_i)$ from the sensitive data x_i. Given the functional key sk_f and the ciphertexts $\mathsf{Enc}(x_1), \dots, \mathsf{Enc}(x_n)$, the decryptor can only learn the value $f(x_1, \dots, x_n)$ while nothing else about $\{x_i\}_{i\in[n]}$. MCFE has many practical applications involving multiple data sources, where the decryption result is a joint function on the sensitive data coming from different parties [25,33].

Decentralized Multi-Client Functional Encryption (DMCFE) [25] represents a distributed adaptation of MCFE, eliminating the need for the trusted third party. In DMCFE, all clients interactively generate the encryption keys $\{\mathsf{ek}_i\}_{i\in[n]}$ and the secret keys $\{\mathsf{sk}_i\}_{i\in[n]}$. For the function f, the client with the secret key sk_i generates the partial functional key $\mathsf{sk}_{i,f}$. The user with n partial functional keys $\{\mathsf{sk}_{i,f}\}_{i\in[n]}$ computes the functional key sk_f to decrypt the ciphertexts $\mathsf{Enc}(x_1), \dots, \mathsf{Enc}(x_n)$. That is, the functional key is no longer generated independently by the master secret key msk, but by n secret keys $\{\mathsf{sk}_i\}_{i\in[n]}$ in a decentralized manner.

Compared to MCFE, DMCFE can better protect the confidentiality of each client's data, since the authority having the master secret key can recover the data of any encryptor [37]. However, a fundamental requirement of DMCFE is that the decryptor must collect the partial functional keys and the ciphertexts from all clients. If a client does not generate the partial functional key or the ciphertext, the decryptor cannot obtain any useful information. We found that this strong requirement limits the application of DMCFE in scenarios such as statistical analysis and machine learning. For example, the work [35] uses the DMCFE scheme to measure the traffic density at each underground station, aiming to detect congestion and predict potential increases in traffic density. Using the DMCFE scheme, each client locally encrypts its location data, which is the value 0 or 1 (1 indicates that the client has visited the station), and provides a partial functional key corresponding to the vector $\boldsymbol{y}$ of 1s (the vector length is equal to the number of clients). Then, the central server collects the partial functional keys and the ciphertexts from all clients and combines all partial functional keys to generate the functional key. The central server decrypts and learns the number of clients traveling through that station, *i.e.*, the value $\langle \boldsymbol{x}, \boldsymbol{y} \rangle$, where the vector $\boldsymbol{x}$ indicates which clients have traveled through that station. However, if a client is unable or unwilling to generate the partial functional key or the ciphertext due to hardware or personal reasons, which we call the negative client, the central server cannot obtain the traffic density. Conversely, a client is said to be a positive one if it is able and willing to generate both the partial functional key and the ciphertext. We expect that even if the central server receives only the partial functional keys and the ciphertexts from positive clients instead of all clients, it can still obtain a traffic density with an error, which indicates the number of positive clients traveling through that station. Furthermore, in order to detect the congestion of that station as realistically as possible, we require that the number of positive clients is not less than a given threshold. Thus, an interesting question arises naturally:

Can decentralized multi-client functional encryption still work even when some clients do not generate partial functional keys for the function or encrypt their sensitive data?

1.1 Our Contributions

This paper gives an affirmative answer to this interesting question. We introduce a new primitive named *Robust Decentralized Multi-Client Functional Encryption* (RDMCFE), which generalizes the notion of DMCFE. In RDMCFE, all clients interactively generate the encryption keys $\{\mathsf{ek}_i\}_{i\in[n]}$ and the secret keys $\{\mathsf{sk}_i\}_{i\in[n]}$. For the function f, the positive client with the secret key sk_i, who knows the positive client set S, generates the partial functional key $\mathsf{sk}_{i,f}$, which helps to eliminate the influence of negative clients. When the cardinality of the set S is not less than a given threshold, the decryptor having the partial functional keys from all the positive clients can evaluate the ciphertexts from all the positive clients.

To present Inner Product RDMCFE (IP-RDMCFE) construction, we first define two key properties on Inner Product MCFE having special key generation (Special IP-MCFE), called robust correctness and robust security, which are the extensions to traditional correctness and traditional indistinguishability-based security. Then, we provide two IP-RDMCFE constructions. The first is a basic construction, in which one set of secret keys can generate the partial functional keys for only one function. To achieve the reusability of the secret keys, we design the enhanced construction at the cost of increasing storage and communication overheads.

1.2 Related Work

All known FE schemes can be roughly grouped into two categories. One is constructions that support general functionalities [19,21,28,31], which often depend on highly strong cryptographic primitives, including multi-linear maps [29] or indistinguishability obfuscation [30]. Neither of these primitives is currently instantiable under extensively studied cryptographic assumptions or with efficient building blocks. The other is constructions for specific functionalities, including linear evaluations [1,2,6,8,13,14,17,24,25] and quadratic functions [9,10,15,18,27,32,39], which is more important in practice.

Inner Product Functional Encryption. Inner product, a special case of functionality, has garnered increased attention due to its widespread use in descriptive statistics and polynomials, *e.g.*, calculating the weighted average of all components of many vectors. Abdalla et al. [1] first constructed an Inner Product Functional Encryption (IP-FE) scheme. The scheme can be instantiated under some standard assumptions, such as Learning With Errors (LWE) assumption or Decisional Diffie-Hellman (DDH) assumption. However, the scheme is limited to achieving selective security. Later on, Agrawal et al. [14] considered the adaptive security of IP-FE scheme, and presented IP-FE schemes under the assumptions of LWE, DDH, and Decisional Composite Residuosity (DCR) respectively.

Multi-input and Multi-client Functional Encryption for Inner Product. Abdalla et al. [8] first considered the multi-user setting of IP-FE. Building upon the first IP-FE scheme [1], Multi-Input Functional Encryption (MIFE) scheme specifically designed for inner product computations in the bilinear groups of prime order. They proved that the scheme has adaptive security under the k-linear assumption within the standard model. As a generalization of MIFE, Chotard et al. [25] designed the first Inner Product MCFE (IP-MCFE) scheme by replacing the public random number with the hash function. Further research on IP-MCFE has focused on enhancing security [2,3] or implementing more fine-grained access control [36].

Decentralized Functional Encryption for Inner Product. Fan et al. [26] introduced the concept of distributed public key FE, wherein the key generation algorithm does not output a single functional key, but n shares of the functional key. One uses each share of the functional key to decrypt the ciphertext $\mathsf{Enc}(m)$ and obtains $\{s_i\}_{i\in[n]}$, which can reconstruct the function value $f(m)$. However, this primitive still needs a trusted third party to set the system and compute the functional keys, and it does not consider the multi-user setting. Chotard et al. [25] completely excluded the trusted third party and proposed the concept of DMCFE. They designed an Inner Product DMCFE (IP-DMCFE) scheme under the assumption of Symmetric eXternal Diffie-Hellman (SXDH). Libert et al. [33] presented an IP-DMCFE scheme under LWE assumption, which is secure in the standard model. However, it is still subject to the same security restriction as [25]. Abdalla et al. [3] designed two compilers. The first compiler can convert any Special IP-MCFE into IP-DMCFE. The second compiler is used to enhance the security of the IP-DMCFE scheme and is modified in the work [2] to be compatible with new construction.

Dynamic Decentralized Functional Encryption for Inner Product. Agrawal et al. [5] defined the concept of Ad Hoc MIFE, in which clients can dynamically join the system, and functional keys are generated by each client in a decentralized manner without interaction. In addition, they give not only the feasibility results for general functions but also the practical structure for inner product. Chotard et al. [23] introduce the concept of Dynamic Decentralized Functional Encryption (DDFE), in which clients can also join the system dynamically and do not need to interact with the trusted third party. In the random oracle model, they constructed an inner product DDFE scheme under the standard assumption in prime order groups. Compared to Ad Hoc MIFE, DDFE is more general due to its key generation algorithm, which does not necessitate a predetermined group of clients. However, these two primitives only consider the dynamic entry of users, and do not consider the dynamic exit of users and the issue of robustness for negative clients.

1.3 Organization

The subsequent sections of this paper are structured in the following manner. First, we give high-level overviews and intuitions of our results in Sect. 2, and introduce the necessary preliminaries in Sect. 3. Then, we formalize the syntax and security notion of RDMCFE in Sect. 4, define the robust correctness and robust security for Special IP-MCFE and construct two IP-RDMCFE constructions in Sect. 5. Finally, we wrap up this paper in Sect. 6.

2 Technical Overview

In this section, we present high-level overviews of our methods and techniques. We first analyse how existing work constructs IP-DMCFE scheme from Special IP-MCFE, and then describe how a new property can be introduced on the Special IP-MCFE to construct the desired IP-RDMCFE scheme.

IP-MCFE allows the user to decrypt the value $\sum_{i\in[n]}\langle \boldsymbol{x}_i, \boldsymbol{y}_i\rangle$ from ciphertexts $\mathsf{Enc}(\boldsymbol{x}_1), \cdots, \mathsf{Enc}(\boldsymbol{x}_n)$ through the functional key sk_y corresponding to $\boldsymbol{y} = (\boldsymbol{y}_1, \cdots, \boldsymbol{y}_n)$. As a special case of IP-MCFE, the master secret key of Special IP-MCFE [3] can be divided into individual keys, *i.e.*, $\mathsf{msk} = \{\mathsf{ek}_i\}_{i\in[n]}$. In addition, the functional key of Special IP-MCFE is generated by performing local function calculations and the sum of inner-products on $\boldsymbol{y}_i$ and ek_i, denoted by $\mathsf{sk}_y = (\{s(\mathsf{ek}_i, \boldsymbol{y}_i)\}_{i\in[n]}, \sum_{i\in[n]}\langle u(\mathsf{ek}_i), \boldsymbol{y}_i\rangle)$. Here, $s(\cdot,\cdot)$ and $u(\cdot)$ are two publicly accessible functions.

Intuitively, IP-DMCFE can be constructed from Special IP-MCFE by letting the client i generate the partial functional key $\mathsf{dk}_{i,y} = (s(\mathsf{ek}_i, \boldsymbol{y}_i), \langle u(\mathsf{ek}_i), \boldsymbol{y}_i\rangle)$ using his/her key ek_i. However, this solution is not secure because the partial functional keys for different functions can be combined in any way, *i.e.*, it suffers the mix-and-match attack. In the IP-DMCFE scheme [3], which is constructed from Special IP-MCFE, noise vectors $\{\boldsymbol{v}_i\}_{i\in[n]}$ satisfying $\sum_{i\in[n]} \boldsymbol{v}_i = \boldsymbol{0}$ are applied to address the security issue. More precisely, each client has the secret key $\mathsf{sk}_i = (\mathsf{ek}_i, \boldsymbol{v}_i)$ and the corresponding partial functional key is generated as $\mathsf{dk}_{i,y} = (s(\mathsf{ek}_i, \boldsymbol{y}_i), \langle u(\mathsf{ek}_i), \boldsymbol{y}_i\rangle + \langle \boldsymbol{v}_i, \boldsymbol{y}\rangle)$. The functional key $\mathsf{sk}_y = (\{s(\mathsf{ek}_i, \boldsymbol{y}_i)\}_{i\in[n]}, \sum_{i\in[n]}\langle u(\mathsf{ek}_i), \boldsymbol{y}_i\rangle)$ of Special IP-MCFE is generated from n partial functional keys through the algorithm KeyComb, because $\sum_{i\in[n]}\langle \boldsymbol{v}_i, \boldsymbol{y}\rangle = \langle \sum_{i\in[n]} \boldsymbol{v}_i, \boldsymbol{y}\rangle = 0$.

Our IP-RDMCFE constructions are also constructed from Special IP-DMCFE but in a different way. There are two steps deployed in our constructions.

- First, without considering the security against mix-and-match attack, we found that the definition of Special IP-MCFE naturally implies a property called *robust correctness*. In this property, if we let the client i generate the partial functional key $\mathsf{dk}_{i,y} = (s(\mathsf{ek}_i, \boldsymbol{y}_i), \langle u(\mathsf{ek}_i), \boldsymbol{y}_i\rangle)$ using his/her key ek_i, then any subset clients S of $[n]$ can generate the functional key $\mathsf{sk}'_y = (\{s(\mathsf{ek}_i, \boldsymbol{y}_i)\}_{i\in S}, \sum_{i\in S}\langle u(\mathsf{ek}_i), \boldsymbol{y}_i\rangle)$ to evaluate their ciphertexts $\{\mathsf{Enc}(\boldsymbol{x}_i)\}_{i\in S}$ and obtain $\sum_{i\in S}\langle \boldsymbol{x}_i, \boldsymbol{y}_i\rangle$, which is the goal of IP-RDMCFE when $|S| \geq t$.
- Second, we found that the mix-and-match attack exists due to the fact that each client in S generates $\langle u(\mathsf{ek}_i), \boldsymbol{y}_i\rangle$ independently for the decryptor to aggregate into $\sum_{i\in S}\langle u(\mathsf{ek}_i), \boldsymbol{y}_i\rangle$ as part of the functional key sk'_y. To solve this security issue, the decryptor cannot receive each individual $\langle u(\mathsf{ek}_i), \boldsymbol{y}_i\rangle$ but the aggregated $\sum_{i\in S}\langle u(\mathsf{ek}_i), \boldsymbol{y}_i\rangle$ only. Unfortunately, we cannot directly borrow the idea in [3] by using the noise vectors $\{\boldsymbol{v}_i\}_{i\in[n]}$ satisfying $\sum_{i\in[n]} \boldsymbol{v}_i = \boldsymbol{0}$ because it is only suitable for $S = [n]$. To realize the secure IP-RDMCFE, we introduce two new methods such that any subset clients S ($|S| \geq t$) of $[n]$ can independently compute $\mathsf{dk}_{i,y}$ for the decryptor who is not allowed to get each individual $\langle u(\mathsf{ek}_i), \boldsymbol{y}_i\rangle$ but only their aggregation $\sum_{i\in S}\langle u(\mathsf{ek}_i), \boldsymbol{y}_i\rangle$.

In the following two subsections, we introduce two different methods for the secure generation of partial functional key $\mathsf{dk}_{i,y}$.

2.1 The Basic IP-RDMCFE Construction

In the basic IP-RDMCFE construction, the secure generation of the partial functional key $\mathsf{dk}_{i,y}$ is achieved by the first method, which is inspired by the work [20]. We protect $\langle u(\mathsf{ek}_i), \boldsymbol{y}_i\rangle$ through the technique of double-masking structure, since one mask will be revealed in Dec while the other mask can still provide protection. Specifically, the positive client i computes

$$mk_i = \langle u(\mathsf{ek}_i), \boldsymbol{y}_i\rangle + \sum_{j\in[n], i>j} v_{i,j} - \sum_{j\in[n], i<j} v_{i,j} + r_i,$$

where $v_{i,j}$ is generated with the private key sk_i and public key pk_j through underlying Non-Interactive Key Exchange (NIKE) scheme, and the mask r_i is selected randomly in Setup. The positive clients show the decryptor the shares of masks r_i of all positive clients, such that masks r_i of all positive clients can be eliminated. In addition, the positive clients show the decryptor the shares of sk_i of all negative clients, such that the decryptor can compute $\{v_{i,j}\}_{j\in[n]}$ through the NIKE scheme and obtain the masks w_i of all negative clients, where

$$w_i = \sum_{j\in[n],i>j} v_{i,j} - \sum_{j\in[n],i<j} v_{i,j}.$$

Specifically, each client i shares the private key sk_i and the mask r_i with all clients through underlying t-out-of-n secret sharing scheme, such that the secret key of client i is $\mathsf{sk}_i = (\mathsf{ek}_i, \{sk_{j,i}\}_{j\in[n]}, r_i, \{r_{j,i}\}_{j\in[n]}, \{v_{i,j}\}_{j\in[n]})$, where ek_i is the part of master secret key of underlying Special IP-MCFE, $sk_{j,i}$ is the i-th share of sk_j from the client j, and $r_{j,i}$ is the i-th share of r_j from the client j. The partial functional key of client i is $\mathsf{dk}_{i,y} = (s(\mathsf{ek}_i, \boldsymbol{y}_i), mk_i, \{sk_{j,i}\}_{j\in[n]\setminus S}, \{r_{j,i}\}_{j\in S})$, where $\{sk_{j,i}\}_{j\in[n]\setminus S}$ is the i-th shares of sk_j of all negative clients, $\{r_{j,i}\}_{j\in S}$ is the i-th shares of masks r_j of all positive clients. As long as the decryptor gets at least t partial functional keys $\mathsf{dk}_{i,y}$, he/she can not only reconstruct $\{r_j\}_{j\in S}$, but also reconstruct $\{sk_j\}_{j\in[n]\setminus S}$ to compute $\{v_{i,j}\}_{i\in[n]\setminus S, j\in[n]}$ and $\{w_i\}_{i\in[n]\setminus S}$. Essentially,

$$\sum_{i\in S}\langle u(\mathsf{ek}_i), \boldsymbol{y}_i\rangle = \sum_{i\in S} mk_i - \sum_{i\in S} r_i - \sum_{i\in S} w_i.$$

Since $\sum_{i\in[n]} w_i = 0$, the decryptor only obtains $\sum_{i\in S}\langle u(\mathsf{ek}_i), \boldsymbol{y}_i\rangle$ by computing

$$\sum_{i\in S}\langle u(\mathsf{ek}_i), \boldsymbol{y}_i\rangle = \sum_{i\in S} mk_i - \sum_{i\in S} r_i + \sum_{i\in[n]\setminus S} w_i.$$

The above construction still suffers the mix-and-match attack because mk_i is only related to $\boldsymbol{y}_i$ of vector $\boldsymbol{y}$ independently. To solve this security issue, inspired by the transformation from Special IP-MCFE to IP-DMCFE scheme [3], we replace $v_{i,j}$ with $\mathsf{PRG}(v_{i,j})$ to compute inner product, *i.e.*,

$$mk_i = \langle u(\mathsf{ek}_i), \boldsymbol{y}_i\rangle + \sum_{j\in[n],i>j} \langle \mathsf{PRG}(v_{i,j}), \boldsymbol{y}\rangle - \sum_{j\in[n],i<j} \langle \mathsf{PRG}(v_{i,j}), \boldsymbol{y}\rangle + r_i,$$

where $\mathsf{PRG}(\cdot)$ is a pseudo-random generator that outputs a vector on the input $v_{i,j}$.

The basic IP-RDMCFE construction is risky if the secret keys $\{\mathsf{sk}_i\}_{i\in[n]}$ were used to generate the partial functional keys for different functions. Specifically, in an instantiation of the basic construction, when the decryptor gets the partial functional keys of one function, he/she can learn either the mask r_i or the private key sk_i, which is part of the secret key. If the partial functional keys for a new function were generated by the same set of secret keys, the above double-masking structure would be degraded to a single-masking structure, which would threaten the security of the construction. Therefore, in the basic construction, one set of secret keys can only be used for one function and cannot be reused for other functions, *i.e.*, the basic construction is not reusable.

2.2 The Reusable IP-RDMCFE Construction

In the reusable IP-RDMCFE construction, the secure generation of the partial functional key $\mathsf{dk}_{i,y}$ is achieved by the second method. This solution includes the following two steps.

- First, to achieve the reusability of the mask, we let the decryptor not receive each individual mask r_i but the aggregated mask $\sum_{i\in S} r_i$ only, which can be achieved through underlying t-out-of-n secret sharing scheme having additively homomorphic property. More precisely, using at least t values $\sum_{j\in S} r_{j,i}$, where $r_{j,i}$ is the i-th share of r_j, the decryptor can reconstruct the sum $\sum_{j\in S} r_j$. Since the decryptor cannot reconstruct each individual mask in Dec, the single-masking structure is sufficient, *i.e.*,

$$mk_i = \langle u(\mathsf{ek}_i), \boldsymbol{y}_i\rangle + \langle \boldsymbol{r}_i, \boldsymbol{y}\rangle,$$

  where the mask was extended the form of vector to compute the inner product to resist the mix-and-match attack. To generate the partial functional key $\mathsf{dk}_{i,y}$, the secret key of client i contains ek_i, $\boldsymbol{r}_i$ and $\{\boldsymbol{r}_{j,i}\}_{j\in[n]}$, where $\boldsymbol{r}_{j,i}$ is the i-th share of $\boldsymbol{r}_j$ in vector form.
- Second, the sum $\sum_{i\in S} \boldsymbol{r}_i$ should not be obtained by the decryptor in plaintext form, because it is possible to learn individual masks by collecting sums for different sets S. To solve this issue, an IP-FE scheme was used to encrypt $\sum_{j\in S} \boldsymbol{r}_{j,i}$ as ct_i and generate the functional key $sk_{i,y}$ for the vector $\boldsymbol{y}$ such that the decryptor learns $\langle \sum_{j\in S} \boldsymbol{r}_{j,i}, \boldsymbol{y}\rangle$ only. Then we set the partial functional key of client i as $\mathsf{dk}_{i,y} = (s(\mathsf{ek}_i, \boldsymbol{y}_i), mk_i, sk_{i,y}, ct_i)$. As long as the decryptor gets at least t partial functional keys $\mathsf{dk}_{i,y}$, he/she can reconstruct $\langle \sum_{j\in S} \boldsymbol{r}_j, \boldsymbol{y}\rangle$ from $\{\langle \sum_{j\in S} \boldsymbol{r}_{j,i}, \boldsymbol{y}\rangle\}_{i\in S}$ through underlying t-out-of-n secret sharing scheme having additively homomorphic property. Then, the decryptor only obtains $\sum_{i\in S}\langle u(\mathsf{ek}_i), \boldsymbol{y}_i\rangle$ by subtracting $\langle \sum_{j\in S} \boldsymbol{r}_j, \boldsymbol{y}\rangle$ from $\sum_{i\in S} mk_i$.

In addition, when presenting reusable IP-RDMCFE construction, we must prohibit the partial functional keys of different functions from decrypting the same set of ciphertexts due to the decryptor can learn the sensitive data by choosing functions painstakingly. To be specific, given ciphertexts $\mathsf{Enc}(\boldsymbol{x}_1), \cdots, \mathsf{Enc}(\boldsymbol{x}_n)$, if $S = [n]$, the decryptor learns $\sum_{i\in[n]}\langle \boldsymbol{x}_i, \boldsymbol{y}_i^1\rangle$ with the partial functional key for $\boldsymbol{y}^1 = (\boldsymbol{y}_1^1, \cdots, \boldsymbol{y}_n^1)$, and $\sum_{i\in[n]}\langle \boldsymbol{x}_i, \boldsymbol{y}_i^2\rangle$ with the partial functional key for $\boldsymbol{y}^2 = (\boldsymbol{y}_1^2, \cdots, \boldsymbol{y}_n^2)$, respectively. If $\boldsymbol{y}^1 + (1, 0, \ldots, 0) = \boldsymbol{y}^2$, the decryptor can learn $x_{1,1}$ by subtracting $\sum_{i\in[n]}\langle \boldsymbol{x}_i, \boldsymbol{y}_i^1\rangle$ from $\sum_{i\in[n]}\langle \boldsymbol{x}_i, \boldsymbol{y}_i^2\rangle$. To solve this issue, we replace the underlying Special IP-MCFE with the Inner Product Identity-based MCFE having special key generation (Special IP-ID-MCFE), which is proposed by Mera et al. [34]. In Special IP-ID-MCFE, the functional key is also associated with a label, and the decryption is valid only when the functional key and ciphertexts correspond to the same label.

Compared to the basic construction, where each client in Setup needs to send a share of sk_i and a share of r_i to $n-1$ clients, each client in the reusable construction needs to send a share of $\boldsymbol{r}_i$ to $n-1$ clients, which contains mn values. Thus, the basic construction exhibits a small communication overhead that remains independent of the vector length m, while the reusable construction incurs a larger communication overhead. Similarly, the storage overhead of the reusable construction is also greater than that of the basic construction. Therefore, the reusable construction achieved the reusability of secret keys at the cost of increasing storage and communication overheads. A reader could now concerned about the additional overhead of the reusable construction. However, although each client must send its share to other clients in the setup phase, this phase is executed only once and the share can be reused, which is similar to the amortized model [7]. Moreover, the client grouping strategy [16] may be helpful for reducing the communication and storage overheads of a single client.

3 Preliminaries

Notations. We represent the set $\{1, \cdots, n\}$ with $[n]$, and denote the size of a set S with $|S|$. Given a set S' ($S' \subseteq S$), we use $S \backslash S'$ to represent the set formed by elements that are present in set S but not in set S'. In this paper, all vectors are treated as column vectors. We represent the vector of mn zeros as $\mathbf{0}$, and denote by x_i the i-th element of the vector $\boldsymbol{x}$. Let $(\boldsymbol{y}_1, \cdots, \boldsymbol{y}_n)$ indicates the vertical concatenation of vectors $\boldsymbol{y}_1, \cdots, \boldsymbol{y}_n$.

3.1 Basic Tools

Definition 1 (Threshold Secret Sharing). *A t-out-of-n threshold secret sharing scheme* $\mathsf{SS} = (\mathsf{Setup}, \mathsf{Share}, \mathsf{Recon})$ *is comprised of the following three algorithms.*

- $\mathsf{Setup}(1^\lambda)$: *Given the security parameter* λ, *the algorithm produces the public parameters pp. We assume that the remaining algorithms implicitly input pp.*
- $\mathsf{Share}(s, t, S)$: *Given a secret s, a set* S $(|S| = n)$, *and a threshold* t $(t \leq n)$, *the algorithm produces a set of shares* $\{s_i\}_{i \in S}$.
- $\mathsf{Recon}(\{s_i\}_{i \in S'}, t)$: *Given the threshold t and the shares corresponding to a subset* S' $(S' \subseteq S)$, *the algorithm produces* s'.

Correctness. *This scheme* SS *is correct if for any* $t, n \in \mathbb{N}$ $(1 \leq t \leq n)$, *any set* S $(|S| = n)$, *and any subset* S' $(S' \subseteq S, |S'| \geq t)$, *we have*

$$\Pr[\mathsf{Recon}(\{s_i\}_{i \in S'}, t) = s] = 1,$$

where the probability is evaluated with respect to $pp \leftarrow \mathsf{Setup}(1^\lambda)$, *and* $\{s_i\}_{i \in S} \leftarrow \mathsf{Share}(s, t, S)$.

IND Security. *The security is defined through the following experiment* $\mathsf{IND}_b^{\mathsf{SS}}(1^\lambda, \mathcal{A})$ *between a challenger and an adversary* $\mathcal{A}$.

1. *The challenger generates* $pp \leftarrow \mathsf{Setup}(1^\lambda)$ *and sends* pp *to the adversary* $\mathcal{A}$.
2. $\mathcal{A}$ *sends* (s^0, s^1) *to the challenger. Then, the challenger runs* $\{s_i^b\}_{i\in S} \leftarrow \mathsf{Share}(s^b, t, S)$ *and sends* $\{s_i^b\}_{i\in S''}$ *to* $\mathcal{A}$, *where* $S'' \subseteq S$ *and* $|S''| < t$.
3. $\mathcal{A}$ *generates a bit* b'. *The challenger takes* b' *as the result of the experiment.*

The scheme SS *is indistinguishability-based (IND) secure if the advantage*

$$\mathsf{Adv}_{\mathsf{SS},\mathcal{A}}^{\mathsf{IND}}(\lambda) = \left|\Pr[\mathsf{IND}_0^{\mathsf{SS}}(1^\lambda, \mathcal{A}) = 1] - \Pr[\mathsf{IND}_1^{\mathsf{SS}}(1^\lambda, \mathcal{A}) = 1]\right|$$

is negligible for every adversary $\mathcal{A}$.

Definition 2 (Additively Homomorphic Threshold Secret Sharing). *A* t*-out-of-*n *threshold secret sharing scheme* $\mathsf{SS} = (\mathsf{Setup}, \mathsf{Share}, \mathsf{Recon})$ *has the additively homomorphic property if for any* $t, n \in \mathbb{N}$ $(1 \leq t \leq n)$, *any* $m \in \mathbb{N}$, *any set* S $(|S| = n)$, *and any subset* S' $(S' \subseteq S, |S'| \geq t)$, *we have*

$$\Pr\left[\mathsf{Recon}(\{\sum_{j\in[m]} s_{j,i}\}_{i\in S'}, t) = \sum_{j\in[m]} s_j\right] = 1,$$

where the probability is evaluated with respect to $pp \leftarrow \mathsf{Setup}(1^\lambda)$, *and* $\{s_{j,i}\}_{i\in S} \leftarrow \mathsf{Share}(s_j, t, S)$ *for* $j \in [m]$.

Definition 3 (Non-Interactive Key Exchange). *A non-interactive key exchange scheme* $\mathsf{NIKE} = (\mathsf{Setup}, \mathsf{Gen}, \mathsf{Agree})$ *for shared key space* $\mathcal{K}$ *is comprised of the following three algorithms.*

- $\mathsf{Setup}(1^\lambda)$: *Given the security parameter* λ, *the algorithm produces the public parameters* pp.
- $\mathsf{Gen}(pp)$: *Given the public parameters* pp, *this algorithm produces the private key* sk_i *and the corresponding public key* pk_i.
- $\mathsf{Agree}(sk_i, pk_j)$: *Given the private key* sk_i *and the public key* pk_j, *this algorithm produces the shared key* $k_{i,j} \in \mathcal{K}$.

Correctness. *This scheme* NIKE *is correct if for any* λ, *we have*

$$\Pr[\mathsf{Agree}(sk_i, pk_j) = \mathsf{Agree}(sk_j, pk_i)] = 1,$$

where the probability is evaluated with respect to $pp \leftarrow \mathsf{Setup}(1^\lambda)$, $(sk_i, pk_i) \leftarrow \mathsf{Gen}(pp)$, *and* $(sk_j, pk_j) \leftarrow \mathsf{Gen}(pp)$.

IND Security. *Consider the following experiment* $\mathsf{IND}_b^{\mathsf{NIKE}}(1^\lambda, \mathcal{A})$ *between a challenger and an adversary* $\mathcal{A}$:

1. *The challenger generates* $pp \leftarrow \mathsf{Setup}(1^\lambda)$ *and sends* pp *to the adversary* $\mathcal{A}$. *The set* $\mathcal{S}$ *was sent to the challenger by* $\mathcal{A}$. *For* $i \in \mathcal{S}$, *the challenger generates* $(sk_i, pk_i) \leftarrow \mathsf{Gen}(pp)$ *and sends* $\{pk_i\}_{i\in\mathcal{S}}$ *to* $\mathcal{A}$.

2. $\mathcal{A}$ sends $i', j' \in \mathcal{S}$ $(i' \neq j')$ to the challenger. When $b = 0$, the challenger runs $k_{i',j'} \leftarrow \mathsf{Agree}(sk_{i'}, pk_{j'})$ and sends $k_{i',j'}$ to $\mathcal{A}$. When $b = 1$, the challenger samples a uniformly random $k_{i',j'}$ from $\mathcal{K}$ and sends it to the adversary $\mathcal{A}$.
3. $\mathcal{A}$ outputs a bit b'. The challenger outputs b' as the final result of the experiment.

The scheme NIKE *is IND secure if the advantage*

$$\mathsf{Adv}^{\mathsf{IND}}_{\mathsf{NIKE},\mathcal{A}}(\lambda) = \left|\Pr[\mathsf{IND}^{\mathsf{NIKE}}_0(1^\lambda, \mathcal{A}) = 1] - \Pr[\mathsf{IND}^{\mathsf{NIKE}}_1(1^\lambda, \mathcal{A}) = 1]\right|$$

is negligible for every adversary $\mathcal{A}$.

3.2 Multi-client Functional Encryption

We recall the standard syntax of IP-MCFE [25] and an additional property known as special key generation [3], and its identity-based version [34].

Definition 4 (Inner Product Multi-client Functional Encryption [25]). *Let $\mathcal{F}^m_{L,n}$ be an inner product function family, $\mathcal{L}$ be a set of labels, and function $f_{\boldsymbol{y}} \in \mathcal{F}^m_{L,n}$ is defined as $f_{\boldsymbol{y}} : (\mathbb{Z}^m_L)^n \to \mathbb{Z}_L$, where $\boldsymbol{y} = (\boldsymbol{y}_1, \cdots, \boldsymbol{y}_n)$ $(\boldsymbol{y}_i \in \mathbb{Z}^m_L)$. An IP-MCFE scheme for $\mathcal{F}^m_{L,n}$ is comprised of the following four algorithms.*

- $\mathsf{Setup}(1^\lambda, \mathcal{F}^m_{L,n})$: *Given the security parameter λ and a description of $\mathcal{F}^m_{L,n}$, the algorithm produces the public parameters pp, the master secret key msk, and n encryption keys ek_i. We assume that the remaining algorithms implicitly input the public parameters pp.*
- $\mathsf{KeyGen}(msk, \boldsymbol{y})$: *Given the master secret key msk and a vector $\boldsymbol{y} \in \mathbb{Z}^{nm}_L$, the algorithm produces a functional key $sk_{\boldsymbol{y}}$.*
- $\mathsf{Enc}(ek_i, \boldsymbol{x}_i, l)$: *Given the encryption key ek_i, a message vector $\boldsymbol{x}_i \in \mathbb{Z}^m_L$, and a label $l \in \mathcal{L}$, the algorithm produces the ciphertext $Ct_{i,l}$.*
- $\mathsf{Dec}(sk_{\boldsymbol{y}}, l, Ct_{1,l}, \cdots, Ct_{n,l})$: *Given the functional key $sk_{\boldsymbol{y}}$, the label l and n ciphertexts, the algorithm produces a value $z \in \mathbb{Z}_L$.*

Correctness. *This IP-MCFE scheme is correct if for any $n, m \in \mathbb{N}$, $f_{\boldsymbol{y}} \in \mathcal{F}^m_{L,n}$, $l \in \mathcal{L}$, we have*

$$\Pr\left[\mathsf{Dec}(sk_{\boldsymbol{y}}, l, Ct_{1,l}, \cdots, Ct_{n,l}) = \sum_{i \in [n]} \langle \boldsymbol{x}_i, \boldsymbol{y}_i \rangle\right] = 1,$$

where the probability is evaluated with respect to $(pp, msk, \{ek_i\}_{i \in [n]}) \leftarrow \mathsf{Setup}(1^\lambda, \mathcal{F}^m_{L,n})$, $sk_{\boldsymbol{y}} \leftarrow \mathsf{KeyGen}(msk, \boldsymbol{y})$, and $Ct_{i,l} \leftarrow \mathsf{Enc}(ek_i, \boldsymbol{x}_i, l)$ for $i \in [n]$.

Remark 1. In the above definition, if $n = 1$ and the label is not considered, and the algorithm Enc does not input the encryption key but the master public key mpk, which is the output of the algorithm Setup, then it corresponds to the (single-input) IP-FE.

Definition 5 (sta-IND Security of IP-MCFE [25]). *For any IP-MCFE scheme for $\mathcal{F}_{L,n}^m$, every adversary $\mathcal{A}$, and every security parameter $\lambda \in \mathbb{N}$, for $b \in \{0,1\}$, consider the following experiments:*

Experiment $\mathsf{IND}_b^{\mathsf{IP\text{-}MCFE}}(1^\lambda, \mathcal{A})$:
$(pp, msk, \{ek_i\}_{i\in[n]}) \leftarrow \mathsf{Setup}(1^\lambda, \mathcal{F}_{L,n}^m)$
$\alpha \leftarrow \mathcal{A}^{\mathsf{QCor}(\cdot),\mathsf{QKeyGen}(\cdot),\mathsf{QEnc}(\cdot,\cdot,\cdot,\cdot)}(pp)$
Output: α

where the corruption oracle $\mathsf{QCor}(\cdot)$ *outputs* ek_i *on input* i, *the key generation oracle* $\mathsf{QKeyGen}(\cdot)$ *outputs* $\mathsf{KeyGen}(msk, \boldsymbol{y})$ *on input* $\boldsymbol{y}$, *the encryption oracle* $\mathsf{QEnc}(\cdot,\cdot,\cdot,\cdot)$ *outputs* $\mathsf{Enc}(ek_i, \boldsymbol{x}_i^b, l)$ *on input* $(i, \boldsymbol{x}_i^0, \boldsymbol{x}_i^1, l)$. *We denote by* $Q_{i,l}$ *the number of queries to* $\mathsf{QEnc}(\cdot,\cdot,\cdot,\cdot)$ *on the slot* i *under the label* l, *by* $\mathcal{CS}$ *the set of corrupted parties, which are queried to* $\mathsf{QCor}(\cdot)$, *by* $\mathcal{HS} = [n]\backslash\mathcal{CS}$ *the set of honest parties. In addition, the queries of* $\mathcal{A}$ *must meet the following conditions.*

1. *For* $i \in \mathcal{CS}$, *the queries* $\mathsf{QEnc}(i, \boldsymbol{x}_i^0, \boldsymbol{x}_i^1, l)$ *must satisfy* $\boldsymbol{x}_i^0 = \boldsymbol{x}_i^1$.
2. *For every label* $l \in \mathcal{L}$, *every query* $\mathsf{QKeyGen}(\boldsymbol{y})$ *and query* $\mathsf{QEnc}(i, \boldsymbol{x}_i^0, \boldsymbol{x}_i^1, l)$ *for* $i \in [n]$, *we require that* $\sum_{i\in[n]}\langle \boldsymbol{x}_i^0, \boldsymbol{y}_i\rangle = \sum_{i\in[n]}\langle \boldsymbol{x}_i^1, \boldsymbol{y}_i\rangle$.
3. *After the adversary* $\mathcal{A}$ *queries* $\mathsf{QEnc}(\cdot,\cdot,\cdot,\cdot)$ *or* $\mathsf{QKeyGen}(\cdot)$, *he/she cannot query* $\mathsf{QCor}(\cdot)$.
4. *For any slot* $i \in [n]$, *any label* $l \in \mathcal{L}$, *we require* $Q_{i,l} \in \{0,1\}$. *In addition, if there is* $Q_{i,l} = 1$, *then* $Q_{j,l} = 1$ *for* $j \in [n]$.

An IP-MCFE for $\mathcal{F}_{L,n}^m$ *has the IND security under static (sta) corruption if the advantage*

$$\mathsf{Adv}_{\mathsf{IP\text{-}MCFE},\mathcal{A}}^{\mathsf{sta\text{-}IND}}(\lambda) = \left|\Pr[\mathsf{IND}_0^{\mathsf{IP\text{-}MCFE}}(1^\lambda, \mathcal{A}) = 1] - \Pr[\mathsf{IND}_1^{\mathsf{IP\text{-}MCFE}}(1^\lambda, \mathcal{A}) = 1]\right|$$

is negligible for every adversary $\mathcal{A}$.

Definition 6 (Special IP-MCFE [3]). *An IP-MCFE scheme for* $\mathcal{F}_{L,n}^m$ *and* $\mathcal{L}$ *has the special key generation property modulo* L *(*L *depends on the public parameters* pp*) if:*

1. *The master secret key* msk *exhibits the following form:* $msk = \{ek_i\}_{i\in[n]}$ *and* $ek_i = (i, s_i, \boldsymbol{u}_i)$, *where* $s_i \in \{0,1\}^*$ *and* $\boldsymbol{u}_i \leftarrow_R \mathbb{Z}_L^m$.
2. *For* $i \in [n]$, $Ct_{i,l} = e(s_i, \boldsymbol{x}_i + h(l)\cdot \boldsymbol{u}_i)$, *where* $e(\cdot,\cdot)$ *and* $h(\cdot)$ *are two public functions.*
3. $\mathsf{KeyGen}(msk, \boldsymbol{y})$ *generates* $sk_y = (\{s_{i,y}\}_{i\in[n]}, dk_y)$, *where* $dk_y = \sum_{i\in[n]}\langle \boldsymbol{u}_i, \boldsymbol{y}_i\rangle$ *and* $s_{i,y}$ *is a function of* s_i, $\boldsymbol{y}_i$ *and* pp.
4. *In* $\mathsf{Dec}(sk_y, l, Ct_{1,l}, \cdots, Ct_{n,l})$, $\{s_{i,y}\}_{i\in[n]}$ *were used to generate* $\sum_{i\in[n]}\langle \boldsymbol{z}_i, \boldsymbol{y}_i\rangle$, *and* $h(l)\cdot dk_y$ *was subtracted from* $\sum_{i\in[n]}\langle \boldsymbol{z}_i, \boldsymbol{y}_i\rangle$, *where* $\boldsymbol{z}_i = \boldsymbol{x}_i + h(l)\cdot \boldsymbol{u}_i$.

Abdalla et al. [3] have shown that existing IP-MCFE schemes from [4,25] all have the property of special key generation.

Definition 7 (Identity-based Multi-client Functional Encryption for Inner Product [34]**).** *The definition of an identity-based IP-MCFE (IP-ID-MCFE) scheme bears resemblance to that of IP-MCFE (Definition 4), except that the algorithms* KeyGen *and* Dec *are now defined as:*

- KeyGen$(msk, \boldsymbol{y}, l)$: *Given the master secret key msk, a vector $\boldsymbol{y} \in \mathbb{Z}_L^{nm}$ and a label (identity) $l \in \mathcal{L}$, the algorithm produces a functional key $sk_{y,l}$.*
- Dec$(l, sk_{y,l}, Ct_{1,l}, \cdots, Ct_{n,l})$: *Given the label $l \in \mathcal{L}$, the functional key $sk_{y,l}$ and n ciphertexts, the algorithm produces a value $z \in \mathbb{Z}_L$.*

Definition 8 (sta-IND Security of IP-ID-MCFE [34]**).** *The sta-IND security notion of an IP-ID-MCFE scheme bears resemblance to that of IP-MCFE (Definition 5), except that the oracle* QKeyGen *is now defined as:*
QKeyGen$(\cdot, \cdot)$: *Inputs $(\boldsymbol{y}, l)$ and outputs* KeyGen$(msk, \boldsymbol{y}, l)$.

4 Robust Decentralized Multi-client Functional Encryption

This section is dedicated to providing a definition of RDMCFE and presenting its security model in the indistinguishability-based setting.

Recall that DMCFE supports the function family, in which every function has n inputs. In DMCFE, the Setup phase is decentralized among n clients that encrypt the sensitive data and generate the partial functional keys, and a combining algorithm combines n partial functional keys into the functional key. If a client is negative, the combining algorithm fails to output the functional key and the user fails to decrypt the ciphertexts.

Compared to DMCFE, RDMCFE supports a more flexible function family, in which every function is still meaningful when some inputs are default. For example, suppose the function f sums the squares of all inputs, *i.e.*, $f(x_1, x_2, x_3) = x_1^2 + x_2^2 + x_3^2$. If the third client does not generate the ciphertext of x_3, the decryptor can still obtain the sum of the squares of the inputs x_1 and x_2, *i.e.*, $f(x_1, x_2, x_0) = x_1^2 + x_2^2 + x_0^2$, where x_0 is a default value and is defined here as 0. The motivation for introducing RDMCFE ensures that the function still makes sense when some inputs are default.

4.1 Syntax of RDMCFE

In RDMCFE, a client is said to be a positive one if it is able and willing to compute both the partial functional key and ciphertext, otherwise it is a negative one. A RDMCFE scheme involving n clients, allows the existence of up to $n-t$ negative clients, and can evaluate the function value associated with the sensitive data of positive clients.

Definition 9 (Robust Decentralized Multi-client Functional Encryption). *Let $\mathcal{F} = \{\mathcal{F}_n\}_{n \in \mathbb{N}}$ be an ensemble, where $\mathcal{F}_n$ represents a collection of n-ary functions, $\mathcal{L}$ be a set of labels, and t be a threshold. A function $f \in \mathcal{F}_n$*

is defined as $f : \mathcal{X}_1 \times \cdots \times \mathcal{X}_n \rightarrow \mathcal{Y}$*, where* $\mathcal{X}_i$ $(i \in [n])$ *contains a pre-defined default value* x_0*. A* RDMCFE *scheme for* $\mathcal{F}$*, the label set* $\mathcal{L}$ *and the threshold* t *is comprised of a setup protocol and three algorithms:*

- $\mathsf{Setup}(1^\lambda, \mathcal{F}_n, t)$*: This is the setup protocol between* n *clients. Given a security parameter* λ*, a description of* $\mathcal{F}_n \in \mathcal{F}$ *and the threshold* t $(t \leq n)$*, the protocol eventually generates the public parameters* pp*, each client's own secret keys* sk_i *and encryption keys* ek_i*. We assume that the remaining algorithms implicitly input the public parameters* pp*.*
- $\mathsf{Enc}(\mathsf{ek}_i, x_i, l)$*: Given the encryption key* ek_i*, the message* $x_i \in \mathcal{X}_i$*, and the label* $l \in \mathcal{L}$*, the algorithm produces the index* i *and the ciphertext* $\mathsf{Ct}_{i,l}$*.*
- $\mathsf{PFunKG}(\mathsf{sk}_i, f, l, S)$*: Given the secret key* sk_i*, the function* $f \in \mathcal{F}_n$*, the label* $l \in \mathcal{L}$*, and the positive client set* $S \subseteq [n]$*, the algorithm produces the index* i *and the partial functional key* $\mathsf{dk}_{i,l}$*.*
- $\mathsf{Dec}(l, \{\mathsf{Ct}_{i,l}\}_{i \in S}, \{\mathsf{dk}_{i,l}\}_{i \in S})$*: Given the label* $l \in \mathcal{L}$*,* $|S|$ *ciphertexts,* $|S|$ *partial functional keys, the algorithm produces a value* $z \in \mathcal{Y}$*.*

Correctness. *This* RDMCFE *scheme is correct, if for any* $t, n \in \mathbb{N}$*,* $t \leq n$*,* $f \in \mathcal{F}_n$*,* $l \in \mathcal{L}$*,* $S \subseteq [n]$*,* $|S| \geq t$*, when* $(\mathsf{pp}, \{\mathsf{sk}_i\}_{i \in [n]}, \{\mathsf{ek}_i\}_{i \in [n]}) \leftarrow \mathsf{Setup}(1^\lambda, \mathcal{F}_n, t)$*,* $(i, \mathsf{Ct}_{i,l}) \leftarrow \mathsf{Enc}(\mathsf{ek}_i, x_i, l)$ *for* $i \in S$*, and* $(i, \mathsf{dk}_{i,l}) \leftarrow \mathsf{PFunKG}(\mathsf{sk}_i, f, l, S)$ *for* $i \in S$*, we have*

$$\Pr\left[\mathsf{Dec}(l, \{\mathsf{Ct}_{i,l}\}_{i \in S}, \{\mathsf{dk}_{i,l}\}_{i \in S}) = f(x'_1, \cdots, x'_n)\right] = 1,$$

where for $i \in [n]$*, if* $i \in S$*,* $x'_i = x_i$*, otherwise* $x'_i = x_0$*, and the probability is evaluated with respect to* Setup*,* Enc *and* PFunKG*.*

The definition of RDMCFE is similar to that of DMCFE [25], but as noted there are the following differences:

1. We set $\mathcal{X}_i$ $(i \in [n])$ to contain a pre-defined default value x_0 to unify the expression of the function value in the robust setting with that in the non-robust setting.
2. In Setup, we additionally input the threshold t, which limits the difference between the function values in the robust and non-robust setting.
3. In PFunKG, we additionally input the positive client set S to declare the state of each client so that the partial functional key $\mathsf{dk}_{i,l}$ helps to eliminate the influence of negative clients.
4. The decryption algorithm Dec implicitly contains the combining algorithm of DMCFE that combines partial functional keys into a functional key, and the algorithm Dec only inputs $|S|$ (instead of n) ciphertexts and partial functional keys.

Remark 2. If the algorithm PFunKG does not input the label l, the Definition 9 corresponds to the unlabeled version of RDMCFE.

Remark 3. The definition of RDMCFE implies that of DMCFE, and the latter is a special case of the former. When $t = n$ and $S = [n]$, the unlabeled version of RDMCFE is just DMCFE.

4.2 Security Definition of RDMCFE

Recall that the IND security of DMCFE roughly states that in the presence of the key generation oracle, the corruption oracle and the encryption oracle, where the key generation oracle outputs the partial functional keys of n slots, no PPT adversary can distinguish ciphertexts of x_i^0 and x_i^1 for $i \in [n]$. Then the security notion of RDMCFE, also known as IND security, should intuitively guarantee that when an adversary is provided with the partial functional keys of the slots in a subset of its choice, the adversary cannot distinguish ciphertexts of x_i^0 and x_i^1 for $i \in [n]$. The security notion is formally captured and demonstrated through the following indistinguishability experiment.

Definition 10 (IND Security of RDMCFE). *For every RDMCFE scheme for* $\mathcal{F}$, $\mathcal{L}$ *and* t, *every adversary* $\mathcal{A}$, *and every security parameter* $\lambda \in \mathbb{N}$, *for* $\mathrm{xx} \in \{\mathsf{one}, \mathsf{many}\}$, $b \in \{0,1\}$, *consider the following experiments:*

Experiment $\mathrm{xx}\text{-}\mathsf{IND}_b^{\mathsf{RDMCFE}}(1^\lambda, \mathcal{A})$:
$(\mathsf{pp}, \{\mathsf{sk}_i\}_{i\in[n]}, \{\mathsf{ek}_i\}_{i\in[n]}) \leftarrow \mathsf{Setup}(1^\lambda, \mathcal{F}_n, t)$
$\alpha \leftarrow \mathcal{A}^{\mathsf{QCor}(\cdot),\mathsf{QEnc}(\cdot,\cdot,\cdot,\cdot),\mathsf{QKeyGen}(\cdot,\cdot,\cdot)}(\mathsf{pp})$
Output: α

The oracles used in the experiment are defined as follows.

Corruption oracle $\mathsf{QCor}(\cdot)$**:** *On input i, it generates* $(\mathsf{sk}_i, \mathsf{ek}_i)$. *We represent the set of corrupted clients as* $\mathcal{CS}$, *which are queried to* $\mathsf{QCor}(\cdot)$, *and the set of honest clients as* $\mathcal{HS} = [n]\backslash\mathcal{CS}$.

Encryption oracle $\mathsf{QEnc}(\cdot,\cdot,\cdot,\cdot)$**:** *On input* (i, x_i^0, x_i^1, l) $(x_i^0, x_i^1 \neq x_0)$, *it outputs* $\mathsf{Enc}(\mathsf{ek}_i, x_i^b, l)$.

Key generation oracle $\mathsf{QKeyGen}(\cdot,\cdot,\cdot)$**:** *On input* (f, l, S), *it computes* $(i, \mathsf{dk}_{i,l}) \leftarrow \mathsf{PFunKG}(\mathsf{sk}_i, f, l, S)$ *for* $i \in S$ *and outputs* $\{(i, \mathsf{dk}_{i,l})\}_{i\in S}$. *We represent the number of queries of the form* $\mathsf{QKeyGen}(\cdot,\cdot,\cdot)$ *as* Q_y.

In addition, the queries of $\mathcal{A}$ must meet the following conditions:

1. *The number of corrupted clients is less than the threshold t, i.e.,* $|\mathcal{CS}| < t$.
2. *For any* $i \in [n]$, *the query* $\mathsf{QEnc}(i, x_i^0, x_i^1, l)$ *has been asked.*
3. *For* $i \in \mathcal{CS}$, *the queries* $\mathsf{QEnc}(i, x_i^0, x_i^1, l)$ *must satisfy* $x_i^0 = x_i^1$.
4. *For every label* $l \in \mathcal{L}$, *every query* $\mathsf{QKeyGen}(f, l, S)$ *and query* $\mathsf{QEnc}(i, x_i^0, x_i^1, l)$ *for* $i \in [n]$, *we require that* $f({x'}_1^0, \cdots, {x'}_n^0) = f({x'}_1^1, \cdots, {x'}_n^1)$, *where for* $i \in [n]$, $b \in \{0,1\}$, *if* $i \in S$, ${x'}_i^b = x_i^b$, *otherwise* ${x'}_i^b = x_0$.
5. *After the adversary $\mathcal{A}$ queries* $\mathsf{QKeyGen}(\cdot,\cdot,\cdot)$ *or* $\mathsf{QEnc}(\cdot,\cdot,\cdot,\cdot)$, *he/she cannot query* $\mathsf{QCor}(\cdot)$.
6. *When* $\mathrm{xx} = \mathsf{one}$, $Q_y = 1$. *When* $\mathrm{xx} = \mathsf{many}$, $Q_y > 1$.

A RDMCFE for $\mathcal{F}_n$ *is* $\mathrm{xx}\text{-}\mathsf{IND}$-secure *if the advantage*

$$\mathsf{Adv}_{\mathsf{RDMCFE},\mathcal{A}}^{\mathrm{xx}\text{-}\mathsf{IND}}(\lambda) = \left|\Pr[\mathrm{xx}\text{-}\mathsf{IND}_0^{\mathsf{RDMCFE}}(1^\lambda, \mathcal{A}) = 1] - \Pr[\mathrm{xx}\text{-}\mathsf{IND}_1^{\mathsf{RDMCFE}}(1^\lambda, \mathcal{A}) = 1]\right|$$

is negligible for every adversary $\mathcal{A}$.

The security notion of RDMCFE is similar to the one defined for DMCFE, but there are the following differences:

1. For robustness, we require that the oracle $\mathsf{QKeyGen}(\cdot,\cdot,\cdot)$ has an additional input S and only outputs $\{(i, \mathsf{dk}_{i,l})\}_{i\in S}$ rather than $\{(i, \mathsf{dk}_{i,l})\}_{i\in[n]}$.
2. Since the threshold t captures the minimum number of positive clients that RDMCFE required, in order to protect the keys of the honest clients, we limit the number of corrupt clients to less than t.
3. Since the adversary can learn $f({x'}^b_1, \cdots, {x'}^b_n)$, we set the security restriction as $f({x'}^0_1, \cdots, {x'}^0_n) = f({x'}^1_1, \cdots, {x'}^1_n)$. Otherwise, the adversary can win the security experiment trivially.
4. We present two IND security definitions for RDMCFE, including one-IND security and many-IND security. In the former, a set of secret keys can generate the partial functional keys for only one function, *i.e.*, the secret keys are not reusable. In the latter, a set of secret keys can generate the partial functional keys for multiple functions, *i.e.*, the secret keys are reusable.

The above IND security model considers the general case, where there are both corrupted clients and honest clients in negative clients, as well as in positive clients. However, recall that the motivation for robustness is to prevent negative clients from crashing the DMCFE system. In this sense, negative clients can be viewed as weakened attackers. Moreover, for a negative client, the system cannot determine whether it is corrupted or not. To resist potential attackers, the system may tend to consider the worst case that it has been corrupted. Therefore, we also consider a special case where all negative clients are corrupted, and present a weaker variant of IND security.

Definition 11 (Constant IND (con-IND) Security of RDMCFE). *The definition is the same as Definition 10, except that the set S has to be chosen before hand by the adversary $\mathcal{A}$ and the queries $\{\mathsf{QEnc}(i, x_i^0, x_i^1, l)\}_{i\in[n]\setminus S}$ must satisfy $\{x_i^0 = x_i^1\}_{i\in[n]\setminus S}$.*

Clearly, this weaker security notion considers all negative clients as corrupted ones, which cannot guarantee the privacy of all negative clients. However, this weaker security still makes sense in some applications of the proposed notion, RDMCFE. For example, in the scenario of electronic voting, each voter should provide eligible proof to show that the encrypted vote is correct, *e.g.*, encrypting 0 means vote for Alice, and 1 for Bob. The final voting result can be obtained by aggregating those encrypted bits (using the RDMCFE scheme). In this case, a voter that maliciously encrypts a value out of $\{0, 1\}$ (*e.g.*, 2) will destroy the final voting result. In this scenario, positive voters are those who always provide correct proof. Negative voters are those who fail to provide correct proof, due to being corrupted or going offline. Then, in order to make the final voting result effective, those negative voters, regardless of whether they are corrupted or offline, must be excluded when counting the final result. In other words, we only consider those positive voters, and do not care about those negative ones, including their privacy, since their presence disrupts the usability of the voting system. Moreover, in such scenarios where the privacy of negative clients does not need to be considered, the use of the weak security model may bring efficiency gains, which may be of independent interest.

5 The RDMCFE Constructions for Inner Product

To present the IP-RDMCFE construction, we first define two new and key properties for the underlying Special IP-MCFE, namely the robust correctness and the robust security. We then present two IP-RDMCFE constructions. The first is a basic construction, in which the secret keys can generate the partial functional keys for only one function. To achieve the reusability of the secret keys, an enhanced construction was designed.

5.1 New Properties of Special IP-MCFE

Definition 12 (Robust Correctness of Special IP-MCFE). *The Special IP-MCFE for $\mathcal{F}_{L,n}^m$ and $\mathcal{L}$ is robust correct if for every $f_y \in \mathcal{F}_{L,n}^m$, $l \in \mathcal{L}$, $S \subseteq [n]$, we have*

$$\Pr\left[\mathsf{Dec}(sk'_y, l, \{Ct_{i,l}\}_{i\in S}) = \sum_{i\in S}\langle \boldsymbol{x}_i, \boldsymbol{y}_i\rangle\right] = 1,$$

where $sk'_y = (\{s_{i,y}\}_{i\in S}, \sum_{i\in S}\langle \boldsymbol{u}_i, \boldsymbol{y}_i\rangle)$ and the probability is evaluated with respect to $(pp, msk, \{ek_i\}_{i\in[n]}) \leftarrow \mathsf{Setup}(1^\lambda, \mathcal{F}_{L,n}^m)$, $sk'_y \leftarrow \mathsf{KeyGen}(\{ek_i\}_{i\in S}, \{\boldsymbol{y}_i\}_{i\in S})$, and $Ct_{i,l} \leftarrow \mathsf{Enc}(ek_i, \boldsymbol{x}_i, l)$ for $i \in S$.

Lemma 1. *If the scheme is a Special IP-MCFE for $\mathcal{F}_{L,n}^m$ and $\mathcal{L}$, then it has the robust correctness.*

Proof. Given a Special IP-MCFE scheme for $\mathcal{F}_{L,n}^m$ and $\mathcal{L}$, when $(pp, msk, \{ek_i\}_{i\in[n]}) \leftarrow \mathsf{Setup}(1^\lambda, \mathcal{F}_{L,n}^m)$, $Ct_{i,l} := e(s_i, \boldsymbol{x}_i + h(l)\cdot \boldsymbol{u}_i) \leftarrow \mathsf{Enc}(ek_i, \boldsymbol{x}_i, l)$ for $i \in [n]$, $sk_y := (\{s_{i,y}\}_{i\in[n]}, dk_y) \leftarrow \mathsf{KeyGen}(msk, \{\boldsymbol{y}_i\}_{i\in[n]})$, where $dk_y = \sum_{i\in[n]}\langle \boldsymbol{u}_i, \boldsymbol{y}_i\rangle$, there are $\mathsf{Dec}(sk_y, \{Ct_{i,l}\}_{i\in[n]}) = \sum_{i\in[n]}\langle \boldsymbol{x}_i, \boldsymbol{y}_i\rangle$. Specifically, in Dec, $\{s_{i,y}\}_{i\in[n]}$ were used to generate $\sum_{i\in[n]}\langle \boldsymbol{z}_i, \boldsymbol{y}_i\rangle$, and $h(l)\cdot dk_y$ was subtracted from $\sum_{i\in[n]}\langle \boldsymbol{z}_i, \boldsymbol{y}_i\rangle$, where $\boldsymbol{z}_i = \boldsymbol{x}_i + h(l)\cdot \boldsymbol{u}_i$.

Assuming that the scheme does not have robust correctness. For any subsets $S_1, S_2 \subseteq [n]$ ($S_1 \cap S_2 = \emptyset$ and $S_1 \cup S_2 = [n]$), there exists $K \in \mathbb{Z}_L$ ($K \neq 0$) such that

$$\mathsf{Dec}(sk_y^1, \{Ct_{i,l}\}_{i\in S_1}) = \sum_{i\in S_1}\langle \boldsymbol{x}_i, \boldsymbol{y}_i\rangle + K, \tag{1}$$

$$\mathsf{Dec}(sk_y^2, \{Ct_{i,l}\}_{i\in S_1}) = \sum_{i\in S_2}\langle \boldsymbol{x}_i, \boldsymbol{y}_i\rangle - K, \tag{2}$$

where $sk_y^1 = (\{s_{i,y}\}_{i\in S_1}, dk_y^1)$, $sk_y^2 = (\{s_{i,y}\}_{i\in S_2}, dk_y^2)$ and $dk_y^1 = \sum_{i\in S_1}\langle \boldsymbol{u}_i, \boldsymbol{y}_i\rangle$, $dk_y^2 = \sum_{i\in S_2}\langle \boldsymbol{u}_i, \boldsymbol{y}_i\rangle$. According to the Eqs. (1) and (2), we have

$$dk_y^1 - \sum_{i\in S_1}\langle \boldsymbol{u}_i, \boldsymbol{y}_i\rangle = -\frac{1}{h(l)}K,$$

$$dk_y^2 - \sum_{i \in S_2} \langle \boldsymbol{u}_i, \boldsymbol{y}_i \rangle = \frac{1}{h(l)} K.$$

Since $dk_y^1 = \sum_{i \in S_1} \langle \boldsymbol{u}_i, \boldsymbol{y}_i \rangle$ and $dk_y^2 = \sum_{i \in S_2} \langle \boldsymbol{u}_i, \boldsymbol{y}_i \rangle$, we have $K = 0$, which contradicts $K \neq 0$. Therefore, the scheme has robust correctness. □

Definition 13 (Robust Security of Special IP-MCFE). *For every Special IP-MCFE for $\mathcal{F}_{L,n}^m$ and $\mathcal{L}$, every adversary $\mathcal{A}$, every security parameter $\lambda \in \mathbb{N}$, and every set $S \subseteq [n]$, for $b \in \{0,1\}$, consider the following experiments:*

<u>*Experiment*</u> $\mathsf{ROB}_b^{\text{IP-MCFE}}(1^\lambda, \mathcal{A})$:
$(pp, msk, \{ek_i\}_{i \in [n]}) \leftarrow \mathsf{Setup}(1^\lambda, \mathcal{F}_{L,n}^m)$
$\alpha \leftarrow \mathcal{A}^{\mathsf{QCor}(\cdot), \mathsf{QEnc}(\cdot,\cdot,\cdot,\cdot), \mathsf{QKeyGen}(\cdot)}(pp)$
Output: α

where $\mathsf{QCor}(\cdot)$ *and* $\mathsf{QEnc}(\cdot,\cdot,\cdot,\cdot)$ *are the same as in Definition 5,* $\mathsf{QKeyGen}(\cdot)$ *outputs* $(\{s_{i,y}\}_{i \in S}, \sum_{i \in S} \langle \boldsymbol{u}_i, \boldsymbol{y}_i \rangle) \leftarrow \mathsf{KeyGen}(\{ek_i\}_{i \in S}, \{\boldsymbol{y}_i\}_{i \in S})$ *on input* $\{\boldsymbol{y}_i\}_{i \in S}$. *The queries of $\mathcal{A}$ must meet the following conditions.*

1. *For $i \in \mathcal{CS}$, the queries $\mathsf{QEnc}(i, \boldsymbol{x}_i^0, \boldsymbol{x}_i^1, l)$ must satisfy $\boldsymbol{x}_i^0 = \boldsymbol{x}_i^1$.*
2. *For any label $l \in \mathcal{L}$, any query $\mathsf{QKeyGen}(\{\boldsymbol{y}_i\}_{i \in S})$ and query $\mathsf{QEnc}(i, \boldsymbol{x}_i^0, \boldsymbol{x}_i^1, l)$ for $i \in S$, we require that $\sum_{i \in S} \langle \boldsymbol{x}_i^0, \boldsymbol{y}_i \rangle = \sum_{i \in S} \langle \boldsymbol{x}_i^1, \boldsymbol{y}_i \rangle$.*
3. *After the adversary $\mathcal{A}$ queries $\mathsf{QKeyGen}(\cdot)$ or $\mathsf{QEnc}(\cdot,\cdot,\cdot,\cdot)$, he/she cannot query $\mathsf{QCor}(\cdot)$.*
4. *For any slot $i \in S$ and any label $l \in \mathcal{L}$, we require $Q_{i,l} \in \{0,1\}$. In addition, if there is $Q_{i,l} = 1$, then $Q_{j,l} = 1$ for $j \in S$.*

A Special IP-MCFE for $\mathcal{F}_{L,n}^m$ and $\mathcal{L}$ is robust secure if the advantage

$$\mathsf{Adv}_{\text{IP-MCFE},\mathcal{A}}^{\mathsf{ROB}}(\lambda) = \left| \Pr[\mathsf{ROB}_0^{\text{IP-MCFE}}(1^\lambda, \mathcal{A}) = 1] - \Pr[\mathsf{ROB}_1^{\text{IP-MCFE}}(1^\lambda, \mathcal{A}) = 1] \right|$$

is negligible for every adversary $\mathcal{A}$.

Lemma 2. *If the Special IP-MCFE has sta-IND security, it also has robust security. Namely, for every adversary $\mathcal{A}$ who can break the robust security of Special IP-MCFE, there is an adversary $\mathcal{B}$ who can break the sta-IND security of Special IP-MCFE such that*

$$\mathsf{Adv}_{\text{IP-MCFE},\mathcal{A}}^{\mathsf{ROB}}(\lambda) \leq \mathsf{Adv}_{\text{IP-MCFE},\mathcal{B}}^{\text{sta-IND}}(\lambda).$$

Proof. (Sketch) In the sta-IND security model, the adversary $\mathcal{B}$ can send the queries to the challenger $\mathcal{C}$, who sets up the Special IP-MCFE system. At the same time, in the robust security model, the adversary $\mathcal{B}$ is simulated as another challenger to respond to the queries from the adversary $\mathcal{A}$. That is, $\mathcal{B}$ interacts with $\mathcal{C}$ as the adversary, while $\mathcal{B}$ interacts with $\mathcal{A}$ as the challenger. Specifically, we show how the adversary $\mathcal{B}$ responds to the queries from the adversary $\mathcal{A}$ with the help of the challenger $\mathcal{C}$.

- Corruption Queries: the adversary $\mathcal{B}$ receives the set $\mathcal{CS}$ from the adversary $\mathcal{A}$ and sends $\mathcal{CS}$ to the challenger $\mathcal{C}$ to obtain $\{ek_i\}_{i\in\mathcal{CS}}$, where $ek_i = (i, s_i, \boldsymbol{u}_i)$. The adversary $\mathcal{B}$ then returns $\{ek_i\}_{i\in\mathcal{CS}}$ to the adversary $\mathcal{A}$.
- Key Generation Queries: after receiving the query $\{\boldsymbol{y}_i\}_{i\in S}$ from the adversary $\mathcal{A}$, the adversary $\mathcal{B}$ sets $\boldsymbol{y}_i = (0, 0, \cdots, 0)$ for $i \in [n]\backslash S$, and sends $\{\boldsymbol{y}_i\}_{i\in[n]}$ to the challenger $\mathcal{C}$ to obtain $sk_y = (\{s_{i,y}\}_{i\in[n]}, dk_y)$, where $dk_y = \sum_{i\in[n]}\langle \boldsymbol{u}_i, \boldsymbol{y}_i\rangle$. Since $\boldsymbol{y}_i = (0, 0, \cdots, 0)$ for $i \in [n]\backslash S$, there is

$$dk_y = \sum_{i\in S}\langle \boldsymbol{u}_i, \boldsymbol{y}_i\rangle + \sum_{i\in[n]\backslash S}\langle \boldsymbol{u}_i, \boldsymbol{y}_i\rangle = \sum_{i\in S}\langle \boldsymbol{u}_i, \boldsymbol{y}_i\rangle + 0,$$

so the adversary $\mathcal{B}$ returns $sk'_y = (\{s_{i,y}\}_{i\in S}, dk_y)$ to the adversary $\mathcal{A}$.
- Encryption Queries: the adversary $\mathcal{B}$ receives $\{(i, \boldsymbol{x}_i^0, \boldsymbol{x}_i^1, l)\}_{i\in[n]}$ from the adversary $\mathcal{A}$, where $\boldsymbol{x}_i^0 = \boldsymbol{x}_i^1$ for $i \in \mathcal{CS}$ and $\sum_{i\in S}\langle \boldsymbol{x}_i^0, \boldsymbol{y}_i\rangle = \sum_{i\in S}\langle \boldsymbol{x}_i^1, \boldsymbol{y}_i\rangle$. Then, the adversary $\mathcal{B}$ sends $\{(i, \boldsymbol{x}_i^0, \boldsymbol{x}_i^1, l)\}_{i\in[n]}$ to the challenger $\mathcal{C}$. For $b \in \{0, 1\}$, since $\boldsymbol{y}_i = (0, 0, \cdots, 0)$ for $i \in [n]\backslash S$, we also have

$$\sum_{i\in[n]}\langle \boldsymbol{x}_i^b, \boldsymbol{y}_i\rangle = \sum_{i\in S}\langle \boldsymbol{x}_i^b, \boldsymbol{y}_i\rangle + 0.$$

Since $\sum_{i\in S}\langle \boldsymbol{x}_i^0, \boldsymbol{y}_i\rangle = \sum_{i\in S}\langle \boldsymbol{x}_i^1, \boldsymbol{y}_i\rangle$, we have $\sum_{i\in[n]}\langle \boldsymbol{x}_i^0, \boldsymbol{y}_i\rangle = \sum_{i\in[n]}\langle \boldsymbol{x}_i^1, \boldsymbol{y}_i\rangle$, so the challenger $\mathcal{C}$ returns $\{Ct_{i,l}\}_{i\in[n]}$ to the adversary $\mathcal{B}$, where $Ct_{i,l} \leftarrow \mathsf{Enc}(ek_i, \boldsymbol{x}_i^b, l)$. Finally, $\mathcal{B}$ returns $\{Ct_{i,l}\}_{i\in[n]}$ to the adversary $\mathcal{A}$.

Therefore, if the adversary $\mathcal{A}$ succeeds against the robust security of Special IP-MCFE, then the adversary $\mathcal{B}$ breaks the sta-IND security of the scheme. □

5.2 The Basic IP-RDMCFE Construction

We rely on a t-out-of-n secret sharing scheme SS = (SS.Setup, SS.Share, SS.Recon), a non-interactive key exchange scheme NIKE = (NIKE.Setup, NIKE.Gen, NIKE.Agree) and a Special IP-MCFE scheme MCFE = (MCFE.Setup, MCFE.KeyGen, MCFE.Enc, MCFE.Dec) for the class $\mathcal{F}_{L,n}^m$. We require a pseudorandom generator PRG that inputs a uniformly random seed, and whose output space is $\mathbb{Z}_L^{mn}$. The basic IP-RDMCFE construction for the class $\mathcal{F}_{L,n}^m$ is as follows:

$\mathsf{Setup}(1^\lambda, \mathcal{F}_{L,n}^m, t)$: Given the security parameter λ, the description of $\mathcal{F}_{L,n}^m$ and the threshold t, do the following:
- Generate $(pp_1, msk, \{mek_i\}_{i\in[n]}) \leftarrow \mathsf{MCFE.Setup}(1^\lambda, \mathcal{F}_{L,n}^m)$, where $msk = \{mek_i\}_{i\in[n]}$, $mek_i = (s_i, \boldsymbol{u}_i)$, $s_i \in \{0,1\}^*$ and $\boldsymbol{u}_i \in \mathbb{Z}_L^m$.
- Generate $pp_2 \leftarrow \mathsf{NIKE.Setup}(1^\lambda)$ and $pp_3 \leftarrow \mathsf{SS.Setup}(1^\lambda)$.
- Each client $i \in [n]$ does the following:
  1. Generates $(sk_i, pk_i) \leftarrow \mathsf{NIKE.Gen}(pp_2)$ and $\{sk_{i,j}\}_{j\in[n]} \leftarrow \mathsf{SS.Share}(sk_i, t, [n])$.
  2. Samples $r_i \leftarrow \mathbb{Z}_L$ and generates $\{r_{i,j}\}_{j\in[n]} \leftarrow \mathsf{SS.Share}(r_i, t, [n])$.
  3. For $j \in [n]\backslash\{i\}$, sends pk_i, $sk_{i,j}$ and $r_{i,j}$ to the client j.

4. For $j \in [n]\backslash\{i\}$, generates $v_{i,j} \leftarrow \mathsf{NIKE.Agree}(sk_i, pk_j)$.
- Output $(\mathsf{pp}, \{\mathsf{sk}_i\}_{i\in[n]}, \{\mathsf{ek}_i\}_{i\in[n]})$, where $\mathsf{pp} := (pp_1, pp_2, pp_3, \{pk_i\}_{i\in[n]})$, $\mathsf{ek}_i := mek_i$ and $\mathsf{sk}_i := (mek_i, \{sk_{j,i}\}_{j\in[n]}, r_i, \{r_{j,i}\}_{j\in[n]}, \{v_{i,j}\}_{j\in[n]})$.

$\underline{\mathsf{Enc}(\mathsf{ek}_i, \boldsymbol{x}_i, l)}$: Given the encryption key ek_i, the vector $\boldsymbol{x}_i \in \mathbb{Z}_L^m$ and the label l, do the following:
- Generate $\mathsf{Ct}_{i,l} \leftarrow \mathsf{MCFE.Enc}(mek_i, \boldsymbol{x}_i, l)$.
- Output $(i, \mathsf{Ct}_{i,l})$.

$\underline{\mathsf{PFunKG}(\mathsf{sk}_i, \boldsymbol{y}, S)}$: Given the secret key sk_i, the vector $\boldsymbol{y} \in \mathbb{Z}_L^{mn}$ and the positive client set S, do the following:
- Generate $(s_{i,y}, dk_i) \leftarrow \mathsf{MCFE.KeyGen}(mek_i, \{\boldsymbol{y}_i\}_{i\in S})$, where $dk_i = \langle \boldsymbol{u}_i, \boldsymbol{y}_i\rangle$ and $s_{i,y}$ is a function of s_i, $\boldsymbol{y}_i$ and pp_1.
- For $j \in [n]\backslash\{i\}$, compute $\boldsymbol{p}_{i,j} = \Delta_{i,j}\mathsf{PRG}(v_{i,j})$, where $\Delta_{i,j} = 1$ when $i > j$, and $\Delta_{i,j} = -1$ when $i < j$.
- Compute $mk_i = dk_i + \sum_{j\in[n]}\langle \boldsymbol{p}_{i,j}, \boldsymbol{y}\rangle + r_i$, where $\boldsymbol{p}_{i,i} = \boldsymbol{0}$.
- Output $(i, \mathsf{dk}_{i,y})$, where $\mathsf{dk}_{i,y} := (s_{i,y}, mk_i, \{sk_{j,i}\}_{j\in[n]\backslash S}, \{r_{j,i}\}_{j\in S})$.

$\underline{\mathsf{Dec}(l, \{\mathsf{Ct}_{i,l}\}_{i\in S}, \{\mathsf{dk}_{i,y}\}_{i\in S})}$: Given the label $l \in \mathcal{L}$, $|S|$ ciphertexts $\{\mathsf{Ct}_{i,l}\}_{i\in S}$ corresponding to the same label l and $|S|$ keys $\{\mathsf{dk}_{i,y}\}_{i\in S}$ under the same vector $\boldsymbol{y}$, do the following:
- If $|S| < t$, abort.
- For $j \in S$, reconstruct $r_j \leftarrow \mathsf{SS.Recon}(\{r_{j,i}\}_{i\in S}, t)$.
- For $j \in [n]\backslash S$, reconstruct $sk_j \leftarrow \mathsf{SS.Recon}(\{sk_{j,i}\}_{i\in S}, t)$.
- For $j \in [n]\backslash S$, $i \in [n]$, compute $v_{j,i} \leftarrow \mathsf{NIKE.Agree}(sk_j, pk_i)$.
- Compute $\mathsf{dk}_y = \sum_{i\in S} mk_i - \sum_{j\in S} r_j + \sum_{j\in[n]\backslash S, i\in[n]}\langle \boldsymbol{p}_{j,i}, \boldsymbol{y}\rangle$, where $\boldsymbol{p}_{j,i} = \Delta_{j,i}\mathsf{PRG}(v_{j,i})$ for $j \neq i$, and $\boldsymbol{p}_{j,i} = \boldsymbol{0}$ for $j = i$.
- Define $\mathsf{sk}_y := (\{s_{i,y}\}_{i\in S}, \mathsf{dk}_y)$, output $\sum_{i\in S}\langle \boldsymbol{x}_i, \boldsymbol{y}_i\rangle \leftarrow \mathsf{MCFE.Dec}(\mathsf{sk}_y, l, \{\mathsf{Ct}_{i,l}\}_{i\in S})$.

Correctness. When $|S| \geq t$, we have the fact that

$$\begin{aligned}
\mathsf{dk}_y &= \sum_{i\in S} mk_i - \sum_{j\in S} r_j + \sum_{j\in[n]\backslash S, i\in[n]} \langle \boldsymbol{p}_{j,i}, \boldsymbol{y}\rangle \\
&= \sum_{i\in S}\langle \boldsymbol{u}_i, \boldsymbol{y}_i\rangle + \sum_{i\in S, j\in[n]}\langle \boldsymbol{p}_{i,j}, \boldsymbol{y}\rangle + \sum_{j\in[n]\backslash S, i\in[n]}\langle \boldsymbol{p}_{j,i}, \boldsymbol{y}\rangle \\
&= \sum_{i\in S}\langle \boldsymbol{u}_i, \boldsymbol{y}_i\rangle + \sum_{j,i\in[n]}\langle \boldsymbol{p}_{j,i}, \boldsymbol{y}\rangle \\
&= \sum_{i\in S}\langle \boldsymbol{u}_i, \boldsymbol{y}_i\rangle + \sum_{j,i\in[n], j\neq i}(\Delta_{j,i}\langle \mathsf{PRG}(v_{j,i}), \boldsymbol{y}\rangle) \\
&= \sum_{i\in S}\langle \boldsymbol{u}_i, \boldsymbol{y}_i\rangle + \sum_{j,i\in[n], j>i}[(\Delta_{j,i} + \Delta_{i,j})\langle \mathsf{PRG}(v_{j,i}), \boldsymbol{y}\rangle] \\
&= \sum_{i\in S}\langle \boldsymbol{u}_i, \boldsymbol{y}_i\rangle.
\end{aligned}$$

Since $(s_{i,y}, dk_i) \leftarrow \mathsf{MCFE.KeyGen}(mek_i, \{\boldsymbol{y}_i\}_{i\in S})$ and $\mathsf{Ct}_{i,l} \leftarrow \mathsf{MCFE.Enc}(mek_i, \boldsymbol{x}_i, l)$ for $i \in S$, and $\mathsf{dk}_y = \sum_{i\in S}\langle \boldsymbol{u}_i, \boldsymbol{y}_i\rangle$, we have $\mathsf{MCFE.Dec}((\{s_{i,y}\}_{i\in S},$

$\mathsf{dk}_y), l, \{\mathsf{Ct}_{i,l}\}_{i\in S}) = \sum_{i\in S}\langle \boldsymbol{x}_i, \boldsymbol{y}_i\rangle$ according to the robust correctness of the scheme MCFE. Then, the correctness of the above construction can be derived directly from the robust correctness of the scheme MCFE.

Theorem 1. *If* MCFE = (MCFE.Setup, MCFE.KeyGen, MCFE.Enc, MCFE.Dec) *be a Special IP-MCFE scheme with sta-IND security,* SS = (SS.Setup, SS.Share, SS.Recon) *be an IND secure t-out-of-n secret sharing scheme,* NIKE = (NIKE.Setup, NIKE.Gen, NIKE.Agree) *be an IND secure non-interactive key exchange scheme,* PRG *be a secure pseudorandom generator, then the basic IP-RDMCFE construction described above is one-IND secure. More precisely,*

$$\begin{aligned}\mathsf{Adv}^{\text{one-IND}}_{\mathsf{RDMCFE}}(\mathcal{A}) \le &\mathsf{Adv}^{\text{sta-IND}}_{\mathsf{MCFE},\mathcal{B}_4}(\lambda) + 2h_2 \cdot \left(\mathsf{Adv}^{\mathsf{IND}}_{\mathsf{NIKE},\mathcal{B}_2}(\lambda) + \mathsf{Adv}_{\mathsf{PRG},\mathcal{B}_3}(\lambda)\right) \\ &+ 4h_1 \cdot \mathsf{Adv}^{\mathsf{IND}}_{\mathsf{SS},\mathcal{B}_1}(\lambda) + 2 \cdot \mathrm{negl}(\lambda),\end{aligned}$$

where $h_1 = |S \cap \mathcal{HS}|$ $(0 \le h_1 \le n)$*,* $h_2 = \frac{h_1(h_1-1)}{2}$.

Proof. We define $\mathcal{U}^* := S \cap \mathcal{HS}$ and $h_1 := |\mathcal{U}^*|$. The proof progresses through the following sequence of games.

Game G_0: is the real game corresponding to $b = 0$.

Game G_1: is the same as the previous game, with the exception that we replace all shares of r_i generated by clients $i \in \mathcal{U}^*$ and given to the corrupted clients with shares of 0 (using a different sharing of 0 for every $i \in \mathcal{U}^*$).

Game G_2: is the same as the previous game, with the exception that we replace all shares of sk_i generated by clients $i \in \mathcal{U}^*$ and given to the corrupted clients with shares of 0 (using a different sharing of 0 for every $i \in \mathcal{U}^*$).

Game G_3: is the same as the previous game, with the exception that, for $i, j \in \mathcal{U}^*$, we replace $v_{i,j} = v_{j,i} \leftarrow \mathsf{NIKE.Agree}(sk_i, pk_j)$ with a uniformly random number.

Game G_4: is the same as the previous game, with the exception that, for $i, j \in \mathcal{U}^*$, we replace $\boldsymbol{p}_{i,j} = \Delta_{i,j}\mathsf{PRG}(v_{i,j})$ with $\boldsymbol{p}_{i,j} = \Delta_{i,j}\boldsymbol{r}_{i,j}$, where $\boldsymbol{r}_{i,j}$ is a fresh random vector (of the appropriate size).

Game G_5: is the same as the previous game, with the exception that, for $i \in \mathcal{U}^*$, we replace

$$\begin{aligned}mk_i &= \langle \boldsymbol{u}_i, \boldsymbol{y}_i\rangle + \sum_{j\in[n]} \langle \boldsymbol{p}_{i,j}, \boldsymbol{y}\rangle + r_i \\ &= \langle \boldsymbol{u}_i, \boldsymbol{y}_i\rangle + \sum_{j\in\mathcal{U}^*} \langle \boldsymbol{p}_{i,j}, \boldsymbol{y}\rangle + \sum_{j\in[n]\setminus\mathcal{U}^*} \langle \boldsymbol{p}_{i,j}, \boldsymbol{y}\rangle + r_i\end{aligned}$$

with

$$mk_i = \langle \boldsymbol{w}_i, \boldsymbol{y}_i\rangle + \sum_{j\in[n]\setminus\mathcal{U}^*} \langle \boldsymbol{p}_{i,j}, \boldsymbol{y}\rangle + r_i,$$

where $\{\boldsymbol{w}_i\}_{i\in\mathcal{U}^*}$ are uniformly random, subject to $\sum_{i\in\mathcal{U}^*}\langle \boldsymbol{w}_i, \boldsymbol{y}_i\rangle = \mathsf{dk}_y - \sum_{i\in S\cap\mathcal{CS}}\langle \boldsymbol{u}_i, \boldsymbol{y}_i\rangle$.

Game G_6**:** is the same as the previous game, with the exception that for $i \in [n]$, we replace $\mathsf{Ct}_{i,l} = \mathsf{Enc}(\mathsf{ek}_i, \boldsymbol{x}_i^0, l)$ with $\mathsf{Ct}_{i,l} = \mathsf{Enc}(\mathsf{ek}_i, \boldsymbol{x}_i^1, l)$.
Game G_7**:** is the real game corresponding to $b = 1$.

Lemma 3. *For every adversary $\mathcal{A}$, there is an adversary $\mathcal{B}_0$ against the IND security of the t-out-of-n secret sharing scheme* $\mathsf{SS} = (\mathsf{SS.Setup}, \mathsf{SS.Share}, \mathsf{SS.Recon})$ *such that*

$$\left|\mathsf{Adv}^0_{\mathcal{A}}(\lambda) - \mathsf{Adv}^1_{\mathcal{A}}(\lambda)\right| \leq h_1 \cdot \mathsf{Adv}^{\mathsf{IND}}_{\mathsf{SS},\mathcal{B}_0}(\lambda).$$

Proof. We can see that the difference between game G_0 and game G_1 lies only in the shares of r_i generated by clients $i \in \mathcal{U}^*$ and given to the corrupted clients. We denote the set $\mathcal{U}^* := \{i_1, \cdots, i_{h_1}\}$ in ascending order. The proof of this lemma employs a series of intermediate games $G_{0,0}$, $G_{0,1}$, $\cdots$, G_{0,h_1}. In the game $G_{0,\mu}$ ($\mu \in \{0, 1, \cdots, h_1\}$),

- for $i \in [n]$, $(sk_i, pk_i) \leftarrow \mathsf{NIKE.Gen}(pp_2)$, $\{sk_{i,j}\}_{j\in[n]} \leftarrow \mathsf{SS.Share}(sk_i, t, [n])$;
- for $i \in [n]$, $r_i \leftarrow \mathbb{Z}_L$, $\{r_{i,j}\}_{j\in[n]} \leftarrow \mathsf{SS.Share}(r_i, t, [n])$, $v_{i,j} \leftarrow \mathsf{NIKE.Agree}(sk_i, pk_j)$ for $j \in [n]\backslash\{i\}$;
- for $i \in \mathcal{U}^*$, $i \leq i_\mu$, $\{r'_{i,j}\}_{j\in[n]} \leftarrow \mathsf{SS.Share}(0, t, [n])$;
- for $i \in \mathcal{HS}$, $\mathsf{sk}_i := (mek_i, \{sk_{j,i}\}_{j\in[n]}, r_i, \{r_{j,i}\}_{j\in[n]}, \{v_{i,j}\}_{j\in[n]})$;
- for $i \in \mathcal{CS}$, $\mathsf{sk}_i := (mek_i, \{sk_{j,i}\}_{j\in[n]}, r_i, \{r_{j,i}\}_{j\in[n]\backslash\mathcal{U}^*}, \{r'_{j,i}\}_{j\in\mathcal{U}^*, j\leq i_\mu}, \{r_{j,i}\}_{j\in\mathcal{U}^*, j>i_\mu}, \{v_{i,j}\}_{j\in[n]})$.

Note that game $G_{0,0}$ is identical to game G_0, and game G_{0,h_1} is identical to game G_1.

We can see that the difference between game $G_{0,\mu-1}$ and game $G_{0,\mu}$ lies only in the shares of r_{i_μ} generated by the client i_μ and given to the corrupted clients, which is either $\{r_{i_\mu,j}\}_{j\in\mathcal{CS}}$ or $\{r'_{i_\mu,j}\}_{j\in\mathcal{CS}}$. Suppose that the adversary $\mathcal{B}_{0,\mu-1}$ attacks the IND security of SS. Note that, in game $G_{0,\mu-1}$ and game $G_{0,\mu}$, the adversary $\mathcal{B}_{0,\mu-1}$ does not receive any additional shares of r_{i_μ} for the client i_μ, because $i_\mu \in S$ and the honest clients do not reveal shares of r_{i_μ}. Thus, the adversary $\mathcal{B}_{0,\mu-1}$ knows only $|\mathcal{CS}| < t$ shares of r_{i_μ}. Therefore, relying on the IND security of SS, we have $\left|\mathsf{Adv}^{0,\mu-1}_{\mathcal{A}}(\lambda) - \mathsf{Adv}^{0,\mu}_{\mathcal{A}}(\lambda)\right| \leq \mathsf{Adv}^{\mathsf{IND}}_{\mathsf{SS},\mathcal{B}_{0,\mu-1}}(\lambda)$ for $\mu \in [h_1]$. To sum up, we have that there is an adversary $\mathcal{B}_0$ such that $\left|\mathsf{Adv}^0_{\mathcal{A}}(\lambda) - \mathsf{Adv}^1_{\mathcal{A}}(\lambda)\right| \leq h_1 \cdot \mathsf{Adv}^{\mathsf{IND}}_{\mathsf{SS},\mathcal{B}_0}(\lambda)$. □

Lemma 4. *For every adversary $\mathcal{A}$, there is an adversary $\mathcal{B}_1$ against the IND security of t-out-of-n secret sharing scheme* $\mathsf{SS} = (\mathsf{SS.Setup}, \mathsf{SS.Share}, \mathsf{SS.Recon})$ *such that*

$$\left|\mathsf{Adv}^1_{\mathcal{A}}(\lambda) - \mathsf{Adv}^2_{\mathcal{A}}(\lambda)\right| \leq h_1 \cdot \mathsf{Adv}^{\mathsf{IND}}_{\mathsf{SS},\mathcal{B}_1}(\lambda).$$

Proof. We can see that the difference between game G_1 and game G_2 lies only in the shares of sk_i generated by clients $i \in \mathcal{U}^*$ and given to the corrupted clients. We denote the set $\mathcal{U}^* := \{i_1, \cdots, i_{h_1}\}$ in ascending order. The proof of this lemma employs a series of intermediate games $G_{1,0}$, $G_{1,1}$, $\cdots$, G_{1,h_1}. In the Game $G_{1,\mu}$ ($\mu \in \{0, 1, \cdots, h_1\}$),

- for $i \in [n]$, $(sk_i, pk_i) \leftarrow \mathsf{NIKE.Gen}(pp_2)$, $\{sk_{i,j}\}_{j\in[n]} \leftarrow \mathsf{SS.Share}(sk_i, t, [n])$;
- for $i \in [n]$, $r_i \leftarrow \mathbb{Z}_L$, $\{r_{i,j}\}_{j\in[n]} \leftarrow \mathsf{SS.Share}(r_i, t, [n])$, $v_{i,j} \leftarrow \mathsf{NIKE.Agree}(sk_i, pk_j)$ for $j \in [n]\backslash\{i\}$;
- for $i \in \mathcal{U}^*$, $\{r'_{i,j}\}_{j\in[n]} \leftarrow \mathsf{SS.Share}(0, t, [n])$;
- for $i \in \mathcal{U}^*$, $i \leq i_\mu$, $\{sk'_{i,j}\}_{j\in[n]} \leftarrow \mathsf{SS.Share}(0, t, [n])$;
- for $i \in \mathcal{HS}$, $\mathsf{sk}_i := (mek_i, \{sk_{j,i}\}_{j\in[n]}, r_i, \{r_{j,i}\}_{j\in[n]}, \{v_{i,j}\}_{j\in[n]})$;
- for $i \in \mathcal{CS}$, $\mathsf{sk}_i := (mek_i, \{sk_{j,i}\}_{j\in[n]\backslash\mathcal{U}^*}, \{sk'_{j,i}\}_{j\in\mathcal{U}^*, j\leq i_\mu}, \{sk_{j,i}\}_{j\in\mathcal{U}^*, j>i_\mu}, r_i, \{r_{j,i}\}_{j\in[n]\backslash\mathcal{U}^*}, \{r'_{j,i}\}_{j\in\mathcal{U}^*}, \{v_{i,j}\}_{j\in[n]})$.

Note that game $G_{1,0}$ is identical to game G_1, and game G_{1,h_1} is identical to game G_2.

We can see that the difference between game $G_{1,\mu-1}$ and game $G_{1,\mu}$ lies only in the shares of sk_{i_μ} generated by the client i_μ and given to the corrupted clients, which is either $\{sk_{i_\mu,j}\}_{j\in\mathcal{CS}}$ or $\{sk'_{i_\mu,j}\}_{j\in\mathcal{CS}}$. Suppose that the adversary $\mathcal{B}_{1,\mu-1}$ attacks the IND security of SS. Note that, in game $G_{1,\mu-1}$ and game $G_{1,\mu}$, the adversary $\mathcal{B}_{1,\mu-1}$ does not receive any additional shares of sk_{j_μ} for the client j_μ, because $i_\mu \in S$ and the honest clients do not reveal shares of sk_{i_μ}. Thus, the adversary $\mathcal{B}_{1,\mu-1}$ knows only $|\mathcal{CS}| < t$ shares of sk_{i_μ}. Therefore, relying on the IND security of SS, we have $\left|\mathsf{Adv}^{1,\mu-1}_{\mathcal{A}}(\lambda) - \mathsf{Adv}^{1,\mu}_{\mathcal{A}}(\lambda)\right| \leq \mathsf{Adv}^{\mathsf{IND}}_{\mathsf{SS},\mathcal{B}_{1,\mu-1}}(\lambda)$ for $\mu \in [h_1]$. To sum up, we have that there is an adversary $\mathcal{B}_1$ such that $\left|\mathsf{Adv}^1_{\mathcal{A}}(\lambda) - \mathsf{Adv}^2_{\mathcal{A}}(\lambda)\right| \leq h_1 \cdot \mathsf{Adv}^{\mathsf{IND}}_{\mathsf{SS},\mathcal{B}_1}(\lambda)$. □

Lemma 5. *For every adversary $\mathcal{A}$, there is an adversary $\mathcal{B}_2$ against the IND security of non-interactive key exchange scheme* NIKE = (NIKE.Setup, NIKE.Gen, NIKE.Agree) *such that*

$$\left|\mathsf{Adv}^2_{\mathcal{A}}(\lambda) - \mathsf{Adv}^3_{\mathcal{A}}(\lambda)\right| \leq \frac{h_1(h_1-1)}{2} \cdot \mathsf{Adv}^{\mathsf{IND}}_{\mathsf{NIKE},\mathcal{B}_2}(\lambda).$$

Proof. We can see that the difference between game G_2 and game G_3 lies only in the generation of $\{v_{i,j}\}_{i,j\in\mathcal{U}^*}$. In the former experiment, Game G_2, for $i, j \in \mathcal{U}^*$, $v_{i,j} = v_{j,i} \leftarrow \mathsf{NIKE.Agree}(sk_i, pk_j)$. While in the latter experiment, Game G_3, for $i, j \in \mathcal{U}^*$, $v_{i,j} = v_{j,i}$ is a uniformly random number. We denote the set $\mathcal{U}' := \{j_1, \cdots, j_{h_2}\}$, where $h_2 = \frac{h_1(h_1-1)}{2}$, for $\mu \in [h_2]$, $j_\mu = (i,j) = (j,i)$ $(i, j \in \mathcal{U}^*, i \neq j)$. The proof of this lemma employs a series of intermediate games, which contains h_2 games. Among them, the difference between two adjacent games lies only in the generation of $v_{i,j}$, which is either $v_{i,j} = v_{j,i} \leftarrow \mathsf{NIKE.Agree}(sk_i, pk_j)$ or a uniformly random number. Note that game $G_{2,0}$ is identical to game G_2, and game G_{2,h_2} is identical to game G_3. Relying on the IND security of NIKE, we have that for $\mu \in [h_2]$, there is an adversary $\mathcal{B}_{2,\mu-1}$ such that $\left|\mathsf{Adv}^{2,\mu-1}_{\mathcal{A}}(\lambda) - \mathsf{Adv}^{2,\mu}_{\mathcal{A}}(\lambda)\right| \leq \mathsf{Adv}^{\mathsf{IND}}_{\mathsf{NIKE},\mathcal{B}_{2,\mu-1}}(\lambda)$. To sum up, we have that there is an adversary $\mathcal{B}_2$ such that $\left|\mathsf{Adv}^2_{\mathcal{A}}(\lambda) - \mathsf{Adv}^3_{\mathcal{A}}(\lambda)\right| \leq \frac{h_1(h_1-1)}{2} \cdot \mathsf{Adv}^{\mathsf{IND}}_{\mathsf{NIKE},\mathcal{B}_2}(\lambda)$. □

Lemma 6. *For every adversary $\mathcal{A}$, there is an adversary $\mathcal{B}_3$ against the security of the pseudorandom generator* PRG *such that*

$$\left|\mathsf{Adv}^3_{\mathcal{A}}(\lambda) - \mathsf{Adv}^4_{\mathcal{A}}(\lambda)\right| \leq \frac{h_1(h_1-1)}{2} \cdot \mathsf{Adv}_{\mathsf{PRG},\mathcal{B}_3}(\lambda).$$

Proof. We can see that the difference between game G_3 and game G_4 lies only in the generation of $\{\boldsymbol{p}_{i,j}\}_{i,j\in\mathcal{U}^*}$. In the former experiment, Game G_3, for $i,j \in \mathcal{U}^*$, $\boldsymbol{p}_{i,j} = \Delta_{i,j}\mathsf{PRG}(v_{i,j})$. While in the latter experiment, Game G_4, for $i,j \in \mathcal{U}^*$, $\boldsymbol{p}_{i,j} = \Delta_{i,j}\boldsymbol{r}_{i,j}$, where $\boldsymbol{r}_{i,j}$ is a fresh random vector (of the appropriate size). We also denote the set $\mathcal{U}' := \{j_1, \cdots, j_{h_2}\}$, where $h_2 = \frac{h_1(h_1-1)}{2}$, for $\mu \in [h_2]$, $j_\mu = (i,j)$ $(i,j \in \mathcal{U}^*, i \neq j)$. The proof of this lemma employs a series of intermediate games, which contains h_2 games. Among them, the difference between two adjacent games lies only in the generation of $\boldsymbol{p}_{i,j}$, which is either $\Delta_{i,j}\mathsf{PRG}(v_{i,j})$ or $\Delta_{i,j}\boldsymbol{r}_{i,j}$. Note that game $G_{3,0}$ is identical to game G_3, and game G_{3,h_2} is identical to game G_4. Relying on the security of PRG, we have that for $\mu \in [h_2]$, there is an adversary $\mathcal{B}_{3,\mu-1}$ such that $\left|\mathsf{Adv}_{\mathcal{A}}^{3,\mu-1}(\lambda) - \mathsf{Adv}_{\mathcal{A}}^{3,\mu}(\lambda)\right| \leq \mathsf{Adv}_{\mathsf{PRG},\mathcal{B}_{3,\mu-1}}(\lambda)$. To sum up, we have that there is an adversary $\mathcal{B}_3$ such that $\left|\mathsf{Adv}_{\mathcal{A}}^{3}(\lambda) - \mathsf{Adv}_{\mathcal{A}}^{4}(\lambda)\right| \leq \frac{h_1(h_1-1)}{2} \cdot \mathsf{Adv}_{\mathsf{PRG},\mathcal{B}_3}(\lambda)$. □

Lemma 7. *For any adversary $\mathcal{A}$ and any security parameter λ, we have that*

$$\left|\mathsf{Adv}_{\mathcal{A}}^{4}(\lambda) - \mathsf{Adv}_{\mathcal{A}}^{5}(\lambda)\right| \leq \mathrm{negl}(\lambda).$$

Proof. We can see that the difference between game G_4 and game G_5 lies only in the generation of $\{mk_i\}_{i\in\mathcal{U}^*}$. In the former experiment, Game G_4, for $i \in \mathcal{U}^*$,

$$mk_i = \langle \boldsymbol{u}_i, \boldsymbol{y}_i\rangle + \sum_{j\in\mathcal{U}^*}\langle \boldsymbol{p}_{i,j}, \boldsymbol{y}\rangle + \sum_{j\in[n]\setminus\mathcal{U}^*}\langle \boldsymbol{p}_{i,j}, \boldsymbol{y}\rangle + r_i.$$

While in the latter experiment, Game G_5, for $i \in \mathcal{U}^*$,

$$mk_i = \langle \boldsymbol{w}_i, \boldsymbol{y}_i\rangle + \sum_{j\in[n]\setminus\mathcal{U}^*}\langle \boldsymbol{p}_{i,j}, \boldsymbol{y}\rangle + r_i,$$

where $\{\boldsymbol{w}_i\}_{i\in\mathcal{U}^*}$ are uniformly random, subject to

$$\sum_{i\in\mathcal{U}^*}\langle \boldsymbol{w}_i, \boldsymbol{y}_i\rangle = \mathsf{dk}_y - \sum_{i\in\mathcal{S}\cap\mathcal{CS}}\langle \boldsymbol{u}_i, \boldsymbol{y}_i\rangle.$$

Since

$$\{\{\boldsymbol{p}_{i,j} \leftarrow \mathbb{Z}_L^m,\ \boldsymbol{p}_{i,j} + \boldsymbol{p}_{j,i} = \boldsymbol{0}\}_{i<j} :\ \{\langle \boldsymbol{u}_i, \boldsymbol{y}_i\rangle + \sum_{j\in\mathcal{U}^*}\langle \boldsymbol{p}_{i,j}, \boldsymbol{y}\rangle\}_{i\in\mathcal{U}^*}\},$$

$$\{\{\boldsymbol{w}_i \leftarrow \mathbb{Z}_L^m\}_{i\in\mathcal{U}^*} \text{ s.t. } \sum_{i\in\mathcal{U}^*}\langle \boldsymbol{w}_i, \boldsymbol{y}_i\rangle = \sum_{i\in\mathcal{U}^*}\langle \boldsymbol{u}_i, \boldsymbol{y}_i\rangle :\ \{\boldsymbol{w}_i\}_{i\in\mathcal{U}^*}\}$$

are identical distributions, we have $\left|\mathsf{Adv}_{\mathcal{A}}^{4}(\lambda) - \mathsf{Adv}_{\mathcal{A}}^{5}(\lambda)\right| \leq \mathrm{negl}(\lambda)$. □

Lemma 8. *For every adversary $\mathcal{A}$, there is an adversary $\mathcal{B}_4$ against the* sta-IND *security of the scheme* MCFE *such that*

$$\left|\mathsf{Adv}_{\mathcal{A}}^{5}(\lambda) - \mathsf{Adv}_{\mathcal{A}}^{6}(\lambda)\right| \leq \mathsf{Adv}_{\mathsf{MCFE},\mathcal{B}_4}^{\mathsf{sta\text{-}IND}}(\lambda).$$

Proof. Since the Lemma 2, the scheme $\mathsf{MCFE} = (\mathsf{MCFE.Setup}, \mathsf{MCFE.KeyGen}, \mathsf{MCFE.Enc}, \mathsf{MCFE.Dec})$ has the robust security. Suppose that the adversary $\mathcal{A}$ possesses a non-negligible advantage in distinguishing between game G_5 and game G_6. Then, we construct an adversary $\mathcal{B}_4'$ that attacks the robust security of MCFE. To generate the partial functional keys for $\boldsymbol{y}$, the adversary $\mathcal{B}_4'$ sends $\boldsymbol{y}$ to the challenger of MCFE, receives the functional key $\mathsf{sk}_y = (\{s_{i,y}\}_{i\in S}, \mathsf{dk}_y)$, and generates $\{mk_i\}_{i\in S}$ as follows:

$$mk_i = \begin{cases} \langle \boldsymbol{u}_i, \boldsymbol{y}_i\rangle + \sum_{j\in[n]}\langle \boldsymbol{p}_{i,j}, \boldsymbol{y}\rangle + r_i, & i \in S \cap \mathcal{CS} \\ \langle \boldsymbol{w}_i, \boldsymbol{y}_i\rangle + \sum_{j\in[n]\setminus\mathcal{U}^*}\langle \boldsymbol{p}_{i,j}, \boldsymbol{y}\rangle + r_i, & i \in \mathcal{U}^*,\ i \neq i^* \\ \langle \boldsymbol{w}_{i^*}, \boldsymbol{y}_{i^*}\rangle + \sum_{j\in[n]\setminus\mathcal{U}^*}\langle \boldsymbol{p}_{i^*,j}, \boldsymbol{y}\rangle + r_{i^*}, & i = i^* \in \mathcal{U}^* \end{cases},$$

where $\boldsymbol{w}_i$ is a random vector, i^* is the last honest client in the set S and $\langle \boldsymbol{w}_{i^*}, \boldsymbol{y}_{i^*}\rangle = \mathsf{dk}_y - \sum_{i\in S\cap\mathcal{CS}}\langle \boldsymbol{u}_i, \boldsymbol{y}_i\rangle - \sum_{i\in\mathcal{U}^*, i\neq i^*}\langle \boldsymbol{w}_i, \boldsymbol{y}_i\rangle$. Then, for $i \in [n]$, the adversary $\mathcal{B}_4'$ sends $(\boldsymbol{x}_i^0, \boldsymbol{x}_i^1)$ to the challenger of MCFE, and receives $\mathsf{Ct}_{i,l} \leftarrow \mathsf{MCFE.Enc}(mek_i, \boldsymbol{x}_i^b, l)$. If $b = 0$, then $\mathcal{B}_4'$ is simulating the game G_5. If $b = 1$, then $\mathcal{B}_4'$ is simulating the game G_6. Thus, we have

$$\left|\mathsf{Adv}^5_{\mathcal{A}}(\lambda) - \mathsf{Adv}^6_{\mathcal{A}}(\lambda)\right| \leq \mathsf{Adv}^{\mathsf{ROB}}_{\mathsf{MCFE},\mathcal{B}_4'}(\lambda).$$

According to Lemma 2, there is $\left|\mathsf{Adv}^5_{\mathcal{A}}(\lambda) - \mathsf{Adv}^6_{\mathcal{A}}(\lambda)\right| \leq \mathsf{Adv}^{\mathsf{sta\text{-}IND}}_{\mathsf{MCFE},\mathcal{B}_4}(\lambda)$. □

The hybrid game of G_6 to G_7 is just the reverse of G_0 to G_5, so we have that

$$\begin{aligned}\left|\mathsf{Adv}^6_{\mathcal{A}}(\lambda) - \mathsf{Adv}^7_{\mathcal{A}}(\lambda)\right| \leq & h_2 \cdot \left(\mathsf{Adv}^{\mathsf{IND}}_{\mathsf{NIKE},\mathcal{B}_2}(\lambda) + \mathsf{Adv}_{\mathsf{PRG},\mathcal{B}_3}(\lambda)\right) \\ & + 2h_1 \cdot \mathsf{Adv}^{\mathsf{IND}}_{\mathsf{SS},\mathcal{B}_1}(\lambda) + \mathrm{negl}(\lambda).\end{aligned}$$

5.3 The Reusable IP-RDMCFE Construction

The reusable IP-RDMCFE construction rely on a t-out-of-n secret sharing scheme $\mathsf{SS} = (\mathsf{SS.Setup}, \mathsf{SS.Share}, \mathsf{SS.Recon})$ having the additively homomorphic property, a Special IP-ID-MCFE scheme $\mathsf{ID\text{-}MCFE} = (\mathsf{ID\text{-}MCFE.Setup}, \mathsf{ID\text{-}MCFE.KeyGen}, \mathsf{ID\text{-}MCFE.Enc}, \mathsf{ID\text{-}MCFE.Dec})$ for the class $\mathcal{F}^m_{L,n}$ and an IP-FE scheme $\mathsf{FE} = (\mathsf{FE.Setup}, \mathsf{FE.KeyGen}, \mathsf{FE.Enc}, \mathsf{FE.Dec})$ for the class $\mathcal{F}^{mn}_L$. The reusable IP-RDMCFE construction for the class $\mathcal{F}^m_{L,n}$ is as follows:

$\underline{\mathsf{Setup}(1^\lambda, \mathcal{F}^m_{L,n}, t)}$: Given the security parameter λ, the description of $\mathcal{F}^m_{L,n}$ and the threshold t, do the following:

- Generate $(pp_1, msk, \{mek_i\}_{i\in[n]}) \leftarrow \mathsf{ID\text{-}MCFE.Setup}(1^\lambda, \mathcal{F}^m_{L,n})$, where $msk = \{mek_i\}_{i\in[n]}$, $mek_i = (s_i, \boldsymbol{u}_i)$, $s_i \in \{0,1\}^*$ and $\boldsymbol{u}_i \in \mathbb{Z}^m_L$.
- Generate $pp_2 \leftarrow \mathsf{SS.Setup}(1^\lambda)$.
- Each client $i \in [n]$ does the following:
  1. Generates $(pk_i, uk_i) \leftarrow \mathsf{FE.Setup}(1^\lambda, \mathcal{F}^{mn}_L)$.

2. Samples $\boldsymbol{r}_i \leftarrow \mathbb{Z}_L^{mn}$ and generates $\{\boldsymbol{r}_{i,j}\}_{j\in[n]} \leftarrow \mathsf{SS.Share}(\boldsymbol{r}_i, t, [n])$[1].
3. For $j \in [n]\backslash\{i\}$, sends $\boldsymbol{r}_{i,j}$ to the client j.

– Output $(\mathsf{pp}, \{\mathsf{sk}_i\}_{i\in[n]}, \{\mathsf{ek}_i\}_{i\in[n]})$, where $\mathsf{pp} := (pp_1, pp_2, \{pk_i\}_{i\in[n]})$, $\mathsf{ek}_i := mek_i$ and $\mathsf{sk}_i := (mek_i, uk_i, \boldsymbol{r}_i, \{\boldsymbol{r}_{j,i}\}_{j\in[n]})$.

$\mathsf{Enc}(\mathsf{ek}_i, \boldsymbol{x}_i, l)$: Given the encryption key ek_i, the vector $\boldsymbol{x}_i \in \mathbb{Z}_L^m$ and the label l, do the following:
– Generate $\mathsf{Ct}_{i,l} \leftarrow \mathsf{ID\text{-}MCFE.Enc}(mek_i, \boldsymbol{x}_i, l)$.
– Output $(i, \mathsf{Ct}_{i,l})$.

$\mathsf{PFunKG}(\mathsf{sk}_i, \boldsymbol{y}, l, S)$: Given the secret key sk_i, the vector $\boldsymbol{y} \in \mathbb{Z}_L^{mn}$, the label l and the positive client set S, do the following:
– Generate $sk_{i,y} \leftarrow \mathsf{FE.KeyGen}(uk_i, \boldsymbol{y})$ and $(s_{i,l}, dk_i) \leftarrow \mathsf{ID\text{-}MCFE.KeyGen}(mek_i, \{\boldsymbol{y}_i\}_{i\in S}, l)$, where $dk_i = \langle \boldsymbol{u}_i, \boldsymbol{y}_i \rangle$ and $s_{i,l}$ is a function of s_i, $\boldsymbol{y}_i$, l and pp_1.
– Compute $mk_i = dk_i + \langle \boldsymbol{r}_i, \boldsymbol{y} \rangle$, $\boldsymbol{g}_i = \sum_{j\in S} \boldsymbol{r}_{j,i}$ and $ct_i \leftarrow \mathsf{FE.Enc}(pk_i, \boldsymbol{g}_i)$.
– Output $(i, \mathsf{dk}_{i,l})$, where $\mathsf{dk}_{i,l} := (mk_i, s_{i,l}, sk_{i,y}, ct_i)$.

$\mathsf{Dec}(l, \{\mathsf{Ct}_{i,l}\}_{i\in S}, \{\mathsf{dk}_{i,l}\}_{i\in S})$: Given the label $l \in \mathcal{L}$, $|S|$ ciphertexts $\{\mathsf{Ct}_{i,l}\}_{i\in S}$ and $|S|$ keys $\{\mathsf{dk}_{i,l}\}_{i\in S}$, do the following:
– If $|S| < t$, abort.
– For $i \in S$, generate $p_i \leftarrow \mathsf{FE.Dec}(ct_i, sk_{i,y})$.
– Reconstruct $p \leftarrow \mathsf{SS.Recon}(\{p_i\}_{i\in S}, t)$ and compute $\mathsf{dk}_y = \sum_{i\in S} mk_i - p$.
– Outputs $\sum_{i\in S}\langle \boldsymbol{x}_i, \boldsymbol{y}_i \rangle \leftarrow \mathsf{ID\text{-}MCFE.Dec}(\mathsf{sk}_y, l, \{\mathsf{Ct}_{i,l}\}_{i\in S})$, where $\mathsf{sk}_y = (\{s_{i,l}\}_{i\in S}, \mathsf{dk}_y)$.

Correctness. For $i \in S$, we have $p_i = \langle \boldsymbol{g}_i, \boldsymbol{y} \rangle$ following from the correctness of the scheme FE. Since $\boldsymbol{g}_i = \sum_{j\in S} \boldsymbol{r}_{j,i}$, when $|S| \geq t$, we have $p = \sum_{j\in S}\langle \boldsymbol{r}_j, \boldsymbol{y} \rangle$ due to the correctness and the additively homomorphic property of the scheme SS. Thus, we have $\mathsf{dk}_y = \sum_{i\in S}\langle \boldsymbol{u}_i, \boldsymbol{y}_i \rangle$, and the correctness of the above construction can be derived directly from the robust correctness of the scheme ID-MCFE.

Theorem 2. *If* ID-MCFE = (ID-MCFE.Setup, ID-MCFE.KeyGen, ID-MCFE.Enc, ID-MCFE.Dec) *be a Special IP-ID-MCFE scheme with sta-IND security,* SS = (SS.Setup, SS.Share, SS.Recon) *be an IND secure t-out-of-n secret sharing scheme having the additively homomorphic property,* FE = (FE.Setup, FE.KeyGen, FE.Enc, FE.Dec) *be an IND secure IP-FE scheme, then the proposed construction above is many-IND secure. More precisely,*

$$\mathsf{Adv}^{\mathsf{many\text{-}IND}}_{\mathsf{RDMCFE}}(\mathcal{A}) \leq 2mnh_1 \cdot \mathsf{Adv}^{\mathsf{IND}}_{\mathsf{SS},\mathcal{B}_1}(\lambda) + 2h_1 \cdot \mathsf{Adv}^{\mathsf{IND}}_{\mathsf{FE},\mathcal{B}_2}(\lambda) + \mathsf{Adv}^{\mathsf{sta\text{-}IND}}_{\mathsf{ID\text{-}MCFE},\mathcal{B}_3}(\lambda),$$

where $h_1 = |S \cap \mathcal{HS}|$ $(0 \leq h_1 \leq n)$.

Proof. We define $\mathcal{U}^* := S \cap \mathcal{HS}$ and $h_1 := |\mathcal{U}^*|$. The proof progresses through the following sequence of games.

Game G_0: is the real game corresponding to $b = 0$.

[1] This form implies that under the same threshold t and the set $[n]$, the algorithm $\mathsf{SS.Share}(\cdot, t, [n])$ is run m times, where each time inputting a component of the vector $\boldsymbol{r}_i$, and m shares with the same subscript are combined into a vector $\boldsymbol{r}_{i,j}$.

Game G_1**:** is the same as the previous game, with the exception that we replace all shares $\{\boldsymbol{r}_{i,j}\}_{j\in\mathcal{CS}}$ of $\boldsymbol{r}_i$ generated by clients $i \in \mathcal{U}^*$ and given to the corrupted clients with shares $\{\boldsymbol{r}'_{i,j}\}_{j\in\mathcal{CS}}$ of $\mathbf{0}$, where $\{\boldsymbol{r}'_{i,j}\}_{j\in[n]} \leftarrow \mathsf{SS.Share}(\mathbf{0}, t, [n])$ (using a different sharing of $\mathbf{0}$ for every $i \in \mathcal{U}^*$).

Game G_2**:** is the same as the previous game except that for $k \in Q_y$, $i \in \mathcal{U}^*$, the challenger calculates $ct_{k,i} \leftarrow \mathsf{FE.Enc}(pk_i, \boldsymbol{g}_{k,i})$ with $\boldsymbol{g}_{k,i} = \sum_{j\in\mathcal{U}^*} \boldsymbol{r}_{k,j,i} + \sum_{j\in\mathcal{S}\cap\mathcal{CS}} \boldsymbol{r}'_{j,i}$, where $\{\boldsymbol{r}_{k,j,i}\}_{j\in\mathcal{U}^*}$ are uniformly sampled such that $\boldsymbol{r}_i \leftarrow \mathsf{SS.Recon}(\{\boldsymbol{r}_{k,i,j}\}_{j\in\mathcal{U}^*}, \{\boldsymbol{r}'_{i,j}\}_{j\in\mathcal{S}\cap\mathcal{CS}}, t)$ and $\sum_{j\in\mathcal{U}^*}\langle \boldsymbol{r}_{k,j,i}, \boldsymbol{y}_k\rangle = \sum_{j\in\mathcal{U}^*}\langle \boldsymbol{r}_{j,i}, \boldsymbol{y}_k\rangle$.

Game G_3**:** is the same as the previous game except that for $i \in [n]$, we replace $\mathsf{Ct}_{i,l} = \mathsf{Enc}(\mathsf{ek}_i, \boldsymbol{x}_i^0, l)$ with $\mathsf{Ct}_{i,l} = \mathsf{Enc}(\mathsf{ek}_i, \boldsymbol{x}_i^1, l)$.

Game G_4**:** is the real game corresponding to $b = 1$.

Lemma 9. *For every adversary $\mathcal{A}$, there is an adversary $\mathcal{B}_1$ against the* IND *security of the t-out-of-n secret sharing scheme* $\mathsf{SS} = (\mathsf{SS.Setup}, \mathsf{SS.Share}, \mathsf{SS.Recon})$ *such that*

$$\left|\mathsf{Adv}^0_{\mathcal{A}}(\lambda) - \mathsf{Adv}^1_{\mathcal{A}}(\lambda)\right| \le mnh_1 \cdot \mathsf{Adv}^{\mathsf{IND}}_{\mathsf{SS},\mathcal{B}_1}(\lambda).$$

Proof. This proof is similar to that of Lemma 3. □

Lemma 10. *For every adversary $\mathcal{A}$, there is an adversary $\mathcal{B}_2$ against the* IND *security of the scheme* FE *such that*

$$\left|\mathsf{Adv}^1_{\mathcal{A}}(\lambda) - \mathsf{Adv}^2_{\mathcal{A}}(\lambda)\right| \le h_1 \cdot \mathsf{Adv}^{\mathsf{IND}}_{\mathsf{FE},\mathcal{B}_2}(\lambda).$$

Proof. We can see that the difference between game G_1 and game G_2 lies only in the generation of $\{ct_{k,i}\}_{k\in Q_y, i\in\mathcal{U}^*}$. In the former experiment, Game G_1, for $k \in Q_y$, $i \in \mathcal{U}^*$, it is

$$ct_{k,i} \leftarrow \mathsf{FE.Enc}(pk_i, \sum_{j\in\mathcal{U}^*} \boldsymbol{r}_{j,i} + \sum_{j\in\mathcal{S}\cap\mathcal{CS}} \boldsymbol{r}'_{j,i}).$$

While in the latter experiment, Game G_2, for $k \in Q_y$, $i \in \mathcal{U}^*$, it is

$$ct_{k,i} \leftarrow \mathsf{FE.Enc}(pk_i, \sum_{j\in\mathcal{U}^*} \boldsymbol{r}_{k,j,i} + \sum_{j\in\mathcal{S}\cap\mathcal{CS}} \boldsymbol{r}'_{j,i}),$$

where $\{\boldsymbol{r}_{k,j,i}\}_{j\in\mathcal{U}^*}$ are uniformly random under the constraints

$$\boldsymbol{r}_i \leftarrow \mathsf{SS.Recon}(\{\boldsymbol{r}_{k,i,j}\}_{j\in\mathcal{U}^*}, \{\boldsymbol{r}'_{i,j}\}_{j\in\mathcal{S}\cap\mathcal{CS}}, t),$$

and $\sum_{j\in\mathcal{U}^*}\langle \boldsymbol{r}_{k,j,i}, \boldsymbol{y}_k\rangle = \sum_{j\in\mathcal{U}^*}\langle \boldsymbol{r}_{j,i}, \boldsymbol{y}_k\rangle$.

We denote the set $\mathcal{U}^* := \{i_1, \cdots, i_{h_1}\}$ in ascending order. We prove the indistinguishability of game G_1 and game G_2 with a sequence of games: $G_{1,0}$, $G_{1,1}$, $\cdots$, G_{1,h_1}. For $\mu \in [h_1]$, $G_{1,\mu}$ is the same as $G_{1,\mu-1}$ except that for $k \in Q_y$,

$$ct_{k,i_\mu} \leftarrow \mathsf{FE.Enc}(pk_{i_\mu}, \sum_{j\in\mathcal{U}^*} \boldsymbol{r}_{j,i_\mu} + \sum_{j\in\mathcal{S}\cap\mathcal{CS}} \boldsymbol{r}'_{j,i_\mu})$$

is substituted with

$$ct_{k,i_\mu} \leftarrow \mathsf{FE.Enc}(pk_{i_\mu}, \sum_{j \in \mathcal{U}^*} \boldsymbol{r}_{k,j,i_\mu} + \sum_{j \in \mathcal{S} \cap \mathcal{CS}} \boldsymbol{r}'_{j,i_\mu}).$$

We can see that the game $G_{1,0}$ is the same as the game G_1, and the game G_{1,h_1} is the same as the game G_2. If the adversary $\mathcal{A}$ can distinguish between the game G_1 and game G_2, and the adversary $\mathcal{A}_\mu$ can distinguish between the game $G_{1,\mu}$ and game $G_{1,\mu-1}$, we have

$$\left|\mathsf{Adv}^1_{\mathcal{A}}(\lambda) - \mathsf{Adv}^2_{\mathcal{A}}(\lambda)\right| \le h_1 \cdot \left|\mathsf{Adv}^{\mu-1}_{\mathcal{A}_\mu}(\lambda) - \mathsf{Adv}^{\mu}_{\mathcal{A}_\mu}(\lambda)\right|.$$

If the adversary $\mathcal{A}_\mu$ can distinguish between the game $G_{1,\mu}$ and game $G_{1,\mu-1}$, we construct an adversary $\mathcal{B}_{2,\mu}$ that attack the IND security of FE. For $k \in Q_y$, to generate the partial functional keys for $\boldsymbol{y}_k$, the adversary $\mathcal{B}_{2,\mu}$ computes $(s_{k,i,l}, dk_{k,i}) \leftarrow \mathsf{ID\text{-}MCFE.KeyGen}(mek_i, \{\boldsymbol{y}_{k,i}\}_{i \in S}, l)$ and $mk_{k,i} = dk_{k,i} + \langle \boldsymbol{r}_i, \boldsymbol{y}_k\rangle$ for $i \in S$, and generates $\{sk_{k,i}\}_{i \in S}$ as follows:

- For $i = i_\mu$, the adversary $\mathcal{B}_{2,\mu}$ sends $\boldsymbol{y}_k$ to the challenger of FE and gets $sk_{k,i_\mu} \leftarrow \mathsf{FE.KeyGen}(uk_{i_\mu}, \boldsymbol{y}_k)$.
- For $i (\neq i_\mu) \in [n]$, the adversary $\mathcal{B}_{2,\mu}$ computes $sk_{k,i} \leftarrow \mathsf{FE.KeyGen}(uk_i, \boldsymbol{y}_k)$.

Then the adversary $\mathcal{B}_{2,\mu}$ generates $\{ct_{k,i}\}_{i \in S \setminus \{i_\mu\}}$ as follows:

- For $i \in S \cap \mathcal{CS}$ and $i (> i_\mu) \in \mathcal{U}^*$, the adversary $\mathcal{B}_{2,\mu}$ computes $\boldsymbol{g}_{k,i} = \sum_{j \in \mathcal{U}^*} \boldsymbol{r}_{j,i} + \sum_{j \in \mathcal{S} \cap \mathcal{CS}} \boldsymbol{r}'_{j,i}$ and $ct_{k,i} \leftarrow \mathsf{FE.Enc}(pk_i, \boldsymbol{g}_{k,i})$.
- For $i (< i_\mu) \in \mathcal{U}^*$, the adversary $\mathcal{B}_{2,\mu}$ computes $\boldsymbol{g}_{k,i} = \sum_{j \in \mathcal{U}^*} \boldsymbol{r}_{k,j,i} + \sum_{j \in \mathcal{S} \cap \mathcal{CS}} \boldsymbol{r}'_{j,i}$ and $ct_{k,i} \leftarrow \mathsf{FE.Enc}(pk_i, \boldsymbol{g}_{k,i})$.

In addition, the adversary $\mathcal{B}_{2,\mu}$ computes $\boldsymbol{g}^0_{k,i_\mu} = \sum_{j \in \mathcal{U}^*} \boldsymbol{r}_{j,i_\mu} + \sum_{j \in \mathcal{S} \cap \mathcal{CS}} \boldsymbol{r}'_{j,i_\mu}$ and $\boldsymbol{g}^1_{k,i_\mu} = \sum_{j \in \mathcal{U}^*} \boldsymbol{r}_{k,j,i_\mu} + \sum_{j \in \mathcal{S} \cap \mathcal{CS}} \boldsymbol{r}'_{j,i_\mu}$, sends $(\boldsymbol{g}^0_{k,i_\mu}, \boldsymbol{g}^1_{k,i_\mu})$ to the challenger of FE, and receives $ct_{k,i_\mu} \leftarrow \mathsf{FE.Enc}(pk_{i_\mu}, \boldsymbol{g}^b_{k,i_\mu})$.

Since $\sum_{j \in \mathcal{U}^*} \langle \boldsymbol{r}_{k,j,i_\mu}, \boldsymbol{y}_k\rangle = \sum_{j \in \mathcal{U}^*} \langle \boldsymbol{r}_{j,i_\mu}, \boldsymbol{y}_k\rangle$, we have $\langle \boldsymbol{g}^0_{k,i_\mu}, \boldsymbol{y}_k\rangle = \langle \boldsymbol{g}^1_{k,i_\mu}, \boldsymbol{y}_k\rangle$. When $b = 0$, the adversary $\mathcal{B}_{2,\mu}$ simulates the game $G_{1,\mu-1}$. When $b = 1$, the adversary $\mathcal{B}_{2,\mu}$ simulates the game $G_{1,\mu}$. Thus, we have

$$\left|\mathsf{Adv}^{\mu-1}_{\mathcal{A}_\mu}(\lambda) - \mathsf{Adv}^{\mu}_{\mathcal{A}_\mu}(\lambda)\right| \le \mathsf{Adv}^{\mathsf{IND}}_{\mathsf{FE},\mathcal{B}_{2,\mu}}(\lambda).$$

To sum up, we have that there is an adversary $\mathcal{B}_2$ such that $\left|\mathsf{Adv}^1_{\mathcal{A}}(\lambda) - \mathsf{Adv}^2_{\mathcal{A}}(\lambda)\right| \le h_1 \cdot \mathsf{Adv}^{\mathsf{IND}}_{\mathsf{FE},\mathcal{B}_2}(\lambda)$. □

Lemma 11. *For every adversary $\mathcal{A}$, there is an adversary $\mathcal{B}_3$ against the sta-IND security of the scheme ID-MCFE such that*

$$\left|\mathsf{Adv}^2_{\mathcal{A}}(\lambda) - \mathsf{Adv}^3_{\mathcal{A}}(\lambda)\right| \le \mathsf{Adv}^{\mathsf{sta\text{-}IND}}_{\mathsf{ID\text{-}MCFE},\mathcal{B}_3}(\lambda).$$

Proof. This proof is similar to that of Lemma 8. □

The hybrid game of G_3 to G_4 is just the reverse of G_0 to G_2, so we have that

$$\left|\mathsf{Adv}^3_{\mathcal{A}}(\lambda) - \mathsf{Adv}^4_{\mathcal{A}}(\lambda)\right| \le mnh_1 \cdot \mathsf{Adv}^{\mathsf{IND}}_{\mathsf{SS},\mathcal{B}_1}(\lambda) + h_1 \cdot \mathsf{Adv}^{\mathsf{IND}}_{\mathsf{FE},\mathcal{B}_2}(\lambda).$$

6 Conclusion

In this paper, we first introduced a new cryptographic primitive named RDM-CFE, which allows the decryptor to evaluate the ciphertexts of a subset of clients. Then, we defined the robust correctness and robust security for Special IP-MCFE. Besides, we proposed two IP-RDMCFE constructions, where the basic construction is not reusable but exhibits small storage and communication overheads that remain independent of the vector length, while the enhanced construction achieves the reusability of secret keys at the cost of increasing storage and communication overheads.

Acknowledgements. We would like to thank the anonymous reviewers for their invaluable comments. This work is supported by the National Natural Science Foundation of China (Nos. 61960206014, 62121001 and 62172434), and China 111 Project (No. B16037). Willy Susilo was partially supported by the Australian Research Council (ARC) Discovery project (DP200100144) and the Australian Laureate Fellowship (FL230100033). Fuchun Guo was partially supported by the Australian Future Fellowship (FT220100046).

References

1. Abdalla, M., Bourse, F., De Caro, A., Pointcheval, D.: Simple functional encryption schemes for inner products. In: Katz, J. (ed.) PKC 2015. LNCS, vol. 9020, pp. 733–751. Springer, Heidelberg (2015). https://doi.org/10.1007/978-3-662-46447-2_33
2. Abdalla, M., Benhamouda, F., Gay, R.: From single-input to multi-client inner-product functional encryption. In: Galbraith, S.D., Moriai, S. (eds.) ASIACRYPT 2019. LNCS, vol. 11923, pp. 552–582. Springer, Cham (2019). https://doi.org/10.1007/978-3-030-34618-8_19
3. Abdalla, M., Benhamouda, F., Kohlweiss, M., Waldner, H.: Decentralizing inner-product functional encryption. In: Lin, D., Sako, K. (eds.) PKC 2019. LNCS, vol. 11443, pp. 128–157. Springer, Cham (2019). https://doi.org/10.1007/978-3-030-17259-6_5
4. Abdalla, M., Catalano, D., Fiore, D., Gay, R., Ursu, B.: Multi-input functional encryption for inner products: function-hiding realizations and constructions without pairings. In: Shacham, H., Boldyreva, A. (eds.) CRYPTO 2018. LNCS, vol. 10991, pp. 597–627. Springer, Cham (2018). https://doi.org/10.1007/978-3-319-96884-1_20
5. Agrawal, S., Clear, M., Frieder, O., Garg, S., O'Neill, A., Thaler, J.: Ad hoc multi-input functional encryption. In: Vidick, T. (ed.) ITCS 2020, vol. 151, pp. 40:1–40:41. Schloss Dagstuhl - Leibniz-Zentrum für Informatik (2022)
6. Abdalla, M., Catalano, D., Gay, R., Ursu, B.: Inner-product functional encryption with fine-grained access control. In: Moriai, S., Wang, H. (eds.) ASIACRYPT 2020. LNCS, vol. 12493, pp. 467–497. Springer, Cham (2020). https://doi.org/10.1007/978-3-030-64840-4_16
7. Angel, S., Chen, H., Laine, K., Setty, S.T.V.: PIR with compressed queries and amortized query processing. In: 2018 IEEE Symposium on Security and Privacy, pp. 962–979. IEEE Computer Society Press (2018)

8. Abdalla, M., Gay, R., Raykova, M., Wee, H.: Multi-input inner-product functional encryption from pairings. In: Coron, J.-S., Nielsen, J.B. (eds.) EUROCRYPT 2017. LNCS, vol. 10210, pp. 601–626. Springer, Cham (2017). https://doi.org/10.1007/978-3-319-56620-7_21
9. Agrawal, S., Goyal, R., Tomida, J.: Multi-input quadratic functional encryption from pairings. In: Malkin, T., Peikert, C. (eds.) CRYPTO 2021. LNCS, vol. 12828, pp. 208–238. Springer, Cham (2021). https://doi.org/10.1007/978-3-030-84259-8_8
10. Agrawal, S., Goyal, R., Tomida, J.: Multi-input quadratic functional encryption: Stronger security, broader functionality. In: Kiltz, E., Vaikuntanathan, V. (eds.) TCC 2022. LNCS, vol. 13747, pp. 711–740. Springer, Cham (2022). https://doi.org/10.1007/978-3-031-22318-1_25
11. Ananth, P., Jain, A.: Indistinguishability obfuscation from compact functional encryption. In: Gennaro, R., Robshaw, M. (eds.) CRYPTO 2015. LNCS, vol. 9215, pp. 308–326. Springer, Heidelberg (2015). https://doi.org/10.1007/978-3-662-47989-6_15
12. Ananth, P., Lombardi, A.: Succinct garbling schemes from functional encryption through a local simulation paradigm. In: Beimel, A., Dziembowski, S. (eds.) TCC 2018. LNCS, vol. 11240, pp. 455–472. Springer, Cham (2018). https://doi.org/10.1007/978-3-030-03810-6_17
13. Agrawal, S., Libert, B., Maitra, M., Titiu, R.: Adaptive simulation security for inner product functional encryption. In: Kiayias, A., Kohlweiss, M., Wallden, P., Zikas, V. (eds.) PKC 2020. LNCS, vol. 12110, pp. 34–64. Springer, Cham (2020). https://doi.org/10.1007/978-3-030-45374-9_2
14. Agrawal, S., Libert, B., Stehlé, D.: Fully secure functional encryption for inner products, from standard assumptions. In: Robshaw, M., Katz, J. (eds.) CRYPTO 2016. LNCS, vol. 9816, pp. 333–362. Springer, Heidelberg (2016). https://doi.org/10.1007/978-3-662-53015-3_12
15. Ananth, P., Sahai, A.: Projective arithmetic functional encryption and indistinguishability obfuscation from degree-5 multilinear maps. In: Coron, J.-S., Nielsen, J.B. (eds.) EUROCRYPT 2017. LNCS, vol. 10210, pp. 152–181. Springer, Cham (2017). https://doi.org/10.1007/978-3-319-56620-7_6
16. Bell, J.H., Bonawitz, K.A., Gascón, A., Lepoint, T., Raykova, M.: Secure single-server aggregation with (poly)logarithmic overhead. In: Ligatti J., Ou X., Katz J., Vigna G. (eds.) ACM CCS 2020, pp. 1253–1269. ACM Press (2020)
17. Benhamouda, F., Bourse, F., Lipmaa, H.: CCA-secure inner-product functional encryption from projective hash functions. In: Fehr, S. (ed.) PKC 2017. LNCS, vol. 10175, pp. 36–66. Springer, Heidelberg (2017). https://doi.org/10.1007/978-3-662-54388-7_2
18. Baltico, C.E.Z., Catalano, D., Fiore, D., Gay, R.: Practical functional encryption for quadratic functions with applications to predicate encryption. In: Katz, J., Shacham, H. (eds.) CRYPTO 2017. LNCS, vol. 10401, pp. 67–98. Springer, Cham (2017). https://doi.org/10.1007/978-3-319-63688-7_3
19. Badrinarayanan, S., Gupta, D., Jain, A., Sahai, A.: Multi-input functional encryption for unbounded arity functions. In: Iwata, T., Cheon, J.H. (eds.) ASIACRYPT 2015. LNCS, vol. 9452, pp. 27–51. Springer, Heidelberg (2015). https://doi.org/10.1007/978-3-662-48797-6_2
20. Bonawitz, K.A., et al.: Practical secure aggregation for privacy-preserving machine learning. In: Thuraisingham, B., Evans, D., Malkin, T., Xu, D. (eds.) ACM CCS 2017, pp. 1175–1191. ACM Press (2017)

21. Brakerski, Z., Komargodski, I., Segev, G.: Multi-input functional encryption in the private-key setting: stronger security from weaker assumptions. In: Fischlin, M., Coron, J.-S. (eds.) EUROCRYPT 2016, Part II. LNCS, vol. 9666, pp. 852–880. Springer, Heidelberg (2016)
22. Boneh, D., Sahai, A., Waters, B.: Functional encryption: definitions and challenges. In: Ishai, Y. (ed.) TCC 2011. LNCS, vol. 6597, pp. 253–273. Springer, Heidelberg (2011). https://doi.org/10.1007/978-3-642-19571-6_16
23. Chotard, J., Dufour-Sans, E., Gay, R., Phan, D.H., Pointcheval, D.: Dynamic decentralized functional encryption. In: Micciancio, D., Ristenpart, T. (eds.) CRYPTO 2020. LNCS, vol. 12170, pp. 747–775. Springer, Cham (2020). https://doi.org/10.1007/978-3-030-56784-2_25
24. Castagnos, G., Laguillaumie, F., Tucker, I.: Practical fully secure unrestricted inner product functional encryption modulo p. In: Peyrin, T., Galbraith, S. (eds.) ASIACRYPT 2018, Part II. LNCS, vol. 11273, pp. 733–764. Springer, Cham (2018)
25. Chotard, J., Dufour Sans, E., Gay, R., Phan, D.H., Pointcheval, D.: Decentralized multi-client functional encryption for inner product. In: Peyrin, T., Galbraith, S. (eds.) ASIACRYPT 2018. LNCS, vol. 11273, pp. 703–732. Springer, Cham (2018). https://doi.org/10.1007/978-3-030-03329-3_24
26. Fan, X., Tang, Q.: Making public key functional encryption function private, distributively. In: Abdalla, M., Dahab, R. (eds.) PKC 2018. LNCS, vol. 10770, pp. 218–244. Springer, Cham (2018). https://doi.org/10.1007/978-3-319-76581-5_8
27. Gay, R.: A new paradigm for public-key functional encryption for degree-2 polynomials. In: Kiayias, A., Kohlweiss, M., Wallden, P., Zikas, V. (eds.) PKC 2020. LNCS, vol. 12110, pp. 95–120. Springer, Cham (2020). https://doi.org/10.1007/978-3-030-45374-9_4
28. Goldwasser, S., Gordon, S.D., Goyal, V., Jain, A., Katz, J., Liu, F.-H., Sahai, A., Shi, E., Zhou, H.-S.: Multi-input functional encryption. In: Nguyen, P.Q., Oswald, E. (eds.) EUROCRYPT 2014. LNCS, vol. 8441, pp. 578–602. Springer, Heidelberg (2014). https://doi.org/10.1007/978-3-642-55220-5_32
29. Garg, S., Gentry, C., Halevi, S.: Candidate multilinear maps from ideal lattices. In: Johansson, T., Nguyen, P.Q. (eds.) EUROCRYPT 2013. LNCS, vol. 7881, pp. 1–17. Springer, Heidelberg (2013). https://doi.org/10.1007/978-3-642-38348-9_1
30. Garg, S., Gentry, C., Halevi, S., Raykova, M., Sahai, A., Waters, B.: Candidate indistinguishability obfuscation and functional encryption for all circuits. In: FOCS 2013, pp. 40–49. IEEE Computer Society Press (2013)
31. Goyal, V., Jain, A., O'Neill, A.: Multi-input Functional Encryption with Unbounded-Message Security. In: Cheon, J.H., Takagi, T. (eds.) ASIACRYPT 2016. LNCS, vol. 10032, pp. 531–556. Springer, Heidelberg (2016). https://doi.org/10.1007/978-3-662-53890-6_18
32. Lin, H., Tessaro, S.: Indistinguishability obfuscation from trilinear maps and block-wise local PRGs. In: Katz, J., Shacham, H. (eds.) CRYPTO 2017. LNCS, vol. 10401, pp. 630–660. Springer, Cham (2017). https://doi.org/10.1007/978-3-319-63688-7_21
33. Libert, B., Ţiţiu, R.: Multi-client functional encryption for linear functions in the standard model from LWE. In: Galbraith, S.D., Moriai, S. (eds.) ASIACRYPT 2019. LNCS, vol. 11923, pp. 520–551. Springer, Cham (2019). https://doi.org/10.1007/978-3-030-34618-8_18
34. Mera, J.M.B., Karmakar, A., Marc, T., Soleimanian, A.: Efficient lattice-based inner-product functional encryption. In: Hanaoka, G., Shikata, J., Watanabe, Y. (eds.) PKC 2022, Part II. LNCS, vol. 13178, pp. 163–193. Springer, Cham (2022). https://doi.org/10.1007/978-3-030-97131-1_6

35. Marc, T., Stopar, M., Hartman, J., Bizjak, M., Modic, J.: Privacy-enhanced machine learning with functional encryption. In: Sako, K., Schneider, S., Ryan, P.Y.A. (eds.) ESORICS 2019. LNCS, vol. 11735, pp. 3–21. Springer, Cham (2019). https://doi.org/10.1007/978-3-030-29959-0_1
36. Nguyen, K., Phan, D.H., Pointcheval, D.: Multi-client functional encryption with fine-grained access control. In: Agrawal, S., Lin, D. (eds.) ASIACRYPT 2022, Part I. LNCS, vol. 13791, pp. 95–125. Springer, Cham (2022). https://doi.org/10.1007/978-3-031-22963-3_4
37. Rogaway, P.: The Moral Character of Cryptographic Work. Cryptology ePrint Archive. Report 2015/1162 (2015). http://eprint.iacr.org/2015/1162
38. Ryffel, T., Pointcheval, D., Bach, F., Dufour-Sans, E., Gay, R.: Partially encrypted deep learning using functional encryption. In: Wallach, H.M., Larochelle, H., Beygelzimer, A., d'Alché-Buc, F., Fox, E.B., Garnett, R. (eds.) NeurIPS 2019, pp. 4519–4530. Canada (2019)
39. Wee, H.: Functional encryption for quadratic functions from k-Lin, revisited. In: Pass, R., Pietrzak, K. (eds.) TCC 2020. LNCS, vol. 12550, pp. 210–228. Springer, Cham (2020). https://doi.org/10.1007/978-3-030-64375-1_8

Cuckoo Commitments: Registration-Based Encryption and Key-Value Map Commitments for Large Spaces

Dario Fiore[1], Dimitris Kolonelos[1,2], and Paola de Perthuis[3,4](✉)

[1] IMDEA Software Institute, Madrid, Spain
{dario.fiore,dimitris.kolonelos}@imdea.org
[2] Universidad Politénica de Madrid, Madrid, Spain
[3] DIENS, École Normale Supérieure, CNRS, Inria, Université PSL, Paris, France
paola.de.perthuis@ens.fr
[4] Cosmian, Paris, France

Abstract. Registration-Based Encryption (RBE) [Garg et al. TCC'18] is a public-key encryption mechanism in which users generate their own public and secret keys, and register their public keys with a central authority called the key curator. Similarly to Identity-Based Encryption (IBE), in RBE users can encrypt by only knowing the public parameters and the public identity of the recipient. Unlike IBE, though, RBE does not suffer the key escrow problem—one of the main obstacles of IBE's adoption in practice—since the key curator holds no secret.

In this work, we put forward a new methodology to construct RBE schemes that support large users identities (i.e., arbitrary strings). Our main result is the first efficient pairing-based RBE for large identities. Prior to our work, the most efficient RBE is that of [Glaeser et al. ePrint' 22] which only supports small identities. The only known RBE schemes with large identities are realized either through expensive non-black-box techniques (ciphertexts of 3.6 TB for 1000 users), via a specialized lattice-based construction [Döttling et al. Eurocrypt'23] (ciphertexts of 2.4 GB), or through the more complex notion of Registered Attribute-Based Encryption [Hohenberger et al. Eurocrypt'23]. By unlocking the use of pairings for RBE with large identity space, we enable a further improvement of three orders of magnitude, as our ciphertexts for a system with 1000 users are 1.7 MB.

The core technique of our approach is a novel use of cuckoo hashing in cryptography that can be of independent interest. We give two main applications. The first one is the aforementioned RBE methodology, where we use cuckoo hashing to compile an RBE with small identities into one for large identities. The second one is a way to convert any vector commitment scheme into a key-value map commitment. For instance, this leads to the first algebraic pairing-based key-value map commitments.

J. Guo and R. Steinfeld (Eds.): ASIACRYPT 2023, LNCS 14442, pp. 166–200, 2023.
https://doi.org/10.1007/978-981-99-8733-7_6

1 Introduction

Registration-Based Encryption (RBE), introduced by Garg et al. [34], is a public key encryption mechanism in which users generate their own public and secret keys, and register their public keys with a central authority called the *Key Curator* (KC). The responsibility of the KC is to maintain the system's public parameters updated every time a new user joins. In RBE, Alice can send an encrypted message to Bob by only knowing the public parameters and Bob's identity. On the other hand, in order to decrypt, Bob uses his secret key and a small piece of information, *the opening*, that can be retrieved from the KC. An RBE scheme should have compact public parameters, and its algorithms for encryption and decryption should be sublinear in the number of registered users. In terms of security, RBE guarantees that messages encrypted under an identity id stay confidential (in a usual semantic security fashion) as long as id is an honest user or id did not register in the system.

Registration-based encryption can be seen as an hybrid between traditional Public-Key Encryption (PKE) [21,56] and Identity-Based Encryption (IBE) [57]. The most appealing feature of RBE is to remove the need of trusted parties, which is a common issue, for different reasons, in PKE and IBE. In IBE, a trusted authority is responsible to generate users' secret keys and thus can decrypt any message in the system, a problem known as key escrow. In traditional PKE, one needs a trusted authority, the PKI, in order to certify ownership of public keys; PKIs are however complex to implement and manage. In contrast, while an RBE system still involves an authority, the key curator, the main benefit is that *the KC does not hold any secret* and *its behavior is completely transparent*, to the point that it can be replicated (and thus audited) by any user in the system. Therefore, RBE can be a promising alternative to realize public key encryption with simple, safe, and transparent key management.

The approaches used to construct the first proposals of RBE [34,35] rely either on indistinguishability obfuscation or the garbled circuit tree technique of [17]. In spite of their power, these techniques are prohibitively expensive. For instance, based on estimations from [18] an RBE based on garbled circuits with a thousand users would have ciphertexts of 3.6 TB (which [18] can reduce by approximately 45%). As observed in [38], this high cost is (partially) due to their *non-black-box* use of cryptographic schemes—an approach that is notoriously expensive.

Two very recent works [24,38] have filled this gap by proposing efficient, *black-box* constructions of RBE that are based on bilinear pairings and lattices respectively. On the good side, the schemes of [24,38] achieve feasible efficiency—both report implementations confirming encryption and decryption time in the order of milliseconds, public parameters in the order of a few MBs. On the other hand, this efficiency profile comes at the price of some limitations. The work of Glaeser et al. [38] achieves their efficiency by limiting the identity space to the set of polynomial-size integers $\{1, \dots, n\}$. Although this identity space fits a few application scenarios (e.g., if identities are phone numbers), it rules out many more. In practice, the desiderata is to support identities that can be arbitrary strings (e.g., email addresses, arbitrary usernames). The work of Döttling et al. [24] manages to solve this issue. They propose an RBE construction for arbitrary identities based on the LWE problem. Nevertheless, their ciphertext size is still far from desirable in practice: for n registered users their ciphertexts consist of $\approx 2\lambda \log n$ LWE ciphertexts (concretely, 2.4 GB for a system with 1024 registered users).

Finally, another recent work, by Hohenberger et al. [40], introduces the notion of Registered Attribute-Based Encryption (R-ABE) and gives *black-box* constructions from composite-order bilinear groups. One can generically transform an R-ABE to an RBE scheme with unbounded identities. Unfortunately, the construction of of [40] inherits the complexity of the enhanced functionality of ABE, therefore the resulting RBE with unbounded identities would be overly complicated and concretely inefficient.

1.1 Our Contributions

In this work, we continue the line of research on constructing efficient and black-box registration-based encryption.

PAIRING-BASED RBE. Our main result is *the first RBE scheme for unbounded identity spaces that is black-box and based on prime-order bilinear groups.* The interest of an RBE from pairings is twofold. First, we show how to support large identities using an algebraic structure that is substantially more limited than lattices. Second, pairings lend themselves to efficient implementations and in fact our scheme achieves much shorter ciphertexts than the state-of-the-art RBE for large identities from [24]. Concretely, a ciphertext of our RBE is 1.67MB for 1024 users and identity space $\{0,1\}^{2\lambda}$. In other words, by unlocking the use of pairings for RBE with large identities we show yet another three-orders-of-magnitude improvement in this research line.

We should highlight that, as mentioned above, an RBE from pairings can also be constructed using the R-ABE scheme of [40]. However, it would be over composite order bilinear groups, where the order has an unknown factorization, making it less efficient and cumbersome for implementations.

We provide a comparison of our schemes with the state-of-the-art black-box constructions in Table 1. A thorough analysis of the table can be found in Sect. 5.1.

NOVEL CONSTRUCTION METHODOLOGY FOR RBE. To achieve this milestone, our technical contribution is a novel methodology to construct black-box RBE schemes that can accommodate exponentially large identity spaces, i.e., $\mathsf{id} \in \{0,1\}^*$. Prior to our work, this was a challenging problem solved either through the use of non-black-box techniques [34,35], via a specialized construction based on LWE [24] or going through the heavier notion of R-ABE. Our approach instead consists of a generic compiler that yields several RBE instantiations based on a variety of assumptions, in the random oracle model.

The core technique of our approach is a *novel use of cuckoo hashing* [51] in cryptography that can be of independent interest. Cuckoo hashing is a powerful

Table 1. Comparison of the schemes resulting from different instantiations of our compiler. n is the maximum number of users to be registered. Parings (P) indicates prime order groups and Pairings (C) composite order groups respectively. $|\mathsf{ct}|$ in the pairing construction is measured in group elements and in the Lattice constructions LWE ciphertexts.

	Setting	$\mathcal{ID}$	Compactness	$\lvert\mathsf{ct}\rvert$	#updates	$\lvert\mathsf{pp}\rvert + \lvert\mathsf{crs}\rvert$
[40]	Pairings (C)	$\{0,1\}^*$	Adaptive	$O(\lambda \log n)$	$\log n$	$O(\lambda n^{2/3} \log n)$
[38]	Pairings (P)	$[1, n]$	Adaptive	$4 \log n$	$\log n$	$O(\sqrt{n} \log n)$
Ours P1	Pairings (P)	$\{0,1\}^*$	Adaptive	$6\lambda \log n$	$\log n$	$O(\sqrt{\lambda n} \log n)$
Ours P2	Pairings (P)	$\{0,1\}^*$	Selective	$12 \log n$	$\log n$	$O(\sqrt{n} \log n)$
[24]	Lattices	$\{0,1\}^*$	Adaptive	$(2\lambda + 1) \log n$	$\log n$	$O(\log n)$
Ours L	Lattices	$\{0,1\}^*$	Selective	$4 \log^2 n$	$\log n$	$O(\log n)$

(probabilistic) technique to store elements from a large universe $\mathcal{X}$ into a small table $\boldsymbol{T}$ so that one can later access them in constant-time. Concretely, the latter means that for an element x the cuckoo hash returns $k = O(1)$ possible locations of $\boldsymbol{T}$ where to find x; the cuckoo hashing algorithms take care of resolving collisions by reallocating elements in $\boldsymbol{T}$ whenever a collision occurs.

In this work, we present a compiler that takes an RBE scheme for a polynomial-size identity space $\overline{\mathcal{ID}} = \{1, \ldots, n\}$ and boosts it to become an RBE for large identity space $\mathcal{ID} = \{0,1\}^*$. We start with the idea of using cuckoo hashing to map identities in $\mathcal{ID}$ to polynomial-size integers in $\overline{\mathcal{ID}}$ so that user id becomes user $H(\mathsf{id})$ in the underlying RBE. Unsurprisingly, this simple idea does not work straightforwardly. The main obstacle is that the cuckoo hashing algorithms "move" elements around different locations during the lifetime of the system. This implies that a user id assigned to location $j = H(\mathsf{id})$ might decrypt ciphertexts that were previously generated for another user id^* that was assigned to the same location j in the past. In our compiler, we resolve these "collisions" thanks to a novel combination of the RBE with *Witness Encryption for Vector Commitments* (WE for VC), and a secret sharing scheme. A Vector Commitment (VC) scheme [15,48] allows one to compute a short commitment to a vector $\boldsymbol{v}$ and later locally open at a specific position j. A WE for VC is a special-purpose witness encryption [33] thanks to which a party can encrypt a message m w.r.t. a commitment C, position j, and value y, and m can be decrypted by anyone holding a valid opening of C at the correct value $y = v_j$. Interestingly, we show how to construct this class of WE based on well established assumptions over pairings (DHE [8]) and lattices (LWE [55]). We refer to our technical overview (Sect. 2) for more details.

Additional contributions. To confirm the power of our cuckoo hashing technique, we show additional results that we discuss hereafter.

New lattice-based RBE. Through our RBE compiler, we also obtain new RBE schemes based on LWE. We do this by instantiating the RBE of [24] with a small identity space and then boosting it to large identities through our compiler. This instantiation though does not improve over the large-identity instantiation of [24]; this is due to the fact that we need a robust[1] cuckoo hash [62] that produces $k = \lambda$ indices for every element and blows our ciphertexts by a factor λ. Interestingly, though, we need the robustness property of cuckoo hashing only to ensure that the public parameters stay polylogarithmic *in the worst case*. Based on this observation, we can also use a (non-robust) cuckoo hashing where $k = 2$ and obtain an LWE-based RBE that has shorter ciphertexts than [24] (ours has of $4 \log^2 n$ LWE encryptions, as opposed to $2\lambda \log n$). Our RBE scheme is correct and secure, but achieves compact parameters only against selective adversaries. We refer to Sect. 4.4 for more details on this compactness model.

APPLICATION TO KEY-VALUE MAP COMMITMENTS AND ACCUMULATORS. Based on the cuckoo hashing idea described above, we present a construction that compiles *any* vector commitment into a key-value map commitment (KVC) [1,7] for arbitrary-size keys. In a nutshell, a KVC is a generalization of VCs in which one commits to a collection of key-value pairs $(\mathsf{k}_i, \mathsf{v}_i)$, i.e., VCs are a special case where keys are integers in $\{1, \ldots, n\}$. Thus the interesting problem is to realize KVCs with large keys, e.g., $\mathsf{k} \in \{0,1\}^*$. Existing schemes are based on hidden-order groups [1,7], Merkle trees or, very recently, lattices [14].[2] In Sect. 6, we present a generic and black-box construction of (updatable) KVC obtained by combining any (updatable) VC and cuckoo hashing. Through this generic construction, we obtain new efficient KVCs; notably, the first updatable KVCs for large keys based on pairings.

Finally, we observe that KVCs (for large keys) imply accumulators (for large universe). By putting this observation together with our VC-to-KVC compiler, we obtain a way to convert VCs into accumulators. This connection was previously shown by Catalano and Fiore in [15] *but only for small universe*. Our results thus bridge this gap. Furthermore, we close the circle in showing the equivalence of VCs and universal accumulators, since the reversed implication (i.e., building VCs from universal accumulators) has been recently shown by Boneh, Bunz and Fisch [7]. An outstanding implication is that our result yields the first accumulator for large universe based on the CDH problem in bilinear groups. Prior to our work, this result could only be achieved by using non-black-box techniques (e.g., a Merkle tree with a CDH-based VC).

CUCKOO HASHING APPLICATIONS. Cuckoo Hashing has been used extensively in many contexts in cryptography, mainly to boost efficiency in oblivious two-party computations (*e.g.* in [2,52–54]). However, in most of these contexts, due to the oblivious security model, the adversary does not have direct access to the cuckoo hash functions. Only recently, a new work has discussed cuckoo hashing in this perspective [62].

---

1 Informally, a CH is robust if its correctness error is negligible for adversarially chosen inputs; standard correctness holds only for inputs chosen before public parameters.

2 One can also use polynomial commitments, e.g., [42], in combination with interpolation but to the best of our knowledge this KVC is not updatable.

In our work, we propose new cryptographic applications where cuckoo hashes can be publicly computed. In a way, our results show how vector commitment techniques can mitigate the shortcomings of publicly computable cuckoo hashing, as combining them with vector commitments enable their use while keeping constructions succinct and efficient. We believe that this approach can serve as inspiration for future applications.

1.2 Related Work

Registered Encryption Primitives. As we mentioned, the first works on registration-based encryption (with large identities) were non-black box: [34] introduced the notion, [35] showed a construction with more efficient registration computational complexity, [39] introduced the notion of *verifiability* for RBE and [18] improved the efficiency of the previous works by replacing the Merkle tree with a form of PATRICIA trie. Lately, there has been an increasing interest in generalizing RBE to registered fine-grained encryption such as Registered Attribute-Based Encryption [40] and Registered Functional Encryption [19,29].

Cuckoo Hashing in Cryptography. Cuckoo hashing has been used in Cryptography in oblivious access primitives such as Oblivious RAM [53], Private Set Intersection [54], Private Information Retrieval [2], and Searchable Encryption [52]. Recently, Yeo gave a formal treatment from a cryptographic perspective [62], again with the objective of discussing applications to PIR. To the best of our knowledge, our work is the first that uses cuckoo hashing in the context of fine-grained encryption and commitment schemes.

Key-Value Map Commitments and Accumulators. The notion Key-Value Map Commitments was introduced by Boneh et al. [7] where they also presented a construction from Groups of Unknown order. Different KVC constructions from Groups of Unknown order exist [1,12]. KVCs can also be realized by Merkle Trees. Recently deCastro and Peikert [14] showed a construction from Lattices.

Accumulators were introduced by Benaloh and de Mare [5]. Constructions for large universe exist from RSA groups [4,10], Groups of Unknown Order [7,49], q-type assumptions in bilinear groups [50], and Merkle trees. The recent work of de Castro and Peikert [14] also implies an accumulator from lattices.

Lite-WE Flavors. Witness Encryption for Merkle trees implicitly appears in [17,22,34], using non-black box techniques (Garbling). Witness Encryption flavors for special purpose relation, with the objective to have a more efficient instantiation, have also been introduced in prior works [6,11,13,23]

2 Technical Overview

We give here an informal overview of the techniques that we introduce in this work to obtain our Registration-Based Encryption (RBE) and Key-Value Map

Commitments (KVC) results. To put some context, we recall first Vector Commitments [15,48] a fundamental primitive for both RBE and KVC.

Vector Commitments. A Vector Commitment (VC) is a cryptographic primitive with which one can commit to a vector of elements in such a way that, at a later point, one can selectively open any position of the vector. Importantly, the commitments and the openings should be succinct (sublinear or polylogarithmic) in the size of the vector. The simplest form of VCs are Merkle trees.

We guide the reader through an example, the Libert-Yung VC [48], that we will also use in this work. It works over pairings, using a common reference string (CRS) $\mathsf{crs} = (g^{\alpha}, \ldots, g^{\alpha^n}, g^{\alpha^{n+2}}, \ldots, g^{\alpha^{2n}})$ and we denote $g_i = g^{\alpha^i}$. Committing to a vector $\boldsymbol{x} = (x_1, \ldots, x_n)$ happens as $C = \prod_{i\in[n]} g_i^{x_i}$. To open the position i (to value x_i) we compute $\Lambda_i = \prod_{j\neq i}(g_{n+1-i+j})^{x_j}$. For the verification of the opening we check if $e(C, g_{n+1-i}) = e(\Lambda_i, g) \cdot e(g_i^{x_i}, g_{n+1-i})$. The VC is position binding under the n-Diffie-Hellman Exponent assumption [8], a well-established q-type (falsifiable) assumption. Observe that C, Λ are just a single group element each, and the verification time is independent of the size of the vector.

2.1 Registration-Based Encryption with Unbounded Identity Space

Prior Black-Box RBE Constructions. To date, the only RBE constructions that are black-box (i.e., they do not encode cryptographic operations in the circuit of another cryptographic primitive such as a Garbled Circuit) are the ones of Glaeser et al. [38] (henceforth GMKMR) and Döttling et al. [24] (henceforth DKLLMR). The former works over pairings and the latter over lattices. For the sake of this overview we are only concerned with the former RBE. Furthermore, to simplify the exposition we omit efficiency tricks that retain the efficiency properties (compactness, number of updates) of RBE. We discuss them extensively in the main body of our work.

The GKMR RBE. The GKMR RBE [38] roughly works as follows. It uses [48] as an underlying vector commitment in order to commit (in a compressing way) to the public keys of all the users.

In more detail, the user i samples a secret key sk_i randomly and sends $\mathsf{pk}_i = g_i^{\mathsf{sk}_i}$ to the Key Curator (KC). Then the KC compresses the public keys of all users by computing $C = \prod_{i\in[n]} \mathsf{pk}_i = \prod_{i\in[n]} g_i^{\mathsf{sk}_i}$, and sets the public parameters as $\mathsf{pp} \leftarrow C$. In essence, C is a vector commitment to the vector of the secret keys $\mathbf{sk} = (\mathsf{sk}_1, \ldots, \mathsf{sk}_n)$ of all registered user.

GKMR introduced a simple technique to encrypt a message $m \in \mathbb{G}_T$ to the user i by only having C and, crucially, without having pk_i: Recalling that $e(C, g_{n+1-i}) = e(\Lambda_i, g) \cdot e(g_i^{\mathsf{sk}_i}, g_{n+1-i})$, one defines the ciphertext as $(\mathsf{ct}_1, \mathsf{ct}_2, \mathsf{ct}_3) = (g^r, e(C, g_{n+1-i})^r, e(g_i, g_{n+1-i})^r \cdot m)$. Observe that $e(C, g_{n+1-i})^r = e(\Lambda_i, g)^r \cdot e(g_i, g_{n+1-i})^{r\cdot\mathsf{sk}_i}$, and thus $\left(\mathsf{ct}_2 \cdot e(\Lambda_i, \mathsf{ct}_1)^{-1}\right)^{\mathsf{sk}_i^{-1}} = \mathsf{ct}_3/m$. Hence, the user i, knowing sk_i and additionally Λ_i, can decrypt as $m^* = \mathsf{ct}_3/\left(\mathsf{ct}_2 \cdot e(\Lambda_i, \mathsf{ct}_1)^{-1}\right)^{\mathsf{sk}_i^{-1}}$.

In RBE terms, Λ_i represents the update information of user i that should be periodically fetched from the KC (whenever it is changed). The final note is that naively computing $\Lambda_i = \prod_{j \neq i}(g_{n+1-i+j})^{\mathsf{sk}_j}$ would need knowledge of **sk** to be computed. However, each user j can compute the cross-terms $(g_{n+1-i+j})^{\mathsf{sk}_j}$ for each $i \neq j$ previously registered, and send them to the KC to enable the KC to compute the Λ_i's. We summarize the GKMR RBE below:

$$\mathsf{crs} = \{g, g^{\alpha}, \ldots, g^{\alpha^N}, g^{\alpha^{N+2}}, \ldots, g^{2N}\}; \qquad \mathsf{pk}_i = g_i^{\mathsf{sk}_i};$$

$$\mathsf{pp} = C := g_1^{\mathsf{sk}_1} g_2^{\mathsf{sk}_2} \ldots g_N^{\mathsf{sk}_N}; \qquad \mathsf{u}_i = \Lambda_i := \prod_{j \neq i}(g_{N+1-i+j})^{\mathsf{sk}_j};$$

$$\mathsf{ct} = \left(g^r, e(C, g_{N+1-i})^r, e(g_i, g^{N+1-i})^r \cdot m\right); \quad m^* = \mathsf{ct}_3 / \left(\mathsf{ct}_2 \cdot e(\Lambda_i, \mathsf{ct}_1)^{-1}\right)^{\mathsf{sk}_i^{-1}}.$$

The Limitation of Bounded Identities. In the scheme above, i plays the role of the user's identity. It is apparent from the construction that i should lie in $[1, n]$ and since the CRS is linear in n, n must be polynomially bounded, and so must be the RBE identity space. This limitation is acknowledged in [38] and is the main drawback of the, otherwise highly efficient, scheme.

In the following we describe our technique to overcome this limitation.

Our Approach: Cuckoo Hashing. One may be tempted to use a hash function to map larger identities to $[1, n]$. However, naively this cannot work because of collisions: since $[1, n]$ is polynomial-size collisions are inevitable.

Our idea is to use Cuckoo Hashing (CH) [51] for the mapping $\{0,1\}^* \rightarrow [1, n]$. Cuckoo Hashing is a powerful (probabilistic) technique to store elements from a large universe $\mathcal{X}$ in a small table $\boldsymbol{T}$ in constant time so that one can later efficiently access them, in constant time. Hence it is an inherent method to deal with collisions in a small space.

To put some context, we describe a simple version of Cuckoo Hashing with a stash [44]. For this, we have 2 hash functions h_1, h_2, a table $\boldsymbol{T}$ of size $4n$ and a (unordered) set S, called the 'stash'. To insert a new element x, one first computes $x^{(1)} = h_1(x)$ and if $\boldsymbol{T}[x^{(1)}] = \mathsf{empty}$ then stores x in $\boldsymbol{T}[x^{(1)}]$. Otherwise, if $\boldsymbol{T}[x^{(1)}] = y$ then x 'evicts' y; namely, x is stored in $\boldsymbol{T}[x^{(1)}]$ and y is inserted in $\boldsymbol{T}[y^{(2)}]$ (assume for this example that y was previously 'sent' to $\boldsymbol{T}[x^{(1)}]$ using h_1). Subsequently, if $\boldsymbol{T}[y^{(2)}]$ is occupied by z then y 'evicts' z, and z gets sent to the location specified by the alternative hash function. Observe that one always begin with h_1 for a new element and when the element is evicted always uses the next hash function (and if the last is reached, then the first one again). This procedure continues until either an empty position is found or M attempts have been made. If the latter event occurs, then the last element that was evicted gets stored in the stash S. It can be shown that for random hash functions h_1, h_2, if $M = O(\lambda \log n)$ then the size of the stash is in $O(\log n)$ with overwhelming probability [3].

There are many variants of the above mechanism: Cuckoo Hashing with $k > 2$ hash functions [27] or having tables where every position/bucket has capacity

$\ell > 1$ [20]. We refer to [61] for an insightful systematization of knowledge and [62] for an overview from a cryptographic perspective.

In our work, we formally define a *Cuckoo Hashing scheme* in a cryptographic manner in Sect. 3.2, closely following the definitions of [62]. For the rest, we mostly treat Cuckoo Hashing as a black-box, assuming that it uses k hash functions with buckets of size $\ell = 1$.

Cuckoo Hashing in RBE. Now let's see how one would use Cuckoo Hashing in the above RBE scheme in order to map large identities $\mathsf{id} \in \{0,1\}^*$ to small representatives in $[1, n]$. From now on, we denote $\mathsf{id}^{(\eta)} = h_\eta(\mathsf{id})$ for short.

A user id who wishes to register in the system, computes $\mathsf{id}^{(1)} = h_1(\mathsf{id}), \ldots, \mathsf{id}^{(k)} = h_k(\mathsf{id})$, samples k different secret keys $\mathsf{sk}^{(1)}, \ldots, \mathsf{sk}^{(k)}$ and sends the corresponding public keys $g_{\mathsf{id}^{(1)}}^{\mathsf{sk}^{(1)}}, \ldots, g_{\mathsf{id}^{(k)}}^{\mathsf{sk}^{(k)}}$ to the KC. Then the KC inserts id in the system by Cuckoo Hashing it (KC keeps the table $\boldsymbol{T}$ of currently hashed identities). Assuming that id is eventually stored in $\boldsymbol{T}$ at position $\mathsf{id}^{(\eta)}$, KC has $\mathsf{pk}_{\mathsf{id}^{(\eta)}}$. To give an example, a potential instance of such a system could be:

$$
\begin{array}{rcccccccc}
C = & g_1^{\mathsf{sk}_b^{(2)}} & \cdot\, 1 \cdot & g_3^{\mathsf{sk}_a^{(1)}} & \cdot\, g_4^{\mathsf{sk}_e^{(3)}} & \cdot\, g_5^{\mathsf{sk}_c^{(1)}} & \cdot\, 1 \cdot 1 \cdot & g_8^{\mathsf{sk}_d^{(2)}} \\
\Big(\mathsf{sk} = (& \mathsf{sk}_b^{(2)}, & 0, & \mathsf{sk}_a^{(1)}, & \mathsf{sk}_e^{(3)}, & \mathsf{sk}_c^{(1)}, & 0, 0, & \mathsf{sk}_d^{(2)})\Big) \\
\boldsymbol{T} = (& b, & 0, & a, & e, & c, & 0, 0, & d) \\
\hline
 & 1 & 2 & 3 & 4 & 5 & 6\ 7 & 8
\end{array}
$$

where $n = 8$, a, b, c, d, e are identities and $h_2(b) = 1$, $h_1(a) = 3$, $h_3(e) = 4$, $h_1(c) = 5$, $h_2(d) = 8$ (recall, sk is not known explicitly to the KC; and to highlight this is written with brackets in the examples).

Until now, we have resolved the collisions in a pragmatic way: thanks to cuckoo hashing, no collisions of identities are stored in the public parameters. This is however not clear from the Encryptor's perspective. The Encryptor wishing to encrypt for id does not have $\boldsymbol{T}$ and thus does not know in which position among $\mathsf{id}^{(1)}, \ldots, \mathsf{id}^{(k)}$ the identity is placed. Hence, she does not know which position to encrypt for, and could compromise security by encrypting for a position occupied by another identity id', in which case id' would read the message intended for id.

The Missing Piece: Witness Encryption for Vector Commitments. To solve the issue explained above, our approach is to use another Vector Commitment, D, this time to commit to the actual table $\boldsymbol{T}$ of identities rather than the secret keys. The above example is modified as follows:

$$
\begin{array}{rcccccccc}
C = & g_1^{\mathsf{sk}_b^{(2)}} & \cdot\, 1 \cdot & g_3^{\mathsf{sk}_a^{(1)}} & \cdot\, g_4^{\mathsf{sk}_e^{(3)}} & \cdot\, g_5^{\mathsf{sk}_c^{(1)}} & \cdot\, 1 \cdot 1 \cdot & g_8^{\mathsf{sk}_d^{(2)}} \\
\Big(\mathsf{sk} = (& \mathsf{sk}_b^{(2)}, & 0, & \mathsf{sk}_a^{(1)}, & \mathsf{sk}_e^{(3)}, & \mathsf{sk}_c^{(1)}, & 0, 0, & \mathsf{sk}_d^{(2)})\Big) \\
D = & g_1^b \cdot & 1 \cdot & g_3^a \cdot & g_4^e \cdot & g_5^c \cdot & 1 \cdot 1 \cdot & g_8^d \\
\boldsymbol{T} = (& b, & 0, & a, & e, & c, & 0, 0, & d) \\
\hline
 & 1 & 2 & 3 & 4 & 5 & 6\ 7 & 8
\end{array}
$$

For such a configuration of the system, the wish is a cryptographic primitive that allows encrypting, when having in hands only D and the target id, and that should work as follows: If $\boldsymbol{T}[\mathsf{id}^{(\eta)}] = \mathsf{id}$ is in the committed vector, then anyone having the corresponding opening $\Psi_{\mathsf{id}^{(\eta)}}$ can decrypt. Otherwise, if $\boldsymbol{T}[\mathsf{id}^{(\eta)}] \neq \mathsf{id}$ then the ciphertext is computationally indistinguishable for everyone.[3]

This mechanism is reminiscent of Witness Encryption (WE) [33], but only for a specific NP language and a slightly different notion of security. We formalize such a primitive and call it *Witness Encryption for Vector Commitments* (VCWE, see Sect. 4.1). Using a VCWE, the encryptor can:

1. Secret share the message m into two shares m_1, m_2
2. Encrypt m_1 for the position $\mathsf{id}^{(1)}$ using the above RBE for small identities.
3. Encrypt m_2 with the VCWE for commitment D, position $\mathsf{id}^{(1)}$, value id.

and repeat this *for every possible position* of id in the table, i.e. $\mathsf{id}^{(2)}, \ldots, \mathsf{id}^{(k)}$.

To argue the security of this idea, we note that:

- If $\boldsymbol{T}[\mathsf{id}^{(\eta)}] = \mathsf{id}$, then *everybody* can decrypt the second part of ciphertext (for security, we consider that $\boldsymbol{T}$ and thus $\Psi_{\mathsf{id}^{(\eta)}}$ are public) and obtain m_2. On the other hand, $\boldsymbol{T}[\mathsf{id}^{(\eta)}] = \mathsf{id}$ means that the 'correct' user is registered in that position, hence only id can obtain the first share m_1.
- If $\boldsymbol{T}[\mathsf{id}^{(\eta)}] \neq \mathsf{id}$ then *nobody* can decrypt the second part of the ciphertext and obtain m_2. This follows from the security of VCWE.

VCWE Constructions. Witness Encryption for all NP is notoriously hard to achieve in efficient ways with currently known constructions from multilinear maps [33,36], indistinguishability obfuscation [32,41] or, recently, non-standard non-falsifiable lattice assumptions [58,59].

Nevertheless, it turns out that for the specific relation above, there are surprisingly simple and efficient black-box solutions. Therefore, the VCWE ciphertext imposes a minimal overhead to the size of the overall ciphertext. In Sect. 5, we provide two simple VCWE schemes, over Pairings and Lattices respectively.

Final RBE Scheme. In conclusion the Cuckoo Hashing technique in combination with the VCWE allow us to have a secure RBE with unbounded identities.

Dealing with the Stash. Finally, if the CH scheme has a stash S, then we demand that this stash is small (polylogarithmic or sublinear). This is because we store $S = \{(\mathsf{pk}_1, \mathsf{id}_1), \ldots, (\mathsf{pk}_s, \mathsf{id}_s)\}$ in the public parameters, and anyone who wants to encrypt w.r.t an id_i in the stash can do it, using a regular Public Key Encryption scheme. As we discuss in Sect. 3.2 there are CH schemes that have $|S| = \log n$ or even $|S| = 0$ even in the worst case.

[3] We note that if $\boldsymbol{T}[\mathsf{id}^{(\eta)}] \neq \mathsf{id}$ then from position-binding of the VC no PPT party can compute a Ψ that verifies for id in position $\mathsf{id}^{(\eta)}$.

2.2 Generalization and Other Implications

General Compiler. It is not difficult to see that the procedure described above, to enlarge the identity space, in a semi-generic way through the GKMR RBE, can be generalized. That is, we give a generic compiler that boosts *any* RBE scheme with small identity to one with large identity space, using Cuckoo Hashing, and Witness Encryption for Vector Commitments.

Lattice-Based RBE with Shorter Ciphertexts. Our general compiler applies naturally to Lattice-Based RBE schemes. As previously mentioned, the DKLLMR RBE scheme [24] already allows for unbounded identities.

In spite of this, their ciphertext size is logarithmic in the size of the identity space: $|\mathsf{ct}| = \log(|\mathcal{ID}|) \log n$ LWE ciphertexts. This stems from the fact that their construction works with a (sparse) Merkle tree with one leaf per element of $\mathcal{ID}$, thus $|\mathcal{ID}|$ leaves, and then the ciphertext is roughly one LWE ciphertext per level of the tree. For a virtually unbounded identity space we need $\mathcal{ID} = \{0,1\}^{2\lambda}$ (so that we can use a collision resistant hash function $H : \{0,1\}^* \to \{0,1\}^{2\lambda}$), meaning $|\mathsf{ct}| = 2\lambda \log n$. This means that there is a Merkle tree with $2^{2\lambda}$ leaves, while only $n = \mathsf{poly}(\lambda)$ are going to be occupied.

Our idea is the following: Say that we want to support $n = \mathsf{poly}(\lambda)$ users, then we could start from a DKLLMR RBE with exactly n leaves (i.e. bounded identities), thus $|\mathsf{ct}| = \log^2 n$. Then we could apply our compiler to boost it to a full-fledged RBE with unbounded identities. Our hope is that, after applying our compiler, we could obtain an RBE with smaller ciphertexts than DKLLMR instantiated for $\mathcal{ID} = \{0,1\}^{2\lambda}$.

Our general compiler yields about $2k|\mathsf{ct}|$-sized ciphertexts (assuming that VCWE has roughly the same size as RBE which turns out to be the case, see the full version [26]). If we desire our RBE to have adversarial compactness then for technical reason related to CH (see the full version [26])we need to fix $k = \lambda$. This unfortunately does not let us achieve an improvement. However, if one relaxes compactness to hold only against selective adversaries, meaning adversaries who need to choose the set of identities they wish to register before seeing the Cuckoo hash functions, one can set $k = 2$ and obtain a significant improvement: $|\mathsf{ct}| \approx 4\log^2$ in constant to $2\lambda \log n$ (initial DKLLMR), which concretely saves an $\frac{\lambda}{2\log n}$ factor from the ciphertext. We defer the discussion and the formal definition of this selective notion to the full version [26].

2.3 Key-Value Map Commitments and Accumulators

Finally, we informally describe how we can use our cuckoo hashing technique in the context of vector commitments, specifically to transform *any* VC scheme into a key-value map commitment for keys from a large space.

Assuming one needs to commit to a key-value map consisting of n key-value pairs $(\mathsf{k}_i, \mathsf{v}_i)$ for $i = 1$ to n, one can "cuckoo hash" all the keys so as to obtain a table $\boldsymbol{T}$, a vector, that stores all the keys at certain positions. Then, one can compute a vector commitment C_T to $\boldsymbol{T}$ and another vector commitment C_V to a vector $\boldsymbol{V}$ built in such a way that $\boldsymbol{V}[j]$ stores a value v if the key k associated to v is stored in $\boldsymbol{T}[j]$. Namely, each pair $(\mathsf{k}_i, \mathsf{v}_i)$ is stored in $\boldsymbol{T}$ and $\boldsymbol{V}$ at the *same* position j. By correctness of cuckoo hashing, for every k such an index j exists. In order to open the commitment (C_T, C_V) to a key k one can use cuckoo hashing to find the set of h candidate indices $(j_1, \ldots, j_h)$ where k is (potentially) stored and open C_T at those positions, to find the index j^* such that $\boldsymbol{T}[j^*] = \mathsf{k}$. One then also opens C_V to position j^* and its value v. The verifier then would run similarly: for a key-value (k, v), she runs the cuckoo hashing to find out $(j_1, \ldots, j_h)$ associated to k, verify the openings of C_T to $(\boldsymbol{T}[j_1], \ldots, \boldsymbol{T}[j_h])$, and the opening of C_V to v in the position j^* such that $\boldsymbol{T}[j^*] = \mathsf{k}$. For security it is essential that all $(j_1, \ldots, j_h$ of (C_T, C_V) are opened so that the fact that k is stored in exactly one position can be verified.

In Sect. 6 we give more details on other technicalities of this construction, such as how to: deal with elements in the stash, prove that a key is not committed, reduce key-binding to the position binding of the VC. Notably, this transformation is black-box, *i.e.*, it works by only invoking the algorithms of the underlying VC. This stands in contrast to, *e.g.*, Verkle tree approaches [16,45].

3 Preliminaries

Notation. An integer $\lambda \in \mathbb{N}$ will denote the security parameter, $\mathsf{poly}(\lambda)$ and $\mathsf{negl}(\lambda)$ polynomial and negligible functions respectively. Vectors are written in bold font (*e.g.* $\boldsymbol{v}$), and given vectors $\boldsymbol{v}_1, \ldots, \boldsymbol{v}_m$, $\mathbf{cat}((\boldsymbol{v}_1, \ldots, \boldsymbol{v}_m))$ will be the vector of concatenated vectors $\boldsymbol{v}_1 \| \ldots \| \boldsymbol{v}_m$. For any positive integer $n \in \mathbb{Z}$ we denote by $[n]$ the set of integers $\{1, \ldots, n\}$ and, more generally, by $[A, B]$ the set $\{A, \ldots, B\}$ for any $A, B \in \mathbb{Z}$, $A \leq B$. $x \xleftarrow{\$} X$ will mean that x is being uniformly sampled from a finite set X. Throughout this work "PPT" stands for Probabilistic Polynomial-Time.

3.1 Public Key Encryption

Public-Key Encryption (PKE) allows all users aware of some public information to encrypt messages that only some users aware of secret information will be able to decrypt to access these messages. It has extensively been used and developed in cryptography during the last fifty years. In short, a PKE scheme PKE consists of three algorithms:

- $\mathsf{PKE.KeyGen}(1^\lambda)$: this algorithm outputs a public key pk and a secret key sk to use in the scheme with security on λ bits;
- $\mathsf{PKE.Enc}(\mathsf{pk}, m)$: the encryption algorithm outputs a ciphertext C encrypting the message m using the public key pk;
- $\mathsf{PKE.Dec}(\mathsf{sk}, C)$: this algorithm returns the message m encrypted in the ciphertext C using the secret key sk.

3.2 Cuckoo Hashing

Cuckoo Hashing (CH) [51] is a technique to store a set of m elements from a large universe $\mathcal{X}$ into a linear-size data structure that allows efficient memory accesses. In our work we abstract away the properties of a family of cuckoo hashing constructions that can be used in our RBE and KVC constructions. We do this by defining the notion of *Cuckoo Hashing schemes*. Our definition is a variant of the one recently offered by Yeo [62]; in our definition, we use *deterministic* Insert algorithms.

In a nutshell, a cuckoo hashing scheme inserts n elements $x_1, \ldots, x_n \in \mathcal{X}$ in a vector $\boldsymbol{T}$ so that each element x_i can be found exactly once in $\boldsymbol{T}$, or in a stash set S. The efficient memory access comes from the fact that for a given x one can efficiently compute the k indices $i_1, \ldots, i_k$ such that $x \in \{\boldsymbol{T}[i_1], \ldots, \boldsymbol{T}[i_k]\} \cup S$. The idea of cuckoo hashing constructions is to sample k random hash functions $H_1, \ldots, H_k : \mathcal{X} \rightarrow [n]$ and use them to allocate x in one of the k indices $H_1(x), \ldots, H_k(x)$. Each construction uses a specific algorithm to search the index allocated to x, requiring to move existing elements whenever a position is going to be allocated to another element. The most efficient algorithms are local search allocation [43] and random walks [28,30,31,60,62].

We define a Cuckoo Hashing scheme with the following algorithms:

Definition 1 (Cuckoo Hashing Schemes Algorithms). *A Cuckoo Hashing scheme* $\mathsf{CH} = (\mathsf{Setup}, \mathsf{Insert}, \mathsf{Lookup})$ *consists of the following algorithms:*

- $\mathsf{Setup}(1^\lambda, \mathcal{X}, n) \rightarrow (\mathsf{pp}, \boldsymbol{T}, S)$: *is a probabilistic algorithm that on input the security parameter, the space of input values* $\mathcal{X}$ *and a bound* n *on the number of insertions, outputs public parameters* pp, $k \geq 2$, *an empty vector* $\boldsymbol{T}$ *with* N *entries (with* N *a multiple of* k*), along with an empty stash set* S*, (denoting* $s \geq 0$ *its size, at this point,* $s = 0$*);*
- $\mathsf{Insert}(\mathsf{pp}, \boldsymbol{T}, S, x_1, \ldots, x_m) \rightarrow (\boldsymbol{T}', S')$: *is a deterministic algorithm that on input vector* $\boldsymbol{T}$ *where each non-empty component contains an element in* $\mathcal{X} \in \mathsf{pp}$*, inserts each* $x_1, \ldots, x_m \in \mathcal{X}$ *in the vector exactly once and returns the updated vector with moved elements,* $\boldsymbol{T}', S'$*.*
- $\mathsf{Lookup}(\mathsf{pp}, x) \rightarrow (i_1, \ldots, i_k)$: *is a deterministic algorithm that on input public parameters* pp *and* $x \in \mathcal{X}$*, returns* $(i_1, \ldots, i_k)$*, the candidate indices where* x *could be stored.*

Remark 1. Our Cuckoo Hashing schemes are, overall, probabilistic with the probability taken over the choice of pp. Once pp is fixed, everything is deterministic; Insert and Lookup, that take pp as input, are deterministic algorithms.

Our definition above differs from the one in [62] in the following aspects. First, we consider dynamic cuckoo hashing schemes in which one can keep inserting elements, while [62] considers the static case in which the set is hashed all at once. Second, in our notion each entry of $\boldsymbol{T}$ can store a single element, whereas [62] considers the more general case where it can store $\ell \geq 1$ elements, which occurs in some constructions.

We define correctness of cuckoo hashing by looking at the probability that either the insertion algorithm fails or, if it does not fail, an inserted element is not stored in the appropriate indices returned by Lookup. To model this notion we give two definitions. The first one is the "classical" correctness definition of cuckoo hashing that takes this probability over any choice of inputs but for a random and independent sampling of the hash functions. Intuitively this models the scenario where an adversary for correctness does not have explicit access to the hash functions, but can still choose any input set.

Definition 2 (Correctness). *A cuckoo hashing scheme* CH *is* ϵ-***correct*** *if for any* n*, any set of* $m \leq n$ *items* $x_1, \ldots, x_m \in \mathcal{X}$ *such that* $x_i \neq x_j$ *for all* $i \neq j$ *and any* $\ell \in [m]$*:*

$$\Pr\left[\begin{array}{c} \boldsymbol{T}' = \bot \\ \vee\, (\boldsymbol{T}' \neq \bot\, \wedge \\ x_\ell \notin \{\boldsymbol{T}'[i_1], \ldots, \boldsymbol{T}'[i_k]\} \cup S') \end{array} : \begin{array}{r} (\mathsf{pp}, \boldsymbol{T}, S) \leftarrow \mathsf{Setup}(1^\lambda, \mathcal{X}, n) \\ (\boldsymbol{T}', S') \leftarrow \mathsf{Insert}(\mathsf{pp}, \boldsymbol{T}, S, x_1, \ldots, x_m) \\ (i_1, \ldots, i_k) \leftarrow \mathsf{Lookup}(\mathsf{pp}, x_\ell) \end{array}\right] \leq \epsilon$$

and one simply says that CH *is* ***correct*** *if it is* ϵ*-correct with* $\epsilon = \mathsf{negl}(\lambda)$*.*

Robust Cuckoo Hashing. The second definition (introduced by Yeo [62]) instead considers the case of inputs that are chosen by a PPT adversary after having seen the hash functions. This models the scenario where an adversary has explicit access to the hash functions before choosing the set of elements.

Definition 3 (Robustness). *A cuckoo hashing scheme* CH *is* ϵ-***robust*** *if for any* n*, any PPT adversary* $\mathcal{A}$*:*

$$\Pr\left[\begin{array}{c} \boldsymbol{T}' = \bot \\ \vee\, (\boldsymbol{T}' \neq \bot\, \wedge \\ x_\ell \notin \{\boldsymbol{T}'[i_1], \ldots, \boldsymbol{T}'[i_k]\} \cup S') \end{array} : \begin{array}{r} (\mathsf{pp}, \boldsymbol{T}, S) \leftarrow \mathsf{Setup}(1^\lambda, \mathcal{X}, n) \\ \{x_1, \ldots, x_m, \ell\} \leftarrow \mathcal{A}(\mathsf{pp}) \\ x_i \neq x_j \forall i \neq j \in [m] \\ (\boldsymbol{T}', S') \leftarrow \mathsf{Insert}(\mathsf{pp}, \boldsymbol{T}, S, x_1, \ldots, x_m) \\ (i_1, \ldots, i_k) \leftarrow \mathsf{Lookup}(\mathsf{pp}, x_\ell) \end{array}\right] \leq \epsilon$$

Efficiency Parameters of Cuckoo Hashing. For our applications, the following parameters will dictate the efficiency of a cuckoo hashing scheme: k, the number of possible indices (and of hash functions); N, the size of the table $\boldsymbol{T}$; s, the size of the stash S; d, the number of changes in the table (i.e., number of evictions) after a single insertion. While in most constructions, the parameters k and N are fixed at Setup time, in some cuckoo hashing schemes the values of s and d may depend on the randomness and the choice of inputs. As in the case of correctness vs. robustness, we define s and d in the average case (i.e., for any set of inputs and for random and independent execution of Setup) or in the worst case (i..e, for adversarial choice of inputs after seeing pp).

Existing Cuckoo Hashing Schemes. The following theorem encompasses a few existing cuckoo hashing schemes.

Theorem 1. *For a security parameter* λ *and an upper bound* n*, there exist the following cuckoo hashing schemes:*

- CH_2 *where* $k = 2$, $N = 2kn$, *that achieves* $\mathsf{negl}(\lambda)$*-correctness, and average case* $s = \log n$, $d = O(1)$ *[44].*
- $\mathsf{CH}_2^{(\mathsf{rob})}$ *where* $k = 2$, $N = 2kn$, *that achieves* $\mathsf{negl}(\lambda)$*-robustness, and worst case* $s = n$, $d = O(1)$ *[44,62] in the Random Oracle Model.*
- $\mathsf{CH}_\lambda^{(\mathsf{rob})}$ *where* $k = \lambda$, $N = 2\lambda n$, *that achieves* $\mathsf{negl}(\lambda)$*-robustness, and worst case* $s = 0$, $d = \lambda$ *[62] in the Random Oracle Model.*

3.3 Vector Commitments

Vector commitment (VC) schemes [15,48] allow a party to compute a commitment to a vector $\boldsymbol{v}$ and later to locally open a specific position v_i. A VC guarantees that it is hard to open a commitment to two distinct values at the same position – what is called "position binding" – and should have short (i.e., polylogarithmic in $|\boldsymbol{v}|$) commitments and openings. Formally:

Definition 4 (Vector Commitment [15]**).** *A Vector Commitment (VC) scheme* $\mathsf{VC} = (\mathsf{Setup}, \mathsf{Com}, \mathsf{Open}, \mathsf{Ver})$ *consists of the following algorithms:*

- $\mathsf{Setup}(1^\lambda, n) \rightarrow \mathsf{crs}$: *on input the security parameter* λ *and an integer* n *expressing the length of the vectors to be committed, returns the common reference string* crs.
- $\mathsf{Com}(\mathsf{crs}, \boldsymbol{v}) \rightarrow (C, \mathsf{aux})$: *on input a common reference string* crs *and a vector* $\boldsymbol{v}$*, returns a commitment* C.
- $\mathsf{Open}(\mathsf{crs}, \mathsf{aux}, i) \rightarrow \Lambda$: *on input an auxiliary information as produced by* Com *and a position* $i \in [n]$*, returns an opening proof* Λ.
- $\mathsf{Ver}(\mathsf{crs}, C, \Lambda, i, v) \rightarrow b$: *on input a commitment* C*, returns a bit* $b \in \{0; 1\}$ *to check whether* Λ *is a valid opening of* C *to* v *at position* i.

Correctness. VC *is* perfectly correct *if for any vector* $\boldsymbol{v}$*:*

$$\Pr\left[\mathsf{Ver}(\mathsf{crs}, C, \mathsf{Open}(\mathsf{crs}, \mathsf{aux}, i), i, v_i)) = 1 : \begin{array}{r} \mathsf{crs} \xleftarrow{\$} \mathsf{Setup}(1^\lambda, n) \\ (C, \mathsf{aux}) \leftarrow \mathsf{Com}(\mathsf{crs}, \boldsymbol{v}) \end{array}\right] = 1$$

Position Binding. VC *satisfies position binding if for any PPT* $\mathcal{A}$

$$\Pr\left[\begin{array}{c} \mathsf{Ver}(\mathsf{crs}, C, \Lambda, i, v)) = 1 \\ \wedge\, \mathsf{Ver}(\mathsf{crs}, C, \Lambda, i, v')) = 1 \\ \wedge\, v \neq v' \end{array} : \begin{array}{r} \mathsf{crs} \xleftarrow{\$} \mathsf{Setup}(1^\lambda, n) \\ (C, i, v, \Lambda, v', \Lambda') \leftarrow \mathcal{A}(\mathsf{crs}) \end{array}\right] = \mathsf{negl}(\lambda)$$

Succinctness. VC *is* succinct *if for any* $\mathsf{crs} \xleftarrow{\$} \mathsf{Setup}(1^\lambda, n)$*, any vector* $\boldsymbol{v}$*, any* $(C, \mathsf{aux}) \leftarrow \mathsf{Com}(\mathsf{crs}, \boldsymbol{v})$*, any* $i \in [n]$ *and* $\Lambda \leftarrow \mathsf{Open}(\mathsf{crs}, \mathsf{aux}, i)$*, the bitsize of* C *and* Λ *is polylogarithmic in* n, i.e., *is bounded by a fixed polynomial* $p(\lambda, \log n)$.

In this work we use the notion of *updatable* vector commitments [15], which informally provides the functionality that, given a commitment C and opening Λ corresponding to a vector $\boldsymbol{v}$, one can update them into values C' and Λ' corresponding to a vector $\boldsymbol{v}'$. Notably, this update should be efficient, i.e., in time proportional to the number of different positions in $\boldsymbol{v}$ and $\boldsymbol{v}'$, and thus faster than recomputing them from scratch. More formally:

Definition 5 (Updatable VCs [15]). *A vector commitment scheme* VC *is updatable if there are two algorithms* (ComUpdate, ProofUpdate) *such that:*

- $\mathsf{ComUpdate}(\mathsf{crs}, C, i, v, v') \rightarrow C'$ *: on input a commitment C, a position i and two values v, v', outputs an updated commitment C'.*
- $\mathsf{ProofUpdate}(\mathsf{crs}, \Lambda, i, v, v') \rightarrow \Lambda'$ *: on input an opening proof Λ (for some position j), a position i and two values v, v', returns an updated opening Λ'.*

Correctness. *An updatable VC is perfectly correct if for honestly generated* $\mathsf{crs} \xleftarrow{\$} \mathsf{Setup}(1^\lambda, n)$*, any vector $\boldsymbol{v}$, initial commitment* $(C, \mathsf{aux}) \leftarrow \mathsf{Com}(\mathsf{crs}, \boldsymbol{v})$*, position $i \in [n]$,* $\Lambda \leftarrow \mathsf{Open}(\mathsf{crs}, \mathsf{aux}, i)$*, and any sequence of valid updates* $\{(i_k, v_{i_k}, v'_{i_k})\}_{k\in[m]}$ *that result into a vector $\boldsymbol{v}^*$, commitment C^* and opening Λ^*,* $\mathsf{Ver}(\mathsf{crs}, C^*, \Lambda^*, i, v_i^*)) = 1$ *holds with probability 1.*

Efficiency. *An updatable VC is* efficient *if its algorithms* ComUpdate *and* Proof Update *run in polylogarithmic time given polylogarithmic inputs.*

3.4 Registration-Based Encryption

We recall the original definition of Registration-Based Encryption [34] with the modification of [38] that allows for a structured common reference string crs and a bound n on the number of users that can be registered. In case a crs is not involved or the scheme allows for an unbounded number of registered users we consider $\mathsf{crs} = \emptyset$ and $N = \infty$ respectively.

For completeness we recall how an RBE system evolves: At the beginning a one-time setup algorithm generates the common reference string. Then there are two types of parties: the Key Curator (KC) and the users, each represented by an identity id from a pre-specified identity space $\mathcal{ID}$. The KC is completely transparent (and deterministic) and her role is solely to ease the computational burden of each user. Each user, upon entering the system generates their own public-secret key-pair (pk, sk) and registers their public key with the Key Curator, who computes the updated public parameters pp after the new registration. Anyone can encrypt a message $m \in \mathcal{M}$ for an identity id by having access to the crs and the current pp (without knowing the corresponding pk of id). Finally the identity can decrypt the ciphertext ct using their secret key sk and an update information u that is computed by the KC and given to the user.[4]

We further enhance the RBE definition with the functionality of deletion of users from the system. We call an RBE that supports this functionality an *RBE with deletions*. Below is the formal definition.

[4] The update information does not have to be secret and is only computed by KC and not by the user for efficiency.

Definition 6 (Registration-Based Encryption (RBE) with deletions). *A registration-based encryption scheme with identity space $\mathcal{ID}$ and message space space $\mathcal{M}$ consists of six/ seven PPT algorithms* (Setup, Gen, Reg, Del, Enc, Upd, Dec) *working as follows.*

- $\mathsf{Setup}(1^\lambda, N) \rightarrow \mathsf{crs}$: *On input the security parameter λ and a positive integer N indicating the maximum number of users that can be registered, the randomized setup algorithm samples a common reference string* crs.
- $\mathsf{Gen}(\mathsf{crs}, \mathsf{id}) \rightarrow (\mathsf{pk}, \mathsf{sk})$: *On input the common reference string* crs *and an identity* id*, the randomized algorithm key generation algorithm outputs a pair of public and secret keys* (pk, sk).
- $\mathsf{Reg}^{[\mathsf{aux}]}(\mathsf{crs}, \mathsf{pp}, \mathsf{id}, \mathsf{pk}) \rightarrow \mathsf{pp}'$: *On input the common reference string* crs*, the current public parameters* pp*, an identity* $\mathsf{id} \in \mathcal{ID}$*, and a public key* pk*, the deterministic registration algorithm outputs the new public parameters* pp′*. The* Reg *algorithm has* read *and* write *oracle access to the auxiliary information* aux *which is updated into* aux′ *during registration. (The system is initialized with public parameters* pp *and auxiliary information* aux *set to* $\perp$*.)*
- $\mathsf{Del}^{[\mathsf{aux}]}(\mathsf{crs}, \mathsf{pp}, \mathsf{id}) \rightarrow \mathsf{pp}'$: *On input the common reference string* crs*, the current public parameters* pp*, and an identity* $\mathsf{id} \in \mathcal{ID}$ *the deterministic registration algorithm outputs the new public parameters* pp′ *or* $\perp$ *if* id *was not registered before. The* Del *algorithm has* read *and* write *oracle access to the auxiliary information* aux *which is updated into* aux′ *during the process.*
- $\mathsf{Enc}(\mathsf{crs}, \mathsf{pp}, \mathsf{id}, m) \rightarrow \mathsf{ct}$: *On input the common reference string* crs*, the current public parameters* pp*, a recipient identity* $\mathsf{id} \in \mathcal{ID}$ *and a message* $m \in \mathcal{M}$*, the randomized encryption algorithm outputs a ciphertext* ct.
- $\mathsf{Upd}^{[\mathsf{aux}]}(\mathsf{pp}, \mathsf{id}) \rightarrow \mathsf{u}$: *On input the current public parameters* pp *and a registered identity* id*, the deterministic update algorithm outputs an update information* u *that can help* id *to decrypt its messages. It has* read only *oracle access to* aux.
- $\mathsf{Dec}(\mathsf{sk}, \mathsf{u}, \mathsf{ct}) \rightarrow m$: *On input the secret* sk*, the (current) update information* u *and a ciphertext* ct*, the deterministic decryption algorithm outputs a message* $m \in \{0,1\}^*$ *or in* $\{\perp, \mathsf{GetUpd}\}$*. The symbol* $\perp$ *indicates a syntax error while* GetUpd *indicates that more recent update information might be needed for decryption.*

Below is the formal definition of completeness and the efficiency requirements of RBE as described in [34] with two modifications: (1) we additionally take into account deletions, (2) and define a computational version, *i.e.* with a PPT adversary instead of an unbounded one.

Definition 7 (Completeness, compactness, and efficiency of RBE). *For any interactive PPT adversary $\mathcal{A}$, consider the following game* $\mathsf{Comp}_{\mathcal{A}}(\lambda)$ *between an adversary $\mathcal{A}$ and a challenger $\mathcal{C}$.*

1. **Initialization.** *$\mathcal{C}$ sets* $\mathsf{pp} \leftarrow \perp$, $\mathsf{aux} \leftarrow \perp$, $\mathsf{u} \leftarrow \perp$, $\mathcal{D} \leftarrow \emptyset$, $\mathsf{id}^* \leftarrow \perp$, $t \leftarrow 0$, $\hat{N} \leftarrow 0$, $\hat{M} \leftarrow 0$ *and* $\mathsf{crs} \leftarrow \mathsf{Setup}(1^\lambda, N)$*, and sends the sampled* crs *to* $\mathcal{A}$.

2. *Until $\mathcal{A}$ continues, proceed as follows. At every iteration, $\mathcal{A}$ chooses exactly one of the actions below to be performed.*
   (a) **Registering new (non-target) identity.** *If $|\mathcal{D}| = N$ skip this step. $\mathcal{A}$ sends some* $\mathsf{id} \notin \mathcal{D}$ *and* pk *in the support of the* $\mathsf{Gen}(\mathsf{crs})$ *algorithm, to $\mathcal{C}$. $\mathcal{C}$ registers* $(\mathsf{id}, \mathsf{pk})$ *by letting* $\mathsf{pp} \leftarrow \mathsf{Reg}^{[\mathsf{aux}]}(\mathsf{crs}, \mathsf{pp}, \mathsf{id}, \mathsf{pk})$ *and* $\mathcal{D} \leftarrow \mathcal{D} \cup \{\mathsf{id}\}$, $\hat{N} \leftarrow \hat{N} + 1$.
   (b) **Deleting existing (non-target) identity.** *$\mathcal{A}$ sends some* $\mathsf{id} \in \mathcal{D}$ *to $\mathcal{C}$. $\mathcal{C}$ un-registers* id *by letting* $\mathsf{pp} \leftarrow \mathsf{Del}^{[\mathsf{aux}]}(\mathsf{crs}, \mathsf{pp}, \mathsf{id})$ *and* $\mathcal{D} \leftarrow \mathcal{D} \setminus \{\mathsf{id}\}$, $\hat{M} \leftarrow \hat{M} + 1$.
   (c) **Registering the target identity.** *If* $\mathsf{id}^* \neq \perp$ *or* $|\mathcal{D}| = N$ *, skip this step. Otherwise, $\mathcal{A}$ sends some* $\mathsf{id}^* \notin \mathcal{D}$ *to $\mathcal{C}$. $\mathcal{C}$ then samples* $(\mathsf{pk}^*, \mathsf{sk}^*) \leftarrow \mathsf{Gen}(\mathsf{crs}, \mathsf{id}^*)$, *updates* $\mathsf{pp} \leftarrow \mathsf{Reg}^{[\mathsf{aux}]}(\mathsf{crs}, \mathsf{pp}, \mathsf{id}^*, \mathsf{pk}^*)$ *and* $\mathcal{D} \leftarrow \mathcal{D} \cup \{\mathsf{id}^*\}$, $\hat{N} \leftarrow \hat{N} + 1$, *and sends* pk^* *to $\mathcal{A}$.*
   (d) **Deleting the target identity.** *If* $\mathsf{id}^* \notin \mathcal{D}$, *skip this step. Otherwise, $\mathcal{C}$ updates* $\mathsf{pp} \leftarrow \mathsf{Del}^{[\mathsf{aux}]}(\mathsf{crs}, \mathsf{pp}, \mathsf{id}^*)$ *and* $\mathcal{D} \leftarrow \mathcal{D} \setminus \{\mathsf{id}^*\}$, $\hat{M} \leftarrow \hat{M} + 1$.
   (e) **Encrypting for the target identity.** *If* $\mathsf{id}^* = \perp$, *skip this step. Otherwise, $\mathcal{C}$ sets $t \leftarrow t + 1$. $\mathcal{A}$ sends some $m_t \in \mathcal{M}$ to $\mathcal{C}$ who sends back a corresponding ciphertext* $\mathsf{ct}_t \leftarrow \mathsf{Enc}(\mathsf{crs}, \mathsf{pp}, \mathsf{id}^*, m_t)$ *to $\mathcal{A}$.*
   (f) **Decryption by target identity.** *$\mathcal{A}$ sends a $j \in [t]$ to $\mathcal{C}$. $\mathcal{C}$ then lets* $m'_j = \mathsf{Dec}(\mathsf{sk}^*, \mathsf{u}, \mathsf{ct}_j)$. *If* $m'_j = \mathsf{GetUpd}$, *then $\mathcal{C}$ obtains the update* $\mathsf{u}^* = \mathsf{Upd}^{[\mathsf{aux}]}(\mathsf{pp}, \mathsf{id}^*)$ *and then lets* $m'_j = \mathsf{Dec}(\mathsf{sk}^*, \mathsf{u}^*, \mathsf{ct}_j)$.
3. *The adversary $\mathcal{A}$ wins the game if there is some $j \in [t]$ for which $m'_j \neq m_j$.*

Let $Q \in \mathsf{poly}(\lambda)$ *be an upper bound on the number of queries issued by $\mathcal{A}$. Let $\mathcal{D}_q$ be the set of identities after the q-th query. We require the following properties to hold for any PPT adversary $\mathcal{A}$.*

Completeness. $\Pr[\mathcal{A} \text{ wins } \mathsf{Comp}_{\mathcal{A}}(\lambda)] = \mathsf{negl}(\lambda)$.

Compactness of public parameters and updates. *For all queries $q \in [Q]$, let* pp_q *be the public parameters after the q-th query. Then* $|\mathsf{pp}_q|$ *is sublinear in $|\mathcal{D}_q|$. Moreover, for all* $\mathsf{id} \in \mathcal{D}$, *the size of the corresponding update* $|\mathsf{u}_q|$ *is also sublinear in $|\mathcal{D}_q|$.*

Efficiency of the number of updates. *The total number of invocations of* Upd *for identity* id^* *in Step 2(f) of the game* $\mathsf{Comp}_{\mathcal{A}}(\lambda)$ *is sublinear in $\hat{N}$.*

Remark 2 (Efficiency of Registration and Updates). The initial work of Garg et al. [34] considers a fourth stringent efficiency requirement, that the running times of Reg, Del and Upd should be $\mathsf{polylog}(N)$. Constructions using iO [34] and garbled circuits [35] satisfy this, however to date there is no black-box construction with this property. Additionally our concrete compilers do not (asymptotically) affect the running times of Reg, Del and Upd. Therefore, to avoid overwhelming the reader we do not consider this property.

For the security of RBE, the adversary can control all users except for a target identity id^* of their choice. Then we demand ciphertext indistinguishability for encrypted messages under this id^*. Below is the formal security definition taken almost verbatim from [34], where we additionally consider deletions.

Definition 8 (Security of RBE). *For any interactive PPT adversary $\mathcal{A}$, consider the following game* $\mathsf{Sec}_{\mathcal{A}}(\lambda)$ *between* $\mathcal{A}$ *and a challenger* $\mathcal{C}$.

1. **Initialization.** $\mathcal{C}$ *sets* $\mathsf{pp} = \perp$, $\mathsf{aux} = \perp$, $\mathcal{D} = \emptyset$, $\mathsf{id}^* = \perp$, $\mathsf{crs} \leftarrow \mathsf{Setup}(1^\lambda)$ *and sends the sampled* crs *to* $\mathcal{A}$.
2. *Until* $\mathcal{A}$ *continues (which is at most* $\mathsf{poly}(\lambda)$ *steps), proceed as follows. At every iteration,* $\mathcal{A}$ *chooses exactly one of the actions below to be performed.*
   (a) **Registering new (non-target) identity.** $\mathcal{A}$ *sends some* $\mathsf{id} \notin \mathcal{D}$ *and* pk *to* $\mathcal{C}$. $\mathcal{C}$ *registers* $(\mathsf{id}, \mathsf{pk})$ *by letting* $\mathsf{pp} \leftarrow \mathsf{Reg}^{[\mathsf{aux}]}(\mathsf{crs}, \mathsf{pp}, \mathsf{id}, \mathsf{pk})$ *and* $\mathcal{D} \leftarrow \mathcal{D} \cup \{\mathsf{id}\}$.
   (b) **Deleting an existing (non-target) identity.** $\mathcal{A}$ *sends some* $\mathsf{id} \in \mathcal{D}$ *to* $\mathcal{C}$. $\mathcal{C}$ *un-registers* id *by letting* $\mathsf{pp} \leftarrow \mathsf{Del}^{[\mathsf{aux}]}(\mathsf{crs}, \mathsf{pp}, \mathsf{id})$ *and* $\mathcal{D} \leftarrow \mathcal{D} \setminus \{\mathsf{id}\}$.
   (c) **Registering the target identity.** *If* $\mathsf{id}^* \neq \perp$*, skip this step. Otherwise,* $\mathcal{A}$ *sends an* $\mathsf{id}^* \notin \mathcal{D}$ *to* $\mathcal{C}$. $\mathcal{C}$ *then samples* $(\mathsf{pk}^*, \mathsf{sk}^*) \leftarrow \mathsf{Gen}(\mathsf{crs}, \mathsf{id}^*)$, *updates* $\mathsf{pp} \leftarrow \mathsf{Reg}^{[\mathsf{aux}]}(\mathsf{crs}, \mathsf{pp}, \mathsf{id}^*, \mathsf{pk}^*)$, $\mathcal{D} \leftarrow \mathcal{D} \cup \{\mathsf{id}^*\}$, *and sends* pk^* *to* $\mathcal{A}$.
   (d) **Deleting the target identity.** *If* $\mathsf{id}^* = \perp$*, skip this step. Otherwise,* $\mathcal{C}$ *updates* $\mathsf{pp} \leftarrow \mathsf{Del}^{[\mathsf{aux}]}(\mathsf{crs}, \mathsf{pp}, \mathsf{id}^*)$ *and* $\mathcal{D} \leftarrow \mathcal{D} \setminus \{\mathsf{id}^*\}$, $\mathsf{id}^* \leftarrow \perp$.
3. **Encrypting for the target identity.** $\mathcal{A}$ *sends some* $\mathsf{id} \notin \mathcal{D} \setminus \{\mathsf{id}^*\}$ *and two messages* (m_0, m_1) *and* $\mathcal{C}$ *generates* $\mathsf{ct} \leftarrow \mathsf{Enc}(\mathsf{crs}, \mathsf{pp}, \mathsf{id}, m_b)$, *where* $b \leftarrow \{0, 1\}$ *is a random bit, and sends* ct *to* $\mathcal{A}$.
4. *The adversary* $\mathcal{A}$ *outputs a bit* b' *and wins the game if* $b = b'$.

We call an RBE scheme secure if there exists a negligible function $\mathsf{negl}(\lambda)$ *such that for all PPT adversaries* $\mathcal{A}$ *it holds that* $\Pr[\mathcal{A}\ \textit{wins}\ \mathsf{Sec}_{\mathcal{A}}(\lambda)] \leq \frac{1}{2} + \mathsf{negl}(\lambda)$.

Remark 3 (RBE with deletions–constructions). Although the notion of deletions has not been previously formally in the context of RBE, all known RBE constructions [24,34,35,38,39] can be enhanced in a straightforward way with this functionality.

Laconic Encryption. Döttling et al. [24] introduced the notion of Laconic Encryption which is essentially the same as RBE but dropping the 'Efficiency of the number of updates' requirement. They additionally showed a generic transformation from any Laconic Encryption scheme to an RBE scheme with Efficient updates, generalizing the transformations of Garg et al. [34] and Glaeser et al. [38]. The same transformation was presented in the context of Registered Attribute-Based Encryption by Hohenberger et al. [40].

We summarize the transformation in the following theorem, slightly extending it to include deletions.

Theorem 2 ([24]). *Assume any Laconic Encryption scheme* LE *with deletions, with worst-case:*

$$\textbf{\textit{Compactness:}}\ |\mathsf{pp}|, |\mathsf{u}| = o(N), \qquad \textbf{\textit{Ciphertext size:}}\ |\mathsf{ct}|,$$

then there exists an RBE scheme (without deletions) with worst-case:

$$\textbf{\textit{Compactness:}}\ |\mathsf{pp}| \log(\hat{N}), |\mathsf{u}|, \qquad \textbf{\textit{Ciphertext size:}}\ |\mathsf{ct}| \log(\hat{N}),$$
$$\textbf{\textit{Number of updates:}}\ \log(\hat{N}).$$

For conciseness in the rest of this work we will consider Laconic Encryption, and then apply the above Theorem 2 to achieve a fully efficient RBE.

4 RBE with Unbounded Identity Space from CH

Here we show our compiler that boosts any RBE scheme with small identity space to an RBE with large identity space. On the core of compiler are Cuckoo Hashing and the notion of Witness Encryption for Vector Commitments that we define next (Sect. 4.1). For the intuition of the transformation we refer to the technical overview of Sect. 2.

4.1 Witness Encryption for Vector Commitments

As mentioned in Sect. 2, a building block of our RBE construction is a specialized witness encryption scheme. We call this primitive VCWE and intuitively it works as follows. One encrypts a message m with respect to a statement consisting of a commitment C, a position i and a value v, and decryption is achieved by using a valid opening that shows that v is indeed the value at position i in the vector committed in C. We notice that VCWE can be seen as a special case of the notion of 'WE for functional commitments' recently proposed by Campanelli, Fiore and Khoshakhlagh [13].

Although VCWE has a witness encryption flavor, its semantic security notion is weaker than standard WE. Notably, in WE semantic security for false statements should hold statistically, whereas in VCWE is computational. Also, we define semantic security in such a way that the experiment is falsifiable and can check whether a statement is true or false. For details, see the definition provided hereafter.

Definition 9 (Witness Encryption for Vector Commitments). *Let* $\mathsf{VC} = (\mathsf{Setup}, \mathsf{Com}, \mathsf{Open}, \mathsf{Ver})$ *be a vector commitment scheme. A witness encryption scheme with respect to* VC, VCWE *for short, consist of PPT algorithms* $(\mathsf{Enc}, \mathsf{Dec})$*:*

- $\mathsf{Enc}(\mathsf{crs}, C, i, v, m) \to \mathsf{ct}$: *on input a vector commitment common reference string* crs*, a commitment* C*, a position* i*, a value* v *and a message* m *outputs a witness-encryption of* m *under the statement* (C, i, v)*.*

- $\mathsf{Dec}(\mathsf{crs}, \Lambda, \mathsf{ct}) \to m^*$: *on input a vector commitment common reference string* crs*, a witness* Λ *and a ciphertext* m *outputs a decryption message* m^*.

Furthermore, VCWE *should satisfy the following properties:*

Correctness. *For any security parameter* $\lambda \in \mathbb{N}$*, any* $N = \mathsf{poly}(\lambda)$*, any* $\boldsymbol{v} = (v_1, \dots, v_N)$ *in the domain of* VC*,* $i \in [N]$*,* $m \in \mathcal{M}$*,* $\mathsf{crs} \leftarrow \mathsf{VC.Setup}(1^\lambda, N)$*,* $C \leftarrow \mathsf{VC.Com}(\mathsf{crs}, \boldsymbol{v})$*, and* $\Lambda \leftarrow \mathsf{Open}(\mathsf{crs}, C, \boldsymbol{v}, i)$*:*

$$\Pr[\mathsf{Dec}(\mathsf{crs}, \Lambda, \mathsf{ct}) = m : \mathsf{ct} \leftarrow \mathsf{Enc}(\mathsf{crs}, C, i, v, m)] = 1$$

Semantic Security. *For any security parameter* $\lambda \in \mathbb{N}$*,* $N = \mathsf{poly}(\lambda)$ *and any PPT adversary* $\mathcal{A}$*:*

$$\left| \Pr\left[b' = b : \begin{array}{l} \mathsf{crs} \leftarrow_{\$} \mathsf{Setup}(1^\lambda, N), \\ (\boldsymbol{v}, i, v, m_0, m_1, \mathsf{st}) \leftarrow \mathcal{A}(\mathsf{crs}), \\ C \leftarrow \mathsf{Com}(\mathsf{crs}, \boldsymbol{v}), b \leftarrow_{\$} \{0,1\}, \\ \textbf{if } \boldsymbol{v}[i] = v \textbf{ then } \mathsf{ct} \leftarrow \bot \\ \textbf{else } \mathsf{ct} \leftarrow \mathsf{Enc}(\mathsf{crs}, C, i, v, m_b), \\ b' \leftarrow \mathcal{A}(\mathsf{st}, \mathsf{ct}) \end{array} \right] - \frac{1}{2} \right| = \mathsf{negl}(\lambda)$$

4.2 RBE with Unbounded Identity Space

Assume any RBE scheme with deletions, $\widetilde{\mathsf{RBE}} = (\mathsf{Setup}, \mathsf{Gen}, \mathsf{Reg}, \mathsf{Enc}, \mathsf{Upd}, = \mathsf{Dec})$ that supports bounded identities, i.e. $\log(|\mathcal{ID}|) < 2\lambda$. We show a transformation that boosts it to an RBE scheme that supports unbounded identities $\mathcal{ID} = \{0,1\}^{2\lambda}$.[5]

For presentational convenience we show the compiler for Laconic Encryption, that is from $\widetilde{\mathsf{LE}}$ with $|\mathcal{ID}| < 2\lambda$ to LE with $\mathcal{ID} = \{0,1\}^{2\lambda}$. Recall from Sect. 3.4 $\widetilde{\mathsf{LE}}$ is essentially $\widetilde{\mathsf{RBE}}$ without the efficiency on the number of updates requirement. Then we make use of Theorem 2 with which we can obtain an RBE with a logarithmic number of updates.

From now on we will be using small n as an upper bound on the number of RBE users and capital $N > n$ as the resulting number of entries of the Cuckoo Hashing table (see Sect. 3.2).

Building Blocks. For our compiler we need the following primitives:

1. A Cuckoo Hashing scheme $\mathsf{CH} = (\mathsf{Setup}, \mathsf{Insert}, \mathsf{Lookup})$.
2. A Witness Encryption scheme $\mathsf{VCWE} = (\mathsf{Enc}, \mathsf{Dec})$ w.r.t. a Vector Commitment scheme $\mathsf{VC} = (\mathsf{Setup}, \mathsf{Com}, \mathsf{Open}, \mathsf{Ver})$.
3. A Public Key Encryption scheme $\mathsf{PKE} = (\mathsf{KeyGen}, \mathsf{Enc}, \mathsf{Dec})$.
4. A Secret Sharing scheme $\mathsf{Sh} = (\mathsf{Share}, \mathsf{Rec})$.

[5] We consider the identity space $\{0,1\}^{2\lambda}$ virtually unbounded since one can always use a collision-resistant hash function $H : \{0,1\}^* \to \{0,1\}^{2\lambda}$ to support unbounded identities.

We note that RBE trivially implies a PKE by registering a single user. Furthermore, any RBE scheme implies a (weakly position binding) VC scheme. For the secret sharing scheme, if the message space of the RBE is a group then there exist simple information-theoretic constructions. Therefore, in essence we only assume a Cuckoo Hashing and a Witness Encryption scheme for the underlying Vector Commitment. However, one may desire to instantiate the primitives with different constructions therefore we explicitly mention them distinctly.

Construction. We denote the initial LE scheme as $\widetilde{\mathsf{LE}}$. Throughout the description of our construction below, for every identity id we use the notation $\mathsf{id}^{(\eta)}$ for η'th coordinate of $\mathsf{Lookup}(\mathsf{pp}, \mathsf{id})$, i.e. by defintion $(\mathsf{id}^{(1)}, \ldots, \mathsf{id}^{(k)}) = \mathsf{Lookup}(\mathsf{pp}, \mathsf{id})$.

Our compiler yields a Laconic Encryption scheme RBE that works as follows:

- $\mathsf{Setup}(1^\lambda, n) \rightarrow \mathsf{crs}$: Sets: $\mathsf{chpp} \leftarrow \mathsf{CH.Setup}(1^\lambda, n)$, $\widetilde{\mathsf{crs}} \leftarrow \widetilde{\mathsf{LE}}.\mathsf{Setup}(1^\lambda, n)$, $\mathsf{vccrs} \leftarrow \mathsf{VC.Setup}(1^\lambda, N)$, and returns: $\mathsf{crs} = (\widetilde{\mathsf{crs}}, \mathsf{chpp}, \mathsf{vccrs})$.
- $\mathsf{Gen}(\mathsf{crs}, \mathsf{id}) \rightarrow (\mathsf{pk}, \mathsf{sk})$:
  1. $(\mathsf{pk}^{(\eta)}, \mathsf{sk}^{(\eta)}) \leftarrow \widetilde{\mathsf{LE}}.\mathsf{Gen}(\widetilde{\mathsf{crs}}, \mathsf{id}^{(\eta)})$ for each $\eta \in [k]$,
  2. $(\mathsf{pk}^{(k+1)}, \mathsf{sk}^{(k+1)}) \leftarrow \mathsf{KeyGen}(1^\lambda)$.

$$\mathsf{pk} = \left((\mathsf{pk}^{(\eta)})_{\eta \in [k]}, \mathsf{pk}^{(k+1)}\right), \quad \mathsf{sk} = \left((\mathsf{sk}^{(\eta)})_{\eta \in [k]}, \mathsf{sk}^{(k+1)}\right)$$

- $\mathsf{Reg}^{[\mathsf{aux}]}(\mathsf{crs}, \mathsf{pp}, \mathsf{id}, \mathsf{pk}) \rightarrow \mathsf{pp}'$:

  Auxiliary information. The auxiliary information of the Key Curator consists of $\mathsf{aux} := (\widetilde{\mathsf{aux}}, \boldsymbol{I})$, where $\boldsymbol{I} := (\mathsf{id}_1, \ldots, \mathsf{id}_N)$ is the vector of the (previously) registered identities in the corresponding positions (if no identity is registered in position j then $\mathsf{id}_j = 0$).

  Public Parameters. The public parameters of the system consist of $\mathsf{pp} := (\widetilde{\mathsf{pp}}, D, S)$, where D is the current vector commitment to the identities $\boldsymbol{I} := (\mathsf{id}_1, \ldots, \mathsf{id}_N)$ and $S = \{(\mathsf{id}_{N+1}, \mathsf{pk}_{N+1}), \ldots, (\mathsf{id}_{N+s}, \mathsf{pk}_{N+s})\}$ is the set of identities that are stored in the stash.

  Insert id. Runs $(\boldsymbol{I}', S') \leftarrow \mathsf{CH.Insert}(\mathsf{chpp}, \boldsymbol{I}, S, \mathsf{id})$ and if CH.Insert failed outputs $\perp$. Otherwise for every identity $\bar{\mathsf{id}}$ that was moved, i.e. its position in $(\boldsymbol{I}', S')$ and $(\boldsymbol{I}, S)$ differs, re-registers it as $\bar{\mathsf{id}}^{(\eta^\dagger)}$ (η^* indicates the hash function with which id was placed before, in $\boldsymbol{I}$, and $\eta^\dagger$ the one after, in $\boldsymbol{I}'$). For every $\bar{\mathsf{id}}$ that was moved:

  1. $\boldsymbol{I}[\bar{\mathsf{id}}^{(\eta^*)}] \leftarrow 0$,
  2. $\widetilde{\mathsf{pp}} \leftarrow \widetilde{\mathsf{LE}}.\mathsf{Del}^{[\widetilde{\mathsf{aux}}]}(\widetilde{\mathsf{crs}}, \widetilde{\mathsf{pp}}, \bar{\mathsf{id}}^{(\eta^{(*)})}, \bar{\mathsf{pk}})$.

  Then for every $\bar{\mathsf{id}}$ that was moved to $\boldsymbol{I}'$ (including id that was freshly inserted):

  3. $\boldsymbol{I}[\bar{\mathsf{id}}^{(\eta^\dagger)}] \leftarrow \bar{\mathsf{id}}$,
  4. $\widetilde{\mathsf{pp}} \leftarrow \widetilde{\mathsf{LE}}.\mathsf{Reg}^{[\widetilde{\mathsf{aux}}]}(\widetilde{\mathsf{crs}}, \widetilde{\mathsf{pp}}, \bar{\mathsf{id}}^{(\eta^{(\dagger)})}, \bar{\mathsf{pk}})$.

  For every $\bar{\mathsf{id}}$ that was moved to the stash:

5. $S \leftarrow S \cup \{(\bar{\mathsf{id}}, \bar{\mathsf{pk}})\}$.

Finally, it computes:

6. $D = \mathsf{VC.Com}(\mathsf{vccrs}, \boldsymbol{I})$.[6]

Output: $\mathsf{pp}' = (\widetilde{\mathsf{pp}}, D, S)$.

- $\mathsf{Enc}(\mathsf{crs}, \mathsf{pp}, \mathsf{id}, m) \rightarrow \mathsf{ct}$: searches the stash S and then, depending on whether $(\mathsf{id}, \cdot) \in S$, proceeds as follows:

  Identity in the table. If $(\mathsf{id}, \cdot) \notin S$ then for each $\eta \in [k]$:

  1. $(m_1^{(\eta)}, m_2^{(\eta)}) \leftarrow \mathsf{Sh.Share}(m)$,
  2. $\mathsf{ct}_1^{(\eta)} \leftarrow \widetilde{\mathsf{LE}}.\mathsf{Enc}(\widetilde{\mathsf{crs}}, \widetilde{\mathsf{pp}}, \mathsf{id}^{(\eta)}, m_1^{(\eta)})$,
  3. $\mathsf{ct}_2^{(\eta)} \leftarrow \mathsf{VCWE.Enc}(\mathsf{crs}, D, \mathsf{id}^{(\eta)}, \mathsf{id}, m_2^{(\eta)})$.

  The final ciphertext is: $\mathsf{ct} = \left((\mathsf{ct}_1^{(1)}, \mathsf{ct}_2^{(1)}), \ldots, (\mathsf{ct}_1^{(k)}, \mathsf{ct}_2^{(k)})\right)$.

  Identity in the stash. If $(\mathsf{id}, \mathsf{pk}) \in S$ for some pk then:
  $\mathsf{ct} = \mathsf{PKE.Enc}(\mathsf{pk}^{(k+1)}, m)$.

- $\mathsf{Upd}^{[\mathsf{aux}]}(\mathsf{pp}, \mathsf{id}) \rightarrow \mathsf{u}$: finds the $\eta^* \in [k]$ such that $\boldsymbol{I}[\mathsf{id}^{(\eta^*)}] = \mathsf{id}$. If such η^* does not exist outputs $\mathsf{u} = \mathsf{Stash}$. Otherwise it computes:

  1. $\widetilde{\mathsf{u}} \leftarrow \widetilde{\mathsf{LE}}.\mathsf{Upd}^{[\widetilde{\mathsf{aux}}]}(\widetilde{\mathsf{pp}}, \mathsf{id}^{(\eta^*)})$,
  2. $\Psi_{\mathsf{id}^{(\eta^*)}} \leftarrow \mathsf{VC.Open}(\mathsf{vccrs}, \boldsymbol{I}, \mathsf{id}^{(\eta^*)})$

  and outputs: $\mathsf{u} = (\tilde{\mathsf{u}}, \Psi_{\mathsf{id}^{(\eta^*)}}, \eta^*)$.

- $\mathsf{Dec}(\mathsf{sk}, \mathsf{u}, \mathsf{ct}) \rightarrow m$ or GetUpd :

  Identity in the table. If the ciphertext is an LE ciphertext:

  1. $m_1^* \leftarrow \widetilde{\mathsf{LE}}.\mathsf{Dec}(\mathsf{sk}^{(\eta^*)}, \tilde{u}, \mathsf{ct}_1^{(\eta^*)})$,
  2. $m_2^* \leftarrow \mathsf{VCWE.Dec}(\mathsf{vccrs}, \Psi, \mathsf{ct}_2^{(\eta^*)})$.

  Output: $m^* = \mathsf{Sh.Rec}(m_1^*, m_2^*)$.

  Identity in the Stash. If ct is a PKE ciphertext then,
  it outputs: $m^* = \mathsf{PKE.Dec}(\mathsf{sk}^{(k+1)}, \mathsf{ct})$.

4.3 Completeness, Security and Efficiency

Completeness. Directly follows from completeness of $\widetilde{\mathsf{LE}}$ and correctness of VC, VCWE and Sh, as long as id is always either in the table or in the stash thoughtout the lifetime of the system. That is, we desire that $\mathsf{Insert}(\boldsymbol{I}, S, \mathsf{id})$ never outputs $\perp$ for any id during the registration algorithm, even if the adversary chooses the identities that register. This is guaranteed by the $\mathsf{negl}(\lambda)$-robustness property of Cuckoo Hashing (see Sect. 3.2).

Theorem 3 (Completeness). *If* CH *is a* $\mathsf{negl}(\lambda)$*-robust Cuckoo Hashing scheme,* VC, VCWE, PKE, Sh *are correct and* $\widetilde{\mathsf{LE}}$ *is a complete Laconic Encryption with deletions then the* LE *scheme presented above is complete against any PPT adversary.*

[6] In case the VC is updatable, the updated D can computed efficiently without having to recompute it from scratch. For simplicity we do not make this explicit in the construction.

Security. The security of our LE follows by the security of the underlying building blocks. If the target identity turns out to be in the stash, then the ciphertext is simply a PKE one, and therefore we rely on the security of PKE.

If not, then the ciphertext has k components, one for each possible position of id^*, *i.e.* the first is w.r.t. position $\mathsf{id}^{(1)}$, the second w.r.t position $\mathsf{id}^{(2)}$, etc. Each component consists of a VCWE ciphertext and a $\widetilde{\mathsf{LE}}$ ciphertext. For the positions $i \in [k]$ such that eventually id^* is in fact not registered we can rely on the fact that $\boldsymbol{I}[i] \neq \mathsf{id}^*$ which allows to argue that the VCWE gives us indistinguishability for one of the two components. On the other hand, for the position(s) $i \in [k]$ such that id^* is registered one can use $\mathsf{id}^{*(i)}$ as a target for the $\widetilde{\mathsf{LE}}$ security, which gives indistinguishability.

In both cases one component is indistinguishable for the adversary, therefore one of the two shares of the secret sharing is "hidden" from the adversary. Thus the privacy of the secret sharing scheme gives us security. Below is the formal security theorem, whose proof is in the full version [26].

Theorem 4 (Security). *If* $\widetilde{\mathsf{LE}}$ *is secure,* VCWE *w.r.t* VC *is (VCWE) semantically secure,* PKE *is (PKE) semantically secure and* Sh *is* $(2,2)$ *private then the* LE *scheme presented above is a secure LE scheme.*

Efficiency. Regarding efficiency, inspecting the scheme gives:

$$|\mathsf{crs}| = |\widetilde{\mathsf{crs}}| + |\mathsf{chpp}| + |\mathsf{vccrs}|; \qquad |\mathsf{pp}| = |\widetilde{\mathsf{pp}}| + |D| + |S|;$$
$$|\mathsf{u}| = |\widetilde{\mathsf{u}}| + |\Psi| + \log(k); \qquad |\mathsf{ct}| = k(|\widetilde{\mathsf{ct}}| + |\mathsf{ct}_{\mathsf{VCWE}}|).$$

Theorem 5 (Efficiency). *If* CH *is a* $\mathsf{negl}(\lambda)$*-robust Cuckoo Hashing scheme with* $s = o(N)$ *in the worst case,* VC *is a succinct VC with sublinear CRS and for any PPT adversary of* $\mathsf{Comp}_{\mathcal{A}}(\lambda)$ $\widetilde{\mathsf{LE}}$ *has:*

Compactness: $|\widetilde{\mathsf{crs}}|, |\widetilde{\mathsf{pp}}|, |\widetilde{\mathsf{u}}|$ ***Ciphertext size:*** $|\widetilde{\mathsf{ct}}|$

then the LE *scheme presented above has (in the worst-case):*

Compactness: $|\mathsf{crs}| = |\widetilde{\mathsf{crs}}| + |\mathsf{chpp}| + |\mathsf{vccrs}|$, $|\mathsf{pp}| = |\widetilde{\mathsf{pp}}| + |D| + |S|$, $|\mathsf{u}| = |\widetilde{\mathsf{u}}| + |\Psi| + \log(k)$;

Ciphertext size: $k(|\widetilde{\mathsf{ct}}| + |\mathsf{ct}_{\mathsf{VCWE}}|)$.

As discussed in Sect. 3.2 and Theorem 1 there exist a CH with $k = \lambda$ and $s = 0$. Furthermore if $|\widetilde{\mathsf{crs}}| \geq |\mathsf{vccrs}|$, $|\widetilde{\mathsf{pp}}| \geq |D|$, $|\widetilde{\mathsf{u}}| \geq |\Psi|$ and $|\mathsf{ct}| \geq \mathsf{ct}_{\mathsf{VCWE}}$ (as one will see in Sect. 5 there are VCs with corresponding VCWE that satisfy these conditions for the known $\widetilde{\mathsf{LE}}$ constructions) then $|\mathsf{crs}| = O(|\widetilde{\mathsf{crs}}|)$, $|\mathsf{pp}| = O(|\widetilde{\mathsf{pp}}|)$, $|\mathsf{u}| = O(|\widetilde{u}|)$[7] and $|\mathsf{ct}| = O(\lambda|\widetilde{\mathsf{ct}}|)$. This means that the only (asymptotic) overhead of our compiler for LE is on the ciphertext size. We elaborate more on the efficiency of concrete RBE constructions resulting from our compiler in Sect. 5.

[7] The $\log k = \log \lambda$ factor is in bits, while the rest are in cryptographic elements (e.g. Group elements or Lattice matrices) therefore $\log \lambda$ bits correspond to one element.

Regarding the sublinear CRS requirement above, although pairing-based VC typically have linear-sized CRS, there is a well known trick [8] that trades sublinear (square-root) CRS to square-root commitments, resulting to overall sublinear parameters $|\mathsf{crs}| + |D|$.

The final step is to show a tranformation from LE to an RBE with $\mathsf{polylog}(\lambda)$ number of u-updates for each user in the worst case. But this comes directly from Theorem 2.

Corollary 1. *If* CH *is a* $\mathsf{negl}(\lambda)$*-robust Cuckoo Hashing scheme with* $s = o(N)$ *in the worst case,* VC *is a succinct VC with sublinear CRS and for any PPT adversary of* $\mathsf{Comp}_{\mathcal{A}}(\lambda)$ $\widetilde{\mathsf{RBE}}$ *is compact then* RBE *is compact and efficient on the number of updates.*

4.4 A More Efficient Compiler with Selective Compactness

As argued previously, assuming that there are efficient instantiations of VC and VCWE, the above compiler adds a minimal efficiency overhead. However, the ciphertext size becomes k times larger, where k is the parameter from CH (number of hash functions). [62] showed that a $\mathsf{negl}(\lambda)$-robust Cuckoo Hashing requires either $k = \lambda$ hash functions, or $s = n$ stash size. We recall that the size of the stash impacts our public parameters as $|\mathsf{pp}| = |\widetilde{\mathsf{pp}}| + |D| + |S|$.

This leads us to the following relaxation: Let CH_2 be the cuckoo hashing scheme from Theorem 1 that has $k = 2$ and an unbounded stash. Theorem 1 indicates that CH_2 achieves $s = \log n$ if the adversary chooses the identities independently of the hash functions' representation (correctness), or $s = n$ in the worst case (robustness). Therefore, when using CH_2, the resulting RBE scheme is secure, complete, has smaller ciphertexts and $\log n$ number of updates (in the worst case). However, it is compact only assuming a selective adversary that chooses the identities independently of chpp.

A way of interpreting selective compactness is saying that public parameters are compact (in the worst case) as long as an adversary is not actively trying to blow them up. [62] presented an attack that requires heavy (but still polynomial) computations to expand the size of the stash, when having oracle access to the hash functions. Hence, though this is possible, the adversary should still dedicate substantial computational resources to blow up the size of the stash (and thus of the parameters). In our view, selective compactness is less weak than selective security (or a notion of selective completeness, where a similar attack could compromise the correct functioning of the system) in view of the fact that there is no clear motive for an adversary to expand the public parameters of the system just to make it inefficient (security and completeness are still computationally impossible to break). We leave as an interesting open problem the investigation of practical ways to mitigate this kind of DoS attacks.

Below we formally define Selective Compactness, similar to compactness but with an adversary who chooses the identities to be registered before seeing chpp.

Definition 10 (Selective Compactness). *An RBE scheme has selective compactness, if in the following* $\mathsf{SelCompactness}_{\mathcal{A}}(\lambda)$ *game:* $|\mathsf{pp}_q|$ *is sublinear in* $|\mathcal{D}_q|$ *and for all* $\mathsf{id} \in \mathcal{D}$, $|\mathsf{u}_q|$ *is also sublinear in* $|\mathcal{D}_q|$.

$\mathsf{SelCompactness}_{\mathcal{A}}(\lambda)$

1. $\mathsf{pp} \leftarrow \perp$; $\mathsf{aux} \leftarrow \perp$; $\mathsf{u} \leftarrow \perp$; $\mathcal{D} \leftarrow \emptyset$; $\mathsf{id}^* \leftarrow \perp$; $t \leftarrow 0$; $\hat{N} \leftarrow 0$;
   $(\widetilde{\mathsf{crs}}, \mathsf{chpp}, \mathsf{vccrs}) \leftarrow \mathsf{Setup}(1^\lambda)$
2. **for** $i = 1$ **to** Q **do** *one of the following:*
   (a) $(\mathsf{id}, \mathsf{pk}) \leftarrow \mathcal{A}(1^\lambda)$;
   if $|\mathcal{D}| < n \wedge \mathsf{id} \notin \mathcal{D} \wedge (\mathsf{pk}, \cdot) \in \mathsf{Gen}(\mathsf{crs}, \mathsf{id})$ ***then***
   $\mathsf{pp} \leftarrow \mathsf{Reg}^{[\mathsf{aux}]}(\mathsf{crs}, \mathsf{pp}, \mathsf{id}, \mathsf{pk})$; $\mathcal{D} \leftarrow \mathcal{D} \cup \{\mathsf{id}\}$; $\hat{N} \leftarrow \hat{N} + 1$
   (b) ***if*** $|\mathcal{D}| < n \wedge \mathsf{id}^* = \perp$ ***then***
   $\mathsf{id}^* \leftarrow \mathcal{A}(1^\lambda)$; $(\mathsf{pk}^*, \mathsf{sk}^*) \leftarrow \mathsf{Gen}(\mathsf{crs}, \mathsf{id}^*)$;
   $\mathsf{pp} \leftarrow \mathsf{Reg}^{[\mathsf{aux}]}(\mathsf{crs}, \mathsf{pp}, \mathsf{id}^*, \mathsf{pk}^*)$; $\mathcal{D} \leftarrow \mathcal{D} \cup \{\mathsf{id}^*\}$; $\hat{N} \leftarrow \hat{N} + 1$
   (c) ***if*** $\mathsf{id}^* \neq \perp$ ***then***
   $m_t \leftarrow \mathcal{A}(\mathsf{crs}, \mathsf{pp}, \mathsf{aux}, \mathsf{pk}^*)$; $t \leftarrow t + 1$;
   $\mathsf{ct}_t \leftarrow \mathsf{Enc}(\mathsf{crs}, \mathsf{id}^*)$
   (d) $j \leftarrow \mathcal{A}(\mathsf{crs}, \mathsf{pp}, \mathsf{aux}, \mathsf{pk}^*)$
   if $j \in [t]$ ***then***
   $m_j \leftarrow \mathsf{Dec}(\mathsf{sk}^*, \mathsf{u}, \mathsf{ct}_j)$
   if $m'_j = \mathsf{GetUpd}$ ***then***
   $\mathsf{u}^* \leftarrow \mathsf{Upd}^{[\mathsf{aux}]}(\mathsf{pp}, \mathsf{id}^*)$; $m_j \leftarrow \mathsf{Dec}(\mathsf{sk}^*, \mathsf{u}^*, \mathsf{ct}_j)$

For all queries $q \in [Q]$, pp_q *are the public parameters after the* q*-th query and* u_q *the corresponding update information of* id.

Theorem 6 (RBE with selective compactness). *There exists a* CH *scheme such that the resulting RBE scheme of the compiler,* RBE, *is secure, complete and has:*

- **Selective Compactness:** $|\mathsf{crs}| = |\widetilde{\mathsf{crs}}| + |\mathsf{chpp}| + |\mathsf{vccrs}|$, $|\mathsf{pp}| = (|\widetilde{\mathsf{pp}}| + |D| + \log n) \log n$, $|\mathsf{u}| = |\widetilde{\mathsf{u}}| + |\Psi| + 1$,
- **Number of Updates:** $\log n$
- **Ciphertext size:** $2\left(|\widetilde{\mathsf{ct}}| + |\mathsf{ct}_{\mathsf{VCWE}}|\right) \log n$

The proof of this theorem is straightforward, adapting the construction of Sect. 4.2 with CH_2. The main difference with Theorem 5 is that in CH_2 the number of hash function is $k = 2$, affecting the ciphertext-size directly.

5 Concrete RBE Schemes

In this section, we discuss two RBE constructions that result from instantiating the compiler of the previous section. The first RBE is from Pairings assuming the hardness of the (decisional) Bilinear Diffie-Hellman Exponent (DBDHE) problem, while the second RBE is from Lattices assuming the hardness the Learning with Errors problem.

To obtain these instantiations, we use that based on DBDHE (resp. LWE), there exist black-box: RBE schemes with small $\mathcal{ID}$ space [38] (resp. [24][8]), and VC schemes [48] (resp. [47]). Additionally, there are PKE schemes from DDH [25] and LWE [37,55]. Therefore, to complete the building blocks of our compiler, in this section we construct two Witness Encryption for Vector Commitments from the respective assumptions. Due to space limitations we present them in the full version [26]. For completeness, and since the resulting RBE scheme over pairings comprises our central result, we also present explicitly our final pairing-based RBE construction in the full version [26].

5.1 Efficiency and Comparison

Putting everything together, we compare the efficiency of the schemes obtained via our compiler, considering both our Robust and Efficient transformation (see Sect. 4.4), with the existing black-box RBE schemes. We summarize the comparison in Table 1 of the introduction Sect. 1.1.

In conclusion, our central RBE scheme from pairings with unbounded identity space and adaptive Compactness has the same efficiency properties as the one from [38], except for a 1.5λ overhead in ciphertext size. On the other hand, if we apply our efficient compiler we get only a $3\times$ overhead in ciphertext size, albeit at the cost of having selective compactness.

For the Lattice-based construction, compared to [24]'s, if one applies the selective compactness compiler, one gets a ciphertext that is $(2\lambda + 1)/4 \log n$ smaller. For example, for 1billion users this yields an $\approx 2\times$ improvement, while for moderate size number of $100,000$ users the improvement is $\approx 4\times$.

As for the construction from the [40] R-ABE, the differences are both quantitative and qualitative. First, the common reference string in [40] is quadratic therefore applying the tradeoff of between $|\mathsf{crs}|$ and $|\mathsf{pp}|$ [18,38] the best one can get is $|\mathsf{crs}| + |\mathsf{pp}| = O(\lambda n^{2/3} \log n)$ while in our case is $\sqrt{n} \log n$. Second, and more importantly, the R-ABE scheme of [40] uses bilinear groups of composite order where the factorization of the order should be unknown. Quantitatively, given the state of affairs in composite order bilinear groups, this leads to severe inefficiency both in running times of the algorithms and group elements' size. Qualitatively the group should be generated by a trusted third party, who afterwards erases the factors of the order of the group.[9]

[8] In [24] $\mathcal{ID}$ can be arbitrarily large. We make use of the scheme with small identities to argue that compiling it to a large $\mathcal{ID}$ with our transformation instead can benefit efficiency.

[9] In theory, this is integrated in the trusted setup of the CRS generation. In practice, though, this type of CRS is highly undesirable, since no efficient MPC ceremony to generate it is currently known, in contrast to the 'powers-of-tau' CRS.

6 Key-Value Map Commitments from Cuckoo Hashing and Vector Commitments

Given a key space $\mathcal{K}$ and a value space $\mathcal{V}$, a key-value map $\mathcal{M} \subseteq \mathcal{K} \times \mathcal{V}$ is a collection of pairs $(\mathsf{k}, \mathsf{v}) \in \mathcal{K} \times \mathcal{V}$. Key-value map commitments (KVC) [1,7] are a cryptographic primitive that allows one to commit to a key-value map $\mathcal{M}$ in such a way that one can later open the commitment at a specific key, i.e., prove that (k, v) is in the committed map $\mathcal{M}$, and do so in a key-binding way. Namely, it is not possible to open the commitment at two distinct values $\mathsf{v} \neq \mathsf{v}'$ for the same key k. KVCs are a generalization of vector commitments [15]: while in VCs the key space is the set of integers $\{1, \dots, n\}$, in a KVC the key space is usually a set of exponential size.

In this section, we present a construction of KVCs based on a combination of vector commitments and cuckoo hashing. The resulting KVC needs to fix at setup time a bound on the cardinality of the key-value map, but otherwise supports a key space and a value space of arbitrary sizes.

6.1 Definition of Key-Value Map Commitments

Given a key-value map $\mathcal{M}$, we write $(\mathsf{k}, \epsilon) \in \mathcal{M}$ to denote that $\mathcal{M}$ does not contain the key k.

Definition 11 (Key-Value Map Commitment). *A Key-Value Map Commitment* $\mathsf{KVM} = (\mathsf{Setup}, \mathsf{Com}, \mathsf{Open}, \mathsf{Ver})$ *consists of the following algorithms:*

- $\mathsf{Setup}(1^\lambda, n, \mathcal{K}, \mathcal{V}) \to \mathsf{crs}$*: on input the security parameter* λ*, an upper bound* n *on the cardinality of the key-value maps to be committed, a key-space* $\mathcal{K}$*, and a value-space* $\mathcal{V}$*, the setup algorithm returns the common reference string* crs.
- $\mathsf{Com}(\mathsf{crs}, \mathcal{M}) \to (C, \mathsf{aux})$ *: on input a key-value map* $\mathcal{M} = \{(\mathsf{k}_1, \mathsf{v}_1), \dots, (\mathsf{k}_m, \mathsf{v}_m)\} \subset \mathcal{K} \times \mathcal{V}$*, computes a commitment* C *and auxiliary information* aux.
- $\mathsf{Open}(\mathsf{crs}, \mathsf{aux}, \mathsf{k}) \to \Lambda$*: on input auxiliary information* aux *as produced by* Com*, and a key* $\mathsf{k} \in \mathcal{K}$*, the opening algorithm returns an opening* Λ.
- $\mathsf{Ver}(\mathsf{crs}, C, \Lambda, (\mathsf{k}, \mathsf{v})) \to b$ *: accepts (*i.e., *outputs* $b \leftarrow 1$*) if* Λ *is a valid opening of the commitment* C *to the key* $\mathsf{k} \in \mathcal{K}$ *and value* $\mathsf{v} \in \mathcal{V} \cup \{\epsilon\}$*, else rejects (*i.e., *outputs* $b \leftarrow 0$*).*

Intuitively, a KVC scheme should be correct in the sense that, for honest execution of the algorithms, an opening to a $(\mathsf{k}, \mathsf{v}) \in \mathcal{M}$ should correctly verify for a commitment to $\mathcal{M}$. While usual definitions for VCs consider perfect correctness, our work aims at also capturing constructions that have a negligible probability of failing correctness. To capture this, we introduce a strong notion called *robust correctness*, which essentially means that the expected correctness condition holds with overwhelming probability even for key-value maps that are adversarially chosen after seeing the public parameters. We note that such definition is strictly stronger than a 'classical' correctness definition that measures the probability over any choice of input but over the random and independent choice of the public parameters.

Definition 12 (Robust Correctness). KVM *is* robust *if for any PPT $\mathcal{A}$ the following probability is overwhelming in λ:*

$$\Pr\left[\mathsf{Ver}(\mathsf{crs}, C, \mathsf{Open}(\mathsf{crs}, \mathsf{aux}, \mathsf{k}), (\mathsf{k}, \mathsf{v})) = 1 : \begin{array}{r} \mathsf{crs} \leftarrow_{\$} \mathsf{Setup}(1^\lambda, n, \mathcal{K}, \mathcal{V}) \\ (\mathcal{M}, \mathsf{k}, \mathsf{v}) \leftarrow \mathcal{A}(\mathsf{crs}) \\ |\mathcal{M}| \leq n, (\mathsf{k}, \mathsf{v}) \in \mathcal{K} \times \mathcal{V} \cup \{\epsilon\} \\ (C, \mathsf{aux}) \leftarrow \mathsf{Com}(\mathsf{crs}, \mathcal{M}) \end{array}\right]$$

Definition 13 (Key-binding). KVM *is* key-value binding *if for any PPT $\mathcal{A}$:*

$$\Pr\left[\begin{array}{c} \mathsf{Ver}(\mathsf{crs}, C, \Lambda, (\mathsf{k}, \mathsf{v})) = 1 \\ \wedge \mathsf{Ver}(\mathsf{crs}, C, \Lambda, (\mathsf{k}, \mathsf{v}')) = 1 \\ \wedge \mathsf{v} \neq \mathsf{v}' \end{array} : \begin{array}{c} \mathsf{crs} \leftarrow_{\$} \mathsf{Setup}(1^\lambda, n, \mathcal{K}, \mathcal{V}) \\ (C, \mathsf{k}, \mathsf{v}, \Lambda, \mathsf{v}', \Lambda') \leftarrow \mathcal{A}(\mathsf{crs}) \end{array}\right] = \mathsf{negl}(\lambda)$$

Below we define an efficiency notion for KVCs, which aim to rule out "uninteresting" constructions, e.g., schemes where either commitments or openings have size linear in the size of the map or the key space. More formally,

Definition 14 (Efficient KVC). *A key-value map commitment* KVM *as defined above is* efficient *if for any* $\mathsf{crs} \leftarrow_{\$} \mathsf{Setup}(1^\lambda, n, \mathcal{K}, \mathcal{V})$*, any key-value map* $\mathcal{M} \subset \mathcal{K} \times \mathcal{V}$*, any* $(C, \mathsf{aux}) \leftarrow \mathsf{Com}(\mathsf{crs}, \mathcal{M})$*, any* $\mathsf{k} \in \mathcal{K}$ *and* $\Lambda \leftarrow \mathsf{Open}(\mathsf{crs}, \mathsf{aux}, \mathsf{k})$*, the bitsize of C and Λ is polylogarithmic in n, i.e., it is bounded by a fixed polynomial* $p(\lambda, \log n)$.

We give definitions for updatable Key-Value Map Commitments in the full version [26], along with the corresponding robust correctness and efficiency notions.

6.2 KVM Construction from Cuckoo Hashing and Vector Commitments

We present a construction of a KVC for keys of arbitrary size. Our scheme is obtained by combining a Cuckoo Hashing scheme CH and a Vector Vommitment one VC. We refer to Sect. 2 for an intuitive description.

- $\mathsf{Setup}(1^\lambda, n, \mathcal{K}, \mathcal{V}) \rightarrow \mathsf{crs}$: runs $(\mathsf{pp}_{\mathsf{CH}}, \hat{\boldsymbol{T}}, \hat{S}) \leftarrow \mathsf{CH.Setup}(1^\lambda, n)$, and generates $\mathsf{crs}_{\mathsf{VC}} \leftarrow \mathsf{VC.Setup}(1^\lambda, N)$, then returns $\mathsf{crs} \leftarrow (\mathsf{crs}_{\mathsf{VC}}, \mathsf{pp}_{\mathsf{CH}})$.
- $\mathsf{Com}(\mathsf{crs}, \mathcal{M}) \rightarrow (C, \mathsf{aux})$: on input a key-value map $\mathcal{M} = \{(\mathsf{k}_i, \mathsf{v}_i)\}_{i=1}^m$:
  1. if there exists $i, j \in [m], i \neq j$ such that $\mathsf{k}_i = \mathsf{k}_j$, it aborts;
  2. $(\boldsymbol{T}, S) \leftarrow \mathsf{CH.Insert}(\mathsf{pp}_{\mathsf{CH}}, \hat{\boldsymbol{T}}, \hat{S}, \mathsf{k}_1, \ldots, \mathsf{k}_m)$; if $\boldsymbol{T} = \perp$ it aborts, else sets $\boldsymbol{T}' \leftarrow \mathbf{cat}(\boldsymbol{T})$;
  3. $(C_{\boldsymbol{T}}, \mathsf{aux}_{\boldsymbol{T}}) \leftarrow \mathsf{VC.Com}(\mathsf{crs}_{\mathsf{VC}}, \boldsymbol{T}')$;
  4. For $j = 1$ to m, let $\mathsf{ind}_j \in [N]$ be the index such that $\boldsymbol{T}'[\mathsf{ind}_j] = \mathsf{k}_j$. If ind_j exists, it sets $\boldsymbol{V}[\mathsf{ind}_j] \leftarrow \mathsf{v}_j$, otherwise, if $\mathsf{k}_j \in S$, adds $(\mathsf{k}_j, \mathsf{v}_j)$ to S^*.
  5. $(C_{\boldsymbol{V}}, \mathsf{aux}_{\boldsymbol{V}}) \leftarrow \mathsf{VC.Com}(\mathsf{crs}_{\mathsf{VC}}, \boldsymbol{V})$

It return $C = (C_T, C_V, S^*)$ and $\mathsf{aux} = (\mathsf{aux}_T, \mathsf{aux}_V, S^*, \boldsymbol{T}', S, \mathcal{M})$.

- $\mathsf{Open}(\mathsf{crs}, \mathsf{aux}, \mathsf{k}) \to \Lambda$:
  1. $(\mathsf{ind}_1, \ldots, \mathsf{ind}_k) \leftarrow \mathsf{CH.Lookup}(\mathsf{pp}_{\mathsf{CH}}, \mathsf{k})$;
  2. if $\mathsf{k} \notin \{\boldsymbol{T}[\mathsf{ind}_1], \ldots, \boldsymbol{T}[\mathsf{ind}_k]\} \cup S$ aborts;
  3. for $j = 1$ to k: $\Lambda_j \leftarrow \mathsf{VC.Open}(\mathsf{crs}_{\mathsf{CH}}, \mathsf{aux}_T, \mathsf{ind}_j)$.
  4. Let $\mathsf{ind}^* \in [N]$ be the index such that $\boldsymbol{T}[\mathsf{ind}^*] = \mathsf{k}$. If ind^* exists, it computes $\Lambda^* \leftarrow \mathsf{VC.Open}(\mathsf{crs}_{\mathsf{CH}}, \mathsf{aux}_V, \mathsf{ind}^*)$, else sets $\Lambda^* = \perp$.

  Return $\Lambda = (\Lambda_1, \boldsymbol{T}[\mathsf{ind}_1], \ldots, \Lambda_k, \boldsymbol{T}[\mathsf{ind}_k], \Lambda^*)$.
- $\mathsf{Ver}(\mathsf{crs}, C, \Lambda, (\mathsf{k}, \mathsf{v})) \to b$: parses $C = (C_T, C_V, S^*)$ and $\Lambda = (\Lambda_1, t_1, \ldots, \Lambda_k, t_k, \Lambda^*)$ and proceeds as follows:
  1. $(\mathsf{ind}_1, \ldots, \mathsf{ind}_k) \leftarrow \mathsf{CH.Lookup}(\mathsf{pp}_{\mathsf{CH}}, \mathsf{k})$;
  2. for $j = 1$ to k: $b_j \leftarrow \mathsf{VC.Ver}(\mathsf{crs}_{\mathsf{CH}}, C_T, \Lambda_j, \mathsf{ind}_j, t_j)$; if $\bigwedge_{j=1}^{k} b_j = 0$ outputs 0, else continues;
  3. if $\mathsf{k} \notin \{t_1, \ldots, t_k\}$, outputs 1 if and S^* is valid (i.e., it does not contain any repeated key and no entry (k, ϵ) and $(\mathsf{k}, \mathsf{v}) \in S^*$, else outputs 0.
  4. Otherwise, let j^* be the first index such that $\mathsf{k} = t_{j^*}$: it computes $b^* \leftarrow \mathsf{VC.Ver}(\mathsf{crs}_{\mathsf{CH}}, C_V, \Lambda^*, \mathsf{ind}_{j^*}, \mathsf{v})$, and returns b^*.

Correctness and Succinctness. One can see by inspection that the proposed KVC scheme is robust (with overwhelming probability) under the assumption that VC is perfectly correct and that the cuckoo hashing scheme CH is robust. Succinctness of our KVC scheme is also easy to see by inspection, under the assumption that VC is succinct and that we use an instantiation of CH that satisfies $k = O(\log n)$.

Theorem 7 (Key binding). *If* VC *is position binding, then* KVM *is a key-binding KVC.*

Proof. Assume by contradiction that there exists a PPT adversary $\mathcal{A}$ that breaks the position binding of our KVC scheme. Then we show how to build a reduction $\mathcal{B}$ that breaks the position binding of VC. $\mathcal{B}$ takes as input $\mathsf{crs}_{\mathsf{VC}}$, generates the CH public parameters and runs $\mathcal{A}$ on input $\mathsf{crs} \leftarrow (\mathsf{crs}_{\mathsf{VC}}, \mathsf{pp}_{\mathsf{CH}})$.

Assume that $\mathcal{A}$ returns a tuple $(C, \mathsf{k}, \mathsf{v}, \Lambda, \tilde{\mathsf{v}}, \tilde{\Lambda})$ that breaks key binding with non-negligible probability. Let

$$\Lambda = (\Lambda_1, t_1, \ldots, \Lambda_k, t_k, \Lambda^*), \quad \tilde{\Lambda} = (\tilde{\Lambda}_1, \tilde{t}_1, \ldots, \tilde{\Lambda}_k, \tilde{t}_k, \tilde{\Lambda}^*)$$

By the winning condition of key binding we have that $\mathsf{v} \neq \tilde{\mathsf{v}}$ and that both opening proofs are accepted by the Ver algorithm. In particular, since Ver is invoked on the same key k, the first step of verification computes the same indices $\mathsf{ind}_1, \ldots, \mathsf{ind}_k$ in the verification of both Λ and $\tilde{\Lambda}$.

First, notice that it must be the case that $\forall j \in [k]$, $t_j = \tilde{t}_j$. Otherwise, one can immediately break the VC position binding with the tuple $(C_T, \mathsf{ind}_j, \Lambda_j, t_j, \tilde{\Lambda}_j, \tilde{t}_j)$.

Second, if $\mathsf{k} \notin \{t_1, \ldots, t_k\}$ then by construction of Ver (step 3), $\mathcal{A}$ cannot break position binding.

Finally, let j^* be the index such that $\mathsf{k} = t_{j^*}$. Then one can break the VC position binding with the tuple $(C_V, \mathsf{ind}_{j^*}, \Lambda^*, \mathsf{v}, \tilde{\Lambda}^*, \tilde{\mathsf{v}})$. □

In the full version [26] we show that this KVC is updatable.

6.3 Key-Value Map Instantiations

We can instantiate the generic construction of the previous section with the CH scheme CH_λ from Theorem 1 (which is robust in the random oracle model) and any of the existing vector commitment schemes. If the VC has constant-size openings, say $O(\lambda)$, then the resulting KVC constructions have openings of size $O(\lambda^2)$. The most interesting implication of this KVC instantiation is that we obtain the first KVCs for unbounded key space based on pairings in a black-box manner. More in detail, we can obtain a variety of updatable KVCs according to which updatable VC we start from, e.g., we can use [15] to obtain a KVC based on CDH, [48] for one based on q-DHE. Prior to this work, an updatable KVC under these assumptions could only be obtained by instantiating the Merkle tree scheme with one of [15,48] VCs. However, Merkle trees with algebraic VCs need to make a non-black-box use of the underlying groups in order to map commitments back to the message space. In contrast, all our KVCs are black-box, if so are the underlying VC (as it is the case for virtually all existing schemes).

6.4 Accumulators from Vector Commitments with Cuckoo Hashing

It is easy to see that a KVC for a key space $\mathcal{K}$ immediately implies a universal accumulator [4,46] for universe $\mathcal{K}$. The idea is simple: to accumulate $\mathsf{k}_1, \ldots, \mathsf{k}_n$ one commits to the key-value map $\{(\mathsf{k}_1, 1), \ldots, (\mathsf{k}_n, 1)\}$; a membership proof for k is an opening to $(\mathsf{k}, 1)$, and a non-membership proof is a KVC opening to (k, ϵ). The security of this construction (i.e., undeniability [49] – the hardness of finding a membership and a non-membership proof for the same element) follows straightforwardly from key binding. Furthermore, if the KVC is updatable, the accumulator is updatable (aka dynamic, in accumulators lingo).

From this, we obtain new accumulators for large universe enjoying properties not known in prior work. For instance, we obtain the first dynamic accumulators for a large universe that are based on pairings in a black-box manner. To the best of our knowledge, prior black-box pairing-based accumulators either support a small universe [9,15], or are not dynamic [42,50]. Notably, using the CDH-based VC of [15] we obtain the first universal accumulator for a large universe that is dynamic, based on the CDH problem over bilinear groups, and black-box.

Acknowledgements. We would like to thank Kevin Yeo for helpful feedback on the robustness of Cuckoo Hashing. The first two authors received funding from projects from the European Research Council (ERC) under the European Union's Horizon 2020 research and innovation program under project PICOCRYPT (grant agreement No. 101001283), from the Spanish Government under projects PRODIGY (TED2021-132464B-I00) and ESPADA (PID2022-142290OB-I00). The last two projects are co-funded by European Union EIE, and NextGenerationEU/PRTR funds.

References

1. Agrawal, S., Raghuraman, S.: KVaC: key-value commitments for blockchains and beyond. In: Moriai, S., Wang, H. (eds.) ASIACRYPT 2020, Part III. LNCS, vol. 12493, pp. 839–869. Springer, Cham (2020). https://doi.org/10.1007/978-3-030-64840-4_28
2. Angel, S., Chen, H., Laine, K., Setty, S.T.V.: PIR with compressed queries and amortized query processing. In: 2018 IEEE Symposium on Security and Privacy, pp. 962–979. IEEE Computer Society Press, May 2018. https://doi.org/10.1109/SP.2018.00062
3. Aumüller, M., Dietzfelbinger, M., Woelfel, P.: Explicit and efficient hash families suffice for cuckoo hashing with a stash. Algorithmica **70**(3), 428–456 (2014)
4. Barić, N., Pfitzmann, B.: Collision-free accumulators and fail-stop signature schemes without trees. In: Fumy, W. (ed.) EUROCRYPT 1997. LNCS, vol. 1233, pp. 480–494. Springer, Heidelberg (1997). https://doi.org/10.1007/3-540-69053-0_33
5. Benaloh, J., de Mare, M.: One-way accumulators: a decentralized alternative to digital signatures. In: Helleseth, T. (ed.) EUROCRYPT 1993. LNCS, vol. 765, pp. 274–285. Springer, Heidelberg (1994). https://doi.org/10.1007/3-540-48285-7_24
6. Benhamouda, F., Lin, H.: Mr NISC: multiparty reusable non-interactive secure computation. In: Pass, R., Pietrzak, K. (eds.) TCC 2020, Part II. LNCS, vol. 12551, pp. 349–378. Springer, Cham (2020). https://doi.org/10.1007/978-3-030-64378-2_13
7. Boneh, D., Bünz, B., Fisch, B.: Batching techniques for accumulators with applications to IOPs and stateless blockchains. In: Boldyreva, A., Micciancio, D. (eds.) CRYPTO 2019, Part I. LNCS, vol. 11692, pp. 561–586. Springer, Cham (2019). https://doi.org/10.1007/978-3-030-26948-7_20
8. Boneh, D., Gentry, C., Waters, B.: Collusion resistant broadcast encryption with short ciphertexts and private keys. In: Shoup, V. (ed.) CRYPTO 2005. LNCS, vol. 3621, pp. 258–275. Springer, Heidelberg (2005). https://doi.org/10.1007/11535218_16
9. Camenisch, J., Kohlweiss, M., Soriente, C.: An accumulator based on bilinear maps and efficient revocation for anonymous credentials. In: Jarecki, S., Tsudik, G. (eds.) PKC 2009. LNCS, vol. 5443, pp. 481–500. Springer, Heidelberg (2009). https://doi.org/10.1007/978-3-642-00468-1_27
10. Camenisch, J., Lysyanskaya, A.: Dynamic accumulators and application to efficient revocation of anonymous credentials. In: Yung, M. (ed.) CRYPTO 2002. LNCS, vol. 2442, pp. 61–76. Springer, Heidelberg (2002). https://doi.org/10.1007/3-540-45708-9_5
11. Campanelli, M., David, B., Khoshakhlagh, H., Konring, A., Nielsen, J.B.: Encryption to the future - a paradigm for sending secret messages to future (anonymous) committees. In: Agrawal, S., Lin, D. (eds.) ASIACRYPT 2022, Part III. LNCS, vol. 13793, pp. 151–180. Springer, Heidelberg (2022). https://doi.org/10.1007/978-3-031-22969-5_6
12. Campanelli, M., Fiore, D., Greco, N., Kolonelos, D., Nizzardo, L.: Incrementally aggregatable vector commitments and applications to verifiable decentralized storage. In: Moriai, S., Wang, H. (eds.) ASIACRYPT 2020, Part II. LNCS, vol. 12492, pp. 3–35. Springer, Cham (2020). https://doi.org/10.1007/978-3-030-64834-3_1
13. Campanelli, M., Fiore, D., Khoshakhlagh, H.: Witness encryption for succinct functional commitments and applications. Cryptology ePrint Archive, Report 2022/1510 (2022). https://eprint.iacr.org/2022/1510

14. de Castro, L., Peikert, C.: Functional commitments for all functions, with transparent setup and from SIS. In: Hazay, C., Stam, M. (eds.) EUROCRYPT 2023, Part III. LNCS, vol. 14006, pp. 287–320. Springer, Heidelberg (2023). https://doi.org/10.1007/978-3-031-30620-4_10
15. Catalano, D., Fiore, D.: Vector commitments and their applications. In: Kurosawa, K., Hanaoka, G. (eds.) PKC 2013. LNCS, vol. 7778, pp. 55–72. Springer, Heidelberg (2013). https://doi.org/10.1007/978-3-642-36362-7_5
16. Catalano, D., Fiore, D., Messina, M.: Zero-knowledge sets with short proofs. In: Smart, N. (ed.) EUROCRYPT 2008. LNCS, vol. 4965, pp. 433–450. Springer, Heidelberg (2008). https://doi.org/10.1007/978-3-540-78967-3_25
17. Cho, C., Döttling, N., Garg, S., Gupta, D., Miao, P., Polychroniadou, A.: Laconic oblivious transfer and its applications. In: Katz, J., Shacham, H. (eds.) CRYPTO 2017, Part II. LNCS, vol. 10402, pp. 33–65. Springer, Cham (2017). https://doi.org/10.1007/978-3-319-63715-0_2
18. Cong, K., Eldefrawy, K., Smart, N.P.: Optimizing registration based encryption. In: Paterson, M.B. (ed.) IMACC 2021. LNCS, vol. 13129, pp. 129–157. Springer, Cham (2021). https://doi.org/10.1007/978-3-030-92641-0_7
19. Datta, P., Pal, T.: Registration-based functional encryption. Cryptology ePrint Archive (2023)
20. Dietzfelbinger, M., Weidling, C.: Balanced allocation and dictionaries with tightly packed constant size bins. Theoret. Comput. Sci. **380**(1–2), 47–68 (2007)
21. Diffie, W., Hellman, M.E.: New directions in cryptography. IEEE Trans. Inf. Theory **22**(6), 644–654 (1976). https://doi.org/10.1109/TIT.1976.1055638
22. Döttling, N., Garg, S.: Identity-based encryption from the Diffie-Hellman assumption. In: Katz, J., Shacham, H. (eds.) CRYPTO 2017, Part I. LNCS, vol. 10401, pp. 537–569. Springer, Cham (2017). https://doi.org/10.1007/978-3-319-63688-7_18
23. Döttling, N., Hanzlik, L., Magri, B., Wohnig, S.: McFly: verifiable encryption to the future made practical. Cryptology ePrint Archive, Report 2022/433 (2022). https://eprint.iacr.org/2022/433
24. Döttling, N., Kolonelos, D., Lai, R.W.F., Lin, C., Malavolta, G., Rahimi, A.: Efficient laconic cryptography from learning with errors. In: Hazay, C., Stam, M. (eds.) EUROCRYPT 2023, Part III. LNCS, vol. 14006, pp. 417–446. Springer, Heidelberg (2023). https://doi.org/10.1007/978-3-031-30620-4_14
25. ElGamal, T.: A public key cryptosystem and a signature scheme based on discrete logarithms. IEEE Trans. Inf. Theory **31**(4), 469–472 (1985)
26. Fiore, D., Kolonelos, D., de Perthuis, P.: Cuckoo commitments: registration-based encryption and key-value map commitments for large spaces. Cryptology ePrint Archive, Paper 2023/1389 (2023). https://eprint.iacr.org/2023/1389
27. Fotakis, D., Pagh, R., Sanders, P., Spirakis, P.G.: Space efficient hash tables with worst case constant access time. Theory Comput. Syst. **38**, 229–248 (2003)
28. Fountoulakis, N., Panagiotou, K., Steger, A.: On the insertion time of cuckoo hashing (2013)
29. Francati, D., Friolo, D., Maitra, M., Malavolta, G., Rahimi, A., Venturi, D.: Registered (inner-product) functional encryption. Cryptology ePrint Archive (2023)
30. Frieze, A.M., Johansson, T.: On the insertion time of random walk cuckoo hashing. CoRR abs/1602.04652 (2016). http://arxiv.org/abs/1602.04652
31. Frieze, A.M., Melsted, P., Mitzenmacher, M.: An analysis of random-walk cuckoo hashing. In: International Workshop and International Workshop on Approximation, Randomization, and Combinatorial Optimization. Algorithms and Techniques (2009)

32. Garg, S., Gentry, C., Halevi, S., Raykova, M., Sahai, A., Waters, B.: Candidate indistinguishability obfuscation and functional encryption for all circuits. In: 54th FOCS, pp. 40–49. IEEE Computer Society Press, October 2013. https://doi.org/10.1109/FOCS.2013.13
33. Garg, S., Gentry, C., Sahai, A., Waters, B.: Witness encryption and its applications. In: Boneh, D., Roughgarden, T., Feigenbaum, J. (eds.) 45th ACM STOC, pp. 467–476. ACM Press, June 2013. https://doi.org/10.1145/2488608.2488667
34. Garg, S., Hajiabadi, M., Mahmoody, M., Rahimi, A.: Registration-based encryption: removing private-key generator from IBE. In: Beimel, A., Dziembowski, S. (eds.) TCC 2018, Part I. LNCS, vol. 11239, pp. 689–718. Springer, Cham (2018). https://doi.org/10.1007/978-3-030-03807-6_25
35. Garg, S., Hajiabadi, M., Mahmoody, M., Rahimi, A., Sekar, S.: Registration-based encryption from standard assumptions. In: Lin, D., Sako, K. (eds.) PKC 2019, Part II. LNCS, vol. 11443, pp. 63–93. Springer, Cham (2019). https://doi.org/10.1007/978-3-030-17259-6_3
36. Gentry, C., Lewko, A., Waters, B.: Witness encryption from instance independent assumptions. In: Garay, J.A., Gennaro, R. (eds.) CRYPTO 2014, Part I. LNCS, vol. 8616, pp. 426–443. Springer, Heidelberg (2014). https://doi.org/10.1007/978-3-662-44371-2_24
37. Gentry, C., Peikert, C., Vaikuntanathan, V.: Trapdoors for hard lattices and new cryptographic constructions. In: Ladner, R.E., Dwork, C. (eds.) 40th ACM STOC, pp. 197–206. ACM Press, May 2008. https://doi.org/10.1145/1374376.1374407
38. Glaeser, N., Kolonelos, D., Malavolta, G., Rahimi, A.: Efficient registration-based encryption. In: Meng, W., Jensen, C.D., Cremers, C., Kirda, E. (eds.) ACM CCS 2023. ACM Press, November 2023. https://doi.org/10.1145/3576915.3616596
39. Goyal, R., Vusirikala, S.: Verifiable registration-based encryption. In: Micciancio, D., Ristenpart, T. (eds.) CRYPTO 2020, Part I. LNCS, vol. 12170, pp. 621–651. Springer, Cham (2020). https://doi.org/10.1007/978-3-030-56784-2_21
40. Hohenberger, S., Lu, G., Waters, B., Wu, D.J.: Registered attribute-based encryption. In: EUROCRYPT 2023, Part III. LNCS, vol. 14006, pp. 511–542. Springer, Cham (2023). https://doi.org/10.1007/978-3-031-30620-4_17
41. Jain, A., Lin, H., Sahai, A.: Indistinguishability obfuscation from well-founded assumptions. In: Khuller, S., Williams, V.V. (eds.) 53rd ACM STOC, pp. 60–73. ACM Press, June 2021. https://doi.org/10.1145/3406325.3451093
42. Kate, A., Zaverucha, G.M., Goldberg, I.: Constant-size commitments to polynomials and their applications. In: Abe, M. (ed.) ASIACRYPT 2010. LNCS, vol. 6477, pp. 177–194. Springer, Heidelberg (2010). https://doi.org/10.1007/978-3-642-17373-8_11
43. Khosla, M.: Balls into bins made faster. In: Embedded Systems and Applications (2013)
44. Kirsch, A., Mitzenmacher, M., Wieder, U.: More robust hashing: cuckoo hashing with a stash. SIAM J. Comput. **39**(4), 1543–1561 (2010)
45. Kuszmaul, J.: Verkle trees: V(ery short m)erkle trees (2018). https://math.mit.edu/research/highschool/primes/materials/2018/Kuszmaul.pdf
46. Li, J., Li, N., Xue, R.: Universal accumulators with efficient nonmembership proofs. In: Katz, J., Yung, M. (eds.) ACNS 2007. LNCS, vol. 4521, pp. 253–269. Springer, Heidelberg (2007). https://doi.org/10.1007/978-3-540-72738-5_17

47. Libert, B., Ling, S., Nguyen, K., Wang, H.: Zero-knowledge arguments for lattice-based accumulators: logarithmic-size ring signatures and group signatures without trapdoors. In: Fischlin, M., Coron, J.-S. (eds.) EUROCRYPT 2016, Part II. LNCS, vol. 9666, pp. 1–31. Springer, Heidelberg (2016). https://doi.org/10.1007/978-3-662-49896-5_1
48. Libert, B., Yung, M.: Concise mercurial vector commitments and independent zero-knowledge sets with short proofs. In: Micciancio, D. (ed.) TCC 2010. LNCS, vol. 5978, pp. 499–517. Springer, Heidelberg (2010). https://doi.org/10.1007/978-3-642-11799-2_30
49. Lipmaa, H.: Secure accumulators from Euclidean rings without trusted setup. In: Bao, F., Samarati, P., Zhou, J. (eds.) ACNS 2012. LNCS, vol. 7341, pp. 224–240. Springer, Heidelberg (2012). https://doi.org/10.1007/978-3-642-31284-7_14
50. Nguyen, L.: Accumulators from bilinear pairings and applications. In: Menezes, A. (ed.) CT-RSA 2005. LNCS, vol. 3376, pp. 275–292. Springer, Heidelberg (2005). https://doi.org/10.1007/978-3-540-30574-3_19
51. Pagh, R., Rodler, F.F.: Cuckoo hashing. J. Algorithms **51**(2), 122–144 (2004)
52. Patel, S., Persiano, G., Yeo, K., Yung, M.: Mitigating leakage in secure cloud-hosted data structures: Volume-hiding for multi-maps via hashing. In: Cavallaro, L., Kinder, J., Wang, X., Katz, J. (eds.) ACM CCS 2019, pp. 79–93. ACM Press, November 2019. https://doi.org/10.1145/3319535.3354213
53. Pinkas, B., Reinman, T.: Oblivious RAM revisited. In: Rabin, T. (ed.) CRYPTO 2010. LNCS, vol. 6223, pp. 502–519. Springer, Heidelberg (2010). https://doi.org/10.1007/978-3-642-14623-7_27
54. Pinkas, B., Schneider, T., Segev, G., Zohner, M.: Phasing: private set intersection using permutation-based hashing. In: Jung, J., Holz, T. (eds.) USENIX Security 2015. pp. 515–530. USENIX Association, August 2015
55. Regev, O.: On lattices, learning with errors, random linear codes, and cryptography. In: Gabow, H.N., Fagin, R. (eds.) 37th ACM STOC, pp. 84–93. ACM Press, May 2005. https://doi.org/10.1145/1060590.1060603
56. Rivest, R.L., Shamir, A., Adleman, L.M.: A method for obtaining digital signatures and public-key cryptosystems. Commun. Assoc. Comput. Mach. **21**(2), 120–126 (1978). https://doi.org/10.1145/359340.359342
57. Shamir, A.: Identity-based cryptosystems and signature schemes. In: Blakley, G.R., Chaum, D. (eds.) CRYPTO'84. LNCS, vol. 196, pp. 47–53. Springer, Heidelberg (Aug (1984)
58. Tsabary, R.: Candidate witness encryption from lattice techniques. In: Dodis, Y., Shrimpton, T. (eds.) CRYPTO 2022, Part I. LNCS, vol. 13507, pp. 535–559. Springer, Heidelberg (2022). https://doi.org/10.1007/978-3-031-15802-5_19
59. Vaikuntanathan, V., Wee, H., Wichs, D.: Witness encryption and null-IO from evasive LWE. In: Agrawal, S., Lin, D. (eds.) ASIACRYPT 2022, Part I. LNCS, vol. 13791, pp. 195–221. Springer, Heidelberg (2022). https://doi.org/10.1007/978-3-031-22963-3_7
60. Walzer, S.: Insertion time of random walk cuckoo hashing below the peeling threshold (2022)
61. Wieder, U., et al.: Hashing, load balancing and multiple choice. Found. Trends® Theor. Comput. Sci. **12**(3–4), 275–379 (2017)
62. Yeo, K.: Cuckoo hashing in cryptography: Optimal parameters, robustness and applications. In: Handschuh, H., Lysyanskaya, A. (eds.) CRYPTO 2023. LNCS, vol. 14084, pp. 197–230. Springer, Cham (2023). https://doi.org/10.1007/978-3-031-38551-3_7

Lattice-Based Functional Commitments: Fast Verification and Cryptanalysis

Hoeteck Wee[1,2] and David J. Wu[3(✉)]

[1] NTT Research, Sunnyvale, CA, USA
[2] ENS, Paris, France
[3] University of Texas at Austin, Austin, TX, USA
dwu4@cs.utexas.edu

Abstract. A functional commitment allows a user to commit to an input $\mathbf{x} \in \{0,1\}^\ell$ and later open up the commitment to a value $y = f(\mathbf{x})$ with respect to some function f. In this work, we focus on schemes that support fast verification. Specifically, after a preprocessing step that depends only on f, the verification time as well as the size of the commitment and opening should be *sublinear* in the input length ℓ, We also consider the dual setting where the user commits to the function f and later, opens up the commitment at an input $\mathbf{x}$.

In this work, we develop two (non-interactive) functional commitments that support fast verification. The first construction supports openings to constant-degree polynomials and has a shorter CRS for a broad range of settings compared to previous constructions. Our second construction is a dual functional commitment for arbitrary bounded-depth Boolean circuits that supports fast verification with security from falsifiable assumptions. Both schemes are lattice-based and avoid non-black-box use of cryptographic primitives or lattice sampling algorithms. Security of both constructions rely on the ℓ-succinct short integer solutions (SIS) assumption, a falsifiable q-type generalization of the SIS assumption (Preprint 2023).

In addition, we study the challenges of extending lattice-based functional commitments to extractable functional commitments, a notion that is equivalent to succinct non-interactive arguments (when considering openings to quadratic relations). We describe a general methodology that heuristically breaks the extractability of our construction and provides evidence for the implausibility of the knowledge k-R-ISIS assumption of Albrecht et al. (CRYPTO 2022) that was used in several constructions of lattice-based succinct arguments. If we additionally assume hardness of the standard inhomogeneous SIS assumption, we obtain a direct attack on a variant of the extractable linear functional commitment of Albrecht et al.

1 Introduction

In a functional commitment scheme [IKO07,BC12,LRY16], a user can commit to a vector $\mathbf{x}$ and at a later point in time, provide a *short* opening to a value $y = f(\mathbf{x})$ with respect to an (arbitrary) function f. We also consider a *dual* notion where a user commits to the function f and opens to

J. Guo and R. Steinfeld (Eds.): ASIACRYPT 2023, LNCS 14442, pp. 201–235, 2023.
https://doi.org/10.1007/978-981-99-8733-7_7

an evaluation at a point $\mathbf{x}$ [BNO21,dCP23]. The efficiency requirement on a functional commitment is both the commitment and the openings are short (i.e., have size that is sublinear or polylogarithmic in the length of $\mathbf{x}$ and the size of the function f). The security requirement is that an adversary cannot open up a commitment σ to two distinct values $y_0 \neq y_1$ with respect to any function f (or in the dual formulation, with respect to an input $\mathbf{x}$). In this work, we focus exclusively on *non-interactive* functional commitments [LRY16,LP20,PPS21,BNO21,ACL+22,BCFL22,dCP23,WW23] in the *standard model* (with a common reference string). Functional commitments generalize notions like vector commitments [LY10,CF13] and polynomial commitments [KZG10,PSTY13] and have found numerous applications to cryptography, most notably, to efficient constructions of succinct non-interactive arguments (SNARGs).

Functional Commitments with Fast Verification. Our focus in this work is on lattice-based functional commitments for general functions. We are specifically interested in constructions that support *fast verification* in the preprocessing model. In this setting, we allow for an initial preprocessing stage that can depend *only* on the function f (which operates on inputs of length ℓ) and outputs a short verification key vk_f. Given the preprocessed verification key vk_f, we then require that the verifier running time (and by extension, the size of the commitment and opening) to be sublinear in the input length ℓ. We can define a similar property in the dual setting where we preprocess the input $\mathbf{x}$ instead of the function f. Note that having succinct commitments and openings alone does not imply fast verification. For instance, the verification time in [WW23] is linear in the size of the function f even though the size of the commitment and the opening only depend on the depth of f.

In applications where the function of interest is known in advance, preprocessing can significantly reduce verification costs. This is common in settings like delegation and outsourcing computation. Specifically, for the closely-related problem of succinct arguments, working in the "preprocessing" model yields the most succinct constructions [GGPR13,BCI+13,PHGR13,Gro16].

Lattice-Based Functional Commitments. Functional commitments from lattice-based assumptions have received extensive study in the last few years. Several works [PPS21,ACL+22,BCFL22,WW23] gave constructions of functional commitments for broad classes of functions from lattice-based assumptions with a structured CRS. De Castro and Peikert [dCP23] gave a dual functional commitment for all circuits from the standard short integer solutions (SIS) problem in the *uniform* random string model. The authors of [KLVW23] consider a closely-related problem of delegation for RAM programs; their techniques can be adapted to obtain a functional commitments scheme for Boolean circuits from the learning with errors (LWE) assumption in the random string model; see Sect. 1.3 for more details. Their construction relies on non-black-box use of cryptographic hash functions (as well as lattice sampling algorithms). Our focus in this work is on constructions that only make black-box use of cryptographic algorithms.

If we restrict our attention to lattice-based functional commitments that only make black-box use of cryptography, the existing constructions with fast verification either support constant-degree polynomials [ACL+22] or bounded-width Boolean circuits [BCFL22]. In the dual setting, we do not have any constructions with fast verification. We refer to Table 1 for a summary of the current state of the art.

Table 1. Summary of succinct *lattice-based* functional commitments. For each scheme, we report the class of functions they support, the size of the common reference string crs, the size of the commitment σ, and the size of an opening π as a function of the function f and the input length ℓ. We assume functions with a single output. For simplicity, we suppress $\mathsf{poly}(\lambda, d, \log \ell)$ terms throughout the comparison (where d refers to either the degree of the polynomial or the depth of the circuit). The first set of constructions (above the solid purple line) are standard functional commitments where one commits to an input $\mathbf{x}$ and opens to a function f while the second set (below the solid purple line) are dual functional commitments where one commits to a function f and opens to an input $\mathbf{x}$. We say that a scheme supports "fast verification" (**FV**) if after an *input-independent* preprocessing step, the verification time is *sublinear* in ℓ and that it is "black-box" (**BB**) if it only makes black-box use of cryptographic algorithms. Note that $\mathsf{BASIS}_{\mathsf{struct}}$ implies ℓ-succinct SIS [Wee23]. In all constructions, the running time of the commitment algorithm is *linear* in the input length.

Scheme	Functions	|crs|	$\|\sigma\|$	$\|\pi\|$	FV	BB	Assumption
[KLVW23]*	Boolean circuits	1	1	1	✓	✗	LWE
[BCFL22]	width-w, depth-d circuits†	w^5	1	1	✓	✓	twin-k-M-ISIS
[WW23]	linear functions	ℓ^2	1	1	✓	✓	$\mathsf{BASIS}_{\mathsf{struct}}$
[WW23]	depth-d Boolean circuits	ℓ^2	1	1	✗	✓	$\mathsf{BASIS}_{\mathsf{struct}}$
[ACL+22]	degree-d polynomials†	ℓ^{2d}	1	1	✓	✓	k-R-ISIS
[BCFL22]	degree-d polynomials§	ℓ^{5d}	1	1	✓	✓	twin-k-M-ISIS
Cons. 3.2	degree-d polynomials§	ℓ^{d+1}	1	1	✓	✓	$O(\ell^d)$-succinct SIS
[KLVW23]*	Boolean circuits	1	1	1	✓	✗	LWE
[dCP23]	depth-d Boolean circuits	ℓ	1	ℓ	✗‡	✓	SIS
Cons. 3.10	depth-d Boolean circuits	ℓ^2	1	1	✓	✓	ℓ-succinct SIS

* While [KLVW23] construct delegation for RAM programs, their construction can be adapted to obtain a functional commitments for all Boolean circuits. We provide more details in Sect. 1.3.

§ Only supports commitments and openings to *small* values.

† The width of the circuit w is always at least the input length ℓ. In the case of an arbitrary *dense* polynomial of degree d (e.g., a polynomial with ℓ^d distinct monomials), then the width of the circuit computing it is ℓ^d.

‡ The [dCP23] construction supports fast verification for certain special cases (e.g., vector commitments and polynomial commitments).

1.1 Our Contributions

In this work, we give two constructions of functional commitments that support fast verification. Security of both construction rely on the ℓ-succinct SIS assumption, a falsifiable "q-type" generalization of the SIS assumption introduced by [Wee23]. Notably, this is a weaker assumption than the more structured $\mathsf{BASIS}_{\mathsf{struct}}$ assumption from [WW23]. Our first construction supports constant-degree polynomials and the second is the first dual functional commitment for (bounded-depth) Boolean circuits with fast verification and only making black-box use of cryptography. We provide a more detailed comparison to previous constructions in Table 1 and summarize the main results here.

Functional Commitment for Constant-Degree Polynomials. Our first construction (Construction 3.2) is a functional commitment for constant-degree polynomials where the size of the CRS scales with $\ell^{d+1} \cdot \mathsf{poly}(\lambda, d, \log \ell)$, where d is the degree of the polynomial, λ is the security parameter, and ℓ is the input length.

For the particular case of opening to quadratic polynomials (an important special case for delegating computations due to the NP-hardness of deciding satisfiability of a system of quadratic functions), our construction has a CRS size of ℓ^3. Previous approaches required a CRS that scale with ℓ^4 [ACL+22] or ℓ^5 [BCFL22]. More broadly, when considering openings to polynomials of constant degree d, we achieve a factor of 2 reduction in the *exponent* for the CRS size compared to [ACL+22]. Namely, the [ACL+22] construction has a CRS of size $\ell^{2d} \cdot \mathsf{poly}(\lambda, d, \log \ell)$, so our construction reduces the exponent from $2d$ to $d+1$. The [BCFL22] scheme has a smaller CRS for the case of sparse polynomials (e.g., when the width w of the circuit computing the polynomial f is roughly the input length $w \approx \ell$). Conversely, for dense polynomials with $\approx \ell^d$ monomials, and which corresponds to a circuit of width ℓ^d, the size of the CRS is significantly worse for their scheme. While the CRS size of our construction is worse than that of [WW23], the latter does not support fast verification (except in the case of linear functions).

On the assumption front, the security of Construction 3.2 follows from the L-succinct SIS assumption (with $L = O(\ell^d)$), a falsifiable "q-type" generalization of the SIS assumption introduced by [Wee23]. This is a weaker assumption than the $\mathsf{BASIS}_{\mathsf{struct}}$ assumption used in [WW23] (i.e., is implied by the $\mathsf{BASIS}_{\mathsf{struct}}$ assumption), and less structured generalizations of SIS compared to the k-R-ISIS and twin-k-M-ISIS assumptions used in [ACL+22,BCFL22]. We refer to Sect. 1.2 and Sect. 3 for an overview of the assumption and construction.

Dual Functional Commitment for Boolean Circuits. Our second construction is a dual functional commitment for arbitrary (bounded-depth) Boolean circuits (Construction 3.10). This is the first dual functional commitment scheme based on falsifiable assumptions that supports *succinct* openings and verification and which does not make non-black-box use of cryptography. Previously, [dCP23] constructed a dual functional commitment from the standard SIS assumption with short commitments but *long* openings and thus, slow verification. Specifically, in their scheme, the size of the opening and the running time of the verification algorithm scaled linearly with the input size ℓ. In our construction, the size of the opening is polylogarithmic in the input length, as is verification (after an initial preprocessing step). On the flip side, the [dCP23] construction has a *transparent* CRS whose size scales linearly with ℓ while our construction has a *structured* CRS whose size scales quadratically with ℓ. The structured CRS is used to "compress" the openings (see Sect. 1.2 and Construction 3.10). Security of our construction also relies on the falsifiable ℓ-succinct SIS assumption.

Extractable Commitments and Cryptanalysis. The authors of [ACL+22] showed that if the binding property on a functional commitment for *quadratic* functions was replaced by a stronger extractability property, then it can be used to obtain a succinct non-interactive argument for NP. A functional commitment is extractable if for any efficient adversary that outputs a commitment σ and an opening π to the value y with respect to a function f, there exists an extractor that outputs an input x such that $f(x) = y$. Extractable functional commitments for quadratic functions can be used to obtain a succinct non-interactive argument (SNARG) for NP (using the fact that satisfiability of quadratic systems is NP-complete). In this work, we describe a general methodology for cryptanalyzing existing approaches for constructing extractable functional commitments. Notably, we show heuristically that our functional commitment for constant-degree polynomials is unlikely to satisfy extractability. We then describe a similar attack on an adaptation of the [ACL+22] functional commitment for linear functions. Here, we show that assuming (non-uniform) hardness of the *standard* inhomogeneous SIS problem, the variant of [ACL+22] we consider is *not* extractable. Alone the way, we also give an oblivious sampling algorithm on a matrix version of the k-R-ISIS knowledge assumption from [ACL+22]. We provide an overview in Sect. 1.2 and the details in Sect. 4.

1.2 Technical Overview

In this section, we provide a high-level overview of our approach for constructing functional commitments with fast verification in the preprocessing model as well as the challenges in extending these constructions to satisfy the stronger extractability notion needed to construct preprocessing succinct non-interactive arguments.

Notation. We start with some basic notation. For a matrix $\mathbf{A} \in \mathbb{Z}_q^{n \times m}$ and a target vector $\mathbf{t} \in \mathbb{Z}_q^n$, we write $\mathbf{A}^{-1}(\mathbf{t})$ to denote a random variable $\mathbf{x} \in \mathbb{Z}_q^m$ whose entries are distributed according to a discrete Gaussian distribution conditioned on $\mathbf{A}\mathbf{x} = \mathbf{t}$. We can efficiently sample from $\mathbf{A}^{-1}(\mathbf{t})$ given a trapdoor for the matrix $\mathbf{A}$. We write $\mathbf{I}_n$ to denote the identity matrix of dimension n. We let $\mathbf{G} \in \mathbb{Z}_q^{n \times m}$ denote the standard gadget matrix (i.e., $\mathbf{G} = \mathbf{I}_n \otimes \mathbf{g}^\intercal$, where $\mathbf{g}^\intercal = [1, 2, \ldots, 2^{\lfloor \log q \rfloor}]$) [MP12], and $\mathbf{G}^{-1}(\cdot) \colon \mathbb{Z}_q^n \to \mathbb{Z}_q^m$ denote the usual binary-decomposition operator.

The ℓ-Succinct SIS Assumption. Our constructions rely on the ℓ-succinct short integer solutions (SIS) assumption [Wee23]. For a matrix $\mathbf{A} \xleftarrow{\mathrm{R}} \mathbb{Z}_q^{n \times m}$, the standard SIS problem [Ajt96] is to find a short non-zero solution $\mathbf{x} \in \mathbb{Z}_q^m$ such that $\mathbf{Ax} = \mathbf{0}$. The ℓ-succinct SIS assumption states that SIS is hard with respect to $\mathbf{A}$ even given a trapdoor for $[\mathbf{I}_\ell \otimes \mathbf{A} \mid \mathbf{W}]$ where $\mathbf{W} \xleftarrow{\mathrm{R}} \mathbb{Z}_q^{\ell n \times m}$ is a random *narrow* matrix. Note that if $\mathbf{W} \in \mathbb{Z}_q^{\ell n \times \ell m}$ is *wide*, then hardness of ℓ-succinct SIS can be reduced to the hardness of SIS using lattice trapdoor extension techniques [Wee23].

The ℓ-succinct SIS assumption is a *weaker* assumption that the structured $\mathsf{BASIS}_{\mathsf{struct}}$ assumption used in [WW23] for constructing functional commitments; notably, the $\mathsf{BASIS}_{\mathsf{struct}}$ assumption from [WW23] is an instance of the ℓ-succinct SIS assumption with a *structured* $\mathbf{W}$. While ℓ-succinct SIS is a new and non-standard assumption, it is a falsifiable assumption, and can be viewed as a "q-type" analog of the SIS assumption. We note that it is also implied by the "evasive LWE" assumption [Wee22, Tsa22], which is an assumption that has been used successfully in several other recent works [WWW22, VWW22].

1.2.1 A Functional Commitment Scheme for Quadratic Polynomials

Here, we describe our approach for constructing a functional commitment for constant-degree polynomials on ℓ-dimensional inputs. Specifically, the committer should be able to commit to an input $\mathbf{x} \in \mathbb{Z}_q^\ell$ and then subsequently open up the commitment to $f(\mathbf{x})$ where f is a constant-degree polynomial. For simplicity of exposition, we will focus on the case of quadratic polynomials, and defer the generalization to higher-degree polynomials to Sect. 3.

The Wee-Wu Scheme. We start with a quick recap of the functional commitment for circuits from [WW23] based on the $\mathsf{BASIS}_{\mathsf{struct}}$ assumption (c.f., [WW23, Remark 4.13]), adapted to the ℓ-succinct SIS assumption.[1] As we explain below, although the [WW23] construction shares a similar verification relation as our construction, it does *not* appear to support fast verification. To describe the construction, we first parse the matrix $\mathbf{W} \in \mathbb{Z}_q^{\ell n \times m}$ from the ℓ-succinct SIS assumption as the vertical concatenation of matrices $\mathbf{W}^{(1)}, \ldots, \mathbf{W}^{(\ell)} \in \mathbb{Z}_q^{n \times m}$. A commitment to a (short) input vector $\mathbf{x} \in \mathbb{Z}_q^\ell$ consists of a short matrix $\mathbf{C} \in \mathbb{Z}^{m \times m}$ along with short matrices $\mathbf{V}_i$ satisfying the following relation:

$$\mathbf{W}^{(i)}\mathbf{C} = x_i\mathbf{G} - \mathbf{A}\mathbf{V}_i$$

Then, for all $i, j \in [\ell]$,

$$\begin{aligned}(\mathbf{W}^{(i)}\mathbf{C}) \cdot \mathbf{G}^{-1}(\mathbf{W}^{(j)}\mathbf{C}) &= x_i\mathbf{W}^{(j)}\mathbf{C} - \mathbf{A}\mathbf{V}_i\mathbf{G}^{-1}(\mathbf{W}^{(j)}\mathbf{C}) \\ &= x_i x_j \cdot \mathbf{G} - \mathbf{A} \cdot \underbrace{(x_i\mathbf{V}_j + \mathbf{V}_i\mathbf{G}^{-1}(\mathbf{W}^{(j)}\mathbf{C}))}_{\tilde{\mathbf{V}}_{ij}}\end{aligned}$$

[1] In the full version of this paper, we provide the formal description and analysis of [WW23] using the ℓ-succinct SIS assumption.

Observe that $\tilde{\mathbf{V}}_{i,j} = x_i\mathbf{V}_j + \mathbf{V}_i\mathbf{C}$ is small since x_i, $\mathbf{V}_i$, $\mathbf{V}_j$, and $\mathbf{C}$ are all small. We now view $\tilde{\mathbf{V}}_{ij}$ as the opening for $\mathbf{C}$ to the quadratic relation $x_i x_j$. Furthermore, this extends readily to circuits following [BGG+14, GVW15b]. For the specific case of a general quadratic polynomial $f(\mathbf{x}) = \sum_{i,j\in[\ell]} \gamma_{ij} x_i x_j$, the left-hand side of the verification relation becomes

$$\sum_{i,j\in[\ell]} \gamma_{ij}(\mathbf{W}^{(i)}\mathbf{C}) \cdot \mathbf{G}^{-1}(\mathbf{W}^{(j)}\mathbf{C}).$$

We do not know how to decompose this computation into a slow preprocessing phase that is *independent* of $\mathbf{C}$, followed by a fast computation on $\mathbf{C}$. The analogous expression in the functional commitment scheme of [ACL+22] is given by $\sum_{i,j\in[\ell]} \gamma_{ij} w^{(i)} c \cdot w^{(j)} c$ where $w^{(i)}, w^{(j)}, c$ are *ring* elements. Since ring multiplication is commutative (unlike matrix multiplication), this can be rewritten as $(\sum \gamma_{i,j\in[\ell]} w^{(i)} w^{(j)}) \cdot c^2$. By precomputing the quantity $(\sum \gamma_{i,j\in[\ell]} w^{(i)} w^{(j)})$, which is *independent* of the commitment, the [ACL+22] construction supports fast verification in the preprocessing model.

Our Approach. To construct a functional commitment scheme that supports fast verification (with preprocessing), we introduce *additional* structure. For the case of quadratic functions, we rely on the $(\ell + \ell^2)$-succinct SIS assumption; contrast this with the [WW23] construction described above which relied on the *smaller* ℓ-succinct SIS assumption. We parse the matrix $\mathbf{W} \in \mathbb{Z}_q^{(\ell+\ell^2)n\times m}$ from the assumption as

$$\mathbf{W} = \begin{bmatrix} \mathbf{W}_1 \\ \mathbf{W}_2 \end{bmatrix} \quad \text{where} \quad \mathbf{W}_1 = \begin{bmatrix} \mathbf{W}_1^{(1)} \\ \vdots \\ \mathbf{W}_1^{(\ell)} \end{bmatrix} \in \mathbb{Z}_q^{n\ell\times m} \quad \text{and} \quad \mathbf{W}_2 = \begin{bmatrix} \mathbf{W}_2^{(1,1)} \\ \vdots \\ \mathbf{W}_1^{(\ell,\ell)} \end{bmatrix} \in \mathbb{Z}_q^{n\ell^2\times m},$$

where $\mathbf{W}_1^{(i)}, \mathbf{W}_2^{(i,j)} \in \mathbb{Z}_q^{n\times m}$. A commitment to a (short) input vector $\mathbf{x} \in \mathbb{Z}_q^{\ell}$ consists of a *short* matrix $\mathbf{C} \in \mathbb{Z}^{m\times m}$ along with short matrices $\mathbf{V}_i, \mathbf{V}_{ij} \in \mathbb{Z}_q^{m\times m}$ satisfying the following relation:

$$\mathbf{W}_1^{(i)}\mathbf{C} = x_i\mathbf{G} - \mathbf{A}\mathbf{V}_i \tag{1.1}$$

$$\mathbf{W}_2^{(i,j)}\mathbf{C} = x_i\mathbf{W}_1^{(j)} - \mathbf{A}\mathbf{V}_{ij} \tag{1.2}$$

Then, for all $i, j \in [\ell]$,

$$\begin{aligned} \mathbf{W}_2^{(i,j)}\mathbf{C}^2 &= x_i\mathbf{W}_1^{(j)}\mathbf{C} - \mathbf{A}\mathbf{V}_{ij}\mathbf{C} \\ &= x_i x_j \cdot \mathbf{G} - \mathbf{A} \cdot \underbrace{(x_i\mathbf{V}_j + \mathbf{V}_{ij}\mathbf{C})}_{\tilde{\mathbf{V}}_{ij}} \end{aligned}$$

Observe that $\tilde{\mathbf{V}}_{i,j} = x_i\mathbf{V}_j + \mathbf{V}_{ij}\mathbf{C}$ is small since $\mathbf{x}$, $\mathbf{V}_j$, $\mathbf{V}_{ij}$, and $\mathbf{C}$ are all small. We now take $\tilde{\mathbf{V}}_{ij}$ to be the opening for $\mathbf{C}$ to the quadratic relation $x_i x_j$. More generally, an opening for a general quadratic polynomial $f(\mathbf{x}) = \sum_{i,j \in [\ell]} \gamma_{ij} x_i x_j$ to the value $y = f(\mathbf{x})$ is a short matrix $\tilde{\mathbf{V}}$ where

$$\underbrace{\left(\sum_{i,j \in [\ell]} \gamma_{ij} \mathbf{W}_2^{(i,j)} \right)}_{\mathbf{W}_f} \cdot \mathbf{C}^2 = y \cdot \mathbf{G} - \mathbf{A} \cdot \tilde{\mathbf{V}}. \tag{1.3}$$

Our Scheme. To complete the description, we publish the following components in the CRS:

$$\begin{bmatrix} \mathbf{T}_{\mathsf{open}} \\ \mathbf{T}_{\mathsf{com}} \end{bmatrix} \leftarrow \left[\begin{array}{cc|c} \mathbf{I}_\ell \otimes \mathbf{A} & & \mathbf{W}_1 \\ & \mathbf{I}_{\ell^2} \otimes \mathbf{A} & \mathbf{W}_2 \end{array}\right]^{-1} \left(\begin{bmatrix} \mathbf{I}_\ell \otimes \mathbf{G} \\ \mathbf{I}_\ell \otimes \mathbf{W}_1 \end{bmatrix} \right), \tag{1.4}$$

where $\mathbf{T}_{\mathsf{open}} \in \mathbb{Z}_q^{(\ell+\ell^2)m \times m\ell}$ and $\mathbf{T}_{\mathsf{com}} \in \mathbb{Z}_q^{m \times m\ell}$. Note that the CRS has size $O(\ell^3)$, improving upon the $O(\ell^4)$-sized CRS in [ACL+22].

To commit to a short $\mathbf{x} \in \mathbb{Z}_q^\ell$, the committer computes $\mathbf{C} \leftarrow \mathbf{T}_{\mathsf{com}}(\mathbf{x} \otimes \mathbf{I}_m)$. By construction this means that

$$\begin{aligned} \mathbf{W}_1\mathbf{C} &= \mathbf{W}_1\mathbf{T}_{\mathsf{com}}(\mathbf{x} \otimes \mathbf{I}_m) = (\mathbf{I}_\ell \otimes \mathbf{G})(\mathbf{x} \otimes \mathbf{I}_m) - (\mathbf{I}_\ell \otimes \mathbf{A})\mathbf{T}_{\mathsf{open}}(\mathbf{x} \otimes \mathbf{I}_m) \\ &= \mathbf{x} \otimes \mathbf{G} - (\mathbf{I}_\ell \otimes \mathbf{A})\mathbf{T}_{\mathsf{open}}(\mathbf{x} \otimes \mathbf{I}_m) \\ \mathbf{W}_2\mathbf{C} &= \mathbf{W}_2\mathbf{T}_{\mathsf{com}}(\mathbf{x} \otimes \mathbf{I}_m) = (\mathbf{I}_\ell \otimes \mathbf{W}_1)(\mathbf{x} \otimes \mathbf{I}_m) - (\mathbf{I}_{\ell^2} \otimes \mathbf{A})\mathbf{T}_{\mathsf{open}}(\mathbf{x} \otimes \mathbf{I}_m) \\ &= \mathbf{x} \otimes \mathbf{W}_1 - (\mathbf{I}_{\ell^2} \otimes \mathbf{A})\mathbf{T}_{\mathsf{open}}(\mathbf{x} \otimes \mathbf{I}_m). \end{aligned}$$

Observe that taking $\mathbf{V}_i$ and $\mathbf{V}_{ij}$ to be the blocks of $\mathbf{T}_{\mathsf{open}}(\mathbf{x} \otimes \mathbf{I}_m)$, we satisfy Eqs. (1.1) and (1.2). To argue binding from the $(\ell^2+\ell)$-succinct SIS assumption, observe that $\mathbf{T}_{\mathsf{open}}$ and $\mathbf{T}_{\mathsf{com}}$ can be sampled using the trapdoor provided by the $(\ell^2+\ell)$-succinct SIS assumption. Suppose now that an adversary outputs two possible openings $\tilde{\mathbf{V}}_0, \tilde{\mathbf{V}}_1$ to values $y_0, y_1 \in \mathbb{Z}_q$ with respect to the *same* quadratic function f. From Eq. (1.3), this means that

$$\mathbf{W}_f\mathbf{C}^2 = y_0\mathbf{G} - \mathbf{A}\tilde{\mathbf{V}}_0 = y_1\mathbf{G} - \mathbf{A}\tilde{\mathbf{V}}_1,$$

or equivalently, that $\mathbf{A}(\tilde{\mathbf{V}}_1 - \tilde{\mathbf{V}}_0) = (y_1 - y_0)\mathbf{G}$. When $y_1 \neq y_0$ and q is prime (so that $y_1 - y_0$ is invertible), this yields a gadget trapdoor [MP12] for $\mathbf{A}$, which the reduction can use to sample a short non-zero SIS solution from $\mathbf{A}^{-1}(\mathbf{0})$. We provide the full details (and extension to higher-degree polynomials) in Sect. 3.

Fast Verification with Preprocessing. It is easy to see that the above construction supports fast verification given preprocessing. For instance, consider the verification relation in Eq. (1.3). If the function f is known in advance, we can precompute the matrix $\mathbf{W}_f = \sum_{i,j \in [\ell]} \gamma_{ij} \mathbf{W}_2^{(i,j)}$. If we do so, then the verification relation simply checks $\mathbf{W}_f\mathbf{C}^2 = f(\mathbf{x}) \cdot \mathbf{G} - \mathbf{A}\tilde{\mathbf{V}}$, which can be computed in time that depends only *polylogarithmically* on ℓ.

Extending to Multiple Outputs. Using a similar technique as [WW23], we can also extend our construction above to functions with multiple outputs. To illustrate, suppose we have a commitment $\mathbf{C}$ and a collection of T openings $\tilde{\mathbf{V}}_1, \ldots, \tilde{\mathbf{V}}_T$ to values $y_1, \ldots, y_T$ and with respect to functions $f_1, \ldots, f_T$. Then, for all $i \in [T]$, we have from Eq. (1.3) that $\mathbf{W}_{f_i}\mathbf{C}^2 = y_i\mathbf{G} - \mathbf{A}\tilde{\mathbf{V}}_1$. To support openings to multiple outputs, we publish random vectors $\mathbf{u}_1, \ldots, \mathbf{u}_T \xleftarrow{\text{R}} \mathbb{Z}_q^n$ in the CRS, and define the "multi-output" verification relation to be

$$\sum_{i \in [T]} \mathbf{W}_{f_i}\mathbf{C}^2\mathbf{G}^{-1}(\mathbf{u}_i) \stackrel{?}{=} \sum_{i \in [T]} y_i\mathbf{u}_i - \sum_{i \in [T]} \mathbf{A}\tilde{\mathbf{V}}_i\mathbf{G}^{-1}(\mathbf{u}_i).$$

The new opening is now $\sum_{i \in [T]} \tilde{\mathbf{V}}_i\mathbf{G}^{-1}(\mathbf{u}_i)$ which remains short. Moreover, the multi-output scheme still supports preprocessing. This is because the left-hand-side of the verification relation is still a linear function in $\mathbf{C}^2$ and can be preprocessed; formally, this is done by "vectorizing" the verification relation (see Remark 3.6). In this case, the verification time with preprocessing is independent of the input length ℓ, but still dependent on the output dimension T (this is anyhow necessary since the verification algorithm needs to read the opened values). In the setting where the target values $y_1, \ldots, y_T$ are also known in advance, we can also precompute the target value $\sum_{i \in [T]} y_i\mathbf{u}_i$. When both the functions and the outputs are preprocessed, the running time of the verification algorithm is polylogarithmic in *both* the input length ℓ and the output dimension T. Finally, security of the multi-output version still reduces to $(\ell^2 + \ell)$-succinct SIS. We provide the full details in Sect. 3.1. Taken together, we obtain a functional commitment for constant-degree polynomials of degree d where the size of the CRS is $\ell^{d+1} \cdot \mathsf{poly}(\lambda, d, \log \ell, \log T)$ and the proof/opening sizes are $\mathsf{poly}(\lambda, d, \log \ell, \log T)$. Compared to [ACL+22], our construction achieves a shorter CRS (reducing from ℓ^{2d} to ℓ^{d+1}) and relies on a less-structured assumption.

Generalizing to Module Lattices. Our functional commitment scheme described here generalizes directly to module lattices and ideal lattices. Security in turn relies on the hardness of ℓ-succinct over module lattices (as opposed to integer lattices). We describe the generalization in the full version of this paper. For a security parameter λ and using module lattices (along with a z-ary gadget matrix), we obtain a functional commitment scheme for constant-degree polynomials where the commitment and the opening for an input of length ℓ (and single output) is $\tilde{O}(\lambda \log \ell)$; this relies on $2^{\tilde{\Omega}(\lambda)}$ hardness of $O(\ell^d)$-succinct module SIS. This matches the commitment size and the opening size of the functional commitment from [ACL+22] which relies on ideal lattices. As noted above, compared to [ACL+22], our construction reduces the CRS size from $\ell^{2d} \cdot \mathsf{poly}(\lambda, d, \log \ell)$ to $\ell^{d+1} \cdot \mathsf{poly}(\lambda, d, \log \ell)$.

1.2.2 A Dual Functional Commitment for Boolean Circuits

Next, we turn our attention to the dual setting where the user commits to a function f and opens to an input $\mathbf{x}$. This is the setting studied in [BNO21, dCP23].

While a functional commitment that supports general functions (e.g., [WW23, BCFL22]) can be used to obtain a dual functional commitment for general functions through the use of universal circuits, the generic transformation necessarily both imposes an *a priori* bound on the size (or description length) of the function. Here, we opt for a more direct construction that avoids the need for universal circuits. Our approach is essentially a hybrid of the dual functional commitment for bounded-depth Boolean circuits from [dCP23] (which has short commitments but openings whose size scales with the input length) and the succinct ABE scheme from [Wee23]. We show how to combine these techniques to obtain a dual functional commitment for bounded-depth Boolean circuits with short commitments *and* openings. As before, our starting point is the ℓ-succinct SIS assumption, where we are given a trapdoor $\mathbf{T}$ satisfying

$$[\mathbf{I}_\ell \otimes \mathbf{A} \mid \mathbf{W}] \cdot \mathbf{T} = \mathbf{I}_\ell \otimes \mathbf{G}. \tag{1.5}$$

We again parse the trapdoor $\mathbf{T}$ as $\mathbf{T} = \begin{bmatrix} \mathbf{T}_{\mathsf{open}} \\ \mathbf{T}_{\mathsf{com}} \end{bmatrix}$ where $\mathbf{T}_{\mathsf{open}} \in \mathbb{Z}_q^{\ell m \times \ell m}$ and $\mathbf{T}_{\mathsf{com}} \in \mathbb{Z}_q^{m \times \ell m}$. If we multiply both sides of Eq. (1.5) by $(\mathbf{x}^{\mathsf{T}} \otimes \mathbf{I}_n)$ and use the fact that $(\mathbf{x}^{\mathsf{T}} \otimes \mathbf{I}_n)(\mathbf{I}_\ell \otimes \mathbf{A}) = (1 \otimes \mathbf{A})(\mathbf{x}^{\mathsf{T}} \otimes \mathbf{I}_m) = \mathbf{A}(\mathbf{x}^{\mathsf{T}} \otimes \mathbf{I}_m)$, we have that

$$[\mathbf{A}(\mathbf{x}^{\mathsf{T}} \otimes \mathbf{I}_m) \mid (\mathbf{x}^{\mathsf{T}} \otimes \mathbf{I}_n)\mathbf{W}] \cdot \begin{bmatrix} \mathbf{T}_{\mathsf{open}} \\ \mathbf{T}_{\mathsf{com}} \end{bmatrix} = \mathbf{x}^{\mathsf{T}} \otimes \mathbf{G}.$$

Take any matrix $\mathbf{W}_0 \in \mathbb{Z}_q^{n \times m}$. Then, we can write

$$[\mathbf{A} \mid \mathbf{W}_0 + (\mathbf{x}^{\mathsf{T}} \otimes \mathbf{I}_n)\mathbf{W}] \cdot \begin{bmatrix} -(\mathbf{x}^{\mathsf{T}} \otimes \mathbf{I}_m)\mathbf{T}_{\mathsf{open}} \\ -\mathbf{T}_{\mathsf{com}} \end{bmatrix} = -\mathbf{W}_0\mathbf{T}_{\mathsf{com}} - \mathbf{x}^{\mathsf{T}} \otimes \mathbf{G}. \tag{1.6}$$

Let us define $\mathbf{B} := -\mathbf{W}_0\mathbf{T}_{\mathsf{com}} \in \mathbb{Z}_q^{n \times \ell m}$. The CRS will contain the elements $(\mathbf{A}, \mathbf{W}, \mathbf{T}_{\mathsf{com}}, \mathbf{T}_{\mathsf{open}}, \mathbf{W}_0, \mathbf{B})$. Now, Eq. (1.6) essentially says we can "recode" the matrix $[\mathbf{A} \mid \mathbf{W}_0 + (\mathbf{x}^{\mathsf{T}} \otimes \mathbf{I}_n)\mathbf{W}]$ to $\mathbf{B} - \mathbf{x}^{\mathsf{T}} \otimes \mathbf{G}$. Following [dCP23], we now define the commitment to a function $f \colon \{0,1\}^\ell \to \{0,1\}$ as the matrix $\mathbf{B}_f$ obtained by homomorphically evaluating f on $\mathbf{B}$ using the lattice-based homomorphic evaluation machinery from [GSW13, BGG+14].[2] To recall, for every matrix $\mathbf{B} \in \mathbb{Z}_q^{n \times \ell m}$, every function $f \colon \{0,1\}^\ell \to \{0,1\}$, and every input $\mathbf{x} \in \{0,1\}^\ell$, there exist a matrix $\mathbf{B}_f \in \mathbb{Z}_q^{n \times m}$ that depends only on $\mathbf{B}$ and f, and a short matrix $\mathbf{H}_{\mathbf{B},f,\mathbf{x}} \in \mathbb{Z}_q^{\ell m \times m}$ such that

$$(\mathbf{B} - \mathbf{x}^{\mathsf{T}} \otimes \mathbf{G}) \cdot \mathbf{H}_{\mathbf{B},f,\mathbf{x}} = \mathbf{B}_f - f(\mathbf{x}) \cdot \mathbf{G} \in \mathbb{Z}_q^{n \times m}.$$

To open at a point $\mathbf{x} \in \{0,1\}^\ell$ to the value $z = f(\mathbf{x})$, the committer then computes

$$\mathbf{V} = \begin{bmatrix} -(\mathbf{x} \otimes \mathbf{I}_m)\mathbf{T}_{\mathsf{open}} \\ -\mathbf{T}_{\mathsf{com}} \end{bmatrix} \cdot \mathbf{H}_{\mathbf{B},f,\mathbf{x}} \in \mathbb{Z}_q^{2m \times m}.$$

[2] In the syntax of [Wee23], the ABE ciphertext is essentially $\mathbf{s}^{\mathsf{T}}[\mathbf{A} \mid \mathbf{W}_0 + (\mathbf{x} \otimes \mathbf{I}_n)\mathbf{W}] +$ error and the secret key is a short Gaussian pre-image of $[\mathbf{A} \mid \mathbf{B}_f]$ where $\mathbf{B}_f$ is derived from $\mathbf{B}$ via homomorphic evaluation [GSW13, BGG+14] of f on $\mathbf{B}$.

Observe that the size of the opening is essentially independent of the input length ℓ.[3] In [dCP23], the opening is the full matrix $\mathbf{H}_{\mathbf{B},f,\mathbf{x}}$. Here, the trapdoor $\mathbf{T}$ from the ℓ-succinct SIS assumption allows us to "compress" the opening. The verification relation is then

$$\mathbf{B}_f - z\mathbf{G} \stackrel{?}{=} [\mathbf{A} \mid \mathbf{W}_0 + (\mathbf{x} \otimes \mathbf{I}_n)\mathbf{W}]\mathbf{V}. \tag{1.7}$$

From Eq. (1.6), we see that

$$\begin{aligned}
[\mathbf{A} \mid \mathbf{W}_0 + (\mathbf{x}^{\mathsf{T}} \otimes \mathbf{I}_n)\mathbf{W}]\mathbf{V} &= [\mathbf{A} \mid \mathbf{W}_0 + (\mathbf{x}^{\mathsf{T}} \otimes \mathbf{I}_n)\mathbf{W}] \begin{bmatrix} -(\mathbf{x}^{\mathsf{T}} \otimes \mathbf{I}_m)\mathbf{T}_{\mathsf{open}} \\ -\mathbf{T}_{\mathsf{com}} \end{bmatrix} \cdot \mathbf{H}_{\mathbf{B},f,\mathbf{x}} \\
&= (-\mathbf{W}_0\mathbf{T}_{\mathsf{com}} - \mathbf{x}^{\mathsf{T}} \otimes \mathbf{G}) \cdot \mathbf{H}_{\mathbf{B},f,\mathbf{x}} \\
&= (\mathbf{B} - \mathbf{x}^{\mathsf{T}} \otimes \mathbf{G}) \cdot \mathbf{H}_{\mathbf{B},f,\mathbf{x}} \\
&= \mathbf{B}_f - f(\mathbf{x}) \cdot \mathbf{G}.
\end{aligned}$$

This yields a dual functional commitment for all (bounded-depth) Boolean circuits on ℓ-length inputs where the size of the commitment and the opening are both $\mathsf{poly}(\lambda, d^{1/\varepsilon}, \log \ell)$, where d is the bound on the depth of the function. The CRS in our construction has size $\ell^2 \cdot \mathsf{poly}(\lambda, d^{1/\varepsilon}, \log \ell)$. We note that this construction also supports preprocessing; namely, if the input $\mathbf{x}$ is known in advance, we can precompute the matrix $[\mathbf{A} \mid \mathbf{W}_0 + (\mathbf{x} \otimes \mathbf{I}_n)\mathbf{W}]$ in Eq. (1.7). Security reduces to the ℓ-succinct SIS with a *sub-exponential* noise bound $2^{\tilde{O}(n^{\varepsilon})}$, where $\varepsilon > 0$ is a constant and n is the lattice dimension. We refer to Sect. 3.2 for the full construction and analysis.

1.2.3 Knowledge Assumptions, Extractable Functional Commitments, and Cryptanalysis

The authors of [ACL+22] showed that if we strengthen the binding property on a functional commitment for *quadratic* functions to an extractability property, then it can be used to obtain a succinct non-interactive argument for NP. More specifically, in an extractable functional commitment, the binding property is replaced by a stronger extractability requirement which says that for any efficient adversary that outputs a commitment σ and an opening π to the value y with respect to a function f, there exists an extractor that outputs an input x such that $f(x) = y$. Extractable functional commitments for quadratic functions can be used to obtain a succinct non-interactive argument (SNARG) for NP (using the fact that satisfiability of quadratic systems is NP-complete).

In Sect. 4, we highlight some of the difficulties in constructing extractable functional commitments from lattices, and more generally, the challenges of formulating lattice-based knowledge assumptions. The difficulties stem from the following fundamental phenomenon about lattices, which has no analog in the pairing world: given sufficiently many independent short vectors in the kernel of a lattice $\mathbf{A}$, we can recover a trapdoor for $\mathbf{A}$ and efficiently sample short preimages for any coset of $\mathbf{A}$. (The pairing analogue would be recovering a trapdoor

[3] Technically, there is a polylogarithmic dependence on ℓ since $\log q$ scales with $\mathsf{poly}(\log \ell)$.

that allows computing discrete logs). In our attacks, we invoke this basic fact for a carefully crafted matrix $\mathbf{A}$ derived from the verification equation of the functional commitment scheme.

Attack on Knowledge k-R-ISIS. As a warm-up, we describe a candidate attack on a matrix variant of the knowledge k-R-ISIS assumption from [ACL+22].[4] Here, the adversary is given

$$\mathbf{A} \xleftarrow{R} \mathbb{Z}_q^{t \times m}, \quad \mathbf{D} \xleftarrow{R} \mathbb{Z}_q^{t \times n}, \quad \forall i \in [\ell] : \mathbf{t}_i \xleftarrow{R} \mathbb{Z}_q^n, \ \mathbf{z}_i \leftarrow \mathbf{A}^{-1}(\mathbf{D}\mathbf{t}_i)$$

where $\ell \gg m + n$ and $t \geq n + 1$. The goal of the adversary is to sample $\mathbf{c} \in \mathbb{Z}_q^t$ along with a low-norm $\mathbf{v} \in \mathbb{Z}^m$ so that

$$\mathbf{A}\mathbf{v} = \mathbf{D}\mathbf{c}.$$

One way to do this is to sample small integers x_i, and then compute $\mathbf{v} = \sum_{i \in [\ell]} x_i \mathbf{z}_i$ and $\mathbf{c} = \sum_{i \in [\ell]} x_i \mathbf{t}_i$. The knowledge assumption basically asserts that this is the only way to sample $(\mathbf{c}, \mathbf{v})$. In particular, if an adversary samples a random low-norm $\mathbf{v}$, then $\mathbf{A}\mathbf{v}$ will lie outside the column span of $\mathbf{D}$ with high probability.

Our candidate attack uses Babai's rounding algorithm to sample small *fractional* x_i's such that $\mathbf{v} = \sum_{i \in [\ell]} x_i \mathbf{z}_i \in \mathbb{Z}^m$ and $\mathbf{c} = \sum_{i \in [\ell]} x_i \mathbf{t}_i \in \mathbb{Z}_q^t$ and satisfies $\mathbf{A}\mathbf{v} = \mathbf{D}\mathbf{c}$. It is a candidate attack in the sense that we do not know how to rule out an extractor that outputs the same distribution for $\mathbf{v}, \mathbf{c}$ using small *integer* x_i's. The attack is fairly simple (in hindsight): we first construct a basis for the lattice $\mathbf{B} = [\mathbf{A} \mid \mathbf{D}\mathbf{G}]$ as follows:

$$[\mathbf{A} \mid \mathbf{D}\mathbf{G}] \cdot \underbrace{\begin{bmatrix} \mathbf{z}_1 & \cdots & \mathbf{z}_\ell \\ -\mathbf{G}^{-1}(\mathbf{t}_1) & \cdots & -\mathbf{G}^{-1}(\mathbf{t}_\ell) \end{bmatrix}}_{\mathbf{T}} = \mathbf{0} \bmod q.$$

Since the $\mathbf{z}_i$'s are independent Gaussians and the $\mathbf{t}_i$'s are uniformly random, we (heuristically) assume that $\mathbf{T} \in \mathbb{Z}^{(m+n) \times \ell}$ is full rank over the *reals*.[5] Now, an adversary can start with an arbitrary (non-zero) solution $\mathbf{y} \in \mathbb{Z}^{m+n}$ where $\mathbf{B}\mathbf{y} = \mathbf{0} \bmod q$, solves for the unique $\mathbf{z} \in \mathbb{Q}^{m+n}$ where $\mathbf{T}\mathbf{z} = \mathbf{y} \in \mathbb{Q}^{m+n}$, and then outputs the integer vector $\mathbf{y}^* = \mathbf{y} - \mathbf{T} \cdot \lfloor \mathbf{z} \rceil$. By construction $\mathbf{B}\mathbf{y}^* = \mathbf{0} \bmod q$ and moreover, $\|\mathbf{y}^*\| \leq \|\mathbf{T}(\mathbf{z} - \lfloor \mathbf{z} \rceil)\|$, which is small. From $\mathbf{y}^*$, we can compute $\mathbf{v}, \mathbf{c}$ as desired.

Attacks on Extractable Functional Commitments. Using a similar methodology, we obtain heuristic attacks on the extractability of our functional commitment for constant-degree polynomials described above as well as on a version of the [ACL+22] functional commitment for the particular case of linear functions. We note that [ACL+22] define their commitment over module and ideal lattices, so

[4] After communicating the attack to the authors of [ACL+22], Albrecht implemented and confirmed the attack [Alb23].

[5] Note that $\mathbf{T}$ does *not* (and cannot) have full rank over $\mathbb{Z}_q$.

when describing our attack, we consider a specific translation of their scheme to the integer case. Our methodology for analyzing the extractability of functional commitments follows the general blueprint:

1. We start by writing down the key verification relation. In all lattice-based functional commitment constructions [ACL+22, WW23, dCP23, BCFL22], the verification relation consists of checking that the opening is a short solution to a linear system. We re-express the verification relation as finding a short non-zero vector in the kernel of some related lattice.
2. Using the components published in the CRS, we derive a basis for this related lattice. We now use the basis to *jointly* sample a (possibly short) commitment and a (short) opening that satisfies the main verification relation.

Importantly, the commitment and the opening are sampled without explicit knowledge of a specific input. We can apply this strategy both to our functional commitment for constant-degree polynomials as well as to an integer variant of the [ACL+22] construction:

- In the case of our functional commitment for quadratic functions, we can use the above procedure to sample a commitment and a set of valid openings that correspond to an *unsatisfiable* constraint system. For instance, we show that the attacker can efficiently come up with a commitment $\mathbf{C}$ together with valid openings asserting that $x_1^2 = 0$ and $x_1 x_2 = 1$.
- When applied to our integer-variant of the [ACL+22] functional commitment for linear functions, we can use this strategy to efficiently sample a commitment together with an opening for an *arbitrary* linear function to an arbitrary vector $\mathbf{y}$. In other words, for *any* (short) matrix $\mathbf{M}$, we can construct an efficient algorithm that samples a commitment $\mathbf{C}$ and an opening $\mathbf{V}$ to *any* target vector $\mathbf{y}$ under the linear function $\mathbf{x} \mapsto \mathbf{M}\mathbf{x}$. Note that this sampler does *not* need an explicit $\mathbf{x}$ to sample $(\mathbf{C}, \mathbf{V})$. If the commitment scheme is extractable, then there would exist an extractor that can output a short $\mathbf{x}$ such that $\mathbf{M}\mathbf{x} = \mathbf{y}$. But this is precisely solving the inhomogeneous SIS problem (with respect to a short matrix $\mathbf{M}$; hardness of inhomogeneous SIS with low-norm matrices follows from the standard setting with uniform $\mathbf{M}$ via the mapping $\mathbf{M} \mapsto \mathbf{G}^{-1}(\mathbf{M})$). Thus, our attacks demonstrates that assuming (non-uniform) hardness of the *standard* inhomogeneous SIS assumption, the variant of [ACL+22] defined over the integers does *not* satisfy extractability (i.e., the existence of an efficient extractor for our adversarial strategy implies a non-uniform polynomial-time algorithm for inhomogeneous SIS). Note that due to the way we construct the basis for the related lattice, our approach can be used to (heuristically) break inhomogeneous SIS, but not necessarily SIS. We refer to Sect. 4.1 for more details.

We describe our methodology and attack algorithms in Sect. 4. We stress that our oblivious sampling attacks only apply to extractability of lattice-based functional commitments; all of the aforementioned schemes still plausibly satisfy the standard notion of binding security for functional commitments. We hope that our techniques will encourage further cryptanalysis of lattice-based knowledge assumptions (and also of the new falsifiable assumptions such as ℓ-succinct SIS) that underlie succinct commitments and arguments from lattices.

1.3 Related Work

Interactive functional commitments were first introduced in [IKO07] (for linear functions) and extended to general functions in [BC12] for realizing (interactive) succinct arguments without relying on traditional probabilistically-checkable proofs. In the interactive setting, we can also obtain a functional commitment from any collision-resistant hash function via Kilian's interactive succinct argument [Kil92]. This can be made non-interactive in the random oracle model [Mic00] through the Fiat-Shamir heuristic. Functional commitments are also generically implied by succinct non-interactive arguments (SNARKs), but constructions of SNARKs either rely on strong non-falsifiable assumptions [GW11] or rely on idealized models (e.g., the random oracle model or the generic group model). Our focus in this work is on non-interactive functional commitments in the plain model from *falsifiable* assumptions.

There have also been numerous constructions of functional commitments (and its specialization to vector and polynomial commitments) from standard pairing-based assumptions [LY10,KZG10,CF13,LRY16,LM19,TAB+20, GRWZ20,BCFL22] as well as assumptions over groups of unknown order such as RSA groups or class groups [CF13,LM19,CFG+20,AR20,TXN20]. We refer to [Nit21] for a survey of recent constructions. Our focus in this work is on functional commitments from lattice assumptions (similar to [PPS21,ACL+22, BCFL22,dCP23,WW23]). The work of [GVW15b] construct *non-succinct* functional commitments for arbitrary functions and fast verification from SIS; non-succinct functional commitments are often referred to as *homomorphic commitments*.

RAM Delegation. A RAM delegation scheme [KP16,BHK17,KPY19,CJJ21, KVZ21,KLVW23] allows a prover to compute a short digest of an input x and later on, convince the verifier that $M(x) = y$ for an arbitrary RAM program M with a proof whose size scales with $\mathsf{poly}(\lambda, \log |x|, \log T)$, where T is the running time of the RAM computation. A RAM delegation scheme can be used to obtain a functional commitment for circuits by having the digest be over the pair (x, C), where x is the input and C is the circuit, and taking M to be the RAM program that evaluates C gate-by-gate. There is a slight syntactic mismatch here because in a functional commitment scheme, the user should be able to commit to the input x (resp., in the dual case, the circuit C) separately, and later on, open the commitment to the circuit C (resp., at the input x). However, if the underlying digest-computation algorithm has the property that the digest for the pair (x, C) can be derived from independent digests for x and C separately, then it is possible to obtain a functional commitment scheme for circuits. In recent RAM delegation schemes [CJJ21,KVZ21,KLVW23], the digest is just a Merkle hash of the inputs [Mer87], which satisfies this requirement.

Taken together, the RAM delegation schemes from [CJJ21, KVZ21] yields a functional commitments from circuits that satisfy the weaker notion of *target binding* security (where binding is only required to hold for *honestly-generated* commitments). The construction of Kalai et al. [KLVW23] yields a functional commitment for general circuits satisfies the standard notion of evaluation binding for functional commitments.[6] This yields a functional commitment scheme for all circuits from the plain LWE assumption; notably, this scheme has a transparent setup and $\mathsf{poly}(\lambda, \log|x|, \log|C|)$ common reference string, commitment, and opening. The main limitation of the RAM delegation approaches is their heavy *non-black-box* use of cryptography. Namely, the constructions require the circuit description of cryptographic hash functions and lattice sampling algorithms. In this work, we focus on constructions that only make black-box use of cryptographic algorithms (and lattice sampling algorithms).

Relation to [Wee23]. The ℓ-succinct SIS assumption we rely on in this work was recently introduced by [Wee23], who showed how to use it (specifically, its extension to ℓ-succinct LWE) to construct succinct attribute-based encryption, reusable garbled circuits, and laconic functional encryption. The main technical result there is an attribute-based encryption scheme that achieves ciphertext overhead and key size $\mathsf{poly}(\lambda, d)$ (independent of both the attribute length and circuit size) for circuits of depth d under the ℓ-succinct LWE assumption. These aforementioned applications exploit the fact that the trapdoor $[\mathbf{I}_\ell \otimes \mathbf{A} \mid \mathbf{W}]$ can be used to "compress" the homomorphic evaluation matrix $\mathbf{H}_{\mathbf{B},f,\mathbf{x}}$, which is also the approach we take for compressing our openings in our dual functional commitment scheme.

We refer to [Wee23] for more discussion on the ℓ-succinct SIS and LWE assumptions, including reductions basing these assumptions on the evasive LWE assumption [Wee22, Tsa22]. In particular, ℓ-succinct SIS is implied by both the $\mathsf{BASIS}_{\mathsf{struct}}$ assumption from [WW23] (the latter is in turn implied by matrix variants of k-R-ISIS, as shown in [WW23, §6]) and the evasive LWE assumption (plus LWE). That is, ℓ-succinct SIS constitutes the "weakest" of recent non-standard lattice assumptions used in functional commitments as well as other advanced lattice-based cryptosystems.

Concurrent Work. Concurrent to this work, [FLV23, CLM23] gave new constructions of lattice-based SNARKs with a linear-size CRS based on the knowledge k-R-ISIS assumption from [ACL+22]. The construction of [FLV23] leverage the k-R-ISIS assumption to construct a polynomial commitment with a linear-size CRS; in conjunction with the knowledge variant of the k-R-ISIS assumption, they obtain a lattice-based preprocessing SNARK for NP with a linear-size CRS and quasilinear prover complexity. The work of [CLM23] introduces the vanishing SIS problem and uses it to construct functional commitments for quadratic functions (and correspondingly, a preprocessing SNARK for NP). They provide

[6] The difference in target binding vs. evaluation binding is due to the soundness properties of the underlying RAM delegation scheme. We refer to [KLVW23, Remark 6.1] for more discussion on the different security definitions for RAM delegation.

two ways to instantiate their SNARK: in the plain model under the knowledge variant of the k-R-ISIS assumption, or in the random oracle model under the new, but falsifiable vanishing SIS assumption. The results we show in this work provide strong evidence against the plausibility of the knowledge k-R-ISIS assumption. It is an interesting question to study whether our approach can be used to directly break soundness of these new SNARK candidates.

2 Preliminaries

We write λ to denote the security parameter. For a positive integer $n \in \mathbb{N}$, we write $[n]$ to denote the set $\{1, \ldots, n\}$. For a positive integer $q \in \mathbb{N}$, we write $\mathbb{Z}_q$ to denote the integers modulo q. We use bold uppercase letters to denote matrices (e.g., $\mathbf{A}, \mathbf{B}$) and bold lowercase letters to denote vectors (e.g., $\mathbf{u}$, $\mathbf{v}$). We use non-boldface letters to refer to their components: $\mathbf{v} = (v_1, \ldots, v_n)$. We write $\mathbf{I}_\ell$ to denote the ℓ-by-ℓ identity matrix.

We write $\mathsf{poly}(\lambda)$ to denote a fixed function that is $O(\lambda^c)$ for some $c \in \mathbb{N}$ and $\mathsf{negl}(\lambda)$ to denote a function that is $o(\lambda^{-c})$ for all $c \in \mathbb{N}$. For functions $f = f(\lambda), g = g(\lambda)$, we write $g \geq O(f)$ to denote that there exists a fixed function $f'(\lambda) = O(f)$ such that $g(\lambda) > f'(\lambda)$ for all $\lambda \in \mathbb{N}$. We say an event occurs with overwhelming probability if its complement occurs with negligible probability. An algorithm is efficient if it runs in probabilistic polynomial time in its input length. We say that two families of distributions $\mathcal{D}_1 = \{\mathcal{D}_{1,\lambda}\}_{\lambda \in \mathbb{N}}$ and $\mathcal{D}_2 = \{\mathcal{D}_{2,\lambda}\}_{\lambda \in \mathbb{N}}$ are computationally indistinguishable if no efficient algorithm can distinguish them with non-negligible probability, and we denote this by writing $\mathcal{D}_1 \stackrel{c}{\approx} \mathcal{D}_2$. We say that $\mathcal{D}_1$ and $\mathcal{D}_2$ are statistically indistinguishable if the statistical distance $\Delta(\mathcal{D}_1, \mathcal{D}_2)$ is bounded by a negligible function $\mathsf{negl}(\lambda)$.

Tensor Products. For matrices $\mathbf{A} \in \mathbb{Z}_q^{n \times m}$ and $\mathbf{B} \in \mathbb{Z}_q^{k \times \ell}$, we write $\mathbf{A} \otimes \mathbf{B}$ to denote the tensor (Kronecker) product of $\mathbf{A}$ and $\mathbf{B}$. For a positive integer $i \in \mathbb{N}$, we write $\mathbf{A}^{\otimes i}$ to denote tensoring $\mathbf{A}$ with itself i times. For matrices $\mathbf{A}, \mathbf{B}, \mathbf{C}, \mathbf{D}$ where the products $\mathbf{AC}$ and $\mathbf{BD}$ are well-defined, the tensor product satisfies the following mixed-product property:

$$(\mathbf{A} \otimes \mathbf{B})(\mathbf{C} \otimes \mathbf{D}) = (\mathbf{AC}) \otimes (\mathbf{BD}). \tag{2.1}$$

The following is a useful consequence of the mixed-product property. For a vector $\mathbf{x}$ and a matrix $\mathbf{A}$,

$$(\mathbf{x} \otimes \mathbf{I})\mathbf{A} = (\mathbf{x} \otimes \mathbf{I})(1 \otimes \mathbf{A}) = \mathbf{x} \otimes \mathbf{A}. \tag{2.2}$$

Vectorization. For a matrix $\mathbf{A} \in \mathbb{Z}_q^{n \times m}$, we write $\mathrm{vec}(\mathbf{A})$ to denote its vectorization (i.e., the vector formed by vertically stacking the columns of $\mathbf{A}$ from leftmost to rightmost). We will use the following useful identity: for matrices $\mathbf{A}, \mathbf{B}, \mathbf{C}$ where the product $\mathbf{ABC}$ is well-defined, then

$$\mathrm{vec}(\mathbf{ABC}) = (\mathbf{C}^{\mathsf{T}} \otimes \mathbf{A}) \cdot \mathrm{vec}(\mathbf{B}).$$

Lattice Preliminaries. Throughout this work, we let χ denote a Gaussian width parameter. We review some preliminaries on lattice-based cryptography in the full version of this paper.

2.1 Functional Commitments

In this section, we recall the formal definition of a (succinct) functional commitment. Our definition is adapted from that of [WW23].

Definition 2.1 (Succinct Functional Commitment [WW23, **Definition 4.1]).** *Let λ be a security parameter. Let $\mathcal{F} = \{\mathcal{F}_\lambda\}_{\lambda \in \mathbb{N}}$ be a family of efficiently-computable functions $f : \mathcal{X}^\ell \to \mathcal{Y}^T$ with domain $\mathcal{X}^\ell$ and range $\mathcal{Y}^T$; here $\ell = \ell(\lambda)$ and $T = T(\lambda)$ denote the input dimension and the output dimension, respectively. A succinct functional commitment for $\mathcal{F}$ is tuple of efficient algorithms $\Pi_{\mathsf{FC}} = (\mathsf{Setup}, \mathsf{Commit}, \mathsf{Eval}, \mathsf{Verify})$ with the following properties:*

- $\mathsf{Setup}(1^\lambda) \to \mathsf{crs}$: *On input the security parameter λ, the setup algorithm outputs a common reference string* crs.
- $\mathsf{Commit}(\mathsf{crs}, \mathbf{x}) \to (\sigma, \mathsf{st})$: *On input the common reference string* crs *and an input $\mathbf{x} \in \mathcal{X}^\ell$, the commitment algorithm outputs a commitment σ and a state* st.
- $\mathsf{Eval}(\mathsf{st}, f) \to \pi_f$: *On input a commitment state* st *and a function $f \in \mathcal{F}$, the evaluation algorithm outputs an opening π_f.*
- $\mathsf{Verify}(\mathsf{crs}, \sigma, f, \mathbf{y}, \pi) \to \{0, 1\}$: *On input the common reference string* crs, *a commitment σ, a function $f \in \mathcal{F}$, a value $\mathbf{y} \in \mathcal{Y}^T$, and an opening π, the verification algorithm outputs a bit $b \in \{0, 1\}$.*

We now define several correctness and security properties on the functional commitment scheme:

- **Correctness:** *For all security parameters λ, all functions $f \in \mathcal{F}$, and all inputs $\mathbf{x} \in \mathcal{X}^\ell$,*

$$\Pr\left[\mathsf{Verify}\big(\mathsf{crs}, \sigma, f, f(\mathbf{x}), \pi_f\big) = 1 : \begin{array}{r} \mathsf{crs} \leftarrow \mathsf{Setup}(1^\lambda); \\ (\sigma, \mathsf{st}) \leftarrow \mathsf{Commit}(\mathsf{crs}, \mathbf{x}); \\ \pi_f \leftarrow \mathsf{Eval}(\mathsf{st}, f) \end{array}\right] = 1 - \mathsf{negl}(\lambda).$$

- **Succinctness:** *There exists a universal polynomial* $\mathsf{poly}(\cdot)$ *such that for all $\lambda \in \mathbb{N}$, $|\sigma| = \mathsf{poly}(\lambda, \log \ell)$ and $|\pi_f| = \mathsf{poly}(\lambda, \log \ell, T)$ in the correctness definition.*
- **Binding:** *We say Π_{FC} satisfies statistical (resp., computational) binding if for all adversaries $\mathcal{A}$ (resp., efficient adversaries $\mathcal{A}$),*

$$\Pr\left[\mathsf{Verify}(\mathsf{crs}, \sigma, f, y_0, \pi_0) = 1 = \mathsf{Verify}(\mathsf{crs}, \sigma, f, y_1, \pi_1)\right] = \mathsf{negl}(\lambda),$$

where $\mathsf{crs} \leftarrow \mathsf{Setup}(1^\lambda, 1^\ell, 1^d)$ *and* $(\sigma, f, (y_0, \pi_0), (y_1, \pi_1)) \leftarrow \mathcal{A}(1^\lambda, 1^\ell, 1^d, \mathsf{crs})$.

Functional Commitments with Preprocessing. In many constructions of functional commitments, verifying an opening with respect to a function f requires time that scales with the running time of f and the size of the opening often *scales* with the output dimension T. In settings where the function f and the target $\mathbf{y}$ are known in advance (e.g., f could encode a list of predicates and the output $\mathbf{y}$ could be the all-ones vector, indicating that every predicate should be satisfied by the committed input)), it is sometimes possible to decompose the verification algorithm into a "slow" offline step that takes as input the function f and the target output $\mathbf{y}$ and outputs a verification key $\mathsf{vk}_{f,\mathbf{y}}$. Importantly, $\mathsf{vk}_{f,\mathbf{y}}$ is independent of the commitment and the opening. Then, there is a fast online verification algorithm that uses the preprocessed verification key to validate the commitment and opening in time that is sublinear in the size of f and the number of outputs T.

In Remark 3.3, we note that it is also possible to preprocess the verification key when only the function f is known in advance. In this case, the online verification algorithm will need to run in time that grows with the output dimension T (since the verifier necessarily has to read the output in this case). Several recent schemes support fast verification with preprocessing [ACL+22, dCP23, BCFL22]. We define this below:

Definition 2.2 (Functional Commitment with Full Preprocessing). *Let λ be a security parameter. Let $\mathcal{F} = \{\mathcal{F}_\lambda\}_{\lambda \in \mathbb{N}}$ be a family of efficiently-computable functions $f \colon \mathcal{X}^\ell \to \mathcal{Y}^T$ where each function f can be computed by a Boolean circuit of size at most $s = s(\lambda)$. Let $\Pi_{\mathsf{FC}} = (\mathsf{Setup}, \mathsf{Commit}, \mathsf{Eval}, \mathsf{Verify})$ be a succinct functional commitment for $\mathcal{F}$. We say that $\mathcal{F}$ supports preprocessing if the verification algorithm can be decomposed into two efficient algorithms $(\mathsf{Preprocess}, \mathsf{OnlineVerify})$ with the following syntax:*

- $\mathsf{Preprocess}(\mathsf{crs}, f, \mathbf{y}) \to \mathsf{vk}_{f,\mathbf{y}}$: *On input the common reference string crs, a function $f \in \mathcal{F}$, and an output $\mathbf{y} \in \mathcal{Y}^T$, the preprocess algorithm outputs a verification key $\mathsf{vk}_{f,\mathbf{y}}$.*
- $\mathsf{OnlineVerify}(\mathsf{vk}, \sigma, \pi) \to \{0,1\}$: *On input a verification key vk, a commitment σ, and an opening π, the online verification algorithm outputs a bit $b \in \{0,1\}$.*

We require that

$$\mathsf{Verify}(\mathsf{crs}, \sigma, f, \mathbf{y}, \pi) := \mathsf{OnlineVerify}(\mathsf{Preprocess}(\mathsf{crs}, f, \mathbf{y}), \sigma, \pi).$$

In addition, we require the additional succinctness property:

- **Fast Online Verification:** *There exists a universal polynomial $\mathsf{poly}(\cdot)$ such that for all $\lambda \in \mathbb{N}$, for $\mathsf{crs} \leftarrow \mathsf{Setup}(1^\lambda)$, all functions $f \in \mathcal{F}$, and all outputs $\mathbf{y} \in \mathcal{Y}^T$, the verification key $\mathsf{vk}_{f,\mathbf{y}}$ output by $\mathsf{Preprocess}(\mathsf{crs}, f, \mathbf{y})$ satisfies $|\mathsf{vk}_{f,\mathbf{y}}| = \mathsf{poly}(\lambda, \log s, \log T)$, and moreover, the running time of $\mathsf{OnlineVerify}$ is $\mathsf{poly}(\lambda, \log s, \log T)$.*

Remark 2.3 (Function-Only Preprocessing). We can also consider functional commitments with a weaker function-only preprocessing where the preprocessing algorithm $\mathsf{Preprocess}$ only takes the crs and the function f as input (but *not* the output $\mathbf{y}$) and outputs a preprocessed function key vk_f. Then, the online verification algorithm $\mathsf{OnlineVerify}$ takes the verification key vk_f, the output $\mathbf{y} \in \mathcal{Y}^T$, the commitment σ, and the opening π as input. In this case, we require that the size of the verification key $\mathsf{vk}_f = \mathsf{poly}(\lambda, \log s)$, and the verification time to be $\mathsf{poly}(\lambda, \log s, T)$. Notably, the online verification algorithm can now depend on the output dimension T (and this is required since the verification algorithm must read the output).

3 Functional Commitments with Fast Verification

In this section, we show how to construct a functional commitment for constant-degree polynomials that support fast verification. Security of our construction relies on the ℓ-succinct short integer solutions problem from [Wee23], which we recall below:

Assumption 3.1 (ℓ-Succinct SIS [Wee23]). Let λ be a security parameter and $n = n(\lambda), m = m(\lambda), q = q(\lambda)$, $\chi = \chi(\lambda)$, and $\beta = \beta(\lambda)$ be lattice parameters. We say that the ℓ-succinct SIS assumption with parameters (n, m, q, χ, β) holds if for all efficient adversaries $\mathcal{A}$,

$$\Pr\left[\mathbf{A}\mathbf{x} = \mathbf{0} \text{ and } 0 < \|\mathbf{x}\| \leq \beta : \begin{array}{c} \mathbf{A} \xleftarrow{\text{R}} \mathbb{Z}_q^{n\times m}, \mathbf{W} \xleftarrow{\text{R}} \mathbb{Z}_q^{n\ell\times m}, \\ \mathbf{R} \leftarrow [\mathbf{I}_\ell \otimes \mathbf{A} \mid \mathbf{W}]_\chi^{-1}(\mathbf{G}_{n\ell}) \\ \mathbf{x} \leftarrow \mathcal{A}(1^\lambda, \mathbf{A}, \mathbf{W}, \mathbf{R}) \end{array}\right] = \mathsf{negl}(\lambda).$$

As suggested in [Wee23], we consider parameter settings for (n, m, q, β) where $\mathsf{SIS}_{n,m,q,\beta}$ hold and where $\chi = \mathsf{poly}(\lambda, m, \ell)$.

Construction 3.2 (Functional Commitment for Constant-Degree Polynomials). Let λ be a security parameter and $n = n(\lambda)$, $m = m(\lambda)$, $q = q(\lambda)$, $\chi = \chi(\lambda)$ be lattice parameters. Let $\ell = \ell(\lambda)$ be an input length parameter, $d_{\max} = O(1)$ be a *constant* degree bound, $B_{\mathsf{in}} = B_{\mathsf{in}}(\lambda)$ be a bound on the magnitude of the inputs, and $B_{\mathsf{out}} = B_{\mathsf{out}}(\lambda)$ be a bound on the magnitude of the outputs. Let $L = \sum_{i \in [d_{\max}]} \ell^i$ and $B = B(\lambda)$ be a verification bound. Let $\mathcal{F}_\lambda$ be the set of functions $f \colon [-B_{\mathsf{in}}, B_{\mathsf{in}}]^\ell \to [-B_{\mathsf{out}}, B_{\mathsf{out}}]$ where f can be computed by a *homogeneous* polynomial[7] with B_{in}-bounded coefficients and degree at most $d_{\max}$. We associate a function $f \in \mathcal{F}_\lambda$ with a vector $\mathbf{f} \in [-B_{\mathsf{in}}, B_{\mathsf{in}}]^{\ell^d}$ for some $d \leq d_{\max}$ and define $f(\mathbf{x}) := \mathbf{f}^\mathsf{T}\mathbf{x}^{\otimes d}$. We construct a functional commitment $\Pi_{\mathsf{FC}} = (\mathsf{Setup}, \mathsf{Commit}, \mathsf{Eval}, \mathsf{Verify})$ for $\mathcal{F} = \{\mathcal{F}_\lambda\}_{\lambda \in \mathbb{N}}$ as follows:

- $\mathsf{Setup}(1^\lambda)$: On input the security parameter λ, the setup algorithm samples $(\mathbf{A}, \mathbf{R}) \leftarrow \mathsf{TrapGen}(1^n, q, m)$ and $\mathbf{W} \xleftarrow{\text{R}} \mathbb{Z}_q^{Ln\times m}$. Next, define the target matrix

[7] A functional commitment scheme for homogeneous polynomials implies one for non-homogeneous polynomial by padding the input with a constant-value 1. See also Remark 3.4.

$$\mathbf{P} = \begin{bmatrix} \mathbf{I}_\ell \otimes \mathbf{G} \\ \mathbf{I}_\ell \otimes \mathbf{W}_1 \\ \vdots \\ \mathbf{I}_\ell \otimes \mathbf{W}_{d_{\max}-1} \end{bmatrix} \in \mathbb{Z}_q^{Ln \times \ell m} \quad \text{where} \quad \mathbf{W} = \begin{bmatrix} \mathbf{W}_1 \\ \vdots \\ \mathbf{W}_{d_{\max}} \end{bmatrix} \in \mathbb{Z}_q^{Ln \times m}, \tag{3.1}$$

where $\mathbf{W}_i \in \mathbb{Z}_q^{\ell^i n \times m}$. Then, compute $\mathbf{T} \leftarrow \mathsf{SamplePre}([\mathbf{I}_L \otimes \mathbf{A} \mid \mathbf{W}], \mathbf{I}_L \otimes \mathbf{R}, \mathbf{P}, \chi) \in \mathbb{Z}_q^{(Lm+m)\times \ell m}$. Parse $\mathbf{T} = \begin{bmatrix} \mathbf{T}_{\mathsf{open}} \\ \mathbf{T}_{\mathsf{com}} \end{bmatrix}$ where $\mathbf{T}_{\mathsf{open}} \in \mathbb{Z}_q^{Lm \times \ell m}$ and $\mathbf{T}_{\mathsf{com}} \in \mathbb{Z}_q^{m \times \ell m}$. Output the common reference string $\mathsf{crs} = (\mathbf{A}, \mathbf{W}, \mathbf{T}_{\mathsf{com}}, \mathbf{T}_{\mathsf{open}})$.

- $\mathsf{Commit}(\mathsf{crs}, \mathbf{x})$: On input the common reference string $\mathsf{crs} = (\mathbf{A}, \mathbf{W}, \mathbf{T}_{\mathsf{com}}, \mathbf{T}_{\mathsf{open}})$ and an input $\mathbf{x} \in [-B_{\mathsf{in}}, B_{\mathsf{in}}]^\ell$, the commit algorithm outputs the commitment $\sigma = \mathbf{C} = \mathbf{T}_{\mathsf{com}}(\mathbf{x} \otimes \mathbf{I}_m) \in \mathbb{Z}_q^{m \times m}$ and the state $\mathsf{st} = \mathbf{x}$.
- $\mathsf{Eval}(\mathsf{crs}, \mathsf{st}, f)$: On input the common reference string $\mathsf{crs} = (\mathbf{A}, \mathbf{W}, \mathbf{T}_{\mathsf{com}}, \mathbf{T}_{\mathsf{open}})$, the state $\mathsf{st} = \mathbf{x}$, and a function $f = \mathbf{f} \in \mathbb{Z}_q^{\ell^d}$ (for some $d \le d_{\max}$) with B_{in}-bounded coefficients, the evaluation algorithm first computes $\mathbf{V} = \mathbf{T}_{\mathsf{open}}(\mathbf{x} \otimes \mathbf{I}_m)$. It then parses

$$\mathbf{V} = \begin{bmatrix} \mathbf{V}_1 \\ \vdots \\ \mathbf{V}_{d_{\max}} \end{bmatrix} \in \mathbb{Z}_q^{Lm \times m} \tag{3.2}$$

where $\mathbf{V}_i \in \mathbb{Z}_q^{\ell^i m \times m}$. Let $\mathbf{V}_1' \leftarrow \mathbf{V}_1$ and for $i \in [d]$, let $\mathbf{V}_i' \leftarrow (\mathbf{x} \otimes \mathbf{I}_{\ell^{i-1}m})\mathbf{V}_{i-1}' + \mathbf{V}_i \mathbf{C}^{i-1} \in \mathbb{Z}_q^{\ell^i m \times m}$. Equivalently, in expanded form, we can write

$$\begin{aligned} \mathbf{V}_i' &= \mathbf{V}_i \mathbf{C}^{i-1} + (\mathbf{x} \otimes \mathbf{I}_{\ell^{i-1}m})\mathbf{V}_{i-1}\mathbf{C} + (\mathbf{x}^{\otimes 2} \otimes \mathbf{I}_{\ell^{i-2}m})\mathbf{V}_{i-2}\mathbf{C}^2 + \cdots + (\mathbf{x}^{\otimes i-1} \otimes \mathbf{I}_{\ell m})\mathbf{V}_1 \\ &= \sum_{j \in [i]} (\mathbf{x}^{\otimes i-j} \otimes \mathbf{I}_{\ell^j m})\mathbf{V}_j \mathbf{C}^{j-1} \end{aligned}$$

Output the opening $\pi_f = \mathbf{V}_f = (\mathbf{f}^\top \otimes \mathbf{I}_m)\mathbf{V}_d' \in \mathbb{Z}_q^{m \times m}$.
- $\mathsf{Verify}(\mathsf{crs}, \sigma, f, y, \pi)$: On input $\mathsf{crs} = (\mathbf{A}, \mathbf{W}, \mathbf{T}_{\mathsf{com}}, \mathbf{T}_{\mathsf{open}})$, the commitment $\sigma = \mathbf{C} \in \mathbb{Z}_q^{m \times m}$, the output $y \in [-B_{\mathsf{out}}, B_{\mathsf{out}}]$, a function $f = \mathbf{f} \in \mathbb{Z}_q^{\ell^d}$ (for some $d \le d_{\max}$) with B_{in}-bounded coefficients, and the proof $\pi = \mathbf{V} \in \mathbb{Z}_q^{m \times m}$, the verification algorithm first parses $\mathbf{W}$ into $\mathbf{W}_1, \ldots, \mathbf{W}_{d_{\max}}$ as in Eq. (3.1) and outputs 1 if

$$\|\mathbf{V}\| \le B \quad \text{and} \quad (\mathbf{f}^\top \otimes \mathbf{I}_m)\mathbf{W}_d \mathbf{C}^d = y \cdot \mathbf{G} - \mathbf{A}\mathbf{V}. \tag{3.3}$$

Remark 3.3 (Supporting Preprocessing). Similar to previous (non-succinct) homomorphic commitments [GVW15b] and succinct functional commitments [ACL+22, dCP23, BCFL22], our functional commitment Construction 3.2 supports fast verification in the preprocessing model. Note that since the output dimension is 1, we do not distinguish between function-only preprocessing (Remark 2.3) and full preprocessing (Definition 2.2). We define the preprocessing and online verification algorithms as follows:

- $\mathsf{Preprocess}(\mathsf{crs}, f)$: On input $\mathsf{crs} = (\mathbf{A}, \mathbf{W}, \mathbf{T}_{\mathsf{com}}, \mathbf{T}_{\mathsf{open}})$ and the function $f = \mathbf{f} \in \mathbb{Z}_q^{\ell^d}$ for some $d \leq d_{\max}$, the preprocess algorithm outputs $\mathsf{vk}_f = \mathbf{F}_d = (\mathbf{f}^{\mathsf{T}} \otimes \mathbf{I}_m)\mathbf{W}_d \in \mathbb{Z}_q^{n \times m}$.
- $\mathsf{OnlineVerify}(\mathsf{vk}, \sigma, y, \pi)$: On input the verification key $\mathsf{vk} = \mathbf{F}_d$, the commitment $\sigma = \mathbf{C} \in \mathbb{Z}_q^{m \times m}$, the value $y \in [-B_{\mathsf{out}}, B_{\mathsf{out}}]$, and the opening $\pi = \mathbf{V} \in \mathbb{Z}_q^{m \times m}$, the online verification algorithm outputs 1 if

$$\|\mathbf{V}\| \leq B \quad \text{and} \quad \mathbf{F}_d \cdot \mathbf{C}^d = y \cdot \mathbf{G} - \mathbf{A}\mathbf{V}.$$

By construction, $|\mathbf{F}_d| = nm \log q$ and similarly, the online verification algorithm runs in time $\mathsf{poly}(n, m, d_{\max}, \log q)$. We can set the parameters for Construction 3.2, so $n, m, \log q$ scale polylogarithmically with the input dimension ℓ.

Remark 3.4 (Supporting Non-homogeneous Polynomials). It is straightforward to extend a functional commitment for homogeneous polynomials (i.e., polynomials where every monomial has the same degree) to a functional commitment for inhomogeneous polynomials. Specifically, to support openings to inhomogeneous polynomials over inputs of dimension ℓ, we instantiate a scheme that supports homogeneous polynomials over inputs of dimension $\ell+1$. Then to commit to an input $\mathbf{x} \in \mathbb{Z}_q^\ell$, the committer commits to the extended vector $\mathbf{x}' = \left[\begin{smallmatrix}1\\ \mathbf{x}\end{smallmatrix}\right]$. Now, every inhomogeneous polynomial $f \colon \mathbb{Z}_q^\ell \to \mathbb{Z}_q$ of degree at most d can be described by a *homogeneous* polynomial $f' \colon \mathbb{Z}_q^{\ell+1} \to \mathbb{Z}_q$ of degree d where $f'(\mathbf{x}') = f(\mathbf{x})$. Now, to open to an inhomogeneous polynomial f, the committer instead open to f'.

Correctness and Security Analysis. We provide the correctness and security analysis of Construction 3.2 in the full version of this paper.

3.1 Opening to Multiple Outputs

In this section, we describe how to extend Construction 3.2 to obtain a functional commitment scheme that supports succinct openings to *multiple* outputs (i.e., the size of the opening scales sub-linearly with the number of functions we open to). Our approach follows the approach from [WW23] for aggregating openings.

Construction 3.5 (Multi-output Functional Commitment for Constant-Degree Polynomials). Let λ be a security parameter. Let $n, m, q, \chi, \ell, d_{\max}, B_{\mathsf{in}}, B_{\mathsf{out}}, B$ be the same parameters as in Construction 3.2. Let $T = T(\lambda)$ be a bound on the number of outputs. Let $\mathcal{F} = \{\mathcal{F}_\lambda\}_{\lambda \in \mathbb{N}}$ be the set of functions $f \colon [-B_{\mathsf{in}}, B_{\mathsf{in}}]^\ell \to [-B_{\mathsf{out}}, B_{\mathsf{out}}]^T$, where each function f can be described by a vector of homogeneous polynomials $(\mathbf{f}_1, \ldots, \mathbf{f}_T)$ with B_{in}-bounded coefficients and of the same degree $d \leq d_{\max}$:[8]

$$f(\mathbf{x}) := \left(\mathbf{f}_1^{\mathsf{T}} \mathbf{x}^{\otimes d}, \ldots, \mathbf{f}_T^{\mathsf{T}} \mathbf{x}^{\otimes d}\right).$$

[8] Our construction also supports the setting where $\mathbf{f}_1, \ldots, \mathbf{f}_T$ have different degrees $d_1, \ldots, d_T \leq d_{\max}$. For simplicity of exposition, we just describe the case where they have equal degree $d \leq d_{\max}$.

We construct a functional commitment $\Pi_{\mathsf{FC}} = (\mathsf{Setup}, \mathsf{Commit}, \mathsf{Eval}, \mathsf{Verify})$ for $\mathcal{F} = \{\mathcal{F}_\lambda\}_{\lambda \in \mathbb{N}}$ as follows:

- $\mathsf{Setup}(1^\lambda)$: Sample $\mathbf{A} \in \mathbb{Z}_q^{n \times m}$, $\mathbf{W} \in \mathbb{Z}_q^{Ln \times m}$, $\mathbf{T}_{\mathsf{open}} \in \mathbb{Z}_q^{Lm \times \ell m}$, and $\mathbf{T}_{\mathsf{com}} \in \mathbb{Z}_q^{m \times \ell m}$ using the same procedure as Setup in Construction 3.2. Sample $\mathbf{D} \xleftarrow{\mathrm{R}} \mathbb{Z}_q^{n \times T}$, and output the common reference string $\mathsf{crs} = (\mathbf{A}, \mathbf{W}, \mathbf{T}_{\mathsf{com}}, \mathbf{T}_{\mathsf{open}}, \mathbf{D})$.
- $\mathsf{Commit}(\mathsf{crs}, \mathbf{x})$: Same as in Construction 3.2.
- $\mathsf{Eval}(\mathsf{crs}, \mathsf{st}, f)$: On input $\mathsf{crs} = (\mathbf{A}, \mathbf{W}, \mathbf{T}_{\mathsf{com}}, \mathbf{T}_{\mathsf{open}}, \mathbf{D})$, the state $\mathsf{st} = \mathbf{x}$, and a function $f = (\mathbf{f}_1, \ldots, \mathbf{f}_T)$ where each $\mathbf{f}_i \in \mathbb{Z}_q^{\ell^d}$ is B_{in}-bounded and $d \le d_{\max}$, the evaluation algorithm first computes an opening $\mathbf{V}_{\mathbf{f}_i} \in \mathbb{Z}_q^{m \times m}$ for $\mathbf{f}_i$ using the same procedure as in Construction 3.2. Then, it outputs the opening $\pi_f = \mathbf{v}_f$ where
$$\mathbf{v}_f = \sum_{i \in [T]} \mathbf{V}_{\mathbf{f}_i} \mathbf{G}^{-1}(\mathbf{d}_i) \in \mathbb{Z}_q^m,$$
and $\mathbf{d}_i \in \mathbb{Z}_q^n$ denotes the ith column of $\mathbf{D}$.
- $\mathsf{Verify}(\mathsf{crs}, \sigma, f, \mathbf{y}, \pi)$: On input $\mathsf{crs} = (\mathbf{A}, \mathbf{W}, \mathbf{T}_{\mathsf{com}}, \mathbf{T}_{\mathsf{open}}, \mathbf{D})$, the commitment $\sigma = \mathbf{C} \in \mathbb{Z}_q^{m \times m}$, the function $f = (\mathbf{f}_1, \ldots, \mathbf{f}_T)$ where each $\mathbf{f}_i \in \mathbb{Z}_q^{\ell^d}$ is B_{in}-bounded and $d \le d_{\max}$, the output $\mathbf{y} \in [-B_{\mathsf{out}}, B_{\mathsf{out}}]^T$, and the proof $\pi = \mathbf{v} \in \mathbb{Z}_q^m$, the verification algorithm parses $\mathbf{W}$ as in Eq. (3.1) and outputs 1 if
$$\|\mathbf{v}\| \le B \quad \text{and} \quad \sum_{i \in [T]} (\mathbf{f}_i^{\mathsf{T}} \otimes \mathbf{I}_m) \mathbf{W}_d \mathbf{C}^d \mathbf{G}^{-1}(\mathbf{d}_i) = \mathbf{D}\mathbf{y} - \mathbf{A}\mathbf{v}, \tag{3.4}$$
where $\mathbf{d}_i \in \mathbb{Z}_q^n$ is the ith column of $\mathbf{D}$.

Remark 3.6 (Supporting Preprocessing). Like Construction 3.2, Construction 3.5 supports full preprocessing (Definition 2.2) and function-only preprocessing (Remark 2.3). Here, we describe the approach for full preprocessing.

- $\mathsf{Preprocess}(\mathsf{crs}, f, \mathbf{y})$: On input $\mathsf{crs} = (\mathbf{A}, \mathbf{W}, \mathbf{T}_{\mathsf{com}}, \mathbf{T}_{\mathsf{open}}, \mathbf{D})$, the function $f = (\mathbf{f}_1, \ldots, \mathbf{f}_T)$ where each $\mathbf{f}_i \in \mathbb{Z}_q^{\ell^d}$ is B_{in}-bounded and $d \le d_{\max}$, and the output $\mathbf{y} \in [-B_{\mathsf{out}}, B_{\mathsf{out}}]^T$, the preprocessing algorithm computes
$$\mathbf{F} = \sum_{i \in [T]} \left(\left(\mathbf{G}^{-1}(\mathbf{d}_i)\right)^{\mathsf{T}} \otimes (\mathbf{f}_i^{\mathsf{T}} \otimes \mathbf{I}_m) \mathbf{W}_d \right) \in \mathbb{Z}_q^{n \times m^2} \tag{3.5}$$
$$\mathbf{y}^* = \mathbf{D}\mathbf{y} \in \mathbb{Z}_q^n, \tag{3.6}$$
and outputs the verification key $\mathsf{vk}_{f,\mathbf{y}} = (\mathbf{F}, \mathbf{y}^*)$.
- $\mathsf{OnlineVerify}(\mathsf{vk}, \sigma, \pi)$: On input the verification key $\mathsf{vk} = (\mathbf{F}, \mathbf{y}^*)$, the commitment $\sigma = \mathbf{C} \in \mathbb{Z}_q^{m \times m}$, and the opening $\pi = \mathbf{v} \in \mathbb{Z}_q^m$, the online verification algorithm outputs 1 if
$$\|\mathbf{v}\| \le B \quad \text{and} \quad \mathbf{F} \cdot \mathrm{vec}(\mathbf{C}^d) = \mathbf{y}^* - \mathbf{A}\mathbf{v}.$$

To show that this is correct, we apply vectorization to the main verification relation in Eq. (3.4):

$$\mathrm{vec}\left(\sum_{i\in[T]}(\mathbf{f}_i^{\mathsf{T}}\otimes\mathbf{I}_m)\mathbf{W}_d\mathbf{C}^d\mathbf{G}^{-1}(\mathbf{d}_i)\right)=\underbrace{\sum_{i\in[T]}\left((\mathbf{G}^{-1}(\mathbf{d}_i))^{\mathsf{T}}\otimes(\mathbf{f}_i^{\mathsf{T}}\otimes\mathbf{I}_m)\mathbf{W}_d\right)}_{\mathbf{F}}\mathrm{vec}(\mathbf{C}^d).$$

Then, the main verification relation in Eq. (3.4) becomes

$$\mathbf{F}\cdot\mathrm{vec}(\mathbf{C}^d)=\mathbf{D}\mathbf{y}-\mathbf{A}\mathbf{v}=\mathbf{y}^*-\mathbf{A}\mathbf{v},$$

and correctness reduces to that of Construction 3.5. By construction, $|\mathsf{vk}_{f,\mathbf{y}}|=(nm^2+n)\log q$ and the running time of $\mathsf{OnlineVerify}$ is $\mathsf{poly}(n,m,d_{\max},\log q)$. As we show below, we can instantiate our scheme so that $n,m,\log q=\mathsf{poly}(\lambda,\log\ell,\log T)$, and so the construction satisfies the required efficiency properties. Finally, the above analysis also applies to function-only preprocessing: namely, the preprocessed function key for a function $f=(\mathbf{f}_1,\ldots,\mathbf{f}_T)$ is the matrix $\mathbf{F}$ from Eq. (3.5). In this case, the running time of verification becomes $\mathsf{poly}(n,m,\log q,T)$.

Correctness and Security Analysis. We provide the correctness and security analysis as well as the parameter instantiation in the full version of this paper. We summarize the results in the following corollary:

Corollary 3.7 (Succinct Functional Commitment for Constant-Degree Polynomials). *Let λ be a security parameter, and let $\mathcal{F}=\{\mathcal{F}_\lambda\}_{\lambda\in\mathbb{N}}$ be a family of functions $f\colon[-B_{\mathsf{in}},B_{\mathsf{in}}]^\ell\to[-B_{\mathsf{out}},B_{\mathsf{out}}]^T$ on inputs of length $\ell=\ell(\lambda)$ and magnitude $B_{\mathsf{in}}=\mathsf{poly}(\lambda)$, and outputs of length $T=T(\lambda)$ and magnitude $B_{\mathsf{out}}=\mathsf{poly}(\lambda)$, and where each function f can be described by a vector of T homogeneous polynomials with B_{in}-bounded coefficients and degree $d\le d_{\max}=O(1)$. Then, under the L-succinct SIS assumption (with $L=O(\ell^{d_{\max}})$) and a polynomial norm bound, there exists a succinct functional commitment for $\mathcal{F}$. The commitment and opening have size $\mathsf{poly}(\lambda,d_{\max},\log\ell,\log T)$ and the CRS has size $\ell^{d_{\max}+1}\cdot\mathsf{poly}(\lambda,d_{\max},\log\ell,\log T)$. The functional commitment supports full preprocessing (Definition 2.2) and function-only preprocessing (Remark 2.3). With full preprocessing, the running time of the online verification algorithm is $\mathsf{poly}(\lambda,d_{\max},\log\ell,\log T)$.*

Remark 3.8 (Shorter Commitment and Openings). We can reduce the commitment size to $O(n^2\log q)$ and the opening size to $O(n\log q)$ in the above construction by using a gadget matrix with a larger decomposition base (specifically, instead of considering a binary decomposition, we consider a z-ary gadget matrix where $z=q^{1/c}$ for a large constant $c\in\mathbb{N}$). This coincides with the approach taken in [ACL+22]. In addition, we can further reduce the size of the commitment by using module lattices instead of integer lattices. We provide the details on extending to modules and using a z-ary gadget decomposition in the full version of this paper.

3.2 A Dual Construction for Committing to Functions

In this section, we construct a functional commitment that supports committing to a *function* $f\colon \{0,1\}^\ell \to \{0,1\}$ and then opening the commitment at a particular input $\mathbf{x} \in \{0,1\}^\ell$. This is a dual notion of Definition 2.1, where the Commit algorithm takes as input the function f and the Eval algorithm takes as input an input vector $\mathbf{x}$. We often refer to this variant of functional commitment as a "dual functional commitment."

Here, we consider a construction for general Boolean functions f on inputs of length $\ell = \ell(\lambda)$ and computable by Boolean circuits with bounded depth $d = d(\lambda)$. Similar to [dCP23, WW23], we allow the length of the commitment and the openings to scale with $\mathsf{poly}(\lambda, d, \log \ell)$. We can view our construction as a hybrid of the dual functional commitment from [dCP23] and the attribute-based encryption (ABE) scheme from [Wee23].

Like the construction of [dCP23], our functional commitment scheme satisfies a weaker notion of binding called "selective-input security" where the adversary is required to first *commit* to the point $\mathbf{x} \in \{0,1\}^\ell$ to which it will construct an opening. The adversary has to commit to this input before seeing the public parameters. The security reduction will then program $\mathbf{x}$ into the public parameters itself. This limitation to a selective notion of security is common to many related lattice-based primitives such as attribute-based encryption [GVW13, BGG+14, GVW15a, Wee23] and constrained PRFs [BV15, BTVW17]. We now give the formal definition of selective-input binding and then show how to use the ℓ-succinct SIS assumption to construct a succinct dual functional commitment for Boolean circuits with succinct commitments, openings, and fast verification (in the preprocessing model).

Definition 3.9 (Selective-Input Binding Security). *Let λ be a security parameter, and let $\mathcal{F} = \{\mathcal{F}_\lambda\}_{\lambda \in \mathbb{N}}$ be a family of efficiently-computable functions $f\colon \mathcal{X}^\ell \to \mathcal{Y}$. Let $\Pi_{\mathsf{FC}} = (\mathsf{Setup}, \mathsf{Commit}, \mathsf{Eval}, \mathsf{Verify})$ be a (dual) functional commitment scheme for $\mathcal{F}$. We now define the selective-input binding game between an adversary $\mathcal{A}$ and a challenger:*

1. *At the beginning of the game, the adversary chooses an input $\mathbf{x} \in \mathcal{X}^\ell$ and sends $\mathbf{x}$ to the challenger.*
2. *The challenger samples $\mathsf{crs} \leftarrow \mathsf{Setup}(1^\lambda)$ and gives crs to $\mathcal{A}$.*
3. *The adversary outputs a commitment σ, values $y_0, y_1 \in \mathcal{Y}$, and openings π_0, π_1.*
4. *The output of the experiment is $b = 1$ if $y_0 \neq y_1$ and $\mathsf{Verify}(\mathsf{crs}, \sigma, \mathbf{x}, y_0, \pi_0) = 1 = \mathsf{Verify}(\mathsf{crs}, \sigma, \mathbf{x}, y_1, \pi_1)$. Otherwise, the output of the experiment is $b = 0$.*

The functional commitment scheme satisfies computational selective-input binding if for all efficient adversaries $\mathcal{A}$, $\Pr[b = 1] = \mathsf{negl}(\lambda)$ in the above security game.

Construction 3.10 (Dual Functional Commitment for Boolean Circuits). Let λ be a security parameter and $n = n(\lambda)$, $m = m(\lambda)$, $q = q(\lambda)$, and $\chi = \chi(\lambda)$ be lattice parameters. Let $\ell = \ell(\lambda)$ be an input length parameter, and

$B = B(\lambda)$ be a bound. Let $\mathcal{F}_\lambda$ be a collection of functions $f\colon \{0,1\}^\ell \to \{0,1\}$ that can be computed by a Boolean circuit of depth at most $d = d(\lambda)$. We construct a dual functional commitment $\Pi_{\mathsf{FC}} = (\mathsf{Setup}, \mathsf{Commit}, \mathsf{Eval}, \mathsf{Verify})$ for $\mathcal{F} = \{\mathcal{F}_\lambda\}_{\lambda\in\mathbb{N}}$ as follows:

- $\mathsf{Setup}(1^\lambda)$: On input the security parameter λ, the setup algorithm samples $(\mathbf{A}, \mathbf{R}) \leftarrow \mathsf{TrapGen}(1^n, q, m)$ and $\mathbf{W} \xleftarrow{R} \mathbb{Z}_q^{\ell n\times m}$. Sample $\mathbf{T} \leftarrow \mathsf{SamplePre}([\mathbf{I}_\ell \otimes \mathbf{A} \mid \mathbf{W}], \mathbf{I}_\ell \otimes \mathbf{R}, \mathbf{G}_{n\ell}, \chi) \in \mathbb{Z}_q^{(\ell m+m)\times \ell m}$. Parse $\mathbf{T} = \begin{bmatrix} \mathbf{T}_{\mathsf{open}} \\ \mathbf{T}_{\mathsf{com}} \end{bmatrix}$ where $\mathbf{T}_{\mathsf{open}} \in \mathbb{Z}_q^{\ell m\times \ell m}$ and $\mathbf{T}_{\mathsf{com}} \in \mathbb{Z}_q^{m\times \ell m}$. Finally, it samples $\mathbf{W}_0 \xleftarrow{R} \mathbb{Z}_q^{n\times m}$, computes $\mathbf{B} = -\mathbf{W}_0\mathbf{T}_{\mathsf{com}} \in \mathbb{Z}_q^{n\times \ell m}$ and outputs the common reference string $\mathsf{crs} = (\mathbf{A}, \mathbf{W}, \mathbf{T}_{\mathsf{com}}, \mathbf{T}_{\mathsf{open}}, \mathbf{W}_0, \mathbf{B})$.
- $\mathsf{Commit}(\mathsf{crs}, f)$: On input $\mathsf{crs} = (\mathbf{A}, \mathbf{W}, \mathbf{T}_{\mathsf{com}}, \mathbf{T}_{\mathsf{open}}, \mathbf{W}_0, \mathbf{B})$ and a function $f\colon \{0,1\}^\ell \to \{0,1\}$, the commit algorithm computes $\mathbf{B}_f \leftarrow \mathsf{EvalF}(\mathbf{B}, f)$ and outputs the commitment $\sigma = \mathbf{B}_f \in \mathbb{Z}_q^{n\times m}$ along with the state $\mathsf{st} = f$.
- $\mathsf{Eval}(\mathsf{crs}, \mathsf{st}, \mathbf{x})$: On input $\mathsf{crs} = (\mathbf{A}, \mathbf{W}, \mathbf{T}_{\mathsf{com}}, \mathbf{T}_{\mathsf{open}}, \mathbf{W}_0, \mathbf{B})$, the state $\mathsf{st} = f$, and the input $\mathbf{x} \in \{0,1\}^\ell$, the evaluation algorithm computes $\mathbf{H}_{\mathbf{B},f,\mathbf{x}} \leftarrow \mathsf{EvalFX}(\mathbf{B}, f, \mathbf{x}) \in \mathbb{Z}_q^{\ell m\times m}$ and outputs

$$\pi = \mathbf{V} = \begin{bmatrix} -(\mathbf{x}^\intercal \otimes \mathbf{I}_m)\mathbf{T}_{\mathsf{open}} \\ -\mathbf{T}_{\mathsf{com}} \end{bmatrix} \cdot \mathbf{H}_{\mathbf{B},f,\mathbf{x}} \in \mathbb{Z}_q^{2m\times m}. \tag{3.7}$$

- $\mathsf{Verify}(\mathsf{crs}, \sigma, \mathbf{x}, y, \pi)$: On input $\mathsf{crs} = (\mathbf{A}, \mathbf{W}, \mathbf{T}_{\mathsf{com}}, \mathbf{T}_{\mathsf{open}}, \mathbf{W}_0, \mathbf{B})$, a commitment $\sigma = \mathbf{B}_f \in \mathbb{Z}_q^{n\times m}$, an input $\mathbf{x} \in \{0,1\}^\ell$, an output $y \in \{0,1\}$, and an opening $\pi = \mathbf{V} \in \mathbb{Z}_q^{2m\times m}$, the verification algorithm outputs 1 if

$$\|\mathbf{V}\| \le B \quad \text{and} \quad \mathbf{B}_f - y\mathbf{G} = [\mathbf{A} \mid \mathbf{W}_0 + (\mathbf{x}^\intercal \otimes \mathbf{I}_n)\mathbf{W}]\mathbf{V}. \tag{3.8}$$

Remark 3.11 (Supporting Preprocessing). Similar to Constructions 3.2 and 3.5, Construction 3.10 also supports fast verification in the preprocessing model. Note that in the dual setting, we preprocess with respect to an *input* $\mathbf{x}$ rather than a function f.

- $\mathsf{Preprocess}(\mathsf{crs}, \mathbf{x})$: On input $\mathsf{crs} = (\mathbf{A}, \mathbf{W}, \mathbf{T}_{\mathsf{com}}, \mathbf{T}_{\mathsf{open}}, \mathbf{W}_0, \mathbf{B})$ and the input $\mathbf{x} \in \{0,1\}^\ell$, the preprocess algorithm outputs $\mathsf{vk}_\mathbf{x} = \mathbf{F}_\mathbf{x} = [\mathbf{A} \mid \mathbf{W}_0 + (\mathbf{x}^\intercal \otimes \mathbf{I}_n)\mathbf{W}] \in \mathbb{Z}_q^{n\times 2m}$.
- $\mathsf{OnlineVerify}(\mathsf{vk}, \sigma, y, \pi)$: On input the verification key $\mathsf{vk} = \mathbf{F}_\mathbf{x} \in \mathbb{Z}_q^{n\times 2m}$, the commitment $\sigma = \mathbf{B}_f \in \mathbb{Z}_q^{n\times 2m}$, a value $y \in \{0,1\}$, and an opening $\pi = \mathbf{V} \in \mathbb{Z}_q^{2m\times m}$, the online verification algorithm outputs 1 if

$$\|\mathbf{V}\| \le B \quad \text{and} \quad \mathbf{B}_f - y\mathbf{G} = \mathbf{F}_\mathbf{x}\mathbf{V}.$$

Correctness and Security Analysis. We provide the correctness, security analysis, and parameter instantiation for Construction 3.10 in the full version of this paper. We summarize the instantiation in the following corollary:

Corollary 3.12 (Dual Functional Commitment for Bounded-Depth Boolean Circuits). *Let λ be a security parameter and let $\mathcal{F} = \{\mathcal{F}_\lambda\}_{\lambda\in\mathbb{N}}$ be* *a family of functions* $f: \{0,1\}^\ell \to \{0,1\}$ *on inputs of length* $\ell = \ell(\lambda)$ *and which can be computed by Boolean circuits of depth at most* $d = d(\lambda)$. *Under the* ℓ*-succinct SIS assumption with a sub-exponential norm bound* $\beta = 2^{\tilde{O}(n^\varepsilon)}$ *for some constant* $\varepsilon > 0$ *and lattice dimension* $n = n(\lambda)$, *there exists a dual functional commitment for* $\mathcal{F}$. *The functional commitment satisfies computational* selective-input *binding and supports preprocessing for fast verification (Definition 2.2). The size of the commitment and the opening have size* $\mathsf{poly}(\lambda, d^{1/\varepsilon}, \log \ell)$ *and the CRS has size* $\ell^2 \cdot \mathsf{poly}(\lambda, d^{1/\varepsilon}, \log \ell)$.

4 Cryptanalysis of Extractable Commitments

In this section, we describe some of the challenges in constructing extractable lattice-based functional commitments. In the full version of this paper, we show that Construction 3.2 is not an extractable functional commitment for quadratic functions. In this section, we show that assuming inhomogeneous SIS, the [ACL+22] approach does not yield an extractable functional commitment for linear functions. The attacks we develop work by using the components in the CRS to derive a basis for a lattice defined by the scheme's verification relation. We then use the basis to *obliviously* sample a solution that satisfies the schemes' verification relation *without* knowledge of a corresponding input. In one case, this can be used to sample a valid opening to an unsatisfiable set of quadratic constraints, while in the other case (Sect. 4.1), we can embed a SIS instance that the extractor must solve in order to output a valid input. We start with the definition of a extractable functional commitment.

Definition 4.1 (Extractability). *Let* λ *be a security parameter. We say that a functional commitment* $\Pi_{\mathsf{FC}} = (\mathsf{Setup}, \mathsf{Commit}, \mathsf{Eval}, \mathsf{Verify})$ *for a function family* $\mathcal{F} = \{\mathcal{F}_\lambda\}_{\lambda \in \mathbb{N}}$ *is extractable if for all efficient adversaries* $\mathcal{A}$, *there exists an efficient extractor* $\mathcal{E}$ *such that*

$$\Pr\left[\begin{array}{c} \mathsf{Verify}(\mathsf{crs}, \sigma, f, y, \pi) = 1 \text{ and} \\ f(\mathbf{x}) \neq y \end{array} : \begin{array}{c} \mathsf{crs} \leftarrow \mathsf{Setup}(1^\lambda) \\ ((\sigma, f, y, \pi), \mathbf{x}) \leftarrow (\mathcal{A} \| \mathcal{E})(1^\lambda, \mathsf{crs}) \end{array}\right] = \mathsf{negl}(\lambda).$$

Here, we write $(\mathcal{A}\|\mathcal{E})(\cdot)$ *to denote invoking algorithm* $\mathcal{A}$ *and the extractor* $\mathcal{E}$ *on the same input* and *randomness. The output of* $\mathcal{A}$ *is* (σ, f, y, π) *and the output of* $\mathcal{E}$ *is* $\mathbf{x}$.

4.1 Analyzing the [ACL+22] Knowledge Assumption

In this section, we analyze one version of the k-ISIS and knowledge k-ISIS family of assumptions from [ACL+22]. While the original assumptions from [ACL+22] were defined over polynomial rings (and module/ideal lattices), we consider the analogous assumptions over the integers. Since ring multiplication is commutative whereas matrix multiplication is not, there are multiple (and similar) ways to translate the [ACL+22] family of assumptions to the integers. We describe one adaptation here, where we "sparsify by left multiplication." We refer to this adaptation as the $\mathsf{MatrixACLMT}$ construction.

Assumption 4.2 (MatrixACLMT k-ISIS **Assumption for Linear Functions).** Let λ be a security parameter and let $(n, m, q, \chi, \ell, \beta)$ be lattice parameters. The MatrixACLMT k-SIS assumption says that for every efficient adversary $\mathcal{A}$, there exists a negligible function $\mathsf{negl}(\cdot)$ such that

$$\Pr\left[\begin{array}{c}\mathbf{A}\mathbf{x} = \alpha\mathbf{u} \bmod q \\ \text{and} \\ 0 < |\alpha|, \|\mathbf{x}\| \leq \beta\end{array} : \begin{array}{c}\mathbf{A} \xleftarrow{\text{R}} \mathbb{Z}_q^{n \times m},\ \mathbf{u} \xleftarrow{\text{R}} \mathbb{Z}_q^n, \\ \forall i \in [\ell] : \mathbf{W}_i \xleftarrow{\text{R}} \mathbb{Z}_q^{n \times n},\ \mathbf{t}_i \leftarrow \mathbf{W}_i^{-1}\mathbf{u}, \\ \forall i \neq j : \mathbf{z}_{i,j} \leftarrow \mathbf{A}_\chi^{-1}(\mathbf{W}_i \mathbf{t}_j), \\ (\alpha, \mathbf{x}) \leftarrow \mathcal{A}(1^\lambda, \mathbf{A}, \mathbf{u}, \{\mathbf{W}_i\}_{i \in [\ell]}, \{\mathbf{z}_{i,j}\}_{i \neq j})\end{array}\right] = \mathsf{negl}(\lambda).$$

Assumption 4.3 (MatrixACLMT **Knowledge Assumption).** Let λ be a security parameter and let $(n, m, q, \chi, t, \ell, \alpha, \beta)$ be lattice parameters where $q^{n-t} = \mathsf{negl}(\lambda)$ and $m \geq O(t \log q)$. The MatrixACLMT knowledge assumption says that for every efficient adversary $\mathcal{A}$, there exists an efficient extractor $\mathcal{E}$ such that $\Pr[b = 1] = \mathsf{negl}(\lambda)$, where $b \in \{0, 1\}$ is the output of the following experiment:

$$\Pr\left[\begin{array}{c}\mathbf{A}\mathbf{v} = \mathbf{D}\mathbf{c} \bmod q \text{ and } \|\mathbf{v}\| \leq \beta \text{ and} \\ (\|\mathbf{x}\| \geq \alpha \text{ or } \mathbf{c} \neq \sum_{i \in [\ell]} x_i \mathbf{t}_i \bmod q)\end{array} : \begin{array}{c}\mathbf{A} \xleftarrow{\text{R}} \mathbb{Z}_q^{t \times m}, \mathbf{D} \xleftarrow{\text{R}} \mathbb{Z}_q^{t \times n}, \\ \forall i \in [\ell] : \mathbf{t}_i \xleftarrow{\text{R}} \mathbb{Z}_q^n,\ \mathbf{z}_i \leftarrow \mathbf{A}_\chi^{-1}(\mathbf{D}\mathbf{t}_i) \\ ((\mathbf{c}, \mathbf{v}), \mathbf{x}) \leftarrow (\mathcal{A} \| \mathcal{E})(1^\lambda, \mathbf{A}, \mathbf{D}, \{(\mathbf{t}_i, \mathbf{z}_i)\}_{i \in [\ell]})\end{array}\right] = \mathsf{negl}(\lambda),$$

where $((\mathbf{c}, \mathbf{v}), \mathbf{x}) \leftarrow (\mathcal{A} \| \mathcal{E})(1^\lambda, \mathbf{A}, \mathbf{D}, \{(\mathbf{t}_i, \mathbf{z}_i)\}_{i \in [\ell]})$ denotes that $\mathcal{A}$ and $\mathcal{E}$ are invoked on the same input *and* randomness, and $(\mathbf{c}, \mathbf{v})$ is the output of $\mathcal{A}$ while $\mathbf{x}$ is the output of $\mathcal{E}$.

The MatrixACLMT knowledge assumption essentially says that any efficient adversarial strategy that produces a short $\mathbf{v} \in \mathbb{Z}_q^m$ where $\mathbf{A}\mathbf{v} \in \mathbb{Z}_q^t$ lies in the image of $\mathbf{D}$ (i.e., $\mathbf{A}\mathbf{v} = \mathbf{D}\mathbf{c}$) can be explained as taking a short linear combination of the given preimages $\mathbf{z}_1, \ldots, \mathbf{z}_\ell$. Indeed, if $\mathbf{c} = \sum_{i \in [\ell]} x_i \mathbf{t}_i$, then $\mathbf{A}\left(\sum_{i \in [\ell]} x_i \mathbf{z}_i\right) = \mathbf{D}\left(\sum_{i \in [\ell]} x_t \mathbf{t}_i\right) = \mathbf{D}\mathbf{c}$. The requirement $q^{n-t} = \mathsf{negl}(\lambda)$ is necessary to prevent the basic oblivious sampling attack where the adversary samples a random short vector $\mathbf{v} \in \mathbb{Z}_q^m$ and solves for a $\mathbf{c} \in \mathbb{Z}_q^n$ satisfying $\mathbf{A}\mathbf{v} = \mathbf{D}\mathbf{c}$. Since the image of $\mathbf{A}$ has q^t elements and the image of $\mathbf{D}$ has q^n elements, all but a negligible fraction of the elements in the image of $\mathbf{A}$ are contained in the image of $\mathbf{D}$.

A Heuristic Oblivious Sampling Algorithm for Assumption 4.3. We start by describing an adversary for Assumption 4.3 that *obliviously samples* a short vector $\mathbf{v} \in \mathbb{Z}_q^m$ such that $\mathbf{A}\mathbf{v}$ is in the image of $\mathbf{D}$. While this by itself does not necessarily falsify Assumption 4.3, we will subsequently show that Assumptions 4.2 and 4.3 cannot simultaneously hold for a broad range of parameter settings (i.e., at least one of Assumption 4.2 or Assumption 4.3 is false).

Algorithm 4.4 (Candidate Oblivious Sampler for MatrixACLMT**).** *Suppose $\ell \gg m + n$ in Assumption 4.3. Our heuristic oblivious sampling algorithm $\mathcal{A}$ for Assumption 4.3 works as follows:*

1. *Let* $\mathbf{A} \xleftarrow{R} \mathbb{Z}_q^{t \times m}$, $\mathbf{D} \xleftarrow{R} \mathbb{Z}_q^{t \times n}$, $\mathbf{t}_i \xleftarrow{R} \mathbb{Z}_q^n$ *and* $\mathbf{z}_i \leftarrow \mathbf{A}_\chi^{-1}(\mathbf{D}\mathbf{t}_i)$ *be the challenge from Assumption 4.3. By construction,*

$$[\mathbf{A} \mid \mathbf{DG}] \cdot \underbrace{\begin{bmatrix} \mathbf{z}_1 & \cdots & \mathbf{z}_\ell \\ -\mathbf{G}^{-1}(\mathbf{t}_1) & \cdots & -\mathbf{G}^{-1}(\mathbf{t}_\ell) \end{bmatrix}}_{\bar{\mathbf{T}}} = \mathbf{0} \bmod q.$$

Since $\mathbf{t}_i$ *and* $\mathbf{z}_i$ *are sampled independently and assuming that* $\ell \gg m + n$ *is sufficiently large (e.g., setting* $\ell = 2(m+n)$ *should suffice), we can heuristically assume that* $\bar{\mathbf{T}} \in \mathbb{Z}^{(m+n) \times \ell}$ *is full rank over the* reals.[9] *Thus, we can use* $\bar{\mathbf{T}}$ *to derive an Ajtai-trapdoor* $\mathbf{T}$ *for the matrix* $\mathbf{B} = [\mathbf{A} \mid \mathbf{DG}]$ *(e.g., by taking a subset of* $m+n$ *columns of* $\bar{\mathbf{T}}$ *that are linearly independent over the reals).*

2. *Using* $\mathbf{T}$*, the algorithm samples a short* $\left[\begin{smallmatrix} \mathbf{v} \\ \mathbf{c} \end{smallmatrix}\right]$ *where* $\mathbf{B} \cdot \left[\begin{smallmatrix} \mathbf{v} \\ \mathbf{c} \end{smallmatrix}\right] = \mathbf{0}$*. The commitment is then* $\mathbf{Gc}$ *and the opening is* $\mathbf{v}$*. For instance, the algorithm might implement Babai's rounding algorithm. Specifically, it starts with an arbitrary (non-zero) solution* $\mathbf{y} \in \mathbb{Z}^{m+n}$ *where* $\mathbf{By} = \mathbf{0} \bmod q$*, solves for the unique* $\mathbf{z} \in \mathbb{Q}^{m+n}$ *where* $\mathbf{Tz} = \mathbf{y} \in \mathbb{Q}^{m+n}$ *and then outputs* $\mathbf{x} = \mathbf{y} - \mathbf{T} \cdot \lfloor \mathbf{z} \rceil$*. By construction* $\mathbf{Bx} = \mathbf{0} \bmod q$ *and moreover* $\|\mathbf{x}\| \leq \|\mathbf{T}(\mathbf{z} - \lfloor \mathbf{z} \rceil)\|$*, which is small.*

The basic question is whether the solution $\mathbf{x}$ derived by rounding off a long solution as in Algorithm 4.4 (or sampled through some alternative trapdoor sampling algorithm) can *always* be explained by a short linear combination of the basis vectors $\mathbf{T}$. In the following, we show that assuming (non-uniform) hardness of inhomogeneous SIS and the matrix-ACLMT assumption for linear functions (Assumption 4.2), then no such extractor exists. One implication of this is that this particular adaptation of [ACL+22] to the integers is not an extractable functional commitment for linear functions.

Attacking the Matrix-ACLMT Commitment for Linear Functions. We now show how we can apply the approach in Algorithm 4.4 to break extractability for the linear functional commitment from [ACL+22] (when instantiated over the integers). We start by recalling their construction (over the integers):

Construction 4.5 (Functional Commitment for Linear Functions). Let λ be a security parameter and n, m, m', q, t, B, χ be lattice parameters. Let $\ell = \ell(\lambda)$ be the input length. For a matrix $\mathbf{M} \in \mathbb{Z}_q^{k \times \ell}$, let $f_\mathbf{M} \colon \mathbb{Z}_q^{k \times \ell} \to \mathbb{Z}_q^k$ be the linear function $\mathbf{x} \mapsto \mathbf{Mx}$. Let $\mathcal{F}_\lambda = \{f_\mathbf{M} \mid \mathbf{M} \in \{0,1\}^{k \times \ell}\}$. We construct a functional commitment $\Pi_{\mathsf{FC}} = (\mathsf{Setup}, \mathsf{Commit}, \mathsf{Eval}, \mathsf{Verify})$ for $\mathcal{F} = \{\mathcal{F}_\lambda\}_{\lambda \in \mathbb{N}}$ as follows:

- $\mathsf{Setup}(1^\lambda, 1^\ell)$: Sample matrices $(\mathbf{A}, \mathbf{R_A}) \leftarrow \mathsf{TrapGen}(1^\lambda, n, m)$, $\mathbf{W}_1, \ldots, \mathbf{W}_\ell \xleftarrow{R} \mathbb{Z}_q^{n \times n}$, $\mathbf{u} \leftarrow \mathbb{Z}_q^n$, and let $\mathbf{t}_i \leftarrow \mathbf{W}_i^{-1}\mathbf{u} \in \mathbb{Z}_q^n$ for each $i \in [\ell]$. For

[9] Note that $\bar{\mathbf{T}}$ does *not* (and cannot) have full rank over $\mathbb{Z}_q$.

each $i \neq j$, sample $\mathbf{z}_{i,j} \leftarrow \mathsf{SamplePre}(\mathbf{A}, \mathbf{R_A}, \mathbf{W}_i\mathbf{t}_j, \chi)$. Let $\widehat{\mathbf{W}} \in \mathbb{Z}_q^{\ell n \times n}$ to be the vertical stacking of the matrices $\mathbf{W}_1, \ldots, \mathbf{W}_\ell$:

$$\widehat{\mathbf{W}} = \begin{bmatrix} \mathbf{W}_1 \\ \vdots \\ \mathbf{W}_\ell \end{bmatrix} \in \mathbb{Z}_q^{\ell n \times n}.$$

Next, sample $(\mathbf{B}, \mathbf{R_B}) \leftarrow \mathsf{TrapGen}(1^\lambda, t, m')$ and a matrix $\mathbf{D} \xleftarrow{\text{R}} \mathbb{Z}_q^{t \times n}$. Sample $\mathbf{z}'_i \leftarrow \mathsf{SamplePre}(\mathbf{B}, \mathbf{R_B}, \mathbf{D}\mathbf{t}_i, \chi)$ for each $i \in [\ell]$. Output the common reference string $\mathsf{crs} = (\mathbf{A}, \mathbf{B}, \mathbf{D}, \mathbf{u}, \{\mathbf{W}_i\}_{i \in [\ell]}, \{\mathbf{z}_{i,j}\}_{i \neq j}, \{\mathbf{z}'_i\}_{i \in [\ell]})$.

- $\mathsf{Commit}(\mathsf{crs}, \mathbf{x})$: On input $\mathsf{crs} = (\mathbf{A}, \mathbf{B}, \mathbf{D}, \mathbf{u}, \{\mathbf{W}_i\}_{i \in [\ell]}, \{\mathbf{z}_{i,j}\}_{i \neq j}, \{\mathbf{z}'_i\}_{i \in [\ell]})$ and an input vector $\mathbf{x} \in \mathbb{Z}_q^\ell$, the commit algorithm outputs the commitment $\mathbf{c} = \sum_{i \in [\ell]} x_i \mathbf{t}_i \in \mathbb{Z}_q^n$ and the state $\mathsf{st} = \mathbf{x}$.
- $\mathsf{Eval}(\mathsf{crs}, \mathsf{st}, f_\mathbf{M})$: On input $\mathsf{crs} = (\mathbf{A}, \mathbf{B}, \mathbf{D}, \mathbf{u}, \{\mathbf{W}_i\}_{i \in [\ell]}, \{\mathbf{z}_{i,j}\}_{i \neq j}, \{\mathbf{z}'_i\}_{i \in [\ell]})$, a commitment state $\mathsf{st} = \mathbf{x}$, and a function $f_\mathbf{M}$ for some matrix $\mathbf{M} \in \mathbb{Z}_q^{k \times \ell}$, the evaluation algorithm computes $\hat{\mathbf{v}}_i \leftarrow \sum_{j \neq i} x_j \mathbf{z}_{i,j}$ for each $i \in [\ell]$ and defines $\hat{\mathbf{v}} \in \mathbb{Z}_q^{\ell m}$ and $\hat{\mathbf{z}} \in \mathbb{Z}_q^{\ell m'}$ as follows:

$$\hat{\mathbf{v}} = \begin{bmatrix} \hat{\mathbf{v}}_1 \\ \vdots \\ \hat{\mathbf{v}}_\ell \end{bmatrix} \in \mathbb{Z}_q^{\ell m} \quad \text{and} \quad \hat{\mathbf{z}} = \begin{bmatrix} \mathbf{z}'_1 \\ \vdots \\ \mathbf{z}'_\ell \end{bmatrix}.$$

It outputs the opening

$$\mathbf{v} = \begin{bmatrix} (\mathbf{M} \otimes \mathbf{I}_m)\hat{\mathbf{v}} \\ (\mathbf{x}^\mathsf{T} \otimes \mathbf{I}_{m'})\mathbf{z}'_i \end{bmatrix} \in \mathbb{Z}_q^{km+m'}.$$

- $\mathsf{Verify}(\mathsf{crs}, \sigma, f_\mathbf{M}, y, \pi)$: On input $\mathsf{crs} = (\mathbf{A}, \mathbf{B}, \mathbf{D}, \mathbf{u}, \{\mathbf{W}_i\}_{i \in [\ell]}, \{\mathbf{z}_{i,j}\}_{i \neq j}, \{\mathbf{z}'_i\}_{i \in [\ell]})$, a commitment $\sigma = \mathbf{c} \in \mathbb{Z}_q^n$, a function $f_\mathbf{M} \colon \mathbb{Z}_q^{k \times \ell} \to \mathbb{Z}_q^k$ where $\mathbf{M} \in \mathbb{Z}_q^{k \times \ell}$, a value $\mathbf{y} \in \mathbb{Z}_q^k$, and an opening $\pi = \mathbf{v} \in \mathbb{Z}_q^{(km+m') \times m}$, the verification algorithm outputs 1 if

$$\|\mathbf{v}\| \leq B \quad \text{and} \quad \begin{bmatrix} \mathbf{I}_k \otimes \mathbf{A} & \mathbf{0} \\ \mathbf{0} & \mathbf{B} \end{bmatrix} \cdot \mathbf{v} = \begin{bmatrix} (\mathbf{M} \otimes \mathbf{I}_n)\widehat{\mathbf{W}} \\ \mathbf{D} \end{bmatrix} \cdot \mathbf{c} - \begin{bmatrix} \mathbf{y} \otimes \mathbf{u} \\ \mathbf{0} \end{bmatrix}. \quad (4.1)$$

Correctness. Correctness follows by the same argument as in [ACL+22], adapted to operate over the integers. We give a sketch here and refer to [ACL+22] for more details. Let $\mathsf{crs} = (\mathbf{A}, \mathbf{B}, \mathbf{D}, \mathbf{u}, \{\mathbf{W}_i\}_{i \in [\ell]}, \{\mathbf{z}_{i,j}\}_{i \neq j}, \{\mathbf{z}'_i\}_{i \in [\ell]})$ be a CRS sampled via the Setup algorithm. Suppose $\mathbf{c} = \sum_{i \in [\ell]} x_i \mathbf{t}_i$ is a commitment to a *short* input $\mathbf{x} \in \mathbb{Z}_q^\ell$. Suppose $\mathbf{v}$ is an opening to a function $f_\mathbf{M}$ where $\mathbf{M} \in \mathbb{Z}_q^{k \times \ell}$ is a matrix with small entries. By construction, if the entries of $\mathbf{M}$ and $\mathbf{x}$ are short, then so is $\mathbf{v}$. Consider now the main verification relation. First, for each $i \in [\ell]$,

$$\mathbf{W}_i \mathbf{c} = \sum_{j \in [\ell]} x_j \mathbf{W}_i \mathbf{t}_j = x_i \mathbf{u} + \sum_{j \neq i} x_j \mathbf{A} \mathbf{z}_{i,j} = x_i \mathbf{u} + \mathbf{A} \hat{\mathbf{v}}_i.$$

Equivalently, this means $\widehat{\mathbf{W}}\mathbf{c} = \mathbf{x} \otimes \mathbf{u} + (\mathbf{I}_\ell \otimes \mathbf{A})\widehat{\mathbf{v}}$. Consider now the main verification relation:

$$\begin{aligned}(\mathbf{M} \otimes \mathbf{I}_n)\widehat{\mathbf{W}}\mathbf{c} &= (\mathbf{M} \otimes \mathbf{I}_n)(\mathbf{x} \otimes \mathbf{u}) + (\mathbf{M} \otimes \mathbf{I}_n)(\mathbf{I}_\ell \otimes \mathbf{A})\widehat{\mathbf{v}} \\ &= (\mathbf{M}\mathbf{x} \otimes \mathbf{u}) + (\mathbf{I}_k \otimes \mathbf{A})(\mathbf{M} \otimes \mathbf{I}_m)\widehat{\mathbf{v}}\end{aligned}$$

$$\mathbf{D}\mathbf{c} = \sum_{i \in [\ell]} x_i \mathbf{D}\mathbf{t}_i = \mathbf{B} \cdot \left(\sum_{i \in [\ell]} x_i \mathbf{z}_i' \right) = \mathbf{B} \cdot (\mathbf{x}^\mathsf{T} \otimes \mathbf{I}_{m'})\hat{\mathbf{z}}.$$

For a sufficiently-large bound B, the verification relations hold and correctness follows.

Extractability. By an analogous argument as in [ACL+22], we can show that under Assumptions 4.2 and 4.3 (with suitable parameter instantiations), if an efficient adversary can produce a commitment $\sigma = \mathbf{c}$ along with a valid opening $\pi = \mathbf{v}$ to a short value $\mathbf{y} \in \mathbb{Z}_q^t$ with respect to a linear function $f_\mathbf{M}$ with short $\mathbf{M} \in \mathbb{Z}_q^{k \times \ell}$, then there exists an efficient extractor that outputs a *short* $\mathbf{x} \in \mathbb{Z}_q^\ell$ where $\mathbf{M}\mathbf{x} = \mathbf{y}$. We give a sketch of the general approach here and refer to [ACL+22] for a formal argument:

- Suppose there exists an efficient adversary $\mathcal{A}$ is able to come up with a commitment $\mathbf{c} \in \mathbb{Z}_q^n$ and a short opening $\mathbf{v} = \left[\begin{smallmatrix}\mathbf{v}_1\\ \mathbf{v}_2\end{smallmatrix}\right]$ that satisfies Eq. (4.1). This means that $\mathbf{B}\mathbf{v}_2 = \mathbf{D}\mathbf{c}$. By Assumption 4.3, there exists an efficient extractor $\mathcal{E}$ that outputs a short $\mathbf{x} \in \mathbb{Z}_q^\ell$ such that $\mathbf{c} = \sum_{i \in [\ell]} x_i \mathbf{t}_i$.
- If the extracted $\mathbf{x}$ satisfies $\mathbf{M}\mathbf{x} = \mathbf{y}$, then the extractor is successful. Consider the case where $\mathbf{M}\mathbf{x} \neq \mathbf{y}$. If this happens with non-negligible probability, we can construct an adversary $\mathcal{B}$ that uses the extractor $\mathcal{E}$ to break Assumption 4.2:
  1. Algorithm $\mathcal{B}$ receives $\left(\mathbf{A}, \mathbf{u}, \{\mathbf{W}_i\}_{i \in [\ell]}, \{\mathbf{z}_{i,j}\}_{i \neq j}\right)$ from the challenger for Assumption 4.2.
  2. It samples $(\mathbf{B}, \mathbf{R}_\mathbf{B}) \leftarrow \mathsf{TrapGen}(1^\lambda, t, m')$, $\mathbf{D} \xleftarrow{\text{R}} \mathbb{Z}_q^{t \times n}$, and $\mathbf{z}_i' \leftarrow \mathsf{SamplePre}(\mathbf{B}, \mathbf{R}_\mathbf{B}, \mathbf{D}\mathbf{t}_i, \chi)$ for each $i \in [\ell]$ as in the real scheme. The reduction algorithm constructs the common reference string $\mathsf{crs} = \left(\mathbf{A}, \mathbf{B}, \mathbf{D}, \mathbf{u}, \{\mathbf{W}_i\}_{i \in [\ell]}, \{\mathbf{z}_{i,j}\}_{i \neq j}, \{\mathbf{z}_i'\}_{i \in [\ell]}\right)$ and gives crs to $\mathcal{A}$.
  3. After $\mathcal{A}$ outputs a commitment $\mathbf{c}$ and opening $\mathbf{v} = \left[\begin{smallmatrix}\mathbf{v}_1\\ \mathbf{v}_2\end{smallmatrix}\right]$, algorithm $\mathcal{B}$ runs the extractor $\mathcal{E}$ on the same input as $\mathcal{A}$ to obtain a short input $\mathbf{x} \in \mathbb{Z}_q^\ell$. Suppose $\mathbf{M}\mathbf{x} = \mathbf{y}' \neq \mathbf{y}$. Then algorithm $\mathcal{A}$ computes an opening $\mathbf{v}' = \begin{bmatrix}\mathbf{v}_1'\\ \mathbf{v}_2'\end{bmatrix}$ by computing $\mathsf{Eval}(\mathsf{crs}, \mathbf{x}, f_\mathbf{M})$. By correctness, $\mathbf{v}'$ is short and moreover satisfies the following verification relation from Eq. (4.1):

$$(\mathbf{I}_k \otimes \mathbf{A})\mathbf{v}_1' = (\mathbf{M} \otimes \mathbf{I}_n)\widehat{\mathbf{W}}\mathbf{c} - \mathbf{M}\mathbf{x} \otimes \mathbf{u} \tag{4.2}$$

     Since $\mathbf{v}$ is also a valid opening, we have that

$$(\mathbf{I}_k \otimes \mathbf{A})(\mathbf{v}_1 - \mathbf{v}_1') = (\mathbf{y}' - \mathbf{y}) \otimes \mathbf{u}.$$

Since $\mathbf{y} - \mathbf{y}' \neq \mathbf{0}$, there is at least one non-zero "block" where $\mathbf{A}(\mathbf{v}_{1,i} - \mathbf{v}'_{1,i}) = (y'_i - y_i)\mathbf{u}$ and $y'_i \neq y_i$. Since $\mathbf{y}, \mathbf{y}'$ are both short, this yields a valid solution to Assumption 4.2.

An Attack on Construction 4.5. To conclude, we describe a (heuristic) attack that breaks extractability of Construction 4.5. Our approach takes the following template:

1. Given the CRS for the functional commitment scheme, we construct an efficient adversary $\mathcal{A}$ that can obliviously sample an opening to an arbitrary vector $\mathbf{y} \in \mathbb{Z}_q^k$ with respect to a function $f_{\mathbf{M}}$ where $\mathbf{M} = [\mathbf{M}_{\mathsf{L}} \mid \mathbf{0}^{k \times \ell_1}]$ and $\mathbf{M}_{\mathsf{L}} \in \mathbb{Z}_q^{k \times \ell_2}$ is short.
2. Extractability of the functional commitment now says that there exists an efficient extractor that outputs a short $\mathbf{x} \in \mathbb{Z}_q^{\ell_1 + \ell_2}$ such that $\mathbf{M}\mathbf{x} = \mathbf{y}$.
3. Since the oblivious sampler is agnostic to the choice of $\mathbf{M}_{\mathsf{L}}$ (as long as it is short), we can embed an (inhomogeneous) SIS instance into $\mathbf{M}_{\mathsf{L}}$. In this case, an extractor for algorithm $\mathcal{A}$ is able to solve inhomogeneous SIS with respect to $\mathbf{M}$, and by extension, $\mathbf{M}_{\mathsf{L}}$.

We defer the details to the the full version of this paper. Taken together, our analysis shows that under the inhomogeneous SIS assumption, either Assumption 4.2 or Assumption 4.3 must be false, and correspondingly, the functional commitment scheme in Construction 4.5 is *not* extractable.

Acknowledgments. We thank Martin Albrecht for helpful discussions about the cryptanalysis of the k-R-ISIS assumption and Daniel Wichs for helpful insights on functional commitments and RAM delegation. David J. Wu is supported in part by NSF CNS-2151131, CNS-2140975, CNS-2318701, a Microsoft Research Faculty Fellowship, and a Google Research Scholar award.

References

ACL+22. Albrecht, M.R., Cini, V., Lai, R.W.F., Malavolta, G., Thyagarajan, S.A.: Lattice-based SNARKs: publicly verifiable, preprocessing, and recursively composable. In: Dodis, Y., Shrimpton, T. (eds.) CRYPTO 2022. LNCS, vol. 13508, pp. 102–132. Springer, Cham (2022). https://doi.org/10.1007/978-3-031-15979-4_4

Ajt96. Ajtai, M.. Generating hard instances of lattice problems (extended abstract). In: STOC (1996)

Alb23. Albrecht, M.: Knowledge K-M-ISIS is false (2023). https://gist.github.com/malb/7c8b86520c675560be62eda98dab2a6f

AR20. Agrawal, S., Raghuraman, S.: KVaC: key-value commitments for blockchains and beyond. In: Moriai, S., Wang, H. (eds.) ASIACRYPT 2020. LNCS, vol. 12493, pp. 839–869. Springer, Cham (2020). https://doi.org/10.1007/978-3-030-64840-4_28

BC12. Bitansky, N., Chiesa, A.: Succinct arguments from multi-prover interactive proofs and their efficiency benefits. In: Safavi-Naini, R., Canetti, R. (eds.) CRYPTO 2012. LNCS, vol. 7417, pp. 255–272. Springer, Heidelberg (2012). https://doi.org/10.1007/978-3-642-32009-5_16

BCFL22. Balbás, D., Catalano, D., Fiore, D., Lai, R.W.F.: Functional commitments for circuits from falsifiable assumptions. IACR Cryptol. ePrint Arch. (2022)

BCI+13. Bitansky, N., Chiesa, A., Ishai, Y., Paneth, O., Ostrovsky, R.: Succinct non-interactive arguments via linear interactive proofs. In: Sahai, A. (ed.) TCC 2013. LNCS, vol. 7785, pp. 315–333. Springer, Heidelberg (2013). https://doi.org/10.1007/978-3-642-36594-2_18

BGG+14. Boneh, D., et al.: Fully key-homomorphic encryption, arithmetic circuit ABE and compact garbled circuits. In: Nguyen, P.Q., Oswald, E. (eds.) EUROCRYPT 2014. LNCS, vol. 8441, pp. 533–556. Springer, Heidelberg (2014). https://doi.org/10.1007/978-3-642-55220-5_30

BHK17. Brakerski, Z., Holmgren, J., Kalai, Y.T.: Non-interactive delegation and batch NP verification from standard computational assumptions. In: STOC (2017)

BNO21. Boneh, D., Nguyen, W., Ozdemir, A.: How to commit to private functions. In: IACR Cryptol. ePrint Arch, Efficient Functional Commitments (2021)

BTVW17. Brakerski, Z., Tsabary, R., Vaikuntanathan, V., Wee, H.: Private constrained PRFs (and more) from LWE. In: Kalai, Y., Reyzin, L. (eds.) TCC 2017. LNCS, vol. 10677, pp. 264–302. Springer, Cham (2017). https://doi.org/10.1007/978-3-319-70500-2_10

BV15. Brakerski, Z., Vaikuntanathan, V.: Constrained key-homomorphic PRFs from standard lattice assumptions. In: Dodis, Y., Nielsen, J.B. (eds.) TCC 2015. LNCS, vol. 9015, pp. 1–30. Springer, Heidelberg (2015). https://doi.org/10.1007/978-3-662-46497-7_1

CF13. Catalano, D., Fiore, D.: Vector commitments and their applications. In: Kurosawa, K., Hanaoka, G. (eds.) PKC 2013. LNCS, vol. 7778, pp. 55–72. Springer, Heidelberg (2013). https://doi.org/10.1007/978-3-642-36362-7_5

CFG+20. Campanelli, M., Fiore, D., Greco, N., Kolonelos, D., Nizzardo, L.: Incrementally aggregatable vector commitments and applications to verifiable decentralized storage. In: Moriai, S., Wang, H. (eds.) ASIACRYPT 2020. LNCS, vol. 12492, pp. 3–35. Springer, Cham (2020). https://doi.org/10.1007/978-3-030-64834-3_1

CJJ21. Choudhuri, A.R., Jain, A., Jin, Z.: SNARGs for $\mathcal{P}$ from LWE. In: FOCS (2021)

CLM23. Cini, V., Lai, R.W.F., Malavolta, G.: Lattice-based succinct arguments from vanishing polynomials: (extended abstract). In: Handschuh, H., Lysyanskaya, A. (eds.) CRYPTO 2023. LNCS, vol. 14082, pp. 72–105. Springer, Cham (2023). https://doi.org/10.1007/978-3-031-38545-2_3

dCP23. de Castro, L., Peikert, C.: Functional commitments for all functions, with transparent setup and from SIS. In: Hazay, C., Stam, M. (eds.) EUROCRYPT 2023. LNCS, vol. 14006, pp. 287–320. Springer, Cham (2023). https://doi.org/10.1007/978-3-031-30620-4_10

FLV23. Fisch, B., Liu, Z., Vesely, P.: Orbweaver: succinct linear functional commitments from lattices. In: Handschuh, H., Lysyanskaya, A. (eds.) CRYPTO 2023. LNCS, vol. 14082, pp. 106–131. Springer, Cham (2023). https://doi.org/10.1007/978-3-031-38545-2_4

GGPR13. Gennaro, R., Gentry, C., Parno, B., Raykova, M.: Quadratic span programs and succinct NIZKs without PCPs. In: Johansson, T., Nguyen, P.Q. (eds.) EUROCRYPT 2013. LNCS, vol. 7881, pp. 626–645. Springer, Heidelberg (2013). https://doi.org/10.1007/978-3-642-38348-9_37

Gro16. Groth, J.: On the size of pairing-based non-interactive arguments. In: Fischlin, M., Coron, J.-S. (eds.) EUROCRYPT 2016. LNCS, vol. 9666, pp. 305–326. Springer, Heidelberg (2016). https://doi.org/10.1007/978-3-662-49896-5_11

GRWZ20. Gorbunov, S., Reyzin, L., Wee, H., Zhang, Z.: Aggregating proofs for multiple vector commitments. In: ACM CCS, Pointproofs (2020)

GSW13. Gentry, C., Sahai, A., Waters, B.: Homomorphic encryption from learning with errors: conceptually-simpler, asymptotically-faster, attribute-based. In: Canetti, R., Garay, J.A. (eds.) CRYPTO 2013. CRYPTO 2013. LNCS, vol. 8042, pp. 75–92. Springer, Heidelberg (2013). https://doi.org/10.1007/978-3-642-40041-4_5

GVW13. Gorbunov, S., Vaikuntanathan, V., Wee, H.: Attribute-based encryption for circuits. In: STOC (2013)

GVW15a. Gorbunov, S., Vaikuntanathan, V., Wee, H.: Predicate encryption for circuits from LWE. In: Gennaro, R., Robshaw, M. (eds.) CRYPTO 2015. LNCS, vol. 9216, pp. 503–523. Springer, Heidelberg (2015). https://doi.org/10.1007/978-3-662-48000-7_25

GVW15b. Gorbunov, S., Vaikuntanathan, V., Wichs, D.: Leveled fully homomorphic signatures from standard lattices. In: STOC (2015)

GW11. Gentry, C., Wichs, D.: Separating succinct non-interactive arguments from all falsifiable assumptions. In: STOC (2011)

IKO07. Ishai, Y., Kushilevitz, E., Ostrovsky, R.: Efficient arguments without short PCPs. In: CCC (2007)

Kil92. Kilian, J.: A note on efficient zero-knowledge proofs and arguments (extended abstract). In: STOC (1992)

KLVW23. Kalai, Y., Lombardi, A., Vaikuntanathan, V., Wichs, D.: Boosting batch arguments and RAM delegation. In: STOC (2023)

KP16. Kalai, Y., Paneth, O.: Delegating RAM computations. In: Hirt, M., Smith, A. (eds.) TCC 2016. LNCS, vol. 9986, pp. 91–118. Springer, Heidelberg (2016). https://doi.org/10.1007/978-3-662-53644-5_4

KPY19. Kalai, Y.T., Paneth, O., Yang, L.: How to delegate computations publicly. In: STOC (2019)

KVZ21. Kalai, Y.T., Vaikuntanathan, V., Zhang, R.Y.: Somewhere statistical soundness, post-quantum security, and SNARGs. In: Nissim, K., Waters, B. (eds.) TCC 2021. LNCS, vol. 13042, pp. 330–368. Springer, Cham (2021). https://doi.org/10.1007/978-3-030-90459-3_12

KZG10. Kate, A., Zaverucha, G.M., Goldberg, I.: Constant-size commitments to polynomials and their applications. In: Abe, M. (ed.) ASIACRYPT 2010. LNCS, vol. 6477, pp. 177–194. Springer, Heidelberg (2010). https://doi.org/10.1007/978-3-642-17373-8_11

LM19. Lai, R.W.F., Malavolta, G.: Subvector commitments with application to succinct arguments. In: Boldyreva, A., Micciancio, D. (eds.) CRYPTO 2019. LNCS, vol. 11692, pp. 530–560. Springer, Cham (2019). https://doi.org/10.1007/978-3-030-26948-7_19

LP20. Lipmaa, H., Pavlyk, K.: Succinct functional commitment for a large class of arithmetic circuits. In: Moriai, S., Wang, H. (eds.) ASIACRYPT 2020. LNCS, vol. 12493, pp. 686–716. Springer, Cham (2020). https://doi.org/10.1007/978-3-030-64840-4_23

LRY16. Libert, B., Ramanna, S.C., Yung, M.: From polynomial commitments to pairing-based accumulators from simple assumptions. In: ICALP, Functional Commitment Schemes (2016)

LY10. Libert, B., Yung, M.: Concise mercurial vector commitments and independent zero-knowledge sets with short proofs. In: Micciancio, D. (ed.) TCC 2010. LNCS, vol. 5978, pp. 499–517. Springer, Heidelberg (2010). https://doi.org/10.1007/978-3-642-11799-2_30

Mer87. Merkle, R.C.: A digital signature based on a conventional encryption function. In: Pomerance, C. (ed.) CRYPTO 1987. LNCS, vol. 293, pp. 369–378. Springer, Heidelberg (1988). https://doi.org/10.1007/3-540-48184-2_32

Mic00. Micali, S.: Computationally sound proofs. SIAM J. Comput. **30**(4), 1253–1298 (2000)

MP12. Micciancio, D., Peikert, C.: Trapdoors for lattices: simpler, tighter, faster, smaller. In: Pointcheval, D., Johansson, T. (eds.) EUROCRYPT 2012. LNCS, vol. 7237, pp. 700–718. Springer, Heidelberg (2012). https://doi.org/10.1007/978-3-642-29011-4_41

Nit21. Nitulescu, A.: SoK: Vector Commitments (2021). https://www.di.ens.fr/~nitulesc/files/vc-sok.pdf

PHGR13. Parno, B., Howell, J., Gentry, C., Raykova, M: Nearly practical verifiable computation. In: IEEE Symposium on Security and Privacy, Pinocchio (2013)

PPS21. Peikert, C., Pepin, Z., Sharp, C.: Vector and functional commitments from lattices. In: Nissim, K., Waters, B. (eds.) TCC 2021. LNCS, vol. 13044, pp. 480–511. Springer, Cham (2021). https://doi.org/10.1007/978-3-030-90456-2_16

PSTY13. Papamanthou, C., Shi, E., Tamassia, R., Yi, K.: Streaming authenticated data structures. In: Johansson, T., Nguyen, P.Q. (eds.) EUROCRYPT 2013. LNCS, vol. 7881, pp. 353–370. Springer, Heidelberg (2013). https://doi.org/10.1007/978-3-642-38348-9_22

TAB+20. Tomescu, A., et al.: Aggregatable subvector commitments for stateless cryptocurrencies. In: Galdi, C., Kolesnikov, V. (eds.) SCN 2020. LNCS, vol. 12238, pp. 45–64. Springer, Cham (2020). https://doi.org/10.1007/978-3-030-57990-6_3

Tsa22. Tsabary, R.: Candidate witness encryption from lattice techniques. In: Dodis, Y., Shrimpton, T. (eds.) CRYPTO 2022. LNCS, vol. 13507, pp. 535–559. Springer, Cham (2022). https://doi.org/10.1007/978-3-031-15802-5_19

TXN20. Tomescu, A., Xia, Y., Newman, Z.: Authenticated dictionaries with cross-incremental proof (dis)aggregation. IACR Cryptol. ePrint Arch. (2020)

VWW22. Vaikuntanathan, V., Wee, H., Wichs, D.: Witness encryption and null-IO from evasive LWE. In: Agrawal, S., Lin, D. (eds.) ASIACRYPT 2022. LNCS, vol. 13791, pp. 195–221. Springer, Cham (2022). https://doi.org/10.1007/978-3-031-22963-3_7

Wee22. Wee, H.: Optimal broadcast encryption and CP-ABE from evasive lattice assumptions. In: Dunkelman, O., Dziembowski, S. (eds.) EUROCRYPT 2022. LNCS, vol. 13276, pp. 217–241. Springer, Cham (2022). https://doi.org/10.1007/978-3-031-07085-3_8

Wee23. Wee, H.: Circuit ABE with small ciphertexts and keys from lattices (2023). Manuscript

WW23. Wee, H., Wu, D.J.: Succinct vector, polynomial, and functional commitments from lattices. In: Hazay, C., Stam, M. (eds.) EUROCRYPT 2023. LNCS, vol. 14006, pp. 385–416. Springer, Cham (2023). https://doi.org/10.1007/978-3-031-30620-4_13

WWW22. Waters, B., Wee, H., Wu, D.J.: Multi-authority ABE from lattices without random oracles. In: Kiltz, E., Vaikuntanathan, V. (eds.) TCC 2022, vol. 13747, pp. 651–679. Springer, Cham (2022). https://doi.org/10.1007/978-3-031-22318-1_23

Non-interactive Zero-Knowledge Functional Proofs

Gongxian Zeng[1], Junzuo Lai[2(✉)], Zhengan Huang[1(✉)], Linru Zhang[3(✉)], Xiangning Wang[3(✉)], Kwok-Yan Lam[3], Huaxiong Wang[3], and Jian Weng[2]

[1] Peng Cheng Laboratory, Shenzhen, China
gxzeng@cs.hku.hk, zhahuang.sjtu@gmail.com

[2] College of Information Science and Technology, Jinan University, Guangzhou, China
laijunzuo@gmail.com

[3] Nanyang Technological University, Singapore, Singapore
{linru.zhang,xiangning.wang,kwokyan.lam,hxwang}@ntu.edu.sg

Abstract. In this paper, we consider to generalize NIZK by empowering a prover to share a witness in a fine-grained manner with verifiers. Roughly, the prover is able to authorize a verifier to obtain extra information of witness, i.e., besides verifying the truth of the statement, the verifier can additionally obtain certain function of the witness from the accepting proof using a secret functional key provided by the prover.

To fulfill these requirements, we introduce a new primitive called *non-interactive zero-knowledge functional proofs (fNIZKs)*, and formalize its security notions. We provide a generic construction of fNIZK for any NP relation $\mathcal{R}$, which enables the prover to share any function of the witness with a verifier. For a widely-used relation about set membership proof (implying range proof), we construct a concrete and efficient fNIZK, through new building blocks (set membership encryption and dual inner-product encryption), which might be of independent interest.

Keywords: non-interactive zero knowledge proof · set membership proof · range proof · inner-product encryption

1 Introduction

The zero-knowledge (ZK) proof system [19] is an interactive protocol in which a prover convinces a verifier of the truth of a statement without disclosing any additional information. A non-interactive zero-knowledge (NIZK) proof [1] is a type of ZK proof without any interactions with a verifier. NIZKs have found numerous applications in cryptography, including but not limited to secure public key encryption resilient against chosen-ciphertext attacks [27], group/ring signatures [7,9], anonymous credentials [7], multi-party computations [18], and some applications in blockchain such as privacy preserving coins (e.g., Zcash

J. Guo and R. Steinfeld (Eds.): ASIACRYPT 2023, LNCS 14442, pp. 236–268, 2023.
https://doi.org/10.1007/978-981-99-8733-7_8

[28]), zero knowledge virtual machine (e.g., zkEVM [32]) and blockchain-based e-voting [21].

In this paper, our objective is to generalize the concept of NIZK by enabling the prover to share a witness in a fine-grained manner with verifiers. Specifically, the prover is granted the ability to authorize a verifier to access additional information of the witness. This means that, in addition to verifying the truth of the statement, the verifier can also gain insights into certain functions of the witness using a secret key provided by the prover. To address these requirements, we propose a new type of NIZKs called *non-interactive zero-knowledge functional proofs (fNIZKs)*.

Our Contributions. We initiate the study of fNIZK. The specific contributions are outlined as follows:

1. We present a formal definition and security notions of non-interactive zero-knowledge functional proof (fNIZK).
2. We provide a generic construction of fNIZK for any NP relation $\mathcal{R}$, which enables the prover to share any function of the witness with a verifier.
3. For a widely-used relation about set membership proof (implying range proof), we construct a concrete and efficient fNIZK, called set membership functional proof (fSMP).

Primitive of fNIZK. A fNIZK scheme consists of seven algorithms: Setup, Prove, Verify, UKGen, FKGen, CheckKey and Extract. Roughly, (Setup, Prove, Verify) are similar to those of NIZK, except that Prove and Verify also input the prover's public key, which is generated by UKGen. The prover invokes FKGen to generate a secret key for some function (secret functional key) and distribute it to a verifier. With this key, the verifier can call Extract to extract the function of the witness from an accepting proof. The validity of the secret functional key can be checked via CheckKey.

If there is no restrictions on the extracting capability of keys, then a verifier with a secret functional key can learn a function of the witnesses in *all* accepting proofs generated by the prover. To address the above issue, we introduce *labels* in some of the above algorithms.

Concretely, in fNIZK, the FKGen algorithm, whose input includes a label $\tau_{\mathtt{f}}$, the secret key sk of the prover, and a function f, generates a secret functional key $sk_{f,\tau_{\mathtt{f}}}$. Similarly, the Prove algorithm, whose input includes a label τ_{p}, the public key pk, and a statement-witness pair (x, w), to generate a proof π. The extraction algorithm Extract can output $f(w)$ from π, only if $\mathsf{P}(\tau_{\mathrm{p}}, \tau_{\mathtt{f}}) = 1$ for some predicate P.

The security properties of fNIZK contains completeness, functional knowledge, adaptive soundness and zero knowledge. Soundness is similar to that of NIZK. Other properties are listed below.

1. Completeness of fNIZK has three requirements. Firstly, any proof π generated by Prove should be verified successfully by Verify. Secondly, any normally generated secret functional key $sk_{f,\tau_{\mathtt{f}}}$ for $(f, \tau_{\mathtt{f}})$ should pass the verification

of CheckKey. Thirdly, for normally generated proof π (associated with τ_{p}) and normally generated secret functional key $sk_{f,\tau_{\mathfrak{f}}}$ (for $(f, \tau_{\mathfrak{f}})$), if $\mathsf{P}(\tau_{\mathrm{p}}, \tau_{\mathfrak{f}}) = 1$, Extract should extract $f(w)$ from π.

2. The functional knowledge property requires that, in general, if the verifier accepts a proof π associated with a label τ_{p} (here π *does not have to be normally generated*), then he/she can be convinced that a function of some witness can be extracted from the proof (with the help of the secret functional key associated with label $\tau_{\mathfrak{f}}$ satisfying $\mathsf{P}(\tau_{\mathrm{p}}, \tau_{\mathfrak{f}}) = 1$).
3. The zero knowledge requires that except for the fact of the truth of the statement and the functions (authorized by the prover) of witness, the verifier cannot obtain any other information about the witness from an accepting proof.

Generic Construction of fNIZK. Based on NIZKs and functional encryption (FE) [2,25], we provide a generic construction of fNIZK for any NP relation $\mathcal{R}$, which enables the prover to share any function (from a function family $\mathbb{F}$) of the witness with a verifier.

When generating a proof for a valid statement-witness pair (x, w), Prove firstly encrypts the witness using the underlying FE scheme, then utilizes the NIZK to prove that "$(x, w) \in \mathcal{R}$ and the well-formedness of the ciphertext", and finally outputs a proof including the ciphertext and the NIZK proof. Extract can be implemented by calling the decryption of FE. We require that the underlying FE supports function family $\widehat{\mathbb{F}}$, where a function $\widehat{f}$ belongs to $\widehat{\mathbb{F}}$, if and only if there exists $(f \in \mathbb{F}, \tau_{\mathfrak{f}})$ satisfying

$$\widehat{f}(w, \tau_{\mathrm{p}}) = \begin{cases} f(w) & \text{if } \mathsf{P}(\tau_{\mathrm{p}}, \tau_{\mathfrak{f}}) = 1 \\ \perp & \text{if } \mathsf{P}(\tau_{\mathrm{p}}, \tau_{\mathfrak{f}}) = 0 \end{cases}$$

The secret functional key generated by FKGen also contains a NIZK proof, which enables the verifier to check the validity of the secret functional key, via CheckKey.

The security properties of this fNIZK construction are derived from the properties of the FE scheme and the NIZK schemes.

Concrete and Efficient Construction of fSMP. Set membership proof (SMP) [5] enables a prover to convince a verifier that a digitally committed value belongs to a specified public set. A special case of SMP is range proof [4,5,13], where the public set is an integer range. SMPs are widely utilized as building blocks in various cryptographic schemes such as anonymous credentials [7,30], Zcash [28], and e-cash [6].

Due to the extensive application value of SMPs, we provide a concrete and efficient fNIZK for relation about set membership proof, called set membership functional proof (fSMP).

In our fSMP, Prove outputs a proof associated with label τ_{p} to demonstrate that the committed value $w \in \Phi$ where Φ is a public set, and a verifier with a secret functional key for $(\Phi_S, \tau_{\mathfrak{f}})$ can additionally check whether $w \in \Phi_S$ or not (where $\Phi_S \subset \Phi$) from the proof, when $\mathsf{P}(\tau_{\mathrm{p}}, \tau_{\mathfrak{f}}) = 1$.

To construct a fSMP, we propose a new primitive, called *set membership encryption* (SME), which is a variant of public-key encryption, including Setup, KGen, Enc and Query. Roughly, Enc takes a set Φ, a message $w \in \Phi$ and a label τ_p as input to generate a ciphertext c. The query algorithm Query takes as input c and a secret functional key for $(\Phi_S \subset \Phi, \tau_\mathrm{f})$ generated by KGen, and outputs a bit. We require that when $\mathsf{P}(\tau_\mathrm{p}, \tau_\mathrm{f}) = 1$, Query outputs 1 if and only if $w \in \Phi_S$. We say that a SME supports Sigma protocols, if there exists a Sigma protocol to prove the well-formedness of a SME ciphertext. Then we show a generic framework of constructing fSMP from a SME and a commitment scheme that both support Sigma protocols[1].

With the help of a new building block called *dual inner-product encryption* (dual IPE), we present a generic construction of SME. Dual IPE is a special two-level hierarchical IPE (2-HIPE) [20,23,24] without delegation capability. In terms of attribute-hiding, our dual IPE requires the first-level vector to be fully attribute-hiding, without requiring the second-level vector to be hidden.

We provide an efficient instantiation of dual IPE, utilizing the techniques in IPE [10,12,31], based on the k-LIN assumption.

When plugging the dual IPE instantiation ($k = 1$) into the generic construction of SME from dual IPE, we can obtain a concrete and efficient SME supporting Sigma protocols. Further, incorporating Pedersen commitment [26], we achieve a concrete and efficient fSMP.

Finally, we improve the size of the proof of fSMP. Note that fSMP contains a NIZK proof, which derives from the Sigma protocols about the SME and Pedersen commitment. We utilize the self-stacking technique [17] to achieve logarithmic size of the NIZK proof, i.e., $O((\log l_1) \cdot \mathsf{poly}(\lambda)) = O(\log l_1)$, where $l_1 = |\Phi|$ and λ is the security parameter.

Applications of fNIZK. In the following, we present examples that illustrate the promising applications of fNIZK.

A scenario where fNIZK can work effectively is in supervision[2], such as anti-money laundering. Typically, individuals generate zero knowledge proofs for their regular activities, such as transferring privacy-preserving cryptocurrencies. In certain cases, the authority may authorize a specific department or institution for supervision purposes. For instance, the authority is able to issue a secret functional key that is only applicable to proofs generated during specific periods (facilitated by labels). Consequently, the department or institution can obtain the specified information from the proofs using the authorized key. This enables them to determine whether a user has violated the rules within certain periods, while ensuring that other information about the witnesses in the proofs remains undisclosed.

[1] A commitment scheme supports Sigma protocols, if there exists a Sigma protocol to prove the well-formedness of a commitment.

[2] In this scenario, the authority generates a public key and a secret key, and all users utilize the public key to generate or verify proofs. The secret functional keys are generated by the authority, using the secret key.

In blockchain-based auction systems, before participation in auctions, users lock a certain amount of coins by transferring them to the auction platform, accompanied by a NIZK proof that verifies the validity of the coins in a zero-knowledge manner. However, when users intend to participate in specific auctions, the auction platform needs to verify if the amount of coins meets the minimum deposit requirement. Without the use of fNIZK, in order to maintain the privacy of the exact amount of coins, users would need to generate NIZK proofs for auctions with different minimum deposit requirements. By employing fNIZK, users only need to generate the proof once when transferring coins to the platform. Subsequently, they can generate secret keys associated with range functions (e.g., greater than the minimum deposit requirement) for the auction organizer, each time they wish to join particular auctions. The auction organizer can extract the function about the amount to verify if the user meets the requirements for participation, while keeping other information about the amount of coins private.

Another application example is anonymous attribute-based credential [7]. Users who obtain credentials for specific attribute sets are required to show different proofs to different verifiers (e.g., service providers) in order to demonstrate possession of a valid credential that satisfies the access policies set by the service providers. We point out that fNIZK offers an alternative approach for constructing anonymous attribute-based credential systems. Firstly, taking all the attributes and the credentials as witness, the user can utilize fNIZK to generate a proof to demonstrate the well-formedness of a valid credential for a specific attribute set without disclosing any attributes. Then, when the user needs to show proofs for different service providers, he/she can simply send different secret keys for different functions associated with the access policies to different service providers, instead of generating multiple NIZK proofs. This approach could reduce computational overhead.

Roadmap. The remaining sections of this paper are structured as follows: Sect. 2 provides a review of the preliminaries. In Sect. 3, we present the formal definitions of syntax and security notions pertaining to fNIZK. A generic construction of fNIZK is presented in Sect. 4. Furthermore, we delve into the specific case of the set membership proof and introduce the construction of set membership functional proof (fSMP) in Sect. 5.

2 Preliminaries

Notations. Throughout this paper, let λ denote the security parameter. For any $k \in \mathbb{N}$, let $[k] := \{1, 2, \cdots, k\}$. For a finite set S, we denote by $|S|$ the number of elements in S, and denote by $a \leftarrow S$ the process of uniformly sampling a from S. For a distribution X, we denote by $a \leftarrow X$ the process of sampling a from X. For any probabilistic polynomial-time (PPT) algorithm Alg, let $\mathcal{RS}_{\mathsf{Alg}}$ be the randomness space of Alg. We write $\mathsf{Alg}(x; r)$ for the process of Alg on input x with inner randomness $r \in \mathcal{RS}_{\mathsf{Alg}}$, and use $y \leftarrow \mathsf{Alg}(x)$ to denote the process of running Alg on input x with $r \leftarrow \mathcal{RS}_{\mathsf{Alg}}$, and assigning y the result.

We write $\mathsf{negl}(\lambda)$ to denote a negligible function in λ and write $\mathsf{poly}(\lambda)$ to denote a polynomial.

For a polynomial-time relation $\mathcal{R} \subset \mathcal{X} \times \mathcal{W}$, where $\mathcal{X}$ is the statement space and $\mathcal{W}$ is the witness space, we say that w is a witness for x if $(x, w) \in \mathcal{R}$. We denote the language associated with $\mathcal{R}$ as $\mathcal{L}_{\mathcal{R}} = \{x \mid \exists w : (x, w) \in \mathcal{R}\}$.

Bold lower-case letters denote vectors, e.g., $\mathbf{a} = (a_1, \dots, a_n)$ is a n-dimension vector, and usually the number of dimensions can be inferred from the context. Let $\langle \mathbf{a}, \mathbf{b} \rangle = \sum_{i \in [n]} a_i \cdot b_i$ denotes the inner product between two vectors $\mathbf{a}$ and $\mathbf{b}$. Bold upper-case letters denote matrices, e.g., $\mathbf{B} \in \mathbb{Z}_p^{n_1 \times n_2}$ is an $n_1 \times n_2$ matrix. We use $\mathbf{I}_n$ to denote the $n \times n$ identity matrix. For simplicity, we sometimes write $\mathbf{I}$ to denote the identity matrix when n is given in the text.

IPE. We recall the definition of inner-product encryption (IPE).

Definition 1. (Inner-product encryption). *An* inner-product encryption (IPE) *scheme for a message space $\mathcal{M}$ consists of four algorithms* $\mathsf{IPE} = (\mathsf{Setup}, \mathsf{KGen}, \mathsf{Enc}, \mathsf{Dec})$.

- $\mathsf{Setup}(1^\lambda, l) \to (pk, msk)$: *On input the security parameter 1^λ and the dimension l of the vector space, the setup algorithm outputs a public key pk and a master secret key msk.*
- $\mathsf{KGen}(msk, \mathbf{x}) \to sk_{\mathbf{x}}$: *On input msk and a vector $\mathbf{x}$, the key generation algorithm outputs a secret key $sk_{\mathbf{x}}$ for $\mathbf{x}$.*
- $\mathsf{Enc}(pk, \mathbf{y}, m) \to c_{\mathbf{y}}$: *On input pk, a vector $\mathbf{y}$ and a message $m \in \mathcal{M}$, the encryption algorithm outputs a ciphertext $c_{\mathbf{y}}$ for $\mathbf{y}$.*
- $\mathsf{Dec}(c_{\mathbf{y}}, sk_{\mathbf{x}}) \to m$: *On input a ciphertext $c_{\mathbf{y}}$ for $\mathbf{y}$ and a secret key $sk_{\mathbf{x}}$ for $\mathbf{x}$ as input, the decryption algorithm outputs a m.*

Correctness requires that for all $m \in \mathcal{M}$ and all vectors $\mathbf{x}, \mathbf{y}$ satisfying $\langle \mathbf{x}, \mathbf{y} \rangle = 0$, it holds that:

$$\Pr\left[\begin{matrix}(pk, msk) \leftarrow \mathsf{Setup}(1^\lambda, l) \\ sk_{\mathbf{x}} \leftarrow \mathsf{KGen}(msk, \mathbf{x})\end{matrix} : \mathsf{Dec}(\mathsf{Enc}(pk, \mathbf{y}, m), sk_{\mathbf{x}}) = m\right] = 1.$$

We recall adaptive security and fully attribute-hiding property for IPE [24].

Definition 2. (Adaptive security and fully attribute-hiding property for IPE). *An IPE scheme* $\mathsf{IPE} = (\mathsf{Setup}, \mathsf{KGen}, \mathsf{Enc}, \mathsf{Dec})$ *for message space $\mathcal{M}$ and dimension l is* adaptively secure and fully attribute-hiding, *if for any PPT adversary $\mathcal{A}$, the advantage $\mathbf{Adv}^{\mathsf{a\text{-}ah}}_{\mathsf{IPE},\mathcal{A}}(\lambda) := |\Pr[\mathsf{Exp}^{\mathsf{a\text{-}ah}}_{\mathsf{IPE},\mathcal{A}}(\lambda) = 1] - \frac{1}{2}|$ is negligible, where $\mathsf{Exp}^{\mathsf{a\text{-}ah}}_{\mathsf{IPE},\mathcal{A}}(\lambda)$ is defined in Fig. 1.*

Due to space limitations, please refer the other preliminaries to the full version of this paper, including the definitions of NIZK and Sigma protocols (including the stackable Sigma protocols), the definition of functional encryption and the definition of commitment.

$\underline{\mathsf{Exp}^{\text{a-ah}}_{\mathsf{IPE},\mathcal{A}}(\lambda)}$:
$(pk, msk) \leftarrow \mathsf{Setup}(1^\lambda, l)$, $b \leftarrow \{0,1\}$, $C_{\mathrm{y,m}} := \emptyset$, $U_{\mathrm{x}} := \emptyset$
$(\mathbf{y}_0, \mathbf{y}_1, m_0, m_1, st) \leftarrow \mathcal{A}_1^{\mathcal{O}^{\mathsf{KGen}}(\cdot)}(pk, l)$
s.t. if $m_0 \neq m_1$, $(\langle \mathbf{x}, \mathbf{y}_0 \rangle \neq 0) \wedge (\langle \mathbf{x}, \mathbf{y}_1 \rangle \neq 0)$ for all $\mathbf{x} \in U_{\mathrm{x}}$; and
if $m_0 = m_1$, $((\langle \mathbf{x}, \mathbf{y}_0 \rangle \neq 0) \wedge (\langle \mathbf{x}, \mathbf{y}_1 \rangle \neq 0)) \vee (\langle \mathbf{x}, \mathbf{y}_0 \rangle = \langle \mathbf{x}, \mathbf{y}_1 \rangle = 0)$ for all $\mathbf{x} \in U_{\mathrm{x}}$
$C_{\mathrm{y,m}} := \{(\mathbf{y}_0, \mathbf{y}_1, m_0, m_1)\}$, $c \leftarrow \mathsf{Enc}(pk, \mathbf{y}_b, m_b)$
$b' \leftarrow \mathcal{A}_2^{\mathcal{O}^{\mathsf{KGen}}(\cdot)}(c, st)$
Return $(b = b')$

$\underline{\mathcal{O}^{\mathsf{KGen}}(\mathbf{x})}$:
If $C_{\mathrm{y,m}} \neq \emptyset$:
Parse $C_{\mathrm{y,m}} = \{(\mathbf{y}_0, \mathbf{y}_1, m_0, m_1)\}$
If $m_0 \neq m_1$:
If $(\langle \mathbf{x}, \mathbf{y}_0 \rangle = 0) \vee (\langle \mathbf{x}, \mathbf{y}_1 \rangle = 0)$: Return $\perp$
If $m_0 = m_1$:
If $((\langle \mathbf{x}, \mathbf{y}_0 \rangle \neq 0) \wedge (\langle \mathbf{x}, \mathbf{y}_1 \rangle = 0)) \vee ((\langle \mathbf{x}, \mathbf{y}_0 \rangle = 0) \wedge (\langle \mathbf{x}, \mathbf{y}_1 \rangle \neq 0))$: Return $\perp$
$U_{\mathrm{x}} := U_{\mathrm{x}} \cup \{\mathbf{x}\}$
Return $sk_{\mathbf{x}} \leftarrow \mathsf{KGen}(msk, \mathbf{x})$

Fig. 1. Game for defining adaptive security and fully attribute-hiding property for IPE

3 Non-interactive Zero-Knowledge Functional Proof

In this section, we introduce a primitive called *non-interactive zero-knowledge functional proof (fNIZK)*, and formalize its security notions. Generally speaking, fNIZK offers the functionalities of NIZK, while also enabling a verifier with a specific secret key, provided by the prover, to extract specific information about the witness from the accepting proof.

Definition 3. (fNIZK). *Let $\mathcal{L}_{\mathcal{R}}$ be an* NP *language associated with an* NP *relation $\mathcal{R}$. Let $\mathbb{F}$ be a function family, and $\mathcal{T}$ be the label space. Let $\mathsf{P} : \mathcal{T} \times (\mathcal{T} \cup \{*\}) \rightarrow \{0,1\}$ be a predicate function satisfying $\mathsf{P}(\tau, *) = 1$ for all $\tau \in \mathcal{T}$.* A non-interactive zero-knowledge functional proof (fNIZK proof) *for $\mathcal{L}_{\mathcal{R}}$, $\mathbb{F}$, $\mathcal{T}$ and* P *consists of a tuple of seven efficient algorithms* fNIZK = (Setup, UKGen, FKGen, CheckKey, Prove, Verify, Extract).

- $\mathsf{Setup}(1^\lambda) \rightarrow \mathsf{crs}$: *On input the security parameter λ, the setup algorithm outputs a common reference string* crs.
- $\mathsf{UKGen}(\mathsf{crs}) \rightarrow (pk, sk)$: *On input a common reference string* crs, *the user key generation algorithm outputs a public key pk and a secret key sk.*
- $\mathsf{FKGen}(\mathsf{crs}, pk, sk, f, \tau_{\mathfrak{f}}) \rightarrow sk_{f,\tau_{\mathfrak{f}}}$: *On input a common reference string* crs, *a user key pair (pk, sk), a function $f \in \mathbb{F}$ and a label $\tau_{\mathfrak{f}} \in \mathcal{T} \cup \{*\}$, the secret functional key generation algorithm outputs a secret functional key $sk_{f,\tau_{\mathfrak{f}}}$. We assume that $sk_{f,\tau_{\mathfrak{f}}}$ implicitly includes the information of f and $\tau_{\mathfrak{f}}$.*

- $\mathsf{CheckKey}(\mathsf{crs}, pk, f, \tau_{\mathfrak{f}}, sk_{f,\tau_{\mathfrak{f}}}) \to b$: *On input a common reference string* crs, *a public key* pk, *a function* $f \in \mathbb{F}$ *and a label* $\tau_{\mathfrak{f}} \in \mathcal{T} \cup \{*\}$ *and a secret functional key* $sk_{f,\tau_{\mathfrak{f}}}$, *the checking algorithm outputs a bit* $b \in \{0,1\}$.
- $\mathsf{Prove}(\mathsf{crs}, pk, \tau_{\mathrm{p}}, x, w) \to \pi$: *On input a common reference string* crs, *a public key* pk, *a label* $\tau_{\mathrm{p}} \in \mathcal{T}$, *a statement* x *and a witness* w, *the proving algorithm outputs a proof* π. *We assume that there exists an efficient algorithm* $\mathsf{Ext}_{\mathcal{T}}$ *such that* $\tau_{\mathrm{p}} \leftarrow \mathsf{Ext}_{\mathcal{T}}(\pi)$.
- $\mathsf{Verify}(\mathsf{crs}, pk, x, \pi) \to b$: *On input the common reference string* crs, *a public key* pk, *a statement* x *and a proof* π, *the verification algorithm outputs a bit* $b \in \{0,1\}$.
- $\mathsf{Extract}(\mathsf{crs}, x, \pi, sk_{f,\tau_{\mathfrak{f}}}) \to y$: *On input a common reference string* crs, *a statement* x, *a proof* π *and a secret functional key* $sk_{f,\tau_{\mathfrak{f}}}$ *(for* f *and* $\tau_{\mathfrak{f}}$*), the extraction algorithm outputs* y.

Moreover, fNIZK *should satisfy the following properties:*

1. ***Completeness.*** *For any* $(x,w) \in \mathcal{R}$, *any* $f \in \mathbb{F}$, *any* $\tau_{\mathrm{p}} \in \mathcal{T}$ *and any* $\tau_{\mathfrak{f}} \in \mathcal{T} \cup \{*\}$,

$$\Pr\left[\begin{array}{l}\mathsf{crs} \leftarrow \mathsf{Setup}(1^\lambda),\ (pk, sk) \leftarrow \mathsf{UKGen}(\mathsf{crs}) \\ \pi \leftarrow \mathsf{Prove}(\mathsf{crs}, pk, \tau_{\mathrm{p}}, x, w)\end{array} : \mathsf{Verify}(\mathsf{crs}, pk, x, \pi) = 1\right] \geq 1 - \mathsf{negl}(\lambda),$$

$$\Pr\left[\begin{array}{l}\mathsf{crs} \leftarrow \mathsf{Setup}(1^\lambda),\ (pk, sk) \leftarrow \mathsf{UKGen}(\mathsf{crs}) \\ sk_{f,\tau_{\mathfrak{f}}} \leftarrow \mathsf{FKGen}(\mathsf{crs}, pk, sk, f, \tau_{\mathfrak{f}})\end{array} : \mathsf{CheckKey}(\mathsf{crs}, pk, f, \tau_{\mathfrak{f}}, sk_{f,\tau_{\mathfrak{f}}}) = 1\right]$$
$$\geq 1 - \mathsf{negl}(\lambda),$$

$$\Pr\left[\begin{array}{l}\mathsf{crs} \leftarrow \mathsf{Setup}(1^\lambda) \\ (pk, sk) \leftarrow \mathsf{UKGen}(\mathsf{crs}) \\ sk_{f,\tau_{\mathfrak{f}}} \leftarrow \mathsf{FKGen}(\mathsf{crs}, pk, sk, f, \tau_{\mathfrak{f}}) \\ \pi \leftarrow \mathsf{Prove}(\mathsf{crs}, pk, \tau_{\mathrm{p}}, x, w)\end{array} : \mathsf{Extract}(\mathsf{crs}, x, \pi, sk_{f,\tau_{\mathfrak{f}}}) = f(w) \middle| \mathsf{P}(\tau_{\mathrm{p}}, \tau_{\mathfrak{f}}) = 1\right]$$
$$\geq 1 - \mathsf{negl}(\lambda).$$

2. ***Functional knowledge.*** *For any PPT adversary* $\mathcal{A}$,

$$\Pr\left[\begin{array}{l}\mathsf{crs} \leftarrow \mathsf{Setup}(1^\lambda),\ (pk, sk) \leftarrow \mathsf{UKGen}(\mathsf{crs}) \\ (\pi, x, f, \tau_{\mathfrak{f}}, sk_{f,\tau_{\mathfrak{f}}}) \leftarrow \mathcal{A}(\mathsf{crs}, pk, sk) \\ \quad s.t.\ (x \in \mathcal{L}_{\mathcal{R}}) \wedge (f \in \mathbb{F}) \wedge \tau_{\mathfrak{f}} \in (\mathcal{T} \cup \{*\}) \\ \quad\ \wedge (\mathsf{Verify}(\mathsf{crs}, pk, x, \pi) = 1) \\ \quad\ \wedge (\mathsf{CheckKey}(\mathsf{crs}, pk, f, \tau_{\mathfrak{f}}, sk_{f,\tau_{\mathfrak{f}}}) = 1) \\ \quad\ \wedge (\mathsf{P}(\mathsf{Ext}_{\mathcal{T}}(\pi), \tau_{\mathfrak{f}}) = 1) \\ y \leftarrow \mathsf{Extract}(\mathsf{crs}, x, \pi, sk_{f,\tau_{\mathfrak{f}}})\end{array} : \begin{array}{l}\exists\, w \in \mathcal{W},\ s.t. \\ ((x,w) \in \mathcal{R}) \\ \wedge (y = f(w))\end{array}\right] \geq 1 - \mathsf{negl}(\lambda).$$

3. ***Adaptive soundness.*** *For any computationally unbounded adversary* $\mathcal{A}$,

$$\Pr\left[\begin{array}{l}\mathsf{crs} \leftarrow \mathsf{Setup}(1^\lambda) \\ (pk, x, \pi) \leftarrow \mathcal{A}(\mathsf{crs})\end{array} : \begin{array}{c}x \notin \mathcal{L}_{\mathcal{R}} \\ \wedge\ \mathsf{Verify}(\mathsf{crs}, pk, x, \pi) = 1\end{array}\right] \leq \mathsf{negl}(\lambda).$$

4. ***Zero knowledge.*** *For any PPT adversary* $\mathcal{A} = (\mathcal{A}_1, \mathcal{A}_2, \mathcal{A}_3)$, *there exists a simulator* $\mathsf{Sim} = (\mathsf{Sim}_1, \mathsf{Sim}_2)$ *such that*

$$\left|\Pr[\mathsf{ExpReal}^{\mathsf{zk}}_{\mathsf{fNIZK},\mathcal{A},n}(\lambda) = 1] - \Pr[\mathsf{ExpIdeal}^{\mathsf{zk}}_{\mathsf{fNIZK},\mathcal{A},\mathsf{Sim},n}(\lambda) = 1]\right| \leq \mathsf{negl}(\lambda)$$

where $\mathsf{ExpReal}^{\mathsf{zk}}_{\mathsf{fNIZK},\mathcal{A},n}(\lambda)$ *and* $\mathsf{ExpIdeal}^{\mathsf{zk}}_{\mathsf{fNIZK},\mathcal{A},\mathsf{Sim},n}(\lambda)$ *are defined in Fig. 2, and* $n = \mathsf{poly}(\lambda)$.

$\underline{\mathsf{ExpReal}^{\mathsf{zk}}_{\mathsf{fNIZK},\mathcal{A},n}(\lambda)}$:

$\mathsf{crs} \leftarrow \mathsf{Setup}(1^\lambda)$, $W := \emptyset$, $Q := \emptyset$
$((pk_i, sk_i) \leftarrow \mathsf{UKGen}(\mathsf{crs}))_{i\in[n]}$
$(U_{\mathrm{cor}}, st_1^{\mathcal{A}}) \leftarrow \mathcal{A}_1(\mathsf{crs}, (pk_i)_{i\in[n]})$
  s.t. $U_{\mathrm{cor}} \subset [n]$
$(i^*, \tau_{\mathrm{p}}, x, w, w', st_2^{\mathcal{A}}) \leftarrow \mathcal{A}_2^{\mathcal{O}^{\mathsf{FKGen}}(\cdot)}((sk_i)_{i\in U_{\mathrm{cor}}}, st_1^{\mathcal{A}})$
  s.t. $(i^* \notin U_{\mathrm{cor}}) \wedge ((x, w) \in \mathcal{R})$
    $\wedge(\forall (i^*, f', \tau'_{\mathrm{f}}) \in Q$ satisfying $\mathsf{P}(\tau_{\mathrm{p}}, \tau'_{\mathrm{f}}) = 1$,
     $f'(w) = f'(w'))$
$W := \{i^*, \tau_{\mathrm{p}}, w, w'\}$
$\pi \leftarrow \mathsf{Prove}(\mathsf{crs}, pk_{i^*}, \tau_{\mathrm{p}}, x, w)$
$b \leftarrow \mathcal{A}_3^{\mathcal{O}^{\mathsf{FKGen}}(\cdot)}(\pi, st_2^{\mathcal{A}})$
Return b

$\underline{\mathcal{O}^{\mathsf{FKGen}}(i', f', \tau'_{\mathrm{f}})}$:

If $W \neq \emptyset$:
  Parse $W = \{i^*, \tau_{\mathrm{p}}, w, w'\}$
  If $(i' = i^*) \wedge (\mathsf{P}(\tau_{\mathrm{p}}, \tau'_{\mathrm{f}}) = 1) \wedge (f'(w) \neq f'(w'))$:
    Return $\perp$
$Q := Q \cup \{(i', f', \tau'_{\mathrm{f}})\}$
Return $sk_{i',f',\tau'_{\mathrm{f}}} \leftarrow \mathsf{FKGen}(\mathsf{crs}, pk_{i'}, sk_{i'}, f', \tau'_{\mathrm{f}})$

$\underline{\mathsf{ExpIdeal}^{\mathsf{zk}}_{\mathsf{fNIZK},\mathcal{A},\mathsf{Sim},n}(\lambda)}$:

$(\mathsf{crs}, st^{\mathsf{Sim}}) \leftarrow \mathsf{Sim}_1(1^\lambda)$, $W := \emptyset$, $Q := \emptyset$
$((pk_i, sk_i) \leftarrow \mathsf{UKGen}(\mathsf{crs}))_{i\in[n]}$
$(U_{\mathrm{cor}}, st_1^{\mathcal{A}}) \leftarrow \mathcal{A}_1(\mathsf{crs}, (pk_i)_{i\in[n]})$
  s.t. $U_{\mathrm{cor}} \subset [n]$
$(i^*, \tau_{\mathrm{p}}, x, w, w', st_2^{\mathcal{A}}) \leftarrow \mathcal{A}_2^{\mathcal{O}^{\mathsf{FKGen}}(\cdot)}((sk_i)_{i\in U_{\mathrm{cor}}}, st_1^{\mathcal{A}})$
  s.t. $(i^* \notin U_{\mathrm{cor}}) \wedge ((x, w) \in \mathcal{R})$
    $\wedge(\forall (i^*, f', \tau'_{\mathrm{f}}) \in Q$ satisfying $\mathsf{P}(\tau_{\mathrm{p}}, \tau'_{\mathrm{f}}) = 1$,
     $f'(w) = f'(w'))$
$W := \{i^*, \tau_{\mathrm{p}}, w, w'\}$
$\pi \leftarrow \mathsf{Sim}_2(\mathsf{crs}, pk_{i^*}, \tau_{\mathrm{p}}, x, w', st^{\mathsf{Sim}})$
$b \leftarrow \mathcal{A}_3^{\mathcal{O}^{\mathsf{FKGen}}(\cdot)}(\pi, st_2^{\mathcal{A}})$
Return b

$\underline{\mathcal{O}^{\mathsf{FKGen}}(i', f', \tau'_{\mathrm{f}})}$:

If $W \neq \emptyset$:
  Parse $W = \{i^*, \tau_{\mathrm{p}}, w, w'\}$
  If $(i' = i^*) \wedge (\mathsf{P}(\tau_{\mathrm{p}}, \tau'_{\mathrm{f}}) = 1) \wedge (f'(w) \neq f'(w'))$:
    Return $\perp$
$Q := Q \cup \{(i', f', \tau'_{\mathrm{f}})\}$
Return $sk_{i',f',\tau'_{\mathrm{f}}} \leftarrow \mathsf{FKGen}(\mathsf{crs}, pk_{i'}, sk_{i'}, f', \tau'_{\mathrm{f}})$

Fig. 2. Games for defining zero knowledge property for fNIZK

Here, we offer some explanations and discussions regarding the above definition.

1. Completeness of fNIZK has three requirements. Firstly, any normally generated proof π (i.e., π is generated by algorithm Prove) can be verified successfully via algorithm Verify with overwhelming probability. Secondly, for normally generated secret functional key $sk_{f,\tau_{\mathrm{f}}}$ for (f, τ_{f}), the checking algorithm $\mathsf{CheckKey}(\mathsf{crs}, pk, f, \tau_{\mathrm{f}}, sk_{f,\tau_{\mathrm{f}}})$ returns 1 with overwhelming probability. Thirdly, for normally generated proof π (associated with τ_{p}) and normally generated secret functional key $sk_{f,\tau_{\mathrm{f}}}$ (for (f, τ_{f})), if $\mathsf{P}(\tau_{\mathrm{p}}, \tau_{\mathrm{f}}) = 1$, $\mathsf{Extract}$ will extract $f(w)$ with overwhelming probability.
2. The functional knowledge property requires that, in general, if the verifier accepts a proof π, then he/she can be convinced that a function of some witness can be extracted from the proof (with the help of a secret key for the function). Note that this property requires that the secret key should pass the verification of $\mathsf{CheckKey}$, and $\mathsf{P}(\tau_{\mathrm{p}}, \tau_{\mathrm{f}}) = 1$ (τ_{p} is the label associated with the proof and τ_{f} is the label associated with the secret functional key). Compared with the third requirement of completeness (which focuses on *normally generated proofs*), the functional knowledge property focuses on *maliciously generated proofs which can successfully go through the verification process of* Verify.
3. The security notion of zero knowledge for fNIZK is formalized in the multi-user setting, and requires that except for the fact $(x, w) \in \mathcal{R}$ and the functions about w (i.e., $f'(w)$ for all $(i^*, f', \tau'_{\mathrm{f}}) \in Q$ when $\mathsf{P}(\tau_{\mathrm{p}}, \tau'_{\mathrm{f}}) = 1$), the verifier

cannot obtain any other information about w from the proof π. Further explanations regarding the details are provided below. In both $\mathsf{ExpReal}^{\mathsf{zk}}_{\mathsf{fNIZK},\mathcal{A},n}(\lambda)$ and $\mathsf{ExpIdeal}^{\mathsf{zk}}_{\mathsf{fNIZK},\mathcal{A},\mathsf{Sim},n}(\lambda)$,

(a) $\mathcal{A}$ is allowed to make secret key generation queries to the oracle $\mathcal{O}^{\mathsf{FKGen}}$ adaptively. In particular, we require that for each query $(i', f', \tau_{\mathtt{f}}') \in [n] \times \mathbb{F} \times (\mathcal{T} \cup \{*\})$ raised by $\mathcal{A}_3$ (note that in this case, $W = \{i^*, \tau_{\mathtt{p}}, w, w'\} \neq \emptyset$), $\mathcal{A}_3$ will receive $sk_{i',f',\tau_{\mathtt{f}}'}$ as a response if and only if $(i' \neq i^*) \vee (\mathsf{P}(\tau_{\mathtt{p}}, \tau_{\mathtt{f}}') = 0) \vee (f'(w) = f'(w'))$. Because if it receives $sk_{i',f',\tau_{\mathtt{f}}'}$ for $(i' = i^*) \wedge (\mathsf{P}(\tau_{\mathtt{p}}, \tau_{\mathtt{f}}') = 1) \wedge (f'(w) \neq f'(w'))$, it can trivially distinguish the two games.

(b) For the challenge tuple $(i^*, \tau_{\mathtt{p}}, x, w, w')$ output by $\mathcal{A}_2$, we require that (i) $i^* \notin U_{\mathtt{cor}}$, (ii) $(x, w) \in \mathcal{R}$, and (iii) for all $(i^*, f', \tau_{\mathtt{f}}') \in Q$, it holds that if $\mathsf{P}(\tau_{\mathtt{p}}, \tau_{\mathtt{f}}') = 1$, then $f'(w) = f'(w')$, where Q denotes all the tuples that have been queried to the oracle $\mathcal{O}^{\mathsf{FKGen}}$ by $\mathcal{A}_2$. We stress that w' is *not* required to be a witness for statement x. The "witness" w', specified by $\mathcal{A}_2$, is used to provide the information (that the simulator Sim is allowed to know) about w to Sim.

We note that the zero knowledge property of fNIZK implies the traditional zero knowledge property. Actually, we have the conclusion that every fNIZK scheme trivially offers a NIZK scheme.

Specifically, for a fNIZK scheme $\mathsf{fNIZK} = (\mathsf{Setup}, \mathsf{UKGen}, \mathsf{FKGen}, \mathsf{CheckKey}, \mathsf{Prove}, \mathsf{Verify}, \mathsf{Extract})$, consider a non-interactive proof scheme $\Pi = (\Pi.\mathsf{Setup}, \Pi.\mathsf{Prove}, \Pi.\mathsf{Verify})$ as in Fig. 3.

$\Pi.\mathsf{Setup}(1^\lambda)$:	$\Pi.\mathsf{Prove}(\mathsf{crs}^{\mathsf{zk}}, x, w)$:	$\Pi.\mathsf{Verify}(\mathsf{crs}^{\mathsf{zk}}, x, \pi)$:
$\mathsf{crs} \leftarrow \mathsf{Setup}(1^\lambda)$	$\tau_{\mathtt{p}} \leftarrow \mathcal{T}$	$b \leftarrow \mathsf{Verify}(\mathsf{crs}, pk, x, \pi)$
$(pk, sk) \leftarrow \mathsf{UKGen}(\mathsf{crs})$	$\pi \leftarrow \mathsf{Prove}(\mathsf{crs}, pk, \tau_{\mathtt{p}}, x, w)$	Return b
Return $\mathsf{crs}^{\mathsf{zk}} = (\mathsf{crs}, pk)$	Return π	

Fig. 3. NIZK Π deduced by fNIZK

We have the following theorem. Due to space limitations, its proof is given in the full version of this paper.

Theorem 1. *If* fNIZK *is a fNIZK scheme for an* NP *language* $\mathcal{L}_{\mathcal{R}}$*, a function family* $\mathbb{F}$*, a label space* $\mathcal{T}$ *and a predicate function* P*, then* Π *is a NIZK scheme for* $\mathcal{L}_{\mathcal{R}}$.

Remark 1. In the definition of zero knowledge for fNIZK, we only consider the single-theorem version. It can be further strengthened to the multi-theorem version, which allows the adversary to generate multiple challenge tuples $(i^*, \tau_{\mathtt{p}}, x, w, w')$. But these tuples should also satisfy $(i^* \notin U_{\mathtt{cor}}) \wedge ((x, w) \in \mathcal{R}) \wedge (\forall (i^*, f', \tau_{\mathtt{f}}') \in Q$ satisfying $\mathsf{P}(\tau_{\mathtt{p}}, \tau_{\mathtt{f}}') = 1, f'(w) = f'(w'))$, and meanwhile any secret functional key generation query $(i', f', \tau_{\mathtt{f}}')$ raised by the adversary should satisfy

$f'(w) = f'(w')$ or $\mathsf{P}(\tau_{\mathrm{p}}, \tau'_{\mathfrak{f}}) = 0$ for all challenge tuples $(i^*, \tau_{\mathrm{p}}, x, w, w')$ (otherwise, the adversary will receive $\perp$ as a response for this query).

4 Generic Construction of fNIZK

In this section, we present a method for constructing a fNIZK proof using a functional encryption (FE) scheme and NIZK schemes. The main idea is straightforward: given a valid pair of statement and witness $(x, w) \in \mathcal{R}$, we encrypt the witness using the functional encryption scheme. Verifiers can then obtain some functions of the witness by decrypting the ciphertext with the corresponding secret keys. In addition to proving the relation about $(x, w) \in \mathcal{R}$, we also need to demonstrate that the ciphertext is well-formed.

We begin by introducing the generic construction, followed by an analysis of its security properties.

Generic Construction. Let $\mathcal{L}_{\mathcal{R}}$ be an NP language associated with an NP relation $\mathcal{R} \subset \mathcal{X} \times \mathcal{W}$. Let $\mathbb{F}$ be a function family. Let $\mathcal{T}$ be the label space, and $\mathsf{P} : \mathcal{T} \times (\mathcal{T} \cup \{*\}) \to \{0, 1\}$ be a predicate function satisfying $\mathsf{P}(\tau, *) = 1$ for all $\tau \in \mathcal{T}$.

We define a function family $\widehat{\mathbb{F}}$ as follows: a function $\widehat{f}$ (with domain $\mathcal{W} \times \mathcal{T}$) belongs to $\widehat{\mathbb{F}}$, if and only if there exists $(f, \tau_{\mathfrak{f}}) \in \mathbb{F} \times (\mathcal{T} \cup \{*\})$ satisfying

$$\widehat{f}(w, \tau_{\mathrm{p}}) = \begin{cases} f(w) & \text{if } \mathsf{P}(\tau_{\mathrm{p}}, \tau_{\mathfrak{f}}) = 1 \\ \perp & \text{if } \mathsf{P}(\tau_{\mathrm{p}}, \tau_{\mathfrak{f}}) = 0 \end{cases}$$

For simplicity, for each pair $(f, \tau_{\mathfrak{f}}) \in \mathbb{F} \times (\mathcal{T} \cup \{*\})$, we denote the corresponding function in $\widehat{\mathbb{F}}$ as $\widehat{f}_{f,\tau_{\mathfrak{f}}}$. We require that there is an efficient algorithm, which takes $(f, \tau_{\mathfrak{f}}) \in \mathbb{F} \times (\mathcal{T} \cup \{*\})$ as input and outputs the corresponding $\widehat{f}_{f,\tau_{\mathfrak{f}}}$.

Let $\mathsf{FE} = (\mathsf{FE.Setup}, \mathsf{FE.KGen}, \mathsf{FE.Enc}, \mathsf{FE.Dec})$ be a functional encryption scheme for $\widehat{\mathbb{F}}$ on message space $\mathcal{M} = \mathcal{W} \times \mathcal{T}$.

Consider the following two NP relations

$$\begin{aligned} \mathcal{R}_{\mathrm{ct}} &= \{((\tau_{\mathrm{p}}, x, mpk, c), (w, r_{\mathrm{enc}})) : (x, w) \in \mathcal{R} \wedge \mathsf{FE.Enc}(mpk, (w, \tau_{\mathrm{p}}); r_{\mathrm{enc}}) = c\}, \\ \mathcal{R}_{\mathrm{k}} &= \{((mpk, \widehat{f}_{f,\tau_{\mathfrak{f}}}, sk_{\widehat{f}_{f,\tau_{\mathfrak{f}}}}), (msk, r_{\mathrm{kg}})) : \mathsf{FE.KGen}(mpk, msk, \widehat{f}_{f,\tau_{\mathfrak{f}}}; r_{\mathrm{kg}}) = sk_{\widehat{f}_{f,\tau_{\mathfrak{f}}}}\}, \end{aligned}$$

where (x, w) is a statement-witness pair, τ_{p} (resp., $\tau_{\mathfrak{f}}$) is a label in $\mathcal{T}$ (resp., $\mathcal{T} \cup \{*\}$), mpk and msk is the master key pair of FE, c is a ciphertext, and r_{enc} and r_{kg} are the corresponding randomness. As stated in [15], we can construct NIZKs for any NP language. Therefore, we can construct two NIZK schemes, $\mathsf{NIZK}_{\mathcal{R}_{\mathrm{ct}}} = (\mathsf{NIZK}_{\mathcal{R}_{\mathrm{ct}}}.\mathsf{Setup}, \mathsf{NIZK}_{\mathcal{R}_{\mathrm{ct}}}.\mathsf{Prove}, \mathsf{NIZK}_{\mathcal{R}_{\mathrm{ct}}}.\mathsf{Verify})$ and $\mathsf{NIZK}_{\mathcal{R}_{\mathrm{k}}} = (\mathsf{NIZK}_{\mathcal{R}_{\mathrm{k}}}.\mathsf{Setup}, \mathsf{NIZK}_{\mathcal{R}_{\mathrm{k}}}.\mathsf{Prove}, \mathsf{NIZK}_{\mathcal{R}_{\mathrm{k}}}.\mathsf{Verify})$, for $\mathcal{L}_{\mathcal{R}_{\mathrm{ct}}}$ and $\mathcal{L}_{\mathcal{R}_{\mathrm{k}}}$, respectively.

We present the generic construction of fNIZK proof $\mathsf{fNIZK} = (\mathsf{Setup}, \mathsf{UKGen}, \mathsf{FKGen}, \mathsf{CheckKey}, \mathsf{Prove}, \mathsf{Verify}, \mathsf{Extract})$ for $\mathcal{L}_{\mathcal{R}}$, $\mathbb{F}$, $\mathcal{T}$ and P from FE, $\mathsf{NIZK}_{\mathcal{R}_{\mathrm{ct}}}$ and $\mathsf{NIZK}_{\mathcal{R}_{\mathrm{k}}}$, as shown in Fig. 4.

Note that for $\pi \leftarrow \mathsf{Prove}(\mathsf{crs}, pk, \tau_{\mathrm{p}}, x, w)$ in Fig. 4, τ_{p} is directly packed into π, so an efficient $\mathsf{Ext}_{\mathcal{T}}$ can be trivially constructed.

<u>$\mathsf{Setup}(1^\lambda)$:</u>
$\mathsf{crs}_{\mathcal{R}_{ct}} \leftarrow \mathsf{NIZK}_{\mathcal{R}_{ct}}.\mathsf{Setup}(1^\lambda)$
$\mathsf{crs}_{\mathcal{R}_{k}} \leftarrow \mathsf{NIZK}_{\mathcal{R}_{k}}.\mathsf{Setup}(1^\lambda)$
Return $\mathsf{crs} := (\mathsf{crs}_{\mathcal{R}_{ct}}, \mathsf{crs}_{\mathcal{R}_{k}})$

<u>$\mathsf{Prove}(\mathsf{crs}, pk, \tau_p, x, w)$:</u>
$r_{enc} \leftarrow \mathcal{RS}_{\mathsf{FE.Enc}}$, $c \leftarrow \mathsf{FE.Enc}(pk, (w, \tau_p); r_{enc})$
$\Pi_{\mathcal{R}_{ct}} \leftarrow \mathsf{NIZK}_{\mathcal{R}_{ct}}.\mathsf{Prove}(\mathsf{crs}_{\mathcal{R}_{ct}}, (\tau_p, x, pk, c), (w, r_{enc}))$
Return $\pi := (\tau_p, \Pi_{\mathcal{R}_{ct}}, c)$

<u>$\mathsf{Verify}(\mathsf{crs}, pk, x, \pi)$:</u>
Parse $\pi = (\tau_p, \Pi_{\mathcal{R}_{ct}}, c)$
Return $b \leftarrow \mathsf{NIZK}_{\mathcal{R}_{ct}}.\mathsf{Verify}(\mathsf{crs}_{\mathcal{R}_{ct}}, (\tau_p, x, pk, c), \Pi_{\mathcal{R}_{ct}})$

<u>$\mathsf{Extract}(\mathsf{crs}, x, \pi, sk_{f,\tau_f})$:</u>
Parse $\pi = (\tau_p, \Pi_{\mathcal{R}_{ct}}, c)$, $sk_{f,\tau_f} = (sk_{\widehat{f}_{f,\tau_f}}, \Pi_{\mathcal{R}_k})$
Return $y \leftarrow \mathsf{FE.Dec}(c, sk_{\widehat{f}_{f,\tau_f}})$

<u>$\mathsf{UKGen}(\mathsf{crs})$:</u>
$(mpk, msk) \leftarrow \mathsf{FE.Setup}(1^\lambda)$
Return $(pk = mpk, sk = msk)$

<u>$\mathsf{FKGen}(\mathsf{crs}, pk, sk, f, \tau_f)$:</u>
$r_{kg} \leftarrow \mathcal{RS}_{\mathsf{FE.KGen}}$, $sk_{\widehat{f}_{f,\tau_f}} \leftarrow \mathsf{FE.KGen}(pk, sk, \widehat{f}_{f,\tau_f}; r_{kg})$
$\Pi_{\mathcal{R}_k} \leftarrow \mathsf{NIZK}_{\mathcal{R}_k}.\mathsf{Prove}(\mathsf{crs}_{\mathcal{R}_k}, (pk, \widehat{f}_{f,\tau_f}, sk_{\widehat{f}_{f,\tau_f}}), (sk, r_{kg}))$
Return $sk_{f,\tau_f} := (sk_{\widehat{f}_{f,\tau_f}}, \Pi_{\mathcal{R}_k})$

<u>$\mathsf{CheckKey}(\mathsf{crs}, pk, f, \tau_f, sk_{f,\tau_f})$:</u>
Parse $sk_{f,\tau_f} = (sk_{\widehat{f}_{f,\tau_f}}, \Pi_{\mathcal{R}_k})$
Return $b \leftarrow \mathsf{NIZK}_{\mathcal{R}_k}.\mathsf{Verify}(\mathsf{crs}_{\mathcal{R}_k}, (pk, \widehat{f}_{f,\tau_f}, sk_{\widehat{f}_{f,\tau_f}}), \Pi_{\mathcal{R}_k})$

Fig. 4. Construction of fNIZK from FE, $\mathsf{NIZK}_{\mathcal{R}_{ct}}$ and $\mathsf{NIZK}_{\mathcal{R}_k}$

Remark 2. We stress that the above generic scheme fNIZK is built for *any* NP language $\mathcal{L}_\mathcal{R}$, *any* function family $\mathbb{F}$ (as long as there is FE for $\widehat{\mathbb{F}}$), and any predicate function $\mathsf{P} : \mathcal{T} \times (\mathcal{T} \cup \{*\}) \rightarrow \{0, 1\}$ satisfying $\mathsf{P}(\tau, *) = 1$ for all $\tau \in \mathcal{T}$.

Security Analysis. Now, we show that the above fNIZK satisfies completeness, functional knowledge property, adaptive soundness, and zero knowledge.

Completeness. Completeness of fNIZK is trivially guaranteed by correctness of the underlying FE and completeness of the underlying $\mathsf{NIZK}_{\mathcal{R}_{ct}}$ and $\mathsf{NIZK}_{\mathcal{R}_k}$.

Functional Knowledge. For any PPT adversary $\mathcal{A}$, for $\mathsf{crs} \leftarrow \mathsf{Setup}(1^\lambda)$, $(pk, sk) \leftarrow \mathsf{UKGen}(\mathsf{crs})$, $(\pi, x, f, \tau_f, sk_{f,\tau_f}) \leftarrow \mathcal{A}(\mathsf{crs}, pk, sk)$ satisfying $(x \in \mathcal{L}_\mathcal{R}) \wedge (f \in \mathbb{F}) \wedge (\tau_f \in \mathcal{T} \cup \{*\}) \wedge (\mathsf{Verify}(\mathsf{crs}, pk, x, \pi) = 1) \wedge (\mathsf{CheckKey}(\mathsf{crs}, pk, f, \tau_f, sk_{f,\tau_f}) = 1) \wedge (\mathsf{P}(\mathsf{Ext}_\mathcal{T}(\pi), \tau_f) = 1)$, and for $y \leftarrow \mathsf{Extract}(\mathsf{crs}, x, \pi, sk_{f,\tau_f})$, we analyze the probability that there is w satisfying $((x, w) \in \mathcal{R}) \wedge (y = f(w))$.

First of all, note that $\mathsf{Verify}(\mathsf{crs}, pk, x, \pi) = 1$ implies that $\mathsf{NIZK}_{\mathcal{R}_{ct}}.\mathsf{Verify}(\mathsf{crs}, (\tau_p, x, pk, c), \Pi_{\mathcal{R}_{ct}}) = 1$. By the adaptive soundness of $\mathsf{NIZK}_{\mathcal{R}_{ct}}$, with overwhelming probability, there are $w \in \mathcal{W}$ and $r_{enc} \in \mathcal{RS}_{\mathsf{FE.Enc}}$ such that $(x, w) \in \mathcal{R}$ and $c = \mathsf{FE.Enc}(mpk, (w, \tau_p); r_{enc})$, where $\tau_p = \mathsf{Ext}_\mathcal{T}(\pi)$.

Parse $sk_{f,\tau_f} = (sk_{\widehat{f}_{f,\tau_f}}, \Pi_{\mathcal{R}_k})$. Note that $\mathsf{CheckKey}(\mathsf{crs}, pk, f, \tau_f, sk_{f,\tau_f}) = 1$ implies that $\mathsf{NIZK}_{\mathcal{R}_k}.\mathsf{Verify}(\mathsf{crs}_{\mathcal{R}_k}, (pk, \widehat{f}_{f,\tau_f}, sk_{\widehat{f}_{f,\tau_f}}), \Pi_{\mathcal{R}_k}) = 1$. By the adaptive soundness of $\mathsf{NIZK}_{\mathcal{R}_k}$, with overwhelming probability, $sk_{\widehat{f}_{f,\tau_f}}$ can be explained as generated for $\widehat{f}_{f,\tau_f}$ with FE.KGen. Since $\mathsf{P}(\tau_p = \mathsf{Ext}_\mathcal{T}(\pi), \tau_f) = 1$, we have $\widehat{f}_{f,\tau_f}(w, \tau_p) = f(w)$. Recall that the algorithm Extract returns $y \leftarrow \mathsf{FE.Dec}(c, sk_{\widehat{f}_{f,\tau_f}})$, so $y = \widehat{f}_{f,\tau_f}(w, \tau_p) = f(w)$.

Hence, the above fNIZK satisfies the functional knowledge property.

Adaptive Soundness. For any computationally unbounded adversary $\mathcal{A}$, let $\mu(\lambda)$ denote the probability that $\mathcal{A}$ outputs pk, $x \notin \mathcal{L}_\mathcal{R}$ and $\pi^* = (\tau_p, \Pi^*_{\mathcal{R}_{ct}}, c)$ such that π^* is an accepting proof, i.e.,

$$\mu(\lambda) = \Pr\left[\begin{array}{l}\mathsf{crs} \leftarrow \mathsf{Setup}(1^\lambda)\\ (pk, x, \pi^*) \leftarrow \mathcal{A}(\mathsf{crs})\\ \quad \text{where } \pi^* = (\tau_\mathrm{p}, \Pi^*_{\mathcal{R}_\mathrm{ct}}, c)\end{array} : \begin{array}{c} x \notin \mathcal{L}_\mathcal{R}\\ \wedge\ \mathsf{Verify}(\mathsf{crs}, pk, x, \pi^*) = 1\end{array}\right].$$

Now, we construct an adversary $\mathcal{A}'$, attacking the adaptive soundness of the underlying NIZK $\mathsf{NIZK}_{\mathcal{R}_\mathrm{ct}}$, from $\mathcal{A}$ as follows.

Upon receiving the common reference string $\mathsf{crs}_{\mathcal{R}_\mathrm{ct}}$, $\mathcal{A}'$ firstly generates $\mathsf{crs}_{\mathcal{R}_\mathrm{k}} \leftarrow \mathsf{NIZK}_{\mathcal{R}_\mathrm{k}}.\mathsf{Setup}(1^\lambda)$, and then sends $\mathsf{crs} = (\mathsf{crs}_{\mathcal{R}_\mathrm{ct}}, \mathsf{crs}_{\mathcal{R}_\mathrm{k}})$ to $\mathcal{A}$.

Receiving $(pk, x, \pi^* = (\tau_\mathrm{p}, \Pi^*_{\mathcal{R}_\mathrm{ct}}, c))$ from $\mathcal{A}$, $\mathcal{A}'$ returns a pair $((\tau_\mathrm{p}, x, pk, c), \Pi^*_{\mathcal{R}_\mathrm{ct}})$ as its final output.

That is the construction of $\mathcal{A}'$. Next, we analyze its success probability. We have the following equations.

$$\begin{aligned}
&\Pr\left[\begin{array}{l}\mathsf{crs}_{\mathcal{R}_\mathrm{ct}} \leftarrow \mathsf{NIZK}_{\mathcal{R}_\mathrm{ct}}.\mathsf{Setup}(1^\lambda)\\ (x^*, \Pi^*_{\mathcal{R}_\mathrm{ct}}) \leftarrow \mathcal{A}'(\mathsf{crs}_{\mathcal{R}_\mathrm{ct}})\\ \quad \text{where } x^* = (\tau_\mathrm{p}, x, pk, c)\end{array} : \begin{array}{c} x^* \notin \mathcal{L}_{\mathcal{R}_\mathrm{ct}}\\ \wedge\ \mathsf{NIZK}_{\mathcal{R}_\mathrm{ct}}.\mathsf{Verify}(\mathsf{crs}_{\mathcal{R}_\mathrm{ct}}, x^*, \Pi^*_{\mathcal{R}_\mathrm{ct}}) = 1\end{array}\right]\\
=\ &\Pr\left[\begin{array}{l}\mathsf{crs}_{\mathcal{R}_\mathrm{ct}} \leftarrow \mathsf{NIZK}_{\mathcal{R}_\mathrm{ct}}.\mathsf{Setup}(1^\lambda)\\ (pk, x, \pi^*) \leftarrow \mathcal{A}'(\mathsf{crs}_{\mathcal{R}_\mathrm{ct}})\\ \quad \text{where } \pi^* = (\tau_\mathrm{p}, \Pi^*_{\mathcal{R}_\mathrm{ct}}, c)\end{array} : \begin{array}{c} (\tau_\mathrm{p}, x, pk, c) \notin \mathcal{L}_{\mathcal{R}_\mathrm{ct}}\\ \wedge\ \mathsf{NIZK}_{\mathcal{R}_\mathrm{ct}}.\mathsf{Verify}(\mathsf{crs}_{\mathcal{R}_\mathrm{ct}}, (\tau_\mathrm{p}, x, pk, c), \Pi^*_{\mathcal{R}_\mathrm{ct}}) = 1\end{array}\right]\\
\geq\ &\Pr\left[\begin{array}{l}\mathsf{crs}_{\mathcal{R}_\mathrm{ct}} \leftarrow \mathsf{NIZK}_{\mathcal{R}_\mathrm{ct}}.\mathsf{Setup}(1^\lambda)\\ (pk, x, \pi^*) \leftarrow \mathcal{A}'(\mathsf{crs}_{\mathcal{R}_\mathrm{ct}})\\ \quad \text{where } \pi^* = (\tau_\mathrm{p}, \Pi^*_{\mathcal{R}_\mathrm{ct}}, c)\end{array} : \begin{array}{c} x \notin \mathcal{L}_{\mathcal{R}}\\ \wedge\ \mathsf{NIZK}_{\mathcal{R}_\mathrm{ct}}.\mathsf{Verify}(\mathsf{crs}_{\mathcal{R}_\mathrm{ct}}, (\tau_\mathrm{p}, x, pk, c), \Pi^*_{\mathcal{R}_\mathrm{ct}}) = 1\end{array}\right]\\
=\ &\Pr\left[\begin{array}{l}\mathsf{crs}_{\mathcal{R}_\mathrm{ct}} \leftarrow \mathsf{NIZK}_{\mathcal{R}_\mathrm{ct}}.\mathsf{Setup}(1^\lambda)\\ \mathsf{crs}_{\mathcal{R}_\mathrm{k}} \leftarrow \mathsf{NIZK}_{\mathcal{R}_\mathrm{k}}.\mathsf{Setup}(1^\lambda)\\ (pk, x, \pi^*) \leftarrow \mathcal{A}(\mathsf{crs}_{\mathcal{R}_\mathrm{ct}}, \mathsf{crs}_{\mathcal{R}_\mathrm{k}})\\ \quad \text{where } \pi^* = (\tau_\mathrm{p}, \Pi^*_{\mathcal{R}_\mathrm{ct}}, c)\end{array} : \begin{array}{c} x \notin \mathcal{L}_{\mathcal{R}}\\ \wedge\ \mathsf{NIZK}_{\mathcal{R}_\mathrm{ct}}.\mathsf{Verify}(\mathsf{crs}_{\mathcal{R}_\mathrm{ct}}, (\tau_\mathrm{p}, x, pk, c), \Pi^*_{\mathcal{R}_\mathrm{ct}}) = 1\end{array}\right]\\
=\ &\Pr\left[\begin{array}{l}\mathsf{crs} \leftarrow \mathsf{Setup}(1^\lambda)\\ (pk, x, \pi^*) \leftarrow \mathcal{A}(\mathsf{crs})\\ \quad \text{where } \pi^* = (\tau_\mathrm{p}, \Pi^*_{\mathcal{R}_\mathrm{ct}}, c)\end{array} : \begin{array}{c} x \notin \mathcal{L}_{\mathcal{R}}\\ \wedge\ \mathsf{Verify}(\mathsf{crs}, pk, x, \pi^*) = 1\end{array}\right]\\
=\ &\mu(\lambda).
\end{aligned}$$

The adaptive soundness of $\mathsf{NIZK}_{\mathcal{R}_\mathrm{ct}}$ guarantees that $\mathcal{A}'$'s success probability is negligible, so we derive that $\mu(\lambda) \leq \mathsf{negl}(\lambda)$, concluding the proof of adaptive soundness.

Remark 3. In fact, for any NP language, we can always construct a NIZK in the hidden-bits model [15], which also satisfies adaptive soundness. Therefore, we can always construct $\mathsf{NIZK}_{\mathcal{R}_\mathrm{ct}}$ satisfying adaptive soundness.

Zero Knowledge. For zero knowledge of fNIZK, we have the following theorem. Due to space limitations, the proof of this theorem is given in the full version of this paper.

Theorem 2. *If* FE *is IND secure,* $\mathsf{NIZK}_{\mathcal{R}_\mathrm{ct}}$ *is single-theorem zero knowledge, and* $\mathsf{NIZK}_{\mathcal{R}_\mathrm{k}}$ *is multi-theorem zero knowledge, then* fNIZK *is zero knowledge.*

5 Set Membership Functional Proof

Set membership proofs (SMPs) [5] are widely utilized as building blocks in various cryptographic schemes such as anonymous credentials [7,30], Zcash [28], and e-cash [6]. Following the definition of [5], the relation about set membership is

$$\mathcal{R}_{\text{sm}} = \{((\mathsf{com}, \varPhi), (w, r_{\text{com}})) : \mathsf{com} = \mathsf{Com}(pp, w; r_{\text{com}}) \wedge w \in \varPhi\},$$

where pp is the public parameter of the commitment scheme in the relation, com is the commitment to the message w, r_{com} denotes the internal randomness, and $\varPhi$ represents a set. Essentially, given a commitment com, the prover must demonstrate knowledge of the message w corresponding to that commitment, as well as prove that w is an element of the set $\varPhi$.

Due to the extensive application value of SMPs, in this section, we provide a concrete and efficient fNIZK for relation about set membership proof. We consider a specific function family as follows: given a public set $\varPhi$, each function f within this family corresponds to a subset $\varPhi_{S_f}$ of $\varPhi$, and $f(w)$ indicates whether w belongs to $\varPhi_{S_f}$ or not. We call fNIZK for $\mathcal{R}_{\text{sm}}$ and the above function family, *set membership functional proof (fSMP)*.

In fSMP, Prove outputs a proof associated with label τ_{p} to demonstrate that the committed value $w \in \varPhi$, and a verifier with a secret functional key for $(\varPhi_{S_f}, \tau_{\text{f}})$ can additionally check whether $w \in \varPhi_{S_f}$ or not from the proof, when $\mathsf{P}(\tau_{\text{p}}, \tau_{\text{f}}) = 1$.

To construct a fSMP, we introduce a new primitive, called *set membership encryption (SME)*, and show a generic framework of constructing fSMP from a SME and a commitment scheme that both support Sigma protocols in Sect. 5.1. Subsequently, we propose another primitive called *dual inner-produce encryption (dual IPE)* and illustrate the construction of SME from dual IPE in Sect. 5.2. In Sect. 5.3, we provide an efficient instantiation of dual IPE, utilizing the techniques in IPE [10,12,31], based on the k-LIN assumption. We plug the dual IPE instantiation ($k = 1$) into the generic construction of SME from dual IPE, obtaining a concrete and efficient SME supporting Sigma protocols, in Sect. 5.4. Lastly, we improve the efficiency of fSMP obtained from the concrete SME and Pedersen commitment [26], by utilizing the self-stacking technique [17], in Sect. 5.5.

5.1 fSMP from SME

Here, we firstly introduce set membership encryption (SME) and its security notion, and then show a generic construction of set membership functional proof (fSMP) from SME.

Set Membership Encryption. Let $\mathcal{W}$ be the message space. We use $\mathcal{S}_{\mathcal{W},l}$ to denote the set of all the sets of size $l = \mathsf{poly}(\lambda)$ in $\mathcal{W}$, i.e., $\mathcal{S}_{\mathcal{W},l} := \{\varPhi \subset \mathcal{W} \mid |\varPhi| = l\}$. For a set $\varPhi \in \mathcal{S}_{\mathcal{W},l}$, without loss of generality, we write that $\varPhi = \{w_1, \cdots, w_l\}$. For a set $S \subset [l]$, let $\varPhi_S := \{w_j \mid j \in S\}$.

For each set $S \subset [l]$, we define a set membership function $\mathsf{func}_{\varPhi_S} : \varPhi_S \to \{0, 1\}$ as follows: $\mathsf{func}_{\varPhi_S}(w) = 1$ if and only if $w \in \varPhi_S$.

Definition 4. (Set membership encryption). *Let* $\mathcal{T}$ *be a label space. Let* $\mathsf{P} : \mathcal{T} \times (\mathcal{T} \cup \{*\}) \to \{0,1\}$ *be a predicate function satisfying* $\mathsf{P}(\tau, *) = 1$ *for all* $\tau \in \mathcal{T}$. *A* set membership encryption (SME) *scheme* SME *(with set of size* $l = \mathsf{poly}(\lambda)$*) for message set* $\mathcal{W}$*, label space* $\mathcal{T}$ *and predicate* P *contains five algorithms* SME = (Setup, KGen, CheckKey, Enc, Query).

- $\mathsf{Setup}(1^\lambda) \to (pk, sk)$*: On input the security parameter* 1^λ*, the setup algorithm outputs a public key* pk *and a secret key* sk.
- $\mathsf{KGen}(pk, sk, S, \tau_{\mathfrak{f}}) \to sk_{S,\tau_{\mathfrak{f}}}$*: On input a key pair* (pk, sk)*, a set* $S \subset [l]$ *and a label* $\tau_{\mathfrak{f}} \in \mathcal{T} \cup \{*\}$*, the key generation algorithm outputs a key* $sk_{S,\tau_{\mathfrak{f}}}$.
- $\mathsf{CheckKey}(pk, S, \tau_{\mathfrak{f}}, sk_{S,\tau_{\mathfrak{f}}}) \to b$*: On input a public key* pk*, a set* $S \subset [l]$ *and a label* $\tau_{\mathfrak{f}} \in \mathcal{T} \cup \{*\}$ *and a secret key* $sk_{S,\tau_{\mathfrak{f}}}$*, the checking algorithm outputs a bit* $b \in \{0,1\}$.
- $\mathsf{Enc}(pk, \Phi, \tau_{\mathrm{p}}, w) \to c$*: On input a public key* pk*, a set* $\Phi \subset \mathcal{W}$ *satisfying* $|\Phi| = l$*, a label* $\tau_{\mathrm{p}} \in \mathcal{T}$*, and a message* $w \in \Phi$*, the encryption algorithm outputs a ciphertext* c*. We assume that there exists an efficient algorithm* $\mathsf{Ext}_{\mathcal{T}}$ *such that* $\tau_{\mathrm{p}} \leftarrow \mathsf{Ext}_{\mathcal{T}}(c)$.
- $\mathsf{Query}(c, sk_{S,\tau_{\mathfrak{f}}}) \to y$*: On input a ciphertext* c *and a secret key* $sk_{S,\tau_{\mathfrak{f}}}$*, the query algorithm outputs a bit* $y \in \{0,1\}$.

Correctness requires that for any $\Phi \subset \mathcal{W}$ *satisfying* $|\Phi| = l$*, any* $w \in \Phi$*, any* $S \subset [l]$*, any* $\tau_{\mathrm{p}} \in \mathcal{T}$ *and any* $\tau_{\mathfrak{f}} \in \mathcal{T} \cup \{*\}$ *satisfying* $\mathsf{P}(\tau_{\mathrm{p}}, \tau_{\mathfrak{f}}) = 1$,

$$\Pr\left[\begin{array}{l}(pk, msk) \leftarrow \mathsf{Setup}(1^\lambda) \\ sk_{S,\tau_{\mathfrak{f}}} \leftarrow \mathsf{KGen}(pk, sk, S, \tau_{\mathfrak{f}}) \\ c \leftarrow \mathsf{Enc}(pk, \Phi, \tau_{\mathrm{p}}, w), y \leftarrow \mathsf{Query}(c, sk_{S,\tau_{\mathfrak{f}}})\end{array} : y = 1\right] = \begin{cases} 1 & \text{if } w \in \Phi_S \\ \mathsf{negl}(\lambda) & \text{otherwise}\end{cases}$$

$$\Pr\left[\begin{array}{l}(pk, sk) \leftarrow \mathsf{Setup}(1^\lambda) \\ sk_{S,\tau_{\mathfrak{f}}} \leftarrow \mathsf{KGen}(pk, sk, S, \tau_{\mathfrak{f}})\end{array} : \mathsf{CheckKey}(pk, S, \tau_{\mathfrak{f}}, sk_{S,\tau_{\mathfrak{f}}}) = 1\right] \geq 1 - \mathsf{negl}(\lambda).$$

We say that a SME scheme SME *supports Sigma protocols*, if there exists an efficient Sigma protocol for the following relation:

$$\mathcal{R}_{\mathrm{c}} = \{((\tau_{\mathrm{p}}, c, pk, \Phi), (w, r_{\mathrm{enc}})) : c = \mathsf{Enc}(pk, \Phi, \tau_{\mathrm{p}}, w; r_{\mathrm{enc}})\}.$$

We now define *IND security* for SME.

Definition 5. (IND security for SME). *A SME scheme* SME = (Setup, KGen, CheckKey, Enc, Query) *(of size* $l = \mathsf{poly}(\lambda)$*) for message set* $\mathcal{W}$*, label space* $\mathcal{T}$ *and predicate* P *is* IND secure, *if for any PPT adversary* $\mathcal{A}$*, the advantage* $\mathbf{Adv}^{\mathrm{ind}}_{\mathsf{SME},\mathcal{A}}(\lambda) := |\Pr[\mathsf{Exp}^{\mathrm{ind}}_{\mathsf{SME},\mathcal{A}}(\lambda) = 1] - \frac{1}{2}|$ *is negligible, where* $\mathsf{Exp}^{\mathrm{ind}}_{\mathsf{SME},\mathcal{A}}(\lambda)$ *is defined in Fig. 5.*

fSMP from SME. Now, we construct a fSMP scheme for the following relation:

$$\mathcal{R}_{\mathrm{sm}} := \{((\mathsf{com}, \Phi), (w, r_{\mathrm{com}})) : \mathsf{com} = \mathsf{Com}(pp, w; r_{\mathrm{com}}) \wedge w \in \Phi\}. \quad (1)$$

$\underline{\mathsf{Exp}^{\mathsf{ind}}_{\mathsf{SME},\mathcal{A}}(\lambda)}$:
$(pk, sk) \leftarrow \mathsf{Setup}(1^\lambda)$, $b \leftarrow \{0,1\}$
$W := \emptyset$, $Q := \emptyset$
$(\Phi, \tau_\mathrm{p}, w_0, w_1, st) \leftarrow \mathcal{A}_1^{\mathcal{O}^{\mathsf{KGen}}(\cdot)}(pk)$
  s.t. $(w_0 \in \Phi) \wedge (w_1 \in \Phi)$
    $\wedge(\forall (S', \tau'_\mathrm{f}) \in Q$ s.t. $\mathsf{P}(\tau_\mathrm{p}, \tau'_\mathrm{f}) = 1$,
      $\mathsf{func}_{\Phi_{S'}}(w_0) = \mathsf{func}_{\Phi_{S'}}(w_1))$
$W := \{\tau_\mathrm{p}, w_0, w_1\}$, $c \leftarrow \mathsf{Enc}(pk, \Phi, \tau_\mathrm{p}, w_b)$
$b' \leftarrow \mathcal{A}_2^{\mathcal{O}^{\mathsf{KGen}}(\cdot)}(c, st)$
Return $(b = b')$

$\underline{\mathcal{O}^{\mathsf{KGen}}(S', \tau'_\mathrm{f})}$:
If $W \neq \emptyset$:
  Parse $W = \{\tau_\mathrm{p}, w_0, w_1\}$
  If $(\mathsf{P}(\tau_\mathrm{p}, \tau'_\mathrm{f}) = 1) \wedge (\mathsf{func}_{\Phi_{S'}}(w_0) \neq \mathsf{func}_{\Phi_{S'}}(w_1))$:
    Return $\perp$
$Q := Q \cup \{(S', \tau'_\mathrm{f})\}$
Return $sk_{S',\tau'_\mathrm{f}} \leftarrow \mathsf{KGen}(pk, sk, S', \tau'_\mathrm{f})$

Fig. 5. Game for defining IND security for SME

We require that the commitment scheme in Eq. (1) also supports Sigma protocols. In other words, there exists an efficient Sigma protocol to prove $\mathsf{com} = \mathsf{Com}(pp, w; r_\mathrm{com})$ with statement com and witness (w, r_com). One example that satisfies our requirements is Pedersen commitment [26], which we can prove by Okamoto's Sigma protocol [22].

Let $\mathcal{T}$ be the label space. Let $\mathsf{P} : \mathcal{T} \times (\mathcal{T} \cup \{*\}) \rightarrow \{0,1\}$ be a predicate function satisfying $\mathsf{P}(\tau, *) = 1$ for all $\tau \in \mathcal{T}$. Let $\mathsf{SME} = (\mathsf{SME.Setup}, \mathsf{SME.KGen}, \mathsf{SME.CheckKey}, \mathsf{SME.Enc}, \mathsf{SME.Query})$ be a SME scheme (with set of size l) for message set $\mathcal{W}$, label space $\mathcal{T}$ and predicate P supporting Sigma protocols. Let $\mathsf{Commit} = (\mathsf{Commit.Setup}, \mathsf{Commit.Com}, \mathsf{Commit.Dec})$ be a commitment scheme supporting Sigma protocols.

Since both SME and Commit support Sigma protocols, a Sigma protocol for relation

$$\widetilde{\mathcal{R}_\mathrm{sm}} = \{((\tau_\mathrm{p}, \mathsf{com}, c, pk, \Phi), (w, r_\mathrm{com}, r_\mathrm{enc})) : \mathsf{com} = \mathsf{Commit.Com}(pp, w; r_\mathrm{com}) \wedge c = \mathsf{SME.Enc}(pk, \Phi, \tau_\mathrm{p}, w; r_\mathrm{enc})\}$$

can be constructed by the composition of Sigma protocols [3]. So a NIZK scheme $\mathsf{NIZK} = (\mathsf{NIZK.Setup}, \mathsf{NIZK.Prove}, \mathsf{NIZK.Verify})$ (with adaptive soundness) can be obtained by applying the Fiat-Shamir transform [16] to the composite Sigma protocol.

We define the function family $\mathbb{F}$ as follows[3]. Each function $f \in \mathbb{F}$ indicates a set $S_f \subset [l]$, such that for any $x = (\mathsf{com}, \Phi = \{w_1, \cdots, w_l\})$ and any $w_x = (w, r_\mathrm{com})$,

$$f(w) = \begin{cases} 1 & \text{if } w \in \Phi_{S_f} \\ 0 & \text{if } w \in \Phi \setminus \Phi_{S_f} \\ \perp & \text{otherwise} \end{cases}$$

We require that there is an efficient algorithm, which takes a $f \in \mathbb{F}$ as input and outputs the corresponding $S_f \subset [l]$. Note that for all $(x, w_x = (w, r_\mathrm{com})) \in \mathcal{R}_\mathrm{sm}$, we have $f(w) = \mathsf{func}_{\Phi_{S_f}}(w) \in \{0,1\}$.

[3] For each $x \in \mathcal{L}_{\mathcal{R}_\mathrm{sm}}$, its witness is in the form of (w, r_com). In fSMP, we are only interested in functions of w (rather than r_com). So we define $\mathbb{F}$ as family of functions whose domain is $\mathcal{W}$ (rather than $\mathcal{W} \times \mathcal{RS}_{\mathsf{Commit.Com}}$).

We present a fSMP scheme $\mathsf{fSMP} = (\mathsf{Setup}, \mathsf{UKGen}, \mathsf{FKGen}, \mathsf{CheckKey}, \mathsf{Prove}, \mathsf{Verify}, \mathsf{Extract})$ for $\mathcal{L}_{\mathcal{R}_{\rm sm}}$, $\mathbb{F}$, $\mathcal{T}$ and P as shown in Fig. 6.

Note that for $\pi \leftarrow \mathsf{Prove}(\mathsf{crs}, pk, \tau_{\rm p}, x, w)$ in Fig. 6, $\tau_{\rm p}$ is directly packed into π, so an efficient Ext_τ can be trivially constructed.

$\underline{\mathsf{Setup}(1^\lambda)}$:
$\mathsf{crs}_{\rm nizk} \leftarrow \mathsf{NIZK.Setup}(1^\lambda)$
$pp \leftarrow \mathsf{Commit.Setup}(1^\lambda)$
Return $\mathsf{crs} := (\mathsf{crs}_{\rm nizk}, pp)$

$\underline{\mathsf{UKGen}(\mathsf{crs})}$:
$(pk, sk) \leftarrow \mathsf{SME.Setup}(1^\lambda)$
Return (pk, sk)

$\underline{\mathsf{FKGen}(\mathsf{crs}, pk, sk, f, \tau_{\rm f})}$:
$sk_{S_f,\tau_{\rm f}} \leftarrow \mathsf{SME.KGen}(pk, sk, S_f, \tau_{\rm f})$ $/\!/ S_f \subset [l]$
Return $sk_{f,\tau_{\rm f}} := sk_{S_f,\tau_{\rm f}}$

$\underline{\mathsf{CheckKey}(\mathsf{crs}, pk, f, \tau_{\rm f}, sk_{f,\tau_{\rm f}})}$:
$b \leftarrow \mathsf{SME.CheckKey}(pk, S_f, \tau_{\rm f}, sk_{f,\tau_{\rm f}})$
Return b

$\underline{\mathsf{Prove}(\mathsf{crs}, pk, \tau_{\rm p}, x, w_x)}$:
Parse $x = (\mathsf{com}, \Phi)$, $w_x = (w, r_{\rm com})$ $/\!/ |\Phi| = l$
$r_{\rm enc} \leftarrow \mathcal{RS}_{\mathsf{SME.Enc}}$
$c \leftarrow \mathsf{SME.Enc}(pk, \Phi, \tau_{\rm p}, w; r_{\rm enc})$
$\pi_{\widetilde{\mathcal{R}_{\rm sm}}} \leftarrow \mathsf{NIZK.Prove}(\mathsf{crs}_{\rm nizk}, (\tau_{\rm p}, \mathsf{com}, c, pk, \Phi), (w, r_{\rm com}, r_{\rm enc}))$
Return $\pi := (\tau_{\rm p}, \pi_{\widetilde{\mathcal{R}_{\rm sm}}}, c)$

$\underline{\mathsf{Verify}(\mathsf{crs}, pk, x, \pi)}$:
Parse $x = (\mathsf{com}, \Phi)$, $\pi = (\tau_{\rm p}, \pi_{\widetilde{\mathcal{R}_{\rm sm}}}, c)$
$b \leftarrow \mathsf{NIZK.Verify}(\mathsf{crs}_{\rm nizk}, (\tau_{\rm p}, \mathsf{com}, c, pk, \Phi), \pi_{\widetilde{\mathcal{R}_{\rm sm}}})$
Return b

$\underline{\mathsf{Extract}(\mathsf{crs}, x, \pi, sk_{f,\tau_{\rm f}})}$:
Parse $x = (\mathsf{com}, \Phi)$, $\pi = (\tau_{\rm p}, \pi_{\widetilde{\mathcal{R}_{\rm sm}}}, c)$
Return $y \leftarrow \mathsf{SME.Query}(c, sk_{f,\tau_{\rm f}})$

Fig. 6. Construction of fSMP from SME

Security Analysis. Now, we show that the fSMP satisfies completeness, functional knowledge property, adaptive soundness, and zero knowledge.

Completeness. The completeness of fSMP is trivially guaranteed by the completeness of the underlying NIZK and the correctness of the underlying SME.

Functional knowledge. For any $x \in \mathcal{L}_{\mathcal{R}_{\rm sm}}$ and any $f \in \mathbb{F}$, let $\mathcal{W}_x := \{w \mid \exists\, r_{\rm com} \text{ s.t. } (x, (w, r_{\rm com})) \in \mathcal{R}_{\rm sm}\}$ and $\mathsf{Rge}_{f(\mathcal{W}_x)} := \{f(w) \mid w \in \mathcal{W}_x\}$.

For any PPT adversary $\mathcal{A}$, for $\mathsf{crs} \leftarrow \mathsf{Setup}(1^\lambda)$, $(pk, sk) \leftarrow \mathsf{UKGen}(\mathsf{crs})$, and $(\pi, x, f, \tau_{\rm f}, sk_{f,\tau_{\rm f}}) \leftarrow \mathcal{A}(\mathsf{crs}, pk, sk)$ satisfying $(x \in \mathcal{L}_{\mathcal{R}_{\rm sm}}) \wedge (f \in \mathbb{F}) \wedge (\tau_{\rm f} \in \mathcal{T} \cup \{*\}) \wedge (\mathsf{Verify}(\mathsf{crs}, pk, x, \pi) = 1) \wedge (\mathsf{CheckKey}(\mathsf{crs}, pk, f, \tau_{\rm f}, sk_{f,\tau_{\rm f}}) = 1) \wedge (\mathsf{P}(\tau_{\rm p}, \tau_{\rm f}) = 1)$ where $\tau_{\rm p} \leftarrow \mathsf{Ext}_\tau(\pi)$, we analyze the probability $\Pr[\mathsf{Extract}(\mathsf{crs}, x, \pi, sk_{f,\tau_{\rm f}}) \notin \mathsf{Rge}_{f(\mathcal{W}_x)}]$ as follows.

First of all, the fact $x \in \mathcal{L}_{\mathcal{R}_{\rm sm}}$ implies that parsing $x = (\mathsf{com}, \Phi)$, there must be some $w_x = (w, r_{\rm com})$ satisfying $\mathsf{com} = \mathsf{Commit.Com}(pp, w; r_{\rm com})$ and $w \in \Phi$. In other words, $\mathcal{W}_x \neq \emptyset$.

Recall that $f \in \mathbb{F}$ indicates a set $S_f \subset [l]$, such that $f(w) = 1$ if $w \in \Phi_{S_f}$, and $f(w) = 0$ if $w \in \Phi \setminus \Phi_{S_f}$.

Parse $\mathsf{crs} = (\mathsf{crs}_{\rm nizk}, pp)$ and $\pi = (\tau_{\rm p}, \pi_{\widetilde{\mathcal{R}_{\rm sm}}}, c)$. Let evt_1 denote the event that $c = \mathsf{SME.Enc}(pk, \Phi, \tau_{\rm p}, w; r_{\rm enc})$ for some $w \in \mathcal{W}_x$ and some $r_{\rm enc}$, and evt_2 denote the event that $c \neq \mathsf{SME.Enc}(pk, \Phi, \tau_{\rm p}, w; r_{\rm enc})$ for all $w \in \mathcal{W}_x$ and all $r_{\rm enc}$. So

$$\begin{aligned} & \Pr[\mathsf{Extract}(\mathsf{crs}, x, \pi, sk_{f,\tau_{\rm f}}) \notin \mathsf{Rge}_{f(\mathcal{W}_x)}] \\ = \; & \Pr[(\mathsf{Extract}(\mathsf{crs}, x, \pi, sk_{f,\tau_{\rm f}}) \notin \mathsf{Rge}_{f(\mathcal{W}_x)}) \wedge \mathsf{evt}_1] \end{aligned}$$

$$+ \Pr[(\mathsf{Extract}(\mathsf{crs}, x, \pi, sk_{f,\tau_f}) \notin \mathsf{Rge}_{f(\mathcal{W}_x)}) \wedge \mathsf{evt}_2]$$
$$\leq \Pr[\mathsf{Extract}(\mathsf{crs}, x, \pi, sk_{f,\tau_f}) \notin \mathsf{Rge}_{f(\mathcal{W}_x)} \mid \mathsf{evt}_1] + \Pr[\mathsf{evt}_2].$$

We note that $\mathsf{Extract}(\mathsf{crs}, x, \pi, sk_{f,\tau_f}) = \mathsf{SME.Query}(c, sk_{f,\tau_f})$. So if evt_1 occurs (i.e., $c = \mathsf{SME.Enc}(pk, \Phi, \tau_p, w; r_{enc})$ for some $w \in \mathcal{W}_x$ and some r_{enc}), the correctness of SME guarantees that $\mathsf{Extract}(\mathsf{crs}, x, \pi, sk_{f,\tau_f}) = f(w)$ with overwhelming probability. So $\Pr[\mathsf{Extract}(\mathsf{crs}, x, \pi, sk_{f,\tau_f}) \neq f(w) \mid \mathsf{evt}_1]$ is negligible.

If evt_2 occurs (i.e., $c \neq \mathsf{SME.Enc}(pk, \Phi, \tau_p, w; r_{enc})$ for all $w \in \mathcal{W}_x$ and all r_{enc}), then $(\tau_p, \mathsf{com}, c, pk, \Phi) \notin \mathcal{L}_{\widetilde{\mathcal{R}_{sm}}}$, where $\mathcal{L}_{\widetilde{\mathcal{R}_{sm}}}$ is denoted as the the NP language for the relation $\widetilde{\mathcal{R}_{sm}}$. Note that $\mathsf{Verify}(\mathsf{crs}, x, \pi) = 1$ implies that $\mathsf{NIZK.Verify}(\mathsf{crs}_{nizk}, (\tau_p, \mathsf{com}, c, pk, \Phi), \pi_{\widetilde{\mathcal{R}_{sm}}}) = 1$. The adaptive soundness of NIZK for $\widetilde{\mathcal{R}_{sm}}$ guarantees that

$$\Pr[((\tau_p, \mathsf{com}, c, pk, \Phi) \notin \mathcal{L}_{\widetilde{\mathcal{R}_{sm}}}) \wedge (\mathsf{NIZK.Verify}(\mathsf{crs}_{nizk}, (\tau_p, \mathsf{com}, c, pk, \Phi), \pi_{\widetilde{\mathcal{R}_{sm}}}) = 1)]$$

is negligible. So $\Pr[\mathsf{evt}_2]$ is also negligible.

Thus, $\Pr[\mathsf{Extract}(\mathsf{crs}, x, \pi, sk_{f,\tau_f}) \notin \mathsf{Rge}_{f(\mathcal{W}_x)}]$ is negligible, concluding the proof of functional knowledge.

Adaptive Soundness. The adaptive soundness of fSMP is guaranteed by the adaptive soundness of the underlying NIZK.

More specifically, assume that there is a computationally unbounded adversary $\mathcal{A}$, which takes crs as input and outputs (pk, x, π) satisfying $x \notin \mathcal{L}_{\mathcal{R}_{sm}}$ and $\mathsf{Verify}(\mathsf{crs}, pk, x, \pi) = 1$. Parse $x = (\mathsf{com}, \Phi)$ and $\pi = (\tau_p, \pi_{\widetilde{\mathcal{R}_{sm}}}, c)$.

Note that $\mathsf{Verify}(\mathsf{crs}, pk, x, \pi) = 1$ guarantees that $\mathsf{NIZK.Verify}(\mathsf{crs}_{nizk}, (\tau_p, \mathsf{com}, c, pk, \Phi), \pi_{\widetilde{\mathcal{R}_{sm}}}) = 1$.

On the other hand, $x \notin \mathcal{L}_{\mathcal{R}_{sm}}$ implies that there is no $w \in \Phi$ satisfying $\mathsf{com} = \mathsf{Com}(pp, w; \cdot)$. As a result, for all $w \in \Phi$, $(\tau_p, \mathsf{com}, \mathsf{SME.Enc}(pk, \Phi, \tau_p, w), pk, \Phi) \notin \mathcal{L}_{\widetilde{\mathcal{R}_{sm}}}$. In other words, for the $(\tau_p, \mathsf{com}, pk, \Phi)$ contained in (x, π), and for all ciphertext c', we have $(\tau_p, \mathsf{com}, c', pk, \Phi) \notin \mathcal{L}_{\widetilde{\mathcal{R}_{sm}}}$. Hence, for the c contained in π, we derive that $(\tau_p, \mathsf{com}, c, pk, \Phi) \notin \mathcal{L}_{\widetilde{\mathcal{R}_{sm}}}$. According to the adaptive soundness of NIZK, this occurs with only negligible probability.

Hence, fSMP is adaptively sound.

Zero knowledge. For zero knowledge of fSMP, we have the following theorem. Due to space limitations, the proof of this theorem is given in the full version of this paper.

Theorem 3. *If the underlying* SME *is IND secure and supports Sigma protocols, then* fSMP *is zero knowledge.*

5.2 SME from Dual IPE

In this part, we introduce a primitive called *dual inner-product encryption (dual IPE)* and leverage it to build a SME scheme.

Dual IPE. For vectors $(\mathbf{x}_1, \mathbf{x}_2), (\mathbf{y}_1, \mathbf{y}_2) \in (\mathbb{Z}_p)^{l_1} \times (\mathbb{Z}_p)^{l_2}$, we define a function $\mathtt{DuIP} : (\mathbb{Z}_p)^{l_1} \times (\mathbb{Z}_p)^{l_2} \times (\mathbb{Z}_p)^{l_1} \times (\mathbb{Z}_p)^{l_2} \to \{0, 1\}$ as follows:

$$\mathtt{DuIP}((\mathbf{x}_1, \mathbf{x}_2), (\mathbf{y}_1, \mathbf{y}_2)) = \begin{cases} 0 & \text{if } \langle \mathbf{x}_1, \mathbf{y}_1 \rangle = \langle \mathbf{x}_2, \mathbf{y}_2 \rangle = 0 \\ 1 & \text{otherwise} \end{cases}$$

Definition 6. (Dual IPE). *A dual inner-product encryption (dual IPE) scheme* DIPE *for a message space* $\mathcal{M}$ *and vector space* $(\mathbb{Z}_p)^{l_1} \times (\mathbb{Z}_p)^{l_2}$ *consists of five algorithms* $\mathsf{DIPE} = (\mathsf{Setup}, \mathsf{KGen}, \mathsf{CheckKey}, \mathsf{Enc}, \mathsf{Dec})$.

- $\mathsf{Setup}(1^\lambda, (l_1, l_2)) \to (pk, msk)$: *On input the security parameter* 1^λ *and the dimension* (l_1, l_2)*, the setup algorithm outputs a public key* pk *and a master secret key* msk.
- $\mathsf{KGen}(msk, \mathbf{x} = (\mathbf{x}_1, \mathbf{x}_2)) \to sk_{\mathbf{x}}$: *On input a master secret key* msk *and two vectors* $(\mathbf{x}_1, \mathbf{x}_2) \in (\mathbb{Z}_p)^{l_1} \times (\mathbb{Z}_p)^{l_2}$*, the key generation algorithm outputs a secret key* $sk_{\mathbf{x}}$ *for these vectors.*
- $\mathsf{CheckKey}(pk, \mathbf{x} = (\mathbf{x}_1, \mathbf{x}_2), sk_{\mathbf{x}}) \to b$: *On input a public key* pk*, two vectors* $(\mathbf{x}_1, \mathbf{x}_2)$ *and a secret key* $sk_{\mathbf{x}}$*, the checking algorithm outputs a bit* b.
- $\mathsf{Enc}(pk, \mathbf{y} = (\mathbf{y}_1, \mathbf{y}_2), m) \to c_{\mathbf{y}}$: *On input* pk*, vectors* $(\mathbf{y}_1, \mathbf{y}_2) \in (\mathbb{Z}_p)^{l_1} \times (\mathbb{Z}_p)^{l_2}$ *and a message* $m \in \mathcal{M}$*, the encryption algorithm outputs a ciphertext* $c_{\mathbf{y}}$ *for* $(\mathbf{y}_1, \mathbf{y}_2)$.
- $\mathsf{Dec}(c_{\mathbf{y}}, sk_{\mathbf{x}}) \to m$: *On input a ciphertext* $c_{\mathbf{y}}$ *and a secret key* $sk_{\mathbf{x}}$ *as input, the decryption algorithm outputs a message* m.

Correctness requires that for all $m \in \mathcal{M}$ *and all vectors* $(\mathbf{x}_1, \mathbf{x}_2)$ *and* $(\mathbf{y}_1, \mathbf{y}_2)$ *satisfying* $\mathtt{DuIP}((\mathbf{x}_1, \mathbf{x}_2), (\mathbf{y}_1, \mathbf{y}_2)) = 0$*, it holds that:*

$$\Pr\left[\begin{matrix}(pk, msk) \leftarrow \mathsf{Setup}(1^\lambda, (l_1, l_2)) \\ sk_{\mathbf{x}} \leftarrow \mathsf{KGen}(msk, (\mathbf{x}_1, \mathbf{x}_2))\end{matrix} : \mathsf{Dec}(\mathsf{Enc}(pk, (\mathbf{y}_1, \mathbf{y}_2), m), sk_{\mathbf{x}}) = m\right] = 1,$$

$$\Pr\left[\begin{matrix}(pk, msk) \leftarrow \mathsf{Setup}(1^\lambda, (l_1, l_2)) \\ sk_{\mathbf{x}} \leftarrow \mathsf{KGen}(msk, (\mathbf{x}_1, \mathbf{x}_2))\end{matrix} : \mathsf{CheckKey}(pk, (\mathbf{x}_1, \mathbf{x}_2), sk_{\mathbf{x}}) = 1\right] \geq 1 - \mathsf{negl}(\lambda).$$

We now define adaptive security for dual IPE.

Definition 7. (Adaptive security). *A dual IPE scheme* $\mathsf{DIPE} = (\mathsf{Setup}, \mathsf{KGen}, \mathsf{CheckKey}, \mathsf{Enc}, \mathsf{Dec})$ *for message space* $\mathcal{M}$ *and vector space* $(\mathbb{Z}_p)^{l_1} \times (\mathbb{Z}_p)^{l_2}$ *is* adaptively secure, *if for any PPT adversary* $\mathcal{A}$*, the advantage* $\mathbf{Adv}^{\mathsf{as}}_{\mathsf{DIPE},\mathcal{A}}(\lambda) := |\Pr[\mathit{Exp}^{\mathsf{as}}_{\mathsf{DIPE},\mathcal{A}}(\lambda) = 1] - \frac{1}{2}|$ *is negligible, where* $\mathsf{Exp}^{\mathsf{as}}_{\mathsf{DIPE},\mathcal{A}}(\lambda)$ *is defined in Fig. 7.*

The adaptive security implies payload-hiding and partial attribute-hiding. More exactly, our dual IPE requires the first-level vector (i.e., $\mathbf{y}_1^{(\beta)}$) to be fully attribute-hiding, without requiring the second-level vector (i.e., $\mathbf{y}_2$) to be hidden. A concrete adaptively secure dual IPE scheme will be presented in Sec. 5.3.

Encoding Algorithms. Before we show how to construct SME from dual IPE, we firstly present two encoding algorithms, as shown in the following:

$\underline{\mathsf{Exp}^{\mathsf{as}}_{\mathsf{DIPE},\mathcal{A}}(\lambda)}$:
$(pk, msk) \leftarrow \mathsf{Setup}(1^\lambda, (l_1, l_2))$, $b \leftarrow \{0,1\}$, $C_{\mathrm{y,m}} := \emptyset$, $U_{\mathrm{x}} := \emptyset$
$(\mathbf{y}_1^{(0)}, \mathbf{y}_1^{(1)}, \mathbf{y}_2, m_0, m_1, st) \leftarrow \mathcal{A}_1^{\mathcal{O}^{\mathsf{KGen}}(\cdot)}(pk, (l_1, l_2))$
  s.t. if $m_0 \neq m_1$, $\mathtt{DuIP}((\mathbf{x}_1, \mathbf{x}_2), (\mathbf{y}_1^{(\beta)}, \mathbf{y}_2)) \neq 0$ for all $\beta \in \{0,1\}$ and all $(\mathbf{x}_1, \mathbf{x}_2) \in U_{\mathrm{x}}$;
  if $m_0 = m_1$, $(\forall \beta \in \{0,1\} : \mathtt{DuIP}((\mathbf{x}_1, \mathbf{x}_2), (\mathbf{y}_1^{(\beta)}, \mathbf{y}_2)) \neq 0)$
    $\vee (\forall \beta \in \{0,1\} : \mathtt{DuIP}((\mathbf{x}_1, \mathbf{x}_2), (\mathbf{y}_1^{(\beta)}, \mathbf{y}_2)) = 0)$ for all $(\mathbf{x}_1, \mathbf{x}_2) \in U_{\mathrm{x}}$
$C_{\mathrm{y,m}} := \{(\mathbf{y}_1^{(0)}, \mathbf{y}_1^{(1)}, \mathbf{y}_2, m_0, m_1)\}$, $c \leftarrow \mathsf{Enc}(pk, (\mathbf{y}_1^{(b)}, \mathbf{y}_2), m_b)$, $b' \leftarrow \mathcal{A}_2^{\mathcal{O}^{\mathsf{KGen}}(\cdot)}(c, st)$
Return $(b = b')$

$\underline{\mathcal{O}^{\mathsf{KGen}}((\mathbf{x}_1, \mathbf{x}_2))}$:
If $C_{\mathrm{y,m}} \neq \emptyset$:
  Parse $C_{\mathrm{y,m}} = \{(\mathbf{y}_1^{(0)}, \mathbf{y}_1^{(1)}, \mathbf{y}_2, m_0, m_1)\}$
  If $m_0 \neq m_1$:
    If $(\exists \beta \in \{0,1\} : \mathtt{DuIP}((\mathbf{x}_1, \mathbf{x}_2), (\mathbf{y}_1^{(\beta)}, \mathbf{y}_2)) = 0)$: Return $\perp$
  If $m_0 = m_1$:
    If $(\exists \beta \in \{0,1\} : (\mathtt{DuIP}((\mathbf{x}_1, \mathbf{x}_2), (\mathbf{y}_1^{(\beta)}, \mathbf{y}_2)) = 0) \wedge (\mathtt{DuIP}((\mathbf{x}_1, \mathbf{x}_2), (\mathbf{y}_1^{(1-\beta)}, \mathbf{y}_2)) \neq 0))$:
      Return $\perp$
$U_{\mathrm{x}} := U_{\mathrm{x}} \cup \{(\mathbf{x}_1, \mathbf{x}_2)\}$
Return $sk_{\mathrm{x}} \leftarrow \mathsf{KGen}(msk, (\mathbf{x}_1, \mathbf{x}_2))$

Fig. 7. Game for defining adaptive security for dual IPE

1. $\mathsf{EncodeW}(\Phi, w)$: Taking $\Phi = \{w_1, \ldots, w_l\}$ and $w \in \mathcal{W}$ as input, it outputs a vector I in $\{0,1\}^l$ as follows:

$$\forall j \in [l] : I_j = \begin{cases} 1 & \text{if } w = w_j \\ 0 & \text{otherwise} \end{cases}$$

   For example, supposing $w = w_{j'}$ for some $j' \in [l]$, I can be represented as follows:

$$I = \underset{1}{\boxed{0}} \boxed{\cdots} \boxed{0} \underset{j'}{\boxed{1}} \boxed{0} \boxed{\cdots} \underset{l}{\boxed{0}}$$

   It is clear that I depends on w. Thus, we also write $I(w)$ for simplicity to denote the vector output by $\mathsf{EncodeW}(\Phi, w)$.
2. $\mathsf{EncodeS}(l, S)$: Taking a value l and a set $S \subset [l]$ as input, it outputs a vector I^* in $\{0,1\}^l$ as follows:

$$\forall j \in [l] : I_j^* = \begin{cases} 0 & \text{if } j \in S \\ 1 & \text{otherwise} \end{cases}$$

   For example, supposing $S = \{3, 5, l\} \subset [l]$, I^* can be represented as follows:

$$I^* = \underset{1}{\boxed{1}} \boxed{1} \underset{3}{\boxed{0}} \boxed{1} \underset{5}{\boxed{0}} \boxed{1} \boxed{\cdots} \boxed{1} \underset{l}{\boxed{0}}$$

It is clear that given l, I^* depends on S. Thus, we also write $I^*(S)$ for simplicity to denote the vector output by $\mathsf{EncodeS}(l, S)$ when l is given in the text.

SME from Dual IPE. Let $\mathcal{I} = \{0,1\}^{l_1}$ denote a vector space with alphabet $\{0,1\}$ and length l_1. Let $\mathcal{T} = (\mathbb{Z}_p)^{l_2}$ denote the label space with alphabet $\{0,\ldots,p-1\}$ and length l_2. Let $\mathsf{P}_{\text{ip}} : \mathcal{T} \times (\mathcal{T} \cup \{*\}) \to \{0,1\}$ be a predicate function satisfying that for any $\tau \in \mathcal{T}$ and $\tau' \in \mathcal{T} \cup \{*\}$,

$$\mathsf{P}_{\text{ip}}(\tau, \tau') = \begin{cases} 1 & \text{if } (\tau' = *) \vee ((\tau' \neq *) \wedge (\langle \tau, \tau' \rangle = 0)) \\ 0 & \text{otherwise} \end{cases}$$

From the perspective of inner product, the symbol $*$ can be regarded as vector 0^{l_2}. In this case, P_{ip} can be rephrased as

$$\mathsf{P}_{\text{ip}}(\tau, \tau') = \begin{cases} 1 & \text{if } \langle \tau, \tau' \rangle = 0 \\ 0 & \text{otherwise} \end{cases}$$

Let $\mathsf{DIPE} = (\mathsf{DIPE.Setup}, \mathsf{DIPE.KGen}, \mathsf{DIPE.CheckKey}, \mathsf{DIPE.Enc}, \mathsf{DIPE.Dec})$ be an adaptively secure dual IPE scheme for vector space $\mathcal{I} \times \mathcal{T}$ and message space $\mathcal{M}_{\mathsf{DIPE}}$, as presented in Sect. 5.3. Let $\mathsf{m}_{\mathsf{dum}}$ be an arbitrary public default message in $\mathcal{M}_{\mathsf{DIPE}}$.

Our SME scheme $\mathsf{SME} = (\mathsf{Setup}, \mathsf{KGen}, \mathsf{CheckKey}, \mathsf{Enc}, \mathsf{Query})$ (with set of size l_1) for message set $\mathcal{W}$, label space $\mathcal{T}$ and predicate P_{ip} is described in Fig. 8.

```
Setup(1^λ):        //set l_1 = poly(λ), l_2 = poly(λ)
(pk, msk) ← DIPE.Setup(1^λ, (l_1, l_2))
Return (pk, sk = msk)

KGen(pk, sk, S, τ_f):                     // S ⊂ [l_1]
I*(S) ← EncodeS(l_1, S)
sk_{I*(S),τ_f} ← DIPE.KGen(msk, (I*(S), τ_f))
Return sk_{S,τ_f} = sk_{I*(S),τ_f}

CheckKey(pk, S, τ_f, sk_{S,τ_f}):
Return b ← DIPE.CheckKey(pk, (I*(S), τ_f), sk_{S,τ_f})

Enc(pk, Φ, τ_p, w):                       // |Φ| = l_1
If w ∉ Φ: Return ⊥
I(w) = EncodeW(Φ, w)
c ← DIPE.Enc(pk, (I(w), τ_p), m_dum)
Return c

Query(c, sk_{S,τ_f}):
m'_dum ← DIPE.Dec(c, sk_{S,τ_f})
If m_dum = m'_dum: Return y = 1
Else: Return y = 0
```

Fig. 8. Construction of SME from DIPE ($\mathsf{m}_{\mathsf{dum}}$ is an arbitrary public default message in $\mathcal{M}_{\mathsf{DIPE}}$)

Security Analysis. Here, we show that the above SME constructed from dual IPE DIPE, is correct and IND secure.

Correctness. For any $\Phi \subset \mathcal{W}$ satisfying $|\Phi| = l$, any $w \in \Phi$ and any $S \subset [l]$, any $\tau_{\mathfrak{f}} \in \mathcal{T} \cup \{*\}$ and any $\tau_{\mathrm{p}} \in \mathcal{T}$ satisfying $\mathsf{P}_{\text{ip}}(\tau_{\mathrm{p}}, \tau_{\mathfrak{f}}) = 1$ (i.e., $\langle \tau_{\mathrm{p}}, \tau_{\mathfrak{f}} \rangle = 0$), for $(pk, sk) \leftarrow \mathsf{Setup}(1^\lambda)$, $sk_{S,\tau_{\mathfrak{f}}} \leftarrow \mathsf{KGen}(pk, sk, S, \tau_{\mathfrak{f}})$, $c \leftarrow \mathsf{Enc}(pk, \Phi, \tau_{\mathrm{p}}, w)$ and $y \leftarrow \mathsf{Query}(c, sk_{S,\tau_{\mathfrak{f}}})$, it holds that

- If $w \in \Phi_S$, then $\langle I^*(S), I(w)\rangle = 0$. So $\mathsf{DIPE.Dec}(c, sk_{S,\tau_\mathfrak{f}}) = \mathsf{m_{dum}}$, which suggests that $y = 1$.
- If $w \notin \Phi_S$, then $\langle I^*(S), I(w)\rangle \neq 0$. The adaptive security of DIPE guarantee that $\mathsf{DIPE.Dec}(c, sk_{S,\tau_\mathfrak{f}}) \neq \mathsf{m_{dum}}$ with overwhelming probability. Hence, the probability that $y = 1$ is negligible.

For $(pk, sk) \leftarrow \mathsf{Setup}(1^\lambda)$ and $sk_{S,\tau_\mathfrak{f}} \leftarrow \mathsf{KGen}(pk, sk, S, \tau_\mathfrak{f})$, we have that $\mathsf{CheckKey}(pk, S, \tau_\mathfrak{f}, sk_{S,\tau_\mathfrak{f}}) = \mathsf{DIPE.CheckKey}(pk, (I^*(S), \tau_\mathfrak{f}), sk_{S,\tau_\mathfrak{f}})$, since CheckKey invokes DIPE.CheckKey to check the keys. By the correctness of DIPE, we know that $\mathsf{DIPE.CheckKey}(pk, (I^*(S), \tau_\mathfrak{f}), sk_{S,\tau_\mathfrak{f}}) = 1$, when $sk_{S,\tau_\mathfrak{f}} \leftarrow \mathsf{DIPE.KGen}(pk, (I^*(S), \tau_\mathfrak{f}))$. Note that the key generation KGen calls $\mathsf{DIPE.KGen}(pk, (I^*(S), \tau_\mathfrak{f}))$ to generate $sk_{S,\tau_\mathfrak{f}}$. Thus, $\mathsf{CheckKey}(pk, S, \tau_\mathfrak{f}, sk_{S,\tau_\mathfrak{f}}) = \mathsf{DIPE.CheckKey}(pk, (I^*(S), \tau_\mathfrak{f}), sk_{S,\tau_\mathfrak{f}}) = 1$.

In all, the SME above is correct.

IND Security. The IND security of SME is guaranteed by the adaptive security of the underlying dual IPE DIPE. Formally, we have the following theorem. Due to space limitations, its proof will be given in the full version of this paper.

Theorem 4. *If the underlying* DIPE *is adaptively secure, then* SME *is IND secure.*

5.3 A Concrete Construction of Dual IPE

Starting from the IPE schemes proposed in [10,12,31], we provide a concrete construction of adaptively secure dual IPE. In this subsection, we first give some notations, assumptions and facts. Then, we provide a *private-key* dual IPE, and upgrade it to *public-key* dual IPE employing the "private-key to public-key" compiler in [31]. Unless otherwise specified, the term "dual IPE" refers to public-key dual IPE.

Notations. A group generator $\mathcal{G}$ takes as input the security parameter λ and outputs group description $\mathbb{G} = (p, \mathbb{G}_1, \mathbb{G}_2, \mathbb{G}_T, e)$, where p is a prime of $\Theta(\lambda)$ bits, $\mathbb{G}_1$, $\mathbb{G}_2$ and $\mathbb{G}_T$ are cyclic groups of order p, and $e : \mathbb{G}_1 \times \mathbb{G}_2 \rightarrow \mathbb{G}_T$ is a nondegenerate bilinear map. We require that group operations in $\mathbb{G}_1$, $\mathbb{G}_2$ and $\mathbb{G}_T$ as well the bilinear map e are computable in deterministic polynomial time with respect to λ. Let $g_1 \in \mathbb{G}_1$, $g_2 \in \mathbb{G}_2$ and $g_T = e(g_1, g_2) \in \mathbb{G}_T$ be the respective generators. We employ the implicit representation of group elements: for a matrix $\mathbf{M}$ over $\mathbb{Z}_p$, we define $[\mathbf{M}]_1 = g_1^{\mathbf{M}}$,$[\mathbf{M}]_2 = g_2^{\mathbf{M}}$,$[\mathbf{M}]_T = g_T^{\mathbf{M}}$, where exponentiations are carried out component-wise. For $[\mathbf{A}]_1$ and $[\mathbf{B}]_2$, we let $e([\mathbf{A}]_1, [\mathbf{B}]_2) = [\mathbf{AB}]_T$. For any matrix $\mathbf{B} \in \mathbb{Z}_p^{n \times m}$, we define an operator $\odot$ as follows: $\alpha \odot [\mathbf{B}]_* = [\alpha \mathbf{B}]_*$, where the star $*$ belongs to $\{1, 2, T\}$ and α could be a constant in $\mathbb{Z}_p$, a row vector in $\mathbb{Z}_p^n$ or a matrix in $\mathbb{Z}_p^{n' \times n}$. $\mathrm{GL}_k(\mathbb{Z}_p)$ denotes the general linear group of degree k over $\mathbb{Z}_p$. Let $\mathbf{A}$ be a $\ell \times k$ matrix over $\mathbb{Z}_p$, where $\ell \geq k$. We use $\mathsf{span}_c(\mathbf{A})$ to denote the column span of $\mathbf{A}$. By $\mathsf{span}_r(\mathbf{A}^\top)$, we are indicating the row span of $\mathbf{A}^\top$. If $\mathbf{A}$ is a basis of $\mathsf{span}_c(\mathbf{A})$, we use $\mathsf{basis}(\mathbf{A})$ to denote another basis of $\mathsf{span}_c(\mathbf{A})$ via $\mathbf{A} \cdot \mathbf{R}$, where $\mathbf{R} \leftarrow \mathrm{GL}_k(\mathbb{Z}_p)$. Given an invertible matrix $\mathbf{B}$, we use $\mathbf{B}^*$ to denote its dual satisfying $\mathbf{B}^\top \mathbf{B}^* = \mathbf{I}$.

Assumptions. We review the matrix Diffie-Hellman (MDDH) assumption on $\mathbb{G}_1$ [14]. The $\text{MDDH}_{k,\ell}$ assumption on $\mathbb{G}_2$ can be defined analogously.

Definition 8. ($\text{MDDH}_{k,\ell}$ assumption). *Let $\ell > k \geq 1$. We say that the $\text{MDDH}_{k,\ell}$ assumption holds with respect to $\mathcal{G}$ if for all PPT adversaries $\mathcal{A}$, the following advantage function is negligible in λ.*

$$\mathbf{Adv}_{\mathcal{A}}^{\text{MDDH}_{k,\ell}}(\lambda) := |\Pr[\mathcal{A}(\mathbb{G}, [\mathbf{M}]_1, [\mathbf{Ms}]_1) = 1] - \Pr[\mathcal{A}(\mathbb{G}, [\mathbf{M}]_1, [\mathbf{u}]_1) = 1]|$$

where $\mathbb{G} \leftarrow \mathcal{G}(1^\lambda)$, $\mathbf{M} \leftarrow \mathbb{Z}_p^{\ell\times k}$, $\mathbf{s} \leftarrow \mathbb{Z}_p^k$ *and* $\mathbf{u} \leftarrow \mathbb{Z}_p^\ell$.

Let $\ell_1, \ell_2, \ell_3 > 1$ and $\ell := \ell_1+\ell_2+\ell_3$. We use basis $\mathbf{B}_1 \leftarrow \mathbb{Z}_p^{\ell\times\ell_1}$, $\mathbf{B}_2 \leftarrow \mathbb{Z}_p^{\ell\times\ell_2}$, $\mathbf{B}_3 \leftarrow \mathbb{Z}_p^{\ell\times\ell_3}$, and its dual basis $(\mathbf{B}_1^*, \mathbf{B}_2^*, \mathbf{B}_3^*)$ such that $\mathbf{B}_i^\top\mathbf{B}_i^* = \mathbf{I}$ (known as *non-degeneracy*) and $\mathbf{B}_i^\top\mathbf{B}_j^* = 0$ if $i \neq j$ (known as *orthogonality*). We review the $\text{SD}^{\mathbb{G}_2}_{\mathbf{B}_1\mapsto\mathbf{B}_1,\mathbf{B}_2}$ assumption as follows. By symmetry, one may permute the indices for subspaces.

Definition 9. ($\text{SD}^{\mathbb{G}_2}_{\mathbf{B}_1\mapsto\mathbf{B}_1,\mathbf{B}_2}$ assumption). *We say that the $\text{SD}^{\mathbb{G}_2}_{\mathbf{B}_1\mapsto\mathbf{B}_1,\mathbf{B}_2}$ assumption holds if for all PPT adversaries $\mathcal{A}$, the following advantage function is negligible in λ.*

$$\mathbf{Adv}_{\mathcal{A}}^{\text{SD}^{\mathbb{G}_2}_{\mathbf{B}_1\mapsto\mathbf{B}_1,\mathbf{B}_2}}(\lambda) := |\Pr[\mathcal{A}(\mathbb{G}, D, [\mathbf{t}_0]_1) = 1] - \Pr[\mathcal{A}(\mathbb{G}, D, [\mathbf{t}_1]_1) = 1]|$$

where $D := ([\mathbf{B}_1]_2, [\mathbf{B}_2]_2, [\mathbf{B}_3]_2, \mathsf{basis}(\mathbf{B}_1^*, \mathbf{B}_2^*), \mathsf{basis}(\mathbf{B}_3^*))$, $\mathbf{t}_0 \leftarrow \mathsf{span}_c(\mathbf{B}_1)$, $\mathbf{t}_1 \leftarrow \mathsf{span}_c(\mathbf{B}_1, \mathbf{B}_2)$.

It is known that k-LIN $\Rightarrow \text{MDDH}_{k,\ell}$ [14] and $\text{MDDH}_{\ell,\ell_1+\ell_2} \Rightarrow \text{SD}^{\mathbb{G}_2}_{\mathbf{B}_1\mapsto\mathbf{B}_1,\mathbf{B}_2}$ [11].

Facts. With basis $(\mathbf{B}_1, \mathbf{B}_2, \mathbf{B}_3)$, we can uniquely decompose $\mathbf{w} \in \mathbb{Z}_p^{1\times\ell}$ as $\mathbf{w} = \Sigma_{\beta\in[3]}\mathbf{w}^{(\beta)}$ where $\mathbf{w}^{(\beta)} \in \mathsf{span}_r(\mathbf{B}_\beta^{*\top})$. Define $\mathbf{w}^{(\beta_1\beta_2)} = \mathbf{w}^{(\beta_1)}+\mathbf{w}^{(\beta_2)}$ for $\beta_1, \beta_2 \in [3]$. We have the following two facts:

1. For $\beta \in [3]$, it holds that $\mathbf{wB}_\beta = \mathbf{w}^{(\beta)}\mathbf{B}_\beta$;
2. For all $\beta^* \in [3]$, it holds that $\{\mathbf{w}^{(\beta^*)}, \{\mathbf{w}^{(\beta)}\}_{\beta\neq\beta^*}\} \equiv \{\mathbf{w}^*, \{\mathbf{w}^{(\beta)}\}_{\beta\neq\beta^*}\}$ when $\mathbf{w} \leftarrow \mathbb{Z}_p^{1\times\ell}$ and $\mathbf{w}^* \leftarrow \mathsf{span}_r(\mathbf{B}_{\beta^*}^{*\top})$.

Construction of Private-Key Dual IPE. In a private-key dual IPE, the Setup algorithm does not output *pk*; the CheckKey algorithm is not needed; and the Enc algorithm takes *msk* instead of *pk* as input. The adaptive security can be defined similar to Definition 7 except that the adversary $\mathcal{A}$ only gets the challenge ciphertext c and has access to KGen. Next, we give a concrete construction of private-key dual IPE skDIPE = (Setup, KGen, Enc, Dec), and the details are shown in Fig. 9.

Correctness. For all vectors $(\mathbf{x}_1, \mathbf{x}_2)$ and $(\mathbf{y}_1, \mathbf{y}_2)$ satisfying $\mathtt{DuIP}((\mathbf{x}_1, \mathbf{x}_2), (\mathbf{y}_1, \mathbf{y}_2)) = 0$, we have

$$((x_{1,1} \cdot C_{1,1} + \cdots + x_{1,l_1} \cdot C_{1,l_1} + x_{2,1} \cdot C_{2,1} + \cdots + x_{2,l_2} \cdot C_{2,l_2}) \odot K_1) \cdot K_0^{-1}$$

$\mathsf{Setup}(1^\lambda, l_1, l_2)$:
$\mathbb{G} := (p, \mathbb{G}_1, \mathbb{G}_2, \mathbb{G}_T, e) \leftarrow \mathcal{G}(1^\lambda)$
$\mathbf{B}_1 \leftarrow \mathbb{Z}_p^{(2k+1)\times k}$
$\mathbf{u}_1, \mathbf{u}_2, \mathbf{w}_{1,1}, \ldots, \mathbf{w}_{1,l_1}, \mathbf{w}_{2,1}, \ldots, \mathbf{w}_{2,l_2} \leftarrow \mathbb{Z}_p^{1\times(2k+1)}$, $\alpha \leftarrow \mathbb{Z}_p$
$msk := (\mathbb{G}, \alpha, \mathbf{u}_1, \mathbf{u}_2, \mathbf{w}_{1,1}, \ldots, \mathbf{w}_{1,l_1}, \mathbf{w}_{2,1}, \ldots, \mathbf{w}_{2,l_2}, \mathbf{B}_1)$
Return msk

$\mathsf{KGen}(msk, (\mathbf{x}_1, \mathbf{x}_2))$:
Parse $\mathbf{x}_1 = (x_{1,1}, \ldots, x_{1,l_1}) \in \mathbb{Z}_p^{l_1}$, $\mathbf{x}_2 = (x_{2,1}, \ldots, x_{2,l_2}) \in \mathbb{Z}_p^{l_2}$
$\mathbf{r} \leftarrow \mathbb{Z}_p^k$
$K_0 := [\alpha + (x_{1,1} \cdot \mathbf{w}_{1,1} + \ldots + x_{1,l_1} \cdot \mathbf{w}_{1,l_1} + x_{2,1} \cdot \mathbf{w}_{2,1} + \ldots + x_{2,l_2} \cdot \mathbf{w}_{2,l_2})\mathbf{B}_1\mathbf{r}]_2$
$K_1 := [\mathbf{B}_1\mathbf{r}]_2$
Return $sk_{\mathbf{x}} := (K_0, K_1)$

$\mathsf{Enc}(msk, (\mathbf{y}_1, \mathbf{y}_2), m \in \mathbb{G}_2)$:
Parse $\mathbf{y}_1 = (y_{1,1}, \ldots, y_{1,l_1}) \in \mathbb{Z}_p^{l_1}$, $\mathbf{y}_2 = (y_{2,1}, \ldots, y_{2,l_2}) \in \mathbb{Z}_p^{l_2}$
For $i \in [l_1]$: $C_{1,i} := y_{1,i} \cdot \mathbf{u}_1 + \mathbf{w}_{1,i}$
For $i \in [l_2]$: $C_{2,i} := y_{2,i} \cdot \mathbf{u}_2 + \mathbf{w}_{2,i}$
$C := [\alpha]_2 \cdot m$
Return $c_{\mathbf{y}} := ((C_{1,i})_{i\in[l_1]}, (C_{2,i})_{i\in[l_2]}, C)$

$\mathsf{Dec}(c_{\mathbf{y}}, sk_{\mathbf{x}})$:
Parse $c_{\mathbf{y}} = ((C_{1,i})_{i\in[l_1]}, (C_{2,i})_{i\in[l_2]}, C)$, $sk_{\mathbf{x}} = (K_0, K_1)$
Return $m' := C \cdot ((x_{1,1} \cdot C_{1,1} + \cdots + x_{1,l_1} \cdot C_{1,l_1} + x_{2,1} \cdot C_{2,1} + \cdots + x_{2,l_2} \cdot C_{2,l_2}) \odot K_1) \cdot K_0^{-1}$

Fig. 9. The algorithms of private-key dual IPE scheme skDIPE

$$
\begin{aligned}
=&[(x_{1,1} \cdot (y_{1,1}\mathbf{u}_1 + \mathbf{w}_{1,1}) + \cdots + x_{1,l_1} \cdot (y_{1,l_1}\mathbf{u}_1 + \mathbf{w}_{1,l_1}) \\
&+ x_{2,1} \cdot (y_{2,1}\mathbf{u}_2 + \mathbf{w}_{2,1}) + \cdots + x_{2,l_2} \cdot (y_{2,l_2}\mathbf{u}_2 + \mathbf{w}_{2,l_2}))\mathbf{B}_1\mathbf{r}]_2 \\
&\cdot [\alpha + (x_{1,1} \cdot \mathbf{w}_{1,1} + \ldots + x_{1,l_1} \cdot \mathbf{w}_{1,l_1} + x_{2,1} \cdot \mathbf{w}_{2,1} + \ldots + x_{2,l_2} \cdot \mathbf{w}_{2,l_2})\mathbf{B}_1\mathbf{r}]_2^{-1} \\
=&[\langle \mathbf{x}_1, \mathbf{y}_1 \rangle \cdot \mathbf{u}_1\mathbf{B}_1\mathbf{r} + \langle \mathbf{x}_2, \mathbf{y}_2 \rangle \cdot \mathbf{u}_2\mathbf{B}_1\mathbf{r}]_2 \\
&\cdot [(x_{1,1} \cdot \mathbf{w}_{1,1} + \ldots + x_{1,l_1} \cdot \mathbf{w}_{1,l_1} + x_{2,1} \cdot \mathbf{w}_{2,1} + \ldots + x_{2,l_2} \cdot \mathbf{w}_{2,l_2})\mathbf{B}_1\mathbf{r}]_2 \\
&\cdot [\alpha]_2^{-1} \cdot [(x_{1,1} \cdot \mathbf{w}_{1,1} + \ldots + x_{1,l_1} \cdot \mathbf{w}_{1,l_1} + x_{2,1} \cdot \mathbf{w}_{2,1} + \ldots + x_{2,l_2} \cdot \mathbf{w}_{2,l_2})\mathbf{B}_1\mathbf{r}]_2^{-1} \\
=&[\alpha]_2^{-1}
\end{aligned}
$$

where the last equality follows from the fact that $\langle \mathbf{x}_1, \mathbf{y}_1 \rangle = 0$ and $\langle \mathbf{x}_2, \mathbf{y}_2 \rangle = 0$. This proves the correctness.

Security. We have the following theorem for the private-key dual IPE scheme. Due to space limitations, the proof is given in the full version of this paper.

Theorem 5. *Under the k-LIN assumption, the private-key dual IPE scheme described in Fig. 9 is adaptively secure.*

Construction of public-key dual IPE. We give a concrete construction of public-key dual IPE $\mathsf{pkDIPE} = (\mathsf{Setup}, \mathsf{KGen}, \mathsf{CheckKey}, \mathsf{Enc}, \mathsf{Dec})$, and the details are shown in Fig. 10.

Setup($1^\lambda, l_1, l_2$):
$\mathbb{G} := (p, \mathbb{G}_1, \mathbb{G}_2, \mathbb{G}_T, e) \leftarrow \mathcal{G}(1^\lambda)$
$\mathbf{A} \leftarrow \mathbb{Z}_p^{(k+1)\times k}$, $\mathbf{B}_1 \leftarrow \mathbb{Z}_p^{(2k+1)\times k}$
$\mathbf{U}_1, \mathbf{U}_2, \mathbf{W}_{1,1}, \ldots, \mathbf{W}_{1,l_1}, \mathbf{W}_{2,1}, \ldots, \mathbf{W}_{2,l_2} \leftarrow \mathbb{Z}_p^{(k+1)\times(2k+1)}$, $\mathbf{k} \leftarrow \mathbb{Z}_p^{k+1}$
$pk := (\mathbb{G}, [\mathbf{A}^\top]_1, [\mathbf{A}^\top\mathbf{U}_1]_1, [\mathbf{A}^\top\mathbf{U}_2]_1, [\mathbf{A}^\top\mathbf{W}_{1,1}]_1, \ldots, [\mathbf{A}^\top\mathbf{W}_{1,l_1}]_1, [\mathbf{A}^\top\mathbf{W}_{2,1}]_1, \ldots, [\mathbf{A}^\top\mathbf{W}_{2,l_2}]_1, [\mathbf{A}^\top\mathbf{k}]_T)$
$msk := (\mathbf{k}, \mathbf{W}_{1,1}, \ldots, \mathbf{W}_{1,l_1}, \mathbf{W}_{2,1}, \ldots, \mathbf{W}_{2,l_2}, \mathbf{B}_1)$
Return (pk, msk)

KGen($msk, (\mathbf{x}_1, \mathbf{x}_2)$):
Parse $\mathbf{x}_1 = (x_{1,1}, \ldots, x_{1,l_1}) \in \mathbb{Z}_p^{l_1}$, $\mathbf{x}_2 = (x_{2,1}, \ldots, x_{2,l_2}) \in \mathbb{Z}_p^{l_2}$
$\mathbf{r} \leftarrow \mathbb{Z}_p^k$
$K_0 := [\mathbf{k} + (x_{1,1}\cdot\mathbf{W}_{1,1} + \ldots + x_{1,l_1}\cdot\mathbf{W}_{1,l_1} + x_{2,1}\cdot\mathbf{W}_{2,1} + \ldots + x_{2,l_2}\cdot\mathbf{W}_{2,l_2})\mathbf{B}_1\mathbf{r}]_2$, $K_1 := [\mathbf{B}_1\mathbf{r}]_2$
Return $sk_{\mathbf{x}} := (K_0, K_1)$

CheckKey($pk, (\mathbf{x}_1, \mathbf{x}_2), sk_{\mathbf{x}}$):
If $[0]_T = e((x_{1,1}\odot[\mathbf{A}^\top\mathbf{W}_{1,1}]_1)\cdots(x_{1,l_1}\odot[\mathbf{A}^\top\mathbf{W}_{1,l_1}]_1)\cdot(x_{2,1}\odot[\mathbf{A}^\top\mathbf{W}_{2,1}]_1)\cdots(x_{2,l_2}\odot[\mathbf{A}^\top\mathbf{W}_{2,l_2}]_1), K_1)$
$\cdot e([\mathbf{A}^\top]_1, K_0)^{-1}\cdot[\mathbf{A}^\top\mathbf{k}]_T$: Return 1
Else Return 0

Enc($pk, (\mathbf{y}_1, \mathbf{y}_2), m \in \mathbb{G}_T$):
Parse $\mathbf{y}_1 = (y_{1,1}, \ldots, y_{1,l_1}) \in \mathbb{Z}_p^{l_1}$, $\mathbf{y}_2 = (y_{2,1}, \ldots, y_{2,l_2}) \in \mathbb{Z}_p^{l_2}$
$\mathbf{s} \leftarrow \mathbb{Z}_p^k$
$C_0 := [\mathbf{s}^\top\mathbf{A}^\top]_1$
For $i \in [l_1]$: $C_{1,i} := [\mathbf{s}^\top\mathbf{A}^\top(y_{1,i}\cdot\mathbf{U}_1 + \mathbf{W}_{1,i})]_1$
For $i \in [l_2]$: $C_{2,i} := [\mathbf{s}^\top\mathbf{A}^\top(y_{2,i}\cdot\mathbf{U}_2 + \mathbf{W}_{2,i})]_1$
$C := [\mathbf{s}^\top\mathbf{A}^\top\mathbf{k}]_T\cdot m$
Return $c_{\mathbf{y}} := (C_0, (C_{1,i})_{i\in[l_1]}, (C_{2,i})_{i\in[l_2]}, C)$

Dec($c_{\mathbf{y}}, sk_{\mathbf{x}}$):
Parse $c_{\mathbf{y}} := (C_0, (C_{1,i})_{i\in[l_1]}, (C_{2,i})_{i\in[l_2]}, C)$, $sk_{\mathbf{x}} := (K_0, K_1)$
Return $m' := C\cdot e((x_{1,1}\odot C_{1,1})\cdots(x_{1,l_1}\odot C_{1,l_1})(x_{2,1}\odot C_{2,1})\cdots(x_{2,l_2}\odot C_{2,l_2}), K_1)\cdot e(C_0, K_0)^{-1}$

Fig. 10. The algorithms of public-key dual IPE scheme pkDIPE

Correctness. For all $m \in \mathcal{M}$ and all vectors $(\mathbf{x}_1, \mathbf{x}_2)$ and $(\mathbf{y}_1, \mathbf{y}_2)$ satisfying $\mathtt{DuIP}((\mathbf{x}_1, \mathbf{x}_2), (\mathbf{y}_1, \mathbf{y}_2)) = 0$, it holds that:

$$\begin{aligned}
&e(\ (x_{1,1}\odot C_{1,1})\cdots(x_{1,l_1}\odot C_{1,l_1})\cdot(x_{2,1}\odot C_{2,1})\cdots(x_{2,l_2}\odot C_{2,l_2}), K_1\ )\cdot e(C_0, K_0)^{-1}\\
=&e(\ [x_{1,1}\cdot\mathbf{s}^\top\mathbf{A}^\top(y_{1,1}\cdot\mathbf{U}_1 + \mathbf{W}_{1,1})]_1\ \cdots\ [x_{1,l_1}\cdot\mathbf{s}^\top\mathbf{A}^\top(y_{1,l_1}\cdot\mathbf{U}_1 + \mathbf{W}_{1,l_1})]_1\\
&\cdot[x_{2,1}\cdot\mathbf{s}^\top\mathbf{A}^\top(y_{2,1}\cdot\mathbf{U}_2 + \mathbf{W}_{2,1})]_1\ \cdots\ [x_{2,l_2}\cdot\mathbf{s}^\top\mathbf{A}^\top(y_{2,l_2}\cdot\mathbf{U}_2 + \mathbf{W}_{2,l_2})]_1,\ [\mathbf{B}_1\mathbf{r}]_2\ )\\
&\cdot e(\ [\mathbf{s}^\top\mathbf{A}^\top]_1,\ [\mathbf{k} + (x_{1,1}\cdot\mathbf{W}_{1,1} + \cdots + x_{1,l_1}\cdot\mathbf{W}_{1,l_1} + x_{2,1}\cdot\mathbf{W}_{2,1} + \cdots + x_{2,l_2}\cdot\mathbf{W}_{2,l_2})\mathbf{B}_1\mathbf{r}]_2\ )^{-1}\\
=&[\langle\mathbf{x}_1, \mathbf{y}_1\rangle\cdot\mathbf{s}^\top\mathbf{A}^\top\mathbf{U}_1\mathbf{B}_1\mathbf{r} + \langle\mathbf{x}_2, \mathbf{y}_2\rangle\cdot\mathbf{s}^\top\mathbf{A}^\top\mathbf{U}_2\mathbf{B}_1\mathbf{r}]_T\cdot[\mathbf{s}^\top\mathbf{A}^\top\mathbf{k}]_T^{-1}\\
&\cdot[\mathbf{s}^\top\mathbf{A}^\top(x_{1,1}\cdot\mathbf{W}_{1,1} + \cdots + x_{1,l_1}\cdot\mathbf{W}_{1,l_1} + x_{2,1}\cdot\mathbf{W}_{2,1} + \cdots + x_{2,l_2}\cdot\mathbf{W}_{2,l_2})\mathbf{B}_1\mathbf{r}]_T\\
&\cdot[\mathbf{s}^\top\mathbf{A}^\top(x_{1,1}\cdot\mathbf{W}_{1,1} + \cdots + x_{1,l_1}\cdot\mathbf{W}_{1,l_1} + x_{2,1}\cdot\mathbf{W}_{2,1} + \cdots + x_{2,l_2}\cdot\mathbf{W}_{2,l_2})\mathbf{B}_1\mathbf{r}]_T^{-1}\\
=&[\mathbf{s}^\top\mathbf{A}^\top\mathbf{k}]_T^{-1}
\end{aligned}$$

The above equation holds because of $\langle\mathbf{x}_1, \mathbf{y}_1\rangle = 0$ and $\langle\mathbf{x}_2, \mathbf{y}_2\rangle = 0$. Thus, the decryption algorithm Dec outputs a correct message, $m' = [\mathbf{s}^\top\mathbf{A}^\top\mathbf{k}]_T\cdot m\cdot[\mathbf{s}^\top\mathbf{A}^\top\mathbf{k}]_T^{-1} = m$. In addition, it also holds that

$$\begin{aligned}
&e((x_{1,1}\odot[\mathbf{A}^\top\mathbf{W}_{1,1}]_1)\cdots(x_{1,l_1}\odot[\mathbf{A}^\top\mathbf{W}_{1,l_1}]_1)\\
&\cdot(x_{2,1}\odot[\mathbf{A}^\top\mathbf{W}_{2,1}]_1)\cdots(x_{2,l_2}\odot[\mathbf{A}^\top\mathbf{W}_{2,l_2}]_1), K_1)\cdot e([\mathbf{A}^\top]_1, K_0)^{-1}\cdot[\mathbf{A}^\top\mathbf{k}]_T\\
=&e([x_{1,1}\cdot\mathbf{A}^\top\mathbf{W}_{1,1}]_1\cdots[x_{1,l_1}\cdot\mathbf{A}^\top\mathbf{W}_{1,l_1}]_1\cdot[x_{2,1}\cdot\mathbf{A}^\top\mathbf{W}_{2,1}]_1\cdots[x_{2,l_2}\cdot\mathbf{A}^\top\mathbf{W}_{2,l_2}]_1, [\mathbf{B}_1\mathbf{r}]_2)\\
&\cdot e([\mathbf{A}^\top]_1, [\mathbf{k} + (x_{1,1}\cdot\mathbf{W}_{1,1} + \cdots + x_{1,l_1}\cdot\mathbf{W}_{1,l_1} + x_{2,1}\cdot\mathbf{W}_{2,1} + \cdots + x_{2,l_2}\cdot\mathbf{W}_{2,l_2})\mathbf{B}_1\mathbf{r}]_2)^{-1}
\end{aligned}$$

$$\begin{aligned}
&\cdot [\mathbf{A}^\top \mathbf{k}]_T \\
=&e([x_{1,1} \cdot \mathbf{A}^\top \mathbf{W}_{1,1}]_1 \cdots [x_{1,l_1} \cdot \mathbf{A}^\top \mathbf{W}_{1,l_1}]_1 \cdot [x_{2,1} \cdot \mathbf{A}^\top \mathbf{W}_{2,1}]_1 \cdots [x_{2,l_2} \cdot \mathbf{A}^\top \mathbf{W}_{2,l_2}]_1, [\mathbf{B}_1 \mathbf{r}]_2) \\
&\cdot e([\mathbf{A}^\top]_1, [(x_{1,1} \cdot \mathbf{W}_{1,1} + \cdots + x_{1,l_1} \cdot \mathbf{W}_{1,l_1} + x_{2,1} \cdot \mathbf{W}_{2,1} + \cdots + x_{2,l_2} \cdot \mathbf{W}_{2,l_2})\mathbf{B}_1 \mathbf{r}]_2)^{-1} \\
&\cdot e([\mathbf{A}^\top]_1, [\mathbf{k}]_2)^{-1} \cdot [\mathbf{A}^\top \mathbf{k}]_T \\
=&[(x_{1,1} \cdot \mathbf{A}^\top \mathbf{W}_{1,1} + \cdots + x_{1,l_1} \cdot \mathbf{A}^\top \mathbf{W}_{1,l_1} + x_{2,1} \cdot \mathbf{A}^\top \mathbf{W}_{2,1} + \cdots + x_{2,l_2} \cdot \mathbf{A}^\top \mathbf{W}_{2,l_2})\mathbf{B}_1 \mathbf{r}]_T \\
&\cdot [(x_{1,1} \cdot \mathbf{A}^\top \mathbf{W}_{1,1} + \cdots + x_{1,l_1} \cdot \mathbf{A}^\top \mathbf{W}_{1,l_1} + x_{2,1} \cdot \mathbf{A}^\top \mathbf{W}_{2,1} + \cdots + x_{2,l_2} \cdot \mathbf{A}^\top \mathbf{W}_{2,l_2})\mathbf{B}_1 \mathbf{r}]_T^{-1} \\
&\cdot [\mathbf{A}^\top \mathbf{k}]_T^{-1} \cdot [\mathbf{A}^\top \mathbf{k}]_T \\
=&[\mathbf{0}]_T.
\end{aligned}$$

Thus, the checking algorithm CheckKey outputs 1.

In all, the dual IPE constructed in Fig. 10 is correct.

Security. We have the following theorem for the public-key dual IPE scheme. Due to space limitations, the proof is given in the full version of this paper.

Theorem 6. *Under the k-LIN assumption and the adaptive secuity of the private-key dual IPE scheme described in Fig. 9, the public-key dual IPE scheme described in Fig. 10 is adaptively secure.*

5.4 A SME Supporting Sigma Protocol

In Sect. 5.2, we show how to construct a SME from a dual IPE. Thus, leveraging the concrete dual IPE in Sect. 5.3, we can obtain a concrete SME. Note that the dual IPE DIPE constructed in Sect. 5.3 is based on the k-LIN assumption (here we pick $k = 1$, i.e., based on the SXDH assumption [12]). In the following, we show that the concrete SME supports Sigma protocols.

We firstly show the main idea of how to transfer the relation $\mathcal{R}_c$ when the underlying SME scheme is constructed from the dual IPE in Sect. 5.3. After that, we give the details of the Sigma protocol.

Main Idea. Recall that the relation of the property of supporting Sigma protocols is as follows:

$$\mathcal{R}_c = \{((\tau_\mathrm{p}, c, pk, \Phi), (w, r_\mathrm{enc})) : c = \mathsf{SME.Enc}(pk, \Phi, \tau_\mathrm{p}, w; r_\mathrm{enc})\}.$$

As shown in Fig. 8, we can know that SME.Enc mainly invokes the encryption algorithm of dual IPE (i.e., DIPE.Enc). Note that when $w \notin \Phi$, SME.Enc would output $\perp$. Thus, directly proving that c is the output by the encryption of DIPE is not enough, since it is also required to guarantee $w \in \Phi$.

A simple idea is to adopt the "OR" technique, such that we can prove that there exists a w in Φ and the ciphertext c for a default message m_dum is generated with a predicate corresponding to w.

Then, what remains is to prove that the ciphertext is well-formed when given a $w \in \Phi$. As introduced in the aforementioned section, the witness w is transferred to $I(w)$. With respect to the algorithm EncodeW, we can know that $I(w)$

only contains a one and other positions are labelled by zeros. Therefore, when adopting DIPE to construct SME, roughly $\mathcal{R}_c$ can be transferred as follows:

$$\mathcal{R}_c^{\mathsf{DIPE}} = \{((\tau_\mathrm{p}, c, pk, \Phi), r_{\mathrm{enc}}) : \vee_{w\in\Phi}(\ (\ c = \mathsf{DIPE.Enc}(pk, (I(w), \tau_\mathrm{p}), \mathsf{m}_{\mathsf{dum}}; r_{\mathrm{enc}}), \text{where } I(w) \text{ has a one and other positions are zeros })\}.$$

Details of the Sigma Protocol. Plugging with the concrete algorithms of DIPE, we can transfer the relation $\mathcal{R}_c^{\mathsf{DIPE}}$ into the following relation $\mathcal{R}'$.

$$\begin{aligned}
\mathcal{R}' = \{((\tau_\mathrm{p}, c, pk, \mathsf{m}_{\mathsf{dum}}, \Phi), \mathbf{s}) : & & /\!/ \ |\Phi| = l_1 \\
(\vee_{i\in[l_1]}\ (\ (C_0 = [\mathbf{s}^\top \mathbf{A}^\top]_1) \wedge (C = [\mathbf{s}^\top \mathbf{A}^\top \mathbf{k}]_T \cdot \mathsf{m}_{\mathsf{dum}}) & & \\
\wedge (C_{1,1} = [\mathbf{s}^\top \mathbf{A}^\top \mathbf{W}_{1,1}]_1) \wedge \ldots & & /\!/ \ I(w)_1 = 0 \ldots \\
\wedge (C_{1,i-1} = [\mathbf{s}^\top \mathbf{A}^\top \mathbf{W}_{1,i-1}]_1) & & /\!/ \ I(w)_{i-1} = 0 \\
\wedge (C_{1,i} = [\mathbf{s}^\top \mathbf{A}^\top (\mathbf{U}_1 + \mathbf{W}_{1,i})]_1) & & /\!/ \ I(w)_i = 1 \\
\wedge (C_{1,i+1} = [\mathbf{s}^\top \mathbf{A}^\top \mathbf{W}_{1,i+1}]_1) \wedge \ \ldots & & /\!/ \ I(w)_{i+1} = 0 \ldots \\
\wedge (C_{1,l_1} = [\mathbf{s}^\top \mathbf{A}^\top \mathbf{W}_{1,l_1}]_1) & & /\!/ \ I(w)_{l_1} = 0 \\
\wedge \ (\wedge_{\iota\in[l_2]} (C_{2,\iota} = [\mathbf{s}^\top \mathbf{A}^\top ((\tau_\mathrm{p})_\iota \mathbf{U}_2 + \mathbf{W}_{2,\iota})]_1))\ )\ )\} & & /\!/ \ \tau_\mathrm{p}
\end{aligned}$$

Then, for each clause, we show that we can construct a Sigma protocol. We denote the jth clause in the relation $\mathcal{R}'$ as $\mathcal{R}'_j$, as shown in the following.

$$\begin{aligned}
\mathcal{R}'_j = \{((\tau_\mathrm{p}, c, pk, \mathsf{m}_{\mathsf{dum}}, j), \mathbf{s}) : & & \\
(C_0 = [\mathbf{s}^\top \mathbf{A}^\top]_1) \wedge (C = [\mathbf{s}^\top \mathbf{A}^\top \mathbf{k}]_T \cdot \mathsf{m}_{\mathsf{dum}}) & & \\
\wedge (C_{1,1} = [\mathbf{s}^\top \mathbf{A}^\top \mathbf{W}_{1,1}]_1) \wedge \ldots & & /\!/ \ I(w)_1 = 0 \ldots \\
\wedge (C_{1,j-1} = [\mathbf{s}^\top \mathbf{A}^\top \mathbf{W}_{1,j-1}]_1) & & /\!/ \ I(w)_{j-1} = 0 \\
\wedge (C_{1,j} = [\mathbf{s}^\top \mathbf{A}^\top (\mathbf{U}_1 + \mathbf{W}_{1,j})]_1) & & /\!/ \ I(w)_j = 1 \\
\wedge (C_{1,j+1} = [\mathbf{s}^\top \mathbf{A}^\top \mathbf{W}_{1,j+1}]_1) \wedge \ \ldots & & /\!/ \ I(w)_{j+1} = 0 \ldots \\
\wedge (C_{1,l_1} = [\mathbf{s}^\top \mathbf{A}^\top \mathbf{W}_{1,l_1}]_1) & & /\!/ \ I(w)_{l_1} = 0 \\
\wedge \ (\wedge_{\iota\in[l_2]} (C_{2,\iota} = [\mathbf{s}^\top \mathbf{A}^\top ((\tau_\mathrm{p})_\iota \mathbf{U}_2 + \mathbf{W}_{2,\iota})]_1))\ \} & & /\!/ \ \tau_\mathrm{p}
\end{aligned}$$

We present our Sigma protocol $\Sigma_{\mathrm{clause}}^{\mathcal{R}'} = (\mathcal{P}, \mathcal{V})$ in Fig. 11 for the relation $\mathcal{R}'_j$, which essentially is an extension of the Chaum-Pedersen protocol [8].

(1) $\mathcal{P}_1(x = (\tau_p, c, pk, \mathsf{m}_{\mathsf{dum}}, j), w = \mathbf{s})$:

$\mathbf{t} \leftarrow \mathbb{Z}_p$, $\mathsf{a}_{C_0} := [\mathbf{t}^\top \mathbf{A}^\top]_1$, $\mathsf{a}_{C_{1,j}} := [\mathbf{t}^\top \mathbf{A}^\top (\mathbf{U}_1 + \mathbf{W}_{1,j})]_1$

For each $i \in [l_1] \backslash \{j\}$: $\mathsf{a}_{C_{1,i}} := [\mathbf{t}^\top \mathbf{A}^\top \mathbf{W}_{1,i})]_1$

For each $\iota \in [l_2]$: $\mathsf{a}_{C_{2,\iota}} := [\mathbf{t}^\top \mathbf{A}^\top ((\tau_p)_\iota \cdot \mathbf{U}_2 + \mathbf{W}_{2,\iota}))]_1$

$\mathsf{a}_C := [\mathbf{t}^\top \mathbf{A}^\top \mathbf{k}]_T$, send $\mathsf{a} := (\mathsf{a}_{C_0}, (\mathsf{a}_{C_{1,i}})_{i\in[l_1]}, (\mathsf{a}_{C_{2,\iota}})_{\iota\in[l_2]}, \mathsf{a}_C)$ to $\mathcal{V}$

(2) $\mathcal{V}_1(\mathsf{a})$: $\mathsf{c} \leftarrow \mathbb{Z}_p$, send c to $\mathcal{P}$

(3) $\mathcal{P}_2(\mathsf{a}, \mathsf{c}, x, w)$: $\mathbf{z_t} := \mathbf{t} - \mathsf{c} \cdot \mathbf{s}$, send $\mathbf{z} := \mathbf{z_t}$ to $\mathcal{V}$

$\mathcal{V}_2(x, \mathsf{a}, \mathsf{c}, \mathbf{z})$:

Parse $x = (\tau_p, c, pk, \mathsf{m}_{\mathsf{dum}}, j)$, $\mathsf{a} = (\mathsf{a}_{C_0}, (\mathsf{a}_{C_{1,i}})_{i\in[l_1]}, (\mathsf{a}_{C_{2,\iota}})_{\iota\in[l_2]}, \mathsf{a}_C)$

$\mathbf{z_t} := \mathbf{z}$, $\mathsf{a}'_{C_0} := [\mathbf{z_t}^\top \mathbf{A}^\top]_1 (\mathsf{c} \odot C_0)$, $\mathsf{a}'_{C_{1,j}} := [\mathbf{z_t}^\top \mathbf{A}^\top (\mathbf{U}_1 + \mathbf{W}_{1,j})]_1 (\mathsf{c} \odot C_{1,j})$

For each $i \in [l_1] \backslash \{j\}$: $\mathsf{a}'_{C_{1,i}} := [\mathbf{z_t}^\top \mathbf{A}^\top \mathbf{W}_{1,i}]_1 (\mathsf{c} \odot C_{1,i})$

For each $\iota \in [l_2]$: $\mathsf{a}'_{C_{2,\iota}} := [\mathbf{z_t}^\top \mathbf{A}^\top ((\tau_p)_\iota \cdot \mathbf{U}_2 + \mathbf{W}_{2,\iota})]_1 (\mathsf{c} \odot C_{2,\iota})$

$\mathsf{a}'_C := [\mathbf{z_t}^\top \mathbf{A}^\top \mathbf{k}]_T \cdot (\mathsf{c} \odot (C/\mathsf{m}_{\mathsf{dum}}))$

If $(\mathsf{a}'_{C_0} = \mathsf{a}_{C_0}) \wedge (\mathsf{a}'_{C_{1,i}} = \mathsf{a}_{C_{1,i}})_{i\in[l_1]} \wedge (\mathsf{a}'_{C_{2,\iota}} = \mathsf{a}_{C_{2,\iota}})_{\iota\in[l_2]} \wedge (\mathsf{a}'_C = \mathsf{a}_C)$: Return 1

Else Return 0

Fig. 11. Algorithms of $\Sigma^{\mathcal{R}'}_{\text{clause}} = (\mathcal{P}, \mathcal{V})$

Due to space limitations, the security analysis of $\Sigma^{\mathcal{R}'}_{\text{clause}}$ is placed in full version of this paper. Recall that we set $k = 1$ for the underlying dual IPE (i.e., based on the SXDH assumption), the communication overhead is listed as follows: 1) the commitment a output by $\mathcal{P}_1$ contains $3(l_1 + l_2) + 2$ elements in $\mathbb{G}_1$ and 1 element in $\mathbb{G}_T$; 2) the challenge c selected by $\mathcal{V}_2$ contains 1 element in $\mathbb{Z}_p$; 3) the response z generated by $\mathcal{P}_2$ contains 1 element in $\mathbb{Z}_p$.

Therefore, the scheme SME constructed above supports Sigma protocols.

5.5 A More Efficient fSMP

Now we discuss a concrete construction for fSMP. More exactly, we adopt Pedersen commitment [26] (for simplicity, the commitment scheme runs over the group $\mathbb{G}_{\mathsf{com}}$ with prime order p, and g and h are two generators of group $\mathbb{G}_{\mathsf{com}}$ where $\log_g h$ is unknown) and the SME scheme introduced in Sect. 5.2 (constructed with a concrete dual IPE introduced in Sect. 5.3).

Firstly, we show that we can construct a Sigma protocol for the internal relation $\widetilde{\mathcal{R}_{\text{sm}}}$ (see in the following). It implies a NIZK for $\widetilde{\mathcal{R}_{\text{sm}}}$ by applying the Fiat-Shamir transform. The size of NIZK proof would be $O(l_1 \cdot \mathsf{poly}(\lambda))$, where l_1 is the size of the set Φ and λ is the security parameter. After that, we discuss how to improve the size of proof for relation $\widetilde{\mathcal{R}_{\text{sm}}}$. Applying self-stacking technique [17], we will show that the size of proof can be logarithmic, i.e., $O((\log l_1) \cdot \mathsf{poly}(\lambda)) = O(\log l_1)$.

A Sigma Protocol for $\widetilde{\mathcal{R}_{\text{sm}}}$. Recall that the relation $\widetilde{\mathcal{R}_{\text{sm}}}$ is as follows:

$$\widetilde{\mathcal{R}_{\text{sm}}} = \{((\tau_{\text{p}}, \mathsf{com}, c, pk, \Phi),(w, r_{\text{com}}, r_{\text{enc}})) : \mathsf{com} = \mathsf{Commit.Com}(pp, w; r_{\text{com}}) \\ \wedge c = \mathsf{SME.Enc}(pk, \Phi, (w, \tau_{\text{p}}); r_{\text{enc}})\}.$$

Following the transformation discussed in Sect. 5.4, the relation $\widetilde{\mathcal{R}_{\text{sm}}}$ can be transferred into the following relation $\mathcal{R}''$.

$$\begin{aligned}
\mathcal{R}'' = \{((g, h, \tau_{\text{p}}, \mathsf{com}, c, pk, \mathsf{m}_{\mathsf{dum}}, \Phi), (r_{\text{com}}, \mathbf{s})) : & \\
(\vee_{i\in[l_1]} \; (\; (\mathsf{com} = g^{\Phi_i} h^{r_{\text{com}}}) & \quad /\!/ \; \Phi_i \text{ is the } i^{th} \text{ element in } \Phi \\
\wedge \; (C_0 = [\mathbf{s}^\top \mathbf{A}^\top]_1) \wedge (C = [\mathbf{s}^\top \mathbf{A}^\top \mathbf{k}]_T \cdot \mathsf{m}_{\mathsf{dum}}) & \\
\wedge \, (C_{1,1} = [\mathbf{s}^\top \mathbf{A}^\top \mathbf{W}_{1,1}]_1) \; \wedge \ldots & \quad /\!/ \; I(w)_1 = 0 \ldots \\
\wedge \, (C_{1,i-1} = [\mathbf{s}^\top \mathbf{A}^\top \mathbf{W}_{1,i-1}]_1) & \quad /\!/ \; I(w)_{i-1} = 0 \\
\wedge \, (C_{1,i} = [\mathbf{s}^\top \mathbf{A}^\top (\mathbf{U}_1 + \mathbf{W}_{1,i})]_1) & \quad /\!/ \; I(w)_i = 1 \\
\wedge \, (C_{1,i+1} = [\mathbf{s}^\top \mathbf{A}^\top \mathbf{W}_{1,i+1}]_1) \; \wedge \; \ldots & \quad /\!/ \; I(w)_{i+1} = 0 \ldots \\
\wedge \, (C_{1,l_1} = [\mathbf{s}^\top \mathbf{A}^\top \mathbf{W}_{1,l_1}]_1) & \quad /\!/ \; I(w)_{l_1} = 0 \\
\wedge \; (\wedge_{\iota\in[l_2]} (C_{2,\iota} = [\mathbf{s}^\top \mathbf{A}^\top ((\tau_{\text{p}})_\iota \mathbf{U}_2 + \mathbf{W}_{2,\iota})]_1)) \;) \;)\} & \quad /\!/ \; \tau_{\text{p}}
\end{aligned}$$

It is clear that we can prove $\mathcal{R}''$ by the composite Sigma protocol. More exactly, we can construct a Sigma protocol for $\mathcal{R}''$ through the following method:

1. Firstly, for each clause $\mathcal{R}''_j$ ($j \in [l_1]$) in $\mathcal{R}''$, we can construct a Sigma protocol $\Sigma^{\mathcal{R}''}_{\text{clause}}$ by adopting the "AND" technique to composite Schnorr's Sigma protocol for the discrete logarithm of the commitment (i.e., knowing the discrete logarithm of (com/g^{Φ_i}) with base h is r_{com}) and the Sigma protocol $\Sigma^{\mathcal{R}'}_{\text{clause}}$ for the SME.
2. Secondly, we can obtain a composite Sigma protocol for relation $\mathcal{R}''$ by adopting the "OR" technique to composite the Sigma protocols for all clause.

We present a Sigma protocol $\Sigma^{\mathcal{R}''}_{\text{clause}}$ in Fig. 12 for a clause $\mathcal{R}''_j$ (see below).

$$\begin{aligned}
\mathcal{R}''_j = \{((g, h, \tau_{\text{p}}, \mathsf{com}, c, pk, \mathsf{m}_{\mathsf{dum}}, \Phi_j, j), (r_{\text{com}}, \mathbf{s})) : & \\
(\mathsf{com} = g^{\Phi_j} h^{r_{\text{com}}}) & \quad /\!/ \; \Phi_j \text{ is the } j^{th} \text{ element in } \Phi \\
\wedge \, (C_0 = [\mathbf{s}^\top \mathbf{A}^\top]_1) \wedge (C = [\mathbf{s}^\top \mathbf{A}^\top \mathbf{k}]_T \cdot \mathsf{m}_{\mathsf{dum}}) & \\
\wedge \, (C_{1,1} = [\mathbf{s}^\top \mathbf{A}^\top \mathbf{W}_{1,1}]_1) \; \wedge \ldots & \quad /\!/ \; I(w)_1 = 0 \ldots \\
\wedge \, (C_{1,j-1} = [\mathbf{s}^\top \mathbf{A}^\top \mathbf{W}_{1,j-1}]_1) & \quad /\!/ \; I(w)_{j-1} = 0 \\
\wedge \, (C_{1,j} = [\mathbf{s}^\top \mathbf{A}^\top (\mathbf{U}_1 + \mathbf{W}_{1,j})]_1) & \quad /\!/ \; I(w)_j = 1 \\
\wedge \, (C_{1,j+1} = [\mathbf{s}^\top \mathbf{A}^\top \mathbf{W}_{1,j+1}]_1) \; \wedge \; \ldots & \quad /\!/ \; I(w)_{j+1} = 0 \ldots \\
\wedge \, (C_{1,l_1} = [\mathbf{s}^\top \mathbf{A}^\top \mathbf{W}_{1,l_1}]_1) & \quad /\!/ \; I(w)_{l_1} = 0 \\
\wedge \; (\wedge_{\iota\in[l_2]} (C_{2,\iota} = [\mathbf{s}^\top \mathbf{A}^\top ((\tau_{\text{p}})_\iota \mathbf{U}_2 + \mathbf{W}_{2,\iota})]_1)) \; \} & \quad /\!/ \; \tau_{\text{p}}
\end{aligned}$$

(1) $\mathcal{P}_1(x = (g, h, \tau_{\mathsf{p}}, \mathsf{com}, c, pk, \mathsf{m_{dum}}, \Phi_j, j), w = (r_{\mathrm{com}}, \mathbf{s}))$:

$t_{\mathsf{com}} \leftarrow \mathbb{Z}_p$, $\mathsf{a_{com}} := h^{t_{\mathsf{com}}}$

$\mathbf{t} \leftarrow \mathbb{Z}_p$, $\mathsf{a}_{C_0} := [\mathbf{t}^\top \mathbf{A}^\top]_1$, $\mathsf{a}_{C_{1,j}} := [\mathbf{t}^\top \mathbf{A}^\top(\mathbf{U}_1 + \mathbf{W}_{1,j})]_1$

For each $i \in [l_1] \backslash \{j\}$: $\mathsf{a}_{C_{1,i}} := [\mathbf{t}^\top \mathbf{A}^\top \mathbf{W}_{1,i})]_1$

For each $\iota \in [l_2]$: $\mathsf{a}_{C_{2,\iota}} := [\mathbf{t}^\top \mathbf{A}^\top((\tau_{\mathsf{p}})_\iota \cdot \mathbf{U}_2 + \mathbf{W}_{2,\iota}))]_1$

$\mathsf{a}_C := [\mathbf{t}^\top \mathbf{A}^\top \mathbf{k}]_T$, send $\mathsf{a} := (\mathsf{a_{com}}, \mathsf{a}_{C_0}, (\mathsf{a}_{C_{1,i}})_{i\in[l_1]}, (\mathsf{a}_{C_{2,\iota}})_{\iota\in[l_2]}, \mathsf{a}_C)$ to $\mathcal{V}$

(2) $\mathcal{V}_1(\mathsf{a})$: $\mathsf{c} \leftarrow \mathbb{Z}_p$, send c to $\mathcal{P}$

(3) $\mathcal{P}_2(\mathsf{a}, \mathsf{c}, x, w)$: $\mathsf{z_{com}} := t_{\mathsf{com}} - \mathsf{c} \cdot r_{\mathrm{com}}$, $\mathbf{z_t} := \mathbf{t} - \mathsf{c} \cdot \mathbf{s}$, send $\mathsf{z} := (\mathsf{z_{com}}, \mathbf{z_t})$ to $\mathcal{V}$

$\mathcal{V}_2(x, \mathsf{a}, \mathsf{c}, \mathsf{z})$:

Parse $x = (g, h, \tau_{\mathsf{p}}, \mathsf{com}, \mathsf{c}, pk, \mathsf{m_{dum}}, \Phi_j, j)$

Parse $\mathsf{a} = (\mathsf{a_{com}}, \mathsf{a}_{C_0}, (\mathsf{a}_{C_{1,i}})_{i\in[l_1]}, (\mathsf{a}_{C_{2,\iota}})_{\iota\in[l_2]}, \mathsf{a}_C)$, $\mathsf{z} = (\mathsf{z_{com}}, \mathbf{z_t})$

$\mathsf{a}'_{\mathsf{com}} := h^{\mathsf{z_{com}}}(\mathsf{com}/g^{\Phi_j})^{\mathsf{c}}$, $\mathsf{a}'_{C_0} := [\mathbf{z_t}^\top \mathbf{A}^\top]_1(\mathsf{c} \odot C_0)$

$\mathsf{a}'_{C_{1,j}} := [\mathbf{z_t}^\top \mathbf{A}^\top(\mathbf{U}_1 + \mathbf{W}_{1,j})]_1(\mathsf{c} \odot C_{1,j})$

For each $i \in [l_1] \backslash \{j\}$: $\mathsf{a}'_{C_{1,i}} := [\mathbf{z_t}^\top \mathbf{A}^\top \mathbf{W}_{1,i}]_1(\mathsf{c} \odot C_{1,i})$

For each $\iota \in [l_2]$: $\mathsf{a}'_{C_{2,\iota}} := [\mathbf{z_t}^\top \mathbf{A}^\top((\tau_{\mathsf{p}})_\iota \cdot \mathbf{U}_2 + \mathbf{W}_{2,\iota})]_1(\mathsf{c} \odot C_{2,\iota})$

$\mathsf{a}'_C := [\mathbf{z_t}^\top \mathbf{A}^\top \mathbf{k}]_T \cdot (\mathsf{c} \odot (C/\mathsf{m_{dum}}))$

If $(\mathsf{a}'_{\mathsf{com}} = \mathsf{a_{com}}) \wedge (\mathsf{a}'_{C_0} = \mathsf{a}_{C_0}) \wedge (\mathsf{a}'_{C_{1,i}} = \mathsf{a}_{C_{1,i}})_{i\in[l_1]} \wedge (\mathsf{a}'_{C_{2,\iota}} = \mathsf{a}_{C_{2,\iota}})_{\iota\in[l_2]}$

$\wedge(\mathsf{a}'_C = \mathsf{a}_C)$: Return 1

Else Return 0

Fig. 12. Algorithms of $\Sigma^{\mathcal{R}''}_{\text{clause}} = (\mathcal{P}, \mathcal{V})$

Since the Sigma protocol $\Sigma^{\mathcal{R}''}_{\text{clause}}$ for $\mathcal{R}''_j$ is obtained by compositing Schnorr's Sigma protocol and $\Sigma^{\mathcal{R}'}_{\text{clause}}$ for relation $\mathcal{R}'_j$ (as shown in Sect. 5.4) using an "AND" combination, the security of $\Sigma^{\mathcal{R}''}_{\text{clause}}$ is well guaranteed. Here we omit the discussions on its security.

Recall that we set $k = 1$ for the underlying dual IPE (i.e., based on the SXDH assumption), so the communication overhead of $\Sigma^{\mathcal{R}''}_{\text{clause}}$ would be 1 element in $\mathbb{G}_{\mathsf{com}}$, $3(l_1 + l_2) + 2$ elements in $\mathbb{G}_1$, 1 element in $\mathbb{G}_T$ and 3 elements in $\mathbb{Z}_p$. Thus, it can be inferred that using the conventional composition method, the total communication overhead would be $O(l_1(l_1 + l_2))$ (since there are l_1 clauses). By applying the Fiat-Shamir transform to the composited Sigma protocol[4], we can obtain a NIZK for $\widetilde{\mathcal{R}_{\text{sm}}}$ and the proof size would be $3l_1$ elements in $\mathbb{Z}_p$, where $2l_1$ elements are the responses (i.e., all z's for all clauses) and l_1 elements are the challenges for all clauses.

Proofs with Shorter Size. In [17], Goel et al. present a general framework for composing *stackable Sigma protocols* for disjunctions in which communication depends on the size of the largest clause. Notably, they also demonstrate the

[4] Note that the Sigma protocol $\Sigma^{\mathcal{R}''}_{\text{clause}}$ supports that the verifier can recover the commitment via the responses and the challenge, so we can save the proof size by only sending the responds to the verifier as the proof.

stackability of several classic Sigma protocols, including Schnorr's Sigma protocol [29] and the Chaum-Pedersen protocol [8].

We will show that the Sigma protocol $\Sigma^{\mathcal{R}''}_{\text{clause}}$ is stackable. Then, according to the theorem of self stacking (see in [17]), we can achieve a compiled Sigma protocol by utilizing the self-stacking technique [17] and we can know that its communication complexity is linearly proportional to the largest communication cost among these clauses. Note that in $\mathcal{R}''$, we can run $\Sigma^{\mathcal{R}''}_{\text{clause}}$ for every clause, so every clause has the same communication cost. Thus, the communication complexity of the compiled Sigma protocol is linearly proportional to the communication overhead of $\Sigma^{\mathcal{R}''}_{\text{clause}}$.

We have the following theorem. Due to space limitations, the proof for Theorem 7 is provided in the full version of this paper.

Theorem 7. *The Sigma protocol* $\Sigma^{\mathcal{R}''}_{\text{clause}}$ *in Fig. 12 is a stackable Sigma protocol.*

Communication Complexity. Here, we follow the analysis in [17]. Let $\mathsf{CC}(\Sigma)$ be the communication complexity of $\Sigma^{\mathcal{R}''}_{\text{clause}}$ for the relation $\mathcal{R}''_j$ and Σ_{l_1} denote the compiled Sigma protocol for $\mathcal{R}''$. Let $|\mathsf{Size}(\mathsf{VCommit})|$ be the size of the 1-out-of-l binding vector commitment scheme (please refer its definition to [17]), which is independent of $\mathsf{CC}(\Sigma)$ and only depends on the security parameter λ. We have $\mathsf{CC}(\Sigma_{l_1}) = \mathsf{CC}(\Sigma) + 2(\log l_1)(|\mathsf{Size}(\mathsf{VCommit})|) = O(\mathsf{CC}(\Sigma) + (\log l_1) \cdot \mathsf{poly}(\lambda))$. Thus, when applying the Fiat-Shamir transform, the proof size would be $O((\log l_1) \cdot \mathsf{poly}(\lambda)) = O(\log l_1)$.

Acknowledgements. We would like to express our sincere appreciation to Junqing Gong for his valuable suggestions on the inner-product encryption! We also want to express our sincere appreciation to the anonymous reviewers for their valuable comments and suggestions! Gongxian Zeng and Zhengan Huang was supported by The Major Key Project of PCL (PCL2023A09). Junzuo Lai was supported by National Natural Science Foundation of China under Grant No. U2001205, Guangdong Basic and Applied Basic Research Foundation (Grant No. 2023B1515040020), Industrial project No. TC20200930001. Jian Weng was supported by National Natural Science Foundation of China under Grant Nos. 61825203, 62332007 and U22B2028, Major Program of Guangdong Basic and Applied Research Project under Grant No. 2019B030302008, Guangdong Provincial Science and Technology Project under Grant No. 2021A0505030033, Science and Technology Major Project of Tibetan Autonomous Region of China under Grant No. XZ202201ZD0006G, National Joint Engineering Research Center of Network Security Detection and Protection Technology, Guangdong Key Laboratory of Data Security and Privacy Preserving, Guangdong Hong Kong Joint Laboratory for Data Security and Privacy Protection, and Engineering Research Center of Trustworthy AI, Ministry of Education. This research is supported by the National Research Foundation, Singapore under its Strategic Capability Research Centres Funding Initiative. Any opinions, findings and conclusions or recommendations expressed in this material are those of the author(s) and do not reflect the views of National Research Foundation, Singapore.

References

1. Blum, M., Feldman, P., Micali, S.: Non-interactive zero-knowledge and its applications (extended abstract). In: STOC 1988, pp. 103–112. ACM (1988)
2. Boneh, D., Sahai, A., Waters, B.: Functional encryption: definitions and challenges. In: Ishai, Y. (ed.) TCC 2011. LNCS, vol. 6597, pp. 253–273. Springer, Heidelberg (2011). https://doi.org/10.1007/978-3-642-19571-6_16
3. Boneh, D., Shoup, V.: A graduate course in applied cryptography. Draft 0.6 (2023)
4. Bunz, B., Bootle, J., Boneh, D., Poelstra, A., Wuille, P., Maxwell, G.: Bulletproofs: short proofs for confidential transactions and more. In: S&P 2018, pp. 315–334. IEEE (2018)
5. Camenisch, J., Chaabouni, R., Shelat, A.: Efficient protocols for set membership and range proofs. In: Pieprzyk, J. (ed.) ASIACRYPT 2008. LNCS, vol. 5350, pp. 234–252. Springer, Heidelberg (2008). https://doi.org/10.1007/978-3-540-89255-7_15
6. Camenisch, J., Hohenberger, S., Lysyanskaya, A.: Compact E-Cash. In: Cramer, R. (ed.) EUROCRYPT 2005. LNCS, vol. 3494, pp. 302–321. Springer, Heidelberg (2005). https://doi.org/10.1007/11426639_18
7. Camenisch, J., Lysyanskaya, A.: An efficient system for non-transferable anonymous credentials with optional anonymity revocation. In: Pfitzmann, B. (ed.) EUROCRYPT 2001. LNCS, vol. 2045, pp. 93–118. Springer, Heidelberg (2001). https://doi.org/10.1007/3-540-44987-6_7
8. Chaum, D., Pedersen, T.P.: Wallet databases with observers. In: Brickell, E.F. (ed.) CRYPTO 1992. LNCS, vol. 740, pp. 89–105. Springer, Heidelberg (1993). https://doi.org/10.1007/3-540-48071-4_7
9. Chaum, D., van Heyst, E.: Group signatures. In: Davies, D.W. (ed.) EUROCRYPT 1991. LNCS, vol. 547, pp. 257–265. Springer, Heidelberg (1991). https://doi.org/10.1007/3-540-46416-6_22
10. Chen, J., Gay, R., Wee, H.: Improved dual system ABE in prime-order groups via predicate encodings. In: Oswald, E., Fischlin, M. (eds.) EUROCRYPT 2015. LNCS, vol. 9057, pp. 595–624. Springer, Heidelberg (2015). https://doi.org/10.1007/978-3-662-46803-6_20
11. Chen, J., Gong, J., Kowalczyk, L., Wee, H.: Unbounded ABE via bilinear entropy expansion, revisited. In: Nielsen, J.B., Rijmen, V. (eds.) EUROCRYPT 2018. LNCS, vol. 10820, pp. 503–534. Springer, Cham (2018). https://doi.org/10.1007/978-3-319-78381-9_19
12. Chen, J., Gong, J., Wee, H.: Improved inner-product encryption with adaptive security and full attribute-hiding. In: Peyrin, T., Galbraith, S. (eds.) ASIACRYPT 2018. LNCS, vol. 11273, pp. 673–702. Springer, Cham (2018). https://doi.org/10.1007/978-3-030-03329-3_23
13. Couteau, G., Kloß, M., Lin, H., Reichle, M.: Efficient range proofs with transparent setup from bounded integer commitments. In: Canteaut, A., Standaert, F.-X. (eds.) EUROCRYPT 2021. LNCS, vol. 12698, pp. 247–277. Springer, Cham (2021). https://doi.org/10.1007/978-3-030-77883-5_9
14. Escala, A., Herold, G., Kiltz, E., Ràfols, C., Villar, J.: An algebraic framework for diffie-hellman assumptions. J. Cryptology **30**, 242–288 (2017)
15. Feige, U., Lapidot, D., Shamir, A.: Multiple noninteractive zero knowledge proofs under general assumptions. SIAM J. Comput. **29**(1), 1–28 (1999)

16. Fiat, A., Shamir, A.: How To prove yourself: practical solutions to identification and signature problems. In: Odlyzko, A.M. (ed.) CRYPTO 1986. LNCS, vol. 263, pp. 186–194. Springer, Heidelberg (1987). https://doi.org/10.1007/3-540-47721-7_12
17. Goel, A., Green, M., Hall-Andersen, M., Kaptchuk, G.: Stacking sigmas: a framework to Compose Σ-protocols for disjunctions. In: EUROCRYPT 2022, pp. 458–487. Springer (2022). https://doi.org/10.1007/978-3-031-07085-3_16
18. Goldwasser, S.: How to play any mental game, or a completeness theorem for protocols with an honest majority. In: STOC 1987, pp. 218–229 (1987)
19. Goldwasser, S., Micali, S., Rackoff, C.: The knowledge complexity of interactive proof systems. SIAM J. Comput. **18**(1), 186–208 (1989)
20. Lewko, A., Okamoto, T., Sahai, A., Takashima, K., Waters, B.: Fully secure functional encryption: attribute-based encryption and (hierarchical) inner product encryption. In: Gilbert, H. (ed.) EUROCRYPT 2010. LNCS, vol. 6110, pp. 62–91. Springer, Heidelberg (2010). https://doi.org/10.1007/978-3-642-13190-5_4
21. McCorry, P., Shahandashti, S.F., Hao, F.: A smart contract for boardroom voting with maximum voter privacy. In: Kiayias, A. (ed.) FC 2017. LNCS, vol. 10322, pp. 357–375. Springer, Cham (2017). https://doi.org/10.1007/978-3-319-70972-7_20
22. Okamoto, T.: An efficient divisible electronic cash scheme. In: Coppersmith, D. (ed.) CRYPTO 1995. LNCS, vol. 963, pp. 438–451. Springer, Heidelberg (1995). https://doi.org/10.1007/3-540-44750-4_35
23. Okamoto, T., Takashima, K.: Hierarchical predicate encryption for inner-products. In: Matsui, M. (ed.) ASIACRYPT 2009. LNCS, vol. 5912, pp. 214–231. Springer, Heidelberg (2009). https://doi.org/10.1007/978-3-642-10366-7_13
24. Okamoto, T., Takashima, K.: Adaptively attribute-hiding (hierarchical) inner product encryption. In: Pointcheval, D., Johansson, T. (eds.) EUROCRYPT 2012. LNCS, vol. 7237, pp. 591–608. Springer, Heidelberg (2012). https://doi.org/10.1007/978-3-642-29011-4_35
25. O'Neill, A.: Definitional issues in functional encryption. Cryptology ePrint Archive (2010)
26. Pedersen, T.P.: Non-interactive and information-theoretic secure verifiable secret sharing. In: Feigenbaum, J. (ed.) CRYPTO 1991. LNCS, vol. 576, pp. 129–140. Springer, Heidelberg (1992). https://doi.org/10.1007/3-540-46766-1_9
27. Sahai, A.: Non-malleable non-interactive zero knowledge and adaptive chosen-ciphertext security. In: FOCS 1999, pp. 543–553. IEEE Computer Society (1999)
28. Sasson, E.B., et al.: Zerocash: decentralized anonymous payments from bitcoin. In: S&P 2014, pp. 459–474. IEEE (2014)
29. Schnorr, C.P.: Efficient identification and signatures for smart cards. In: Brassard, G. (ed.) CRYPTO 1989. LNCS, vol. 435, pp. 239–252. Springer, New York (1990). https://doi.org/10.1007/0-387-34805-0_22
30. Tan, S.-Y., Groß, T.: MoniPoly—an expressive q-SDH-based anonymous attribute-based credential system. In: Moriai, S., Wang, H. (eds.) ASIACRYPT 2020. LNCS, vol. 12493, pp. 498–526. Springer, Cham (2020). https://doi.org/10.1007/978-3-030-64840-4_17
31. Wee, H.: Attribute-hiding predicate encryption in bilinear groups, revisited. In: Kalai, Y., Reyzin, L. (eds.) TCC 2017. LNCS, vol. 10677, pp. 206–233. Springer, Cham (2017). https://doi.org/10.1007/978-3-319-70500-2_8
32. Zhang, Y.: Introducing zkEVM (2022). https://scroll.io/blog/zkEVM

Zero-Knowledge Functional Elementary Databases

Xinxuan Zhang[1,2] and Yi Deng[1,2(✉)]

[1] State Key Laboratory of Information Security, Institute of Information Engineering, Chinese Academy of Sciences, Beijing, China
{zhangxinxuan,deng}@iie.ac.cn

[2] School of Cyber Security, University of Chinese Academy of Sciences, Beijing, China

Abstract. Zero-knowledge elementary databases (ZK-EDBs) enable a prover to commit a database D of key-value (x, v) pairs and later provide a convincing answer to the query "send me the value $D(x)$ associated with x" without revealing any extra knowledge (including the size of D). After its introduction, several works extended it to allow more expressive queries, but the expressiveness achieved so far is still limited: only a relatively simple queries–range queries over the keys and values– can be handled by known constructions.

In this paper we introduce a new notion called *zero knowledge functional elementary databases* (ZK-FEDBs), which allows the most general functional queries. Roughly speaking, for any Boolean circuit f, ZK-FEDBs allows the ZK-EDB prover to provide convincing answers to the queries of the form "send me all records (x, v) in D satisfying $f(x, v) = 1$," without revealing any extra knowledge (including the size of D). We present a construction of ZK-FEDBs in the random oracle model and generic group model, whose proof size is only linear in the length of record and the size of query circuit, and is independent of the size of input database D.

Our technical contribution is two-fold. Firstly, we introduce a new variant of zero-knowledge sets (ZKS) which supports combined operations on sets, and present a concrete construction that is based on groups with unknown order. Secondly, we develop a transformation that transforms the query of Boolean circuit into a query of combined operations on related sets, which may be of independent interest.

1 Introduction

Zero-knowledge sets (ZKS) are a valuable primitive introduced by Micali *et al.* [31], which enable a prover to commit a finite set S and later prove the membership or non-membership of any element without revealing any extra knowledge (including the size of the set). An Elementary Database (EDB) D is a partial function mapping a (sub)set of keys into values (i.e., a set of key-value pairs (x, v) such that no two pairs have equivalent keys but different values). As described

J. Guo and R. Steinfeld (Eds.): ASIACRYPT 2023, LNCS 14442, pp. 269–303, 2023.
https://doi.org/10.1007/978-981-99-8733-7_9

in [31], the concept of ZKS can be extended to the one called zero-knowledge elementary databases (ZK-EDBs), which allows the prover to commit an EDB D and later prove that "x belongs to the support of D and $D(x) = v$" or that "x does not belong to the support of D" without revealing any knowledge beyond that. A number of ZK-EDB constructions have since emerged such as updatable ZK-EDBs [29], independent ZK-EDBs [22] and efficient ZK-EDBs [11,28], but, most constructions follow the paradigm of Chase *et al.* [13], which relies on a Merkle tree and mercurial commitment and is not suitable to support richer queries.

Libert *et al.* [27] recently introduced zero-knowledge expressive elementary databases (ZK-EEDBs) that support the following richer queries: a) range query $[a_x, b_x]$, to which prover responds with all records $(x, v) \in D$ whose key x lies within $[a_x, b_x]$; b) range query $[a_v, b_v]$, to which prover responds with all records $(x, v) \in D$ whose value v is within the range $[a_v, b_v]$, and c) natural combination of range query $[a_x, b_x] \times [a_v, b_v]$. These techniques can be further exploited to support several other interesting queries such as k-nearest neighbours and k-minimum/maximum.

Despite the advancements made thus far, the expressivity of the known ZK-EDBs constructions is still very limited. For example, known constructions cannot even handle the simple query "send me all records $(x, v) \in D$ where the last bit of value v is zero", let alone the general Boolean circuit f query that requests to return all records $(x, v) \in D$ satisfying $f(x, v) = 1$.

Besides the theoretical value in ZK-EDB, enabling general function queries will have many practical applications. For instance, append-only ZK-EDBs are recently used to construct Key Transparency (KT) systems [12,15], which maintain an auditable directory of the pairs of user's ID and their public keys while securely answer the queries for public key associated with certain ID in a consistent manner, even when the service provider is untrusted. ZK-EDBs with more expressive queries can improve the functionality of the KT system, allowing clients to more flexibly query public keys. Specifically, users can add labels or other short information to their IDs, such as a CV of a job hunter. Clients can then send queries to the service provider to obtain all public keys associated with IDs that meet their requirements, e.g., an HR can query the service provider to get all job hunters' public keys whose CVs satisfy certain requirement.

1.1 Our Contribution

In this paper, we introduce a new concept called zero-knowledge functional elementary databases (ZK-FEDBs), which allows the most general function queries. Specifically, ZK-FEDBs enable one to commit an elementary database D of key-value pairs $(x, v) \in \{0,1\}^\ell \times \{0,1\}^\ell$ and then, for any Boolean circuit $f : \{0,1\}^{2\ell} \to \{0,1\}$, convincingly answer the query "Send me all records $(x, v) \in D$ satisfying $f(x, v) = 1$", without revealing any extra knowledge (including the size of D).

We present a construction of ZK-FEDBs based on groups of unknown orders, and prove its security in the random oracle model and generic group model.

Its proof size is only linear in the length of record and the size of circuit f, independent of the size of input database D. Prior to our approach, the most expressive queries achievable were limited to range queries over keys and values, as demonstrated by Libert *et al.* [27].

Our technical contribution is two-fold (explained in detail below). Firstly, we introduce a new variant of zero-knowledge sets (ZKS) which supports combined operations on sets, and present a concrete construction that is based on groups with unknown order. Secondly, we develop a transformation that transforms the query of Boolean circuit into a query of combined operations on related sets, which may be of independent interest.

1.2 Technique Overview

A naive attempt to construct ZK-FEDBs is to use zero-knowledge succinct non-interactive arguments of knowledge (zk-SNARKs). Specifically, one can use a SNARK-friendly hash function alone or, like most existing ZK-EDBs, use a Merkle tree to create a commitment for the database, and then use zk-SNARKs to generate proofs for queries. However, almost all zk-SNARKs expose the length of the witness. And for the commitment methods mentioned above, the witness must include all records in database to ensure the correctness of function queries. Therefore, this attempt would fail due to the potential revelation of the database size. The same issue will also arise when using other general-purpose zero-knowledge protocols.

RSA Accumulator as ZKS and Its Limitations. Our start point is RSA accumulator, which is close to ZKS except that it offers no privacy. Let $\mathcal{H}_{prime}$ be a hash function mapping an element in set S into a prime. RSA accumulator computes $\mathsf{g}^{\Pi_{i\in[m]}p_i}$ to commit set $S = \{x_i\}_{i\in[m]}$, where $p_i = \mathcal{H}_{prime}(x_i)$.

Now we consider the three basic set operations, i.e., intersection, union and set-difference, on accumulators. It is a widely used approach to reduce set operation relations to several simpler set relations [23,35,46]. Taking intersection as an example. Note that, $I = S_0 \cap S_1$ if and only if there exists $J_0 := S_0 \backslash I$ and $J_1 := S_1 \backslash I$ such that (J_0, J_1) belongs to disjoint relation $\{(J_0, J_1) | J_0 \cap J_1 = \emptyset\}$, and both (S_0, I, J_0) and (S_1, I, J_1) belong to union among disjoint relation $\{(U, J_0, J_1) | \ U = J_0 \cup J_1 \ \wedge \ J_0 \cap J_1 = \emptyset\}$.

Thus, given three RSA accumulators $\mathsf{C}_I, \mathsf{C}_{S_0}, \mathsf{C}_{S_1}$ to sets I, S_0, S_1, proving $I = S_0 \cap S_1$ is equivalent to prove the following statements: there exist accumulators $\mathsf{C}_{J_0}, \mathsf{C}_{J_1}$ to sets J_0 and J_1 such that a) the *committed* sets (J_0, J_1) belongs to disjoint relation, and b) the *committed* sets (S_0, I, J_0) and (S_1, I, J_1) belong to union among disjoint relation. It is easy to verify that these two items a) and b) are equivalent to the following two conditions respectively:

a′) $(\mathsf{C}_{J_0}, \mathsf{C}_{J_1})$ belongs to co-prime relations $\{(\mathsf{C}_1, \mathsf{C}_2) | \exists a, b \in \mathbb{Z} \ s.t. \ \gcd(a, b) = 1 \wedge (\mathsf{C}_1, \mathsf{C}_2) = (\mathsf{g}^a, \mathsf{g}^b)\}$.

b′) Both $(\mathsf{C}_I, \mathsf{C}_{J_0})$ and $(\mathsf{C}_I, \mathsf{C}_{J_1})$ belong to co-prime relations, and both $(\mathsf{C}_{S_0}, \mathsf{C}_I, \mathsf{C}_{J_0})$ and $(\mathsf{C}_{S_0}, \mathsf{C}_I, \mathsf{C}_{J_1})$ are DDH tuples.

All of them can be proved easily relying on Boneh's PoKE (Proof of knowledge of exponent) protocol and its variants [4]. The other two basic set-operation relations on accumulators, can also be proved in a similar manners.

As in [41,42], one can achieve privacy and obtain a ZKS scheme by using randomness r in computing the commitment $\mathsf{g}^{r\Pi_{i\in[m]}p_i}$ to S. However, the introduction of randomness would invalidate the proof of basic set-operation relations on commitments. Specifically, for this ZKS, the disjoint relations and the union among disjoint sets relations on *committed* sets can no longer be equivalent to co-prime relations and DDH relations over RSA groups.

Zero-Knowledge Sets with Set-Operation Queries. Our key observation is that the randomness r in above ZKS scheme can be chosen from small and bounded range of $[0, B]$. This leads to that, for sets S_0, S_1, U satisfying $S_0 \cap S_1 = \emptyset, S_0 \cup S_1 = U$ and their commitments $\mathsf{C}_{S_0}, \mathsf{C}_{S_1}, \mathsf{C}_U$, we have:

$a'')$ The greatest common divisor of the exponents of commitments $\mathsf{C}_{S_0}, \mathsf{C}_{S_1}$ is small. We call such a tuple $(\mathsf{C}_{S_0}, \mathsf{C}_{S_1})$ as a *pseudo-coprime exponent* tuple.

$b'')$ The commitment tuple $(\mathsf{C}_{S_0}, \mathsf{C}_{S_1}, \mathsf{C}_U)$ is close to a DDH tuple. We call such a tuple $(\mathsf{C}_{S_0}, \mathsf{C}_{S_1}, \mathsf{C}_U)$ as a *pseudo-DDH* tuple.

We present a series of NIZK protocols to prove the above pseudo-relations. Though these NIZK protocols achieve somewhat weaker soundness, they are sufficient for our applications.

We further consider more general combined operations on sets, and regard it as a "circuit" with gates "intersection", "union" and "set-difference" in a natural way. To construct a ZKS supporting combined operations on sets (i.e., a ZKS that allows prover to convincingly answer the query "send me all records in $\mathcal{Q}(S_1, \cdots, S_m)$" for any "circuit" $\mathcal{Q}$ and committed sets $\{S_i\}_{i\in[m]}$), the prover can use above NIZK proofs to demonstrate that each gate/set-operation is performed honestly.

From Boolean Circuit Queries to Set-Operation. A crucial step toward our construction of ZK-FEDBs is a transformation that transform a query of Boolean circuit f over a set S (requesting $S_{output} := \{x | x \in S \wedge f(x) = 1\}$) into a query of combined operations $\mathcal{Q}$ on related sets $S_i^b = \{x | x \in S \wedge \text{the i-th bit of "}x\text{" is } b\}$ (requesting $S_{output} := \mathcal{Q}(\{S_i^b\})$).

This transformation proceeds as follows. Let the number of input wires of f be n. We first associate each input wire i of f with two subsets $\{S_i^b\}_{b\in\{0,1\}}$ of S, which are defined as above. Sequentially, for each gate in f, we associate its output wire i $(i > n)$ with two subsets $\{S_i^b\}_{b\in\{0,1\}}$, which are defined in the following way:

- For an AND gate with two input wires a, b and an output wire c, the two sets associated with wire c are set to be $S_c^0 = S_a^0 \cup S_b^0$ and $S_c^1 = S_a^1 \cap S_b^1$.
- For an OR gate with two input wires a, b and an output wire c, the two sets associated with wire c are set to be $S_c^0 = S_a^0 \cap S_b^0$ and $S_c^1 = S_a^1 \cup S_b^1$.
- For a NOT gate with an input wire a and an output wire b, the two sets associated with wire c are set to be $S_b^0 = S_a^1$ and $S_b^1 = S_b^0$.

In the ending, the second set S_ℓ^1 associated with the output wire ℓ of f is now a result of a circuit $\mathcal{Q}$ of combined operations on the sets $\{S_i^b\}$ associated with the input wires, i.e., $S_\ell^1 = \mathcal{Q}(\{S_i^b\})$.

One can check that the above resulting set S_ℓ^1 is exactly the set $S_{output} := \{x | x \in S \wedge f(x) = 1\}$. A crucial observation here is that, for each x belonging to S and each wire i, $x \in S_i^b$ if and only if the value of i-th wire of $f(x)$ is b. Therefore S_ℓ^b is the set of x that makes the output wire of f equaling to b, which means that $S_\ell^1 = \{x | x \in S \wedge f(x) = 1\}$.

A simple example of transforming $f(x) = \bar{x}_1 \wedge \bar{x}_2 \vee (\neg \bar{x}_3)$ (where $x = \bar{x}_1 \| \bar{x}_2 \| \bar{x}_3 \in \{0,1\}^3$) is shown in Fig. 1.

$$S_4^0 = S_1^0 \cup S_2^0$$
$$S_4^1 = S_1^1 \cap S_2^1$$
$$S_5^0 = S_3^1$$
$$S_5^1 = S_3^0$$
$$S_6^0 = S_4^0 \cap S_5^0 = S_1^0 \cup S_2^0 \cap S_3^1$$
$$S_6^1 = S_4^1 \cup S_5^1 = S_1^1 \cap S_2^1 \cup S_3^0$$

Output set :
$$S_{output} = S_6^1 = S_1^1 \cap S_2^1 \cup S_3^0$$

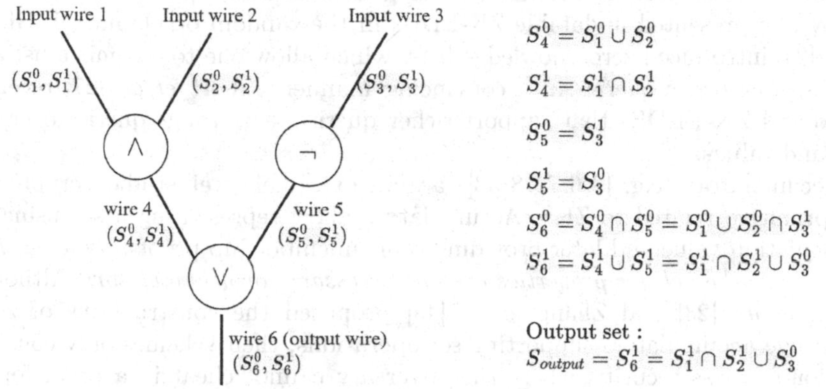

Fig. 1.

Finally, we construct ZK-FEDBs using ZKS with set-operation queries and standard ZK-EDBs. Roughly, we use the former to ensure the correctness of function queries and the latter to ensure the correctness of associated values. Furthermore, we construct a constant-size ZK-EDB in conjunction with standard batch techniques, and achieve a ZK-FEDB with a proof size that is only linear in the length of the record and the size of the circuit f, and is independent of the size of the input database D.

1.3 Related Work

Since the notion of ZK-EDB was first introduced by Micali et al. [31], numerous works concentrating on the performance, security, and functionality of ZK-EDB have been developed.

In [13], Chase et al. introduced the notion of mercurial commitments and presented a widely used paradigm to construct a ZK-EDB. Mercurial commitments (and thus ZK-EDBs) can be constructed through one-way functions [9], and efficient mercurial commitments (and thus efficient ZK-EDBs) can be constructed through DL, Factoring, RSA or LWE assumption [9,27,47]. The notion of q-mercurial commitments were introduced and developed in [10,11,28] to further compress the (non-)membership proof size of ZK-EDBs. Li *et al.* [26] introduced concise mercurial subvector commitments and achieved batch verifiable ZK-EDBs.

There are also several works focusing on developing the security definition of ZK-EDBs, such as independent ZK-EDBs [22] and secure database commitments [14]. Prabhakaran and Xue [36] put forward statistically hiding set and present its construction from RSA accumulators. Following [36,41,42] constructed a constant-size ZKS.

Another research point of ZK-EDBs is how to extend its functionality. Ostrovsky et al. [34] explored generating consistency proofs for queries on a committed database and present a concrete construction for range queries over the keys. Liskov [29] presented updatable ZK-EDBs in the random oracle model. Ghosh *et al.* [24] introduced zero-knowledge lists, which allow one to commit a list and later answer order queries in a convincing manner. Libert *et al.* [27] recently introduced ZK-EEDBs that support richer queries, e.g., range queries over the keys and values.

Accumulators (e.g. [3,6,7,18,33]) are an extremely well-studied cryptography primitive related to ZKS. Accumulators allow representing a set using an accumulation value and later providing (non-)membership proofs; however, *hiding and zero-knowledge properties are not necessary for accumulators.* Although Ghosh *et al.* [23] and Zhang *et al.* [46] proposed the constructions of zero-knowledge accumulators supporting set operations, their schemes only consider collision-freeness security, where the adversary cannot cheat in a proof for an *honestly* generated accumulation value. In contrast, ZKS prevent the adversary from cheating in a proof even for a *maliciously* generated commitment. Agrawal and Raghuraman [1] proposed a commitment scheme for databases of key-value pairs. Their scheme does not provide privacy.

Authenticated data structures (ADS) (e.g., [32,35,38]) also allow a trusted database owner to commit its database, and an untrusted server can answer the queries on behalf of trusted database owners to any clients knowing the commitment. However, as a three-party scheme in which the committer (database owner) is always trusted, ADS is incomparable to ZK-EDB.

Key Transparency (KT) systems (e.g. [25,30,39,40]) allow service providers to maintain an auditable directory of their users' public keys, producing proofs that all participants have a consistent view of those keys, and allowing each user to check updates to their own keys. Recently, Chase *et al.* [12] show how to construct privacy-preserving KT systems from append only ZKS and Chen *et al.* [15] develop it and achieve post compromise security.

Recently, there are several works [19,21,43,44] of lookup arguments studying how to efficiently prove subset relation and achieving constant proof size. Lookup arguments can be zero-knowledge and can be used alongside zk-SNARKs to prove that "all records in D_{output} satisfy the query function f and $D_{output} \subset D$" without revealing any extra knowledge. However, constructing ZK-FEDBs from lookup arguments and zk-SNARKs is considerably more challenging. The reason is that, to achieve ZK-FEDBs, one must also prove that any record in $D\backslash D_{output}$ does not satisfy the query function f. Utilizing zk-SNARKs in this context would leak the size of the remaining database $D\backslash D_{output}$ as we discussed in Technique Overview, and therefore leak the size of D.

1.4 Organization

Preliminaries are described in Sect. 2. In Sect. 3, we introduce several new building blocks. In Sect. 4 we introduce and construct ZKS with set-operation queries. In Sect. 5 we show how to transform a Boolean circuit and introduce the notion of ZK-FEDBs, while also providing a concrete construction. Due to space constraints, the construction of constant-size standard ZK-EDBs and several security proofs are deferred to the full version of this paper [45].

2 Preliminaries

In this paper, we denote by λ the security parameter, by $[m]$ the set $\{1, 2, \cdots, m\}$ and by $[m_1, m_2]$ the set $\{m_1 + 1, m_1 + 2, \cdots, m_2\}$. A non-negative function $f : \mathbb{N} \to \mathbb{R}$ is negligible if $f(\lambda) = \lambda^{-w(1)}$. We use the standard abbreviation PPT to denote probabilistic polynomial time.

An elementary database D is a set of key-value pairs $(x, v) \in \{0,1\}^{\ell} \times \{0,1\}^{\ell}$ such that if $(x, v) \in D$ and $(x, v') \in D$, then $v = v'$. Here ℓ is a public polynomial in λ. We denote by $Sup(D)$ the support of D, i.e., the set of $x \in \{0,1\}^{\ell}$ for which $\exists v$ such that $(x, v) \in D$. We denote such unique v as $D(x)$, and if $x \notin Sup(D)$, we then also write $D(x) =\perp$. For consistency, for any set S of elements $x \in \{0,1\}^{\ell}$, we write $S(x) = 1$ if $x \in S$ and write $S(x) =\perp$ if $x \notin S$.

2.1 Zero-Knowledge Elementary Databases and Sets

ZKS allow one to commit a set S and later prove the (non-)membership of any elements without revealing any extra knowledge (including the size of the set). The notion of ZKS can be extended to ZK-EDBs, which allow one to commit an elementary database D. Due to that ZKS can be seen as a special case of ZK-EDBs, where $D(x) = 1$ if $x \in Sup(D)$, we skip the definition of ZKS here. Following [22,27,31], we present the following formal definition of ZK-EDBs:

Definition 1 (Zero-Knowledge Elementary Database). *A zero-knowledge elementary database consists of four algorithms* (Setup, Com, Prove, Verify)*:*

- $\delta \leftarrow \mathsf{Setup}(1^{\lambda})$*: On input the security parameter* 1^{λ}, Setup *outputs a random string (or a structured reference string)* δ *as the CRS.*
- $(com, \tau) \leftarrow \mathsf{Com}(\delta, D)$*: On input the CRS* δ *and an elementary database* D, Com *outputs a commitment of database com and an opening information* τ.
- $\pi \leftarrow \mathsf{Prove}(\delta, com, \tau, x, v)$*: On input the CRS* δ*, the pairing of the commitment and opening information* (com, τ)*, and a key* x *and its associated value* v *(i.e.,* $(x, v) \in D$ *or* $x \notin Sup(D), v =\perp$*),* Prove *outputs a proof* π *of* $v = D(x)$

- $0/1 \leftarrow \mathsf{Verify}(\delta, com, x, v, \pi)$: *On input the CRS* δ*, commitment* com*, key-value pair* (x, v) *and proof* π*,* Verify *either outputs* 1 *(denoting accept) or* 0 *(denoting reject).*

It satisfies the following three properties:

- **Completeness:** *For any elementary database* D *and any* x*,*

$$\Pr\left[\mathsf{Verify}(\delta, com, x, D(x), \pi) = 1 \;\middle|\; \begin{array}{c} \delta \leftarrow \mathsf{Setup}(1^\lambda); (com, \tau) \leftarrow \mathsf{Com}(\delta, D); \\ \pi \leftarrow \mathsf{Prove}(\delta, com, \tau, x, D(x)) \end{array}\right] = 1$$

- **Soundness:** *For any PPT adversary* $\mathcal{A}$*, there exists a negligible function* $negl(\cdot)$ *such that:*

$$\Pr\left[\begin{array}{c} v \neq v' \wedge \\ \mathsf{Verify}(\delta, com, x, v, \pi) = 1 \wedge \\ \mathsf{Verify}(\delta, com, x, v', \pi') = 1 \end{array} \;\middle|\; \begin{array}{c} \delta \leftarrow \mathsf{Setup}(1^\lambda); \\ (com, x, v, v', \pi, \pi') \leftarrow \mathcal{A}(\delta) \end{array}\right] \leq negl(\lambda)$$

- **Zero-Knowledge:** *There exists a simulator Sim such that for any PPT adversary* $\mathcal{A}$*, the absolute value of the difference*

$$\Pr\left[\mathcal{A}^{\mathcal{O}_P}(\delta, state_{\mathcal{A}}, com) = 1 \;\middle|\; \begin{array}{c} \delta \leftarrow \mathsf{Setup}(1^\lambda), (D, state_{\mathcal{A}}) \leftarrow \mathcal{A}(\delta), \\ (com, \tau) \leftarrow \mathsf{Com}(\delta, D) \end{array}\right]$$
$$- \Pr\left[\mathcal{A}^{\mathcal{O}_S}(\delta, state_{\mathcal{A}}, com) = 1 \;\middle|\; \begin{array}{c} (\delta, state_{\delta}) \leftarrow Sim(1^\lambda), (D, state_{\mathcal{A}}) \leftarrow \mathcal{A}(\delta), \\ (com, state_S) \leftarrow Sim(\delta, state_{\delta}) \end{array}\right]$$

is negligible in λ*, where* $\mathcal{O}_P$ *and* $\mathcal{O}_S$ *are defined as follows:*
$\mathcal{O}_P$*: On input a string* x*,* $\mathcal{O}_P$ *outputs* $\pi \leftarrow \mathsf{Prove}(\delta, com, \tau, x, D(x))$.
$\mathcal{O}_S$*: On input a string* x*,* $\mathcal{O}_S$ *outputs* $\pi \leftarrow Sim(state_S, x, D(x))$.

2.2 Groups of Unknown-Order and Assumptions

In this paper, the schemes are constructed on groups of unknown order, for which the order is difficult to compute for the committer. Groups of unknown order are a useful tool in the construction of polynomial commitments, integer commitments, and accumulators, among other aspects.

The strong RSA assumption is a useful assumption for groups of unknown orders. We introduce it in the following.

Assumption 1 *(Strong RSA Assumption) [1,2]. The strong RSA assumption states that an efficient adversary cannot compute* ℓ*-th roots for a given random group element, where* ℓ *is an odd prime chosen by the adversary. Specifically, it holds for GGen if for any probabilistic polynomial time adversary* $\mathcal{A}$*,*

$$\Pr\left[\mathsf{u}^\ell = \mathsf{g} \text{ and } \ell \text{ is an odd prime} \;\middle|\; \begin{array}{c} \mathbb{G} \leftarrow GGen(\lambda), \mathsf{g} \xleftarrow{\$} \mathbb{G}, \\ (\mathsf{u}, \ell) \in \mathbb{G} \times \mathbb{N} \leftarrow \mathcal{A}(\mathbb{G}, \mathsf{g}) \end{array}\right] \leq negl(\lambda).$$

Generic Group Model. In this paper, we use the generic group model for groups of unknown order as defined by Damgård and Koprowski [17], and as used in [4]. Portions of the definition of the generic group model are taken verbatim from [4].

In the generic group model, the group is parameterized by two public integers A and B, and the group order is sampled uniformly from $[A, B]$. The group $\mathbb{G}$ is defined by a random injective function $\sigma : \mathbb{Z}_{|\mathbb{G}|} \rightarrow \{0,1\}^l$ for some l, where $2^l \gg |\mathbb{G}|$. The group elements are $\sigma(0), \cdots, \sigma(|\mathbb{G}|)$. A generic group algorithm $\mathcal{A}$ is a probabilistic algorithm. Let $\mathcal{L}$ be a list that is initialized with the encodings given to $\mathcal{A}$ as input. $\mathcal{A}$ can query two generic group oracles. The first oracle $\mathcal{O}_1$ samples a random $r \in \mathbb{Z}_{|\mathbb{G}|}$ and returns $\sigma(r)$, which is appended to the list of encodings $\mathcal{L}$. The second oracle $\mathcal{O}_2(i, j, \pm)$ takes two indices $i, j \in [p]$, where p is the size of $\mathcal{L}$, as well as a sign bit, and returns $\sigma(i \pm j)$, which is appended to $\mathcal{L}$. Note that herein $\mathcal{A}$ is not given the order of $\mathbb{G}$.

As shown in [17], the strong RSA assumption holds in the generic group model.

Zero-Knowledge Protocol for Bounded Discrete-Log. The classical Schnorr Σ-protocol can be used to prove the discrete-log relation when the exponent is small (i.e., $\mathcal{R}_{boundedDL} = \{(\mathsf{u}, \mathsf{w}, T; x) | \mathsf{u}^x = \mathsf{w} \wedge |x| \leq T\}$). It only provides a weak soundness that, a proof for $(\mathsf{u}, \mathsf{w}, T)$ can convince verifier that $(\mathsf{u}, \mathsf{w}, T)$ belongs to a relaxed relation $\mathcal{R}^*_{boundedDL} = \{(\mathsf{u}, \mathsf{w}, T; x, t) | \mathsf{u}^x = \mathsf{w}^t \wedge |x| \leq 2^{2\lambda}T, |t| \leq 2^{\lambda}\}$, which is sufficient for our goal. Following [8,16,20], the construction is as follows (Fig. 2).

Protocol $\mathsf{ZK}_{boundedDL}$ (Zero-knowledge protocol for $\mathcal{R}_{boundedDL}$)

Params: $\mathbb{G} \leftarrow GGen(\lambda)$; Common Input: $\mathsf{u}, \mathsf{w} \in \mathbb{G}, T \in \mathbb{N}$;
Private Input for $\mathcal{P}$: $x \in \mathbb{Z}$

1. $\mathcal{P}$ samples $r \xleftarrow{\$} [2^{2\lambda}T]$ and sends $\mathsf{z} = \mathsf{u}^r \in \mathbb{G}$ to $\mathcal{V}$.
2. $\mathcal{V}$ sends challenge $c \xleftarrow{\$} [2^{\lambda}]$.
3. $\mathcal{P}$ computes $s = r + cx$ and sends s to $\mathcal{V}$.
4. $\mathcal{V}$ accepts if $\mathsf{u}^s = \mathsf{z}\mathsf{w}^c$ and $s \leq 2^{2\lambda}T$.

Fig. 2. Protocol $\mathsf{ZK}_{boundedDL}$ [8,20]

Lemma 1. Protocol $\mathsf{ZK}_{boundedDL}$ *is an honest-verifier statistically zero-knowledge protocol for* $\mathcal{R}_{boundedDL}$, *achieving a weak knowledge soundness defined as follows: There exists an extractor such that for any polynomial* p *and any prover* $\mathcal{P}^*$ *convincing verifier of statement* $(\mathsf{u}, \mathsf{w}, T)$ *with probability* p^{-1}, *the extractor can extract* (x', t) *within an expected polynomial time such that* $|x'| \leq 2^{2\lambda}T, |t| \leq 2^{\lambda}$ *and* $\mathsf{u}^{x'} = \mathsf{w}^t$.

Note that the honest-verifier statistically zero-knowledge property of the above lemma directly follows [16]. And the weak knowledge soundness can be easily proved by rewinding.

Furthermore, above zero-knowledge protocol can be easily extend to multidimensional discrete-log relation with small exponents (i.e., $\mathcal{R} = \{(\{\mathsf{u}_i\}_{i\in[n]}, \mathsf{w}, T; \{x_i\}_{i\in[n]}) | \Pi_{i\in[n]} \mathsf{u}_i^{x_i} = \mathsf{w} \wedge \forall i \in [n], |x_i| \leq T\}$), resulting in a similar weak knowledge soundness.

Proof of Knowledge of Exponent (PoKE). Recently, Boneh *et al.* [4] introduced a way to present an argument of knowledge protocol for the following relation.

$$\mathcal{R}_{PoKE} := \{(\mathsf{u}, \mathsf{w} \in \mathbb{G}; x \in \mathbb{Z}) | \mathsf{w} = \mathsf{u}^x \in \mathbb{Z}\}$$

Let $\mathcal{P}$ be the prover and $\mathcal{V}$ be the verifier. Let $\mathsf{Primes}(\lambda)$ denote the set of odd prime numbers in $[0, 2^\lambda]$. Their protocol is as follows (Fig. 3):

Protocol PoKE (Proof of knowledge of exponent)

Params: $\mathbb{G} \leftarrow GGen(\lambda), \mathsf{g} \in \mathbb{G}$; Common Input: $\mathsf{u}, \mathsf{w} \in \mathbb{G}$;
Private Input for $\mathcal{P}$: $x \in \mathbb{Z}$

1. $\mathcal{P}$ sends $\mathsf{z} = \mathsf{g}^x \in \mathbb{G}$ to $\mathcal{V}$.
2. $\mathcal{V}$ samples $l \stackrel{\$}{\leftarrow} \mathsf{Primes}(\lambda)$ and sends l to $\mathcal{P}$.
3. $\mathcal{P}$ finds the quotient $q \in \mathbb{Z}$ and residue $r \in [l]$ such that $x = ql + r$. $\mathcal{P}$ sends $\mathsf{Q} = \mathsf{u}^q$, $\mathsf{Q}' = \mathsf{g}^q$, and r to $\mathcal{V}$.
4. $\mathcal{V}$ accepts if $r \in [l]$, $\mathsf{Q}^l \mathsf{u}^r = \mathsf{w}$, and $\mathsf{Q}'^l \mathsf{g}^r = \mathsf{z}$.

Fig. 3. PoKE protocol [4]

Theorem 1 ([4] Theorem 3). Protocol PoKE *is an argument of knowledge for the relation* $\mathcal{R}_{PoKE}$ *in the generic group model.*

Our constructions will use above PoKE protocol as a subroutine, and that's why our results rely on the generic group model. In practice, there are two common methods used to instantiate groups of unknown order.

RSA Group: The multiplicative group $\mathbb{Z}_n^*$ of integers modulo a product $n = pq$ of large primes p and q. Any efficient algorithm that calculates the order can be transformed into an efficient algorithm factoring n. In addition, we need to point out that it is difficult to generate the RSA group in a publicly verifiable way without exposing the order. Therefore, we need a trusted party to generate the group.

Class Group: The class group of an imaginary quadratic order with discriminant Δ where $-\Delta$ is a prime and $\Delta \equiv 1 \mod 4$. As an important property, one can choose a security class group $Cl(\Delta)$ by choosing the "good" discriminant Δ randomly without a trusted party. For more details, one can refer to Buchmann and Hamdy's survey [5] and Straka's accessible blog post [37] for more details.

At the end of this section, we provide several simple lemmas used for our construction.

Lemma 2. *For any positive integers a, A, and B satisfying $B > A$, we have:*

$$\mathsf{Dist}(\{x \xleftarrow{\$} \mathbb{Z}_a\}, \{x \mod a | x \xleftarrow{\$} [A, B]\}) \leq \frac{a}{B - A}$$

where Dist *indicates the statistical distance between distributions.*

Lemma 3. *For any integers s_1, s_2 and positive integers a, A, B satisfying $B > A$, $\gcd(s_1, s_2) = 1$, we have:*

$$\mathsf{Dist}(\{x \xleftarrow{\$} \mathbb{Z}_a\}, \{xs_1 + ys_2 \mod a | x, y \xleftarrow{\$} [A, B]\}) \leq \frac{3a}{B - A}$$

where Dist *indicates the statistical distance between distributions.*

Lemma 4. *For any multiplicative group $\mathbb{G}$ and group elements $\mathsf{g}, \mathsf{h} \in \mathbb{G}$, if there exists* coprime *integers a, p satisfying $\mathsf{g}^a = \mathsf{h}^p$, then one can easily compute h' satisfying $\mathsf{g} = \mathsf{h}'^p$ from a, p, g and h.*

The proofs of the above three lemmas are shown in the full version of this paper [45].

3 New Building Blocks

This section introduces several building blocks that we use in our construction. It comprises of two parts. In the first part, we present a new variant of Boneh *et al.*'s zero-knowledge protocol for multidimensional discrete-log relation and lightly modify the standard ZKS scheme [36,41,42]. In the second part, we construct two new zero-knowledge protocols for pseudo-coprime exponent relation and pseudo-DDH relation over the groups of unknown orders.

3.1 Zero-Knowledge Protocol for Multidimensional Discrete-Log and Standard ZKS Scheme

In [4], Boneh *et al.* combined the classical Schnorr Σ-protocol and the batched PoKE protocol to present a zero-knowledge argument of knowledge protocol (called Protocol ZKPoKRep) for the relation $\mathcal{R}_{multiDL} = \{(\{\mathsf{u}_i\}_{i \in [n]}, \mathsf{w}; \{x_i\}_{i \in [n]}) | \Pi_{i \in [n]} \mathsf{u}_i^{x_i} = \mathsf{w}\}$. Their protocol satisfies soundness only when $\{\mathsf{u}_i\}_{i \in [n]}$ is a base specified in the CRS. However, our constructions require the prover to generate such a set $\{\mathsf{u}_i\}_{i \in [n]}$.

Therefore, we construct a new variant of Boneh *et al.*'s protocol. We call it Protocol $\mathsf{ZK}_{multiDL}$. Compared to the origin protocol, the prover in our new protocol uses n PoKE protocols to prove the relation $\mathsf{z}\mathsf{w}^c = \Pi_{i \in [n]} \mathsf{u}_i^{s_i}$. Here, we require the prover to send $\mathsf{u}_i^{s_i}$ additionally, which doesn't affect the proof of statistical honest verifier zero-knowledge. This allows the extractor to extract

s_i even when $\{u_i\}_{i\in[n]}$ is generated by the prover. As a result, we obtain a zero-knowledge protocol for $\mathcal{R}_{multiDL}$ where $\{u_i\}_{i\in[n]}$ can be generated by the prover. However, this benefit comes at a price: This protocol only satisfies a weak knowledge soundness that a valid proof can convince the verifier that the statement belongs to a *relaxed* relation $\mathcal{R}^*_{multiDL} = \{(\{u_i\}_{i\in[n]}, w; \{x_i\}_{i\in[n]}, t) | \Pi_{i\in[n]} u_i^{x_i} = w^t, |t| \leq 2^\lambda\}$. The concrete construction is shown in Fig. 4.

Protocol $\mathsf{ZK}_{multiDL}$ (Zero-knowledge protocol for $\mathcal{R}_{multiDL}$)

Params: $\mathbb{G} \leftarrow GGen(\lambda), B \geq |\mathbb{G}|$; Common Input: $\{u_i\}_{i\in[n]}, w \in \mathbb{G}$;
Private Input for $\mathcal{P}$: $\{x_i\}_{i\in[n]}$

1. $\mathcal{P}$ samples $r_i \xleftarrow{\$} [2^{2\lambda} B]$ for each $i \in [n]$ and sends $z = \Pi_{i\in[n]} u_i^{r_i} \in \mathbb{G}$ to $\mathcal{V}$.
2. $\mathcal{V}$ sends challenge $c \xleftarrow{\$} [2^\lambda]$.
3. $\mathcal{P}$ computes $s_i = r_i + cx_i$ for each $i \in [n]$ and sends $\hat{u}_i = u_i^{s_i}$ to $\mathcal{V}$.
4. $\mathcal{P}$ and $\mathcal{V}$ run $\mathsf{PoKE}(u, \hat{u}_i; s_i)$, and $\mathcal{V}$ output 1 if and only if all PoKE accept and $\Pi_{i\in[n]} \hat{u}_i = zw^c$.

Fig. 4. Protocol $\mathsf{ZK}_{multiDL}$ [4]

Lemma 5. *In the generic group model,* Protocol $\mathsf{ZK}_{multiDL}$ *is an honest-verifier statistically zero-knowledge protocol for* $\mathcal{R}_{multiDL}$*, achieving a weak knowledge soundness defined as follows: There exists an extractor such that for any prover* $\mathcal{P}^*$ *convincing the verifier of statement* $(\{u_i\}_{i\in[n]}, w)$ *with inverse-polynomial probability, the extractor can extract* $(\{x'_i\}_{i\in[n]}, t)$ *within an expected polynomial time such that* $|t| \leq 2^\lambda$ *and* $\Pi_{i\in[n]} u_i^{x'_i} = w^t$.

proof sketch. The honest-verifier statistically zero-knowledge property can be proved in the same manner as [4] and the weak knowledge soundness follows Lemma 1 (the extension version for multidimensional DL) and the argument of knowledge property of PoKE (used for extracting s_i) directly.

A complete proof is shown in the full version of this paper [45].

In the remainder of this paper, we only use the protocol $\mathsf{ZK}_{multiDL}$ for the cases when $n = 1$ or 2. For convenience, we shall refer to these protocols as ZK_{DL} and ZK_{2DL}. Additionally, we denote their non-interactive versions obtained via the Fiat-Shamir heuristic as NIZK_{DL} and NIZK_{2DL}.

Standard Zero-Knowledge Sets. Here we introduce the construction of standard ZKS in [36,41,42], but with some modifications. Instead of using RSA groups, we now use general groups of unknown orders. Furthermore, we use ZK_{DL} and ZK_{2DL} as sub-routine zero-knowledge protocol.

Let $\mathcal{H}_{prime}$ be a hash function that upon inputting a string outputs a large prime. And let $\mathcal{R}_{DL} = \{(u, w; x) | u^x = w\}$, $\mathcal{R}_{2DL} = \{(u_1, u_2, w; x_1, x_2) | u_1{}^{x_1} u_2{}^{x_2} = w\}$. The modified construction is shown below.

Standard zero-knowledge set scheme

Setup(1^λ): On input the security parameter 1^λ, Setup generates the description of an unknown-order group $\mathbb{G} \leftarrow GGen(\lambda)$ and a random group element $\mathsf{g} \xleftarrow{\$} \mathbb{G}$. Let B be the upper bound of $\mathbb{G}$ (i.e., $B \geq |\mathbb{G}|$). Sample the description of a hash function $\mathcal{H}_{prime}$ that on input a string, outputs a random prime larger than $2^{8\lambda}B^3$. Output CRS $\delta = (\mathbb{G}, \mathsf{g}, B, \mathcal{H}_{prime})$.

Commit(δ, S): On input the set $S = \{x_1, \cdots, x_m\}$, Commit hashes them into large primes, i.e., for $i \in [m]$, $p_i \leftarrow \mathcal{H}_{prime}(x_i)$. Then Commit samples $r \xleftarrow{\$} [2^\lambda B]$, and outputs the commitment $\mathsf{C} = \mathsf{g}^{r\Pi_{i\in[m]}p_i}$ and the open information $\tau = (r, p_1, \cdots, p_m, S)$.

Prove($\delta, (C, \tau), x, S(x)$): Parse the input τ as $(r, p_1, \cdots, p_m, S)$.

a) If $S(x) = 1$, which means that $x \in S$, $p = \mathcal{H}_{prime}(x) \in \{p_1, \cdots, p_m\}$, Prove outputs the proof $\pi \leftarrow \mathsf{NIZK}_{DL}(\mathsf{g}^p, \mathsf{C}; r\Pi_{i\in[m]}p_i/p)$.

b) If $S(x) = \perp$, which means that $x \notin S$, $p = \mathcal{H}_{prime}(x) \notin \{p_1, \cdots, p_m\}$ and $\gcd(p, r\Pi_{i\in[m]}p_i) = 1$, Prove finds a, b such that $ap + br\Pi_{i\in[m]}p_i = 1$ and outputs $\pi \leftarrow \mathsf{NIZK}_{2DL}(\mathsf{g}^p, \mathsf{C}, \mathsf{g}; a, b)$.

Verify($\delta, \mathsf{C}, x, S(x), \pi$): If $S(x) = 1$, check whether π is a valid NIZK_{DL} proof for statement $(\mathsf{g}^p, \mathsf{C}) \in \mathcal{R}_{DL}$. If $S(x) = \perp$, check whether π is a valid NIZK_{2DL} proof for statement $(\mathsf{g}^p, \mathsf{C}, \mathsf{g}) \in \mathcal{R}_{2DL}$. Verify outputs 1 if the check passes and outputs 0 otherwise.

Fig. 5. Protocol ZKS

Theorem 2. *The protocol constructed in Fig. 5 is a ZKS scheme in the generic group model and random oracle model.*

The proof follows from [36, 41, 42]. We present a detailed proof in the full version of this paper [45].

Remark 1. One can use the batch technique put forward in [4] to batch the (non-)membership proofs. For example, to prove that $x'_1, \cdots, x'_t \in S$, the prover hashes them into primes $p'_1, \cdots p'_t$ by $\mathcal{H}_{prime}$ and then generates the proof $\pi \leftarrow \mathsf{NIZK}_{DL}(\mathsf{g}^{\Pi_{i\in[t]}p'_i}, \mathsf{C}; r\Pi_{i\in[m]}p_i/\Pi_{i\in[t]}p'_i)$. To prove that $x'_1, \cdots, x'_t \notin S$, the prover hashes them into primes $p'_1, \cdots p'_t$ by $\mathcal{H}_{prime}$ and finds $a, b \in \mathbb{Z}$ such that $a\Pi_{i\in[t]}p'_i + br\Pi_{i\in[m]}p_i = 1$, and then outputs $\pi \leftarrow \mathsf{NIZK}_{2DL}(\mathsf{g}^{\Pi_{i\in[t]}p'_i}, \mathsf{C}, \mathsf{g}; a, b)$.

3.2 Zero-Knowledge Protocols for Pseudo-Coprime Exponent Relation and Pseudo-DDH Relation

As shown in the technique overview subsection, due to the introduction of randomness in ZKS commitment, the basic set-operation relations on committed set can only be reduced to pseudo-coprime exponent relation and pseudo-DDH relation over group elements. Here pseudo-coprime exponent relation means that the greatest common divisor of the exponents of two group elements are small and pseudo-DDH relation means that a group element triple is close to a DDH tuple.

In this subsection, we construct two new zero-knowledge protocols for these two relations. Similar to Schnorr Σ-protocol, both protocols only provide a weak knowledge soundness, which are sufficient for our construction of ZKS with set-operation query.

Zero-Knowledge Protocol for Pseudo-coprime Exponents Relation. Let u, v be ZKS commitments to sets X, Y respectively, i.e., $\mathsf{u} = \mathsf{g}^{r_u \Pi_{x \in X} \mathcal{H}_{prime}(x)}$, $\mathsf{v} = \mathsf{g}^{r_v \Pi_{x \in Y} \mathcal{H}_{prime}(x)}$. If $X \cap Y = \emptyset$, it yields that the exponents of u, v are almost coprime. We call such a tuple (u, v) as a pseudo-coprime exponents tuple and denote the **pseudo-coprime exponents relation** as follows:

$$\mathcal{R}_{coprime} = \left\{ (\mathsf{u}, \mathsf{v}, T; a_1, a_2) \middle| \begin{array}{ll} \gcd(a_1, a_2) \leq T & \wedge \\ \mathsf{u} = \mathsf{g}^{a_1}, \mathsf{v} = \mathsf{g}^{a_2} & \end{array} \right\}$$

We provide a zero-knowledge protocol for $\mathcal{R}_{coprime}$ in Fig. 6. This protocol only satisfies a weak soundness that, a valid proof can convince the verifier that the statement belongs to a *relaxed* relation $\mathcal{R}^*_{coprime} = \{(\mathsf{u}, \mathsf{v}, T; t_1, t_2, c) | c \leq 2^{4\lambda} BT \wedge \mathsf{u}^{t_1} \mathsf{v}^{t_2} = \mathsf{g}^c\}$.

Protocol $\mathsf{ZK}_{coprime}$ (Zero-knowledge protocol for $\mathcal{R}_{coprime}$)

Params: $\mathbb{G} \leftarrow GGen(\lambda), B \geq |\mathbb{G}|$; Common Input: $\mathsf{u}, \mathsf{v} \in \mathbb{G}, T \in \mathbb{Z}$;
Private Input for $\mathcal{P}$: $a_1, a_2 \in \mathbb{Z}$

1. $\mathcal{P}$ finds integers t_1, t_2 such that $t_1 a_1 + t_2 a_2 = \gcd(a_1, a_2)$. $\mathcal{P}$ samples $r \xleftarrow{\$} [2^\lambda B]$ and sends $\mathsf{Q} = \mathsf{g}^{r \gcd(a_1, a_2)} = \mathsf{u}^{r t_1} \mathsf{v}^{r t_2}$ to $\mathcal{V}$.
2. $\mathcal{P}$ and $\mathcal{V}$ run $\mathsf{ZK}_{boundedDL}(\mathsf{g}, \mathsf{Q}, 2^\lambda BT; r \gcd(a_1, a_2))$ and $\mathsf{ZK}_{2DL}(\mathsf{u}, \mathsf{v}, \mathsf{Q}; r t_1, r t_2)$

Fig. 6. Protocol $\mathsf{ZK}_{coprime}$

Lemma 6. *In the generic group model,* $\mathsf{ZK}_{coprime}$ *is an honest-verifier statistically zero-knowledge protocol for* $\mathcal{R}_{coprime}$*, achieving a weak knowledge soundness defined as follows: There exists an extractor such that for any prover* P^* *convincing the verifier with inverse-polynomial probability over statement* $(\mathsf{u}, \mathsf{v}, T)$*, the extractor can extract* $t_1, t_2, c \in \mathbb{Z}$ *within an expected polynomial time such that* $|c| \leq 2^{4\lambda} BT$ *and* $\mathsf{u}^{t_1} \mathsf{v}^{t_2} = \mathsf{g}^c$.

Proof. **Completeness** is obvious.

Weak knowledge soundness follows from the weak knowledge soundness of $\mathsf{ZK}_{boundedDL}$ and ZK_{2DL}. Specifically, the weak knowledge soundness of $\mathsf{ZK}_{boundedDL}$ allows us to extract $x, t \in \mathbb{Z}$ satisfying that $|x| \leq 2^{3\lambda}BT, |r'| \leq 2^{\lambda}$ and $\mathsf{Q}^{r'} = \mathsf{g}^{x}$. And the weak knowledge soundness of ZK_{2DL} enables the extraction of $t'_1, t'_2, r'' \in \mathbb{Z}$ such that $|r''| \leq 2^{\lambda}$ and $\mathsf{Q}^{r''} = \mathsf{u}^{t'_1}\mathsf{v}^{t'_2}$. With this, we obtain $\mathsf{u}^{r't'_1}\mathsf{v}^{r't'_2} = \mathsf{g}^{r''x}$. By setting $t_1 = r't'_1, t_2 = r't'_2, c = r''x$, we obtain $\mathsf{u}^{t_1}\mathsf{v}^{t_2} = \mathsf{g}^{c}$ and $|c| \leq 2^{4\lambda}BT$.

The simulator Sim of the **honest-verifier statistically zero-knowledge** property can be constructed as follows: Sim samples $r_1, r_2 \xleftarrow{\$} [2^{\lambda}B]$, sets $\mathsf{Q} = \mathsf{u}^{r_1}\mathsf{v}^{r_2}$, and then simulates the remaining zero-knowledge protocol to conclude the simulation.

Due to that both $\mathsf{ZK}_{boundedDL}$ and ZK_{2DL} are honest-verifier statistically zero-knowledge, we only need to prove that the distributions of $(\mathsf{u}, \mathsf{v}, \mathsf{Q})$ generated by the simulator and the honest prover are statistically indistinguishable. In other words, we need to show the following: For any fixed $\mathsf{u} = \mathsf{g}^{a_1}, \mathsf{v} = \mathsf{g}^{a_2}$, the statistical distance of the distributions $\{\mathsf{g}^{r \gcd(a_1,a_2)} | r \xleftarrow{\$} [2^{\lambda}B]\}$ and $\{\mathsf{u}^{r_1}\mathsf{v}^{r_2} = \mathsf{g}^{r_1a_1+r_2a_2} | r_1, r_2 \xleftarrow{\$} [2^{\lambda}B]\}$ is exponentially small.

Let b be the order of $\mathsf{g}^{\gcd(a_1,a_2)}$, i.e., $b = \mathsf{Ord}(\mathsf{g}^{\gcd(a_1,a_2)}) \leq B$. From Lemma 2, $\{r \bmod b | r \xleftarrow{\$} [2^{\lambda}B]\}$ is exponentially close to the uniform distribution over $\mathbb{Z}_b$. Therefore the distribution $\{\mathsf{g}^{r \gcd(a_1,a_2)} | r \xleftarrow{\$} [2^{\lambda}B]\}$ is exponential close to the distribution $\{(\mathsf{g}^{\gcd(a_1,a_2)})^{r} | r \xleftarrow{\$} \mathbb{Z}_b\}$. From Lemma 3, $\{r_1 \cdot \frac{a_1}{\gcd(a_1,a_2)} + r_2 \cdot \frac{a_2}{\gcd(a_1,a_2)} \bmod b | r_1, r_2 \xleftarrow{\$} [2^{\lambda}B]\}$ is exponentially close to the uniform distribution over $\mathbb{Z}_b$. Therefore, we have that the distribution $\{\mathsf{g}^{r_1a_1+r_2a_2} | r_1, r_2 \xleftarrow{\$} [2^{\lambda}B]\}$, which equals $\{(\mathsf{g}^{\gcd(a_1,a_2)})^{r_1 \cdot \frac{a_1}{\gcd(a_1,a_2)} + r_2 \cdot \frac{a_2}{\gcd(a_1,a_2)} \bmod b} | r_1, r_2 \xleftarrow{\$} [2^{\lambda}B]\}$, is also exponentially close to the distribution $\{(\mathsf{g}^{\gcd(a_1,a_2)})^{r} | r \xleftarrow{\$} \mathbb{Z}_b\}$. This concludes the lemma. □

Zero-Knowledge Protocol for Pseudo-DDH Relation. Let $\mathsf{u}, \mathsf{v}, \mathsf{w}$ be ZKS commitments to sets A, B, C, i.e., $\mathsf{u} = \mathsf{g}^{r_u \Pi_{x \in A} \mathcal{H}_{prime}(x)}, \mathsf{v} = \mathsf{g}^{r_v \Pi_{x \in B} \mathcal{H}_{prime}(x)}$, $\mathsf{w} = \mathsf{g}^{r_w \Pi_{x \in C} \mathcal{H}_{prime}(x)}$. If $C = A \cup B$ and $A \cap B = \emptyset$, it yields that the tuple $(\mathsf{u}, \mathsf{v}, \mathsf{w})$ is close to a DDH tuple. We call such a tuple $(\mathsf{u}, \mathsf{v}, \mathsf{w})$ as a pseudo-DDH tuple and denote the **pseudo-DDH relation** as follows:

$$\mathcal{R}_{pseudo-DDH} = \left\{ (\mathsf{u}, \mathsf{v}, \mathsf{w}, T; x, y, a_1, a_2, a_3) \;\middle|\; \begin{array}{ll} |a_1|, |a_2|, |a_3| \leq T & \wedge \\ \gcd(xy, \Pi_{i=1}^{2^{\lambda}|\mathbb{G}|} i) = 1 & \wedge \\ \mathsf{u} = \mathsf{g}^{a_1 x}, \mathsf{v} = \mathsf{g}^{a_2 y}, \mathsf{w} = \mathsf{g}^{a_3 xy} & \end{array} \right\}.$$

In above relation, we require that the integers x and y are products of large primes (the second condition), which is necessary for our distance analysis in the proof of zero-knowledge property. We provide a zero-knowledge protocol for $\mathcal{R}_{pseudo-DDH}$ in Fig. 7, which partially relies on Boneh et al.'s protocol. This protocol only satisfies a weak soundness that, a valid proof can convince the verifier that the statement belongs to a *relaxed* relation $\mathcal{R}^*_{pseudo-DDH} =$

$\{(\mathsf{u},\mathsf{v},\mathsf{w},T;x,y,\{a_i,c_i\}_{i\in[3]})| \; |a_1|,|a_2|,|a_3| \le 2^{4\lambda}BT, |c_1|,|c_2| \le 2^{6\lambda}B^2, |c_3| \le 2^{8\lambda}B^3 \wedge \mathsf{u}^{c_1} = \mathsf{g}^{a_1 x}, \mathsf{v}^{c_2} = \mathsf{g}^{a_2 y}, \mathsf{w}^{c_3} = \mathsf{g}^{a_3 xy}\}$.

Protocol $\mathsf{ZK}_{pseudo-DDH}$ (Zero-knowledge protocol for $\mathcal{R}_{pseudo-DDH}$)

Params: $\mathbb{G} \leftarrow GGen(\lambda), B \ge |\mathbb{G}|$; Common Input: $\mathsf{u},\mathsf{v},\mathsf{w} \in \mathbb{G}, T \in \mathbb{Z}$;
Private Input for $\mathcal{P}$: $a_1, a_2, a_3, x, y \in \mathbb{Z}$

1. $\mathcal{P}$ samples $r_1, r_2 \xleftarrow{\$} [2^{2\lambda}B]$ and sends $\mathsf{u}' = \mathsf{g}^{r_1 x}, \mathsf{v}' = \mathsf{g}^{r_2 y}, \mathsf{w}' = \mathsf{g}^{r_1 r_2 xy}$ to $\mathcal{V}$.
2. $\mathcal{V}$ sends $l_1 \xleftarrow{\$} \mathsf{Primes}(\lambda), l_2 \xleftarrow{\$} \mathsf{Primes}(\lambda)$.
3. $\mathcal{P}$ finds the quotient $q_1, q_2 \in \mathbb{Z}$ and residue $t_1 \in [l_1], t_2 \in [l_2]$ such that $r_1 x = q_1 l_1 + t_1$ and $r_2 y = q_2 l_2 + t_2$. $\mathcal{P}$ sends $\mathsf{Q}_1 = \mathsf{g}^{q_1}$, $\mathsf{Q}_1' = \mathsf{v}'^{q_1}$ and $\mathsf{Q}_2 = \mathsf{g}^{q_2}$, t_1 and t_2 to $\mathcal{V}$.
4. $\mathcal{V}$ checks $t_1 \in [l_1], t_2 \in [l_2]$, $\mathsf{Q}_1^{l_1}\mathsf{g}^{t_1} = \mathsf{u}'$, $\mathsf{Q}_1'^{l_1}\mathsf{v}'^{t_1} = \mathsf{w}'$, and $\mathsf{Q}_2^{l_2}\mathsf{g}^{t_2} = \mathsf{v}'$.
5. $\mathcal{P}$ samples $r_u, r_v, r_w \xleftarrow{\$} [2^{\lambda}B]$ and sends $\mathsf{u}'' = \mathsf{u}^{r_1 r_u}, \mathsf{v}'' = \mathsf{v}^{r_2 r_y}, \mathsf{w}'' = \mathsf{w}^{r_1 r_2 r_w}$ to $\mathcal{V}$.
6. $\mathcal{P}$ and $\mathcal{V}$ run $\mathsf{ZK}_{boundedDL}(\mathsf{u}, \mathsf{u}'', 2^{3\lambda}B^2; r_1 r_u)$, $\mathsf{ZK}_{boundedDL}(\mathsf{u}', \mathsf{u}'', 2^{\lambda}BT; a_1 r_u)$, $\mathsf{ZK}_{boundedDL}(\mathsf{v}, \mathsf{v}'', 2^{3\lambda}B^2; r_2 r_v)$, $\mathsf{ZK}_{boundedDL}(\mathsf{v}', \mathsf{v}'', 2^{\lambda}BT; a_2 r_v)$, $\mathsf{ZK}_{boundedDL}(\mathsf{w}, \mathsf{w}'', 2^{5\lambda}B^3; r_1 r_2 r_w)$ and $\mathsf{ZK}_{boundedDL}(\mathsf{w}', \mathsf{w}'', 2^{\lambda}BT; a_3 r_w)$.

Fig. 7. Protocol $\mathsf{ZK}_{pseudo-DDH}$

Lemma 7. *In the generic group model,* $\mathsf{ZK}_{pseudo-DDH}$ *is an honest-verifier statistically zero-knowledge protocol for* $\mathcal{R}_{pseudo-DDH}$*, achieving a weak knowledge soundness defined as follows: There exists an extractor such that for any prover* $\mathcal{P}^*$ *convincing the verifier with inverse-polynomial probability over statement* $(\mathsf{u},\mathsf{v},\mathsf{w},T)$*, the extractor can extract* $x, y, a_1, a_2, a_3, c_1, c_2, c_3 \in \mathbb{Z}$ *such that* $|a_1|,|a_2|,|a_3| \le 2^{4\lambda}BT$ $|c_1|,|c_2| \le 2^{6\lambda}B^2$, $|c_3| \le 2^{8\lambda}B^3$*, and* $\mathsf{u}^{c_1} = \mathsf{g}^{a_1 x}, \mathsf{v}^{c_2} = \mathsf{g}^{a_2 y}, \mathsf{w}^{c_3} = \mathsf{g}^{a_3 xy}$.

Proof. **Completeness** is obvious.

Weak knowledge soundness can be prove through the weak knowledge soundness of $\mathsf{ZK}_{boundedDL}$ and the knowledge extractor of PoKE. It is worth noting that steps 2 through 4 in our protocol are the same as in Boneh et al.'s PoDDH protocol [4], which roughly consists of two PoKE protocols. We can use the knowledge extractor provided in [4] to extract x, y satisfying $\mathsf{u}' = \mathsf{g}^x$, $\mathsf{v}' = \mathsf{g}^y$ and $\mathsf{w}' = \mathsf{g}^{xy}$. Meanwhile, the weak knowledge soundness of $\mathsf{ZK}_{boundedDL}$ allows us to extract a_u, c_u, a_u', c_u' from the first two $\mathsf{ZK}_{boundedDL}$ protocols such that $|c_u|, |c_u'| \le 2^{\lambda}, |a_u| \le 2^{5\lambda}B^2, |a_u'| \le 2^{3\lambda}BT$ and $\mathsf{u}^{a_u} = \mathsf{u}''^{c_u}, \mathsf{u}'^{a_u'} = \mathsf{u}''^{c_u'}$. Hence, we have $\mathsf{u}^{a_u c_u'} = \mathsf{g}^{a_u' c_u x}$. By setting $c_1 = a_u c_u'$, $a_1 = a_u' c_u$, we obtain $|c_1| \le 2^{6\lambda}B^2, |a_1| \le 2^{4\lambda}BT$ and $\mathsf{u}^{c_1} = \mathsf{g}^{a_1 x}$. Using the same strategy, we can extract c_2, c_3, a_2, a_3, thus meeting our goal.

The simulator Sim of **honest-verifier statistically zero-knowledge** property can be constructed as follows: Initially, Sim samples $r_1, r_2 \xleftarrow{\$} [2^{2\lambda}B]$ and sets $\mathsf{u}' = \mathsf{g}^{r_1}, \mathsf{v}' = \mathsf{g}^{r_2}, \mathsf{w}' = \mathsf{g}^{r_1 r_2}$. In step 3, Sim finds the quotient $q_1, q_2 \in \mathbb{Z}$ and residue t_1, t_2 such that $r_1 = q_1 l_1 + t_1$ and $r_2 = q_2 l_2 + t_2$, and then applies the same action as an honest prover. Subsequently, Sim samples $r_u, r_v, r_w \xleftarrow{\$} [2^{\lambda}B]$, sets $\mathsf{u}'' = \mathsf{u}^{r_1 r_u}, \mathsf{v}'' = \mathsf{v}^{r_2 r_v}, \mathsf{w}'' = \mathsf{w}^{r_1 r_2 r_w}$, and simulates the $\mathsf{ZK}_{boundedDL}$ protocols to conclude the simulation.

Due to the honest-verifier statistically zero-knowledge of $\mathsf{ZK}_{boundedDL}$, we only need to prove that for any fixed statement $(\mathsf{u}, \mathsf{v}, \mathsf{w}, T)$ and challenges l_1, l_2 (note that $l_1, l_2 \le 2^{\lambda}$), the distributions of $(\mathsf{u}', \mathsf{v}', \mathsf{w}', \mathsf{Q}_1, \mathsf{Q}_1', \mathsf{Q}_2, t_1, t_2, \mathsf{u}'', \mathsf{v}'', \mathsf{w}'')$ generated by the simulator and the honest prover are exponentially close. We denote these two distributions by $\mathcal{D}_{sim}$ and $\mathcal{D}_P$ respectively. Thus, for any fixed statement $(\mathsf{u}, \mathsf{v}, \mathsf{w}, T)$ and challenges l_1, l_2, we have the following:

$$\mathcal{D}_{sim} = \{(\mathsf{g}^{r_1}, \mathsf{g}^{r_2}, \mathsf{g}^{r_1 r_2}, \mathsf{g}^{\lfloor r_1/l_1 \rfloor}, (\mathsf{g}^{r_2})^{\lfloor r_1/l_1 \rfloor}, \mathsf{g}^{\lfloor r_2/l_2 \rfloor}, r_1 \mod l_1,$$

$$r_2 \mod l_2, \mathsf{u}^{r_1 r_u}, \mathsf{v}^{r_2 r_v}, \mathsf{w}^{r_1 r_2 r_w}) | r_1, r_2 \xleftarrow{\$} [2^{2\lambda}B], r_u, r_v, r_w \xleftarrow{\$} [2^{\lambda}B]\}$$

$$\mathcal{D}_P = \{(\mathsf{g}^{r_1 x}, \mathsf{g}^{r_2 y}, \mathsf{g}^{r_1 r_2 x y}, \mathsf{g}^{\lfloor r_1 x/l_1 \rfloor}, (\mathsf{g}^{r_2 y})^{\lfloor r_1 x/l_1 \rfloor}, \mathsf{g}^{\lfloor r_2 y/l_2 \rfloor}, r_1 x \mod l_1,$$

$$r_2 y \mod l_2, \mathsf{u}^{r_1 r_u}, \mathsf{v}^{r_2 r_v}, \mathsf{w}^{r_1 r_2 r_w}) | r_1, r_2 \xleftarrow{\$} [2^{2\lambda}B], r_u, r_v, r_w \xleftarrow{\$} [2^{\lambda}B]\}$$

Denote $f(r_1, r_2, r_u, r_v, r_w) := (\mathsf{g}^{r_1}, \mathsf{g}^{r_2}, \mathsf{g}^{r_1 r_2}, \mathsf{g}^{\lfloor r_1/l_1 \rfloor}, (\mathsf{g}^{r_2})^{\lfloor r_1/l_1 \rfloor}, \mathsf{g}^{\lfloor r_2/l_2 \rfloor}, r_1 \mod l_1, r_2 \mod l_2, \mathsf{u}^{r_1 r_u}, \mathsf{v}^{r_2 r_v}, \mathsf{w}^{r_1 r_2 r_w})$. As a key observation, $f(r_1, r_2, r_u, r_v, r_w) = f(r_1 \mod l_1|\mathbb{G}|, r_2 \mod l_2|\mathbb{G}|, r_u \mod |\mathbb{G}|, r_v \mod |\mathbb{G}|, r_w \mod |\mathbb{G}|)$. We thus have that $\mathcal{D}_{sim} = \{f(r_1 \mod l_1|\mathbb{G}|, r_2 \mod l_2|\mathbb{G}|, r_u \mod |\mathbb{G}|, r_v \mod |\mathbb{G}|, r_w \mod |\mathbb{G}|) |\ r_1, r_2 \xleftarrow{\$} [2^{2\lambda}B], r_u, r_v, r_w \xleftarrow{\$} [2^{\lambda}B]\}$. Let x' (resp. y') be the element in $\mathbb{Z}_{|\mathbb{G}|}$ satisfying $xx' \equiv 1 \mod |\mathbb{G}|$ (resp. $yy' \equiv 1 \mod |\mathbb{G}|$). This is possible due to $\gcd(xy, |\mathbb{G}|) = 1$. Then, we obtain that $\mathcal{D}_P = \{f(r_1 x \mod l_1|\mathbb{G}|, r_2 y \mod l_1|\mathbb{G}|, r_u x' \mod |\mathbb{G}|, r_v y' \mod |\mathbb{G}|, r_w x' y' \mod |\mathbb{G}|) | r_1, r_2 \xleftarrow{\$} [2^{2\lambda}B], r_u, r_v, r_w \xleftarrow{\$} [2^{\lambda}B]\}$. From Lemma 2 and the fact that $\gcd(x, l_1|\mathbb{G}|) = 1$, $\gcd(y, l_2|\mathbb{G}|) = 1$, we have that both of the distributions $\mathcal{D}_{sim}$ and $\mathcal{D}_P$ are exponentially close to the distribution $\{f(r_1, r_2, r_u, r_v, r_w) | r_1 \xleftarrow{\$} \mathbb{Z}_{l_1|\mathbb{G}|}, r_2 \xleftarrow{\$} \mathbb{Z}_{l_2|\mathbb{G}|}, r_u, r_v, r_w \xleftarrow{\$} \mathbb{Z}_{|\mathbb{G}|}\}$, which concludes the proof. □

Note that both of the protocols provided in this subsection are constant-round public-coin protocols. One can use the Fiat-Shamir heuristic to obtain the non-interactive version of these zero-knowledge protocols. These non-interactive protocols satisfy zero-knowledge property and the same weak knowledge soundness property in the random oracle model. We denote these two non-interactive protocols as $\mathsf{NIZK}_{coprime}$ and $\mathsf{NIZK}_{pseudo-DDH}$.

4 Zero-Knowledge Set with Set-Operation Queries

In this section, we introduce the notion of ZKS with set-operation queries, which is the key ingredient for achieving our end goal of ZK-FEDBs. Moreover, we provide a concrete construction of ZKS with set-operation queries based on groups of unknown orders.

4.1 Definition

Informally, ZKS with set-operation queries allow one to commit to several sets $\{S_i\}_{i\in[m]}$, and then convincingly answer a) the (non-)membership queries and b) for any combined operation $\mathcal{Q}$ represented as a "circuit" of unions, intersections and set-differences, the queries in the form as "send me all records x in $\mathcal{Q}(S_1, \cdots, S_m)$," without revealing any extra knowledge. The formal definition of ZKS with set-operation queries is as follows:

Definition 2 (ZKS with Set-Operation Queries). *A ZKS with set-operation queries consists of six algorithms,* (Setup, Com, Prove, Verify, SO.Prove, SO.Verify), *where* Setup, Com, Prove, Verify *are in the same form as a standard ZKS and*

- $\pi \leftarrow \mathsf{SO.Prove}(\delta, \widetilde{com}, \widetilde{\tau}, \mathcal{Q}, S_{output})$: *On input the CRS δ, the list of set commitments and the associated opening information $\widetilde{com} = (com_1, \cdots, com_m)$, $\widetilde{\tau} = (\tau_1, \cdots, \tau_m)$ where $(com_i, \tau_i) \in \mathsf{Com}(\delta, S_i)$, a combined operation $\mathcal{Q}$, and the output set S_{output},* SO.Prove *outputs a proof π of $S_{output} = \mathcal{Q}(S_1, \cdots, S_m)$.*
- $0/1 \leftarrow \mathsf{SO.Verify}(\delta, \widetilde{com}, \mathcal{Q}, S_{output}, \pi)$: *On input the CRS δ, the list of commitments $\widetilde{com}$, the combined operation $\mathcal{Q}$, the output S_{output}, and the proof π,* SO.Verify *either outputs* 1 *(denoting accept) or* 0 *(denoting reject).*

and satisfies the following properties:

- **Completeness:** *Completeness consists of two parts,*
  a) For any set S and any x,

$$\Pr\left[\mathsf{Verify}(\delta, com, x, S(x), \pi) = 1 \;\middle|\; \begin{array}{c} \delta \leftarrow \mathsf{Setup}(1^\lambda); (com, \tau) \leftarrow \mathsf{Com}(\delta, S); \\ \pi \leftarrow \mathsf{Prove}(\delta, com, \tau, x, S(x)) \end{array}\right] = 1$$

  b) For any sets $\{S_i\}_{i\in[m]}$ and any combined operation $\mathcal{Q}$ which takes m sets as input and outputs one set, let $S_{output} = \mathcal{Q}(S_1, \cdots, S_m)$, and thus

$$\Pr\left[\begin{array}{r} \mathsf{SO.Verify}(\delta, \widetilde{com}, \mathcal{Q}, \\ S_{output}, \pi) = 1 \end{array} \;\middle|\; \begin{array}{c} \delta \leftarrow \mathsf{Setup}(1^\lambda); \\ \forall i \in [m], (com_i, \tau_i) \leftarrow \mathsf{Com}(\delta, S_i); \\ \pi \leftarrow \mathsf{SO.Prove}(\delta, \widetilde{com}, \widetilde{\tau}, \mathcal{Q}, S_{output}) \end{array}\right] = 1$$

  where $\widetilde{com} = (com_1, \cdots, com_m)$ and $\widetilde{\tau} = (\tau_1, \cdots, \tau_m)$.
- **Function Binding:** *For any PPT adversary $\mathcal{A}$, the probability that $\mathcal{A}$ wins the following game is negligible:*
  1. *The challenger generates a CRS δ by running* $\mathsf{Setup}(1^\lambda)$ *and gives δ to the adversary $\mathcal{A}$.*

2. *The adversary $\mathcal{A}$ outputs a set of commitments $\{com_i\}_{i\in[m]}$ and the following tuples:*
   (a) *A series of (non-)membership query-proof tuples $\{(com'_j, x_j, v_j, \pi_j)\}_{j\in[n_1]}$, where $com'_j \in \{com_i\}_{i\in[m]}$ (supposing that $com'_j = com_{t_j}$).*
   (b) *A series of set-operation query-proof tuples $\{(\widetilde{com}_j, \mathcal{Q}_j, S'_j, \pi'_j)\}_{j\in[n_2]}$, where $\widetilde{com}_j$ is a list of commitments contained in $\{com_i\}_{i\in[m]}$ (supposing that $\widetilde{com}_j = (com_{t_{j1}}, com_{t_{j2}}, \cdots)$).*
3. *The adversary $\mathcal{A}$ wins the game if the following hold:*
   (a) *For each $j \in [n_1]$, $\mathsf{Verify}(com'_j, x_j, v_j, \pi_j) = 1$*
   (b) *For each $j \in [n_2]$, $\mathsf{SO.Verify}(\widetilde{com}_j, \mathcal{Q}_j, S'_j, \pi'_j) = 1$.*
   (c) *There do **not** exist sets $\{S_i\}_{i\in[m]}$ satisfying $S_{t_j}(x_j) = v_j$ for each $j \in [n_1]$ and $\mathcal{Q}_j(\widetilde{S}_j) = S'_j$ for each $j \in [n_2]$, where $\widetilde{S}_j = (S_{t_{j1}}, S_{t_{j2}}, \cdots)$.*

- **Zero-Knowledge:** *There exists a simulator Sim such that for any PPT adversary $\mathcal{A}$, the absolute value of the difference*

$$\Pr\left[\mathcal{A}^{\mathcal{O}_P}(\delta, st_{\mathcal{A}}, \{com_i\}_{i\in[m]})=1 \;\middle|\; \begin{array}{c}\delta \leftarrow \mathsf{Setup}(1^\lambda),\\ (\{S_i\}_{i\in[m]}, st_{\mathcal{A}}) \leftarrow \mathcal{A}(\delta),\\ \text{for } i\in[m], (com_i,\tau_i)\leftarrow \mathsf{Com}(\delta, S_i)\end{array}\right]$$
$$-\Pr\left[\mathcal{A}^{\mathcal{O}_S}(\delta, st_{\mathcal{A}}, \{com_i\}_{i\in[m]})=1 \;\middle|\; \begin{array}{c}(\delta, st_\delta) \leftarrow Sim(1^\lambda),\\ (\{S_i\}_{i\in[m]}, st_{\mathcal{A}}) \leftarrow \mathcal{A}(\delta),\\ (\{com_i\}_{i\in[m]}, st_S)\leftarrow Sim(\delta, m, st_\delta)\end{array}\right]$$

is negligible in λ, where $\mathcal{O}_P$ and $\mathcal{O}_S$ are defined as follows:

$\mathcal{O}_P$: *On input (com_i, x) for some $i \in [m]$, $\mathcal{O}_P$ outputs $\pi \leftarrow \mathsf{Prove}(\delta, com_i, \tau_i, x, S_i(x))$. On input $(\widetilde{com}, \mathcal{Q})$ where $\widetilde{com} = (com_{t_1}, \cdots, com_{t_n})$ for some $t_1, \cdots, t_n \in [m]$, $\mathcal{O}_P$ outputs $\pi \leftarrow \mathsf{SO.Prove}(\delta, \widetilde{com}, \widetilde{\tau}, \mathcal{Q}, \mathcal{Q}(S_{t_1}, \cdots, S_{t_n}))$ where $\widetilde{\tau} = (\tau_{t_1}, \cdots, \tau_{t_n})$. In other cases, $\mathcal{O}_P$ outputs $\perp$.*

$\mathcal{O}_S$: *On input (com_i, x) for some $i \in [m]$, $\mathcal{O}_S$ outputs $\pi \leftarrow Sim(\delta, com, st_S, x, S_i(x))$. On input $(\widetilde{com}, Q)$ where $\widetilde{com} = (com_{t_1}, \cdots, com_{t_n})$ for some $t_1, \cdots, t_n \in [m]$, $\mathcal{O}_S$ outputs $\pi \leftarrow Sim(\delta, \widetilde{com}, st_S, \mathcal{Q}, \mathcal{Q}(S_{t_1}, \cdots, S_{t_n}))$. In other cases, $\mathcal{O}_S$ outputs $\perp$.*

4.2 Construction of ZKS with Set-Operation Queries

This subsection describes our construction of a ZKS scheme with set-operation queries. Our construction builds on the standard ZKS described in Sect. 3.1. The Setup, Commit, Prove, Verify algorithms remain the same as Fig. 5, and we only show how to construct SO.Prove and SO.Verify algorithms.

Combined Operations. In this paper, we denote a combined operation $\mathcal{Q}$ by a "circuit" of intersection "$\cap$", union "$\cup$", and set-difference "$\setminus$". Firstly, we demonstrate how to prove a basic set operation (namely the intersection, union or set-difference) on committed sets.

Algorithm for Intersection. Here we present a non-interactive protocol to prove that a commitment C_I commits to the intersection of two sets committed in C_{S_1} and C_{S_2}. Our protocol satisfies a special-purpose knowledge soundness, which roughly ensures the following:

- If one can generate a membership proof showing that x belongs to the set committed in C_I, then the extractor can generate membership proofs showing that x belongs to the sets committed in C_{S_1} and C_{S_2}.
- If one can generate a non-membership proof showing that x does not belong to the set committed in C_I, then the extractor can generate a non-membership proof showing that x does not belong to either the set committed in C_{S_1} or the set committed in C_{S_2}

Follow the fact that, for any S_1 and S_2, proving $I = S_1 \cap S_2$ only requires to show that I is a subset of S_1 and S_2, and $J_1 = S_1 \backslash I, J_2 = S_2 \backslash I$ are disjointed. We construct the zero-knowledge protocol Intersection-NIZK shown in Fig. 8. For any set $S = \{x_1, \cdots, x_m\}$, we denote by $\mathcal{H}_{prime}(S) = \{\mathcal{H}_{prime}(x_1), \cdots, \mathcal{H}_{prime}(x_m)\}$.

Protocol Intersection-NIZK

Common Input: $\delta = (\mathbb{G}, \mathsf{g}, B, \mathcal{H}_{prime})$, $\mathsf{C}_{S_1}, \mathsf{C}_{S_2}, \mathsf{C}_I$;
Private Input for Prover: $S_1, S_2, I, \tau_{S_1}, \tau_{S_2}, \tau_I$ satisfying that
$(\mathsf{C}_{S_1}, \tau_{S_1}) \in \mathsf{Commit}(\delta, S_1)$; $(\mathsf{C}_{S_2}, \tau_{S_2}) \in \mathsf{Commit}(\delta, S_2)$;
$(\mathsf{C}_I, \tau_I) \in \mathsf{Commit}(\delta, I)$ and $S_1 \cap S_2 = I$.

Prover:

1. Generate the commitments C_{J_1} and C_{J_2} to the sets $J_1 = S_1 \backslash I$ and $J_2 = S_2 \backslash I$.
2. Run $\pi_1 \leftarrow \mathsf{NIZK}_{pseudo-DDH}(\mathsf{C}_I, \mathsf{C}_{J_1}, \mathsf{C}_{S_1}, 2^\lambda B)$ and $\pi_2 \leftarrow \mathsf{NIZK}_{pseudo-DDH}(\mathsf{C}_I, \mathsf{C}_{J_2}, \mathsf{C}_{S_2}, 2^\lambda B)$ using the required witness contained in the opening information.
3. Run $\pi_3 \leftarrow \mathsf{NIZK}_{coprime}(\mathsf{C}_{J_1}, \mathsf{C}_{J_2}, 2^\lambda B)$ using the required witness contained in the opening information.
4. Output $\pi = (\mathsf{C}_{J_1}, \mathsf{C}_{J_2}, \pi_1, \pi_2, \pi_3)$

Verifier: Output 1 iff. the proofs contained in π are valid.

Fig. 8. Protocol Intersection-NIZK

Lemma 8. Intersection-NIZK *is a zero-knowledge protocol, achieving a special purpose knowledge soundness defined as follows: There exists an extractor $E = (E_1, E_2)$ such that for any prover $\mathcal{P}^*$ convincing the verifier with inverse-polynomial probability over input $(\delta, \mathsf{C}_{S_1}, \mathsf{C}_{S_2}, \mathsf{C}_I)$, $E_1^{\mathcal{P}^*}$ can extract w in expected polynomial time such that the following holds:*

1. *On input w, $\mathsf{g}_a \in \mathbb{G}$ and prime $p \in \mathbb{Z}$ satisfying $p \geq 2^{8\lambda}B^3$ and $\mathsf{C}_I = \mathsf{g}_a^p$, $E_2(w, (\mathsf{g}_a, p))$ can output g_b and g_c such that $\mathsf{C}_{S_1} = \mathsf{g}_b^p$ and $\mathsf{C}_{S_2} = \mathsf{g}_c^p$.*
2. *On input w and $a, b, p \in \mathbb{Z}$ such that prime $p \geq 2^{8\lambda}B^3$ and $\mathsf{C}_I^a \cdot \mathsf{g}^{bp} = \mathsf{g}$, $E_2(w, (a, b, p))$ can output $a', b' \in \mathbb{Z}$ such that $\mathsf{C}_{S_1}^{a'} \cdot \mathsf{g}^{b'p} = \mathsf{g}$ or $\mathsf{C}_{S_2}^{a'} \cdot \mathsf{g}^{b'p} = \mathsf{g}$.*

Proof. **Completeness** directly follows the structure of ZKS commitment, therefore we skip it here.

The simulator of the **zero-knowledge** property only needs to generate $\mathsf{C}_{J_1} = \mathsf{g}^{r_1}$ and $\mathsf{C}_{J_2} = \mathsf{g}^{r_2}$ by sampling $r_1, r_2 \xleftarrow{\$} [2^\lambda B]$, and generate π_1, π_2, π_3 using the simulator of $\mathsf{NIZK}_{pseudo-DDH}$ and $\mathsf{NIZK}_{coprime}$. Then the zero-knowledge property follows from the fact that the distributions of $\mathsf{C}_{J_1}, \mathsf{C}_{J_2}$ generated by the simulator are statistically indistinguishable from those generated by an honest prover and the zero-knowledge property of $\mathsf{NIZK}_{pseudo-DDH}$ and $\mathsf{NIZK}_{coprime}$.

The proof of the **special purpose knowledge soundness** is as follows.

From the weak knowledge soundness of $\mathsf{NIZK}_{pseudo-DDH}$, E_1 can extract $w_1 = (x, y, a_1, a_2, a_3, c_1, c_2, c_3)$ such that $|a_1|, |a_2|, |a_3| \leq 2^{5\lambda}B^2$, $|c_1|, |c_2| \leq 2^{6\lambda}B^2$, $|c_3| \leq 2^{8\lambda}B^3$, and $\mathsf{C}_I^{c_1} = \mathsf{g}^{a_1x}, \mathsf{C}_{J_1}^{c_2} = \mathsf{g}^{a_2y}, \mathsf{C}_{S_1}^{c_3} = \mathsf{g}^{a_3xy}$; and $w_2 = (x', y', a_1', a_2', a_3', c_1', c_2', c_3')$ such that $|a_1'|, |a_2'|, |a_3'| \leq 2^{5\lambda}B^2$, $|c_1'|, |c_2'| \leq 2^{6\lambda}B^2$, $|c_3'| \leq 2^{8\lambda}B^3$, and $\mathsf{C}_I^{c_1'} = \mathsf{g}^{a_1'x'}, \mathsf{C}_{J_2}^{c_2'} = \mathsf{g}^{a_2'y'}, \mathsf{C}_{S_2}^{c_3'} = \mathsf{g}^{a_3'x'y'}$. From the weak knowledge soundness of $\mathsf{NIZK}_{coprime}$, E_1 can extract $w_3 = (t_1, t_2, c)$ such that $|c| \leq 2^{5\lambda}B^2$ and $\mathsf{C}_{J_1}^{t_1}\mathsf{C}_{J_2}^{t_2} = \mathsf{g}^c$. Here, E_1 outputs $w = (\mathsf{C}_{J_1}, \mathsf{C}_{J_2}, w_1, w_2, w_3)$.

Nextly, we show how E_2 works to conclude the proof:

1. On input w, $\mathsf{g}_a \in \mathbb{G}$ and prime $p \in \mathbb{Z}$ satisfying $p \geq 2^{8\lambda}B^3$ and $\mathsf{C}_I = \mathsf{g}_a^p$, E_2 firstly parses w as $(\mathsf{C}_{J_1}, \mathsf{C}_{J_2}, w_1, w_2, w_3)$ and parses w_1 as $(x, y, a_1, a_2, a_3, c_1, c_2, c_3)$. Since $\mathsf{C}_I^{c_1} = \mathsf{g}^{a_1x}$, it follows that $\mathsf{g}_a^{c_1p} = \mathsf{g}^{a_1x}$. We claim that $p|a_1x$, otherwise, from Lemma 4, an attacker could easily find a p-root of g and break the strong RSA assumption. Since p is a prime larger than a_1, it follows that $p|x$ and $\mathsf{C}_{S_1}^{c_3} = \mathsf{g}^{a_3xy} = (\mathsf{g}^{a_3x_py})^p$ where $x_p = x/p \in \mathbb{Z}$. As $\gcd(p, c_3) = 1$, from Lemma 4, E_2 can easily compute g_b from $(c_3, \mathsf{g}^{a_3xy/p})$ such that $\mathsf{C}_{S_1} = \mathsf{g}_b^p$. Using the same strategy, E_2 can also compute g_c such that $\mathsf{C}_{S_2} = \mathsf{g}_c^p$.
2. On input w and $a, b, p \in \mathbb{Z}$ satisfying that p is a prime larger than $2^{8\lambda}B^3$ and $\mathsf{C}_I^a \cdot \mathsf{g}^{bp} = \mathsf{g}$, E_2 firstly parses w as $(\mathsf{C}_{J_1}, \mathsf{C}_{J_2}, w_1, w_2, w_3)$ and further parses w_1 as $(x, y, a_1, a_2, a_3, c_1, c_2, c_3)$. We claim that $\gcd(p, x) = 1$, since it is known that $\mathsf{C}_I^a \cdot \mathsf{g}^{bp} = \mathsf{g}$ and $\mathsf{C}_I^{c_1} = \mathsf{g}^{a_1x}$; otherwise, an attacker could easily break the strong RSA assumption. If $\gcd(p, y) = 1$ (or equivalently, $\gcd(p, a_3xy) = 1$), E_2 can easily find integers α, β satisfying $\alpha p + \beta a_3xy = 1$, and output $a' = \beta c_3$ and $b' = \alpha$ such that $\mathsf{C}_{S_1}^{a'} \cdot \mathsf{g}^{b'p} = \mathsf{C}_{S_1}^{\beta c_3}\mathsf{g}^{\alpha p} = \mathsf{g}^{\beta a_3xy}\mathsf{g}^{\alpha p} = \mathsf{g}$. Similarly, parsing $w_2 = (x', y', a_1', a_2', a_3', c_1', c_2', c_3')$, if $\gcd(p, y') = 1$, E_2 can also compute $a', b' \in \mathbb{Z}$ such that $\mathsf{C}_{S_2}^{a'} \cdot \mathsf{g}^{b'p} = \mathsf{g}$. The construction of E_2 concludes by claiming that at least one of the $\gcd(p, y) = 1$, $\gcd(p, y') = 1$ must happen. Otherwise, an attacker could easily break the strong RSA assumption as follows: Since p is a large prime and $\gcd(p, y) \neq 1, \gcd(p, y') \neq 1$, it follows that $p|y$, $p|y'$. Then, from Lemma 4 and the fact $\mathsf{C}_{J_1}^{c_2} = \mathsf{g}^{a_2y}, \mathsf{C}_{J_2}^{c_2'} = \mathsf{g}^{a_2'y'}$, it can compute $\mathsf{h}_1, \mathsf{h}_2$ such that $\mathsf{C}_{J_1} = \mathsf{h}_1^p$ and $\mathsf{C}_{J_2} = \mathsf{h}_2^p$. Subsequently, from Lemma 4 and the

fact $\mathsf{C}_{J_1}^{t_1}\mathsf{C}_{J_2}^{t_2} = \mathsf{g}^c$ where $w_3 = (t_1, t_2, c)$, it can compute h such that $\mathsf{h}^p = \mathsf{g}$, breaking the strong RSA assumption. □

Algorithm for Union. Herein we present a non-interactive protocol to prove that a commitment C_U commits to the union of two sets committed in C_{S_1} and C_{S_2}. Our protocol satisfies a special-purpose knowledge soundness, which roughly ensures the following:

- If one can generate a membership proof showing that x belongs to the set committed in C_U, the extractor can generate a membership proof showing that x belongs to the set committed in either C_{S_1} or C_{S_2}.
- If one can generate a non-membership proof showing that x does not belong to the set committed in C_I, then the extractor can generate non-membership proofs showing that x does not belong to the sets committed in C_{S_1} and C_{S_2}.

We construct the zero-knowledge protocol Union-NIZK in Fig. 9.

Protocol Union-NIZK

Common Input: $\delta = (\mathbb{G}, \mathsf{g}, B, \mathcal{H}_{prime}), \mathsf{C}_{S_1}, \mathsf{C}_{S_2}, \mathsf{C}_U$;
Private Input for Prover: $S_1, S_2, U, \tau_{S_1}, \tau_{S_2}, \tau_U$ satisfying that $(\mathsf{C}_{S_1}, \tau_{S_1}) \in \mathsf{Commit}(\delta, S_1)$; $(\mathsf{C}_{S_2}, \tau_{S_2}) \in \mathsf{Commit}(\delta, S_2)$; $(\mathsf{C}_U, \tau_U) \in \mathsf{Commit}(\delta, U)$ and $S_1 \cup S_2 = U$.

Prover
1. Generates the commitment $\mathsf{C}_I, \mathsf{C}_{J_1}, \mathsf{C}_{J_2}$ to the sets $I = S_1 \cap S_2, J_1 = U \backslash S_1, J_2 = U \backslash S_2$.
2. Run $\pi_1 \leftarrow \mathsf{NIZK}_{pseudo-DDH}(\mathsf{C}_I, \mathsf{C}_{J_1}, \mathsf{C}_{S_2}, 2^\lambda B)$ using the required witness contained in the opening information.
3. Run $\pi_2 \leftarrow \mathsf{NIZK}_{pseudo-DDH}(\mathsf{C}_{S_1}, \mathsf{C}_{J_1}, \mathsf{C}_U, 2^\lambda B)$ and $\pi_3 \leftarrow \mathsf{NIZK}_{pseudo-DDH}(\mathsf{C}_{S_2}, \mathsf{C}_{J_2}, \mathsf{C}_U, 2^\lambda B)$ using the required witness contained in the opening information.
4. Output $\pi = (\mathsf{C}_I, \mathsf{C}_{J_1}, \mathsf{C}_{J_2}, \pi_1, \pi_2, \pi_3)$

Verifier: Output 1 iff. the proofs contained in π are valid.

Fig. 9. Protocol Union-NIZK

Lemma 9. Union-NIZK *is a zero-knowledge protocol, achieving a special purpose knowledge soundness defined as follows: There exists an extractor $E = (E_1, E_2)$ such that for any prover $\mathcal{P}^*$ convincing the verifier with inverse-polynomial probability over input $(\delta, \mathsf{C}_{S_1}, \mathsf{C}_{S_2}, \mathsf{C}_I)$, $E_1^{\mathcal{P}^*}$ can extract w within an expected time such that the following hold:*

1. *On input w and $\mathsf{g}_a \in \mathbb{Z}$ and prime p satisfying $p \geq 2^{8\lambda}B^3$ and $\mathsf{C}_U = \mathsf{g}_a^p$, $E_2(w, (\mathsf{g}^a, p))$ can output g_b such that $\mathsf{C}_{S_1} = \mathsf{g}_b^p$ or $\mathsf{C}_{S_2} = \mathsf{g}_b^p$.*

2. *On input w and $a, b, p \in \mathbb{Z}$ such that prime $p \geq 2^{8\lambda}B^3$ and $\mathsf{C}_U^a \cdot \mathsf{g}^{bp} = \mathsf{g}$, $E_2(w, (a, b, p))$ can output $a', b', a'', b'' \in \mathbb{Z}$ such that $\mathsf{C}_{S_1}^{a'} \cdot \mathsf{g}^{b'p} = \mathsf{g}$ and $\mathsf{C}_{S_2}^{a''} \cdot \mathsf{g}^{b''p} = \mathsf{g}$.*

The proof of this lemma is similar to Lemma 8. We defer it to the full version of this paper [45].

Algorithm for Set-Difference. We present a non-interactive protocol to prove that the difference D between two sets S_1, S_2 committed in C_{S_1} and C_{S_2} (i.e., $D = S_1 \backslash S_2$) is committed in C_D. Our protocol satisfies a special-purpose knowledge soundness, which roughly ensures the following:

- If one can generate a membership proof showing that x belongs to the set committed in C_D, the extractor can generate a membership proof showing that x belongs to the set committed in C_{S_1} and a non-membership proof showing that x doesn't belong to the set committed in C_{S_2}.
- If one can generate a non-membership proof showing that x does not belong to the set committed in C_D, the extractor can generate a non-membership proof showing that x does not belong to the set committed in C_{S_1} or a membership proof showing that x belongs to the set committed in C_{S_2}.

We construct the zero-knowledge protocol Difference-NIZK in Fig. 10.

Protocol Difference-NIZK

Common Input: $\delta = (\mathbb{G}, \mathsf{g}, B, \mathcal{H}_{prime})$, $\mathsf{C}_{S_1}, \mathsf{C}_{S_2}, \mathsf{C}_D$;
Private Input for Prover: $S_1, S_2, S_D, \tau_{S_1}, \tau_{S_2}, \tau_D$ satisfying that $(\mathsf{C}_{S_1}, \tau_{S_1}) \in \mathsf{Commit}(\delta, S_1)$; $(\mathsf{C}_{S_2}, \tau_{S_2}) \in \mathsf{Commit}(\delta, S_2)$; $(\mathsf{C}_D, \tau_D) \in \mathsf{Commit}(\delta, D)$ and $S_1 \backslash S_2 = D$.

Prover:

1. Generate the commitments $\mathsf{C}_I, \mathsf{C}_J$ to the sets $I = S_1 \cap S_2, J = S_2 \backslash I$.
2. Run $\pi_1 \leftarrow \mathsf{NIZK}_{pseudo-DDH}(\mathsf{C}_I, \mathsf{C}_D, \mathsf{C}_{S_1}, 2^\lambda B)$ and $\pi_2 \leftarrow \mathsf{NIZK}_{pseudo-DDH}(\mathsf{C}_I, \mathsf{C}_J, \mathsf{C}_{S_2}, 2^\lambda B)$ using the required witness contained in the opening information.
3. Run $\pi_3 \leftarrow \mathsf{NIZK}_{coprime}(\mathsf{C}_D, \mathsf{C}_{S_2}, 2^\lambda B)$ using the required witness contained in the opening information.
4. Output $\pi = (\mathsf{C}_I, \mathsf{C}_J, \pi_1, \pi_2, \pi_3)$

Verifier: Output 1 iff. the proofs contained in π are valid.

Fig. 10. Protocol Difference-NIZK

Lemma 10. Difference-NIZK *is a zero-knowledge protocol, achieving a special purpose knowledge soundness defined as follows: There exists a extractor $E = (E_1, E_2)$ such that for any prover $\mathcal{P}^*$ convincing the verifier with inverse-polynomial probability over input $(\delta, \mathsf{C}_{S_1}, \mathsf{C}_{S_2}, \mathsf{C}_D)$, $E_1^{\mathcal{P}^*}$ can extract w such that the following holds:*

1. *On input* w, $\mathsf{g}_a \in \mathbb{G}$ *and prime* $p \in \mathbb{Z}$ *such that* $p \geq 2^{8\lambda} B^3$ *and* $\mathsf{C}_D = \mathsf{g}_a^p$, $E_2(w, (\mathsf{g}_a, p))$ *can output* g_b *and* a, b *such that* $\mathsf{C}_{S_1} = \mathsf{g}_b^p$ *and* $\mathsf{C}_{S_2}^a \mathsf{g}^{pb} = \mathsf{g}$.
2. *On input* w *and* $a, b, p \in \mathbb{Z}$ *such that prime* $p \geq 2^{8\lambda} B^3$ *and* $\mathsf{C}_D^a \cdot \mathsf{g}^{bp} = \mathsf{g}$, $E_2(w, (a, b, p))$ *can output* g_a *or* a', b' *such that* $\mathsf{C}_{S_2} = \mathsf{g}_a^p$ *or* $\mathsf{C}_{S_1}^{a'} \cdot \mathsf{g}^{b'p} = g$.

The proof of this lemma is similar to Lemma 8, and we defer it to the full version of this paper [45].

Algorithm for Combined Operations. Using above algorithms, we now construct the SO.Prove and SO.Verify algorithms to conclude the construction of ZKS with set-operation queries. Remind that a combined operation $\mathcal{Q}$ is a circuit comprised of gates and wires. Each gate corresponds to an intersection, union, or set difference operation. Just like in Boolean circuits, when given a string as input, each wire in Boolean circuit has a deterministic bit in $\{0, 1\}$. Each wire in the set-operation circuit corresponds to a deterministic set when provided with a specific input.

Therefore, to prove that a combined operation $\mathcal{Q}$ on (committed) sets is performed honestly, we only need to show that each gate in $\mathcal{Q}$ is performed honestly, i.e., for each gate corresponding a basic set operation, the (committed) set corresponding to the output wire is the result of applying this set operation to the (committed) sets corresponding to the input wires.

Without loss of generality, assume that the gates of $\mathcal{Q}$ are numbered based on their execution order. That is to say, the input wires of the gate i are either the output wire of some gate $j < i$ or an input wire of $\mathcal{Q}$, and the output wire of the last gate is also the output wire of $\mathcal{Q}$. The protocol is shown in Fig. 11:

Theorem 3. *The algorithms* (Setup, Com, Prove, Verify) *in Fig. 5 together with the algorithms* (SO.Prove, SO.Verify) *in Fig. 11 consist a ZKS with set-operation queries in the generic group model and random oracle model.*

Proof. **Completeness** is oblivious.

To prove the **function binding** property, we will show the existence of a extractor E satisfying that, for any PPT adversary $\mathcal{A}$ generating a series of valid query-proof tuples with a noticeable probability, E can either extract a series of sets satisfying all queries or break the strong RSA assumption. Here, E is constructed as follows.

1. First, E invokes $\mathcal{A}$ to obtain m commitments, $\mathsf{C}_1, \cdots, \mathsf{C}_m$. Then, E initializes $2m+1$ sets, labeled as $S_0, S_1, S_1', \cdots, S_m, S_m'$. Here, S_0 is used to record all the elements x appearing in the query-proof queries generated by $\mathcal{A}$ (including the elements in the output set of a set-operation query). In addition, for any $i \in [m]$, S_i is the sets of elements that, believed by E, are contained in the set committed in C_i; S_i' is the sets of elements that, believed by E, are not contained in the set committed in C_i. Here, E invokes $\mathcal{A}$ to obtain the query-proof tuples and adds all appearing elements to S_0.
2. For each membership proof proving that x belongs to the set committed in C_i, E adds x to S_i, and extracts and records the tuple $(x, \mathsf{g}_x, p, \mathsf{C}_i)$ from the proof such that $\mathsf{g}_x^p = \mathsf{C}_i$ and $p = \mathcal{H}_{prime}(x)$. (The extraction of the tuple is trivial).

Algorithm for Verifiable Combined Operations

$\mathsf{SO.Prove}(\delta, \widetilde{com}, \widetilde{\tau}, \mathcal{Q}, S_{output})$: On input the CRS δ, the list of commitments and the associated opening information $\widetilde{com} = (\mathsf{C}_1, \cdots, \mathsf{C}_m)$, $\widetilde{\tau} = (\tau_1, \cdots, \tau_m)$ where $(\mathsf{C}_i, \tau_i) \in \mathsf{Com}(\delta, S_i)$, a combined operation $\mathcal{Q}$ and the target output set S_{output}. SO.Prove runs as follows.

1. Recover the sets $\{S_i\}_{i\in[m]}$ from the opening information. Regard $\mathcal{Q}$ as a "circuit" and let l be the number of gates. Run $\mathcal{Q}(S_1, \cdots, S_m)$ to obtain the sets $S_1', \cdots, S_l'$ corresponding to the output wires of l gates in $\mathcal{Q}$ (note that $S_l' = S_{output}$). Generate the commitments $\mathsf{C}_1', \cdots, \mathsf{C}_l'$ to the sets $S_1', \cdots, S_l'$. (Note that the sets corresponding to the input wires of circuit are already committed by $\{\mathsf{C}_i\}_{i\in[m]}$.)
2. For each gate i, suppose S_{a_i}, S_{b_i} are the sets corresponding to its input wires, S_{c_i} is the set corresponding to its output wire and $\mathsf{C}_{a_i}, \mathsf{C}_{b_i}, \mathsf{C}_{c_i}$ are their commitments.
   (a) If the gate corresponds to "interaction", SO.Prove runs $\pi_i \leftarrow \mathsf{Intersection\text{-}NIZK}(\delta, \mathsf{C}_{a_i}, \mathsf{C}_{b_i}, \mathsf{C}_{c_i})$.
   (b) If the gate corresponds to "union", SO.Prove runs $\pi_i \leftarrow \mathsf{Union\text{-}NIZK}(\delta, \mathsf{C}_{a_i}, \mathsf{C}_{b_i}, \mathsf{C}_{c_i})$.
   (c) If the gate corresponds to "set-difference", SO.Prove runs $\pi_i \leftarrow \mathsf{Difference\text{-}NIZK}(\delta, \mathsf{C}_{a_i}, \mathsf{C}_{b_i}, \mathsf{C}_{c_i})$.
3. Output $\pi = (\mathsf{C}_1', \cdots, \mathsf{C}_l', \pi_1, \cdots, \pi_l, \tau_l')$, where τ_l' is the opening information of C_l'.

$\mathsf{SO.Verify}(\delta, \widetilde{com}, \mathcal{Q}, S_{output}, \pi)$: Parse π as $(\mathsf{C}_1', \cdots, \mathsf{C}_l', \pi_1, \cdots, \pi_l, \tau_l')$. Regard $\mathcal{Q}$ as a "circuit" in the same way as the prover. For each gate i, suppose $\mathsf{C}_{a_i}, \mathsf{C}_{b_i}$ are the commitments that commit to the sets corresponding to the input wires and C_{c_i} is the commitment that commits to the set corresponding to the output wire. If this gate corresponds to "interaction" (resp. "union", "set-difference"), check whether π_i is a valid Intersection-NIZK (resp. Union-NIZK, Difference-NIZK) proof over the statement $\delta, \mathsf{C}_{a_i}, \mathsf{C}_{b_i}, \mathsf{C}_{c_i}$. Use τ_l' to check whether C_l' is a commitment to the set S_{output}. Output 1 iff. all checks pass.

Fig. 11. Protocol for Verifiable Combined Operations

We call such a tuple as membership tuple. For each non-membership proof proving that x does not belong to the set committed in C_i, E adds x to S_i', and extracts and records $(x, a, b, p, \mathsf{C}_i)$ such that $\mathsf{C}_i^a \mathsf{g}^{pb} = \mathsf{g}$ and $p = \mathcal{H}_{prime}(x)$. We call such a tuple as non-membership tuple. Furthermore, for each set-operation query-proof tuple, E uses the extractors E_1 of Intersection-NIZK, Union-NIZK and Difference-NIZK to extract the corresponding w.

3. For each element $x \in S_0$, E applies the following. For each set-operation query-proof tuple, if x belongs to the output set S_{output} whose commitment

is C'_l, E can obtain a membership tuple $(x, \mathsf{g}_x, p, \mathsf{C}'_l)$ from proof. On the other hand, if x does not belong to the output set, then E can obtain a non-membership tuple $(x, a, b, p, \mathsf{C}'_l)$. According to the special purpose knowledge soundness of Intersection-NIZK, Union-NIZK, and Difference-NIZK, for each gate, when given a (non-)membership tuple associated to the output wires (we call a (non-)membership tuple associated to a wire if the commitment in this tuple is the one committing to the set corresponding to this wire), one can extract one or two (non-)membership tuples associated to the input wires. E can hence recursively obtain a series of tuples associated to input wires of the combined operation. As a result, for each obtained tuple of the form $(x, \mathsf{g}', p, \mathsf{C}_i)$, E adds x to S_i, and for each obtained tuple of the form $(x, a, b, p, \mathsf{C}_i)$, E adds x to S'_i.

4. If there are no contradictions (that is, there are no elements x and $i \in [m]$ such that $x \in S_i \wedge x \in S'_i$), then E outputs $S_1, \cdots, S_m$. Otherwise, it means that there exists $(x, \mathsf{g}_x, p, \mathsf{C}_i)$ and $(x, a, b, p, \mathsf{C}_i)$ such that $\mathsf{g}_x^p = \mathsf{C}_i$ and $\mathsf{C}_i^a \mathsf{g}^{pb} = \mathsf{g}$, breaking the strong RSA Assumption.

Now we only need to show that the sets $S_1, \cdots, S_m$ outputted by E satisfy all queries. From step 2, we can see that these sets already satisfy the (non-)membership queries. As for set-operation queries, we need to show that: For each set-operation query-proof $(\mathsf{C}_{t_1}, \cdots, \mathsf{C}_{t_k}, \mathcal{Q}, S_{output}, \pi)$, $\mathcal{Q}(S_{t_1}, \cdots, S_{t_k}) = S_{output}$.

Let l be the number of the gates of $\mathcal{Q}$, parse π as $(\mathsf{C}'_1, \cdots, \mathsf{C}'_l, \pi_1, \cdots, \pi_l, \tau'_l)$. Run $\mathcal{Q}(S_{t_1}, \cdots, S_{t_k})$ to obtain the sets $S'_1, \cdots, S'_l$ corresponding to the output wires of the gates in $\mathcal{Q}$ (thus, $S'_l = \mathcal{Q}(S_{t_1}, \cdots, S_{t_k})$). Denote by $(S''_1, \cdots, S''_{k+l}) = (S_{t_1}, \cdots, S_{t_k}, S'_1, \cdots, S'_l)$ and $(\mathsf{C}''_1, \cdots, \mathsf{C}''_{k+l}) = (\mathsf{C}_{t_1}, \cdots, \mathsf{C}_{t_k}, \mathsf{C}'_1, \cdots, \mathsf{C}'_l)$. Remind that E will extract lots of tuples associated to the wires in $\mathcal{Q}$ in step 3. Here, we recursively prove the following statements are true for each $i \in [k + l]$:

For each $x \in S_0$, if E used to extract a tuple of the form $(x, \mathsf{g}', p, \mathsf{C}''_i)$ in step 3, then $x \in S''_i$; And if E used to extract a tuple of the form $(x, a, b, p, \mathsf{C}''_i)$ in step 3, then $x \notin S''_i$.

Firstly, from the definition of $S_1, \cdots, S_m$, above statements are true for $i \in [k]$. Suppose above statements are true for $i \in [k + t - 1]$. Then for gate t with sets S''_{j_1}, S''_{j_2} $(j_1, j_2 \leq k + t - 1)$ corresponding to the input wires, if the gate corresponding to "interactive" and $(x, \mathsf{g}_a, p, \mathsf{C}''_{k+t})$ (resp. $(x, a, b, p, \mathsf{C}''_{k+t})$) is extracted, then from the knowledge soundness of Intersection-NIZK, $(x, \mathsf{g}_b, p, \mathsf{C}''_{j_1})$ and $(x, \mathsf{g}_c, p, \mathsf{C}''_{j_2})$ (resp. $(x, a', b', \mathsf{C}''_{j_1})$ or $(x, a', b', \mathsf{C}''_{j_2})$) are extracted by E. Since $j_1, j_2 \leq k + t - 1$, it follows that $x \in S''_{j_1}, x \in S''_{j_2}$ (resp. $x \notin S''_{j_1}$ or $x \notin S''_{j_2}$), and therefore $x \in S''_{k+t} = S''_{j_1} \cap S''_{j_2}$ (resp. $x \notin S''_{k+t} = S''_{j_1} \cap S''_{j_2}$). The case that gate t corresponds to "union" or "set-difference" can be proved similarly. Therefore above statement is also true for $i = k + t$. Recursively, the above statements are true for each $i \in [k + l]$. Note that S''_{k+l} is the output set. Remind that if $x \in S_{output}$ (resp. $x \notin S_{output}$), E will extract $(x, \mathsf{g}', p, \mathsf{C}''_{l+k})$ (resp. $(x, a, b, p, \mathsf{C}''_{l+k})$), which means that $x \in S''_{k+l}$ (resp. $x \notin S''_{m+l}$). Therefore we have $\mathcal{Q}(S_{t_1}, \cdots, S_{t_k}) = S'_l = S''_{k+l} = S_{output}$, which concludes the proof of function binding.

For the **zero-knowledge** property, due to that the distribution of the ZKS commitment is statistically indistinguishable from $\{g^r | r \leftarrow [2^\lambda B]\}$, the simulator can sample element from $\{g^r | r \leftarrow [2^\lambda B]\}$ as the commitments and then use the simulators of Intersection-NIZK, Union-NIZK and Difference-NIZK to conclude the simulations.

Remark 2. One can use the randomness r'_l applied in the commitment C'_l to replace the opening information τ'_l, which is also sufficient to check whether C'_l is a commitment to S_{output}. Therefore the proof size of a set-operation query is only linear in the size of combined operation $\mathcal{Q}$ and the length of elements in S.

5 Zero-Knowledge Functional Elementary Databases

This section consists of three parts. Firstly, we describe the definition of ZK-FEDBs. Secondly, we show how to transform a Boolean circuit query into a set-operation query on related sets. Finally we show how to construct a ZK-FEDBs from standard ZE-EDBs and ZKS with set-operation queries.

5.1 Definition of Zero-Knowledge Functional Elementary Databases

Informally, a ZK-FEDB allows one to commit an elementary database D of key-value pairs (x, v) and then, for any Boolean circuit f, convincingly answer the queries in the form of "send me all records (x, v) in D satisfying $f(x, v) = 1$". Here we write the output database as $D(f)$ (i.e., $D(f) = \{(x, v) \in D | f(x, v) = 1\}$) and regard the membership queries (supported by the standard ZK-EDB) as a type of special function query.

Definition 3 (Zero-Knowledge Functional Elementary Databases). *A Zero-Knowledge Functional Elementary Database consists of four algorithms* (Setup, Com, Prove, Verify),

- $\delta \leftarrow \mathsf{Setup}(1^\lambda)$*: On input a security parameter* 1^λ, Setup *outputs a random string (or a structured reference string)* δ *as the CRS.*
- $(com, \tau) \leftarrow \mathsf{Com}(\delta, D)$*: On input a CRS* δ *and an elementary database* D, Com *outputs a commitment of database com and opening information* τ.
- $\pi \leftarrow \mathsf{Prove}(\delta, com, \tau, f, D_{output})$*: On input the CRS* δ*, the database commitment and the associated opening information* (com, τ)*, a Boolean circuit* f*, and the target output* D_{output}, Prove *outputs a proof* π *for* $D_{output} = D(f)$.
- $0/1 \leftarrow \mathsf{Verify}(\delta, com, f, D_{output}, \pi)$*: On input the CRS* δ*, the commitment com, the boolean circuit* f*, the target output* D_{output} *and the proof* π, Verify *accepts or rejects.*

It satisfies the following three properties:

- **Completeness:** *For any elementary database D and any Boolean circuit f,*

$$\Pr\left[\mathsf{Verify}(\delta, com, f, D(f), \pi) = 1 \,\middle|\, \begin{array}{c}\delta \leftarrow \mathsf{Setup}(1^\lambda); (com, \tau) \leftarrow \mathsf{Com}(\delta, D);\\ \pi \leftarrow \mathsf{Prove}(\delta, com, \tau, f, D(f))\end{array}\right] = 1$$

- **Function binding:** *For any PPT adversary $\mathcal{A}$, the probability that $\mathcal{A}$ wins in the following game is negligible:*
  1. *The challenger generates a CRS δ by running* $\mathsf{Setup}(1^\lambda)$ *and gives δ to adversary $\mathcal{A}$.*
  2. *The adversary $\mathcal{A}$ outputs a commitment com and a series of function query-proof tuples $\{(f_i, D_i, \pi_i)\}_{i\in[n]}$.*
  3. *The adversary $\mathcal{A}$ wins the game if the following hold: a) For each $i \in [n]$,* $\mathsf{Verify}(\delta, com, f_i, D_i, \pi_i) = 1$ *and b) there does not exist a database D satisfying $D(f_i) = D_i$ for each $i \in [n]$.*
- **Zero-Knowledge:** *There exists a simulator Sim such that for any PPT adversary $\mathcal{A}$, the absolute value of the difference*

$$\Pr\left[\mathcal{A}^{\mathcal{O}_P}(\delta, st_{\mathcal{A}}, com) = 1 \,\middle|\, \begin{array}{c}\delta \leftarrow \mathsf{Setup}(1^\lambda), (D, st_{\mathcal{A}}) \leftarrow \mathcal{A}(\delta),\\ (com, \tau) \leftarrow \mathsf{Com}(\delta, D)\end{array}\right] -$$

$$\Pr\left[\mathcal{A}^{\mathcal{O}_S}(\delta, st_{\mathcal{A}}, com) = 1 \,\middle|\, \begin{array}{c}(\delta, st_\delta) \leftarrow Sim(1^\lambda), (D, st_{\mathcal{A}}) \leftarrow \mathcal{A}(\delta),\\ (com, st_S) \leftarrow Sim(\delta, st_\delta)\end{array}\right]$$

is negligible in λ. where $\mathcal{O}_P$ and $\mathcal{O}_S$ are defined as follows:
$\mathcal{O}_P$: On input a Boolean circuit f, $\mathcal{O}_P$ outputs $\pi \leftarrow \mathsf{Prove}(\delta, com, \tau, f, D(f))$.
$\mathcal{O}_S$: On input a Boolean circuit f, $\mathcal{O}_S$ outputs $\pi \leftarrow Sim(st_S, f, D(f))$.

5.2 Circuit Transformation

In this subsection, we show how to transform a Boolean circuit query into a set-operation query.

Roughly, we construct a deterministic algorithm that on input a Boolean circuit f output a combined operation $\mathcal{Q}$ (a 'circuit' of unions, intersections and set-differences) such that, for any database D, the set of keys belonging to the output database of querying Boolean circuit f, (i.e., $\{x|\exists v, (x, v) \in D \wedge f(x, v) = 1\}$) equals to the output of combined operation $\mathcal{Q}$ on the corresponding related sets $\{S_i^b\}_{b\in[0,1], i\in[n]}$, which are defined as follows:

$$S_i^b = \{x \in Sup(D)| \text{ the } i\text{-th bit of "}x||v\text{" is } b\}.$$

The construction of above deterministic algorithm is as follows.
Algorithm $\mathcal{Q} \leftarrow \mathsf{Tran}(f)$: On input the boolean circuit $f : \{0,1\}^n \rightarrow \{0,1\}$, $\mathsf{Tran}(f)$ outputs $\mathcal{Q}$, a combined operation having an input of $2n$ sets $(S_1^0, S_1^1, \cdots, S_n^0, S_n^1)$, and outputs a set S'. Here, $\mathcal{Q}$ is constructed as follows:

Tran first associates the i-th input wires of f with the two sets (S_i^0, S_i^1). Supposing that f contains l gates $(n_1, \cdots, n_l)$, without loss of generality, we require the input wires of n_i to be either the input wires of f or the output wires of gates $(n_1, \cdots, n_{i-1})$, and the output of gate n_l is also the output of f. Then for i from 1 to l, we have the following:

1. If gate n_i is "AND" gate, and the sets associated with the two input wires are $(S^0_{input1}, S^1_{input1}), (S^0_{input2}, S^1_{input2})$, then denote the sets associated with the output wire as $(S^1_{input1} \cap S^1_{input2}, S^0_{input1} \cup S^0_{input2})$.
2. If gate n_i is "OR" gate, and the sets associated with the two input wires are $(S^0_{input1}, S^1_{input1}), (S^0_{input2}, S^1_{input2})$, then denote the sets associated with the output wire as $(S^1_{input1} \cup S^1_{input2}, S^0_{input1} \cap S^0_{input2})$.
3. If gate n_i is "NOT" gate, and the sets associated with the two input wires are $(S^0_{input}, S^1_{input})$, then denote the sets associated with the output wire as $(S^1_{input}, S^0_{input})$.

Supposing that (S^0, S^1) are the sets associated with the output wire of gate n_l, $\mathcal{Q}$ outputs S^1.

Denote by *Sup* the algorithm that on input a key-value database $D = \{(x_1, v_1), \cdots, (x_m, v_m)\}$, outputs the set of keys belonging to D, i.e., $Sup(D) = \{x_1, \cdots, x_m\}$. We then have the following:

Lemma 11. Tran *is a deterministic algorithm satisfying that for any Boolean circuit* f *and any key-value databases* D,

$$\mathcal{Q}(S^0_1, S^1_1, \cdots, S^0_n, S^1_n) = Sup(D(f))$$

where $S^b_i = \{x \in Sup(D) |$ *the i-th bit of* "$x||v$" *is* $b\}$, $\mathcal{Q} = \mathsf{Tran}(f)$ *and* $D(f) = \{(x, v) \in D | f(x, v) = 1\}$.

proof sketch. Suppose S^0_i, S^1_i are the sets associated to the i-th wire defined as in Tran (remind that for input wire $i \in [2n]$, $S^b_i = \{x \in Sup(D) | \text{ the } i\text{-th bit of "}x||v\text{" is } b\}$), then one can conclude the correctness of above lemma by recursively checking that for each wire i in f, $S^b_i = \{x | \exists v \text{ s.t. } (x, v) \in D \wedge \text{the value of the } i\text{-th wire of } f(x, v) \text{ is } b\}$, which means that $\mathcal{Q}(S^0_1, S^1_1, \cdots, S^0_n, S^1_n) = \{x | \exists v \text{ s.t. } (x, v) \in D \wedge \text{the value of the output wire of } f(x, v) \text{ is } 1\} = Sup(D(f))$.

5.3 Construction

In this section, we present a construction of the ZK-FEDB from a standard ZK-EDB ($\mathsf{Setup}_D, \mathsf{Com}_D, \mathsf{Prove}_D, \mathsf{Verify}_D$) and a ZKS with set-operation queries ($\mathsf{Setup}_S, \mathsf{Com}_S, \mathsf{Prove}_S, \mathsf{Verify}_S, \mathsf{SO.Prove}_S, \mathsf{SO.Verify}_S$).

The construction of ZK-FEDBs is shown in Fig. 12.

Theorem 4. *The scheme shown in Fig. 12 is a zero-knowledge functional elementary database scheme.*

Proof. The **completeness** follows from Lemma 11 directly.

To prove the **function binding** property, we will show that, supposing there exists a PPT adversary $\mathcal{A}$ that on input a random CRS δ, outputs a commitment C and a series of valid query-proof tuples $\{f_i, D_i, \pi_{f_i}\}_{i \in [t]}$ such that $\mathsf{Verify}(\delta, C, f_i, D_i, \pi_{f_i}) = 1$ with noticeable property. Then $D = \cup_{i \in [t]} D_i$ is a database satisfying $D(f_i) = D_i$.

Zero-Knowledge Functional Elementary Databases

$\mathsf{Setup}(1^\lambda)$: On input the security parameter 1^λ, Setup generates $\delta_D \leftarrow \mathsf{Setup}_D(1^\lambda)$ and $\delta_S \leftarrow \mathsf{Setup}_S(1^\lambda)$. Output CRS $\delta = (\delta_D, \delta_S)$.

$\mathsf{Commit}(\delta, D)$: On input the database D and $\delta = (\delta_D, \delta_S)$, Commit runs $(C_D, \tau_D) \leftarrow \mathsf{Com}_D(\delta_D, D)$. For each $b \in \{0,1\}$, $i \in [2l]$, denote by $S_i^b = \{x \in Sup(D) |$ the i-th bit of $x||v$ is $b\}$. Commit S_i^b using the ZKS scheme, i.e., $(\mathsf{C}_i^b, \tau_i^b) \leftarrow \mathsf{Com}_S(\delta_S, S_i^b)$. Output the commitment $C = (C_D, \{\mathsf{C}_i^b\}_{b\in\{0,1\}, i\in[2l]})$ and the open information $\tau = (\tau_D, \{\tau_i^b\}_{b\in\{0,1\}, i\in[2l]})$.

$\mathsf{Prove}(\delta, C, \tau, f, D(f))$: Prover transforms Boolean circuit f into a combined operations $\mathcal{Q}$ using the algorithm Tran. Run $\pi_{\mathcal{Q}} \leftarrow \mathsf{SO.Prove}_S(\delta_S, \{\mathsf{C}_i^b\}, \{\tau_i^b\}, \mathcal{Q}, Sup(D(f)))$. For each $x \in Sup(D(f))$, run $\pi_x \leftarrow \mathsf{Prove}_D(\delta_D, C_D, \tau_D, x, D(x))$ and for $b \in \{0,1\}, i \in [2l]$, run $\pi_{x,i}^b \leftarrow \mathsf{Prove}_S(\delta_S, \mathsf{C}_i^b, \tau_i^b, x, S_i^b(x))$. Output $\pi = (\pi_{\mathcal{Q}}, \{\pi_x, \pi_{x,i}^b\}_{x\in Sup(D(f)), b\in\{0,1\}, i\in[2l]})$.

$\mathsf{Verify}(\delta, C, f, D(f), \pi)$: Parse C as $(C_D, \{\mathsf{C}_i^b\}_{b\in\{0,1\}, i\in[2l]})$, parse the input π as $(\pi_{\mathcal{Q}}, \{\pi_x, \pi_{x,i}^b\}_{x\in Sup(D(f)), b\in\{0,1\}, i\in[2l]})$ and run $Q = \mathsf{Tran}(f)$. Output 1 iff. the following checks pass:
1. $\mathsf{SO.Verify}_S(\delta_S, \{\mathsf{C}_i^b\}, \mathcal{Q}, Sup(D(f)), \pi_{\mathcal{Q}}) = 1$
2. For each $x \in Sup(\mathcal{D}(f))$, $\mathsf{Verify}_D(\delta_D, C_D, x, D(x), \pi_x) = 1$.
3. For each $x \in Sup(\mathcal{D}(f))$ and $b \in \{0,1\}, i \in [2l]$, $\mathsf{Verify}_S(\delta_S, \mathsf{C}_i^b, x, S_i^b(x), \pi_{x,i}^b) = 1$

Fig. 12. ZK-FEDB

First, we claim that D is indeed a database (that is, for each $x \in Sup(D)$, there is at most one value v satisfying $(x, v) \in D$), otherwise, one can break the soundness of the ZK-EDB scheme $(\mathsf{Setup}_D, \mathsf{Com}_D, \mathsf{Prove}_D, \mathsf{Verify}_D)$.

Second, we claim that for each $i \in [t]$, $D(f_i) = D_i$. Denote by $S_i^b = \{x \in Sup(D) |$ the i-th bit of $x||v$ is $b\}$. From the function binding of ZKS with set-operation queries, we know that there exists sets $S_i'^b$ satisfying the first and third checks of the verifier in each proof, which means the following:

1. $\mathcal{Q}_i(S_1'^0, S_1'^1, \cdots, S_n'^0, S_n'^1) = Sup(D_i)$ where $\mathcal{Q}_i = \mathsf{Tran}(f_i)$.
2. For each $i \in [2l]$ and $x \in Sup(D)$, $x \in S_i'^{b_{x,i}}$ and $x \notin S_i'^{1-b_{x,i}}$ where $b_{x,i}$ is the i-th bit of $x||D(x)$.

From the second property above, we have $S_i^b = S_i'^b \cap Sup(D)$. Now, from the first property, we have that $\mathcal{Q}_i(S_1^0, S_1^1, \cdots, S_{2l}^0, S_{2l}^1) = \mathcal{Q}_i(S_1'^0 \cap Sup(D), S_1'^1 \cap Sup(D), \cdots, S_{2l}'^0 \cap Sup(D), S_{2l}'^1 \cap Sup(D)) = D_i \cap Sup(D) = D_i$. From Lemma 11, we have $D(f_i) = D_i$, which concludes the proof.

The **zero-knowledge** property directly follows the zero-knowledge property of ZK-EDB and ZKS with set-operation queries. □

Performance. As shown in Remark 1, our ZKS scheme supports standard batch technique. In the full version of this paper [45], we additionally present a construction of ZK-EDB, which achieves constant-size batched proofs. When utilizing this ZK-EDB and our ZKS, and using the standard batch technique, the performance of our ZK-FEDB is as follows (Table 1):

Table 1. Performance of our ZK-FEDB

	Prover's work	Verifier's work	Communication
Commit	$O(\ell\|D\|)\mathsf{EXT} + O(\|D\|)h$	N/A	$O(\ell)\mathbb{G}$
Query	$O(\ell\|D\| + \|D\|\|f\|)\mathsf{EXT}$ $+O(\|D\| + \ell + \|f\|)h$	$O(\ell + \|f\|)\mathsf{EXT}$ $+O(\|D_{output}\| + \ell + \|f\|)h$	$O(\ell + \|f\|)\mathbb{G}$

where ℓ is the bit length of record, $|D|$ and $|D_{output}|$ denote the size of committed database and output database respectly, $|f|$ is the size of query function (for example, a search query can be expressed as a circuit of l AND gates, while a range query can be expressed as a circuit containing no more than 2ℓ AND/OR gates), $\mathbb{G}$ represents a group element, h denotes hashing to a prime and EXT is a λ-bit exponentiation.

Furthermore, by utilizing Boneh et al.'s PoE protocol to reduce the verifier's computation cost, the proof size is approximately $(28\ell + 122|f|)\mathbb{G}$ and the verify cost is approximately $(24\ell + 131|f|)\mathsf{EXT} + (3\ell + 43|f| + |D_{output}|)h$. We hope our work will stimulate more research in this field and bring more efficient constructions of ZK-FEDB.

Applications. Our construction of the ZK-FEDB can be used to construct a Key Transparency system via [12]'s paradigm. It is easy to see that our construction also satisfies the append-only property. The resulting Key Transparency system achieves enhanced functionality, which enables clients to query public keys in a more flexible manner.

Acknowledgments. We would like to thank the anonymous reviewers for their valuable suggestions. We are supported by the National Natural Science Foundation of China (Grant No. 62372447 and No. 61932019) and Beijing Natural Science Foundation (Grant No. M22003).

References

1. Agrawal, S., Raghuraman, S.: KVaC: key-value commitments for blockchains and beyond. In: Moriai, S., Wang, H. (eds.) ASIACRYPT 2020. LNCS, vol. 12493, pp. 839–869. Springer, Cham (2020). https://doi.org/10.1007/978-3-030-64840-4_28
2. Barić, N., Pfitzmann, B.: Collision-free accumulators and fail-stop signature schemes without trees. In: Fumy, W. (ed.) EUROCRYPT 1997. LNCS, vol. 1233, pp. 480–494. Springer, Heidelberg (1997). https://doi.org/10.1007/3-540-69053-0_33
3. Benaloh, J., de Mare, M.: One-way accumulators: a decentralized alternative to digital signatures. In: Helleseth, T. (ed.) EUROCRYPT 1993. LNCS, vol. 765, pp. 274–285. Springer, Heidelberg (1994). https://doi.org/10.1007/3-540-48285-7_24
4. Boneh, D., Bünz, B., Fisch, B.: Batching techniques for accumulators with applications to IOPs and stateless blockchains. In: Boldyreva, A., Micciancio, D. (eds.) CRYPTO 2019. LNCS, vol. 11692, pp. 561–586. Springer, Cham (2019). https://doi.org/10.1007/978-3-030-26948-7_20
5. Buchmann, J., Hamdy, S.: A survey on IQ cryptography. In: Alster, K., Urbanowicz, J., Williams, H.C. (eds.) Public-Key Cryptography and Computational Number Theory: Proceedings of the International Conference organized by the Stefan Banach International Mathematical Center Warsaw, Poland, 11–15 September 2000, pp. 1–16. De Gruyter, Berlin, New York (2001). https://doi.org/10.1515/9783110881035.1
6. Camacho, P., Hevia, A., Kiwi, M., Opazo, R.: Strong accumulators from collision-resistant hashing. In: Wu, T.-C., Lei, C.-L., Rijmen, V., Lee, D.-T. (eds.) ISC 2008. LNCS, vol. 5222, pp. 471–486. Springer, Heidelberg (2008). https://doi.org/10.1007/978-3-540-85886-7_32
7. Camenisch, J., Lysyanskaya, A.: Dynamic accumulators and application to efficient revocation of anonymous credentials. In: Yung, M. (ed.) CRYPTO 2002. LNCS, vol. 2442, pp. 61–76. Springer, Heidelberg (2002). https://doi.org/10.1007/3-540-45708-9_5
8. Camenisch, J., Stadler, M.: Efficient group signature schemes for large groups. In: Kaliski, B.S. (ed.) CRYPTO 1997. LNCS, vol. 1294, pp. 410–424. Springer, Heidelberg (1997). https://doi.org/10.1007/BFb0052252
9. Catalano, D., Dodis, Y., Visconti, I.: Mercurial commitments: minimal assumptions and efficient constructions. In: Halevi, S., Rabin, T. (eds.) TCC 2006. LNCS, vol. 3876, pp. 120–144. Springer, Heidelberg (2006). https://doi.org/10.1007/11681878_7
10. Catalano, D., Fiore, D.: Vector commitments and their applications. In: Kurosawa, K., Hanaoka, G. (eds.) PKC 2013. LNCS, vol. 7778, pp. 55–72. Springer, Heidelberg (2013). https://doi.org/10.1007/978-3-642-36362-7_5
11. Catalano, D., Fiore, D., Messina, M.: Zero-knowledge sets with short proofs. In: Smart, N. (ed.) EUROCRYPT 2008. LNCS, vol. 4965, pp. 433–450. Springer, Heidelberg (2008). https://doi.org/10.1007/978-3-540-78967-3_25
12. Chase, M., Deshpande, A., Ghosh, E., Malvai, H.: Seemless: secure end-to-end encrypted messaging with less trust. In: Proceedings of the 2019 ACM SIGSAC Conference on Computer and Communications Security, CCS 2019m pp. 1639–1656. ACM, New York (2019). https://doi.org/10.1145/3319535.3363202
13. Chase, M., Healy, A., Lysyanskaya, A., Malkin, T., Reyzin, L.: Mercurial commitments with applications to zero-knowledge sets. In: Cramer, R. (ed.) EUROCRYPT 2005. LNCS, vol. 3494, pp. 422–439. Springer, Heidelberg (2005). https://doi.org/10.1007/11426639_25

14. Chase, M., Visconti, I.: Secure database commitments and universal arguments of quasi knowledge. In: Safavi-Naini, R., Canetti, R. (eds.) CRYPTO 2012. LNCS, vol. 7417, pp. 236–254. Springer, Heidelberg (2012). https://doi.org/10.1007/978-3-642-32009-5_15
15. Chen, B., et al.: Rotatable zero knowledge sets. Post compromise secure auditable dictionaries with application to key transparency. In: Agrawal, S., Lin, D. (eds.) Advances in Cryptology, ASIACRYPT 2022. LNCS, vol. 13793, pp. 547–580. Springer, Cham (2022). https://doi.org/10.1007/978-3-031-22969-5_19
16. Damgård, I., Fujisaki, E.: A statistically-hiding integer commitment scheme based on groups with hidden order. In: Zheng, Y. (ed.) ASIACRYPT 2002. LNCS, vol. 2501, pp. 125–142. Springer, Heidelberg (2002). https://doi.org/10.1007/3-540-36178-2_8
17. Damgård, I., Koprowski, M.: Generic lower bounds for root extraction and signature schemes in general groups. In: Knudsen, L.R. (ed.) EUROCRYPT 2002. LNCS, vol. 2332, pp. 256–271. Springer, Heidelberg (2002). https://doi.org/10.1007/3-540-46035-7_17
18. Derler, D., Hanser, C., Slamanig, D.: Revisiting cryptographic accumulators, additional properties and relations to other primitives. In: Nyberg, K. (ed.) CT-RSA 2015. LNCS, vol. 9048, pp. 127–144. Springer, Cham (2015). https://doi.org/10.1007/978-3-319-16715-2_7
19. Eagen, L., Fiore, D., Gabizon, A.: cq: cached quotients for fast lookups. Cryptology ePrint Archive, Paper 2022/1763 (2022). https://eprint.iacr.org/2022/1763
20. Fujisaki, E., Okamoto, T.: Statistical zero knowledge protocols to prove modular polynomial relations. In: Kaliski, B.S. (ed.) CRYPTO 1997. LNCS, vol. 1294, pp. 16–30. Springer, Heidelberg (1997). https://doi.org/10.1007/BFb0052225
21. Gabizon, A., Williamson, Z.J.: plookup: a simplified polynomial protocol for lookup tables. Cryptology ePrint Archive, Paper 2020/315 (2020)
22. Gennaro, R., Micali, S.: Independent zero-knowledge sets. In: Bugliesi, M., Preneel, B., Sassone, V., Wegener, I. (eds.) ICALP 2006. LNCS, vol. 4052, pp. 34–45. Springer, Heidelberg (2006). https://doi.org/10.1007/11787006_4
23. Ghosh, E., Ohrimenko, O., Papadopoulos, D., Tamassia, R., Triandopoulos, N.: Zero-knowledge accumulators and set algebra. In: Cheon, J.H., Takagi, T. (eds.) ASIACRYPT 2016. LNCS, vol. 10032, pp. 67–100. Springer, Heidelberg (2016). https://doi.org/10.1007/978-3-662-53890-6_3
24. Ghosh, E., Ohrimenko, O., Tamassia, R.: Zero-knowledge authenticated order queries and order statistics on a list. In: Malkin, T., Kolesnikov, V., Lewko, A.B., Polychronakis, M. (eds.) ACNS 2015. LNCS, vol. 9092, pp. 149–171. Springer, Cham (2015). https://doi.org/10.1007/978-3-319-28166-7_8
25. Hu, Y., Hooshmand, K., Kalidhindi, H., Yang, S.J., Popa, R.A.: Merkle^2: a low-latency transparency log system. In: 42nd IEEE Symposium on Security and Privacy, SP 2021, pp. 285–303. IEEE (2021). https://doi.org/10.1109/SP40001.2021.00088
26. Li, Y., Susilo, W., Yang, G., Phuong, T.V.X., Yu, Y., Liu, D.: Concise mercurial subvector commitments: definitions and constructions. In: Baek, J., Ruj, S. (eds.) ACISP 2021. LNCS, vol. 13083, pp. 353–371. Springer, Cham (2021). https://doi.org/10.1007/978-3-030-90567-5_18
27. Libert, B., Nguyen, K., Tan, B.H.M., Wang, H.: Zero-knowledge elementary databases with more expressive queries. In: Lin, D., Sako, K. (eds.) PKC 2019. LNCS, vol. 11442, pp. 255–285. Springer, Cham (2019). https://doi.org/10.1007/978-3-030-17253-4_9

28. Libert, B., Yung, M.: Concise mercurial vector commitments and independent zero-knowledge sets with short proofs. In: Micciancio, D. (ed.) TCC 2010. LNCS, vol. 5978, pp. 499–517. Springer, Heidelberg (2010). https://doi.org/10.1007/978-3-642-11799-2_30
29. Liskov, M.: Updatable zero-knowledge databases. In: Roy, B. (ed.) ASIACRYPT 2005. LNCS, vol. 3788, pp. 174–198. Springer, Heidelberg (2005). https://doi.org/10.1007/11593447_10
30. Melara, M.S., Blankstein, A., Bonneau, J., Felten, E.W., Freedman, M.J.: CONIKS: bringing key transparency to end users. In: 24th USENIX Security Symposium, USENIX Security 2015, pp. 383–398. USENIX Association, Washington, D.C. (2015)
31. Micali, S., Rabin, M.O., Kilian, J.: Zero-knowledge sets. In: Proceedings of the 44th Annual IEEE Symposium on Foundations of Computer Science, FOCS 2003, pp. 80–91. IEEE Computer Society (2003). https://doi.org/10.1109/SFCS.2003.1238183
32. Naor, M., Ziv, A.: Primary-secondary-resolver membership proof systems. In: Dodis, Y., Nielsen, J.B. (eds.) TCC 2015. LNCS, vol. 9015, pp. 199–228. Springer, Heidelberg (2015). https://doi.org/10.1007/978-3-662-46497-7_8
33. Nguyen, L.: Accumulators from bilinear pairings and applications. In: Menezes, A. (ed.) CT-RSA 2005. LNCS, vol. 3376, pp. 275–292. Springer, Heidelberg (2005). https://doi.org/10.1007/978-3-540-30574-3_19
34. Ostrovsky, R., Rackoff, C., Smith, A.: Efficient consistency proofs for generalized queries on a committed database. In: Díaz, J., Karhumäki, J., Lepistö, A., Sannella, D. (eds.) ICALP 2004. LNCS, vol. 3142, pp. 1041–1053. Springer, Heidelberg (2004). https://doi.org/10.1007/978-3-540-27836-8_87
35. Papamanthou, C., Tamassia, R., Triandopoulos, N.: Optimal verification of operations on dynamic sets. In: Rogaway, P. (ed.) CRYPTO 2011. LNCS, vol. 6841, pp. 91–110. Springer, Heidelberg (2011). https://doi.org/10.1007/978-3-642-22792-9_6
36. Prabhakaran, M., Xue, R.: Statistically hiding sets. In: Fischlin, M. (ed.) CT-RSA 2009. LNCS, vol. 5473, pp. 100–116. Springer, Heidelberg (2009). https://doi.org/10.1007/978-3-642-00862-7_7
37. Straka, M.: Class groups for cryptographic accumulators (2019). https://www.michaelstraka.com/posts/classgroups/
38. Tamassia, R.: Authenticated data structures. In: Di Battista, G., Zwick, U. (eds.) ESA 2003. LNCS, vol. 2832, pp. 2–5. Springer, Heidelberg (2003). https://doi.org/10.1007/978-3-540-39658-1_2
39. Tomescu, A., Bhupatiraju, V., Papadopoulos, D., Papamanthou, C., Triandopoulos, N., Devadas, S.: Transparency logs via append-only authenticated dictionaries. In: Cavallaro, L., Kinder, J., Wang, X., Katz, J. (eds.) Proceedings of the 2019 ACM SIGSAC Conference on Computer and Communications Security, CCS 2019, pp. 1299–1316. ACM (2019). https://doi.org/10.1145/3319535.3345652
40. Tzialla, I., Kothapalli, A., Parno, B., Setty, S.T.V.: Transparency dictionaries with succinct proofs of correct operation. In: 29th Annual Network and Distributed System Security Symposium, NDSS 2022. The Internet Society (2022)
41. Xue, R., Li, N., Li, J.: A new construction of zero-knowledge sets secure in Random oracle Model. In: The First International Symposium on Data, Privacy, and E-Commerce, ISDPE 2007, pp. 332–337 (2007). https://doi.org/10.1109/ISDPE.2007.8
42. Xue, R., Li, N., Li, J.: Algebraic construction for zero-knowledge sets. J. Comput. Sci. Technol. **23**(2), 166–175 (2008). https://doi.org/10.1007/s11390-008-9119-x

43. Zapico, A., Buterin, V., Khovratovich, D., Maller, M., Nitulescu, A., Simkin, M.: Caulk: lookup arguments in sublinear time. In: Yin, H., Stavrou, A., Cremers, C., Shi, E. (eds.) Proceedings of the 2022 ACM SIGSAC Conference on Computer and Communications Security, CCS 2022, pp. 3121–3134. ACM (2022). https://doi.org/10.1145/3548606.3560646
44. Zapico, A., Gabizon, A., Khovratovich, D., Maller, M., Ràfols, C.: Baloo: nearly optimal lookup arguments. Cryptology ePrint Archive, Paper 2022/1565 (2022). https://eprint.iacr.org/2022/1565
45. Zhang, X., Deng, Y.: Zero-knowledge functional elementary databases. Cryptology ePrint Archive, Paper 2023/156 (2023). https://eprint.iacr.org/2023/156
46. Zhang, Y., Katz, J., Papamanthou, C.: An expressive (zero-knowledge) set accumulator. In: 2017 IEEE European Symposium on Security and Privacy (EuroS&P), pp. 158–173 (2017). https://doi.org/10.1109/EuroSP.2017.35
47. Zhu, H.: Mercurial commitments from general RSA moduli and their applications to zero-knowledge databases/sets. In: 2009 Second International Workshop on Computer Science and Engineering, vol. 2, pp. 289–292 (2009). https://doi.org/10.1109/WCSE.2009.815

Secure Messaging and Broadcast

WhatsUpp with Sender Keys? Analysis, Improvements and Security Proofs

David Balbás[1,2(✉)], Daniel Collins[3], and Phillip Gajland[4,5]

[1] IMDEA Software Institute, Madrid, Spain
[2] Universidad Politécnica de Madrid, Madrid, Spain
david.balbas@imdea.org
[3] EPFL, Lausanne, Switzerland
[4] Max Planck Institute for Security and Privacy, Bochum, Germany
[5] Ruhr University Bochum, Bochum, Germany

Abstract. Developing end-to-end encrypted instant messaging solutions for group conversations is an ongoing challenge that has garnered significant attention from practitioners and the cryptographic community alike. Notably, industry-leading messaging apps such as WhatsApp and Signal Messenger have adopted the *Sender Keys* protocol, where each group member shares their own symmetric encryption key with others Despite its widespread adoption, Sender Keys has never been formally modelled in the cryptographic literature, raising the following natural question:

What can be proven about the security of the Sender Keys protocol, and how can we practically mitigate its shortcomings?

In addressing this question, we first introduce a novel security model to suit protocols like Sender Keys, deviating from conventional group key agreement-based abstractions. Our framework allows for a natural integration of two-party messaging within group messaging sessions that may be of independent interest. Leveraging this framework, we conduct the first formal analysis of the Sender Keys protocol, and prove it satisfies a weak notion of security. Towards improving security, we propose a series of efficient modifications to Sender Keys without imposing significant performance overhead. We combine these refinements into a new protocol that we call Sender Keys+, which may be of interest both in theory and practice.

1 Introduction

Messaging applications like WhatsApp, Facebook Messenger, Signal, and Telegram have witnessed remarkable global adoption, serving as essential communication tools for billions of users. All of these applications rely, to a varying degree, on cryptography to provide diverse forms of authenticity and secrecy. Among end-to-end encrypted messaging services (this excludes, among others, Telegram and Facebook Messenger by default), numerous cryptographic solutions

J. Guo and R. Steinfeld (Eds.): ASIACRYPT 2023, LNCS 14442, pp. 307–341, 2023.
https://doi.org/10.1007/978-981-99-8733-7_10

have emerged, each with its own merits. Notably, for two-party messaging, Signal's Double Ratchet Protocol [41] stands out as the dominant choice in practice. In the context of group messaging, Signal [43][1] and later WhatsApp [48] have adopted the so-called *Sender Keys* protocol [40], which has enjoyed widespread adoption for numerous years. Besides these, other popular solutions such as Matrix [2] and Session [37] implement variants of this protocol. In Sender Keys, messages are encrypted using a user-specific symmetric key (which is then hashed forward) and then authenticated with a signature. Additionally, parties rely on secure two-party channels (instantiated in practice with the Double Ratchet) to share key material between them. Looking ahead, two-party channels will be central to determine the security attained by any instantiation of Sender Keys.

A baseline for secure group messaging has been recently established by the IETF Messaging Layer Security (MLS) [16] standard, a joint effort between academia and industry[2]. The protocol provides sub-linear complexity for group operations (adding/removing members and updating key material). Academic works have also explored so-called continuous group key agreement (CGKA) [7–9,18,39], although these are only a component of a fully-fledged group messaging protocol. So far, in terms of complete messaging protocols, only the modular construction from [8] building on CGKA (which includes MLS), DCGKA [47] in the decentralised setting and very recently Matrix [2] have been formalised to date.

Despite being the most complete and well-studied protocol to-date in the literature, MLS (and CGKAs in general) still present some drawbacks. While some exhibit sub-linear performance in specific executions (and this class of executions is not well-characterised in the literature), their performance can degrade to linear in general, which is unavoidable at least when using off-the-shelf cryptographic primitives [19]. Moreover, they tend to be complex, increasing their attack surface and making them more susceptible to design and implementation bugs. Finally, given the standardisation of MLS only occurred recently, MLS is yet to be widely deployed.

Hence, Sender Keys and similar approaches to group messaging remain an essential and practical alternative with different security / performance tradeoffs. Firstly, Sender Keys stands out for its relative simplicity, which reduces its potential attack surface, making the protocol less susceptible to vulnerabilities in both its design and implementation. Secondly, Sender Keys offers good performance in small to moderate-sized groups, as demonstrated by its successful adoption for groups of up to 1024 parties in WhatsApp and Signal [43,48]. While the main group operations (adding and removing users) respectively have $\mathcal{O}(n)$ and $\mathcal{O}(n^2)$ total communication complexity for groups of size n, concrete effi-

[1] Contrary to the folklore understanding that the Signal Messenger uses the pairwise channels approach for group messaging in small groups, Signal currently uses Sender Keys whenever possible.

[2] Recent academic works and ongoing discussions in mailing lists have identified and addressed several security issues that emerged during the standardisation of MLS [7, 11,35].

ciency suffices in practice. Thirdly, Sender Keys offers forward-secure confidentiality and robust support for concurrent and out-of-order application message exchange.

Surprisingly, despite having the widest adoption and an open source implementation of its core cryptographic operations [43], Sender Keys has not been formally studied in the literature, prompting the following natural question:

Can we formalise the Sender Keys protocol in a meaningful security model?

To answer this question we start by introducing a new cryptographic primitive, along with a security model, to capture a broad class of group messaging protocols that do not necessarily employ CGKA [7] at their core. Our framework provides native support for group messaging protocols that utilise secure two-party communication channels under the hood, for which we introduce a clean level of abstraction. This novel framework proves instrumental in our analysis, as existing literature predominately focuses on CGKA-oriented models that do not suit Sender Keys and similar protocols.

Subsequently, we present a detailed description of the core Sender Keys protocol within our framework and provide a security proof validating the soundness of the protocol. In our analysis, we observe that Sender Keys presents several deficiencies that, despite not being easily exploitable flaws, prevent several desirable and fundamental security notions, such as secure group membership, from being met. These include forward security under message injections, resilience against injections impacting group membership changes[3], and fast recovery from state compromise. These findings call into question the widespread use of the term "secure messaging" by commercial messaging solutions, motivating the need for more detailed discussion about the nuances around these protocols.

In this regard we propose an improved version of Sender Keys, that we call Sender Keys+, where we only employ readily available cryptographic primitives that have minimal impact on efficiency[4]. This addresses the following pertinent question:

How can we improve the security of Sender Keys
whilst preserving its practical efficiency?

Overall, we believe that the formalisation and establishment of a provably secure variant of Sender Keys, such as the Sender Keys+ protocol proposed in this work, can serve as a valuable foundation for future implementations of the protocol.

---

[3] Note that Signal uses a dedicated private group management solution in practice [25] that we do not capture and is less affected by this attack vector than WhatsApp [46]; we refer to our full version for further details.

[4] Our approach veers away from a theoretically systematic exploration to determine the "optimal" security for a Sender Keys-like protocol, as this would require non-standard primitives that considerably degrade performance [9,15].

1.1 Contributions

In summary, the main scientific contributions of our paper are the following:

- We introduce a new cryptographic primitive that we call *Group Messenger* (GM). We establish a modular security model for GM designed to capture messaging protocols like Sender Keys that are not necessarily based on group key agreement. It accounts for an active adversary capable of controlling the network and adaptively learning the secret states of different parties.
- We develop a general framework for composing two-party channels with group messaging protocols that use them. Our approach parameterises the security of the Group Messenger primitive based on the underlying two-party channels, presenting a novel perspective that, to the best of our knowledge, has not been explored previously.
- We formally describe Sender Keys, based on an analysis of Signal's source code [43], WhatsApp's security white paper [48], and the yowsup library [33].
- We prove the security of Sender Keys in our model and describe several shortcomings. These force us to restrict the capabilities of the adversary substantially for the proof to be carried out.
- We propose security fixes and improvements, several of which result in the improved protocol Sender Keys+. In particular, we secure group membership changes, improve the forward security of the protocol, and introduce an efficient key update mechanism. We also formalise the additional security guarantees in our model.

Full Version. Due to space constraints, some parts of the modelling, all proofs, some additional clarifications and the full protocol description are only available in the full version of this work [13].

1.2 Paper Overview

Security in Group Messaging. Besides standard notions such as confidentiality, authenticity, and integrity of sent messages, two security properties are commonly considered in the messaging literature: forward security (FS) and post-compromise security (PCS) [28]. Both properties require some form of key updating mechanism, and forward security requires secure state erasures to achieve. Additionally, protocols must secure group membership updates, namely removed members must not be able to read messages sent after their removal, and newly added members must not (by default) be able to read past messages.

Most of the different formalisations of security in the literature model an adversarial Delivery Service (DS), the entity responsible for delivering messages between parties over the network. The adversary (modelling the DS) can act as an eavesdropper with extended capabilities, e.g., that can schedule messages to be consistently delivered by users, as in [7], as a semi-active adversary that can schedule messages arbitrarily [39], or as an active adversary that can inject messages [9,14]. In many protocols, including Sender Keys and MLS, the DS relies mainly on some centralised infrastructure (the *central server* hereafter).

Sender Keys. In a Sender Keys group $\boldsymbol{G}$, every user $ID \in \boldsymbol{G}$ owns a so-called *sender key* which is shared with all group members. A sender key is a tuple $\mathsf{SK} = (\mathsf{spk}, \mathsf{ck})$, where spk is a public signature key (with a private counterpart ssk), and ck is a symmetric *chain key.* Every time ID sends a message m to the group, ID encrypts m using a *message key* mk that is deterministically derived (via a key derivation function H_1) from its chain key ck and erased immediately after being used. Upon message reception, group members derive mk to decrypt the corresponding ciphertext, which can also be delivered out-of-order as we discuss in later sections. Messages are authenticated by appending the sender's signature to them. In Fig. 1, we show a high-level abstraction of what occurs in a three-member group $G = \{A, B, C\}$ when A sends a message that parties B and C receive.

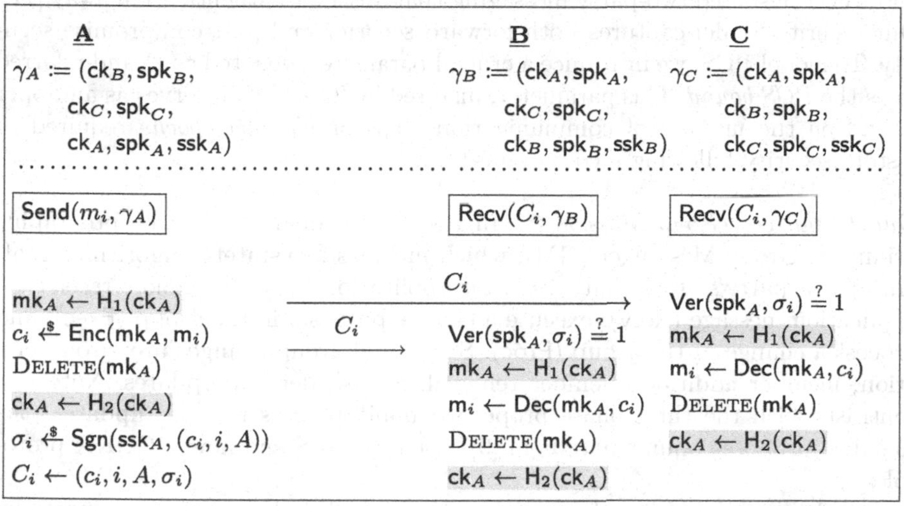

Fig. 1. Simplified diagram for sending/receiving messages between three group members. For $ID \in \{A, B, C\}$, ID's initial sender key is $(\mathsf{ck}_{ID}, \mathsf{spk}_{ID})$. The state γ_{ID} of ID contains the sender keys of all group members.

Informally, forward security is provided by using a fresh message key for every message: every time a message is sent, the chain key is symmetrically ratcheted, i.e., hashed forward using a key derivation function H_2. The protocol, that we describe further in Sect. 4, also requires that there exist confidential and authenticated two-party communication channels between each pair of group members. These are used for sharing sender keys when parties are added or removed from the group, or when some party updates their key material. For example, in the event that some ID leaves the group, members erase their own sender key and start over. This mechanism provides a form of PCS when a user is removed as the key material is refreshed.

Modelling Two-party Channels. Formally capturing the security of two-party channels is central to our analysis of Sender Keys in particular since fresh sender keys are sent over these channels. Two-party channels that are not regularly used can undermine security. For example, if a group member *ID*'s state is compromised, there is no guarantee that fresh keys sent by other members (via two-party channels) are not leaked, since *ID*'s two-party channels may not yet have healed yet. Moreover, two-party channels can take more than one round trip to heal when using the Double Ratchet, as is the case for WhatsApp and the Signal Messenger [6].

Our modelling starts in Sect. 2 with the introduction of a primitive 2PC for two-party channels. We define a two-party channel with initialisation (Init), channel initialisation (InitCh) send (Send) and receive (Recv) algorithms. Notably, InitCh allows parties to adaptively bootstrap channels, and deviates from works on ratcheting-based two-party messaging that abstract authentication away [17]. Our security model captures both forward security and post-compromise security. To model PCS, we introduce a crucial parameter, denoted as Δ and referred to as the *PCS bound*. This parameter, inspired by [6] and [22], serves as an upper bound on the number of communication steps or *channel epochs* required to restore security following a compromise.

Our Primitive: Group Messenger. In Sect. 3, we define a new cryptographic primitive, Group Messenger (GM), which includes five stateful algorithms that: initialise a party's state (Init), send an application message (Send), receive an application message (Recv), execute a change proposal in the group (Exec), and process a change in the group (Proc). Supported group changes are: group creation, member addition, member removal, and sender key updates. Note this contrasts with the three-phase propose/commit/process flow for updates (the so-called propose-commit paradigm [9]) used by MLS and newer CGKA protocols.

We define a game-based security notion for GM that captures a partially active adversary with control over the Delivery Service, taking inspiration from previous CGKA modelling [9,14]. In our model in Sect. 3.1, we capture the security of each protocol by parameterising the game with a *cleanness predicate* (sometimes safety predicate in other work), which excludes trivial attacks and reflects security weaknesses.

Security Analysis of Sender Keys. With this formalism established, in Sect. 5.1 we define cleanness predicates for Sender Keys that precisely capture its security. We define three sub-predicates that restrict the capabilities of the adversary for message *challenges*, capturing confidentiality; for message *injections*, capturing integrity and authenticity; and for re-orderings and forgeries of control messages (*concurrency*), capturing the message ordering provided by the central server.

Notably, the restrictions that we impose via our cleanness predicates are necessary for the security proof to go through and reveal several shortcomings in the protocol. Examples include:

- Sender Keys achieves only a weak form of PCS through key updates. Healing from a compromise requires multiple messages (at least $\Delta + 1$), even if a user is removed during healing.
- Control messages lack proper authentication and are malleable. An adversary with partial control over the network, such as the server, can make arbitrary changes in the group membership (such as adding new users without any member's authorisation), which is a significant practical concern.
- Forward security is sub-optimal, as messages are malleable after they are sent if a state exposure occurs.

In our full version, we also compare our description of Sender Keys with the implementations in WhatsApp and Signal, clarifying the extent to which our findings are applicable to these popular apps. We remark that our core analysis is nevertheless implementation-agnostic, and the fact that we model the underlying two-party channels in a fine-grained fashion allows us to capture their impact on security of Sender Keys in the face of state exposure (i.e., FS and PCS).

Shortcomings and Proposed Improvements. Leaving aside the security limitations that are intrinsic to the design of the protocol, we find that one can improve both its security and efficiency in several aspects. Hence, in Sect. 6 we propose modifications to the protocol with the aim of securing group membership, strengthening the (weaker than expected) forward security for authentication, and integrating efficient post-compromise security updates. Notably, our novel PCS update mechanism improves the key update mechanism implemented by our core protocol and performed in Signal, bringing down the total communication complexity from quadratic to linear in the group size. Moreover, as a result of our modular approach with respect to modelling two-party channels, our modelling can capture the security improvement (or weakening) that results from replacing the Double Ratchet by an alternative two-party messaging protocol.

We extend the techniques used in the original proof to establish the security of our modified protocol, called Sender Keys+. The main technical step involves redefining the cleanness predicates, which are strictly less restrictive compared to those used for the original protocol. Notably, the adversary is now allowed to inject control messages (given the group has recovered from any state exposures). We also allow the adversary to mount more fine-grained attacks for application message forgeries, and allow *arbitrary* challenges after some party has updated over a refreshed channel (before, we could only allow challenges on the *updater*).

1.3 Additional Related Work

A notable recent research direction revolves around the MLS protocol [16] and the CGKA abstraction [7]. This line of work started with asynchronous ratchet trees [27] and quickly led to TreeKEM [18] and its variants [5,9,11,39]. [10] considers CGKA where the central server 'splits' ciphertexts for receiving parties, reducing bandwidth overhead. The CGKA of [34] has $\mathcal{O}(n)$-sized ciphertexts in all cases, but its relative simplicity makes them attractive and for smaller groups can be concretely competitive in performance. We provide a more thorough comparison between CGKA-based protocols and Sender Keys in Sect. 6.4.

The formal extension of CGKA to group messaging was explored in [8], while the key schedule of MLS was proven secure in [23]. The work of [29] shares some similarities with ours as it also constructs group messaging from two-party channels and achieves $\mathcal{O}(n)$ key update complexity. However, they do not model two-party channels as a standalone primitive nor dynamic groups formally, and their protocols require more interaction than ours (e.g., the initial group key agreement protocol can take several rounds).

Concurrency, a crucial aspect in CGKA-based protocols, has been a central topic in works such as [4,5,20]. Secure administration in CGKAs was explored in [14]. In [47] a Sender Keys-like approach is utilized to construct a decentralised CGKA protocol but they do not capture group messaging, and their security model does not support message injections (hence considering a passive adversary). Moreover, the theorems in their work assume a non-adaptive adversary where the adversary must announce all queries at the game's outset. This work nonetheless extends the scope of modern messaging to decentralised networks without a central authority, diverging from existing approaches that target centralised networks. A simplified (notably lacking forward security) decentralised variant of Sender Keys is implemented by the Session app [37].

Also relevant to our work are secure two-party messaging protocols that propose alternatives to the Double Ratchet [41], such as [6,15,32,36,44,45]. Inspired by more practical-oriented endeavors, we acknowledge recent cryptographic audits conducted on Telegram [3], Matrix [1], Threema [38], and WhatsApp's backup service [31].

Sender Keys. While some works on Sender Keys lack formalism and security proofs, they offer valuable insights. In [46] the authors evaluate Sender Keys, provide a high-level description of the protocol, and examine practical vulnerabilities in WhatsApp group chats. Multi-group security and key update mechanisms for Sender Keys are informally discussed in [30]. In [12], a preliminary analysis of the security of Sender Keys is carried out. While the paper only includes informal discussions and no proofs, it serves as an initial exploration for the ideas in the present work. We remark that the scope of [12] is limited, as it does not formally develop a security model, and assumes that all two-party channels used by Sender Keys are *perfectly secure*, which is unrealistic and impossible to develop in practice.

Concurrent work by Albrecht, Dowling and Jones [2] develops a device-oriented security model and a proof for a recent specification of Matrix (i.e., for the updated protocol that mitigates the issues described in [1]). For group messaging, Matrix implements the Megolm protocol, which is Sender Keys-inspired but still deviates significantly from our description in this work, particularly regarding server interaction. Remarkably, [2] and our work arrive to similar conclusions in our analysis, such as the insecurity of group management and the challenges imposed by message ordering. Our works are complimentary and open new research directions. Examples include exploring whether the improvements behind Sender Keys+ can also be applied to Megolm, as well as extending our modelling to consider the (challenging) multi-device setting as they do.

2 Preliminaries

Notation. Unless otherwise stated, all algorithms are probabilistic, and $(x_1, \dots) \xleftarrow{\$} \mathcal{A}(y_1, \dots)$ is used to denote that $\mathcal{A}$ returns $(x_1, \dots)$ when run on input $(y_1, \dots)$. Blank values are represented by $\perp$, which we return in case of algorithm failure. We denote the security parameter by λ and its unary representation by 1^λ. We also define the state γ of a user ID as the data required by ID for protocol execution, including message records, group-related variables, and cryptographic material. We store such material in dictionaries $M[\cdot]$ and write $a \leftarrow M[b]$ to assign, to a, the value stored in M under key b. All dictionaries can optionally be indexed by an oracle query q to represent the state of a dictionary at the time q is made, e.g., $\mathcal{E}[ID; q]$ denotes the value of $\mathcal{E}[ID]$ at the beginning of query q. We define the clause **require** P on a logical predicate P that immediately returns $\perp$ if P is not satisfied (or **false** if the algorithm returns a boolean value). For two sets $\mathcal{S}$ and $\mathcal{T}$, let $\mathcal{S} \xleftarrow{\cup} \mathcal{T}$ denote the reassignment of $\mathcal{S}$ to the set $\mathcal{S} \cup \mathcal{T}$, and let $\mathcal{S} \xleftarrow{-} \mathcal{T}$ denote the reassignment of $\mathcal{S}$ to the set $\mathcal{S} \setminus \mathcal{T}$. To indicate that certain variable values are not crucial to the algorithm's logic, we use "·" notation. For instance, `Receive`$(ID, C) = (\cdot, ID', e''_{\mathsf{2pc}}, i''_{\mathsf{2pc}})$ denotes that the first variable can take any value. We defer the definitions of standard cryptographic primitives used throughout this work to the full version.

2.1 Two-Party Channels

Towards defining our Group Messenger primitive with support for two-party channels, we define them below as a standalone primitive.

Definition 1 (Two-Party Channel). *A two-party channel scheme* $\mathsf{2PC} := (\mathsf{Init}, \mathsf{InitCh}, \mathsf{Send}, \mathsf{Recv})$ *is defined as the following tuple of* PPT *algorithms.*

$\gamma \xleftarrow{\$} \mathsf{Init}(ID)$: *Given a user identity ID, the probabilistic initialisation algorithm returns an initial state* γ.

$b \xleftarrow{\$} \mathsf{InitCh}(ID^*, \gamma)$: *Given a state* γ *and a user identity* ID^*, *the probabilistic channel initialisation algorithm returns an acceptance bit* $b \in \{0, 1\}$ *and updates the caller's state.*

$(C, e_{\mathsf{2pc}}, i_{\mathsf{2pc}}) \xleftarrow{\$} \mathsf{Send}(\mathsf{m}, ID^*, \gamma)$: *Given a message* m, *the intended message recipient* ID^* *and a state* γ, *the probabilistic sending algorithm returns a ciphertext* C *and a channel epoch-index pair* $(e_{\mathsf{2pc}}, i_{\mathsf{2pc}})$ *corresponding to* m *(or* $\perp$ *upon failure), and updates the state.*

$(\mathsf{m}, ID^*, e_{\mathsf{2pc}}, i_{\mathsf{2pc}}) \leftarrow \mathsf{Recv}(C, \gamma)$: *Given a ciphertext* C *and a state* γ, *the deterministic receiving algorithm returns a message* m, *a user identity* ID^* *corresponding to the sender of* m *and a channel epoch-index pair* $(e_{\mathsf{2pc}}, i_{\mathsf{2pc}})$ *corresponding to* m *(or* $\perp$ *upon failure), and updates the state.*

Our $\mathsf{2PC} := (\mathsf{Init}, \mathsf{InitCh}, \mathsf{Send}, \mathsf{Recv})$ primitive captures two initialisation functions. The first function initialises the state of a party by taking its ID as input, while the second function is used to initialise a communication channel with a counterpart ID^*. Consider two parties, ID and ID^* who intend to communicate over a two-party channel. Both parties initialise their states, γ_{ID} and γ_{ID^*} using the Init function. Subsequently, ID (or ID^*) initiates the communication channel by invoking the $\mathsf{InitCh}(\gamma_{ID}, ID^*)$ (or $\mathsf{InitCh}(\gamma_{ID^*}, ID)$) function. It is worth noting that, similar to DCGKA [47], our two-party channel primitive assumes the presence of a public-key infrastructure, which is omitted here for simplicity.

We adopt the notion of channel epochs from [6], such that in each two-party channel, ID and ID' are associated with a channel epoch e_{2pc}, indicating the number of times the direction of communication has changed (alongside a message index i_{2pc}).

Security. The Double Ratchet protocol has been the subject of several academic works [6,21,24,26] that analyse its security on a fine-grained level for two-party communication. When used by multiple parties in a group during the execution of Sender Keys, analysing the Double Ratchet protocol becomes complex, making it difficult to replace it with other protocols. To tame this complexity, we adopt a comparatively simpler notion of two-party communication in similar complexity to the formalism of Weidner et al. for their DCGKA protocol [47].

In the game-based security notion that we define for two-party channels, that we formalise in our full version, we parameterise security by a cleanness predicate $\mathsf{C}_{\mathsf{2pc}}$ and a PCS bound $\Delta > 0$. Broadly, the cleanness predicate prevents the adversary from winning the game by making a trivial attack, i.e., via a bit guess (resp. forgery) based on a challenge (resp. delivery) using exposed key material. PCS after an exposure is parameterised by Δ, which is the number of message round-trips (i.e. number of times that the sender-receiver roles alternate) that the channel requires for healing. In our modelling, out-of-order delivery is also supported.

Instantiations. By previous work [6], the Double Ratchet can be seen to achieve a PCS bound of $\Delta = 3$. However, by replacing the Diffie Hellman key exchange component in the Double Ratchet (referred to as continuous key agreement [6]) with a KEM, the PCS bound can be improved to $\Delta = 2$. This is optimal since if a user is exposed in channel epoch e_{2pc} and acts as the sender, then they can decrypt a message from channel epoch $e_{\mathsf{2pc}}+1$ based on correctness requirements. While we do consider protocols with weak PCS and hence larger values of Δ, including $\Delta = \infty$ if new randomness is never injected in key derivation, protocols lacking forward security are considered insecure within our model.

For channel initialisation InitCh, an initial key exchange between the parties needs to be carried out. Typically this is done via the asynchronous X3DH protocol [42] and by relying on a PKI, that we abstract away in this work.

3 Group Messenger

We introduce our main cryptographic primitive called *Group Messenger* that captures sending and receiving application messages between members of a dynamic group. We note that our primitive captures a single group; extending it to multiple groups is straightforward by using group identifiers (see e.g. [14]).

Definition 2 (Group Messenger). *A Group Messenger* $\mathsf{GM} :=$ $(\mathsf{Init}, \mathsf{Send}, \mathsf{Recv}, \mathsf{Exec}, \mathsf{Proc})$ *is defined as the following tuple of* PPT *algorithms.*

$\gamma \xleftarrow{\$} \mathsf{Init}(ID)$: *Given a user identity ID, the probabilistic initialisation algorithm returns an initial state* γ.

$C \xleftarrow{\$} \mathsf{Send}(\mathsf{m}, \gamma)$: *Given a message* m *and a state* γ*, the probabilistic sending algorithm returns a ciphertext C (or* $\perp$ *upon failure) and updates the state.*

$(\mathsf{m}, ID^*, e, i) \leftarrow \mathsf{Recv}(C, \gamma)$: *Given a ciphertext C and a state* γ*, the deterministic receiving algorithm returns a message* m*, an identity* ID^* *corresponding to the sender, a group epoch e and index i both corresponding to* m *(or* $\perp$ *upon failure), and updates the state.*

$T \xleftarrow{\$} \mathsf{Exec}(\mathtt{cmd}, \boldsymbol{IDs}, \gamma)$: *Given a command* $\mathtt{cmd} \in \{\mathtt{crt}, \mathtt{add}, \mathtt{rem}, \mathtt{upd}\}$*, a list of identitics* $\boldsymbol{IDs}$ *and a state* γ*, the probabilistic execution algorithm returns a control message T (or* $\perp$ *upon failure) and updates the state.*

$b \leftarrow \mathsf{Proc}(T, \gamma)$: *Given a control message T and a state* γ*, the deterministic processing algorithm outputs an acceptance bit* $b \in \{0, 1\}$ *and updates the state.*

In our syntax, a distinction is made between application messages and control messages. Specifically, distinct algorithms are employed for the transmission and reception of application messages, as well as for the execution and processing of group modifications. These modifications, executed via Exec, are parameterised by a command cmd that encompasses various operations such as user addition add, removal rem, group creation crt, or user key material update upd. Moreover, in scenarios where two-party messaging protocols are necessitated for the implementation of the group primitive (although not applicable to CGKAs such as TreeKEM [7]), two-party messages are formally assumed to be sent alongside or within ciphertexts or control messages. Consequently, they are abstracted away from our syntax. Looking ahead, we will enforce that ciphertexts and control messages are sent alongside two-party channel ciphertexts (and can be received with a different ciphertext or control message) when we define security in Sect. 3.1.

Message Epochs. We define a message epoch as a pair of integers (e, i), internal to the state γ of a party *ID*, that captures time and synchronisation between parties. Message epochs are central to our description of Sender Keys and security model. Each application message sent by *ID* corresponds to a single message epoch (e, i), which is output by the Recv algorithm at the receiver's end. The *epoch e* advances whenever *ID* processes a new group change (i.e., a control message). The *index* i advances when ID sends a new message. If control messages are delivered to group members in lockstep (i.e. sequentially in the same order), parties who have the same epoch e will have the same view of the group membership. We define a total ordering $(e, i) \leq (e', i')$ when $e < e'$, or $e = e'$ and $i < i'$. Nevertheless, we remark that 2PC channel epochs are independent from GM message epochs.

Oracles for Correctness and Security. We introduce game-based notions for GM correctness and security, where the adversary $\mathcal{A}$ will have access to various oracles that we outline below.

$\texttt{Create}(ID, \boldsymbol{IDs})$: creates a group by executing $\mathsf{Exec}(\texttt{crt}, \boldsymbol{IDs}, \gamma)$ with ID as the initiator, generating a control message T.
$\texttt{Challenge}(ID, \mathsf{m}_0, \mathsf{m}_1)$: outputs a ciphertext C_b corresponding to the message m_b sent by ID, where b is the bit that parametrises the game. Namely, $\mathcal{A}$ obtains $C_b \leftarrow \mathsf{Send}(\mathsf{m}_b, \gamma[ID])$.
$\texttt{Send}(ID, \mathsf{m})$: ID sends an application-level message m using the Send algorithm, producing a ciphertext C.
$\texttt{Receive}(ID, C)$: ID receives a ciphertext C by calling $\mathsf{Recv}(C, \gamma[ID])$. The sender ID' is inferred from the message as output by Recv. In the event of a successful forgery, $\mathcal{A}$ obtains the value of b.
$\texttt{Add}(ID, ID')/\texttt{Remove}(ID, ID')/\texttt{Update}(ID)$: ID adds ID' / removes ID' / refreshes ID's secrets by calling $\mathsf{Exec}(\texttt{add}, ID', \gamma[ID])$ / $\mathsf{Exec}(\texttt{rem}, ID', \gamma[ID])$ / $\mathsf{Exec}(\texttt{upd}, ID, \gamma[ID])$, generating control message T.
$\texttt{Deliver}(ID, T)$: ID is delivered a control message T via $\mathsf{Proc}(T, \gamma[ID])$.
$\texttt{Expose}(ID)$: Leaks the state γ of ID to $\mathcal{A}$.

Correctness. To ensure correctness, several properties must be satisfied given that all messages are generated honestly.

- *Message delivery*: Application messages (generated by `Send`) must be received correctly by all group members.
- *Group evolution*: Group operations, such as `crt` (group creation), `add` (user addition), `rem` (user removal), and `upd` (key update), must have their intended effects on the group when received and processed.
- *Group membership consistency*: The list of group members must be consistent among all group members, assuming they process the same sequence of control messages.
- *Out-of-order delivery*: Messages corresponding to past epochs must be decryptable if delivered out-of-order. Messages corresponding to future epochs must be rejected upon reception.

To formally capture correctness, a game-based correctness notion can be considered between a challenger and a computationally unbounded adversary. In the correctness game, the adversary initiates the protocol by calling the `Create` oracle once. The adversary can use the `Send` and `Receive` oracles as usual, and also has access to the `Add`, `Remove`, `Update`, `Deliver` and `Expose` oracles. However, the `Challenge` oracle may not be called, and `Send` and `Deliver` can only be called on honestly generated ciphertexts or control messages.

Looking ahead, the predicates used in the correctness analysis need to be modified from those used in security to suit the context. Notably, there is no need for a challenge predicate since the challenge oracle is not allowed. However, the concurrency predicate (defined later) is essential, addressing situations where members propose concurrent group changes or process group changes in different orders.

3.1 Security Model

We introduce a game-based model of security for our Group Messenger primitive that captures the main desirable security properties of a group messaging scheme. In brief, our game $\mathbf{M\text{-}IND}_{\mathsf{GM},\mathsf{C}}$ captures a partially active adversary who can, in particular, expose the state of users and inject (possibly malformed) messages at any time. We consider the confidentiality of application messages with FS and PCS, and we also model the out-of-order delivery of application and control messages.

Definition 3 (Message indistinguishability of GM). Let $\mathsf{GM} := (\mathsf{Init}, \mathsf{Send}, \mathsf{Recv}, \mathsf{Exec}, \mathsf{Proc})$ be a group messenger. *Message indistinguishability* with $b \in \{0,1\}$ and cleanness predicate C for GM is defined via the game $\mathbf{M\text{-}IND}_{\mathsf{GM},\mathsf{C}}$ depicted in Fig. 2. We define the advantage of adversary $\mathcal{A}$ in $\mathbf{M\text{-}IND}_{\mathsf{GM},\mathsf{C}}$ as

$$\mathsf{Adv}^{\mathbf{m\text{-}ind}}_{\mathsf{GM},\mathsf{C}}(\mathcal{A}) := \left|\Pr[\mathbf{M\text{-}IND}^{\mathcal{A}}_{\mathsf{GM},1,\mathsf{C}} \Rightarrow 1] - \Pr[\mathbf{M\text{-}IND}^{\mathcal{A}}_{\mathsf{GM},0,\mathsf{C}} \Rightarrow 1]\right|.$$

We say that GM is (q,ϵ)-$\mathbf{M\text{-}IND}_{\mathsf{GM},\mathsf{C}}$ if for all PPT adversaries $\mathcal{A}$ who make at most q oracle queries we have $\mathsf{Adv}^{\mathbf{m\text{-}ind}}_{\mathsf{GM},\mathsf{C}}(\mathcal{A}) \leq \epsilon$.

Game Description. The $\mathbf{M\text{-}IND}_{\mathsf{GM},\mathsf{C}}$ game that we introduce in Fig. 2, is played between a PPT adversary $\mathcal{A}$ and a challenger. The game is parameterised by a bit b that has to be guessed by $\mathcal{A}$, as in a message indistinguishability game. The adversary wins the game if it directly guesses b correctly, or if it carries out a successful forgery. The game is further parameterised by a protocol-specific *cleanness* predicate (sometimes safety predicate [7]) that rules out trivial attacks and captures the exact security of the protocol.

Message Epochs. We define a function $\mathsf{m\text{-}ep}(ID, ID', q)$ that indicates the highest message epoch (e,i), as output by the Recv algorithm, for which a user ID has received a message from ID' at the time of query q for $ID \neq ID'$. For $ID = ID'$, this indicates the local state value for $(\mathcal{E}[ID], \mathcal{I}[ID])$. The $\mathsf{m\text{-}ep}$ function reflects the view of user ID' by user ID.

320   D. Balbás et al.

Game M-IND$_{GM,b,C}^{\mathcal{A}}$

01   for all ID :
02       $\gamma[ID] \xleftarrow{\$} \mathsf{Init}(1^\lambda, ID)$
03    $\mathcal{T}[\cdot], \mathcal{M}[\cdot], \mathcal{CH}[\cdot], \mathcal{SM}[\cdot] \leftarrow \bot$
04   ep $\leftarrow 0$
05    $\mathcal{E}[\cdot], \mathcal{I}[\cdot] \leftarrow 0$
06    $b' \leftarrow \mathcal{A}^{\mathsf{Create},...,\mathsf{Receive}}$
07   **require** C
08   **return** b'

Oracle Create($ID, \boldsymbol{IDs}$)   // Called only once

09   **require** $ID \in \boldsymbol{IDs}$
10   **require** ep $= 0$
11    $T \xleftarrow{\$} \mathsf{Exec}(\mathtt{crt}, \boldsymbol{IDs}, \gamma[ID])$
12    $\mathcal{T}[\mathrm{ep}] \leftarrow T$; ep $\leftarrow$ ep $+ 1$
13   **return** T

Oracle Send(ID, m)

14    $C \xleftarrow{\$} \mathsf{Send}(m, \gamma[ID])$
15   **require** $C \neq \bot$
16    $\mathcal{I}[ID] \leftarrow \mathcal{I}[ID] + 1$
17    $\mathcal{M}[ID, \mathcal{E}[ID], \mathcal{I}[ID]] \leftarrow C$
18   **return** C

Oracle Challenge(ID, m_0, m_1)

19   **require** $|m_0| = |m_1|$
20    $C^* \xleftarrow{\$} \mathsf{Send}(m_b, \gamma[ID])$
21   **require** $C^* \neq \bot$
22    $\mathcal{I}[ID] \leftarrow \mathcal{I}[ID] + 1$
23    $\mathcal{CH}[ID, \mathcal{E}[ID], \mathcal{I}[ID]] \leftarrow C^*$
24   **return** C^*

Oracle Expose(ID)

25   **return** $\gamma[ID]$

Oracle Add(ID, ID')

26    $T \xleftarrow{\$} \mathsf{Exec}(\mathtt{add}, \{ID'\}, \gamma[ID])$
27   **require** $T \neq \bot$
28    $\mathcal{T}[\mathrm{ep}] \leftarrow T$; ep $\leftarrow$ ep $+ 1$
29   **return** T

Oracle Remove(ID, ID')

30    $T \xleftarrow{\$} \mathsf{Exec}(\mathtt{rem}, \{ID'\}, \gamma[ID])$
31   **require** $T \neq \bot$
32    $\mathcal{T}[\mathrm{ep}] \leftarrow T$; ep $\leftarrow$ ep $+ 1$
33   **return** T

Oracle Update(ID)

34    $T \xleftarrow{\$} \mathsf{Exec}(\mathtt{upd}, \{ID\}, \gamma[ID])$
35   **require** $T \neq \bot$
36    $\mathcal{T}[\mathrm{ep}] \leftarrow T$; ep $\leftarrow$ ep $+ 1$
37   **return** T

Oracle Deliver(ID, T)

38   acc $\leftarrow \mathsf{Proc}(T, \gamma[ID])$
39   **require** acc
40    $\mathcal{E}[ID] \leftarrow \mathcal{E}[ID] + 1$
41    $\mathcal{I}[ID] \leftarrow 0$
42   **if** proc-forgery(T) :
43   **return** b // $\mathcal{A}$ wins
44   **return**

Oracle Receive(ID, C)

45    $(m, ID', e, i) \leftarrow \mathsf{Recv}(C, \gamma[ID])$
46   **if** $m \neq \bot$:
47   Update $\mathcal{SM}[ID, ID']$
48   **if** recv-forgery(C) :
49   **return** b // $\mathcal{A}$ wins
50   **return**

Fig. 2. Game defining **M-IND$_{GM,b,C}^{\mathcal{A}}$** with adversary $\mathcal{A}$ and cleanness predicate C. Lines in teal correspond only to bookkeeping and state update operations. All oracles except for Create and Expose can only be called when ep > 0.

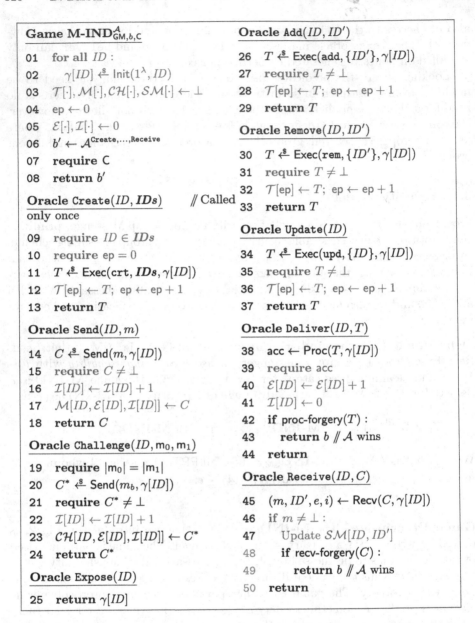

Dictionaries. The challenger keeps a record of messages and game variables in several dictionaries. The state of each party is stored in $\gamma[\cdot]$ and updated when an algorithm is called on a given $\gamma[ID]$. Ciphertexts and challenged ciphertexts are

stored in $\mathcal{M}$ and $\mathcal{CH}$, respectively, each of them indexed by an ID and a message epoch (e, i). The unique honest control message that starts a given epoch e is stored in $\mathcal{T}[e]$, and the most recent epoch of the group is stored in variable ep (note that we implicitly assume a total ordering of control messages). The current message epoch of ID is stored in $\mathcal{E}[ID], \mathcal{I}[ID]$. Even if each control message in $\mathcal{T}$ corresponds to a single epoch, different parties can be in different epochs. We say ID is in epoch e before query q if the last control message processed by ID before query q is $\mathcal{T}[e]$.

The message epochs corresponding to skipped messages from sender ID' stored by ID are kept in $\mathcal{SM}[ID, ID']$. We keep $\mathcal{SM}$ updated in the `Receive` oracle as follows: given a message epoch (e, i) and an ID' output by Recv, if $(e, i) \in \mathcal{SM}[ID, ID']$ then (e, i) is erased from $\mathcal{SM}[ID, ID']$. Otherwise, we add all pairs (e', i') such that $(e', i') < (e, i)$ and (e', i') corresponds to all messages sent by ID' not delivered to ID.

Outcome. After q oracle queries, $\mathcal{A}$ outputs a guess b' of b if the cleanness predicate C is satisfied (otherwise the game aborts). $\mathcal{A}$ can win the game in three different ways: by directly guessing the challenge bit correctly, by injecting a forged application message via `Receive` successfully, or by injecting a forged control message via `Deliver`. The cleanness predicate C parameterises the security of a given protocol by restricting the capabilities of the adversary to exclude a class of attacks. Additionally, we explicitly state predicates $\mathsf{recv\text{-}forgery}$ and $\mathsf{proc\text{-}forgery}$ in our game, which model the (general, not protocol-specific) conditions under which a `Receive` or `Deliver` call result in a successful forgery (leaking b to $\mathcal{A}$). We expand on these predicates in Sect. 3.2.

Related Security Notions. Our security model takes inspiration from the game-based modelling developed for MLS and for CGKA [7,39]. Nevertheless, it is not possible to adopt these models as they consider a single group key, which is not compatible with a Sender Keys (or similar) approach to group messaging. The closest security model to ours in the literature comes from the DCGKA scheme [47], which however does not consider message injections nor adaptive security.

Limitations. Our security game allows a single successful injection to occur, since after this point the adversary is given the secret key for free. That is, we do not allow 'trivial' message forgeries that do not result in the adversary winning the game. Hence, full active security cannot be captured by our modelling. Like several other models in the literature (e.g., [7,39,47]), our security model considers a single group (see [30] for an analysis of cross-group security) and ignores randomness exposure or manipulation [15].

3.2 Modelling Two-Party Channel Ciphertexts

Given that the GM protocol uses two-party channels (as Sender Keys does), these need to be modelled accurately within the GM security game, particularly to describe forgeries via the recv-forgery and proc-forgery predicates. We introduce additional notation to define how two-party ciphertexts can be sent alongside GM messages; we opt for such modelling for convenience, as in this way the adversary gets access to all two-party channels explicitly. We remark that this subsection can be skipped for GM protocols that do not employ two-party channels.

Essentially, we want to capture the fact that an Exec or Send call can output *several* two-party channel ciphertexts, whereas Proc and Recv should only take as input a *single* two-party channel ciphertext (i.e., the one intended for the caller) for efficiency. We thus assume input/output ciphertexts and control messages for group messenger algorithms take the following form. Let C_{2pc} be a 2PC ciphertext and let T_{core} (resp. C_{core}) be the remaining part of a control (resp. application) message in the GM primitive. For output, we assume control messages output by Exec are of the form $(T_{\mathsf{core}}, C^1_{\mathsf{2pc}}, \ldots, C^k_{\mathsf{2pc}})$, and ciphertexts output by Send are of the form $(C_{\mathsf{core}}, C^1_{\mathsf{2pc}}, \ldots, C^k_{\mathsf{2pc}})$ for some k. For input, we assume control messages input to Exec (resp. to Recv) are of the form $(T_{\mathsf{core}}, C_{\mathsf{2pc}})$ (resp. $(C_{\mathsf{core}}, C_{\mathsf{2pc}})$).

Forgery Predicates. We define the predicates proc-forgery and recv-forgery in Fig. 3 used in Fig. 2 using the input/output semantics introduced above. The purpose of these predicates is to handle ciphertext 'splitting' resulting from the use of two-party channels. Without accounting for this splitting, forgeries could be defined as usual, i.e. any ciphertext input to Proc (resp. Recv) that was not previously output by Exec (resp. Proc) would be considered a forgery. Essentially, we consider that a control message $T^* = (T^*_{\mathsf{core}}, C^*_{\mathsf{2pc}})$ is a forgery whenever either T^*_{core} or C^*_{2pc} are not part of an honestly generated message (i.e. in $\mathcal{T}[\cdot]$). Forgeries for Recv are defined analogously.

$$\boxed{\mathsf{proc\text{-}forgery}(T^* = (T^*_{\mathsf{core}}, C^*_{\mathsf{2pc}})):}\ \nexists \{(T, \boldsymbol{C}), (T', \boldsymbol{C}')\} \subseteq \mathcal{T}[\cdot]:$$
$$(T^*_{\mathsf{core}}, C^*_{\mathsf{2pc}}) \in \{(T, C_i), (T', C_i), (T, C'_j)\} \wedge (C_i \in \boldsymbol{C}) \wedge (C'_j \in \boldsymbol{C}')$$
$$\boxed{\mathsf{recv\text{-}forgery}(C = (C^*_{\mathsf{core}}, C^*_{\mathsf{2pc}})):}\ \nexists \{(C_0, \boldsymbol{C}), (C'_0, \boldsymbol{C}')\} \subseteq \mathcal{CH}[\cdot] \cup \mathcal{M}[\cdot]:$$
$$(C^*_{\mathsf{core}}, C^*_{\mathsf{2pc}}) \in \{(C_0, C_i), (C'_0, C_i), (C_0, C'_j)\} \wedge (C_i \in \boldsymbol{C}) \wedge (C'_j \in \boldsymbol{C}')$$

Fig. 3. Predicates that determine what is considered a forgery in Fig. 2 for algorithms Proc and Recv.

The predicates imply that it is *not* considered a forgery if a two-party ciphertext is received with a different control message/ciphertext than it was sent with. That is, the adversary is allowed to mix-and-match ciphertexts, i.e., by replacing the C_i corresponding to some T (resp. C_0) by C'_i corresponding to some other T' (resp. C'_0).

4 Sender Keys

Two-Party Channels and the Server. The Sender Keys protocol assumes the existence of authenticated and secure two-party communication channels between each pair of users, which can be achieved through the use of Signal's Double Ratchet protocol [41] also used by WhatsApp [48]. Additionally, the protocol relies on a central server to distribute both control messages and application messages. We assume that the server provides a *total ordering for control messages*, ensuring that all parties process control messages in the correct order.[5] Total ordering is not required for application messages. User authentication is initially performed via the central server (modelled here with 2PC.InitCh), after which users authenticate other group members through the underlying two-party communication channel. We note that this deviates from other work in the literature such as [11] where the *authentication service* is different to the *delivery service.*

4.1 Protocol

We describe the Sender Keys protocol in our GM syntax according to the details inferred from [48] and [43], although we acknowledge that our interpretation may not precisely match the closed-source implementation of WhatsApp. In this section we present a detailed overview of the main algorithms depicted in Fig. 4. For Exec and Proc, we only present the remove operation as it involves key refreshing and is considered the most complex, while the create, add, and update operations follow a similar approach. For the sake of clarity, we make some simplifications in this section, and refer to the full version for the complete protocol logic and description.

Primitives. The protocol relies on standard primitives including a symmetric encryption scheme $\mathsf{SymEnc} = (\mathsf{Gen}, \mathsf{Enc}, \mathsf{Dec})$, a signature scheme $\mathsf{Sig} = (\mathsf{Gen}, \mathsf{Sgn}, \mathsf{Ver})$, and two different key derivation functions $\mathsf{H}_1, \mathsf{H}_2$ (our improved protocol also uses message authentication codes).

State Initialisation. Each user is assumed to maintain a state γ containing: a secret key used for signing ssk, a list of current group members $\boldsymbol{G}$, the current epoch ep, the current index of their chain key i_{ck} (indicating the number of times the user's sender key has been ratcheted forward), a list of key counters kc (indicating the number of times that a sender key has been re-sampled since ID initialised their state), a dictionary of sender keys $\mathsf{SK}[\cdot] := (\mathsf{spk}_{ID}, \mathsf{ck}_{ID}, \mathsf{i}_{\mathsf{ck}})$ indexed by a user ID and a key counter, and a list of message keys $\mathcal{MK}$. The Init algorithm initialises the state variable of users; in practice this is done by a user when they install the messaging application.

Group Creation. This occurs via $\mathsf{Exec}(\mathtt{crt}, \boldsymbol{IDs}, \gamma)$, which takes a list of users $\boldsymbol{G} := \{ID_1, \ldots, ID_{|G|}\}$ as input; two-party channels are initialised by users upon processing the control message via 2PC.InitCh.

[5] We remark that total ordering is a standard assumption in the CGKA line of work [7–9,11,39] and is assumed by MLS.

Init($ID, 1^\lambda$)

01 $\gamma.ME \leftarrow ID$
02 $\gamma.(\mathsf{ssk}, G, \mathsf{ep}, i_{ME}) \leftarrow \bot$
03 $\gamma.(\mathsf{SK}[\cdot], \mathcal{MK}[\cdot], \mathsf{kc}[\cdot]) \leftarrow \bot$
04 **return** γ

Send(m, γ)

05 **require** $ME \in G$
06 **if** $\mathsf{SK}[ME, \mathsf{kc}[ME]] = \bot$:
// Sample fresh sender key
07     $C \leftarrow \textsc{PreSendFirst}()$
08 **if** $i_{ME} = 0$:
09     $C \leftarrow (C, \textsc{SendToMissing}())$
10 $\mathsf{mk} \leftarrow H_1(\mathsf{SK}[ME, \mathsf{kc}[ME]].\mathsf{ck})$
11 $c \xleftarrow{\$} \mathsf{Enc}(\mathsf{mk}, \mathsf{m})$
12 $\textsc{UpdateCK}(ME, \mathsf{kc}[ME])$
// This also updates i_{ME}
13 $M \leftarrow (c, (\mathsf{ep}, i_{ME}), \mathsf{kc}[ME], i_{\mathsf{ck}}, ME)$
14 $\sigma \xleftarrow{\$} \mathsf{Sig.Sgn}(\mathsf{ssk}, M)$
15 **return** $C := ((M, \sigma), C)$

Exec($\mathsf{cmd} = \mathsf{rem}, ID, \gamma$)

16 **require** $ID \in G$
17 $C[\cdot] \leftarrow \bot$
18 $T \leftarrow (\mathsf{rem}, ME, ID, \mathsf{ep} + 1)$
19 **return** (T, C)

Recv($C = ((M, \sigma), C_{\mathsf{2pc}}), \gamma$)

20 **parse** M **as** $(c, (e, i), \mathsf{kc}', i_{\mathsf{ck}}', ID)$
21 **require** $ID \in G$
22 **if** $\mathsf{SK}[ID, \mathsf{kc}'] = \bot$:
23     $(\mathsf{SK}[ID, \mathsf{kc}'], \mathsf{kc}^*, \mathsf{ep}', \mathsf{aux}, ID^*) \leftarrow$ 2PC.Recv(C_{2pc}, γ)
24   **require** $(ID, e, \mathsf{kc}') = (ID^*, \mathsf{ep}', \mathsf{kc}^*)$
25        $\textsc{DeleteOldCK}(ID, \mathsf{aux})$
26 **else require** $C_{\mathsf{2pc}} = \bot$
27 **require** $e \leq \mathsf{ep}$
28 **require** $\mathsf{Sig.Ver}(\mathsf{SK}[ID, \mathsf{kc}'].\mathsf{spk}, \sigma, M)$
29 $\mathsf{mk} \leftarrow \textsc{UpdateKeysRecv}()$
30 $\mathsf{m} \leftarrow \mathsf{Dec}(\mathsf{mk}, c)$
31 **return** (m, ID, e, i)

Proc($(T = (\mathsf{rem}, ID, ID', \mathsf{ep}'), C_{\mathsf{2pc}}), \gamma$)

32 **require** $ID \in G \wedge C_{\mathsf{2pc}} = \bot$
33 **require** $\mathsf{ep}' = \mathsf{ep} + 1$
34 $G \xleftarrow{-} \{ID'\}$
35 $\mathsf{ep} \leftarrow \mathsf{ep} + 1$; $i_{ME} \leftarrow 0$
36 **for all** $ID^* \in G$:
37     $\mathsf{kc}[ID^*] \leftarrow \mathsf{kc}[ID^*] + 1$
38 $\mathsf{SK}[ID', \cdot] \leftarrow \bot$
39 **if** $ID = ME$: $\gamma \leftarrow \bot$
40 **return** true

Fig. 4. Sender Keys protocol description (main operations). For conditions of the form "**require** T" when T is false, the function outputs $\bot$ and all computation is reverted. The full protocol is available in the full version.

Message Sending. To send an application message m to the group, every $ID \in G$ must have the caller's (ME) sender key. The process is as follows:

- If ME does not have a sender key, ME generates a fresh sender key $((\gamma.\mathsf{ssk}, \mathsf{spk}) \xleftarrow{\$} \mathsf{Sig.Gen}(1^\lambda)$ and $\mathsf{ck} \xleftarrow{\$} \{0,1\}^\lambda)$. The sender key is then set as $\mathsf{SK}[ME, \mathsf{kc}[ME]] \leftarrow (\mathsf{spk}, \mathsf{ck}, i_{\mathsf{ck}})$ where $i_{\mathsf{ck}} = 0$. ME shares this key with each $ID \in G$ using 2PC.Send, resulting in a vector of ciphertexts C.
- If ME has a non-empty sender key but not all parties have it, ME shares the key with them via 2PC.Send and updates C.

Then ME generates a new message key mk from their chain key $\mathsf{SK}[ME, \mathsf{kc}[ME]].\mathsf{ck}$, encrypts m using mk, and ratchets its chain key forward by setting $\mathsf{ck} \leftarrow H_2(\mathsf{SK}[ME, \mathsf{kc}'].\mathsf{ck})$. Finally, ME signs the ciphertext and sends it together with C.

Message Receiving. To receive a message from ID, ME follows these steps:

- ME checks if they have ID's sender key $\mathsf{SK}[ID, \mathsf{kc}']$ corresponding to the key counter kc' indicated in the received message. If ME does not have it, they retrieve it from the two-party ciphertext $C_{2\mathsf{pc}}$ using 2PC.Recv, aborting the Recv call if the sender key cannot be found.
- ME performs epoch consistency checks and verifies the signature on the ciphertext using the signature public key $\mathsf{SK}[ID, \mathsf{kc}'].\mathsf{spk}$.
- The message key mk required to decrypt the message is computed from the chain keys as $\mathsf{mk} \leftarrow \mathsf{H}_1(\mathsf{SK}[ID, \mathsf{kc}'].\mathsf{ck})$, and is deleted after use.

Out-of-Order Messages. In the scenario of out-of-order message delivery (handled by UPDATEKEYSRECV), the following cases arise (we let $\mathsf{i_{ck}} := \mathsf{SK}[ID, \mathsf{kc}'].\mathsf{i_{ck}}$):

- If the received message comes from a past epoch $(e, i) < (\mathsf{ep}, \mathsf{i_{ck}})$, ME searches for the relevant skipped message key in $\mathcal{MK}$.
- If $e = \mathsf{ep}$ and $i > \mathsf{i_{ck}}$, ME ratchets ID's chain key $i - \mathsf{i_{ck}}$ times, and stores the skipped message keys in $\mathcal{MK}$.
- If $e > e$, the message reception fails since ME is not synchronised with the latest group epoch and cannot (even) determine whether the sender is still a member of the group.

Handling out-of-order message delivery constitutes a significant portion of the protocol's logic. For instance, parties must keep track of (and announce) the highest $\mathsf{i_{ck}}$ associated with a given kc. Failing to do so can result in correctness and security issues, as parties may overlook the need to store and delete keys in $\mathcal{MK}$.

Key Updates. In certain implementations of Sender Keys (although not specified in [48]) a simple (but weak) on-demand key update mechanism is supported. A party ME can update its key material via $\mathsf{Exec}(\mathtt{crt}, ME, \gamma)$. This operation lazily samples a fresh sender key $(\mathsf{spk}, \mathsf{ck}, 0)$ and distributes it over the two-party channels. All users sample a fresh key after processing a removal.

Membership Changes. The protocol allows individual group members to be added or removed from the group via $\mathsf{Exec}(\mathtt{add}, ID, \gamma)$ and $\mathsf{Exec}(\mathtt{rem}, ID, \gamma)$. These operations result in the distribution of a control message T to the group sent in clear. Newly added members are also sent a welcome 2PC ciphertext containing group information. Note that we model single adds/removes for simplicity but this can be extended in a straightforward manner to handle batched group changes.

Upon processing a control message via $\mathsf{Proc}(T, \gamma)$, ME proceeds as follows:

- If some ID^* is being removed at epoch e, ME erases all sender keys corresponding to ID^* (except for skipped message keys).[6] For other users, old

[6] A different deletion schedule may be applied as long as these keys are clearly marked as being no longer valid, e.g., if ID^* announces its maximum $\mathsf{i_{ck}}$ value over two-party channels when it processes its own removal.

sender keys are replaced with new ones when receiving messages from epoch $e' \geq e$, ensuring messages sent concurrently with the removal can be received.
- If some ID^* is being added, ME initialises its 2PC with ID^* via 2PC.InitCh.
- If ME is itself removed, it erases its state. If it is added to some group (or processes a create message), it initialises two-party channels with every $ID \in \boldsymbol{G}$.

Note that after either updating or adding or removing a user, new sender keys are only distributed once a party sends his first message.

5 Security

In this section, we argue that Sender Keys as described in Sect. 4 is secure with respect to our security model in Sect. 3.1. However, the security captured by our cleanness predicate is far from theoretically optimal since Sender Keys is relatively weak in security, and so in Sect. 6 we strengthen it by modifying the protocol in different ways. Our predicates are parameterised by the security of the underlying two-party channels. We first state our main theorem below.

Theorem 1. *Let* SymEnc := (Enc, Dec) *be a* $(q, \epsilon_{\mathsf{sym}})$-$\mathbf{IND\text{-}CPA}_{\mathsf{SymEnc},b}$ *symmetric encryption scheme,* Sig := (Gen, Sgn, Ver) *a* $(q, \epsilon_{\mathsf{sig}})$-$\mathbf{SUF\text{-}CMA}_{\mathsf{Sig}}$ *signature scheme,* $\mathsf{H} : \{0,1\}^\lambda \to \{0,1\}^\lambda \times \{0,1\}^\lambda$ *(where* $\mathsf{H}(x) := (\mathsf{H}_1(x), \mathsf{H}_2(x))$*) a* $(q, \epsilon_{\mathsf{prg}})$-$\mathbf{PRG}_{\mathsf{H}}$ *function and* 2PC *a* $(q, \epsilon_{\mathsf{2pc}})$-$\mathbf{2PC\text{-}IND}_{\mathsf{2PC},\mathsf{C}_{\mathsf{2pc}},\Delta}$ *two-party channels scheme for PCS bound* $\Delta > 0$*. Then Sender Keys (Fig. 4) is*

$$(q, 2 \cdot \epsilon_{\mathsf{2pc}} + q^2 \cdot (\epsilon_{\mathsf{2pc}} + \epsilon_{\mathsf{sym}} + q \cdot \epsilon_{\mathsf{prg}}) + q \cdot \epsilon_{\mathsf{sig}})\text{-}\mathbf{M\text{-}IND}_{\mathsf{GM},\mathsf{C}}$$

with respect to cleanness predicate $\mathsf{C} = \mathsf{C}_{\mathsf{sk}}^{\Delta}$ *(Fig. 8), where two-party channels cleanness predicate* $\mathsf{C}_{\mathsf{2pc}}$ *is defined in the full version.*

We define C_{sk} in Sect. 5.1 and prove the theorem in the full version. A proof sketch is provided in Sect. 5.2. Our security notion is adaptive as users can adaptively call oracles and in particular compromise users. Security is tighter when we restrict the game to consider non-adaptive adversaries as described below.

Corollary 1. *Under the same conditions of Theorem 1, and considering a non-adaptive security game, Sender Keys (Fig. 4) is* $(q, 2 \cdot \epsilon_{\mathsf{2pc}} + q \cdot (\epsilon_{\mathsf{sym}} + q \cdot \epsilon_{\mathsf{prg}}) + q \cdot \epsilon_{\mathsf{sig}})$-$\mathbf{M\text{-}IND}_{\mathsf{GM},\mathsf{C}}$ *with respect to cleanness predicate* $\mathsf{C} = \mathsf{C}_{\mathsf{sk}}$ *(Fig. 8).*

Sender Keys and Two-Party Channels. To illustrate how the cleanness predicates for Sender Keys must depend on the underlying two-party channels, consider a strongly secure two-party channel 2PC that provides optimal FS and PCS. Now, consider an execution of Sender Keys where all parties share the same view of the group $G = \{ID_1, ID_2, ID_3\}$, in which

1. ID_1 generates a control message $(T_{\mathsf{core}}, \boldsymbol{C})$ to remove party ID_3 ($q_1 = \texttt{Remove}(ID_1, ID_3)$),

2. ID_1 and ID_2 process T ($q_{2,1} = \texttt{Deliver}(ID_1, (T_{\text{core}}, C[ID_1]))$, $q_{2,2} = \texttt{Deliver}(ID_2, (T_{\text{core}}, C[ID_2]))$),
3. $\mathcal{A}$ exposes ID_2 ($q_3 = \texttt{Expose}(ID_2)$);
4. ID_1 sends an application message ($q_4 = \texttt{Send}(ID_1, m)$).

Recall that in step 4, ID_1 samples a new sender key that it sends to ID_2 over 2PC, since processing remove messages results in the sender keys of all parties being refreshed. Even with optimally-secure 2PC, the adversary will be able to decrypt the key sent over 2PC (by the correctness of the channel) and thus decrypt the ciphertext output in query q_4.

5.1 Cleanness

Our goal is to describe a suitable cleanness predicate C_{sk} for Sender Keys. The intuition behind this cleanness predicate is based on the following observations about the protocol:

- The exposure of a group member compromises the security of subsequent chain and message keys[7] until a secure key refresh takes place. This enables the adversary to forge messages since they also gain access to the exposed signature keys.
- Control messages can be trivially forged and injected by a network adversary as they are not authenticated.
- Forward-secure confidentiality holds except for messages delivered out-of-order since parties only delete message keys after using them, so a message that is delayed forever results in the corresponding message key never being deleted.[8]
- All parties recover from state exposure (via $\texttt{Expose}(ID)$) after security on the two-party channels is restored (considering the PCS bound Δ) and then either a) a removal is made effective, or b) all parties update their keys successfully.

To formalise the security predicate we introduce conventions for tracking the channel epochs of each user's two-party channels. We assume the game $\textbf{M-IND}_{\mathsf{GM,C}}$ maintains the largest channel epoch-index for each user's two-party channels over time. The game obtains this information by observing the channel epoch-index pairs generated by the 2PC.Send and 2PC.Recv operations within the group messenger. Specifically, we use a variable of the form $\texttt{EI}[ID, ID']$, where $\texttt{EI}[ID, ID']$ represents the largest channel epoch-index pair from ID's perspective for the channel between them and user ID', as for two-party channels. More generally, two-party state variables that we use below can be tracked easily by an $\textbf{M-IND}_{\mathsf{GM,C}}$ adversary such that our predicates are well-defined.

[7] Although it is not captured in our model, note that the exposure of a message key alone only compromises the message it refers to and does not (computationally) leak information about the chain key or other message keys.

[8] In practice, applications like WhatsApp and Signal bound the amount of (logical) time that keys are active for and the total number of keys that can be stored at once.

The Refresh$_\Delta$ Predicate. We define the predicate $\mathsf{refresh}_\Delta(ID, ID', q_i, e)$, parameterised by the PCS bound $\Delta > 0$ of the underlying two-party channels. Informally, given that ID' is exposed in query q_i ($q_i = \texttt{Expose}(ID')$), $\mathsf{refresh}_\Delta(ID, ID', q_i, e)$ is true if the (ID, ID') channel has healed and *then* ID has sampled a fresh sender key in or by epoch e (or will do so upon their next Send call). If the predicate is true, ID has recovered from the exposure in q_i.

More formally, let $(e_{\mathsf{2pc}}, i_{\mathsf{2pc}}) = \max\{\texttt{EI}[ID', ID; q_i], \texttt{EI}[ID, ID'; q_i]\}$. Then $\mathsf{refresh}_\Delta(ID, ID', q_i, e)$ is true if a) for $(e'_{\mathsf{2pc}}, i'_{\mathsf{2pc}}) = \texttt{EI}[ID', ID; q_j]$ for some $j > i$, $e'_{\mathsf{2pc}} \geq e_{\mathsf{2pc}} + \Delta$ holds; and b) during query q_k with $k \geq j$, member ID processes one of the following control messages corresponding to epoch e:

1. a removal of some member ID^*,
2. an addition of ID itself,
3. a group creation message, or
4. an update from ID itself.

In particular, if ID executes (and processes) an update that involves sending new key material over a refreshed two-party channel, this key material should be safe. We also define a simpler predicate $\mathsf{refresh\text{-}s}(ID, e)$ which is true if member ID processes one of the aforementioned control messages corresponding to epoch e. Observe that both $\mathsf{refresh}_\Delta$ and $\mathsf{refresh\text{-}s}$ events may only happen when ID moves to a new group epoch e.

Cleanness for Sender Keys. We divide our cleanness predicate into three components (challenge, injection, concurrency) that we specify below. The final predicate is defined in Fig. 8.

Challenge (Fig. 5). The effect of this predicate is to prevent challenges on exposed users (i.e., due to `Expose` calls). After exposing (with query q_i) *any* user ID', adversarial queries to `Challenge` are disallowed for every ID in the group until $\mathsf{refresh}_\Delta(ID, ID', q_i, e)$ occurs for some later epoch $e > \mathcal{E}[ID'; q_i]$. Note that this only restricts challenge queries q_j where $i < j$. To capture forward security precisely, some challenges made before an exposure ($i > j$) are also forbidden. These affect messages sent by some ID in epochs $(e, i) \geq \mathsf{m\text{-}ep}(ID', ID, q_i)$, which correspond to keys that ID' still stores (including skipped message keys stored at exposure time) or can derive due to being in a previous message epoch (for example if the user is offline).

Injection (Fig. 6). Firstly, let us recall the two-party ciphertext splitting semantics defined in Sect. 3.2. Namely, a GM ciphertext C naturally splits into $C = (C_{\mathsf{core}}, C_{\mathsf{2pc}})$ where C_{2pc} is processed by the two-party channels. An injection is said to have occurred when a message with a forged C_{core} and/or C_{2pc} was successfully processed.

We define the injection predicate to prevent injections of *application messages* coming from a user that has been exposed and has not refreshed its keys. We start with the definition for C_{core}. After exposing *a specific* user ID' with query q_i, $\mathcal{A}$ cannot make a query $q_j = \texttt{Receive}(ID, C)$ to impersonate ID' with a forgery

$$\boxed{\mathsf{C}^{\Delta}_{\text{sk-chall}}:} \ \forall(i,j,ID,ID') : q_i = \texttt{Expose}(ID') \wedge q_j = \texttt{Challenge}(ID,\cdot,\cdot),$$
$$(i > j \wedge \text{m-ep}(ID', ID, q_i) > (\mathcal{E}[ID;q_j], \mathcal{I}[ID;q_j]) \wedge$$
$$(\mathcal{E}[ID;q_j], \mathcal{I}[ID;q_j]) \notin \mathcal{SM}[ID', ID; q_i])$$
$$\vee\ (i < j \wedge \exists e : \mathcal{E}[ID';q_i] < e \leq \mathcal{E}[ID;q_j] \wedge \text{refresh}_{\Delta}(ID, ID', q_i, e))$$

Fig. 5. Challenge cleanness predicate for Sender Keys where the adversary makes oracle queries $q_1, \ldots, q_q$.

ciphertext C corresponding to some epoch e^* (i.e., such that tuple (ID', e^*) is output by $\mathsf{Recv}(C, \gamma[ID])$ in the game) in the following situations:

1. $e^* \geq \mathcal{E}[ID';q_i]$ and there hasn't been a $\text{refresh}_{\Delta}(ID', ID, q_i, e')$ event for the sender ID' at some epoch e' such that $\mathcal{E}[ID';q_i] < e' \leq e^*$, where the receiver ID has also processed the key update from ID''s message at injection time, i.e., $\mathcal{E}[ID;q_j] \geq e'$.
2. $e^* < \mathcal{E}[ID';q_i]$ but the signature key of ID' at epoch e^* was the same key as in the exposure epoch $\mathcal{E}[ID';q_i]$. Formally, this is expressed by the condition that there has not been any event $\text{refresh-s}(ID', e')$ for an epoch $e^* < e' \leq \mathcal{E}[ID';q_i]$.

For C_{2pc}, we directly adopt the injection cleanness predicate $\mathsf{C}_{\text{2pc-inj}}$ used to define two-party channel security (see full version). For additional clarity, we parametrize the predicates by the ciphertexts $C_{\text{core}}, C_{\text{2pc}}$. We also define the auxiliary predicate $\mathsf{C}^{\Delta}_{\text{sk-inj-core}}(C_{\text{core}})$ in Fig. 6.

$$\boxed{\mathsf{C}^{\Delta}_{\text{sk-inj-core}}(C_{\text{core}}):} \ \forall(i,j,ID,ID'):$$
$$(C_{\text{core}},\cdot) \notin \mathcal{M}[ID',\cdot;q_j] \wedge (i < j) \wedge q_i = \texttt{Expose}(ID') \wedge$$
$$q_j = \texttt{Receive}(ID, (C_{\text{core}},\cdot)) \wedge (\cdot, e^*, \cdot, ID') \leftarrow \mathsf{Recv}((C_{\text{core}},\cdot), \gamma[ID]) \text{ in } q_j,$$
$$\exists e' : \big[\ (\mathcal{E}[ID';q_i] < e' \leq e^* \wedge \text{refresh}_{\Delta}(ID', ID, q_i, e'))$$
$$\vee\ (e^* < e' \leq \mathcal{E}[ID';q_i] \wedge \text{refresh-s}(ID', e'))\ \big]$$

$$\boxed{\mathsf{C}^{\Delta}_{\text{sk-inj}}:} \ \forall\ C_{\text{core}}, C_{\text{2pc}}, \mathsf{C}^{\Delta}_{\text{sk-inj-core}}(C_{\text{core}}) \wedge \mathsf{C}_{\text{2pc-inj}}(C_{\text{2pc}})$$

Fig. 6. Auxiliary core injection cleanness predicate (top) and injection cleanness predicate (bottom) for Sender Keys, where the adversary makes oracle queries $q_1, \ldots, q_q$. The injection cleanness predicate additionally uses the $\mathsf{C}_{\text{2pc-inj}}$ defined in the full version.

Concurrency (Fig. 7). This predicate ensures several properties in the protocol. Firstly, it enforces that users process control message in the same order (albeit they need not be synchronised beyond this restriction). Additionally, it prevents the injection of *all* control messages. It is important to note that control messages are not signed in the core protocol, making injections trivial. Furthermore, the predicate guarantees that every user proposing a group change (via the Exec, Add, Remove or Update oracles) is in the most recent epoch. In practice, this predicate ensures that there is a unique honest control message in each epoch of the game.

The concurrency predicate ensures both security and correctness by addressing scenarios where members propose concurrent group changes or process group changes in different orders. Without enforcing this predicate, the protocol's behaviour becomes ill-defined.

$$\boxed{\mathsf{C}_{\text{sk-con}}:} \ \forall(i, ID) : q_i = \texttt{Deliver}(ID, (T_{\text{core}}, C_{\text{2pc}})), \exists j < i : q_j = (\texttt{Add} \text{ or } \texttt{Remove} \text{ or } \texttt{Update} \text{ or } \texttt{Create})(ID, \cdot) \wedge \exists e' : (T, \boldsymbol{C}) = \mathcal{T}[e'] \wedge (C_{\text{2pc}} \in \boldsymbol{C}) \wedge (\mathcal{E}[ID; q_i] = e' - 1 = \mathcal{E}[ID; q_j])$$

Fig. 7. Concurrency cleanness predicate in the ideal case where the adversary makes oracle queries $q_1, \ldots, q_q$.

$$\boxed{\mathsf{C}^{\Delta}_{\text{sk}}:} \ \mathsf{C}^{\Delta}_{\text{sk-chall}} \wedge \mathsf{C}^{\Delta}_{\text{sk-inj}} \wedge \mathsf{C}_{\text{sk-con}}$$

Fig. 8. Sender Keys cleanness predicate which makes use of sub-predicates defined in Figs. 5 to 7.

Limitations and Extensions. Our cleanness predicate enforces a total ordering on control messages, in contrast to considering causal ordering such as in [47] or no ordering at all. This assumption is consistent with real-world protocols (as in WhatsApp) where a central server is trusted to provide such an ordering, but makes our model unsuitable for decentralized protocols. If our security model allowed for it, one could modify our cleanness predicates to allow for 'trivial' injections that are non-winning, by not giving the adversary the challenger's bit b given that the forgery is trivial (i.e., it violates the injection predicate). Our concurrency predicate and security model could be strengthened to allow several Exec calls in an epoch, from which the network chooses one that is processed to all parties, which has been modelled for TreeKEM in the past [7].

5.2 Proof Sketch for Theorem 1

Towards proving the theorem we construct a series of hybrids. We first transition to a game where injections on the two-party channels are disallowed, following from their underlying security. After that, we transition to a game where oracle

`Receive` never outputs challenge bit b, reducing the transition to SUF-CMA signature security, while still excluding trivial injections due to cleanness. Then, we move to a game where the adversary is limited to a single `Challenge` query, losing a factor of q in the resulting reduction. Subsequently, we transition to a game where the message key used in the `Challenge` query (if it exists) is replaced by a uniformly random key that remains unknown to the adversary due to cleanness, and the two-party ciphertexts that send the key's ancestor chain key are replaced by dummy ciphertexts, which follows from the 2PC security and the PRG security of (H_1, H_2). Finally, we directly reduce to the IND-CPA security of the symmetric encryption scheme.

6 Analysis and Improvements

For the proof of security of Sender Keys (Theorem 1) to go through, we need to impose severe restrictions on the adversarial behaviour through the cleanness predicate C_{sk}. Hence, even if we manage to prove Sender Keys secure, we do so under a weak model that reveals important security shortcomings of the protocol. In this section, we elaborate on these limitations and propose changes to enhance security while maintaining efficiency. Some of these findings were presented in a preliminary analysis in [12].

6.1 Security Analysis and Limitations

Injection of Control Messages. Our first observation is that control messages lack user authentication, necessitating a high level of trust in the server to prevent the crafting of its own messages. To address this, in predicate $\mathsf{C}_{\mathsf{sk\text{-}con}}$ we need to enforce that every delivered control message has been honestly generated. A server deviating from standard behavior could mount a host of attacks. Here are three examples.

Censorship attack: The server can remove any member(s) ID from $\boldsymbol{G}$ such that all remaining members assume ID left the group by himself, whilst ID believes a different user ID' removed him.

- The server delivers a control message $T := (\mathtt{rem}, ID, ID, \cdot) \leftarrow \mathsf{Exec}(\mathtt{rem}, ID, \perp)$ to every $ID' \in \boldsymbol{G} \setminus \{ID\}$.
- The server delivers a control message $T' := (\mathtt{rem}, ID', ID, \cdot) \leftarrow \mathsf{Exec}(\mathtt{rem}, ID, \perp)$ to $ID \in \boldsymbol{G}$.

Burgle into the group attack: This attack, observed in [46], allows the server to add any member(s) ID to $\boldsymbol{G}$. For this, the server just delivers a control message $T := (\mathtt{add}, \cdot, ID, \cdot) \leftarrow \mathsf{Exec}(\mathtt{add}, ID, \perp)$ to every $ID' \in \boldsymbol{G}$.

Unsafe group administration: In general, administration cannot be enforced or trusted due to the lack of authentication of control messages, similarly to what has been observed for CGKA-based protocols in [14].

Weak Post-compromise Security. Sender Keys offers a very limited form of PCS. Essentially, a $\mathsf{refresh}_\Delta$ event is the only possibility for ID to recover from a state compromise. This event only occurs whenever another user is removed or whenever ID triggers an on-demand update (or trivially when ID is new to the group). On-demand updates are supported by our primitive syntax and protocol description, but it is not clear whether they are implemented in practice (for instance, there is no mention to them in [48]).

Moreover, the update mechanism is not satisfactory. Since only the updater ID refreshes its sender key, this allows a passive adversary to eavesdrop on messages sent by any other group member due to the adversary's knowledge of the chain keys corresponding to those members. Extending the update mechanism to the entire group in a naive manner would result in a total communication complexity of $\mathcal{O}(n^2)$.

PCS and Two-Party Channels. PCS guarantees are even weaker due to the reliance of Sender Keys on two-party channels. As parametrized by $\mathsf{refresh}_\Delta$, if ID sends new key material over a two-party channel with ID' that has not been healed (after Δ round-trip messages) since the last exposure of either ID or ID', then such key material is still compromised. In practice, if the state of ID is compromised, both the group and the two-party sessions will be exposed. Therefore, unless parties refresh their individual two-party channels consciously (by sending each other messages), executing updates or removals in the group session will not have the desired healing effect.

In the real world, usually not all pairs of members of a group exchange private messages regularly, hence not refreshing their two-party channels. The fact that even manually triggering a key update does not necessarily heal the group from a state compromise conveys an important security limitation.

Lack of Forward Security on Authentication. Beyond PCS limitations, we observe that the forward security guarantees for authentication provided by Sender Keys are sub-optimal. Consider a simple group $G = \{ID_1, ID_2\}$ and the attack described in Fig. 9. Note that q_3 is a forbidden query by $\mathsf{C}_{\mathsf{sk\text{-}inj}}$. q_3 attempts to inject a message that corresponds to key material used *before* the state exposure, hence one can envision stronger FS where queries like q_3 are allowed. This attack can occur naturally if ID_2 is offline when m is first sent.

01 $q_1 = \mathtt{Send}(ID_1, \mathsf{m})$ generates ciphertext C encrypted under mk and signed under ssk_1.
02 $q_2 = \mathtt{Expose}(ID_1)$, where $\mathcal{A}$ obtains ssk_1, but not mk.
03 $\mathcal{A}$ modifies C and signs it again under ssk_1 to create a forgery C' corresponding to the same message epoch as C.
04 $q_3 = \mathtt{Receive}(ID_2, ID_1, C')$, which is a successful injection.

Fig. 9. Attack on authentication forward security in Sender Keys.

An attack of a similar nature can also occur in a messaging scheme where the same signature keys are re-used across groups, and are refreshed at different times, as pointed out in [30].

Additional Remarks. In the full version, we introduce additional discussions on trade-offs between concurrency and efficiency, randomness manipulation, stronger notions of security, and multi-group security. With respect to the latter, our formalism can be adapted to capture multi-group security formally via the use of group identifiers, which we leave for future work.

6.2 Proposed Improvements: Sender Keys+

We propose several improvements to Sender Keys below. Our improvements are constrained by the desire to retain the performance characteristics and structure of Sender Keys. In particular, we retain $\mathcal{O}(1)$-sized ciphertexts, do not increase key sizes, and utilize only standard cryptographic primitives. Our improved version of Sender Keys, which we call Sender Keys+, is presented fully in our full version. We formalise security by introducing several modifications to our cleanness predicate, which we describe here but also relegate their specification to the full version.

Secure Control Messages. A simple way of resolving the attacks in Sect. 6.1 would be for users to sign their own control messages and verify signatures before processing control messages. Additional protocol logic for correctness is required, namely that users who craft a control message but have not shared their sender key yet (because they have not spoken in the group) generate a signature key pair and share their public key over the two-party channels.

By introducing this tweak, we can weaken the cleanness predicate such that it no longer enforces honest control message delivery ($\mathsf{C}_{\mathsf{sk+\text{-}con}}$). On the other hand, we need to introduce the restriction that no secret signature key ssk can be known to the adversary at delivery time, similar as in the injection predicate. We do so by introducing a new control predicate $\mathsf{C}^{\Delta}_{\mathsf{sk+\text{-}ctr}}$ that follows the blueprints of the injection predicate (Fig. 6).

Improved Forward-Secure Authentication. We propose two possible improvements that address the attack in Sect. 6.1 to varying extents.

MACing from the Chain Key. The first improvement, which has minimal overhead, is to MAC the application messages with a MAC key $\tau\mathsf{k}$ that we derive via an additional $\mathsf{H}_3(\mathsf{ck})$. The modification is done in the Send algorithm as follows: given an unsigned ciphertext $\tilde{C} = (c, (e, i), ME)$, we obtain the MAC tag $\tau \leftarrow \mathsf{MAC.Tag}(\tau\mathsf{k}, \tilde{C})$. Then, we sign the ciphertext with the appended tag $\sigma \leftarrow \mathsf{Sig.Sgn}(\mathsf{ssk}, (\tilde{C}, \tau))$. The verification of the MAC tag is easily carried out at the receiver's end. We include this simple tweak in our improved protocol.

Naturally, symmetric encryption can alternatively be replaced with an AEAD to achieve the same effect.

The main security improvement that results from this upgrade is that, in the attack in Sect. 6.1, the adversary additionally needs knowledge of $\tau\mathsf{k}$ to forge the MAC tag. Hence, one of the following situations must occur before delivery:

- The sender ID is exposed before the message is sent. Then, both $\tau\mathsf{k}$ and ssk are compromised.
- The sender ID is exposed after the message is sent (leaking ssk), and another group member ID' is exposed before the message is delivered (leaking $\tau\mathsf{k}$).

In particular, the attack of Fig. 9 no longer results in a successful message delivery. The MAC key can be stored together with the message key for out-of-order messages, such that the MAC can always be verified in a correct execution of the protocol. We note that insider attacks (forgeries from other group members) cannot be prevented by MACing, but we do not model these.

The modified injection predicate that results from this improvement is roughly as follows. Essentially, we define an auxiliary predicate $\mathsf{C}^{\Delta}_{\mathsf{sk+\text{-}inj\text{-}extra}}$ that considers the security given by the message/MAC keys (similarly as in Fig. 5). Then, the modified $\mathsf{C}_{\mathsf{sk+\text{-}inj}}$ is the logical disjunction of the former injection predicate with $\mathsf{C}^{\Delta}_{\mathsf{sk+\text{-}inj\text{-}extra}}$, and hence strictly weaker.

Ratcheting Signature Keys. An alternative mitigation strategy for the attack of Fig. 9 is to ratchet signature keys. Let $(\mathsf{ssk}, \mathsf{spk})$ be ID's signature key pair, where spk is part of its sender key. Before sending a new message m to the group, ID can generate a new key pair $(\mathsf{ssk}', \mathsf{spk}') \xleftarrow{\$} \mathsf{Gen}(1^\lambda)$. Then, ID can attach the new spk' to the ciphertext corresponding to encrypting m, and sign the package using ssk. This (by now standard) countermeasure not only provides strong forward security but also post-compromise security for the authentication of messages. Nevertheless, it involves larger overhead, so it may not be desirable in all scenarios and we refrain from including it in Sender Keys+.

Efficient PCS Updates. We propose an asynchronous update mechanism to refresh all chain keys at once, recovering PCS on-demand for the whole group with a single update (and $\mathcal{O}(n)$ complexity for a group of n users). Recall that our Group Messenger primitive supports updates via $\mathsf{Exec}(\mathsf{upd}, \{ID\})$.

A Naive Solution. Let ID be the updating party. ID generates a new sender key for himself as in the case of a remove operation; namely samples a fresh ck and a fresh $(\mathsf{ssk}, \mathsf{spk}) \xleftarrow{\$} \mathsf{Sig.Gen}(1^\lambda)$. Additionally, ID samples randomness $r \xleftarrow{\$} \{0,1\}^\lambda$. Then, it distributes $(\mathsf{ck}, \mathsf{spk}, r)$ over the two-party channels. Upon reception, every group member (including ID itself) sets $\mathsf{SK}[ID] \leftarrow (\mathsf{ck}, \mathsf{spk})$; and then for every $ID' \in \boldsymbol{G}$, set $\mathsf{SK}[ID'].\mathsf{ck} \leftarrow \mathsf{H}_r(\mathsf{SK}[ID'].\mathsf{ck}, r)$, where $\mathsf{H}_r : \{0,1\}^{2\lambda} \to \{0,1\}^\lambda$ is a secure key derivation function. Since r is freshly sampled and distributed securely, all chain keys recover from exposure. Note that r must be used and erased immediately, as all updated chain keys are exposed if r is leaked at any future time.

Our Solution. The previous solution fails in out-of-sync scenarios such as the following. Suppose that ID' is in message epoch $(1,1)$ when ID sends an update message T. Then, ID' speaks in the group before receiving T (for example, while being offline), ratcheting its key to $(1,2)$. All group members will update the chain key $\mathsf{ck}_{ID'}^{1,1}$ (i.e. corresponding to the message epoch $(e,i) = (1,1)$) in $\mathsf{SK}[ID']$, but ID' will be in message epoch $(1,2)$ (and therefore will have erased $\mathsf{ck}_{ID'}^{1,1}$). In general, if there are application messages in transit concurrently with the update, users will be out-of-sync.

To support asynchronicity, we propose that all parties ratchet their chain key N times forward, where N is a fixed constant that we call the *concurrency bound* (for example $N = 100$; in practice the cost of executing 100 hash function calls sequentially is negligible). In the event that ℓ messages have been sent out-of-sync, then the chain key is ratcheted $N - \ell$ times instead. Then, parties update the ratcheted chain keys with the sent randomness r. To synchronise between them and with the update initiator ID, the latter sends a list with his view of the key indices of each group member (in the control message). Our update mechanism, included in Sender Keys+, requires the assumption of total ordering of control messages to avoid overlapping updates.

The security improvement is reflected in the challenge cleanness predicate as follows. The predicate is as the challenge predicate for Sender Keys (Fig. 5), except that now it also suffices that *some* arbitrary member ID^* that has a healed channel with ID' updates after the exposure, and that ID processes such update before the challenge.

Efficient Remove Operations. The previous update mechanism can be extended to improve the efficiency of group removals from $\mathcal{O}(n^2)$ (everyone needs to generate and distribute a new key) to $\mathcal{O}(n)$ in terms of communication complexity. Note a removal can be made effective if the party that sends the remove message T distributes update material among all group members except for the removed party ID'. If ID' leaves, the next member that speaks in the group must also trigger an update. This tweak, like our solution above, has the drawback that the signature keys are not refreshed. Thus, we do not include this tweak in Sender Keys+. Furthermore, considering the minimal overhead of updates, they could potentially become the preferred method for sharing sender keys in the group under all circumstances. This approach allows the group to achieve PCS almost for free.

6.3 Security of Sender Keys+

Following similar steps as the proof for Theorem 1, we can prove the security of our Sender Keys+ protocol with respect to the modified cleanness predicate. The proof is provided in the full version.

Theorem 2. *Let* $\mathsf{SymEnc} := (\mathsf{Enc}, \mathsf{Dec})$ *be a* $(q, \epsilon_{\mathsf{sym}})$-$\mathbf{IND\text{-}CPA}_{\mathsf{SymEnc},b}$ *symmetric encryption scheme,* $\mathsf{Sig} := (\mathsf{Gen}, \mathsf{Sgn}, \mathsf{Ver})$ *a* $(q, \epsilon_{\mathsf{sig}})$-$\mathbf{SUF\text{-}CMA}_{\mathsf{Sig}}$ *signature scheme,* $\mathsf{H} : \{0,1\}^{\lambda} \to \{0,1\}^{\lambda} \times \{0,1\}^{\lambda}$ *a* $(q, \epsilon_{\mathsf{prg}})$-$\mathbf{PRG}_{\mathsf{H}}$ *function,*

F *a* $(q, \epsilon_{\mathsf{dprf}})$-**dual-PRF**$_{\mathsf{F}}$ *function,* MAC *a* $(q, \epsilon_{\mathsf{mac}})$-**SUF-CMA**$_{\mathsf{MAC}}$ *message authentication code and* $\mathsf{2PC}$ *a* $(q, \epsilon_{\mathsf{2pc}})$-**2PC-IND**$_{\mathsf{2PC},\mathsf{C}_{\mathsf{2pc}},\Delta}$ *two-party channels scheme for PCS bound* $\Delta > 0$*. Then Sender Keys+ is*

$$(q, 2 \cdot \epsilon_{\mathsf{2pc}} + q^3 \cdot (\epsilon_{\mathsf{2pc}} + \epsilon_{\mathsf{sym}} + q \cdot \epsilon_{\mathsf{prg}} + N \cdot q \cdot \epsilon_{\mathsf{dprf}} + q \cdot \epsilon_{\mathsf{mac}}) + q \cdot \epsilon_{\mathsf{sig}})\text{-}\mathbf{M\text{-}IND}_{\mathsf{GM},\mathsf{C}}$$

with respect to predicate $\mathsf{C} =:= \mathsf{C}^{\Delta}_{\mathsf{sk+\text{-}chall}} \wedge \mathsf{C}^{\Delta}_{\mathsf{sk+\text{-}inj}} \wedge \mathsf{C}^{\Delta}_{\mathsf{sk+\text{-}con}} \wedge \mathsf{C}^{\Delta}_{\mathsf{sk+\text{-}ctr}}$ *and concurrency bound* N*.*

6.4 Sender Keys+ Vs CGKA

As remarked in the introduction, Sender Keys (and especially Sender Keys+) offers different efficiency and security trade-offs over CGKA-based protocols. We provide a detailed comparison below.

PCS. When a user *ID* is exposed, the confidentiality of all subsequent messages is lost in both CGKA and Sender Keys(+). For an update to take effect in Sender Keys(+), all two-party channels must have healed. In this case, an update by ID' only heals the confidentiality of messages sent by ID' in Sender Keys, as opposed to the confidentially of messages sent by *all* members in Sender Keys+.

It is worth noting that both Sender Keys and Sender Keys+ require up to PCS bound Δ messages (or rounds) to heal after a compromise (due to the two-party channels) in addition to the update message. In contrast, a single message suffices for some CGKA protocols [7,9,10,39].

Update Efficiency. In Sender Keys+, an update message requires $O(n)$ communication by the updating user, where each member is sent a constant-size message. In TreeKEM variants, or in general binary-tree-based CGKAs, updates involve best-case $O(\log n)$ size for the updating user and have to be entirely downloaded by each member, involving a total $O(n \log n)$ download overhead. Nevertheless, this can be degrade to $O(n)$ per member. The multi-recipient PKE approach in [34] achieves the same asymptotic complexity as Sender Keys+, although with larger concrete costs.

Insider Security. The attack in [11] that reveals the need for IND-CCA (and not only IND-CPA) encryption in TreeKEM also applies to Sender Keys, but can be fixed with the use of a MAC. Following the analysis in [11], it is not clear how to mount fake group attacks as they do, although if different users process different control messages, they may end up with different views of the group. This attack however also applies to CGKAs in general.

Separately, we note that Sender Keys(+) does not suffer from the forward security issues from MLS's CGKA [7].

7 Conclusion and Future Work

In conclusion, our modular approach to modelling Sender Keys has allowed us to identify its main security limitations, some of which we can mitigate while preserving efficiency. We have demonstrated that the protocol at its core is sound, although it does have notable shortcomings that can be remedied without sacrificing performance. We propose Sender Keys+ as a viable alternative for group messaging when strong PCS is not a critical requirement or regular updates are performed. Interestingly, our modelling of two-party channels has revealed the difficulty of achieving PCS in Sender Keys, even after updates or removals, contradicting folklore assumptions.

In practice, it is common for two-party channels between group members to remain stagnant for extended periods if private communication is not frequent. This degrades the overall group security, underscoring the importance of implementing a regular refresh mechanism by default, especially if PCS updates are implemented. Additionally, Sender Keys is commonly supplemented by additional mechanisms not considered in our study, such as support for multiple devices and encrypted cloud backups that increase the attack surface.

Looking forward, several research directions emerge. Firstly, our security model can be extended to encompass randomness manipulation, successful message injections, insider threats, and other relevant scenarios. Investigating the practical behaviour of Sender Keys would provide valuable insights for improved modelling and the identification of potential vulnerabilities. Benchmarking both the baseline and extended Sender Keys protocols would also contribute to assessing their practicality. Additionally, it is important to address the challenges that arise when total order is violated, and to design a protocol that avoids the drawbacks associated with decentralised continuous group key agreement (DCGKA) such as the need for multi-round communication [47]. Towards a more concurrency-friendly Sender Keys protocol, an important direction is the design of a mechanism for resolving ties in control messages that are sent concurrently.

Acknowledgments. This work is supported by the PICOCRYPT project that has received funding from the European Research Council (ERC) under the European Union's Horizon 2020 research and innovation programme (Grant agreement No. 101001283), partially supported by PRODIGY Project (TED2021-132464B-I00) funded by MCIN/AEI/10.13039/501100011033/ and the European Union NextGenerationEU / PRTR, partially funded by Ministerio de Universidades (FPU21/00600), and funded by the Deutsche Forschungsgemeinschaft (DFG, German Research Foundation) under Germany's Excellence Strategy - EXC 2092 CASA - 390781972.

References

1. Albrecht, M.R., Celi, S., Dowling, B., Jones, D.: Practically-exploitable cryptographic vulnerabilities in matrix. In: 2023 IEEE Symposium on Security and Privacy (2023)
2. Albrecht, M.R., Dowling, B., Jones, D.: Device-oriented group messaging: a formal cryptographic analysis of matrix' core. In: 2024 IEEE Symposium on Security and Privacy (to appear) (2024)
3. Albrecht, M.R., Mareková, L., Paterson, K.G., Stepanovs, I.: Four attacks and a proof for telegram. In: 2022 IEEE Symposium on Security and Privacy, pp. 87–106. IEEE Computer Society Press, May 2022. https://doi.org/10.1109/SP46214.2022.9833666
4. Alwen, J., Auerbach, B., Noval, M.C., Klein, K., Pascual-Perez, G., Pietrzak, K.: DeCAF: Decentralizable continuous group key agreement with fast healing. Cryptology ePrint Archive, Report 2022/559 (2022). https://eprint.iacr.org/2022/559
5. Alwen, J., Auerbach, B., Noval, M.C., Klein, K., Pascual-Perez, G., Pietrzak, K., Walter, M.: CoCoA: Concurrent continuous group key agreement. In: Dunkelman, O., Dziembowski, S. (eds.) EUROCRYPT 2022, Part II. LNCS, vol. 13276, pp. 815–844. Springer, Heidelberg (2022). https://doi.org/10.1007/978-3-031-07085-3_28
6. Alwen, J., Coretti, S., Dodis, Y.: The double ratchet: security notions, proofs, and modularization for the Signal protocol. In: Ishai, Y., Rijmen, V. (eds.) EUROCRYPT 2019, Part I. LNCS, vol. 11476, pp. 129–158. Springer, Heidelberg (2019). https://doi.org/10.1007/978-3-030-17653-2_5
7. Alwen, J., Coretti, S., Dodis, Y., Tselekounis, Y.: Security analysis and improvements for the IETF MLS standard for group messaging. In: Micciancio, D., Ristenpart, T. (eds.) CRYPTO 2020, Part I. LNCS, vol. 12170, pp. 248–277. Springer, Heidelberg (2020). https://doi.org/10.1007/978-3-030-56784-2_9
8. Alwen, J., Coretti, S., Dodis, Y., Tselekounis, Y.: Modular design of secure group messaging protocols and the security of MLS. In: Vigna, G., Shi, E. (eds.) ACM CCS 2021, pp. 1463–1483. ACM Press (2021). https://doi.org/10.1145/3460120.3484820
9. Alwen, J., Coretti, S., Jost, D., Mularczyk, M.: Continuous group key agreement with active security. In: Pass, R., Pietrzak, K. (eds.) TCC 2020, Part II. LNCS, vol. 12551, pp. 261–290. Springer, Heidelberg (2020). https://doi.org/10.1007/978-3-030-64378-2_10
10. Alwen, J., Hartmann, D., Kiltz, E., Mularczyk, M.: Server-aided continuous group key agreement. In: Yin, H., Stavrou, A., Cremers, C., Shi, E. (eds.) ACM CCS 2022, pp. 69–82. ACM Press (Nov 2022). https://doi.org/10.1145/3548606.3560632
11. Alwen, J., Jost, D., Mularczyk, M.: On the insider security of MLS. In: Dodis, Y., Shrimpton, T. (eds.) CRYPTO 2022, Part II. LNCS, vol. 13508, pp. 34–68. Springer, Heidelberg (2022). https://doi.org/10.1007/978-3-031-15979-4_2
12. Balbás, D., Collins, D., Gajland, P.: Analysis and improvements of the sender keys protocol for group messaging. XVII Reunión española sobre criptología y seguridad de la información. RECSI 2022 265, 25 (2022)
13. Balbás, D., Collins, D., Gajland, P.: WhatsUpp with sender keys? Analysis, improvements and security proofs. Cryptology ePrint Archive, Paper 2023/1385 (2023). https://eprint.iacr.org/2023/1385. (Full version)
14. Balbás, D., Collins, D., Vaudenay, S.: Cryptographic administration for secure group messaging. In: 2023 USENIX Security Symposium (2023)

15. Balli, F., Rösler, P., Vaudenay, S.: Determining the core primitive for optimally secure ratcheting. In: Moriai, S., Wang, H. (eds.) ASIACRYPT 2020, Part III. LNCS, vol. 12493, pp. 621–650. Springer, Heidelberg (2020). https://doi.org/10.1007/978-3-030-64840-4_21
16. Barnes, R., Beurdouche, B., Robert, R., Millican, J., Omara, E., Cohn-Gordon, K.: The Messaging Layer Security (MLS) Protocol. RFC 9420 (2023). https://doi.org/10.17487/RFC9420, https://www.rfc-editor.org/info/rfc9420
17. Bellare, M., Singh, A.C., Jaeger, J., Nyayapati, M., Stepanovs, I.: Ratcheted encryption and key exchange: the security of messaging. In: Katz, J., Shacham, H. (eds.) CRYPTO 2017, Part III. LNCS, vol. 10403, pp. 619–650. Springer, Heidelberg (2017). https://doi.org/10.1007/978-3-319-63697-9_21
18. Bhargavan, K., Barnes, R., Rescorla, E.: TreeKEM: asynchronous decentralized key management for large dynamic groups a protocol proposal for messaging layer security (MLS). Research report, Inria Paris, May 2018. https://hal.inria.fr/hal-02425247
19. Bienstock, A., Dodis, Y., Garg, S., Grogan, G., Hajiabadi, M., Rösler, P.: On the worst-case inefficiency of CGKA. In: Kiltz, E., Vaikuntanathan, V. (eds.) TCC 2022, Part II. LNCS, vol. 13748, pp. 213–243. Springer, Heidelberg (2022). https://doi.org/10.1007/978-3-031-22365-5_8
20. Bienstock, A., Dodis, Y., Rösler, P.: On the price of concurrency in group ratcheting protocols. In: Pass, R., Pietrzak, K. (eds.) TCC 2020, Part II. LNCS, vol. 12551, pp. 198–228. Springer, Heidelberg (2020). https://doi.org/10.1007/978-3-030-64378-2_8
21. Bienstock, A., Fairoze, J., Garg, S., Mukherjee, P., Raghuraman, S.: A more complete analysis of the Signal double ratchet algorithm. In: Dodis, Y., Shrimpton, T. (eds.) CRYPTO 2022, Part I. LNCS, vol. 13507, pp. 784–813. Springer, Heidelberg (2022). https://doi.org/10.1007/978-3-031-15802-5_27
22. Blazy, O., Boureanu, I., Lafourcade, P., Onete, C., Robert, L.: How fast do you heal? A taxonomy for post-compromise security in secure-channel establishment. Cryptology ePrint Archive, Report 2022/1090 (2022). https://eprint.iacr.org/2022/1090
23. Brzuska, C., Cornelissen, E., Kohbrok, K.: Security analysis of the MLS key derivation. In: 2022 IEEE Symposium on Security and Privacy, pp. 2535–2553. IEEE Computer Society Press (2022). https://doi.org/10.1109/SP46214.2022.9833678
24. Canetti, R., Jain, P., Swanberg, M., Varia, M.: Universally composable end-to-end secure messaging. In: Dodis, Y., Shrimpton, T. (eds.) CRYPTO 2022, Part II. LNCS, vol. 13508, pp. 3–33. Springer, Heidelberg (2022). https://doi.org/10.1007/978-3-031-15979-4_1
25. Chase, M., Perrin, T., Zaverucha, G.: The signal private group system and anonymous credentials supporting efficient verifiable encryption. In: Ligatti, J., Ou, X., Katz, J., Vigna, G. (eds.) ACM CCS 2020, pp. 1445–1459. ACM Press (2020). https://doi.org/10.1145/3372297.3417887
26. Cohn-Gordon, K., Cremers, C., Dowling, B., Garratt, L., Stebila, D.: A formal security analysis of the signal messaging protocol. J. Cryptol. **33**(4), 1914–1983 (2020). https://doi.org/10.1007/s00145-020-09360-1
27. Cohn-Gordon, K., Cremers, C., Garratt, L., Millican, J., Milner, K.: On ends-to-ends encryption: asynchronous group messaging with strong security guarantees. In: Lie, D., Mannan, M., Backes, M., Wang, X. (eds.) ACM CCS 2018, pp. 1802–1819. ACM Press (2018). https://doi.org/10.1145/3243734.3243747

28. Cohn-Gordon, K., Cremers, C.J.F., Garratt, L.: On post-compromise security. In: Hicks, M., Köpf, B. (eds.) CSF 2016 Computer Security Foundations Symposium, pp. 164–178. IEEE Computer Society Press (2016). https://doi.org/10.1109/CSF.2016.19
29. Cong, K., Eldefrawy, K., Smart, N.P., Terner, B.: The key lattice framework for concurrent group messaging. Cryptology ePrint Archive, Report 2022/1531 (2022). https://eprint.iacr.org/2022/1531
30. Cremers, C., Hale, B., Kohbrok, K.: The complexities of healing in secure group messaging: why cross-group effects matter. In: Bailey, M., Greenstadt, R. (eds.) USENIX Security 2021, pp. 1847–1864. USENIX Association (2021)
31. Davies, G.T., et al.: Security analysis of the whatsapp end-to-end encrypted backup protocol. In: Handschuh, H., Lysyanskaya, A. (eds.) Advances in Cryptology. CRYPTO 2023. LNCS, vol. 14084. Springer, Cham (2023). https://doi.org/10.1007/978-3-031-38551-3_11
32. Durak, F.B., Vaudenay, S.: Bidirectional asynchronous ratcheted key agreement with linear complexity. In: Attrapadung, N., Yagi, T. (eds.) IWSEC 2019. LNCS, vol. 11689, pp. 343–362. Springer, Heidelberg (2019). https://doi.org/10.1007/978-3-030-26834-3_20
33. Galal, T.: yowsup, Code Repository (2021). https://github.com/tgalal/yowsup
34. Hashimoto, K., Katsumata, S., Postlethwaite, E., Prest, T., Westerbaan, B.: A concrete treatment of efficient continuous group key agreement via multi-recipient PKEs. In: Vigna, G., Shi, E. (eds.) ACM CCS 2021, pp. 1441–1462. ACM Press (2021). https://doi.org/10.1145/3460120.3484817
35. Internet Engineering Task Force, I.: Messaging layer security, mailing list (2023). https://mailarchive.ietf.org/arch/browse/mls/
36. Jaeger, J., Stepanovs, I.: Optimal channel security against fine-grained state compromise: the safety of messaging. In: Shacham, H., Boldyreva, A. (eds.) CRYPTO 2018, Part I. LNCS, vol. 10991, pp. 33–62. Springer, Heidelberg (2018). https://doi.org/10.1007/978-3-319-96884-1_2
37. Jefferys, K.: Session Protocol: Technical implementation details (2020). https://getsession.org/blog/session-protocol-technical-information. Accessed 4 July 2023
38. Kenneth G. Paterson, Matteo Scarlata, K.T.T.: Three lessons from threema: analysis of a secure messenger. In: 2023 USENIX Security Symposium (2023)
39. Klein, K., et al.: Keep the dirt: Tainted TreeKEM, adaptively and actively secure continuous group key agreement. In: 2021 IEEE Symposium on Security and Privacy, pp. 268–284. IEEE Computer Society Press, May 2021. https://doi.org/10.1109/SP40001.2021.00035
40. Marlinspike, M.: Private Group Messaging (2014). https://signal.org/blog/private-groups/. Accessed 5 Sep 2023
41. Marlinspike, M., Perrin, T.: The double ratchet algorithm (2016). https://signal.org/docs/specifications/doubleratchet/doubleratchet.pdf
42. Marlinspike, M., Perrin, T.: The x3dh key agreement protocol. Open Whisper Syst. **283**, 10 (2016)
43. Marlinspike, M., et al.: Signal protocol (2016). https://github.com/signalapp/libsignal-protocol-java/tree/master/java/src/main/java/org/whispersystems/libsignal
44. Pijnenburg, J., Poettering, B.: On secure ratcheting with immediate decryption. In: Agrawal, S., Lin, D. (eds.) ASIACRYPT 2022, Part III. LNCS, vol. 13793, pp. 89–118. Springer, Heidelberg (2022). https://doi.org/10.1007/978-3-031-22969-5_4

45. Poettering, B., Rösler, P.: Towards bidirectional ratcheted key exchange. In: Shacham, H., Boldyreva, A. (eds.) CRYPTO 2018, Part I. LNCS, vol. 10991, pp. 3–32. Springer, Heidelberg (2018). https://doi.org/10.1007/978-3-319-96884-1_1
46. Rösler, P., Mainka, C., Schwenk, J.: More is less: on the end-to-end security of group chats in signal, WhatsApp, and Threema. In: 2018 IEEE European Symposium on Security and Privacy (EuroS&P), pp. 415–429. IEEE, London, UK (2018). https://doi.org/10.1109/EuroSP.2018.00036
47. Weidner, M., Kleppmann, M., Hugenroth, D., Beresford, A.R.: Key agreement for decentralized secure group messaging with strong security guarantees. In: Vigna, G., Shi, E. (eds.) ACM CCS 2021, pp. 2024–2045. ACM Press (2021). https://doi.org/10.1145/3460120.3484542
48. WhatsApp: WhatsApp Encryption Overview Technical white paper, vol. 3, October 2020. https://www.whatsapp.com/security/WhatsApp-Security-Whitepaper.pdf

Efficient Updatable Public-Key Encryption from Lattices

Calvin Abou Haidar[1,2](✉), Alain Passelègue[1,2,3], and Damien Stehlé[1,3]

[1] ENS de Lyon, Lyon, France
[2] INRIA, Paris, France
calvin.abou-haidar@ens-lyon.fr
[3] CryptoLab Inc, Lyon, France
{alain.passelegue,damien.stehle}@cryptolab.co.kr

Abstract. Updatable public key encryption has recently been introduced as a solution to achieve forward-security in the context of secure group messaging without hurting efficiency, but so far, no efficient lattice-based instantiation of this primitive is known.

In this work, we construct the first LWE-based UPKE scheme with polynomial modulus-to-noise rate, which is CPA-secure in the standard model. At the core of our security analysis is a generalized reduction from the standard LWE problem to (a stronger version of) the Extended LWE problem. We further extend our construction to achieve stronger security notions by proposing two generic transforms. Our first transform allows to obtain CCA security in the random oracle model and adapts the Fujisaki-Okamoto transform to the UPKE setting. Our second transform allows to achieve security against malicious updates by adding a NIZK argument in the update mechanism. In the process, we also introduce the notion of Updatable Key Encapsulation Mechanism (UKEM), as the updatable variant of KEMs. Overall, we obtain a CCA-secure UKEM in the random oracle model whose ciphertext sizes are of the same order of magnitude as that of CRYSTALS-Kyber.

1 Introduction

Secure group messaging aims to allow secure, long-lasting, communication for a large group of users. The larger the group and the longer the communication, the likelier one of the group member gets compromised. When the latter happens, ideally, one would like to guarantee that messages sent before the attack occurred remain hidden to the attacker. This corresponds to the notion of forward security [5,9,13,17,19,29,35] and can be achieved by relying on forward-secure public key encryption (FS-PKE), but it vastly hurts efficiency compared to relying on standard PKE. FS-PKE generates an initial key pair (pk_0, sk_0) which allows to derive a chain of key pairs $(pk_1, sk_1), (pk_2, sk_2), \ldots$ where each pk_{t+1} can be derived publicly from pk_t (and sk_{t+1} from sk_t). Hence, the first epoch key pair of an FS-PKE scheme implicitly defines all the subsequent epoch key pairs. Forward security further requires that it should be hard to go back in the secret

J. Guo and R. Steinfeld (Eds.): ASIACRYPT 2023, LNCS 14442, pp. 342–373, 2023.
https://doi.org/10.1007/978-981-99-8733-7_11

key chain, as compromising sk_j should not hurt the confidentiality of messages encrypted under pk_t for $t < j$. Therefore, FS-PKE can be seen as a simple form of hierarchical identity-based encryption (HIBE) [17,28], and tight connections between the notions have been observed [26]. As of today, FS-PKE schemes have similar performances as HIBE constructions, and therefore relying on FS-PKE for building secure group messaging seems inherently inefficient. The extreme alternative is to rely on standard PKE and to require every user to refresh their key pair on a regular basis. This assumes users to be active and online, which is an undesirable assumption in the context of group messaging. Moreover, a user refreshing its own key only guarantees confidentiality of messages it receives (and therefore messages sent by other users) but does not provide any guarantee about messages it sent. For the latter, users have to rely on the willingness of receivers to update their keys.

Updatable public-key encryption (UPKE), recently introduced in [4,30], offers a compromise between the above two approaches by relaxing the update mechanism of FS-PKE: in a UPKE scheme, any user can update any other user's key pair by running an update algorithm with (high-entropy) private coins. As a consequence, a key pair does not need to contain any information about the next epoch key pair as this information can be provided by the external user who proceeds in the update. This change allows to hope for UPKE constructions with similar efficiency as standard PKE, but a sender can now protect the messages it sent by updating the receiver's key.

To be formal, a UPKE scheme consists in a standard PKE scheme (KeyGen, Enc, Dec) augmented with two additional algorithms (UpdatePk, UpdateSk). The UpdatePk algorithm can be run by any user on inputs a target public key pk_t^U of a user U used at epoch t and fresh private coins r. It produces a public key pk_{t+1}^U for user U for epoch $t+1$ as well as an update ciphertext up (encrypted under pk_t^U). The UpdateSk algorithm then allows user U, given an update ciphertext up and its secret key sk_t^U to update the latter to obtain secret key sk_{t+1}^U corresponding to pk_{t+1}^U. Security of UPKE guarantees that ciphertexts encrypted under U's public key pk_t^U at any epoch t remain secret to an attacker which compromises sk_j^U for $j > t$, as long as any of the updates which occurred between epoch t and epoch j was performed by an honest user (i.e., using private coins unknown to the attacker). This is formalized by the notion of IND-CR-CPA security, in which the adversary can impose updates of the target user's public key with Chosen Randomness (CR) (i.e., providing the private coins used by the update mechanism to the challenger). This has been the main security notion studied so far [4,22,30]. For practical applications, stronger notions are desirable, and were introduced in [22]: first, the adversary could have access to a decryption oracle (using the secret key of the current epoch), which corresponds to CCA security. Second, the adversary could generate malicious updates. The latter notion corresponds to IND-CU-CPA/CCA security, where the adversary provides Chosen Updates (CU) by providing (possibly malicious) updates to the challenger rather than providing private coins (used to honestly generate updates in the chosen randomness setting).

UPKE has been constructed from various assumptions over the past years. An efficient IND-CR-CPA construction based on the Computational Diffie-Hellman (CDH) assumption and in the random oracle model (ROM) was proposed in [4, 30]. Constructions in the standard model were first proposed in [22] from the Learning with Errors (LWE) assumption and from the Decisional Diffie-Hellman (DDH) assumption, but the latter two constructions are mainly of theoretical interest as they rely on bit-by-bit encryption, and circular-secure and leakage-resilient PKE. The LWE-based construction notably relies on super-polynomial modulus-to-noise rate due to the use of the noise flooding technique. Generic transforms from IND-CR-CPA security to IND-CU-CCA security are described in [22] but rely on heavy tools, namely one-time, strong, true-simulation f-extractable Non-Interactive Zero-Knowledge (NIZK) arguments [21]. In [1], an efficient construction based on the Decisional Composite Residuosity (DCR) assumption was proposed. The authors show that a variant of the ElGamal Paillier encryption scheme [16] can be turned into a (standard model) IND-CR-CPA UPKE scheme, and achieve IND-CR-CCA and IND-CU-CCA UPKE by further adding NIZK proofs using the Naor-Yung paradigm [38]. Concrete instantiations of the latter NIZKs are proposed in the random oracle model, resulting in the first efficient IND-CR-CCA and IND-CU-CCA instantiations from the DCR assumption and the strong RSA assumption [8], in the ROM.

1.1 Contributions

We provide the first efficient UPKE instantiation based on the LWE assumption with polynomial modulus-to-noise rate.

First, we construct a UPKE encryption scheme which follows the lines of the PKE scheme from [34], which underlies CRYSTALS-Kyber [11]. The main technicalities lie in its security analysis: (i) we prove our construction to achieve IND-CR-CPA security in the standard model, based on a new assumption which generalizes the extended-LWE assumption defined in [39], and (ii) we show that the latter assumption reduces to the standard LWE assumption by extending the results from [15].

Second, we provide two simple generic transforms which allow to convert any IND-CR-CPA UPKE construction into IND-CR-CCA and IND-CU-CCA UPKE schemes in the ROM. As we aim for practical constructions, we focus on constructing updatable key encapsulation mechanism (UKEM), which we introduce as the updatable variant of KEM. Our first transformation is an adaption of the Fujisaki-Okamoto transform [24] to the context of UPKE and allows to generically transform an IND-CR-CPA UPKE into an IND-CR-CCA UKEM with a minimal cost, in the ROM. The second transformation relies on the existence of a NIZK argument for a specific language. As an important remark, the underlying NIZK only plays a role in the update mechanism and should only satisfy basic properties (namely, a single-theorem NIZK with computational soundness and computational zero-knowledge is sufficient) while prior constructions [1,22] relied on strong NIZK notions (e.g., statistical-simulation-sound NIZKs for instantiating Naor-Yung). The latter NIZK argument can be efficiently instantiated from [33].

1.2 Technical Overview

We now present our contributions in more details, starting with our IND-CR-CPA UPKE construction.

IND-CR-CPA UPKE from Lattices. Our IND-CR-CPA construction follows the LWE-variant of [34]: a public key is an LWE instance $(\mathbf{A}, \mathbf{b})$ with $\mathbf{b} = \mathbf{As} + \mathbf{e}$ for $\mathbf{A} \in \mathbb{Z}_q^{n \times n}$ and $\mathbf{s}, \mathbf{e} \hookleftarrow \mathcal{D}_{\mathbb{Z}^n,\sigma}$, the LWE secret $\mathbf{s}$ being the corresponding secret key. An encryption of a message $\boldsymbol{\mu} \in \mathbb{Z}_p^n$ is a pair $(\mathsf{ct}_0, \mathsf{ct}_1)$ of the form $(\mathbf{XA} + \mathbf{E}, \mathbf{Xb} + \mathbf{f} + \lfloor q/p \rfloor \cdot \boldsymbol{\mu} \bmod q)$ with $\mathbf{X}, \mathbf{E} \hookleftarrow \mathcal{D}_{\mathbb{Z}^{n \times n},\sigma}, \mathbf{f} \hookleftarrow \mathcal{D}_{\mathbb{Z}^n,\sigma}$. Such a ciphertext can be decrypted by rounding $\mathsf{ct}_1 - \mathsf{ct}_0\mathbf{s}$ since:

$$\mathsf{ct}_1 - \mathsf{ct}_0\mathbf{s} = \mathbf{Xb} + \mathbf{f} + \lfloor q/p \rfloor \cdot \boldsymbol{\mu} - (\mathbf{XA} + \mathbf{E})\mathbf{s} = \mathbf{Xe} + \mathbf{f} - \mathbf{Es} + \lfloor q/p \rfloor \cdot \boldsymbol{\mu}$$

where the term $\mathbf{Xe} + \mathbf{f} - \mathbf{Es}$ is small. Updating a key pair is done by sampling small vectors $\mathbf{r}, \boldsymbol{\eta} \hookleftarrow \mathcal{D}_{\mathbb{Z}^n,\sigma}$. The public key is updated to $(\mathbf{A}, \mathbf{b} + \mathbf{Ar} + \boldsymbol{\eta}) = (\mathbf{A}, \mathbf{A}(\mathbf{s} + \mathbf{r}) + \mathbf{e} + \boldsymbol{\eta})$. The corresponding update ciphertext *up* is an encryption of $\mathbf{r}$ (which fits in the plaintext space) under the original public key $(\mathbf{A}, \mathbf{b})$. The updated secret key is then $\mathbf{s} + \mathbf{r}$. Correctness follows from the correctness of the PKE scheme. We emphasize that the secret key and noise term might have increased in norm, which can hurt correctness of decryption. We provide more details about how we handle this issue later, when we mention concrete instantiations.

Let us now focus on the security analysis. An IND-CR-CPA attacker first sees a public key $(\mathbf{A}, \mathbf{b} = \mathbf{As} + \mathbf{e})$ and can make a first sequence of updates with private coins of its choice $(\mathbf{r}_1, \boldsymbol{\eta}_1), \ldots, (\mathbf{r}_{chall}, \boldsymbol{\eta}_{chall})$ before asking for a challenge ciphertext for a pair of plaintexts $(\boldsymbol{\mu}_0, \boldsymbol{\mu}_1)$ at epoch *chall*. The challenge ciphertext is then encrypted under public key $pk_{chall} = (\mathbf{A}, \mathbf{b} + \mathbf{A}\Delta^{\mathbf{r}}_{chall} + \Delta^{\eta}_{chall})$, where $\Delta^{\mathbf{r}}_{chall} = \sum_{i=1}^{chall} \mathbf{r}_i$ and $\Delta^{\eta}_{chall} = \sum_{i=1}^{chall} \boldsymbol{\eta}_i$. It can then ask for an additional sequence of updates $(\mathbf{r}_{chall+1}, \boldsymbol{\eta}_{chall+1}), \ldots, (\mathbf{r}_{last}, \boldsymbol{\eta}_{last})$ until it decides to compromise the secret key. When the latter happens, an honest update is performed by the challenger using randomness $\mathbf{r}^*, \boldsymbol{\eta}^*$. Let $\Delta^{\mathbf{r}}_{last}$ and Δ^{η}_{last} denote respectively $\sum_{i=1}^{last} \mathbf{r}_i$ and $\sum_{i=1}^{last} \boldsymbol{\eta}_i$. Then, the adversary's goal is to guess which plaintext was encrypted, given the compromised secret key $\mathbf{s} + \Delta^{\mathbf{r}}_{last} + \mathbf{r}^*$ and the last update ciphertext which encrypts $\mathbf{r}^*$ under public key $(\mathbf{A}, \mathbf{b} + \mathbf{A}\Delta^{\mathbf{r}}_{last} + \Delta^{\eta}_{last})$.

The prior lattice-based construction from [22] has a similar structure (though it is based on the Dual-Regev PKE scheme [25]) and the authors argue about security by using the following observation, which we adapt to our construction for the exposition. First, notice that the final update ciphertext, which encrypts $\mathbf{r}^*$, can be transformed into an encryption of $-\mathbf{s}$ as we are given $\mathbf{s} + \Delta^{\mathbf{r}}_{last} + \mathbf{r}^*$ and $\Delta^{\mathbf{r}}_{last}$ is known. It then suffices to argue that the scheme is circular-secure, given the compromised secret key (which is additional leakage about $\mathbf{s}$).

To do so, observe that, for a ciphertext $(\mathsf{ct}_0, \mathsf{ct}_1) = (\mathbf{XA} + \mathbf{E}, \mathbf{Xb} + \mathbf{f} + \lfloor q/p \rfloor \cdot \boldsymbol{\mu})$, the second term can be re-written as $(\mathbf{XA} + \mathbf{E})\mathbf{s} + \mathbf{Xe} + \mathbf{f} + \lfloor q/p \rfloor \cdot \boldsymbol{\mu} - \mathbf{Es}$, where $\mathbf{XA} + \mathbf{E}$ is the first part ct_0 of the ciphertext. That is, we have:

$$\mathsf{ct}_1 = \mathsf{ct}_0\mathbf{s} + \mathbf{f} + \mathbf{Xe} - \mathbf{Es} + \lfloor q/p \rfloor \cdot \boldsymbol{\mu} \ .$$

Therefore, assuming $\mathbf{f}$ is much larger than $\mathbf{Xe} - \mathbf{Es}$, the ciphertext distribution is statistically close to $(\mathsf{ct}_0, \mathsf{ct}_0\mathbf{s} + \mathbf{f} + \lfloor q/p \rfloor \cdot \boldsymbol{\mu})$. Under the LWE assumption, ct_0 is pseudorandom, and then any (linear) information about the secret $\mathbf{s}$ contained in $\boldsymbol{\mu}$ can be absorbed by the term $\mathsf{ct}_0\mathbf{s}$. The Leftover Hash Lemma allows to complete the security analysis by proving that the latter term is statistically close to uniform, as long as $\mathbf{s}$ retains enough min-entropy (in this case, conditioned on the leaked key $\mathbf{s} + \Delta^{\mathbf{r}}_{last} + \mathbf{r}^*$). Hence, using noise-flooding and assuming LWE, the scheme is proven secure. The proof additionally relies on the (key)-homomorphism of Dual-Regev to incorporate updates required by the adversary in the challenge/update ciphertext and keys.

Our analysis deviates from the above and avoids the noise-flooding step. Instead, we directly prove pseudorandomness of the above $\mathbf{XA} + \mathbf{E}$ term. It seems that the LWE assumption for the instance $(\mathbf{A}, \mathbf{XA} + \mathbf{E})$ would suffice, but the issue is that the second term $\mathsf{ct}_1 = (\mathbf{XA} + \mathbf{E})\mathbf{s} + \mathbf{Xe} + \mathbf{f} + \lfloor q/p \rfloor \cdot \boldsymbol{\mu} - \mathbf{Es}$ of the above tuple contains information about $\mathbf{X}$ and $\mathbf{E}$, namely the terms $\mathbf{Xe}$ and $-\mathbf{Es}$. This is similar to the Extended-LWE assumption [39], which claims that pseudorandomness of an LWE instance $(\mathbf{A}, \mathbf{As} + \mathbf{e})$ still holds when the adversary is given an additional hint h computed as $\langle \mathbf{z}, \mathbf{e} \rangle \bmod q$ for a small $\mathbf{z}$ chosen by the adversary independently of $\mathbf{A}$. However, the latter assumption is not sufficient: in our case, the sample contains a hint about both the error and the secret and, additionally, as we are interested in updatable encryption, the adversary can make update queries before asking for the challenge. To answer such queries, one needs to know $\mathbf{A}$, which is part of the public key, in advance. We introduce the Hermite Normal Form Adaptive Extended LWE assumption HNF-AextLWE, which precisely states that pseudorandomness of $(\mathbf{A}, \mathbf{As} + \mathbf{e})$ still holds, provided an additional hint of the form $\langle \mathbf{z}_0, \mathbf{s} \rangle + \langle \mathbf{z}_1, \mathbf{e} \rangle + g \bmod q$, with $\mathbf{z}_0, \mathbf{z}_1$ being small vectors arbitrarily chosen by the adversary after it sees $\mathbf{A}$ and g being a small Gaussian noise. Equipped with this assumption, the rest of the proof can be adapted and we are able to prove the IND-CR-CPA security of our UPKE scheme under the HNF-AextLWE assumption. It remains to show that the latter assumption is implied by the standard LWE assumption.

Reduction from LWE. We first make a reduction from the adaptive extended-LWE (AextLWE) problem to the HNF-AextLWE problem. AextLWE generalizes the Extended-LWE problem by allowing the adversary to choose a small vector $\mathbf{z}$ arbitrarily given $\mathbf{A}$. The reduction adapts the one from LWE to HNF-LWE given in [6] to our setting. It relies on the observation made in [15] that, if $\mathbf{A} \in \mathbb{Z}_q^{m \times n}$ for $m \geq 16n + 4 \log \log q$, one can extract an invertible matrix $\mathbf{A}_0$ from $\mathbf{A}$ together with another matrix $\mathbf{A}_1 \in \mathbb{Z}_q^{m' \times n}$ with $m' = m - 16n - 4 \log \log q$ such that the matrix $\mathbf{A}_1 \cdot \mathbf{A}_0^{-1}$ is uniformly distributed. Importantly, a hint

$\langle \mathbf{z}_0, \mathbf{s}^* \rangle + \langle \mathbf{z}_1, \mathbf{e}^* \rangle + g \bmod q$ for an HNF-AextLWE instance using $\mathbf{A}^*$ can be computed as a hint $\langle \mathbf{z}, \mathbf{e} \rangle + g \bmod q$ for an AextLWE instance using $\mathbf{A}$.

We then show that LWE reduces to this new adaptive version by showing that taking a larger standard deviation allows the additional Gaussian noise g in the hint $h = \langle \mathbf{z}, \mathbf{e} \rangle + g \bmod q$ to hide the information given by it. Precisely, the standard deviation must be taken larger by a factor $\|\mathbf{z}\|_2$ (which has to be small by definition). The proof technique is similar to that of [18,31], except that we need to show that the adaptive nature of our assumption still allows for a reduction.

The reduction goes as follows: Given an LWE instance $(\mathbf{A}, \mathbf{b})$, first send $\mathbf{A}$ to the AextLWE adversary to receive its choice of small hint vector $\mathbf{z}$. In response, sample an additional error $\mathbf{e}'$ and Gaussian term g' from a well-chosen distribution that depends on the small vector $\mathbf{z}$ chosen by the adversary, and return $\mathbf{b}' = \mathbf{b} + \mathbf{e}'$ and a hint $h = \langle \mathbf{z}, \mathbf{e}' \rangle + g'$.

One can rewrite the hint as $h = \langle \mathbf{z}, \mathbf{e} + \mathbf{e}' \rangle - \langle \mathbf{z}, \mathbf{e} \rangle + g' = \langle \mathbf{z}, \mathbf{e} + \mathbf{e}' \rangle + g$ for $g = -\langle \mathbf{z}, \mathbf{e} \rangle + g'$. If the vector $\mathbf{b}$ is equal to $\mathbf{As} + \mathbf{e}$, as we have $\mathbf{b}' = \mathbf{As} + (\mathbf{e} + \mathbf{e}')$ and $h = \langle \mathbf{z}, \mathbf{e} + \mathbf{e}' \rangle + g$, it suffices to show that the joint distribution of $\mathbf{e} + \mathbf{e}'$ and g is a spherical Gaussian. This is achieved by applying a convolution lemma to the sum

$$\begin{pmatrix} \mathbf{e} + \mathbf{e}' \\ -\mathbf{z}^T \mathbf{e} + g' \end{pmatrix} = \begin{pmatrix} \mathbf{Id} \\ -\mathbf{z}^T \end{pmatrix} \mathbf{e} + \begin{pmatrix} \mathbf{e}' \\ g' \end{pmatrix},$$

which is possible if the standard deviation is larger by a factor of $\|\mathbf{z}\|_2$. The analysis for the case where of uniform $\mathbf{b}$ is identical.

Combining the above two results, we then obtain an IND-CR-CPA UPKE construction based on the standard LWE assumption, leading to the first lattice-based UPKE with polynomial modulus-to-noise ratio. We now explain how we transform this construction in order to achieve IND-CU-CCA security.

A Fujisaki-Okamoto Transform for UPKE. Prior works [1,22] have relied on the Naor-Yung paradigm [38] to achieve CCA-security, which requires simulation-sound NIZK proofs. While this allows to remain in the standard model, efficient instantiations of NIZKs rely on random oracles, which motivates us to consider a ROM-based transform following the Fujisaki-Okamoto transform [24]. As we aim for practical efficiency, we focus on constructing IND-CR-CCA updatable key encapsulation mechanism (UKEM), a notion we introduce in this work. Our transform allows to construct IND-CR-CCA UKEM in the ROM with similar efficiency as that of the underlying IND-CR-CPA UPKE. To encapsulate a key for a target user with public key pk_t (at epoch t), one produces a ciphertext ct as an encryption of a uniform message m with randomness extracted from applying a hash function G (modeled as a random oracle) to the public key pk_t and the message m. The encapsulated key is defined as $\mathsf{H}(\mathsf{ct}, m)$ for another hash function (also modeled as a random oracle). Decapsulation recovers m by decrypting ct and re-encrypts it to check that ct was properly generated, in which case one computes the key $\mathsf{H}(\mathsf{ct}, m)$. The update mechanism $\mathsf{UpdatePk}, \mathsf{UpdateSk}$ are exactly the same as that of the underlying IND-CR-CPA UPKE scheme. Overall, this is the same transform as for PKE [27] except that pk_t is fed as input to G. The security analysis follows the standard route for FO analyses: we modify oracles to allow the challenger to simulate the decapsulation oracle without knowledge of the secret key sk. The main change is that we rely on the additional pk_t which is fed as an additional input to the hash function G in order to keep track of possibly valid ciphertexts known by the adversary for each epoch t.

In a concurrent work, Asano et al. [7] define a similar FO transform to build IND-CR-CCA secure UPKEs. The authors point out a weakness in the generic CCA transform from [22]: the latter work does not consider the possibility of updates of the public key that would allow the adversary to come back to the challenge public key and then trivially break security by querying the CCA decryption oracle on the ciphertext. This is allowed as in [22], this query is forbidden only at the challenge epoch. This is solved in [7] by generalizing the technique of [1], which adjoins a counter to the public key that is incremented at each update. The construction of [7] relies on using this counter in the derandomization step of their FO transform, which then makes any ciphertext generated in a previous epoch invalid for decryption queries. Our security model for IND-CR-CCA UKEM deals with this problem by adding another sanity check in the decapsulation oracle: we require that the adversary is not allowed to make a decapsulation query of the challenge ciphertext only if it current public key is the same as the challenge one.

Adding Security Against Malicious Updates. Next, we extend our IND-CR-CCA construction to achieve IND-CU-CCA security. This is achieved via the standard Naor-Yung "double-encrypt + NIZK" paradigm [38] applied (only) to the update mechanism: a user's public key is now a pair of public keys (pk_0^L, pk^R). The first one is an evolving key, for which the user keeps the corresponding secret key sk_0^L, while the second one is never updated and its corresponding secret key is discarded after generation. To update a target public key (pk_t^L, pk^R) used at epoch t, one updates the first key as before by revealing the next epoch public key pk_{t+1}^L and encrypting the private coins r used for the update. However, rather than encrypting r under pk_t^L only, one also encrypts it under pk^R. Additionally, one produces a NIZK argument that the private coins underlying each ciphertext and used for updating the public key match. The encapsulation and decapsulation mechanisms are unchanged (and only use pk_t^L).

These changes allow us to argue about IND-CU-CCA security using standard techniques. Let $up^* = (\mathsf{ct}_L^*, \mathsf{ct}_R^*, \pi^*)$ denote the honest update generated by the challenger before leaking the secret key, and r^* denote the underlying private coins. In the IND-CU-CCA security reduction, one can then replace π^* by a simulated proof and ct_R^* by an encryption of 0 using the zero-knowledge property and the IND-CPA security of the underlying PKE, since no information about sk^R is revealed to the adversary. The soundness of the NIZK argument guarantees that the adversary cannot produce an accepting argument for invalid updates. Hence, security can be reduced to that of the underlying IND-CR-CCA UKEM: the IND-CR-CCA attacker can use the additional key sk_R to decrypt the private coins r used by the IND-CU-CCA adversary in its valid updates queries, and forward r to its IND-CR-CCA challenger for producing the same update. A crucial remark is that the adversary gets to see an update (and then a NIZK argument) generated by the challenger only at the very end of the game, when it compromises the key. In particular, it can no longer query oracles from this point and therefore cannot use this proof as part of oracle queries. This allows us to rely on a NIZK argument which is only computational zero-knowledge.

Concrete Parameters. We provide concrete parameters for our (IND-CR-CPA / IND-CR-CCA) scheme, following design choices of CRYSTALS-Kyber [11]: we instantiate our construction in the module lattices setting, using binomial distributions. In particular, we assume that our scheme is secure in the module setting though our security analysis does not immediately carries over to the Module Learning With Errors (MLWE) setting [14,32]. To extend it, one would need a similar reduction from decision entropic-MLWE to MLWE, which is currently lacking though a recent work from [12] shows a reduction for the search variants, providing a first step in this direction.

Notice that, as our modulus is small and the key can keep growing with (adversarially generated) updates, we can only guarantee correctness for a bounded number of updates as the decryption error might become too large at some point. We introduce a parameter k which is the maximal number of updates for which correctness is guaranteed with probability extremely close to 1. This parameter affects the size of the modulus q and forces us to use a larger modulus compared to Kyber (which uses $q = 3329$ and achieves a ciphertext size of 0.8 KB for 128 bit CCA security). Note that in practice, if randomness is honestly sampled from centered distribution (e.g., $\mathbf{r} \leftarrow U(\{-1, 0, 1\}^n)$), the expected number of supported updates is $O(k^2)$. In Table 1, we provide parameters for our IND-CR-CPA/CCA UKEM schemes, for $k \in \{2^5, 2^{10}, 2^{15}, 2^{20}\}$, and for a security of λ close to 128 bits.

Table 1. Concrete parameters for our IND-CR-CCA UKEM.

	λ	q	k	$\|ct\|$	$\|up\|$
DCR-based construction [1]	128	-	∞	8.3 KB	1.5 KB
Estimate for [22]	120	$\approx 2^{85}$	2^5	33 KB	360 KB
This work	128	$\approx 2^{21}$	2^5	1.8 KB	5.4 KB
	128	$\approx 2^{26}$	2^{10}	3.0 KB	12 KB
	116	$\approx 2^{31}$	2^{15}	5.8 KB	12 KB
	128	$\approx 2^{36}$	2^{20}	9.1 KB	27 KB

We provide a brief comparison with the DCR-based (IND-CR-CPA) construction of [1], whose ciphertext/update size is about 1.5 KB. Note that in the latter work, the authors achieve CCA-security by adding NIZKs, which hurts their ciphertext size for the CCA setting (about 8.3 KB for 128 bits of security), while using our FO transform leaves us with the same numbers for our IND-CR-CCA construction. In order to give an insight on the efficiency gain compared to the construction of [22] (which was not meant to be efficient), we provide estimates of practical parameters for their scheme. As it requires flooding, we first make the assumption that flooding by 64 bits suffices (see [37]). In order to give optimistic parameters, we relax their statistical leftover hash lemma to a computational one, i.e., we use an adaptation of the scheme from [34] rather than dual Regev encryption. This leads to considering parameters for our scheme but with flooding. Also, to achieve IND-CR-CCA security, we apply our efficient FO transform and not their generic one.

2 Preliminaries

We start by giving out the mathematical background and some useful lemmas needed in this paper.

Throughout this paper, we use bold upper case letters to denote matrices ($\mathbf{A}$), bold lower case letters for vectors ($\mathbf{a}$) and italic letters for scalars (a). For any vector $\mathbf{x} = (x_1, \dots, x_n)$, we use the ℓ_2-norm $\|\mathbf{x}\|_2 = \sqrt{\sum x_i^2}$, the ℓ_1-norm $\|\mathbf{x}\|_1 = \sum |x_i|$ and the ℓ_∞-norm $\|\mathbf{x}\|_\infty = \max |x_i|$. For any matrix $\mathbf{A} = (\mathbf{a}_1 \| \dots \| \mathbf{a}_n)$, we define $\|\mathbf{F}\|_2 = \max \|\mathbf{a}_i\|_2$, $\|\mathbf{F}\|_1 = \max \|\mathbf{a}_i\|_1$ and $\|\mathbf{F}\|_\infty = \max \|\mathbf{a}_i\|_\infty$. We let $\lfloor\cdot\rfloor$ denote the floor function and $\lfloor\cdot\rceil$ denote the rounding to the closest integer with ties being rounded up, which are extended to vectors by considering their coefficient-wise application. For $\mathbf{x} \in \mathbb{Q}^n$ and $q > p > 0$, we write $\lfloor \mathbf{x} \rceil_{p,q}$ for $\lfloor p/q \cdot \mathbf{x} \bmod q \rceil$. In this work, the modulus q will always be implicit and omitted.

For a distribution $\mathcal{S}$, we note $s \hookleftarrow S$ the fact that s is sampled using distribution $\mathcal{S}$. For a random variable X, we write $X \sim \mathcal{S}$ if X follows the distribution $\mathcal{S}$. We let $\mathcal{B}(p)$ denote the Bernouilli distribution of parameter p. We write $a \approx_\delta b$ for $a, b, \delta > 0$ if there exists $\varepsilon < \delta$ such that $|a - b| = \varepsilon$.

We say an algorithm is PPT if it is probabilistic, polynomial-time. We use log to denote the logarithm in base 2 and ln to denote the logarithm in base e.

We use the convolution product to express the distribution of a sum of random variables, which we remind below as well as some additional basic operations and properties of probability distributions and discrete Gaussian distributions.

Definition 1 (Convolution). *Let $m \in \mathbb{N}$. Let $\mathcal{S}_1, \mathcal{S}_2$ be two probability distribution on $\mathbb{Z}^m$. We define the convolution product $\mathcal{S}_1 * \mathcal{S}_2$ as:*

$$\mathcal{S}_1 * \mathcal{S}_2(x) = \sum_{y \in \mathbb{Z}^m} \mathcal{S}_1(x - y)\mathcal{S}_2(y).$$

If $X \sim \mathcal{S}_1$ and $Y \sim \mathcal{S}_2$ are independent random variables, then $X + Y \sim \mathcal{S}_1 * \mathcal{S}_2$.

We recall the definition of min-entropy.

Definition 2 (Min-entropy). *Let X, Y be random variables. We define the min-entropy*

$$\mathsf{H}_\infty(X) = -\log\left(\max_x \mathbb{P}\left[X = x\right]\right)$$

and the average conditional min-entropy:

$$\mathsf{H}_\infty(X \mid Y) = -\log\left(\mathbb{E}_y[\max_x \mathbb{P}[X = x \mid Y = y]]\right).$$

Definition 3 (Statistical distance). *Let $\mathcal{S}_1, \mathcal{S}_2$ be two distributions on $\mathbb{Z}^n$. We define the statistical $\Delta(\mathcal{S}_1, \mathcal{S}_2)$ as:*

$$\Delta(\mathcal{S}_1, \mathcal{S}_2) = \frac{1}{2} \sum_{x \in \mathbb{Z}^n} |\mathcal{S}_1(x) - \mathcal{S}_2(x)| .$$

2.1 Gaussian Distributions

We give the definition of Gaussian distribution and several useful lemmas that are used afterwards.

Definition 4 (Gaussian distribution). *Let $m \in \mathbb{N}$. For any symmetric positive-definite matrix $\mathbf{\Sigma} \in \mathbb{R}^{m \times m}$, define the function $g_{\mathbf{\Sigma}} : \mathbb{R}^m \to \mathbb{R}$ as*

$$\rho_{\mathbf{\Sigma}}(\mathbf{x}) = \exp\left(-\pi \frac{\mathbf{x}^T \mathbf{\Sigma}^{-1} \mathbf{x}}{2}\right).$$

We define the Gaussian distribution on $\mathbb{Z}^m$ with center parameter $\mathbf{c}$ and covariance matrix parameter $\mathbf{\Sigma}$ as $\mathcal{D}_{\mathbb{Z}^m,\mathbf{\Sigma},\mathbf{c}}(\mathbf{x}) = \rho_{\mathbf{\Sigma}}(\mathbf{x}-\mathbf{c})/\rho_{\mathbf{\Sigma}}(\mathbb{Z}^m - \mathbf{c})$. We will also use, for $\sigma > 0$, the notation $\mathcal{D}_{\mathbb{Z}^m,\sigma}$ to denote $\mathcal{D}_{\mathbb{Z}^m,\sigma^2\mathbf{Id},\mathbf{0}}$. Additionally, we will let $\mathcal{D}_{\mathbb{Z}^{m\times n},\sigma}$ denote the distribution obtained by sampling n vectors from $\mathcal{D}_{\mathbb{Z}^m,\sigma}$ and viewing them as the columns of a matrix in $\mathbb{Z}^{m\times n}$.

Lemma 1 (Gaussian tail-bound, [20, Lemma 2.13]). *Let $\mathbf{x} \sim \mathcal{D}_{\mathbb{Z}^m,\sigma}$, then for all $t > 1$, we have*

$$\mathbb{P}\left[\|\mathbf{x}\|_2 \geq t\sigma\sqrt{\frac{m}{2\pi}}\right] \leq e^{-\frac{m}{2}(1-t)^2} .$$

Lemma 2 (Gaussian convolution, [10, Lemma 4.12]). *Let $\mathbf{c}_1, \mathbf{c}_2 \in \mathbb{Z}^n$. Let $X \sim \mathcal{D}_{\mathbb{Z}^n,\sigma,\mathbf{c}_1}$, $Y \sim \mathcal{D}_{\mathbb{Z}^n,\sigma',\mathbf{c}_2}$ and let $\mathcal{S}$ be the distribution followed by $X+Y$. Then, if*

$$\left(\frac{1}{\sigma^2} + \frac{1}{\sigma'^2}\right)^{-1/2} > \sqrt{\frac{\ln(2n(1+\frac{1}{\varepsilon}))}{\pi}},$$

then we have the following inequality

$$\Delta\left(\mathcal{S}, \mathcal{D}_{\mathbb{Z}^n,\sqrt{\sigma^2+\sigma'^2},\mathbf{c}_1+\mathbf{c}_2}\right) < \frac{2\varepsilon}{1-\varepsilon} .$$

We now state a discrete Gaussian decomposition result.

Lemma 3 (Gaussian decomposition, instantiated from [36, Lemma 1]). *For $m \geq n$, let $\mathbf{F} \in \mathbb{Z}^{m \times n}$ be a matrix and let $s_1(\mathbf{F})$ be the largest singular value of $\mathbf{F}$. Take $\sigma, \sigma_1 > 0$. Let $\mathbf{e}_1 \sim \mathcal{D}_{\mathbb{Z}^n, \sigma_1}$ and $\mathbf{e}_2 \sim \mathcal{D}_{\mathbb{Z}^m, \mathbf{\Sigma}}$ for*

$$\mathbf{\Sigma} = \sigma^2 \mathbf{Id} - \sigma_1^2 \mathbf{F}^T \mathbf{F} \ .$$

Then, if $\sigma > \sqrt{2}\sigma_1 s_1(\mathbf{F})$ and $\sigma_1 > \sqrt{2\ln(2n(1 + 1/\varepsilon))/\pi}$, we have:

$$\Delta\left(\mathcal{S}, \mathcal{D}_{\mathbb{Z}^m, \sigma}\right) < \frac{2\varepsilon}{1 - \varepsilon} \ ,$$

where $\mathcal{S}$ is the distribution of $\mathbf{F}\mathbf{e}_1 + \mathbf{e}_2$.

In order to apply Lemma 3, one needs to control the ratio $s_1(\mathbf{F})$. This is the purpose of the following result.

Lemma 4 (Adapted from [2, Lemma 8]). *There exists a constant $K > 1$ such that the following holds. For $m \geq 2n$, $\sigma > K\sqrt{n}$ and $\mathbf{F} \hookleftarrow \mathcal{D}_{\mathbb{Z}^{m \times n}, \sigma}$*

$$\mathbb{P}\left[s_1(\mathbf{F}) > K\sigma\sqrt{m}\right] < e^{-m/K} \ ,$$

where $s_1(\mathbf{F})$ denotes the largest singular value of $\mathbf{F}$

2.2 Updatable Public Key Encryption

We recall the syntax of Updatable Public Key Encryption (UPKE) and adapt the underlying IND-CR-CPA security notion defined in [22], with a minor modification: we define correctness and security with a bound on the number of updates. This is motivated by the fact that, in our LWE-based scheme, updates make the key slightly larger and then after a (large but polynomial) number of updates, correctness of decryption is no longer guaranteed. This results from the fact that we are able to work over a (small) polynomial modulus.

Definition 5. *(Updatable Public Key Encryption) An updatable public key encryption scheme is a tuple* UPKE = (KeyGen, Enc, Dec, UpdatePk, UpdateSk) *of PPT algorithms with the following syntax:*

- KeyGen(1^λ) *takes as input a security parameter 1^λ and outputs a pair (pk, sk).*
- Enc(pk, m) *takes as input a public key pk and a message m and outputs a ciphertext ct.*
- Dec(sk, ct) *takes as input a secret key sk and a ciphertext ct and outputs a message m'.*
- UpdatePk(pk) *takes as input a public key pk and outputs an update up and a new public key pk'.*
- UpdateSk(sk, up) *takes as input a secret key sk and an update up and outputs a new secret key sk'.*

(k, δ)-Correctness: *Let $(pk_0, sk_0) \leftarrow \mathsf{KeyGen}(1^\lambda)$ be a key pair and $k > 0$ be an integer. For $t < k$, define*

$$(up_{t+1}, pk_{t+1}) \leftarrow \mathsf{UpdatePk}(pk_t) \text{ and } sk_{t+1} \leftarrow \mathsf{UpdateSk}(sk_t, up_{t+1}).$$

The UPKE scheme is said to be (k, δ)-correct, for $\delta > 0$, if for all messages m and $t \leq k$

$$\mathbb{P}\left[\mathsf{Dec}(sk_t, \mathsf{Enc}(pk_t, m)) \neq m\right] < \delta \ ,$$

where the probability is over the coins of the underlying algorithms.

We give the definition from [22] which we adapt to the bounded number of updates setting by adding a parameter k for the number of updates.

Definition 6 (k-IND-CR-CPA security). *Let $k > 0$ be an integer and* (KeyGen, Enc, Dec, UpdatePk, UpdateSk) *be a UPKE scheme. Let $\mathcal{R}$ be the randomness space of*

UpdatePk. *We give the k-IND-CR-CPA security game in Fig. 1.*

The advantage of $\mathcal{A}$ in winning the above game is

$$\mathsf{Adv}_{\mathrm{UPKE}}^{\mathsf{IND\text{-}CR\text{-}CPA}}(\mathcal{A}) = \left|\Pr\left[\beta = \beta'\right] - \frac{1}{2}\right| .$$

A UPKE scheme is k-IND-CR-CPA-secure if for all PPT attackers $\mathcal{A}$, the advantage $\mathsf{Adv}_{\mathrm{UPKE}}^{\mathsf{IND\text{-}CR\text{-}CPA}}(\mathcal{A})$ is negligible.

Parameters: λ, k.

GAME($\mathcal{A}$):
- $t = 0$; ▷ Epoch counter
- $\beta \hookleftarrow \mathcal{U}(\{0, 1\})$;
- $(pk_0, sk_0) \leftarrow \mathsf{KeyGen}(1^\lambda)$;
- $(m_0^\star, m_1^\star, st) \leftarrow \mathcal{A}^{\mathcal{O}_{up}}(pk_0)$;
- $c^\star \leftarrow \mathsf{Enc}(pk_t, m_\beta^\star)$;
- $st \leftarrow \mathcal{A}^{\mathcal{O}_{up}}(c^\star, st)$;
- $r^\star \hookleftarrow \mathcal{U}(\mathcal{R})$;
- $(pk^\star, up^\star) \leftarrow \mathsf{UpdatePk}(pk_t, r^\star)$;
- $sk^\star \leftarrow \mathsf{UpdateSk}(sk_t, up^\star)$;
- $\beta' \leftarrow \mathcal{A}(pk^\star, sk^\star, up^\star, c^\star, st)$;
- $\mathcal{A}$ wins if $\beta = \beta'$.

$\mathcal{O}_{up}(r)$:
- $t = t + 1$;
- **if** $t > k$ **then**
  - **return** $\perp$;
- **end**
- $(pk_t, up_t) \leftarrow \mathsf{UpdatePk}(pk_{t-1}; r)$;
- $sk_t \leftarrow \mathsf{UpdateSk}(sk_{t-1}, up_t)$;

Fig. 1. k-IND-CR-CPA security game.

We also recall the definition of γ-spreadness, which allows to bound the probability that a specific randomness r was used to produce a valid encryption. It is used in Sect. 5 for our FO transform.

Definition 7 (γ-spreadness, adapted from [23, Sect. 2.1]). *Let $\gamma > 0$. We say that a UPKE* (KeyGen, Enc, Dec, UpdatePk, UpdateSk) *is γ-spread if for all m, c and $(pk, sk) \leftarrow \mathsf{KeyGen}(1^\lambda)$, we have*

$$\mathbb{P}[\mathsf{Enc}(pk, m) = c] \leq \gamma.$$

2.3 Updatable Key Encapsulation Mechanism

We introduce the KEM variant of UPKE, which we term Updatable KEM or UKEM. Defining the KEM equivalent of UPKE seems particularly relevant considering that UPKE was introduced as a group messaging primitive, hence requiring real-world efficiency.

We adapt the definitions of IND-CR-CCA and IND-CU-CCA security notions defined by [22] for UPKEs.

Definition 8 (Updatable KEM (UKEM)). *An updatable KEM is a tuple* (KeyGen, Encaps, Decaps, UpdatePk, UpdateSk) *of algorithms with the following syntax:*

- $\mathsf{KeyGen}(1^\lambda)$ *takes as input a security parameter 1^λ and outputs a pair (pk, sk).*
- $\mathsf{Encaps}(pk)$ *takes as input a public key pk and outputs an encapsulation c and a key K.*
- $\mathsf{Decaps}(sk, c)$ *takes as input a secret key sk and an encapsulation c and outputs a key K'.*
- $\mathsf{UpdatePk}(pk)$ *takes as input a public key pk and outputs an update up and a new public key pk'.*
- $\mathsf{UpdateSk}(sk, up)$ *takes as input a secret key sk and an update up and outputs a new secret key sk'.*

(k, δ)-Correctness: *Let $(pk_0, sk_0) \leftarrow \mathsf{KeyGen}(1^\lambda)$ be a key pair and $k > 0$ be an integer. For $t < k$, define*

$$(up_{t+1}, pk_{t+1}) \leftarrow \mathsf{UpdatePk}(pk_t) \text{ and } sk_{t+1} \leftarrow \mathsf{UpdateSk}(sk_t, up_{t+1}).$$

The UKEM scheme is said to be (k, δ)-correct, for $\delta > 0$, if for all $t \leq k$

$$\mathbb{P}[\mathsf{Decaps}(sk_t, c_t) \neq K_t \mid (c_t, K_t) \leftarrow \mathsf{Encaps}(pk_t)] < \delta \ ,$$

where the probability is over the coins of the underlying algorithms.

The k-IND-CR-CCA security corresponds to a variant of k-IND-CR-CPA where the adversary is given access to a decapsulation oracle. We define k-IND-CR-CCA in the Random Oracle Model (ROM), as we make use of the Fujisaki-Okamato transform in Sect. 5 in order to build our IND-CR-CCA UKEM.

Definition 9 (k-IND-CR-CCA KEM security in the ROM). *Let* (KeyGen, Encaps, Decaps, UpdatePk, UpdateSk) *be a UKEM with key space $\mathcal{K}$. Let $\mathcal{R}$ denote the randomness space of* UpdatePk*. We give the game for k-IND-CR-CCA security for an adversary that has access to a random oracle* H *in Fig. 2.*

Parameters: λ, k.

GAME($\mathcal{A}$):
$t = 0$; ▷ Epoch counter
$\beta \leftarrow\!\!\!\!\!\$\ \mathcal{U}(\{0,1\})$;
$(pk_0, sk_0) \leftarrow \mathsf{KeyGen}(1^\lambda)$;
$st \leftarrow \mathcal{A}^{\mathcal{O}_{up},\mathcal{O}_{dec},\mathsf{H}}(pk_0)$;
$(c^\star, K^\star) \leftarrow \mathsf{Encaps}(pk_t)$;
if $\beta = 1$ **then**
$K^\star = \mathcal{U}(\mathcal{K})$;
end
$pk^{chall} = pk_t$;
$st \leftarrow \mathcal{A}^{\mathcal{O}_{up},\mathcal{O}_{dec},\mathsf{H}}(c^\star, st)$;
$r^\star \leftarrow \mathcal{U}(\mathcal{R})$;
$(up^\star, pk^\star) \leftarrow \mathsf{UpdatePk}(pk_t, r^\star)$;
$sk^\star \leftarrow \mathsf{UpdateSk}(sk_t, up^\star)$;
$\beta' \leftarrow \mathcal{A}^{\mathsf{H}}(pk^\star, sk^\star, up^\star, c^\star, st)$;
$\mathcal{A}$ wins if $\beta = \beta'$.

$\mathcal{O}_{up}(r)$:
$t = t + 1$;
if $t > k$ **then**
return $\perp$;
end
$(pk_t, up_t) \leftarrow \mathsf{UpdatePk}(pk_{t-1}; r)$;
$sk_t \leftarrow \mathsf{UpdateSk}(sk_{t-1}, up_t)$;

$\mathcal{O}_{dec}(c)$:
if $pk_t = pk^{chall} \wedge c = c^\star$ **then**
return $\perp$;
end
return $\mathsf{Decaps}(sk_t, c)$.

Fig. 2. k-IND-CR-CCA security game in the ROM. Note that if $\beta = 0$, then the value of the key $K^\star$ is the output of Encaps.

The advantage of $\mathcal{A}$ in winning the above game is

$$\mathsf{Adv}_{\mathrm{UKEM}}^{\mathsf{IND\text{-}CR\text{-}CCA}}(\mathcal{A}) = \left| \Pr[\beta = \beta'] - \frac{1}{2} \right|.$$

A UKEM scheme is k-IND-CR-CCA-secure if for all PPT attackers $\mathcal{A}$, the advantage $\mathsf{Adv}_{\mathrm{UKEM}}^{\mathsf{IND\text{-}CR\text{-}CCA}}(\mathcal{A})$ is negligible.

Notice that compared to the IND-CR-CCA definition for UPKE given in [22], we add a check in the $\mathcal{O}_{dec}$ oracle that the current public key pk_t is different from the challenge public key pk^{chall}. This disallows trivial attacks in which an adversary might make carefully chosen updates that would cancel out in order to get back to the challenge public key and issue a decryption query on the challenge. Another approach to solve this is given in [7], which generalizes the one considered in [1].

In order to define the stronger k-IND-CU-CCA security notions for UKEM, we add an algorithm VerifyUpdate to the UKEM syntax that allows a user to check the validity of an update. Specifically, VerifyUpdate$(pk, (pk', up))$ takes as input the current epoch public key pk and a proposed update (pk', up) and returns a Boolean value. k-IND-CU-CCA security aims to guarantee security against adversaries who makes malicious updates.

Definition 10 (k-IND-CU-CCA KEM security in the ROM). *Let* (KeyGen, Encaps, Decaps, UpdatePk, UpdateSk, VerifyUpdate) *be a UKEM. The security game for* IND-CU-CCA *is identical to the* IND-CR-CCA *game, except for the modified $\mathcal{O}_{up}(\cdot)$ oracle. We present the modified $\mathcal{O}_{up}$ oracle in Fig. 3.*

$\mathcal{O}_{up}(pk', up)$:
  if $\mathsf{VerifyUpdate}(pk_t, (pk', up)) = \bot$ **then**
    return $\bot$;
  end
  $pk_{t+1} = pk'$;
  $sk_{t+1} \leftarrow \mathsf{UpdateSk}(sk_t, up_{t+1})$;
  $t = t + 1$.

Fig. 3. k-IND-CU-CCA security game in the ROM.

A UKEM scheme is k-IND-CU-CCA-*secure if for all PPT attackers* $\mathcal{A}$*, its advantage* $\mathsf{Adv}_{\mathrm{UKEM}}^{\mathsf{IND\text{-}CU\text{-}CCA}}(\mathcal{A})$ *is negligible.*

In the rest of the paper, we omit the k in k-IND-CR-CPA/k-IND-CR-CCA/k-IND-CU-CCA when it is implicit.

3 Extended LWE

We start by recalling the Learning With Errors (LWE) assumption.

Definition 11. *(Learning With Errors - LWE) Let* $\lambda \geq 0$ *be a security parameter. Let* $q = q(\lambda), n = n(\lambda), m = m(\lambda) \geq 0$*,* $\mathcal{S}$ *be a distribution on* $\mathbb{Z}_q^n$ *and* χ *be an error distribution on* $\mathbb{Z}^m$*. The goal of* $\mathsf{LWE}_{q,n,m,\chi}(\mathcal{S})$ *for an adversary* $\mathcal{A}$ *is to distinguish between* $(\mathbf{A}, \mathbf{b} = \mathbf{As} + \mathbf{e})$ *and* $(\mathbf{A}, \mathbf{u})$*, for* $\mathbf{A} \hookleftarrow \mathcal{U}(\mathbb{Z}_q^{m \times n})$*,* $\mathbf{s} \hookleftarrow \mathcal{S}$*,* $\mathbf{e} \hookleftarrow \chi^m$ *and* $\mathbf{u} \hookleftarrow \mathcal{U}(\mathbb{Z}_q^m)$*. We define the advantage of* $\mathcal{A}$ *in the* LWE *game as*

$$\mathsf{Adv}^{\mathsf{LWE}}(\mathcal{A}) := \left| \mathbb{P}\left[\mathcal{A}(\mathbf{A}, \mathbf{As} + \mathbf{e}) \to 1\right] - \mathbb{P}\left[\mathcal{A}(\mathbf{A}, \mathbf{u}) \to 1\right] \right| .$$

To keep the notations simple, we write $\mathsf{LWE}_{q,n,m,\sigma}$ *for* $\sigma > 0$*, to denote* $\mathsf{LWE}_{q,n,m,\mathcal{D}_{\mathbb{Z}^m,\sigma}}(\mathcal{U}(\mathbb{Z}_q^n))$*.*

The extended-LWE assumption claims that pseudorandomness of an LWE instance $(\mathbf{A}, \mathbf{As} + \mathbf{e})$ still holds when the adversary is given an additional hint h computed as $\langle \mathbf{z}, \mathbf{e} \rangle \bmod q$ for a small $\mathbf{z}$ chosen by the adversary independently of $\mathbf{A}$. We define Adaptive extended-LWE, an adaptive version of this assumption. As the name suggests, it allows the adversary to choose the hint vector $\mathbf{z}$ adaptively, i.e. after having seen the matrix $\mathbf{A}$, which is not allowed in the definition of the extended-LWE from [39]. In Theorem 1, we prove that LWE reduces to this adaptive version.

Definition 12 (Adaptive extended-LWE - AextLWE). *Let* $\lambda \geq 0$ *be a security parameter. Let* $q = q(\lambda), n = n(\lambda), m = m(\lambda), B = B(\lambda) \in \mathbb{N}$ *and* χ *be an error distribution on* $\mathbb{Z}^m$*. The goal of* $\mathsf{AextLWE}_{q,n,m,\chi,B}$ *for an adversary* $\mathcal{A}$ *is to distinguish between the case where* $\beta = 0$ *and* $\beta = 1$ *in the interactive game depicted in Fig. 4. We define the advantage of* $\mathcal{A}$ *in the* AextLWE *game as*

$$\mathsf{Adv}^{\mathsf{AextLWE}}(\mathcal{A}) := \left| \mathbb{P}\left[\mathcal{A}(\mathbf{A}, \mathbf{As} + \mathbf{e}, \mathbf{z}, h) \to 1\right] - \mathbb{P}\left[\mathcal{A}(\mathbf{A}, \mathbf{u}, \mathbf{z}, h) \to 1\right] \right| ,$$

where the elements are distributed as shown in Fig. 4.

To keep the notations simple, we write $\mathsf{AextLWE}_{q,n,m,\sigma,B}$, *for* $\sigma > 0$, *to denote* $\mathsf{AextLWE}_{q,n,m,\mathcal{D}_{\mathbb{Z}^m,\sigma},B}$.

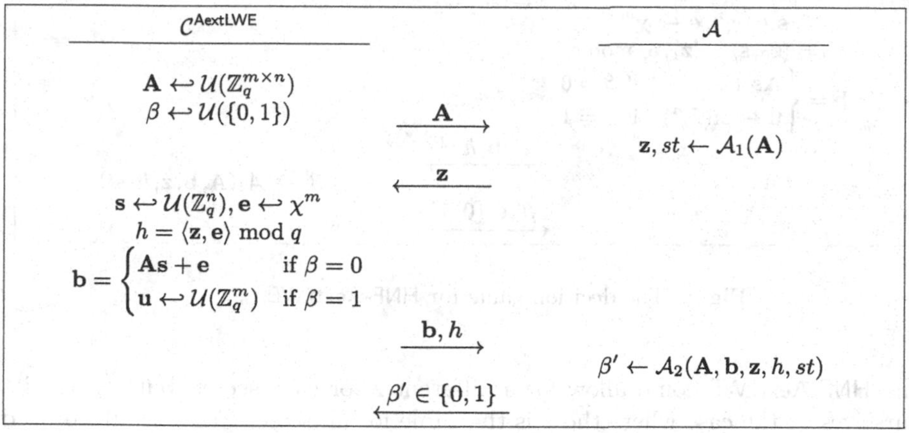

Fig. 4. The decision game for $\mathsf{AextLWE}_{q,n,m,\chi}$.

We define the Hermite Normal Form (HNF) variant of Adaptive extended-LWE, based on the normal form reduction from [6, Lemma 2]. Lemma 5 shows that the HNF variant reduces to the standard Adaptive extended-LWE.

Definition 13 (HNF Adaptive extended-LWE - HNF-AextLWE). *Let* $\lambda \in \mathbb{N}$ *be a security parameter. Let* $q = q(\lambda), n = n(\lambda), m = m(\lambda), B = B(\lambda) \in \mathbb{N}$ *and* χ *be an error distribution on* $\mathbb{R}^m$. *The goal of* $\mathsf{HNF\text{-}AextLWE}_{q,n,m,\chi,B}$ *for an adversary* $\mathcal{A}$ *is to distinguish between the case where* $\beta = 0$ *and* $\beta = 1$ *in the interactive game depicted in Fig. 5. We define the advantage of* $\mathcal{A}$ *in the* HNF-AextLWE *game as*

$$\mathsf{Adv}^{\mathsf{HNF\text{-}AextLWE}}(\mathcal{A}) = |\mathbb{P}[\mathcal{A}(\mathbf{A}, \mathbf{As}+\mathbf{e}, \mathbf{z}_0, \mathbf{z}_1, h) \to 1] - \mathbb{P}[\mathcal{A}(\mathbf{A}, \mathbf{u}, \mathbf{z}_0, \mathbf{z}_1, h) \to 1]|$$

where the elements are distributed as shown in Fig. 5.

To keep the notations simple, we write $\mathsf{HNF\text{-}AextLWE}_{q,n,m,\sigma,B}$, *for* $\sigma > 0$, *to denote* $\mathsf{HNF\text{-}AextLWE}_{q,n,m,\mathcal{D}_{\mathbb{Z}^m,\sigma},B}$.

Multiple-secret Variants. We consider the multiple-secret variants of all our assumptions $\mathsf{Asp} \in \{\mathsf{LWE}, \mathsf{AextLWE}, \mathsf{HNF\text{-}AextLWE}\}$ which consist in considering k distinct secrets for the same public matrix $\mathbf{A}$, thus replacing the secret vector $\mathbf{s} \in \mathbb{Z}_q^n$ by a secret matrix $\mathbf{S} \in \mathbb{Z}_q^{n\times k}$ and the error vector $\mathbf{e}$ by an error matrix $\mathbf{E} \in \mathbb{Z}_q^{m\times k}$. Note that for AextLWE and HNF-AextLWE, the hint $h \in \mathbb{Z}_q$ also becomes a vector $\mathbf{h} \in \mathbb{Z}_q^k$. Also, the multiple-secret variants for AextLWE

$\mathcal{C}^{\mathsf{HNF\text{-}AextLWE}}$		$\mathcal{A}$
$\mathbf{A} \hookleftarrow \mathcal{U}(\mathbb{Z}_q^{m\times n})$ $\beta \hookleftarrow \mathcal{U}(\{0,1\})$	$\xrightarrow{\mathbf{A}}$	
		$\mathbf{z}_0, \mathbf{z}_1, st \leftarrow \mathcal{A}_1(\mathbf{A})$
	$\xleftarrow{\mathbf{z}_0, \mathbf{z}_1}$	
$\mathbf{s} \hookleftarrow \chi^n, \mathbf{e} \hookleftarrow \chi^m$ $h = \langle \mathbf{z}_0, \mathbf{s}\rangle + \langle \mathbf{z}_1, \mathbf{e}\rangle \bmod q$ $\mathbf{b} = \begin{cases} \mathbf{As}+\mathbf{e} & \text{if } \beta = 0 \\ \mathbf{u} \hookleftarrow \mathcal{U}(\mathbb{Z}_q^m) & \text{if } \beta = 1 \end{cases}$		
	$\xrightarrow{\mathbf{b}, h}$	
		$\beta' \leftarrow \mathcal{A}_2(\mathbf{A}, \mathbf{b}, \mathbf{z}, h, st)$
	$\xleftarrow{\beta' \in \{0,1\}}$	

Fig. 5. The decision game for $\mathsf{HNF\text{-}AextLWE}_{q,n,m,\chi}$.

and HNF-AextLWE could allow for a different $\mathbf{z}$ for each secret, but we restrict ourselves to the case where the $\mathbf{z}$ is the same for all secrets, as it is all we need for our proofs.

Using a hybrid argument, one can show that for every adversary $\mathcal{A}$ for the multiple-secret variant of Asp with k secrets, there exists an adversary $\mathcal{B}$ with a similar run-time against the single-secret problem Asp such that $\mathcal{A}$'s advantage is bounded by $k \cdot \mathsf{Adv}^{\mathsf{Asp}}(\mathcal{B})$.

Lemma 5. *Let $q \geq 25, n \geq 1, m \geq 16n + 4\log\log q$, then any adversary $\mathcal{A}$ for* $\mathsf{HNF\text{-}AextLWE}_{q,n,m',\sigma,B}$ *, where $m' = m - 16n - 4\log\log q$, running in time T can be used to build an adversary $\mathcal{B}$ for* $\mathsf{AextLWE}_{q,n,m,\sigma,B}$ *running in time $\approx T$, with advantage*

$$\mathsf{Adv}^{\mathsf{HNF\text{-}AextLWE}}(\mathcal{A}) \leq 4 \cdot \mathsf{Adv}^{\mathsf{AextLWE}}(\mathcal{B}) \ .$$

Proof. Assume $\mathcal{A}$ is an adversary against HNF-AextLWE. We construct an adversary $\mathcal{B}$ against AextLWE with the claimed advantage as follows.

Adversary $\mathcal{B}$ receives a matrix $\mathbf{A} = \left(\mathbf{A}_0^T \| \mathbf{A}_1^T\right)^T \in \mathbb{Z}_q^{m\times n}$ from the AextLWE challenger, with $\mathbf{A}_0 \in \mathbb{Z}_q^{n\times n}$ and $\mathbf{A}_1 \in \mathbb{Z}_q^{m-n\times n}$. According to [15, Claim 2.13], with probability at least $1 - 2e^{-1} \geq 1/4$, there exist n linearly independent rows within the first $16n + 4\log\log q$ rows of $\mathbf{A}$ and an efficient way to find them, so that $\mathcal{B}$ can reorder the matrix so that $\mathbf{A}_0$ is invertible. If it cannot find such n rows, adversary $\mathcal{B}$ aborts. To avoid keeping track of the indices for the reordering, assume that $\mathbf{A}$ is such that $\mathbf{A}_0$ is invertible and denote by $\mathbf{A}_d$ the last $15n + 4\log\log q$ rows of $\mathbf{A}_1$ so that $\mathbf{A}_1 = (\tilde{\mathbf{A}}_1^T \| \mathbf{A}_d^T)^T$ with $\tilde{\mathbf{A}}_1 \in \mathbb{Z}_q^{m'\times n}$.

It then computes $\mathbf{A}^* = -\tilde{\mathbf{A}}_1 \mathbf{A}_0^{-1} \in \mathbb{Z}_q^{m'\times n}$ and sends $\mathbf{A}^*$ to adversary $\mathcal{A}$. Adversary $\mathcal{A}$ responds with the hint vectors $\mathbf{z}_0 \in \mathbb{Z}_q^n, \mathbf{z}_1 \in \mathbb{Z}_q^{m'}$. Then, adversary $\mathcal{B}$ forwards $\mathbf{z} = (\mathbf{z}_0^T \| \mathbf{z}_1^T \| 0^{m-m'-n})^T \in \mathbb{Z}_q^m$ to its challenger and receives a vector $\mathbf{b} = \left(\mathbf{b}_0^T \| \mathbf{b}_1^T \| \mathbf{d}^T\right)^T$ and a hint $h = \langle \mathbf{z}, \mathbf{e}\rangle + g \bmod q$ from the AextLWE challenger, with $\mathbf{b}_0 \in \mathbb{Z}_q^n$, $\mathbf{b}_1 \in \mathbb{Z}_q^{m'}$, $\mathbf{d} \in \mathbb{Z}_q^{m-m'}$ and $g \hookleftarrow \mathcal{D}_{\mathbb{Z},\sigma}$. It then computes $\mathbf{b}^* = \mathbf{b}_1 + \mathbf{A}^*\mathbf{b}_0$ and sends $(\mathbf{b}^*, h)$ to $\mathcal{A}$. Finally, it receives a response bit β from $\mathcal{A}$, which it forwards to its challenger.

In the case where $\mathbf{b}$ was a uniform vector, as $\mathbf{A}_0$ is an invertible matrix, matrix $\mathbf{A}^*$ is uniform and so is $\mathbf{b}^* = \mathbf{b}_1 + \mathbf{A}^*\mathbf{b}_0$.

If we are in the case where

$$\begin{pmatrix}\mathbf{b}_0\\ \mathbf{b}_1\\ \mathbf{d}\end{pmatrix} = \begin{pmatrix}\mathbf{A}_0\\ \tilde{\mathbf{A}}_1\\ \mathbf{A}_d\end{pmatrix}\mathbf{s} + \begin{pmatrix}\mathbf{e}_0\\ \mathbf{e}_1\\ \mathbf{e}_d\end{pmatrix}$$

for $\mathbf{s} \hookleftarrow \mathcal{D}_{\mathbb{Z}^n,\sigma}, \mathbf{e}_0 \hookleftarrow \mathcal{D}_{\mathbb{Z}^n,\sigma}, \mathbf{e}_1 \hookleftarrow \mathcal{D}_{\mathbb{Z}^{m'},\sigma}$ and $\mathbf{e}_d \hookleftarrow \mathcal{D}_{\mathbb{Z}^{m-m'},\sigma}$, then

$$\mathbf{b}^* = \tilde{\mathbf{A}}_1\mathbf{s} + \mathbf{e}_1 - \tilde{\mathbf{A}}_1\mathbf{A}_0^{-1}\mathbf{A}_0\mathbf{s} + \mathbf{A}^*\mathbf{e}_0 = \mathbf{A}^*\mathbf{e}_0 + \mathbf{e}_1.$$

Furthermore, the hint is exactly

$$\begin{aligned}\langle \mathbf{z}, \mathbf{e}\rangle + g &= \left\langle \mathbf{z}_0^T \| \mathbf{z}_1^T \| 0^{m-m'}, \mathbf{e}_0^T \| \mathbf{e}_1^T \| \mathbf{e}_d^T \right\rangle + g \\ &= \langle \mathbf{z}_0, \mathbf{e}_0\rangle + \langle \mathbf{z}_1, \mathbf{e}_1\rangle + g \bmod q.\end{aligned}$$

Consequently, adversary $\mathcal{A}$ receives a valid HNF Adaptive extended-LWE instance.

Adversary $\mathcal{B}$ runs $\mathcal{A}$ only once and has to compute the reordering which is feasible in time $\mathsf{poly}(\lambda)$. It has advantage at least $\mathsf{Adv}^{\mathsf{HNF\text{-}AextLWE}}(\mathcal{A})/4$, completing the proof of the lemma. □

We now show that LWE reduces to Adaptive extended-LWE .

Theorem 1. *Let q be a prime, $\varepsilon > 0$ and $n, m, B, \gamma, \sigma \geq 0$. Assume that $\sigma > \sqrt{2\ln(2(n+1)(1+1/\varepsilon))/\pi}$ and $\gamma > \sigma\sqrt{2(1+nB^2)}$. Then for any adversary $\mathcal{A}$ for $\mathsf{AextLWE}_{q,n,m,\sigma,B}$ running in time T, there exists an adversary $\mathcal{B}$ for $\mathsf{LWE}_{q,n,m,\gamma,B}$ running in time $\mathsf{poly}(m, \log q) \cdot T$ such that:*

$$\mathsf{Adv}^{\mathsf{AextLWE}}(\mathcal{A}) \leq \mathsf{Adv}^{\mathsf{LWE}}(\mathcal{B}) + 2\frac{2\varepsilon}{1-\varepsilon}\ .$$

Proof. Let $\mathcal{A}$ be an adversary against $\mathsf{AextLWE}_{q,n,m,\sigma}$. We build an adversary $\mathcal{B}$ against $\mathsf{LWE}_{q,n,m,\gamma}$ as follows. Adversary $\mathcal{B}$ receives from its LWE challenger a tuple $(\mathbf{A}, \mathbf{b})$. It forwards $\mathbf{A}$ to $\mathcal{A}$ and receives a small hint vector $\mathbf{z}$ such that $\|\mathbf{z}\|_\infty \leq B$.

It then samples $[\mathbf{e}'^T \| g']^T \hookleftarrow \mathcal{D}_{\mathbb{Z}^{n+1},\mathbf{\Sigma}}$, for some $\mathbf{\Sigma}$ defined later on. It sets $\mathbf{b}' = \mathbf{b} + \mathbf{e}'$ and $h = \langle \mathbf{z}, \mathbf{e}'\rangle + g'$ and sends $(\mathbf{b}', h)$ to $\mathcal{A}$. Adversary $\mathcal{B}$ receives a final bit from $\mathcal{A}$ which it forwards to its challenger.

Assume we are in the $\beta = 0$ case of the LWE game. Then $\mathbf{b} = \mathbf{A}\mathbf{s} + \mathbf{e}$ and $\mathbf{b}' = \mathbf{A}\mathbf{s} + (\mathbf{e} + \mathbf{e}')$. The hint $h = \langle \mathbf{z}, \mathbf{e}'\rangle + g'$ can be rewritten as $h = \langle \mathbf{z}, (\mathbf{e} + \mathbf{e}')\rangle - \langle \mathbf{z}, \mathbf{e}\rangle + g'$. Notice that if

$$\begin{pmatrix}\mathbf{e} + \mathbf{e}'\\ -\langle \mathbf{z}, \mathbf{e}\rangle + g'\end{pmatrix} = \begin{pmatrix}\mathbf{e}\\ -\mathbf{z}^T\mathbf{e}\end{pmatrix} + \begin{pmatrix}\mathbf{e}'\\ g'\end{pmatrix} \sim \mathcal{D}_{\mathbb{Z}^{n+1},\gamma} \tag{1}$$

this corresponds to the $\beta = 0$ case of the AextLWE game.

It thus suffices to set $\mathbf{\Sigma}$ accordingly. Notice that as $\mathbf{e} \sim \mathcal{D}_{\mathbb{Z}^n,\sigma}$, we have

$$\begin{pmatrix} \mathbf{e} \\ -\mathbf{z}^T\mathbf{e} \end{pmatrix} = \begin{pmatrix} \mathbf{Id} \\ -\mathbf{z}^T \end{pmatrix} \mathbf{e} \sim \mathcal{D}_{\mathbb{Z}^{n+1},\sigma^2\mathbf{F}\mathbf{F}^T}$$

for $\mathbf{F} = [\mathbf{Id}\| - \mathbf{z}]^T$. Let us then take $\mathbf{\Sigma} = \gamma^2\mathbf{Id} - \sigma^2\mathbf{F}\mathbf{F}^T$. Note that $s_1(\mathbf{F})^2 = 1 + \|z\|_2^2 \leq 1 + nB^2$. By assumption, we have $\gamma > \sqrt{2}\sigma s_1(\mathbf{F})$. By applying Lemma 3, we get

$$\begin{pmatrix} \mathbf{e} \\ -\mathbf{z}^T\mathbf{e} \end{pmatrix} + \begin{pmatrix} \mathbf{e}' \\ g' \end{pmatrix} \approx_\delta \mathcal{D}_{\mathbb{Z}^{n+1},\gamma} \tag{2}$$

for $\delta = 2\varepsilon/(1-\varepsilon)$.

In the $\beta = 1$ case of the LWE game, the vector $\mathbf{b}$ is uniform and so is $\mathbf{b}'$. The same analysis holds for the distribution of the hint h, so this case matches with the $\beta = 1$ case of the AextLWE game for $\mathcal{A}$. □

4 IND-CR-CPA UPKE from LWE

We now describe a UPKE scheme with security based on the HNF-AextLWE assumption. As already shown, it is implied by the standard LWE assumption. Our scheme, detailed in Fig. 6, avoid noise flooding by taking advantage of the HNF-AextLWE assumption defined in Sect. 3. We then provide the first efficient UPKE scheme based on lattices. Our construction follows the lines of [34] which underlies Kyber [11].

In contrast, the only prior lattice-based construction, proposed in [22] and based on the Dual-Regev PKE from [25], is highly inefficient: (i) it supports only binary plaintexts, (ii) updates are done via bit-by-bit encryption of the private coins, and (iii) the security analysis relies on noise flooding, which requires a super-polynomial modulus.

Theorem 2. *Let* $\varepsilon, \delta \in (0,1), k > 0$. *Let* q, p *be primes and* $n, m > 0$ *and* $\sigma, \sigma_c > 0$ *such that* $\sigma \geq \sqrt{2\ln(2n(1+1/\varepsilon))/\pi}$ *and* $\sigma_c > 2\sigma\sqrt{1 + n((k+1)y\sigma)^2}$, *where* $y = \sqrt{-2\log(\delta/(4n))}$.

Assuming the hardness of HNF-AextLWE, *the scheme presented in Fig. 6 is* k-IND-CR-CPA *secure. More precisely, for any adversary* $\mathcal{A}$ *for the* k-IND-CR-CPA *game, there exists an adversary* $\mathcal{B}$ *for* HNF-AextLWE *running in similar time as* $\mathcal{A}$ *such that:*

$$\mathsf{Adv}_{\mathsf{UPKE}}^{\mathsf{IND\text{-}CR\text{-}CPA}}(\mathcal{A}) \leq (2n+8) \cdot \frac{2\varepsilon}{1-\varepsilon} + (2n+1) \cdot \mathsf{Adv}^{\mathsf{HNF\text{-}AextLWE}}(\mathcal{B}) \; .$$

Furthermore, assuming $q > 2p\sigma_c \cdot (2y^2\sigma nk + y)$ *and* $p > 2y\sigma$, *the scheme is* (k, δ)-*correct.*

Public parameters: (n, q, p, σ)

KeyGen(1^λ):
  $\mathbf{A} \hookleftarrow \mathcal{U}(\mathbb{Z}_q^{n\times n})$, $\mathbf{s}, \mathbf{e} \hookleftarrow \mathcal{D}_{\mathbb{Z}^n,\sigma}$;
  $pk = (\mathbf{A}, \mathbf{b} = \mathbf{A}\mathbf{s} + \mathbf{e})$, $sk = \mathbf{s}$;
  return (pk, sk).

Enc$(pk, \boldsymbol{\mu} \in \mathbb{Z}_p^n)$:
  $\mathbf{X}, \mathbf{E} \hookleftarrow \mathcal{D}_{\mathbb{Z}^{n\times n},\sigma}$ and $\mathbf{f} \hookleftarrow \mathcal{D}_{\mathbb{Z}^n,\sigma}$;
  return $\mathbf{ct} = (\mathbf{X}\mathbf{A} + \mathbf{E}, \mathbf{X}\mathbf{b} + \mathbf{f} + \lfloor q/p \rfloor \cdot \boldsymbol{\mu} \bmod q)$.

Dec$(sk = \mathbf{s}, ct = (\mathbf{ct}_0, ct_1))$:
  $\mathbf{v} = ct_1 - \mathbf{ct}_0\mathbf{s}$;
  return $\lfloor p/q \cdot \mathbf{v} \rceil_p$.

UpdatePk$(pk = (\mathbf{A}, \mathbf{b}))$:
  $\mathbf{r}, \boldsymbol{\eta} \hookleftarrow \mathcal{D}_{\mathbb{Z}^n,\sigma}$;
  return $(pk' = (\mathbf{A}, \mathbf{b} + \mathbf{A}\mathbf{r} + \boldsymbol{\eta}), up = \text{Enc}(pk, \mathbf{r}))$.

UpdateSk(sk, up):
  return $sk' = sk + \text{Dec}(sk, up)$.

Fig. 6. LWE-based IND-CR-CPA UPKE construction.

Proof. The proof of correctness is detailed in the full version of the paper. We also provide a proof of γ-spreadness there, which is relevant for the next section.

We show the IND-CR-CPA security of the scheme. Let us start by defining all the security games.

Game G_0: This is the original IND-CR-CPA game. Adversary $\mathcal{A}$ receives $pk_0 = (\mathbf{A}, \mathbf{b}_0 = \mathbf{A}\mathbf{s} + \mathbf{e})$ and queries the $\mathcal{O}_{up}(\cdot)$ oracle with randomness $(\mathbf{r}_1, \boldsymbol{\eta}_1), \ldots, (\mathbf{r}_{chall}, \boldsymbol{\eta}_{chall})$ until it asks for a challenge at epoch *chall* for a pair of plaintexts $(\boldsymbol{\mu}_0, \boldsymbol{\mu}_1)$. At this epoch, the secret key is $sk_{chall} = \mathbf{s} + \Delta^{\mathbf{r}}_{chall}$ where $\Delta^{\mathbf{r}}_{chall} = \sum_{i=1}^{chall} \mathbf{r}_i$ and the public key is

$$pk_{chall} = \Big(\mathbf{A},\ \mathbf{b}_{chall} = \mathbf{A}(\mathbf{s} + \Delta^{\mathbf{r}}_{chall}) + \mathbf{e} + \Delta^{\boldsymbol{\eta}}_{chall}\Big),$$

with $\Delta^{\boldsymbol{\eta}}_{chall} = \sum_{i=1}^{chall} \boldsymbol{\eta}_i$. It receives a challenge

$$\mathbf{c}^* = \left(\mathbf{T}_{chall} = \mathbf{X}_{chall}\mathbf{A} + \mathbf{E}_{chall},\ \mathbf{pad}_{chall} = \mathbf{X}_{chall}\mathbf{b}_{chall} + \mathbf{f}_{chall} + \lfloor q/p \rfloor \cdot \boldsymbol{\mu}_\beta\right),$$

for $\beta \in \{0, 1\}$ uniform.

Then the adversary queries the $\mathcal{O}_{up}(\cdot)$ oracle until the last epoch *last*. At this epoch, the secret key is $sk_{last} = \mathbf{s} + \Delta^{\mathbf{r}}_{last}$, where $\Delta^{\mathbf{r}}_{last} = \sum_{i=1}^{last} \mathbf{r}_i$ and the public key is $pk_{last} = (\mathbf{A}, \mathbf{b}_{last} = \mathbf{A}(\mathbf{s} + \Delta^{\mathbf{r}}_{last}) + \mathbf{e} + \Delta^{\boldsymbol{\eta}}_{last})$, where $\Delta^{\boldsymbol{\eta}}_{last} = \sum_{i=1}^{last} \boldsymbol{\eta}_i$.

The challenger samples the final update $\mathbf{r}^*, \boldsymbol{\eta}^* \hookleftarrow \mathcal{D}_{\mathbb{Z}^n,\sigma}$ and sends

$$\begin{aligned} up^* &= \mathsf{Enc}(pk_{last}, \mathbf{r}^*) \\ &= (\mathbf{T}_{last} = \mathbf{X}_{last}\mathbf{A} + \mathbf{E}_{last}, \ \mathbf{pad}_{last} = \mathbf{X}_{last}\mathbf{b}_{last} + \mathbf{f}_{last} + \lfloor q/p \rfloor \cdot \mathbf{r}^*) \end{aligned}$$

together with $pk^* = (\mathbf{A}, \mathbf{b}_{last} + \mathbf{A}\mathbf{r}^* + \boldsymbol{\eta}^*)$ and $sk^* = \mathbf{s} + \Delta^{\mathbf{r}}_{last} + \mathbf{r}^*$ to the adversary.

Game G_1: In this game we modify the update up^*. Instead of computing it as

$$up^* = (\mathbf{T}_{last} = \mathbf{X}_{last}\mathbf{A} + \mathbf{E}_{last}, \ \mathbf{pad}_{last} = \mathbf{X}_{last}\mathbf{b}_{last} + \mathbf{f}_{last} + \lfloor q/p \rfloor \cdot \mathbf{r}^*),$$

the challenger sets

$$up^* = (\mathbf{T}_{last} = \mathbf{X}_{last}\mathbf{A} + \mathbf{E}_{last}, \ \mathbf{pad}_{last} = \mathbf{X}_{last}\mathbf{b}_{last} + \mathbf{f}_{last} + \lfloor q/p \rfloor \cdot (-\mathbf{s})).$$

This modification results in a computationally equivalent game. Indeed adversary receives up^* together with $sk^* = \mathbf{s} + \Delta^{\mathbf{r}}_{last} + \mathbf{r}^*$ with $\Delta^{\mathbf{r}}_{last}$ known to the adversary. This modification is just a subtraction of $\lfloor q/p \rfloor \cdot (\mathbf{s} + \mathbf{r}^*)$ in $\mathbf{pad}_{last}$.

Game G_2: In this game, we again modify the update. This time the challenger computes the update up^* as

$$\begin{aligned} \mathbf{T}_{last} &= \mathbf{X}_{last}\mathbf{A} + \mathbf{E}_{last} - \lfloor q/p \rfloor \cdot \mathbf{Id}, \\ \mathbf{pad}_{last} &= \mathbf{T}_{last}(\mathbf{s} + \Delta^{\mathbf{r}}_{last}) - \mathbf{E}_{last}(\mathbf{s} + \Delta^{\mathbf{r}}_{last}) + \mathbf{X}_{last}(\mathbf{e} + \Delta^{\eta}_{last}) \\ &\quad + \mathbf{f}_{last} + \lfloor q/p \rfloor \cdot \Delta^{\mathbf{r}}_{last}. \end{aligned}$$

Notice that

$$\mathbf{pad}_{last} = \mathbf{X}_{last}\mathbf{b}_{last} + \mathbf{f}_{last} + \lfloor q/p \rfloor \cdot (-\mathbf{s}).$$

Therefore, the only difference with the previous game is that we subtract a publicly computable element $\lfloor q/p \rfloor \cdot \mathbf{Id}$ in $\mathbf{T}_{last}$, which implies that this game is computationally equivalent to the last one.

Game G_3: In this game, instead of computing $\mathbf{T}_{last}$ as $\mathbf{T}_{last} = \mathbf{X}_{last}\mathbf{A} + \mathbf{E}_{last} - \lfloor q/p \rfloor \cdot \mathbf{Id}$ the challenger sets $\mathbf{T}_{last}$ uniformly, i.e., $\mathbf{T}_{last} \hookleftarrow \mathcal{U}(\mathbb{Z}_q^{n \times n})$.

Lemma 6 below states that games G_2 and G_3 are computationally indistinguishable. The proof relies on the hardness of HNF-AextLWE. In particular, any adversary $\mathcal{B}$ has advantage at most $\mathsf{Adv}(\mathcal{B}) \leq n \cdot \mathsf{Adv}^{\mathsf{HNF\text{-}AextLWE}}$ at distinguishing games G_2 and G_3.

Game G_4: Here, instead of having the challenger sample $\mathbf{s}, \mathbf{e} \hookleftarrow \mathcal{D}_{\mathbb{Z}^n,\sigma}$ at the start of the game, and $\mathbf{r}^*, \boldsymbol{\eta}^* \hookleftarrow \mathcal{D}_{\mathbb{Z}^n,\sigma}$ at the end and setting $sk^* = \mathbf{s} + \mathbf{r}^* + \Delta^{\mathbf{r}}_{last}$ and $pk^* = (\mathbf{A}, \mathbf{A}(\mathbf{s} + \Delta^{\mathbf{r}}_{last} + \mathbf{r}^*) + \mathbf{e} + \Delta^{\eta}_{last} + \boldsymbol{\eta}^*)$, we do the following.

Let us define distributions $\mathcal{S}$, $\mathcal{S}_{\mathbf{t}}$ and $\mathcal{S}_{\tilde{\mathbf{e}}}$ as:

$$\mathcal{S} = \mathcal{D}_{\mathbb{Z}^n, \sigma\sqrt{2}}, \quad \mathcal{S}_{\mathbf{t}} = \mathcal{D}_{\mathbb{Z}^n, \frac{\sigma}{\sqrt{2}}, \frac{\mathbf{t}}{2}}, \quad \text{and } \mathcal{S}_{\tilde{\mathbf{e}}} = \mathcal{D}_{\mathbb{Z}^n, \frac{\sigma}{\sqrt{2}}, \frac{\tilde{\mathbf{e}}}{2}}.$$

Then, in game G_4, the challenger samples $\mathbf{t}, \tilde{\mathbf{e}} \hookleftarrow \mathcal{S}$ at the beginning of the game, then samples $\mathbf{s} \hookleftarrow \mathcal{S}_{\mathbf{t}}, \mathbf{e} \hookleftarrow \mathcal{S}_{\tilde{\mathbf{e}}}$ and finally sets $sk^* = \mathbf{t} + \Delta^{\mathbf{r}}_{last}$ and $pk^* = (\mathbf{A}, \mathbf{At} + \tilde{\mathbf{e}} + \mathbf{A}\Delta^{\mathbf{r}}_{last} + \Delta^{\eta}_{last})$.

Let $\delta = 2\varepsilon/(1-\varepsilon)$. Lemma 2 shows that this change only induces a statistically negligible bias. Specifically, assuming $\sigma \geq \sqrt{2\ln(2n(1+1/\varepsilon))/\pi}$, $\mathbf{t}$ is within statistical distance at most δ from the distribution of $\mathbf{s} + \mathbf{r}^*$ in game G_3, and the marginal distribution of $\mathbf{s}$ in game G_4 with respect to the adversary's view is:

$$\begin{aligned}
\mathbb{P}[\mathbf{s} = \mathbf{x}] &= \sum_{\mathbf{y} \in \mathbb{Z}^n} \mathbb{P}[\mathbf{s} = \mathbf{x} | \mathbf{t} = \mathbf{y}] \, \mathbb{P}[\mathbf{t} = \mathbf{y}] \\
&= \sum_{\mathbf{y} \in \mathbb{Z}^n} \mathcal{D}_{\mathbb{Z}^n, \frac{\sigma}{\sqrt{2}}} \left(\mathbf{x} - \frac{\mathbf{y}}{2}\right) \mathcal{D}_{\mathbb{Z}^n, \sigma\sqrt{2}}(\mathbf{y}) \\
&= \sum_{\mathbf{y} \in \mathbb{Z}^n} \mathcal{D}_{\mathbb{Z}^n, \sigma\sqrt{2}}(2\mathbf{x} - \mathbf{y}) \, \mathcal{D}_{\mathbb{Z}^n, \sigma\sqrt{2}}(\mathbf{y}) \\
&\approx_{\delta} \mathcal{D}_{\mathbb{Z}^n, 2\sigma}(2\mathbf{x}) = \mathcal{D}_{\mathbb{Z}^n, \sigma}(\mathbf{x}).
\end{aligned}$$

The fourth equality comes from applying Lemma 2 for the convolution of two Gaussian distributions with the same standard deviation. The same argument applies for $\tilde{\mathbf{e}}$ and $\mathbf{e}$. Hence any adversary $\mathcal{B}$ has advantage at most $4\delta = 8\varepsilon/(1-\varepsilon)$ in distinguishing games G_3 and G_4.

Game G_5: In this game, we replace $\mathbf{b}_0$ and $up^* = (\mathbf{T}_{last}, \mathbf{pad}_{last})$ by uniform elements. Note that $\mathbf{T}_{last}$ is already uniform since game G_3. Hence, the challenger samples $\mathbf{b}_0, \mathbf{pad}_{last} \hookleftarrow \mathcal{U}(\mathbb{Z}_q^n)$, and sets $pk_0 = (\mathbf{A}, \mathbf{b}_0)$ at the start of the game, and returns $up^* = (\mathbf{T}_{last}, \mathbf{pad}_{last})$ as the last update message.

Lemma 7 below states that this game and the previous one are computationally indistinguishable under the LWE assumption.

Game G_6: This is the final game. Here, the challenger replaces the challenge $\mathbf{c}^*$ to make it uniform: it samples $\mathbf{T}_{chall} \hookleftarrow \mathcal{U}(\mathbb{Z}_q^{n\times n})$ and $\mathbf{pad}_{chall} \hookleftarrow \mathcal{U}(\mathbb{Z}_q^n)$, and then sets $\mathbf{c}^* = (\mathbf{T}_{chall}, \mathbf{pad}_{chall})$.

Remember that in game G_5, we have $\mathbf{c}^* = (\mathbf{X}_{chall}\mathbf{A} + \mathbf{E}_{chall}, \mathbf{X}_{chall}\mathbf{b}_{chall} + \mathbf{f}_{chall} + \lfloor q/p \rfloor \cdot \boldsymbol{\mu}_\beta)$. We can rewrite $\mathbf{c}^*$ in a matrix form as:

$$\mathbf{X}_{chall}\left(\mathbf{A} \| \mathbf{b}_{chall}\right) + \left(\mathbf{E}_{chall} \| \mathbf{f}_{chall}\right) + \lfloor q/p \rfloor \cdot (\mathbf{0} \| \boldsymbol{\mu}_\beta) \tag{3}$$

with $\mathbf{A} \hookleftarrow \mathcal{U}(\mathbb{Z}_q^{n\times n})$ and $\mathbf{b}_{chall} = \mathbf{b}_0 + \mathbf{A}\Delta^{\mathbf{r}}_{chall} + \Delta^{\eta}_{chall}$. Recall that we have $\mathbf{b}_0 \hookleftarrow \mathcal{U}(\mathbb{Z}_q^n)$ since game G_5. The last column of Equation (3) is

$$(\mathbf{X}_{chall}\mathbf{b}_0 + \mathbf{f}_{chall}) + (\mathbf{X}_{chall}(\mathbf{A}\Delta^{\mathbf{r}}_{chall} + \Delta^{\eta}_{chall})) + \lfloor q/p \rfloor \cdot \boldsymbol{\mu}_\beta.$$

and can be rewritten as

$$\begin{aligned}
&(\mathbf{X}_{chall}\mathbf{b}_0 + \mathbf{f}_{chall,0}) \\
&+ \mathbf{T}_{chall}\Delta^{\mathbf{r}}_{chall} - \mathbf{E}_{chall}\Delta^{\mathbf{r}}_{chall} + \mathbf{X}_{chall}\Delta^{\eta}_{chall} + \mathbf{f}_{chall,1} \\
&+ \lfloor q/p \rfloor \cdot \boldsymbol{\mu}_\beta \,,
\end{aligned}$$

where $\mathbf{f}_{chall} = \mathbf{f}_{chall,0} + \mathbf{f}_{chall,1}$ for $\mathbf{f}_{chall,0}, \mathbf{f}_{chall,1} \hookleftarrow \mathcal{D}_{\mathbb{Z}^n,\sigma_c/\sqrt{2}}$. Consider we are working with standard deviation $\sigma_c/\sqrt{2}$ instead of σ_c. The first term is a multiple-secret LWE sample that is independent of any adversarially chosen value. The second one can be computed from $\mathbf{T}_{chall}$. The next three can be viewed as an HNF-AextLWE hint on the secret $\mathbf{X}_{chall}$ and the error $\mathbf{E}_{chall}$ with hint vector $\mathbf{z}_0 = \Delta^{\eta}_{chall}$ and $\mathbf{z}_1 = \Delta^{\mathbf{r}}_{chall}$, which are small vectors. The difference in standard deviation can be handled as in Lemma 7 by adding terms sampled from $\mathcal{D}_{\mathbb{Z}^n,\sigma_c/\sqrt{2}}$ to the matrices $\mathbf{X}_{chall}$ and $\mathbf{E}_{chall}$. Applying Lemma 2 proves this change to be statistically unnoticeable.

The above indicates that the modification between games G_5 and G_6 can be analyzed by using the multiple-secret variant of $\mathsf{HNF\text{-}AextLWE}_{q,n,n+1,\frac{\sigma_c}{\sqrt{2}},ky\sigma}$ with n secrets and hint vector $\mathbf{z} = [(\Delta^{\eta}_{chall})^T \| (\Delta^{\mathbf{r}}_{chall})^T]^T$. Consequently, any adversary $\mathcal{A}$ has advantage at most $n \cdot \mathsf{Adv}^{\mathsf{HNF\text{-}AextLWE}} + (2n+1) \cdot 2\varepsilon/(1-\varepsilon)$ in distinguishing between games G_5 and G_6.

Note that in game G_6, the adversary has no information on the challenge $\boldsymbol{\mu}_\beta$. Hence $\mathsf{Adv}^{G_6}(\mathcal{A}) = 0$. We obtain

$$\mathsf{Adv}^{\mathsf{IND\text{-}CR\text{-}CPA}}_{\mathsf{UPKE}}(\mathcal{A}) \leq (2n+8) \cdot \frac{2\varepsilon}{1-\varepsilon} + (2n+1) \cdot \mathsf{Adv}^{\mathsf{HNF\text{-}AextLWE}}.$$

This completes the proof, up to Lemmas 6 and 7 below. □

Lemma 6. *For any adversary $\mathcal{A}$ that distinguishes between games G_2 and G_3, there exists an efficient algorithm $\mathcal{B}$ for $\mathsf{HNF\text{-}AextLWE}_{q,n,n,\sigma_c,B}$ (for $B = (k+1)y\sigma$), calling $\mathcal{A}$ once, such that $\mathsf{Adv}^{\mathsf{dist}}_{G_2,G_3}(\mathcal{A}) \leq n \cdot \mathsf{Adv}^{\mathsf{HNF\text{-}AextLWE}}(\mathcal{B})$.*

Proof. This proof constructs an algorithm $\mathcal{B}$ for the multiple-secret variant of the HNF-AextLWE assumption with n secrets, using a distinguisher $\mathcal{A}$ for games G_2 and G_3.

Algorithm $\mathcal{B}$ receives a matrix $\mathbf{A} \in \mathbb{Z}_q^{n\times n}$ from the HNF-AextLWE challenger. Then it samples $\mathbf{s}, \mathbf{e} \hookleftarrow \mathcal{D}_{\mathbb{Z}^n,\sigma}$ and sets $pk_0 = (\mathbf{A}, \mathbf{b}_0 = \mathbf{A}\mathbf{s} + \mathbf{e})$, forwards pk_0 to $\mathcal{A}$ and acts as $\mathcal{A}$'s challenger until the last update phase where it has to send up^* and sk^* to $\mathcal{A}$. At this stage, algorithm $\mathcal{B}$ knows the sum of all the updates $\Delta^{\mathbf{r}}_{last}$ and the sum of all the noises used for each updates Δ^{η}_{last} as $\mathcal{A}$ has finished querying the $\mathcal{O}_{up}$ oracle.

The HNF-AextLWE challenger expects small vectors $\mathbf{z}_0, \mathbf{z}_1$ for which to send a hint $\mathbf{h}$. Let $\mathbf{X}_{last} \hookleftarrow \mathcal{D}_{\mathbb{Z}^{n\times n},\sigma_c}$ be the secret matrix and $\mathbf{E}_{last} \hookleftarrow \mathcal{D}_{\mathbb{Z}^{n\times n},\sigma_c}$ be the error matrix sampled by the challenger in the multiple-secret variant of HNF-AextLWE. Algorithm $\mathcal{B}$ sets $\mathbf{z}_0 = \mathbf{e} + \Delta^{\eta}_{last}$ and $\mathbf{z}_1 = -(\mathbf{s} + \Delta^{\mathbf{r}}_{last})$.

It then receives from the challenger a matrix $\mathbf{B} \in \mathbb{Z}_q^{n\times n}$ and a hint

$$\mathbf{h} = \mathbf{X}_{last}\mathbf{z}_0 + \mathbf{E}_{last}\mathbf{z}_1 = (\mathbf{X}_{last} \| \mathbf{E}_{last})\mathbf{z} + \mathbf{f}_{last} ,$$

where $\mathbf{z} = \left(\mathbf{z}_0^T \| \mathbf{z}_1^T\right)^T$ and $\mathbf{f}_{last} \hookleftarrow \mathcal{D}_{\mathbb{Z}^n,\sigma_c}$. The matrix $\mathbf{B}$ is either uniform or of the form $\mathbf{X}_{last}\mathbf{A} + \mathbf{E}_{last}$.

Adversary $\mathcal{B}$ sets

$$\begin{aligned} up^* &= (\mathbf{T}_{last} = \mathbf{B} - \lfloor q/p \rfloor \cdot \mathbf{Id},\ \mathbf{T}_{last}(\mathbf{s} + \Delta^{\mathbf{r}}_{last}) + \mathbf{h} + \lfloor q/p \rfloor \Delta^{\mathbf{r}}_{last}) \\ &= \Big(\mathbf{T}_{last},\ \mathbf{T}_{last}(\mathbf{s} + \Delta^{\mathbf{r}}_{last}) + \mathbf{X}_{last}(\mathbf{e} + \Delta^{\eta}_{last}) - \mathbf{E}_{last}(\mathbf{s} + \Delta^{\mathbf{r}}_{last}) \\ &\quad + \mathbf{f}_{last} + \lfloor q/p \rfloor \Delta^{\mathbf{r}}_{last}\Big). \end{aligned}$$

It also sets $pk^* = (\mathbf{A}, \mathbf{b}_0 + \mathbf{A}(\Delta^{\mathbf{r}}_{last} + \mathbf{r}^*) + \Delta^{\eta}_{last} + \boldsymbol{\eta}^*)$ and $sk^* = \mathbf{s} + \Delta^{\mathbf{r}}_{last} + \mathbf{r}^*$, where $\mathbf{r}^*, \boldsymbol{\eta}^* \hookleftarrow \mathcal{D}_{\mathbb{Z}^n,\sigma}$.

The case where $\mathbf{B}$ is uniform corresponds to adversary $\mathcal{A}$ playing game G_3 and the case where $\mathbf{B} = \mathbf{X}_{last}\mathbf{A} + \mathbf{E}_{last}$ corresponds to $\mathcal{A}$ playing game G_2. Hence $\mathcal{B}$ has the same advantage as $\mathcal{A}$.

By a hybrid argument, there exists an adversary $\mathcal{B}'$ for $\mathsf{HNF\text{-}AextLWE}_{q,n,n,\sigma,B}$ such that the advantage of $\mathcal{B}$ in the multiple-secret variant of HNF-AextLWE with n secrets can be bounded by $n \cdot \mathsf{Adv}^{\mathsf{HNF\text{-}AextLWE}}(\mathcal{B}')$, completing the proof. □

Lemma 7. *For any adversary $\mathcal{A}$ that distinguishes between games G_4 and G_5, there exists an adversary $\mathcal{B}$ for $\mathsf{LWE}_{q,n,2n,\sigma/2}$ calling $\mathcal{A}$ once, such that:*

$$\mathsf{Adv}^{\mathsf{dist}}_{G_4,G_5}(\mathcal{A}) \leq \mathsf{Adv}^{\mathsf{LWE}}(\mathcal{B}) + \frac{6\varepsilon}{1-\varepsilon}.$$

Proof. Let us build an adversary $\mathcal{B}$ for $\mathsf{LWE}_{q,n,2n,\sigma/2}$ that uses any distinguisher $\mathcal{A}$ between games G_4 and G_5.

Adversary $\mathcal{B}$ receives a uniform $\mathbf{B} \in \mathbb{Z}_q^{2n\times n}$ and a vector $\mathbf{c} \in \mathbb{Z}_q^{2n}$ from the LWE challenger. The vector $\mathbf{c}$ is either uniform or computed as an LWE sample with secret $\mathbf{s} \hookleftarrow \mathcal{D}_{\mathbb{Z}^n,\sigma/2}$. Now adversary $\mathcal{B}$ samples $\mathbf{E}_{last}, \mathbf{X}_{last} \hookleftarrow \mathcal{D}_{\mathbb{Z}^{n\times n},\sigma_c}$. It then computes

$$\mathbf{B}' = \mathbf{M}\mathbf{B} + \begin{pmatrix} \mathbf{0} \\ \mathbf{E}_{last} \end{pmatrix}, \quad \text{with} \quad \mathbf{M} = \begin{pmatrix} \mathbf{Id} & \mathbf{0} \\ \mathbf{X}_{last} & \mathbf{Id} \end{pmatrix} \in \mathbb{Z}_q^{2n\times 2n}$$

and parses $\mathbf{B}'$ as $\left(\mathbf{A}^T \| \mathbf{T}_{last}^T\right)^T$. Let $\mathbf{t}, \tilde{\mathbf{e}} \hookleftarrow \mathcal{S} = \mathcal{D}_{\mathbb{Z}^n,\sigma\sqrt{2}}$. After that, it samples elements $\mathbf{s}' \hookleftarrow \mathcal{D}_{\mathbb{Z}^n,\sigma/2,\mathbf{t}/2}$, $\boldsymbol{\eta} \hookleftarrow \mathcal{D}_{\mathbb{Z}^n,\sigma/2,\tilde{\mathbf{e}}/2}$ and $\mathbf{f}' \hookleftarrow \mathcal{D}_{\mathbb{Z}^n,(\sigma_c^2-\sigma^2/4)\mathbf{Id}}$ that are used to adjust the standard deviations of the discrete Gaussian distributions involved in the proof. Then it sets $\mathbf{e}' = \left(\boldsymbol{\eta}^T \| \mathbf{f}'^T\right)^T$ and $\mathbf{c}' = \mathbf{M}(\mathbf{c} + \mathbf{e}') + \mathbf{M}\mathbf{B}\mathbf{s}'$ and parses $\mathbf{c}'$ as $\left(\mathbf{b}_0^T \| \mathbf{u}_1^T\right)^T$.

From there, adversary $\mathcal{B}$ runs as $\mathcal{A}$'s challenger and sets $pk_0 = (\mathbf{A}, \mathbf{b}_0)$. At epoch *last*, it computes

$$up^* = (\mathbf{T}_{last}, \mathbf{u}_1 + (\mathbf{T}_{last} - \mathbf{E}_{last} + \lfloor q/p \rfloor \cdot \mathbf{Id})\Delta^{\mathbf{r}}_{last}) + \mathbf{X}_{last}\Delta^{\eta}_{last}.$$

If $\mathcal{A}$ returns G_4 then $\mathcal{B}$ guesses that $\mathbf{c}$ is an LWE sample and if $\mathcal{A}$ returns G_5 it guesses that it is uniform.

If $\mathbf{c}$ is uniform, as $\mathbf{M}$ is invertible, $\mathbf{B}'$ and $\mathbf{c}'$ are also uniformly distributed and adversary $\mathcal{A}$ is playing game G_5.

If $\mathbf{c} = \mathbf{B}\mathbf{s} + (\mathbf{e}^T \| \mathbf{f}^T)^T$, for $\mathbf{s} \hookleftarrow \mathcal{D}_{\mathbb{Z}^n,\sigma/2}$ and $\mathbf{e}, \mathbf{f} \hookleftarrow \mathcal{D}_{\mathbb{Z}^n,\sigma/2}$, then

$$\begin{aligned}\mathbf{c}' &= \mathbf{M}\left(\mathbf{B}\mathbf{s} + \begin{pmatrix}\mathbf{e}+\boldsymbol{\eta}\\ \mathbf{f}+\mathbf{f}'\end{pmatrix}\right) + \mathbf{M}\mathbf{B}\mathbf{s}' \\ &= \begin{pmatrix}\mathbf{A}\\ \mathbf{T}_{last} - \mathbf{E}_{last}\end{pmatrix}(\mathbf{s}+\mathbf{s}') + \begin{pmatrix}\mathbf{e}+\boldsymbol{\eta}\\ \mathbf{X}_{last}(\mathbf{e}+\boldsymbol{\eta}) + \mathbf{f} + \mathbf{f}'\end{pmatrix} = \begin{pmatrix}\mathbf{b}_0\\ \mathbf{u}_1\end{pmatrix}.\end{aligned}$$

Let us set $\bar{\mathbf{s}} = \mathbf{s} + \mathbf{s}'$, $\bar{\mathbf{e}} = \mathbf{e} + \boldsymbol{\eta}$, $\bar{\mathbf{f}} = \mathbf{f} + \mathbf{f}'$. Then, using the equation above, we have the following:

$$\begin{aligned}up^* &= (\mathbf{T}_{last}, \mathbf{u}_1 + (\mathbf{T}_{last} - \mathbf{E}_{last} + \lfloor q/p \rfloor \cdot \mathbf{Id})\Delta^{\mathbf{r}}_{last} + \mathbf{X}_{last}\Delta^{\eta}_{last}) \\ &= (\mathbf{T}_{last}, (\mathbf{T}_{last} - \mathbf{E}_{last})\bar{\mathbf{s}} + \mathbf{X}_{last}(\bar{\mathbf{e}} + \Delta^{\eta}_{last}) + \bar{\mathbf{f}} \\ &\quad + (\mathbf{T}_{last} - \mathbf{E}_{last} + \lfloor q/p \rfloor \cdot \mathbf{Id})\Delta^{\mathbf{r}}_{last}) \\ &= (\mathbf{T}_{last}, (\mathbf{T}_{last} - \mathbf{E}_{last})(\bar{\mathbf{s}} + \Delta^{\mathbf{r}}_{last}) + \mathbf{X}_{last}(\bar{\mathbf{e}} + \Delta^{\eta}_{last}) + \bar{\mathbf{f}} + \lfloor q/p \rfloor \cdot \Delta^{\mathbf{r}}_{last}).\end{aligned} \tag{4}$$

Let $\delta = 2\varepsilon/(1-\varepsilon)$, for $\varepsilon \in (0,1)$. As $\mathbf{s} \hookleftarrow \mathcal{D}_{\mathbb{Z}^n,\sigma/2}$ and $\mathbf{s}' \hookleftarrow \mathcal{D}_{\mathbb{Z}^n,\sigma/2,\mathbf{t}/2}$, Lemma 2 gives that the distribution of $\bar{\mathbf{s}}$ has statistical distance at most δ from $\mathcal{D}_{\mathbb{Z}^n,\sigma/\sqrt{2},\mathbf{t}/2}$. Similarly, errors $\boldsymbol{\eta}$ and $\mathbf{f}'$ were chosen such that $\bar{\mathbf{e}}$ and $\bar{\mathbf{f}}$ are within statistical distance at most δ from $\mathcal{D}_{\mathbb{Z}^n,\sigma/\sqrt{2},\bar{\mathbf{e}}}$ and $\mathcal{D}_{\mathbb{Z}^n,\sigma_c}$. The equation above shows that up^* is statistically close (at distance at most 3δ) from its value in game G_4, thus $\mathcal{A}$ can be viewed as playing game G_4.

Overall, algorithm $\mathcal{B}$ has advantage at least $\mathsf{Adv}^{\mathsf{dist}}_{G_4,G_5}(\mathcal{A}) - 3\delta$, completing the proof. □

5 A UPKE Fujisaki-Okamoto Transform

In this section, we describe a transform from an IND-CR-CPA UPKE into an IND-CR-CCA UKEM following the Fujisaki-Okamoto [24] technique.

Definition 14 (FO-transform for UPKEs). *Let* UPKE *be a UPKE, and* G *and* H *be two functions modeled as random oracles. We define the transform* FO(UPKE, G, H) *in Fig. 7.*

```
KeyGen = UPKE.KeyGen.

Encaps(pk):
    m ←$ U(M);
    c ← UPKE.Enc(pk, m; G(pk, m));
    K = H(m, c);
    return (c, K).

Decaps(sk, c):
    m' ← UPKE.Dec(sk, c);
    if c ≠ UPKE.Enc(pk, m'; G(pk, m'))
      then return ⊥;
    return K' = H(m', c).

UpdatePk = UPKE.UpdatePk.

UpdateSk = UPKE.UpdateSk.
```

Fig. 7. Transform FO(UPKE, G, H) for a UPKE using random oracles G, H.

Our FO transform is essentially the $\mathsf{KEM}^{\perp}$ construction from [27]. We add pk to the inputs of the hash function used to determinize the Enc algorithm in order to prevent trivial attacks, given the ability of the adversary to update the key pair.

Theorem 3 (FO Transform for UPKEs). *Let $\gamma, \delta \in (0,1), k > 0$. Let $\mathsf{UPKE} = (\mathsf{Enc}, \mathsf{Dec}, \mathsf{UpdatePk}, \mathsf{UpdateSk})$ denote a γ-spread and (k, δ)-correct k-IND-CR-CPA UPKE scheme. Then the UPKE $\mathsf{FO}(\mathsf{UPKE}, \mathsf{G}, \mathsf{H})$ is a (k, δ)-correct k-IND-CR-CCA UKEM in the ROM.*

More precisely, for any adversary $\mathcal{A}$ for the k-IND-CR-CCA UKEM game in the ROM making at most q_{G} queries to oracle G, q_{H} queries to oracle H and q_{D} queries to oracle $\mathcal{O}_{dec}$, there exists an adversary $\mathcal{B}$ for the k-IND-CR-CPA game of UPKE with a similar running time such that:

$$\mathsf{Adv}^{\mathsf{IND\text{-}CR\text{-}CCA}}(\mathcal{A}) \leq q_{\mathsf{G}} \cdot \delta + q_{\mathsf{D}} \cdot \gamma + 2\left(\mathsf{Adv}^{\mathsf{IND\text{-}CR\text{-}CPA}}(\mathcal{B}) + \frac{q_{\mathsf{G}} + q_{\mathsf{H}}}{|\mathcal{M}|}\right).$$

The proof of the above theorem follows standard techniques for FO analysis (e.g., [27]), and is detailed in the full version of this paper.

Note that we rely on the γ-spreadness of the underlying UPKE scheme. We prove this property for the scheme from Sect. 4 in the full version of this paper.

6 Obtaining IND-CU-CCA Security

In this section, we further boost security in order to achieve IND-CU-CCA-security. As in [1], we use a NIZK argument that two keys encrypt the same message in order to make a reduction from IND-CU-CCA to IND-CR-CCA. This technique allows to extract the randomness used by the adversary for the oracle queries to $\mathcal{O}_{up}(\cdot)$, to forward it to the update oracle of the IND-CR-CCA challenger. We give the definitions about Non Interactive Zero Knowledge (NIZK) argument in the ROM in the full version of the paper.

Let $\mathsf{UPKE} = (\mathsf{KeyGen}, \mathsf{Enc}, \mathsf{Dec}, \mathsf{UpdatePk}, \mathsf{UpdateSk})$ be a k-IND-CR-CPA UPKE, for some $k > 0$. Define $\mathsf{UKEM} = (\mathsf{KeyGen}, \mathsf{Encaps}, \mathsf{Decaps}, \mathsf{UpdatePk}, \mathsf{UpdateSk})$ as the k-IND-CR-CCA UKEM scheme obtained by applying our FO transform from Sect. 5 to UPKE, using G, H modeled as random oracles. Let F be a third function, also modeled as a random oracle. We assume that UpdatePk proceeds in two parts (this is the case for all known constructions, including the one from Sect. 4): $\mathsf{UpdatePk}(pk) = (\mathsf{Enc}(pk, r), \mathsf{NewPk}(pk, r))$, i.e., a first part which encrypts the randomness of the update using the UKEM encryption algorithm, and a second one which returns the updated public key. Let us define the language

$$\begin{aligned}\mathcal{L}_{up}^{\mathsf{UKEM}} &= \{(pk_0, pk_1, pk', \mathsf{ct}_0, \mathsf{ct}_1) \mid \exists r_0, r_1, r, \\ &\mathsf{ct}_0 = \mathsf{Enc}(pk_0, r; r_0) \wedge \mathsf{ct}_1 = \mathsf{Enc}(pk_1, r; r_1) \wedge (pk', ct_0) = \mathsf{UpdatePk}(pk_0; r)\}.\end{aligned}$$

$\overline{\text{KeyGen}}(1^\lambda)$:
  $(pk_0, sk_0) \leftarrow \text{KeyGen}(1^\lambda)$;
  $(pk_1, sk_1) \leftarrow \text{KeyGen}(1^\lambda)$;
  return $\overline{pk} = (pk_0, pk_1)$, $\overline{sk} = sk_0$.

$\overline{\text{Encaps}}(\overline{pk})$:
  parse $\overline{pk}$ as (pk_0, pk_1);
  $(c, K) \leftarrow \text{Encaps}(pk_0)$;
  return (c, K).

$\overline{\text{Decaps}}(\overline{sk}, c) = \text{Decaps}(\overline{sk}, c)$.

$\overline{\text{UpdatePk}}(\overline{pk})$:
  parse $\overline{pk}$ as (pk_0, pk_1);
  sample $r \hookleftarrow R$;
  $pk_0' \leftarrow \text{NewPk}(pk_0, r)$;
  $\text{ct}_0 \leftarrow \text{Enc}(pk_0, r)$;
  $\text{ct}_1 \leftarrow \text{Enc}(pk_1, r)$;
  $\pi \leftarrow \text{Prove}^{\text{F}}(pk_0, pk_1, pk_0', \text{ct}_0, \text{ct}_1, r)$;
  return $\overline{up} = (\text{ct}_0, \text{ct}_1, \pi)$, $\overline{pk}' = (pk_0', pk_1)$.

$\overline{\text{VerifyUpdate}}(\overline{up}, \overline{pk}')$:
  parse $\overline{up}$ as $(\text{ct}_0, \text{ct}_1, \pi)$ and $\overline{pk}'$ as (pk_0', pk_1);
  return $\text{Verify}^{\text{F}}((pk_0, pk_1, pk_0', \text{ct}_0, \text{ct}_1), \pi)$;

$\overline{\text{UpdateSk}}(\overline{up}, \overline{pk}')$:
  if $\text{VerifyUpdate}(\overline{up}, \overline{pk}') = 0$ **then**
    return $\perp$;
  end
  parse $\overline{up}$ as $(\text{ct}_0, \text{ct}_1, \pi)$;
  run $\text{UpdateSk}(\overline{sk}, \text{ct}_0)$.

Fig. 8. Construction of a IND-CU-CCA UKEM.

Let $\Pi = (\text{Prove}^{\text{F}}, \text{Verify}^{\text{F}})$ a NIZK argument in the random oracle for $\mathcal{L}_{up}^{\text{UKEM}}$. We construct an k-IND-CU-CCA UKEM as described in Fig. 8.

Theorem 4. *Let* UPKE, UKEM, Π *be defined as above. Then, the construction* $\overline{\text{UKEM}}$ *described in Fig. 8 is an* k-IND-CU-CCA *UKEM. Specifically, for any adversary* $\mathcal{A}$ *against the* k-IND-CU-CCA *security of* $\overline{\text{UKEM}}$, *there exist adversaries* $\mathcal{B}, \mathcal{C}, \mathcal{D}, \mathcal{E}$ *with running times similar to* $\mathcal{A}$*'s such that:*

$$\text{Adv}^{\text{IND-CU-CCA}}(\mathcal{A}) \leq \text{Adv}_{\text{UKEM}}^{\text{IND-CR-CCA}}(\mathcal{B}) + \text{Adv}_{\text{UPKE}}^{\text{IND-CR-CPA}}(\mathcal{C}) + \text{Adv}_{\Pi}^{\text{zk}}(\mathcal{D}) + \text{Adv}_{\Pi}^{\text{sound}}(\mathcal{E}) \ .$$

The proof closely follows the one of IND-CU-CCA security of the construction from [1] and is detailed in the full version of the paper.

7 Concrete Parameters

In this section, we give some concrete parameters for the scheme presented in Sect. 4, which can directly be transformed into an IND-CR-CCA UKEM by applying the FO transform from Sect. 5. We focus on the latter. We conjecture that security holds in the module setting and use the lattice-estimator SAGE module (commit fd4a460) from [3] to estimate the security of the given parameter sets. For our UPKE/UKEM, we consider the module variant of the scheme presented in Sect. 4, i.e., we define $\mathcal{R} = \mathbb{Z}[X]/(X^d + 1)$ and $\mathcal{R}_q = \mathcal{R}/q\mathcal{R}$ and we consider the base ring to be $\mathcal{R}$ instead of $\mathbb{Z}$.

Note that, for $p > 0$ a prime, the message space of Enc for the module variant is $\mathcal{M} = \mathcal{R}_p^n$ which is of size p^{dn}. For optimization purposes, we drop the last $n-1$ rows of the whole ciphertext computed by Enc in our encapsulation mechanism, so that an encapsulation is just:

$$c = (\mathbf{x}^T\mathbf{A} + \mathbf{e}^T, \mathbf{x}\mathbf{b} + f + \lfloor q/p \rfloor m)$$

for $\mathbf{x}, \mathbf{e} \in \mathcal{R}_q^n$, $f \in \mathcal{R}_q$ and $m \in \mathcal{R}_p$. The message space is now $\mathcal{M} = \mathcal{R}_p$, of size p^d. This optimization is made possible by considering the UKEM, which only require a message space with at least λ bits of entropy, which is the case when setting $d = 256$. The whole message space $\mathcal{R}_p^n$ is only used to encrypt updates, as an update changes all components of the secret key.

Also, as done in [11], we replace Gaussian distributions by the centered binomial distributions B_η, which for $\eta > 0$, samples elements $(a_i, b_i)_{i \le \eta} \hookleftarrow \mathcal{U}(\{0,1\}^2)$ and returns $\sum_{i=1}^{\eta}(a_i - b_i)$. Samples from B_η are contained in $[-\eta, \eta]$, and we choose the modulus q such that perfect correctness ($\delta = 0$) is guaranteed up to a bounded number of (possibly malicious) updates. We let k denote this bound, and provide parameters for $k \in \{2^5, 2^{10}, 2^{15}, 2^{20}\}$. We are assuming worst-case updates and then make q scale linearly with k. It could be tempting to make it scale with $\sqrt{k}$ as updates are symmetric and centered in 0 though we should not, as they are chosen by the attacker. Due to this requirement, our UPKE/UKEM suffers from a loss compared to Kyber, which can take q as small as 3329 and then have ciphertexts of size 0.8 KB.

As we are working in the UPKE setting, we consider that the adversary gets a leakage $\mathbf{s}+\mathbf{r}$ on the initial secret key $\mathbf{s}$, which roughly halves the variance of the distribution of $\mathbf{s}$ in the adversary's view (as shown in the proof of Theorem 2). We use a script to compute the average variance left on $\mathbf{s}$ conditioned on the value of $\mathbf{s} + \mathbf{r}$. We obtain that for $\mathbf{s} \hookleftarrow B_{2\eta}^n$, we are left on average as if $\mathbf{s}$ was sampled from B_η^n. This is taken into account for the security estimates.

Our parameters are given in Table 2. Note that as done in Kyber, in order to have fast multiplication using the Number Theoretic Transform in the ring, we take modulus $q = 1 \bmod 2d$. This is the first practical lattice-based construction of UPKE/UKEM, hence there are no equivalent constructions to compare our results to. We achieve similar efficiency as the IND-CR-CPA construction of [1], which is based on the DCR assumption achieves a ciphertext and update size of 1.5 KB (for the CPA case only, although our FO transform applies to their scheme). Note that by increasing d, the matrices involved become smaller. Hence, a tradeoff can be made to reduce the sizes of the updates at the cost of increasing ciphertext size. For small number of updates, we also apply the bit-dropping technique from Kyber to improve parameters. This optimization drops parts of the least significant bits of the ciphertexts to reduce their size. We use the script provided at https://github.com/pq-crystals/security-estimates to estimate the correctness loss implied by using this technique.

Table 2. Parameter sets for the module variant of our IND-CR-CCA UKEM.

	λ	q	n	d	p	η	δ	k	$\lvert ct\rvert$	$\lvert up\rvert$
DCR-based construction [1]	128	-	-	-	-	-	0	∞	8.3 KB	1.5 KB
Estimate for [22]	120	$\approx 2^{85}$	11	256	21	10	0	2^5	33 KB	360 KB
This work	128	$\approx 2^{21}$	3	256	5	2	2^{-136}	2^5	1.8 KB	5.4 KB
	128	$\approx 2^{26}$	4	256	5	2	0	2^{10}	3.0 KB	12 KB
	116	$\approx 2^{31}$	2	512	5	2	0	2^{15}	5.8 KB	12 KB
	128	$\approx 2^{36}$	3	512	5	2	0	2^{20}	9.1 KB	27 KB

IND-CU-CCA Instantiation. In order to add security against chosen updates via our transform from Sect. 6, we can further add a computationally sound NIZK argument for $\mathcal{L}_{up}^{\mathsf{UKEM}}$ in the updates. In the module setting, the language $\mathcal{L}_{up}^{\mathsf{UKEM}}$ can be defined as:

$$\begin{aligned}\mathcal{L}_{up}^{\mathsf{UKEM}} &= \{(pk_0, pk_1, pk', \mathsf{ct}_0, \mathsf{ct}_1) \mid \exists \mathbf{X}_0, \mathbf{X}_1, \mathbf{E}_0, \mathbf{E}_1 \in \mathcal{R}^{n\times n}, \mathbf{f}_0, \mathbf{f}_1, \mathbf{r} \in \mathcal{R}^n \\ \mathsf{ct}_0 &= (\mathbf{X}_0\mathbf{A} + \mathbf{E}_0, \mathbf{X}_0\mathbf{b} + \mathbf{f}_0 + \lfloor q/p \rfloor \cdot \mathbf{r}) \bmod q \ \wedge \|\mathbf{X}_0\|_2, \|\mathbf{E}_0\|_2, \|\mathbf{f}_0\|_2 < B_0 \\ \wedge\ \mathsf{ct}_1 &= (\mathbf{X}_1\tilde{\mathbf{A}} + \mathbf{E}_1, \mathbf{X}_1\tilde{\mathbf{b}} + \mathbf{f}_1 + \lfloor q/p \rfloor \cdot \mathbf{r}) \bmod q \ \wedge \|\mathbf{X}_1\|_2, \|\mathbf{E}_1\|_2, \|\mathbf{f}_1\|_2 < B_0 \\ \wedge\ &\|\mathbf{b}' - (\mathbf{b} + \mathbf{A}\mathbf{r})\|_2 \le B_1 \wedge \|\mathbf{r}\|_2 < B_1 \}.\end{aligned}$$

where $pk_0 = (\mathbf{A}, \mathbf{b})$, $pk_1 = (\tilde{\mathbf{A}}, \tilde{\mathbf{b}})$, $pk' = (\mathbf{A}, \mathbf{b}')$ and B_0, B_1 are bounds for correctness.

Proving membership in $\mathcal{L}_{up}^{\mathsf{UKEM}}$ then corresponds to proving 4 norm bounds for matrices, 4 norm bounds for vectors and $2n^2 + 2n$ linear equations over $\mathcal{R}_q$. This can be achieved by applying [33], which allows to prove exact norm bounds and linear relations using a commit-and-prove protocol. This only affects the size of the updates, since the ciphertext remains the same as in the IND-CR-CCA setting.

Acknowledgments. We thank Michael Rosenberg for pointing out a flaw in a prior version of this work. The first author is funded by the Direction Générale de l'Armement (Pôle de Recherche CYBER). This work was supported by the France 2030 ANR Project ANR-22-PECY-003 SecureCompute and the France 2030 ANR Project ANR-22-PETQ-0008 PQ-TLS.

References

1. Abou Haidar, C., Libert, B., Passelègue, A.: Updatable public key encryption from DCR: efficient constructions with stronger security. In: CCS (2022)
2. Agrawal, S., Gentry, C., Halevi, S., Sahai, A.: Sampling discrete gaussians efficiently and obliviously. In: ASIACRYPT (2013)
3. Albrecht, M.R., Player, R., Scott, S.: On the concrete hardness of learning with errors. ePrint 2015/046 (2015)
4. Alwen, J., Coretti, S., Dodis, Y., Tselekounis, Y.: Security analysis and improvements for the IETF MLS standard for group messaging. In: Micciancio, D., Ristenpart, T. (eds.) CRYPTO 2020. LNCS, vol. 12170, pp. 248–277. Springer, Cham (2020). https://doi.org/10.1007/978-3-030-56784-2_9
5. Anderson, R.: Two remarks on public-key cryptology. In: CCS (1997). invited talk
6. Applebaum, B., Cash, D., Peikert, C., Sahai, A.: Fast cryptographic primitives and circular-secure encryption based on hard learning problems. In: Halevi, S. (ed.) CRYPTO 2009. LNCS, vol. 5677, pp. 595–618. Springer, Heidelberg (2009). https://doi.org/10.1007/978-3-642-03356-8_35
7. Asano, K., Watanabe, Y.: Updatable public key encryption with strong CCA security: Security analysis and efficient generic construction. Cryptology ePrint Archive 2023/976 (2023)
8. Barić, N., Pfitzmann, B.: Collision-free accumulators and fail-stop signature schemes without trees. In: Fumy, W. (ed.) EUROCRYPT 1997. LNCS, vol. 1233, pp. 480–494. Springer, Heidelberg (1997). https://doi.org/10.1007/3-540-69053-0_33
9. Bellare, M., Miner, S.K.: A forward-secure digital signature scheme. In: Wiener, M. (ed.) CRYPTO 1999. LNCS, vol. 1666, pp. 431–448. Springer, Heidelberg (1999). https://doi.org/10.1007/3-540-48405-1_28
10. Boneh, D., Freeman, D.M.: Linearly homomorphic signatures over binary fields and new tools for lattice-based signatures. In: Catalano, D., Fazio, N., Gennaro, R., Nicolosi, A. (eds.) PKC 2011. LNCS, vol. 6571, pp. 1–16. Springer, Heidelberg (2011). https://doi.org/10.1007/978-3-642-19379-8_1
11. Bos, J.W., et al.: CRYSTALS - Kyber: a CCA-secure module-lattice-based KEM. In: EuroS&P (2018)
12. Boudgoust, K., Jeudy, C., Roux-Langlois, A., Wen, W.: Entropic hardness of module-LWE from module-NTRU. In: Isobe, T., Sarkar, S. (eds.) INDOCRYPT 2022. LNCS, vol. 13774. Springer, Cham (2022)
13. Boyen, X., Shacham, H., Shen, E., Waters, B.: Forward-secure signatures with untrusted update. In: CCS (2006)
14. Brakerski, Z., Gentry, C., Vaikuntanathan, V.: (Leveled) fully homomorphic encryption without bootstrapping. In: ITCS (2012)
15. Brakerski, Z., Langlois, A., Peikert, C., Regev, O., Stehle, D.: Classical hardness of learning with errors. In: STOC (2013)
16. Camenisch, J., Shoup, V.: Practical verifiable encryption and decryption of discrete logarithms. In: Boneh, D. (ed.) CRYPTO 2003. LNCS, vol. 2729, pp. 126–144. Springer, Heidelberg (2003). https://doi.org/10.1007/978-3-540-45146-4_8
17. Canetti, R., Halevi, S., Katz, J.: A forward-secure public-key encryption scheme. In: Biham, E. (ed.) EUROCRYPT 2003. LNCS, vol. 2656, pp. 255–271. Springer, Heidelberg (2003). https://doi.org/10.1007/3-540-39200-9_16
18. Cheon, J.H., Kim, D., Kim, D., Lee, J., Shin, J., Song, Y.: Lattice-based secure biometric authentication for hamming distance. In: Baek, J., Ruj, S. (eds.) ACISP

2021. LNCS, vol. 13083, pp. 653–672. Springer, Cham (2021). https://doi.org/10.1007/978-3-030-90567-5_33

19. Cronin, E., Jamin, S., Malkin, T., McDaniel, P.: On the performance, feasibility, and use of forward-secure signatures. In: CCS (2003)
20. Dadush, D., Regev, O., Stephens-Davidowitz, N.: On the closest vector problem with a distance guarantee. In: CCC (2014)
21. Dodis, Y., Haralambiev, K., López-Alt, A., Wichs, D.: Efficient public-key cryptography in the presence of key leakage. In: Abe, M. (ed.) ASIACRYPT 2010. LNCS, vol. 6477, pp. 613–631. Springer, Heidelberg (2010). https://doi.org/10.1007/978-3-642-17373-8_35
22. Dodis, Y., Karthikeyan, H., Wichs, D.: Updatable public key encryption in the standard model. In: Nissim, K., Waters, B. (eds.) TCC 2021. LNCS, vol. 13044, pp. 254–285. Springer, Cham (2021). https://doi.org/10.1007/978-3-030-90456-2_9
23. Duman, J., Hövelmanns, K., Kiltz, E., Lyubashevsky, V., Seiler, G.: Faster lattice-based KEMs via a generic Fujisaki-Okamoto transform using prefix hashing. In: CCS (2021)
24. Fujisaki, E., Okamoto, T.: Statistical zero knowledge protocols to prove modular polynomial relations. In: Kaliski, B.S. (ed.) CRYPTO 1997. LNCS, vol. 1294, pp. 16–30. Springer, Heidelberg (1997). https://doi.org/10.1007/BFb0052225
25. Gentry, C., Peikert, C., Vaikunthanathan, V.: Trapdoors for hard lattices and new cryptographic constructions. In: STOC (2008)
26. Gentry, C., Silverberg, A.: Hierarchical ID-based cryptography. In: ASIACRYPT (2002)
27. Hofheinz, D., Hövelmanns, K., Kiltz, E.: A modular analysis of the Fujisaki-Okamoto transformation. In: Kalai, Y., Reyzin, L. (eds.) TCC 2017. LNCS, vol. 10677, pp. 341–371. Springer, Cham (2017). https://doi.org/10.1007/978-3-319-70500-2_12
28. Horwitz, J., Lynn, B.: Toward hierarchical identity-based encryption. In: Knudsen, L.R. (ed.) EUROCRYPT 2002. LNCS, vol. 2332, pp. 466–481. Springer, Heidelberg (2002). https://doi.org/10.1007/3-540-46035-7_31
29. Itkis, G., Reyzin, L.: Forward-secure signatures with optimal signing and verifying. In: Kilian, J. (ed.) CRYPTO 2001. LNCS, vol. 2139, pp. 332–354. Springer, Heidelberg (2001). https://doi.org/10.1007/3-540-44647-8_20
30. Jost, D., Maurer, U., Mularczyk, M.: Efficient ratcheting: almost-optimal guarantees for secure messaging. In: Ishai, Y., Rijmen, V. (eds.) EUROCRYPT 2019. LNCS, vol. 11476, pp. 159–188. Springer, Cham (2019). https://doi.org/10.1007/978-3-030-17653-2_6
31. Kim, D., Lee, D., Seo, J., Song, Y.: Toward practical lattice-based proof of knowledge from Hint-MLWE. In: CRYPTO (2023)
32. Langlois, A., Stehlé, D.: Worst-case to average-case reductions for module lattices. Des. Codes Cryptogr. **75**(3), 565–599 (2014). https://doi.org/10.1007/s10623-014-9938-4
33. Lyubashevsky, V., Nguyen, N.K., Planç on, M.: Lattice-based zero-knowledge proofs and applications: shorter, simpler, and more general. In: Dodis, Y., Shrimpton, T. (eds.) CRYPTO 2022. LNCS, vol. 13508. Springer, Cham (2022). https://doi.org/10.1007/978-3-031-15979-4_3
34. Lyubashevsky, V., Palacio, A., Segev, G.: Public-key cryptographic primitives provably as secure as subset sum. In: Micciancio, D. (ed.) TCC 2010. LNCS, vol. 5978, pp. 382–400. Springer, Heidelberg (2010). https://doi.org/10.1007/978-3-642-11799-2_23

35. Malkin, T., Micciancio, D., Miner, S.: Efficient generic forward-secure signatures with an unbounded number of time periods. In: Knudsen, L.R. (ed.) EUROCRYPT 2002. LNCS, vol. 2332, pp. 400–417. Springer, Heidelberg (2002). https://doi.org/10.1007/3-540-46035-7_27
36. Mera, J.M.B., Karmakar, A., Marc, T., Soleimanian, A.: Efficient lattice-based inner-product functional encryption. In: Hanaoka, G., Shikata, J., Watanabe, Y. (eds.) PKC 2022. LNCS, vol. 13178. Springer, Cham (2022). https://doi.org/10.1007/978-3-030-97131-1_6
37. Micciancio, D., Walter, M.: On the bit security of cryptographic primitives. In: Nielsen, J.B., Rijmen, V. (eds.) EUROCRYPT 2018. LNCS, vol. 10820, pp. 3–28. Springer, Cham (2018). https://doi.org/10.1007/978-3-319-78381-9_1
38. Naor, M., Yung, M.: Public-key cryptosystems provably secure against chosen ciphertext attacks. In: STOC (1990)
39. O'Neill, A., Peikert, C., Waters, B.: Bi-deniable public-key encryption. In: Rogaway, P. (ed.) CRYPTO 2011. LNCS, vol. 6841, pp. 525–542. Springer, Heidelberg (2011). https://doi.org/10.1007/978-3-642-22792-9_30

CCA-1 Secure Updatable Encryption with Adaptive Security

Huanhuan Chen[1], Yao Jiang Galteland[2(✉)], and Kaitai Liang[1]

[1] Delft University of Technology, Delft, The Netherlands
{h.chen-2,kaitai.liang}@tudelft.nl
[2] Qredo, London, UK
yao.jiang@qredo.com

Abstract. Updatable encryption (UE) enables a cloud server to update ciphertexts using client-generated tokens. There are two types of UE: *ciphertext-independent (c-i)* and *ciphertext-dependent (c-d)*. In terms of construction and efficiency, c-i UE utilizes a single token to update all ciphertexts. The update mechanism relies mainly on the homomorphic properties of exponentiation, which limits the efficiency of encryption and updating. Although c-d UE may seem inconvenient as it requires downloading parts of the ciphertexts during token generation, it allows for easy implementation of the Dec-then-Enc structure. This methodology significantly simplifies the construction of the update mechanism. Notably, the c-d UE scheme proposed by Boneh et al. (ASIACRYPT'20) has been reported to be 200 times faster than prior UE schemes based on DDH hardness, which is the case for most existing c-i UE schemes. Furthermore, c-d UE ensures a high level of security as the token does not reveal any information about the key, which is difficult for c-i UE to achieve. However, previous security studies on c-d UE only addressed selective security; the studies for adaptive security remain an open problem.

In this study, we make three significant contributions to ciphertext-dependent updatable encryption (c-d UE). Firstly, we provide stronger security notions compared to previous work, which capture adaptive security and also consider the adversary's decryption capabilities under the adaptive corruption setting. Secondly, we propose a new c-d UE scheme that achieves the proposed security notions. The token generation technique significantly differs from the previous Dec-then-Enc structure, while still preventing key leakages. At last, we introduce a packing technique that enables the simultaneous encryption and updating of multiple messages within a single ciphertext. This technique helps alleviate the cost of c-d UE by reducing the need to download partial ciphertexts during token generation.

Keywords: Updatable Encryption · Adaptive Security · Lattice

J. Guo and R. Steinfeld (Eds.): ASIACRYPT 2023, LNCS 14442, pp. 374–406, 2023.
https://doi.org/10.1007/978-981-99-8733-7_12

1 Introduction

Regularly changing encryption keys is widely recognized as an effective approach to mitigate the risk of key compromise, especially when outsourcing encrypted data to a semi-honest cloud server. Updatable encryption (UE), introduced by Boneh et al. [5], offers a practical solution to this challenge. In UE schemes, in addition to the usual $\mathsf{KG}, \mathsf{Enc}, \mathsf{Dec}$ algorithms, two core algorithms, $\mathsf{TokenGen}$ and Update, are employed. Essentially, $\mathsf{TokenGen}$ takes the old and new encryption keys, along with *possibly* a small fraction of the ciphertext, and generates an update token on the client side. This token is then sent to the cloud server, which utilizes the Update algorithm to convert ciphertexts from the old keys to the new keys.

c-d/c-i UE. Depending on if a part of ciphertext (called ciphertext header) is needed in the token generation algorithm $\mathsf{TokenGen}$, UE schemes have two variants: *ciphertext-independent* (c-i) UE [6,15,17,18,20,23] and *ciphertext-dependent* (c-d) UE [4,5,10,11]. In the former, tokens are independent of ciphertexts, and a single update token is used to update all old ciphertexts. In the latter, update tokens depend on the specific ciphertext to be updated and a tiny part of the ciphertexts is downloaded by the client when generating the update tokens.

In this paper, we specifically focus on ciphertext-dependent UE (c-d UE) due to its notable advantages in terms of efficiency and security. First of all, c-d UE schemes have been reported to be more efficient than ciphertext-independent (c-i) constructions. For instance, the nested c-d UE construction presented in [4], which relies solely on symmetric cryptographic primitives, approaches the performance of AES. In contrast, c-i UE schemes imply the use of public key encryption, as proven by Alamati et al. [3], and most c-i constructions require costly exponentiation operations to update ciphertexts. With regard to UE security, Jiang [15] demonstrated that there are no c-i UE schemes stronger than those with no-directional key updates, as defined in Sect. 3. However, constructing such schemes remains an open problem, primarily due to the requirement that update tokens should not reveal any information about either the old key or the new key. Consequently, only two c-i UE schemes with no-directional key updates have been proposed thus far. One is presented by Slamanig [23], which is based on the SXDH assumption, thus necessitating expensive exponential operations. The other is introduced by Nishimaki [20], relying on the existence of indistinguishability obfuscation, but remains purely theoretical. On the other hand, for c-d UE, the construction of no-directional key update schemes is considerably easier and practical. In fact, the token generation algorithm in all existing c-d UE constructions [4,5,10,11] benefits from a "Dec-then-Enc" process. This involves decrypting the ciphertext header using the old key to recover the secret information, and then computing the token by encrypting the secret information using the new key. As a result, the old key remains independent of the token, while the new key is safeguarded by the underlying encryption scheme. The update token does not divulge any information about the old and new keys.

Security Notions (c-d UE). The primary security objective of UE is to ensure the confidentiality of ciphertexts even when the keys are exposed. Extensive research on this topic has been conducted in [4,10,11]. Previous security models provide guarantees that adversaries cannot differentiate between a freshly generated ciphertext in the current epoch and an updated ciphertext rotated to the current epoch. In practical scenarios, this property safeguards the confidentiality of the *age* of ciphertext, i.e., the number of times it has been updated, from being leaked to an adversary. For instance, consider a situation where a client stores its encrypted medical records with a cloud provider. The existing security notions ensure that the adversary observing the records cannot determine which records are new and which ones are old, thereby preserving the sort of privacy.

Limitation. Unfortunately, prior work on c-d UE has the following limitations:

1. The current security notions for c-d UE solely capture selective security, where the adversary is provided with certain keys at the beginning of the security experiment. It is needed to introduce a stronger notion of adaptive security, which guarantees security in the model where the adversary can corrupt keys throughout the experiment.
2. Prior notions for c-d UE only apply to randomized ciphertext updates (see Sect. 2.1 for details), whereas the ciphertext update procedure can be also deterministic[1], which can be seen in our construction in Sect. 5.1. It is still an open problem how could we capture confidentiality for both types of ciphertext updates.
3. The current security notions for c-d UE are complex, requiring multiple simulations of oracles that the adversary has access to in the security analysis. A simpler and more compact notion can help one simplify the proof.

1.1 Related Work

Constructions of UE. Since the introduction of updatable encryption by Boneh et al. [5], various constructions have been proposed. All c-d UE schemes in [4,5,10,11] benefit from a *Dec-then-Enc* structure in token generation, whether they are treated in a symmetric manner to deploy double encryption or rely on *key-homomorphic PRFs*. As a consequence, tokens only contain the ciphertext under the new key, avoiding the issue of leaking neither old nor new key.

By comparison, all c-i UE schemes in [6,17,18] are based on the DDH or SXDH assumption and rely on the homomorphic properties of exponentiation to rotate ciphertexts. Tokens are the division of the new key and the old key; therefore, one of the two successive keys key can be inferred if the other is leaked. Such a leakage limitation is also applied to the scheme proposed by Jiang [15],

[1] Note this case does not require the server to generate randomness for ciphertext updates, which is required in the former case.

because tokens are the subtraction of new and old keys, even though this scheme avoids the expensive exponentiation but is instead lattice-based.

Two promising c-i UE schemes have been proposed to overcome this leakage limitation. Nishimaki [20] presented a construction that utilizes *indistinguishability obfuscation (IO)* for an update circuit, which operates as a Dec-then-Enc process taking a ciphertext as input. This scheme relies on an assumption that there exists a practical IO. Slamanig and Striecks [23] gave a pairing-based scheme and defined an *expiry* model: each ciphertext is associated with an expiry epoch, after

	Schemes	Dir. Key	s/a	Prob.	Enc.	Token Gen.	Update
c-i UE	*SHINE [6]	bi	a	DDH	1 exp.	1 division	1 exp.
	LWEUE [15]	bi	a	LWE	(n, m, l)	1 subtract.	(n, m, l)
	UNIUE [13]	bk.	a	LWE	$(n, m, l) \times l_e$	l_e subtract.	$(n, m, l) \times l_e$
	Nishimaki [20]	bk.	a	LWE	$(1, m, l)$	$(nk, m, n + l)$	$(1, m, n + l)$
	Nishimaki [20]	no	a	IO, OWF	–	–	–
	SS [23]	no	a	SXDH	–	–	–
c-d UE	KSS [11]	no	s	Symmetry	1 AE.Enc	1 AE.Enc	1 vect. addition
	ReCrypt [11]	no	s	KH-PRF	1 KH-PRF	1 KH-PRF	1 KH-PRF
	ReCrypt$^+$ [10]	no	s	HomHash	1 HomHash	1 HomHash	1 HomHash
	Nested [4]	no	s	Symmetry	1 AE.Enc	1 AE.Enc	1 AE.Enc
	BEKS [4]	no	s	KH-PRF	1 KH-PRF	1 AE.Enc	1 KH-PRF
	TDUE (5.1)	no	a	LWE	$(1, n, \bar{m} + 2l)$	$\bar{m} + 2l$ sampling	$(1, \bar{m} + 2l, \bar{m} + 2l)$
	Packing UE (5.4)	no	a	LWE	$(1, n, \bar{m} + l + Nl)$	$\bar{m} + l + Nl$ sampling	$(1, \bar{m} + l + Nl, \bar{m} + l + Nl)$

Fig. 1. A comparison of c-i UE which can avoid the leakage of "ciphertext age" and all existing c-d UE. The second column set states the direction of key updates, achieved security, and the underlying assumptions, where bk. stands for the backward directional key updates, s and a represent the selective and adaptive security, respectively, and KH-PRF, IO, OWF, HomHash represent key-homomorphic PRF, indistinguishability obfuscation, one-way function, and homomorphic hash function respectively. The third column set shows the computational efficiency in terms of the most expensive cost of encryption, token generation, and update for one-block ciphertext ([20,23] are omitted here as the first is theoretical and the second is built on a different expiry model). For lattice-based schemes, (a, b, c) denotes the major computation cost by the multiplication of two matrices of size $a \times b$ and $b \times c$, and m and n denote the size of the matrix generated on $\mathbb{Z}_q$ in the setup, for which $m = O(nk)$, $k = \lceil q \rceil$, message bit length $l = nk$, $\bar{m} = O(nk)$, and the maximum number of updates l_e. In our UE schemes, tokens are generated with multiple calls to a preimage sampling oracle, and N is a power of 2 that defines the associated cyclotomic ring. AE represents authenticated encryption, [10] instantiates HomHash from DDH groups, and KH-PRFs are constructed from the Ring-LWE problem in [4].

which the updated ciphertext cannot be decrypted anymore. Their scheme consumes expensive group operations and moreover, the key size increases linearly to the maximum number of updates.

In Fig. 1, we provide a comparison of UE schemes in terms of security and efficiency. Our c-d UE constructions offer several advantages compared to c-i UE schemes. Regarding security, we achieve no-directional key updates to protect keys being derived by tokens, in comparison to the difficulty in constructing such c-i UE, as discussed above. In terms of efficiency, we utilize lattice encryption to circumvent expensive group operations that are used in [6,23]. Compared to lattice-based c-i UE Schemes, our works are the first to achieve CCA-1 security, and TDUE exhibits equivalent complexity to that of [20] for both the encryption and update algorithms, an improvement by a factor n over the algorithms in [15][2]. Our packing UE further reduces the encryption and update algorithms' complexity of TDUE by a factor N, leading to more efficient encryption and update compared to [13,15,20]. Nevertheless, it is worth noting that [15] provides the most efficient token generation using a simple vector subtraction. In comparison with c-d UE schemes, our constructions ensure the confidentiality that hides ciphertext age, whereas [10,11] only capture message confidentiality and re-encryption indistinguishability. Note that Boneh et al. [4] demonstrated that, for c-d UE, even the combination of the above two notions cannot prevent the leakage of ciphertext age (see Fig. 3 for more details). Moreover, our schemes are the first c-d UE schemes to achieve adaptive security.

Relative Primitives. Proxy Re-encryption (PRE) and Homomorphic Encryption (HE) are two highly related primitives to updatable encryption.

Proxy Re-encryption (PRE) enables a ciphertext to be decryptable by the new key after re-encryption. Compared to UE, it does not necessarily require the updated ciphertext to be indistinguishable from fresh encryption, thereby not covering the confidentiality requirement inherent in UE. However, PRE schemes have served as a source of inspiration for the construction of UE due to the similar ciphertext update process, for example, the ElGamal-based proxy re-encryption scheme is adapted to RISE [18] and Sakurai et al. [22] to SHINE [6].

The PRE scheme proposed by Kirshanova [16] is based on lattices and only uses the old secret key (serving as the trapdoor) to sample a matrix as the update token to rotate ciphertexts, which are LWE samples. Such a matrix leaks neither the old nor the new keys, since it does not involve any function of old and new keys (recall the key leakage caused the division or subtraction of two keys in the token of c-i UE schemes). However, Fan and Liu [12] pointed out a mistake in the security proof of [16] that the simulated game in the proof is not indistinguishable from the real game. In this work, a new UE scheme that leverages a part of the techniques in [16] is constructed with a detailed reduction proof.

[2] Note that, for lattice-based schemes, the cost is determined by the multiplication of two matrices, which takes $O(nml)$ for matrices of size $n \times m$ and $m \times l$ by a naive multiplication, for example.

Fully Homomorphic Encryption (FHE) develops a key-switching technique [7,8] that takes as input the old ciphertext and the encryption of the old key under the new key (called the key-switching key) and outputs a new ciphertext that is decryptable by the new key. Such a technique has been used in [13,17] to construct UE schemes with so-called backward directional key updates. In our UE construction, the matrix in the token is called a key-switching matrix as it achieves the same functionality as the key-switching key in FHE.

1.2 Our Approaches

We propose new UE schemes that achieve the new confidentiality notion. To achieve this, we first build a new PKE scheme inspired by [19] that utilizes lattice trapdoor techniques as the underlying encryption scheme. For the UE construction, we leverage the "re-encryption key generation" process in [16] to generate a key-switching matrix, which is used to update ciphertexts from the old to the new key. However, the key-switching matrix alone is not sufficient to achieve our confidentiality notion, which will be discussed later in this section. A detailed proof of our construction is presented in Sect. 5.3.

A New PKE Scheme. This scheme is based on lattice trapdoor techniques. The public key is a 1×3 block matrix $\mathbf{A}_\mu = [\mathbf{A}_0 \mid \mathbf{A}_0\mathbf{R} + \mathbf{H}_\mu\mathbf{G} \mid \mathbf{A}_1] \in \mathbb{Z}^{\bar{m}+2nk}$ where $\mathbf{A}_0$ and $\mathbf{A}_1$ are two random matrices, and $\mathbf{H}_\mu$ is an invertible matrix. The secret key is the trapdoor $\mathbf{R}$ for the first two block matrices of $\mathbf{A}_\mu$, which allows for an efficient algorithm for inverting LWE samples related to $\mathbf{A}_\mu$ (see Sect. 4.1 for more details). The ciphertext is a tuple $c = (\mathbf{H}_\mu, \mathbf{b})$ where $\mathbf{b}$ is a LWE sample as follows:

$$\mathbf{b}^t = \mathbf{s}^t\mathbf{A}_\mu + (\mathbf{e}_0, \mathbf{e}_1, \mathbf{e}_2)^t + (\mathbf{0}, \mathbf{0}, \mathsf{encode}(\mathbf{m}))^t \mod q, \quad (1)$$

for a proper encoding algorithm encode, error items $(\mathbf{e}_0, \mathbf{e}_1, \mathbf{e}_2)$, and integer q. To decrypt a ciphertext, one first recovers $\mathbf{s}$ and $(\mathbf{e}_0, \mathbf{e}_1)$ from the first two blocks of $\mathbf{b}$ using the trapdoor $\mathbf{R}$ and an inversion algorithm. Then $\mathbf{m}$ and $\mathbf{e}_2$ are recovered from the last block of $\mathbf{b}$ with the recovered $\mathbf{s}$ and the inverse of encode.

Key-Switching Matrix. The key-switching matrix enables the transition of a ciphertext in Eq. (1) to a new ciphertext with the same form, denoted as $c' = (\mathbf{H}_\mu, \mathbf{b}')$, where

$$\mathbf{b}'^t = \mathbf{s}^t\mathbf{A}'_\mu + \mathbf{e}'^t + (\mathbf{0}, \mathbf{0}, \mathsf{encode}(\mathbf{m}))^t \mod q, \quad (2)$$

for new public matrix $\mathbf{A}'_\mu$ and new error items $\mathbf{e}'$. This matrix is essentially the transition matrix from $\mathbf{A}_\mu$ to $\mathbf{A}'_\mu$, with the last row block matrix $[\mathbf{0}\ \mathbf{0}\ \mathbf{I}]$, i.e., $\mathbf{A}_\mu \cdot \mathbf{M} = \mathbf{A}'_\mu$. The old ciphertext c is updated by multiplying $\mathbf{b}^t$ and $\mathbf{M}$, that is

$$\begin{aligned}\mathbf{b}^t\mathbf{M} &= \mathbf{s}^t\mathbf{A}_\mu \cdot \mathbf{M} + \mathbf{e}^t \cdot \mathbf{M} + (\mathbf{0}, \mathbf{0}, \mathsf{encode}(\mathbf{m}))^t \cdot \mathbf{M} \\ &= \mathbf{s}^t\mathbf{A}'_\mu + \mathbf{e}'^t + (\mathbf{0}, \mathbf{0}, \mathsf{encode}(\mathbf{m}))^t \mod q,\end{aligned}$$

which matches the desired form in Eq. (2). The matrix $\mathbf{M}$ can be efficiently generated by the trapdoor (secret key) $\mathbf{R}$ and the preimage sampling algorithm, as presented in Sect 2.2.

Challenges and a New UE Scheme. We state that there are two technical challenges in directly using the key-switching matrix as the update token to construct a secure UE scheme satisfying our confidentiality notion, which requires the indistinguishability between "fresh" and updated ciphertexts. The first observation is that $\mathbf{H}_\mu$, as part of the ciphertext, is never rotated in the update process. The adversary can distinguish the challenge ciphertexts by comparing $\mathbf{H}_\mu$ extracted from the challenge output and input. Beyond that, $\mathbf{s}$ is also never changed during the update process. With the known $\mathbf{s}$ used in the challenge input ciphertext, the adversary may attempt to decrypt the challenge output (note that the last step in the decryption algorithm in PKE only requires $\mathbf{s}$). If it fails, then the adversary knows the challenge output is a fresh encryption of the challenge input message. Otherwise, that is an update of the challenge input ciphertext.

Our solution to address the challenges is to change the invertible matrix $\mathbf{H}_\mu$ and the variable $\mathbf{s}$ in each update. Specifically, a new invertible matrix $\mathbf{H}'_\mu$ and a fresh encryption of message $\mathbf{0}$ under the new key with $\mathbf{H}'_\mu$, denoted by $\mathbf{b}_0$, are generated in the token generation algorithm to improve the randomness. In summary, the update token is a triple $\Delta = (\mathbf{M}, \mathbf{b}_0, \mathbf{H}'_\mu)$, and the update of ciphertext $c = (\mathbf{H}_\mu, \mathbf{b})$ works by multiplying $\mathbf{b}$ by $\mathbf{M}$ and then adding $\mathbf{b}_0$. That is, $c' = (\mathbf{H}'_u, \mathbf{b}')$, where

$$\begin{aligned}(\mathbf{b}')^t &= \mathbf{b}^t \cdot \mathbf{M} + \mathbf{b}_0^t \\ &= \left[\mathbf{s}^t \mathbf{A}_\mu + \mathbf{e}^t + (\mathbf{0}, \mathbf{0}, \mathsf{encode}(\mathbf{m}))^t\right] \mathbf{M} + (\mathbf{s}')^t \mathbf{A}'_\mu + (\mathbf{e}')^t \\ &= (\mathbf{s} + \mathbf{s}')^t \mathbf{A}'_\mu + \left(\mathbf{e}^t \mathbf{M} + (\mathbf{e}')^t\right) + (\mathbf{0}, \mathbf{0}, \mathsf{encode}(\mathbf{m}))^t \mod q.\end{aligned}$$

Thus, the updated ciphertext shares the same form as the old ciphertext, but has a new independent invertible matrix and new random factor $\mathbf{s} + \mathbf{s}'$, thereby avoiding the two problems mentioned above. Note that even if an adversary corrupts the update token and the old key (or new key), it can only recover $\mathbf{A}'_\mu$ (or $\mathbf{A}_\mu$, resp.) that is actually public. Therefore, the UE scheme does not leak any information about secret keys, and its token generation process is different from the previously commonly used Dec-then-Enc method.

Regarding the CCA-1 security, at a high level, the decryption procedure allows the adversary to recover at most $\mathbf{A}_\mu$ before the challenge phase, while ensuring that the secret key $\mathbf{R}$ (i.e., the trapdoor) remains statistically hidden from the adversary. We state that the scheme cannot achieve CCA-2 security as the decryption of a challenge ciphertext with extra small noise, which is also a valid ciphertext, reveals the information of the challenge plaintext.

A Packing UE. Our packing UE scheme allows for the simultaneous encryption and update of multiple messages in a single ciphertext. It is based on our UE scheme with the main difference in the encoding algorithm as follows:

$$\mathsf{encode}(\mathbf{m}_0, \ldots, \mathbf{m}_{N-1}) = \mathsf{encode}(\mathbf{m}_0) + \mathsf{encode}(\mathbf{m}_1) X + \cdots + \mathsf{encode}(\mathbf{m}_{N-1}) X^{N-1},$$

for messages $\mathbf{m}_0, \ldots, \mathbf{m}_{N-1}$, where the encode in the right side is the same as that in the PKE scheme. Multiple message blocks are encrypted into one single ciphertext, which can then be recovered degree by degree. This packing scheme enhances efficiency by requiring only one ciphertext header to be downloaded during the update process.

1.3 Summary of Contributions

We strengthen the confidentiality notions for c-d UE to address the above limitations 1–3 of existing work and provide efficient UE schemes that achieve the confidentiality we define. First, we simplify the description of the confidentiality model by reducing the number of oracles available to the adversary, while maintaining the same level of security. This simplification facilitates the security analysis of UE schemes. Our new definition "maximizes" the capability of the adversary, including the ability to corrupt keys in an adaptive manner and gain access to the decryption oracle, thus providing stronger security than prior work.

We then propose a new construction that is the first c-d UE to achieve adaptive security under the LWE assumption. It is built on our lattice-based PKE scheme and rotates ciphertext with a key-switching matrix, which differs from the Dec-then-Enc structure used in existing c-d UE schemes. We also propose a new packing method to further enhance the efficiency of c-d UE. Our approach enables multiple messages to be encrypted and updated simultaneously, reducing the overhead associated with downloading ciphertext headers during the update process.

2 Preliminaries

We use upper-case and lower-case bold letters to denote matrices and column vectors, respectively. For a vector $\mathbf{x}$, we denote the 2-norm of $\mathbf{x}$ by $\|\mathbf{x}\|$ and the infinity norm by $\|\mathbf{x}\|_\infty$. The largest singular value of a matrix $\mathbf{B}$ is denoted by $s_1(\mathbf{B}) := \max_{\mathbf{u}} \|\mathbf{B}^t\mathbf{u}\|$, where the maxima is taken over all unit vectors $\mathbf{u}$ and $\mathbf{B}^t$ is the transpose of $\mathbf{B}$. For two matrices $\mathbf{A}$ and $\mathbf{B}$, $[\mathbf{A} \mid \mathbf{B}]$ denotes the concatenation of the columns of $\mathbf{A}$ and $\mathbf{B}$. We also use standard asymptotical notations such as ω, Ω and O.

2.1 Updatable Encryption

We briefly review the syntax of ciphertext-dependent UE and prior confidentiality notions for c-d UE.

Definition 1 ([4,5,11]). *A ciphertext-dependent UE scheme includes a tuple of PPT algorithms* {KG, Enc, Dec, TokenGen, Update} *that operate in epochs starting from 0.*

- $\mathsf{KG}(1^\lambda)$*: the key generation algorithm outputs an epoch key* $\mathsf{k_e}$.

- $\mathsf{Enc}(\mathsf{k_e}, \mathsf{m})$: *the encryption algorithm takes as input an epoch key* $\mathsf{k_e}$ *and a message* m *and outputs a ciphertext header* $\hat{\mathsf{ct}}_\mathsf{e}$ *and a ciphertext body* $\mathsf{ct_e}$*, i.e.,* $\mathsf{ct} = (\hat{\mathsf{ct}}_\mathsf{e}, \mathsf{ct_e})$.
- $\mathsf{Dec}(\mathsf{k_e}, (\hat{\mathsf{ct}}_\mathsf{e}, \mathsf{ct_e}))$: *the decryption algorithm takes as input an epoch key* $\mathsf{k_e}$ *and a ciphertext* $(\hat{\mathsf{ct}}_\mathsf{e}, \mathsf{ct_e})$ *and outputs a message* m' *or* $\perp$.
- $\mathsf{TokenGen}(\mathsf{k_e}, \mathsf{k_{e+1}}, \hat{\mathsf{ct}}_\mathsf{e})$: *the token generation algorithm takes as input two epoch keys* $\mathsf{k_e}$ *and* $\mathsf{k_{e+1}}$ *and a ciphertext header* $\hat{\mathsf{ct}}_\mathsf{e}$*, and outputs an update token* $\Delta_{\mathsf{e+1},\hat{\mathsf{ct}}_\mathsf{e}}$ *or* $\perp$.
- $\mathsf{Update}(\Delta_{\mathsf{e+1},\hat{\mathsf{ct}}_\mathsf{e}}, (\hat{\mathsf{ct}}_\mathsf{e}, \mathsf{ct_e}))$: *the update algorithm takes as input a token* $\Delta_{\mathsf{e+1},\hat{\mathsf{ct}}}$ *related to the ciphertext* $(\hat{\mathsf{ct}}_\mathsf{e}, \mathsf{ct_e})$*, and outputs an updated ciphertext* $(\hat{\mathsf{ct}}_\mathsf{e+1}, \mathsf{ct_{e+1}})$ *or* $\perp$.

In an updatable encryption scheme, there are two ways to generate a ciphertext: either via the encryption algorithm to produce the fresh ciphertext, or via the update algorithm to produce an updated ciphertext. The *correctness* of a UE scheme requires both types of ciphertexts to decrypt correctly to the underlying message, except with a low failure probability.

Prior Notions of Confidentiality. To capture the security under key leakage, the challenger in prior confidentiality games [4,11] provides the adversary selective keys in the setup phase. In the query phase, the adversary is given access to query the algorithms involved in UE schemes, including {Enc, TokenGen, Update}, to obtain the encryption of messages, update tokens, and updates of ciphertexts, respectively. The adversary then submits two challenge inputs in the challenge phase based on the information it has acquired and receives the challenge output from the challenger. The goal of the adversary is to guess which challenge input the challenge output is related to (encrypted or updated from). The adversary can continue querying those oracles as long as the combination of queries would not lead to a trivial win, and eventually submits a guess bit.

Prior confidentiality notions have three variants with the only difference in challenge inputs: UP-IND [11] has inputs of two messages $(\bar{\mathsf{m}}_0, \bar{\mathsf{m}}_1)$ to capture the security of fresh encryptions, UP-REENC [11] uses inputs of two ciphertexts $(\bar{\mathsf{c}}_0, \bar{\mathsf{c}}_1)$ to protect the confidentiality after updating, and Confidentiality [4], which is stronger the former two, takes one message and one ciphertext as input $(\bar{\mathsf{m}}_0, \bar{\mathsf{c}}_1)$ to protect against the leakage of the *age* of ciphertext, i.e., the number of update times, to the adversary. We rewrite the confidentiality game of Confidentiality in Fig. 2 with two modifications.

First, we describe oracles that operate in consecutive epochs $\{\ldots, \mathsf{e}-1, \mathsf{e}, \mathsf{e}+1, \ldots\}$, which is more consistent with the practical periodic updating of ciphertexts and differs from the node-based oracles originating from proxy re-encryption in prior work. Second, we introduce a new lookup table in the game to track non-challenge ciphertexts (as defined in Definition 2) to address the insufficient analysis of trivial win conditions for deterministic UE schemes in prior work [4,5,10,11]. Our main observation is that for UE schemes with deterministic updates, the adversary should be prevented from querying $\mathcal{O}_{\mathsf{Update}}$ and $\mathcal{O}_{\mathsf{TokenGen}}$ on the challenge input ciphertext in the challenge epoch before querying the challenge oracle, as this would enable the adversary to know one of the

$\mathsf{Expt}_{\mathsf{UE}}^{\mathsf{Confidentiality}}(\lambda, l, \mathcal{A}, b)$:

$\mathsf{k}_1, \ldots, \mathsf{k}_l \leftarrow \mathsf{KG}(1^\lambda)$
$b' \leftarrow \mathcal{A}^{\mathcal{O}}(\mathcal{K})$
return $b' = b$

$\mathcal{O}_{\mathsf{Enc}}(\mathsf{e}, \mathsf{m})$:

$(\hat{\mathsf{ct}}, \mathsf{ct}) \leftarrow \mathsf{Enc}(\mathsf{k_e}, \mathsf{m})$
$\mathsf{TC}_{\mathsf{non}}[\mathsf{e}, \hat{\mathsf{ct}}] \leftarrow \mathsf{ct}$
return $(\hat{\mathsf{ct}}, \mathsf{ct})$

$\mathcal{O}_{\mathsf{Update}}(\mathsf{e}, (\hat{\mathsf{ct}}, \mathsf{ct}))$:

if $\mathsf{TC}_{\mathsf{chall}}[\mathsf{e}-1, \hat{\mathsf{ct}}] = \perp$ **and**
  $\mathsf{TC}_{\mathsf{non}}[\mathsf{e}-1, \hat{\mathsf{ct}}] = \perp$ **then**
  return $\perp$
$\Delta_{\mathsf{e},\hat{\mathsf{ct}}} \leftarrow \mathsf{TokenGen}(\mathsf{k_{e-1}}, \mathsf{k_e}, \hat{\mathsf{ct}})$
if $\mathsf{TC}_{\mathsf{chall}}[\mathsf{e}-1, \hat{\mathsf{ct}}] \neq \perp$ **then**
  if $\mathsf{e} \in \mathcal{K}$ **return** $\perp$
  else $\mathsf{ct} \leftarrow \mathsf{TC}_{\mathsf{chall}}[\mathsf{e}-1, \hat{\mathsf{ct}}]$
    $(\hat{\mathsf{ct}}', \mathsf{ct}') \leftarrow \mathsf{Update}(\Delta_{\mathsf{e},\hat{\mathsf{ct}}}, (\hat{\mathsf{ct}}, \mathsf{ct}))$
    $\mathsf{TC}_{\mathsf{chall}}[\mathsf{e}, \hat{\mathsf{ct}}'] \leftarrow \mathsf{ct}'$
else $\mathsf{ct} \leftarrow \mathsf{TC}_{\mathsf{non}}[\mathsf{e}-1, \hat{\mathsf{ct}}]$
    $(\hat{\mathsf{ct}}', \mathsf{ct}') \leftarrow \mathsf{Update}(\Delta_{\mathsf{e},\hat{\mathsf{ct}}}, (\hat{\mathsf{ct}}, \mathsf{ct}))$
    $\mathsf{TC}_{\mathsf{non}}[\mathsf{e}, \hat{\mathsf{ct}}'] \leftarrow \mathsf{ct}'$
return $(\hat{\mathsf{ct}}', \mathsf{ct}')$

$\mathcal{O}_{\mathsf{TokenGen}}(\mathsf{e}, \hat{\mathsf{ct}})$:

if $\mathsf{e} \in \mathcal{K}$ **and** $\mathsf{TC}_{\mathsf{chall}}[\mathsf{e}-1, \hat{\mathsf{ct}}] \neq \perp$
  return $\perp$
$\Delta_{\mathsf{e},\hat{\mathsf{ct}}} \leftarrow \mathsf{TokenGen}(\mathsf{k_{e-1}}, \mathsf{k_e}, \hat{\mathsf{ct}})$
if $\mathsf{e} \notin \mathcal{K}$ **and** $\mathsf{TC}_{\mathsf{chall}}[\mathsf{e}-1, \hat{\mathsf{ct}}] \neq \perp$
  $\mathsf{ct} \leftarrow \mathsf{TC}_{\mathsf{chall}}[\mathsf{e}-1, \hat{\mathsf{ct}}]$
  $(\hat{\mathsf{ct}}', \mathsf{ct}') \leftarrow \mathsf{Update}(\Delta_{\mathsf{e},\hat{\mathsf{ct}}}, (\hat{\mathsf{ct}}, \mathsf{ct}))$
  $\mathsf{TC}_{\mathsf{chall}}[\mathsf{e}, \hat{\mathsf{ct}}'] \leftarrow \mathsf{ct}'$
elseif $\mathsf{TC}_{\mathsf{non}}[\mathsf{e}-1, \hat{\mathsf{ct}}] \neq \perp$
  $\mathsf{ct} \leftarrow \mathsf{TC}_{\mathsf{non}}[\mathsf{e}-1, \hat{\mathsf{ct}}]$
  $(\hat{\mathsf{ct}}', \mathsf{ct}') \leftarrow \mathsf{Update}(\Delta_{\mathsf{e},\hat{\mathsf{ct}}}, (\hat{\mathsf{ct}}, \mathsf{ct}))$
  $\mathsf{TC}_{\mathsf{non}}[\mathsf{e}, \hat{\mathsf{ct}}'] \leftarrow \mathsf{ct}'$
else return $\perp$
return $\Delta_{\mathsf{e},\hat{\mathsf{ct}}}$

$\mathcal{O}_{\mathsf{Chall}}(\mathsf{e}, \mathsf{m}, (\hat{\mathsf{ct}}, \mathsf{ct}))$:

if $\mathsf{e} \in \mathcal{K}$ **return** $\perp$
$(\hat{\mathsf{ct}}_0', \mathsf{ct}_0') \leftarrow \mathsf{Enc}(\mathsf{k_e}, \mathsf{m})$
if $(\hat{\mathsf{ct}}_0', \mathsf{ct}_0') = \perp$ or $\mathsf{TC}_{\mathsf{non}}[\mathsf{e}-1, \hat{\mathsf{ct}}] \neq \mathsf{ct}$
  return $\perp$
$\Delta_{\mathsf{e},\hat{\mathsf{ct}}} \leftarrow \mathsf{TokenGen}(\mathsf{k_{e-1}}, \mathsf{k_e}, \hat{\mathsf{ct}})$
$(\hat{\mathsf{ct}}_1', \mathsf{ct}_1') \leftarrow \mathsf{Update}(\Delta_{\mathsf{e},\hat{\mathsf{ct}}}, (\hat{\mathsf{ct}}, \mathsf{ct}))$
if $|\hat{\mathsf{ct}}_0'| \neq |\hat{\mathsf{ct}}_1'|$ or $|\mathsf{ct}_0'| \neq |\mathsf{ct}_1'|$
  return $\perp$
if $(\mathsf{xx} = \mathsf{det}$ and $\mathsf{TC}_{\mathsf{non}}[\mathsf{e}, \hat{\mathsf{ct}}_1'] = \mathsf{ct}_1')$
  return $\perp$
$\mathsf{TC}_{\mathsf{chall}}[\mathsf{e}, \hat{\mathsf{ct}}_b'] \leftarrow \mathsf{ct}_b'$
return $(\hat{\mathsf{ct}}_b', \mathsf{ct}_b')$

Fig. 2. Security game for Confidentiality. The adversary in the startup is provided with selective keys whose epochs are recorded by the set $\mathcal{K}$, and the other keys are kept private from the adversary. Initially set to be empty, the table $\mathsf{T}_{\mathsf{chall}}$ (or $\mathsf{T}_{\mathsf{non}}$) maps an epoch and challenge-equal (or non-challenge, respectively) ciphertext header pair to the corresponding challenge-equal (or non-challenge, respectively) ciphertext body. $\mathsf{xx} = \mathsf{det}$ means the update algorithm is deterministic.

possible challenge output ciphertexts in advance due to the determinism of the update. Such conditions are not analyzed in prior notions, which are therefore only applicable to UE with randomized updates; however, the update algorithm can be deterministic as in our construction, even though the encryption algorithm must be randomized.

Definition 2. *A ciphertext is called challenge-equal ciphertext, if the adversary learns it via querying the challenge oracle $\mathcal{O}_{\mathsf{Chall}}$, or obtains it by updating the challenge ciphertext using $\mathcal{O}_{\mathsf{Update}}$ or tokens acquired from $\mathcal{O}_{\mathsf{TokenGen}}$. Any ciphertext that is not obtained through these methods is referred to as a non-challenge ciphertext.*

The functionalities and restrictions of oracles used in the Confidentiality game in Fig. 2 are as follows.

- $\mathcal{O}_{\mathsf{Enc}}$: returns an encryption of a message.
- $\mathcal{O}_{\mathsf{Update}}$: returns an update of a valid (lines 1–3) ciphertext, recorded by $\mathsf{TC}_{\mathsf{chall}}$ (line 9) or $\mathsf{TC}_{\mathsf{non}}$ (line 12) according to the input. But the update of challenge-equal ciphertexts in epochs with known epoch keys is not allowed (line 6).
- $\mathcal{O}_{\mathsf{TokenGen}}$: returns a token related to a valid ciphertext, and updates $\mathsf{TC}_{\mathsf{chall}}$ (line 7) or $\mathsf{TC}_{\mathsf{non}}$ (line 11). But tokens related to challenge-equal ciphertexts in epochs with known epoch keys are not allowed to be acquired (lines 1–2).
- $\mathcal{O}_{\mathsf{Chall}}$: returns the challenge output, either a fresh encryption of the input message or an update of input valid ciphertext (lines 2–4). However, this oracle should not be queried in epochs with known epoch keys (line 1), and for deterministic UE, the input ciphertext should not be updated in advance (lines 9–10).

In fact, the adversary may infer more ciphertexts, tokens, and keys from corrupted information, aside from the recorded sets, and the extended leakages cannot be tracked (but can be computed) by look-up tables. For example, a token can be inferred if two successive epoch keys are known. We will show in Lemmas 3 to 5 that trivial win conditions on recorded leakages and extended leakages are actually the same for no-directional UE (Definition 5). Therefore, it is sufficient to check the above restrictions on recorded look-up tables to avoid trivial win.

2.2 Gaussians and Lattices

Given a matrix $\mathbf{A} \in \mathbb{Z}_q^{n\times m}$, we first review the Learning With Errors (LWE) and Short Integer Solution (SIS) problems as follows:

- $\mathsf{LWE}_{q,\alpha}$: for arbitrary $\mathbf{s} \in \mathbb{Z}_q^n$ and error $\mathbf{e}$ from the discrete Gaussian distribution $D_{\mathbb{Z}^m,\alpha q}$ (Definition 4), let $\mathbf{b}^t = \mathbf{s}^t\mathbf{A}+\mathbf{e}^t \bmod q \in \mathbb{Z}_q^m$. The *search*-$\mathsf{LWE}_{q,\alpha}$ is to find $\mathbf{s}$ and $\mathbf{e}$ from $(\mathbf{A}, \mathbf{b})$; the *decision*-$\mathsf{LWE}_{q,\alpha}$ is to distinguish between $\mathbf{b}$ and a uniformly random sample from $\mathbb{Z}_q^m$.
- $\mathsf{SIS}_{q,\beta}$: find a nonzero $\mathbf{x} \in \mathbb{Z}^m$ such that $\mathbf{A}\mathbf{x} = \mathbf{0} \bmod q$ and $\|\mathbf{x}\| \leq \beta$.

When $\mathbf{A}$ is a uniformly random matrix, solving the above two problems is computationally intractable under some parameter settings [2,21]. However, for a random matrix $\mathbf{A}$ with a $\mathbf{G}$-trapdoor (Definition 3), those two problems can be solved immediately (Lemma 1 and Lemma 2).

For the rest of the paper, let $q \geq 2$ be an integer modulus with $k = \lceil \log_2 q \rceil$, and $\mathbf{G}$ is defined as $\mathbf{G} := \mathbf{I}_n \otimes \mathbf{g}^t \in \mathbb{Z}_q^{n \times nk}$, i.e.,

$$\mathbf{G} = diag(\mathbf{g}^t, \ldots, \mathbf{g}^t),$$

where $\mathbf{g}^t = [1\ 2\ 4\ \ldots\ 2^{k-1}] \in \mathbb{Z}_q^{1 \times k}$ and integer $n \geq 1$.

Definition 3 (G-trapdoor). *Let $\mathbf{A} \in \mathbb{Z}_q^{n \times m}$ for some $m \geq nk \geq n$. A* **G***-trapdoor for* $\mathbf{A}$ *is a matrix* $\mathbf{R} \in \mathbb{Z}_q^{(m-nk) \times nk}$ *such that* $\mathbf{A}\left[\begin{smallmatrix}\mathbf{R}\\ \mathbf{I}\end{smallmatrix}\right] = \mathbf{HG}$ *for some invertible matrix* $\mathbf{H} \in \mathbb{Z}_q^{n \times n}$.

As an example in [19], $\mathbf{R}$ is a $\mathbf{G}$-trapdoor for a random matrix $\mathbf{A} = [\mathbf{A}_0 | -\mathbf{A}_0\mathbf{R} + \mathbf{HG}]$, where $\mathbf{A}_0$ is a uniform matrix in $\mathbb{Z}_q^{n \times m}$, $\mathbf{H} \in \mathbb{Z}_q^{n \times n}$ is an invertible matrix and $\mathbf{R}$ is chosen from a distribution over $\mathbb{Z}_q^{m \times nk}$.

Lemma 1 **([19], Theorem 5.4).** *Given a* **G***-trapdoor* $\mathbf{R}$ *for* $\mathbf{A} \in \mathbb{Z}_q^{n \times m}$ *and an* LWE *instance* $\mathbf{b}^t = \mathbf{s}^t\mathbf{A} + \mathbf{e}^t$, *if* $\|[\mathbf{R}^t\ \mathbf{I}] \cdot \mathbf{e}\|_\infty \leq q/4$ *, then there is an efficient algorithm called* $\mathsf{Invert}^{\mathcal{O}}(\mathbf{R}, \mathbf{A}, \mathbf{H}, \mathbf{b})$ *that recovers* $\mathbf{s}$ *and* $\mathbf{e}$ *from the* $\mathbf{b}^t = \mathbf{s}^t\mathbf{A} + \mathbf{e}^t$.

Lemma 2 **([19], Theorem 5.5).** *Given a* **G***-trapdoor* $\mathbf{R}$ *for* $\mathbf{A} \in \mathbb{Z}_q^{n \times m}$ *with invertible matrix* $\mathbf{H}$ *and any* $\mathbf{u} \in \mathbb{Z}_q^n$, *there is an efficient algorithm called* $\mathsf{SampleD}^{\mathcal{O}}(\mathbf{R}, \mathbf{A}, \mathbf{H}, \mathbf{u}, s)$ *that samples a Gaussian vector* $\mathbf{x}$ *from* $D_{\mathbb{Z}^m, s}$ *such that* $\mathbf{Ax} = \mathbf{u}$, *where* s *can be as small as* $\sqrt{s_1(\mathbf{R})^2 + 1} \cdot \sqrt{s_1(\sum_\mathbf{G}) + 1} \cdot \omega(\sqrt{\log n})$ *and* $s_1(\sum_\mathbf{G})$ *is a constant for given* $\mathbf{G}$ *(equal to 4 if* q *is a power of 2, and 5 otherwise).*

Definition 4 **([1]).** *For a positive real* s, *the discrete Gaussian distribution over a countable set* A *is defined by the density function*

$$D_{A,s}(x) := \frac{\rho_s(x)}{\sum_{y \in A} \rho_s(y)},$$

where $\rho_s(x) = \exp\left(-\pi\|x\|^2/s^2\right)$.

Lemma 1 and Lemma 2 work for $\mathbf{G}$ as well. More conclusions related to Gaussians and lattices are provided in Appendix B of the full version [9].

3 New Confidentiality Notions for Updatable Encryption

To simplify the security notion given in [4], we define a new confidentiality notion called sConfidentiality, where we replace $\mathcal{O}_{\mathsf{TokenGen}}$ and $\mathcal{O}_{\mathsf{Update}}$ in the security game with a single $\mathcal{O}_{\mathsf{sUpd}}$ that returns both the update token and updated ciphertext to the adversary simultaneously. We prove in Theorem 1 that sConfidentiality and Confidentiality are equal for UE schemes with no-directional key updates.

Meanwhile, to provide the adversary with maximum power, we introduce a new stronger confidentiality notion than sConfidentiality, called xxIND-UE-atk[3], where the adversary is given extra access to $\mathcal{O}_{\mathsf{Dec}}$ and $\mathcal{O}_{\mathsf{Corr}}$, which enables it to corrupt epoch keys at any time during the game. To avoid making the security game trivial, we fully analyze the conditions for any trivial win in this game model. A brief comparison of the proposed notions with those of prior work is presented in Fig. 3.

Notions	Oracles	Compromised Key	Challenge Input	Update
UP-IND [11]	$\mathcal{O}_{\mathsf{Enc}}, \mathcal{O}_{\mathsf{TokenGen}}, \mathcal{O}_{\mathsf{Update}}$	Selective	$(\bar{\mathsf{m}}_0, \bar{\mathsf{m}}_1)$	rand
UP-REENC [11]	$\mathcal{O}_{\mathsf{Enc}}, \mathcal{O}_{\mathsf{TokenGen}}, \mathcal{O}_{\mathsf{Update}}$	Selective	$(\bar{\mathsf{c}}_0, \bar{\mathsf{c}}_1)$	rand
Confidentiality [4]	$\mathcal{O}_{\mathsf{Enc}}, \mathcal{O}_{\mathsf{TokenGen}}, \mathcal{O}_{\mathsf{Update}}$	Selective	$(\bar{\mathsf{m}}_0, \bar{\mathsf{c}}_1)$	rand
sConfidentiality Sect. 3.2	$\mathcal{O}_{\mathsf{Enc}}, \mathcal{O}_{\mathsf{sUpd}}$	Selective	$(\bar{\mathsf{m}}_0, \bar{\mathsf{c}}_1)$	rand
xxIND-UE-CPA Sect. 3.3	$\mathcal{O}_{\mathsf{Enc}}, \mathcal{O}_{\mathsf{sUpd}}, \mathcal{O}_{\mathsf{Corr}},$	Adaptive	$(\bar{\mathsf{m}}_0, \bar{\mathsf{c}}_1)$	xx
xxIND-UE-CCA Sect. 3.3	$\mathcal{O}_{\mathsf{Enc}}, \mathcal{O}_{\mathsf{sUpd}}, \mathcal{O}_{\mathsf{Corr}}, \mathcal{O}_{\mathsf{Dec}}$	Adaptive	$(\bar{\mathsf{m}}_0, \bar{\mathsf{c}}_1)$	xx

Fig. 3. A summary of confidentiality notions, where xx $\in$ {rand, det} represents the update procedure can be either randomized or deterministic. The adversary in each confidentiality game provides two challenge inputs based on the oracles it has access to and tries to distinguish the challenge outputs. Confidentiality is proven stronger than both UP-IND and UP-REENC in [4], and $\mathcal{O}_{\mathsf{sUpd}}$ is defined in Sect. 3.2. Chen et al. [10] proposed strengthened UP-IND and UP-REENC to capture malicious update security, with the modification in the oracle $\mathcal{O}_{\mathsf{Update}}$ that enables the adversary to query the update of maliciously generated ciphertexts, instead of only honestly generated ciphertexts as in [11].

3.1 UE Schemes with No-Directional Key Updates

In c-i UE schemes, update tokens are generated by two successive epoch keys: $\Delta = \mathsf{TokenGen}(\mathsf{k_e}, \mathsf{k_{e+1}})$, e.g., $\Delta = \mathsf{k_{e+1}}/\mathsf{k_e}$ in [6] or $\Delta = \mathsf{k_{e+1}} - \mathsf{k_e}$ in [15]); therefore, one key may be derived by the other if the token is known by the adversary. However, in c-d UE schemes, tokens are also determined by the ciphertext header: $\Delta = \mathsf{TokenGen}(\mathsf{k_e}, \mathsf{k_{e+1}}, \hat{\mathsf{ct}}_\mathsf{e})$, so keys may not be derived via corrupted tokens. We generalize the definition of no-directional key updates from c-i UE to c-d UE as follows.

Definition 5. *A UE scheme, either ciphertext-independent or ciphertext-dependent, is said to have no-directional key updates if epoch keys cannot be inferred from known tokens.*

[3] The same notion for the c-i UE scheme was proposed in [6]. We aim to unify the notions for c-i/c-d UE that both capture adaptive security and prevent the leakage of ciphertext age. Note that, as analyzed in the introduction, there are intrinsic differences between c-i UE and c-d UE. The disparity is evident in the confidentiality notion, specifically in the approach to recording leakage sets.

Jiang [15] proposed the open problem of constructing no-directional c-i UE schemes. However, all known c-d UE schemes in [4,5,10,11] (as well as our construction in Sect. 5) have no-directional key updates, which benefit from a Dec-then-Enc process as discussed in the introduction. In contrast, there are only two c-i UE schemes with no-directional key update: one is not practical [17] and the other is less efficient [23]. In the following, we focus on c-d UE schemes with no-directional key updates.

3.2 A Simplified Confidentiality Notion

Based on our refinement on Confidentiality, we now define a new simplified confidentiality notion by substituting the oracles $\mathcal{O}_{\mathsf{TokenGen}}$ and $\mathcal{O}_{\mathsf{Upd}}$ in the Confidentiality game with a single $\mathcal{O}_{\mathsf{sUpd}}$ that returns both the token and update simultaneously. We call this new notion sConfidentiality. In Theorem 1, we prove sConfidentiality is equivalent to Confidentiality for UE schemes with no-directional key updates, as defined in [4].

$\mathrm{Expt}^{\mathsf{sConf}}_{\mathsf{UE}}(\lambda, l, \mathcal{A}, b)$:

$k_1, \ldots, k_l \leftarrow \mathsf{KG}(1^\lambda)$
$b' \leftarrow \mathcal{A}^{\mathcal{O}}(\mathcal{K})$
return $b' = b$

$\mathcal{O}_{\mathsf{sUpd}}(\mathsf{e}, (\hat{\mathsf{ct}}, \mathsf{ct}))$:

if $\mathsf{TC}_{\mathsf{chall}}[\mathsf{e}-1, \hat{\mathsf{ct}}] = \perp$ and
  $\mathsf{TC}_{\mathsf{non}}[\mathsf{e}-1, \hat{\mathsf{ct}}] = \perp$ **then**
  return $\perp$
$\Delta_{\mathsf{e},\hat{\mathsf{ct}}} \leftarrow \mathsf{TokenGen}(k_{\mathsf{e}-1}, k_{\mathsf{e}}, \hat{\mathsf{ct}})$
if $\mathsf{TC}_{\mathsf{chall}}[\mathsf{e}-1, \hat{\mathsf{ct}}] \neq \perp$ **then**
  if $\mathsf{e} \in \mathcal{K}$ **return** $\perp$
  else $\mathsf{ct} \leftarrow \mathsf{TC}_{\mathsf{chall}}[\mathsf{e}-1, \hat{\mathsf{ct}}]$
    $(\hat{\mathsf{ct}}', \mathsf{ct}') \leftarrow \mathsf{Update}(\Delta_{\mathsf{e},\hat{\mathsf{ct}}}, (\hat{\mathsf{ct}}, \mathsf{ct}))$
    $\mathsf{TC}_{\mathsf{chall}}[\mathsf{e}, \hat{\mathsf{ct}}'] \leftarrow \mathsf{ct}'$
else $\mathsf{ct} \leftarrow \mathsf{TC}_{\mathsf{non}}[\mathsf{e}-1, \hat{\mathsf{ct}}]$
    $(\hat{\mathsf{ct}}', \mathsf{ct}') \leftarrow \mathsf{Update}(\Delta_{\mathsf{e},\hat{\mathsf{ct}}}, (\hat{\mathsf{ct}}, \mathsf{ct}))$
    $\mathsf{TC}_{\mathsf{non}}[\mathsf{e}, \hat{\mathsf{ct}}'] \leftarrow \mathsf{ct}'$
return $(\Delta_{\mathsf{e},\hat{\mathsf{ct}}}, (\hat{\mathsf{ct}}', \mathsf{ct}'))$

$\mathcal{O}_{\mathsf{Enc}}(\mathsf{e}, \mathsf{m})$:

$(\hat{\mathsf{ct}}, \mathsf{ct}) \leftarrow \mathsf{Enc}(k_{\mathsf{e}}, \mathsf{m})$
$\mathsf{TC}_{\mathsf{non}}[\mathsf{e}, \hat{\mathsf{ct}}] \leftarrow \mathsf{ct}$
return $(\hat{\mathsf{ct}}, \mathsf{ct})$

$\mathcal{O}_{\mathsf{Chall}}(\mathsf{e}, \mathsf{m}, (\hat{\mathsf{ct}}, \mathsf{ct}))$:

if $\mathsf{e} \in \mathcal{K}$ **return** $\perp$
$(\hat{\mathsf{ct}}'_0, \mathsf{ct}'_0) \leftarrow \mathsf{Enc}(k_{\mathsf{e}}, \mathsf{m})$
if $(\hat{\mathsf{ct}}'_0, \mathsf{ct}'_0) = \perp$ or $\mathsf{TC}_{\mathsf{non}}[\mathsf{e}-1, \hat{\mathsf{ct}}] \neq \mathsf{ct}$
  return $\perp$
$\Delta_{\mathsf{e},\hat{\mathsf{ct}}} \leftarrow \mathsf{TokenGen}(k_{\mathsf{e}-1}, k_{\mathsf{e}}, \hat{\mathsf{ct}})$
$(\hat{\mathsf{ct}}'_1, \mathsf{ct}'_1) \leftarrow \mathsf{Update}(\Delta_{\mathsf{e},\hat{\mathsf{ct}}}, (\hat{\mathsf{ct}}, \mathsf{ct}))$
if $|\hat{\mathsf{ct}}'_0| \neq |\hat{\mathsf{ct}}'_1|$ or $|\mathsf{ct}'_0| \neq |\mathsf{ct}'_1|$
  return $\perp$
if ($\mathsf{xx} = \mathsf{det}$ and $\mathsf{TC}_{\mathsf{non}}[\mathsf{e}, \hat{\mathsf{ct}}'_1] = \mathsf{ct}'_1$)
  return $\perp$
$\mathsf{TC}_{\mathsf{chall}}[\mathsf{e}, \hat{\mathsf{ct}}'_b] \leftarrow \mathsf{ct}'_b$
return $(\hat{\mathsf{ct}}'_b, \mathsf{ct}'_b)$

Fig. 4. Security game for sConfidentiality in Definition 6.

Definition 6 (sConfientiality). *Let* $\mathsf{UE} = \{\mathsf{KG}, \mathsf{Enc}, \mathsf{Dec}, \mathsf{TokenGen}, \mathsf{Update}\}$ *be an updatable encryption scheme. For a security parameter* λ*, an integer* l*, an adversary* $\mathcal{A}$*, and a binary bit* $b \in \{0, 1\}$*, we define the confidentiality experiment* $\mathrm{Expt}^{\mathsf{sConf}}_{\mathsf{UE}}(\lambda, l, \mathcal{A}, b)$ *and oracles* $\mathcal{O} = \{\mathcal{O}_{\mathsf{Enc}}, \mathcal{O}_{\mathsf{sUpd}}, \mathcal{O}_{\mathsf{Chall}}\}$ *as described in Fig. 4.*

The experiment maintains two look-up tables $\mathsf{TC}_{\mathsf{non}}$ *and* $\mathsf{TC}_{\mathsf{chall}}$ *that record non-challenge and challenge-equal ciphertexts known to the adversary, respectively, and an epoch set* $\mathcal{K}$ *in which epoch keys are provided to the adversary in setup.*

We say that an updatable encryption scheme UE *satisfies* sConfidentiality *if there exists a negligible function* $\mathsf{negl}(\lambda)$ *such that for all* $\mathcal{K} \subseteq [0, \ldots, l]$ *and efficient adversaries* $\mathcal{A}$, *we have*

$$\left|\Pr\left[\mathrm{Expt}_{\mathsf{UE}}^{\mathsf{sConf}}(\lambda, l, \mathcal{A}, 0) = 1\right] - \Pr\left[\mathrm{Expt}_{\mathsf{UE}}^{\mathsf{sConf}}(\lambda, l, \mathcal{A}, 1) = 1\right]\right| \leq \mathrm{negl}(\lambda).$$

Theorem 1. *Let* $\mathsf{UE} = (\mathsf{KG}, \mathsf{Enc}, \mathsf{Dec}, \mathsf{TokenGen}, \mathsf{Update})$ *be an updatable encryption scheme with no-directional key updates. For any* sConfidentiality *adversary* $\mathcal{A}$ *against* UE, *there is a* Confidentiality *adversary* $\mathcal{B}$ *against* UE *such that*

$$\mathsf{Adv}_{\mathsf{UE},\mathcal{A}}^{\mathsf{sConf}}(1^\lambda) \leq \mathsf{Adv}_{\mathsf{UE},\mathcal{B}}^{\mathsf{Conf}}(1^\lambda). \tag{3}$$

In addition, for any Confidentiality *adversary* $\mathcal{B}$ *against* UE, *there is a* sConfidentiality *adversary* $\mathcal{A}$ *against* UE *such that*

$$\mathsf{Adv}_{\mathsf{UE},\mathcal{B}}^{\mathsf{Conf}}(1^\lambda) = \mathsf{Adv}_{\mathsf{UE},\mathcal{A}}^{\mathsf{sConf}}(1^\lambda).$$

Proof. In general, we construct a reduction that runs the Confidentiality (or sConfidentiality) game and simulates all responses to the queries of the adversary in the sConfidentiality (or Confidentiality game, respectively), as shown in Fig. 5. The details are presented in Appendix A of the full version [9]. □

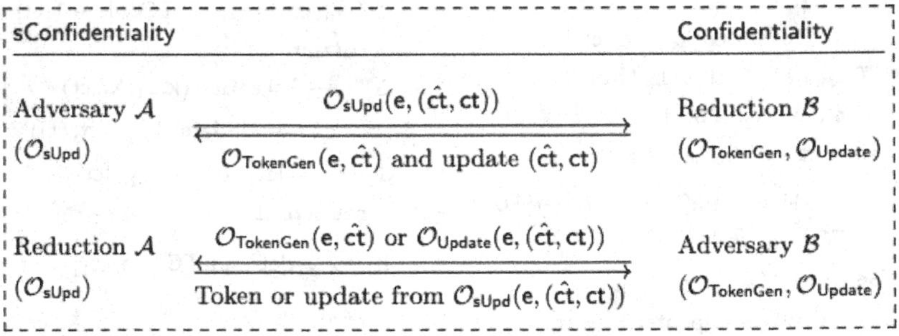

Fig. 5. Reductions in the proof of Theorem 1. When the adversary makes queries to specific oracles, indicated above the arrow, the reduction forwards to the adversary the corresponding responses from its own challenger, marked below the arrow.

3.3 A Stronger Confidentiality Notion

We now provide a stronger confidentiality notion, called xxIND-UE-atk for c-d UE in Definition 7, which provides the adversary with more power than the notion of sConfidentiality in Sect. 3.2. All available oracles that the adversary has access to are described in Fig. 8. The stronger notion allows the adversary to corrupt keys at any time during the game by querying $\mathcal{O}_{\mathsf{Corr}}$, instead of selecting the compromised keys in the setup phrase. In addition, the adversary is provided with an extra ability to query the decryption oracle compared with sConfidentiality. Prior to defining xxIND-UE-atk, we first analyze the conditions that lead the adversary to trivially win the game through a combination of queries, which therefore should be excluded from the game.

Leakage Information. To track the information leaked to the adversary, we similarly record two look-up tables $\mathsf{TC}_{\mathsf{non}}$ and $\mathsf{TC}_{\mathsf{chall}}$ as defined in Sect. 3.2, and an epoch set $\mathcal{K}$ in which the epoch key is corrupted via $\mathcal{O}_{\mathsf{Corr}}$. We define $\mathsf{TC}_{\mathsf{chall}}[0]$ as the set of epochs in which the adversary learns a challenge-equal ciphertext, and $\mathcal{T}$ as the set of epochs in which the adversary learns a token corresponding to a challenge-equal ciphertext, which are exactly the epochs stored in $\mathsf{TC}_{\mathsf{chall}}$ and $\Delta_{\mathsf{e},\hat{\mathsf{ct}}}$, respectively. A summary of notations is shown in Table 1.

Table 1. Summary of leakage set notations

Notations	Descriptions
$\mathsf{TC}_{\mathsf{non}}$	Look-up table recording leaked non-challenge ciphertexts
$\mathsf{TC}_{\mathsf{chall}}$	Look-up table recording leaked challenge-equal ciphertexts
$\mathsf{TC}_{\mathsf{chall}}[0]$	Set of epochs in which a challenge-equal ciphertext is learned
$\mathcal{K}$	Set of epochs in which the adversary learned the epoch key
$\mathcal{T}$	Set of epochs in which a token w.r.t. a challenge-equal ct is learned

Leakage Extension. Note that the adversary possibly extends its corrupted information $\mathsf{TC}_{\mathsf{non}}, \mathsf{TC}_{\mathsf{chall}}, \mathcal{K}$ via corrupted tokens, and the former leakages may also in turn help to corrupt more tokens. We denote $\mathsf{TC}^*_{\mathsf{chall}}[0], \mathcal{K}^*, \mathcal{T}^*$ as the extended sets of $\mathsf{TC}_{\mathsf{chall}}[0], \mathcal{K}, \mathcal{T}$, respectively. Following the analysis in [18], the extended leakage sets are computed as follows:

$$\mathcal{K}^* = \mathcal{K} \text{ (no-directional key updates)}, \tag{4}$$

$$\mathcal{T}^* = \{\mathsf{e} \in \{0, \ldots, l\} \mid (\mathsf{e} \in \mathcal{T}) \vee (\mathsf{e} \in \mathcal{K}^* \wedge \mathsf{e}-1 \in \mathcal{K}^*\}, \tag{5}$$

$$\begin{aligned}\mathsf{TC}^*_{\mathsf{chall}}[0] = \{\mathsf{e} \in \{0, \ldots, l\} \mid (\mathsf{e} \in \mathsf{TC}_{\mathsf{chall}}[0]) \vee (\mathsf{e}-1 \in \mathsf{TC}_{\mathsf{chall}}[0] \wedge \mathsf{e} \in \mathcal{T}^*) \vee \\ (\mathsf{e}+1 \in \mathsf{TC}_{\mathsf{chall}}[0] \wedge \mathsf{e}+1 \in \mathcal{T}^*)\}.\end{aligned} \tag{6}$$

An example is shown in Fig. 6. Assume the adversary queries $\mathcal{O}_{\mathsf{sUpd}}$ only in epoch $\mathsf{e}-5$ and corrupts epoch keys in epochs $\mathsf{e}-5$ and $\mathsf{e}-4$. Even though it cannot

Epoch	...	e − 5	e − 4	...
$\mathsf{TC}_{\mathsf{chall}}[0]$		✓	×	
$\mathcal{K}$		✓	✓	
$\mathcal{T}$	✓		×	
$\mathsf{TC}^*_{\mathsf{chall}}[0]$		✓	✓	
$\mathcal{K}^*$		✓	✓	
$\mathcal{T}^*$	✓		✓	

Fig. 6. Example of leakage sets. Marks ✓ and × indicate if an epoch key/token is corrupted. The green mark ✓ indicates an epoch key/token can be inferred from other corrupted keys and tokens. (Color figure online)

Abilities	Trivial Win Conditions
Keys and ciphertexts	$\mathcal{K}^* \cap \mathsf{TC}^*_{\mathsf{chall}}[0] \neq \emptyset$
Updates	rand-UE : – det-UE : $\tilde{\mathsf{e}} \in \mathcal{T}^*$ or $\mathcal{O}_{\mathsf{sUpd}}(\tilde{\mathsf{e}}, (\hat{\mathsf{ct}}, \mathsf{ct}))$ is queried (line 8-9 of $\mathcal{O}_{\mathsf{Chall}}$)
Decryptions	rand-UE : $\mathsf{e} \in \mathsf{TC}^*_{\mathsf{chall}}[0]$ and ($\mathsf{m}' = \mathsf{m}$ or m_1) (line 3-4 of $\mathcal{O}_{\mathsf{Dec}}$) det-UE : $\mathsf{TC}^*_{\mathsf{chall}}[\mathsf{e}, \hat{\mathsf{ct}}] = \mathsf{ct}$ (line 2 of $\mathcal{O}_{\mathsf{Dec}}$)

Fig. 7. A summary of trivial win conditions, where $\tilde{\mathsf{e}}$ is the challenge epoch, $(\hat{\mathsf{ct}}, \mathsf{ct})$ is the challenge input ciphertext whose underlying message is m_1, m is the challenge input message, and m' is the returned message of decryption algorithm. Oracles are given in Fig. 8.

learn the token in epoch $\mathsf{e} - 4$ by $\mathcal{O}_{\mathsf{sUpd}}$, it can infer that token via corrupted keys in $\mathsf{e} - 5$ and $\mathsf{e} - 4$, which further infers the ciphertexts in $\mathsf{e} - 4$.

Trivial Win Conditions. We follow the analysis of trivial win conditions for c-i UE in [6,15,17,18], as shown in Fig. 7. Our analysis for c-d UE in Lemmas 3 to 5 shows that it is sufficient to check trivial win conditions on recorded leakages $\mathcal{K}, \mathsf{TC}_{\mathsf{chall}}, \mathcal{T}$, eliminating the need to calculate extended leakages $\mathcal{K}^*, \mathsf{TC}^*_{\mathsf{chall}}, \mathcal{T}^*$ and check trivial win conditions on them.

I. Trivial win by keys and ciphertexts

If the adversary knows the epoch key and a valid challenge-equal ciphertext in the same epoch, it can recover the underlying message by a direct decryption with its corrupted key and therefore win the game. Namely, we should ensure $\mathcal{K}^* \cap \mathsf{TC}^*_{\mathsf{chall}}[0] = \emptyset$. The following lemma shows this condition is equal to $\mathcal{K} \cap \mathsf{TC}_{\mathsf{chall}}[0] = \emptyset$ for c-d UE with no-directional key updates.

Lemma 3. *For c-d UE schemes with no-directional key updates, we have* $\mathcal{K}^* \cap \mathsf{TC}^*_{\mathsf{chall}}[0] = \emptyset \iff \mathcal{K} \cap \mathsf{TC}_{\mathsf{chall}}[0] = \emptyset$.

Proof. By the definition of no-directional key updates, we have $\mathcal{K}^* = \mathcal{K}$. In addition, we have $\mathsf{TC}_{\mathsf{chall}}[0] \subseteq \mathsf{TC}^*_{\mathsf{chall}}[0]$. Therefore, we only need to prove $\mathsf{TC}_{\mathsf{chall}}[0] = \mathsf{TC}^*_{\mathsf{chall}}[0]$ when $\mathcal{K} \cap \mathsf{TC}_{\mathsf{chall}}[0] = \emptyset$.

Suppose $\mathsf{TC}_{\mathsf{chall}}[0] = \cup\{\mathsf{e}_{start}, \ldots, \mathsf{e}_{end}\}$. We prove that the adversary cannot learn a challenge-equal ciphertext in epoch e_{end+1} either by querying or inferring. First, the adversary cannot learn a challenge-equal ciphertext in epoch e_{end+1} via querying $\mathcal{O}_{\mathsf{sUpd}}$, since e_{end} is the last epoch in the epoch continuum; otherwise, the received updated ciphertext will be recorded in the table $\mathsf{TC}_{\mathsf{chall}}$, which conflicts with the condition that e_{end} is the last epoch in the epoch continuum. Alternatively, it can update challenge-equal ciphertext in epoch e_{end} with its inferred token as Eq. (6). But from $\mathcal{K} \cap \mathsf{TC}_{\mathsf{chall}}[0] = \emptyset$, we know the epoch key k_{end} is unknown to the adversary, which is needed to infer the token in e_{end+1} (see Eq. (5)).

The proof is the same for the challenge-equal ciphertext in epoch e_{start}. Therefore, the adversary cannot learn a challenge-equal ciphertext in any epoch outside of the set $\mathsf{TC}_{\mathsf{chall}}[0]$, which implies that $\mathsf{TC}_{\mathsf{chall}}[0] = \mathsf{TC}^*_{\mathsf{chall}}[0]$. □

Remark 1. Lemma 3 shows that the adversary cannot infer a challenge-equal ciphertext in an epoch that is not recorded in the look-up table, i.e., $\mathsf{TC}_{\mathsf{chall}}[0] = \mathsf{TC}^*_{\mathsf{chall}}[0]$. But that does not mean all the ciphertexts known to the adversary are stored in the table $\mathsf{TC}_{\mathsf{chall}}$, or equally $\mathsf{TC}_{\mathsf{chall}} = \mathsf{TC}^*_{\mathsf{chall}}$, which is only true for deterministic UE. For randomized UE schemes, the adversary can create an arbitrary number of valid challenge-equal ciphertexts in any epoch in $\mathsf{TC}_{\mathsf{chall}}[0]$ by performing the update with its known ciphertexts and tokens.

II. Trivial Win by Updates

For UE schemes with randomized updates, there are no restrictions on the update oracle. However, for UE schemes with deterministic updates, the adversary can learn one of the possible challenge outputs by querying the oracle $\mathcal{O}_{\mathsf{sUpd}}$ on the challenge input $(\hat{\mathsf{ct}}, \mathsf{ct})$, or infer the update of $(\hat{\mathsf{ct}}, \mathsf{ct})$ if $\bar{\mathsf{e}} \in \mathcal{T}^*$, in advance before the challenge phase. In the first case, all known ciphertext leakages before the challenge are recorded by $\mathsf{TC}_{\mathsf{non}}$, so that we can set lines 8–9 in challenge oracle to check for this, as shown in Fig. 8. In the second case, if $\bar{\mathsf{e}} \in \mathcal{T}(\subseteq \mathcal{T}^*)$, i.e., the token is learned by querying $\mathcal{O}_{\mathsf{sUpd}}$, it goes back to the first case ($\mathcal{O}_{\mathsf{sUpd}}$ also returns the updated ciphertext, which is recorded in $\mathsf{TC}_{\mathsf{non}}$). If $\bar{\mathsf{e}} \in \mathcal{T}^* \backslash \mathcal{T}$, the following lemma shows the impossibility.

Lemma 4. *For c-d UE schemes with no-directional key updates, if* $\mathcal{K} \cap \mathsf{TC}_{\mathsf{chall}}[0] = \emptyset$*, then the challenge epoch* $\bar{\mathsf{e}} \notin \mathcal{T}^* \backslash \mathcal{T}$.

Proof. Note that since the adversary queries the challenge oracle in $\bar{\mathsf{e}}$, then $\bar{\mathsf{e}} \in \mathsf{TC}_{\mathsf{chall}}[0]$. Due to $\mathcal{K} \cap \mathsf{TC}_{\mathsf{chall}}[0] = \emptyset$, we know the epoch key $\mathsf{k}_{\bar{\mathsf{e}}}$ is unknown to the adversary, which is necessary to infer $\Delta_{\bar{\mathsf{e}},\hat{\mathsf{ct}}}$ (see Eq. (5)). □

III. Trivial win by decryptions

Table $\mathsf{TC}^*_{\mathsf{chall}}$ records all the challenge-equal ciphertexts known to the adversary in the game. By Remark 1, we first have the following lemma.

$\mathcal{O}_{\mathsf{Enc}}(\mathsf{e}, \mathsf{m})$:

```
(ĉt, ct) ← Enc(k_e, m)
TC_non[e, ĉt] ← ct
return (ĉt, ct)
```

$\mathcal{O}_{\mathsf{sUpd}}(\mathsf{e}, (\hat{\mathsf{ct}}, \mathsf{ct}))$:

```
if TC_chall[e − 1, ĉt] =⊥ and
    TC_non[e − 1, ĉt] =⊥ then
    return ⊥
Δ_{e,ĉt} ← TokenGen(k_{e−1}, k_e, ĉt)
(ĉt′, ct′) ← Update(Δ_{e,ĉt}, (ĉt, ct))
if TC_chall[e − 1, ĉt] ≠⊥
    TC_chall[e, ĉt′] ← ct′
else TC_non[e, ĉt′] ← ct′
return (Δ_{e,ĉt}, (ĉt′, ct′))
```

$\mathcal{O}_{\mathsf{Corr}}(\mathsf{e})$:

```
𝒦 = 𝒦 ∪ {e}
return k_e
```

$\mathcal{O}_{\mathsf{Dec}}(\mathsf{e}, (\hat{\mathsf{ct}}, \mathsf{ct}))$:

```
1 : m′ or ⊥ ← Dec(k_e, (ĉt, ct))
2 : if (xx = det and TC_chall[e, ĉt] = ct) or
3 :     ((xx = rand and e ∈ TC_chall[0]) and
4 :     (m′ = m or m_1)) then
5 :     return ⊥
6 : return Dec (k_e, (ĉt, ct))
```

$\mathcal{O}_{\mathsf{Chall}}(\bar{\mathsf{e}}, \mathsf{m}, (\hat{\mathsf{ct}}, \mathsf{ct}))$:

```
(ĉt′_0, ct′_0) ← Enc (k_ē, m)
if (ĉt′_0, ct′_0) =⊥ or TC_non[ē − 1, ĉt] ≠ ct
    return ⊥
Δ_{ē,ĉt} ← TokenGen (k_{ē−1}, k_ē, ĉt)
(ĉt′_1, ct′_1) ← Update(Δ_{ē,ĉt}, (ĉt, ct))
if |ĉt′_0| ≠ |ĉt′_1| or |ct′_0| ≠ |ct′_1|
    return ⊥
if (xx = det and TC_non[ē, ĉt′_1] = ct′_1)
    return ⊥
TC_chall[ē, ĉt′_b] ← ct′_b
return (ĉt′_b, ct′_b)
```

Fig. 8. An overview of the oracles that the adversary has access to in Definition 7. In the decryption oracle, m is the challenge input message and m_1 is the underlying message of the challenge input ciphertext.

Lemma 5. *For c-d UE schemes with no-directional key updates, if* $\mathcal{K} \cap \mathsf{TC}_{\mathsf{chall}}[0] = \emptyset$, *then* $\mathsf{TC}^*_{\mathsf{chall}} = \mathsf{TC}_{\mathsf{chall}}$ *for deterministic UE, and* $\mathsf{TC}^*_{\mathsf{chall}}[0] = \mathsf{TC}_{\mathsf{chall}}[0]$ *for randomized UE.*

For UE schemes with deterministic ciphertext updates, table $\mathsf{TC}_{\mathsf{chall}}$ records all leaked challenge-equal ciphertexts in the game. The adversary can trivially win the game by querying the decryption oracle on the challenge-equal ciphertexts recorded on the table $\mathsf{TC}_{\mathsf{chall}}$ (line 2 in $\mathcal{O}_{\mathsf{Dec}}$, Fig. 8).

For UE schemes with randomized ciphertext updates, the epoch set $\mathsf{TC}_{\mathsf{chall}}[0]$ records all the epochs in which the adversary can generate a valid challenge-equal ciphertext. The adversary can trivially win the game if the returned message of the decryption oracle in epochs in $\mathsf{TC}_{\mathsf{chall}}[0]$ is the challenge message or the plaintext of the challenge input ciphertext (lines 3–4).

In summary, the above analysis shows trivial win conditions for c-d UE can be checked immediately based on the recorded leakages during the confidentiality game, without the need for extra calculations and further checks of the extended leaked sets of keys, tokens and ciphertext as in previous work for c-i UE in

[6,15,18]. After all the queries, if $\perp$ is not returned, only one condition remains to be checked: $\mathcal{K} \cap \mathsf{TC}_{\mathsf{chall}}[0] = \emptyset$. This advantage is due to both the no-directional key update setting and the proper ways of recording leakage information via look-up tables. Finally, we introduce the definition of xxIND-UE-atk.

Definition 7 (xxIND-UE-atk). *Let* $\mathsf{UE} = (\mathsf{KG}, \mathsf{Enc}, \mathsf{Dec}, \mathsf{TokenGen}, \mathsf{Update})$ *be a ciphertext-dependent updatable encryption scheme with no-directional key updates. For an adversary* $\mathcal{A}$ *and* $\mathrm{b} \in \{0,1\}$, *we define the confidentiality experiment* $\mathbf{Exp}_{\mathsf{UE},\mathcal{A}}^{\mathsf{xxIND\text{-}UE\text{-}atk\text{-}b}}$ *in Fig. 9 for* $\mathsf{xx} \in \{\mathsf{det}, \mathsf{rand}\}$ *and* $\mathsf{atk} \in \{\mathsf{CPA}, \mathsf{CCA\text{-}1}, \mathsf{CCA}\}$.

We say UE *meets the* xxIND-UE-atk *confidentiality if there is a negligible function* $\mathsf{negl}(\lambda)$ *such that* $\mathsf{Adv}_{\mathsf{UE},\mathcal{A}}^{\mathsf{xxIND\text{-}UE\text{-}atk}}(\lambda) \le \mathsf{negl}(\lambda)$, *where*

$$\mathsf{Adv}_{\mathsf{UE},\mathcal{A}}^{\mathsf{xxIND\text{-}UE\text{-}atk}}(\lambda) = \left| \Pr\left[\mathbf{Exp}_{\mathsf{UE},\mathcal{A}}^{\mathsf{xxIND\text{-}UE\text{-}atk\text{-}1}} = 1 \right] - \Pr\left[\mathbf{Exp}_{\mathsf{UE},\mathcal{A}}^{\mathsf{xxIND\text{-}UE\text{-}atk\text{-}1}} = 0 \right] \right|.$$

$\mathsf{Exp}_{\mathsf{UE},\mathcal{A}}^{\mathsf{xxIND\text{-}UE\text{-}atk\text{-}b}}$:

$(\mathsf{m}, (\hat{\mathsf{ct}}, \mathsf{ct})) \leftarrow \mathcal{A}^{\mathcal{O}_1}(1^\lambda)$ // setup phase

$\mathcal{A}$ queries $\mathcal{O}_{\mathsf{chall}}$ on $(\mathsf{m}, (\hat{\mathsf{ct}}, \mathsf{ct}))$ // challenge phase

$\mathrm{b}' \leftarrow \mathcal{A}^{\mathcal{O}_2}(1^\lambda)$ // response phase

if $(\mathcal{K} \cap \mathsf{TC}_{\mathsf{chall}}[0] \neq \emptyset)$ **then**

  $\mathrm{b}' \xleftarrow{\$} \{0,1\}$

return b'

Fig. 9. The confidentiality game $\mathbf{Exp}_{\mathsf{UE},\mathcal{A}}^{\mathsf{xxIND\text{-}UE\text{-}atk\text{-}b}}$ where $\mathsf{xx} \in \{\mathsf{det}, \mathsf{rand}\}$ indicates the type of UE scheme (deterministic or randomized) and $\mathsf{atk} \in \{\mathsf{CPA}, \mathsf{CCA\text{-}1}, \mathsf{CCA}\}$ indicates the type of attack model. In the game, the adversary is given access to a set of oracles, denoted by $\mathcal{O}_1$ and $\mathcal{O}_2$ which are shown in Fig. 8 and Fig. 10. During the setup phase, the adversary generates a challenge plaintext and a challenge ciphertext using the oracles in $\mathcal{O}_1$, and submits them to the challenger in the challenge phase. The adversary continues to query the oracles in $\mathcal{O}_2$ and eventually provides a guess bit. The only condition for the adversary to lose the game is $\mathcal{K} \cap \mathsf{TC}_{\mathsf{chall}}[0] \neq \emptyset$.

Future Extensions. In our security model, the adversary is only allowed to query the update oracle with "correctly" generated ciphertexts throughout the experiment. An interesting future work is to investigate security notions that capture both adaptive security and protection against malicious updates.

3.4 Firewall Techniques

Firewall Technique. In c-i UE, the firewall technique was developed in [17,18] to facilitate security proof by separating epochs into different regions. Inside an insulated region, the simulation in the proof should appropriately respond to the

atk	$\mathcal{O}_1$	$\mathcal{O}_2$
CPA	$\mathcal{O}_{\mathsf{Enc}}, \mathcal{O}_{\mathsf{sUpd}}, \mathcal{O}_{\mathsf{Corr}}$	$\mathcal{O}_{\mathsf{Enc}}, \mathcal{O}_{\mathsf{sUpd}}, \mathcal{O}_{\mathsf{Corr}}$
CCA-1	$\mathcal{O}_{\mathsf{Enc}}, \mathcal{O}_{\mathsf{sUpd}}, \boxed{\mathcal{O}_{\mathsf{Dec}}}, \mathcal{O}_{\mathsf{Corr}}$	$\mathcal{O}_{\mathsf{Enc}}, \mathcal{O}_{\mathsf{sUpd}}, \mathcal{O}_{\mathsf{Corr}}$
CCA	$\mathcal{O}_{\mathsf{Enc}}, \mathcal{O}_{\mathsf{sUpd}}, \boxed{\mathcal{O}_{\mathsf{Dec}}}, \mathcal{O}_{\mathsf{Corr}}$	$\mathcal{O}_{\mathsf{Enc}}, \mathcal{O}_{\mathsf{sUpd}}, \boxed{\mathcal{O}_{\mathsf{Dec}}}, \mathcal{O}_{\mathsf{Corr}}$

Fig. 10. Oracles that the adversary has access to before and after the challenge phase in the confidentiality game for different attacks. It can corrupt keys at any time during the game in all attacks via querying $\mathsf{O}_{\mathsf{Corr}}$, but is not allowed to query the decryption oracle in the CPA attack, limited to query the decryption oracle before the challenge in the CCA-1 attack, and free to query the decryption oracle in the CCA attack.

queries of the adversary, since it corrupts all tokens within this region. While outside, the simulation can generate tokens and epoch keys freely.

In c-d UE, we similarly define the insulated region, inside which all tokens related to challenge-equal ciphertexts (called challenge-equal tokens) are corrupted but no epoch key is corrupted.

Definition 8 (Firewall). *In ciphertext-dependent UE schemes, an insulated region with firewalls* fwl *and* fwr, *denoted by* $\mathcal{FW}$, *is a consecutive sequence of epochs* $(\mathsf{fwl}, \ldots, \mathsf{fwr})$ *for which:*

- *no key in the sequence of epochs* $\{\mathsf{fwl}, \ldots, \mathsf{fwr}\}$ *is corrupted;*
- *no challenge-equal tokens in epochs* fwl *and* $\mathsf{fwr}+1$ *is corrupted;*
- *all challenge-equal tokens in epochs* $\{\mathsf{fwl}+1, \ldots, \mathsf{fwr}\}$ *are corrupted.*

Suppose an xxIND-UE-atk adversary $\mathcal{A}$ queries the challenge oracle in the epoch $\bar{\mathsf{e}}$ and does not trigger trivial win conditions in the game, and $\mathsf{TC}_{\mathsf{chall}}[0] = \cup\{\mathsf{e}_{start}, \ldots, \mathsf{e}_{end}\}$. The proof of Lemma 3 shows $\mathcal{A}$ cannot update a ciphertext from the epoch e_{end} to the start epoch e'_{start} of the next continuum. Thus, we have $\mathsf{TC}_{\mathsf{chall}}[0] = \{\mathsf{e}_{start}, \ldots, \mathsf{e}_{end}\}$, meaning that the epoch set in which $\mathcal{A}$ knows a challenge-equal ciphertext is only a consecutive continuum starting from the challenge epoch ($\mathsf{e}_{start} = \bar{\mathsf{e}}$), and ending in the epoch e_{end}, the last epoch that the adversary queries the update oracle $\mathcal{O}_{\mathsf{sUpd}}$ on the challenge-equal ciphertext. The epoch keys and tokens in the epoch in $\mathsf{TC}_{\mathsf{chall}}[0]$ have the following properties.

- $\mathcal{A}$ does not know the challenge-equal token in epochs e_{start} and $\mathsf{e}_{end}+1$, following from the proof of Lemma 3;
- $\mathcal{A}$ knows all challenge-equal tokens in epochs in $\{\mathsf{e}_{start}+1, \ldots, \mathsf{e}_{end}\}$, obtained when $\mathcal{A}$ queries the updates of challenge-equal ciphertexts via $\mathcal{O}_{\mathsf{sUpd}}$;
- $\mathcal{A}$ does not know any key in epochs in $\{\mathsf{e}_{start}, \ldots, \mathsf{e}_{end}\}$, as $\mathcal{K} \cap \mathsf{TC}_{\mathsf{chall}}[0] = \emptyset$;

We thus have the Lemma 6, following from the discussion above, and Lemma 7, as a corollary of Lemma 6, both of which provide important tools in the confidentiality proof for c-d UE.

Lemma 6. *Let* $\mathsf{UE} = (\mathsf{KG}, \mathsf{Enc}, \mathsf{TokenGen}, \mathsf{Update}, \mathsf{Decrypt})$ *be a c-d UE scheme with no-directional key updates, and* $\mathsf{xx} \in \{\mathsf{det}, \mathsf{rand}\}$ *and* $\mathsf{atk} \in$

{CPA, CCA-1, CCA}. *For an* xxIND-UE-atk *adversary* $\mathcal{A}$ *against* UE, *the set of epochs in which* $\mathcal{A}$ *knows a challenge-equal ciphertext is an insulated region (Definition 8), starting from the challenge epoch and ending at the last epoch in which the adversary queries the* $\mathcal{O}_{\mathsf{sUpd}}$.

Lemma 7. *For a c-d UE with no-directional key updates, if the* xxIND-UE-atk *adversary knows a challenge-equal ciphertext in epoch* e, *then* e *must be in an insulated region.*

4 A CCA-1 Secure PKE Scheme

In this section, we propose a new PKE scheme called TDP, which is based on the lattice trapdoor techniques. We will use this scheme in Sect. 5 as the underlying encryption scheme to build our UE scheme.

4.1 A New PKE Scheme

Our overall idea is to construct a 1×3 block matrix $\mathbf{A}_\mu$ in the encryption algorithm, with the secret key serving as the trapdoor for the first two blocks of $\mathbf{A}_\mu$ to ensure the correctness of decryption.

We introduce some parameters involved in the construction in Fig. 11, where we use standard asymptotic notations of O, Ω, ω. Let λ be the security parameter, $\omega(\sqrt{\log n})$ is a fixed function that grows asymptotically faster than $\sqrt{\log n}$, and $\Lambda(\mathbf{G}^t)$ is the lattice generated by $\mathbf{G}^t$.

Notations	Functionalities
$\mathbf{G} = \mathbb{Z}_q^{n\times nk}$ (Sect. 2.2) $k = \lceil \log_2 q \rceil = O(\log n)$, $q = \mathsf{poly}(\lambda)$	Make oracles $\mathsf{Invert}^{\mathcal{O}}$ and $\mathsf{SampleD}^{\mathcal{O}}$ efficient for the random matrix with a **G**-trapdoor
$\bar{m} = O(nk)$, $\mathcal{D} = D_{\mathbb{Z}^{\bar{m}\times nk},\omega(\sqrt{\log n})}$	Ensure $(\mathbf{A}, \mathbf{AR})$ is $\mathsf{negl}(\lambda)$-far from uniform for $\mathbf{A} \xleftarrow{\$} \mathbb{Z}_q^{n\times \bar{m}}$ and $\mathbf{R} \leftarrow \mathcal{D}$, due to leftover hash lemma
$\mathsf{encode} : \{0,1\}^{nk} \to \Lambda(\mathbf{G}^t)$ by $\mathsf{encode}(\mathbf{m}) = \mathbf{Bm} \in \mathbb{Z}^{nk}$, and **B** is any basis of $\Lambda(\mathbf{G}^t)$	Ensure an efficient decoding for decryption
LWE error rate α such that : $1/\alpha = 4 \cdot O(nk) \cdot \omega(\sqrt{\log n})$	Control the magnitude of error in ciphertext

Fig. 11. A summary of notations used in PKE construction and their functionalities.

The PKE scheme TDP is described as follows. On a first reading, we suggest readers to neglect the error parameter settings that are used to control the error bound within the decryption capability, in order to have a simpler view at a high level.

- TDP.KG(1^λ): choose $\mathbf{A}_0 \xleftarrow{\$} \mathbb{Z}_q^{n\times\bar{m}}$, $\mathbf{R}_1, \mathbf{R}_2 \xleftarrow{\$} \mathcal{D}$ and let $\mathbf{A} = [\mathbf{A}_0 \mid \mathbf{A}_1 \mid \mathbf{A}_2] = [\mathbf{A}_0 \mid -\mathbf{A}_0\mathbf{R}_1 \mid -\mathbf{A}_0\mathbf{R}_2] \in \mathbb{Z}_q^{n\times m}$ where $m = \bar{m} + 2nk$. The public key is $\mathsf{pk} = \mathbf{A}$ and the secret key is $\mathsf{sk} = \mathbf{R}_1$.

- TDP.Enc($\mathsf{pk} = \mathbf{A}, \mathbf{m} \in \{0,1\}^{nk}$): choose an invertible matrix $\mathbf{H}_\mu \in \mathbb{Z}_q^{n\times n}$, and let $\mathbf{A}_\mu = [\mathbf{A}_0 \mid \mathbf{A}_1 + \mathbf{H}_\mu\mathbf{G} \mid \mathbf{A}_2]$. Choose a random vector $\mathbf{s} \in \mathbb{Z}_q^n$ and an error vector $\mathbf{e} = (\mathbf{e}_0, \mathbf{e}_1, \mathbf{e}_2) \in D_{\mathbb{Z}^{\bar{m}},\alpha q} \times D_{\mathbb{Z}^{nk},d} \times D_{\mathbb{Z}^{nk},d}$ where $d^2 = (\|\mathbf{e}_0\|^2 + \bar{m}\cdot(\alpha q)^2)\cdot\omega(\sqrt{\log n})^2$. Let

$$\mathbf{b}^t = \mathbf{s}^t\mathbf{A}_\mu + \mathbf{e}^t + (\mathbf{0}, \mathbf{0}, \mathsf{encode}(\mathbf{m}))^t \mod q, \tag{7}$$

where the first $\mathbf{0}$ has dimension $\bar{m}$ and the second has dimension nk. Output the ciphertext $c = (\mathbf{H}_\mu, \mathbf{b})$. Notice that $\mathbf{R}_1$ is a trapdoor for $[\mathbf{A}_0 \mid \mathbf{A}_1 + \mathbf{H}_\mu\mathbf{G}]$.

- TDP.Dec($\mathsf{sk} = \mathbf{R}_1, c = (\mathbf{H}_\mu, \mathbf{b})$): let $\mathbf{A}_\mu = [\mathbf{A}_0 \mid \mathbf{A}_1 + \mathbf{H}_\mu\mathbf{G} \mid \mathbf{A}_2]$. The decryption first recovers $\mathbf{s}$ from the first two blocks via the invert algorithm and then the message $\mathbf{m}$ from the third block by decoding (when $\mathbf{s}$ is known):

$$\begin{aligned}(\mathbf{b}_0, \mathbf{b}_1, \mathbf{b}_2)^t =& \mathbf{s}^t[\mathbf{A}_0 \mid \mathbf{A}_1 + \mathbf{H}_\mu\mathbf{G} \mid \mathbf{A}_2] \\ &+ (\mathbf{e}_0, \mathbf{e}_1, \mathbf{e}_2)^t + (\mathbf{0}, \mathbf{0}, \mathsf{encode}(\mathbf{m}))^t \mod q.\end{aligned}$$

  1. If c or $\mathbf{b}$ does not parse, or $\mathbf{H}_\mu = \mathbf{0}$, output $\perp$. Otherwise parse $\mathbf{b}^t = (\mathbf{b}_0, \mathbf{b}_1, \mathbf{b}_2)^t$.
  2. **Recover s.** Call $\mathsf{Invert}^{\mathcal{O}}(\mathbf{R}_1, [\mathbf{A}_0 \mid \mathbf{A}_1 + \mathbf{H}_\mu\mathbf{G}], [\mathbf{b}_0, \mathbf{b}_1], \mathbf{H}_\mu)$ by Lemma 1, which returns $\mathbf{s}$ and $(\mathbf{e}_0, \mathbf{e}_1)$ such that

$$(\mathbf{b}_0, \mathbf{b}_1)^t = \mathbf{s}^t[\mathbf{A}_0 \mid \mathbf{A}_1 + \mathbf{H}_\mu\mathbf{G}] + (\mathbf{e}_0, \mathbf{e}_1)^t \mod q.$$

  If $\mathsf{Invert}^{\mathcal{O}}$ fails, output $\perp$. Invert $\mathbf{b}_2^t - \mathbf{s}^t\mathbf{A}_2$ again and find the unique solution $\mathbf{u}, \mathbf{e}_2$ to the equation

$$\mathbf{b}_2^t - \mathbf{s}^t\mathbf{A}_2 = \mathbf{u}^t\mathbf{G} + \mathbf{e}_2^t \mod q,$$

  3. If $\|\mathbf{e}_0\| \geq \alpha q\sqrt{\bar{m}}$ or $\|\mathbf{e}_j\| \geq \alpha q\sqrt{2\bar{m}nk}\cdot\omega(\sqrt{\log n})$ for $j = 1, 2$, output $\perp$ (Lemma 12 in the full version [9]).
  4. **Recover the plaintext.** Output the following result

$$\mathsf{encode}^{-1}\left(\mathbf{b}_2^t - \mathbf{s}^t\mathbf{A}_2 - \mathbf{e}_2^t\right) \in \mathbb{Z}_2^{nk},$$

  if it exists, otherwise output $\perp$.

4.2 Correctness and Security

We provide a full proof of the correctness (Lemma 8) and security (Lemma 9) of the updatable encryption scheme TDUE in Sect. 5, which is based on TDP as a subcase of TDUE.

Lemma 8. *Our* TDP *decrypts correctly except with* $2^{-\Omega(n)}$ *failure probability.*

Proof. The proof is the same as that of Lemma 10, except the bound for the error vectors. The secret key $\mathbf{R}$ serves as the trapdoor for the first two blocks of $\mathbf{A}_\mu$, which ensures the proper recovery of $\mathbf{s}$ in Step 2 as long as the error bound is within the capability of Invert. That is $\|\mathbf{e}^t(\begin{smallmatrix}\mathbf{R}\\ \mathbf{I}\end{smallmatrix})\| \leq q/4$ by Lemma 1. By Lemma 14 in the full version [9], we have $s_1(\mathbf{R}) = \omega(\sqrt{\log n}) \cdot O(\sqrt{nk})$. By Lemma 12 in the full version [9], we have $\|\mathbf{e}_0\| \leq \alpha q\sqrt{\bar{m}}$ and $\|\mathbf{e}_i\| \leq \alpha q\sqrt{2\bar{m}nk} \cdot \omega(\sqrt{\log n})$ for $j = 1, 2$, except with negligible probability $2^{-\Omega(n)}$, where $\bar{m} = O(nk)$. Therefore,

$$\left\|(\mathbf{e}_0, \mathbf{e}_1)^t \left[\begin{smallmatrix}\mathbf{R}\\ \mathbf{I}\end{smallmatrix}\right]\right\|_\infty \leq \left\|(\mathbf{e}_0, \mathbf{e}_1)^t \left[\begin{smallmatrix}\mathbf{R}\\ \mathbf{I}\end{smallmatrix}\right]\right\| \leq \left\|\mathbf{e}_0^t\mathbf{R}\right\| + \|\mathbf{e}_1\| \leq \alpha q \cdot O(nk) \cdot \omega(\sqrt{\log n}),$$

which is further smaller than $q/4$ since $1/\alpha = 4 \cdot O(nk) \cdot \omega(\sqrt{\log n})$, and $\|\mathbf{e}_2\|_\infty \leq q/4$ for the same reason, which ensures the correct recovery of $\mathbf{s}$, $\mathbf{u}$ and $\mathbf{m}$. □

Lemma 9. *Our PKE scheme* TDP *is* CCA-1 *secure if the* LWE *problem is hard.*

Proof. We provide a detailed CCA-1 proof for our UE scheme in Theorem 2. Note that, if the adversary is disallowed to query the token generation and update algorithm, the CCA-1 game for UE is exactly the standard CCA-1 game for the underlying PKE. Therefore, CCA-1 security of TDP follows from Theorem 2. □

5 A CCA-1 Secure Updatable Encryption Scheme

Based on our PKE scheme in Sect. 4, we construct a new UE scheme, which is IND-UE-CCA-1 secure under the assumption of the LWE hardness.

5.1 Construction

Our UE scheme uses the same encryption and decryption algorithm in TDP, i.e., the ciphertext of a plaintext $\mathbf{m}$ is of the form $(\hat{\mathsf{ct}}, \mathsf{ct}) = (\mathbf{H}_\mu, \mathbf{s}^t\mathbf{A}_\mu + \mathbf{e}^t + (\mathbf{0}, \mathbf{0}, \mathsf{encode}(\mathbf{m})^t)$. To update a ciphertext, at a high level, the update algorithm first generates a key-switching matrix $\mathbf{M}$ with the last row block matrix $[\mathbf{0}\ \mathbf{0}\ \mathbf{I}]$, such that $\mathbf{A}_\mu\mathbf{M} = \mathbf{A}'_\mu$ for the aimed $\mathbf{A}'_\mu$ in the new ciphertext. This step is feasible since the secret key is the trapdoor for the first two blocks of $\mathbf{A}_\mu$, ensuring an efficient preimage sampling algorithm (Lemma 2). To increase the randomness of $\mathbf{s}$, then we add a fresh encryption of message $\mathbf{0}$ to the ciphertext. Figure 12 shows an overview of the ciphertext update.

We use the same parameters as in Sect. 4.1 except the following. We also suggest readers on the first reading to neglect the parameter setting for error items which are used to control the updated error bound.

- $1/\alpha = 4l \cdot \omega(\sqrt{\log n})^{2l+2} O(\sqrt{nk})^{3l+3}$ where l is the maximal number of updates that the scheme can support.
- $\tau = \sqrt{s_1(\mathbf{R})^2 + 1} \cdot \sqrt{s_1(\Sigma_\mathbf{G}) + 1} \cdot \omega(\sqrt{\log n})$ is the smallest Gaussian parameter for the discrete Gaussian distribution from which the sampling algorithm $\mathsf{SampleD}^\mathcal{O}$ can sample vectors, where $s_1(\Sigma_\mathbf{G}) = 5$ by Theorem 1.

$$(\mathbf{H}_\mu,\ \mathbf{s}^t\mathbf{A}_\mu + \mathbf{e}^t + (\mathbf{0}, \mathbf{0}, \text{encode}(\mathbf{m})^t)$$

$$\Big\Downarrow \quad \text{Multiplied by } \mathbf{M} \text{ (generated by Lemma 2)}$$

$$(\mathbf{H}'_\mu,\ \mathbf{s}^t\mathbf{A}'_\mu + \mathbf{e}'^t + (\mathbf{0}, \mathbf{0}, \text{encode}(\mathbf{m})^t)$$

$$\Big\Downarrow \quad \text{Add } \mathbf{s}'^t\mathbf{A}'_\mu + \mathbf{e}''^t, \text{ an encryption of } \mathbf{0}$$

$$(\mathbf{H}'_\mu,\ \mathbf{s}''^t\mathbf{A}'_\mu + \mathbf{e}'''^t + (\mathbf{0}, \mathbf{0}, \text{encode}(\mathbf{m})^t)$$

Fig. 12. An overview of ciphertext update in our UE construction. The first step mainly updates $\mathbf{A}_\mu$ to $\mathbf{A}'_\mu$, and the second step refreshes the randomness $\mathbf{s}$.

The UE scheme TDUE is described as follows.

- TDUE.KG(1^λ): output TDP.KG(1^λ).
- TDUE.Enc$(\mathsf{pk} = \mathbf{A}, \mathbf{m} \in \{0,1\}^{nk})$: output TDP.Enc$(\mathbf{A}, \mathbf{m})$.
- TDUE.Dec$(\mathsf{sk} = \mathbf{R}_1, c = (\mathbf{H}_\mu, \mathbf{b}))$: output TDP.Dec$(\mathbf{R}_1, (\mathbf{H}_\mu, \mathbf{b}))$.
- TDUE.TokenGen$(\mathsf{pk}, \mathsf{sk}, \mathsf{pk}', \mathbf{H}_\mu)$: parse $\mathsf{pk} = [\mathbf{A}_0 \mid \mathbf{A}_1 \mid \mathbf{A}_2] = [\mathbf{A}_0 \mid -\mathbf{A}_0\mathbf{R}_1 \mid -\mathbf{A}_0\mathbf{R}_2]$, $\mathsf{sk} = \mathbf{R}_1$, and $\mathsf{pk}' = [\mathbf{A}'_0 \mid \mathbf{A}'_1 \mid \mathbf{A}'_2]$.
  1. Generate a random invertible matrix $\mathbf{H}'_\mu$ and let $\mathbf{A}'_\mu = [\mathbf{A}'_0 \mid \mathbf{A}'_1 + \mathbf{H}'_\mu\mathbf{G} \mid \mathbf{A}'_2]$. We first generate a transition matrix $\mathbf{M}$ for which $\mathbf{A}_\mu\mathbf{M} = \mathbf{A}'_\mu$ in the following steps 2, 3, and 4, and then compute the encryption of the message $\mathbf{0}$ under $\mathbf{A}'_\mu$ in step 5.
  2. Call $\mathsf{Sample}^{\mathcal{O}}(\mathbf{R}_1, [\mathbf{A}_0 \mid -\mathbf{A}_0\mathbf{R}_1 + \mathbf{H}_\mu\mathbf{G}], \mathbf{H}_\mu, \mathbf{A}'_0, \tau)$ (Lemma 2 and $\mathbf{R}_1$ is a trapdoor for $[\mathbf{A}_0 \mid -\mathbf{A}_0\mathbf{R}_1 + \mathbf{H}_\mu\mathbf{G}]$), which returns an $(\bar{m} + nk) \times \bar{m}$ matrix, parsed as $\mathbf{X}_{00} \in \mathbb{Z}^{\bar{m}\times\bar{m}}$ and $\mathbf{X}_{10} \in \mathbb{Z}^{nk\times\bar{m}}$ with Gaussian entries of parameter τ, satisfying
$$[\mathbf{A}_0 \mid -\mathbf{A}_0\mathbf{R}_1 + \mathbf{H}_\mu\mathbf{G}] \begin{bmatrix} \mathbf{X}_{00} \\ \mathbf{X}_{10} \end{bmatrix} = \mathbf{A}'_0. \tag{8}$$
  3. Call $\mathsf{Sample}^{\mathcal{O}}(\mathbf{R}_1, [\mathbf{A}_0 \mid -\mathbf{A}_0\mathbf{R}_1 + \mathbf{H}_\mu\mathbf{G}], \mathbf{H}_\mu, \mathbf{A}'_1 + \mathbf{H}'_\mu\mathbf{G}, \tau\sqrt{\bar{m}/2})$, which returns $\mathbf{X}_{01} \in \mathbb{Z}_q^{\bar{m}\times nk}$ and $\mathbf{X}_{11} \in \mathbb{Z}_q^{nk\times nk}$ with Gaussian entries of parameter $\tau\sqrt{\bar{m}/2}$ such that
$$[\mathbf{A}_0 \mid -\mathbf{A}_0\mathbf{R}_1 + \mathbf{H}_\mu\mathbf{G}] \begin{bmatrix} \mathbf{X}_{01} \\ \mathbf{X}_{11} \end{bmatrix} = \mathbf{A}'_1 + \mathbf{H}'_\mu\mathbf{G}. \tag{9}$$
  4. Continue calling the sample oracle $\mathsf{Sample}^{\mathcal{O}}(\mathbf{R}_1, [\mathbf{A}_0 \mid -\mathbf{A}_0\mathbf{R}_1 + \mathbf{H}_\mu\mathbf{G}], \mathbf{H}_1, \mathbf{A}'_2 - \mathbf{A}_2, \tau\sqrt{\bar{m}/2})$ and obtain $\mathbf{X}_{02} \in \mathbb{Z}_q^{\bar{m}\times nk}$ and $\mathbf{X}_{12} \in \mathbb{Z}_q^{nk\times nk}$ with Gaussian entries of parameter $\tau\sqrt{\bar{m}/2}$ such that
$$[\mathbf{A}_0 \mid -\mathbf{A}_0\mathbf{R}_1 + \mathbf{H}_\mu\mathbf{G}] \begin{bmatrix} \mathbf{X}_{02} \\ \mathbf{X}_{12} \end{bmatrix} = \mathbf{A}'_2 - \mathbf{A}_2. \tag{10}$$

Let $\mathbf{M}$ be the key-switching matrix as follows:

$$\mathbf{M} = \begin{bmatrix} \mathbf{X}_{00} & \mathbf{X}_{01} & \mathbf{X}_{02} \\ \mathbf{X}_{10} & \mathbf{X}_{11} & \mathbf{X}_{12} \\ \mathbf{0} & \mathbf{0} & \mathbf{I} \end{bmatrix}. \tag{11}$$

Note that $\mathbf{A}_\mu = [\mathbf{A}_0 \mid \mathbf{A}_1 + \mathbf{H}_\mu \mathbf{G} \mid \mathbf{A}_2]$. Then we have $\mathbf{A}_\mu \mathbf{M} = \mathbf{A}'_\mu$ from Eqs. (8) to (10).

5. Let $\mathbf{b}_0$ be the ciphertext of message $\mathbf{m} = \mathbf{0}$ under the public key pk' with the invertible matrix $\mathbf{H}'_\mu$ generated in step 1. That is,

$$\mathbf{b}_0^t = (\mathbf{s}')^t \mathbf{A}'_\mu + (\mathbf{e}')^t \mod q.$$

6. Output the update token $\Delta = (\mathbf{M}, \mathbf{b}_0, \mathbf{H}'_\mu)$.

– $\mathsf{TDUE.Update}(\Delta, c = (\mathbf{H}_\mu, \mathbf{b}))$: parse $\Delta = (\mathbf{M}, \mathbf{b}_0, \mathbf{H}'_\mu)$ and compute

$$(\mathbf{b}')^t = \mathbf{b}^t \cdot \mathbf{M} + \mathbf{b}_0^t \mod q,$$

and output $c' = (\mathbf{H}'_\mu, \mathbf{b}')$.

No-Directional Key Updates. TDUE has no-directional key updates since one can only learn from the update token about the value of $\mathbf{A}'_\mu$ (or $\mathbf{A}_\mu$) through $\mathbf{A}_\mu \mathbf{M} = \mathbf{A}'_\mu$ even if sk (or sk', resp.) is corrupted, whereas $\mathbf{A}'_\mu$ and $\mathbf{A}_\mu$ are random due to the leftover hash lemma and the distribution of the secret key. Therefore, the adversary cannot infer any information about the secret key from the update tokens.

5.2 Correctness

We prove that the decryption algorithm in our scheme can perform correctly with overwhelming probability. Note that the second component in the ciphertext generated by the update algorithm (updated ciphertext) is as follows:

$$\begin{aligned}(\mathbf{b}')^t &= \mathbf{b}^t \cdot \mathbf{M} + \mathbf{b}_0^t \\ &= \left[\mathbf{s}^t \mathbf{A}_\mu + \mathbf{e}^t + (\mathbf{0}, \mathbf{0}, \mathsf{encode}(\mathbf{m}))^t\right] \mathbf{M} + (\mathbf{s}')^t \mathbf{A}'_\mu + (\mathbf{e}')^t \\ &= (\mathbf{s} + \mathbf{s}')^t \mathbf{A}'_\mu + \left(\mathbf{e}^t \mathbf{M} + (\mathbf{e}')^t\right) + (\mathbf{0}, \mathbf{0}, \mathsf{encode}(\mathbf{m}))^t \mod q. \end{aligned} \tag{12}$$

The third equation holds because $\mathbf{A}_\mu \mathbf{M} = \mathbf{A}'_\mu$ and the last nk rows in $\mathbf{M}$ is $[\mathbf{0}\ \mathbf{0}\ \mathbf{I}]$. Therefore the item $(\mathbf{0}, \mathbf{0}, \mathsf{encode}(\mathbf{m}))^t$ stays the same when multiplied by $\mathbf{M}$. Then the updated ciphertext shares the same form with the fresh ciphertext (generated by the encryption algorithm), except that the update algorithm enlarges the error terms by $\mathbf{e}^t \mathbf{M} + (\mathbf{e}')^t$, which may cause the failure in the invert algorithm $\mathsf{Invert}^{\mathcal{O}}$ and further influence the correctness of the decryption algorithm. In the following, we show that the decryption algorithm can tolerate the accumulated errors in the updated ciphertexts by choosing an appropriate value for the parameter α.

Lemma 10. *Our UE scheme* TDUE *decrypts correctly except with* $2^{-\Omega(n)}$ *failure probability.*

Proof. Since the decryption on the fresh ciphertext (from Enc) is a subcase of that on the updated ciphertext (from Update), we choose to prove that the decryption algorithm can output a correct plaintext after performing l updates from epoch 0, where l is the maximum update number.

Let $(\mathsf{pk_e}, \mathsf{sk_e} = \mathbf{R_e})_{0 \leq e \leq l} \leftarrow \mathsf{KG}(1^n)$ be the public and secret key in epoch e. For a random plaintext $\mathbf{m} \in \{0,1\}^{nk}$, let c_e be the ciphertext of $\mathbf{m}$ in epoch e, which is updated from $c_0 = \mathsf{Enc}(\mathbf{m}) = (\mathbf{H}_{\mu,0}, \mathbf{s}_0^t\mathbf{A}_{\mu,0} + \mathbf{e}_0^t + (\mathbf{0}, \mathbf{0}, \mathsf{encode}(\mathbf{m}))^t)$. For $1 \leq i \leq l$, let the token in epoch i be $\Delta_i = (\mathbf{M}_i, \mathbf{b}_{0,i}, \mathbf{H}_{\mu,i})$, where $\mathbf{b}_{0,i}$ is the fresh ciphertext of message $\mathbf{0}$ in epoch i, i.e., $\mathbf{b}_{0,i}^t = \mathbf{s}_i^t\mathbf{A}_{\mu,i} + \mathbf{e}_i^t$ in which $\mathbf{A}_{\mu,i} = [\mathbf{A}_{0,i} \mid \mathbf{A}_{1,i} + \mathbf{H}_{\mu,i}\mathbf{G} \mid \mathbf{A}_{2,i}]$. Iteratively by Eq. (12), we know the updated ciphertext of $\mathbf{m}$ in epoch l is $c_l = (\mathbf{H}_{\mu,l}, \mathbf{b}_l)$ where

$$\mathbf{b}_l^t = (\sum_{i=0}^{l} \mathbf{s}_i)^t\mathbf{A}_{\mu,l} + \sum_{i=0}^{l}(\mathbf{e}_i^t \prod_{j=i+1}^{l} \mathbf{M}_j) + (\mathbf{0}, \mathbf{0}, \mathsf{encode}(\mathbf{m}))^t.$$

Let $\sum_{i=0}^{l}(\mathbf{e}_i^t \prod_{j=i+1}^{l} \mathbf{M}_j) = (\mathbf{e}_0^{(l)}, \mathbf{e}_1^{(l)}, \mathbf{e}_2^{(l)})^t = (\mathbf{e}^{(l)})^t$. In Appendix C of the full version [9], we provide the upper bound for the error $\mathbf{e}^{(l)}$ such that

$$\left\| (\mathbf{e}_0^{(l)}, \mathbf{e}_1^{(l)}, \mathbf{e}_2^{(l)})^t \cdot \begin{bmatrix} \mathbf{R}_l \\ \mathbf{I} \\ \mathbf{0} \end{bmatrix} \right\|_\infty < q/4 \text{ and } \left\| \mathbf{e}_2^{(l)} \right\|_\infty < q/4, \tag{13}$$

except with probability $2^{-\Omega(n)}$ via the appropriate parameter selection for the scheme. Let $\mathbf{b}_l^t = (\mathbf{b}_0^{(l)}, \mathbf{b}_1^{(l)}, \mathbf{b}_2^{(l)})^t$. Then by Lemma 1, the call to $\mathsf{Invert}^{\mathcal{O}}$ made by $\mathsf{Dec}(\mathsf{sk}_l, (\mathbf{H}_{\mu,l}, \mathbf{b}_l))$ returns $\mathbf{s}$ $(=\sum_{i=0}^{l} \mathbf{s}_i)$ and $(\mathbf{e}_0^{(l)}, \mathbf{e}_1^{(l)})$ correctly, for which

$$(\mathbf{b}_0^{(l)}, \mathbf{b}_1^{(l)})^t = \mathbf{s}^t[\mathbf{A}_{0,l} \mid \mathbf{A}_{1,l} + \mathbf{H}_{\mu,l}\mathbf{G}] + (\mathbf{e}_0^{(l)}, \mathbf{e}_1^{(l)})^t \mod q.$$

It follows that

$$(\mathbf{b}_2^{(l)})^t - \mathbf{s}^t\mathbf{A}_{2,l} = (\mathbf{e}_2^{(l)})^t + \mathsf{encode}(\mathbf{m})^t, \tag{14}$$

where $\left\| \mathbf{e}_2^{(l)} \right\| < q/4$ by Inequality (13) and $\mathsf{encode}(\mathbf{m})^t = \mathbf{u}^t\mathbf{G}$ for some $\mathbf{u} \in \mathbb{Z}_q^{nk}$ by the definition of encode. Inverting $(\mathbf{b}_2^{(l)})^t - \mathbf{s}^t\mathbf{A}_{2,l}$, we can find the unique solution $\mathbf{e}_2^{(l)}$ and $\mathbf{u}$ to Eq. (14). Finally, we have

$$\mathsf{encode}^{-1}\left((\mathbf{u}^t\mathbf{G})^t\right) = \mathsf{encode}^{-1}(\mathsf{encode}(\mathbf{m})) = \mathbf{m}.$$

Therefore, the decryption algorithm Dec outputs $\mathbf{m}$ as desired. □

5.3 Security Proof

In this section, we show that our scheme is IND-UE-CCA-1 secure under the hardness assumption of LWE.

Theorem 2. *For any* IND-UE-CCA-1 *adversary* $\mathcal{A}$ *against* TDUE, *there exists an adversary* $\mathcal{B}$ *against* $\mathsf{LWE}_{n,q,\alpha}$ *such that*

$$\mathsf{Adv}^{\mathsf{IND\text{-}UE\text{-}CCA\text{-}1}}_{\mathsf{TDUE},\mathcal{A}}(1^\lambda) \le 2(l+1)^3 \cdot \Big[(l+2)\cdot \mathsf{negl}(\lambda) + (n_{\mathsf{Dec}} + n_{\mathsf{sUpd}}) \cdot 2^{-\Omega(n)} + \mathsf{Adv}^{\mathsf{LWE}}_{n,q,\alpha}(\mathcal{B})\Big],$$

where l *is the maximum number of ciphertext updates that the scheme* TDUE *supports, and* n_{Dec} *and* n_{sUpd} *are the number of queries to the oracles* $\mathcal{O}_{\mathsf{Dec}}$ *and* $\mathcal{O}_{\mathsf{sUpd}}$*, respectively.*

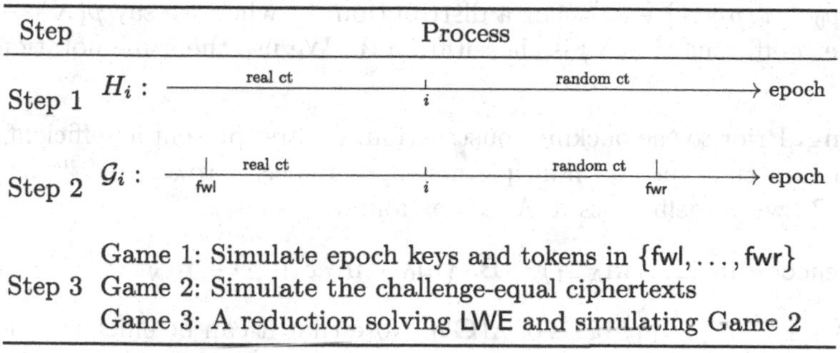

Fig. 13. Steps in the security proof of TDUE. Within an insulated region, the reduction should appropriately respond to all the queries made by the adversary. Outside the region, the reduction can generate epoch keys and tokens freely. ct is the abbreviation of ciphertext.

Proof. In general, we take three steps, see Fig. 13, to bound the advantage of the adversary. In the first step, we build a hybrid game H_i for each epoch i, following [15,20]. To the left of i, the game H_i returns the real challenge-equal ciphertexts and real generated tokens to respond to $\mathcal{O}_{\mathsf{Chall}}$ and $\mathcal{O}_{\mathsf{sUpd}}$ queries; while, to the right of i, H_i returns random ciphertexts and tokens as responses. To distinguish games H_i and H_{i+1}, we assume the adversary queries a challenge-equal ciphertext in epoch i, otherwise the response of both games will be the same. Therefore, the epoch i must be in an insulated region by Lemma 7. In Step 2, we then set up a modified game of H_i, called $\mathcal{G}_i$ that is the same as H_i except for the two randomly chosen epochs fwr, fwl to simulate the insulated region around epoch i: if the adversary queries keys inside the region $[\mathsf{fwr}, \cdots, \mathsf{fwl}]$ or challenge-equal tokens in epochs fwr or $\mathsf{fwl}+1$, $\mathcal{G}_i$ aborts. In the last step, we play three games to bound the advantage of distinguishing games $\mathcal{G}_i$ and $\mathcal{G}_{i+1}$. In Game 1, we simulate keys inside the insulated region, which are unknown to the adversary, and show how to simulate the response to queries on challenge-equal and non-challenge ciphertexts with the simulated keys. We then simulate the challenge-equal ciphertext in the second game, which allows for the construction of a reduction that solves the LWE by simulating the second game to the adversary. We provide the details in Appendix D of the full version [9]. □

5.4 A Packing UE

We now introduce a packing method to further improve the efficiency of c-d UE, which allows us to encrypt multiple messages into one ciphertext and execute ciphertext updates simultaneously.

Let N be a power of 2, $\mathcal{R} = \mathbb{Z}[X]/(X^N+1)$, and $\mathcal{R}_q = \mathcal{R}/(q\mathcal{R})$ be the residue ring of $\mathcal{R}$ modulo q. Any polynomial $p(X)$ in $\mathcal{R}$ can be represented by $p(X) = \sum_{i=0}^{N-1} p_i X^i$ with degree less than N, which is associated with its coefficient vector $\{p_0, \ldots, p_{N-1}\} \in \mathbb{Z}^N$. For a distribution $\mathcal{X}$, when we say $p(X) \xleftarrow{\$} \mathcal{X}$, we mean the coefficient of $p(X)$ is chosen from $\mathcal{X}$. We use the same notations as in Sect. 5.1

Encoding. Prior to the packing construction, we first present an efficient encoding algorithm that encodes multiple messages $\mathbf{m}_0, \ldots, \mathbf{m}_{N-1} \in \mathbb{Z}_2^{nk}$ as an element in $\mathcal{R}_q$ with coefficients in $\Lambda(\mathbf{G}^t)$ as follows:

$$\mathsf{encode}(\mathbf{m}_0, \ldots, \mathbf{m}_{N-1}) = \mathbf{B} \cdot \left(\mathbf{m}_0 + \mathbf{m}_1 x + \cdots + \mathbf{m}_{N-1} x^{N-1}\right),$$

where $\mathbf{B} \in \mathbb{Z}^{nk \times nk}$ is any basis of $\Lambda(\mathbf{G}^t)$. Note that it can be efficiently decoded.

At a high level, multiple message blocks are encrypted in the following form:

$$\begin{aligned}(\mathbf{b}_0, \mathbf{b}_1, \mathbf{b}_2(x))^t &= \mathbf{s}^t[\mathbf{A}_0 \mid \mathbf{A}_0\mathbf{R} + \mathbf{H}_\mu \mathbf{G} \mid \mathbf{A}_2(x)] \\ &+ (\mathbf{e}_0, \mathbf{e}_1, \mathbf{e}_2(x))^t + (\mathbf{0}, \mathbf{0}, \mathsf{encode}(\mathbf{m}_0, \ldots, \mathbf{m}_{N-1}))^t \mod q. \quad (15)\end{aligned}$$

Compared to TDUE, the major modification in this approach is in the third block that uses polynomial matrices and vectors. The secret key $\mathbf{R}$ is still the trapdoor for $[\mathbf{A}_0 \mid \mathbf{A}_0\mathbf{R} + \mathbf{H}_\mu \mathbf{G}]$. Therefore, the decryption procedure is able to properly recover $\mathbf{s}$ from the first two blocks in Eq. (15) as $\mathsf{TDUE.Dec}$, and then call $\mathsf{Invert}^{\mathcal{O}}$ over $\mathbf{b}_2(x) - \mathbf{s}^t\mathbf{A}_2(x)$ degree by degree to recover every message. Moreover, the token generation is feasible due to a generalized preimage sampling algorithm in Lemma 11.

Lemma 11. *Given a* $\mathbf{G}$*-trapdoor* $\mathbf{R}$ *for* $\mathbf{A} \in \mathbb{Z}_q^{n \times m}$ *with invertible matrix* $\mathbf{H}$ *and any polynomial vector* $\mathbf{u}(X) \in \mathcal{R}_q^n$*, there is an efficient algorithm called* $\mathsf{GSampleD}^{\mathcal{O}}(\mathbf{R}, \mathbf{A}, \mathbf{H}, \mathbf{u}(X), s)$ *that samples a Gaussian polynomial vector* $\mathbf{p}(X) \in \mathcal{R}_q^m$ *with coefficients from* $D_{\mathbb{Z},s}$ *such that* $\mathbf{A} \cdot \mathbf{p}(X) = \mathbf{u}(X)$*, where* s *is the smallest Gaussian parameter defined in Lemma 2.*

Proof. Calling the oracle $\mathsf{SampleD}^{\mathcal{O}}$ on each coefficient vector of $\mathbf{u}(X)$ returns a vector $\mathbf{p}_i$ such that

$$\mathbf{A}\mathbf{p}_i = \mathbf{u}_i,$$

for $0 \le i \le N$ and $\mathbf{u}(X) = \sum_{i=0}^{N-1} \mathbf{u}_i X^i$. Denote $\mathbf{p}(X) = \sum_{i=0}^{N-1} \mathbf{p}_i X^i$, then we know $\mathbf{A}\mathbf{p}(X) = \mathbf{u}(X)$. □

Packing UE. Our packing UE scheme is described as follows.

- $\mathsf{KG}(1^\lambda)$: choose $\mathbf{A}_0 \xleftarrow{\$} \mathbb{Z}_q^{n\times\bar{m}}$, $\mathbf{R}_1$, $\mathbf{R}_2(X) \xleftarrow{\$} \mathcal{D}$ and let $\mathbf{A} = [\mathbf{A}_0 \mid \mathbf{A}_1 \mid \mathbf{A}_2] = [\mathbf{A}_0 \mid -\mathbf{A}_0\mathbf{R}_1 \mid -\mathbf{A}_0\mathbf{R}_2(X)] \in \mathcal{R}_q^{n\times m}$ where $m = \bar{m} + 2nk$. The public key is $\mathsf{pk} = \mathbf{A}$ and the secret key is $\mathsf{sk} = \mathbf{R}_1$.
- $\mathsf{Enc}(\mathsf{pk} = \mathbf{A}, \mathbf{m}_0, \ldots, \mathbf{m}_{N-1} \in \{0,1\}^{nk})$: choose an invertible matrix $\mathbf{H}_\mu \in \mathbb{Z}_q^{n\times n}$, and let $\mathbf{A}_\mu = [\mathbf{A}_0 \mid \mathbf{A}_1 + \mathbf{H}_\mu\mathbf{G} \mid \mathbf{A}_2]$. Choose a random vector $\mathbf{s} \in \mathbb{Z}_q^n$ and an error vector $\mathbf{e} = (\mathbf{e}_0, \mathbf{e}_1, \mathbf{e}_2(X)) \in D_{\mathbb{Z}^{\bar{m}},\alpha q} \times D_{\mathbb{Z}^{nk},d} \times D_{\mathbb{Z}^{nk},d}$ where $d^2 = (\|\mathbf{e}_0\|^2 + \bar{m}\cdot(\alpha q)^2)\cdot\omega(\sqrt{\log n})^2$. Let
$$\mathbf{b}^t = \mathbf{s}^t\mathbf{A}_\mu + \mathbf{e}^t + (\mathbf{0}, \mathbf{0}, \mathsf{encode}(\mathbf{m}_0, \ldots, \mathbf{m}_{N-1})^t \mod q, \tag{16}$$
where $\mathsf{encode}(\mathbf{m}_0, \ldots, \mathbf{m}_{N-1}) = \mathbf{B}\cdot(\mathbf{m}_0 + \mathbf{m}_1 X + \cdots + \mathbf{m}_{N-1}X^{N-1})$.
- $\mathsf{Dec}(\mathsf{sk} = \mathbf{R}_1, c = (\mathbf{H}_\mu, \mathbf{b}))$: Recover $\mathbf{s}$ as the steps 1 to 3 in the decryption algorithm of TDP. Parse $\mathbf{b}^t = (\mathbf{b}_0, \mathbf{b}_1, \mathbf{b}_2(X))^t$, invert $\mathbf{b}_2(X)^t - \mathbf{s}^t\mathbf{A}_2$ degree by degree, and find the unique solution $\mathbf{u}_i, \mathbf{e}_{2,i}$ to the equation
$$\mathbf{b}_{2,i}^t - \mathbf{s}^t\mathbf{A}_{2,i} = \mathbf{u}_i^t\mathbf{G} + \mathbf{e}_{2,i}^t \mod q,$$
by Lemma 1 if they exist, where $\mathbf{b}_2(X) = \sum \mathbf{b}_{2,i}X^i$ and $\mathbf{A}_2 = \sum \mathbf{A}_{2,i}X^i$. Output the following result as $\mathbf{m}_i$ if it exists,
$$\mathsf{encode}^{-1}\left((\mathbf{u}_i^t\mathbf{G})^t\right) \in \mathbb{Z}_2^{nk},$$
for $0 \le i \le N-1$, otherwise output $\perp$.
- $\mathsf{TokenGen}(\mathsf{pk}, \mathsf{sk}, \mathsf{pk}', \mathbf{H}_\mu)$: Generate block matrices $\mathbf{M}_{00}$, $\mathbf{M}_{01}$, $\mathbf{M}_{10}$, $\mathbf{M}_{11}$ of $\mathbf{M}$ as in steps 2 and 3 of $\mathsf{TDUE.TokenGen}$, and call the algorithm $\mathsf{GSampleD}^{\mathcal{O}}$ in Lemma 11 to find $\mathbf{M}_{02}(X) \in \mathcal{R}_q^{\bar{m}\times nk}$, $\mathbf{M}_{12}(X) \in \mathcal{R}_q^{nk\times nk}$ such that
$$[\mathbf{A}_0 \mid -\mathbf{A}_0\mathbf{R}_1 + \mathbf{H}_\mu\mathbf{G}]\begin{bmatrix}\mathbf{M}_{02}(X)\\ M_{12}(X)\end{bmatrix} - \mathbf{A}_2' - \mathbf{A}_2.$$
Generate $\mathbf{b}_0$ a fresh encryption of message 0. Output the update token $\Delta = (\mathbf{M}, \mathbf{b}_0, \mathbf{H}_\mu')$.
- $\mathsf{TDUE.Update}(\Delta, c = (\mathbf{H}_\mu, \mathbf{b}))$: parse $\Delta = (\mathbf{M}, \mathbf{b}_0, \mathbf{H}_\mu')$ and compute
$$(\mathbf{b}')^t = \mathbf{b}^t\cdot\mathbf{M} + \mathbf{b}_0^t \mod q,$$
and output $c' = (\mathbf{H}_\mu', \mathbf{b}')$.

Remark. The correctness and IND-UE-CCA-1 security of packing UE is analogous to those of TDUE (as shown in Lemma 10 and Theorem 2). We omit the details. For a message of bit length Nnk, packing UE, compared to TDUE, reduces the number of ciphertexts by a factor of N, and only one ciphertext header is required to be downloaded in the token generation procedure.

6 Conclusion and Future Work

In this paper, we propose a stronger confidentiality notion than prior work for ciphertext-dependent updatable encryption, which captures adaptive security and is applied to both types of UE schemes: deterministic and randomized updates. We also provide a new public key encryption scheme, based on which we construct our updatable encryption scheme. Moreover, we propose a cost-effective packing UE scheme that is able to execute ciphertext updates simultaneously.

Future Work. The first FHE scheme introduced by Gentry [14] and all its subsequent works require a "circular security" assumption, namely that it is safe to encrypt old secret keys with new keys. Such an idea has inspired the UE construction with backward directional key updates. In turn, we suggest an open problem that if no-directional updatable encryption, which is able to update ciphertext without revealing old and new keys, can be used to construct FHE that does not rely on the assumption.

Acknowledgment. We would like to thank the anonymous reviewers for their valuable comments and Hao Lin for the technical discussions. This work was partly supported by the EU Horizon Europe Research and Innovation Programme under Grant No. 101073920 (TENSOR), No. 101070627 (REWIRE), and No. 101070052 (TANGO).

References

1. Agrawal, S., Gentry, C., Halevi, S., Sahai, A.: Discrete Gaussian leftover hash lemma over infinite domains. In: Sako, K., Sarkar, P. (eds.) ASIACRYPT 2013, Part I. LNCS, vol. 8269, pp. 97–116. Springer, Heidelberg (2013). https://doi.org/10.1007/978-3-642-42033-7_6
2. Ajtai, M.: Generating hard instances of lattice problems. In: STOC, pp. 99–108 (1996). https://doi.org/10.1145/237814.237838
3. Alamati, N., Montgomery, H., Patranabis, S.: Symmetric primitives with structured secrets. In: Boldyreva, A., Micciancio, D. (eds.) CRYPTO 2019, Part O. LNCS, vol. 11692, pp. 650–679. Springer, Cham (2019). https://doi.org/10.1007/978-3-030-26948-7_23
4. Boneh, D., Eskandarian, S., Kim, S., Shih, M.: Improving speed and security in updatable encryption schemes. In: Moriai, S., Wang, H. (eds.) ASIACRYPT 2020, Part III. LNCS, vol. 12493, pp. 559–589. Springer, Cham (2020). https://doi.org/10.1007/978-3-030-64840-4_19
5. Boneh, D., Lewi, K., Montgomery, H., Raghunathan, A.: Key homomorphic PRFs and their applications. In: Canetti, R., Garay, J.A. (eds.) CRYPTO 2013, Part I. LNCS, vol. 8042, pp. 410–428. Springer, Heidelberg (2013). https://doi.org/10.1007/978-3-642-40041-4_23
6. Boyd, C., Davies, G.T., Gjøsteen, K., Jiang, Y.: Fast and secure updatable encryption. In: Micciancio, D., Ristenpart, T. (eds.) CRYPTO 2020, Part I. LNCS, vol. 12170, pp. 464–493. Springer, Cham (2020). https://doi.org/10.1007/978-3-030-56784-2_16

7. Brakerski, Z., Gentry, C., Vaikuntanathan, V.: (Leveled) fully homomorphic encryption without bootstrapping. In: Goldwasser, S. (ed.) ITIC 2012, pp. 309–325. ACM (2012). https://doi.org/10.1145/2090236.2090262
8. Brakerski, Z., Vaikuntanathan, V.: Efficient fully homomorphic encryption from (standard) LWE. In: Ostrovsky, R. (ed.) FOCS 2011, pp. 97–106. IEEE Computer Society (2011). https://doi.org/10.1109/FOCS.2011.12
9. Chen, H., Galteland, Y.J., Liang, K.: CCA-1 secure updatable encryption with adaptive security. Cryptology ePrint Archive, Paper 2022/1339 (2022). https://eprint.iacr.org/2022/1339
10. Chen, L., Li, Y., Tang, Q.: CCA updatable encryption against malicious re-encryption attacks. In: Moriai, S., Wang, H. (eds.) ASIACRYPT 2020, Part III. LNCS, vol. 12493, pp. 590–620. Springer, Cham (2020). https://doi.org/10.1007/978-3-030-64840-4_20
11. Everspaugh, A., Paterson, K., Ristenpart, T., Scott, S.: Key rotation for authenticated encryption. In: Katz, J., Shacham, H. (eds.) CRYPTO 2017, Part III. LNCS, vol. 10403, pp. 98–129. Springer, Cham (2017). https://doi.org/10.1007/978-3-319-63697-9_4
12. Fan, X., Liu, F.-H.: Proxy re-encryption and re-signatures from lattices. In: Deng, R.H., Gauthier-Umaña, V., Ochoa, M., Yung, M. (eds.) ACNS 2019. LNCS, vol. 11464, pp. 363–382. Springer, Cham (2019). https://doi.org/10.1007/978-3-030-21568-2_18
13. Galteland, Y.J., Pan, J.: Backward-leak uni-directional updatable encryption from (homomorphic) public key encryption. In: Boldyreva, A., Kolesnikov, V. (eds.) PKC 2023, Part II. LNCS, vol. 13941, pp. 399–428. Springer, Cham (2023). https://doi.org/10.1007/978-3-031-31371-4_14
14. Gentry, C.: Fully homomorphic encryption using ideal lattices. In: Mitzenmacher, M. (ed.) STOC 2009, pp. 169–178. ACM (2009). https://doi.org/10.1145/1536414.1536440
15. Jiang, Y.: The direction of updatable encryption does not matter much. In: Moriai, S., Wang, H. (eds.) ASIACRYPT 2020, Part III. LNCS, vol. 12493, pp. 529–558. Springer, Cham (2020). https://doi.org/10.1007/978-3-030-64840-4_18
16. Kirshanova, E.: Proxy re-encryption from lattices. In: Krawczyk, H. (ed.) PKC 2014. LNCS, vol. 8383, pp. 77–94. Springer, Heidelberg (2014). https://doi.org/10.1007/978-3-642-54631-0_5
17. Klooß, M., Lehmann, A., Rupp, A.: (R)CCA secure updatable encryption with integrity protection. In: Ishai, Y., Rijmen, V. (eds.) EUROCRYPT 2019, Part I. LNCS, vol. 11476, pp. 68–99. Springer, Cham (2019). https://doi.org/10.1007/978-3-030-17653-2_3
18. Lehmann, A., Tackmann, B.: Updatable encryption with post-compromise security. In: Nielsen, J.B., Rijmen, V. (eds.) EUROCRYPT 2018, Part III. LNCS, vol. 10822, pp. 685–716. Springer, Cham (2018). https://doi.org/10.1007/978-3-319-78372-7_22
19. Micciancio, D., Peikert, C.: Trapdoors for lattices: simpler, tighter, faster, smaller. In: Pointcheval, D., Johansson, T. (eds.) EUROCRYPT 2012. LNCS, vol. 7237, pp. 700–718. Springer, Heidelberg (2012). https://doi.org/10.1007/978-3-642-29011-4_41
20. Nishimaki, R.: The direction of updatable encryption does matter. In: Hanaoka, G., Shikata, J., Watanabe, Y. (eds.) PKC 2022, Part II. LNCS, vol. 13178, pp. 194–224. Springer, Cham (2022). https://doi.org/10.1007/978-3-030-97131-1_7

21. Regev, O.: On lattices, learning with errors, random linear codes, and cryptography. In: Gabow, H.N., Fagin, R. (eds.) ACM 2005, pp. 84–93. ACM (2005). https://doi.org/10.1145/1060590.1060603
22. Sakurai, K., Nishide, T., Syalim, A.: Improved proxy re-encryption scheme for symmetric key cryptography. In: IWBIS 2017, pp. 105–111. IEEE (2017). https://doi.org/10.1109/IWBIS.2017.8275110
23. Slamanig, D., Striecks, C.: Puncture 'em all: stronger updatable encryption with no-directional key updates. IACR Cryptology ePrint Archive, p. 268 (2021). https://eprint.iacr.org/2021/268

Distributed Broadcast Encryption from Bilinear Groups

Dimitris Kolonelos[1,2](✉), Giulio Malavolta[3,4], and Hoeteck Wee[5,6]

[1] IMDEA Software Institute, Madrid, Spain
dimitris.kolonelos@imdea.org
[2] Universidad Politécnica de Madrid, Madrid, Spain
[3] Bocconi University, Milan, Italy
giulio.malavolta@hotmail.it
[4] Max Planck Institute for Security and Privacy, Bochum, Germany
[5] NTT Research, Palo Alto, CA, USA
wee@di.ens.fr
[6] École Normale Supérieure - PSL, Paris, France

Abstract. Distributed broadcast encryption (DBE) improves on the traditional notion of broadcast encryption by eliminating the key-escrow problem: In a DBE system, users generate their own secret keys non-interactively without the help of a trusted party. Then anyone can broadcast a message for a subset S of the users, in such a way that the resulting ciphertext size is sublinear in (and, ideally, independent of) $|S|$. Unfortunately, the only known constructions of DBE requires heavy cryptographic machinery, such as general-purpose indistinguishability obfuscation, or come without a security proof.

In this work, we formally show that obfuscation is not necessary for DBE, and we present two practical DBE schemes from standard assumptions in prime-order bilinear groups. Our constructions are conceptually simple, satisfy the strong notion of adaptive security, and are concretely efficient. In fact, their performance, in terms of number of group elements and efficiency of the algorithms, is comparable with that of traditional (non distributed) broadcast encryption schemes from bilinear groups.

Keywords: Pairing-based Cryptography · Broadcast Encryption · Key-Escrow

1 Introduction

In a broadcast encryption (BE) scheme [14] a broadcaster encrypts a message for some subset S of the users who are listening on a broadcast channel. Any user that belongs to the set S can recover the message using their own secret key. The security requirement stipulates that, even if all users not in S collude, they learn nothing about the broadcasted message.

Broadcast encryption has been an active area of research since their introduction in the 1990 s, where a major goal is to obtain schemes with short parameters,

J. Guo and R. Steinfeld (Eds.): ASIACRYPT 2023, LNCS 14442, pp. 407–441, 2023.
https://doi.org/10.1007/978-981-99-8733-7_13

notably ciphertext size that is sublinear in the total number of users L, so as to minimize bandwidth consumption. In a celebrated work from 2005, Boneh, Gentry and Waters (BGW) [4] presented a pairing-based broadcast encryption scheme with constant-size ciphertext (ignoring the contribution from the set S). A series of follow-up works [5,11,21] showed how to achieve constant-size ciphertext under the standard k-Lin assumption, improving upon the q-type assumption used in BGW, while additionally strengthening the security guarantees from selective to adaptive security. More recent works [1,2,10,35], improving upon [6,7], showed how to achieve $\text{poly}(\log L)$ total parameter size under stronger, non-falsifiable assumptions.

All of the aforementioned broadcast encryption schemes suffer from the notorious *key escrow* problem: the schemes require a central authority holding a master secret key, that generates and distributes keys for all users of the system. Moreover, the central authority can decrypt *any ciphertext* ever encrypted using this master secret key. Another security concern is that the central authority needs to remain online with a long-term secret key, which constitutes a recurrent single point of failure.

Distributed Broadcast Encryption. To circumvent the key escrow problem [7,38] introduced the notion of *distributed* broadcast encryption (DBE),[1] where users choose their own public/secret key pairs, and replacing the central authority with a bulletin board of user public keys. This not only solves the key escrow problem, but also captures many applications such as peer-to-peer networks, on-the-fly data sharing, and group messaging.

Wu, Qin, Zhang and Domingo-Ferrer [38] (henceforth WQZD), present a pairing-based scheme for L users with a transparent set-up where each user's public key comprises $O(L^2)$ group elements, and the ciphertext comprises $O(1)$ group elements (more discussion on this in Sect. 1.2), however without a security proof. Shortly after, Boneh and Zhandry [7] construct a distributed broadcast encryption scheme with $\text{poly}(\log L)$-sized public keys and ciphertext assuming indistinguishability obfuscation, in a stronger model with a one-time trusted sampling of a common reference string (CRS). We stress that the trusted setup only needs to be done once (e.g., with an MPC), that the same CRS can be reused across different systems, and that there is no need to store any long-term secrets, thereby also circumventing the key escrow problem. We regard this mostly as a feasibility result, given the state of affairs for obfuscation [8,9,20,26,27,36]. In this work, we address the following question:

Can we construct *simple* and *efficient* distributed broadcast encryption with small ciphertexts?

In particular, we focus on pairing-based schemes, due to the increasing support (e.g., high-quality implementations with strong assurance and performance, on-going IETF standardization) and deployment of pairing-based cryptography.

---

[1] In [38] under the name'Ad Hoc Broadcast Encryption'.

1.1 Our Results

We construct simple pairing-based distributed broadcast encryption (DBE) schemes where, for a bound of L users:

- Ciphertexts comprise a constant number of group elements, like in BGW;
- Encryption to a set S only requires retrieving $O(|S|)$ group elements from the bulletin board;
- Users only need to store $O(L)$ group elements for decryption;
- Both encryption and decryption take time linear in $|S|$.

In particular, our schemes achieve similar efficiency as the state-of-the-art vanilla (non-distributed) pairing-based broadcast encryption schemes (cf. Table 2).

Our schemes rely on standard assumptions in bilinear groups, such as the bilinear Diffie-Hellman Exponent (BDHE) [4], or the k-Lin assumption [3,24,32]. Two of our schemes satisfy strong security guarantees, which ensure that the message is hidden even against an adversary that *adaptively* corrupts honest users and can register malformed public keys to the bulletin board. For the case of the BDHE scheme, this is achieved by a generic transformation that turns any scheme that satisfies a very weak notion of security (that we refer to as semi-selective) to an adaptively secure scheme, following the approach of [21].

Furthermore, we show how to achieve two strengthenings of DBE inspired by recent works on registration-based encryption [12,16,17,22,25]:

- The first is that of dynamic joins, where users can register public keys and join the bulletin board at any time, and secret keys may require to be updated once a new user joins. We show a generic transformation (following [12,16,22,25]) where users need to check the bulletin board for updates at most $\text{poly}(\log L)$ times throughout the lifetime of the system, while increasing the ciphertext size by a $O(\log L)$ factor.
- The second is that of malicious corruptions, where malicious users can register (possibly-malformed) keys. We show that as long as public keys pass a simple validity check, then the presence of malicious users do not comprise correctness or privacy of our schemes.

1.2 Discussion and Related Works

Prior Works. Besides "trivial" schemes, where one simply encrypts the message in parallel for all users in the subsets, the only DBE schemes proposed in the literature are from Wu, Qin, Zhang and Domingo-Ferrer [38] and Boneh and Zhandry [7]. We present an explicit comparison of known DBE schemes, along with their underlying assumptions in Table 1. We mention here that the conference version of [38] presents a construction without a proof of security. On the other hand, the full version [37] presents a *different construction*, along with a security proof. In the full version of this paper [28] we show, unfortunately,

Table 1. Comparison with existing DBE schemes. The notation in the table ignores constants and factors that depend only on the security parameters. |BB| denotes the size of the bulletin board, whereas L denotes the maximum number of users allowed in the system. Encryption and decryption take time $O(|S|)$ in all cases. (First two rows are the "naive" constructions with $O(L)$ ciphertext where we encrypt to all public keys in the set.)

	Assumption	$|\mathsf{pp}|$	$|\mathsf{usk}_j|$	$|\mathsf{upk}_j|$	$|\mathsf{ct}|$	$|\mathrm{BB}|$	#Updates
Folklore	PKE	–	1	1	$|S|$	L	–
Folklore	RBE	$\log L$	$\log L$	1	$|S|$	$L \log L$	$\log L$
Boneh-Zhandry	iO and OWF	L	1	1	1	L	L
WQZD	BDHE	L	L	L^2	1	L^3	L
Scheme 1	BDHE	L	1	L	1	L^2	L
Scheme 1 (Log. Updates)	BDHE	L	1	L	$\log L$	L^2	$\log L$
Scheme 2	k-Lin	L^2	1	L	1	L^2	L
Scheme 2 (Log. Updates)	k-Lin	L^2	1	L	$\log L$	L^2	$\log L$

that their argument is flawed by presenting an attack against their full-version construction. For completeness, we also provide a proof (although only for the weaker notion of selective security) for a slight variant of the conference version [38].

We shall mention here explicitly that neither work explicitly considered the settings with dynamic joins, and therefore the resulting schemes also have a linear (in L) number of updates. However, we stress that a similar transformation as the one that we present in this work can be applied also to their schemes to reduce the number of updates to $\log L$, while increasing the ciphertext size to $\log L$.

Decentralized Broadcast Encryption. Phan, Pointcheval, and Strefler [31] put forth the notion of decentralized broadcast encryption, which relies on *interactive* key generation to solve the key-escrow problem in broadcast encryption. That is, upon a new user's arrival, a subset of the users should be online to involve in an interactive protocol with the new user, in order for the keys of the system–new user's key and (part of) the previous ones–to be updated. Furthermore, the ciphertext is not always succinct on the set size, it can vary from 1 to $O(|S|)$, depending on the structure of S. They provided efficient instantiations based on the DDH assumption in pairing-free groups.

In contrast, the model of [7,38] (which is also the one that we adopt in this work) insist on a *non-interactive* key generation procedure, apart from a single write access to the public bulletin board and up to $O(\log L)$ reads per user and it is required that the ciphertexts are poly-logarithmic in $|S|$ for every possible broadcast-set S.

Registration-Based Encryption. Another related (but different) notion is that of registration-based encryption [16]. Also in registration-based encryption (RBE) users sample their own secret keys and there is no key authority that knows a master secret key. However RBE assumes the existence of a semi-trusted key curator that aggregates the public keys of the users and generates a short *master public key* that anyone can use to encrypt with respect to identities. On the other hand, in DBE there is no key curator, but just an append-only bulletin board (alternatively, one can think of the key curator as doing nothing). These settings entail two different technical challenges:

- In RBE, the non-triviality of the scheme comes from the size of the master public key, which is required to be sublinear, ideally independent, of the number of users. (No requirement on the size of the ciphertext)
- In DBE, the challenge stems from the size of the ciphertext, which is required to be sublinear, ideally independent, of the size of the set. (No requirement on the size of the master public key)

Because of the above differences the two primitives are formally incomparable, i.e., RBE does not imply DBE and vice-versa. We also point out that DBE (and in fact broadcast encryption) does not support the functionality of encryption "with respect to identity" as in RBE, which is rather a property of *identity-based* broadcast encryption.

Recently Hohenberger et al. introduced the relevant to RBE notion of Registered (ciphertext-policy) attribute-based encryption [25] and, as Agrawal and Yamada [2] observed, CP-ABE implies broadcast encryption. However, the same comparison with RBE applies; R-ABE's objective is to have sublinear master public key, which is orthogonal to sublinear ciphertexts. In fact, their ciphertext is linear in the size of policy, therefore naively using the R-ABE as an DBE yields $O(|S|)$-sized ciphertexts.

User Identifiers. We discuss possible choices for assigning user identifiers to participants. For the static settings, where all users are fixed at the beginning of the system, one can simply identify users in the set by their lexicographical ordering. This is what is done in traditional (non-distributed) broadcast encryption systems. In the dynamic settings, where users can post public keys on the bulletin board at different times, one can envision different mechanisms. The simplest one is to identify users by their time of arrival: The bulletin board specifies a counter corresponding to how many users have joined the system so far as well as the identifiers of all the users who have joined the system so far, in order. When a user joins, it checks the counter first, increments it by 1 to j and runs keygen with j and submits her public key, upk_j, with its identifier that also gets appended to the bulletin board; the identifier is now associated with index/time j. When a sender comes along, it looks up the bulletin board to check the identifiers and the corresponding indices, and uses that to determine a set $S \subseteq [L]$. When we say that our scheme supports $\text{poly}(\log L)$ updates, we mean that a decryptor will only need to look up the bulletin board at most $\text{poly}(\log L)$ times for public key updates, even if L users join the system.

Common Reference String. We point out explicitly that, similarly to recent works on RBE [22] and R-ABE [25] and R-FE [15], two of our schemes are in the common reference string model, where a reference string must be sampled in such a way that the underlying trapdoor is kept secret. We argue that this assumption is still substantially better than having a trusted authority distributing secret keys for all parties. This is because the common reference string is sampled once and for all and there is no *long term secret* that needs to be stored. Additionally, availability-wise, no trusted authority must remain online to send secret keys and no secure communication channels are needed.

One way to sample a common reference string is to have a one-time ceremony, where a group of non-colluding parties run a multi-party computation protocol to compute the common reference string, each supplying their own randomness. Furthermore, the common reference string can be reused across different instances of the scheme. We also point out that our first scheme has an *updatable* common reference string [23] of the form

$$[\alpha], \ldots, [\alpha^L], [\alpha^{L+2}], \ldots, [\alpha^{2L}]$$

for a secret scalar α. This class of common reference strings can be easily updated using the techniques in [23,30], where each update can be verified via a simple proof of knowledge of discrete logarithm. This highly mitigates the trust in the common reference string since anyone can update it and even one honest update (the underlying update trapdoor is destroyed) suffices.

Efficiency Comparison with Non-distributed BE. In Table 2 we provide a comparison of our DBE with traditional BE from bilinear groups. Although we compare primitives with different objectives and functionalities, our objective is to show the cost of getting rid of the trusted authority in broadcast encryption. For fairness, we compare with the variant of our schemes in the *static settings*, i.e., where the set of users is fixed, which is the same as traditional BE. The conclusion is that in comparison to [4] and [21] we achieve essentially the same efficiency properties except for a $\log L$ overhead on the size of the ciphertext (for the variant with efficient updates). [34] achieves the best tradeoff between parameters that we do not achieve. We note that in the case of DBE, due to absence of the trusted authority, we have a quadratic-sized Bulletin Board.

1.3 Open Problems

We view our work as opening a promising new line of research in pairing-based broadcast encryption. In fact there is a number of problems that our work leaves open: For example, we ask what are the optimal parameters for pairing-based DBE, and whether we can achieve similar tradeoffs as for the case of vanilla broadcast encryption [34]. Furthermore, an outstanding open problem is whether we can construct distributed broadcast encryption from other assumptions, such as lattice-based computational problems.

Table 2. Comparison with existing BE schemes with $O(1)$-size ciphertexts from Bilinear Groups. The notation in the table ignores constants and factors that depend only on the security parameters, except for $|\mathsf{ct}|$ which is concrete in number group elements. $|\mathrm{Enc}|$ denotes the overall size of information needed to encrypt a message (e.g. mpk or crs), and $|\mathrm{Dec}|$ the overall size of information to decrypt (e.g. usk_j or sk). $|\mathrm{BB}|$ denotes the size of the bulletin board (for DBE), whereas L denotes the maximum number of users allowed in the system. We omit from the comparison schemes like [34] which achieves $O(N^{1/3})$ parameters but not $O(1)$-size ciphertexts. Recall SXDH = 1-Lin.

	Assumption	Dist	Security	$\lvert\mathrm{Enc}\rvert$	$\lvert\mathrm{Dec}\rvert$	$\lvert\mathsf{ct}\rvert$	$\lvert\mathrm{BB}\rvert$	#Updates
BGW05 [4]	BDHE	No	Selective	L	L	3	–	N/A
Scheme 1a	BDHE	Yes	Selective	L	L	3	L^2	L
GW09 [21]	BDHE	No	Adaptive	L	L	6	–	N/A
GKW18 [19]	SXDH	No	Adaptive	L	L	4	–	N/A
Scheme 1b	BDHE	Yes	Adaptive	L	L	6	L^2	L
Scheme 2	SXDH	Yes	Adaptive	L	L	4	L^2	L

2 Technical Overview

2.1 High-Level Overview

Syntax for Distributed Broadcast Encryption. We begin with the syntax for distributed broadcast encryption in the simplest setting. There are L users in the system and a public parameter pp given to all users.

- User j given pp, generates a public/private key pair $(\mathsf{upk}_j, \mathsf{usk}_j)$ and posts upk_j to a public bulletin board.
- Encryption to a set S takes as input $\{\mathsf{upk}_j\}_{j\in S}$ and a message M and outputs a ciphertext ct.
- Decryption takes as input a set S, a ciphertext ct, the public keys $\{\mathsf{upk}_j\}_{j\in S}$, and a secret key usk_i for some $i \in S$.

The basic semantic security requirement says that given an encryption ct of M for any set S, along with $\{\mathsf{upk}_j\}_{j\in[N]}$ and $\{\mathsf{usk}_j\}_{j\notin S}$, the message M remains hidden. The stronger notion of adaptive security (where the adversary can choose S after seeing some of the public keys) can be achieved with a semi-generic transformation due to [21], which we adapt to the distributed setting. However, to keep things simple, in this overview we focus on selective security, where the set S is fixed in advance.

Looking ahead, we present two constructions of DBE satisfying these basic requirements, one based on DBHE and the second based on k-Lin. These two schemes constitute the basic building blocks for our "full fledged"–enhanced with additional requirements described below–DBE schemes. We defer an overview of both constructions for now, and proceed instead to describe the additional requirements for DBE and how we achieve them via a series of generic transformations.

Malicious Corruptions. Next, we strengthen our security requirements to allow for malicious corruptions, where a user j controlled by an adversary may post an arbitrary, malformed upk_j^* to the bulletin board, as long as upk_j^* passes some validity check. We have two requirements: first, we want functionality to hold even amidst malicious corruptions, namely an honest user i should correctly decrypt an honestly generated encryption for a set S where $i \in S$, even if S contains malformed public keys. Next, we require that semantic security holds even if all keys outside S (i.e., $[L] \setminus S$) are corrupted. We note that, as typically in Broadcast Encryption, it's meaningless to assume corruptions inside S; an adversary controlling a user inside S can trivially decrypt.

We show that any scheme that is semantically secure without malicious corruptions is also semantically secure with malicious corruptions. The reduction is fairly straight-forward, crucially relying on the fact that our syntax for encryption takes as input only the public keys of users in S, and since we do not allow malicious corruptions inside S, malicious coruptions do not affect the distribution of the challenge ciphertext.

Reducing the Number of Updates. It is typical in dynamic settings without a private key generator authority that the users have to update their decryption keys. Following similar settings, such as Registration-based Encryption, we put forward a generic transformation to any DBE scheme that allows users to update their decryption keys only logarithmic number—in the total number of users, L—times throughout the history of the system. We defer to Sect. 4.3 for the technical details.

2.2 Scheme from BDHE

We rely on an asymmetric bilinear group $(\mathbb{G}_1, \mathbb{G}_2, \mathbb{G}_T, e)$ of prime order p where $e : \mathbb{G}_1 \times \mathbb{G}_2 \rightarrow \mathbb{G}_T$. We use $[\cdot]_1, [\cdot]_2, [\cdot]_T$ to denote component-wise exponentiations in respective groups $\mathbb{G}_1, \mathbb{G}_2, \mathbb{G}_T$. For this overview we implicitly assume that all algorithms take the description of the group (together with corresponding random generators) as input, $(p, \mathbb{G}_1, \mathbb{G}_2, \mathbb{G}_T, [1]_1, [1]_2, e)$.

BGW Broadcast Encryption. Our starting point is the BGW broadcast encryption scheme [4] which we recap below:

$$\begin{aligned}
\mathsf{pp} &= ([\alpha]_1, \ldots, [\alpha^L]_1, [\alpha]_2, \ldots, [\alpha^L]_2, [\alpha^{L+2}]_2, \ldots, [\alpha^{2L}]_2) \\
\mathsf{msk} &= t, && t \leftarrow_{\$} \mathbb{Z}_p^* \\
\mathsf{mpk} &= ([t]_1) \\
\mathsf{ct} &= \left([s]_1, [s(t + \sum_{j \in S} \alpha^j)]_1, [s\alpha^{L+1}]_T \cdot M \right), && s \leftarrow_{\$} \mathbb{Z}_p^* \\
\mathsf{sk}_i &= [t\alpha^{L+1-i}]_2
\end{aligned}$$

Decryption by a user $i \in S$ is based on the following equation:

$$e\left([s(t+\sum_{j\in S}\alpha^j)]_1, [\alpha^{L+1-i}]_2\right) =$$

$$= e\left([s]_1, \overbrace{\boxed{[t\alpha^{L+1-i}]_2}}^{\mathsf{sk}_i}\cdot[\sum_{j\in S, j\neq i}\alpha^{L+1+j-i}]_2\right)[s\alpha^{L+1}]_T$$

Observe that the secret keys of all users depend on the same secret value: the master secret key t. It is worth noting that this is a technique that is common even among all subsequent broadcast encryption schemes. The natural question when adapting BGW to the distributed setting is: who chooses t?

Our DBE. Our core technique is the following: let t be $t = \sum_{i\in S} t_i$ where t_i is chosen by the i'th user. This transforms the above decryption equation to:

$$e\left([s\sum_{i\in S}(t_j+\alpha^j)]_1, [\alpha^{L+1-i}]_2\right) =$$

$$= e\left([t_i\alpha^{L+1-i} + \sum_{j\in S, j\neq i}(t_j\alpha^{L+1-i} + \alpha^{L+1+j-i})]_1, [s]_2\right)[s\alpha^{L+1}]_T =$$

$$= e\left(\overbrace{\boxed{[t_i\alpha^{L+1-i}]_1}}^{\mathsf{sk}_{i,i}}\prod_{j\in S, j\neq i}\left\{\overbrace{\boxed{[t_j\alpha^{L+1-i}]_1}}^{\mathsf{sk}_{i,j}}\cdot[\alpha^{L+1+j-i}]_1\right\}, [s]_2\right)[s\alpha^{L+1}]_T$$

Now, as it is evident, the cross-terms $t_j\alpha^{L+1-i}$ appear in the decryption equation. Therefore, in order to make decryption possible, it is inevitable that the decryptor i knows these terms.

This affects the efficiency of the scheme (making the user's necessary information to decrypt linear in L), but is very convenient for the distributed setting. The intuition is that each user i can be attached to one distinct t_i that she can sample locally. Then user i publishes the cross-terms of all the other users $\mathsf{sk}_{i,j} = t_i\alpha^{L+1-j}$, except of course for $\mathsf{sk}_{i,i} = t_i\alpha^{L+1-i}$ which is her secret key. In terms of correctness, observe that $\mathsf{sk}_{i,i}$ is only used in the decryption equation of i, i.e. it never plays the role of a cross-term. Additionally, publishing $\mathsf{sk}_{i,j}$ doesn't affect security as long as $\mathsf{sk}_{i,i}$ remains secret.

To summarize, our DBE is given as follows:

$$\begin{aligned}
\mathsf{pp} &= ([\alpha]_1, \ldots, [\alpha^L]_1, [\alpha]_2, \ldots, [\alpha^L]_2, [\alpha^{L+2}]_2, \ldots, [\alpha^{2L}]_2) \\
\mathsf{usk}_j &= [t_j \alpha^{L+1-j}]_2, & t_j \leftarrow_\$ \mathbb{Z}_p^* \\
\mathsf{upk}_j &= ([t_j]_1, [t_j\alpha]_2, \ldots, [t_j\alpha^{L+1-j-1}]_2, [t_j\alpha^{L+1-j+1}]_2, \ldots, [t_j\alpha^L]_2) \\
\mathsf{ct} &= \left([s]_1, [s(\sum_{j \in S} t_j + \alpha^j)]_1, [s\alpha^{L+1}]_T \cdot M \right), & s \leftarrow_\$ \mathbb{Z}_p^*
\end{aligned}$$

It is worth noting that in terms of efficiency the public parameters and the ciphertext remain unaffected. Futhermore, from the point of view of the encryptor the (asymptotic) storage overhead is the same as BGW: In BGW (translated to asymmetric groups) an encryptor needs $\mathsf{pp} = (\{[\alpha^i]_1\}_{i \in [L]}, \{[\alpha^i]_2\}_{i \in [2L] \setminus \{L+1\}})$ and $[t]_1$ while in our case the same pp and $[t_1]_1, \ldots, [t_L]_1$, therefore both are $O(L)$.

Security Proof Sketch. The decision Blinear Diffie-Hellman Exponent assumption [4] says that $[s\alpha^{L+1}]_T$ is pseudorandom given $(\{[\alpha^i]_1\}_{i \in [L]}, \{[\alpha^i]_2\}_{i \in [2L] \setminus \{L+1\}}) := \mathsf{pp}$ and $[s]_1 := \mathsf{ct}_1$. The security reduction for selective security given S^* proceeds as follows:

- for all $j \notin S^*$, reduction samples t_j "in the clear";
- for all $j \in S^*$, reduction samples $\tilde{t}_j$ and implicitly sets $t_j := \tilde{t}_j - \alpha^j$.

Now, observe that

$$\mathsf{ct} = \left([s]_1, [s \sum_{j \in S} \tilde{t}_j]_1, [s\alpha^{L+1}]_T \cdot M \right)$$

the reduction can simulate:

- the public parameters using the input of the assumption;
- the challenge ct given $[s]$ and the target of the assumption.
- terms $[t_j\alpha^{L+1-i}]_2, j \notin S^*$ and any i, we can simulate using t_j
- terms $[t_j\alpha^{L+1-i}]_2, j \in S^*, i \neq j$: we can simulate using $\tilde{t}_j$ and $[\alpha^{L+1-i+j}]_2$
- terms $[t_j\alpha^{L+1-j}]_2, j \in S^*$: appear only in sk_j, which the adversary is not allowed to query

Interestingly, our modification described above allows us to prove our DBE scheme semi-statically secure, something that is not possible for BGW. Semi-static security is a strengthening of static security in the sense that the adversary still outputs the target set S^* a-priori but at the challenge stage is allowed to ask a ciphertext for any subset $S^{**} \subseteq S^*$. This security notion is interesting since Gentry and Waters showed a generic transformation (in the Random Oracle model) from a semi-statically secure scheme to fully adaptive [21]. We adapt this transformation in the distributed broadcast encryption setting in Sect. 4.2.

2.3 Scheme from k-Lin

Our k-Lin Distributed Broadcast Encryption conceptually follows the framework of Gay et al. [19] that construct (plain) Broadcast Encryption from k-Lin. The [19] scheme itself conceptually holds similarities with the Broadcast Encryption scheme of Gentry and Waters (GW) [21]. In order to ease the presentation, first we give some context to the reader on the GW construction.

GW Broadcast Encryption. The GW scheme works as follows:

$$\begin{aligned}
\mathsf{pp} &= \left([w_1]_1, \dots, [w_L]_1\right), w_i \leftarrow \mathbb{Z}_p^* \\
\mathsf{msk} &= \left([\alpha]_2, [w_1]_2, \dots, [w_L]_2\right), \alpha \leftarrow_\$ \mathbb{Z}_p^* \\
\mathsf{mpk} &= [\alpha]_T \\
\mathsf{ct} &= \left([s]_1, [s\sum_{j\in S} w_j]_1, [s\alpha]_T \cdot M\right), s \leftarrow \mathbb{Z}_p^* \\
\mathsf{sk}_i &= \left([\alpha + w_i r_i]_2, [r_i]_2, \{[r_i w_j]_2\}_{j\in[L]\setminus\{i\}}\right), r_i \leftarrow \mathbb{Z}_p^*
\end{aligned}$$

Decryption uses the fact that if $i \in S$, then:

$$e\left([s]_1, \overbrace{\boxed{[\alpha + r_i w_i]_2}}^{\mathsf{sk}_{i,i}} \cdot \prod_{j\in S, j\neq i} \overbrace{\boxed{[r_i w_j]_2}}^{\mathsf{sk}_{i,j}}\right) = e\left([s\sum_{i\in S} w_j]_1, [r_i]_2\right) [s\alpha]_T$$

GKW Broadcast Encryption. The observation of Gay et al. [19] is that one can 'push' $\mathsf{sk}_{i,j}$ to the parameters (sampling a-priori all r_i's). This makes the public parameters quadratic, but achieves constant-sized decryption keys. This gives us:

$$\begin{aligned}
\mathsf{pp} &= \left(\{[w_i]_1\}_{i\in[L]}, \{[r_i]_2\}_{i\in[L]}, \{[r_i w_j]_2\}_{i,j\in[L], i\neq j}\right), w_i, r_i \leftarrow \mathbb{Z}_p^* \\
\mathsf{msk} &= \left([\alpha]_2, [w_1]_2, \dots, [w_L]_2, r_1, \dots, r_L\right) \\
\mathsf{mpk} &= [\alpha]_T \\
\mathsf{ct} &= \left([s]_1, [s\sum_{j\in S} w_j]_1, [s\alpha]_T \cdot M\right), s \leftarrow \mathbb{Z}_p^* \\
\mathsf{sk}_i &= [\alpha + w_i r_i]_2
\end{aligned}$$

Looking ahead, GKW (almost) generically transforms the scheme to the k-Lin setting to achieve adaptive security (without the use of random oracles). For presentational purposes we postpone this to the end of the section and continue with the traditional setting, stated above.

Towards Our DBE. In the distributed case we crucially rely on the fact that $\mathsf{sk}_{i,j}$'s can be 'pushed' to the public parameters, since there is no private key generator authority to sample r_i on-the-fly to extract the decryption key of the user i.

However, we're not done, there still remains the natural question: who samples α, or in more general, how are the secret keys sk_i formed so that they do not depend on a (universal) master secret key? We resolve this as follows: As in our previous DBE scheme, user i samples a fresh $t_i \leftarrow \mathbb{Z}_p^*$. Then, we replace w_j in ct with $t_j + w_j$, which yields

$$\mathsf{ct} = \left([s]_1, [s \sum_{j \in S} (t_j + w_j)]_1, [s\alpha]_T \cdot M \right)$$

Doing the same with sk_i and the corresponding entries of the public parameters (the GW parts of sk_i that were 'pushed' to the pp) yields:

$$\mathsf{sk}_i = [\alpha + (w_i + t_i) r_i]_2$$
$$\mathsf{pp}^{(3)} = \{[(t_j + w_j) r_i]_2\}_{i,j \in [L], i \neq j}$$

This leads us naturally to the following DBE scheme:

$$\mathsf{pp} = ([\alpha]_T, \{[w_i]_1\}_{i \in [L]}, \{[r_i]_2\}_{i \in [L]}, \{[\alpha + r_i w_i]_2\}_{i \in [L]}, \{[r_i w_j]_2\}_{i,j \in [L], i \neq j})$$
$$\mathsf{usk}_j = [t_j r_j]_2, \quad t_j \leftarrow \mathbb{Z}_p^*$$
$$\mathsf{upk}_j = ([t_j]_1, [t_j r_1]_2, \ldots, [t_j r_{j-1}]_2, [t_j r_{j+1}]_2, \ldots, [t_j r_L]_2)$$
$$\mathsf{ct} = \left([s]_1, [s \sum_{j \in S} (t_j + w_j)]_1, [s\alpha]_T \cdot M \right) \quad s \leftarrow \mathbb{Z}_p^*$$

Regarding efficiency, the above Distributed Broadcast Encryption Scheme preserves the decryption and encryption key sizes, $O(L)$, of the GW scheme, but at the cost of having quadratic public parameters instead of linear.

Security Intuition. To gain some intuition about security, consider an adversary that tries to recover $[s\alpha]_T$ by computing $e([s \sum_{j \in S} (t_j + w_j)]_1, [r_i]_2)$ and $e([s], [\alpha + w_i r_i])$. Then notice that:

- if $i \notin S$, it can't cancel out $[s w_i r_i]_T$.
- if $i \in S$, it can't cancel out $[s t_i r_i]_T$ without usk_i, which of course is not allowed to query in the security game of a (distributed) broadcast encryption (otherwise it trivially recovers the message).

Final Scheme from k-Lin. To obtain a scheme under k-Lin following [11,19], we sample $\mathbf{A} \leftarrow \mathbb{Z}_p^{k\times(k+1)}$ and make the following substitutions:

$$\begin{aligned} s &\mapsto \mathbf{s}^\top \mathbf{A} \in \mathbb{Z}_p^{1\times(k+1)}, \ \alpha \mapsto \mathbf{k} \in \mathbb{Z}_p^{k+1}, \\ w_j &\mapsto \mathbf{W}_j \in \mathbb{Z}_q^{(k+1)\times k}, \\ t_j &\mapsto \mathbf{T}_j \in \mathbb{Z}_q^{(k+1)\times k}, \\ [w_j]_1, [\alpha]_T &\mapsto [\mathbf{A}\mathbf{W}_j]_1, [\mathbf{A}\mathbf{k}]_T \end{aligned}$$

We defer further details to Sect. 6.

3 Preliminaries

Notation. We write λ for the security parameter. By $[N]$ we denote the set of integers $\{1, \ldots, N\}$ and, more generally, by $[A, B]$ the set $\{A, \ldots, B\}$ for any $A, B \in \mathbb{Z}, A \leq B$. With $x \leftarrow_\$ X$ we denote the procedure of x being uniformly sampled from a finite set X. Throughout our work "PPT" stands for probabilistic polynomial-time algorithm.

3.1 Bilinear Groups

A generator $\mathcal{BG}$ takes as input a security parameter 1^λ and outputs a description $\mathbb{G} := (p, \mathbb{G}_1, \mathbb{G}_2, \mathbb{G}_T, g_1, g_2, e)$, where p is a prime of $\Theta(\lambda)$ bits, $\mathbb{G}_1$, $\mathbb{G}_2$ and $\mathbb{G}_T$ are cyclic groups of order p, and $e : \mathbb{G}_1 \times \mathbb{G}_2 \rightarrow \mathbb{G}_T$ is a non-degenerate bilinear map. We require that the group operations in $\mathbb{G}_1$, $\mathbb{G}_2$, $\mathbb{G}_T$ and the bilinear map e are computable in deterministic polynomial time in λ. Let $g_1 \in \mathbb{G}_1$, $g_2 \in \mathbb{G}_2$ and $g_T = e(g_1, g_2) \in \mathbb{G}_T$ be the respective generators. We employ the *implicit representation* of group elements: for a matrix $\mathbf{M}$ over $\mathbb{Z}_p$, we define $[\mathbf{M}]_1 := g_1^{\mathbf{M}}, [\mathbf{M}]_2 := g_2^{\mathbf{M}}, [\mathbf{M}]_T := g_T^{\mathbf{M}}$, where exponentiation is carried out component-wise. We denote $[A]_s \cdot [B]_s = [A + B]_s$ for $s = 0, 1, T$. We further define, for any $\mathbf{A} \in \mathbb{Z}_p^{n\times m}$ and $\mathbf{B} \in \mathbb{Z}_{m\times\ell}$,

$$e([\mathbf{A}]_1, [\mathbf{B}]_2) := [\mathbf{A}\mathbf{B}]_T \in \mathbb{G}_T^{n\times\ell}.$$

We recall two standard assumptions over Bilinear Groups, that we will use in the following sections. First, the (decision) Bilinear Diffie-Hellman Exponent assumption introduced by Boneh et. al. [4].

Assumption 1 (Decision BDHE assumption). *Let $\mathcal{BG}$ be a bilinear group generator,* $\mathsf{bg} := (p, \mathbb{G}_1, \mathbb{G}_2, \mathbb{G}_T, [1]_1, [1]_2, e) \leftarrow_\$ \mathcal{BG}(1^\lambda)$, $\alpha, s \leftarrow_\$ \mathbb{Z}_p^*$ *and define*

$$\mathcal{D} = \left(\left\{[\alpha^j]_1\right\}_{j\in[q]}, \left\{[\alpha^j]_2\right\}_{j\in[2q], j\neq q+1}, [s]_1\right)$$

and $T \leftarrow_\$ \mathbb{G}_T$. Then for any PPT adversary $\mathcal{A}$ and any positive integer q:

$$\mathbf{Adv}^{\mathsf{dBDHE}}_{\mathcal{BG},q,\mathcal{A}}(\lambda) := \left|\Pr[\mathcal{A}\left(\mathsf{bg}, \mathcal{D}, [s\alpha^{q+1}]_T\right) = 1] - \Pr[\mathcal{A}\left(\mathsf{bg}, \mathcal{D}, T\right) = 1]\right| = \mathrm{negl}(\lambda)$$

where the above probabilities are taken over the choices of bg, α, s *and* T.

We also recall the k-Lin assumption [3,24,32] which belongs to the more general family of Matrix Diffie-Hellman Assumptions [13]. Define the distribution $\mathcal{L}_k$ outputting a matrix $\mathbf{A} \in \mathbb{Z}_p^{(k+1)\times k}$ as:

$$\mathbf{A} = \begin{pmatrix} a_1 & 0 & \dots & 0 \\ 0 & a_2 & \dots & 0 \\ \vdots & \vdots & \ddots & \vdots \\ 0 & 0 & \dots & a_k \\ 1 & 1 & \dots & 1 \end{pmatrix}$$

where $a_1, \dots, a_k \leftarrow_\$ \mathbb{Z}_p$. The k-Lin assumption is stated below.

Assumption 2 (k-Lin assumption). *Let $\mathcal{BG}$ be a bilinear group generator,* $\mathsf{bg} := (p, \mathbb{G}_1, \mathbb{G}_2, \mathbb{G}_T, [1]_1, [1]_2, e) \leftarrow_\$ \mathcal{BG}(1^\lambda)$, *$k$ any positive integer,* $\mathbf{v} \leftarrow_\$ \mathbb{Z}_p^k$, $\mathbf{u} \leftarrow_\$ \mathbb{Z}_p^{k+1}$ *and* $\mathbf{A} \leftarrow_\$ \mathcal{L}_k$ *Then for any PPT adversary $\mathcal{A}$:*

$$\mathbf{Adv}^{k\text{-}Lin}_{\mathcal{BG},q,\mathcal{A}}(\lambda) := |\Pr[\mathcal{A}(\mathsf{bg}, [\mathbf{A}]_s, [\mathbf{Av}]_s) = 1] - \Pr[\mathcal{A}(\mathsf{bg}, [\mathbf{A}]_s, [\mathbf{u}]_s) = 1]| = \mathrm{negl}(\lambda)$$

where the above probabilities are taken over the choices of $\mathsf{bg}, \mathbf{A}, \mathbf{v}, \mathbf{u}$.

We note that if $s = 1$ we have the k-Lin assumption for group $\mathbb{G}_1$ and similarly $s = 2$ for $\mathbb{G}_2$.

4 Definitions

We consider a model where the system is initialized with some public parameters, given an upper bound on the number of users, L. Users are indexed by a unique identifier $j \in [L]$ which can be, e.g., their time of arrival. Upon each user joining the system, they append their public key on a bulletin board that we assume all users in the system have access to. Importantly, the bulletin board is append-only, and we implicitly assume that all parties involved scrutinize that the public keys of the other parties are well-formed. If not, the public key is simply discarded. By looking at the public parameters and at the users public keys, it is then possible to encrypt a message for a subset $S \subseteq [L]$ of the public keys. What makes the scheme non-trivial is the fact that the size of the ciphertext must be sublinear (and ideally independent) of the size of S.

4.1 Distributed Broadcast Encryption

We present the formal definitions in the following. The syntax is canonical for broadcast encryption, except that each user samples locally a key pair $(\mathsf{usk}, \mathsf{upk})$ and, consequently, the encryption and decryption will take as input the public keys corresponding to the users in the set S. For starters, we define a minimal notion of security, where the adversary is allowed to choose a set S^* for the challenge ciphertext at the beginning of the experiment, but it is otherwise not allowed to corrupt honest users. Later in this Section, we will show how to generically lift this definition to the more challenging settings with adaptive corruptions.

To prevent the adversary from registering public keys that would sabotage the decryption of honest users, we define a validity-check predicate that ensures that the keys are well-formed. Then the correctness guarantee is that, if the check succeeds, then correctness must hold unconditionally.

Definition 1 (Distributed Broadcast Encryption). *Let λ be a security parameter and let $\mathbb{M} = \{\mathbb{M}_\lambda\}_{\lambda \in \mathbb{N}}$ be the message space. A distributed broadcast encryption scheme with message space $\mathbb{M}$ is a tuple of efficient algorithms $\Pi_{\mathsf{DBE}} = (\mathsf{Setup}, \mathsf{KeyGen}, \mathsf{Enc}, \mathsf{Dec})$ with the following properties:*

- $\mathsf{Setup}(1^\lambda, 1^L) \to \mathsf{pp}$*: On input the security parameter λ and the number of slots L, the setup algorithm returns some public parameters* pp.
- $\mathsf{KeyGen}(\mathsf{pp}, j) \to (\mathsf{usk}_j, \mathsf{upk}_j)$*: On input the public parameters and a slot index $j \in [L]$, the key generation algorithm generates a secret key usk_j and a public key upk_j for the j-th slot.*
- $\mathsf{Enc}(\mathsf{pp}, \{\mathsf{upk}_j\}_{j\in S}, S, M) \to \mathsf{ct}$*: On input the public parameters* pp*, the public keys $\{\mathsf{upk}_j\}_{j\in S}$, a subset $S \subseteq [L]$, and a message $M \in \mathbb{M}$, the encryption algorithm returns a ciphertext* ct.
- $\mathsf{Dec}(\mathsf{pp}, \{\mathsf{upk}_j\}_{j\in S}, \mathsf{usk}_i, \mathsf{ct}, S, i) \to M$*: On input the public parameters* pp*, the public keys $\{\mathsf{upk}_j\}_{j\in S}$, a secret key usk_i a ciphertext* ct*, a subset S, and an index i, the decryption algorithm returns a message M.*

Moreover, the algorithms must satisfy the following properties.

- ***Correctness:*** *For all $\lambda \in \mathbb{N}$, $L \in \mathbb{N}$, $j \in [L]$, all* pp *in the support of* $\mathsf{Setup}(1^\lambda, 1^L)$*, all $(\mathsf{usk}_i, \mathsf{upk}_i)$ in the support of $\mathsf{KeyGen}(\mathsf{pp}, i)$, all $\{\mathsf{upk}_j\}_{j\neq i}$ such that $\mathsf{isValid}(\mathsf{pp}, \mathsf{upk}_j, j) = 1$, all $M \in \mathbb{M}$, all $S \subseteq [L]$ such that $i \in S$, it holds that*

$$\Pr\left[\mathsf{Dec}(\mathsf{pp}, \{\mathsf{upk}_j\}_{j\in S}, \mathsf{usk}_i, \mathsf{ct}, S, i) = M : \mathsf{Enc}(\mathsf{pp}, \{\mathsf{upk}_j\}_{j\in S}, S, M)\right] = 1.$$

- ***Verifiable Keys:*** *There exists an efficient algorithm* $\mathsf{isValid}$ *such that for all $\lambda \in \mathbb{N}$, $L \in \mathbb{N}$, $j \in [L]$, all* pp *in the support of* $\mathsf{Setup}(1^\lambda, 1^L)$*, it holds that*

$$(\cdot, \mathsf{upk}_j) \in \mathsf{KeyGen}(\mathsf{pp}, j) \Longrightarrow \mathsf{isValid}(\mathsf{pp}, \mathsf{upk}_j^*, j) = 1$$

- ***(Selective) Security:*** *Define the following experiment between an adversary $\mathcal{A}$ and a challenger, parameterized by a bit b.*
  - ***Setup Phase:*** *The adversary $\mathcal{A}$ sends a set $S^* \subseteq [L]$ to the challenger, who samples $\mathsf{pp} \leftarrow \mathsf{Setup}(1^\lambda, 1^L)$ and gives* pp *to $\mathcal{A}$.*
  - ***Key Generation Phase:*** *For all $j \in S^*$, the challenger samples a key pair $(\mathsf{usk}_j, \mathsf{upk}_j) \leftarrow \mathsf{KeyGen}(\mathsf{pp}, j)$ and sends $\{\mathsf{upk}_j\}_{j\in S^*}$ to $\mathcal{A}$.*
  - ***Challenge Phase:*** *The adversary sends a pair of messages $M_0^*, M_1^* \in \mathbb{M}$. The challenger computes*

$$\mathsf{ct}^* \leftarrow \mathsf{Enc}(\mathsf{pp}, \{\mathsf{upk}_j\}_{j\in S^*}, S^*, M_b^*)$$

  and sends it over to $\mathcal{A}$.

- ***Output Phase:*** *At the end of the experiment, algorithm $\mathcal{A}$ outputs a bit $b' \in \{0,1\}$, which is the output of the experiment.*

We say that a distributed broadcast encryption scheme Π_{dRBE} is selectively secure if for all polynomials $L = L(\lambda)$ and all efficient adversaries $\mathcal{A}$, there exists a negligible function negl *such that for all $\lambda \in \mathbb{N}$:*

$$\left|\Pr[b = b'] - \frac{1}{2}\right| = \text{negl}(\lambda).$$

4.2 Semi-selective to Adaptive

In the following we show a series of transformation that allow us to compile a scheme that satisfies a weak notion of security into one that satisfies adaptive security. We proceed in three steps:

- First, we define a stronger notion of selective security, called *semi-selective* security.
- Second, we show how the transformation described in [21] allows us to build a scheme with adaptive security, albeit only for honestly generated keys.
- Third we show how to handle maliciously generated keys.

Let us first define the notion of *semi-selective* security. The experiment is unchanged, except that the adversary in the challenge phase can specify any $S^{**} \subseteq S^*$ and the challenge ciphertext is defined as

$$\mathsf{ct}^* \leftarrow \mathsf{Enc}(\mathsf{pp}, \{\mathsf{upk}_j\}_{j \in S^{**}}, S^{**}, M_b^*).$$

From Semi-selective to Passive-Adaptive. Before showing the generic transformation, we provide the formal definition of passive-adaptive security below.

Definition 2 (Passive-Adaptive Security). *Define the following experiment between an adversary $\mathcal{A}$ and a challenger, parameterized by a bit b.*

- ***Setup Phase:*** *The challenger samples $\mathsf{pp} \leftarrow \mathsf{Setup}(1^\lambda, 1^L)$ and gives pp to $\mathcal{A}$.*
- ***Key Query Phase:*** *The adversary $\mathcal{A}$ is provided with access to the following oracles.*
  - ***Key Generation Oracle:*** *On input an index $j \in [L]$, check if this index was queried before to this oracle, and return $\perp$ if this is the case. Otherwise, sample $(\mathsf{usk}_j, \mathsf{upk}_j) \leftarrow \mathsf{KeyGen}(\mathsf{pp}, j)$ and sent upk_j to $\mathcal{A}$.*
  - ***Key Corrupt Oracle:*** *On input an index $j \in [L]$, check if upk_j was sampled in the key generation oracle and return the corresponding usk_j to $\mathcal{A}$. In this case, we refer to the index j as "corrupted". Otherwise, return $\perp$.*

- ***Challenge Phase:*** *The adversary sends a pair of messages* $M_0^*, M_1^* \in \mathbb{M}$ *and a set* S^*. *If there exists some index* $j \in S^*$ *such that* j *was corrupted, then the challenger aborts the experiment. Otherwise it computes*

$$\mathsf{ct}^* \leftarrow \mathsf{Enc}(\mathsf{pp}, \{\mathsf{upk}_j\}_{j \in S^*}, S^*, M_b^*)$$

and sends it over to $\mathcal{A}$.
- ***Output Phase:*** *At the end of the experiment, algorithm* $\mathcal{A}$ *outputs a bit* $b' \in \{0, 1\}$, *which is the output of the experiment.*

We say that a distributed broadcast encryption scheme Π_{dRBE} *is passive-adaptively secure if for all polynomials* $L = L(\lambda)$ *and all efficient adversaries* $\mathcal{A}$, *there exists a negligible function* negl *such that for all* $\lambda \in \mathbb{N}$:

$$\left| \Pr\left[b = b'\right] - \frac{1}{2} \right| = \mathrm{negl}(\lambda).$$

We are now ready to state the intermediate result, which follows immediately by a transformation from [21]. Although this transformation was originally presented in the context of (non-distributed) broadcast encryption, we observe that the same proof strategy works here.

Lemma 1 (Semi-selective to Passive-Adaptive). *Let* Π_{DBE} *be a semi-selectively secure distributed broadcast encryption scheme. Then there exists a scheme* Π'_{DBE} *that is passive-adaptively secure.*

Proof (Proof Sketch). The transformation is identical to [21] and we sketch it here only for completeness.

- Setup: Run the setup of the original scheme except that we double the number of users $2L$.
- Key Generation: On input an index $j \in [L]$, the user generates two keys

$$(\mathsf{usk}_{2j}, \mathsf{upk}_{2j}) \leftarrow \mathsf{KeyGen}(\mathsf{pp}, 2j) \text{ and } (\mathsf{usk}_{2j-1}, \mathsf{upk}_{2j-1}) \leftarrow \mathsf{KeyGen}(\mathsf{pp}, 2j-1)$$

then it flips a coin and throws away one of the two secret keys.
- Encryption: For all $j \in S$, sample a random bit t_j, then define two sets

$$S_0 = \{2j - t_j\}_{j \in S} \text{ and } S_1 = \{2j - (1 - t_j)\}_{j \in S}.$$

Encrypt the message M with respect to both S_0 and S_1 and attach $\{t_j\}_{j \in S}$ to the ciphertext.
- Decryption: Decrypt one of the two ciphertexts, depending on which secret key was kept.

Remark 1. Observe that the compiled scheme has public parameters and ciphertext doubled, when compared to the original scheme. Furthermore, the ciphertext is augmented with a string of $|S|$ bits. As already observed in [21], this can be reduced to λ bits in the random oracle model.

Next, we show that the scheme is passive-adaptively secure. The proof proceeds in two steps, first we switch the encryption of under the set S_0 to encrypt a random message and then the encryption under S_1. Since the argument is identical, we only outline the reduction for the first case.

- Sample a random string $T = (t_1, \ldots, t_L) \leftarrow \{0,1\}^L$. Set $S^* = \{2j - t_j\}_{j \in [L]}$ as the initial set for the semi-selective security.
- Receive pp from the challenger, along with the keys $\{\mathsf{upk}_j^*\}_{j \in S^*}$.
- Activate the passive-adaptive adversary on input pp.
- Answer the queries of the adversary on index j as follows:
  - Key Generation Oracle: On input an index j, set $\mathsf{upk}_{2j-t_j} = \mathsf{upk}_j^*$ and sample $\mathsf{upk}_{2j-(1-t_j)}$ with the knowledge of the secret key.
  - Key Corrupt Oracle: On input an index j, check if a key was created for this index and return $\mathsf{usk}_{2j-(1-t_j)}$ in case.
- In the challenge phase, the adaptive adversary specifies a set $S^{**} \subseteq [L]$, which must be a subset of the S^* and furthermore must not include any corrupted index. The reduction sets Set $S_0 = \{2i - t_i\}_{i \in S^{**}}$ and send S_0 to the challenger, who responds with ct^*. Then it samples the other ciphertext honestly for the set $S_1 = \{2i - (1 - t_i)\}_{i \in S^{**}}$ and sends both to the adversary.
- In the output phase, return whatever the adversary returns.

Observe that the reduction perfectly simulates the view of the adversary and therefore they have the same advantage.

From Passive to Active Security. Next, we show that any scheme that satisfies passive-adaptive security also satisfies active-adaptive security, which we define below. The difference with respect to the previous notion, is that we now allow the adversary to register malicious keys, captured by an additional "Malicious Corrupt Oracle".

Definition 3 (Active-Adaptive Security). *Define the following experiment between an adversary $\mathcal{A}$ and a challenger, parameterized by a bit b.*

- ***Setup Phase:*** *The challenger samples* $\mathsf{pp} \leftarrow \mathsf{Setup}(1^\lambda, 1^L)$ *and gives* pp *to* $\mathcal{A}$.
- ***Key Query Phase:*** *The adversary $\mathcal{A}$ is provided with access to the following oracles.*
  - ***Key Generation Oracle:*** *On input an index $j \in [L]$, check if this index was queried before to this oracle or to the malicious corrupt oracle, and return $\perp$ if this is the case. Otherwise sample* $(\mathsf{usk}_j, \mathsf{upk}_j) \leftarrow \mathsf{KeyGen}(\mathsf{pp}, j)$ *and send* upk_j *to* $\mathcal{A}$.
  - ***Key Corrupt Oracle:*** *On input an index $j \in [L]$, check if* upk_j *was sampled in the key generation oracle and return the corresponding* usk_j *to* $\mathcal{A}$*. In this case, we refer to the index j as "corrupted". Otherwise, return* $\perp$.

  - ***Malicious Corrupt Oracle:*** *On input* (j, upk_j^*) *check if this index* $j \in [L]$ *was queried before to this oracle or to the key generation oracle, and return* $\perp$ *if this is the case. Otherwise Store* upk_j^* *and label the index* j *as "corrupted".*
- ***Challenge Phase:*** *The adversary sends a pair of messages* $M_0^*, M_1^* \in \mathbb{M}$ *and a set* S^**. If there exists some index* $j \in S^*$ *such that* j *was corrupted, then the challenger aborts the experiment. Otherwise it computes*

$$\mathsf{ct}^* \leftarrow \mathsf{Enc}(\mathsf{pp}, \{\mathsf{upk}_j\}_{j \in S^*}, S^*, M_b^*)$$

and sends it over to $\mathcal{A}$*.*
- ***Output Phase:*** *At the end of the experiment, algorithm* $\mathcal{A}$ *outputs a bit* $b' \in \{0, 1\}$*, which is the output of the experiment.*

We say that a distributed broadcast encryption scheme Π_{dRBE} *is adaptively secure if for all polynomials* $L = L(\lambda)$ *and all efficient adversaries* $\mathcal{A}$*, there exists a negligible function* negl *such that for all* $\lambda \in \mathbb{N}$*:*

$$\left|\Pr\left[b = b'\right] - \frac{1}{2}\right| = \mathrm{negl}(\lambda).$$

We now show that any scheme that is passive-adaptively secure is also active-adaptively secure. The intuition here is that the challenge ciphertext cannot depend on public keys for which the attacker knows the secret (since otherwise the scheme would be trivially broken), so the queries to the malicious-corrupt oracles have no effect on the distribution of the challenge ciphertext.

Lemma 2 (Passive-Adaptive to Active-Adaptive). *Let* Π_{dRBE} *be a passive-adaptively secure distributed broadcast encryption scheme. Then* Π_{dRBE} *is also active-adaptively secure.*

Proof (Proof Sketch). The reduction only forwards the messages of the adversary to the challenger, except for the queries to the malicious corrupt oracle, which the reduction simply discards. Since the challenge ciphertext is computed as

$$\mathsf{ct}^* \leftarrow \mathsf{Enc}(\mathsf{pp}, \{\mathsf{upk}_j\}_{j \in S^*}, S^*, M_b^*).$$

and the set S^* does not contain any corrupted index, the distribution simulated by the reduction is identical to the view that the adversary is expecting. Thus any advantage of the active-adaptive adversary immediately carries over to the (passive-adaptive) reduction.

4.3 Logarithmic Updates

One drawback of the current syntax for distributed broadcast encryption is that the decrypter has to constantly check the public bulletin board for public keys, since every time a new user joins a new public key is added to the system. It is desirable to minimize the number of updates that each user must receive, without affecting the functionality. More precisely, in the current model, all users need to know $\{\mathsf{upk}_i : i \in [S]\}$ in order to decrypt a ciphertext encrypted with respect to S. In the following we show that we can get away with checking the bulletin board $\log L$ times, with a modest increase in ciphertext size. Before discussing how to turn a scheme into one with logarithmic updates, let us make the notion of update somewhat more formal: We now define the notion of U-updates and we say that a scheme has logarithmic updates if $U = O(\log L)$. The following definition implicitly assumes that users are indexed by their time of arrival.

Definition 4 (U-updates). *A DBE scheme with parameter L has U-updates if, for all $i \in [L]$ there exists a series of subsets*

$$S_1 \subseteq \cdots \subseteq S_U \subseteq [L]$$

such that for any $T \in [L]$ and for any $S^* \subseteq [T]$ it holds that

$$\Pr\left[\mathsf{Dec}(\mathsf{pp}, \{\mathsf{upk}_j\}_{j \in S_i}, \mathsf{usk}_i, \mathsf{ct}, S^*, i) = M : \mathsf{Enc}(\mathsf{pp}, \{\mathsf{upk}_j\}_{j \in S^*}, S^*, M) = \mathsf{ct}\right] = 1.$$

where i is the largest index such that $|S_i| \leq T$.

The Transformation. In the following we describe a simple transformation that achieves exactly this. This transformation has been used many times in the literature [12,16,22,25] and we report it here for completeness. For convenience, we are going to assume that the total number of users in the system is

$$L = 1 + 2 + 4 + \cdots + 2^\ell$$

which is without loss of generality, since we can always pad the number of users to that L is of this form. Let us describe the algorithms of the scheme.

- Setup: Sample the public parameter pp for a distributed broadcast encryption scheme with parameter L, and initialize $k = \ell + 1$ "master public keys" $\{\mathsf{mpk}_k = \emptyset\}_{k \in [\ell+1]}$.
- Key Generation: When the user indexed by j joins the system, it runs the key generation algorithm $\mathsf{KeyGen}(\mathsf{pp}, j)$ as prescribed by the scheme.
- Update: Upon each user joining the system, we will assign a k such that their public key is added to mpk_k. Let k be the smallest integer such that $\mathsf{mpk}_k = \emptyset$, the update algorithm proceeds as follows:
  - If $k = 1$, then we are simply going to assign $\mathsf{mpk}_1 = \{\mathsf{upk}_j\}$.
  - Else, we are going to set

    $$\mathsf{mpk}_k = \mathsf{mpk}_{k-1} \cup \cdots \cup \mathsf{mpk}_1 \cup \{\mathsf{upk}_j\}$$

    and reset $\mathsf{mpk}_{k-1} = \cdots = \mathsf{mpk}_1 = \emptyset$.

  Note that, by construction, the cardinality of mpk_k is either 0 or 2^{k-1}. Therefore, each user will only have to keep track of the master public key he currently resides into, along with its secret key.

- Encryption: Let S be the encryption subset and let us define $\{S_k = \emptyset\}_{k\in[\ell+1]}$. For each $j \in S$, based on the current number of users, we can derive the master public key where upk_j currently resides, which we denote by mpk_{k_j}. We then add $S_{k_j} \cup \{j\}$. The encrypter computes $\ell + 1$ ciphertexts as

$$\left\{\mathsf{ct}_k \leftarrow \mathsf{Enc}(\mathsf{pp}, \{\mathsf{upk}_j\}_{j\in S_k}, S_k, M)\right\}_{k\in[\ell+1]}.$$

- Decryption: The j-th user decrypts the ciphertext corresponding to the mpk_k where their key currently resides.

It is important to observe that each user only has to keep track of the keys inside of her master public key (i.e., the bundle), so it will only have to update their keys whenever the public key is moved up to the next bundle. Since there are at most $\ell + 1 \approx \log(L)$ bundles, it follows that each user receives at most logarithmically many updates throughout the lifetime of the system.

As for the correctness of the scheme, it suffices to observe that, by construction $S = S_1 \cup \cdots \cup S_{\ell+1}$ and therefore correctness follow from the correctness of the underlying distributed broadcast encryption scheme. Security also follows from a standard hybrid argument.

5 Distributed Broadcast Encryption from Decision Bilinear Diffie-Hellman Exponent

In this section we present our first Distributed Broadcast Encryption scheme from the decision Bilinear Diffie-Hellman Exponent assumption. For a more intuitive overview we refer to Sect. 2.2.

5.1 Our Distributed Broadcast Encryption Scheme

Below we describe our Distributed Broadcast Encryption scheme $\Pi_{\mathsf{DBE},1}$.

- $\mathsf{Setup}(1^\lambda, 1^L)$: On input the security parameter λ and the number of slots L, generate a bilinear group $\mathsf{bg} := (p, \mathbb{G}_1, \mathbb{G}_2, \mathbb{G}_T, [1]_1, [1]_2, e) \leftarrow \mathcal{BG}(1^\lambda)$, sample $\alpha \leftarrow_\$ \mathbb{Z}_p^*$ and output the public parameters as:

$$\mathsf{pp} = \left(\mathsf{bg}, [\alpha]_1, \ldots, [\alpha^L]_1, [\alpha]_2, \ldots, [\alpha^L]_2, [\alpha^{L+2}]_2, \ldots, [\alpha^{2L}]_2\right)$$

We denote $\mathsf{pp} := (\mathsf{pp}_0, \mathsf{pp}_1, \ldots, \mathsf{pp}_{3L})$ (defining $\mathsf{pp}_{2L+1} = [0]_2$).

- $\mathsf{KeyGen}(\mathsf{pp}, j)$: on input the public parameters $\mathsf{pp} := \Big(\mathsf{bg}, \left\{[\alpha^j]_1\right\}_{j\in[L]}, \left\{[\alpha^j]_2\right\}_{j\in[2L], j\neq L+1}\Big)$ and a slot j , sample the secret $\kappa_j \leftarrow_\$ \mathbb{Z}_p^*$ and output:

$$\mathsf{usk}_j = [t_j\alpha^{L+1-j}]_2$$
$$\mathsf{upk}_j = \left([t_j]_1, [t_j\alpha]_2, \ldots, [t_j\alpha^{L+1-j-1}]_2, [t_j\alpha^{L+1-j+1}]_2, \ldots, [t_j\alpha^L]_2\right)$$

- $\mathsf{Enc}(\mathsf{pp}, \{\mathsf{upk}_j\}_{j\in S}, S, M)$: on input the public parameters $\mathsf{pp} := (\mathsf{bg}, \{[\alpha^j]_1\}_{j\in[L]}, \{[\alpha^j]_2\}_{j\in[2L], j\neq L+1})$, a set $S \subseteq [L]$, the corresponding users' public keys $\mathsf{upk}_j := ([t_j]_1, [t_j\alpha^\ell]_2)_{\ell\in[L],\ell\neq L+1-j}$ for each $j \in S$ and a message $M \in \mathbb{G}_T$, sample $s \leftarrow_\$ \mathbb{Z}_p^*$, compute $[s\alpha^{L+1}]_T = e([s\alpha]_1, [\alpha^L]_2)$ and output:

$$\mathsf{ct} = \left([s]_1, [s\sum_{j\in S}(t_j + \alpha^j)]_1, [s\alpha^{L+1}]_T \cdot M\right)$$

  where $[s\sum_{j\in S}(t_j + \alpha^j)]_1$ is computed as $\prod_{j\in S}([st_j]_1 \cdot [\alpha^j]_1)$ using upk_j and pp.
- $\mathsf{Dec}(\mathsf{pp}, \{\mathsf{upk}_j\}_{j\in S}, \mathsf{usk}_i, \mathsf{ct}, S, i) \rightarrow M$: on input the public parameters $\mathsf{pp} := \left(\mathsf{bg}, \{[\alpha^j]_1\}_{j\in[L]}, \{[\alpha^j]_2\}_{j\in[2L], j\neq L+1}\right)$, a set $S \subseteq [L]$, the corresponding users' public keys $\mathsf{upk}_j := ([t_j]_1, [t_j\alpha^\ell]_2)_{\ell\in[L],\ell\neq L+1-j}$ for each $j \in S$, a slot index $i \in S$, the user's corresponding secret key $\mathsf{usk}_i := [t_i\alpha^{L+1-i}]_2$ and a ciphertext $\mathsf{ct} = (\mathsf{ct}_1, \mathsf{ct}_2, \mathsf{ct}_3)$ output:

$$M' = \mathsf{ct}_3 \cdot e\left(\mathsf{ct}_2^{-1}, \mathsf{pp}_{2L+1-i}\right) \cdot e\left(\mathsf{ct}_1, \mathsf{usk}_i \cdot \prod_{j\in S, j\neq i}(\mathsf{upk}_{j,L+1-i} \cdot \mathsf{pp}_{2L+1+j-i})\right)$$

  where $\mathsf{pp}_{2L+1-i} := [-\alpha^{L+1-i}]_2$, $\mathsf{usk}_i := [t_i\alpha^{L+1-i}]_2$, $\mathsf{upk}_{j,L+1-i} := [t_j\alpha^{L+1-i}]_2$, $\mathsf{pp}_{2L+1+j-i} := [\alpha^{L+1+j-i}]_2$

Remark 2 (Storage requirements for the encryptor and decryptor). Syntactically speaking, in DBE to be able to encrypt and decrypt with respect to any arbitrary set $S \subseteq [L]$ one needs to store all public keys $\{\mathsf{upk}_j\}_{j\in[L]}$, of size $O(L^2)$ in the above scheme. However, concretely in our scheme it suffices to have linear size of information from $\{\mathsf{upk}_j\}_{j\in[L]}$:

Encryptor: $[t_1]_1, \ldots, [t_L]_1$
Decryptor i: $[t_1\alpha^{L+1+1-i}]_2, \ldots, [t_{i-1}\alpha^L]_2, [t_{i+1}\alpha^{L+2}]_2, \ldots, [t_L\alpha^{L+1+L-i}]_2$.

To ease the presentation of the definition of DBE we do not formalize this aspect of our concrete scheme, letting $\{\mathsf{upk}_j\}_{j\in S}$ to be the inputs of Enc and Dec in the formal description of the construction.

5.2 Correctness

As noted in the definition of DBE correctness, in Sect. 4.1, to prove correctness we first need to prove that there exists an isValid algorithm. We prove existence of such an algorithm for our scheme above by concretely constructing it.

Verifiable Keys. We define $\mathsf{isValid}(\mathsf{pp}, \mathsf{upk}_j^*, j)$ as follows:

- Parse $\mathsf{upk}_j^* := (\mathsf{upk}_{j,0}^*, \ldots, \mathsf{upk}_{j,L+1-j-1}^*, \mathsf{upk}_{j,L+1-j+1}^*, \ldots, \mathsf{upk}_{j,L}^*)$.
- Then if the following holds output 1.

$$e\left(\mathsf{upk}_{j,0}^*, [\alpha^L]_2\right) = e\left([\alpha^{L-1}]_1, \mathsf{upk}_{j,1}^*\right) = \ldots = e\left([\alpha^j]_1, \mathsf{upk}_{j,L+1-j-1}^*\right) = \\ = e\left([\alpha^{j-2}]_1, \mathsf{upk}_{j,L+1-j+1}^*\right) = \ldots = e\left([1]_1, \mathsf{upk}_{j,L}^*\right)$$

otherwise output 0.

Since $\mathsf{upk}_{j,k}^* \in \mathbb{G}_2$ ($\mathsf{upk}_{j,0}^* \in \mathbb{G}_1$ resp.) and $\mathbb{G}_2$ ($\mathbb{G}_1$ resp.) has prime order, p, there exist $u_k \in \mathbb{Z}_p^*$ such that $\mathsf{upk}_{j,k}^* = [u_k]_2$ for all $k \in [L]$ ($\mathsf{upk}_{j,0}^* = [u_0]_1$ resp.). From this and the above paring checks we get that:

$$[u_0\alpha^L]_T = [u_1\alpha^{L-1}]_T = \ldots = [u_{j-1}\alpha^j]_T = [u_{j+1}\alpha^{j-2}]_T = \ldots = [u_L]_T$$

Which gives us that:

$$\mathsf{upk}_j^* = \left([u_0]_1, [u_0\alpha]_2, \ldots, [u_0\alpha^{L-j}]_2, [u_0\alpha^{L-j+2}]_2, \ldots, [u_0\alpha^L]_2\right).$$

Therefore if $\mathsf{isValid}(\mathsf{pp}, \mathsf{upk}_j^*, j) = 1$ then upk_j^* is in the support of KeyGen: $(\cdot, \mathsf{upk}_j^*) \leftarrow \mathsf{KeyGen}(\mathsf{pp}, j)$ for $t_j := u_0 \in \mathbb{Z}_p^*$ and $\mathsf{usk}_j = [u_0\alpha^{L+1-j}]_2$.

Correctness. Let arbitrary $\lambda \in \mathbb{N}$, $L \in \mathbb{N}$, $\mathsf{pp} := \left(\mathsf{bg}, \{[\alpha^j]_1\}_{j\in[L]}, \{[\alpha^j]_2\}_{j\in[2L], j\neq L+1}\right)$ for some $\alpha \in \mathbb{Z}_p^*$, $\mathsf{usk}_i = [t_i\alpha^{L+1-i}]_2$, $\mathsf{upk}_i := ([t_i]_1 [t_i\alpha^k]_2)_{k\in[L], k\neq L+1-i}$ for some $t_i \in \mathbb{Z}_p^*$, upk_j such that $\mathsf{isValid}(\mathsf{pp}, \mathsf{upk}_j, j) = 1$ and for all $j \in [L]$. Furthermore, let $S \subseteq [L]$ such that $i \in S$ and $M \in \mathbb{M}$. Then $\mathsf{Enc}(\mathsf{pp}, \{\mathsf{upk}_j\}_{j\in S}, S, M)$ gives:

$$\mathsf{ct} = \left([s]_1, [s\sum_{j\in S}(t_j + \alpha^j)]_1, [s\alpha^{L+1}]_T \cdot M\right)$$

and $\mathsf{Dec}(\mathsf{pp}\{\mathsf{upk}_j\}_{j\in S}, \mathsf{usk}_i, \mathsf{ct}, S, i)$ gives:

$$\begin{aligned}
M' &= \mathsf{ct}_3 \cdot e\left(\mathsf{ct}_2^{-1}, \mathsf{pp}_{2L+1-i}\right) \cdot e\left(\mathsf{ct}_1, \mathsf{usk}_i \cdot \prod_{j\in S, j\neq i} (\mathsf{upk}_{j,L+1-i} \cdot \mathsf{pp}_{2L+1+j-i})\right)\\
&= \mathsf{ct}_3 \cdot e\left(\mathsf{ct}_2, [-\alpha^{L+1-i}]_2\right) \cdot\\
&\qquad \cdot e\left(\mathsf{ct}_1, [t_i\alpha^{L+1-i}]_2 \cdot [\sum_{j\in S, j\neq i} (t_j\alpha^{L+1-i} + \alpha^{L+1+j-i})]_2\right) =\\
&= M \cdot [s\alpha^{L+1}]_T \cdot e\left([s\sum_{j\in S}(t_j + \alpha^j)]_1, [-\alpha^{L+1-i}]_2\right) \cdot\\
&\qquad \cdot e\left([s]_1, [t_i\alpha^{L+1-i} + \sum_{j\in S, j\neq i} (t_j\alpha^{L+1-i} + \alpha^{N+1+j-i})]_2\right) =\\
&= M \cdot [s\alpha^{L+1}]_T \cdot [s\sum_{j\in S}(t_j + \alpha^j)(-\alpha^{L+1-i})]_T \cdot\\
&\qquad \cdot [s(t_i\alpha^{L+1-i} + \sum_{j\in S, j\neq i} (t_j\alpha^{L+1-i} + \alpha^{N+1+j-i}))]_T =\\
&= M \cdot [s\alpha^{L+1} - s\sum_{j\in S}(t_j\alpha^{L+1-i} + \alpha^{L+1+j-i}) + st_i\alpha^{L+1-i} +\\
&\qquad + s\sum_{j\in S, j\neq i} (t_j\alpha^{L+1-i} + \alpha^{N+1+j-i})]_T =\\
&= M \cdot [s\alpha^{L+1} - s\alpha^{L+1}]_T =\\
&= M \cdot [1]_T =\\
&= M
\end{aligned}$$

In the above equations we used the fact that since $\mathsf{isValid}(\mathsf{pp}, \mathsf{upk}_j, j) = 1$ the key upk_j is in the support of KeyGen (for some t_j).

5.3 Security

For the security of our scheme we rely on the (decisional) Bilinear Diffie Hellman Exponent assumption [4] (see Sect. 3.1).

We prove our scheme semi-selectively secure (see Sect. 4.2). Looking ahead, we can transform our semi-selective DBE scheme to a fully adaptive using the generic transformation of 4.2 (which extends the standard transformation of Gentry and Waters [21] to the distributed setting).

A more intuitive description of the security proof can be found in Sect. 2.2. Below we formally state our main security theorem together with its proof.

Theorem 3. *If the decisional Bilinear Diffie-Hellman Exponent assumption holds, then* $\Pi_{\mathsf{DBE},1}$ *is a semi-selectively secure Distributed Broadcast Encryption* *scheme. More specifically for every PPT adversary $\mathcal{A}$ against the semi-selective security of the above DBE construction, $\Pi_{\mathsf{DBE},1}$, there exists a PPT adversary $\mathcal{B}$ against the decisional Bilinear Diffie-Hellman Exponent assumption such that:*

$$\mathbf{Adv}_{L,\mathcal{A}}^{\Pi_{\mathsf{DBE},1}}(\lambda) \leq \mathbf{Adv}_{\mathcal{BG},L,\mathcal{B}}^{\mathsf{dBDHE}}(\lambda).$$

Proof. Assume a PPT adversary $\mathcal{A}$ that wins the semi-selective security of the above Distributed Broadcast Encryption scheme with a non-negligible probability $\epsilon > 1/\operatorname{poly}(\lambda)$. Moreover let $\mathcal{B}$ be an adversary to the dBHE assumption. $\mathcal{B}$ plays the role of the challenger in the DBE semi-selective security game with $\mathcal{A}$ in order to win the game of the assumption (parametrized by $q = L$).

$\mathcal{B}$ takes as input bg, $\{[\alpha^j]_1\}_{j\in[L]}$, $\{[\alpha^j]_2\}_{j\in[2L],j\neq q+1}$, $[s]_1$ and T. The adversary $\mathcal{A}$ sends to $\mathcal{B}$ the target set S^* and then $\mathcal{B}$ responds with $\mathsf{pp} = \left(\mathsf{bg}, \{[\alpha^j]_1\}_{j\in[L]}, \{[\alpha^j]_2\}_{j\in[2L],j\neq L+1}\right)$, which is identically distributed to an honestly generated pp.

Key Generation Phase: Recall that in our security definition (Definition 1) we are only concerned about keys for $j \in S^*$, thus it is sufficient for $\mathcal{B}$ to simulate those keys. For each $j \in S^*$, $\mathcal{B}$ samples $\tilde{t}_j \leftarrow_\$ \mathbb{Z}_p^*$ and implicitly sets $t_j = \tilde{t}_j - \alpha^j$ (without knowing α). That is, using the assumption's inputs $[\alpha^j]_1$ and $\{[\alpha_j]_2\}_{j\in[2L],j\neq L+1}$, it computes:

$$\begin{aligned}\mathsf{upk}_j &= \left([\tilde{t}_j - \alpha^j]_1, \{[\tilde{t}_j\alpha^\ell - \alpha^{\ell+j}]_2\}_{\ell\in[L],\ell\neq L+1-j}\right) := \\ &:= \left([\tilde{t}_j - \alpha^j]_1, \{[(\tilde{t}_j - \alpha^j)\alpha^\ell]_2\}_{\ell\in[L],\ell\neq L+1-j}\right) := \\ &:= \left([t_j]_1, \{[t_j\alpha^\ell]_2\}_{\ell\in[L],\ell\neq L+1-j}\right)\end{aligned}$$

and sends upk_j to $\mathcal{A}$. Since $\tilde{t}_j$ is uniformly random so is $t_j := \tilde{t}_j - \alpha^j$, therefore upk_j is identically distributed to an honestly generated one.

Challenge Phase: $\mathcal{A}$ sends $M_0^*, M_1^* \in \mathbb{G}_T$ and a new target set $S^{**} \subseteq S^*$. $\mathcal{B}$ samples a bit $b \leftarrow_\$ \{0,1\}$ and sets

$$\mathsf{ct}^* = \left([s]_1, [s\sum_{j\in S^{**}} \tilde{t}_j]_1, T\cdot M_b^*\right)$$

using the assumption's input and the previously sampled $\tilde{t}_j$'s. Note that since $S^{**} \subseteq S^*$ all the corresponding upk_j are simulated by $\mathcal{B}$. Thus $[s\sum_{j\in S^{**}} \tilde{t}_j]_1 := [s\sum_{j\in S^{**}}(t_j + \alpha^j)]_1$ which means that ct^* is identically distributed to an honestly generated ciphertext. Finally, $\mathcal{B}$ sends ct^* to $\mathcal{A}$.

At the end $\mathcal{A}$ sends her guess b'.

Note that if $T = [s\alpha^{L+1}]_T$ then the ciphertext ct^* is perfectly indistinguishable from a real one so $\Pr[b = b'] = \epsilon$. On the other hand if T is uniformly random then the ciphertext leaks nothing about M_b, so $\Pr[b = b'] = 1/2$. It follows directly that $\mathcal{B}$ has advantage ϵ in distinguishing between $T = [s\alpha^{L+1}]_T$ and a random T. In conclusion:

$$\mathbf{Adv}^{\mathsf{dBDHE}}_{\mathcal{BG},L,\mathcal{B}}(\lambda) = \epsilon$$

which contradicts the dBDHE assumption.

After that, from lemmata 1 and 2 of Sect. 4.2 we get a distributed broadcast encryption construction with adaptive security. We summarize this result in corollary 1 stated below:

Corollary 1. *Let $\Pi'_{\mathsf{DBE},1}$ be the Distributed Broadcast Encryption (*DBE*) scheme after applying the transformation of lemma 1 to the $\Pi_{\mathsf{DBE},1}$* DBE *scheme described above. Then $\Pi'_{\mathsf{DBE},1}$ is an adaptively secure* DBE *scheme in the random oracle model, assuming that the decisional Bilinear Diffie-Hellman Exponent assumption holds.*

Remark 3. As stated in Remark 1 we can instead achieve an adaptively secure DBE in the standard model, at the cost of an $|S|$-bit overhead on the size of the ciphertext.

5.4 Efficiency

Here we describe the efficiency and the possible trade-offs of our scheme after the transformations of Sect. 4.2 (Lemma 1) to achieve adaptive security. Also we assume a random oracle is used to output the S-sized bit-string and is given in the ciphertext.

The public parameters consist of $2L$ $\mathbb{G}_1$ and $4L$ $\mathbb{G}_2$-elements: $|\mathsf{pp}| = O(L)$. The secret key of a user is 2 $\mathbb{G}_2$-element: $|\mathsf{usk}_j| = O(1)$. The public key of each user is 2 $\mathbb{G}_1$ and $2(L-2)$ $\mathbb{G}_2$-elements: $|\mathsf{upk}_j| = O(L)$. The ciphertext size is 4 $\mathbb{G}_1$ and 2 $\mathbb{G}_T$-elements, independently of the size of the set of users S that encrypts the message for: $|\mathsf{ct}| = O(1)$. Finally both Enc and Dec run in time $O(|S|)$.

The overall information that has to be stored in the bulletin board has size $O(L^2)$, dominated by the L public keys $\{\mathsf{usk}_j\}_{j\in[L]}$ each of size $O(L)$. The storage overhead of an encryptor and any decryptor $i \in [L]$ is $O(L)$ (see remark 2).

Concretely: $|\mathsf{pp}| = 6L \cdot |\mathbb{G}_1|$, $|\mathsf{usk}_i| = 2 \cdot |\mathbb{G}_2|$, $|\mathsf{upk}_j| = 2 \cdot |\mathbb{G}_1| + (2L-2) \cdot |\mathbb{G}_2|$, $|\mathsf{ct}| = 4|\mathbb{G}_1| + 2|\mathbb{G}_T|$, $|\text{Encryptor}| = 2L|\mathbb{G}_1|$, $|\text{Decryptor}| = (2L-2)|\mathbb{G}_2|$, $|\text{BB}| = 2L|\mathbb{G}_1| + L(2L-2)|\mathbb{G}_2|$.

Logarithmic Updates. As discussed in Sect. 4.3, without further care, each decryptor needs to update her view after each new public key is entering the system, which trivially results in $O(L)$ updates. In order to reduce the maximum necessary number of these updates to $O(\log L)$ we need to apply a standard transformation [16], which gives an $O(\log L)$ overhead to the size of the ciphertext.

Concretely: $|\mathsf{ct}| = 4\log L|\mathbb{G}_1| + 2\log L|\mathbb{G}_T|$, $|\text{Decryptor}| \in \{0, 2, 6, \ldots, 2 \cdot 2^k - 2, \ldots, 2L/2 - 2\}|\mathbb{G}_2|$ (worst case $(L-2)|\mathbb{G}_2|$) and the rest of the values remain as above.

Square-Root Trade-off. Another, standard in Broadcast Encryption, transformation [4,18] that provides a trade-off between ciphertext size and storage requirements (i.e. pp and upk_j size) is to consider L^ϵ, $0 \leq \epsilon < 1$ number of sets of users. That is 'divide' $[L] = 1, \ldots, L$ in $B = L^\epsilon$ (assume wlog that B divides L) sets

$$A_1 = \{1, \ldots, \frac{L}{B}\}, A_2 = \{\frac{L}{B} + 1, \ldots, \frac{2L}{B}\}, \ldots, A_B = \{\frac{(B-1)L}{B} + 1, \ldots, L\}.$$

This results in $O(L^\epsilon)$-sized ciphertexts but smaller parameters and public keys, $O(L^{1-\epsilon})$. We note that, interestingly for the case of Distributed Broadcast Encryption, this additionally results in $O(L^{1-\epsilon})$ number of updates for the decryptor. One can also consider a combination of both the above transformations to reduce the number of decryptor's updates to $\log(L^{1-\epsilon})$ at the cost of increasing the ciphertext size to $O(L^\epsilon \log(L^{1-\epsilon}))$.

Concrete Numbers. For the sake of concreteness, we consider an example use case where we have a relatively small number of users $L = 1024$ and the BLS12-381 curve instantiating the bilinear group. Then our (logarithmic updates) variant has:

- $|\mathsf{pp}| = 288$KB
- $|\mathsf{usk}_i| = 0.19$KB
- $|\mathsf{upk}_j| = 191.9$KB
- $|\mathrm{BB}| = 191.9$MB
- $|\mathrm{Encryptor}| = 96$KB
- $|\mathrm{Decryptor}| = 95.1$KB (worst case)
- $|\mathsf{ct}| = 13$KB
- Number of decryptor updates: 10

6 Distributed Broadcast Encryption from k-Lin

Now we present our second Distributed Broadcast Encryption scheme from a static assumption, k-Lin. We prove this scheme adaptively secure in the standard model using the standard "dual-system" methodology [29,33]. For a more intuitive overview we refer to Sect. 2.3.

6.1 Our Construction

Below we provide the description of our second Distributed Broadcast Encryption scheme $\Pi_{\mathsf{DBE},2}$.

- $\mathsf{Setup}(1^\lambda, 1^L)$: On input the security parameter λ and the number of slots L, generate a bilinear group $\mathsf{bg} := (p, \mathbb{G}_1, \mathbb{G}_2, \mathbb{G}_T, [1]_1, [1]_2, e) \leftarrow \mathcal{BG}(1^\lambda)$, sample

$\mathbf{A}^\top \leftarrow_\$ \mathcal{L}_k$, $\mathbf{k} \leftarrow_\$ \mathbb{Z}_p^{k+1}$ and $\mathbf{W} \leftarrow_\$ \mathbb{Z}_p^{(k+1)\times k}$, $\mathbf{r}_j \leftarrow_\$ \mathbb{Z}_p^k$ for each $j \in [L]$ and output the public parameters as:

$$\begin{aligned}\mathsf{pp} = \big(&\mathsf{bg}, [\mathbf{A}]_1, \{[\mathbf{A}\mathbf{W}_j]_1\}_{j\in[L]}, \{[\mathbf{r}_j]_2\}_{j\in[L]},\\ &\{[\mathbf{W}_\ell \mathbf{r}_j]_2\}_{\ell,j\in[L],\ell\neq j}, \{[\mathbf{k}+\mathbf{W}_j\mathbf{r}_j]_2\}_{j\in[L]}, [\mathbf{A}\mathbf{k}]_T\big)\end{aligned}$$

We denote $\mathsf{pp} = \left(\mathsf{pp}^{(0)}, \mathsf{pp}^{(1)}, \mathsf{pp}^{(2)}, \mathsf{pp}^{(3)}, \mathsf{pp}^{(4)}, \mathsf{pp}^{(5)}, \mathsf{pp}^{(6)}\right)$

- $\mathsf{KeyGen}(\mathsf{pp}, j)$: on input the public parameters pp and a slot j , sample the secret $\mathbf{T}_j \leftarrow_\$ \mathbb{Z}_p^{(k+1)\times k}$ and output:

$$\begin{aligned}\mathsf{usk}_j &= [\mathbf{T}_j\mathbf{r}_j]_2\\ \mathsf{upk}_j &= ([\mathbf{A}\mathbf{T}_j]_1[\mathbf{T}_j\mathbf{r}_1]_2, \ldots, [\mathbf{T}_j\mathbf{r}_{j-1}]_2, [\mathbf{T}_j\mathbf{r}_{j+1}]_2, \ldots, [\mathbf{T}_j\mathbf{r}_L]_2)\end{aligned}$$

- $\mathsf{Enc}(\mathsf{pp}, \{\mathsf{upk}_j\}_{j\in S}, S, M)$: on input the public parameters pp, a set $S \subseteq [L]$, the corresponding users' public keys upk_j for each $j \in S$ and a message $M \in \mathbb{G}_T$, sample $\mathbf{s} \leftarrow_\$ \mathbb{Z}_p^k$ and output:

$$\mathsf{ct} = \left([\mathbf{s}^\top \mathbf{A}]_1, [\mathbf{s}^\top \mathbf{A} \sum_{j\in S}(\mathbf{T}_j + \mathbf{W}_j)]_1, [\mathbf{s}^\top \mathbf{A}\mathbf{k}]_T \cdot M \right)$$

where $[\mathbf{s}\sum_{j\in S}(\mathbf{T}_j + \mathbf{A}_j)]_1$ is computed as $= \prod_{j\in S}([\mathbf{s}^\top \mathbf{A}\mathbf{T}_j]_1 \cdot [\mathbf{s}^\top \mathbf{A}\mathbf{W}_j]_1)$ using $\mathsf{upk}_{j,0}$ and pp.

- $\mathsf{Dec}(\mathsf{pp}, \{\mathsf{upk}_j\}_{j\in S}, \mathsf{usk}_i, \mathsf{ct}, S, i)$: on input the public parameters pp, a set $S \subseteq [L]$, the corresponding users' public keys upk_j for each $j \in S$, a slot index $i \in S$, the user's corresponding secret key $\mathsf{usk}_i := [\mathbf{T}_i\mathbf{r}_i]_2$ and a ciphertext $\mathsf{ct} = (\mathsf{ct}_1, \mathsf{ct}_2, \mathsf{ct}_3)$ output:

$$M' = \mathsf{ct}_3 \cdot e\left(\mathsf{ct}_1^{-1}, \mathsf{pp}_i^{(5)} \cdot \mathsf{usk}_i \cdot \prod_{j\in S, j\neq i} (\mathsf{upk}_{j,i} \cdot \mathsf{pp}_{j,i}^{(5)})\right) \cdot e\left(\mathsf{ct}_2, \mathsf{pp}_i^{(3)}\right)$$

where $\mathsf{pp}_i^{(5)} := [\mathbf{k} + \mathbf{W}_i\mathbf{r}_i]_2$, $\mathsf{usk}_i := [\mathbf{T}_i\mathbf{r}_i]_2$, $\mathsf{upk}_{j,i} := [\mathbf{T}_j\mathbf{r}_i]_2$, $\mathsf{pp}_{j,i}^{(5)} = [\mathbf{W}_j\mathbf{r}_i]$, $\mathsf{pp}_i^{(3)} := [\mathbf{r}_i]_2$

6.2 Correctness

Verifiable Keys. We define $\mathsf{isValid}(\mathsf{pp}, \mathsf{upk}_j^*, j)$ as follows:

- Parse $\mathsf{upk}_j^* := (\mathsf{upk}_{j,0}^*, \ldots, \mathsf{upk}_{j,j-1}^*, \mathsf{upk}_{j,j+1}^*, \ldots, \mathsf{upk}_{j,L}^*)$.
- Then if the following holds output 1.

$$\begin{aligned} e\left(\mathsf{upk}_{j,0}^*, [\mathbf{r}_1]_2\right) &= e\left([\mathbf{A}]_1, \mathsf{upk}_{j,1}^*\right)\\ &\vdots\\ e\left(\mathsf{upk}_{j,0}^*, [\mathbf{r}_{j-1}]_2\right) &= e\left([\mathbf{A}]_1, \mathsf{upk}_{j,j-1}^*\right)\\ e\left(\mathsf{upk}_{j,0}^*, [\mathbf{r}_{j+1}]_2\right) &= e\left([\mathbf{A}]_1, \mathsf{upk}_{j,j+1}^*\right)\\ &\vdots\\ e\left(\mathsf{upk}_{j,0}^*, [\mathbf{r}_L]_2\right) &= e\left([\mathbf{A}]_1, \mathsf{upk}_{j,L}^*\right)\end{aligned}$$

otherwise output 0.

It is easy to see that of $(\cdot, \mathsf{upk}^*_j) \in \mathsf{KeyGen}(\mathsf{pp}, j)$ then $\mathsf{isValid}(\mathsf{pp}, \mathsf{upk}^*_j, j) = 1$.

On the other hand, if $\mathsf{isValid}(\mathsf{pp}, \mathsf{upk}^*_j, j) = 1$ then we get the following: Since $\mathsf{upk}^*_{j,k} \in \mathbb{G}_2^{k+1}$ ($\mathsf{upk}^*_{j,0} \in \mathbb{G}_1^{k \times k}$ resp.) and $\mathbb{G}_2$ ($\mathbb{G}_1$ resp.) has prime order, p, there exist $\mathbf{u}_{j,\ell} \in \mathbb{Z}_p^{k+1}$ such that $\mathsf{upk}^*_{j,\ell} = [\mathbf{u}_{j,\ell}]_2$ for all $\ell \in [L], \ell \neq j$ ($\mathsf{upk}^*_{j,0} = [\mathbf{U}_j]_1$ resp.). From this and the above paring checks we get that:

$$\begin{aligned}
[\mathbf{U}_j \mathbf{r}_1]_T &= [\mathbf{A}\mathbf{u}_{j,1}]_T \\
&\vdots \\
[\mathbf{U}_j \mathbf{r}_{j-1}]_T &= [\mathbf{A}\mathbf{u}_{j,j-1}]_T \\
[\mathbf{U}_j \mathbf{r}_{j+1}]_T &= [\mathbf{A}\mathbf{u}_{j,j+1}]_T \\
&\vdots \\
[\mathbf{U}_j \mathbf{r}_L]_T &= [\mathbf{A}\mathbf{u}_{j,L}]_T
\end{aligned}$$

Correctness. Let arbitrary $\lambda \in \mathbb{N}$, $L \in \mathbb{N}$,

$$\begin{aligned}
\mathsf{pp} = \big(&\mathsf{bg}, [\mathbf{A}]_1, \{[\mathbf{A}\mathbf{W}_j]_1\}_{j \in [L]}, \{[\mathbf{r}_j]_2\}_{j \in [L]}, \\
&\{[\mathbf{W}_\ell \mathbf{r}_j]_2\}_{\ell, j \in [L], \ell \neq j}, \{[\mathbf{k} + \mathbf{W}_j \mathbf{r}_j]_2\}_{j \in [L]}, [\mathbf{A}\mathbf{k}]_T\big)
\end{aligned}$$

for some $\mathbf{A} \in \mathbb{Z}_p^{k \times (k+1)}$, $\mathbf{k} \in \mathbb{Z}_p^{k+1}$ and $\mathbf{W} \in \mathbb{Z}_p^{(k+1) \times k}$, $\mathbf{r}_j \in \mathbb{Z}_p^k$ for each $j \in [L]$, $\mathsf{usk}_i = [\mathbf{T}_j \mathbf{r}_j]_2$ and $\mathsf{upk}_i := ([\mathbf{A}\mathbf{T}_i]_1, [\mathbf{T}_i \mathbf{r}_\ell])_{\ell \in [L], \ell \neq i}$ for some $\mathbf{T}_i \in \mathbb{Z}_p^{(k+1) \times k}$. Moreover, let $\{\mathsf{upk}_j\}_{j \in [L], j \neq i}$ such that $\mathsf{isValid}(\mathsf{pp}, \mathsf{upk}_j, j) = 1$, $S \subseteq [L]$ such that $i \in S$ and $M \in \mathbb{M}$. Then $\mathsf{Enc}(\mathsf{pp}, \{\mathsf{upk}_j\}_{j \in S}, S, M)$ gives:

$$\mathsf{ct} = \left([\mathbf{s}^\top \mathbf{A}]_1, [\sum_{j \in S} (\mathbf{s}^\top \mathbf{U}_j + \mathbf{s}^\top \mathbf{A}\mathbf{W}_j)]_1, [\mathbf{s}^\top \mathbf{A}\mathbf{k}]_T \cdot M \right)$$

where $[\mathbf{U}_j]_1 = \mathsf{upk}_{j,0}$, and $\mathsf{Dec}(\mathsf{pp}\{\mathsf{upk}_j\}_{j \in S}, \mathsf{usk}_i, \mathsf{ct}, S, i)$ gives:

$$\begin{aligned}
M' &= \mathsf{ct}_3 \cdot e\left(\mathsf{ct}_2, \mathsf{pp}_i^{(3)}\right) \cdot e\left(\mathsf{ct}_1^{-1}, \mathsf{pp}_i^{(5)} \cdot \mathsf{usk}_i \cdot \prod_{j \in S, j \neq i} (\mathsf{upk}_{j,i} \cdot \mathsf{pp}_{j,i}^{(5)})\right) = \\
&= M \cdot [\mathbf{s}^\top \mathbf{A}\mathbf{k}]_T \cdot e\left([\sum_{j \in S} (\mathbf{s}^\top \mathbf{U}_j + \mathbf{s}^\top \mathbf{A}\mathbf{W}_j)]_1, [\mathbf{r}_i]_2\right) \cdot \\
&\quad \cdot e\left([-\mathbf{s}^\top \mathbf{A}]_1, [\mathbf{k} + \mathbf{W}_i \mathbf{r}_i]_2 \cdot [\mathbf{T}_i \mathbf{r}_i]_2 \cdot \prod_{j \in S, j \neq i} ([\mathbf{u}_{j,i}]_2 \cdot [\mathbf{W}_j \mathbf{r}_i])\right) = \\
&= M \cdot [\mathbf{s}^\top \mathbf{A}\mathbf{k}]_T \cdot [\sum_{j \in S} (\mathbf{s}^\top \mathbf{A}\mathbf{u}_{j,i} + \mathbf{s}^\top \mathbf{A}\mathbf{W}_j \mathbf{r}_i)]_T \cdot
\end{aligned}$$

$$\cdot [-\mathbf{s}^\top \mathbf{A}\mathbf{k} - \mathbf{s}^\top \mathbf{A}\mathbf{W}_i \mathbf{r}_i - \mathbf{s}^\top \mathbf{A}\mathbf{T}_i \mathbf{r}_i - \sum_{j\in S, j\neq i} (\mathbf{s}^\top \mathbf{A}\mathbf{u}_{j,i} + -\mathbf{s}^\top \mathbf{A}\mathbf{W}_j \mathbf{r}_i)]_T =$$

$$= M \cdot [\mathbf{s}^\top \mathbf{A}\mathbf{k}]_T \cdot [-\mathbf{s}^\top \mathbf{A}\mathbf{k}]_T =$$
$$= M$$

where in the above we used that $\mathbf{U}_j \mathbf{r}_i = \mathbf{A}\mathbf{u}_{j,i}$, since $\mathsf{isValid}(\mathsf{pp}, \mathsf{upk}_j, j) = 1$

6.3 Security

We base the security of our scheme to the k-Lin assumption [3,24,32], the statement of which is given in Sect. 3.1.

We prove adaptive security, following the techniques of [19, Sect. 6]. Interestingly, we achieve adaptive security without the need of the [21] transformation, therefore our scheme is adaptively secure (while maintaining constant-sized ciphertexts) in the standard model.

Theorem 4. *If the k-Lin assumption holds, then $\Pi_{\mathsf{DBE},2}$ is an adaptively secure Distributed Broadcast Encryption scheme. More specifically for every PPT adversary $\mathcal{A}$ against the active-adaptive security of the above DBE construction, $\Pi_{\mathsf{DBE},2}$, there exists a PPT adversary $\mathcal{B}$ against the k-Lin assumption such that:*

$$\mathbf{Adv}^{\Pi_{\mathsf{DBE},2}}_{\mathcal{BG},L,\mathcal{A}}(\lambda) \leq (2L+1) \cdot \mathbf{Adv}^{k\text{-}Lin}_{\mathcal{BG},k,\mathcal{B}}(\lambda) + \frac{1}{p}.$$

Proof. We prove the theorem using a sequence of Hybrids: Game_0, $\mathsf{Game}_1, \ldots,$ Game_L. In Game_0 we switch to a "semi-functional" ciphertext. In Game_i ($1 \leq i \leq L$) we switch to "semi-functional" keys $\mathsf{usk}_1, \ldots, \mathsf{usk}_i$ while maintaining the rest of the keys functional. In Game_L we have both the ciphertext and all the keys being semi-functional and it follows M_b is information-theoretically masked (unless with a negligible probability $1/p$).

Hybrid 0. The Game_0 is the same as the (adaptive) security game of definition 2 except we switch the ciphertext to "semi-functional". That is

$$\mathsf{ct} = \left([\mathbf{c}^\top]_1, [\mathbf{c}^\top \sum_{j\in S} (\mathbf{T}_j + \mathbf{W}_j)]_1, [\mathbf{c}^\top \mathbf{k}]_T \cdot M \right)$$

where $\mathbf{c} \leftarrow_\$ \mathbb{Z}_p^{k+1}$.

It is straightforward to show that Game_0 is negligibly close to the original game: Then there is an PPT adversary $\mathcal{B}_0$ such that

$$|\mathbf{Adv}^{\Pi_{\mathsf{DBE},2}}_{\mathcal{BG},L,\mathcal{A}}(\lambda) - \mathbf{Adv}^{\mathsf{Game}_0}_{\mathcal{BG},L,\mathcal{A}}(\lambda)| \leq \mathbf{Adv}^{k\text{-Lin}}_{\mathcal{BG},L,\mathcal{B}_0}(\lambda).$$

Let $\mathcal{B}_0$ be an adversary to k-Lin, receiving $(\mathsf{bg}, [\mathbf{A}^\top]_1, [\mathbf{c}]_1)$, where $[\mathbf{c}]_1$ is either $[\mathbf{A}^\top \mathbf{s}]$ (for some random $\mathbf{s} \in \mathbb{Z}_p^k$) or random. $\mathcal{B}_0$ will use an adversary $\mathcal{A}'$ that can distinguish with probability $\epsilon > 1/\operatorname{poly}(\lambda)$ between Game_0 and the original game. $\mathcal{B}_0$ samples $\mathbf{W}_j, \mathbf{r}_j, \mathbf{k}, \mathbf{T}_j$ and computes the public parameters and all the keys of the system according to $\Pi_{\mathsf{DBE},2}$ honestly. Now if $\mathbf{c} = \mathbf{A}^\top \mathbf{s}$ then $\mathcal{B}_0$ perfectly simulates the original game otherwise if $\mathbf{c}$ is random perfectly simulates Game_0, which means that by answering the same bit as $\mathcal{A}'$, $\mathcal{B}_0$ gains advantage ϵ against the k-Lin game.

It will be useful for the next Hybrids to state that with probability $1 - 1/p$ over $\mathbf{c}$: $\mathbf{c}$ lies outside the row span of $\mathbf{A}$, so there exists a non-zero $\mathbf{a}^\perp \in \mathbb{Z}_p^{k+1}$ such that $\mathbf{A} \cdot \mathbf{a}^\perp = \mathbf{0}$ and $\mathbf{c} \cdot \mathbf{a}^\perp \neq 0$. Moreover, we can efficiently compute $\mathbf{a}^\perp$ given $\mathbf{A}, \mathbf{c}$.

Hybrid i Game_i is the same as Game_{i-1} except we replace $[\mathbf{k} + \mathbf{W}_i\mathbf{r}_i]_2$ with $[\mathbf{k} + \mathbf{W}_i\mathbf{r}_i + \delta_i\mathbf{a}^\perp]_2$, where $\delta_i \leftarrow \mathbb{Z}_p$. We claim that hybrids $i-1$ and i are computationally indistinguishable assuming k-Lin in $\mathbb{G}_2$, which tells us

$$(\mathbf{A}, \mathbf{A}\mathbf{W}_i, [\mathbf{W}_i\mathbf{r}_i]_2, [\mathbf{r}_i]_2, [\mathbf{W}_i\mathbf{B}]_2, [\mathbf{B}]_2) \approx_c (\mathbf{A}, \mathbf{A}\mathbf{W}_i, [\mathbf{W}_i\mathbf{r}_i + \delta_i\mathbf{a}^\perp]_2, [\mathbf{r}_i]_2, [\mathbf{W}_i\mathbf{B}]_2, [\mathbf{B}]_2)$$

where $\mathbf{B} \leftarrow \mathbb{Z}_p^{k\times k}$.[2] Then, as in the previous case, we build a reduction that reduces distinguishing between Hybrid $i-1$ and Hybrid i to k-Lin. In particular:

$$|\mathbf{Adv}^{\mathsf{Game}_{i-1}}_{\mathcal{BG},L,\mathcal{B}_{i-1}}(\lambda) - \mathbf{Adv}^{\mathsf{Game}_i}_{\mathcal{BG},L,\mathcal{B}_i}(\lambda)| \leq 2 \cdot \mathbf{Adv}^{k\text{-Lin}}_{\mathcal{BG},L,\mathcal{B}_0}(\lambda).$$

We proceed via a case analysis:

- $i \notin S$: the reduction samples $\mathbf{c}, \mathbf{k}, \mathbf{T}_1, \ldots, \mathbf{T}_L$ at random, and for all $j \neq i$: samples $\mathbf{W}_j, \tilde{\mathbf{r}}_j \leftarrow \mathbb{Z}_p^k$ and implicitly sets $\mathbf{r}_j := \mathbf{B}\tilde{\mathbf{r}}_j$. In particular, it can
  1. simulate the challenge ciphertext without knowing $\mathbf{W}_i$ since $i \notin S$;
  2. compute $[\mathbf{r}_j]_2, [\mathbf{T}_i\mathbf{r}_j]_2$ for all i, j using $[\mathbf{B}]_2, \tilde{\mathbf{r}}_j, \mathbf{T}_i$
  3. compute $[\mathbf{W}_j\mathbf{r}_i]_2, j \neq i$ using $[\mathbf{r}_i]_2, \mathbf{W}_j$
  4. compute $[\mathbf{W}_i\mathbf{r}_j]_2, j \neq i$ using $[\mathbf{W}_i\mathbf{B}], \tilde{\mathbf{r}}_j$
  5. compute $\mathsf{pp}, \mathsf{upk}_1, \ldots, \mathsf{upk}_L, \mathsf{usk}_1, \ldots, \mathsf{usk}_L$.
- $i \in S$: the reduction proceeds as in the previous case, with the following changes:
  1. samples $\tilde{\mathbf{T}}_i \leftarrow \mathbb{Z}_p^{(k+1)\times k}$ (instead of $\mathbf{T}_i$ at random) and implicitly sets $\mathbf{T}_i := \tilde{\mathbf{T}}_i - \mathbf{W}_i$;
  2. simulates $\mathbf{c}(\mathbf{T}_i + \mathbf{W}_i)$ in the challenge ciphertext using $\mathbf{c}\tilde{\mathbf{T}}_i$;
  3. simulates $[\mathbf{T}_i\mathbf{r}_j]_2 = [\tilde{\mathbf{T}}_i\mathbf{B}\tilde{\mathbf{r}}_j - \mathbf{W}_i\mathbf{B}\tilde{\mathbf{r}}_j]_2, j \neq i$ using $[\mathbf{W}_i\mathbf{B}]_2, [\mathbf{B}]_2$ along with $\tilde{\mathbf{T}}_i, \tilde{\mathbf{r}}_j$.

  In particular, we do not need to simulate $\mathsf{usk}_i = [\mathbf{T}_i\mathbf{r}_i]_2$ since the query is not allowed.

Formally, the reduction guesses at random which case we will fall into, and abort if the guess is wrong, incuring a factor 2 security loss. This step is essentially the same as [19, Lemma 6.3].

---

[2] k-Lin tells us that

$$[\mathbf{B}]_2, [\mathbf{r}_i]_2, [\mathbf{t}^\top\mathbf{B}]_2, [\mathbf{t}^\top\mathbf{r}_i] \approx_c [\mathbf{B}]_2, [\mathbf{r}_i]_2, [\mathbf{t}^\top\mathbf{B}]_2, [\mathbf{t}^\top\mathbf{r}_i + \delta_i]$$

Now, the reduction samples a random $\tilde{\mathbf{W}}_i$ and programs $\mathbf{W}_i = \tilde{\mathbf{W}}_i + \mathbf{a}^\perp\mathbf{t}$.

Hybrid 3. We complete the proof using an information-theoretic argument, which states that $\mathbf{ck}$ is uniformly random (and in turn perfectly masks M_b) given

$$\mathbf{A}, \mathbf{Ak}, \mathbf{c}, \mathbf{k} + \delta_i \mathbf{a}^\perp, i = 1, \ldots, L$$

This comes directly from [19, Lemma 6.4].

6.4 Efficiency

We compute the efficiency of our scheme for $k = 1$. As can be seen by the construction's description, the public parameters of our scheme are dominated by $O(L^2)$ vectors in $(\mathbb{G}_2)^2$, upk_j consists of $O(L)$ elements (1 in $\mathbb{G}_1$ and $L-1$ in $(\mathbb{G}_2)^2$) and usk_j is one vector of groups elements in $(\mathbb{G}_2)^2$. The cipertext has size $O(1)$ independently of the size of the set S. The remark 2 of the BDHE construction applies here as well giving $O(L)$-size storage for both the Encryptor and the Decryptor. Finally the overall information that has to be stored in the bulletin board is $O(L^2)$, which is the L upk_j's.

Acknowledgments. We would like to thank Brent Waters and David Wu for helpful discussions on [25]. We would, also, like to thank Duong Hieu Phan and Ji Luo for helpful discussions on prior works. G.M. was partially funded by the German Federal Ministry of Education and Research (BMBF) in the course of the 6GEM research hub under grant number 16KISK038 and by the Deutsche Forschungsgemeinschaft (DFG, German Research Foundation) under Germany's Excellence Strategy - EXC 2092 CASA - 390781972. D.K. received funding from projects from the European Research Council (ERC) under the European Union's Horizon 2020 research and innovation program under project PICOCRYPT (grant agreement No. 101001283) and from the Spanish Government under projects PRODIGY (TED2021-132464B-I00) and ESPADA (PID2022-142290OB-I00). The last two projects are co-funded by European Union EIE, and NextGenerationEU/PRTR funds.

References

1. Agrawal, S., Wichs, D., Yamada, S.: Optimal broadcast encryption from LWE and pairings in the standard model. In: Pass, R., Pietrzak, K. (eds.) TCC 2020, Part I. LNCS, vol. 12550, pp. 149–178. Springer, Heidelberg (2020). https://doi.org/10.1007/978-3-030-64375-1_6
2. Agrawal, S., Yamada, S.: Optimal broadcast encryption from pairings and LWE. In: Canteaut, A., Ishai, Y. (eds.) EUROCRYPT 2020, Part I. LNCS, vol. 12105, pp. 13–43. Springer, Heidelberg (2020). https://doi.org/10.1007/978-3-030-45721-1_2
3. Boneh, D., Boyen, X., Shacham, H.: Short group signatures. In: Franklin, M. (ed.) CRYPTO 2004. LNCS, vol. 3152, pp. 41–55. Springer, Heidelberg (2004). https://doi.org/10.1007/978-3-540-28628-8_3
4. Boneh, D., Gentry, C., Waters, B.: Collusion resistant broadcast encryption with short ciphertexts and private keys. In: Shoup, V. (ed.) CRYPTO 2005. LNCS, vol. 3621, pp. 258–275. Springer, Heidelberg (2005). https://doi.org/10.1007/11535218_16

5. Boneh, D., Waters, B.: A fully collusion resistant broadcast, trace, and revoke system. In: Juels, A., Wright, R.N., De Capitani di Vimercati, S. (eds.) ACM CCS 2006, pp. 211–220. ACM Press (2006). https://doi.org/10.1145/1180405.1180432
6. Boneh, D., Waters, B., Zhandry, M.: Low overhead broadcast encryption from multilinear maps. In: Garay, J.A., Gennaro, R. (eds.) CRYPTO 2014, Part I. LNCS, vol. 8616, pp. 206–223. Springer, Heidelberg (2014). https://doi.org/10.1007/978-3-662-44371-2_12
7. Boneh, D., Zhandry, M.: Multiparty key exchange, efficient traitor tracing, and more from indistinguishability obfuscation. In: Garay, J.A., Gennaro, R. (eds.) CRYPTO 2014, Part I. LNCS, vol. 8616, pp. 480–499. Springer, Heidelberg (2014). https://doi.org/10.1007/978-3-662-44371-2_27
8. Brakerski, Z., Döttling, N., Garg, S., Malavolta, G.: Candidate iO from homomorphic encryption schemes. In: Canteaut, A., Ishai, Y. (eds.) EUROCRYPT 2020, Part I. LNCS, vol. 12105, pp. 79–109. Springer, Heidelberg (2020). https://doi.org/10.1007/978-3-030-45721-1_4
9. Brakerski, Z., Döttling, N., Garg, S., Malavolta, G.: Factoring and pairings are not necessary for IO: circular-secure LWE suffices. In: Bojanczyk, M., Merelli, E., Woodruff, D.P. (eds.) 49th International Colloquium on Automata, Languages, and Programming, ICALP 2022, July 4–8, 2022, Paris, France. LIPIcs, vol. 229, pp. 28:1–28:20. Schloss Dagstuhl - Leibniz-Zentrum für Informatik (2022). https://doi.org/10.4230/LIPIcs.ICALP.2022.28
10. Brakerski, Z., Vaikuntanathan, V.: Lattice-inspired broadcast encryption and succinct ciphertext-policy abe. In: 13th Innovations in Theoretical Computer Science Conference (ITCS 2022). Schloss Dagstuhl-Leibniz-Zentrum für Informatik (2022)
11. Chen, J., Gay, R., Wee, H.: Improved dual system ABE in prime-order groups via predicate encodings. In: Oswald, E., Fischlin, M. (eds.) EUROCRYPT 2015, Part II. LNCS, vol. 9057, pp. 595–624. Springer, Heidelberg (2015). https://doi.org/10.1007/978-3-662-46803-6_20
12. Döttling, N., Kolonelos, D., Lai, R.W.F., Lin, C., Malavolta, G., Rahimi, A.: Efficient laconic cryptography from learning with errors. In: EUROCRYPT 2023, Part III, pp. 417–446. LNCS, Springer, Heidelberg (2023). https://doi.org/10.1007/978-3-031-30620-4_14
13. Escala, A., Herold, G., Kiltz, E., Ràfols, C., Villar, J.: An algebraic framework for Diffie-Hellman assumptions. In: Canetti, R., Garay, J.A. (eds.) CRYPTO 2013, Part II. LNCS, vol. 8043, pp. 129–147. Springer, Heidelberg (2013). https://doi.org/10.1007/978-3-642-40084-1_8
14. Fiat, A., Naor, M.: Broadcast encryption. In: Stinson, D.R. (ed.) CRYPTO'93. LNCS, vol. 773, pp. 480–491. Springer, Heidelberg (1994). https://doi.org/10.1007/3-540-48329-2_40
15. Francati, D., Friolo, D., Maitra, M., Malavolta, G., Rahimi, A., Venturi, D.: Registered (inner-product) functional encryption. IACR Cryptol. ePrint Arch. p. 395 (2023), https://eprint.iacr.org/2023/395
16. Garg, S., Hajiabadi, M., Mahmoody, M., Rahimi, A.: Registration-based encryption: removing private-key generator from IBE. In: Beimel, A., Dziembowski, S. (eds.) TCC 2018, Part I. LNCS, vol. 11239, pp. 689–718. Springer, Heidelberg (2018). https://doi.org/10.1007/978-3-030-03807-6_25
17. Garg, S., Hajiabadi, M., Mahmoody, M., Rahimi, A., Sekar, S.: Registration-based encryption from standard assumptions. In: Lin, D., Sako, K. (eds.) PKC 2019, Part II. LNCS, vol. 11443, pp. 63–93. Springer, Heidelberg (2019). https://doi.org/10.1007/978-3-030-17259-6_3

18. Gay, R., Kerenidis, I., Wee, H.: Communication complexity of conditional disclosure of secrets and attribute-based encryption. In: Gennaro, R., Robshaw, M.J.B. (eds.) CRYPTO 2015, Part II. LNCS, vol. 9216, pp. 485–502. Springer, Heidelberg (2015). https://doi.org/10.1007/978-3-662-48000-7_24
19. Gay, R., Kowalczyk, L., Wee, H.: Tight adaptively secure broadcast encryption with short ciphertexts and keys. In: Catalano, D., De Prisco, R. (eds.) SCN 18. LNCS, vol. 11035, pp. 123–139. Springer, Heidelberg (2018). https://doi.org/10.1007/978-3-319-98113-0_7
20. Gay, R., Pass, R.: Indistinguishability obfuscation from circular security. In: STOC 2021: Proceedings of the 53rd Annual ACM SIGACT Symposium on Theory of Computing, pp. 736–749. ACM Press (2021). https://doi.org/10.1145/3406325.3451070
21. Gentry, C., Waters, B.: Adaptive security in broadcast encryption systems (with short ciphertexts). In: Joux, A. (ed.) EUROCRYPT 2009. LNCS, vol. 5479, pp. 171–188. Springer, Heidelberg (2009). https://doi.org/10.1007/978-3-642-01001-9_10
22. Glaeser, N., Kolonelos, D., Malavolta, G., Rahimi, A.: Efficient registration-based encryption. In: Meng, W., Jensen, C.D., Cremers, C., Kirda, E. (eds.) ACM CCS 2023. ACM Press (2023). https://doi.org/10.1145/3576915.3616596
23. Groth, J., Kohlweiss, M., Maller, M., Meiklejohn, S., Miers, I.: Updatable and universal common reference strings with applications to zk-SNARKs. In: Shacham, H., Boldyreva, A. (eds.) CRYPTO 2018, Part III. LNCS, vol. 10993, pp. 698–728. Springer, Heidelberg (2018). https://doi.org/10.1007/978-3-319-96878-0_24
24. Hofheinz, D., Kiltz, E.: Secure hybrid encryption from weakened key encapsulation. In: Menezes, A. (ed.) CRYPTO 2007. LNCS, vol. 4622, pp. 553–571. Springer, Heidelberg (2007). https://doi.org/10.1007/978-3-540-74143-5_31
25. Hohenberger, S., Lu, G., Waters, B., Wu, D.J.: Registered attribute-based encryption. In: EUROCRYPT 2023, Part III, pp. 511–542. LNCS, Springer, Heidelberg (2023). https://doi.org/10.1007/978-3-031-30620-4_17
26. Jain, A., Lin, H., Sahai, A.: Indistinguishability obfuscation from well-founded assumptions. In: STOC 2021: Proceedings of the 53rd Annual ACM SIGACT Symposium on Theory of Computing, pp. 60–73. ACM Press (2021). https://doi.org/10.1145/3406325.3451093
27. Jain, A., Lin, H., Sahai, A.: Indistinguishability obfuscation from LPN over $\mathbb{F}\_p$, DLIN, and PRGs in NC^0. In: Dunkelman, O., Dziembowski, S. (eds.) EUROCRYPT 2022, Part I. LNCS, vol. 13275, pp. 670–699. Springer, Heidelberg (2022). https://doi.org/10.1007/978-3-031-06944-4_23
28. Kolonelos, D., Malavolta, G., Wee, H.: Distributed broadcast encryption from bilinear groups. Cryptology ePrint Archive (2023)
29. Lewko, A.B., Waters, B.: New techniques for dual system encryption and fully secure HIBE with short ciphertexts. In: Micciancio, D. (ed.) TCC 2010. LNCS, vol. 5978, pp. 455–479. Springer, Heidelberg (2010). https://doi.org/10.1007/978-3-642-11799-2_27
30. Maller, M., Bowe, S., Kohlweiss, M., Meiklejohn, S.: Sonic: zero-knowledge SNARKs from linear-size universal and updatable structured reference strings. In: Cavallaro, L., Kinder, J., Wang, X., Katz, J. (eds.) ACM CCS 2019, pp. 2111–2128. ACM Press (2019). https://doi.org/10.1145/3319535.3339817
31. Phan, D.H., Pointcheval, D., Strefler, M.: Decentralized dynamic broadcast encryption. In: Visconti, I., Prisco, R.D. (eds.) SCN 12. LNCS, vol. 7485, pp. 166–183. Springer, Heidelberg (2012). https://doi.org/10.1007/978-3-642-32928-9_10

32. Shacham, H.: A cramer-shoup encryption scheme from the linear assumption and from progressively weaker linear variants. Cryptology ePrint Archive, Report 2007/074 (2007). https://eprint.iacr.org/2007/074
33. Waters, B.: Dual system encryption: Realizing fully secure IBE and HIBE under simple assumptions. In: Halevi, S. (ed.) CRYPTO 2009. LNCS, vol. 5677, pp. 619–636. Springer, Heidelberg (2009). https://doi.org/10.1007/978-3-642-03356-8_36
34. Wee, H.: Broadcast encryption with size $N^{1/3}$ and more from k-lin. In: Malkin, T., Peikert, C. (eds.) CRYPTO 2021, Part IV. LNCS, vol. 12828, pp. 155–178. Springer, Heidelberg, Virtual Event (2021). https://doi.org/10.1007/978-3-030-84259-8_6
35. Wee, H.: Optimal broadcast encryption and CP-ABE from evasive lattice assumptions. In: Dunkelman, O., Dziembowski, S. (eds.) EUROCRYPT 2022, Part II. LNCS, vol. 13276, pp. 217–241. Springer, Heidelberg (2022). https://doi.org/10.1007/978-3-031-07085-3_8
36. Wee, H., Wichs, D.: Candidate obfuscation via oblivious LWE sampling. In: Canteaut, A., Standaert, F.X. (eds.) EUROCRYPT 2021, Part III. LNCS, vol. 12698, pp. 127–156. Springer, Heidelberg (2021). https://doi.org/10.1007/978-3-030-77883-5_5
37. Wu, Q., Qin, B., Zhang, L., Domingo-Ferrer, J.: Ad hoc broadcast encryption. In: Proceedings of the 17th ACM Conference on Computer and Communications Securit, pp. 741–743 (2010). https://crises-deim.urv.cat/web/docs/publications/conferences/318.pdf
38. Wu, Q., Qin, B., Zhang, L., Domingo-Ferrer, J.: Ad hoc broadcast encryption (poster presentation). In: Al-Shaer, E., Keromytis, A.D., Shmatikov, V. (eds.) ACM CCS 2010, pp. 741–743. ACM Press (2010). https://doi.org/10.1145/1866307.1866416

Author Index

A
Abou Haidar, Calvin 342

B
Balbás, David 307

C
Chen, Huanhuan 374
Chen, Jie 3
Chen, Xiaofeng 134
Chu, Qiaohan 3
Collins, Daniel 307

D
Deng, Yi 269

F
Fiore, Dario 166
Francati, Danilo 98
Friolo, Daniele 98

G
Gajland, Phillip 307
Galteland, Yao Jiang 374
Gao, Ying 3
Gong, Junqing 66
Guo, Fuchun 134

H
Huang, Zhengan 236

K
Kolonelos, Dimitris 166, 407

L
Lai, Junzuo 236
Lam, Kwok-Yan 236
Li, Yamin 134
Liang, Kaitai 374

M
Maitra, Monosij 98
Malavolta, Giulio 98, 407

N
Nguyen, Dinh Duy 33
Ning, Jianting 3

P
Passelègue, Alain 342
Perthuis, Paola de 166
Phan, Duong Hieu 33
Pointcheval, David 33

Q
Qian, Haifeng 66

R
Rahimi, Ahmadreza 98

S
Stehlé, Damien 342
Susilo, Willy 134

V
Venturi, Daniele 98

W
Wang, Huaxiong 236
Wang, Luping 3
Wang, Xiangning 236
Wee, Hoeteck 201, 407
Wei, Jianghong 134
Weng, Jian 236
Wu, David J. 201

Z
Zeng, Gongxian 236
Zhang, Kai 66
Zhang, Linru 236
Zhang, Xinxuan 269
Zhu, Ziqi 66

J. Guo and R. Steinfeld (Eds.): ASIACRYPT 2023, LNCS 14442, p. 443, 2023.
https://doi.org/10.1007/978-981-99-8733-7

Author Index

Printed in the United States
by Baker & Taylor Publisher Services